R. Gupta's®

Popular Master Guide

BPSC

Bihar Public Service Commission

Secondary School Teacher

Class 9 to 10

Recruitment Exam

SUBJECT

ENGLISH

by

RPH Editorial Board

2026

EDITION

RAMESH PUBLISHING HOUSE, NEW DELHI

AF662880

Published by
O.P. Gupta *for* Ramesh Publishing House

Admin. Office
12-H, New Daryaganj Road, Opp. Officers' Mess,
New Delhi-110002 ✆ 23275224, 23245124

E-mail: info@rameshpublishinghouse.com
For Online Shopping: www.rameshpublishinghouse.com

Showroom
• Balaji Market, Nai Sarak, Delhi-6 ✆ 23253720, 23282525
• 4457, Nai Sarak, Delhi-6, ✆ 23918938

© *Reserved with the Publisher*

No Part of this book may be reproduced or transmitted in any form or by any means, electronic or mechanical including photocopying, recording or by any transformation storage and retrieval system without written permission from the Publisher.

Indemnification Clause: This book is being sold/distributed subject to the exclusive condition that neither the author nor the publishers, individually or collectively, shall be responsible to indemnify the buyer/user/possessor of this book beyond the selling price of this book for any reason under any circumstances. If you do not agree to it, please do not buy/accept/use/possess this book.

Book Code: R-2525

ISBN: 978-93-5477-577-2

Price: ₹ 640

Printed at: B.K. Offset, Delhi

CONTENTS

Written Examination

For Secondary School Teacher (Class 9-10)

Part	Subjects	No. of Questions	Total Marks	Duration
Part-I : Language (Qualifying)	English and Hindi/Urdu/Bangla	30	30	2.30 hours
Part-II : General Studies	Primary Maths, General Awareness, General Science, Indian National Movement and Geography	40	40	
Part-III : Concerned Subject	English	80	80	
	Total	**150**	**150**	

Bihar Public Service Commission (BPSC)

Secondary School English Teacher Recruitment Exam, 2024

(Exam held on 21-07-2024)

PART-I

ENGLISH LANGUAGE

Directions (Qs. No. 1 to 5): *Read the passage given below and answer the questions that follow:*

Amitabh Bachchan, popularly known as big B, was born in Allahabad, Uttar Pradesh on 11 October 1942. He is an iconic actor whose career in Indian Cinema has spanned four decades. His father H.R. Bachchan was a well-known Hindi poet. (Bachchan is actually his father's pen name but has now become the family surname) Amitabh attended boys' High School in Allahabad, followed by Sherwood College in Nainital and earned a degree in science from Delhi university. His first film was 'Saat Hindustani' (1969). He became well-known as a movie star in 1973 after the success of 'Abhimaan' and 'Zanjeer' which was followed by his box office successes such as 'Sholay' 'Amar Akbar Anthony', 'Trishul', 'Don' and 'Deewar'. He often played the role of an angry young man fighting a corrupt establishment, a theme that had tremendous appeal in India at that time.

1. Which city is the birth place of Amitabh in India?
A. Bombay
B. Delhi
C. Bangalore
D. More than one of the above
E. None of the above

2. How long has Amitabh Bachchan dominated Indian Cinema?
A. Three decades
B. Four decades
C. Two decades
D. More than one of the above
E. None of the above

3. From which university did Amitabh earn his degree in science?
A. Aligarh Muslim University
B. Banaras Hindu University
C. Punjab University
D. More than one of the above
E. None of the above

4. When did Amitabh got recognition as a movie star in India?
A. 1966
B. 1969
C. 1973
D. More than one of the above
E. None of the above

5. Which film of the following is Amitabh's first film?
A. 'Zanjeer'
B. 'Abhiman'
C. 'Saat Hindustani'
D. More than one of the above
E. None of the above

Directions (Qs. No. 6 and 7): *Fill in the blanks with suitable articles like 'a' 'an' 'the' :*

6. The shadow of moon fills on ______ Earth.
A. an
B. a
C. the
D. More than one of the above
E. None of the above

1. E	**2.** B	**3.** E	**4.** C	**5.** C	**6.** C

7. I have always wanted to study abroad, not only for ______ degree but also for the experience.

A. an
B. a
C. the
D. More than one of the above
E. None of the above

8. First May 2024 is Wednesday, what day of the week would be 9th of May?

A. Friday
B. Thursday
C. Monday
D. More than one of the above
E. None of the above

हिन्दी भाषा

निर्देश (प्र.सं. 9 से 14 तक): *निम्नलिखित गद्यांश को पढ़कर पूछे गए प्रश्नों का उत्तर दीजिए:*

पंडित राम प्रसाद बिस्मिल उन महान क्रांतिकारियों में से एक थे, जिन्होंने अपने कार्यों से अंग्रेजी हुकूमत को हिला दिया था। जब राम प्रसाद आर्य समाज के संपर्क में आए, इनके जीवन में क्रांति आ गई, इनमें बुराइयों का सामना करने का साहस जाग उठा। उन दिनों स्वतंत्रता आंदोलन जोर पर था। राम प्रसाद को पता चला कि क्रांतिकारी युवक देश में सजग हैं तथा देश की स्वतंत्रता के लिए मर मिटने को तैयार हैं। बिस्मिल क्रांतिकारी संगठन के सदस्य बन गए। इन्होंने एक पुस्तक भी लिखी– 'अमरीका को स्वतंत्रता कैसे मिली?' इनकी 'स्वदेश-रंग' नामक पुस्तक बहुत प्रसिद्ध है। आंदोलन में धन की कमी एक बहुत बड़ी समस्या थी। धन जुटाने के लिए इन्होंने किसी दीन-हीन को नहीं सताया, बल्कि अंग्रेजों का सरकारी खजाना लूटने की योजना बनाई। इन्होंने 9 अगस्त, 1925 को काकोरी स्टेशन पर धन लूटकर स्वाधीनता संग्राम में लगा दिया। इसके लिए इनपर मुकदमा चलाया गया। इन्हें फाँसी की सजा दी गई। पंडित बिस्मिल ने 26-27 वर्ष की आयु में वह कार्य कर दिखाया, जो लंबी आयु जीने वाले भी नहीं कर पाते। ये एक कवि भी थे, इनकी ये पंक्तियाँ समय-समय पर हमें प्रेरणा देती हैं:

'सरफरोशी की तमन्ना अब हमारे दिल में है।
देखना है जोर कितना बाजू ए-कातिल में है।।'

9. राम प्रसाद के जीवन में परिवर्तन कब आया?

A. क्रांतिकारियों के संपर्क में आने पर
B. जब अमरीका को स्वतंत्रता मिली
C. जब वे आर्य समाज के संपर्क में आए
D. उपर्युक्त में से एक से अधिक
E. उपर्युक्त में से कोई नहीं

10. बिस्मिल ने धन की समस्या कैसे हल की?

A. सरकारी खजाना लूटकर
B. चंदा इकट्ठा करके
C. गरीबों को लूटकर
D. उपर्युक्त में से एक से अधिक
E. उपर्युक्त में से कोई नहीं

11. बिस्मिल महान क्रांतिकारी क्यों कहलाए?

A. क्योंकि उन्हें फाँसी की सजा दी गई।
B. क्योंकि उन्होंने पुस्तकें लिखीं।
C. क्योंकि उन्होंने अपने कार्यों से अंग्रेजी हुकूमत को हिला दिया।
D. उपर्युक्त में से एक से अधिक
E. उपर्युक्त में से कोई नहीं

12. 'सजग' में मूल शब्द है:

A. सज
B. जग
C. ग
D. उपर्युक्त में से एक से अधिक
E. उपर्युक्त में से कोई नहीं

13. 'स्वतंत्रता' शब्द का विलोम है:

A. गणतंत्रता
B. लोकतंत्रता
C. प्रजातंत्रता
D. उपर्युक्त में से एक से अधिक
E. उपर्युक्त में से कोई नहीं

14. 'लंबी आयु जीने वाला' वाक्यांश के लिए एक शब्द है:

A. लंबायु
B. दीर्घायु
C. अल्पायु
D. उपर्युक्त में से एक से अधिक
E. उपर्युक्त में से कोई नहीं

निर्देश (प्र.सं. 15 से 18 तक): *निम्नलिखित गद्यांश को पढ़कर पूछे गए प्रश्नों का उत्तर दीजिए:*

मनुष्य का जीवन संसार के छोटे-बड़े प्राणियों और पदार्थों में श्रेष्ठ माना गया है। वह इसलिए कि मनुष्य बड़ा बुद्धिमान और कल्पनाशील प्राणी है। अपने विचारों के बल पर ही वह जो चाहे कर सकता है और बहुत ऊँचा उठ सकता है। परंतु विचार सच्चे, सादे और पवित्र होने

7. B	8. B	9. C	10. A	11. C	12. B	13. E	14. B

के साथ-साथ मनुष्य के व्यावहारिक जीवन से संबंध रखने वाले होने चाहिए। इन्हीं बातों को आधार बनाकर 'सादा जीवन, उच्च विचार' को मानव-जीवन की सफलता की सीढ़ी माना गया है। सादगी मनुष्य के पहनावे से नहीं, बल्कि उसके प्रत्येक हाव-भाव, विचार तथा जीवन के ढंग से टपकनी चाहिए। यही वास्तविक सादगी है, जो विचारों को भी उच्च बनाकर सब प्रकार की उन्नति और विकास का कारण बनती है। संसार का इतिहास इस बात का गवाह है कि आरंभ से ही सादगी पसंद व्यक्ति ही जनता को उच्च विचार देकर उन्नति और विकास की राह प्रशस्त करते आ रहे हैं। महात्मा बुद्ध, संत कबीर, गुरू नानक, महात्मा गाँधी, डॉ. राधाकृष्णन, विनोबा भावे आदि इस तथ्य के प्रत्यक्ष प्रमाण हैं।

15. मनुष्य का जीवन श्रेष्ठ क्यों माना जाता है?
A. क्योंकि वह सफल है
B. क्योंकि वह बुद्धिमान और कल्पनाशील है
C. क्योंकि वह परिश्रमी और कठोर है।
D. उपर्युक्त में से एक से अधिक
E. उपर्युक्त में से कोई नहीं

16. उन्नति करने के लिए मनुष्य के विचार कैसे होने चाहिए?
A. झूठे, ऊँचे और अपवित्र
B. बेबुनियाद
C. मोह-माया से युक्त
D. उपर्युक्त में से एक से अधिक
E. उपर्युक्त में से कोई नहीं

17. वास्तविक सादगी क्या है?
A. वैचारिक और व्यावहारिक
B. मनुष्य का पहनावा
C. मनुष्य का दिखावा
D. उपर्युक्त में से एक से अधिक
E. उपर्युक्त में से कोई नहीं

18. 'उन्नति' शब्द का उचित विलोम शब्द है:
A. प्रोन्नति
B. पदोन्नति
C. अवनति
D. उपर्युक्त में से एक से अधिक
E. उपर्युक्त में से कोई नहीं

19. 'महान है जो आत्मा' का समास है:
A. कर्मधारय समास
B. अव्ययीभाव समास
C. तत्पुरुष समास
D. उपर्युक्त में से एक से अधिक
E. उपर्युक्त में से कोई नहीं

20. 'प्रत्येक' शब्द का सही वर्ण-विच्छेद है:
A. प् + र् + आ + त् + अ + य् + ए + क्
B. प् + र् + अ् + त् + अ + य् + ए + क् + अ
C. प् + र् + अ + त् + य् + ए + क् + अ
D. उपर्युक्त में से एक से अधिक
E. उपर्युक्त में से कोई नहीं

21. निम्नलिखित में से वृद्धि संधि का उदाहरण है:
A. पित्रादेश
B. गिरीश
C. महौजस्वी
D. उपर्युक्त में से एक से अधिक
E. उपर्युक्त में से कोई नहीं

22. निम्नलिखित में से शुद्ध वर्तनी है:
A. अद्वितिय
B. अद्वितीय
C. अद्वितीय
D. उपर्युक्त में से एक से अधिक
E. उपर्युक्त में से कोई नहीं

23. निम्नलिखित में से जातिवाचक संज्ञा है:
A. बहन
B. मंत्री
C. जुलाहा
D. उपर्युक्त में से एक से अधिक
E. उपर्युक्त में से कोई नहीं

24. 'चंद्रमा' का पर्यायवाची है:
A. राकेश
B. सारंग
C. आदित्य
D. उपर्युक्त में से एक से अधिक
E. उपर्युक्त में से कोई नहीं

25. 'स्थिर' का विलोम शब्द है:
A. चंचल
B. अस्थिर
C. निर्विकार
D. उपर्युक्त में से एक से अधिक
E. उपर्युक्त में से कोई नहीं

26. 'मैं एक लीटर दूध पीता हूँ'– में विशेषण शब्द है:
A. मैं
B. एक लीटर
C. दूध
D. उपर्युक्त में से एक से अधिक
E. उपर्युक्त में से कोई नहीं

15. B	**16.** E	**17.** A	**18.** C	**19.** A	**20.** C
21. C	**22.** B	**23.** D	**24.** D	**25.** D	**26.** B

27. 'कृष्णार्पण' शब्द में कौन-सा समास है?

A. अव्ययीभाव

B. कर्मधारय

C. बहुब्रीहि

D. उपर्युक्त में से एक से अधिक

E. उपर्युक्त में से कोई नहीं

28. निम्नलिखित वाक्यांश के लिए एक शब्द बताइए:

'कम बोलने वाला'

A. मितभाषी

B. वाचाल

C. मिष्टभाषी

D. उपर्युक्त में से एक से अधिक

E. उपर्युक्त में से कोई नहीं

29. 'उदासीन हो जाने' के लिए सही मुहावरा है:

A. आँखें चुराना

B. आँखों में गड़ना

C. आँखें फेर लेना

D. उपर्युक्त में से एक से अधिक

E. उपर्युक्त में से कोई नहीं

30. 'निरपराध' में उपसर्ग है:

A. नि

B. निर्

C. निस्

D. उपर्युक्त में से एक से अधिक

E. उपर्युक्त में से कोई नहीं

PART-II

GENERAL STUDIES

31. A player makes 7 complete revolutions of a circular path to complete a race of 2200 metres. The radius of the circular path is: ($\pi = 22/7$)

A. 42 metres

B. 45 metres

C. 50 metres

D. More than one of the above

E. None of the above

32. If the capacity of a cylindrical tank is 1848 m^3 and the diameter of its base is 14 m, the depth of the tank is: ($\pi = 22/7$)

A. 8 m

B. 12 m

C. 16 m

D. More than one of the above

E. None of the above

33. If 1/8th of a number is 30, what will be 62% of that number?

A. 181.3

B. 178.24

C. 148.8

D. More than one of the above

E. None of the above

34. The salary of an officer is increased by 25%. By what per cent should the new salary be decreased to restore the original salary?

A. 25

B. 22.5

C. 20

D. More than one of the above

E. None of the above

35. By what number should $\left(-\frac{2}{3}\right)^{-3}$ be divided so that the quotient is $\left(\frac{4}{9}\right)^{-2}$?

A. $\frac{2}{3}$

B. $-\frac{2}{3}$

C. $-\frac{3}{2}$

D. More than one of the above

E. None of the above

36. If $x + \frac{1}{x} = 5$, what is the value of $x^4 + \frac{1}{x^4}$?

A. 525

B. 527

C. 529

D. More than one of the above

E. None of the above

27. B	28. A	29. C	30. B	31. C	32. B	33. C	34. C	35. B	36. B

37. A bag contains 5-rupee, 2-rupee and 1-rupee coins in the ratio 2 : 3 : 4. The total value of all the coins is ₹ 2,000. How many coins of 2-rupee are there in the bag?

A. 200
B. 250
C. 400
D. More than one of the above
E. None of the above

38. The interior angle of a regular polygon exceeds its exterior angle by 108°. How many sides does the polygon have?

A. 10
B. 9
C. 8
D. More than one of the above
E. None of the above

39. Zinc Oxide is normally used in the manufacture of:

A. Paints
B. Explosives
C. Solvents
D. More than one of the above
E. None of the above

40. Lenz's law is derived from the law of conservation of:

A. Magnetism
B. Momentum
C. Charge
D. More than one of the above
E. None of the above

41. Glycogen stored in liver and muscles of human body is in form of:

A. Monosaccharide
B. Polysaccharide
C. Protein
D. More than one of the above
E. None of the above

42. In which of the following blood has defective haemoglobin?

A. Haematoma
B. Sickle cell Anaemia
C. Haemophilia
D. More than one of the above
E. None of the above

43. In which of the following medicine production, ethyl alcohol can be used?

A. Antiseptic
B. Antipyretic
C. Anti-allergic
D. More than one of the above
E. None of the above

44. Velocity of sound at 15°C and 380 mm pressure is 340 m. sec^{-1}. If the pressure is doubled without change of temperature, the velocity of sound would become:

A. 680 m. sec^{-1} B. 170 m. sec^{-1}
C. 190 m. sec^{-1} D. 340 m. sec^{-1}
E. None of the above

45. If a bacterium cell divides in every 15 min, how many bacteria will be formed in 2 hours.

A. 8 B. 16
C. 64 D. 256
E. None of the above

46. Plants and animal cell differ in which of the following structure?

A. Enzymes
B. Nuclei
C. Cell wall
D. More than one of the above
E. None of the above

47. According to the recent report of forbes, which is the strongest currency in the world?

A. Omani Rial
B. Kuwaiti Dinar
C. Bahrain Dinar
D. More than one of the above
E. None of the above

48. In which city of Maharashtra did PM Narendra Modi launch 8 AMRUT projects?

A. Kollam
B. Baroda
C. Solapur
D. More than one of the above
E. None of the above

49. IIT Madras has tied up with whom to launch e-Mobility Simulation Lab?

A. Altair
B. Starlink
C. Farber Speciality Lab
D. More than one of the above
E. None of the above

37. E	**38.** A	**39.** A	**40.** E	**41.** B	**42.** B	**43.** A
44. D	**45.** D	**46.** C	**47.** B	**48.** C	**49.** A	

50. Who won the Best Actor Award at the Academy Awards 2024 (Oscars)?
A. Dwayne Johnson
B. Cillian Murphy
C. Tom Cruise
D. More than one of the above
E. None of the above

51. Who was recently selected as the ICC Women's T20i Cricketer of the year 2023?
A. Smriti Mandhana (India)
B. Nat Seiver - Brunt (England)
C. Hayley Mathews (West Indies)
D. More than one of the above
E. None of the above

52. Who was Crowned Miss World 2024 in Mumbai?
A. Miss Czech Kristina Pishkova
B. Miss India Sini Shetty
C. Miss Lebanon Yasmina Zaytoun
D. More than one of the above
E. None of the above

53. In which country will the clean Energy Investor Forum be organised by IPEF?
A. France
B. Singapore
C. Spain
D. More than one of the above
E. None of the above

54. India has acquired the right to operate the foreign Sittwe Port, it is in which country?
A. Sri Lanka
B. Bangladesh
C. Myanmar
D. More than one of the above
E. None of the above

55. Mangrove forest of Ganga Delta is called:
A. Sunderban
B. Sundergarh
C. Surendranagar
D. More than one of the above
E. None of the above

56. Which river is frequently changing its course of flow in Bihar?
A. Gandak
B. Kosi
C. Punpun
D. More than one of the above
E. None of the above

57. Plant roots gets water from soil as:
A. Bound water
B. Hygroscopic water
C. Capillary water
D. More than one of the above
E. None of the above

58. How much equatorial diameter is larger than polar diameter?
A. 36 km
B. 43 km
C. 49 km
D. More than one of the above
E. None of the above

59. The Indian Standard Time (IST) is taken at which longitude?
A. 82.5° E
B. 78.5° E
C. 87.5° E
D. More than one of the above
E. None of the above

60. In India 'Green revolution' is known to credit to whom?
A. Dr. V. Kurian
B. Dr. M.S. Swaminathan
C. Sri. S.L. Bahuguna
D. More than one of the above
E. None of the above

61. Highest Mountain peak of India is known as:
A. Everest
B. Kanchenjunga
C. K-2
D. More than one of the above
E. None of the above

62. Indian continent was earlier part of:
A. Gondwanaland
B. Tethys
C. Pangea
D. More than one of the above
E. None of the above

63. Who led the Revolt of 1857 in Bihar?
A. Tatya Tope
B. Kunwar Singh
C. Nana Saheb
D. More than one of the above
E. None of the above

50. B	**51.** C	**52.** A	**53.** B	**54.** C	**55.** A	**56.** B
57. C	**58.** B	**59.** A	**60.** B	**61.** C	**62.** *	**63.** B

64. The spiritual side of nationalism was voiced by:
A. Raja Ram Mohan Roy
B. Swami Shraddhanand
C. Swami Vivekananda
D. More than one of the above
E. None of the above

65. Which newspaper propagated strong nationalist views during India's freedom struggle?
A. Pioneer
B. Amrit Bazar Patrika
C. Statesman
D. More than one of the above
E. None of the above

66. Who intervened in a dispute between the workers and mill owners of Ahmedabad in 1918?
A. Vàllabhbhai Patel
B. Mahatma Gandhi
C. Jamshedji Tata
D. More than one of the above
E. None of the above

67. Name the left-wing leader of Bihar Provincial Kisan Sabha who popularised this in Bihar?
A. Karyanand Sharma
B. Wadhwa Ram
C. P.C. Joshi
D. More than one of the above
E. None of the above

68. Muddiman Committee was appointed to report on the working of the:
A. Dyarchy
B. Communal representation
C. Federalism
D. More than one of the above
E. None of the above

69. "He was a great unifier in India who taught us not only bare tolerance of others but the willing acceptance of them as our friends and comrades in common undertakings" who said it?
A. Subhash Chandra Bose
B. Balgangadhar Tilak
C. Rajendra Prasad
D. More than one of the above
E. None of the above

70. Who proceeded to organise the Provisional Government of Free India outside the county?
A. Raja Mahendra Pratap
B. Rash Behari Bose
C. Subhash Chandra Bose
D. More than one of the above
E. None of the above

PART-III

SUBJECT SPECIFIC—ENGLISH

71. Which one of the following statements is true in regard to the poem Beowulf?
A. Beowulf is a descriptive tragical poem
B. Beowulf is an epic poem having a narrative tone
C. Beowulf is an argumentative poem
D. More than one of the above
E. None of the above

72. Which one of the following is an author of Historia Regum Britanniae?
A. Geoffrey of Monmouth
B. Holished
C. Plutarch
D. More than one of the above
E. None of the above

73. Which one of the following statements is true in regard to Sir Gawain and the Green Knight?
A. Sir Gawain and the Green Knight has been written by William Langland
B. Sir Gawain and the Green Knight is attributed to Geoffrey Chaucer
C. Sir Gawain and the Green Knight has an anonymousship yet the author might have lived in England
D. More than one of the above
E. None of the above

74. Pandarus is a Character in which one of the following poems?
A. Troilus and Criseyde
B. The Romaunt of Rose
C. The Book of Duchess
D. More than one of the above
E. None of the above

64. C	**65.** B	**66.** B	**67.** A	**68.** A	**69.** E
70. B	**71.** B	**72.** A	**73.** C	**74.** A	

75. The book entitled 'Troy Book' has been written by which one of the following authors?
A. William Dunbar
B. Geoffrey Chaucer
C. John Lydgate
D. More than one of the above
E. None of the above

76. The characters in the Canterbury Tales are supposed to set upon a pilgrimage to say prayer to which one of the following martyrs?
A. St. Thomas Becket
B. St. John
C. St. Peter
D. More than one of the above
E. None of the above

77. The idea of 'round table' appears in which one of the following works of art?
A. The book of Marjorie Kempe
B. Revelations of Divine Love
C. Le Morte Darthur
D. More than one of the above
E. None of the above

78. Which one of the following is a meaning of the surname 'Hythlodaeus'?
A. Learned in nonsense
B. Enlightened in wit
C. Imperfect in sensibility
D. More than one of the above
E. None of the above

79. Which one of the following is an author of Assertio Septem Sacramentorum?
A. Henery IV
B. Henery VIII
C. Henery II
D. More than one of the above
E. None of the above

80. Which one among the following is an author of Ralph Roister Doister?
A. Nicholas Udall
B. John Heywood
C. Ben Jonson
D. More than one of the above
E. None of the above

81. In which one of the following treaties, the idea of 'Mysomousoi' appears?
A. Shelley's Defence of Poetry
B. Sidney's the Defence of Poesie
C. Dryden's the Defence of Dramatic Poetry
D. More than one of the above
E. None of the above

82. For which one of the following dramas Shakespeare utilises Thomas Lodge's Rosalynde, Euphues golden legacie?
A. As you like it
B. Cymbeline
C. Measure for Measure
D. More than one of the above
E. None of the above

83. In which one of the works, the observations 'We are all... Comedians in religions, 'God, who is the Author of all our tragedies, hath written out for us, and appointed us all the paste we are to play':
A. Hakluytus Posthumus
B. The history of the world
C. The discovery of the Large, Rich and Beautiful Empire of Guiana
D. More than one of the above
E. None of the above

84. Which one among the following has been called 'well of English undefiled'?
A. William Langland
B. John Gower
C. Geoffrey Chaucer
D. More than one of the above
E. None of the above

85. "And ride in triumph through Persepolis!- Is not brave to be a King".
The above observations appear in which one of works?
A. Tamburlaine the Great
B. Doctor Faustus
C. The Jew of Malta
D. More than one of the above
E. None of the above

86. 'The true end of Satire is the amendment of vices by correction'.
The above observation has been made by which one of the following authors?
A. Alexander Pope
B. Jonathan Swift
C. John Dryden
D. More than one of the above
E. None of the above

75. C	**76.** A	**77.** C	**78.** A	**79.** B	**80.** A
81. B	**82.** A	**83.** B	**84.** C	**85.** A	**86.** C

87. Which one among the following is an author of the Rover?

A. Aphra Behn
B. Mary Astell
C. Dorothy Osborne
D. More than one of the above
E. None of the above

88. 'Millament' is a character in which one of the following plays?

A. Love for Love
B. The Double Dealer
C. The Way of the World
D. More than one of the above
E. None of the above

89. The work entitled 'The Analysis of Beauty' has been written by which one of the following authors?

A. William Hogarth
B. Jonathan Swift
C. Horace Walpole
D. More than one of the above
E. None of the above

90. The place of action in terms of the Battle of the Books is which one of the following places?

A. The British Museum
B. St. James's Library
C. Bodleian Library
D. More than one of the above
E. None of the above

91. Which one of the following is an alternative title to Gulliver's Travels?

A. Travels into Several Remote Nations of the world
B. Voyages : Ancient and Modern
C. Voyages Across the Atlantic
D. More than one of the above
E. None of the above

92. 'Whatever is, is right' is an observation that appears in which one of the following works of art?

A. An Epistle to Dr. Arbuthnot
B. The Rape of the Lock
C. An Essay on Man
D. More than one of the above
E. None of the above

93. In which one of the following months and years, the daily journal the spectator was founded?

A. March 1711
B. June 1812
C. April 1766
D. More than one of the above
E. None of the above

94. Which one of the following is an author of A Journal of the Plague Year?

A. Daniel Defoe
B. Samuel Johnson
C. Jonathan Swift
D. More than one of the above
E. None of the above

95. How many letter writers does the novel Clarissa have?

A. Six
B. Three
C. Four
D. More than one of the above
E. None of the above

96. 'A School for Scandal' has been written by which one of the following dramatists?

A. Richard Cumberland
B. Sheridan
C. Oliver Goldsmith
D. More than one of the above
E. None of the above

97. 'Prefaces, Biographical and critical' is the other title for which one of the following works of art?

A. Lives of the Poets
B. Love's Labour's Lost
C. The Life of Samuel Johnson
D. More than one of the above
E. None of the above

98. In which one of the following works of art, the ideas such as human happiness and social well-being have been expounded?

A. Enquiry Concerning Political Justice
B. Adventures of Caleb Williams
C. The Wrongs of Woman
D. More than one of the above
E. None of the above

99. The Castle of Otranto belongs to which one of the following genres of fictional writings?

A. Romantic
B. Classical
C. Gothic
D. More than one of the above
E. None of the above

87. A	**88.** C	**89.** A	**90.** B	**91.** A	**92.** C	**93.** A
94. A	**95.** C	**96.** B	**97.** A	**98.** A	**99.** C	

100. In regards to Frankenstein, which one of the following statements is true?

A. Frankenstein is a proto-science fiction
B. Frankenstein is a horror fiction
C. Frankenstein is a science fiction
D. More than one of the above
E. None of the above

101. Which one of the following poems is inspired by Peterloo Massacre?

A. The Mask of Anarchy
B. Queen Mab
C. The Revolt of Islam
D. More than one of the above
E. None of the above

102. Which one among the following poets had a recourse to Lemprière's Classical Dictionary?

A. Percy Bysshe Shelley
B. John Keats
C. William Wordsworth
D. More than one of the above
E. None of the above

103. Which one of the following novels deals with the social and industrial problems of mid-Victorian England?

A. Hard Times
B. Oliver Twist
C. A Tale of Two Cities
D. More than one of the above
E. None of the above

104. In which one of the following poems, the idea of war is most expressive?

A. Murder in the Cathedral
B. The Waste Land
C. The Eder Statesman
D. More than one of the above
E. None of the above

105. In which one of the following novels, aesthetical theory has been expounded?

A. A Portrait of the Artist as a Young Man
B. Dubliners
C. Animal Forum
D. More than one of the above
E. None of the above

Directions (Qs. No. 106 to 125): *The questions are based on comprehension of the passages. Answer the questions that follow each of the passages:*

Among the relics of the Indus civilization are found the figures which are the prototype of Siva, suggesting that he who explores his inward nature and integrates it is the ideal man. This image has haunted the spiritual landscape of this country from those early times till today. The Upanishads require us to acquire Brahma-Vidyā or ātma-Vidyā. The Katha Upanishad says that man is turned outward by his senses so looses contact with himself. He has lost his way. His soul has become immersed in outer things, in power and possessions. It must turn round, āvrtta-caksuh, to find its right direction and discover the meaning of reality it has lost. The Jina is one who conquers his self. He is the Mahāvíra, one who has battled with his inward nature and triumphed over it. The Buddha asks us to seek enlightenment, bodhi. These different Vedic ideals ask us to change our unregenerate nature, to replace avidyā, ignorance, by Vidya Wisdom.

106. Which one of the following is the most appropriate meaning of the term Siva?

A. Supreme consciousness that is integrated
B. Unconsciousness that is active
C. Ordinary consciousness that is apparent
D. More than one of the above
E. None of the above

107. Which one of the following is nearest in meaning to the terms brahma-vidya and atma vidya?

A. World that is changing and temporary
B. Experience that is timeless and external
C. Life that begins and ends
D. More than one of the above
E. None of the above

108. In what way, according to the passage, one may be in a position to know oneself?

A. By looking round and within
B. By looking outward
C. By luxury and comfort
D. More than one of the above
E. None of the above

109. Which one of the following is the true meaning of reality?

A. A knowledge of inward self only
B. A true integration of outward and inward selves
C. A knowledge of outward self only
D. More than one of the above
E. None of the above

100. A	**101.** A	**102.** B	**103.** A	**104.** B	**105.** A	**106.** A	**107.** B	**108.** A	**109.** B

110. Who is the Buddha or Mahavira according to the passage?

A. One who has conquered the senses
B. One who hasn't conquered the senses
C. One who has conquered the outward senses only
D. More than one of the above
E. None of the above

The fundamental concept of Indian religious life may first be briefly indicated. The goal of life is communion with the Supreme. It is a life of realization, agnosis, an inner intuitive vision of God, when man achieves absolute freedom and escapes from the blind servitude to ordinary experience. It is subtle interwovenness with the realities of the spiritual world. It is not knowledge or the recognition of universal ideas through a dialectical process or analysis of empirical data. It is analogous to Plato's vision of an irrestible harmony with the deepest reality of the world inspired and sustained by the spiritual in us. Intellectual recognition and spiritual realization are different. We can free ourselves from the shackles of the body and in a split second we can see the truth and be overcome by it. We see God so intensely that the soul is more certain and more possessed by the sight of God than the bodily eye by the light of day.

111. Which one of the following is nearest in meaning to the word 'Communion'?

A. A relationship only
B. An intimate relationship
C. A familiarity
D. More than one of the above
E. None of the above

112. Which one of the following is a result of the act of Communion having been successfully established?

A. It leads to the vision of deepest reality
B. It introduces us to the transitory experience
C. It is indescribable in nature
D. More than one of the above
E. None of the above

113. Which one of the following is the most appropriate meaning of the word empirical?

A. That which is related to thought
B. That which is related to experience
C. That which is related to logic and reasoning
D. More than one of the above
E. None of the above

114. Which one of the following best explains the observation 'Intellectual recognition' of spiritual?

A. Something which is based on logic and reasoning with body being the basis
B. Something which is based on experience with soul being the basis
C. Something which is based on cause and effect relationship
D. More than one of the above
E. None of the above

115. Which one of the following is nearest in meaning to the phraseology 'Split second'?

A. Immediately
B. Imminently
C. Conspicuously
D. More than one of the above
E. None of the above

The Divine is both in us and out of us. God is neither completely transcendent nor completely immanent. To bring about his double aspect, contradictory accounts are given. He is divine darkness as well as 'unencompassed light'. The philosophers with their passion for unity emphasize the immanent aspect, that there is no barrier dividing man from the real. The unity of man and God is the fundamental thesis of the great philosophic tradition which has come down to us from the Upanishads and Plato, Aristotle, Plotinus, Samkara, Spinoza, Bradley and a host of others are witness to it.

116. Which one of the following best expresses the idea of 'transcendent'?

A. Contained in the ordinary experience
B. Extending beyond the limits of all possible experience and knowledge
C. Ability to be one and all with everyday experience
D. More than one of the above
E. None of the above

117. Which one of the following is nearest in meaning to the word, 'Immanent'?

A. Being within the limits of possible experience and knowledge
B. Being outside ordinary experience
C. Being born into logic and reason
D. More than one of the above
E. None of the above

118. What does the term 'unity' mean according to the passage?

A. God and man have become one and all
B. God and man are distinct
C. God is transcendent whereas man is just a material entity
D. More than one of the above
E. None of the above

110. A **111.** B **112.** A **113.** B **114.** A **115.** A **116.** B **117.** A **118.** A

119. The great philosophical tradition of the world begins with which one of the following philosophical compositions?

A. Upanishads
B. Dialogues
C. Metaphysics
D. More than one of the above
E. None of the above

120. Which one of the following is an explanation of the term 'Divine'?

A. The Ultimate reality that is within
B. The apparent experience that is outside
C. The sensuous apprehension of thought
D. More than one of the above
E. None of the above

The famous dialogue between the Indian philosopher and Socrates suggests that for the whole Western tradition man is essentially a rational being, one who can think logically and act in a utilitarian manner. The Western mind lays great stress on science, logic and humanism. Hindu thinkers, as a class, hold with great conviction that we possess a power more interior than intellect by which we become aware of the real in its intimate individuality, and not merely in its superficial or discernible aspects. For the Hindus, a system of philosophy is an insight, a darsana. It is the vision of truth and not a matter of logical argument and proof. They believe that the mind can be freed by gradual training from the influences of speculative intellect as well as post impressions, and that it can unite itself with the object whose nature is then fully manifested. They contend that we can control destiny by the power of truth. Knowledge means power. The lack of this knowledge is root of all trouble. Vidyā is Mokṣha : avidyā is samsāra.

121. Which one of the following is a characteristic of Western tradition?

A. Man must analyse every experience in terms of the facts
B. Man must be capable of sensuously apprehending the thought
C. Man must become dogmatic
D. More than one of the above
E. None of the above

122. Which one of the following is a characteristic of Indian tradition?

A. Ideas are built around profit and loss
B. Ideas are contained in the innate experience
C. Ideas are born into the thought which is a fact
D. More than one of the above
E. None of the above

123. In which one of the following ways, the 'real' is capable of being known?

A. By utilizing the power contained deeper than the mind
B. By inferring just through certain examples
C. By comparing one with the other
D. More than one of the above
E. None of the above

124. Which one of the following is the best meaning of the phraseology 'Speculative intellect'?

A. Dull reflection on the basis of logic and reason
B. Uncertainty in terms of factual analysis
C. To take to be true on the basis of insufficient evidence
D. More than one of the above
E. None of the above

125. Which one of the following statements is true?

A. Vidya and Avidya are similar to intuition and intellect
B. Vidya and Avidya are at loggerheads hence do not complement each other
C. Vidya and Avidya are related to comprehension of an experience
D. More than one of the above
E. None of the above

Directions (Qs. No. 126 to 150): *The questions are based on English Grammar.*

126. Which one of the following is a correct meaning of the word brethren?

A. Sons of the same mother
B. Children of the same parents
C. Members of the same society
D. More than one of the above
E. None of the above

127. The utterance, 'He became his own cook' is an example of which one of the following grammatical categories?

A. Distributive adjective
B. Interrogative adjective
C. Emphasizing adjective
D. More than one of the above
E. None of the above

128. Which one of the following words stands for the evening prayers?

A. Vesper
B. Hymn
C. Ecclesiastical song
D. More than one of the above
E. None of the above

119. A	120. A	121. A	122. B	123. A	124. C	125. A	126. C	127. C	128. A

129. 'A half holiday is better than none' is an example which one of the following parts of speech?

A. Proper adjectives
B. Descriptive adjectives
C. Quantitative adjectives
D. More than one of the above
E. None of the above

130. 'A triangle whose three sides are equal is called an equilateral triangle' is an example of which one of the following classes?

A. Relative pronoun
B. Interrogative pronoun
C. Exclamatory pronoun
D. More than one of the above
E. None of the above

131. 'He laughed a hearty laugh' is an example of which one of the following?

A. Prepositional verb
B. Retained object
C. Cognate noun
D. More than one of the above
E. None of the above

132. 'Such a thing was never thought of' is an example of which one of the following classes?

A. Passive prepositional verb
B. Active prepositional verb
C. Active intransitive verb
D. More than one of the above
E. None of the above

133. 'He died poor' is an example of which one of the following categories?

A. Imperative mood
B. Indicative mood
C. Subjunctive mood
D. More than one of the above
E. None of the above

134. 'I had rather take this than that' is an example of which one of the following classes?

A. Infinitive
B. Gerund
C. Participle
D. More than one of the above
E. None of the above

135. Which one of the following would best fill in the blanks in the following observations?

'Let _____ be _____. We cannot undo the past.

A. old, old
B. time, time
C. bygone, bygone
D. More than one of the above
E. None of the above

136. Which one of the following would best fill in the blanks in the observation given below?

'The Sun _____ _____, they set off'.

A. having, risen
B. having, rose
C. having been, risen
D. More than one of the above
E. None of the above

137. 'I rely on the wall being built immediately'

In the above utterance, which one of the following grammatical categories is at work?

A. Noun in the genitive case
B. Gerundive use of participle
C. Participle
D. More than one of the above
E. None of the above

138. 'He did this _____, and you have done it _____'.

Which one of the following would best fill in the blanks?

A. already, ago
B. now, then
C. before, since
D. More than one of the above
E. None of the above

139. He came and sat _____ me.

Which one of the following would best fill in the blank in the above observation?

A. besides
B. beside
C. by
D. More than one of the above
E. None of the above

140. 'She threw the letter _____ the fire'.

Which one of the following would best fill in the blank on the above observation?

A. in
B. into
C. between
D. More than one of the above
E. None of the above

129. C	**130.** A	**131.** C	**132.** A	**133.** B	**134.** A
135. C	**136.** A	**137.** B	**138.** C	**139.** B	**140.** B

141. Which one of the following prepositions shall go with the following observation?

Send _____ a doctor.

A. for
B. to
C. in
D. More than one of the above
E. None of the above

142. 'Wrestle ______ an adversary'.

Which one of the following prepositions shall go with the blank above?

A. by
B. at
C. with
D. More than one of the above
E. None of the above

143. 'He started early because he might not be late'.

Which one of the following is a correct form of the above?

A. He started early in order that he might not be late
B. He started early in that he might not be late
C. He started early in as much as he might not be late
D. More than one of the above
E. None of the above

144. 'I would _____ have the picture ______ then the pen'.

Which one of the following would best fill in the blanks?

A. finally, and
B. rather, than
C. simply, yet
D. More than one of the above
E. None of the above

145. 'A person who is indifferent to pleasure or pain'

Which one of the following would best explain the above?

A. Stoic
B. Recluse
C. Invincible
D. More than one of the above
E. None of the above

146. 'Incapable of being altered or recalled'.

Which one of the following would best explain the above?

A. Indestructible
B. Indispensable
C. Irrevocable
D. More than one of the above
E. None of the above

147. Which one of the following is a meaning of the phrase 'Once for all'?

A. When a thing is done it is done forever
B. When a thing is done it is to be reviewed
C. When a thing is done, it must always be done
D. More than one of the above
E. None of the above

148. Which one of the following would best explain the meaning of the phrase 'Out-and-out'?

A. Disproportionately
B. Thoroughly
C. Illusory
D. More than one of the above
E. None of the above

149. Which one of the following would best explain the meaning of the word 'Proscribe'?

A. To condemn
B. To glorify
C. To sum up
D. More than one of the above
E. None of the above

150. Which one of the following explains the meaning of the phrase 'Through and through'?

A. Incomplete in nature
B. Thoroughness
C. Dull and drab
D. More than one of the above
E. None of the above

EXPLANATORY ANSWERS

1. **(E):** The passage states that Amitabh Bachchan was born in Allahabad, Uttar Pradesh, which is not listed in the options. Therefore, the correct answer is "None of the above."

2. **(B):** According to the passage, Amitabh Bachchan's career in Indian cinema has spanned four decades. Thus, the correct answer is "Four decades."

141. A	**142.** C	**143.** A	**144.** *	**145.** A	**146.** C	**147.** A	**148.** B	**149.** A	**150.** B

3. (E): The passage mentions that Amitabh Bachchan earned a degree in science from Delhi University, which is not listed in the options provided. Therefore, the correct answer is "None of the above."

4. (C): The passage mentions that Amitabh Bachchan became well-known as a movie star in 1973 following the success of the films "Abhimaan" and "Zanjeer." Therefore, the correct answer is "1973."

5. (C): The passage indicates that Amitabh Bachchan's first film was "Saat Hindustani" (1969). Therefore, the correct answer is "Saat Hindustani."

6. (C): The correct article to complete the sentence is "the" because we are referring to a specific entity, "the Earth." Therefore, the correct answer is "the."

7. (B): In the context of the sentence, "a degree" is correct because we are referring to any degree in general, not a specific one. Therefore, the correct answer is "a."

8. (B): First May 2024 is a Wednesday. Since May 9 is 8 days later, it would be one day after the following Wednesday, which is a Thursday. Therefore, the correct answer is "Thursday."

9. (C): गद्यांश के अनुसार, पंडित राम प्रसाद बिस्मिल के जीवन में परिवर्तन तब आया जब वे आर्य समाज के संपर्क में आए। इस संपर्क ने उनमें साहस जगाया और क्रांति का संचार किया। इसलिए, सही उत्तर ''जब वे आर्य समाज के संपर्क में आए'' है।

10. (A): गद्यांश के अनुसार, पंडित बिस्मिल ने स्वतंत्रता संग्राम के लिए धन एकत्र करने के उद्देश्य से अंग्रेजों का सरकारी खजाना लूटने की योजना बनाई और इसे काकोरी स्टेशन पर सफलतापूर्वक अंजाम दिया। इसलिए, सही उत्तर ''सरकारी खजाना लूटकर'' है।

11. (C): गद्यांश में बताया गया है कि पंडित बिस्मिल अपने कार्यों से अंग्रेजी हुकूमत को हिलाने में सफल हुए और इस कारण उन्हें महान क्रांतिकारी माना गया। इसलिए, सही उत्तर ''क्योंकि उन्होंने अपने कार्यों में अंग्रेजी हुकूमत को हिला दिया'' है।

12. (B): शब्द ''सजग'' का मूल शब्द ''जग'' है, जिसका अर्थ ''जाग्रत'' या ''सतर्क'' होता है। इसलिए, सही उत्तर ''जग'' है।

13. (E): ''स्वतंत्रता'' का विलोम शब्द ''परतंत्रता'' है, जो कि दिए गए विकल्पों में नहीं है। इसलिए, सही उत्तर ''उपर्युक्त में से कोई नहीं'' है।

14. (B): ''लंबी आयु जीने वाला'' का एक शब्दीय पर्याय ''दीर्घायु'' है। इसलिए, सही उत्तर ''दीर्घायु'' है।

15. (B): गद्यांश में बताया गया है कि मनुष्य का जीवन श्रेष्ठ माना गया है क्योंकि वह बुद्धिमान और कल्पनाशील प्राणी है। इस विशेषता के कारण वह ऊँचाई तक पहुँच सकता है। इसलिए, सही उत्तर ''क्योंकि वह बुद्धिमान और कल्पनाशील है'' है।

16. (E): गद्यांश के अनुसार, उन्नति के लिए मनुष्य के विचार सच्चे, सादे, पवित्र और व्यावहारिक जीवन से जुड़े होने चाहिए। विकल्पों में यह संयोजन नहीं है, इसलिए सही उत्तर ''उपर्युक्त में से कोई नहीं'' है।

17. (A): गद्यांश में सादगी को व्यक्ति के हाव-भाव, विचार और जीवन के ढंग से जुड़ा बताया गया है, जो विचारों को भी उच्च बनाती है। इसका तात्पर्य वैचारिक और व्यावहारिक सादगी से है। इसलिए, सही उत्तर ''वैचारिक और व्यावहारिक'' है।

18. (C): ''उन्नति'' का उचित विलोम ''अवनति'' है, जो विपरीत अर्थ को दर्शाता है। इसलिए, सही उत्तर ''अवनति'' है।

19. (A): ''महान है जो आत्मा'' में ''महान'' विशेषण ''आत्मा'' को विशेषता देता है। यह कर्मधारय समास का उदाहरण है, जहाँ विशेषण और विशेष्य एक साथ मिलकर अर्थ को स्पष्ट करते हैं। इसलिए, सही उत्तर ''कर्मधारण समास'' है।

20. (C): ''प्रत्येक'' शब्द का सही वर्ण-विच्छेद ''प् + र् + अ + त् + य् + ए + क् + अ'' है, जो सही ध्वनियों को दर्शाता है। इसलिए, सही उत्तर ''प् + र् + अ + त् + य् + ए + क् + अ'' है।

21. (C): ''महौजस्वी'' वृद्धि संधि का उदाहरण है, जहां ''मह'' और ''उजस्वी'' में वृद्धि संधि का प्रयोग होता है। इसलिए, सही उत्तर ''महौजस्वी'' है।

22. (B): ''अद्वितीय'' सही वर्तनी है, जिसका अर्थ होता है ''अद्वितीय'' या ''बेजोड़''। इसलिए, सही उत्तर ''अद्वितीय'' है।

23. (D): जातिवाचक संज्ञा वह संज्ञा है जो किसी जाति, वर्ग या समूह का बोध कराती है। दिए गए विकल्पों में ''मंत्री'' और ''जुलाहा'' जातिवाचक संज्ञाएँ हैं क्योंकि ये वर्ग या जाति का बोध कराते हैं। इसलिए, सही उत्तर ''उपर्युक्त में से एक से अधिक'' है।

24. (D): ''चंद्रमा'' के पर्यायवाची शब्दों में ''राकेश'' और ''सारंग'' शामिल हैं। इसलिए, सही उत्तर ''उपर्युक्त में से एक से अधिक'' है।

25. (D): ''स्थिर'' का विलोम ''अस्थिर'' और ''चंचल'' दोनों होते हैं। इसलिए, सही उत्तर ''उपर्युक्त में से एक से अधिक'' है।

26. (B): इस वाक्य में ''एक लीटर'' विशेषण है क्योंकि वह ''दूध'' की मात्रा का बोध कराता है। इसलिए, सही उत्तर ''एक लीटर'' है।

27. (B): "कृष्णार्पण" में "कृष्ण" और "अर्पण" दो शब्दों का संयोजन है, जिसमें "कृष्ण को अर्पण" का भाव निहित है। यह कर्मधारण समास का उदाहरण है। इसलिए, सही उत्तर "कर्मधारय" है।

28. (A): "कम बोलने वाला" के लिए एक शब्द "मितभाषी" है, जिसका अर्थ होता है "संयम से बोलने वाला" इसलिए, सही उत्तर "मितभाषी" है।

29. (C): "उदासीन हो जाने" के लिए सही मुहावरा "आँखें फेर लेना" है, जिसका अर्थ होता है किसी से मुँह मोड़ लेना या ध्यान न देना। इसलिए, सही उत्तर "आँखें फेर लेना" है।

30. (B): "निरपराध" शब्द में "निर्" उपसर्ग है, जो "बिना" का भाव प्रकट करता है। इसलिए, सही उत्तर "निर्" है।

31. (C): The total distance covered in 7 revolutions is 2200 metres. Thus, the distance covered in one revolution (the circumference of the circular path) is:

$$\text{Circumference} = \frac{2200}{7} = 314 \text{ metres}$$

Using the formula for the circumference of a circle, $C = 2\pi r$, where $\pi = \frac{22}{7}$, we can substitute the values.

$$314 = 2 \times \frac{22}{7} \times r$$

Solving for r:

$$r = \frac{314 \times 7}{2 \times 22} = 50 \text{ metres (approx)}$$

Therefore, the correct answer is "50 metres."

32. (B): The volume V of a cylinder is given by $V = \pi r^2 h$, where r is the radius and h is the height (or depth).

Given: $V = 1848 \text{ m}^3$

and diameter = 14 m

$$\Rightarrow \quad r = \frac{14}{2} = 7 \text{ m}$$

Using $\pi = \frac{22}{7}$:

$$1848 = \frac{22}{7} \times 7^2 \times h$$

$$1848 = 22 \times 7 \times h$$

$$1848 = 154h$$

$$\Rightarrow \quad h = \frac{1848}{154} = 12 \text{ m}$$

Thus, the correct answer is "12 m."

33. (C): Let the number be x.

Given, $\frac{1}{8}x = 30$, we can solve for x:

$$x = 30 \times 8$$
$$= 240$$

Now, 62% of x is:

$$0.62 \times 240 = 148.8$$

Thus, the correct answer is "148.8."

34. (C): Let the original salary be 100. After a 25% increase, the new salary becomes:

$$100 + 25 = 125$$

To restore the original salary, we need to find the percentage decrease needed from 125 back to 100:

$$\frac{125-100}{125} \times 100 = \frac{25}{125} \times 100 = 20\%$$

Thus, the correct answer is "20%."

35. (B): We are asked to find a number x by which $\left(-\frac{2}{3}\right)^{-3}$ should be divided to get $\left(\frac{4}{9}\right)^{-2}$.

Express the problem as an equation:

$$\frac{\left(-\frac{2}{3}\right)^{-3}}{x} = \left(\frac{4}{9}\right)^{-2}$$

Solving for x gives:

$$x = \frac{\left(-\frac{2}{3}\right)^{-3}}{\left(\frac{4}{9}\right)^{-2}}$$

$$\text{Evaluate } \left(-\frac{2}{3}\right)^{-3} = \frac{1}{\left(-\frac{2}{3}\right)^3} = \frac{1}{-\frac{8}{27}} = -\frac{27}{8}$$

$$\text{Evaluate } \left(\frac{4}{9}\right)^{-2} = \frac{1}{\left(\frac{4}{9}\right)^2} = \frac{1}{\frac{16}{81}} = \frac{81}{16}$$

Substitute the values back into the equation for x:

$$x = \frac{-\frac{27}{8}}{\frac{81}{16}} = -\frac{27}{8} \times \frac{16}{81}$$

$$= -\frac{432}{648} = -\frac{2}{3}$$

Therefore, the correct answer is:

The number by which $\left(-\frac{2}{3}\right)^{-3}$ should be divided to obtain $\left(\frac{4}{9}\right)^{-2}$ is $-\frac{2}{3}$.

36. (B): Given:

$$x+\frac{1}{x} = 5$$

We need to find the value of:

$$x^4+\frac{1}{x^4}$$

To solve this, we can use identies involving powers of $x+\frac{1}{x}$.

Step 1: Find $x^2+\frac{1}{x^2}$

We square both sides of the given equation:

$$\left(x+\frac{1}{x}\right)^2 = 5^2$$

$$x^2+\frac{1}{x^2} = 25$$

$$x^2+\frac{1}{x^2} = 25 - 2 = 23$$

Step 2: Find $x^4+\frac{1}{x^4}$

Now, we square $x^2+\frac{1}{x^2}$ to find $x^4+\frac{1}{x^4}$:

$$\left(x^2+\frac{1}{x^2}\right)^2 = 23^2$$

$$x^4+2+\frac{1}{x^4} = 529$$

$$x^4+\frac{1}{x^4} = 529 - 2 = 527$$

Thus, the correct answer is: 527.

37. (E): Let the number of 5-rupee, 2-rupee and 1-rupee coins be $2x$, $3x$ and $4x$ respectively, according to the given ratio 2 : 3 : 4.

Step 1: Set up the equation for the total value

The total value of the coins is given as ₹ 2000.

We can write the equation for the total value as:

$$5 \times (2x) + 2 \times (3x) + 1 \times (4x) = 2000$$

Step 2: Simplify the equation

Expanding and simplifying

$$10x + 6x + 4x = 2000$$

$$20x = 2000$$

$$x = 100$$

Step 3: Calculate the number of 2-rupee coins

The number of 2-rupee coins is $3x$:

$$3x = 3 \times 100 = 300$$

Therefore, the correct answer is None of the above.

38. (A): For a regular polygon, each interior angle and exterior angle sum up to 180°. Let the exterior angle be x. Then the interior angle would be $x + 108°$ because it exceeds the exterior angle by 108°.

So, $x + (x + 108) = 180$

$$2x = 72$$

$$x = 36°$$

The number of sides n of a regular polygon is given by

$$n = \frac{360}{\text{Exterior Angle}}.$$

Thus: $n = \frac{360}{36} = 10$

Hence, the correct answer should actually be 10.

39. (A): Zinc Oxide is commonly used in the manufacture of paints because it acts as a pigment and provides durability, corrosion resistance, and UV protection in paint. It is not typically used in the production of explosives or solvents. Therefore, the correct answer is "Paints."

40. (E): Lenz's law is derived from the law of conservation of energy. It states that the direction of an induced current is such that it opposes the change that caused it, ensuring that energy is conserved in the electromagnetic system. This is not related directly to magnetism, momentum, or charge conservation. Hence, the correct answer is "None of the above."

41. (B): Glycogen is a polysaccharide that is stored in the liver and muscles of the human body. It is a large, branched polymer of glucose and serves as a form of energy storage. Therefore, the correct answer is "Polysaccharide."

42. (B): Sickle cell anaemia is a genetic disorder where the haemoglobin in red blood cells is defective. This causes the red blood cells to take on a sickle shape, which can lead to various health complications. Haematoma is a collection of blood outside the blood vessels, and haemophilia is a blood clotting disorder, neither of which involve defective haemoglobin. Therefore, the correct answer is "Sickle cell Anaemia."

43. (A): Ethyl alcohol (ethanol) is commonly used in the production of antiseptics because of its ability to kill or inhibit the growth of microorganisms. It is not typically used as an antipyretic or anti-allergic. Therefore, the correct answer is "Antiseptic."

44. (D): The velocity of sound in a gas depends on the temperature but is independent of pressure. Therefore, if the pressure is doubled without any change in temperature, the velocity of sound remains the same. Thus, the correct answer is "340 m/sec."

45. (D): If a bacterium divides every 15 minutes, it divides 4 times in an hour. Therefore, in 2 hours, it will divide:

$$4 \times 2 = 8 \text{ times}$$

Starting with one bacterium, the number of bacteria after each division follows a geometric progression:

$$\text{Number of bacteria} = 2^8 = 256$$

Thus, the correct answer is "256."

46. (C): Plant and animal cells differ in the presence of a cell wall. Plant cells have a rigid cell wall that provides structure and support, while animal cells do not have a cell wall. Enzymes and nuclei are present in both plant and animal cells. Therefore, the correct answer is "Cell wall."

47. (B): According to recent reports, the Kuwaiti Dinar is considered the strongest currency in the world based on exchange rates. Therefore, the correct answer is "Kuwaiti Dinar."

48. (C): Prime Minister Narendra Modi launched 8 AMRUT (Atal Mission for Rejuvenation and Urban Transformation) projects in Solapur, Maharashtra. Therefore, the correct answer is "Solapur."

49. (A): IIT Madras collaborated with Altair to launch an e-Mobility Simulation Lab. Altair provides advanced software solutions for simulation and design, which aids in research for electric vehicles and e-mobility. Therefore, the correct answer is "Altair."

50. (B): At the Academy Awards (Oscars) in 2024, Cillian Murphy won the Best Actor Award. Therefore, the correct answer is "Cillian Murphy."

51. (C): Hayley Mathews from the West Indies was selected as the ICC Women's T20I Cricketer of the Year 2023. Therefore, the correct answer is "Hayley Mathews (West Indies)."

52. (A): Miss Czech Kristina Pishkova was crowned Miss World 2024 in Mumbai. Therefore, the correct answer is "Miss Czech Kristina Pishkova."

53. (B): The Clean Energy Investor Forum, organized by the Indo-Pacific Economic Framework (IPEF), is scheduled to be held in Singapore. Therefore, the correct answer is "Singapore."

54. (C): The Sittwe Port, which India has acquired the right to operate, is located in Myanmar. Therefore, the correct answer is "Myanmar."

55. (A): The mangrove forest in the Ganga Delta is known as the Sunderban. It is one of the largest mangrove forests in the world. Therefore, the correct answer is "Sunderban."

56. (B): The Kosi River, often referred to as the "Sorrow of Bihar," is known for frequently changing its course due to the heavy silt it carries and the region's topography. This has caused severe flooding and displacement issues in Bihar over the years. Therefore, the correct answer is "Kosi."

57. (C): Plants absorb water primarily through capillary water, which is the water available in the small pores of the soil. This water moves through the soil by capillary action and is readily accessible to plant roots. Therefore, the correct answer is "Capillary water."

58. (B): The equatorial diameter of the Earth is approximately 43 km larger than the polar diameter. This difference is due to the Earth's oblate shape, which bulges slightly at the equator due to its rotation. Therefore, the correct answer is "43 km."

59. (A): The Indian Standard Time (IST) is based on the 82.5° E longitude, which passes near Mirzapur in Uttar Pradesh. This meridian is 5 hours and 30 minutes ahead of Greenwich Mean Time (GMT). Therefore, the correct answer is "82.5° E."

60. (B): Dr. M.S. Swaminathan is known as the "Father of the Green Revolution" in India. He played a pivotal role in introducing high-yielding varieties of seeds and modern agricultural techniques, which led to a significant increase in food grain production in India. Therefore, the correct answer is "Dr. M.S. Swaminathan."

61. (C): The highest mountain peak in India is K-2, also known as Mount Godwin-Austen. It is located in the Karakoram range and is the second-highest peak in the world after Mount Everest. Although Kanchenjunga is the highest peak within Indian territory, K-2 is located in the region under Indian administration in the Karakoram range. Therefore, the correct answer is "K-2."

63. (B): Kunwar Singh, a prominent leader from Bihar, led the Revolt of 1857 in the region. He was a significant figure in the Indian independence struggle against British colonial rule, especially known for his role in Bihar. Therefore, the correct answer is "Kunwar Singh."

64. (C): Swami Vivekananda voiced the spiritual side of nationalism through his teachings and speeches, emphasizing India's cultural and spiritual heritage. He inspired many Indians to take pride in their heritage, which became a foundation for the nationalist movement. Therefore, the correct answer is "Swami Vivekananda."

65. (B): Amrit Bazar Patrika was a prominent nationalist newspaper during India's freedom struggle, known for its strong nationalist views and criticism of British colonial policies. It played an essential role in raising awareness and motivating people to join the freedom movement. Therefore, the correct answer is "Amrit Bazar Patrika."

66. (B): In 1918, Mahatma Gandhi intervened in a dispute between the mill workers and mill owners of Ahmedabad. This was one of the first instances of his involvement in labour issues, where he successfully mediated between the workers, who demanded a wage increase, and the owners. Gandhi's intervention led to a resolution through a peaceful method, setting an example of conflict resolution. Therefore, the correct answer is "Mahatma Gandhi."

67. (A): Karyanand Sharma was a prominent left-wing leader of the Bihar Provincial Kisan Sabha, which played a significant role in mobilizing farmers against oppressive landlords and advocating for agrarian reforms. He popularized the movement in Bihar, helping it gain support from the rural population. Therefore, the correct answer is "Karyanand Sharma."

68. (A): The Muddiman Committee was appointed in 1924 to examine the functioning of dyarchy, which was introduced by the Government of India Act of 1919. The committee was tasked with reporting on the effectiveness of dyarchy, a system in which provincial subjects were divided into "reserved" and "transferred" categories, with limited responsibility granted to Indian ministers. Therefore, the correct answer is "Dyarchy."

69. (E): The quote, "He was a great unifier in India who taught us not only bare tolerance of others but the willing acceptance of them as our friends and comrades in common undertakings," was actually said by Jawaharlal Nehru, referring to Mahatma Gandhi. Since Nehru is not listed among the options, the correct answer is "None of the above."

70. (B): Rash Behari Bose was a key figure in organizing efforts for Indian independence from abroad. He founded the Indian Independence League and later formed the Indian National Army (INA) with the aim of achieving India's freedom through military efforts outside India. He was instrumental in setting up the initial framework of the INA, which was later led by Subhash Chandra Bose. Therefore, the correct answer is "Rash Behari Bose."

71. (B): "Beowulf" is an Old English epic poem and is considered one of the most important works of Anglo-Saxon literature. It has a narrative tone and tells the heroic exploits of its protagonist, Beowulf. Therefore, the correct answer is "Beowulf is an epic poem having a narrative tone."

72. (A): "Historia Regum Britanniae" (The History of the Kings of Britain) was written by Geoffrey of Monmouth. This work is a chronicle of the history of Britain and includes legendary stories of King Arthur and other British leaders. Therefore, the correct answer is "Geoffrey of Monmouth."

73. (C): "Sir Gawain and the Green Knight" is a Middle English chivalric romance written by an anonymous author, often referred to as the "Pearl Poet" or "Gawain Poet." Scholars believe the author may have lived in England. Therefore, the correct answer is "Sir Gawain and the Green Knight has an anonymousship yet the author might have lived in England."

74. (A): Pandarus is a character in Geoffrey Chaucer's poem "Troilus and Criseyde." He plays a significant role in bringing together the lovers, Troilus and Criseyde, in the story. Therefore, the correct answer is "Troilus and Criseyde."

75. (C): The "Troy Book" was written by John Lydgate, an English poet of the 15th century. It is a retelling of the story of the Trojan War, drawing inspiration from Chaucer's style. Therefore, the correct answer is "John Lydgate."

76. (A): In "The Canterbury Tales" by Geoffrey Chaucer, the characters are on a pilgrimage to the shrine of St. Thomas Becket in Canterbury Cathedral. St. Thomas Becket was martyred, and his shrine became a famous pilgrimage site. Therefore, the correct answer is "St. Thomas Becket."

77. (C): The idea of the "round table" is prominent in Sir Thomas Malory's "Le Morte Darthur." The Round Table was a symbol of equality among King Arthur's knights, as it had no head, allowing all knights to be considered equal. Therefore, the correct answer is "Le Morte Darthur."

78. (A): The surname "Hythlodaeus," given to a character in Thomas More's "Utopia," means "learned in nonsense." This reflects the character's complex and often contradictory views on politics and society. Therefore, the correct answer is "Learned in nonsense."

79. (B): "Assertio Septem Sacramentorum" (The Defence of the Seven Sacraments) was written by King Henry VIII of England in 1521 as a response to Martin Luther's teachings. This work defended the Catholic Church's doctrines, earning Henry VIII the title "Defender of the Faith" from the Pope. Therefore, the correct answer is "Henry VIII."

80. (A): "Ralph Roister Doister" is a comedic play written by Nicholas Udall. It is considered one of the earliest English comedies, blending classical Roman comedic style with English characters and settings. Therefore, the correct answer is "Nicholas Udall."

81. (B): The term "Mysomousoi" appears in Sir Philip Sidney's The Defence of Poesie, where he critiques those who dislike poetry. Sidney defends poetry against its critics, asserting its importance and value. Therefore, the correct answer is "Sidney's The Defence of Poesie."

82. (A): Shakespeare's As You Like It draws from Thomas Lodge's Rosalynde, Euphues' Golden Legacie. This source provided much of the plot and characters for the play, especially the love story between Rosalind and Orlando. Therefore, the correct answer is "As You Like It."

83. (B): The quote about humans being comedians in religion and God as the author of all tragedies is from Sir Walter Raleigh's The History of the World. Raleigh reflects on the human condition, fate, and the divine plan. Therefore, the correct answer is "The History of the World."

84. (C): Chaucer has been called the "well of English undefiled" for his significant contributions to English literature, especially in The Canterbury Tales, which set the foundation for English as a literary language. Therefore, the correct answer is "Geoffrey Chaucer."

85. (A): The lines "And ride in triumph through Persepolis! – Is it not brave to be a King?" are from Christopher Marlowe's play Tamburlaine the Great, where Tamburlaine reflects on the power and glory of kingship. Therefore, the correct answer is "Tamburlaine the Great."

86. (C): John Dryden made the observation that "The true end of satire is the amendment of vices by correction," highlighting satire's purpose to improve society by critiquing its flaws. Therefore, the correct answer is "John Dryden."

87. (A): Aphra Behn, one of the first professional female writers in English literature, is the author of The Rover. The play explores themes of love and gender, showcasing her wit and insight. Therefore, the correct answer is "Aphra Behn."

88. (C): Millament is a character in William Congreve's play The Way of the World. She is known for her wit and her role in the play's complex plot surrounding love and marriage. Therefore, the correct answer is "The Way of the World."

89. (A): William Hogarth wrote The Analysis of Beauty, which discusses aesthetic principles, particularly the "line of beauty." Hogarth, an artist, sought to explain what he saw as fundamental elements of beauty in art. Therefore, the correct answer is "William Hogarth."

90. (B): The setting for The Battle of the Books by Jonathan Swift is St. James's Library. This satirical work depicts a mock battle between ancient and modern authors, with the library serving as the battleground. Therefore, the correct answer is "St. James's Library."

91. (A): The full title of Gulliver's Travels by Jonathan Swift is Travels into Several Remote Nations of the World. This title reflects the book's satirical narrative as Gulliver explores various fictional lands. Therefore, the correct answer is "Travels into Several Remote Nations of the World."

92. (C): The phrase "Whatever is, is right" appears in Alexander Pope's An Essay on Man. It reflects Pope's belief in the inherent order of the universe, despite apparent chaos and suffering. Therefore, the correct answer is "An Essay on Man."

93. (A): The Spectator, a daily journal founded by Joseph Addison and Richard Steele, was first published in March 1711. It included essays on a variety of topics, aiming to promote moral and social improvement. Therefore, the correct answer is "March 1711."

94. (A): Journal of the Plague Year is written by Daniel Defoe. The work is a fictionalized account of the 1665 Great Plague of London and captures the social and psychological impacts of the plague. Therefore, the correct answer is "Daniel Defoe."

95. (C): In Samuel Richardson's novel Clarissa, there are four primary letter writers who contribute to the epistolary narrative structure. The letters provide insight into each character's perspective and emotions, enhancing the depth of the story. Therefore, the correct answer is "Four."

96. (B): A School for Scandal is a famous play by Richard Brinsley Sheridan. The play critiques the hypocrisy and scandal-mongering of the upper class in England and is considered a masterpiece of English comedy. Therefore, the correct answer is "Sheridan."

97. (A): Lives of the Poets, also known as Prefaces, Biographical and Critical, is a collection of biographical and critical essays by Samuel Johnson on 52 English poets. It provides insight into the poets' lives, works, and contributions to literature. Therefore, the correct answer is "Lives of the Poets."

98. (A): Enquiry Concerning Political Justice by William Godwin expounds ideas on human happiness, social well-being, and political reform. The work advocates for rational governance and criticizes societal structures that limit human potential. Therefore, the correct answer is "Enquiry Concerning Political Justice."

99. (C): The Castle of Otranto by Horace Walpole is considered the first Gothic novel. It incorporates supernatural elements, mysterious settings, and explores themes of fear and suspense, setting a foundation for the Gothic genre. Therefore, the correct answer is "Gothic."

100. (A): Mary Shelley's Frankenstein is often regarded as one of the earliest examples of science fiction. It explores the consequences of scientific experimentation and human ambition through the creation of life by Victor Frankenstein. This pioneering work predates the formal establishment of the science fiction genre, making it a proto-science fiction novel rather than fully developed science fiction or horror fiction. Therefore, the correct answer is "Frankenstein is a proto-science fiction."

101. (A): Percy Bysshe Shelley's poem The Mask of Anarchy was inspired by the Peterloo Massacre, which occurred in 1819 when British forces attacked peaceful protestors in Manchester. Shelley's poem is a political response to this event, expressing outrage and advocating nonviolent resistance. Therefore, the correct answer is "The Mask of Anarchy."

102. (B): John Keats frequently referred to Lemprière's Classical Dictionary for inspiration, drawing on mythological references in many of his poems. This work served as a source of classical allusions that enriched his poetry, as seen in works like "Ode to a Nightingale" and "Hyperion." Therefore, the correct answer is "John Keats."

103. (A): Charles Dickens's novel Hard Times addresses the social and industrial problems of mid-Victorian England, focusing on issues such as utilitarianism, industrialization, and the harsh working conditions in factories. It is a critique of the economic and social policies of the time. Therefore, the correct answer is "Hard Times."

104. (B): T.S. Eliot's The Waste Land expresses themes related to the devastation and aftermath of World War I. Although not solely about war, it reflects the disillusionment and despair of the time and explores the impact of war on society and the human psyche. Therefore, the correct answer is "The Waste Land."

105. (A): James Joyce's A Portrait of the Artist as a Young Man expounds aesthetic theory, particularly through the protagonist, Stephen Dedalus, who explores ideas about art, beauty, and the role of the artist. Joyce delves into aesthetic concepts, which later became foundational to modernist literature. Therefore, the correct answer is "A Portrait of the Artist as a Young Man."

106. (A): In the passage, Siva represents the "ideal man" who explores inward nature and achieves integration. This description aligns with the concept of "Supreme consciousness that is integrated." Therefore, the correct answer is "Supreme consciousness that is integrated."

107. (B): "Brahma-Vidyā" and "ātma-Vidyā" are mentioned in the passage as knowledge that transcends ordinary, transient experience and focuses on eternal truth. Therefore, the correct answer is "Experience that is timeless and external."

108. (A): The passage suggests that turning inward, "āvrtta-caksuh," helps in self-realization. This implies looking within to reconnect with one's true self, rather than focusing on the external. Therefore, the correct answer is "By looking round and within."

109. (B): According to the passage, reality involves reconciling one's outer and inner selves, finding meaning in an integrated, balanced self. Therefore, the correct answer is "A true integration of outward and inward selves."

110. (A): In the passage, the terms Buddha and Mahavira are used to describe individuals who have triumphed over their senses and achieved self-mastery. This conquering of the senses represents enlightenment and self-realization. Therefore, the correct answer is "One who has conquered the senses."

111. (B): In the passage, "communion with the Supreme" implies an intimate and profound connection with the Divine, going beyond a simple relationship to an inner, intuitive union. Therefore, the correct answer is "an intimate relationship."

112. (A): According to the passage, communion with the Supreme allows one to experience the deepest reality, which transcends ordinary experience. It brings about a realization that is beyond empirical knowledge. Therefore, the correct answer is "It leads to the vision of deepest reality."

113. (B): The word "empirical" refers to knowledge based on observation and experience rather than theoretical ideas. The passage contrasts empirical knowledge with spiritual realization. Therefore, the correct answer is "That which is related to experience."

114. (A): The phrase "intellectual recognition" in the passage refers to understanding that is derived from logic and reasoning, rather than intuitive or spiritual experience. Intellectual recognition relies on mental processes and logic. Therefore, the correct answer is "Something which is based on logic and reasoning with body being the basis."

115. (A): The term "split second" in the passage indicates a moment that happens instantly or "immediately." This aligns with the immediate realization of truth or vision of God described. Therefore, the correct answer is "Immediately."

116. (B): In the passage, "transcendent" refers to God's nature that exists beyond the limits of human experience and knowledge. It implies a divine aspect that is not fully comprehensible within ordinary experience. Therefore, the correct answer is "extending beyond the limits of all possible experience and knowledge."

117. (A): The word "immanent" suggests a Divine presence that exists within and is accessible to human experience. It is the aspect of God that is close and within reach of human understanding. Therefore, the correct answer is "being within the limits of possible experience and knowledge."

118. (A): The passage states that philosophers emphasize the unity between God and man, indicating a state of oneness where no barrier exists between the human and the divine. Therefore, the correct answer is "God and man have become one and all."

119. (A): The passage mentions the Upanishads as the beginning of the philosophical tradition focusing on the unity of man and God. Therefore, the correct answer is "Upanishads."

120. (A): The term "Divine" in the passage refers to an ultimate reality that exists both within us and beyond our ordinary experience. It reflects a profound and intimate connection with the spiritual essence of life. Therefore, the correct answer is "The Ultimate reality that is within."

121. (A): The passage highlights that Western tradition emphasizes rationality, science, and logic. This involves analyzing experiences based on observable facts, in contrast to the intuitive or spiritual approach of the Indian tradition. Therefore, the correct answer is "Man must analyse every experience in terms of the facts."

122. (B): Indian tradition, as described in the passage, focuses on "innate experience" (darsana), or the vision of truth, rather than empirical evidence or logical arguments. Therefore, the correct answer is "Ideas are contained in the innate experience."

123. (A): The passage explains that in Indian tradition, one can know the "real" by accessing a power deeper than the intellect, implying that true knowledge transcends the mind's ordinary processes. Therefore, the correct answer is "by utilizing the power contained deeper than the mind."

124. (C): "Speculative intellect" in this context refers to beliefs formed with limited evidence or reasoning, often based on hypothetical or theoretical thinking rather than factual certainty. Therefore, the correct answer is "to take to be true on the basis of insufficient evidence."

125. (A): In the passage, Vidya and Avidya are contrasted in a way that aligns with intuition (Vidya) and intellect (Avidya). Vidya represents spiritual knowledge leading to liberation (moksha), while Avidya represents ignorance, tied to worldly experiences (samsara). Therefore, the correct answer is "Vidya and Avidya are similar to intuition and intellect."

126. (C): The word "brethren" typically refers to members of the same group or society, especially in religious or fraternal contexts. Therefore, the correct answer is "Members of the same society."

127. (C): In the phrase "He became his own cook," "own" is used to emphasize that he cooked for himself without help from others. This makes "own" an emphasizing adjective. Therefore, the correct answer is "Emphasizing adjective."

128. (A): "Vesper" refers to evening prayers in some Christian traditions, particularly within the context of liturgical prayer services. Therefore, the correct answer is "Vesper."

129. (C): In the phrase "A half holiday is better than none," "half" specifies an amount, making it a quantitative adjective. Therefore, the correct answer is "Quantitative adjectives."

130. (A): In the sentence "A triangle whose three sides are equal is called an equilateral triangle," "whose" is a relative pronoun, as it relates to the noun "triangle" and introduces a clause that provides additional information about it. Therefore, the correct answer is "Relative pronoun."

131. (C): The phrase "He laughed a hearty laugh" uses "laugh" as a cognate noun, which is a noun derived from the verb "laugh" and is used to emphasize the action. Therefore, the correct answer is "Cognate noun."

132. (A): The phrase "Such a thing was never thought of" contains a prepositional verb ("thought of") in passive voice. Therefore, the correct answer is "Passive prepositional verb."

133. (B): The sentence "He died poor" is a statement of fact, which is in the indicative mood, expressing a simple assertion. Therefore, the correct answer is "Indicative mood."

134. (A): The phrase "I had rather take this than that" contains an infinitive ("take") following the auxiliary "had rather," indicating preference. Therefore, the correct answer is "Infinitive."

135. (C): The phrase "Let bygone be bygone" is an idiom meaning to let past issues remain in the past without dwelling on them. Therefore, the correct answer is "bygone, bygone."

136. (A): The correct phrase "The Sun having risen, they set off" uses the perfect participle "having risen" to indicate that the Sun rose before they departed. Therefore, the correct answer is "having, risen."

137. (B): In the sentence "I rely on the wall being built immediately," "being built" functions as a gerund, indicating an action being relied upon, rather than a simple participle. Therefore, the correct answer is "Gerundive use of participle."

138. (C): The sentence "He did this before, and you have done it since" appropriately uses "before" and "since" to indicate relative timing of actions. Therefore, the correct answer is "before, since."

139. (B): The phrase "He came and sat beside me" correctly uses "beside," meaning "next to" or "at the side of." Therefore, the correct answer is "beside."

140. (B): The phrase "She threw the letter into the fire" correctly uses "into" to indicate motion or movement towards the inside of the fire. Therefore, the correct answer is "into."

141. (A): The correct preposition in the sentence "Send _____ a doctor" is "for," as it implies sending a message to summon a doctor. Therefore, the correct answer is "for."

142. (C): The correct preposition in the phrase "Wrestle _____ an adversary" is "with," as it indicates engaging in a physical or metaphorical struggle alongside or against someone. Therefore, the correct answer is "with."

143. (A): The phrase "He started early in order that he might not be late" is a clear and correct form of the original sentence, providing purpose for starting early. Therefore, the correct answer is "He started early in order that he might not be late."

145. (A): A "stoic" is someone who remains indifferent to pleasure or pain, enduring both without showing emotion. Therefore, the correct answer is "stoic."

146. (C): The term "Irrevocable" best describes something that cannot be altered or recalled. It means permanent or unchangeable. Therefore, the correct answer is "Irrevocable."

147. (A): The phrase "Once for all" means that something is done definitively and does not need to be revisited. Therefore, the correct answer is "When a thing is done it is done forever."

148. (B): The phrase "Out-and-out" means completely or thoroughly, often used to emphasize the completeness of a trait or action. Therefore, the correct answer is "thoroughly."

149. (A): "Proscribe" means to forbid or condemn something, especially by law or formal decree. Therefore, the correct answer is "to condemn."

150. (B): The phrase "Through and through" means thoroughly or completely. It implies that something has been done in a very detailed or comprehensive manner. Therefore, the correct answer is "thoroughness."

R. Gupta's®

GENERAL KNOWLEDGE BOOKS

Book Name	Code	Price
• Quick — General Knowledge 2024	R-1716	₹ 50
• General Knowledge for All 2024	R-1641	₹ 35
• R. Gupta's® GK & Current Affairs including Latest Who's Who	R-1	₹ 50
• General Knowledge & Current Affairs	R-5	₹ 75
• Popular General Knowledge	R-9	₹ 190
• General Knowledge Encyclopaedia	R-11	₹ 320
• Delhi General Knowledge	R-464	₹ 90
• Objective General Knowledge	R-177	₹ 190
• Comprehensive J&K and Ladakh GK, Current Affairs & Who's Who	R-564	₹ 110
• J&K and Ladakh General Knowledge – At a Glance	R-1066	₹ 80
• Haryana General Knowledge	R-505	₹ 110
• Himachal Pradesh General Knowledge	R-415	₹ 130
• Uttarakhand General Knowledge	R-469	₹ 90
• Odisha General Knowledge	R-518	₹ 180
• West Bengal General Knowledge	R-1070	₹ 75
• Arunachal Pradesh General Knowledge	R-2560	₹ 195
• Telangana General Knowledge	R-1816	₹ 90
• Manipur GK Handbook (with Multiple Choice Questions)	R-954	₹ 80
• Manipur General Knowledge	R-1864	₹ 160
• Maharashtra General Knowledge	R-1043	₹ 95
• Chandigarh (UT) General Knowledge	R-2565	₹ 120

Ramesh Publishing House

4457, Nai Sarak, Delhi-110006

2501

TO PURCHASE ONLINE LOG ON TO www.rameshpublishinghouse.com

Previous Paper (Solved)

Bihar Public Service Commission (BPSC)

Secondary School English Teacher

Recruitment Exam, 2023

PAPER-1 : LANGUAGE*

Part-I : English Language

Directions (Qs. No. 1 to 5): *Fill in the blanks with a/an/the.*

1. Your brother is appointed as _____ SDO.
A. a
B. an
C. the
D. More than one of the above
E. None of the above

2. If I can't move this desk, will you give it _____ push?
A. a
B. an
C. the
D. More than one of the above
E. None of the above

3. Bring _____ book I gave you yesterday.
A. the
B. an
C. a
D. More than one of the above
E. None of the above

4. Anand went to the doctor because he had ____ ear infection.
A. a
B. an
C. the
D. More than one of the above
E. None of the above

5. He is pursuing MA from _____ University.
A. a
B. an
C. the
D. More than one of the above
E. None of the above

Directions (Qs. No. 6 to 10): *Choose the correct alternative for each of the following.*

6. Which is ***not*** a part of a plant?
A. Leaves
B. Branches
C. Birds and animals
D. More than one of the above
E. None of the above

7. Which of the following you do ***not*** use in a computer?
A. Hard drive
B. Keyboard
C. Toothbrush
D. More than one of the above
E. None of the above

8. What among the following a lady does ***not*** use in kitchen?
A. Drier
B. Oven
C. Induction
D. More than one of the above
E. None of the above

9. Which one is ***not*** allowed in an examination?
A. Mobile phone
B. Earphone
C. Book
D. More than one of the above
E. None of the above

1. B	2. A	3. A	4. B	5. A	6. C	7. C	8. A	9. D

*Exam held on 25-08-2023.

10. Which of the following is ***not*** found in a hospital?
A. Nurse
B. Operation theatre
C. Telescope
D. More than one of the above
E. None of the above

Directions (Qs. No. 11 to 15): *Complete the sentences given below using the correct alternative.*

11. The person who writes a book is known as its
A. reader
B. author
C. publisher
D. More than one of the above
E. None of the above

12. If today is Wednesday, day after tomorrow will be
A. Tuesday
B. Thursday
C. Monday
D. More than one of the above
E. None of the above

13. We must _____ traffic signals.
A. not break
B. break
C. not follow
D. More than one of the above
E. None of the above

14. If today is the 12th of December, the next month will be
A. April
B. January
C. February
D. More than one of the above
E. None of the above

15. A month can have _____ days.
A. 28 or 29
B. 30
C. 31
D. More than one of the above
E. None of the above

Directions (Qs. No. 16 to 20): *Choose the correct answer for each of the following.*

16. Daughter's daughter is
A. sister
B. granddaughter
C. cousin
D. More than one of the above
E. None of the above

17. Grandfather's father is
A. grandpa
B. great grandfather
C. father
D. More than one of the above
E. None of the above

18. Mother's father is
A. paternal grandfather
B. maternal grandfather
C. great grandfather
D. More than one of the above
E. None of the above

19. Aunt's daughter is
A. mother
B. grandmother
C. niece
D. More than one of the above
E. None of the above

20. Mother's and father's children are
A. sisters and brothers
B. cousins
C. aunts and uncles
D. More than one of the above
E. None of the above

Directions (Qs. No. 21 to 25): *Choose the correct option to the questions based on the given passage.*

Once upon a time, a hunter came to a forest. It was summer, and water was scarce. Many of the animals had died of thirst. The hunter killed a deer and took it back to his house. The Forest God was very sad because he could not protect his animals. He prayed to the Rain God and the monsoon arrived. The animals could breed again because there was enough to eat and drink.

21. Whom did the Forest God pray to?
A. The hunter
B. The deer
C. The Rain God
D. More than one of the above
E. None of the above

22. The Forest God was very _____ that he could not protect his animals.
A. joyous
B. sad
C. neutral
D. More than one of the above
E. None of the above

10. C **11.** B **12.** E **13.** A **14.** B **15.** D **16.** B **17.** B **18.** B **19.** E **20.** A **21.** C **22.** B

23. In which season did the animals have enough to eat and drink?
A. Summer
B. Monsoon
C. All through the year
D. More than one of the above
E. None of the above

24. When the hunter came to the forest, it was
A. winter
B. monsoon
C. summer
D. More than one of the above
E. None of the above

25. Who killed the deer?
A. Rain God
B. Forest God
C. A hunter
D. More than one of the above
E. None of the above

भाग-II : हिन्दी भाषा

26. निम्नलिखित में से कौन-सा शब्द अव्यय **नहीं** है?
A. जूता
B. आज
C. भीतर
D. उपर्युक्त में से एक से अधिक
E. उपर्युक्त में से कोई नहीं

27. ह्रस्व, दीर्घ और प्लुत किसके प्रकार हैं?
A. संधि
B. व्यंजन
C. स्वर
D. उपर्युक्त में से एक से अधिक
E. उपर्युक्त में से कोई नहीं

28. तालव्य ध्वनियाँ कौन-सी हैं?
A. च, छ
B. ज, झ
C. ट, ढ
D. उपर्युक्त में से एक से अधिक
E. उपर्युक्त में से कोई नहीं

29. निम्नलिखित में से कौन-सा उत्तम पुरुषवाची शब्द **नहीं** है?
A. तुम
B. हमको
C. मुझमें
D. उपर्युक्त में से एक से अधिक
E. उपर्युक्त में से कोई नहीं

30. 'मरुभूमि में कहीं धान उगता है?' वाक्य में कौन-सा क्रिया-विशेषण है?
A. समयवाचक
B. रीतिवाचक
C. स्थानवाचक
D. उपर्युक्त में से एक से अधिक
E. उपर्युक्त में से कोई नहीं

31. निम्नलिखित में से कौन-सी लक्षणा की विशेषता है?
A. व्यंग्यार्थ
B. मुख्यार्थ
C. रूढ़ि का प्रयोग
D. उपर्युक्त में से एक से अधिक
E. उपर्युक्त में से कोई नहीं

32. विभाव किसे कहते हैं?
A. स्थायी भाव के उद्‌बोधक कारक
B. जिसमें रस उत्पन्न हो
C. जिसको रस उत्पन्न हो
D. उपर्युक्त में से एक से अधिक
E. उपर्युक्त में से कोई नहीं

33. 'लड़के ने कुत्ते को मारा।' वाक्य में कौन-सा कारक है?
A. करण और अपादान
B. संबंध और करण
C. अधिकरण और करण
D. उपर्युक्त में से एक से अधिक
E. उपर्युक्त में से कोई नहीं

34. कौन-सी संक्षिप्ति की विशेषता **नहीं** है?
A. संक्षिप्ति एक स्वतंत्र शब्द है
B. संक्षिप्ति मूल शब्द का अर्थ वहन करती है
C. यह शब्द अपने आप में पूर्णता नहीं रखता
D. उपर्युक्त में से एक से अधिक
E. उपर्युक्त में से कोई नहीं

23. B **24.** C **25.** C **26.** A **27.** C **28.** D **29.** A **30.** E **31.** D **32.** A **33.** E **34.** C

35. 'महाशय' शब्द में कौन-सी स्वर संधि है?
A. स्वर संधि
B. दीर्घ स्वर संधि
C. यण स्वर संधि
D. उपर्युक्त में से एक से अधिक
E. उपर्युक्त में से कोई नहीं

निर्देश (प्र.सं. 36 से 40 तक) : *अशुद्ध वाक्य दिए गए हैं, अतः शुद्ध वाक्य का चयन कर (A), (B), (C), (D) और (E) में से सही विकल्प का चयन कीजिए।*

36. हमने जो कहे थे वही सत्य है।
A. हमने कहे थे वहीं सत्य है।
B. हमने जो कहे रहे वह सत्य है।
C. हमने जो कहा था वही सत्य है।
D. उपर्युक्त में से एक से अधिक
E. उपर्युक्त में से कोई नहीं

37. आपका पत्र धन्यवाद सहित मिला।
A. आपका पत्र धन्यवाद के साथ मिला।
B. आपका पत्र मिला धन्यवाद।
C. धन्यवाद के साथ आपका पत्र मिला।
D. उपर्युक्त में से एक से अधिक
E. उपर्युक्त में से कोई नहीं

38. कृपया करके कार्यक्रम में पधारें।
A. कृपया कार्यक्रम में पधारें।
B. कृपा कर कार्यक्रम में पधारे।
C. कार्यक्रम में पधारे।
D. उपर्युक्त में से एक से अधिक
E. उपर्युक्त में से कोई नहीं

39. मुझसे बेफिजूल बात मत करो।
A. मुझसे फिजूल बात मत करे।
B. मुझसे बेफिजूल में बात मत करो।
C. बेफिजूल में मुझसे बात मत करो।
D. उपर्युक्त में से एक से अधिक
E. उपर्युक्त में से कोई नहीं

40. बिहारी ने गागर में सागर भर दिया है।
A. बिहारी गागर में सागर भर दिए है।
B. बिहारी ने गागर में सागर भरा है।
C. बिहारी ने गागर में सागर भर दिए रहे।
D. उपर्युक्त में से एक से अधिक
E. उपर्युक्त में से कोई नहीं

निर्देश (प्र.सं. 41 से 45 तक) : *निम्नलिखित शब्द किस भाषा का है? (A), (B), (C), (D) और (E) में से सही विकल्प का चयन कीजिए।*

41. बेगम
A. अरबी
B. फारसी
C. पुर्तगाली
D. उपर्युक्त में से एक से अधिक
E. उपर्युक्त में से कोई नहीं

42. सिनेमा
A. पुर्तगाली
B. फारसी
C. अंग्रेजी
D. उपर्युक्त में से एक से अधिक
E. उपर्युक्त में से कोई नहीं

43. अर्दली
A. अरबी
B. फारसी
C. पुर्तगाली
D. उपर्युक्त में से एक से अधिक
E. उपर्युक्त में से कोई नहीं

44. तौलिया
A. देशी भाषा
B. पुर्तगाली
C. फारसी
D. उपर्युक्त में से एक से अधिक
E. उपर्युक्त में से कोई नहीं

45. रिक्शा
A. जापानी
B. चीनी
C. अरबी
D. उपर्युक्त में से एक से अधिक
E. उपर्युक्त में से कोई नहीं

निर्देश (प्र.सं. 46 से 50 तक) : *दिए गए शब्दों के पर्यायवाची शब्द जो नहीं हैं, उनके लिए (A), (B), (C), (D) और (E) में से सही विकल्प का चयन कीजिए।*

46. दुर्जन
A. शठ
B. कपटी
C. कंजूस
D. उपर्युक्त में से एक से अधिक
E. उपर्युक्त में से कोई नहीं

35. B **36.** C **37.** B **38.** A **39.** A **40.** B **41.** E **42.** C **43.** E **44.** B **45.** A **46.** C

47. देह
A. काया
B. शरीर
C. तन
D. उपर्युक्त में से एक से अधिक
E. उपर्युक्त में से कोई नहीं

48. स्त्री
A. वनिता
B. कांता
C. सविता
D. उपर्युक्त में से एक से अधिक
E. उपर्युक्त में से कोई नहीं

49. बिजली
A. विद्युत्
B. आभा
C. चंचला
D. उपर्युक्त में से एक से अधिक
E. उपर्युक्त में से कोई नहीं

50. लक्ष्मी
A. उमा
B. रमा
C. कमला
D. उपर्युक्त में से एक से अधिक
E. उपर्युक्त में से कोई नहीं

निर्देश (प्र.सं. 51 से 55 तक) : *निम्नलिखित वाक्यों में ऐसी हिन्दी का प्रयोग कीजिए जो बोलचाल की भाषा है तथा (A), (B), (C), (D) और (E) में से सही विकल्प का चयन कीजिए।*

51. परीक्षाएँ सन्निकट हैं।
A. परीक्षाएँ दूर है।
B. परीक्षाएँ पास है।
C. परीक्षाएँ भविष्य में है।
D. उपर्युक्त में से एक से अधिक
E. उपर्युक्त में से कोई नहीं

52. बरसात में सरिताओं में बाढ़ आ जाती है।
A. बरसात में नदियों में बाढ़ आ जाती है।
B. बरसात में पहाड़ों पर भी बाढ़ आ जाती है।
C. बरसात में पूरी सृष्टि बाढ़ में डूब जाती है।
D. उपर्युक्त में से एक से अधिक
E. उपर्युक्त में से कोई नहीं

53. मैं आपसे नितांत अपरिचित हूँ।
A. मैं आपसे बिल्कुल अपरिचित हूँ।
B. मैं आपसे एकदम अपरिचित हूँ।
C. मैं आपसे सर्वथा अपरिचित हूँ।
D. उपर्युक्त में से एक से अधिक
E. उपर्युक्त में से कोई नहीं

54. दूरदर्शन की अनेक शृंखलाएँ प्रसिद्ध हैं।
A. दूरदर्शन के अनेक नाटक प्रसिद्ध हैं।
B. दूरदर्शन के अनेक फिल्में प्रसिद्ध हैं।
C. दूरदर्शन के अनेक धारावाहिक प्रसिद्ध हैं।
D. उपर्युक्त में से एक से अधिक
E. उपर्युक्त में से कोई नहीं

55. वे अभी नवधनाढ्य हुए हैं।
A. वह अभी धनी हुए हैं।
B. वह अभी नए अमीर हुए हैं।
C. वह अभी नौ दौलत मंद हुए हैं।
D. उपर्युक्त में से एक से अधिक
E. उपर्युक्त में से कोई नहीं

निर्देश (प्र.सं. 56 से 60 तक) : *दिए गए शब्दों के विलोम शब्द चुनकर (A), (B), (C), (D) और (E) में से सही विकल्प का चयन कीजिए।*

56. इच्छा
A. अइच्छा
B. आशा
C. अनिच्छा
D. उपर्युक्त में से एक से अधिक
E. उपर्युक्त में से कोई नहीं

57. उन्मूलन
A. उन्नयन
B. अवमूल्यन
C. रोपण
D. उपर्युक्त में से एक से अधिक
E. उपर्युक्त में से कोई नहीं

58. कर्कश
A. मधुर
B. कोमल
C. कठोर
D. उपर्युक्त में से एक से अधिक
E. उपर्युक्त में से कोई नहीं

47. E **48.** C **49.** B **50.** A **51.** B **52.** A **53.** D **54.** C **55.** B **56.** C **57.** C **58.** D

59. जंगम
A. वन
B. स्थावर
C. जंगल
D. उपर्युक्त में से एक से अधिक
E. उपर्युक्त में से कोई नहीं

60. शासक
A. शासित
B. पोषक
C. सत्ताधारी
D. उपर्युक्त में से एक से अधिक
E. उपर्युक्त में से कोई नहीं

निर्देश (प्र.सं. 61 से 65 तक) : *निम्नलिखित प्रत्येक वाक्य में एक शब्द रेखांकित है। प्रत्येक रेखांकित शब्द के लिए (A), (B), (C), (D) और (E) के सामने एक-एक विकल्प दिया गया है। इनमें से रेखांकित शब्द के लिए अर्थ की दृष्टि से उपयुक्त विकल्प चुनकर उत्तर-पुस्तिका में चिह्नित कीजिए।*

61. <u>शिशु</u> तेरी अनुपम छवि निहार
A. युवक
B. बालक
C. युवती
D. उपर्युक्त में से एक से अधिक
E. उपर्युक्त में से कोई नहीं

62. <u>युद्ध</u> निरंतर युद्ध विश्व है
A. शांति
B. अंधकार
C. संग्राम
D. उपर्युक्त में से एक से अधिक
E. उपर्युक्त में से कोई नहीं

63. गुमी हुई <u>आजादी</u> की कीमत सबने पहचानी थी
A. स्वाधीनता
B. गुलाम
C. गुलामी
D. उपर्युक्त में से एक से अधिक
E. उपर्युक्त में से कोई नहीं

64. जिसको सुन <u>रिपु</u> के दिल टूटे
A. शत्रु
B. आरि
C. आराति
D. उपर्युक्त में से एक से अधिक
E. उपर्युक्त में से कोई नहीं

65. सोम <u>सुधा</u> बरसाता
A. अमृत
B. अमरित
C. पियूष
D. उपर्युक्त में से एक से अधिक
E. उपर्युक्त में से कोई नहीं

निर्देश (प्र.सं. 66 से 70 तक) : *निम्नलिखित तत्सम शब्दों के लिए पाँच-पाँच विकल्प (A), (B), (C), (D) और (E) दिए गए हैं। इनमें से सर्वाधिक उपयुक्त विकल्प चुनकर उत्तर-पुस्तिका में चिह्नित कीजिए।*

66. खग
A. विहग
B. द्विज
C. खगी
D. उपर्युक्त में से एक से अधिक
E. उपर्युक्त में से कोई नहीं

67. गणेश
A. एकदन्त
B. नन्दी
C. नन्दन
D. उपर्युक्त में से एक से अधिक
E. उपर्युक्त में से कोई नहीं

68. काक
A. फिसफिस
B. काग
C. पिशुन
D. उपर्युक्त में से एक से अधिक
E. उपर्युक्त में से कोई नहीं

69. ठक
A. जालसाज
B. खौफ
C. त्रास
D. उपर्युक्त में से एक से अधिक
E. उपर्युक्त में से कोई नहीं

70. देह
A. वपु
B. क्षीर
C. पय
D. उपर्युक्त में से एक से अधिक
E. उपर्युक्त में से कोई नहीं

59. B **60.** A **61.** B **62.** C **63.** A **64.** A **65.** A **66.** D **67.** A **68.** D **69.** A **70.** A

निर्देश (प्र.सं. 71 से 75 तक) : *निम्नलिखित वाक्य के लिए एक शब्द चुनिए तथा (A), (B), (C), (D) और (E) में से सही विकल्प का चयन कीजिए।*

71. जिसके आने की तिथि न हो

A. अतिथि
B. पोषक
C. सत्ताधारी
D. उपर्युक्त में से एक से अधिक
E. उपर्युक्त में से कोई नहीं

72. जो लज्जा से रहित हो

A. निर्मम
B. निर्लज्ज
C. बेशर्म
D. उपर्युक्त में से एक से अधिक
E. उपर्युक्त में से कोई नहीं

73. जो सिंहासन का अधिकारी हो

A. युवराज
B. युग निर्माता
C. गद्दीधारी
D. उपर्युक्त में से एक से अधिक
E. उपर्युक्त में से कोई नहीं

74. वर्ष में एक बार होने वाला

A. वर्ष भर
B. वार्षिक
C. सालों तक
D. उपर्युक्त में से एक से अधिक
E. उपर्युक्त में से कोई नहीं

75. जो स्वेच्छा से सेवा करे

A. नौकर
B. स्वयं पाकी
C. स्वयं सेवक
D. उपर्युक्त में से एक से अधिक
E. उपर्युक्त में से कोई नहीं

निर्देश (प्र.सं. 76 से 80 तक) : *निम्नलिखित मुहावरों के उपयुक्त अर्थ का चयन कर (A), (B), (C), (D) और (E) में से सही विकल्प का चयन कीजिए।*

76. अंक भरना

A. खाली स्थानों को भरना
B. भाग्य चमकना
C. स्नेह से लिपटा लेना
D. उपर्युक्त में से एक से अधिक
E. उपर्युक्त में से कोई नहीं

77. आस्तीन का साँप

A. कपटी मित्र
B. मित्र को खतरा
C. मित्र को साँप काटना
D. उपर्युक्त में से एक से अधिक
E. उपर्युक्त में से कोई नहीं

78. किस खेत की मूली

A. अधिकारहीन
B. शक्तिहीन
C. हैसियत वाला
D. उपर्युक्त में से एक से अधिक
E. उपर्युक्त में से कोई नहीं

79. घड़ों पानी पड़ना

A. विजयी होना
B. पराजित होना
C. गर्वित होना
D. उपर्युक्त में से एक से अधिक
E. उपर्युक्त में से कोई नहीं

80. नाच नचाना

A. तंग करना
B. नृत्य सिखाना
C. नाच के लिए प्रेरित करना
D. उपर्युक्त में से एक से अधिक
E. उपर्युक्त में से कोई नहीं

निर्देश (प्र.सं. 81 से 85 तक) : *निम्नलिखित अशुद्ध शब्दों के लिए शुद्ध शब्द चुनिए तथा (A), (B), (C), (D) और (E) में से सही विकल्प का चयन कीजिए।*

81. अनाधिकार

A. अनधिकार
B. अनाधीकार
C. अन अधिकार
D. उपर्युक्त में से एक से अधिक
E. उपर्युक्त में से कोई नहीं

82. परलौकिक

A. परालौकिक
B. पारलौकिक
C. परालोकिक
D. उपर्युक्त में से एक से अधिक
E. उपर्युक्त में से कोई नहीं

71. A **72.** D **73.** A **74.** B **75.** C **76.** C **77.** A **78.** D **79.** E **80.** A **81.** A **82.** B

83. चांद
A. चॉन्द
B. चान्द
C. चाँद
D. उपर्युक्त में से एक से अधिक
E. उपर्युक्त में से कोई नहीं

84. सौंदर्यता
A. सौंदर्य
B. सोन्दरता
C. सुदर्य
D. उपर्युक्त में से एक से अधिक
E. उपर्युक्त में से कोई नहीं

85. परसाद
A. प्रशाद
B. प्रसाद
C. प्रषाद
D. उपर्युक्त में से एक से अधिक
E. उपर्युक्त में से कोई नहीं

निर्देश (प्र.सं. 86 से 90 तक) : *निम्नलिखित वाक्यों के सही प्रकार चुनिए तथा (A), (B), (C), (D) और (E) में से सही विकल्प का चयन कीजिए।*

86. उसने कहा कि मैं कल आऊँगी।
A. सरल वाक्य
B. संयुक्त वाक्य
C. मिश्र वाक्य
D. उपर्युक्त में से एक से अधिक
E. उपर्युक्त में से कोई नहीं

87. तुम जाओ और अपने पिताजी से कहना।
A. सरल वाक्य
B. संयुक्त वाक्य
C. मिश्र वाक्य
D. उपर्युक्त में से एक से अधिक
E. उपर्युक्त में से कोई नहीं

88. यह चित्र इस दीवार पर असंगत है।
A. आज्ञावाचक
B. निषेधवाचक
C. विधिवाचक
D. उपर्युक्त में से एक से अधिक
E. उपर्युक्त में से कोई नहीं

89. अरे! तुम अभी यहीं खड़े हो।
A. विस्मयबोधक
B. आश्चर्यबोधक
C. आज्ञार्थक
D. उपर्युक्त में से एक से अधिक
E. उपर्युक्त में से कोई नहीं

90. तुम सदा सुखी रहो।
A. इच्छार्थक
B. आज्ञार्थक
C. विधिवाचक
D. उपर्युक्त में से एक से अधिक
E. उपर्युक्त में से कोई नहीं

निर्देश (प्र.सं. 91 से 95 तक) : *निम्नलिखित शब्दों में प्रयुक्त प्रत्यय को पहचानकर सही विकल्प को उत्तर-पुस्तिका में चिह्नित कीजिए।*

91. स्वाधीन
A. धीन
B. न
C. अधीन
D. उपर्युक्त में से एक से अधिक
E. उपर्युक्त में से कोई नहीं

92. भुलौवल
A. वल
B. औवल
C. ल
D. उपर्युक्त में से एक से अधिक
E. उपर्युक्त में से कोई नहीं

93. बढ़िया
A. या
B. इया
C. ईया
D. उपर्युक्त में से एक से अधिक
E. उपर्युक्त में से कोई नहीं

94. झगड़ालू
A. ड़ालू
B. लू
C. आलू
D. उपर्युक्त में से एक से अधिक
E. उपर्युक्त में से कोई नहीं

83. C **84.** A **85.** B **86.** C **87.** B **88.** B **89.** D **90.** A **91.** C **92.** B **93.** B **94.** C

95. मनौती
A. औती
B. ती
C. औति
D. उपर्युक्त में से एक से अधिक
E. उपर्युक्त में से कोई नहीं

निर्देश (प्र.सं. 96 से 100 तक) : *निम्नलिखित अवतरण को ध्यानपूर्वक पढ़िए और पूछे गए प्रश्नों के सही विकल्प चुनकर उत्तर-पुस्तिका में चिह्नित कीजिए।*

संकटों से वीर घबराते नहीं,
आपदाएँ देख छिप जाते नहीं।
लग गए जिस काम में पूरा किया,
काम करके व्यर्थ पछताते नहीं।।
कठिन पथ को देख मुस्कुराते सदा,
संकटों के बीच वे गाते सदा।
है असंभव कुछ नहीं उनके लिए,
सरल-संभव कर दिखाते वे सदा।।

96. पद्यांश के लिए उपयुक्त शीर्षक है :
A. संकट के बादल
B. वीर
C. कठिन पथ
D. उपर्युक्त में से एक से अधिक
E. उपर्युक्त में से कोई नहीं

97. वीर संकटों को देखकर क्या करते हैं?
A. छिप जाते हैं
B. रोते हैं
C. सोते हैं
D. उपर्युक्त में से एक से अधिक
E. उपर्युक्त में से कोई नहीं

98. वीर सभी कार्य को कैसे करते हैं?
A. सोचते हुए
B. छिपते हुए
C. मुस्कुराते हुए
D. उपर्युक्त में से एक से अधिक
E. उपर्युक्त में से कोई नहीं

99. वीर किसे देखकर मुस्कुराते हैं?
A. मित्र
B. कठिन पथ
C. असंभव
D. उपर्युक्त में से एक से अधिक
E. उपर्युक्त में से कोई नहीं

100. 'आपदाएँ' शब्द का अर्थ क्या है?
A. विपत्ति
B. सम्मति
C. अनुमति
D. उपर्युक्त में से एक से अधिक
E. उपर्युक्त में से कोई नहीं

EXPLANATORY ANSWERS

1. **(B):** "An" is used before words that start with a vowel sound. In the phrase "SDO," which likely stands for a title like "Sub-Divisional Officer," the initial sound is a vowel sound (ess-dee-oh), hence "an SDO" is correct.

2. **(A):** The indefinite article "a" is used before words that begin with a consonant sound. In this sentence, "push" starts with a consonant sound, so "a push" is appropriate. The use of "a" suggests any push, not a specific one.

3. **(A):** "The" is the definite article used before a specific noun which is already known to the listener or reader. In this case, "the book I gave you yesterday" refers to a specific book that was given yesterday, making "the" the correct choice.

4. **(B):** "An" is used before words that start with a vowel sound. "Ear infection" starts with a vowel sound (ee-), so "an ear infection" is correct. This indicates Anand had a type of ear infection, but not a specific, previously known one.

5. **(A):** "A" is used before words that begin with a consonant sound. Since "University" starts with a 'yoo-' sound, which is a consonant sound, "a University" is correct. The use of "a" here suggests the name of the university is not specified or known to the listener.

6. **(C):** Birds and animals are not a part of a plant. Plants consist of parts like leaves and branches, but birds and animals are separate entities that may interact with plants but are not components of them.

95. A	**96.** B	**97.** E	**98.** C	**99.** B	**100.** A

7. **(C):** A toothbrush is not used in a computer. Computers typically include hardware components like hard drives and input devices like keyboards. A toothbrush, being a personal hygiene item, has no function in the operation or maintenance of a computer.

8. **(A):** A drier is not typically used in a kitchen. Kitchens usually contain appliances for cooking and food preparation, such as ovens and induction cooktops. A drier, more commonly associated with laundry and clothes drying, is not a standard kitchen appliance.

9. **(D):** More than one of the above options are not allowed in an examination. Mobile phones, earphones, and books are generally prohibited in exam settings to prevent cheating and distractions, ensuring the integrity of the examination.

10. **(C):** A telescope is not found in a hospital. Hospitals are equipped with medical personnel like nurses and facilities like operation theatres for patient care. A telescope, being an instrument for observing distant objects, typically in astronomy, has no relevance in a hospital setting.

11. **(B):** The person who writes a book is known as its author. An author is someone who creates and writes the content of a book. Readers, publishers, and others may be involved in the book's lifecycle, but the author is the one who actually writes it.

12. **(E):** If today is Wednesday, the day after tomorrow will be Friday. The progression of days follows a set order, so two days after Wednesday is Friday.

13. **(A):** We must not break traffic signals. Following traffic signals is a fundamental aspect of road safety and law. "Not break" means to adhere to the rules and signals while driving.

14. **(B):** If today is the 12th of December, the next month will be January. The sequence of months is fixed, with January coming after December in the Gregorian calendar.

15. **(D):** A month can have 28, 29, 30, or 31 days. Different months have varying numbers of days: February has 28 or 29 days (29 in a leap year), April, June, September, and November have 30 days, and the remaining months have 31 days.

16. **(B):** A daughter's daughter is her granddaughter. This term specifically refers to the female grandchild of a person.

17. **(B):** A grandfather's father is a great-grandfather. This term denotes the father of one's grandfather.

18. **(B):** A mother's father is referred to as a maternal grandfather. The term "maternal" indicates the relationship through the mother's side of the family.

19. **(E):** An aunt's daughter is neither a mother, grandmother, nor niece in relation to the person in question. The correct term for an aunt's daughter is a cousin, which describes the children of one's parents' siblings.

20. **(A):** Mother's and father's children are their sons and daughters, or in other terms, sisters and brothers to each other. This describes the sibling relationship within a family.

21. **(C):** The Forest God prayed to the Rain God. This is stated directly in the passage, indicating the Forest God's appeal for help to bring rain and alleviate the drought conditions in the forest.

22. **(B):** The Forest God was very sad that he could not protect his animals. The passage explicitly mentions this emotional response to the situation where animals were dying due to lack of water.

23. **(B):** The animals had enough to eat and drink in the monsoon season. The passage mentions that the arrival of the monsoon, which was a result of the Forest God's prayer to the Rain God, provided sufficient food and water for the animals.

24. **(C):** When the hunter came to the forest, it was summer. This is specified at the beginning of the passage, highlighting the challenging conditions due to water scarcity during this season.

25. **(C):** A hunter killed the deer. This is clearly stated in the passage, describing the action of the hunter in the forest during the summer.

26. **(A):** 'जूता' (shoe) अव्यय नहीं है। अव्यय वे शब्द होते हैं जो संज्ञा, सर्वनाम, विशेषण या क्रिया की तरह कार्य नहीं करते हैं। जूता एक संज्ञा है, जबकि 'आज' और 'भीतर' अव्यय हैं।

27. **(C):** 'ह्रस्व, दीर्घ और प्लुत' स्वरों के प्रकार हैं। ये तीनों शब्द वर्णमाला के स्वर खंड से संबंधित हैं, जहाँ स्वरों की विभिन्न अवधि को दर्शाया गया है।

28. **(D):** 'तालव्य ध्वनियाँ' वे ध्वनियाँ हैं जो तालु (जीभ के ऊपरी भाग) की सहायता से उत्पन्न होती हैं। 'च, छ' (च-वर्ग) और 'ज, झ' (ज-वर्ग) दोनों ही तालव्य ध्वनियाँ हैं।

29. **(A):** 'तुम' उत्तम पुरुष वाची शब्द नहीं है। उत्तम पुरुष वह होता है जो वक्ता को संबोधित करता है, जैसे 'मैं' या 'हम'।

'तुम' मध्यम पुरुष में आता है, जो संबोधित किए जाने वाले व्यक्ति को दर्शाता है। 'हमको' और 'मुझमें' उत्तम पुरुष वाची शब्द हैं।

30. (E): वाक्य 'मरुभूमि में कहीं धान उगता है?' में कोई क्रिया-विशेषण नहीं है। क्रिया-विशेषण वे शब्द होते हैं जो क्रिया की विशेषता बताते हैं, जैसे समय, स्थान, तरीका आदि। इस वाक्य में 'मरुभूमि' (रेगिस्तान) स्थान का उल्लेख करता है, लेकिन यह क्रिया-विशेषण नहीं है, बल्कि यह सिर्फ स्थान का संज्ञानात्मक वर्णन करता है।

31. (D): लक्षणा की विशेषता में 'व्यंग्यार्थ', 'मुख्यार्थ', और 'रूढ़ि का प्रयोग' सभी शामिल हैं। लक्षणा तब होती है जब शब्द का अर्थ इसके मूल अर्थ से अलग होता है, और यह व्यंग्य, मुख्यार्थ और रूढ़ि प्रयोग के जरिए हो सकता है।

32. (A): विभाव को 'स्थायी भाव के उद्‌बोधक कारक' के रूप में परिभाषित किया जाता है। नाट्यशास्त्र में, विभाव वह तत्व होता है जो रस की अनुभूति के लिए आवश्यक स्थायी भाव को जागृत करता है। इसमें अलंकार, पात्र, और परिस्थितियाँ शामिल हो सकती हैं।

33. (E): वाक्य 'लड़के ने कुत्ते को मारा' में 'लड़के' 'कर्ता' कारक है, और 'कुत्ते को' 'कर्म' कारक है। इस वाक्य में करण या अपादान कारक नहीं है।

34. (C): 'संक्षिप्ति' की विशेषता यह नहीं है कि यह शब्द अपने आप में पूर्णता नहीं रखता। संक्षिप्ति एक स्वतंत्र और मूल शब्द का अर्थ वहन करने वाला शब्द होता है, जो उसका संक्षेपित रूप होता है।

35. (B): 'महाशय' शब्द में 'दीर्घ स्वर संधि' है। यह शब्द 'महा' और 'आशय' के मिलन से बना है, जहां 'महा' के अंतिम 'अ' और 'आशय' के प्रारंभिक 'आ' का मेल होकर 'आ' बनता है, जो दीर्घ स्वर संधि का एक उदाहरण है।

36. (C): शुद्ध वाक्य है 'हमने जो कहा था वही सत्य है।' यहाँ 'कहे थे' की जगह 'कहा था' का प्रयोग होना चाहिए, क्योंकि वाक्य भूतकाल में है और 'हमने' के साथ 'कहा था' का प्रयोग उचित है।

37. (B): शुद्ध वाक्य है 'आपका पत्र मिला धन्यवाद।' 'धन्यवाद सहित' की जगह 'धन्यवाद' का प्रयोग वाक्य को अधिक स्पष्ट और सही बनाता है।

38. (A): शुद्ध वाक्य है 'कृपया कार्यक्रम में पधारें।' 'कृपया करके' का प्रयोग अतिरिक्त है, और 'पधारें' शिष्टाचारपूर्ण आमंत्रण हेतु सही शब्द है।

39. (A): शुद्ध वाक्य है 'मुझसे फिजूल बात मत करो।' 'बेफिजूल' का प्रयोग अशुद्ध है, और सही शब्द 'फिजूल' है।

40. (B): शुद्ध वाक्य है 'बिहारी ने गागर में सागर भरा है।' यहाँ 'भर दिया है' की जगह 'भरा है' का प्रयोग उचित है, जो किसी काम को पूर्ण करने की क्रिया को दर्शाता है।

41. (E): 'बेगम' शब्द तुर्की भाषा का है। यह शब्द मुख्य रूप से उच्च स्थान पर आसीन महिलाओं या रानियों के लिए प्रयोग किया जाता है।

42. (C): 'सिनेमा' शब्द अंग्रेजी भाषा का है। सिनेमा शब्द ग्रीक भाषा के किनेमेटोग्राफोस–किनेमा और ग्रामो से बना है। किनेमा का अर्थ आंदोलन और ग्रामो का अर्थ है लिखना या रिकॉर्ड करना।

43. (E): 'अर्दली' शब्द का मूल न तो अरबी, फारसी, न ही पुर्तगाली भाषा में है। यह शब्द तुर्की भाषा से आया है और सैन्य सहायक या व्यक्तिगत सहायक के लिए प्रयोग किया जाता है।

44. (B): 'तौलिया' शब्द पुर्तगाली भाषा का है। यह शब्द वस्त्र या तौलिये के संदर्भ में प्रयोग किया जाता है।

45. (A): 'रिक्शा' शब्द जापानी भाषा का है। यह शब्द एक प्रकार के छोटे वाहन के लिए प्रयोग किया जाता है जिसे मानव द्वारा खींचा जाता है।

46. (C): 'कंजूस' दुर्जन का पर्यायवाची शब्द नहीं है। दुर्जन का अर्थ होता है दुष्ट या बुरे व्यक्ति, जिसके पर्यायवाची शब्द हैं 'शठ' और 'कपटी'। 'कंजूस' का अर्थ है मितव्ययी या कृपण, जो दुर्जन के अर्थ से भिन्न है।

47. (E): 'काया', 'शरीर', और 'तन' सभी देह के पर्यायवाची शब्द हैं। देह का अर्थ होता है शरीर, और इन सभी शब्दों का प्रयोग शरीर के लिए किया जाता है।

48. (C): 'सविता' स्त्री का पर्यायवाची शब्द नहीं है। स्त्री का अर्थ होता है महिला या नारी, जिसके पर्यायवाची शब्द हैं 'वनिता' और 'कांता'। 'सविता' सूर्य देवता की पत्नी या देवी का नाम है, जो स्त्री के अर्थ से भिन्न है।

49. (B): 'आभा' बिजली का पर्यायवाची शब्द नहीं है। बिजली का अर्थ होता है विद्युत, जिसके पर्यायवाची शब्द हैं 'विद्युत्' और 'चंचला'। 'आभा' का अर्थ होता है प्रकाश या चमक, जो बिजली के अर्थ से भिन्न है।

50. (A): 'उमा' लक्ष्मी का पर्यायवाची शब्द नहीं है। लक्ष्मी धन और समृद्धि की देवी हैं, जिनके पर्यायवाची शब्द हैं 'रमा' और 'कमला'। 'उमा' हिन्दू धर्म में पार्वती या शक्ति का एक नाम है, जो लक्ष्मी से भिन्न है।

51. (B): 'परीक्षाएँ पास है' वाक्य 'परीक्षाएँ सन्निकट हैं' के समान अर्थ रखता है। 'पास' शब्द का इस्तेमाल बोलचाल की भाषा में 'निकट' या 'सन्निकट' के समान अर्थ में होता है।

52. (A): 'बरसात में नदियों में बाढ़ आ जाती है' वाक्य 'बरसात में सरिताओं में बाढ़ आ जाती है' के समान अर्थ रखता है। 'नदियों' शब्द का इस्तेमाल बोलचाल में 'सरिताओं' के समान अर्थ में होता है।

53. (D): 'मैं आपसे बिल्कुल अपरिचित हूँ' वाक्य 'मैं आपसे नितांत अपरिचित हूँ' के समान अर्थ रखता है। 'बिल्कुल' शब्द का प्रयोग बोलचाल की भाषा में 'नितांत' के समान अर्थ में होता है।

54. (C): 'दूरदर्शन के अनेक धारावाहिक प्रसिद्ध हैं' वाक्य 'दूरदर्शन की अनेक शृंखलाएँ प्रसिद्ध हैं' के समान अर्थ रखता है। धारावाहिक का प्रयोग बोलचाल की भाषा में टीवी शो या सीरीज के लिए किया जाता है।

55. (B): 'वह अभी नए अमीर हुए हैं' वाक्य 'वे अभी नवधनाढ्य हुए हैं' के समान अर्थ रखता है। 'नए अमीर' का प्रयोग बोलचाल की भाषा में हाल ही में धनी बने लोगों के लिए होता है।

56. (C): 'इच्छा' का विलोम 'अनिच्छा' है। इच्छा का अर्थ है चाहना या चाह, और अनिच्छा का अर्थ है न चाहना या न चाह।

57. (C): 'उन्मूलन' का विलोम 'रोपण' है। उन्मूलन का अर्थ होता है जड़ से उखाड़ना या नष्ट करना, जबकि रोपण का अर्थ है पौधे लगाना या रोपना।

58. (D): कर्कश का अर्थ होता है कठोर या रूखा, इसलिए इसका विलोम मधुर एवं कोमल होगा।

59. (B): 'जंगम' का विलोम 'स्थावर' है। जंगम का अर्थ है चलायमान या गतिशील, और स्थावर का अर्थ है स्थिर या अचल।

60. (A): 'शासक' का विलोम 'शासित' है। शासक का अर्थ है वह जो शासन करता है, और शासित का अर्थ है वह जिस पर शासन किया जाता है।

61. (B): 'शिशु' का अर्थ होता है बालक या छोटा बच्चा। इसलिए यहाँ सही विकल्प 'बालक' है।

62. (C): 'युद्ध' का अर्थ होता है संग्राम या लड़ाई। इसलिए यहाँ सही विकल्प 'संग्राम' है।

63. (A): 'आजादी' का अर्थ होता है स्वाधीनता या स्वतंत्रता। इसलिए यहाँ सही विकल्प 'स्वाधीनता' है।

64. (A): 'रिपु' का अर्थ होता है 'शत्रु या दुश्मन। इसलिए यहाँ सही विकल्प 'शत्रु' है।

65. (A): 'सोम' का एक अर्थ होता है अमृत, जो देवताओं का पेय होता है। इसलिए यहाँ सही विकल्प 'अमृत' है।

66. (D): 'खग' का अर्थ होता है पक्षी, और इसके पर्यायवाची शब्द हैं 'विहग' और 'खगी'। 'द्विज' भी पक्षियों के लिए प्रयोग किया जाता है, लेकिन इसका प्राथमिक अर्थ ब्राह्मण या दूसरी बार जन्मा हुआ होता है।

67. (A): 'गणेश' के लिए सर्वाधिक उपयुक्त तत्सम शब्द 'एकदन्त' है, जो गणेश जी का एक नाम है और उनके एक दांत के होने का संदर्भ देता है।

68. (D): 'काक' का अर्थ होता है कौवा, और इसके पर्यायवाची शब्द हैं 'फिसफिस' और 'पिशुन'। 'काग' भी कौवे के लिए प्रयोग किया जाता है।

69. (A): 'ठग' का अर्थ होता है धोखेबाज या चालाक, और इसके पर्यायवाची शब्द में 'जालसाज' शामिल है।

70. (A): 'देह' का अर्थ होता है शरीर, और इसके पर्यायवाची शब्द में 'वपु' शामिल है। 'क्षीर' और 'पय' का संबंध दूध या तरल पदार्थ से है, जो देह के अर्थ से अलग है।

71. (A): 'जिसके आने की तिथि न हो' के लिए सही शब्द 'अतिथि' है। अतिथि का अर्थ होता है वह व्यक्ति जिसके आने की कोई निश्चित तिथि न हो।

72. (D): 'जो लज्जा से रहित हो' के लिए सही शब्द निर्लज्ज और 'बेशर्म' है। इसका अर्थ होता है वह व्यक्ति जिसमें लज्जा या शर्म की कमी हो।

73. (A): 'जो सिंहासन का अधिकारी हो' के लिए सही शब्द 'युवराज' है। युवराज का अर्थ होता है वह व्यक्ति जो सिंहासन या राज-पद का अधिकारी हो।

74. (B): 'वर्ष में एक बार होने वाला' के लिए सही शब्द 'वार्षिक' है। वार्षिक का अर्थ होता है कुछ ऐसा जो हर साल एक बार होता है।

75. (C): 'जो स्वेच्छा से सेवा करे' के लिए सही शब्द 'स्वयंसेवक' है। स्वयंसेवक का अर्थ होता है वह व्यक्ति जो अपनी इच्छा से, बिना किसी बाध्यता के, सेवा करता है।

76. (C): 'अंक भरना' मुहावरे का अर्थ होता है स्नेह से लिपटा लेना या गले लगाना। यह प्यार या आत्मीयता दर्शाने के लिए प्रयोग किया जाता है।

77. (A): 'आस्तीन का साँप' मुहावरे का अर्थ होता है कपटी मित्र या धोखेबाज दोस्त। यह ऐसे व्यक्ति के लिए प्रयोग किया जाता है जो दिखावे में तो मित्र है पर वास्तव में शत्रुता रखता है।

78. (D): 'किस खेत की मूली' मुहावरे का अर्थ होता है अधिकारहीन या शक्तिहीन या ऐसा व्यक्ति जिसका कोई महत्व नहीं होता। इसका प्रयोग किसी की अहमियत या स्थिति को कम करके आंकने के लिए किया जाता है।

79. (E): 'घड़ों पानी पड़ना' मुहावरे का अर्थ उपलब्ध विकल्पों में से किसी से मेल नहीं खाता। इस मुहावरे का अर्थ होता है अचानक बहुत अधिक नुकसान होना या किसी बड़ी आपदा का होना।

80. **(A):** 'नाच नचाना' मुहावरे का अर्थ होता है तंग करना या किसी काम में असमर्थ होना। इसका प्रयोग अक्सर उस स्थिति में किया जाता है जब कोई व्यक्ति अपनी अक्षमता के लिए बहाने बनाता है और दूसरों को तंग करता है।

81. **(A):** 'अनाधिकार' का शुद्ध रूप 'अनधिकार' है।

82. **(B):** 'परलौकिक' का शुद्ध रूप 'पारलौकिक' है, जिसका अर्थ होता है परलोक से संबंधित या दिव्य।

83. **(C):** 'चांद' का शुद्ध रूप 'चाँद' है।

84. **(A):** 'सौंदर्यता' का शुद्ध रूप 'सौंदर्य' है।

85. **(B):** 'परसाद' का शुद्ध रूप 'प्रसाद' है। यह शब्द आमतौर पर देवताओं को अर्पित भोजन या पदार्थों के बाद भक्तों को दिए जाने वाले पवित्र भोजन या वस्तु के लिए प्रयोग किया जाता है।

86. **(C):** 'उसने कहा कि मैं कल आऊँगी।' यह वाक्य मिश्र वाक्य है।

87. **(B):** 'तुम जाओ और अपने पिताजी से कहना।' यह वाक्य संयुक्त वाक्य है क्योंकि इसमें दो सरल वाक्यों को 'और' के माध्यम से जोड़ा गया है।

88. **(B):** 'यह चित्र इस दीवार पर असंगत है।' यह वाक्य निषेधवाचक है क्योंकि इसमें चित्र के दीवार पर होने की अनुपयुक्तता या असंगतता का वर्णन किया गया है।

89. **(D):** 'अरे! तुम अभी यहीं खड़े हो।' इस वाक्य में विस्मयबोधक और आश्चर्यबोधक दोनों तत्व मौजूद हैं। इसमें आश्चर्य और विस्मय का भाव व्यक्त होता है।

90. **(A):** 'तुम सदा सुखी रहो।' यह वाक्य इच्छार्थक है क्योंकि इसमें किसी के लिए सुखी रहने की कामना या इच्छा व्यक्त की गई है।

91. **(C):** 'स्वाधीन' शब्द में प्रयुक्त प्रत्यय 'अधीन' है। इसमें 'स्व' उपसर्ग है और 'अधीन' मूल शब्द है।

92. **(B):** 'भुलौवल' शब्द में प्रयुक्त प्रत्यय 'औवल' है। 'भुल' मूल शब्द है और 'औवल' प्रत्यय है।

93. **(B):** 'बढ़िया' शब्द में प्रयुक्त प्रत्यय 'इया' है। 'बढ़' मूल शब्द है और 'इया' प्रत्यय है।

94. **(C):** 'झगड़ालू' शब्द में प्रयुक्त प्रत्यय 'आलू' है। 'झगड़' मूल शब्द है और 'आलू' प्रत्यय है।

95. **(A):** 'मनौती' शब्द में प्रयुक्त प्रत्यय 'औती' है। 'मन' मूल शब्द है और 'औती' प्रत्यय है।

96. **(B):** इस पद्यांश का उपयुक्त शीर्षक 'वीर' है, क्योंकि यह पूरे पद्यांश में वीरता और साहसिकता की भावना को दर्शाता है।

97. **(E):** वीर संकटों को देखकर न तो छिपते हैं, न रोते हैं, और न ही सोते हैं। इसलिए उपलब्ध विकल्पों में से कोई भी सही नहीं है।

98. **(C):** वीर सभी कार्यों को मुस्कराते हुए पूरा करते हैं और व्यर्थ पछताते नहीं हैं।

99. **(B):** वीर कठिन पथ को देखकर मुस्कुराते हैं, जो उनकी साहसिकता और सकारात्मक दृष्टिकोण को दर्शाता है।

100. **(A):** 'आपदाएँ' शब्द का अर्थ 'विपत्ति' या संकट होता है।

PAPER-3*

Part-I : General Studies

1. 10 years ago the ratio of ages of Ramesh and Rajeev was 1 : 3. 5 years hence this ratio will become 2 : 3. What is the ratio of their ages at present?

A. 2 : 5
B. 3 : 5
C. 1 : 2
D. More than one of the above
E. None of the above

2. If I walk with a speed of 5 km per hour from my house to the station, my train would have left the station 7 minutes before my arrival. But, if I walk with a speed of 6 km per hour, I will reach the station 5 minutes before the departure of my train. Accordingly, what is the distance between my house and the station?

A. 7 km
B. 6.5 km
C. 6 km
D. More than one of the above
E. None of the above

3. The average monthly income of P and Q is ₹ 5,050. The average monthly income of Q and R is ₹ 6,250 and the average monthly income of P and R is ₹ 5,200. The monthly income of P is:

A. ₹ 3,500
B. ₹ 4,050
C. ₹ 4,000
D. More than one of the above
E. None of the above

4. If 30% of P is added to 40% of Q, it becomes 80% of Q. Accordingly, what is the percentage of Q with respect to P?

A. 40%
B. 50%
C. 75%
D. More than one of the above
E. None of the above

5. A sum of money is to be distributed among A, B, C, D in the proportion of 5 : 2 : 4 : 3. If C gets ₹ 1,000 more than D, what is B's share?

A. ₹ 500
B. ₹ 1,500
C. ₹ 2,000
D. More than one of the above
E. None of the above

6. A shopkeeper gives a discount of 5% on the selling price of a watch. If he gives a discount of 6%, he will earn a profit which is ₹ 15 less than the before. Accordingly, what is the marked selling price of that watch?

A. ₹ 1,400
B. ₹ 1,500
C. ₹ 1,800
D. More than one of the above
E. None of the above

7. Three numbers are in the ratio 3 : 4 : 5. The total of the largest and the smallest numbers is equal to the other number plus 52. Accordingly, which is the smallest number?

A. 27
B. 39
C. 52
D. More than one of the above
E. None of the above

8. If $2^{2n-1} = \frac{1}{8^{n-3}}$, then the value of n is:

A. 3
B. 2
C. −2
D. More than one of the above
E. None of the above

9. Which of the following photoelectric devices is the most suitable for digital applications?

A. Photo-voltaic cell
B. Photo-emissive cell
C. Photo-diode
D. More than one of the above
E. None of the above

1. B	2. C	3. C	4. C	5. C	6. B	7. B	8. B	9. A

*Exam held on 26-08-2023.

10. The critical mass of a fissionable material is:
A. one kilogram equivalent
B. the minimum mass needed for chain reaction
C. the rest mass equivalent to 10^{10} joules
D. More than one of the above
E. None of the above

11. Which of the following gases is used to force the ripening of fruits?
A. Ethane
B. Ethylene
C. Methylene
D. More than one of the above
E. None of the above

12. Which one of the following has zero octane number?
A. Iso-octane
B. Neo-octane
C. *n*-octane
D. More than one of the above
E. None of the above

13. The edible part of Litchis is:
A. aril
B. thalamus
C. seed coat
D. More than one of the above
E. None of the above

14. The physical process involved in the release of molecular oxygen from leaves is:
A. diffusion
B. transpiration
C. osmosis
D. More than one of the above
E. None of the above

15. The process of finding the relative location of genes on a chromosome is called:
A. genome walking
B. chromosome walking
C. gene mapping
D. More than one of the above
E. None of the above

16. Spore mother cell in bryophytes is:
A. haploid
B. diploid
C. triploid
D. More than one of the above
E. None of the above

17. In which year was NGT (National Green Tribunal) for protection of environment and forest established by the Government of India?
A. 2010
B. 2011
C. 2012
D. More than one of the above
E. None of the above

18. Which city of India started first under-water metro?
A. Kochi
B. Visakhapatnam
C. Bengaluru
D. More than one of the above
E. None of the above

19. Under India's G20 Presidency, where was the Tourism Working Group Meeting held?
A. Patna (Bihar)
B. Srinagar (Jammu and Kashmir)
C. Ramnagar (Uttarakhand)
D. More than one of the above
E. None of the above

20. Who among the following got the Silver Medal in the National Under-17 Girls Wrestling Championship?
A. Liza Tomar
B. Nirjala
C. Pushpa Yadav
D. More than one of the above
E. None of the above

21. Who won the International Booker Prize, 2022 for the novel, *Tomb of Sand*?
A. Geetanjali Shree and Daisy Rockwell
B. David Diop and Anna Moschovakis
C. Marilyn Booth and Jokha Alharthi
D. More than one of the above
E. None of the above

22. Who was the Chief Guest on India's 74th Republic Day?
A. Mohammed bin Salman
B. Abdel Fattah El-Sisi
C. Sheikh Mohammed bin Rashid Al Maktoum
D. More than one of the above
E. None of the above

23. In which district of Bihar, the first floating solar power plant has been built?
A. Darbhanga
B. West Champaran
C. Madhubani
D. More than one of the above
E. None of the above

10. B	**11.** B	**12.** E	**13.** A	**14.** A	**15.** C	**16.** B
17. A	**18.** E	**19.** B	**20.** B	**21.** A	**22.** B	**23.** A

24. Which of the following has got GI Tag in Bihar?
A. Maghai Paan
B. Basmati Rice
C. Chanderi Saree
D. More than one of the above
E. None of the above

25. Match List–I with List–II:

List-I	List-II
(*a*) Char	1. Punjab plain
(*b*) Kankar	2. Delta
(*c*) Kayal	3. Bangar
(*d*) Mand	4. Coastal plain

Select the correct answer using the codes given below.

	(*a*)	(*b*)	(*c*)	(*d*)
A.	1	4	2	3
B.	2	3	4	1
C.	3	1	4	2

D. More than one of the above
E. None of the above

26. Which of the following tributaries does ***not*** join Brahmaputra river from north?
A. Subansiri
B. Belsiri
C. Manas
D. More than one of the above
E. None of the above

27. Likhapani glacier is located in which State of India?
A. Arunachal Pradesh
B. Himachal Pradesh
C. Sikkim
D. More than one of the above
E. None of the above

28. Magadha and Anga plains are parts of:
A. upper Ganga plain
B. middle Ganga plain
C. lower Ganga plain
D. More than one of the above
E. None of the above

29. Which of the following pairs of waterfalls and rivers is ***not*** correctly matched?
A. Jog — Sharavati
B. Kapildhara — Kaveri
C. Dhuandhar — Godavari
D. More than one of the above
E. None of the above

30. Arrange the following seaports of India from north to south:
1. Kakinada
2. Machilipatnam
3. Nagapattinam
4. Visakhapatnam

Select the correct answer using the codes given below.
A. 1, 2, 3, 4
B. 4, 1, 2, 3
C. 1, 3, 2, 4
D. More than one of the above
E. None of the above

31. The Agreement of Kosi Irrigation and Hydro-electricity Plan in 1954 was signed between which two countries?
A. India and Bangladesh
B. India and China
C. India and Nepal
D. More than one of the above
E. None of the above

32. In which climatic division does Bihar fall as per R.L. Singh's classification scheme?
A. Humid south-east
B. Subhumid transitional
C. Subhumid continental
D. More than one of the above
E. None of the above

33. In which Session of the Indian National Congress was the resolution of 'Purna Swaraj' adopted?
A. Kanpur Session, 1925
B. Lahore Session, 1929
C. Karachi Session, 1931
D. More than one of the above
E. None of the above

34. What was an initial objective of 'Kuka Movement' in Punjab?
A. To purify the Sikh religion
B. To gain political power in Punjab
C. Organization of peasant movement
D. More than one of the above
E. None of the above

35. Who described the Revolt of 1857 as the 'First Indian War of Independence'?
A. V.D. Savarkar
B. Bal Gangadhar Tilak
C. Bipin Chandra Pal
D. More than one of the above
E. None of the above

24. A **25.** B **26.** E **27.** A **28.** B **29.** D **30.** B **31.** C **32.** B **33.** B **34.** A **35.** A

36. Where was the first instance of organized non-cooperation in the history of Indian peasantry held?

A. Bihar and Bengal
B. Madras Presidency
C. Punjab Province
D. More than one of the above
E. None of the above

37. Which portfolio did Dr. Rajendra Prasad hold during the Interim Government of 1946?

A. Defence
B. Home
C. Food and Agriculture
D. More than one of the above
E. None of the above

38. Who among the following particularly urged Gandhiji to visit Champaran to witness the miseries of the Ryots?

A. Brijkishore Prasad
B. Rajkumar Shukla
C. Sukhram Ganesh
D. More than one of the above
E. None of the above

39. The 'Day of Deliverance' was observed by the Muslim League on which date?

A. 22nd December, 1939
B. 17th October, 1939
C. 22nd December, 1940
D. More than one of the above
E. None of the above

40. Who laid the foundation stone of National College and Bihar Vidyapeeth?

A. Dr. Rajendra Prasad
B. Maulana Abdul Bari
C. Mahatma Gandhi
D. More than one of the above
E. None of the above

Part-II : English

Directions (Q. Nos. 41 to 65): *Read the passage given below and answer the questions that follow.*

It is a cold night in December and in a remote village, an old storyteller is sitting by the hearth-fire with a group of students who have come home for the winter holidays. They love visiting her to listen to her stories, but tonight Granny is not her usual chirpy self; she looks much older and seems to be agitated over something. One of the boys asks her whether she is not feeling well and tells her that if so, they can come back another night. But instead of answering the question, the old woman starts talking and tells them that on a certain night a peculiar wind blows through the village, which seems to start from the region of the graveyard and which sounds like a hymn. She also tells them that tonight is that kind of a night. At first the youngsters are skeptical and tell her that they cannot hear anything and that such things are not possible, but the old woman rebukes them by saying that they are not paying attention to what is happening around them. She tells them that youngsters of today have forgotten how to listen to the voice of the earth and the wind. They feel chastised and make a show of straining their ears to listen more attentively and to their utter surprise, they hear the beginning of a low hum in the distance. They listen for some time and tell her, almost in triumph, that they can hear only an eerie sound. 'No', the storyteller almost shouts, 'Listen carefully. Tonight is the anniversary of that dreadful Sunday.' There is a death-like silence in the room and some of them begin to look uneasy because they too had heard vague rumours of army atrocities that took place in the village on a Sunday long before they were born. Storyteller and audience strain to listen more attentively and suddenly a strange thing happens : as the wind whirls past the house, it increases in volume and for the briefest of moments, seems to hover above the house. Then it resumes its whirling as though hurrying away to other regions beyond human habitation. The young people are stunned because they hear the new element in the volume and a certain uncanny lilt lingers on in the wake of its departure. The old woman jumps up from her seat and looking at each one in turn asks, 'You heard it, didn't you? Didn't I tell you? It was Apenyo's last song' and she hums a tune softly, almost to herself. The youngsters cannot deny that they heard the note but are puzzled because they do not know what she is talking about. As the old woman stands apart humming the tune, they look at her with wonder. There is a peculiar glow on her face and she seems to have changed into a new self, more alive and animated than earlier. After a while a young girl timidly approaches her and asks, 'Grandmother, what are you talking about? Whose last song?'

The old storyteller whips around and surveys the group as though seeing them for the first time. She then heaves a deep sigh and with infinite sadness in her voice, spreads her arms wide and whispers, 'You have not heard about that song? You do not know about Apenyo? Then come and listen carefully ...'

36. A	37. C	38. B	39. A	40. C

Thus, on a cold December night in a remote village, an old storyteller gathers the young of the land around the leaping flames of a hearth and squats on the bare earth among them to pass on the story of that Black Sunday when a young and beautiful singer sang her last song even as one more Naga village began weeping for her ravaged and ruined children.

[An extract from 'The Last Song' in These Hills Called Home, by Temsula Ao, Penguin Books, New Delhi : 2006, p. 31–33]

41. Why was the grandmother listless that night?
A. She was unwell
B. She was too old
C. She was anxious
D. More than one of the above
E. None of the above

42. How best can one describe the character of the storyteller?
A. Garrulous and cantankerous old woman
B. Cheerful and lively old lady
C. Indolent and grumpy old lady
D. More than one of the above
E. None of the above

43. What does the term 'hearth-fire' indicate?
A. Fireplace
B. Stove
C. Grate
D. More than one of the above
E. None of the above

44. What was so special about 'that night'?
A. It was a stormy night with incessant thunder and rain
B. It was that fateful night when a peculiar wind blew
C. It was a silent night when the moon had a lurid glow
D. More than one of the above
E. None of the above

45. What is the trajectory that the song takes in the story?
A. The song arises from the graveyard filling the whole village and disappears beyond human habitation
B. The song arises from the graveyard filling the whole village with good cheer and dissipates into nothingness
C. The song arises from the graveyard filling the whole village with sadness and fades away gradually
D. More than one of the above
E. None of the above

46. Why do listeners gather to hear stories at night in remote villages upon the hills of North-East India?
A. They are engaged in factories and offices during the day
B. They are engaged in their farms, collection of firewood and water, and other mundane affairs
C. They are engaged in the textile and mining industry
D. More than one of the above
E. None of the above

47. Pick out a synonym for the word 'rebuke' from the extract.
A. Chastised
B. Agitated
C. Ravaged
D. More than one of the above
E. None of the above

48. Which word in the story indicates supernatural elements?
A. Eerie
B. Uncanny
C. Uneasy
D. More than one of the above
E. None of the above

49. Describe the look on the storyteller's face when they all clearly hear the tune of the song.
A. Stunned
B. Alive and animated
C. Puzzled
D. More than one of the above
E. None of the above

50. How would you describe the listeners?
A. As casual and irresponsible
B. As carefree and lighthearted
C. As polite and considerate
D. More than one of the above
E. None of the above

51. What is the role of the storyteller in Naga society?
A. A bearer of traditional lore
B. A bearer of history
C. A bearer of truth
D. More than one of the above
E. None of the above

52. Which colloquial word is an equivalent of the term 'grandmother' that has been used in the extract?
A. Grandma
B. Granny
C. Matriarch
D. More than one of the above
E. None of the above

41. C **42.** B **43.** D **44.** B **45.** A **46.** E **47.** A **48.** D **49.** B **50.** C **51.** D **52.** B

53. Why does the storyteller feel that the 'youngsters of today have forgotten how to listen to the voice of the earth and the wind'?
A. As they are skeptical
B. As they are inattentive
C. As they are disbelievers
D. More than one of the above
E. None of the above

54. What is the initial note of the song compared to in the extract of the story?
A. A hymn
B. Blowing of a peculiar wind
C. A low hum
D. More than one of the above
E. None of the above

55. Pick up an equivalent of the word 'cadence' or 'rhythm' from the extract of the story.
A. Hum
B. Lilt
C. Tune
D. More than one of the above
E. None of the above

56. Which phrase in the extract of the story describes the feeling of surprise or astonishment with reference to the storyteller?
A. Peculiar glow on her face
B. More alive and animated
C. As though seeing them for the first time
D. More than one of the above
E. Nonc of the above

57. The narrator seemed out of joint because
A. she was unwell
B. she was listless
C. she was trapped in dark thoughts
D. More than one of the above
E. None of the above

58. Which phrase in the extract is a close equivalent of 'pin-drop silence'?
A. Death-like silence
B. Haunted silence
C. Icy silence
D. More than one of the above
E. None of the above

59. What made the listeners 'skeptical'?
A. They were educated
B. They were rational
C. They could hear nothing
D. More than one of the above
E. None of the above

60. Which elemental feeling is most prominent in the story?
A. Tragic
B. Elegiac
C. Ghostly
D. More than one of the above
E. None of the above

61. Which word in the extract is closest in meaning to the phrase 'whips around'?
A. Whirling
B. Hover
C. Blows
D. More than one of the above
E. None of the above

62. Why is the narrator described as 'chirpy'?
A. As she chirps like a bird
B. As she is cheerful
C. As she is ill-tempered
D. More than one of the above
E. None of the above

63. What memories did the song bring back to the narrator and the listeners?
A. Anniversary of that dreadful Sunday
B. Death anniversary of Apenyo
C. An incidence of violence
D. More than one of the above
E. None of the above

64. Why is that particular day referred to as 'Black Sunday'?
A. Death of Apenyo and atrocities suffered by the villagers on a certain Sunday
B. Religious associations with the crucifixion of Lord Jesus Christ
C. Atrocities suffered by the villagers on a certain Sunday
D. More than one of the above
E. None of the above

65. Why do you think the narrator 'squats on the bare earth'?
A. She was too poor to have furniture
B. She didn't like sitting on stools and chairs
C. It was a common way of sitting by the village folk of Nagaland
D. More than one of the above
E. None of the above

Directions (Q. Nos. 66 to 75): *Read each of the following sentences to find out whether there is an error or errors in any underlined part(s). If you feel that there is no error in a sentence, write (E) to signify 'None of the above'.*

53. D	**54.** A	**55.** D	**56.** C	**57.** C	**58.** A	**59.** D
60. B	**61.** E	**62.** B	**63.** A	**64.** A	**65.** C	

66. Distribute these (A)/ mangoes between all (B)/ the fifty students. (C)/ More than one of the above (D)/ None of the above (E)

67. Unless you don't (A)/ work hard, (B)/ you can't get success. (C)/ More than one of the above (D)/ None of the above (E)

68. Start early, (A)/ lest you should (B)/ miss the train. (C)/ More than one of the above (D)/ None of the above (E)

69. He talked (A)/ as if he (B)/ was a mad. (C)/ More than one of the above (D)/ None of the above (E)

70. My watch, (A)/ which was damaged (B)/ is now useless. (C)/ More than one of the above (D)/ None of the above (E)

71. She ought (A)/ to have obey (B)/ her parents. (C)/ More than one of the above (D)/ None of the above (E)

72. You will get wet (A)/ if you will (B)/ go out in the rain. (C)/ More than one of the above (D)/ None of the above (E)

73. He is one (A)/ of greatest (B)/ leader of my country. (C)/ More than one of the above (D)/ None of the above (E)

74. Neither you (A)/ nor he (B)/ are guilty. (C)/ More than one of the above (D)/ None of the above (E)

75. Neither of the (A)/ three pens (B)/ will do. (C)/ More than one of the above (D)/ None of the above (E)

76. She _____ alone in the city for almost a decade now. (Use past perfect continuous)

A. has been living
B. had been living
C. was living
D. More than one of the above
E. None of the above

77. He fled where his pursuers could not follow.
The underlined section is:

A. an adjective clause
B. an adverb clause
C. an adverb phrase
D. More than one of the above
E. None of the above

78. The umbrella with a wooden handle is mine. (Identify the correct clause/phrase for the underlined part)

A. An adjective clause
B. An adverb clause
C. An adverb phrase
D. More than one of the above
E. None of the above

79. I have some duties. I must perform them. (Use an infinitive to join the sentences)

A. I must perform the duties that I have.
B. I must perform some of the duties that I have.
C. I have some duties to perform.
D. More than one of the above
E. None of the above

80. He deserved to succeed. He failed. (Use an adverb or an adverbial phrase to join the sentences)

A. He deserved to succeed but he failed.
B. He failed undeservedly.
C. He failed though he deserved to succeed.
D. More than one of the above
E. None of the above

81. Her husband died. She heard the news. She fainted. (Use a preposition with a noun or gerund to join the sentences)

A. She fainted when she heard the news of her husband's death.
B. On hearing the news of her husband's death she fainted.
C. As soon as she heard the news of her husband's death she fainted.
D. More than one of the above
E. None of the above

82. He jumped up. He ran away. (Use a participle to join the sentences)

A. Jumping up he ran away.
B. He jumped up and ran away.
C. He ran away after jumping up.
D. More than one of the above
E. None of the above

83. Insert the punctuation marks in the following:

She read the short story Kafan and adapted it to a radio play

A. She read the short story ''Kafan'' and adapted it to a radio play.
B. She read the short story 'Kafan' and adapted it to a radio play
C. She read the short story 'Kafan' and adapted it to a radio play
D. More than one of the above
E. None of the above

66. B	**67.** A	**68.** E	**69.** C	**70.** E	**71.** B	**72.** B	**73.** D	**74.** C
75. D	**76.** B	**77.** B	**78.** E	**79.** C	**80.** B	**81.** B	**82.** A	**83.** C

84. If he is at home, I shall see him. It is a:
A. simple sentence
B. compound sentence
C. complex sentence
D. More than one of the above
E. None of the above

85. You must hurry or you will miss the train. It is a:
A. simple sentence
B. compound sentence
C. complex sentence
D. More than one of the above
E. None of the above

Directions (Q. Nos. 86 to 95): *Choose the correct option of the following questions.*

86. 'You ate fish' is an example of:
A. clause
B. phrase
C. sentence
D. More than one of the above
E. None of the above

87. Which one of the following options is correct about the sentence, "That which cannot be read."?
A. Illegible
B. Ineligible
C. Invisible
D. More than one of the above
E. None of the above

88. The antonym of the word 'scurrilous' is:
A. outrageous
B. decent
C. moderate
D. More than one of the above
E. None of the above

89. "I left <u>that</u> house."

What is the underlined word 'that', according to the English grammar?
A. Demonstrative pronoun
B. Adverb
C. Noun
D. More than one of the above
E. None of the above

90. The correctly spelt word in the following is:
A. Synchronize
B. Synchromize
C. Syncronize
D. More than one of the above
E. None of the above

91. The misspelt word in the following is:
A. Irrepressible
B. Beaurocracy
C. Pussilanimity
D. More than one of the above
E. None of the above

92. A person who is bad in spelling is known as:
A. philogynist
B. phonologist
C. cacographist
D. More than one of the above
E. None of the above

93. The word most nearly opposite to the word 'opprobrious' is:
A. Vituperative
B. Complimentary
C. Truculent
D. More than one of the above
E. None of the above

94. The term 'quinquennial' stands for:
A. happening in four years
B. happening in six years
C. happening in seven years
D. More than one of the above
E. None of the above

95. A compound sentence consists of:
A. two principal clauses
B. one principal clause
C. one principal clause and one subordinate clause
D. More than one of the above
E. None of the above

96. The Prince said, "It gives me great pleasure to be here this evening." (Change into reported speech)
A. The Prince said, it gives me great pleasure to be here this evening.
B. The Prince said, it gave me great pleasure to be here this evening.
C. The Prince said, it had given him great pleasure to be here this evening.
D. More than one of the above
E. None of the above

97. He inquired whether his name was not Ahmed. (Change into direct speech)
A. He said to him, 'Is not your name Ahmed?'
B. He said to him, "Is not your name Ahmed?"
C. He said to him, 'Is your name not Ahmed?'
D. More than one of the above
E. None of the above

84. C	**85.** B	**86.** C	**87.** A	**88.** D	**89.** E	**90.** A
91. D	**92.** C	**93.** B	**94.** E	**95.** A	**96.** E	**97.** B

98. dot your is and cross your ts then add two 5s and four 2s (Use punctuation marks)

A. Dot your is and cross your ts; then add two 5's and four 2's.

B. Dot your is and cross your t's; then add two 5's and four 2's

C. Dot your i's and cross your t's; then add two 5's and four 2's.

D. More than one of the above

E. None of the above

99. 'Moonlight' is a compound word that is formed by:

A. noun + noun

B. adjective + noun

C. noun + gerund

D. More than one of the above

E. None of the above

100. 'Red-hot' is a compound word that is formed by:

A. noun + noun

B. adjective + adjective

C. noun + gerund

D. More than one of the above

E. None of the above

101. He who has suffered most in the cause, let him speak.

The correct sentence is

A. Let him who has suffered most in the cause speak.

B. He who has suffered most in the cause should speak.

C. Let him speak as has suffered most in the cause.

D. More than one of the above

E. None of the above

102. What a terrible fire this is (Use punctuation mark)

A. Full stop

B. Exclamation mark

C. Question mark

D. More than one of the above

E. None of the above

103. He <u>broke</u> the glass. (Change the underlined word into intransitive verb)

A. The glass was broken.

B. The glass breaked.

C. The glass broke.

D. More than one of the above

E. None of the above

104. I <u>am reading</u> *David Copperfield*. (Point out the tense used in the underlined part)

A. Past continuous

B. Present continuous

C. Future continuous

D. More than one of the above

E. None of the above

105. Why did your brother write such a letter? (Change into passive voice)

A. Why was such a letter written by your brother?

B. How could such a letter be written by your brother?

C. What made your brother write such a letter?

D. More than one of the above

E. None of the above

Directions (Q. Nos. 106 to 110): *Choose the most appropriate meaning of the underlined idioms or phrases given below.*

106. <u>A bolt from the blue</u>

A. Sudden calamity

B. A strange person

C. Blue sky

D. More than one of the above

E. None of the above

107. <u>Do away with</u>

A. To obey

B. To do honestly

C. To destroy

D. More than one of the above

E. None of the above

108. <u>To cast a slur on</u>

A. To praise

B. To blame

C. To accuse

D. More than one of the above

E. None of the above

109. <u>To be at sea</u>

A. Known

B. Confused

C. Forced

D. More than one of the above

E. None of the above

110. <u>In almost no time</u>

A. Quickly

B. Hardly

C. Lately

D. More than one of the above

E. None of the above

98. C	**99.** A	**100.** B	**101.** D	**102.** B	**103.** C	**104.** B
105. A	**106.** A	**107.** C	**108.** D	**109.** B	**110.** A	

Directions (Q. Nos. 111 to 115): *Fill in the blanks with suitable words.*

111. He has been ill _____ Tuesday.
A. for
B. on
C. in
D. More than one of the above
E. None of the above

112. She writes _____ a pen.
A. with
B. by
C. from
D. More than one of the above
E. None of the above

113. The car was running _____ 40 km/h.
A. on
B. up
C. at
D. More than one of the above
E. None of the above

114. He died _____ cholera.
A. from
B. of
C. with
D. More than one of the above
E. None of the above

115. There is a river _____ my residence.
A. to
B. at
C. beside
D. More than one of the above
E. None of the above

116. "Yesterday I saw the film *Macbeth*. I found the story interesting. The film's hero, Macbeth, assassinates King Duncan and ascends the throne of Scotland. But he is dissatisfied. He finds himself in a dangerous situation. He executes those he suspects of plotting against him. Eventually, some of the lords revolted and dethroned him and killed him. The message it conveys is that excessive ambition destroys a man. The actor and actress who played Macbeth and Lady Macbeth had exceptional performances, which significantly increased the film's impact."

The extract is an example of a
A. film review
B. summary
C. paraphrase
D. More than one of the above
E. None of the above

117. Delineate the qualities of a good paragraph.
A. It has to be short
B. It has to be precise
C. It has to be to the point
D. More than one of the above
E. None of the above

118. Read the extract given below :
Student : Good morning Sir, how are you?
Teacher : I am completely fine. What about you?
Student : I was wondering which course to learn in my vacation.
Teacher : It can be confusing with so many options online. You should make a list and narrow it down as per your interest.
Student : I have tried that but still I am left with three options—Artificial Intelligence, Machine Learning or Data Science.
Teacher : Well! All of them are very interesting courses, but as far as I remember you have always been interested in Artificial Intelligence.
Student : Yes ! I do because I feel it is our future.
Teacher : Well then its no harm in pursuing it and later if you find it less interesting you can always switch.
Student : Yes it sounds like a great idea. Thanks !

The above extract is an example of
A. a conversation
B. a dialogue
C. a monologue
D. More than one of the above
E. None of the above

119. Point out the error in the extract given in Q. No. 118.
A. Use of tenses
B. Use of adverbial clauses
C. Use of prepositions
D. More than one of the above
E. None of the above

120. bought/few/several/like/medicines/items/vegetables/kinds/many/of/a/and/he/avocados. (Arrange the words to make a meaningful sentence)
A. He bought a few items like medicines, several vegetables and many kinds of avocados.
B. He bought several items like medicines, a few vegetables and many kinds of avocados.
C. He bought several items like medicines, many kinds of vegetables and a few avocados.
D. More than one of the above
E. None of the above

111. E	112. A	113. C	114. B	115. C	116. D	117. D	118. D	119. E	120. C

EXPLANATORY ANSWERS

1. (B): Let 10 years ago the ages of Ramesh and Rajeev was x years and $3x$ years

Then, present age of Ramesh and Rajeev are $x + 10$ years and $3x + 10$ years

5 years hence,

$(x + 10 + 5) : (3x + 10 + 5) = 2 : 3$

$\Rightarrow \quad (x + 15) : (3x + 15) = 2 : 3$

$\Rightarrow \quad (x + 15) \times 3 = (3x + 15) \times 2$

$\Rightarrow \quad 3x + 45 = 6x + 30$

$\Rightarrow \quad 6x - 3x = 45 - 30$

$\Rightarrow \quad 3x = 15 \Rightarrow x = 5$

$\therefore$ The ratio of their present ages

$= (x + 10) : (3x + 10)$

$= 15 : 25$

$= 3 : 5.$

2. (C): Let the distance between house and the station be d km.

Then, $\dfrac{d}{5} - \dfrac{7}{60} = \dfrac{d}{6} + \dfrac{5}{60}$

$\Rightarrow \quad \dfrac{d}{5} - \dfrac{d}{6} = \dfrac{7}{60} + \dfrac{5}{60}$

$\Rightarrow \quad \dfrac{d}{30} = \dfrac{12}{60}$

$\Rightarrow \quad \dfrac{d}{30} = \dfrac{1}{5} \Rightarrow d = 6$ km

Hence, the distance between my house and the station is 6 km.

3. (C): The total income of

$P + Q = 2 \times ₹\ 5050 = ₹\ 10100 \quad ...(i)$

$Q + R = 2 \times ₹\ 6250 = ₹\ 12500 \quad ...(ii)$

$P + R = 2 \times ₹\ 5200 = ₹\ 10400 \quad ...(iii)$

From adding (*i*), (*ii*) and (*iii*), we obtain

$\therefore\ 2(P + Q + R) = ₹\ 10100 + ₹\ 12500 + ₹\ 10400$

$\Rightarrow \quad P + Q + R = \dfrac{33000}{2}$

$\Rightarrow \quad P + Q + R = ₹\ 16500 \quad ...(iv)$

Subtracting (*ii*) from (*iv*), we obtain

$P = 16500 - 12500 = ₹\ 4000$

Hence, the monthly income of P is ₹ 4000.

4. (C): Given,

$P \times \dfrac{30}{100} + Q \times \dfrac{40}{100} = Q \times \dfrac{80}{100}$

$\Rightarrow \quad 3P + 4Q = 8Q$

$\Rightarrow \quad 3P = 8Q - 4Q$

$\Rightarrow \quad 3P = 4Q$

$\Rightarrow \quad \dfrac{P}{Q} = \dfrac{4}{3}$

Now, $\quad P \times \dfrac{x}{100} = Q$

$\Rightarrow \quad 4 \times \dfrac{x}{100} = 3$

$\Rightarrow \quad x = 75\%$

Hence, Q is 75% with respect to P.

5. (C): Let the share of A, B, C and D are ₹ $5x$, ₹ $2x$, ₹ $4x$ and ₹ $3x$

Then, $\quad 4x - 3x = ₹\ 1000$

$\Rightarrow \quad x = ₹\ 1000$

$\therefore \quad$ B's share $= 2x = 2 \times 1000 = ₹\ 2000.$

6. (B): Let the marked selling price of watch be ₹ x

Then, $\quad x \times \dfrac{100-5}{100} - x \times \dfrac{100-6}{100} = ₹\ 15$

$\Rightarrow \quad x \times \dfrac{95}{100} - x \times \dfrac{94}{100} = ₹\ 15$

$\Rightarrow \quad \dfrac{x}{100} = ₹\ 15$

$\Rightarrow \quad x = ₹\ 1500$

$\therefore$ The marked selling price of watch = ₹ 1500.

7. (B): Let three numbers are $3x$, $4x$ and $5x$

Then, $\quad 5x + 3x = 4x + 52$

$\Rightarrow \quad 8x = 4x + 52$

$\Rightarrow \quad 8x - 4x = 52$

$\Rightarrow \quad 4x = 52$

$\Rightarrow \quad x = 13$

Hence, the smallest number $= 3x = 3 \times 13 = 39.$

8. (B): Given, $\quad 2^{2n-1} = \dfrac{1}{8^{n-3}}$

$\Rightarrow \quad 2^{2n-1}\ 8^{n-3} = 1$

$\Rightarrow \quad 2^{2n-1} . 2^{3(n-3)} = 1$

$\Rightarrow \quad 2^{2n-1} . 2^{3n-9} = 1$

$\Rightarrow \quad 2^{2n-1} + 3^{n-9} = 1$

$\Rightarrow \quad 2^{5n-10} = 1$

$\Rightarrow \quad 2^{5n-10} = 2^0$

$\Rightarrow \quad 5^{n-10} = 0$

$\Rightarrow \quad n = 2.$

9. (A): Among the options provided, the photo-diode is the most suitable for digital applications. Photo-diodes are semiconductor devices that convert light into electrical current. They are fast, sensitive, and capable of operating in a wide range of light wavelengths, making them ideal for various digital and optical applications, such as in sensors, communication devices, and photometers. This makes them more suitable for digital applications compared to photo-voltaic cells and photo-emissive cells, which are typically used for different purposes.

10. **(B):** The critical mass of a fissionable material is indeed the minimum mass necessary for a sustained nuclear chain reaction. It is a precise quantity at which a fissionable material, such as uranium or plutonium, can maintain a chain reaction under specific conditions without an additional neutron source. This critical mass depends on several factors, including the material's purity, its shape, and the conditions under which it's held.

11. **(B):** Ethylene is the gas typically used to expedite the ripening process of fruits. It is a naturally occurring plant hormone and is employed commercially to trigger the ripening of fruits after harvesting. Ethylene affects the ripening by influencing various biochemical pathways. Ethane and methylene are not used for this purpose, making ethylene the correct choice for the gas used to force the ripening of fruits.

12. **(E):** In the context of octane ratings, iso-octane is defined as having an octane rating of 100, but *n*-octane does not have a zero octane number; it has a lower octane number than iso-octane, but it is not zero. Octane number is a measure of a fuel's performance in internal combustion engines, specifically its resistance to knocking or pinging. There is no commonly used compound in this context that would have a zero octane number. Therefore, the correct option is E, None of the above.

13. **(A):** The edible part of lychees is the aril. The aril is the fleshy part surrounding the seed inside the lychee fruit. This part is sweet, juicy, and is commonly eaten fresh. The other parts of the lychee, such as the seed coat and the thalamus, are not eaten.

14. **(A):** The physical process involved in the release of molecular oxygen from leaves is diffusion. In the process of photosynthesis, oxygen is produced as a byproduct in the leaves' chloroplasts. This oxygen then diffuses out of the leaves into the atmosphere. Transpiration is the process of water vapor loss from plants, and osmosis is the movement of water across a semipermeable membrane, but neither of these processes involves the release of oxygen.

15. **(C):** The process of determining the relative locations of genes on a chromosome is known as gene mapping. Gene mapping is used to assign/identify the location of genes and the distances between genes on a chromosome. Genome walking and chromosome walking are techniques used in molecular genetics for isolating long sequences of DNA, but they are not specifically about determining the relative location of genes.

16. **(B):** In bryophytes, the spore mother cell is diploid. These cells undergo meiosis to produce haploid spores, which is a part of the reproductive cycle of bryophytes. Bryophytes, like all plants, have a life cycle that includes both diploid and haploid stages. The spore mother cell is part of the diploid generation, known as the sporophyte.

17. **(A):** The National Green Tribunal (NGT) was established in 2010 by the Government of India. It was created for effective and expeditious disposal of cases relating to environmental protection and conservation of forests and other natural resources. The NGT Act, 2010 was enacted for this purpose, and the Tribunal has been empowered to handle cases relating to environmental issues.

18. **(E):** The first under-water metro in India was started in Kolkata, not in any of the cities listed in the options. Kolkata's East-West Metro includes a section that runs under the Hooghly River, making it the first underwater metro project in India. Therefore, the correct answer is not among the given options.

19. **(B):** Under India's G20 Presidency, the Tourism Working Group Meeting was held in Srinagar, Jammu and Kashmir. This event was part of the series of meetings and events organized in different locations across India during its G20 Presidency.

20. **(B):** Nirjala was the one who got the Silver Medal in the National Under-17 Girls Wrestling Championship. This question is very specific, and the correct answer would be based on the latest available information or specific knowledge about this event. Assuming the given answer is correct, Nirjala is the athlete who won the silver medal in this category.

21. **(A):** Geetanjali Shree and Daisy Rockwell won the International Booker Prize in 2022 for the novel "Tomb of Sand." This novel, originally written in Hindi by Geetanjali Shree and titled "Ret Samadhi," was translated into English by Daisy Rockwell. It is noteworthy for being the first Hindi language work to win the prestigious International Booker Prize.

22. **(B):** The Chief Guest on India's 74th Republic Day was Abdel Fattah El-Sisi, the President of Egypt. Each year, India invites a prominent international leader to be the chief guest at the Republic Day celebrations in New Delhi. In 2023, President El-Sisi was accorded this honor, marking a significant event in the diplomatic relations between India and Egypt.

23. **(A):** The first floating solar power plant in Bihar has been built in Darbhanga district. Floating solar power plants are an innovative form of solar energy generation where solar panels are mounted on a structure that floats on a body of water, typically a reservoir or a lake. This setup is beneficial in regions where land availability is limited or land use is prioritized for other purposes.

24. **(A):** Maghai Paan from Bihar has received the Geographical Indication (GI) tag. A GI tag is a sign used on products that have a specific geographical origin and possess qualities or a reputation that are due to that origin. Maghai Paan is known for its unique taste and qualities and is associated with the Magadh region of Bihar. Basmati Rice and Chanderi Saree have also received GI tags, but they are associated with other regions of India, not Bihar.

25. **(B):** Matching geographical terms with their respective regions, we have:

- Char refers to the sandbanks in river deltas, matching with Delta.
- Kankar is a type of calcareous soil found in the Indo-Gangetic Plain, particularly associated with Bangar, the older alluvial deposits.
- Kayal refers to backwaters, which are typically found along the Coastal plain.
- Mand is related to floodplains in Punjab, hence it corresponds to Punjab plain.

Therefore, the correct match is (*a*)-2, (*b*)-3, (*c*)-4, (*d*)-1, which is option B.

26. **(E):** Among the given tributaries, Subansiri, Belsiri, and Manas, all join the Brahmaputra river from the north. Therefore, none of the listed tributaries are incorrect; they all join the Brahmaputra from the north.

27. **(A):** The Likhapani glacier is located in Arunachal Pradesh, India. This state in the northeastern part of India is known for its diverse topography, including a significant portion of the Himalayas and various glaciers.

28. **(B):** Magadha and Anga plains are part of the middle Ganga plain. The Ganga plain is divided into upper, middle, and lower plains based on their geographical location and characteristics. The Magadha and Anga regions, historically significant areas in India, fall into the middle Ganga plain category.

29. **(D):** The waterfalls and their respective rivers need to be correctly matched:

- Jog Falls is indeed on the Sharavati River.
- Kapildhara Falls is on the Narmada River, not the Kaveri, making option B incorrect.
- Dhuandhar Falls is on the Narmada River as well, not the Godavari, making option C incorrect.

Since both options B and C are incorrect, the answer is D (More than one of the above).

30. **(B):** Arranging the seaports from north to south:

- Visakhapatnam is the northernmost among the given options.
- Kakinada is south of Visakhapatnam.
- Machilipatnam is further south of Kakinada.
- Nagapattinam is the southernmost among these.

Therefore, the correct order is 4 (Visakhapatnam), 1 (Kakinada), 2 (Machilipatnam), 3 (Nagapattinam), which corresponds to option B.

31. **(C):** The Agreement of Kosi Irrigation and Hydroelectricity Plan in 1954 was a bilateral agreement between India and Nepal. This agreement was for the construction and maintenance of a barrage and related works on the Kosi River, which flows through both countries. Thus, the correct answer is C.

32. **(B):** According to R. L. Singh's classification scheme of climatic regions in India, Bihar falls under the 'Subhumid Transitional' climate zone. This classification is based on various climatic parameters, including temperature, rainfall, and humidity. Bihar's climate features a transition between the humid eastern parts of India and the drier western regions. Hence, the correct answer is B (Subhumid transitional).

33. **(B):** The resolution of 'Purna Swaraj' (complete independence) was adopted at the Lahore Session of the Indian National Congress in December 1929. The Congress declared 26th January 1930 as Independence Day. This session was a significant event in the Indian freedom struggle. The correct answer is B (Lahore Session, 1929).

34. **(A):** The initial objective of the 'Kuka Movement' in Punjab was to purify the Sikh religion. It was a socio-religious reform movement in the mid-19th century, led by Guru Ram Singh. The Kukas sought to remove corrupt practices and restore Sikhism to its original purity. Thus, the correct answer is A (To purify the Sikh religion).

35. **(A):** The Revolt of 1857 was described as the 'First Indian War of Independence' by Vinayak Damodar Savarkar. He wrote a book with this title, emphasizing the national and unified nature of the rebellion. Therefore, the correct answer is A (V. D. Savarkar).

36. **(A):** The first instance of organized non-cooperation in Indian peasantry is widely recognized as the Champaran Satyagraha in Bihar, in 1917, led by Mahatma Gandhi. This movement was against the oppressive plantation system in the Champaran district of Bihar. There was also significant peasant movement in Bengal during this period. Thus, the correct answer is A (Bihar and Bengal).

37. **(C):** Dr. Rajendra Prasad held the portfolio of Food and Agriculture during the Interim Government of 1946. He later became the first President of India after independence. The correct answer is C (Food and Agriculture).

38. **(B):** Rajkumar Shukla, a farmer from Champaran, was instrumental in urging Mahatma Gandhi to visit

Champaran to witness the miseries of the ryots (tenants) and to address the issue of forced indigo cultivation. Shukla persistently followed Gandhi to various meetings to convince him to go to Champaran. The correct answer is B (Rajkumar Shukla).

39. **(A):** The 'Day of Deliverance' was observed by the Muslim League on 22nd December, 1939. This was in celebration of the resignation of all members of the Indian National Congress from provincial and central offices in protest against the Viceroy's decision to enter World War II without consulting them. The correct answer is A (22nd December, 1939).

40. **(C):** Mahatma Gandhi laid the foundation stone of the National College and Bihar Vidyapeeth. These institutions were established as part of the national education movement and played a significant role in the freedom struggle by providing alternative education to Indians. The correct answer is C (Mahatma Gandhi).

41. **(C):** In the passage, it's mentioned that the grandmother, who is usually chirpy, appears to be agitated to that question but instead begins talking about a peculiar wind in the village. This diversion from the question suggests that there is something on her mind, and she later reveals that it is the anniversary of a dreadful Sunday, hinting at past tragic events in the village. Therefore, the most accurate interpretation is that she was anxious about the anniversary of the tragic events linked to the peculiar wind and the village history.

42. **(B):** While she appears different on the cold December night, being agitated and not her usual chirpy self, her transformation later in the story, when she jump up, hums a tune, and seems more alive and animated, suggestes a lively and animated, character. Therefore, "Cheerful and lively old lady" is a more fitting description in the context of the passage.

43. **(D):** The term 'hearth-fire' refers to more than one thing, such as a fireplace, stove, or grate. While the term is generally associated with a fireplace, it can sometimes be used more broadly to encompass the broader concept of a place where a fire is kept, which could include a stove or grate.

44. **(B):** The passage mentions that the storyteller tells the students that on a certain night, a peculiar wind blows through the village, starting from the region of the graveyard and sounding like a hymn. This wind is associated with significant events, and on the specific night in question, the storyteller reveals that it is the anniversary of a dreadful Sunday, linking it to past tragic events in the village.

45. **(A):** According to the passage, as the wind (associated with the song) whirls past the house, it increases in volume, seems to hover above the house for the briefest of moments, and then resumes its whirling as though hurrying away to other regions beyond human habitation. The trajectory of the song is described as emanating from the graveyard, filling the whole village, and then disappearing beyond human habitation.

46. **(E):** The passage doesn't provide explict information about why listeners gather to hear stories at night in remote villages upon the hills of North-East India.

47. **(A):** The term "rebuke" is used when the old woman scolds or admonishes the youngsters for not paying attention to what is happening around them. It implies a strong disapproval or criticism of their behaviour. In the context, the synonum "chastised" is appropriate because it also denotes a form of reprimand or correction for their lack of attentiveness.

48. **(D):** The term "eerie" is explicitly used: "they hear only an eerie sound." The word "eerie" typically conveys a sense of the mysterious or supernatural, contributing to the overall atmosphere of the story.

The term "uncanny" is used to describe something strange or mysterious, sometimes with a supernatural undertone. So, both "eerie" and "uncanny" are words that, in a broader sense, indicate a supernatural or mysterious element in the story.

49. **(B):** The passage describes the storyteller's transformation after the young people clearly hear the tune of the song. It mentions that there is a peculiar glow on her face, and she seems to have changed into a new self, more alive and animated than earlier. Therefore, "Alive and animated" is the most fitting description of the look on the storyteller's face in that moment.

50. **(C):** The passage portrays the listeners as initially skeptical, later chastised by the storyteller, and ultimately stunned when they hear the tune of the song. The listeners do engage with the storyteller, with the specific qualities of being "polite" and "considerate". The passage mainly focuses on the listeners' reactions to the storyteller's tale and the mysterious events unfolding in the story.

51. **(D):** In the context of the passage, the storyteller serves multiple roles in Naga society. The old woman is not only a bearer of traditional lore, as she recounts stories about the peculiar wind and the events associated with it, but she also imparts historical information by mentioning the anniversary of a dreadful Sunday and the army atrocities that took place in the village. Additionally, the storyteller is portrayed as someone who conveys a sense of truth or significance to the events she narrates, creating a connection between the past and the present.

So, the storyteller in Naga society can be seen as fulfilling the roles of a bearer of traditional lore, a bearer of history, and a conveyer of truths.

52. **(B):** In the given extract, the term used for "grandmother" is "Granny." This is a colloquial and informal word commonly used to refer to a grandmother. Colloquial language often involves informal, everyday expressions used in ordinary conversation, and "Granny" falls into this category as a familiar term for addressing or mentioning one's grandmother.

53. **(D):** The storyteller expresses the sentiment that the "youngsters of today have forgotten how to listen to the voice of the earth and the wind." This feeling seems to be rooted in the skepticism and inattention displayed by the youngsters in the passage. They initially dismiss the storyteller's mention of the peculiar wind and express disbelief in such things. Therefore, both skepticism and inattention contribute to the storyteller's perception that the younger generation is disconnected from the natural elements and traditional understanding conveyed by the wind and the earth.

54. **(A):** The storyteller describes the peculiar wind that blows through the village, especially on certain nights. This wind, associated with the song, is likened to a hymn. The specific comparison is made in the following part of the passage:

    "...on a certain night a peculiar wind blows through the village, which seems to start from the region of the graveyard and which sounds like a hymn."

55. **(D):** The term "lilt" is used to describe the rhythm or cadence of the song. When the wind, associated with the song, passes by the house, it leaves behind a certain uncanny lilt. The use of "lilt" suggests a distinctive and lively rhythm or cadence in the sound of the wind or the song.

    Additionally, the word "tune" can also be associated with the melody or rhythm of a song. In the context of the passage, when the old woman asks the youngsters if they heard Apenyo's last song, "tune" is mentioned, and it refers to the specific musical quality or melody of the song.

56. **(C):** In the passage, after the young people express surprise at hearing the tune of the song, the old woman, or storyteller, is described as looking at each one in turn "as though seeing them for the first time." This phrase implies a sense of astonishment or fresh perception on the part of the storyteller. It suggests that the unexpected events have had a profound impact on her, causing her to view the young people with renewed attention or a changed perspective. So, this expression conveys the storyteller's response of surprise or astonishment after the listeners hear the song, and it signifies a shift in her demeanor or perception.

57. **(C):** In the passage, the narrator, described as the old storyteller, appears agitated and not her usual chirpy self. The text doesn't explicitly state that she was unwell or listless, but it does suggest that she looks much older and seems to be agitated over something. The phrase "she was trapped in dark thoughts" captures the idea that there is a deeper emotional or mental disturbance affecting the narrator's usual demeanor.

58. **(A):** The phrase "death-like silence" is a vivid and strong expression that describes an absolute and profound quietness, as if in the presence of death itself. It suggests a silence so deep and intense that it is almost palpable, comparable to the silence in a room or space where every sound is hushed and barely perceptible. In the context of the passage, the use of "death-like silence" serves a similar purpose, conveying the gravity and stillness in the room as the storyteller and the audience listens attentively to the mysterious events.

59. **(D):** The listeners' skepticism could be influenced by multiple factors, such as education and rationality. While these factors may contribute to skepticism in some individuals, the passage explicitly mentions that their initial skepticism is based on the fact that they could hear nothing and thought such things were not possible.

60. **(B):** The most prominent elemental feeling in the story appears to be elegiac. The passage revolves around the old storyteller recounting events associated with a peculiar wind and a song, particularly on the anniversary of a dreadful Sunday. The tone is reflective, mournful, and nostalgic, evoking a sense of sadness or lamentation. This elegiac feeling is tied to the tragic events in the village's history, creating a poignant atmosphere throughout the narrative.

61. **(E):** The phrase "whips around" isn't directly mirrored by a single word in the options. The phrase "whips around" typically suggests a sudden and forceful movement, almost as if something is rapidly turning or changing direction. So the options provided are not directly related to the word 'whips around'.

62. **(B):** In the context of the passage, the term "chirpy" is used to describe the usual demeanor of the narrator. It suggests that the narrator is typically cheerful or lively. The word "chirpy" is often used informally to describe someone who is in good spirits or has an animated and lively manner.

63. **(A):** In the passage, the storyteller mentions that the peculiar wind and the associated song bring back memories, specifically tied to the anniversary of a dreadful Sunday. The storyteller hints at past events, alluding to an incidence of violence that occurred in

the village on a Sunday long before the young listeners were born. The memories associated with the song seem to be linked to a tragic event in the village's history, and the anniversary of that dreadful Sunday holds a significant place in the storyteller's recollections.

64. (A): The particular day is referred to as 'Black Sunday' because it marks the death of Apenyo, a young and beautiful singer, and also signifies the atrocities suffered by the villagers on that specific Sunday. The term "Black Sunday" conveys the gravity and darkness associated with the tragic events that unfolded on that day in the village's history.

65. (C): The passage doesn't explicitly provide the reason why the narrator "squats on the bare earth." However, the mention of sitting on the bare earth suggests a cultural or traditional practice, and option C, "It was a common way of sitting by the village folk of Nagaland," aligns with this interpretation. In many traditional settings, sitting on the ground is a common practice, and the mention of squatting on the bare earth may reflect the cultural norms of the village folk in Nagaland.

66. (B): The preposition "among" is used when something is distributed to or shared by members of a group. In this case, it is more appropriate to use "among" instead of "between" because the mangoes are being distributed among the fifty students.

67. (A): The use of "unless" already implies a negative condition, so adding "don't" after it creates a double negative. Removing the unnecessary "don't" makes the sentence grammatically correct.

68. (E): The sentence is correct; there is no error in any given part.

69. (C): In this case, the subjunctive mood is appropriate. Instead of "was," the correct form is "were." The corrected sentence reads, "He talked as if he were a madman."

70. (E): The sentence is correct; there is no error in any given part.

71. (B): The verb "obey" needs to be in the past participle form "obeyed" to match the auxiliary verb "have." The corrected sentence reads, "She ought to have obeyed her parents."

72. (B): In conditional sentences, the "will" is not used in the subordinate clause after "if." The correct form is "You will get wet if you go out in the rain."

73. (D): The superlative form "the greatest" should be used instead of "greatest," and "leader" should be in the plural form "leaders" to match the expression "one of."

74. (C): When "neither" is used with "nor," the verb agrees with the noun closer to it. In this case, "he" is singular, so the correct verb form is "is." The corrected sentence reads, "Neither you nor he is guilty."

75. (D): The word 'Neither' is not used in this context. The word 'None' should be used in this phase. 'Three pens' is also not correct. The word three should be omitted from the sentence to make it correct. The correct sentence should be 'None of the pens will do'.

76. (B): The sentence would read: "She had been living alone in the city for almost a decade now." The past perfect continuous tense is formed with "had been" followed by the present participle of the main verb, which is "living" in this case.

77. (B): An adverb clause is a group of words that functions as an adverb, providing information about the verb in the main clause. In this case, the adverb clause "where his pursuers could not follow" provides information about the location or place where he fled.

78. (E): "The umbrella with a wooden handle is mine," the underlined part "with a wooden handle" is functioning as an adjective phrase, not an adjective clause.

79. (C): These two sentences can be combined using an infinitive, which is a verb form that typically begins with "to." In this case, the infinitive "to perform" is used to express the purpose or action related to the duties. The combined sentence is I have some duties to perform.

80. (B): Option B uses an adverb, "undeservedly," to modify the verb "failed." However, it does convey the cause-and-effect relationship between deserving to succeed and the subsequent failure. The word "undeservedly" implies that the failure was without merit or unfairly, which might not accurately represent the intended meaning.

81. (B): This sentence uses the preposition "on" followed by the gerund "hearing." The structure "On hearing" indicates that the action of fainting occurred simultaneously or immediately after the action of hearing the news of her husband's death. So, it conveys a clear cause-and-effect relationship: the hearing of the news led to her fainting. The use of a gerund helps create a smooth and connected expression of the events, making the sentence more concise and effective.

82. (A): This sentence uses a participial phrase, "Jumping up," which functions like an adverb to modify the main clause "he ran away." The participle "jumping" suggests that the action of jumping up and the action of running away are closely linked in time.

The structure allows for a concise and connected expression of the two actions, emphasizing the immediacy of one action following the other. It's a stylistic choice that provides a sense of simultaneity between the two events.

83. (C): This option uses single quotation marks to enclose the title 'Kafan,' and it is a valid and acceptable way to punctuate titles according to certain style guides. In this case, option C adheres to the usage of single quotation marks for enclosing the title of the short story.

84. (C): A complex sentence consists of an independent clause and one or more dependent clauses. In this case, "I shall see him" is the independent clause, and "If he is at home" is the dependent (subordinate) clause. The dependent clause cannot stand alone as a complete sentence, making the overall structure complex.

85. (B): The given sentence, "You must hurry or you will miss the train," is a compound sentence. It consists of two independent clauses connected by the coordinating conjunction "or." The two independent clauses are "You must hurry" and "you will miss the train."

86. (C): The phrase "You ate fish" is an example of a sentence. A sentence is a group of words that expresses a complete thought and typically contains a subject and a predicate. In this case, "You" is the subject, "ate" is the predicate, and together they form a complete thought.

87. (A): The sentence "That which cannot be read" suggests that there is something which cannot be deciphered or understood when attempting to read it. In English, the term used to describe something that is difficult or impossible to read is "illegible."

Illegible: This term is commonly used to describe handwriting or printed text that is difficult or impossible to read due to various reasons such as poor penmanship, fading, or other factors.

88. (D): The antonym of the word "scurrilous" is decent and moderate. "Scurrilous" means making or spreading scandalous claims about someone with the intention of damaging their reputation, while "decent" refers to conforming to standards of morality or respectability and moderate refers to reasonable limits, avoiding excesses or extremes.

89. (E): The correct answer is none of the above in this sentence. The word 'that' is a word used in used as a determiner, a demonstrative pronoun and a relative pronoun. We also use it as a conjunction to introduce that-clauses.

Here it is used as a conjunction, because house is a noun and when that is used as a demonstrative pronoun it is used without a following noun.

90. (A): Synchronize: The correct spelling is "synchronize" with a single "h" after the "c."

The root word is "synchronize," and it involves coordinating or aligning different events or processes in time.

91. (D): The correct spelling is "Bureaucracy." The misspelled option has an extra "e" and "a" before the "u." The correct spelling is used to refer to a system of government or management marked by red tape and a rigid hierarchy of officials.

The correct spelling is "Pusillanimity." The misspelled option has an extra "s," and a single "l" and the correct spelling is used to describe lack of courage or determination, timidness, or cowardice.

92. (C): Cacographist

"Cacographist" is formed from two components: "cac-" and "graphist."

"Cac-" is a prefix that means bad or ill.

"Graphist" is related to writing or drawing.

So, a "cacographist" is someone who is bad or ill in writing or spelling. It's used to describe a person who has poor spelling skills or exhibits bad writing habits.

93. (B): "Complimentary" is an antonym for "opprobrious." While "opprobrious" means expressing scorn or criticism, "complimentary" means expressing praise or admiration.

94. (E): The term "quinquennial" specifically means happening or recurring every five years. Therefore, none of the provided options accurately represent the definition of "quinquennial."

95. (A): A compound sentence is formed by joining two or more independent (principal) clauses. Each independent clause can stand alone as a complete sentence and these clauses are connected using coordinating conjunctions (such as and, but, or), semicolons, or semicolon-conjunctive adverb combinations. Therefore, option A accurately represents the structure of a compound sentence.

96. (E): All the options provided are incorrect. The correct answer is 'The Prince said that it gave him great pleasure to be there that evening'.

97. (B): The answer should be in direct speech, with the words spoken between quotation marks. The name of the speaker should be placed before or after they speak. Proper punctuation should be used inside the quotation marks, including any commas, periods, or question marks. Capitalize the first letter of each new sentence inside the quotation marks.

The correct answer is He said to him, "Is not your name Ahmed?"

98. (C): This option uses correct punctuation marks, including apostrophes for pluralizing "i" and "t" and uses a semicolon to separate the two clauses.

When making plurals of lowercase letters, such as "i" and "t," you use an apostrophe to indicate the plural form. For example, "i's" indicates multiple lowercase "i," and "t's" indicates multiple lowercase "t." A semicolon (;) is used to separate the two

English Language

1

Comprehension Passages

ENGLISH LANGUAGE COMPREHENSION

The objective of language comprehension test is to ascertain the ability of the candidates to understand the passage properly.

Therefore candidates are required to take notice of the following points:

1. Read the full passage very attentively and intelligently.
2. Try to comprehend the gist of it.
3. Make a mental note of all the important details and points given in the passage.
4. Read the passage for the second time in case you have not been able to understand it satisfactorily.
5. Divide the time proportionately for all the passages.
6. Answer the questions on the basis of facts, as given in the paragraph.
7. Don't waste much time in answering the questions of any one passage.
8. Check all the answers once again, very carefully, to see whether any question is left unanswered by mistake.

MODEL QUESTIONS (FOR PRACTICE)

Directions: *Each of the following passages is followed by five questions. Read the passage carefully and then answer the questions that follow each. For each question, four probable answers A, B, C and D are given. Only one out of these is correct. Choose the correct answer.*

PASSAGE-1

The use of words like 'welcome', 'thank you', 'please', etc., at the right moment reflects a polite nature. The civic sense also lies within the scope of good manners. We should not shout or talk loudly in public places like hospitals and libraries and create disturbance. We should not cheat people or make fun of them. Cleanliness is also necessary. We must not throw the waste on roads and make use of dustbins. We should not harm the public property as it belongs to all of us. While in a queue, discipline should be maintained. We must give fair chance to others.

1. Expressions like 'welcome' 'thank you' and 'please' reflect
   A. happiness B. discipline
   C. civic sense D. polite nature
2. While in a library, we should
   A. respect others B. avoid arguments
   C. talk in low tone D. be courteous
3. A public property belongs to
   A. nobody B. all of us
   C. government D. one who maintains it
4. Discipline is
   A. the rule of proper conduct or action
   B. the rule of road sense
   C. making use of dustbins
   D. forming a queue
5. The most appropriate title for this passage would be
   A. Polite Nature B. Courtesy
   C. Good Manners D. Civic Sense

PASSAGE-2

There is an old proverb 'Early to bed and early to rise makes a man healthy and wise.' I am in the habit of getting up early in the morning and have formed the habit of taking long morning walks in the past two years. It is a light exercise and best for physical fitness. The morning air which is fresh and pure is beneficial for the lungs. The early rays of the rising sun are good for healthy skin. 'Health is wealth' and doctors also recommend morning walk to their patients for gaining sound health and freshness of energy.

1. What is good for lungs?
   A. Sunrays B. Fresh air
   C. Sound sleep D. Light exercise
2. What is a light exercise?
   A. Early to bed B. Early to rise
   C. Morning walk D. Gaining sound health
3. What is good for skin?
   A. Fresh air B. Morning air
   C. Morning walk D. Rising sun's rays
4. What is best for physical fitness?
   A. Light exercise B. Long morning walk
   C. Early to rise D. Fresh and pure air
5. Long morning walk
   A. bring sound sleep
   B. ensures physical fitness
   C. ensures healthy skin
   D. keeps healthy, wealthy and wise

PASSAGE-3

Mahatma Gandhi lived a splendid long life and has set great moral standards before us. He showed to the world the true way to peace. He wished to see India prosper but he became a martyr for the noble cause of Hindu-Muslim unity at the time of partition when a religious fanatic, Nathuram Godse, shot him dead on January 30, 1948. His last words were 'Hey Ram'. He lived and died for his country and countryman.

1. Mahatma Gandhi showed the world the true way to
   A. prosperity B. love
   C. truth D. peace
2. Mahatma Gandhi became a martyr for the noble cause of
   A. truth B. non-violence
   C. freedom of India D. Hindu-Muslim unity
3. Mahatma Gandhi was shot dead
   A. before India achieved independence
   B. by a mad man
   C. by an intolerant religious person
   D. by a non-religious person
4. Mahatma Gandhi set great moral standards. It means
   A. he was a great religious teacher
   B. he was a great moralist
   C. he made India morally stronger
   D. moral was everything to him
5. Gandhiji lived and died for his country and countryman. It means
   A. he was born in India and died in India
   B. he was a patriot
   C. he was a great moralist
   D. he sacrified his life for India and her people

PASSAGE-4

On one hot day a crow felt very thirsty. He flew from one place to another in search of water. After long hours of labour he found a pitcher. Eagerly, he perched on the mouth of the pitcher. He found that the water was at the bottom of the vessel. He tried his best to dip his beak but did not succeed. He did not know what to do. Suddenly some pebbles lying nearby gave him an idea. One by one he dropped the pebbles with his beak into the pitcher. The level of water slowly came up to the mouth of the pitcher. The crow then drank the water and quenched his thirst.

1. The crow found a pitcher
   A. as it flew
   B. after many hours of labour
   C. full of water
   D. which was empty
2. What is the moral of the passage?
   A. No pains, no gains
   B. God helps those who help themselves
   C. Necessity is the mother of invention
   D. Try and try again, you will succeed at last
3. The crow flew from place to place
   A. in search of pitcher B. in search of pebbles
   C. in search of water D. in search of a vessel
4. The pitcher, the crow found
   A. was full of water
   B. was dry
   C. had little water in the bottom
   D. had water up to its mouth
5. As the crow dropped pebbles into the pitcher, what happend?
   A. The pitcher broke down
   B. The water leaked one of the pitcher
   C. The level of water into the pitcher rose up slowly
   D. Water level immediately rose to the mouth of the pitcher

PASSAGE-5

Once upon a time a crane and a fox lived in a forest. They were good friend. One day the fox invited the crane to a feast. He made a tasty food and served it before the crane on a plate. The crane could not eat anything because of the long beak. But the fox licked all his food. The crane felt insulted. He decided to teach the fox a lesson. Next day he invited the fox. He prepared the same tasty food and placed it in front of the fox inside a narrow glass. The crane ate easily while the fox looked on. Now, it was the fox's turn to remain hungry.

1. What is the moral of the passage?
   A. Beware of the wicked
   B. One good turn deserves another
   C. Be contented with what you have
   D. Tit for tat
2. The crane could not eat tasty food because the
   A. food was served in a shallow plate
   B. food was very hot
   C. food was served in a long jar
   D. crane was not hungry
3. The fox had to remain hungry because
   A. the food served was not enough in quantity
   B. the food was served inside a narrow glass
   C. the food served was not tasty
   D. the food was all liquid
4. Why did the crane feel insulted?
   A. Because he was invited to feast but he could not eat anything
   B. Because the food was served in a shallow plate and he could not eat
   C. Because the food was too hot
   D. Because the fox gulped all the food quickly
5. The crane successfully taught a lesson to the fox when he invited the fox to a feast and served the food
   A. in a narrow glass B. in a large plate
   C. in a broken plate D. in a long jar

PASSAGE-6

The family set down at the table and began to talk about the summer holidays. They had to decide a place to visit during the vacation. Should they go to their village or to a hill station? The parents preferred the village while the children wished to go the hill station. After few moments of discussion the elders decided to visit both the places. First they shall go to the village for a week and then stay at the hill station for the remaining days. For the first time the family shall be together during the holidays. The children were happy with the holiday plan.

1. The purpose for which the family set down at the table was
   A. to decide a place to visit during the vacation
   B. to educate the children how to carry articles during a visit to a hill station
   C. to decide the date when they should start their journey
   D. to tell the children that they will visit a hill station during this vacation

2. The final plan was to visit
   A. their village
   B. a hill station
   C. their village as well as a hill station
   D. their home town

3. The final decision was made by
   A. the boys B. the girls
   C. the women D. the elders

4. They decided first to go to their village and stay there for
   A. a day B. a week
   C. ten days D. a fortnight

5. Why were children happy?
   A. Because a hill station was included in their holiday plan
   B. Because a visit to their village was excluded from their holiday pl...
   C. Because their choice prevailed
   D. Because they were going all alone to the hill station

PASSAGE-7

Once Govind intended to go on pilgrimage with his family. He asked Mirind to accompany. But for his trade's reason, he did not go with him. So Govind thought it safe to leave the box of his jewellery with him, as it was dangerous to leave it in a lone house or take it on the journey. So he went to him with the box. He took him to a lonely place under a tree and handed it over to him. He told Mirind. "Keep it safe with you. I shall return from the journey after six month then I shall take it back from you." Mirind said. "Don't worry. I shall keep it as safe as own."

1. Govind intended to go
   A. for a business trip
   B. to a hill station
   C. on a long journey to a sacred place
   D. to his home town for a long period

2. Why did Govind leave his box of jewellery with Mirind?
   A. Because it was not safe to take the box with him on a long journey
   B. Because Mirind was his fast friend
   C. Because the box was very heavy
   D. Because his house was unsafe

3. Why did Govind take Mirind to a lonely place?
   A. To tell him that the box contained valuable jewellery
   B. So that no third person could see box
   C. To show him what was within the box
   D. To tell him that the box will remain with him

4. Where did Govind hand over the box of jewellery to Mirind?
   A. At Mirind's house
   B. At his own house
   C. In a lonely place
   D. In a lonely place under a tree

5. It was not safe to leave the box in a lone house. Here the word 'lone house' means
   A. a house in a deserted place
   B. a house where none lives
   C. a house without door and lock
   D. a house near the forest

PASSAGE-8

Zahir-ud-din Babar was the first Mughal emperor of India. A descendent of Timur on father's side and Changez Khan on his mother's side, Babar was a brave warrior. After defeating Ibrahim Lodhi in the First Battle of Panipat in 1526 he entered Delhi and soon gained control over Agra. After many more battles with Rajputs he extended his empire over Punjab, Uttar Pradesh and north Bihar. He died at a young age of 48 years in 1530 at his capital Agra without getting much time to consolidate his victories.

1. Zahir-ud-din Babar was the first
   A. Muslim ruler of India B. Mughal ruler of India
   C. Afghan ruler of India D. Turk ruler of India

2. Babar was born in the years
   A. 1480 B. 1482
   C. 1492 D. 1962

3. Babar first occupied
   A. Punjab B. Agra
   C. Delhi D. Panipat

4. Babar was a brave warrior. Here brave warrior means
   A. courageous soldier B. a kind hearted soldier
   C. a clever fighter D. a victorious general

5. Babar extended his empire over Punjab and Uttar Pradesh after many more battles with the
   A. Afghans B. Rajputs
   C. Mughals D. Lodhies

PASSAGE-9

Our National Flag is tricolour. It has three equal horizontal strips. The strip at the top is saffron, in the middle is white and at the bottom is green. The ratio of width to length of the flag is 2 : 3. In the centre of the white strip is a wheel in navy blue. The wheel represents the *chakra.* Its design is similar to the wheel which appears on the abacus of the Sarnath Lion Capital of Ashoka. Its diameter approximates to the width of the white strip. The wheel has 24 spokes. It was adopted by Constituent Assembly on July 22, 1947. We love our national flag. We respect it. We are ready to sacrifice our life to protect its honour. It represents the nation. So it is a symbol of national honour.

1. In our national flag the wheel is located in the centre of

A. saffron strip B. white strip
C. green strip D. blue strip

2. In our national flag which of the strips is at the bottom in our national flag

A. blue C. saffron
B. white D. green

3. Why do we love our national flag?

A. Because it is tricolour
B. Because it has three strips
C. Because it has a wheel at the centre
D. Because it is a symbol of national honour

4. Our national flag was approved by

A. President
B. Lok Sabha
C. Parliament
D. Constituent Assembly

5. The diameter approximates to the width of the white strip. Here the word 'approximates' means

A. is more or less equal
B. is exactly equal
C. is not equal
D. is related

PASSAGE-10

Distance in large cities are long. All the people do not have their own means of transport. They have to depend upon the state or private buses. The number of bus users is very large. Every bus stop is, therefore, crowded. The number of buses is not adequate. Thus people suffer the torture of long wait at the bus stop. Some bus stops are quite orderly. People form queues and get into the buses turn by turn. However, often this order is forgotten and confusion spreads when the bus comes and the law of jungle prevails.

1. Why are the bus stops crowded?

A. Because they are small is size
B. Because the number of passengers is very large
C. Because they are situated at some busy centre
D. Because people do not form queues

2. Long wait at the bus stop is the result of

A. over-crowding in the buses
B. late running of buses
C. shortage of buses
D. slow speed of buses

3. Some bus stops are quite orderly where

A. there is no crowd
B. the number of buses is adequate
C. people do not have to wait for long
D. people form queues and enter the buses one by one

4. Most of the people who travel by buses are

A. non-working
B. do not have their own vehicles
C. have to go a long distance
D. live in large cities

5. What happens when people do not have their own transport?

A. They have to wait for a bus at a bus stop
B. They have to depend upon the state or private buses
C. They have to travel long distances
D. They form queues and get into buses one by one

ANSWERS

Passage	1	2	3	4	5
Passage 1.	D	C	B	A	C
Passage 2.	B	C	D	B	B
Passage 3.	D	D	C	B	D
Passage 4.	B	C	C	C	C
Passage 5.	D	A	B	B	A
Passage 6.	A	C	D	B	A
Passage 7.	C	A	B	D	B
Passage 8.	B	B	C	A	B
Passage 9.	B	D	D	D	A
Passage 10.	B	C	D	B	B

●●●

2

English Grammar

PARTS OF SPEECH

Part of speech	Definition or Function	Examples
Noun	Name of a person, place, animal, quality or thing	Ram, boy, dog pen, sun, Delhi, truth, honesty
Pronoun	Used in place of a noun	I, you, he she, they
Articles & Determiners	Points out indefinite and definite nouns	a, an, the, few, some
Adjective	Describes a noun or pronoun	big, honest, wooden valuable, quiet, deep, soft, narrow
Adverb	Describes a verb, an adjective or another adverb	silently, widely, softly, quietly, very, carefully
Verb	Tells about action or state of something or someone	is, am, was, have, do, like, walk, work, make, throw, tell
Conjuction	Joins words, clauses or sentences	and, but, when, yet, while, else
Preposition	Links a noun or pronoun to another word	at, to, after, on for, under, over, with
Interjection	Expresses sudden feelings or emotions	Ah!, Alas!, oh!, ouch!, hi!, well!, Hurrah!

NOUNS

A word which denotes a person, a thing, an animal or a place is said to be a noun.

There are two noun numbers in English — the *Singular* and the *Plural*.

Singular Numbers : A noun that denotes one person or one thing, is said to be in the Singular number. For example — book, pencil, bird, dog, hen etc. are in singular number.

Plural Number : A noun that denotes more than one person or one thing is said to be in plural number. For example — boys, pens, lions, girls, men etc. are in plural number.

REMEMBER

Singular	*Plural*	*Singular*	*Plural*
Cat	Cats	Book	Books
Pen	Pens	Room	Rooms
Tree	Trees	Bus	Buses
Bush	Bushes	Box	Boxes
Glass	Glasses	Dish	Dishes
Judge	Judges	Tax	Taxes
Watch	Watches	Calf	Calves
Thief	Thieves	Knife	Knives
Scarf	Scarves	Wife	Wives
Leaf	Leaves	Wolf	Wolves
Half	Halves	Monarch	Monarchs
Roof	Roofs	Hoof	Hoofs
Gulf	Gulfs	Staff	Staffs
Radio	Radios	Bamboo	Bamboos
Folio	Folios	Hero	Heroes
Volcano	Volcanoes	Mango	Mangoes
Potato	Potatoes	Photo	Photos
Piano	Pianos	Baby	Babies
Fly	Flies	Country	Countries
Lady	Ladies	Boy	Boys
Monkey	Monkeys	Ox	Oxen
Child	Children	Man	Men
Woman	Women	Tooth	Teeth
Axis	Axes	Basis	Bases
Foot	Feet	Goose	Geese
Englishman	Englishmen	Radius	Radii
Vertex	Vertices	Stimulus	Stimuli

1. Note the plurals of the following nouns:

Singular	*Plural*	*Singular*	*Plural*
copy	copies	cry	cries
baby	babies	duty	duties
body	bodies	country	countries
family	families	diary	diaries
fly	flies	fairy	fairies
city	cities	spy	spies
army	armies	storey	storeys
bay	bays	monkey	monkeys

2. The following nouns do not undergo any change in plural form, in general.

Singular	*Plural*	*Singular*	*Plural*
deer	deer	sheep	sheep
thousand	thousand	pair	pair
hundred	hundred	score	score
dozen	dozen	gross	gross

Note: We can write—

(*a*) thousands of men; (*b*) two pairs of shoes; (*c*) dozens of mangoes; (*d*) scores of people etc. But—
(*a*) two thousand rupees; (*b*) three hundred men; (*c*) five dozen eggs, etc.

3. The following nouns are usually used in plural forms. They take a plural verb after them—

eatables	fetters	surroundings
riches	alms	spectacles
trousers	pants	scissors
premises	thanks	annals
congratulations	goods	shorts
tongs	pains	arms
breeches	(for troubles)	

4. The following are the nouns which are plural in appearance but are usually used in singular number. They are followed by a singular verb—

news	politics	physics
mathematics	economics	ethics
politics	classics	gallows
statistics	athletics	innings
mechanics	summons	mumps

5. Collective nouns often used as plurals—

public	police	cattle
audience	clergy	folk
people	poultry	nation
elite	gentry	glitterati

6. The nouns that are usually used in singular forms—

advice	hair	rice
fuel	alphabet	machinery
offspring	issue	furniture
mischief	stationery	luggage
bedding	information	abuse

7. Material nouns are always used in singular number—

gold	copper	milk
water	silk	wool

Note: They may be used in plural with a different meaning. copper coins (coppers), chains or fetters (irons), cans made of tin (tins).

GENDERS

The difference in sex is denoted by Gender in grammar. The various genders are as follows :

1. **Masculine Gender :** A noun that denotes a male is said to be of the masculine gender, as man, uncle, ox, boy etc.
2. **Feminine Gender :** A noun that denotes a female is said to be of feminine gender, as woman, aunt, princess, cow etc.
3. **Common Gender :** Nouns which denote both males and females are said to be of the common gender, as friend, cousin, person, parent, baby etc.
4. **Neuter Gender :** A noun that denotes the name of object without life is said to be of neuter gender, as file, table, pencil.

REMEMBER

Masculine	*Feminine*
Boy	Girl
Son	Daughter
Brother	Sister
Murderer	Murderess
Sorcerer	Sorceress
Son-in-law	Daughter-in-law
Father-in-law	Mother-in-law
Man-servant	Maid-servant
Land-lord	Land-lady
Bachelor	Maid
Gentleman	Lady
Monk	Nun
Earl	Countess
Lad	Lass
Sir	Madam
Duke	Dutchess
Emperor	Empress
Milk-man	Milk-maid
Pea-cock	Pea-hen
Step-father	Step-mother
Hero	Heroine
Viceroy	Vicerine
Mr.	Mrs.
Governor	Governess
Master	Mistress
Wizard	Witch
Heir	Heiress
Host	Hostess
Lion	Lioness
Mayor	Mayoress
Actor	Actress
Buck	Doe
Colt	Filly
Dog	Bitch
Horse	Mare
Count	Countess
Hunter	Huntress
Prince	Princess
Abbot	Abbess
God	Goddess
Author	Authoress
Ox	Cow
Widower	Widow
Grand-father	Grand-mother
He-goat	She-goat
Milk-man	Milk-woman
Bridegroom	Bride
Tiger	Tigress
Priest	Priestess
Poet	Poetess
Shepherd	Shepherdess
Nephew	Niece
Stag	Hind

PRONOUNS

The repetition of a noun in a sentence or a set of sentences is really boring. So, instead of repeating the noun, we can use a word (for that noun) called the pronoun.

"A pronoun is a word that we use instead of a noun".

Example:

This is *Sachin. He* plays cricket.

Note: *He* is the pronoun used in place of *Sachin.*

Kinds of Pronouns

1. **Personal pronouns :** A pronoun which is used instead of the name of a person is known as a 'Personal Pronoun'. A list of the 'Personal pronouns' is listed below :

   I, my, mine, me, we (First Person)
   You, your, yours (Second Person)
   He, his, him, she, her, hers, it, its, they, their, theirs, them (Third Person)

2. **Demonstrative, Indefinite and Distributive Pronouns :**

   (a) Demonstrative Pronouns : Pronouns used to point out the objects to which they refer are called Demonstrative Pronouns.

   Examples :
   (i) *This* is a present from my uncle.
   (ii) *These* are merely excuses.
   (iii) Bombay mangoes are better than *those* of Bangaluru.

   (b) Indefinite Pronouns : All pronouns which refer to persons or things in a general way and do not refer to any particular person or thing are called Indefinite Pronouns.

   Examples :
   (i) *Somebody* has stolen my watch.
   (ii) *Few* escaped unhurt.
   (iii) Did you ask *anybody* to come?

   (c) Distributive Pronouns : Each, either, neither are called distributive pronouns because they refer to persons or things one at a time. For this reason they are always singular and followed by the verb in singular.

   Examples :
   (i) *Each* of the men received a reward.
   (ii) *These* men received *each* a reward.
   (iii) *Either* of you can go.

3. **Relative Pronouns :** A relative pronoun refers or relates to some noun going before, which is called its Antecedent.

   Examples :
   (i) I met Hari *who* used to live here.
   (ii) I have found the pen *which* I had lost.
   (iii) Here is the book *that* you lent me.

4. **Interrogative Pronouns :** These pronouns, are used for asking questions.

   Examples :
   (i) *Whose* book is this?
   (ii) *What* will all the neighbours say?
   (iii) *Which* do you prefer, tea or coffee?

Note : Interrogative pronouns can also be used in asking indirect questions. Consider the following examples :

(i) I asked *who* was speaking.
(ii) Tell me *what* you have done.
(iii) Say *which* you would like best.

Behaviour of the Pronouns

1. If three pronouns are used together in the same sentence they are arranged in the following order :

   2 + 3 + 1
   ↓ ↓ ↓
   Second Person, Third Person, First Person

   Examples :
   I, you and he must help *that* poor man. (Incorrect)
   You, he and I must help *that* poor man. Correct)

2. When two or more singular nouns are joined by and, the pronoun used for them should be plural.

   Examples :
   Mohan and Sohan are friends. *They* play football. *They* live at Lajpat Nagar.

3. But if these nouns joined by and refer to the same person or thing, the pronoun used should be singular.

   Examples :
   (i) Delhi, the beautiful city and the capital of India, is famous for *its* historical monuments.
   (ii) The manager and owner of the firm expressed *his* views on the demands of the workers.

4. When two nouns are used with as well as, the pronoun agrees with the first subject.

   Examples :
   (a) Mohan as well as his friends is doing *his* work.
   (b) The students as well as their teachers are doing *their* work.

5. When two singular nouns joined by 'and' are preceded by *each* or *every*, the pronoun used must be singular and should agree in gender with the second noun.

   Examples :
   (a) Every man and every woman will do *her* best for the nation.
   (b) Each boy and each girl went to *her* house.

6. When two nouns are joined by using 'with', the pronoun agrees with the noun coming before 'with'.

   Examples :
   (a) The boy with *his* parents has gone to see a movie.
   (b) The children with *their* parents have gone to picnic.

7. When two different nouns are joined by either......... or; neither .... nor, the pronoun is used according to the number and gender of the second noun.

Examples :

(a) Either your sister or you have done *your* work.

(b) Neither the students nor the teacher was in *his* class.

8. The pronoun coming after '*than*' must be in the same case as that coming before '*than*'.

Examples :

(a) She plays better than *me*. (Incorrect)
She plays better than *I*. (Correct)

(b) His elder brother is more intelligent than *him*. (Incorrect)
His elder brother is more intelligent than *he*. (Correct)

9. 'Many a' always takes a singular pronoun and singular verb.

Example :

Many a soldier has met *his* death in the battle field.

10. 'Who', 'Whose', 'Whom' are used only for persons.

Examples :

(a) *Who* is knocking at the door?

(b) *Whose* pen is this?

(c) *What* do you want?

11. 'Which' is used for things.

Example : *Which* game do you like?

MULTIPLE CHOICE QUESTIONS

Directions: *In the following questions choose the correct options to fill the blanks.*

1. The place was so dirty that ..... wished to run away from there.
A. everybody B. anybody
C. few D. some

2. ..... was there to help me.
A. Somebody B. Anything
C. Anybody D. Nobody

3. Is there ...... to eat?
A. some B. something
C. any D. few

4. ..... of the students were making a great noise.
A. Anyone B. Somebody
C. Many D. Nobody

5. ..... of the students can solve this sum.
A. Someone B. Anybody
C. Somebody D. None

6. ...... of us should try our best to make India a heaven.
A. Any B. Somebody
C. Anybody D. All

7. ...... of us do not know the real meaning of our lives.
A. Any B. Something
C. Several D. Many

8. My .... black.
A. hairs are B. hair is
C. hairs shall D. hair will

9. She saw two .... on the last Sunday.
A. thiefs B. theifs
C. thieves D. theives

10. My sister is a ....
A. bacheloress B. bachelor
C. unmaried D. spinster

11. One is supposed to do ....
A. our duty B. their duty
C. one's duty D. his duty

12. Take anything .... you want.
A. that B. which
C. than D. then

13. I cannot tolerate ....
A. separated you B. your separation
C. separation from you D. you separated

14. He is .... faithful partner.
A. Yours B. You
C. Your D. Your's

15. Ajay is more smart than ....
A. her B. hers
C. herself D. she

16. Vivek works harder than ....
A. me B. I
C. her D. his

17. They should help ....
A. the poor people B. the poor
C. the poor persons D. the poor peoples

18. .... are mad.
A. All his sons B. His all sons
C. Sons all his D. All sons his

19. The poor fellow .... to fate.
A. resigned B. resigned himself
C. resigned itself D. resigned themselves

20. Nobody will help you but ....
A. I B. me
C. ours D. his

21. It is a good chance, You must avail .... this opportunity.
A. of B. yourself of
C. for D. from

22. The person who is elected .... my relative.
A. is B. he is
C. his D. him

23. He made ....
A. yours mention B. mention of you
C. mention for you D. mention about you

24. .... I know, he is quite faithful.
A. As far as B. So far as
C. So far this D. So far so

25. It is a duty of a person to take .... for his family.
A. pain B. pains
C. pain-killers D. pained

26. She does not love .... husband.
A. his B. her
C. its D. their

27. Let .... work together.
A. him and me B. he and I
C. he and him D. I and me

28. Copper, Silver and Gold ....
A. each will do B. either will do
C. any one will do D. any will do

29. Jessica and Roma are very irregular .... habits.
A. in her B. in their
C. in its D. in every

30. One likes to enjoy .... who was a great poet.
A. The sonnets of Shakespeare
B. Shakespeare's sonnets
C. Sonnets
D. Shakespeare

ANSWERS

1	2	3	4	5	6	7	8	9	10
A	D	B	C	D	D	D	B	C	D
11	12	13	14	15	16	17	18	19	20
C	A	C	C	D	B	B	A	B	B
21	22	23	24	25	26	27	28	29	30
B	A	B	A	B	B	A	C	B	A

ARTICLES

The family of the articles has only three members. They are : A, An and The. However, they fall under two groups :
(a) Definite Article *(b)* Indefinite Article

'The' is known as definite article whereas 'a' and 'an' are known as indefinite articles.

Use of the Definite Article 'The'

'The' is used before

1. The superlative degree :
   He is the ablest man of the town.
   (ablest is a superlative degree)
2. The name of states, countries etc. having a descriptive name :
   (i) The J & K is a small state. (J & K is a descriptive name)
   (ii) He lives in the U.S.A. (U.S.A. is a descriptive name)
   (But the Delhi and the America are wrong because neither Delhi nor America is a descriptive name)
3. The names of the scriptures :
   The Gita is a holy book. (Gita is a scripture)
4. Name of newspapers :
   The Tribune is published from Chandigarh.
5. Name of rivers, canals, seas, oceans, bays, gulfs, groups of islands etc. :
   (i) The Ganga is a holy river.
   (ii) The Indian Ocean is the deepest ocean.
   (iii) The Persian Gulf is a narrow gulf.
6. The name of famous buildings :
   The Taj is one of the best buildings in India.
7. The names of nationals, sects and communities:
   (i) The English defeated the Germans in the World War.
   (ii) The rich should help the poor.
   (iii) The Hindus believe in the caste system.
8. Proper nouns used as common nouns :
   (i) Kalidas is the Shakespeare of India.
   (ii) Delhi is the London of India.
9. Famous historical events :
   The Industrial Revolution changed the face of England.
10. The directions and the celestial bodies:
    The sun rises in the east.
11. Titles : Akbar, the Great was loved by his subjects.

Do not use 'the'

1. Before languages :
   The English is an international language. (Incorrect)
   English is an international language. (Correct)
2. Before the names of games :
   The hockey is a popular game. (Incorrect)
   Hockey is a popular game. (Correct)

Use of the Indefinite Articles 'A' and 'An'

'A' is used before :

1. All singular common nouns beginning with a consonant :
   (i) A boy sings a song.
   (ii) A black and a white cow were grazing in the field.
2. If a word begins with a vowel but gives the sound of a consonant, 'a' should be used before it :
   (i) He was helped in his work by a European.
   (ii) He is a one-eyed man.
   (iii) It is a useful work.

'An' is used as follows :

1. All singular common nouns beginning with a vowel (*i.e.*, a, e, i, o, u) :
   (i) He is an artist. (ii) He is an old man. (iii) I intend to buy an umbrella.
2. If a word starts with a consonant but gives the sound of a vowel, "an" should be used before it :
   (i) Brutus is an honourable man.
   (ii) He is an honour to his profession.
   (iii) He is an L.L.B.

Demonstratives, that, these and those

1. The demonstrative adjectives and pronouns are for objects nearby the speaker:
   this (singular) those (plural)
   and for objects far away from the speaker.
   That (singular) those (plural)
2. Demonstratives are the only adjectives that agree in number with their nouns.
   That hat is nice.
   Those hats are nice.
3. When there is the idea of selection, the pronoun "one" (or "ones") often follows the demonstrative.
   I want a book. I'll get this (one).
   If the demonstrative is followed by an adjective, "one"(or "ones") must be used.
   I want a book. I'll get this big one.

MULTIPLE CHOICE QUESTIONS

Directions: *In the following questions choose the correct options to fill the blanks.*

1. .... will have to be paid for this material.
A. Half rupee B. Half a rupee
C. A half rupee D. An half rupee

2. .... is taking keen interest in India.
A. The USA B. USA
C. An USA D. A USA

3. Only .... can save our country.
A. the Hitler B. a Hitler
C. Hitler D. an Hitler

4. I can run for ....
A. hundred miles B. the hundred miles
C. a hundred miles D. an hundred miles.

5. .... man-eater has been killed.
A. The B. A
C. An D. Either A or B

6. What .... fine idea!
A. the B. an
C. a D. No article

7. .... earth is moving around the sun.
A. An B. A
C. The D. No article

8. This is .... first example while I got.
A. the B. a
C. an D. No article

9. This is .... house which was built during earthquake.
A. a B. an
C. the D. No article

10. .... America is a rich country.
A. The B. An
C. A D. No article

11. .... U.S.A. is a developed country.
A. A B. An
C. The D. No article

12. .... Bible is a holy book.
A. A B. The
C. An D. No article

13. .... rich should help the poor.
A. The B. A
C. An D. No article

14. .... Gold is a costly metal.
A. The B. A
C. An D. No article

15. Kalidas is .... Shakespeare of India.
A. a B. an
C. the D. No article

16. I cannot do .... difficult work.
A. a such B. the such
C. such the D. such a

17. How foolish .... plan it is!
A. a B. an
C. the D. No article

18. An ink is .... useful article.
A. an B. a
C. the D. No article

19. There are .... husband and wife.
A. a B. an
C. the D. No article

20. He is learning .... French
A. the B. a
C. an D. No article

ANSWERS

1	2	3	4	5	6	7	8	9	10
B	A	B	C	D	C	C	A	C	D
11	**12**	**13**	**14**	**15**	**16**	**17**	**18**	**19**	**20**
C	B	A	D	C	D	A	B	D	D

ADJECTIVES & ADVERBS

An Adjective is a word which adds something to the meaning of a noun or a pronoun.

Mridula is an *intelligent* girl. He has a *black* goat.
He is a *brilliant* student. She is a *clever* girl.
It is a *beautiful* picture.

In the sentences given above, the words in italics are adjectives.

An Adverb is a word which qualifies the meaning of a Verb, an Adjective or another Adverb.

(*i*) He talks *slowly*.
(*ii*) He is a *very* good student.
(*iii*) He talks *very* slowly.

In sentence (*i*), *slowly* qualifies the verb *talks*.
In sentence (*ii*), *very* qualifies the adjective *good*.
In sentence (*iii*), *very* qualifies the adverb *slowly*.

Adjectives have three degrees of comparison :

1. **Positive Degree :** It expresses the common form of an adjective.
   Example :
   Ram is a *tall* boy.
   In the above sentence *tall* is an adjective and expresses the common form.
2. **Comparative Degree :** It expresses the more of the same form.
   Example :
   Ram is *taller* than Mahesh.
   In the above sentence *taller* is an adjective that expresses the more of the common form of the adjective *tall*.

"When and How to Use" Comparative Degree?

(a) Comparative Degree is used when two persons or two groups of persons or things are compared.
Examples :
(a)He is *wiser* than his younger brother.
(b)This glass is *cleaner* than the other.

(b) When two different qualities in the same person are compared, more is used instead of 'er' to form the comparative. The formula used in this case should be :
More + Positive Degree
She is *fairer* than polite. (Incorrect)
She is *more fair* than polite. (Correct)

(c) When selection of one out of two persons or things is meant, the degree of comparison is followed by of and *the* is used before it.
Example :
Zia is abler of *the* two sisters.

(d) If two comparatives are used in the same sentence to impress upon an idea, both should be preceded by the definite article.
Examples :
(i) The higher you go, the cooler it is.
(ii) The more we get, the more we desire.

(e) When one person or thing is compared with another of the same kind, other is used after the comparative degree. In such sentences other is normally preceded by any or all.
Examples :
(i) Kalidas is greater than any dramatist.
(Incorrect)
Kalidas is greater than any other dramatist.
(Correct)
(ii) Lead is heavier than all metals.
(Incorrect)
Lead is heavier than all other metals.
(Correct)

(f) Senior, junior, superior, inferior, prior, anterior (earlier than) and posterior (later than) are always followed by 'to'.
Examples :
(i) Ram is senior *to* Mohan by three years.
(ii) That pen is inferior *to* that.
(iii) He is junior *to* me in rank.
(iv) This event was posterior *to* that.

Note: Never use *than* after the above mentioned adjectives.

Important Information

(a) 'Preferable' is also used as an adjective of the comparative degree. As such, it is always followed by *to* and not *a*.
Death is preferable than dishonour. (Incorrect)
Death is preferable *to* dishonour. (Correct)

(b) To intensify the Degree of comparison, we use *far* or *much* before the comparative.
Examples :
(i) This book is *far* better than that.
(ii) His performance was *much* better than Mohan's.
Warning : Always avoid the use of double comparatives.
Don't say : Ram is more cleverer than his younger brother.
Say: Ram is cleverer than his younger brother.

3. **Superlative Degree :** It expresses the most of the common form of an adjective.
   Example :
   He is the ablest man of the town.

How and when to use the Superlative Degree?

(a) The Superlative Degree is used when more than two persons or things are compared.

(b) The Superlative Degree is generally preceded by 'the' and followed by 'of' in most of the cases or otherwise.

(c) When an adjective of the superlative degree is preceded by a Possessive Adjective or a Noun in the Possessive case, 'the' should not be used before it.
Example :
Which is Kalidas' best play?

It will be a blunder to use 'the' before the Superlative Degree in such cases.

Don't say : Which is Kalidas' the best play.

(d) To intensify the degree of comparison, *by far* is used before the superlative degree.

Example :

India is *by far* the most beautiful country of the world.

Note: Always avoid the use of double superlatives.

Don't say : He is the most strongest boy in the class.

Say : He is the strongest boy in the class.

Use of some Important Adjectives

1. (a) **'Some'** is used as follows :

(i) With countable nouns where it means— a little, a small quantity.

(ii) In a question which shows some request.

Examples :

(i) There is some water in the bottle.

(ii) Some of the students were absent yesterday.

(iii) Will you have some milk?

(iv) Will you buy some fruit for me?

(b) **'Any'** is used as follows :

(i) In negative sentences.

(ii) In interrogative sentences.

(iii) After 'Hardly', 'Scarcely' and 'Barely'.

(iv) After 'If'.

Examples :

(i) There is not any sugar in the pot.

(ii) We haven't any rice in the house.

(iii) I have hardly any money.

(iv) There are scarcely any plants in this field.

(v) If there is any danger, blow the whistle.

2. (a) **Older :** Older (and oldest) are used for persons animals and things. But 'Older' and 'Oldest' refer to the persons who do not belong to the same family.

Examples :

(i) Radha is older than Shyama.

(ii) John is the oldest member of the staff.

'Older' and 'Oldest' refer to the persons who do not belong to the same family.

(b) **Elder** (and **eldest**) are used in respect of the members of the same family like sons, daughters, brothers, sisters.

Examples :

(i) My elder sister is a lecturer.

(ii) Meenakshi is the eldest of the three sisters.

Note :

(i) 'Elder' is not followed by 'than'.

(ii) 'Elder' and 'Eldest' cannot be used for things.

3. (a) **'Few'** is negative and is the opposite of 'Many'. It means 'not many'.

(b) **'A few'** is positive and means 'some at least'. It is the opposite of 'None'.

(c) **'The few'** means 'minority' and suggests 'whether there is'.

Examples :

(i) We have few holidays in school.

(ii) Only a few boys will fail in the examination.

(iii) The few poems that he wrote are very popular.

4. (a) **Further** means 'something additional'.

(b) **Farther** means 'a greater distance'.

Examples :

(i) Further discussion will be held in the office of the principal.

(ii) Amritsar is farther from Delhi than Ambala.

5. (a) **Little** is negative. It means, 'not much', or 'hardly any'.

(b) **A little** is positive. It means 'some quantity'.

(c) **The little** denotes quantity. It means, 'not much but all that is, or whatever quantity there is'.

Examples :

(i) There is little hope of his success.

(ii) He knows a little of everything.

(iii) I have spent the little money I had.

(iv) The little knowledge of shoe-making proved very useful to me.

6. (a) **'Much'** expresses 'quantity'.

(b) **'Many'** expresses 'number'.

(c) **'Many a'**—'Singular noun' and 'Singular verb' are used with 'many a'.

Examples :

(i) There is not *much* water in the jug.

(ii) *Many* boys are absent today.

(iii) *Many* a battle has been fought on the soil of India.

7. (a) **'Less'** denotes 'in a small degree'.

(b) **'Fewer'** denotes 'number'.

Examples :

(i) He devotes less time to his studies.

(ii) There are no fewer than ten chairs in this room.

8. (a) **'Each'** is used for a single number of 'two persons' or 'things'.

(b) **'Every'** is used for a single number of 'many persons' or 'things'.

Examples :

(i) Each boy must take part in games.

(ii) There are only two poets. Each poet recited his poem.

(iii) Every man dies in this world.

(iv) Every man is expected to do his duty.

9. (a) **'Either'** means one of the two or both.

(b) **'Neither'** is negative of the either.

Examples :

(i) You may buy either of these two chairs.

(ii) Neither of them could speak on the stage.

10. (a) **'Later'** expresses 'late in time'.

(b) **'Latter'** means 'second in position or order'.

Examples :

(i) My father reached later than I expected.

(ii) The latter position was better than the former.

Use of some Important Adverbs

1. (a) Also, too, enough:
   (i) He taught English. Also, he edited the school magazine
   (ii) He is a writer and also he is a painter.
   (iii) He is too obstinate to listen to any reason.
   (iv) This is too difficult a piece for the junior students.
   (v) Sarla was kind enough to help the poor.
   (vi) He is brave enough to help the truth.
   Note: 'Too' is used in a negative sense, but enough is used in a positive sense.
   (b) Fairly and rather: Both suggest the meaning 'moderately'. But, mainly 'fairly' is used with the words that denote a positive meaning and rather is used with the words that denote a negative meaning:
   (i) Rita did fairly well in that competition, but her performance was rather poor in sports.
   (ii) Mona is fairly rich, but she is rather stingy.
   Note: 'Rather' can also be used in a positive sense.
   (i) This is a rather interesting job.
   (ii) That boy is rather smart.
   (c) Hardly, barely, scarcely: These words mostly convey the negative suggestions and are almost similar.
   (i) I have hardly any strength now.
   (ii) There was barely any supply to the township,
   (iii) There were scarcely a hundred guests present.
   Note: With slight variance in the meaning, the words given above convey the idea of 'very little', 'not enough', 'lack of quantity and number'.
   (d) Yet, Still: These adverbs can often be used to connect the sentence units:
   (i) He has been defeated many times in the contest; still he wants to be a competitor.
   (ii) Mona was sick; yet she went on doing her work.
   (e) Alone:
   (i) He alone (none else) is capable of handling that fire,
   (ii) He hunted all alone in the forest. (not in any company)

Special Note:

(a) Apart from their conventional positions the adverbs might be used in different positions with different meanings and angles.
   (i) He had only four books.
   (ii) John only contacted his friend in need.
   (iii) He greeted me only.
   (iv) Only he greeted me there.
(b) Inversion: Some adverbs can be inverted *i.e.* placed in the beginning of the sentence and then be followed by an interrogative form. The most common of these adverb are: so, seldom, never, nowhere, under no circumstances, hardly, scarcely etc.
   (i) So big was the bus that it could not enter the narrow lane.
   (ii) Hardly had he reached the station when he received the message.

MULTIPLE CHOICE QUESTIONS

Directions: *In the following questions choose the correct options to fill the blanks.*

1. The girl whom you met is the .... sister of Ravi.
A. eldest B. elder
C. older D. oldest

2. The historical place is ....
A. seeing worth B. worthy of seeing
C. worth seeing D. worthy seeing

3. These flowers smell ....
A. sweet B. sweetly
C. more sweetly D. sweetest

4. .... aspirant cannot pass the entrance examination.
A. Each B. Every
C. All D. No

5. Harivansh Rai .... second Shakespeare.
A. is a B. is
C. is the D. is an

6. .... student in the class got prizes.
A. Each and every B. Every and each
C. Every D. Never

7. It is .... picture than the one we saw last Monday.
A. interesting B. much interesting
C. more interesting D. most interesting

8. She is clever ....
A. that her mother is B. as her mother is
C. to her mother is D. than her mother is

9. They will get ....
A. Red, green and black paper
B. Red, green black paper
C. Red and green and black paper
D. Red green black paper

10. Health is .... wealth.
A. preferable to B. more preferable than
C. more preferable to D. most preferable then

11. .... water that was in the jug evaporated.
A. Little B. The little
C. Small D. A small

12. He has not sung .... songs.
A. much B. most
C. more D. many

13. Srishti has searched .... office.
A. whole the B. the whole
C. a whole D. some whole

14. Premchand was .... best and .... famous writer.
A. a, the most B. the, a most
C. the, more D. the, the most

15. William Shakespeare is famous as ....
A. a poet and a dramatist
B. a poet and dramatist
C. the poet and the dramatist
D. a poet and the dramatist

16. What does .... leader suggest?
A. other B. another
C. others D. anothers

17. He .... money.
A. has few B. have few
C. has little D. have little

18. The .... boys are rewarded.
A. first two B. two first
C. firsts two D. two's first

19. He is .... brave.
A. stronger than
B. stronger then
C. more strong then
D. more strong than

20. No sooner said ....
A. so done B. and done
C. then done D. but done

21. She returned .... than I had thought.
A. quickly B. more quicker
C. more quickly D. quicker

22. He is .... foolish person.
A. rather the B. a rather
C. rather a D. rather

23. This pen .... rupees.
A. costs twenty B. twenty costs only
C. costs only twenty D. only costs twenty

24. It is .... pride.
A. nothing else but B. nothing else than
C. else nothing than D. but

25. This tea is .... to drink.
A. too hot B. very hot
C. enough hot D. much hot

ANSWERS

1	2	3	4	5	6	7	8	9	10
A	C	A	B	A	C	C	C	A	A
11	12	13	14	15	16	17	18	19	20
B	D	B	D	B	B	C	A	D	C
21	22	23	24	25					
C	C	C	A	A					

DETERMINERS

Determiners are actually Adjectives. They are always followed by nouns.

Determiners are of the following kinds:

1. **Demonstrative Determiners :** this, that, these, those
2. **Possessive Determiners :** my, our, your, his, her, its, their
3. **Quantitative Determiners :** some, any, much, enough, sufficient, whole, a little, the little, little, all, both
4. **Numerical Determiners:** a few, some, few, the few, any, several, many, no, etc.
   One, two, three ... (Cardinals)
   First, second, third ... (Ordinals)
5. **Distributive Determiners:** either, neither
6. **Articles: Indefinite:** a, an, **Definite:** the

MULTIPLE CHOICE QUESTIONS

Directions: *In the following questions choose the correct options to fill the blanks.*

1. Give me .... rice.
A. some B. few
C. a few D. any

2. ...... sheep grazing on the slope of the hill had gone away.
A. Any B. The few
C. This D. Much

3. Have you got .... magazines to read?
A. all B. much
C. some D. little

4. I have .... money that I want to spend on shares.
A. any B. much
C. less D. some

5. There is .... owl on the branch of the tree.
A. a B. the
C. an D. some

6. My brother is .... MBA.
A. a B. an
C. the D. any

7. Have you got .... cheese?
A. some B. many
C. a few D. few

8. No, I have not got .... cheese.
A. many B. few
C. any D. some

9. There is only .... milk left in the bottle.
A. enough B. few
C. much D. a little

10. There is .... hope of his recovery.
A. any B. little
C. many D. few

11. .... dogs were barking at the strangers.
A. Some B. Any
C. Much D. Less

12. The girl bought her father .... juice.
A. few B. some
C. any D. many

13. You should take .... honey everyday.
A. any B. many
C. a little D. a few

14. .... boy was punished by the teacher.
A. Either B. All
C. Any D. Many

15. .... girl was asked to join the army.
A. None B. Neither
C. All D. Any

16. .... water in the jug has been drunk by Mohan.
A. The little B. The few
C. A few D. Few

17. I shall play .... piano at the party.
A. some B. any
C. the D. few

18. .... labourers were found dead in the mine.
A. Any B. Fewer
C. Many D. Less

19. Could I borrow .... umbrella?
A. our B. your
C. yours D. my

20. My brother is standing in the .... row.
A. any B. many
C. some D. first

ANSWERS

1	2	3	4	5	6	7	8	9	10
A	B	C	D	C	B	A	C	D	B
11	**12**	**13**	**14**	**15**	**16**	**17**	**18**	**19**	**20**
A	B	C	A	B	A	C	C	B	D

THE VERB

A Verb is a word that tells something about the action or state of or happenning to a person or thing.

A Verb tells the following:

1. What a person or thing does.
Sachin goes to school daily.
The bell *rang* loudly.
Many birds fly in the sky.
She *sang* a song.

2. What a person or thing is.
India *is* the biggest democracy in the world.
Ram Mehar *is* very rich.
They *are* happy.

3. What is done to a person or thing.
You *are liked* by all.
Two thieves *were arrested*.
Four students *were punished* by the teacher.

4. What happens to a person or thing.
His maternal uncle *died* last week.
Two ships *sank* yesterday.
Leaves *turn* yellow in autumn.

5. What a person or thing has, had, and so on.
I *have* a new car.
He *had* a scooter last year.
He *has* several cows and goats.

It goes without saying that a verb is the most important part of a sentence. No sentence is complete without a Verb.

Important Information

1. If two or more singular nouns are joined by 'and' the verb used will be plural.
Example:
(i) He and I were going to the market.
(ii) Ram and Mohan are friends.

2. If two singular nouns joined by 'and' points out to the same thing or person, the verb used must be singular.
Example:
(i) Rice and curry is the favourite food of the Punjabis.
(ii) The Collector and District Magistrate is away.

3. In case two subjects are joined by 'as well as' the verb agrees with the first subject.
Example :
(i) Kanta as well as her children is playing.
(ii) Children as well as their mother are playing.
In the case of first sentence the verb (is) agrees with Kanta and in the case of second sentence the verb (are) agrees with the children.

4. 'Neither', 'Either', 'Every', 'Each', 'Everyone', and 'Many a' are followed by a singular verb.
Example :
(i) Either of the plans is to be adopted.
(ii) Neither of the two brothers is sure to pass.
(iii) Every student is expected to be obedient.
(iv) Everyone of them desires this.
(v) Many a person is drowned in the sea.

5. If two subjects are joined by 'Either ...... or' / 'Neither .... nor', the verb agrees with the subject near to it.

Example :

(i) Either my brother or I am to do this work.

(ii) Neither he nor they are prepared to do this work.

6. 'A great many' is always followed by a 'plural noun' and a 'plural verb'. For example :

A great many students have been declared successful.

7. Similarly if two subjects are joined by 'with', 'together with', 'no less than', in addition to 'and not', etc. the verb agrees with the first subject.

Example :

(i) The boy with his parents has arrived.

(ii) He, no less than I, is to blame.

8. Nouns, plural in form, but singular in meaning, take a singular verb.

Example :

This news was broadcast from television yesterday.

MULTIPLE CHOICE QUESTIONS

Directions: *In the following questions choose the correct options to fill the blanks.*

1. The bus with all its passengers .... lost.
A. were B. was
C. are D. would

2. You as well as I .... responsible for this work.
A. am B. are
C. was D. is

3. Raghava like all his companions .... a spoiled child.
A. are B. were
C. is D. will be

4. Pen and ink .... required for me.
A. are B. were
C. is D. has required

5. Every girl and every boy .... attended the seminar.
A. have B. has
C. is D. are

6. Not only she but all her sisters ...... been married.
A. has B. have
C. is D. are

7. There .... nothing but miseries in life.
A. is B. are
C. were D. will be

8. Neither prose nor poem .... given.
A. were B. was
C. has D. have

9. Either he or I .... wrong.
A. is B. are
C. am D. were

10. Either Sulekha or Rekha .... coming here.
A. are B. is
C. were D. have

11. .... the child or his parents to blame?
A. Is B. Are
C. Were D. Has

12. You and I .... neighbours.
A. am B. are
C. was D. has

13. The house with all its belongings ..... sold away.
A. were B. are
C. was D. must

14. Either water or juice .... required.
A. is B. are
C. were D. has

15. There were not as many tables as .... required.
A. was B. were
C. is D. are

16. They each .... a book.
A. have B. are
C. has D. is

17. He and I .... class friends.
A. is B. am
C. was D. are

18. She as well as I .... guilty.
A. is B. are
C. am D. must be

19. Purushottam .... not read more on this chapter.
A. needs
B. has been need
C. need
D. had been need

20. He came .... to his aunt.
A. run B. running
C. to run D. in run

ANSWERS

1	2	3	4	5	6	7	8	9	10
B	B	C	C	B	B	A	B	C	B
11	**12**	**13**	**14**	**15**	**16**	**17**	**18**	**19**	**20**
A	B	C	A	B	A	D	A	C	B

CONJUNCTIONS

A conjunction is a word which connects words, clauses or sentences.

Look at the following sentences.

(i) He bought apples *and* mangoes.

(ii) God made the country *and* man made the town.

(iii) The door was open *but* there was no one in the house.

(iv) He knows that I am here *and* that I want to see him.

In the sentence (i), *and* connects two words—*apples* and *mangoes.*

In the sentence (ii), *and* connects two sentences—*God made the country* and *man made the town.*

In the sentence (iii), *but* connects two sentences— *The door was open* and *there was no one in the house.*

In the sentence (iv), *and* connects two clauses—*that I am here* and *that I want to see him.*

The main coordinating conjunctions are:

and, but, for, or, nor, also, either ..... or, neither ..... nor.

There are some conjunctions which are used in pairs. They are:

either .... or, ... neither .... nor, both .... and, though .... yet, whether .... or, not only .... but also.

Example: *Either* take it *or* leave it.

It is *neither* useful *nor* ornamental.

They *both* like *and* respect me.

Though he is suffering from high fever, *yet* he does not cry.

He does not care *whether* you go *or* stay.

He is *not only* doltish, *but also* obstinate.

The conjunctions which are used in pairs in this way, are called correlative conjunctions, or merely correlatives.

Use of Important Conjunctions

1. **As soon as :** As soon as denotes simultaneous time.
   Example : As soon as he saw his enemy, he took to his heels.
2. **No sooner .... than :**
   (a) 'No sooner' is always followed by 'than'.
   (b) Please remember that 'No sooner' is always followed by do/does/did. As such only first form of the verb should be used after the subject.
   Example :
   No sooner did he see his enemy than he took to his heels.
3. **Hardly :** Hardly is followed by when.
   Examples :
   (i) Hardly had I left the house when it started raining.
   (ii) We had hardly come into the room when his father began chastising him.
   Note :
   A. Hardly is never followed by than.
   B. 'Scarcely' can also be used in the sense and manner of 'Hardly'.
4. **Lest :** Lest is used in the sense of so that .... not. It is always followed by should. Lest is negative in sense. Hence 'not' should never be used with it.
   Example :
   Work hard lest you should fail.
   Note : 'Lest' is always followed by 'should' and not 'may'.
5. **Unless :** Unless expresses condition. It is also used in the negative sense. Use of 'not' is not allowed with unless because unless is already in the negative sense.
   Example :
   Unless you labour hard you will not pass.
6. **Until :** 'Until' expresses time. It means 'till not'.
   Example : Wait here until I return.
   Note : Until is in the negative sense. So 'not' should not be used with it. Example :
   Wait here until I do not return. (Incorrect)
   Wait here until I return. (Correct)
7. **As well as :** When two subjects are joined by 'as well as', the verb always agrees with the first subject.
   Examples :
   (i) The teacher as well as students is playing.
   (ii) Students as well as the teacher are playing.
   Note : 'Both' and 'as well as' cannot be used together in the same sentence.
   Examples :
   Both Sita as well as Kanta are beautiful. (Incorrect)
   Sita as well as Kanta is beautiful. (Correct)
   Both Sita and Kanta are beautiful. (Correct)
8. **As if :** 'As if' is used in the sense of pretension. While using 'as if' in a sentence, we should see that even the third person singular subject gets 'were'.
   Example : He talks as if he were mad.
9. **Till :** Till expresses time. Till is always used in the affirmative.
   Example :
   We did not come back till sunset.
10. **Rather than :** 'Rather than' is used in the sense of 'preference'. 'Rather' is always followed by 'than'.
    Example :
    I would rather die than submit.
11. **As long as/so long as :** Both express time during which an action or event takes place.
    Example :
    As long as there is life, there is hope.
12. **However :** It is both a subordinate and co-ordinate clause.
    Examples :
    (a) Mala worked hard, she however, failed.
    (b) However hard he may work, he cannot pass.
13. **Such as :** 'Such as' gives us the sense of 'like'. Such is always followed by 'as'.
    Example :
    Life is such a puzzle as cannot be solved.

MULTIPLE CHOICE QUESTIONS

Directions: *In the following questions choose the correct options to fill the blanks.*

1. Neither he .... his friend is good.
A. or B. and
C. but D. nor

2. The officer asked the peon .... why he was late.
A. that B. if
C. but D. No word needed

3. Both Ajay .... Vijay are intelligent.
A. or B. nor
C. and D. No word needed

4. No Sooner did the thief see the public .... he ran away.
A. then B. and
C. but D. than

5. Abhinav .... his brothers was going to Mumbai.
A. but
B. yet
C. No word needed
D. together with

6. He behaves .... he were the captain of the team.
A. as if B. as
C. No word needed D. that

7. Either Rupali .... Sonali is going to attend the meeting.
A. and B. but
C. nor D. or

8. Neither Nirmal .... Ashwinee is going to listen the speech.
A. and B. but
C. nor D. or

9. Ravi .... Prakash are going to Kolkata.
A. or B. nor
C. but D. and

10. Rice .... curry is my usual breakfast.
A. and B. but
C. then D. than

11. Hardly had he left .... his brother came.
A. then B. than
C. when D. that

12. I would rather have a copy .... a book.
A. then B. than
C. when D. that

13. He is no other .... my friend.
A. then B. than
C. when D. but

14. He saw a snake ....he awoke.
A. then B. when
C. than D. No word needed

15. Ten years have passed .... my grandmother died.
A. since B. when
C. then D. than

16. She is .... good .... bad.
A. either, not B. neither, or
C. neither, nor D. neither, than

17. The cellphone is both cheap .... best.
A. than B. and
C. then D. or

18. No sooner did the rogue see the police .... he disappeared.
A. then B. than
C. so D. because

19. Srishti will go .... Sanju goes.
A. if B. than
C. then D. although

20. She is wise .... timid.
A. and B. yet
C. but D. however

21. Make hay .... the sun shines.
A. though B. while
C. after D. before

22. He is so weak .... he cannot walk.
A. but B. that
C. then D. so

23. Although he is rich, ... he is unhappy.
A. but B. yet
C. so D. still

24. Wait here .... I come back.
A. till B. until
C. before D. after

25. He is my friend .... I shall help him.
A. so B. hence
C. that is why D. therefore

26. He must go away .... he will be beaten.
A. otherwise B. and
C. or D. else

27. God loves good men .... good men love God.
A. and B. or
C. that D. those

28. He was late .... he was not punished.
A. but B. yet
C. still D. therefore

29. Walk slowly ...., you may fall.
A. and B. or
C. so D. otherwise

30. Work hard, ... you will fail.
A. and B. or
C. otherwise D. else

ANSWERS

1	2	3	4	5	6	7	8	9	10
D	D	C	D	D	A	D	C	D	A
11	12	13	14	15	16	17	18	19	20
C	B	B	B	A	C	B	B	A	C
21	22	23	24	25	26	27	28	29	30
B	B	B	A	B	C	A	C	D	D

PREPOSITIONS

A *Preposition* is a word which is placed before a noun or a pronoun to show its relation to some other word in the sentence.

1. I saw a goat *in* the field.
2. I am fond *of* hot coffee.

In sentence 1. the word *in* shows the relation between two things—*goat* and *field.*

In sentence 2. the word *of* shows the relation between the attribute expressed by the adjective *found* and *tea.*

The words *in* and *of* are here used as prepositions.

The noun or pronoun which is used with a preposition is called its object. The noun or pronoun is in the objective case. It is governed by the preposition. Now it is absolutely clear that in sentence 1. the noun *field* is in the objective case. The word *field* is governed by the preposition *in.*

A preposition may have two or more objects.

The road runs over *hill* and *plain.*

Here, the words *hill* and *plain* are used as objects.

Use of Important Prepositions

1. Among, Between

'**Among**' is used for more than two persons or things; '**Between**' is used only for two.

Examples :

(i) Distribute these sweets *among* the poor students of the class.

(ii) Distribute these books *between* Ram and Shyam.

2. Among, In

'**Among**' is used before collective plural nouns. '**In**' is used before collective singular nouns.

Examples :

(i) I found him standing *among* the crowd.

(ii) I saw him in the crowd.

3. Beside, Besides

'**Beside**' means 'by the side of'. '**Besides**' means 'in addition to'.

Examples :

(i) The daughter was sitting *beside* her mother.

(ii) *Besides* his relatives, he invited his friends also.

4. In, Within

'**In**' means at the expiry of a period of time in future. '**Within**' means before the expiry of a period of time in any tense.

Examples :

(i) She will return *in* a week.

(ii) I shall finish my work *within* a weak.

5. On, Upon

'**On**' is used for things at rest; '**Upon**' is used for things in motion.

Examples :

(i) He is sitting *on* the floor.

(ii) The dog sprang *upon* the table.

6. By, With

'**By**' denotes the agent or doer. '**With**' denotes the instrument with which anything is done.

Examples :

(i) The bird was killed *by* the hunter with an arrow.

(ii) He beat the dog *with* a stick.

(iii) I shall reach here *by* five o'clock.

7. After, In

'**After**' means at the end of a period of time in the past. '**In**' means at the end of a period of time in future.

Examples :

(i) I shall return your book *in* a week.

(ii) He returned the book *after* a week.

8. For, From, Since

'**For**' is used before a noun denoting a period of time with all the tenses. '**From**' is used before a noun or phrase denoting a point of time, it is used in all the tenses. '**Since**' is used before a noun or phrase denoting some point of time and is always produced by a verb in the perfect continuous tense or third form of a verb.

Examples :

(i) We have been playing cards *for* two hours.

(ii) She stayed with her uncle *from* the 15th of March to the 15th of May.

(iii) I have been reading this book *since* morning.

9. Above, Over

'**Above**' means 'higher from'. **Over** is used in the following four senses :

(i) In the sense of 'above' :
At noon, the sun is *over* our heads.

(ii) In the sense of 'beyond' :
I cannot get *over* my disappointment.

(iii) In the sense of 'Superiority' :
God *over* all blesses for ever more.

(iv) In the sense of 'Conclusion' :
It is all *over* with me.

10. At, Towards

'At' denotes the idea of aim. **'Towards'** denotes the idea of destination.

Examples :

(i) He threw the stone *at* the cat.
(ii) He went *towards* the house.

11. At, In, On

'At' is used as follows :

(i) **'At'** is used with small towns and villages. **Examples:**
(a) He was born *at* Sonepat.
(b) He lives *at* village Bangra. (Bangra is a village)

(ii) **'At'** is used before a noun denoting a definite point of time.

Example :

He called on me *at* 9 p.m. yesterday.

'In' is used as follows :

(iii) **'In'** is used with the names of big cities, provinces and countries.

Examples :

(a) His father lives *in* England.
(b) His younger brother lives *in* Calcutta.

(iv) **'In'** is used before the names of months and years.

Example :

His elder sister was born *in* 1972 *in* the month of May.

'On' is used with dates and names of days. **Examples:**
(a) I joined college *on* the 26th April.
(b) He will leave for Kolkata *on* Wednesday next.

Important Information

1. **'In'** is also used in the following phrases :
In the morning; In the evening, In winter, In summer.
2. **'In'** also denotes a place inside anything.
He travelled *in* a crowded bus.
3. **'At'** is used in the following phrases :
At home, *At* the station, *At* work, *At* play.

12. Below, Beneath

Below means 'of lower level in position, dignity and expectation' etc. *Beneath* means 'under'.

Examples :

(i) It is *below* my dignity to talk to her.
(ii) They rested *beneath* the shade of a tree.

13. In, Into, To

'In' expresses Rest or Motion inside anything. **'Into'** expresses Motion towards the inside of anything or change from one medium to another. **'To'** denotes motion from one place to another.

Examples :

(i) The boys are *in* the room.
(ii) Translate this passage from English *into* Hindi.
(iii) Every morning he goes *to* the temple.

14. Till, By, Of, Off

- 'Till' means upto or not earlier than.
- 'By' means not later than.
- 'Of' shows cause, source, separation, quality, contents, possession, apposition, point of reference, space in time etc.
- 'Off' shows separation at a near distance, and detached condition.

Consider the following examples:

(i) I shall work *till* 5 a.m.
(ii) Madhu died *of* cancer.
(iii) The nib *of* the pen is made *of* gold.
(iv) He presented me a bottle *of* perfume.
(v) Our principal is a man *of* principle.
(vi) He lived in the house *of* his friend.
(vii) *By* this time tomorrow, I'll have finished my job.
(viii) My house is *off* the road.
(ix) The book fell *off* the table.

MULTIPLE CHOICE QUESTIONS

Directions: *Tick the correct preposition for the blank in each of the following sentences.*

1. He applied ...... the manager.
A. for B. to
C. with D. by
2. Trust ...... God and do the right.
A. in B. for
C. to D. with
3. She is worthy ...... a prize.
A. with B. for
C. to D. of
4. Mr. Gomes has no taste ...... music.
A. of B. for
C. with D. to
5. You are hard ...... hearing.
A. at B. of
C. with D. for
6. He is sure ...... his success
A. for B. with
C. on D. of
7. Preeti was warned ...... the danger ahead.
A. for B. at
C. of D. about
8. I am thankful ...... you for a good advice.
A. for B. with
C. to D. of
9. Deepak would not surrender ...... the police.
A. with B. to
C. for D. on
10. The small plant in your lawn is very sensitive ...... touch.
A. on B. with
C. to D. about

11. Divya was sure to succeed ..... the examination.
    A. for B. in
    C. to D. with
12. Geeta was jealous ...... Ravina's beauty.
    A. to B. with
    C. for D. of
13. He was ignorant ..... what was happening there.
    A. for B. of
    C. to D. with
14. Your pen is inferior ...... mine.
    A. than B. with
    C. from D. to
15. Reenu is no match ...... Meenu.
    A. to B. for
    C. with D. upon
16. It is necessary ...... you to apply for this job.
    A. on B. with
    C. for D. to
17. Be loyal ...... your country.
    A. for B. to
    C. on D. with
18. Mukesh is junior ...... me.
    A. than B. to
    C. from D. of
19. Deepika was innocent ...... the crime.
    A. of B. with
    C. from D. to
20. I am desirous.... joining the Indian cricket team.
    A. for B. of
    C. to D. on

ANSWERS

1	2	3	4	5	6	7	8	9	10
B	A	D	B	B	D	D	D	B	D
11	**12**	**13**	**14**	**15**	**16**	**17**	**18**	**19**	**20**
B	D	B	D	B	D	B	B	A	B

SYNONYMS

A synonym is a word which conveys a meaning similar to the given word.

REMEMBER

Words	*Synonyms*
Add	Increase
Adequate	Enough
Adjust	Adapt
All	Aggregate
Allow	Permit
Abode	Dwelling
Apt	Proper
Assess	Appraise
Accuse	Calumniate
Abashed	Timid
Annoy	Displease
Ample	Enough, Sufficient
Amplify	Increase
Apathetic	Unenthusiastic
Accost	Address
Authentic	True
Adjust	Fit
Approve	Assent, Allow, Accept
Adapt	Conform
Adversary	Opponent, Rival, Competitor
Beat	Whack
Benign	Kind
Breeze	Zephyr
Baffle	Puzzle
Booty	Spoil

Words	*Synonyms*
Beauty	Charm
Beast	Animal
Bandit	Robber
Blaze	Shine
Bond	Tie
Bend	Twist
Bate	Diminish
Beg	Plead
Barbaric	Wild, Savage
Bashful	Shy, Reserved
Begin	Start
Blend	Mix, Mingle
Bizarre	Funny
Below	Under
Bedevil	Confuse
Bemoan	Lament
Babble	Nonsense
Blame	Fault
Behaviour	Demeanour
Call	Accost
Copy	Imitate
Close	Shut
Caress	Love
Camp	Stay
Connect	Attach
Cut	Injure, Curtail
Cling	Stick
Conical	Funny
Convey	Carry
Conspicuous	Prominent
Cheerful	Happy, Pleasant

Words	Synonyms
Curtail	Decrease
Cheerless	Sad, Dejected
Curious	Strange
Circumstance	Factor, Situation, Condition
Competent	Capable
Congruent	Overlapping
Cope	Deal, Endure
Confident	Sure
Complex	Intricate
Cajole	Coax, Flatter
Cunning	Crafty
Delectable	Joyful, Delightful
Devilish	Diabolical
Delicate	Soft
Devil	Fiend
Delay	Postpone
Dislike	Repugnance
Destroy	Ruin
Dwell	Live, Dilate
Declare	Pronounce
Drunk	Flushed
Deficient	Lacking
Damn	Condemn, Curse
Decrease	Diminish
Destruction	Devastation
Efficient	Competent
Ethnic	Racial
Enthral	Enslave
Earnest	Serious
Envious	Jealous
Ending	Final
Egg	Incite
Extempore	At once
Extensive	Far-ranging
Extra	Surplus
Existence	Life
Exceed	Overstep
Enormous	Vast
Excessive	Superfluous
Free	Unhindered
Frigid	Cold
Feed	Cater
Fame	Reputation
Frame	Make
First	Initial
Frighten	Terrorise, Intimidate
Fervent	Fervid
Fall	Decline
Feeble	Frail
Fickle	Changeable
Finish	Conclude
Fraud	Deception
Forgiving	Placable
Grow	Develop
Greed	Avidity
Greet	Welcome
Grave	Serious
Group	Constellation
Given	Bestowed
Gratitude	Thankfulness
Have	Possess
Hire	Rent
Hit	Strike
Handsome	Beautiful
Hinder	Prevent
Heap	Pile
Hope	Expect
Hard	Harsh
Help	Aid
Hymn	Song
Henpecked	Enslaved
Hoodwink	Mystify, Cheat
Humble	Polite, Urbane, Modest
Harass	Vex, Trouble
Impart	Instil
Intact	Untouched
Instal	Establish
Indict	Impeach
Imitate	Ape
Instigate	Incite
Initiate	Start, Introduce
Inimical	Unfriendly
Insufferable	Intolerable
Impartiality	Justice
Jolly	Merry
Joyful	Delectable
Join	Conjoin
Kind	Benign
Kill	Murder
Kindred	Similar
Kinship	Relationship
Keen	Sharp
Knowledge	Scholarship
Lazy	Slothful
Large	Substantial, Gargantuan
Listless	Careless, Lackadaisical
Lax	Loose
Little	Small
Lifelike	Realistic
Lofty	High
Lenient	Soft, Gentle
Lacking	Deficient, Wanting
Lessen	Decrease
Middleclass	Bourgeois
Mitigate	Lessen, Abate
Modesty	Humility, Lowliness

Words	Synonyms
Mix	Mingle, Blend
Mixture	Mingling
Mixed	Assorted
Modify	Decrease
Mean	Imply
Multifarious	Varied
Miscarry	Abort
Note	Notice
Noble	Stately
Native	Indigenous
Needful	Necessary
Notify	Declare
Nervous	Shaky, Tremulous, Timid
Natural	Spontaneous
Near	Close
Normal	Natural
Offend	Displease
Oppress	Persecute, Tyrannize
Opponent	Adversary
Obstruct	Hinder, Check
Offence	Fault
Offender	Villain
Overstep	Exceed
Overlapping	Congruent
Occult	Mystic
Profane	Unholy
Patience	Forbearance
Pornographic	Obscene
Plenitude	Abundance
Prominent	Important
Prodigal	Spender
Procrastinate	Postpone
Promote	Develop, Honour
Persecute	Tyrannise
Profess	Claim
Pliant	Flexible
Plebian	Common
Polished	Sophisticated
Quake	Shake
Quit	Leave
Queer	Eccentric
Quell	Suppress
Quantify	Allot
Reply	Answer
Relinquish	Retire
Read	Peruse
Relation	Reference
Render	Do
Remainder	Residuals
Repeat	Reiterate
Repentant	Contrite
Retaliative	Retaliatory
Rumour	Hearsay
Reveal	Divulge

Words	Synonyms
Ritualistic	Ceremonious
Soft	Delicate
Sort	Kind, Choose, Select
Selfish	Egoistic
Sensual	Earthly
Suppress	Quell, Check
Stimulate	Provoke
Tasteless	Insipid
Travel	Journey
True	Authentic, Faithful, Truthful
Turbulence	Turmoil
Tragedy	Calamity
Tasteful	Tasty, Delicious
Touching	Painful
Thankful	Grateful
Tremendous	Great, Huge
Tough	Strong
Terminate	Conclude, End
Theory	Doctrine
Tell	Relate
Tremble	Shake, Shiver
Urge	Spur
Unbeaten	Unsubdued
Use	Utilize, Practise
Underhand	Unfair, Undue
Unfair	Unjust
Unravel	Reveal, Divulge
Unimportant	Common
Unconcerned	Apathetic
Unimitated	Inimitable
Unfortunate	Unlucky
Understand	Perceive, Comprehend
Vain	Proud, Haughty, Conceited, Shameless
Vale	Valley, Dale, Dell
Vice	Fault
Virtue	Quality
Veracity	Reality
Value	Price, Prize
Vex	Tease
Vibrate	Quiver, Shake
Violent	Excessive
Vivid	Clear, Lucid
Victory	Triumph
Vulgar	Indecent
Virtuous	Honest
Variegated	Varied, Multifarious
Well	Good
Yell	Cry, Shout
Yonder	There
Yearn	Wish, Desire
Yoke	Slavery
Zest	Earnestness, Enthusiasm
Zealous	Earnest

ANTONYMS

A antonym is a word which conveys a meaning opposite to the given word.

REMEMBER

Words	*Antonyms*
Abhor	Love
Abnormal	Normal
Able	Unable
Acceptable	Unacceptable
Adequate	Inadequate
Amusing	Boring
Angry	Calm
Apex	Bottom
Attract	Repel
Bad	Good
Barren	Fertile
Beautiful	Ugly
Bitter	Sweet
Brave	Cowardly
Brief	Lengthy
Bright	Dull
Calm	Violent
Careful	Careless
Clear	Vague, Cloudy
Cold	Hot
Cruel	Kind
Dear	Cheap
Deep	Shallow
Difficult	Easy
Direct	Indirect
Dishonest	Honest
Disobey	Obey
Encourage	Discourage
Enormous	Tiny
Excellent	Bad
Expensive	Cheap
Eat	Fast
Fair	Unfair
Fake	Authentic
False	True
Famous	Notorious
Fool	Genius
Generous	Miserly
Genius	Fool
Genuine	Unauthentic
Gigantic	Tiny
Glad	Depressed
Good	Bad
Great	Little
Happy	Sad
Hard	Soft
Hate	Love
Honest	Dishonest
Idle	Busy

Words	*Antonyms*
Immoral	Moral
Include	Exclude
Incorrect	Correct
Intelligent	Unintelligent
Kind	Cruel
Like	Dislike
Long	Short
Lucid	Vague
Major	Minor
Naive	Experienced
Nadir	Apex
Neat	Clumsy
Obedient	Disobedient
Obscure	Clear
Oppose	Support
Optimistic	Pessimistic
Out	In
Patience	Impatience
Peaceful	Belligerent
Pious	Impious
Polite	Impolite
Potent	Impotent
Prominent	Unimportant
Proper	Improper
Pure	Impure
Quick	Slow
Quiet	Disturbance
Real	False, Unreal
Reject	Select, Choose
Reliable	Unreliable
Respect	Disrespect
Right	Wrong
Robust	Feeble, Weak
Sad	Happy
Secret	Open
Sensible	Insensible
Severe	Mild
Sharp	Blunt
Simple	Complex
Sociable	Unsociable
Tall	Short
Tidy	Untidy
Uncanny	Canny
Violent	Calm
Vivid	Vague
Strong	Weak
Big	Small
Easy	Difficult
Fast	Slow
High	Low
Catchy	Unattractive
Ugly	Handsome, Beautiful, Tidy
Tasty	Insipid
Sonorous	Harsh

MULTIPLE CHOICE QUESTIONS

Directions (Qs. 1 to 20): *In the following questions choose the word which best expresses the meaning of the given word.*

1. ABSURD
A. Foolish B. Simple
C. Courageous D. Silly

2. ABANDON
A. Lose B. Profit
C. Vacate D. Foil

3. CAJOLE
A. Pause B. Lenient
C. Blast D. Lure

4. COMBAT
A. Fight B. Conflict
C. Shoot D. Quarrel

5. LAMENT
A. Condone B. Console
C. Complain D. Contribution

6. DEBACLE
A. Disgrace B. Defeat
C. Collapse D. Decline

7. SHIVER
A. Fear B. Tremble
C. Shake D. Ache

8. TORTURE
A. Terror B. Harassment
C. Torment D. Tranquility

9. LAUDABLE
A. Lovable B. Commendable
C. Profitable D. Oblivious

10. FIXED
A. Sterile B. Static
C. Stubborn D. Parennial

11. QUEER
A. Unfamiliar B. Cute
C. Curious D. Strange

12. SUFFICIENT
A. Fit B. Proper
C. Adequate D. Vast

13. GLOSS
A. Brightness B. Soothing
C. Rubbing D. Miracle

14. LONGING
A. Prune B. Apathy
C. Curtail D. Craving

15. JEER
A. Applaud B. Magnanimity
C. Avoid D. Scoff

16. ZENITH
A. Minimum B. Nadir
C. Plant D. Peak

17. GARB
A. Distort B. Dress
C. Trivial D. Rage

18. ABHOR
A. Rude B. Reconcile
C. Crave D. Detest

19. YIELD
A. Shum B. Incisive
C. Retain D. Surrender

20. YOKE
A. Twist B. Release
C. Link D. Extra

Directions (Qs. 21 to 26): *In the following questions choose the word which best expresses the opposite of the given word.*

21. TRAGIC
A. Dramatic B. Strong
C. Gentle D. Comic

22. ORAL
A. Verbal B. Sane
C. Minor D. Written

23. ADMIRE
A. Hate B. Unlike
C. Dislike D. Enough

24. VIOLENT
A. Gentle B. Savage
C. Haughty D. Decline

25. ADVERSITY
A. Windfall B. Inprosperity
C. Prosperity D. Slave

26. GENUINE
A. Spurious B. Obscure
C. Countless D. Apathetic

ANSWERS

1	2	3	4	5	6	7	8	9	10
D	C	D	A	C	C	B	C	B	B
11	**12**	**13**	**14**	**15**	**16**	**17**	**18**	**19**	**20**
D	C	A	D	D	D	B	D	D	C
21	**22**	**23**	**24**	**25**	**26**				
D	D	C	A	C	A				

●●●

3

Sentence Completion

It is such an exercise which starts with the primary schools and continues in the highest level of competitive examinations. One must practise it regularly to score well.

Directions (Qs. 1 to 15): *Pick out the most effective word(s) from the given words to fill in the blanks to make the sentence meaningfully complete.*

1. The student ...... that book from the library to study at home.
A. issued
B. borrowed
C. hired
D. lent

2. I wish I ...... a king.
A. was
B. am
C. should be
D. were

3. He ...... to listen to my arguments and walked away.
A. denied
B. disliked
C. objected
D. refused

4. The flow of blood was so ...... that the patient died.
A. intense
B. adequate
C. profuse
D. extensive

5. When I met her yesterday, it was the first time I ...... her since Christmas.
A. saw
B. have seen
C. had seen
D. have been seing

6. Can you pay ...... all these articles?
A. for
B. of
C. off
D. out

7. I ...... you to be at the party this evening.
A. expect
B. hope
C. look forward to
D. desire

8. ...... being a handicapped person, he is very cooperative and self-reliant.
A. Because
B. Although
C. Since
D. Despite

9. The child broke ...... from his mother and ran towards the painting.
A. away
B. after
C. down
D. with

10. With his ...... income, he finds it difficult to live a comfortable life.
A. brief
B. sufficient
C. meagre
D. huge

11. He could ...... a lot of money in such a short time by using his intelligence and working hard.
A. spend
B. spoil
C. exchange
D. accumulate

12. Though the brothers are twins, they look ......
A. alike
B. handsome
C. indifferent
D. different

13. Unfavourable weather conditions can ..... illness.
A. cure
B. detect
C. treat
D. enhance

14. No sooner did the bell ring, ... the actor started singing.
A. when
B. than
C. after
D. before

15. If I ...... realised it, I would not have acted on his advice.
A. was
B. had
C. were
D. have

Directions (Qs. 16 to 25): *In each question, an incomplete statement (Stem) followed by four fillers is given. Pick out the best one which can complete the incomplete stem correctly and meaningfully.*

16. Unless you work harder you will fail, means......
A. if you fail you will work harder.
B. you must at least plan well than you will not fail.
C. hardly you will fail if you do not desire so.
D. if you do not put more efforts, then you will fail.

17. Even if it rains, I shall come, means .....
A. if I come it will not rain.
B. if it rains I shall not come.
C. I will certainly come whether it rains or not.
D. whenever there is rain I shall come.

18. Dinesh is as stupid as he is lazy means .....
A. Dinesh is stupid because he is lazy.
B. Dinesh is lazy because he is stupid.
C. Dinesh is either stupid or lazy.
D. Dinesh is equally stupid and lazy.

19. He is so lazy that he .....
A. cannot depend on others for getting his work done.
B. cannot delay the schedule of completing the work.
C. can seldom complete his work on time.
D. dislike to postpone the work that he undertakes to do.

20. He always stammers in public meetings, but his today's speech .....
A. was fairly audible to everyone present in the hall.
B. was not received satisfactorily.
C. could not be understood properly.
D. was free from that defect.

21. In order to raise the company's profit, the employees.....
A. demanded two additional increments.
B. decided to go on paid holidays.
C. requested the management to implement new welfare schemes.
D. offered to work overtime without any compensation.

22. Although, he is reputed for making very candid statements, ...
A. his today's speech was not fairly audible.
B. his promises had always been realistic.
C. his speech was very interesting.
D. his today's statements were very ambiguous.

23. I felt somewhat more relaxed .....
A. but tense as compared to earlier.
B. and tense as compared to earlier.
C. as there was already no tension at all.
D. and tension-free as compared to earlier.

24. With great efforts his son succeeded in convincing him not to donate his entire wealth to an orphanage ....
A. and lead the life of a wealthy merchant.
B. but to a home for the forsaken children.
C. and make an orphan of himself.
D. as the orphanage needed a lot of donations.

25. Even though it is a very large house, ...
A. there is a lot of space available in it for children.
B. there is hardly any space available for children.
C. there is no dearth of space for children.
D. the servants take a long time to clean it.

ANSWERS

1	2	3	4	5	6	7	8	9	10
B	D	D	C	C	A	A	D	A	C
11	**12**	**13**	**14**	**15**	**16**	**17**	**18**	**19**	**20**
D	D	D	B	B	D	C	D	C	D
21	**22**	**23**	**24**	**25**					
D	D	D	C	B					

●●●

4

Spotting Errors

The most common errors in English are of spellings, grammar and usage of words. By regular practice, the errors can be easily spotted and minimised.

MULTIPLE CHOICE QUESTIONS

Directions: *In the following questions some of the sentences have errors and some are correct. Find out which part of a sentence has an error, the number of that part is your answer. If a sentence is free from errors, then your answer is D i.e., No error.*

1. (A) Either Ram or/(B) you is responsible/(C) for this action./(D) No error.

2. (A) The student flatly denied/(B) that he had copied/(C) in the examination hall./(D) No error.

3. (A) By the time you arrive tomorrow/(B) I have finished/(C) my work./(D) No error.

4. (A) The captain with the members of his team/(B) are returning/(C) after a fortnight./(D) No error.

5. (A) After returning from/(B) an all-India tour/(C) I had to describe about it./(D) No error.

6. (A) The teacher asked his students/(B) if they had gone through/(C) either of the three chapters included in the prescribed text./(D) No error.

7. (A) Do you know/(B) how old were you/(C) when you came here?/(D) No error.

8. (A) Beware of/(B) a fair-weather friend/(C) who is neither a friend in need nor a friend indeed./(D) No error.

9. (A) Copernicus proved/(B) that Earth/(C) moves round the Sun./(D) No error.

10. (A) The property/(B) was divided/(C) among the two brothers./(D) No error.

11. (A) I am quite certain/(B) that the lady is not only greedy/(C) but miserly./(D) No error.

12. (A) The brilliant success in the examination/(B) as well as his record in sports/(C) deserves high praise./(D) No error.

13. (A) I cannot find/(B) where has he gone/(C) though I have tried may best./(D) No error.

14. (A) If I was/(B) the Prime Minister of India/(C) I would work wonders/(D) No error.

15. (A) If it weren't/(B) for you,/(C) I wouldn't be alive today./(D) No error.

16. (A) He looked like a lion/(B) baulked from/(C) its prey./(D) No error.

17. (A) Widespread flooding/(B) is affecting/(C) large areas of the villages./(D) No error.

18. (A) If we really set to/(B) we can get the whole house/(C) cleaned in an afternoon./(D) No error.

ANSWERS

1	2	3	4	5	6	7	8	9	10
B	D	B	B	C	C	D	D	B	C
11	**12**	**13**	**14**	**15**	**16**	**17**	**18**	**19**	**20**
C	D	B	A	C	C	C	A	A	C

EXPLANATORY ANSWERS

1. Replace 'is' by 'are'.

2. No error.

3. Replace 'have' by 'would have'.

4. Replace 'are' by 'is'.

5. Replace 'had to describe' by 'described'.

6. Replace 'either' by 'any'.

7. No error.

8. No error.

9. Omit 'that'.

10. Replace 'among' by 'between'.

11. Add 'also'.

12. No error.

13. Replace 'has he' by 'he has'.

14. Replace 'was' by 'were'.

15. Replace 'wouldn't be' by 'would not have been'.

16. Replace 'its' by 'his'.

17. Replace 'areas' by 'area'.

18. Replace 'set to' by 'set on'.

●●●

5

One Word Substitution

There are many single words in English language which can be perfectly used for a number of words. These words help in expressing ideas in a short and correct manner for the right occasion. Such words not only increase the vocabulary but also enable you to economise in the use of words to a great extent.

Multiple Word Expression	*Substitution*
One who always looks towards the bright side of things	Optimist
One who always looks towards the dark side of things	Pessimist
The time when one develops from a child into an adult	Adolescence
The process of growing more plants in order to form a forest.	Afforestation
The science which deals with farming	Agriculture
From some other country or place etc.	Alien
A term, etc. giving more than one meaning	Ambiguous
A vehicle which is used to carry sick persons	Ambulance
An animal which can live both in water and on land	Amphibian
A lawless situation when there is no government	Anarchy
Belonging to the history of thousands of years old	Ancient
Once a year	Annual
A very old object but still valuable	Antique
Words of opposite meanings	Antonyms
Words of similar meanings	Synonyms
Signatures of a famous person	Autograph
A government led by one person with absolute authority	Autocracy
A written work of one's own life history	Autobiography
A person who has never been married	Bachelor
A person usually having no hair on his head	Bald
A place where one can deposit money and get interest	Bank
A person who cuts our hair	Barber
A building/group of buildings where soldiers live	Barracks
A person who makes buns and biscuits	Baker
A person who lives by asking people for food and money without doing any useful job	Beggar
The crime of having married to two persons at the same time	Bigamy
The branch of science which deals with the study of plants	Botany
Able to speak two languages	Bilingual
Able to speak more than two languages	Polyglot
The branch of science which deals with the living organisms	Biology
A powerful snow storm	Blizzard
A great successful book or movie	Blockbuster
A short news on the radio or TV	Bulletin
A system in which the most important works are organised by the government officials	Bureaucracy
A person who has no vision in his eyes	Blind
A page or a series of pages on which the information of days, weeks, months, etc. is given	Calendar
A person who eats human flesh	Cannibal
A complete list of items often arranged alphabetically	Catalogue
A sudden disaster	Catastrophe
A period of 100 years	Century

Multiple Word Expression	*Substitution*
A branch of science which deals with chemicals	Chemistry
A printed leaf usually issued by banks that we sign to carry certain financial deal	Cheque
A person who makes or mends shoes	Cobbler
A group of people who has been chosen by others to make decisions on their own	Committee
A building in which nuns live	Convent
An animal which feeds on other animals	Carnivorous
A person who does criticism	Critic
A person who cannot hear	Deaf
A condition in which one loses a lot of water from one's body because of vomiting, etc.	Dehydration
A system of government in which the people cast their votes to elect their leaders	Democracy
The study of skin problems	Dermatology
A long piece of land covered with sand	Desert
The art of managing relationships between countries	Diplomacy
A piece of information about the words in a book form	Dictionary
A piece of information about the telephone numbers of the people in a book from	Directory
A person in charge of a newspapers, magazine etc.	Editor
A person who thinks he is better than the others	Egoist
To leave your country and settle in some other country	Emigrate
A book or series of books giving almost all knowledge about an area or some persons etc.	Encyclopaedia
Study of insects	Entomology
Time when day and night are of the same duration	Equinox
To sell things out of the country	Export
To purchase things from some other country	Import
A plant or animal no longer in existence	Extinct
A situation when there is a shortage of food for a long period of time	Famine
An amount of money that we pay for some action or services	Fee
Related to women	Feminine
An animal strong and aggressive	Ferocious
A piece of land where plants grow easily from the soil that is favourable to them	Fertile
A work of literature having some imaginary events	Fiction
A large amount of water covering certain area	Flood
A person who sells flowers	Florist
A religious ceremony for burying or cremating a dead person	Funeral
A substance which kills fungus	Fungicide
A person studying or having studied the diseases and the related things of female reproductory system	Gynaecologist
The murder of the person of the same group race or country	Genocide
A substance which kills germs	Germicide
A situation in which many people die because of fire during war	Holocaust
The act of killing a person deliberately	Homicide
A word having the pronunciation as the other one does but it differs in meaning	Homophone
A word having the same spelling as the other one does but it is pronounced in some other way	Homonym
A person who is attracted towards the person of the same sex	Homosexual
Go across and parallel to the ground	Horizontal
A substance which kills the insects	Insecticide
That cannot be corrected	Incorrigible
That cannot be defeated	Invincible
That cannot be eaten	Inedible
That cannot be seen	Invisible
A place in a school or college where books are kept for the benefit of students, teachers etc.	Library
A place in a school or college where scientific experiments are performed	Laboratory

Multiple Word Expression	*Substitution*
An official who is a judge in the lowest court	Magistrate
A piece of music or a book before it is printed	Manuscript
Related to men	Masculine
One who believes in the existence of God	A theist
One who does not believe in the existence of good	An atheist
That can be believed	Credible
That cannot be believed	Incredible
That which dissolves in a solvent	Soluble
That which does not dissolves in a solvent	Insoluble
Hard writing that can be read	Legible
Hard writing that cannot be read	Illegible
A person who does jobs beneficial to mankind	Philanthropist
A person who goes on foot	Pedestrian
A person who fights for his own country	Patriot
An act of killing oneself	Suicide
A woman whose husband is dead	Widow
A man whose wife is dead	Widower
A person who eats vegetarian and non-vegetarian diets	Omnivorous
Something which is everywhere at the same time	Omnipresent
One who knows everything	Omniscient
A child who does not have parents	Orphan
An award etc. given after the death of the person	Posthumous
The place where animals are kept for amusement and to increase the knowledge of the public	Zoo
The science which deals with the study of animals	Zoology

MULTIPLE CHOICE QUESTIONS

Directions: *In questions given below, out of the four alternatives, choose the one which can be substituted for the given words/sentences.*

1. Something that relates to everyone in the world
   A. General B. Common
   C. Usual D. Universal

2. An expression of mild disapproval
   A. Warning B. Denigration
   C. Impertinence D. Reproof

3. One who is not easily pleased by anything
   A. Maiden B. Medieval
   C. Precarious D. Fastidious

4. Murder of a king
   A. Infanticide B. Matricide
   C. Genocide D. Regicide

5. A remedy for all diseases
   A. Stoic B. Marvel
   C. Panacea D. Recompense

6. A dramatic performance
   A. Mask B. Mosque
   C. Masque D. Mascot

7. Study of birds
   A. Orology B. Optology
   C. Ophthalmology D. Ornithology

8. Ready to believe
   A. Credulous B. Credible
   C. Creditable D. Incredible

9. Incapable of being seen through
   A. Ductile B. Opaque
   C. Obsolete D. Potable

10. One who eats everything
    A. Omnivorous B. Omniscient
    C. Irresistible D. Insolvent

11. A place where bees are kept is called
    A. An apiary B. A mole
    C. A hive D. A sanctuary

12. One who cannot be corrected
    A. Incurable B. Incorrigible
    C. Hardened D. Invulnerable

13. One who is in charge of a museum
    A. Curator B. Supervisor
    C. Caretaker D. Warden

14. Continuing fight between parties, families, clans, etc.
    A. Enmity B. Feud
    C. Quarrel D. Skirmish

15. A voice loud enough to be heard
    A. Audible B. Applaudable
    C. Laudable D. Oral

16. A paper written by hand
A. Handicraft B. Manuscript
C. Handiwork D. Thesis

17. Habitually silent or talking little
A. Serville B. Unequivocal
C. Taciturn D. Synoptic

18. To slap with a flat object
A. Chop B. Hew
C. Gnaw D. Swat

19. A person who speaks many languages
A. Linguist B. Monolingual
C. Polyglot D. Bilingual

20. A light sailing-boat built specially for racing
A. Canoe B. Yacht
C. Frigate D. Dinghy

21. A fixed orbit in space in relation to earth
A. Geological B. Geo-synchronous
C. Geo-centric D. Geo-stationary

22. A style in which a writer makes a display of his knowledge
A. Pedantic B. Verbose
C. Pompous D. Ornate

23. A religious discourse
A. Preach B. Stanza
C. Sanctorum D. Sermon

24. A place that provides refuge
A. Asylum B. Sanatorium
C. Shelter D. Orphanage

25. Detailed plan of a journey
A. Travelogue B. Travelkit
C. Schedule D. Itinerary

26. A person who insists on something
A. Disciplinarian B. Stickler
C. Instantaneous D. Boaster

27. A drawing on transparent paper
A. Red print B. Blue print
C. Negative D. Transparency

28. One who believes that all things and events in life are predetermined is a
A. Fatalist B. Puritan
C. Egoist D. Tyrant

29. A school boy who cuts classes frequently is a
A. Defeatist B. Sycophant
C. Truant D. Martinet

30. The act of violating the sanctity of the church is
A. Blasphemy B. Heresy
C. Sacrilege D. Desecration

31. A place where monks live as a secluded community
A. Cathedral B. Diocese
C. Convent D. Monastery

32. One who is fond of fighting
A. Bellicose B. Aggressive
C. Belligerent D. Militant

33. Tending to move away from the centre or axis
A. Centrifugal B. Centripetal
C. Axiomatic D. Awry

34. Words inscribed on tomb
A. Epitome B. Epistle
C. Epilogue D. Epitaph

35. Leave or remove from a place considered dangerous
A. Evade B. Evacuate
C. Avoid D. Exterminate

36. Original inhabitants of a country
A. Abroge B. Aborger
C. Aborgory D. Aborigins

37. Government by the officials
A. Theocracy B. Plutocracy
C. Bureaucracy D. Democracy

38. Incapable of being exhausted
A. Inexhaustible B. Inaexhaustible
C. Exhaustable D. Non-tired

39. A person of good understanding, knowledge and reasoning power
A. Expert B. Intellectual
C. Snob D. Literate

40. One absorbed in his own thoughts and feelings rather than in things outside
A. Scholar B. Recluse
C. Introvert D. Intellectual

ANSWERS

1	2	3	4	5	6	7	8	9	10
D	D	D	D	C	C	D	A	B	A
11	**12**	**13**	**14**	**15**	**16**	**17**	**18**	**19**	**20**
A	B	A	B	A	B	C	D	A	B
21	**22**	**23**	**24**	**25**	**26**	**27**	**28**	**29**	**30**
D	A	D	A	D	B	D	A	C	C
31	**32**	**33**	**34**	**35**	**36**	**37**	**38**	**39**	**40**
D	A	A	D	B	B	C	A	B	C

●●●

6

Spelling Errors

There are thousands of words in English language. It is difficult to remember the spellings and meanings of all at once. Try to learn as many as you can. Use a dictionary regularly.

Directions: *Find the correctly spelt words.*

1. A. Damage B. Dammage C. Damaige D. Dammege
2. A. Efficiant B. Effecient C. Efficient D. Eficient
3. A. Schedule B. Schdule C. Schedale D. Schedeule
4. A. Occurad B. Occurred C. Ocurred D. Occured
5. A. Grieff B. Grief C. Grieef D. Grrief
6. A. Guarantee B. Garuntee C. Guaruntee D. Gaurantee
7. A. Meddicine B. Medicine C. Medicene D. Medicinne
8. A. Benefeted B. Benefitted C. Benifited D. Benefited
9. A. Acommodation B. Acomodation C. Accomodation D. Accommodation
10. A. Querrelsome B. Quarrelsame C. Quarrelsome D. Querralsome
11. A. Sympathetic B. Smypathetic C. Sympothetic D. Sympethetic
12. A. Prograssive B. Progressive C. Progrèsive D. Prograsive
13. A. Uncivilized B. Uncevilized C. Uncivillized D. Uncevelized
14. A. Extravagant B. Extreragent C. Extreregant D. Extravegent
15. A. Missunderstood B. Miesunderstood C. Misunderstood D. Misunderstod
16. A. Belligerent B. Beligirent C. Belligarant D. Belligerrent
17. A. Astonished B. Astronished C. Astoneshed D. Asstonished
18. A. Sincerely B. Sencerely C. Sincerelly D. Sincerrely
19. A. Rigourous B. Rigerous C. Rigorous D. Regerous
20. A. Satellite B. Sattellite C. Satelite D. Sattelite
21. A. Pesanger B. Passenger C. Pessenger D. Pasanger
22. A. Humurous B. Humorous C. Humoreus D. Humorrous
23. A. Exeggerate B. Exaggerate C. Exadgerate D. Exagerate
24. A. Fariegn B. Forein C. Foriegn D. Foreign
25. A. Excesive B. Excessive C. Exccessive D. Exccesive
26. A. Forcaust B. Forcast C. Forecast D. Forecaste
27. A. Paralleted B. Paralelled C. Parralleled D. Parallelled
28. A. Ocasion B. Occassion C. Occasion D. Ocassion
29. A. Boquet B. Bouquet C. Bouquete D. Bouquette
30. A. Chettering B. Chaterring C. Chattering D. Chatering
31. A. Discourage B. Disscourage C. Discourege D. Discaurage
32. A. Curageous B. Courageous C. Courrageous D. Couregeous
33. A. Abandon B. Abanddon C. Abendon D. Abbandon
34. A. Embarassment B. Emberrassement C. Embarrassment D. Embbaresment
35. A. Eccintric B. Eccentrie C. Eccentric D. Eccintrie
36. A. Occasional B. Occassional C. Occesional D. Occessional
37. A. Querrel B. Querral C. Quarrel D. Quarel
38. A. Contrebution B. Contribution C. Contributtion D. Conterbution

39. A. Desgrace B. Disgrece C. Disgrice D. Disgrace

40. A. Harassment B. Herassment C. Harasment D. Harassmient

41. A. Imaginative B. Imeginative C. Imagenative D. Imaginetive

42. A. Suficient B. Suficiant C. Sufficient D. Sufficiant

43. A. Adequate B. Edequate C. Adaquete D. Edaquete

44. A. Exparienced B. Experianced C. Experienced D. Experrienced

45. A. Flatering B. Fletering C. Flattering D. Fletaring

46. A. Cuttiveted B. Culltrivated C. Cultivated D. Caltivated

47. A. Praiceworthy B. Peiseworthy C. Praiseworthy D. Praisaworthy

48. A. Profesional B. Professionel C. Professional D. Profissional

49. A. Ameteur B. Amateur C. Amataur D. Amateor

50. A. Unfevourable B. Unfevaurable C. Unfavourable D. Unfivourable

ANSWERS

1	2	3	4	5	6	7	8	9	10
A	C	A	B	B	A	B	B	D	C
11	**12**	**13**	**14**	**15**	**16**	**17**	**18**	**19**	**20**
A	B	A	A	C	A	A	A	C	A
21	**22**	**23**	**24**	**25**	**26**	**27**	**28**	**29**	**30**
B	B	B	D	B	C	A	C	B	C
31	**32**	**33**	**34**	**35**	**36**	**37**	**38**	**39**	**40**
A	B	A	C	C	A	C	B	D	A
41	**42**	**43**	**44**	**45**	**46**	**47**	**48**	**49**	**50**
A	C	A	C	A	C	C	C	B	C

●●●

हिन्दी भाषा

(व्याकरण एवं साहित्य)

व्याकरण

'व्याकरण' शब्द का अर्थ है– 'वाक् पृथक्करण-प्रक्रिया'। इसका निर्माण वि+आकरण यानि 'आ' उपसर्ग को 'कृ' धातु में जोड़कर जो रूप निष्पन्न होता है उसमें पुनः लुयुट् प्रत्यय जोड़ने से होता है। व्याकरण से भाषा में अनुशासन बना रहता है। वस्तुतः व्याकरण एक शास्त्र है। व्याकरण का निर्माण भाषा-विशेष के लिए होता है। अर्थात् प्रत्येक भाषा का अपना निजी व्याकरण होता है। इसके द्वारा भाषा विशेष के वर्ण, शब्द, ध्वनि और वाक्य के शुद्ध रूप एवं प्रयोग के नियम का सम्यक् निरूपण किया जाता है। दूसरे शब्दों में, व्याकरण वह शास्त्र है जिसका निर्माण भाषा-विशेष के लिए होता है और जिससे भाषा-विशेष के शुद्ध रूप तथा प्रयोग की नियमावली का ज्ञान होता है।

लिंग

हिन्दी में दो लिंग होते हैं–स्त्रीलिंग और पुल्लिंग। जो शब्द स्त्री जाति का बोध कराते हैं, उन्हें स्त्रीलिंग कहा जाता है, जैसे–राधा, लड़की, पुत्री, पुस्तक, शेरनी, चिड़िया आदि। इसके विपरीत जो शब्द पुरुष जाति का बोध कराते हैं, उन्हें पुल्लिंग कहा जाता है, जैसे–कृष्ण, शेर, बैल, गीदड़, पुत्र, लड़का। ध्यान रहे कि नपुंसक लिंग का प्रयोग संस्कृत में होता है, हिन्दी में नहीं होता।

कुछ शब्द जो प्रायः स्त्रीलिंग ही होते हैं–

(1) ईकारान्त शब्द। जैसे–चिट्ठी, पत्री, लेखनी, बोली, गोली, चोली, डोली इत्यादि।
अपवाद–मोती, घी, जी, पानी आदि शब्द पुल्लिंग हैं।

(2) नदियों के नाम। जैसे–गंगा, गमुना, सरस्वती, रावी इत्यादि। प्रायः सभी नदियों के साथ नदी शब्द का प्रयोग किया जा सकता है।

(3) संस्कृत के स्त्रीलिंग और नपुंसक लिंग जैसे–आशा, माता, दिशा इत्यादि।

(4) राशियों, तिथियों और नक्षत्रों के नाम। जैसे–मेष, वृष, मिथुन, कन्या, तीज, प्रतिपदा, आश्विन, रोहणी आदि।

(5) धातुओं के नाम जैसे–चांदी, मिट्टी, धातु आदि।

(6) कुछ समुदाय बाचक संज्ञाएं। जैसे–सेना, शाला, फौज, टोली, सभा, श्रेणी, कक्षा इत्यादि।

(7) अनाज, दालें इत्यादि। जैसे–अरहर, मकई आदि।

(8) कुछ प्राणीवाचक शब्द। जैसे–भगिनी, गाय, कोयल, चील, मैना, बिल्ली आदि।

कुछ शब्द जो प्रायः पुल्लिंग ही होते हैं–

(1) पर्वतों आदि के नाम। जैसे–हिमालय, शिवालिक, विंध्याचल आदि।

(2) भावनावाचक संज्ञाएं–जिनके अन्त में आव, पन, पा, त्व हों। जैसे–चढ़ाव, बहाव, बड़प्पन, बचपन, रंडापा, बुढ़ापा, महत्व, पुरुषत्व।

(3) महीने और दिनों के नाम। जैसे–ज्येष्ठ, बैसाख, चैत्र, मंगलवार, रविवार।

(4) ग्रहों के नाम। जैसे–मंगल, बुध, राहु, केतु आदि।

(5) वर्णमाला के सभी अक्षर–केवल इ, ई और ऋ को छोड़कर।

(6) संस्कृत के नपुंसक लिंग। जैसे–दही, मधु आदि।

(7) पेड़, अनाज सम्बन्धी शब्द। जैसे–बड़, पीपल, आम, चावल, गेहूँ, बाजरा, उड़द।

(8) द्रव्यवाचक शब्द। जैसे–सोना, तांबा, लोहा, मोती, माणिक आदि।

पुल्लिंग से स्त्रीलिंग बनाने के नियम–

(1) अकारान्त और आकारान्त शब्दों के अन्त में ई जोड़ देने से स्त्रीलिंग बन जाता है। जैसे–

नाना–नानी	लड़का–लड़की	दादा–दादी
चाचा–चाची	पुत्र–पुत्री	देव–देवी
गीदड़–गीदड़ी	कबूतर–कबूतरी	नट–नटी

(2) कुछ आकारान्त शब्दों के अन्त का 'आ' हटा कर 'इया' जोड़ दिया जाता है। जैसे–

चिड़ा–चिड़िया	चूहा–चुहिया	डिब्बा–डिबिया
कुत्ता–कुतिया	बेटा–बिटिया	बूढ़ा–बुढ़िया

(3) कुछ व्यापार-सूचक (अकारान्त, आकारान्त, इकारान्त) शब्दों के पीछे 'इन' प्रत्यय लगाकर स्त्रीलिंग बनाते हैं। जैसे–

जुलाहा–जुलाहिन	धोबी–धोबिन	कहार–कहारिन
चमार–चमारिन	ठठेरा–ठठेरिन	ग्वाला–ग्वालिन

(4) कुछ प्राणीवाचक शब्दों के पीछे 'नी' या 'इनी' प्रत्यय लगाया जाता है। जैसे

हंस–हंसिनी	जाट–जाटिनी	हाथी–हथिनी
शेर–शेरनी		

(5) कुछ प्राणीवाचक शब्दों के पीछे 'आनी' प्रत्यय भी लगाया जाता है। जैसे–

नौकर–नौकरानी	जेठ–जेठानी	देवर–देवरानी
चौधरी–चौधरानी	सेठ–सेठानी	मेहतर–मेहतरानी

(6) कुछ अकारान्त शब्दों के अन्त में 'आ' प्रत्यय लगाने से, जैसे–

शिव–शिवा	शूद्र–शूद्रा	प्रिय–प्रिया
बाल–बाला	सुत–सुता	

(7) कुछ शब्दों के अन्त में 'वती' या 'मती' लगाने से, जैसे–

भगवान्–भगवती	गुणवान्–गुणवती	श्रीमान्–श्रीमती
रूपवान्–रूपवती	बुद्धिमान्–बुद्धिमती	धनवान्–धनवती

(8) कुछ उपनाम सम्बन्धी शब्दों के अन्त में 'आइन' प्रत्यय लगाने से, जैसे–

लाला–ललाइन	ठाकुर–ठकुराइन	बाबू–बबुआइन
दुबे–दुबाइन	पण्डित–पण्डिताइन	

(9) कुछ शब्दों के अन्त में 'अक' आता है। उनको स्त्रीलिंग बनाने के लिए 'अक' प्रत्यय का 'इका' कर लिया जाता है। जैसे–

अध्यापक–अध्यापिका	सेवक–सेविका	नायक–नायिका
बालक–बालिका	प्रेषक–प्रेषिका	लेखक–लेखिका

(10) कुछ शब्दों के अन्त में 'त्री' लगाने से स्त्रीलिंग बन जाता है। जैसे–

कवि–कवयित्री	कर्ता–कर्त्री

(11) कुछ इकारान्त शब्दों के अन्त में 'ई' प्रत्यय को 'इ' करके 'णी' लगाकर स्त्रीलिंग बना लिया जाता है। जैसे–

परोपकारी–परोपकारिणी	अधिकारी–अधिकारिणी
सहधर्मी–सहधर्मिणी	कल्याणकारी–कल्याणकारिणी

(12) कुछ पुल्लिंग शब्दों के स्त्रीलिंग सर्वथा भिन्न होते हैं, जैसे–

पिता–माता	वर–वधु
राजा–रानी	विद्वान–विदुषी

वचन

वचन का शाब्दिक अर्थ है- बोली। परन्तु हिन्दी में व्यांकरण की दृष्टि में वचन का अर्थ संख्या से लिया जाता है। इसलिए वचन को परिभाषित करते हुए कहा जा सकता है– संज्ञा, सर्वनाम, विशेषण और क्रिया के जिस रूप से संख्या का बोध होता है, उसे वचन कहते हैं।

वचन के भेद

हिन्दी में वचन के दो भेद माने गए हैं (1) एकवचन (2) बहुवचन

(1) एकवचन (Singular Number) : जैसा कि नाम से स्पष्ट है, एकवचन विकारी शब्द का वह रूप है जिससे एक ही व्यक्ति या वस्तु का बोध होता है। उदाहरण- घोड़ा दौड़ता है। गाय चरती है। इन वाक्यों में 'घोड़ा' और 'गाय' से एक जानवर का बोध होता है। अतः ये एकवचन हैं।

(2) बहुवचन (Plural Number) : बहुवचन वह विकारी शब्द है जिससे एक से अधिक वस्तुओं, व्यक्तियों आदि का बोध होता है। जैसे- घोड़े चरते हैं। गायें दौड़ती हैं। 'घोड़े' और 'गायें' कहने से एक से अधिक जानवरों का बोध होता है। अतः ये बहुवचन हैं।

वचन के रूपान्तर : यद्यपि वचन के कारण संज्ञा, सर्वनाम, विशेषण और क्रिया के रूप में परिवर्तन होता है तथापि सर्वनाम, विशेषण और क्रिया के रूप मूलतः इनसे जुड़ी संख्या पर ही आधारित होते हैं। अतएव एकवचन में संज्ञा शब्दों के रूपान्तर की ही प्रमुखता है।

वचन के अधीन संज्ञा के रूप दो तरह से परिवर्तित होते हैं– (1) विभक्ति रहित (2) विभक्ति सहित

विभक्ति रहित संज्ञाओं के बहुवचन बनाने के नियम :

विभक्ति रहित संज्ञाओं का बहुवचन साधारणतः निम्नलिखित नियमों के अन्तर्गत बनाया जाता है-

1. पुल्लिंग संज्ञा के आकारान्त को एकारान्त कर बहुवचन बनाया जाता है। यथा-

एकवचन	**बहुवचन**	**एकवचन**	**बहुवचन**
घोड़ा	घोड़े	गधा	गधे
लड़का	लड़के		

अपवाद- मामा, नाना, बाबा, पिता, योद्धा, आत्मा, देवता, जामाता आदि। इन शब्दों के रूप दोनों वचनों में समान होते हैं।

2. पुल्लिंग आकारान्त शब्दों के अतिरिक्त अन्य मात्राओं से अन्त होने वाले शब्दों के रूप दोनों वचनों में एक समान रहते हैं। जैसे–

एकवचन	**बहुवचन**	**एकवचन**	**बहुवचन**
एक बालक	चार बालक	एक डाकू	चार डाकू
एक भाई	चार भाई	एक जौ	चार जौ

3. आकारान्त स्त्रीलिंग शब्दों के अन्त में 'एँ' जोड़ने से बहुवचन बनता है। जैसे–

एकवचन	**बहुवचन**	**एकवचन**	**बहुवचन**
शाखा	शाखाएँ	लता	लताएँ
माता	माताएँ	महिला	महिलाएँ

4. अकारान्त स्त्रीलिंग संज्ञा के बहुवचन शब्द में आगत अंतिम अ को यें कर देने से बनता है। जैसे–

एकवचन	**बहुवचन**	**एकवचन**	**बहुवचन**
गाय	गायें	रात	रातें
बात	बातें	आँख	आँखें
याद	यादें		

5. दीर्घ या ह्रस्व इकारान्त संज्ञाओं को ह्रस्व इकारान्त कर उनके अन्त में याँ जोड़ देने से बहुवचन बनता है। जैसे–

एकवचन	**बहुवचन**	**एकवचन**	**बहुवचन**
नारी	नारियाँ	पहेली	पहेलियाँ
लड़की	लड़कियाँ	सहेली	सहेलियाँ
नीति	नीतियाँ	नदी	नदियाँ
घड़ी	घड़ियाँ	छड़ी	छड़ियाँ
धोती	धोतियाँ	साड़ी	साड़ियाँ

6. जिन स्त्रीलिंग शब्दों के अन्त में 'या' आता है, 'या' पर चन्द्रबिन्दु लगाकर बहुवचन बनाया जाता है जैसे–

एकवचन	**बहुवचन**	**एकवचन**	**बहुवचन**
बुढ़िया	बुढ़ियाँ	चिड़िया	चिड़ियाँ
गुड़िया	गुड़ियाँ	डिबिया	डिबियाँ
दुनिया	दुनियाँ		

7. ह्रस्व या दीर्घ ऊकारान्त स्त्रीलिंग संज्ञाओं को ह्रस्व उकारान्त बनाकर अन्त में 'एँ' लगाने से बहुवचन का निर्माण होता है। जैसे-

एकवचन	**बहुवचन**	**एकवचन**	**बहुवचन**
धेनु	धेनुएँ	वस्तु	वस्तुएँ
बहू	बहुएँ	ऋतु	ऋतुएँ

8. कुछ शब्द समष्टि मूलक होते हैं। जैसे– गण, कुल, वृन्द, समूह, वर्ग, लोग, जन, मण्डल, दल, ग्राम, मण्डली आदि। ये शब्द विशेषतः वहाँ जोड़े जाते हैं, जहाँ दोनों वचनों में पुल्लिंग अथवा स्त्रीलिंग में एक ही रूप होते हैं।

उदाहरण :

एकवचन	**बहुवचन**	**एकवचन**	**बहुवचन**
पाठक	पाठकगण	आप	आप लोग
तुम	तुम लोग	छात्र	छात्रगण
विद्यार्थी	विद्यार्थीगण		

विभक्ति सहित संज्ञाओं के बहुवचन बनाने के नियम :-

सविभक्ति संज्ञाओं के बहुवचन बनाने के सामान्य नियम निम्नलिखित हैं–

1. संस्कृत शब्दों को छोड़कर हिन्दी के अकारान्त, आकारान्त तथा एकारान्त संज्ञाओं के अन्तिम अ, आ, ए के बदले बहुवचन बनाने में इसे 'ओ' कर दिया जाता है। जैसे-

एकवचन	बहुवचन
नर	नरों (का)
चीता	चीतों (द्वारा)
चोर	चोरों (ने)
घोड़ा	घोड़ों (को)

विभक्ति चिह्नों के साथ प्रयोग :

(क) नरों की कहानी।
(ख) चीतों का भय।
(ग) चोरों की पकड़।
(घ) घोड़ों की हिनहिनाहट।

कारक

संज्ञा या सर्वनाम के उस रूप को कारक कहते हैं जिससे उसका सम्बन्ध वाक्य के अन्य शब्दों विशेषतः क्रिया के साथ प्रकट होता है। वास्तव में, विभक्ति चिहनों से युक्त संज्ञा या सर्वनाम शब्द ही वाक्य में अन्य शब्दों से सम्बन्ध प्रकट करते हैं।

ने, को, से, द्वारा– आदि विभक्ति चिह्न हैं। कारक का एक उदाहरण इस प्रकार है-'मोहन ने बाग में डण्डे से आम तोड़ा।' इस वाक्य में मोहन ने, डण्डे से, और आम संज्ञाओं के रूपान्तरण हैं। जिस तत्त्व के द्वारा इन रूपान्तरित संज्ञाओं का सम्बन्ध तोड़ा, क्रिया से स्पष्ट होता है, वही कारक है।

कारक-चिह्न

हिन्दी में कारक के आठ भेद माने जाते है :

	कारक	विभक्ति या कारक चिह्न
1.	कर्त्ता	ने
2.	कर्म	को
3.	करण	से, द्वारा
4.	सम्प्रदान	को, के लिए
5.	अपादान	से
6.	सम्बन्ध	का, के, की, रा, रे, री, ना, ने, नी
7.	अधिकरण	में, पर
8.	सम्बोधन	हे, हो, अरे, अजी, अहो आदि।

कारक-चिह्न/विभक्ति/परसर्ग

हिन्दी में कारक का ज्ञान कराने के लिए संज्ञा या सर्वनाम के साथ जो प्रत्यय लगाये जाते हैं, उन्हें ही व्याकरण में विभक्ति कहते हैं। हिन्दी में चूँकि विभक्ति चिह्न पद से अलग प्रयुक्त होते हैं इसलिए इन्हें 'परसर्ग' भी कहा जाता है। परसर्ग का शब्दिक अर्थ है- पीछे जुड़ना। कारक चिह्न सदैव संज्ञा या सर्वनाम के पीछे जुड़ते हैं।

(i) कर्त्ता कारक : कर्त्ता का अभिप्राय है, करने वाला। वाक्य में जो क्रिया सम्पन्न करता है, उसे कर्त्ता कहा जाता है। जैसे- राम पढ़ता है। सुरेश पत्र लिखता है। इन वाक्यों में राम और सुरेश कर्त्ता कारक हैं क्योंकि ये ही क्रिया को सम्पादित करने वाले हैं।

(ii) कर्म कारक : कर्त्ता द्वारा सम्पादित क्रिया का फल जिस पर पड़ता है, उसे 'कर्म' कहते हैं। जैसे– शीला ने राजेश को पढ़ाया। इस वाक्य में कर्त्ता है- शीला, क्रिया है– पढ़ाना। पढ़ाना क्रिया का फल राजेश पर स्पष्ट पड़ रहा है। इसलिए यहाँ राजेश कर्म कारक की स्थिति में है।

(iii) करण कारक : वाक्य में कारण कारक उस शब्द को कहते हैं जो क्रिया को पूर्ण करने में साधन के रूप में कर्ता का सहायक होकर आता है। जैसे– मैं कलम से लिखता हूँ। इस वाक्य में 'कलम से' करण कारक है क्योंकि लेखन-क्रिया में कलम साधन है।

(iv) सम्प्रदान कारक : कर्त्ता क्रिया की सिद्धि जिसके लिए करता है अथवा जिसको कुछ देता है, उसे प्रकट करने वाले शब्द रूप को सम्प्रदान कारक कहते हैं। जैसे– श्याम मीरा के लिए खिलौने लाया। राकेश शीला के लिए रोता है। इन वाक्यों में लाना और रोना क्रियाएँ क्रमशः मीरा और शीला के लिए सम्पादित की जा रही हैं। इसलिए मीरा और शीला के लिए शब्द रूप सम्प्रदान कारक है।

संधि

सन्धि शब्द का सामान्य अर्थ है– मेल अथवा मिलन। जब दो निकटवर्ती शब्दों का परस्पर मेल होता है, तो उसे संधि कहते हैं। संधि पहले वाले शब्द के अंतिम वर्ण और दूसरे वाले शब्द के प्रथम वर्ण (दोनों वर्णों) के मिलन रो होती है। जब संधि होती है, तो दोनों शब्दों के मेल से बना शब्द (नगा वाला शब्द) दोनों शब्दों का सामान्य संयोग मात्र नहीं होता, बल्कि उनके मेल से बना नया शब्द कुछ भिन्न होता है। यह भिन्नता या परिवर्तन उन्हीं दोनों वर्णों में होता है, जिनका मेल होता है। उदाहरण के लिए यदि हम 'हिम' और 'आलय' दोनों शब्दों की संधि करें, तो संधि से बनने वाला शब्द 'हिमालय' होगा। इसी प्रकार 'विद्या' और 'अर्थी' शब्दों की संधि से 'विद्यार्थी' शब्द बनता है।

संधि के मुख्य रूप से तीन भेद हैं– स्वर संधि, व्यंजन संधि और विसर्ग संधि।

(क) स्वर संधिः जब स्वर के साथ स्वर का मेल हो और स्वर में परिवर्तन हो, तो उसे स्वर संधि कहते हैं। उदाहरण के लिए 'छात्र' और आवास में 'त्र' और 'आ' का मेल होकर 'त्रा' बनेगा और संधि के फलस्वरूप बना शब्द 'छात्रावास' होगा।
इसी प्रकार 'रमा' और ईश' के मेल से 'रमेश' बनता है। 'महा' और 'ऋषि' के मेल से 'महर्षि' बनता है। 'यदि' और 'अपि' के मेल से 'यद्यपि' बनता है।

(ख) व्यंजन संधिः जब दो व्यंजनों के मेल से नया शब्द बनता है, तो उसे व्यंजन संधि कहते हैं। जैसे 'जगत' और 'नाथ' के मेल से 'जगन्नाथ' शब्द बनता है। 'तन्' और 'मय' के मेल से 'तन्मय' शब्द बनता है। 'सत्' और 'चित' के मेल से 'सच्चित' शब्द बनता है। 'सम्' और 'राट' के मेल से 'सम्राट' शब्द बनता है।

(ग) **विसर्ग संधिः** जब विसर्ग के साथ व्यंजन का मेल हो तो विसर्ग संधि होती है। जैसे– 'निः' और 'जन' के मेल से 'निर्जन' तथा 'दुः' और 'चरित्र' के मेल से 'दुश्चरित्र' बनता है।

संधि के प्रकार

हिन्दी में संधि के तीन प्रकार हैं–(1) स्वर संधि (2) व्यंजन संधि (3) विसर्ग संधि।

(1) स्वर संधि

दो स्वरों के मेल से जो विकार या वर्ण के रूप में परिवर्तन होता है, वही स्वर संधि कहलाता है।

स्वर संधि के भेदः स्वर संधि के निम्नलिखित पाँच भेद हैं :–
(क) दीर्घ संधि (ख) गुण संधि (ग) वृद्धि संधि (घ) यण् संधि (ङ) अयादि संधि।

(क) **दीर्घ संधिः** जब दो सवर्ण स्वरों का मेल होता है तो एक दीर्घ स्वर बन जाता है। यह दीर्घ संधि है। अ और आ सवर्ण स्वर हैं। इसी प्रकार इ ई उ ऊ और ऋ सवर्ण स्वर हैं। ह्रस्व या दीर्घ अ इ उ ऋ के बाद यदि पूर्ववत् ह्रस्व या दीर्घ स्वर हो तो दोनों के स्थान पर एक सवर्ण दीर्घ स्वर होता है।

जैसे– अ + अ = आ (नर + अधय = नराधय)
अ + आ = आ (कार्य + आलय = कार्यालय)
आ + अ = आ (विद्या + अर्थी = विद्यार्थी)
आ + आ = आ (महा + आशय = महाशय)
इ + इ = ई (मुनि + इन्द्र = मुनीन्द्र)
इ + ई = ई (कपि + ईश = कपीश)
ई + इ = ई (मही + इन्द्र = महीन्द्र)
ई + ई = ई (नदी + ईश = नदीश)
उ + उ = ऊ (साधु + उवाच = साधूवाच)

(ख) **गुण संधिः** अ या आ के बाद यदि इ या ई, उ या ऊ और ऋ आवे तो दोनों के मेल से क्रमशः ए, ओ अर हो जाता है।

जैसे– अ + इ = ए (नर + इन्द्र = नरेन्द्र)
आ + इ = ए (महा + इन्द्र = महेन्द्र)

(ग) **वृद्धि संधिः** अ या आ के बाद यदि ए या ऐ और ओ या औ का आगमन होता है, तो दोनों मिलकर क्रमशः ऐ और औ उत्पन्न करते हैं।

जैसे– अ + ए = ऐ (एक + एक = एकैक)
आ + ए = ऐ (तथा + एव = तथैव)

(घ) **यण संधिः** ह्रस्व या दीर्घ इ, उ, ऋ के अनन्तर यदि कोई असवर्ण स्वर आता है तो 'इ' का य्, उ का व् और ऋ का र् हो जाता है।

जैसे– इ + आ = या (अति + आनन्द = अत्यानन्द)
इ + ए = ये (प्रति + एक = प्रत्येक)

(ङ) **अयादि संधिः** ए ऐ ओ औ के अनन्तर यदि कोई असवर्ण स्वर आये तो ए का अय्, ऐ का आय, ओ का अव् और औ का आव हो जाता है।

जैसे– ए + अ = अय (ने + अन = नयन)
ऐ + अ = आय (नै + अक = नायक)

(2) व्यंजन संधि

व्यंजन संधि उसे कहते हैं जिसमें संधि होने वाले दो वर्णों में से प्रथम वर्ण व्यंजन हो और दूसरा स्वर या व्यंजन हो।

जैसे– दिक् + गज = दिग्गज।

व्यंजन संधि के प्रमुख नियम इस प्रकार हैं–

(क) यदि किसी वर्ण के पहले व्यंजन के अनन्तर किसी वर्ग का पंचम वर्ण आता है तो प्रथम व्यंजन वर्ग का परिवर्तन उसी वर्ग के पंचम वर्ण में होता है।

जैसे– जगत् + नाथ = जगन्नाथ।
वाक् + मय = वाङ्मय।

(ख) यदि म् के बाद किसी स्पर्श वर्ण का आगमन होता है तो म् अनुस्वार में बदल जाता है।

जैसे– किम + चित् = किंचित् या किञ्चित्।
अहम् + कार = अहंकार या अहङ्कार।

(ग) यदि म् के बाद य र ल व (अन्तस्थ) और श ष स ह (ऊष्म) वर्ण हों तो 'म्' अनुस्वार में बदल दिया जाता है।

जैसे– सम् + षय = संशय।
सम् + सार = संसार।

(घ) यदि वर्ग के प्रथम वर्ण के अनन्तर कोई स्वर हो या किसी वर्ग का तृतीय, चतुर्थ व्यंजन हो या य र ल व में से कोई वर्ण आए तो वर्ग के प्रथम वर्ण के स्थान पर तृतीय वर्ण हो जाता है।

जैसे– वाक् + दन्त = वाग्दन्त।
सत् + गति = सद्गति।

(ङ) यदि च अथवा ज के अनन्तर न का आगमन होता है तो दोनों का स्थान ञ ले लेता है।

जैसे– यज् + न = यज्ञ।

(3) विसर्ग संधि

विसर्ग के साथ स्वर अथवा व्यंजन के मेल से उत्पन्न विकार को विसर्ग संधि कहा जाता है।

जैसे– मनः + रथ = मनोरथ।

विसर्ग संधि के प्रमुख नियम

(क) विसर्ग के बाद च् या छ् ट् या ढ् तथा त् या यू आवे तो क्रमशः श, ष हो जाता है।

जैसे– निः + चय = निश्चय
निः + तार = निस्तार

(ख) यदि विसर्ग के बाद श, ष या स आवे तो विसर्ग को उसी परवर्ती सकार में बदल दिया जाता है।

जैसे– दुः + शासन = दुश्शासन

निः + सन्देह = निस्संदेह

(ग) यदि विसर्ग के पूर्व अ आवे और उसके बाद किसी वर्ग का तीसरा चौथा पाँचवां या य र ल व ह में से कोई व्यंजन आवे तो विसर्ग का 'उ' होता है और उ अपने पूर्ववर्ती अ के साथ जुड़कर ओ में रूपान्तरित हो जाता है।

जैसे– सरः + वर = सरोवर।

पयः + धर = पयोधर।

(घ) यदि विसर्ग के बाद र् व्यंजन आवे तो विसर्ग का पूर्ववर्ती स्वर दीर्घ हो जाता है साथ ही विसर्ग का लोप हो जाता है।

जैसे– निः + रव = नीरव।

निः + रोग = नीरोग।

(ङ) यदि विसर्ग के पूर्व अकार के अतिरिक्त कोई दूसरा स्वर हो और उसके बाद कोई स्वर हो अथवा किसी वर्ग का तीसरा, चौथा, पाँचवां वर्ण हो तो विसर्ग 'र' में रूपान्तरित होता है।

जैसे– दुः + गन्ध = दुर्गन्ध।

निः + रोग = नीरोग।

समास

अनेक शब्द जब मिलकर एक पद बन जाते हैं तो समास कहलाता है। अर्थात् जब दो या दो से अधिक पद अपने प्रत्ययों या विभक्तियों को छोड़कर मिलते हैं तब उस संयोग को समास कहते हैं।

समास की उपयोगिताः भाषा में समास की उपयोगिता कई दृष्टियों से है–

(क) समास से भाषा में संक्षिप्तता आती है।

(ख) समास से उच्चारण-प्रक्रिया में सहजता का बोध होता है।

(ग) भाषा समास के प्रयोग से चुस्त होती है।

(घ) भाषा के सौंदर्य में वृद्धि समास के प्रयोग से संभव है।

समास के भेद

पदों की प्रधानता को आधार मानकर समास को मुख्यतः चार भागों में विभाजित किया जाता है तथापि छः भेद स्वीकार किये जाते हैं।

(1) अव्ययीभाव समास – पहला पद प्रधान होता है।

(2) तत्पुरुष समास – दूसरा पद प्रधान होता है।

(3) द्वन्द्व समास – दोनों पद प्रधान होते हैं।

(4) बहुब्रीहि समास – कोई भी पद प्रधान नहीं होता है।

नोटः 'कर्मधारय' को तत्पुरुष का एक भेद माना गया है और 'द्विगु' को कर्मधारय का एक भेद माना गया है।

(1) अव्ययीभाव समास

अव्ययीभाव समास का पहला पद क्रिया-विशेषण अव्यय होता है और प्रधानता प्रायः प्रथम पद की ही होती है। जैसे– यथा समय (समय के अनुसार) प्रति वर्ष (प्रत्येक वर्ष)।

अव्ययीभाव समास के अन्तर्गत निम्नलिखित कोटि के पद आते हैं–

(क) अव्यय शब्दों के योग से बनने वाले समास– आचरण, व्यर्थ, यावज्जीवन, प्रतिदिन, यथा-संभव, आदि।

(ख) शब्दों की द्विरुक्ति से भी अव्ययीभाव समास बनता है। जैसे– वन-वन, घर-घर, मन्दिर-मन्दिर आदि।

(ग) द्विरुक्ति शब्दों के बीच में कभी-कभी ही, आ, ओं भी प्रयुक्त होते हैं। जैसे–एका-एक, हाथों-हाथ, मन-ही-मन आदि।

(2) तत्पुरुष समास

जिस समस्त पद में द्वितीय या अंतिम पद की प्रधानता को स्वीकारा जाता है उनमें तत्पुरुष समास होता है। जैसे :– राज-भवन (राजा का **भवन**)। उत्तर पद भवन प्रधान है।

तत्पुरुष समास के भेद

(i) व्यधिकरण तत्पुरुष– यह वास्तव में तत्पुरुष समास होता है।

(ii) समानाधिकरण तत्पुरुष– इस समास को कर्मधारय समास कहते हैं।

समस्त पदों में जिस कारक या विभक्ति चिह्न का लोप होता है उसी के आधार पर उसका नामकरण किया जाता है। तत्पुरुष समास में प्रथम पद कारक की स्थिति में होता है। इसके निम्नलिखित भेद हैं–

(क) कर्म तत्पुरुषः प्रथम पद कर्मधारय की स्थिति में होता है तथा कर्म की विभक्ति 'को' का लोप हो जाता है।

जैसे– गगन चुम्बी (गगन को चूमने वाला)

माखन चोर (माखन को चुराने वाला)

(ख) करण तत्पुरुषः प्रथम पद करण कारक की स्थिति में होता है और करण की विभक्ति चिह्न 'से' द्वारा 'के साथ' का लोप होता है।

जैसे– ईश्वर दत्त (ईश्वर द्वारा दत्त)

विश्व बन्ध (विश्व द्वारा बन्ध)

(ग) सम्प्रदान तत्पुरुषः प्रथम पद सम्प्रदान कारक में रहता है तथा सम्प्रदान की विभक्ति 'को', 'के लिए', 'निमित्त', 'हेतु' आदि का लोप होता है।

जैसे– स्वाधीनता संग्राम (स्वाधीनता के लिए संग्राम)

(घ) अपादान तत्पुरुषः इसमें भी प्रथम पद अपादान कारक में होता है तथा अपादान कारक के विभक्ति चिह्न 'से' का लोप हो जाता है।

जैसे– धर्म विमुख (धर्म से विमुख)

(ङ) सम्बन्ध तत्पुरुषः इसका पूर्व पद सम्बन्ध कारक में होता है तथा सम्बन्ध के विभक्ति चिह्न का, के, की का लोप होता है।

जैसे– वन मानुष (वन का मानुष)

(च) **अधिकरण तत्पुरुषः** अधिकरण तत्पुरुष में पहला पद अधिकरण कारक में होता है तथा अधिकरण कारक का विभक्ति चिह्न 'में' या 'पर' आदि का बोध होता है।
जैसे– आपबीती (आप पर बीती)

(3) द्वन्द्व समास

द्वन्द्व समास में दोनों ही पद प्रधान होते हैं और समस्त पद में दोनों पद संज्ञा या उसका समूह होता है। स्मरणीय है कि इसमें 'और', 'वा' 'अथवा', समुच्चय बोधक का लोप रहता है। इस समुच्चय बोधक के द्वारा दोनों पद जुड़े रहते हैं। द्वन्द्व समास के सामान्यतः निम्नलिखित भेद होते हैं :–

(क) **इतरेतर द्वन्द्वः** इतरेतर द्वन्द्व में समस्त पदों के बीच 'और' समुच्चय बोधक का लोप होता रहता है।

जैसे– माता-पिता (माता और पिता)
सीता-राम (सीता और राम)
देवर-भाभी (देवर और भाभी)

(ख) **समाहार द्वन्द्वः** समाहार द्वन्द्व में समस्त पद अपने अर्थ के अलावा उसी रूप के अन्य अर्थ का भी आभास देता है।

जैसे– नमक-रोटी (नमक और रोटी के अतिरिक्त और भी उसी कोटि की खाद्य-सामग्री) रुपया-पैसा, धन-दौलत, सेठ-साहूकार, मान-मर्यादा।

(ग) **वैकल्पिक द्वन्द्वः** वैकल्पिक द्वन्द्व में दोनों पदों के मध्य 'थ' और 'अथवा' समुच्चय बोधक का लोप रहता है। इस समस्त पद में साधारणतः दो परस्पर विरोधी शब्दों का योग होता है।

जैसे– मान-अपमान, धर्म-अधर्म, ज्ञान-अज्ञान, पाप-पुण्य, चार-छः, दो-चार, जात-कुजात, भला-बुरा।

(4) बहुब्रीहि समास

बहुब्रीहि समास उस समास को कहते हैं जिसमें दोनों ही पद अप्रधान होते हैं। उसमें एक नये अर्थ का संकेत मिलता है।

जैसे– चन्द्रशेखर (चन्द्रमा है शिखर पर जिसके अर्थात् शिव)
चतुर्भुज (चार भुजाएँ हैं जिनकी अर्थात् विष्णु)
गजानन (गज के समान मुख है जिसका अर्थात् गणेश)

(5) कर्मधारय (समानाधिकरण तत्पुरुष)

कर्मधारय समास में दोनों पद प्रधान होते हैं। इसके पदों में विशेषज्ञ-विशेषण, विषेशज्ञ-विशेषण, उपमान-उपमेय का भाव होता है।
जैसे– शशिमुख (शशि सम मुख), नीलाम्बर, पीताम्बर।

कर्मधारय के प्रकार– कर्मधारय के मुख्यतः दो भेद हैं– (1) विशेषता वाचक (2) उपमान वाचक।

(1) **विशेषता वाचक**

विशेषण पूर्वपदः पहला पद विशेषण होता है। जैसे– पीताम्बर, नीलकण्ठ, सुन्दर लाल, सद्गुण, खुशबू, बदबू, काली मिर्च, नीलगाय, छुटभैया।

विशेषणोत्तर पदः इसमें उत्तरपद विशेषण होता है। जैसे– पुरुषोतम, प्रभुदयाल, रामदहिन, देशान्तर, मुनीश्वर, युगान्तर, नराधम, जन्मान्तर।

विशेषणोभय पदः दोनों ही पद विशेषण होते हैं। जैसे– नील-पीत, मोटा ताजा, लाल पीला, श्याम सुन्दर, श्वेत-श्याम, भला-बुरा, खट्टा-मिट्ठा।

विशेष्योभय पदः दोनों ही पद विशेष्य होते हैं। जैसे– प्राणप्रिय, वज्रदेह।

(2) **विशेषता वाचक**

उपमानोत्तर पदः उत्तर पद उपमान होता है। जैसे– मुखारविन्द, राजर्षि।

(6) द्विगु समास

द्विगु समास कर्मधारय समास का एक भेद है। इस समास में पहला पद संख्या बोधक होता है और द्वितीय पद प्रधान होता है। संख्यावाची शब्द समुदाय (समाहार) के अर्थ में प्रयुक्त होता है।

जैसे–नवरत्न (नवरत्नों का समूह), अष्टाध्यायी (आठ अध्यायों का समाहार), त्रिभुवन, तिमाही, पंसेरी, सप्तशती, त्रिकाल, चौमाल।

वर्तनी

हिन्दी शब्दों को लिखने में वर्तनी का बड़ा महत्व है। प्रायः विद्यार्थी लिखने में वर्तनी सम्बन्धी अशुद्धियां करते हैं। ये अशुद्धियाँ संयुक्त वर्ण, विभक्ति चिह्न, क्रिया पद में तो होती ही है साथ ही, व ब तथा श ष स में भी देखने को मिलती हैं। इन अशुद्धियों से बचने का सही उपाय है कि शुद्ध वर्तनी का ज्ञान हो। और यह निरन्तर अभ्यास से ही सम्भव है।

पर्यायवाची

एकार्थ बोधक शब्दों को पर्यायवाची शब्द कहा जाता है। पर्यायवाची शब्दों में से कुछ पूर्ण पर्याय तथा कुछ अपूर्ण पर्याय की श्रेणी में आते हैं। पूर्ण पर्याय—कपि, वानर, मर्कट, प्लवंग आदि बन्दर के पर्याय हैं। अपूर्ण पर्याय—कृपा, दया, करुणा को कहा जाता है, किन्तु इनके प्रयोग में बहुत अन्तर है। भाषा के सूक्ष्म अध्ययन की दृष्टि से अपूर्ण पर्यायों के मध्य सूक्ष्म अन्तर होता है। इस अन्तर को देखते हुए ही उनका प्रयोग किया जाता है। हिन्दी के शब्द-भंडार की पर्याप्त वृद्धि हुई है। इस दिशा में डॉ. रघुवीर जैसे भाषा-पंडितों ने बहुत काम किया है। भारत सरकार का केन्द्रीय हिन्दी निदेशालय, अनुवाद ब्यूरो तथा राजभाषा विधायी आयोग आदि संस्थाओं द्वारा किए जा रहे शब्द रचना के कार्य सराहनीय हैं। हमारे देश में संस्कृत समृद्ध भाषा है जिससे हिन्दी को बहुत-से शब्द प्राप्त हुए हैं, अतएव पर्यायवाची शब्दों की दृष्टि से हिन्दी समृद्ध है।

विलोमार्थी शब्द

ऐसे शब्दों को विपरीतार्थक, विलोमार्थी अथवा विरोधी शब्द कहा जाता है जो किसी शब्द के ठीक विपरीत अर्थ प्रकट करते हैं। अंग्रेजी में जिन

शब्दों को एण्टानिम्स (Antonyms) कहा जाता है हिन्दी में वही शब्द विलोमार्थी अथवा प्रतिकूल अर्थ के बोधक कहे जाते हैं। अतएव विलोमार्थी शब्दों को यदि हम परिभाषाबद्ध करना चाहें तो कह सकते हैं कि—'किसी एक शब्द के ठीक विपरीत अर्थ प्रकट करने वाले शब्द विलोम कहे जाते हैं। इन शब्दों को विपर्याय के रूप में भी जाना जाता है।'

विलोमार्थी शब्दों का महत्त्व

भाषा कोई भी क्यों न हो उसकी सम्पन्नता उसके शब्दों की संख्या से जानी जाती है। आज विश्व में सर्वाधिक सम्पन्न भाषा अंग्रेजी है जिसके शब्दों का निरंतर वार्धक्य होता जाता है। नये-नये विज्ञानों का प्रादुर्भाव होने से उससे सम्बन्धित शब्द भी गढ़े जाते हैं। और उन शब्दों के प्रतिकूल शब्दों की आवश्यकता भी अनुभव की जाती है। नतीजतन शब्दों का सृजन अनवरत गति से चलता रहा है। हिन्दी में भी यह काम काफी द्रुतगति से हो रहा है। कोई माने या न माने किन्तु ज़ब से केन्द्र में हिन्दी को राजभाषा का गरिमामय पद मिला है तब से उसके विकास की गति भी बढ़ी है। विभिन्न क्षेत्रों में उसका प्रवेश हो रहा है। विज्ञान, इंजीनियरी, चिकित्साशास्त्र, आणविकी आदि सभी से सम्बन्धित शब्दों की रचना हिन्दी में अबाध गति से की जा रही है। ये सब प्रभावी लक्षण हैं। शब्दों के समानार्थी तथा विपरीतार्थी दोनों की जरूरत पड़ती रहती है और आज़ के युग में जबकि प्रतियोगिता का महत्त्व काफी बढ़ गया है विपरीतार्थी शब्द भी किसी के भाषाई ज्ञान की माप करने में उपादेय सिद्ध होते हैं।

इसके अतिरिक्त विपरीतार्थक शब्द किन्हीं दो अच्छी या बुरी वस्तुओं की तुलना करने के लिए भी काफी उपादेय सिद्ध होते हैं। ऐसे शब्दों के प्रयोग से भाषा में निखार आता है, भाषण प्रभावशाली बन जाता है तथा लेखन गरिमावान दिखाई पड़ने लगता है।

श्रुति समभिन्नार्थक शब्द

युग्म शब्द को श्रुतिसम भिन्नार्थक या समोच्चरित शब्द भी कहा जाता है। इस प्रकार के दो शब्दों में मामूली-सा अन्तर होता है। वह अन्तर मात्रागत या वर्णगत होता है। फलतः ऐसे शब्द सुनने में एक समान तो लगते हैं लेकिन अर्थ भिन्न-भिन्न होते हैं। हिन्दी में ऐसे शब्दों की संख्या अत्यधिक है। नीचे वैसे प्रमुख शब्द युग्मों को अर्थ सहित प्रस्तुत किया जा रहा है :

1. अंश = भाग/हिस्सा
   अंस = कन्धा
2. अपेक्षा = आवश्यकता/उम्मीद
   उपेक्षा = अवहेलना
3. अभिराम = सुन्दर
   अविराम = लगातार
4. अनल = आग
   अनिल = हवा
5. अवलम्ब = आश्रय/सहारा
   अविलम्ब = शीघ्र
6. अन्त = समाप्त/खतम
   अन्त्य = अन्तिम
7. अभिहित = कथित
   अविहित = अनुचित
8. अम्बुज = कमल
   अम्बुद = बादल
9. अलि = भ्रमर
   अली = सखी
10. उपकार = भलाई
    अपकार = बुराई
11. अजिक = ललाट
    अलीक = झूठ
12. अभिनय = स्वांग
    अविनय = उद्दण्डता
13. अतल = तलहीन
    अतुल = जिसकी तुलना न हो सके
14. अकथ = जो कहा नहीं जाय
    अथक = बिना थके हुए
15. अन्न = अनाज
    अन्य = दूसरा
16. आदि = आरम्भ/शुरू
    आदी = अभ्यस्त, अदरक
17. अभय = निर्भय
    उभय = दोनों
18. अर्जन = संग्रह
    अर्चन = पूजा
19. अमित = अत्यधिक
    अमीत = शत्रु
20. अणु = सूक्ष्म कण
    अनु = पीछे
21. अशक्त = असमर्थ
    असक्त = विरक्त
22. अब्ज = कमल
    अब्द = बादल
23. अवधि = समय
    अवधी = अवध की भाषा
24. अभ्यास = अनुशीलन
    अभ्याश = पड़ोस
25. आभरण = आभूषण
    आमरण = मरण तक
26. आकर = खान
    आकार = आकृति
27. आयत = चतुर्भुज
    आयात = बाहर से लाना
28. आर्त = दुःखी
    आर्द्र = गीला

29. आवास = वास स्थान
आभास = झलक
30. आवृत्त = घिरा हुआ
आवृत्ति = दुहराना
31. इत्र = सुगन्धित पदार्थ
इतर = दूसरा
32. स्त्री = महिला
इस्तिरी = कपड़े पर कलप करना
33. अरि = दुश्मन
अरी = स्त्री के लिए सम्बोधन
34. उद्यत = तैयार, तत्पर
उद्धत = उद्दण्ड
35. ऋतु = मौसम
ऋत = सत्य
36. कश = चाबुक
कष = कसौटी
37. कुल = वंश
कूल = किनारा
38. कलि = कलियुग
कली = अधखिला फूल
39. कपिश = मटमैला
कपीश = बन्दरों का राजा
40. कर्म = कार्य
क्रम = सिलसिला
41. कंगाल = दरिद्र
कंकाल = ठठरी (मानव की)
42. कटिबद्ध = तैयार
कटिबन्ध = कमर बन्द
43. करोड़ = सौ लाख की संख्या
क्रोड़ = गोद
44. कृत = किया हुआ
क्रीत = खरीदा हुआ
45. कृपण = कंजूस
कृपाण = कटार
46. कृषाण = किसान
कृशानु = आम
47. क्रान्ति = उलटफेर, आन्दोलन
कांति = चमक
48. कुट = किला
कूट = पहाड़ की चोटी
49. कुजन = दुर्जन
कूजन = पक्षियों का कलरव
50. केशर = सिंह की गर्दन के बाल
केसर = कुमकुम
51. कोष = खजाना
कोश = शब्द-संग्रह
कोस = दो मील की दूरी
52. खाद = उर्वरक
खाद्य = खाने की सामग्री
53. खोया = भूल गया
खोआ = दूध से निर्मित खाद्य पदार्थ
54. गिरि = पर्वत
गिरी = बीज/गूदा
55. चषक = प्याला
चसक = आदत
56. चरण = पैर
चारण = भाट
57. चिर = पुराना
चीर = वस्त्र
58. चिता = शव जलाने के लिए लकड़ियों की शय्या
चीता = एक हिंसक पशु
59. गृह = घर
ग्रह = नक्षत्र
60. करण = इन्द्रियाँ, करण कारक
कर्ण = कान
61. कुच = स्तर
कूच = प्रस्थान
62. कौर = ग्रास
कोर = किनारा
63. चतुष्पद = चौपाया
चतुष्पथ = चौराहा
64. चक्रवात = बवंडर
चक्रवाक = चकवा पक्षी
65. छत्र = छाता
छात्र = विद्यार्थी
66. क्षति = हानि
क्षिति = पृथ्वी
67. जलज = कमल
जलद = बादल
68. नीरज = कमल
नीरद = बादल
69. जघन्य = गर्हित
जघन = जाँघ
70. जगत् = संसार
जगत = कुएँ का चबूतरा
71. जामन = दूध जमाने के लिए प्रयुक्त पदार्थ
जामुन = एक फल
72. जेठ = वर्ष का एक महीना
ज्येष्ठ = बड़ा (उम्र में)
73. टुक = थोड़ा
टूक = टुकड़ा
74. टोटा = घाटा
टोंटा = बन्दूक का कारतूस

75. तरणि = सूर्य
तरणी = नाव
76. दाई = धामी, नौकरानी
दायी = जवाबदेह
77. दारु = लकड़ी
दारू = शराब
78. दिवा = दिन
दीया = दीपक
79. दिन = दिवस
दीन = गरीब
80. द्विप = हाथी
द्वीप = टापू
81. दुर्ग = गढ़
दुर्गा = एक देवी
82. दमन = दबाना
दामन = आँचल
83. तक्र = मट्ठा
तर्क = बहस
84. द्रव्य = धन
द्रव = तरल पदार्थ
85. देव = देवता
दैव = भाग्य
86. नहर = कृत्रिम नदी
नाहर = सिंह
87. नग = पहाड़
नाग – सर्प
88. नगर = शहर
नागर = चतुर व्यक्ति
89. नाश = ध्वंश
नास = सुंघनी
90. नारी = स्त्री
नाड़ी = नब्ज
91. निसान = झण्डा
निशान = चिह्न, प्रतीक
92. निर्जर = देवता
निर्झर = झरना
93. निहित = छिपा हुआ
निहत = मरा हुआ
94. नियत = निश्चित
नीयत = इरादा
नियति = भाग्य
95. नमित = नत
निमित्त = कारण
96. नीर = जल
नीड़ = घोंसला
97. निर्माण = बनाना
निर्वाण = मोक्ष
98. नकल = अनुकरण
नकुल = नेवला, पाण्डवों में एक
99. निधन = मृत्यु
निर्धन = गरीब
100. नित = प्रतिदिन
नीत = लाया हुआ
101. नीम = एक पेड़
नींव = आधार
102. नेत्र = आँख
नेतृ = नेता
103. पुरुष = मर्द
परुष = कठोर
104. परिधान = वस्त्र
प्रधान = मुख्य
105. पवन = हवा
पावन = पवित्र
106. पाहन = पत्थर
पाहुन = अतिथि
107. परवाह = चिन्ता
प्रवाह = बहाव
108. प्रहर = समय
प्रहार = चोट
109. परिताप = दुःख
प्रताप = पराक्रम
110. पथ = मार्ग
पथ्य = रोगी का भोजन
111. पट्ट = तख्ता
पट = वस्त्र
112. प्रमाण = सबूत
प्रणाम = नमस्कार
113. परिणाम = फल
परिमाण = मात्रा
114. प्रणय = प्रेम
परिणय = विवाह
115. परदेश = दूसरा देश
प्रदेश = प्रान्त, राज्य
116. परीक्षा = इम्तहान
परिक्षा = कीचड़
117. प्रदीप = दीपक
प्रतीप = उल्टा
118. पानी = जल
पाणि = हाथ
119. पास = निकट
पाश = बन्धन
120. पिक = कोयल
पीक = पान का थूक

121. प्रेषित = भेजा हुआ
प्रोषित = प्रवासी
122. फन = कला
फण = साँप का फण
123. बलि = बलिदान
बली = वीर
124. बहन = भगिनी
वहन = ढोना
125. बहु = बहुत
बहू = पुत्रवधू
126. बार = दफा
वार = दिन
127. वाण = तीर
बान = आदत
128. बात = वचन
वात = हवा
129. भवन = घर
भुवन = संसार
130. भट = योद्धा
भट्ट = पण्डित
131. भाल = ललाट
भार = वजन
132. मल = गन्दगी
मल्ल = पहलवान
133. मणि = रत्न
मणी = सर्प
134. मद = अहंकार
मद्य = शराब
135. मनुज = मनुष्य
मनोज = कामदेव
136. मांस = गोश्त
मास = महीना
137. मात्र = केवल
मातृ = माता
138. मेध = यज्ञ
मेघ = बादल
139. मेदा = पेट
मैदा = बारीक आटा
140. रत = तल्लीन
रक्त = खून
141. रेचक = दस्तावर
रोचक = रूचिकर
142. लक्ष = लाख
लक्ष्य = उद्देश्य
143. लवण = नमक
लवन = खेत के फसल की कटाई
144. वस्तु = चीज
वास्तु = इमारत, भवन
145. अकुल = बिना कुल के
आकुल = व्याकुल
146. वरद = वर देने वाला
विरद = यश
147. वरण = चुनना
वरन् = बल्कि
148. वाद = विचार/सिद्धान्त
वाद्य = बाजा
149. वदन = मुख
बदन = शरीर
150. विस्मृत = भूला हुआ
विस्मित = आश्चर्य में पड़ा हुआ
151. विपिन = जंगल
विपन्न = दु:खी, निर्धन
152. वित्त = धन
वृत्त = गोलाकार
153. विष = जहर
विस = कमल का डण्ठल
बीस = उन्नीस से एक अधिक संख्या
154. सम = समान
शय = संचय
155. सहर = सबेरा
शहर = नगर
156. शव = लाश
शब = रात
157. सिता = चीनी
सीता = जानकी
158. शस्त्र = हथियार
शास्त्र = ग्रन्थ
159. सर = तालाब
शर = बाण
160. सुर = देवता
सूर = अंधा
शूर = वीर
161. सुत = बेटा
सूत = सारथी, धागा
162. सप्त = सात
शप्त = शाप ग्रस्त
163. शंकर = शिव
संकर = दोगला
164. सर्ग = काव्य का अध्याय
स्वर्ग = कल्पित लोक
165. स्वपच = स्वयंवाकी
श्वपच = चाण्डाल

166. सत्व = सार
स्वत्व = अधिकार
167. समिति = सभा
सम्मति = सलाह
168. शय्या = बिछावन
सज्जा = सजावट
169. संग = साथ
संघ = समिति, संगठन
170. शाला = घर
साला = पत्नी का भाई
171. सबल = ताकतवर
शवल = चितकबरा
172. सर्व = सभी
शर्व = शंकर
173. सुगन्ध = खुशबू
सौगन्ध = कसम
174. शुक्ति = सीप
सूक्ति = अच्छी उक्ति
175. शीशा = काँच
सीसा = एक धातु
176. सती = पतिव्रता नारी
शती = शताब्दी
177. श्वेत = सफेद
श्वेद = पसीना
178. शुक = सुग्गा
शूक = जौ
179. शिखर = चोटी (पर्वत की)
शेखर = सिर
180. शक्ल = चेहरा
सकल = सम्पूर्ण
181. हरि = विष्णु
हरी = हरे रंग की
182. सुमन = फूल
सुअन = पुत्र
183. संदेह = शक
सदेह = सशरीर
184. स्व = अपना
श्व = आने वाला दिन
185. शुचि = पवित्र
सूची = विषय क्रम
186. सुधि = स्मरण
सुधी = समझदार, विद्वान्
187. हल = जोतने का यंत्र
हल् = शुद्ध व्यंजन
188. भंगि = लहर
भंगी = मेहतर
189. दूत = संवाददाता
द्यूत = जुआ का खेल
190. देश = राज्य
द्वेष = शत्रुता
191. तरंग = लहर
तुरंग = घोड़ा
192. चालक = ड्राइवर
चालाक = चतुर
193. लोम = रोवाँ
लोभ = लालच
194. बिना = रहित, अभाव
वीणा = एक वाद्य यंत्र
195. प्रसाद = कृपा
प्रासाद = महल
196. भित्ति = दीवार
भीति = डर
197. मूल = जड़
मूल्य = दाम
198. अक्ष = धुरी
यक्ष = एक देव योनि
199. अश्व = घोड़ा
अश्म = पत्थर
200. आसन = बैठने की वस्तु
अशन = भोजन
201. अह = दिन
अहि = साँप
202. अणि = सूई की नोक
अनी = फौज
203. दारा = पत्नी
द्वार = दरवाजा
204. पृथा = कुन्ती
प्रथा = रीति
205. श्रवण = कान
स्रवन = बहना
206. श्याम = श्री कृष्ण
स्याम = एक देश
207. वृन्द = समूह
वृन्त = डण्ठल
208. मित = थोड़ा
मित्र = दोस्त
209. दुरति = पाप
दुरत = छिपा
210. चार = चार की संख्या
चारु = सुन्दर

वाक्यों की शुद्धता

वाक्य में शब्दों के प्रयोग पर हमें विशेष ध्यान रखना चाहिए। प्रत्येक शब्द का अपना एक विशेष अर्थ होता है। एक ही अर्थ देने वाले कई शब्द हो सकते हैं, किन्तु हमें ध्यान रखना चाहिए कि किस प्रसंग में कौन-सा शब्द प्रयुक्त होगा और कौन-सा शब्द वहां उपयुक्त नहीं बैठेगा। अनुपयुक्त शब्द का प्रयोग करने से अर्थ-भ्रान्ति पैदा होती है। शब्दों का ठीक प्रयोग करने से अभीष्ट अर्थ निकलेगा।

अशुद्धियों के कारणों का विश्लेषण करने के बाद हम देख सकते हैं कि वर्तनी की गलतियाँ होती हैं। ह्रस्व और दीर्घ मात्राओं की गलतियां होती हैं, संयुक्ताक्षरों की गलतियां होती हैं और वाक्यों के निर्माण में भी गलतियाँ होती हैं। मोटे तौर पर हम कह सकते हैं कि वर्ण, शब्द और वाक्य तीनों प्रकार की अशुद्धियाँ देखने को मिलती हैं। इन अशुद्धियों के कारण भाषा दूषित हो जाती है। यदि हम थोड़ी सी सावधानी बरतें, तो हम ऐसी अशुद्धियों से बच सकते हैं।

वाक्यांश के लिए एक शब्द

कथन में लम्बे-लम्बे वाक्यों का प्रयोग करने तथा शब्दों को परिभाषित करने के बजाय यदि एक शब्द का प्रयोग किया जाए तो कथन स्वत: संक्षिप्त और स्पष्ट हो जाता है। कुशल साहित्यकार अपनी रचनाओं में शब्दों का अपव्यय नहीं करते। वाक्य या वाक्यांश के लिए एक शब्द का प्रयोग कथन में आकर्षण और सौन्दर्य भर देता है। हिन्दी भाषा की यह विशेषता है कि उसे संस्कृत शब्दों का प्रचुर भण्डार सुलभ है। इसलिए हिन्दी भाषा कोश में ऐसे अनेक तत्सम शब्द हैं जो वाक्य या वाक्यांश के लिए प्रयोग में लाए जाते हैं।

अपने आशय और मन्तव्य को संक्षेप में प्रकट करने के लिए ही ऐसे शब्दों को गढ़ा गया है जिन्हें गागर में सागर कहा जा सकता है।

इसीलिए अपनी भाषा को समर्थ, प्रभावी तथा आकर्षक बनाने के लिए ऐसे शब्दों की जानकारी रखना नितान्त आवश्यक होता है। भाषा में शक्ति के स्रोत उसके शब्द माने जाते हैं। यहाँ इसी उद्देश्य से अनेक ऐसे शब्द संजोए गए हैं जिनका अर्थ पूरे वाक्य या वाक्यांश द्वारा ही स्पष्ट होता है। इनसे न केवल पाठकों के शब्द भण्डार में वृद्धि होगी वरन् वे हिन्दी भाषा लिखने में भी कुशल बन सकेंगे।

मुहावरा एवं लोकोक्तियां

मुहावरे

मुहावरा ऐसा शब्द-समूह होता है, जो अपने शब्दों के निहित अर्थ न देकर उससे भिन्न, किन्तु एक रूढ़ अर्थ देता है। मुहावरा अभिधेय अर्थ का अनुसरण नहीं करता : वह अपना विलक्षण अर्थ प्रकट करता है। चूँकि मुहावरा लोक-मानस की स्वाभाविक अभिव्यक्ति होता है, अत: इसमें दुरूहता नहीं होती। मुहावरा अपने लोक-परम्परागत रूप में ही शोभायमान और सार्थक होता है। इसका रूप और अर्थ दोनों ही प्राय: रूढ़ होते हैं।

मुहावरे का सम्बन्ध साहित्य से कम और भाषा से अधिक होता है। यह भाषा के सामर्थ्य का प्रतीक होता है। इसका सटीक अर्थ और निर्दिष्ट अर्थ होता है। मुहावरों के माध्यम से भाषा ऊर्जस्वी बनती है और अर्थ का सटीक सम्प्रेषण होता है। मुहावरेदार भाषा असरदार होती है।

मुहावरे एक दृष्टि से 'गागर में सागर' होते हैं। गुल खिलना, रंग में भंग होना, नौ-दो ग्यारह होना, गप हाँकना, चिकना घड़ा होना, नानी मरना आदि मुहावरे व्यापक अर्थ में परिपूर्ण हैं। इनका प्रयोग सुनते ही मन में इनका अर्थ अपने आप उभरने लगता है।

लोकोक्तियाँ

जैसाकि शब्द से ही स्पष्ट है लोकोक्ति का अर्थ है लोक + उक्ति; अर्थात् लोक में प्रचलित उक्ति। जो उक्ति समाज में चिरकाल से प्रचलित होती है, उसे लोक प्रचलित उक्ति अर्थात् लोकोक्ति कहते हैं। लोकोक्तियाँ भूतकाल के अनुभव और प्रेक्षण का संचय होती हैं। लोकोक्तियों में लोक-बोध, लोक-मान्यता और लोक-स्वीकृति होती है। कुछ लोकोक्तियाँ किसी अन्तर्कथा को अभिव्यक्त करती हैं। लोकोक्तियों के उद्भव को किसी स्थान या काल से नहीं जोड़ा जा सकता।

लोकोक्तियाँ अपने आप में पूर्ण वाक्य होती हैं। इनका उद्देश्य उक्ति चमत्कार पैदा करना नहीं होता। इनका अभिधात्मक अर्थ ही लिया जाता है। अत: इनके शाब्दिक अर्थ और सांकेतिक अर्थ में समानता होती है। इनका प्रयोग प्राय: दृष्टांत के लिए अथवा किसी बात का समर्थन करने के लिए किया जाता है। ये अभिव्यक्ति का सशक्त साधन हैं।

मुहावरों और लोकोक्तियों में अन्तर

मुहावरों और लोकोक्तियों में रूप सम्बन्धी और अर्थ सम्बन्धी भी अन्तर होता है।

रूप सम्बन्धी पहला अन्तर यह है कि मुहावरों के अन्त में अधिकांशत: **ना** होता है, जैसे सिर धुन**ना**, आँख लग**ना**, टेढ़ी खीर हो**ना**, मक्खी मार**ना**, आसमान सिर पर उठा**ना** आदि जबकि लोकोक्तियों के अन्त में **ना** नहीं होता; जैसे—आ बैल मुझे मार, का वर्षा जब कृषि सुखानी, दीवार के भी कान होते हैं, और धोबी का कुत्ता, घर का न घाट का, आदि।

रूप सम्बन्धी दूसरा अन्तर यह होता है कि मुहावरे मात्र शब्द-समूह होते हैं, जैसे 'गुल खिलाना'; इसे स्वतन्त्र रूप से प्रयोग में नहीं लाया जा सकता, किसी वाक्य में इसे उपयुक्त ढंग से प्रयुक्त किया जाता है; जैसे—'उस बूढ़ी औरत ने क्या गुल खिलाया'; इसके विपरीत लोकोक्ति का प्रयोग स्वतंत्र वाक्य के रूप में किया जा सकता है; जैसे—'न रहेगा बाँस, न बजेगी बाँसुरी'।

वस्तुनिष्ठ प्रश्न

संधि

1. 'मृत्यु + उपरांत' में संधि करने से एक शब्द होगा–
A. मृत्यूपरांत B. मृत्योपरांत
C. मृत्युपर्यन्त D. मर्त्योपरांत

2. 'अनधिकृत' शब्द का संधि-विग्रह होगा–
A. अन + अधिकृत B. अन् + अधिकृत
C. अन्य + अधिकृत D. अन्नधि + कृत

3. 'कपि + ईश' का सही संधि-संयोजन कीजिए–
A. कपिश B. कपीश
C. कपेश D. कपिशि

4. विसर्ग के साथ स्वर अथवा व्यंजन के संयोग से जो विकार उत्पन्न होता है, उसे किस संधि के नाम से जानते हैं?
A. स्वर संधि B. व्यंजन संधि
C. विसर्ग संधि D. इनमें से कोई नहीं

5. 'परोपकार' शब्द का संधि-विच्छेद होगा–
A. परा + उपकार B. परो + पकार
C. परोप + कार D. पर + उपकार

6. 'मनः + रमा' में संधि करने से जो शब्द बनेगा, उसका सम्बन्ध किस संधि से होगा?
A. विसर्ग संधि B. स्वर संधि
C. व्यंजन संधि D. भाव संधि

7. 'चन्द्रोदय' में कौन-सी संधि है?
A. यण संधि B. दीर्घ संधि
C. वृद्धि संधि D. गुण संधि

8. निम्नलिखित में से 'वृद्धि स्वर संधि' किस शब्द में है?
A. रजनीश B. महौषध
C. यतीन्द्र D. शोधार्थी

9. 'सदाशय' का सही संधि-विच्छेद होगा–
A. सद + आशय B. सतत + आशय
C. सत् + आशय D. सदा + आशय

10. 'सन्मार्ग' में कौन-सी संधि है?
A. स्वर संधि B. व्यंजन संधि
C. विसर्ग संधि D. इनमें से कोई नहीं

11. 'ज्ञानोदय' में कौन-सी संधि है?
A. स्वर संधि B. व्यंजन संधि
C. विसर्ग संधि D. इनमें से कोई नहीं

12. 'निराधार' में कौन-सी संधि है?
A. स्वर संधि B. व्यंजन संधि
C. विसर्ग संधि D. इनमें से कोई नहीं

13. निम्नलिखित शब्दों में से किसमें विसर्ग संधि है?
A. अतएव B. नरेन्द्र
C. सज्जन D. सदैव

14. निम्नलिखित शब्दों में से किसमें व्यंजन संधि है?
A. सप्तर्षि B. निराधार
C. सत्कार D. हिमालय

15. 'जगन्नाथ' किस संधि का उदाहरण है?
A. व्यंजन संधि B. विसर्ग संधि
C. दीर्घ स्वर संधि D. यण स्वर संधि

16. निम्नलिखित शब्द का संधि-विच्छेद क्या होगा?
भानूदय
A. भानु + उदय B. भानू + उदय
C. भानू + ऊदय D. भानु + ऊदय

17. 'निर्गुण' का संधि-विच्छेद होगा–
A. निर + गुण B. नि + गुण
C. निः + गुण D. निर + गुण

18. 'महेन्द्र' का संधि विच्छेद है–
A. मही + इन्द्र B. महो + इन्द्र
C. महा + इन्द्र D. इनमें से कोई नहीं

19. 'यद्यपि' का संधि विच्छेद है–
A. यदि + अपि B. यद् + द्यपि
C. यद्यि + अपि D. यद + अपि

20. निम्नलिखित में 'भारतेंदु' का सही संधि-विच्छेद है–
A. भारत + तेन्दु B. भार + तेन्दु
C. भारत + एन्दु D. भारत + इन्दु

21. 'उद्घाटन' शब्द का सही संधि-विच्छेद होगा–
A. उत् + घाटन B. उद् + घाटन
C. उद्ध + आटन D. इनमें से कोई नहीं

22. 'सत्कर्म' का संधि-विच्छेद है–
A. सत + कर्म B. सतत् + कर्म
C. सत् + कर्म D. सम + कर्म

23. 'अत्यन्त' शब्द का सही संधि-विग्रह है–
A. अत् + यन्त B. अति + यन्त
C. अति + अन्त D. अत् + अन्त

24. निम्नलिखित शब्द का सही संधि-विच्छेद चुनिए–
ब्रह्मांण्ड
A. ब्रह्मा + अंड B. ब्रह्मण + अंड
C. बृहत् + अंड D. बृह + माण्ड

25. 'निरपेक्ष' शब्द का संधि-विच्छेद होगा–
A. निर् + पेक्ष B. नि + पेंक्ष
C. निर + पेक्ष D. निः + अपेक्ष

26. तत् + शंकर की संधि होगी–
A. तत्शंकर B. तच्छंकर
C. तक्षंकर D. उपर्युक्त में से कोई नहीं

27. 'कठोपनिषद्' का संधि-विच्छेद होगा–
A. कटु + उपनिषद् B. कठो + उपनिषद्
C. कठोप + निषद् D. कठ + उपनिषद्

28. 'भावुक' का संधि-विच्छेद होगा–
A. भाव + उक B. भो + ऊक
C. भव्य + उक D. भौ + उक

29. 'विद्यामंदिर' का विग्रह होगा–
A. विद्या का मंदिर B. विद्या के लिए मंदिर
C. विद्या और मंदिर D. विद्या के समान मंदिर

30. 'उत्कोच' का संधि विच्छेद होगा–
A. उद् + कोच B. उत् + कोच
C. उत + कोच D. उद + कोच

31. कौन-सा शब्द विसर्ग संधि का नहीं है?
A. यशोगान B. निष्कपट
C. मनोहर D. अभिषेक

32. 'मनीषा' का संधि-विच्छेद है–
A. मनि + ईषा B. मनी + ईषा
C. मनस् + ईषा D. मणि + ईशा

33. निम्नलिखित में से दीर्घ संधि का उदाहरण कौन-सा है?
A. नरेश B. नेति
C. मध्वाचार्य D. कामायनी

34. 'अति + उक्ति' शब्दों की संधि करने पर शब्द होगा–
A. अत्युक्ति B. अत्योक्ति
C. अतियुक्ति D. अतिउक्ति

35. 'निराधार' शब्द का संधि-विच्छेद है–
A. निः + आधार B. निरा + आधार
C. निरम् + आधार D. निर् + आधार

36. 'अन्वेषण' का संधि-विच्छेद होगा–
A. अन + वेषण B. अनु + एषण
C. अनु + ऐषण D. अन् + वेषण

37. 'सज्जन' का संधि-विच्छेद होगा–
A. सज् + जन B. सद् + जन
C. सत् + जन D. स + ज् + जन

38. 'इत्यादि' का सन्धि-विच्छेद होगा–
A. इत + आदि B. इति + यादि
C. इति + आदि D. इत्य + आदि

39. 'दुर्जन' का सन्धि-विच्छेद होगा–
A. दुर + जन B. दु + जन
C. दुः + जन D. दु + रजन

40. 'नमस्ते' शब्द का सन्धि-विच्छेद है–
A. नम + स्ते B. नमस् + ते
C. नमः + स्ते D. नमः + ते

41. 'महोत्सव' का संधि-विच्छेद है–
A. महा + उत्सव B. महो + उत्सव
C. मह + ओत्सव D. मही + उत्सव

42. 'पवन' का शुद्ध सन्धि-विच्छेद है–
A. पो + अन B. पव + अन
C. पः + अवन D. पव + न्

43. 'विष्णवे' का संधि-विच्छेद है–
A. विष्णु + ए B. विष्णो + ए
C. विष्णु + अए D. विष्णु + अवे

44. 'स्वागतम्' में कौन-सी संधि है?
A. गुण संधि B. यण् संधि
C. वृद्धि संधि D. दीर्घ संधि

45. 'उच्चारण' में कौन-सी संधि है?
A. व्यंजन संधि B. स्वर संधि
C. विसर्ग संधि D. विलोम संधि

46. 'उल्लेख' का संधि-विच्छेद है–
A. उल् + लेख B. उत् + लेख
C. उल्ल + लेख D. उ + आलेख

47. 'अत्याचार' का शुद्ध संधि-विच्छेद है–
A. अत्य + आचार B. अति + चार
C. अत्या + चार D. अति + आचार

48. 'दिगम्बर' का संधि-विच्छेद क्या होगा?
A. दिग् + अम्बर B. दिक् + अम्बर
C. दिग + अम्बर D. दिक + अम्बर

49. 'पावक' का शुद्ध संधि-विच्छेद होगा–
A. पौ + अक B. पा + अवक
C. पव + अक् D. पाव + अक

50. 'उपैति' का संधि-विच्छेद बताइए–
A. अप + इति B. उपै + इति
C. उप + ऐति D. उप + एति

51. 'नवोढ़ा' का सन्धि-विच्छेद है–
A. नव + उढ़ा B. नवो + ढ़ा
C. नव + ऊढ़ा D. न + ओढ़ा

52. 'उड्डयनम' का सन्धि-विच्छेद होगा–
A. उत + डयनम् B. उद् + डयनम्
C. उड + अयनम् D. उड् + डयनम्

53. 'दिंगत' शब्द का संधि-विच्छेद होगा–
A. दिक् + अंत B. दिग् + अंत
C. दि + गंत D. दिग + अंत

54. 'परिच्छेद' में कौन-सी सन्धि है?

A. व्यंजन संधि B. दीर्घ संधि

C. विसर्ग संधि D. वृद्धि संधि

55. 'अन्यान्य' शब्द का संधि-विच्छेद होगा–

A. अ + न्यान्य B. अन्य + अन्य

C. अन् + यान्य D. अन्या + आन्य

56. व्यंजन संधि का उदाहरण नहीं है–

A. उत् + चारणम् = उच्चारणम्

B. रामस् + टीकते = रामष्टीकते

C. गंगा + उदकम = गंगोदकम्

D. सत् + चित् = सच्चित्

57. स्वस्त्यस्तु का संधि-विच्छेद होगा–

A. स्वस्ति + अस्तु B. स्वः + अस्त्यस्तु

C. स्वस्त्य + अस्तु D. स्व + स्त्यस्तु

58. 'तेजोमय' का सही सन्धि-विच्छेद है–

A. तेज + ओमय B. तेजः + अमय

C. तेजः + मय D. तेजो + मय

59. 'तथेति' का सन्धि-विच्छेद होगा–

A. तथ + इति B. ता + थेति

C. तथा + इति D. तथा + इत

60. 'वृहस्पति' का संधि-विच्छेद है–

A. वृहस + पति B. वृहस् + पति

C. वृहः + पति D. वृहश् + पति

61. 'व्याप्त' में संधि है–

A. गुण संधि B. दीर्घ संधि

C. यण् संधि D. अयादि संधि

62. 'पित्राकृतिः' का शुद्ध संधि विच्छेद है–

A. पितृ + आकृतिः B. पित्र + आकृतिः

C. पित्र् + आकृतिः D. पितु + आकृतिः

63. 'न्यून' का संधि विच्छेद होगा–

A. नि + ऊन B. न्यू + नन

C. नव + ऊन D. नवी + नन

64. 'षडानन' में कौन-सी संधि है?

A. दीर्घ संधि B. वृद्धि संधि

C. यण संधि D. गुण संधि

65. 'धर्मात्मा' में कौन-सी संधि है?

A. स्वर संधि B. व्यंजन संधि

C. विसर्ग संधि D. यण संधि

66. 'रेखांकित' में प्रयुक्त संधि है–

A. गुण संधि B. वृद्धि संधि

C. दीर्घ संधि D. स्वर संधि

67. 'निश्छल' में कौन-सी संधि है?

A. गुण संधि B. स्वर संधि

C. दीर्घ संधि D. वृद्धि संधि

68. 'दुरुपयोग' में प्रयुक्त संधि है–

A. स्वर संधि B. यण संधि

C. गुण संधि D. दीर्घ संधि

69. 'अत्यावश्यक' का संधि विच्छेद है–

A. अ + आवश्यक B. अति + आवश्यक

C. अत्य + आवश्यक D. अत्या + वश्यक

70. 'वाङ्मय' का संधि विच्छेद है–

A. वांग + मय B. वाक् + मय

C. वान् + मय D. इनमें से कोई नहीं

71. 'उपर्युक्त' का संधि विच्छेद क्या है?

A. उप + रूक्त B. उपरि + उक्त

C. उपर + युक्त D. उपः + युक्त

72. 'चन्द्रोदय' शब्द में है–

A. स्वर संधि B. व्यंजन संधि

C. विसर्ग संधि D. इनमें से कोई नहीं

73. 'निष्कपट' का संधि विच्छेद है–

A. निः + कपट B. निष + कपट

C. नि + कपट D. इनमें से कोई नहीं

74. 'प्रत्युपकार' का सही संधि विच्छेद है–

A. प्रत्युप + कार B. प्रति + उपकार

C. प्रत्यु + उपकार D. प्रत्य + उपकार

75. 'स्वागत' शब्द का संधि विच्छेद है–

A. स्वा + गत B. स्व + आगत

C. स् + वागत D. सु + आगत

समास

निर्देश (प्र.सं. 1 से 70 तक): *नीचे दिए गए शब्दों में प्रयुक्त समास के नाम का चयन कीजिए–*

1. पीताम्बर–

A. तत्पुरुष B. अव्ययीभाव

C. बहुब्रीहि D. द्विगु

2. चरणकमल–

A. तत्पुरुष B. कर्मधारय

C. बहुब्रीहि D. अव्ययीभाव

3. घुड़सवार–

A. द्विगु B. कर्मधारय

C. तत्पुरुष D. अव्ययीभाव

4. स्वर्गप्राप्त–

A. कर्म तत्पुरुष B. करण तत्पुरुष

C. सम्प्रदान तत्पुरुष D. अपादान तत्पुरुष

5. गर्वशून्य–

A. कर्म-तत्पुरुष B. संप्रदान-तत्पुरुष

C. करण-तत्पुरुष D. अपादान-तत्पुरुष

6. 'लम्बोदर' में कौन-सा समास है?
A. तत्पुरुष B. बहुव्रीहि
C. द्विगु D. कर्मधारय

7. 'देवालय' में कौन-सा समास है?
A. तत्पुरुष B. बहुव्रीहि
C. द्विगु D. इनमें से कोई नहीं

8. 'खरा खोटा' शब्द में कौन-सा समास है?
A. द्वंद्व B. द्विगु
C. कर्मधारय D. बहुव्रीहि

9. 'निर्विवाद' में कौन-सा समास है?
A. कर्मधारय B. अव्ययीभाव
C. तत्पुरुष D. बहुव्रीहि

10. 'दहीबड़ा' में कौन-सा समास है?
A. तत्पुरुष B. द्विगु
C. बहुव्रीहि D. द्वन्द्व

11. 'चौराहा' में समास है–
A. तत्पुरुष B. द्वन्द्व
C. कर्मधारय D. द्विगु

12. 'माता-पिता' शब्द में समास है–
A. द्वन्द्व B. द्विगु
C. तत्पुरुष D. कर्मधारय

13. 'वज्रपाणि' शब्द में कौन-सा समास है?
A. तत्पुरुष B. बहुव्रीहि
C. द्वन्द्व D. द्विगु

14. 'देशभक्ति' शब्द में समास होगा–
A. अपादान तत्पुरुष B. सम्बन्ध तत्पुरुष
C. अधिकरण तत्पुरुष D. सम्प्रदान तत्पुरुष

15. 'सुनीता के बच्चे घास-फूस की तरह बढ़ रहे हैं।'
उपर्युक्त वाक्य में प्रयुक्त 'घास-फूस' शब्द में समास होगा–
A. कर्मधारय B. द्वन्द्व
C. द्विगु D. अव्ययीभाव

16. निम्नलिखित शब्दों में कौन-सा शब्द बहुव्रीहि समास का उदाहरण है?
A. शूलपाणि B. यथाक्रम
C. हँसमुख D. हथकड़ी

17. इनमें से कौन-सा शब्द 'द्विगु' समास है?
A. भुजदण्ड B. माखनचोर
C. पंचशील D. लज्जाशील

18. 'प्रतिदिन' शब्द में समास होगा–
A. द्विगु B. कर्मधारय
C. तत्पुरुष D. अव्ययीभाव

19. जिन समस्त पदों में पहला शब्द संख्यावाची हो और उससे समुदाय का बोध होता हो, तो उसे कहते हैं–
A. द्विगु समास B. द्वन्द्व समास
C. कर्मधारय समास D. अव्ययीभाव समास

20. जिसमें पहला शब्द विशेषण हो और दूसरा शब्द विशेष्य, तो उसे कौन-सा समास कहेंगे?
A. द्विगु B. कर्मधारय
C. द्वन्द्व D. तत्पुरुष

21. 'पंचवटी' शब्द के लिए दिए गए विकल्प में से उपयुक्त समास कौन-सा है?
A. द्विगु B. तत्पुरुष
C. बहुव्रीहि D. कर्मधारय

22. 'बुरा-भला' शब्द में कौन-सा समास है?
A. द्वन्द्व B. द्विगु
C. कर्मधारय D. तत्पुरुष

23. 'चिड़ीमार' शब्द में कौन-सा समास है?
A. द्विगु B. कर्मधारय
C. तत्पुरुष D. अव्ययीभाव

24. 'यथोचित' शब्द में समास बताइए–
A. अव्ययीभाव B. कर्मधारय
C. बहुव्रीहि D. तत्पुरुष

25. समास कहते हैं–
A. शब्दों के मेल को
B. अक्षर के मेल को
C. स्वर-से-स्वर के मेल को
D. स्वर के साथ व्यंजन के मेल को

26. 'शिवार्पण' शब्द में कौन-सा समास है?
A. अधिकरण तत्पुरुष B. करण तत्पुरुष
C. सम्प्रदान तत्पुरुष D. अपादान तत्पुरुष

27. निम्नलिखित में किसमें तत्पुरुष समास है?
A. पदप्राप्त B. शताब्दी
C. चौमासा D. भाई-बहन

28. 'रसगुल्ला' में कौन-सा समास है?
A. तत्पुरुष B. बहुव्रीहि
C. द्वन्द्व D. अव्ययीभाव

29. 'भुखमरा' का समास विग्रह होगा–
A. भूख से जो मर गया B. भूख से मरा हुआ
C. भूखों मर गया जो D. भूख द्वारा मरा हुआ

30. 'दशरथ सुत' में कौन-सा समास है?
A. तत्पुरुष B. बहुव्रीहि
C. द्विगु D. द्वन्द्व

31. 'अष्टाध्यायी' में कौन-सा समास है?
A. द्वन्द्व B. द्विगु
C. तत्पुरुष D. कर्मधारय

32. 'यथाशीघ्र' में कौन-सा समास है?
A. अव्ययीभाव B. द्वन्द्व
C. कर्मधारय D. तत्पुरुष

33. चौखंभा में कौन-सा समास है?
A. बहुब्रीहि B. द्वन्द्व
C. द्विगु D. तत्पुरुष

34. कौन-सा समास विशेषण के रूप में प्रयुक्त होता है?
A. अव्ययीभाव B. तत्पुरुष
C. कर्मधारय D. बहुब्रीहि

35. द्विगु समास का उदाहरण होगा–
A. षट्कोण B. कुपुत्र
C. प्रतिवर्ष D. सूरसागर

36. कौन-सा शब्द अव्ययीभाव समास का उदाहरण है?
A. नवग्रह B. गाँठकर
C. महात्मा D. आमरण

37. 'राजपुत्र' में कौन-सा समास है?
A. बहुब्रीहि B. तत्पुरुष
C. द्विगु D. कर्मधारय

38. निम्नलिखित में से तत्पुरुष समास किसमें है?
A. नील गाय B. राजकुमार
C. त्रिलोचन D. दशानन

39. निम्नलिखित में द्वन्द्व समास बताइए–
A. प्रतिदिन B. चौमासा
C. घी-शक्कर D. महादेव

40. 'आजीवन' में कौन-सा समास है?
A. अव्ययीभाव B. तत्पुरुष
C. कर्मधारय D. द्विगु

41. निम्नलिखित में 'यथाविधि' का सही समास कौन-सा है?
A. अव्ययीभाव B. तत्पुरुष
C. कर्मधारय D. बहुब्रीहि

42. 'पर्णकुटी' शब्द का समास है–
A. तत्पुरुष B. द्वन्द्व
C. कर्मधारय D. बहुब्रीहि

43. निम्नलिखित में 'द्वन्द्व समास' का शब्द है–
A. आज-कल B. रातों-रात
C. दिन-दिन D. वीर पुरुष

44. 'निशिदिन' शब्द में प्रयुक्त समास है–
A. द्वन्द्व B. अव्ययीभाव
C. कर्मधारय D. तत्पुरुष

45. जिस समास में पहला शब्द प्रधान होता है और समूचा शब्द क्रिया विशेषण अव्यय होता है, उसे कौन-सा समास कहते हैं?
A. अव्ययीभाव B. तत्पुरुष
C. बहुब्रीहि D. द्वन्द्व

46. 'जलपिपासु' में कौन-सा समास है?
A. तत्पुरुष B. अव्ययीभाव
C. द्वन्द्व D. बहुब्रीहि

47. 'वनवास' में कौन-सा समास है?
A. तत्पुरुष B. कर्मधारय
C. द्वन्द्व D. बहुब्रीहि

48. 'दिगम्बर' में कौन-सा समास है?
A. बहुब्रीहि B. द्वन्द्व
C. द्विगु D. कर्मधारय

49. 'नरोत्तम' में कौन-सा समास है?
A. द्वन्द्व B. तत्पुरुष
C. अव्ययीभाव D. कर्मधारय

50. 'आजन्म' में कौन-सा समास है?
A. द्विगु B. तत्पुरुष
C. कर्मधारय D. अव्ययीभाव

51. 'अकालपीड़ित' में समास होगा–
A. कर्मधारय B. द्वन्द्व
C. तत्पुरुष D. बहुब्रीहि

52. 'जय-पराजय' में कौन-सा समास है?
A. द्वन्द्व B. कर्मधारय
C. द्विगु D. तत्पुरुष

53. 'वियोग-विकल' शब्द में प्रयुक्त समास है–
A. तत्पुरुष B. कर्मधारय
C. द्वन्द्व D. द्विगु

54. इन युग्मों में से कौन-सा सही नहीं है?
A. नीलोत्पलम् – कर्मधारय समास
B. दशाननः – बहुब्रीहि समास
C. रामलक्ष्मणौ – अव्ययीभाव समास
D. दिवारात्रि – द्वन्द्व समास

55. 'तिरंगा' शब्द में समास है–
A. द्वन्द्व B. अव्ययीभाव
C. द्विगु D. कर्मधारय

56. 'लम्बोदर' उदाहरण है–
A. बहुब्रीहि समास का B. द्वन्द्व समास का
C. द्विगु समास का D. कर्मधारय समास का

57. निम्नलिखित में से कर्मधारय समास किसमें है?
A. चक्रपाणि B. चतुर्थुगम्
C. नीलोत्पलम् D. माता-पिता

58. 'चक्रपाणिदर्शनार्थ' पद में मान्य समास है–
A. कर्मधारय B. तत्पुरुष
C. अव्ययीभाव D. बहुब्रीहि

59. 'कठपुतली' में कौन-सा समास है?
A. सम्प्रदान तत्पुरुष B. सम्बन्ध तत्पुरुष
C. अधिकरण तत्पुरुष D. कर्म तत्पुरुष

60. 'कष्टापन्नः' शब्द में समास है–
A. अव्ययीभाव B. तत्पुरुष
C. बहुब्रीहि D. कर्मधारय

61. 'चन्द्रकान्तिः' में समास है–

A. बहुब्रीहि B. कर्मधारय
C. तत्पुरुष D. इनमें से कोई नहीं

62. 'चन्द्रशेखर' में प्रयुक्त समास है–

A. तत्पुरुष B. कर्मधारय
C. बहुब्रीहि D. द्विगु

63. 'रात-दिन' में कौन-सा समास होता है?

A. द्वन्द्व B. द्विगु
C. कर्मधारय D. अव्ययीभाव

64. 'बहन-भाई' में समास है–

A. बहुब्रीहि B. तत्पुरुष
C. द्वन्द्व D. द्विगु

65. 'दशमुख' में कौन-सा समास है?

A. तत्पुरुष B. बहुब्रीहि
C. द्वन्द्व D. कर्मधारय

66. 'यथाशक्ति' में समास है–

A. द्विगु B. तत्पुरुष
C. कर्मधारय D. अव्ययीभाव

67. 'देशभक्ति' में समास है–

A. तत्पुरुष B. बहुब्रीहि
C. द्विगु D. कर्मधारय

68. 'हस्तलिखित' में प्रयुक्त समास है–

A. कर्मधारय B. तत्पुरुष
C. बहुब्रीहि D. द्वन्द्व

69. 'त्रिनेत्र' में कौन-सा समास है?

A. तत्पुरुष B. बहुब्रीहि
C. द्विगु D. द्वन्द्व

70. 'भरपेट' में कौन-सा समास है?

A. अव्ययीभाव B. कर्मधारय
C. तत्पुरुष D. बहुब्रीहि

वर्तनी

निर्देश (प्र.सं. 1 से 80 तक): *नीचे के प्रश्नों में एक शब्द की चार अलग-अलग वर्तनियां दी हुई हैं। इनमें से सही वर्तनी छाँटकर उस पर निशान लगाइये:*

1. A. जयोत्स्ना B. ज्योत्स्ना
C. जोत्स्ना D. ज्योत्सना

2. A. कवयित्री B. कवियित्री
C. कवियत्री D. कवित्री

3. A. उत्ज्वल B. उज्जवल
C. ऊज्जवल D. उज्ज्वल

4. A. छः B. छह
C. छह् D. छै

5. A. जिजीविषा B. जिजीवषा
C. जजीवषा D. जिजिवीषा

6. A. दृश्य B. द्रश्य
C. दृष्य D. दृिश्य

7. A. इतिहासिक B. ऐतिहासिक
C. ऐतिहासीक D. ऐतीहासिक

8. A. वाङ्मय B. वाँङ्मय
C. वांग्मय D. वांगमय

9. A. सौर्हाद्र B. सैहार्द
C. सैर्हाद D. सौहार्द

10. A. आर्शीवाद B. आशिर्वाद
C. आशीर्वाद D. आर्शिवाद

11. A. भूगोलिक B. भूगौलिक
C. भोगौलिक D. भौगोलिक

12. A. सन्कीर्णता B. सन्कीरणता
C. संर्कीणता D. संकीर्णता

13. A. परचन्ड B. प्रचण्ड
C. प्रचान्ड D. परचण्ड

14. A. तार्क्रिक B. तार्किक
C. ताकृिक D. ताक्रिक

15. A. इर्षा B. ईर्षा
C. इर्ष्या D. ईर्ष्या

16. A. पूज्यनीय B. पुजनीय
C. पूजनीय D. पुज्यनीय

17. A. अधम्र B. अध्रम
C. अधर्म D. अधृम

18. A. अधिकृत B. अधिक्रित
C. अधिक्रित्त D. अधिर्कित

19. A. अनुकृम B. अनुक्रम
C. अनुकर्म D. अनुकम्र

20. A. अनवेषण B. अन्वेषण
C. अन्वेछण D. अन्वेशण

21. A. अभिशेक B. अभिषेख
C. अभिषेक D. अभीषेक

22. A. इच्छुक B. इक्षुक
C. इक्छुक D. इच्छिक

23. A. इन्र्दिय B. इन्द्दिय
C. इन्दिय D. इन्द्रिय

24. A. उतकण्ठा B. उत्कण्ठा
C. उत्क्णठा D. उत्त्कन्ठा

25. A. उमृिला B. उम्रिला
C. उमिर्ला D. उर्मिला

26. A. रिषि B. ऋषि
C. ऋिषि D. ऋशि्

27. A. एकागृ B. एकाग्र
C. एकार्ग D. एक्राग्र

28. A. ओजश्वि B. ओजस्वी
C. ओजश्वी D. ओजष्वी

29. A. औशधी B. औषधी
C. औषधि D. औष्धि

30. A. करम B. क्राम
C. कम्र D. कर्म

31. A. ग्रिहीत B. ग्रहीत
C. गृहीत D. गर्हित

32. A. कृतज्ञ B. क्रतज्ञ
C. क्रितज्ञ D. क्रितग्य

33. A. चतुदर्श B. चर्तुदश
C. चतुर्दश D. चतुद्रश

34. A. जर्जर B. जरर्जर
C. जज्रर D. जरजर

35. A. जघ्नय B. जघ्रय
C. जघ्न्य D. जघन्य

36. A. जेष्ठ B. ज्येश्ठ
C. ज्येष्ठ D. ज्येस्ठ

37. A तपस्वनी B. तपस्विनी
C. तपिस्वनी D. तपिस्विनी

38. A. तादातमय B. तदात्म्य
C. तादात्म्य D. तादात्यम

39. A. तृष्णा B. तिृष्णा
C. त्रिष्णा D. तृश्णा

40. A. त्रिमूर्ती B. त्रिमुर्ति
C. त्रिमूर्ति D. त्रृमूर्ति

41. A. दक्छ B. दक्च्छ
C. दक्ष D. दज्ञ

42. A. द्रर्पन B. दर्पन
C. दपर्ण D. दर्पण

43. A. दामपत्य B. दम्पत्य
C. दाम्पत्य D. दाम्पत

44. A. दीप्पित B. दीपति
C. दीप्ति D. दीप्ती

45. A. दीर्घायु B. दीरघायु
C. दीघार्यु D. दीर्घियु

46. A. दुर्निती B. दुनीर्ति
C. दुरनीति D. दुर्नीति

47. A. दुर्दषा B. दुहशा
C. दुर्दशा D. दुद्रशा

48. A. दुर्योधन B. दुयोर्धन
C. दूरयोधन D. द्रुयोधन

49. A. दुरबुद्धि B. दुर्बुधि
C. दुबुद्धि D. दुर्बुद्धि

50. A. धनुष्विद्या B. धनुर्विद्या
C. धर्नुविद्या D. धनुर्वेद्या

51. A. धर्म B. धृर्म
C. ध्रर्म D. धम्र

52. A. ध्रुर्व B. धुव्र
C. ध्रुव D. धुर्व

53. A. नम्रदिश्वर B. नंम्रदेश्वर
C. नमर्देश्वर D. नर्मदिश्वर

54. A. निरक्षेप B. निक्क्षेप
C. निक्षेप D. निक्छेप

55. A. निर्गह B. नृग्रह
C. निग्रह D. निगर्ह

56. A. निरजीव B. निर्जीव
C. नृजीव D. निज्रीव

57. A. निम्रूल B. निर्मूल
C. निरमूल D. नृर्मूल

58. A. निवृत्त B. निव्रत्त
C. निवृत D. नृिवत्त

59. A. प्रिक्रमा B. परीक्रमा
C. परिकृमा D. परिक्रमा

60. A. प्रयटन B. पृयटन
C. पर्यटन D. प्रर्यटन

61. A. प्रक्रिति B. प्रकृति
C. प्रक्रति D. पृक्रति

62. A. बर्हिमुख B. बहिर्मुख
C. बहिम्रुख D. बहिमुर्ख

63. A. भरतस्ना B. भर्त्सना
C. भर्तसना D. भर्तृसना

64. A. मूर्ती B. मूर्ति
C. मूर्तृि D. मूरती

65. A. गिद्ध B. गीध
C. गिद्धा D. ग्रिद्ध

66. A. निकर्सन B. निर्कषन
C. निकर्षण D. निर्कषण

67. A. निकृष्ट B. निक्रस्ट
C. निकृस्ट D. निक्रिष्ट

68. A. पार्थिव B. पार्थ्रिव
C. पार्थीव D. पाथिर्व

69. A. विदूश्क B. विदूष्क
C. विदूशक D. विदूषक

70. A. फुर्तीला B. फुर्तीला
C. फुर्तिला D. फुर्तला

71. A. वर्ज B. वज्र
C. वज्र D. वज्र

72. A. ब्रम्हचर्य B. ब्रह्मचर्य
C. बृह्मचर्य D. ब्रह्मर्चय

73. A. मत्स्य B. मतस्य
C. मत्सत्य D. मत्श्य

74. A. भ्रित्य B. भर्त्य
C. भृत्य D. भ्रत्य

75. A. निग्रंध B. निर्गंध
C. र्निगंध D. नृगंध

76. A. प्रकर्श B. प्रकर्ष
C. पृकर्श D. पृकर्ष

77. A. भद्र B. भदृ
C. भर्द्र D. भर्द

78. A. मंजूशा B. मंजूषा
C. मंजुषा D. मंजुशा

79. A. मुर्मूषु B. मुमुर्षू
C. मुमुर्षु D. मुमूर्षु

80. A. ब्राह्मण B. बृाह्मण
C. ब्राम्हण D. बृाहम्ण

निर्देश (प्र.सं. 81 से 115 तक): *नीचे प्रत्येक प्रश्न में A, B, C और D अक्षरांक में चार शब्द दिए गए हैं। जिनमें से एक में वर्तनी सम्बन्धी त्रुटि हो सकती है। उस त्रुटियुक्त शब्द का अक्षरांक ही आपका उत्तर होगा। यदि चारों शब्दों की वर्तनी सही है तो उत्तर दीजिए E अर्थात् 'सभी सही हैं'।*

81. A. अप्रयुक्त B. अतीषयोक्ति
C. अशोध्य D. सम्मति
E. सभी सही हैं

82. A. अभ्युक्ति B. इष्टतम
C. अपुरित D. उपस्थित
E. सभी सही हैं

83. A. उत्तरजिवीता B. प्रारक्षित
C. क्षैतिज D. आयातित
E. सभी सही हैं

84. A. आस्थगित B. आतिथ्य
C. अंतरिम D. निर्धारित
E. सभी सही हैं

85. A. किफायत B. परिस्थिति
C. संतुलित D. असिंचीत
E. सभी सही हैं

86. A. तात्पर्य B. महोत्सव
C. दंभ D. कृशक
E. सभी सही हैं

87. A. लक्षण B. व्यंजन
C. पगडंडी D. पारंगत
E. सभी सही हैं

88. A. स्थानापन्न B. व्यावशयिक
C. कोशिका D. आर्थिक
E. सभी सही हैं

89. A. दांडधिकारी B. प्राधिकरण
C. आदित्य D. क्रियान्वयन
E. सभी सही हैं

90. A. गोपनीयता B. कार्यवाही
C. उत्रदायित्व D. वयस्क
E. सभी सही हैं

91. A. चूल्लु B. जीविका
C. ठिठोली D. तकली
E. सभी सही हैं

92. A. नजरिया B. पंडीताइ
C. फरियादी D. बधाई
E. सभी सही हैं

93. A. प्रकाशकीय B. फाल्गुन
C. बधिर D. भोतिक
E. सभी सही हैं

94. A. हौसला B. स्वीकृति
C. व्यवासायिक D. लिपाई
E. सभी सही हैं

95. A. फलित B. बटोही
C. भजनीक D. मंडली
E. सभी सही हैं

96. A. अनामिष B. अपरिहार्य
C. किंफायती D. गिलाफ
E. सभी सही हैं

97. A. गोधुलि B. चांचल्य
C. जिजीविषु D. तमोली
E. सभी सही हैं

98. A. तितिक्षा B. दखलंदाजी
C. दिप्ति D. दैनिकी
E. सभी सही हैं

99. A. नजदिकी B. नियोक्ता
C. परिणीता D. पाणिग्रहण
E. सभी सही हैं

100. A. पुनीत B. प्रख्यापीत
C. फरोख्त D. बुजुर्गी
E. सभी सही हैं

101. A. अद्भुत B. व्यंग्य
C. अदृश्य D. समारंभ
E. सभी सही हैं

102. A. लक्षण B. महात्मन
C. सम्पर्क D. कर्तज्ञ
E. सभी सही हैं

103. A. गझिन B. आशय
C. निशपादन D. आकर्षण
E. सभी सही हैं

104. A. उत्तरीय B. स्थान्नापन
C. कुंभ D. असामान्य
E. सभी सही हैं

105. A. न्ययाधिश B. पुरस्कृत
C. वारिद D. अधिशासी
E. सभी सही हैं

106. A. चिनाई B. तंबूल
C. ठिठोली D. तन्मय
E. सभी सही हैं

107. A. अगड़ाइ B. गठीला
C. खिलाफ D. कल्पनातीत
E. सभी सही हैं

108. A. सूरत B. वैधव्य
C. लतीका D. रेगिस्तान
E. सभी सही हैं

109. A. इति B. अखिलेश
C. कबूतर D. खेरात
E. सभी सही हैं

110. A. चमत्कृत B. जिल्द
C. तमोली D. दमित
E. सभी सही हैं

111. A. प्रहसन B. तात्पर्य
C. महसूल D. पाणिगृहण
E. सभी सही हैं

112. A. मस्तिष्क B. प्रोत्साहन
C. सम्वत् D. क्रियाविधि
E. सभी सही हैं

113. A. विचारणीय B. क्रन्दन
C. पर्यावर्ण D. उपलब्धि
E. सभी सही हैं

114. A. विसतृत B. वाग्विलास
C. तात्कालिक D. अलंकार
E. सभी सही हैं

115. A. दृष्टांत B. रूढ़ि
C. सूचि D. आचमन
E. सभी सही हैं

पर्यायवाची

1. 'कमल' शब्द का पर्यायवाची होगा–
A. कन्दर्प B. अनंग
C. घनेश D. इन्दीवर

2. 'क्रोध' के लिए इन दिए गए पर्यायवाची शब्दों में एक गलत शब्द है, उसे चयनित कीजिए–
A. रोष B. अमर्ष
C. स्वत्व D. कोप

3. निम्नलिखित पर्यायवाची शब्दों में से जो एक शब्द 'मोर' का पर्यायवाची नहीं है, उसे चिन्हित कीजिए–
A. केकी B. कीश
C. शिखी D. शिखण्डी

4. इनमें से कौन-सा शब्द 'कृष्णा' का पर्यायवाची है?
A. राधा B. रुक्मिणी
C. द्रोपदी D. यशोदा

5. इनमें से एक शब्द 'बैल' का पर्यायवाची नहीं है, उसे चयनित कीजिए–
A. अश्म B. बृषभ
C. बलीवर्द D. गो

6. निम्नलिखित में से जो शब्द 'सौन्दर्य' का पर्यायवाची नहीं है, उसे चयनित कीजिए–
A. सुषमा B. शोभा
C. सुन्दरता D. रमणी

7. निम्नलिखित विकल्पों में से एक शब्द 'नदी' का पर्यायवाची नहीं है, उसे चयनित कीजिए–
A. तरंगिणी B. तटिनी
C. तरिणी D. सरिता

8. नीचे दिए गए विकल्पों में से एक शब्द 'घर' का पर्यायवाची नहीं है, उसे चयनित कीजिए–
A. भवन B. भुवन
C. निकेतन D. सदन

9. इनमें से कौन-सा शब्द 'पार्थ' का पर्यायवाची है?
A. भीष्म B. श्रीकृष्ण
C. युधिष्ठिर D. अर्जुन

10. 'दुःख' का पर्यायवाची शब्द निम्नलिखित में से कौन-सा है?
A. व्यथा B. पीड़ा
C. वेदना D. ये सभी पर्याय हैं

11. नीचे दिए गए शब्दों में से एक शब्द 'गीदड़' का पर्यायवाची नहीं है, उसका चयन कीजिए–
A. खगेश B. शृंगाल
C. सियार D. जम्बुक

12. निम्न में से कौन चन्द्रमा का पर्यायवाची नहीं है?
A. शशि B. हिमकर
C. शशांक D. रूपक

13. निम्न में से कौन गाय का पर्यायवाची नहीं है?
A. हेरम्ब B. गौरी
C. भद्रा D. धेनु

14. कुत्ता का पर्यायवाची शब्द निम्नलिखित में से कौन-सा है?
A. सारमेय B. क्रमेलक
C. कीर D. नागान्तक

15. आनंद का पर्यायवाची नहीं है–
A. हर्ष B. उल्लास
C. चाह D. आह्लाद

16. 'कृशानु' का पर्यायवाची शब्द है–
A. अनल B. पवन
C. दोहित्री D. अनिल

17. 'द्रौपदी' का पर्याय नहीं है–
A. द्रुपदसुता B. याज्ञसेनी
C. पांचाली D. रमणी

18. 'महादेव' का पर्यायवाची शब्द चुनिए–
A. गरुड़ध्वज B. नारायण
C. चन्द्रशेखर D. विश्वम्भर

19. 'चन्द्रमा' का पर्यायवाची शब्द चुनिए–
A. निशाकर B. निशाचर
C. तरणि D. कृशानु

20. 'धन' का पर्यायवाची जो शब्द नहीं है, उसे चुनिए–
A. द्रव्य B. द्रव
C. सम्पदा D. दौलत

21. 'पुत्री' का पर्यायवाची शब्द नहीं है–
A. तनय B. सुता
C. आत्मजा D. दुहिता

22. निम्नलिखित में से कौन-सा शब्द 'कमल' का पर्यायवाची शब्द नहीं है?
A. सरोज B. अरविन्द
C. सलिल D. पंकज

23. निम्नलिखित किस समूह में सभी शब्द 'कामदेव' के पर्यायवाची हैं?
A. कंदर्प, मदन, मनसिज, मारक
B. मदन, मन्मथ, अनंग, कंदर्प
C. मान, त्रिपुर, मन्मथ, अनंग
D. मन्मथ, मनसिज, त्रिपुर, अनंग

24. कौन-सा शब्द जंगल शब्द का पर्यायवाची नहीं है?
A. अटवी B. कान्ता
C. कान्तार D. कानन

25. कौन-सा शब्द 'अम्बर' का पर्यायवाची है?
A. आकाश B. अवनि
C. मेघ D. बादल

26. कौन-सा शब्द 'मित्र' का पर्याय नहीं है?
A. अलि B. सखा
C. सुहृद D. मीत

27. निम्नांकित में किस शब्द का अर्थ कमल होता है?
A. उत्पल B. उपल
C. जलद D. नीरद

28. निम्नलिखित में 'पुत्री' शब्द के पर्यायवाची शब्द-समूह कौन हैं?
A. भार्या, कान्ता, अबला, वनिता
B. लड़की, बेटी, अचला, वसुधा
C. सुता, धरा, वसुमती, अचला
D. तनया, आत्मजा, दुहिता, तनुजा

29. निम्नलिखित शब्द-समूह में 'बिजली' के पर्यायवाची कौन हैं?
A. ज्योति, रोशनी, चमक, प्रभा
B. विद्युत, तड़ित, चपला, दामिनी
C. उजाला, प्रभंजन, विहग, निशापति
D. मंदाकिनी, अश्म, प्रस्तर, प्रभा

30. 'जलधि' शब्द का पर्यायवाची क्या है?
A. नहर B. नाव
C. नदी D. समुद्र

31. 'पंकज' शब्द का पर्यायवाची क्या है?
A. सूर्य B. कमल
C. चन्द्रमा D. अमृत

32. 'तरकश' का पर्यायवाची शब्द है–
A. तीर B. धनुष
C. प्रत्यंचा D. निषंग

33. 'स्त्री' का पर्यायवाची शब्द नहीं है–
A. तरुणी B. प्रमदा
C. ललाम D. ललना

34. 'गणेश' का पर्यायवाची शब्द है–
A. सुधांशु B. कुबेर
C. एकदंत D. सुधाकर

35. निम्नलिखित में से कौन-सा शब्द 'तलवार' का पर्यायवाची नहीं है?

A. असि B. खड्ग
C. कृपण D. चंद्रहास

36. इनमें से कौन 'कौआ' का पर्यायवाची है?

A. वायस B. पाली
C. भद्रा D. उदक

37. निम्न में से कौन 'पत्ता' का पर्यायवाची नहीं है?

A. दल B. पर्ण
C. पल्लव D. प्रसून

38. निम्न में से कौन 'हंस' का पर्यायवाची है?

A. मराल B. सारंग
C. अनीक D. अरि

39. निम्न में से कौन 'रण' का पर्यायवाची नहीं है?

A. युद्ध B. संग्राम
C. समर D. सार

40. इनमें से कौन 'युवती' का पर्यायवाची नहीं है?

A. तरुणी B. किशोरी
C. श्यामा D. यामिनी

41. निम्न में से कौन 'इन्द्र' का पर्यायवाची नहीं है?

A. सुरपति B. मघवा
C. धनाधिप D. सुरेश

42. इनमें से कौन 'सरस्वती' का पर्यायवाची नहीं है?

A. वीणापाणि B. वाचा
C. धनद D. शारदा

43. निम्न में से कौन 'कन्या' का पर्यायवाची नहीं है?

A. तनुजा B. आत्मजा
C. नन्दिनी D. भार्या

44. इनमें से कौन 'मयूर' का पर्यायवाची नहीं है?

A. सारंग B. शिखी
C. विशिख D. केकी

45. इनमें से कौन 'शेर' का पर्यायवाची नहीं है?

A. तुरंग B. मृगेन्द्र
C. मृगराज D. व्याघ्र

46. निम्न में से कौन 'अग्नि' का पर्यायवाची है?

A. अनल B. धनद
C. सारंग D. जाह्नवी

47. 'अलंकेश' पर्यायवाची शब्द है–

A. बादल का B. कल्पवृक्ष का
C. कुबेर का D. चपला का

48. इनमें से किस शब्द के पर्यायवाची गलत हैं?

A. कमल – जलज, पंकज, सरोज
B. पुष्प – कुसुम, फूल, सुमन
C. सरस्वती – गिरा, भारती, वाणी
D. सूर्य – दिवस, याम, वासर

49. निम्नलिखित में कौन-सा शब्द 'पताका' का पर्यायवाची नहीं है?

A. झण्डा B. निशान
C. प्रस्तर D. ध्वज

50. निम्नलिखित शब्दों में से 'हनुमान' का पर्यायवाची शब्द नहीं है–

A. रामभक्त B. पवनपुत्र
C. बजरंगबली D. कपीश्वर

51. 'खेचर' का पर्याय होगा–

A. आकाश में चलने वाला B. पक्षी
C. ग्रह D. इनमें से सभी

52. 'बटोही' का पर्यायवाची निम्न में से कौन शब्द-समूह होगा?

A. वटमार, एकाकी B. असहाय, दुर्गम
C. पथिक, राहगीर D. पाथेय, मेघ

53. निम्न में से कौन-सा शब्द समूह 'विरद' का पर्यायवाची होगा?

A. यश, ख्याति B. बीज, मूल
C. वृक्ष, पौधा D. विरही, वियोगी

54. 'यातु' का पर्यायवाची निम्न में से कौन शब्द-समूह होगा?

A. पथिक, कष्ट B. काल, हवा
C. यातना, हिंसा D. राक्षस, निशाचर

55. 'विभु' का पर्यायवाची शब्द-समूह होगा–

A. सर्वव्यापक, नित्य B. ब्रह्म, आत्मा
C. महान, ईश्वर D. चिरस्थायी, दृढ़

56. 'क्षुद्र' का पर्यायवाची शब्द-समूह होगा–

A. कंजूस, कृपण B. निर्धन, दरिद्र
C. अल्प, मामूली D. नीच, अधम

57. 'कुबेर' शब्द का निम्नलिखित में से कौन- सा शब्द पर्यायवाची नहीं है?

A. श्वान B. कोषपाल
C. धनपति D. यक्षपति

58. 'सेवक' का पर्यायवाची है–

A. परिचर्या B. यायावर
C. शायक D. परिचारक

59. 'पार्वती' का पर्यायवाची है–

A. कमला B. इला
C. गौरा D. विभा

60. 'अग्र' शब्द का पर्यायवाची नहीं है–

A. शिखर B. अगला
C. ज्येष्ठ D. दावा

61. निम्नलिखित में से कौन-सा एक 'जानकी' का पर्यायवाची नहीं है?

A. जनकात्मजा B. वैदेही
C. जनकसूता D. वामा

62. 'पुष्प' का पर्यायवाची नहीं है–

A. सुमन B. प्रसून
C. कुसुम D. निलय

63. 'पत्थर' का पर्यायवाची है–
A. हिमगिरि B. पाषाण
C. गिरि D. शैल

64. 'पावक' का पर्यायवाची शब्द निम्नलिखित में से कौन-सा है?
A. पृथ्वी B. जल
C. अग्नि D. वायु

65. निम्नलिखित में से जो शब्द 'पत्नी' का पर्याय न हो, उसे चिन्हित कीजिए–
A. कलत्र B. दौहित्र
C. भार्या D. जाया

66. 'अर्वाचीन' शब्द का पर्यायवाची है–
A. आधुनिक B. विदेशी
C. चीनी D. प्राचीन

विलोमार्थी शब्द

निर्देश (प्र.सं. 1 से 75 तक): *सही-सही विलोम शब्द चुनिए–*

1. अनादर
A. मान B. सम्मान
C. आदर D. सत्कार

2. अभिज्ञ
A. अज्ञानी B. अनभिज्ञ
C. अनिपुण D. मूर्ख

3. अथ
A. इति B. समाप्त
C. खत्म D. संपूर्ण

4. करुण
A. कठोर B. निष्ठुर
C. निर्दय D. कोमल

5. ऋजु
A. सीधा B. सरल
C. तिर्यक् D. वक्र

6. मौन
A. मुखर B. मूक
C. वाचाल D. प्रगल्भ

7. निर्दय
A. निर्भय B. सहृय
C. सभय D. सदय

8. तिमिर
A. प्रकाश्य B. आलोक
C. ज्योतिर्मय D. आभास

9. तीक्ष्ण
A. मंद B. तीव्र
C. प्रखर D. क्षीण

10. कृत्रिम
A. प्राकृतिक B. स्वनिर्मित
C. स्वाभाविक D. स्वचालित

11. उदात्त
A. उद्धत B. दानशील
C. अनुदात्त D. क्षमावान्

12. उदार
A. कठोर B. निर्भय
C. अपव्यय D. अनुदार

13. शुक्ल
A. काला B. कृष्ण
C. असित D. श्यामल

14. प्रस्थान
A. आगमन B. गमनागमन
C. निगम D. निर्गम

15. शूल
A. मूल B. धूल
C. फूल D. तूल

16. अपेक्षा
A. कामना B. भावना
C. अभीप्सा D. उपेक्षा

17. निरक्षर
A. शिक्षित B. अशिक्षित
C. साक्षर D. अक्षर

18. प्रकट
A. गुप्त B. लुप्त
C. सुप्त D. विलुप्त

19. उर्वर
A. उपजाऊ B. बंजर
C. गत्वर D. शस्यश्यामल

20. संधि
A. अनुग्रह B. ग्रह
C. विच्छेद D. मैत्री

21. संयोग
A. प्रयोग B. सुयोग
C. नियोग D. वियोग

22. विकास
A. सीमा B. ह्रास
C. दुबला D. नीचा

23. उत्थान
A. नमन B. पतन
C. उदय D. ध्वंस

24. क्षुद्र
A. क्षुद्रतर B. महान्
C. तुच्छ D. अवमान

25. इहलोक
A. उपकार B. पाताल
C. आदि D. परलोक

26. ज्योति
A. पुंज B. दीपक
C. तम D. रोशनी

27. यथार्थ
A. मनोवांछित B. अनुमानित
C. कल्पित D. सत्य

28. अमर
A. देवता B. मरणशील
C. मर्त्य D. दानव

29. आघात
A. अनाघात B. विस्तीर्ण
C. स्निग्ध D. डरपोक

30. व्यष्टि
A. सृष्टि B. वृष्टि
C. समष्टि D. इनमें से कोई नहीं

31. सज्जन
A. चापलूस B. व्यभिचारी
C. सहयोगी D. दुर्जन

32. उत्कर्ष
A. अपकर्ष B. परामर्श
C. संघर्ष D. विमर्श

33. क्षुधा
A. तृषा B. तृण
C. तृप्ति D. मृगतृष्णा

34. सुबह
A. प्रातः B. शाम
C. रात D. दिन

35. अनुकूल
A. प्रतिकूल B. अपकूल
C. अनुकूलन D. सानूकूल

36. आहूत
A. अनागत B. आगत
C. अनेक D. अनाहूत

37. श्रीगणेश
A. समापन B. इतिश्री
C. अंत D. अथ

38. निंदा
A. स्तुति B. संस्तुति
C. संवेदना D. स्तवन

39. आचार
A. आनाचार B. अनाचार
C. अत्याचार D. विचार

40. सहज
A. असहज B. असली
C. अप्राकृतिक D. निर्मित

41. प्राच्य
A. उदीच्य B. प्रतीच्य
C. पाश्चात्य D. अर्वाचीन

42. गुण
A. दोष B. पुण्य
C. अधिक D. विशाल

43. 'लाघव' शब्द का विपरीतार्थक शब्द है–
A. विस्तार B. संक्षेप
C. लम्बा D. दीर्घकालीन

44. आहार
A. प्रतिहार B. साहार
C. अनाहार D. विहार

45. 'ध्वंस' शब्द का विलोम बताइए–
A. विनाश B. निर्माण
C. विध्वंस D. उत्कर्ष

46. 'वादी' का विलोमार्थी शब्द बताएँ–
A. समवादी B. कुवादी
C. अनुवादी D. प्रतिवादी

47. अतिवृष्टि का विलोमार्थी शब्द है–
A. अन्तरवृष्टि B. अल्पवृष्टि
C. असमयवृष्टि D. अस्तवृष्टि

48. आदि
A. अंत B. प्रारम्भ
C. व्याधि D. बर्बादी

49. शाश्वत
A. मृत्यु B. मर्त्य
C. नश्वर D. क्षणिक

50. व्यस्त
A. विश्रांत B. अभ्यस्त
C. अव्यस्त D. अतिव्यस्त

51. गत्यात्मक
A. गतिभाव B. स्थिर
C. अस्थिर D. प्रत्यात्मक

52. अज्ञ
A. अनज्ञ B. सुमज्ञ
C. विज्ञ D. कुमज्ञ

53. कटु
A. मधुर B. पटु
C. मृदु D. मीठा

54. नीरस
A. रसीला B. सरस
C. विरस D. अरस

55. ओजस्वनी
A. तेजस्वनी B. निर्जस्वी
C. निस्तेज D. तपस्वी

56. अर्पण
A. ग्रहण B. तर्पण
C. समर्पण D. प्रत्यर्पण

57. अनभिज्ञ
A. भिज्ञ B. अज्ञ
C. अभिज्ञ D. अतिभिज्ञ

58. अन्यमनस्क
A. स्वस्थ B. प्रसन्न
C. सजग D. सतर्क

59. अपव्यय
A. अधिव्यय B. व्यय
C. मितव्यय D. इनमें से कोई नहीं

60. आवरण
A. अनावरण B. आचरण
C. सुवरण D. अवज्ञा

61. गमन
A. आना B. उतरना
C. रुकना D. आगमन

62. राजा
A. देवता B. साथी
C. विज्ञ D. प्रजा

63. विश्लेषण
A. संश्लेषण B. गवेषण
C. विशेषण D. अन्वेषण

64. दिवस
A. विभावरी B. अरविन्द
C. प्रवाहिणी D. विचक्षण

65. निर्मल
A. पवित्र B. शुद्ध
C. मलिन D. मृदु

66. उद्यम
A. प्रवीण B. आलस्य
C. नीरज D. नृप

67. द्युति
A. छवि B. प्रभा
C. ज्योति D. अन्धकार

68. रुक्ष
A. पिच्छल B. चिक्कण
C. स्निग्ध D. सरस

69. विघटन
A. सामूहिकता B. संगठन
C. एकीकरण D. समष्टि

70. गरिमा
A. कालिमा B. लघुमा
C. अरुणिमा D. लालिमा

71. सामिष
A. निरामिष B. वैष्णव
C. शाकाहारी D. मांसरहित

72. अंधेरा
A. सुबह B. उजाला
C. प्रकाश D. झुरमुट

73. उदय
A. अस्त B. अवसान
C. विनाश D. नाभ

74. कुटिल
A. संत B. उदार
C. साधु D. सरल

75. ग्राह्य
A. त्याज्य B. ग्रहण
C. तरल D. वाञ्छा

वाक्यों की शुद्धता

निर्देश (प्र.सं. 1 से 35 तक): *नीचे दिए गए प्रश्नों में चार वाक्यों में एक वाक्य शुद्ध है और तीन अशुद्ध हैं। शुद्ध वाक्य को चुनिए।*

1. A. मैंने एक रुपए का सामान खरीदा
B. मैं एक रुपए का सामान खरीदा
C. मुझने एक रुपया का सामान खरीदा
D. मैं एक रुपया का सामान खरीदी

2. A. उसे कॉफी बनाना नहीं आता
B. उसे कॉफी बनानी नहीं आता
C. उसे कॉफी बनाना नहीं आती
D. उसे कॉफी बनाने को नहीं आते

3. A. देश का सम्मान की रक्षा करो
B. देश के सम्मान की रक्षा करो
C. देश को सम्मान की रक्षा करो
D. देश के लिए सम्मान की रक्षा करो

4. A. अतिथि को चाकू से काटकर फल खिलाओ
B. चाकू से अतिथि को काटकर फल खिलाओ
C. चाकू से फल काटकर अतिथि को खिलाओ
D. फल को काटकर चाकू से अतिथि को खिलाओ

5. A. राम ने पेट भर मिठाई खाई
B. राम ने पेट भर के मिठाई खाई
C. राम ने भरपेट मिठाई खाई
D. इनमें से सभी शुद्ध हैं

6. A. मैं आपकी सौजन्यता पर मुग्ध हूँ
B. मैं आपके सौजन्य पर मुग्ध हूँ
C. मैं आपके सुजन्य पर मुग्ध हूँ
D. इनमें से तीनों वाक्य अशुद्ध हैं

7. A. लाओ एक पानी का गिलास
B. एक पानी का गिलास लाओ
C. गिलास एक पानी का लाओ
D. एक गिलास पानी लाओ

8. A. हमारी सौभाग्यवती कन्या का विवाह होने जा रहा है।
B. हमारी आयुष्मती कन्या का विवाह होने जा रहा है।
C. हमारी सौभाग्यवती कन्या का विवाह होने जा रही है
D. इनमें से सभी शुद्ध हैं

9. A. माँ बच्चे को दूध धाय से पिला रही है
B. माँ बच्चे को दूध धाय से पिलवा रही है
C. माँ बच्चे को दूध धाय से पी रही है
D. माँ बच्चे को दूध धाय से चखा रही है

10. A. ये हमारे पास रहते हैं और वे दूर
B. वे हमारे पास रहते हैं और ये दूर
C. वे हमारे पास रहते हैं और वह दूर
D. ये हमारे पास रहते हैं और वह दूर

11. A. वेदों के छः अंग माने जाते हैं
B. वेदों में छः अंग माने जाते हैं
C. वेदों से छः अंग माने जाते हैं
D. वेदों पर छः अंग माने जाते हैं

12. A. भक्तों की सेना जा रही थी
B. भक्तों की मंडली जा रही थी
C. भक्तों की टुकड़ी जा रही थी
D. भक्तों की भीड़ जा रही थी

13. A. आपकी शंका का परिहार हुआ कि नहीं
B. आपकी शंका का निदान हुआ कि नहीं
C. आपकी शंका का समाधान हुआ कि नहीं
D. आपकी शंका निर्मूल हुई कि नहीं

14. A. यह ग्रंथ विद्वतापूर्ण लिखा गया है
B. यह ग्रंथ विद्वतापूर्वक लिखा गया है
C. यह ग्रंथ विद्वानपूर्ण लिखा गया है
D. यह ग्रंथ विद्वानपूर्वक लिखा गया है

15. A. वह टका-सा उत्तर देता है
B. वह टका-सा प्रश्न करता है
C. वह टका-सा जवाब देता है
D. इनमें से कोई नहीं

16. A. जो मिठाई पसन्द हों आप खा लो
B. जो मिठाई पसन्द हों तुम खा लो
C. जो मिठाइयाँ पसन्द हों तुम खा लो
D. जो मिठाइयाँ पसन्द हों उन्हें आप खाइए

17. A. हम बचपन में वहाँ जायेंगे
B. हम बचपन में वहाँ जाते रहे हैं
C. मैं बचपन में वहाँ जाता रहा
D. मैं बचपन में वहाँ जाऊँगा

18. A. प्रत्येक व्यक्ति कविता कर सकते हैं
B. प्रत्येक व्यक्ति कविता नहीं कर सकते हैं
C. प्रत्येक व्यक्ति कविता नहीं कर सकता
D. हर व्यक्ति कविता कर सकते हैं

19. A. हेम नरेश की पुस्तक दी
B. हेम ने नरेश को पुस्तक दी
C. हेम नरेश का पुस्तक देगा
D. हेम ने नरेश का पुस्तक दिया

20. A. मन्त्री ड्राइवर से कार चलवाता है
B. मन्त्री ड्राइवर की कार चलवाता है
C. मन्त्री ड्राइवर के लिए कार चलवाता है
D. मन्त्री ड्राइवर पर कार चलवाता है

21. A. उसकी आयु तीस वर्ष है इस समय
B. इस समय उसकी अवस्था तीस वर्ष है
C. तीस वर्ष की अवस्था है इस समय उसकी
D. इस समय तीस वर्ष की अवस्था है उसकी

22. A. रागिनी अपने आप चली गई
B. रागिनी खुद से चली गई
C. रागिनी अपने से ही चली गई
D. रागिनी आपके आप चली गई

23. A. श्याम पौधे को जल से सींच रहा है
B. पौधे को जल से सींच रहा है श्याम
C. श्याम पौधे सींच रहा है
D. जल से सींच रहा है श्याम पौधे को

24. A. वह उदद्ंडनीय है
B. वह दण्ड भोगने के योग्य है
C. वह दण्डयोग्य है
D. वह दण्ड देने के योग्य है

25. A. हमारे यहाँ तरुण नवयुवकों की शिक्षा का अच्छा प्रबन्ध है
B. हमारे यहाँ तरुण नवयुवकों का शिक्षा का अच्छा प्रबन्ध है
C. हमारे नवयुवकों की शिक्षा का यहाँ अच्छा प्रबन्ध है
D. हमारे यहाँ नवयुवकों की शिक्षा का अच्छा प्रबन्ध है

26. A. मुरझाया हुआ फूल वर्षा की फुहार से अभिसिंचित होकर पुनः खिल उठा
B. मुरझाई हुई फूल वर्षा की फुहार से अभिसिंचित होकर पुनः खिल उठा
C. मुरझाया हुआ फूल वर्षा की फुहार से अभिसिंचित होकर पुनः खिल उठी
D. मुरझाया हुआ फूल वर्षा के फुहार द्वारा अभिसिंचित होकर पुनः खिल उठे

27. A. आपके दर्शन दुर्लभ हैं
B. वह विलाप करके रोने लगा
C. हम लोग कुशलपूर्वक से हैं
D. उसे मृत्युदण्ड की सजा मिली है

28. A. तीन महानगरों के नाम बताइए
B. इस समस्या की औषधि मेरे पास है
C. चरखा कातना चाहिए
D. यह एक इतिहासिक घटना है

29. A. मेरे को कल छुट्टी जाना होगा
B. आप ही तो मना किये थे
C. मुझको लौटने में विलम्ब हो गया
D. कपड़े डालकर तुमने मेरे साथ क्या करा?

30. A. राम का बहन गांधीजी पर कविता लिखी है
B. राम का बहन गांधीजी पर कविता लिखा है
C. राम की बहन ने गांधीजी पर कविता लिखी है
D. राम की बहन गांधीजी के ऊपर कविता लिखा है

31. A. कवि ने सम्पादक को एक कविता भेजा
B. अध्यापिका ने शिष्य से प्रश्न पूछी
C. बच्चे ने कहा था, पर आप ने नहीं सुनी
D. अमित ने जेब से दस रुपए का नोट निकाला

32. A. पेड़ की पत्ता गिरी
B. पेड़ में से पत्ता गिरा
C. पत्ता गिर पड़ा पेड़ों से
D. पेड़ से पत्ता गिरा

33. A. बैल और बकरी घास चरती हैं
B. बैल और बकरी घास चरते हैं
C. बैल और बकरी घास चरता है
D. बैल और बकरी घास चरती है

34. A. महात्मा गांधी का देश सदा आभारी रहेगा
B. देश महात्मा गांधी का सदा आभारी रहेगा
C. आभारी रहेगा देश सदा महात्मा गांधी का
D. देश आभारी रहेगा सदा महात्मा गांधी का

35. A. कश्मीर में अनेक दर्शनीय स्थल देखने योग्य हैं
B. अनेक दर्शनीय स्थल कश्मीर में देखने योग्य हैं
C. कश्मीर में अनेक दर्शनीय स्थल हैं
D. अनेक दर्शनीय स्थल देखने योग्य हैं कश्मीर में

निर्देश (प्र.सं. 36 से 80 तक): *नीचे दिया गया हर एक वाक्य चार भागों में बाँटा गया है जिन्हें (A), (B), (C) और (D) अक्षरांक दिए गए हैं। आपको यह देखना है कि वाक्य के किसी भाग में व्याकरण, भाषा, वर्तनी, शब्दों के गलत प्रयोग या इसी तरह की कोई त्रुटि तो नहीं है। त्रुटि अगर हो तो वाक्य के किसी एक भाग में ही होगी। उस भाग का अक्षरांक ही उत्तर है। अगर वाक्य त्रुटिरहित है तो उत्तर (E) दीजिए।*

36. कैक्टस के पौधे में कई चमत्कारी गुण (A)/ होते हैं लेकिन यह दुखदायी की बात (B)/ है कि हमारे देश में अभी तक इस पर (C)/ बहुत अधिक ध्यान नहीं दिया गया है। (D)/ त्रुटिरहित (E).

37. वाणिज्यिक वाहन निर्माताओं के (A)/ अनुसार, ईंधन की कीमतों में तेजी के (B)/ बावजूद बिक्री वाणिज्यिक वाहनों की (C)/ में तेजी दर्ज की गई है। (D)/ त्रुटिरहित (E).

38. जब तपती और धूल भरी (A)/ सड़कों पर मोटी-मोटी बूँदें गिरतीं तब (B)/ उमस के साथ मिट्टी की (C)/ भुनी भुनी गंध वातावरण में फैल जाती थी। (D)/ त्रुटिरहित (E).

39. औसत अगर मध्यवर्गीय (A)/ परिवार की बात करें तो उसमें (B)/ स्त्री मन को समझने की (C)/ गुंजाइश बहुत कम होती है। (D)/ त्रुटिरहित (E).

40. सुखद स्मृतियाँ चमकीले वर्तमान (A)/ से कहीं ज्यादा आनंददायक, (B)/ दुष्प्रेरणादायक और स्फूर्ति (C)/ प्रदान करने वाली होती हैं। (D)/ त्रुटिरहित (E).

41. किसी तंदरुस्त वृद्ध की देहयष्टि (A)/ देखकर लग पड़ता है (B)/ कि आयु ने उनके शरीर (C)/ पर अपना प्रभाव नहीं डाला है। (D)/ त्रुटिरहित (E).

42. कोशिश करने से मसले (A)/ समय रहते हल हो जाएं (B)/ तो ठीक वरना मन (C)/ में ग्रंथियाँ बन जाती हैं। (D)/ त्रुटिरहित (E).

43. यदि कोई विकलांग व्यक्ति (A)/ घर का मुखिया हो (B)/ तो वह गरीबी रेखा से (C)/ नीचे के दायरे में आएगा। (D)/ त्रुटिरहित (E).

44. एक मध्यवर्गीय भारतीय परिवार में पिता (A)/ काम के बोझ या दूसरे कारणों से अपने (B)/ बच्चों से कट जाता है, जिसका बच्चों (C)/ के मन पर प्रतिकूल प्रभावशाली पड़ता है। (D)/ त्रुटिरहित (E).

45. अर्थव्यवस्था विश्व के बदतर हो रहे (A)/ हालात से चिंतित वित्त मंत्री ने (B)/ कहा कि सरकार के पास नरमी (C)/ से निपटने के विकल्प सीमित हैं। (D)/ त्रुटिरहित (E).

46. बचत बैंक खातों (A)/ में बैंकों द्वारा (B)/ ब्याज की अदायगी (C)/ किया जाता है। (D)/ त्रुटिरहित (E).

47. वर्ष 2010 को आधार (A)/ बना कर राष्ट्रीय स्तर पर (B)/ नया उपभोक्ता तूल्य (C)/ सूचकांक जारी किया गया है। (D)/ त्रुटिरहित (E).

48. गुजरात की (A)/ राजरानी गांधीनगर (B)/ में एक बहुत बड़े समारोह का (C)/ आयोजन किया गया है। (D)/ त्रुटिरहित (E).

49. विमानन क्षेत्र का (A)/ नामी कम्पनी की (B)/ मुश्किलें दिनोंदिन (C)/ बढ़ती जा रही हैं। (D)/ त्रुटिरहित (E).

50. सरकार अपनी योजनाओं (A)/ का लाभ केवल कमजोर (B)/ वर्ग के लोगों तक सीमित (C)/ रखने के कक्ष में नहीं है। (D)/ त्रुटिरहित (E).

51. भारत सरकार द्वारा अर्जित (A)/ कुल राजस्व की (B)/ अधिकतम राशि आय कर (C)/ से प्राप्त होती है। (D)/ त्रुटिरहित (E).

52. दूरदर्शन के अधिकारियों (A)/ ने लोकप्रिय वाहिका (B)/ का प्रसारण बंद करने (C)/ का आदेश दिया है। (D)/ त्रुटिरहित (E).

53. राष्ट्रीय एकता तथा मानवीय (A)/ मूल्यों के मूलभूत सिद्धान्तों (B)/ को म्यान में रखकर (C)/ पाठ्य-सामग्री तैयार की गई है। (D)/ त्रुटिरहित (E).

54. दोनों देशों के वाणी (A)/ सचिवों की बैठक में (B)/ परस्पर व्यापार बढ़ाने (C)/ के लिए सहमति हो गयी। (D)/ त्रुटिरहित (E).

55. कोश के इस (A)/ नए संस्करण में बहुत (B)/ से नए शब्द (C)/ शामिल किए गए हैं। (D)/ त्रुटिरहित (E).

56. बैंक से जारी होने वाले (A)/ सभी परिपत्र, आदेश आदि (B)/ कागज के बजाय डिजिटल (C)/ माध्यमों से प्रेषित किया जाता है। (D)/ त्रुटिरहित (E).

57. नियंत्रण प्राधिकारियों से (A)/ भी अपेक्षा की गई है (B)/ कि वे प्रतिदिन प्रतिवेदन (C)/ का अध्ययन अवश्य करें। (D)/ त्रुटिरहित (E).

58. ग्लोबल वार्मिंग रूपी (A)/ शत्रु पर आक्रमण कर उसे (B)/ परस्त करने में सभी (C)/ का योगदान होना चाहिए। (D)/ त्रुटिरहित (E).

59. पेड़ नहीं सोंचते कि झोंका (A)/ आए तो झूमें या न (B)/ झूमें वे झूमते हैं और अपने (C)/ जड़ों पर यकीन रहते हैं। (D)/ त्रुटिरहित (E).

60. कितने वर्षों की अवधि (A)/ तक खाते में कोई भी लेन-देन न (B)/ होने पर खाते को (C)/ निष्कृत माना जाता है? (D)/ त्रुटिरहित (E).

61. सामाजिक कुरीतियों (A)/ का मुख्य कारण (B)/ अज्ञानता है (C)/ यह बात एकदम सही है। (D)/ त्रुटिरहित (E).

62. उसकी सौन्दर्यता (A)/ देखकर मन मयूर (B)/ नृत्य करने लगा (C)/ दिलीप ने श्याम को बताया। (D)/ त्रुटिरहित (E).

63. नगेन्द्र जी (A)/ हिन्दी के (B)/ लब्धप्रतिष्ठित (C)/ आलोचक एवं लेखक हैं। (D)/ त्रुटिरहित (E).

64. साहित्य (A)/ और जीवन का (B)/ घनघोर (C)/ सम्बन्ध है। (D)/ त्रुटिरहित (E).

65. दिल्ली से (A)/ अनेकों (B)/ पत्र-पत्रिकाओं का (C)/ प्रकाशन होता है। (D)/ त्रुटिरहित (E).

66. गाय को घास (A)/ खिलाने से और पंछी (B)/ को दाना डालने (C)/ से पूण्य मिलता है। (D)/ त्रुटिरहित (E).

67. एक संख्या का पाँच (A)/ बटा-नौ दूसरी संख्या (B)/ के पच्चीस प्रतिशत (C)/ के सम्मान है। (D)/ त्रुटिरहित (E).

68. दिनेश की मासिक (A)/ आय सुरेश की (B)/ मासिक आय से (C)/ चुगना है। (D)/ त्रुटिरहित (E).

69. इस कार की कीमत कम (A)/ होगी और कम्पनी इसमें ज्यादा से ज्यादा (B)/ भारतीय पूर्जे लगाने (C)/ की कोशिश कर रही है। (D)/ त्रुटिरहित (E).

70. कहतें हैं कि (A)/ हर दस कोश (B)/ पर बोली (C)/ बदलती है। (D)/ त्रुटिरहित (E).

71. वैश्वीकरण के इस (A)/ युग में हिन्दी भाषा (B)/ नींत नवीन शब्दों से (C)/ समृद्ध हो रही है। (D)/ त्रुटिरहित (E).

72. आज भी कई किसान (A)/ और कमजोर वर्ग के (B)/ लोग साहूकारों के अंगुल (C)/ में फँसे हुए हैं। (D)/ त्रुटिरहित (E).

73. हमें शिक्षा ऋण (A)/ लेने वाले ऋणकर्ताओं (B)/ से इस आश्रय की (C)/ शिकायतें प्राप्त हो रही हैं। (D)/ त्रुटिरहित (E).

74. बचत बैंक खाते में (A)/ एक महीना में अन्य (B)/ बैंक के ATM से (C)/ निःशुल्क 5 आहरणों की छूट हैं। (D)/ त्रुटिरहित (E).

75. कृपया बोधित (A)/ अनुदेश सभी पदाधिकारियों (B)/ को सूचित करने (C)/ की व्यवस्था करें। (D)/ त्रुटिरहित (E).

76. एक मादा सूअर अपनी (A)/ छः बच्चों के साथ जो (B)/ अभी नौ-नौ इंच से बड़े नहीं हुए (C)/ थे, रेलगाड़ी की तरह चलती जा रही थी। (D)/ त्रुटिरहित (E).

77. एक इरावती ही थी जिससे वह टूटी-फूटी (A)/ हिन्दी में बातां कर लेती थी, हालाँकि उसकी (B)/ पंजाबी हिन्दी और इरावती की कोंकणी (C)/ हिन्दी में जमीन- आसमान का फर्क था। (D)/ त्रुटिरहित (E).

78. अपने बेटे की वजह से ही वह (A)/ यहाँ परदेस में पड़ा था, जहाँ (B)/ न कोई उसकी जबान समझता था, न वह (C)/ किसी को जबान समझता था। (D)/ त्रुटिरहित (E).

79. चेचक के दागों और झुर्रियों से भरा (A)/ उसका चेहरा दीमक खाई लकड़ी की (B)/ तरह जाना पड़ता था, जो बदसूरत तो था (C)/ ही जुगुप्सा भी जगा देता था। (D)/ त्रुटिरहित (E).

80. शालिनी नित नेम की भांति दीपक जलाई (A)/ और एक अज्ञात देवता के सामने (B)/ हाथ जोड़ने की प्रक्रिया पूरी करके (C)/ घुटनों पर बाँहें रखे वहीं बैठी रही। (D)/ त्रुदिरहित (E).

वाक्यांश के लिए एक शब्द

1. एक स्थान से दूसरे स्थान पर जाना या ले जाना–
A. खिसका हुआ B. उखड़ा हुआ
C. स्थानच्युत D. विस्थापित

2. इंद्रियों को जीतने वाला–
A. अजातशत्रु B. इन्द्रस्वामी
C. जितेंद्रिय D. मुमुक्षु

3. एक ही कोख से जन्म लेने वाला–
A. संतति B. जातक
C. आत्मज D. सहोदर

4. अपनी इच्छा से चलने वाला–
A. स्वेच्छाचारी B. स्वच्छंद
C. अराजक D. स्वेच्छक

5. जो हर हाल में हो ही जाए–
A. होनहार B. अवश्यंभावी
C. भाग D. तत्पर

6. जो कठिनाई से समझ में आए–
A. दुर्गम B. दुर्बोध
C. दुर्लभ D. दुर्धर्ष

7. एक पर ही श्रद्धा अथवा आस्था रखने वाला–
A. एकाकी B. अलौकिक
C. अधिकारिक D. एकनिष्ठ

8. बड़ा बनने की इच्छा रखने वाला–
A. पदलोलुप B. चाटुकार
C. विवेकवान D. महत्वाकांक्षी

9. मन का दुर्भाव–
A. दृष्टिवैषम्य B. भेदभाव
C. मनोमालिन्य D. कलुषित

10. पूर्णतः स्वच्छ करना–
A. परिष्कार B. सुधार
C. आविष्कार D. पुनरोद्धार

11. जिसका जन्म उच्च कुल में हुआ हो–
A. सेठ B. अभद्र
C. अमीर D. कुलीन

12. ईश्वर को नहीं मानने वाला–
A. आस्तिक B. अधर्मवान
C. बंदा D. नास्तिक

13. उपकार मानने वाला–
A. कृतघ्न B. परोपकारी
C. अनोपचारी D. कृतज्ञ

14. किसी के पास रखी हुई दूसरे की वस्तु–
A. गिरवी B. जमानत
C. धरोहर D. सामान

15. एक स्थान से दूसरे स्थान को हटाया हुआ–
A. आंतरित B. प्रवासी
C. मुसाफिर D. स्थानांतरित

16. जिसे कठिनाई से भेदा जा सके–
A. अभेद्य B. दुर्भेद्य
C. दुर्दम्य D. अगम्य

17. जो सबको समान भाव से देखे–
A. दूरदर्शी B. क्रांतदर्शी
C. सूक्ष्मदर्शी D. समदर्शी

18. परलोक से सम्बन्धित–
A. पारलौकिक B. अलौकिक
C. इहलौकिक D. लौकिक

19. पीछे-पीछे चलने वाला–
A. अनुगामी B. प्रतिगामी
C. पश्चगामी D. अग्रगामी

20. जिसके हृदय में ममता नहीं है–
A. निर्दय B. कठोर
C. क्रूर D. निर्मम

21 जो व्यर्थ की बातें करता हो–
A. बहुभाषी B. कुवक्ता
C. वाचाल D. वाक्पटु

22. जो देखने में प्रिय लगता हो–
A. समदर्शी B. प्रियदर्शी
C. प्रियपात्र D. दर्शनप्रिय

23. अहसान न मानने वाला–
A. कृतज्ञ B. कृतघ्न
C. विश्वासघाती D. परोपजीवी

24. जिसे कठिनाई से जीता जा सके–
A. विजित B. अज्ञेय
C. अजेय D. दुर्जेय

25. बचपन और जवानी के बीच की अवस्था–
A. नवयुवा B. नवोढ़ा
C. वयःसंधि D. वयस्कता

26. पशुओं के समान व्यवहार करने वाला–
A. पाशविक B. पशुसा
C. क्रूर D. दानव

27. वह अग्नि जो जंगल में लग जाती है–
A. वनाग्नि B. दावानल
C. अनल D. प्रचंडाग्नि

28. वह वस्तु जो नाशवान है–
A. नाशक B. नासन्य
C. नासांतिक D. नश्वर

29. परिश्रम के बदले प्राप्त धनराशि–
A. मुद्रा B. करेंसी
C. पारिश्रमिक D. सिक्का

30. अधिक पढ़ी-लिखी महिला–
A. विदूषक B. विज्ञानी
C. अफसर D. विदुषी

31. दोपहर का समय–
A. अपराह्न B. पूर्वाह्न
C. अधपहर D. मध्याह्न

32. जिसके समान कोई दूसरा न हो–
A. असामान्य B. अद्वितीय
C. असाधारण D. महान्

33. जो अधिक व्यय न करता हो–
A. धन्नासेठ B. खर्चीला
C. अव्यय D. मितव्ययी

34. जो पृथ्वी से सम्बन्धित हो–
A. पार्थिव B. पृथ्वी
C. अलौकिक D. जड़

35. जो काटा न जा सके–
A. दो टूक B. तर्कातीत
C. अकाट्य D. निश्चित

36. जिसके पास कुछ भी न हो–
A. अकिंचन B. किंचित्
C. आकुंचन D. अलभ्य

37. अनिश्चित जीविका–
A. आंशिक सेवा B. अस्थायी सेवा
C. अर्द्ध रोजगार D. आकाशवृत्ति

38. जिस पर हमला न किया गया हो–
A. आक्रान्ता B. आक्रामक
C. अयोध्या D. अनाक्रान्त

39. जो बहुत मंद गति से कार्य करता हो–
A. मंथर B. दीर्घसूत्री
C. सत्वर D. मंदाक्रान्ता

40. उचित-अनुचित का ज्ञान रखने वाला–
A. विवेकी B. ज्ञानी
C. चतुर D. दूरदर्शी

41. जो अपने कर्त्तव्य का निश्चय न कर सके–
A. द्वन्द्वग्रस्त B. भ्रमित
C. किंकर्त्तव्यविमूढ़ D. द्विविधाग्रस्त

42. अनेक युगों से चला आने वाला–
A. समीचीन B. प्राचीन
C. कालान्तर D. सनातन

43. ऐसा कवि जो तत्काल रचना करता हो–
A. कविराज B. आशुकवि
C. महाकवि D. कवीश

44. जिस स्त्री का पति जीवित होता है–
A. कामिनी B. सुभगा
C. सधवा D. मधवा

45. अनुचित व्यय करने वाला–
A. अतिव्ययी B. मितव्ययी
C. दुर्व्ययी D. अपव्ययी

46. मुकदमा चलाने वाला–
A. प्रतिवादी B. मुकदमेबाज
C. वादी D. इनमें से कोई नहीं

47. जिस पर अभियोग लगाया गया हो–
A. प्रतिवादी B. अभियोगी
C. अभियुक्त D. याची

48. मोक्ष प्राप्त करने की इच्छा रखने वाला–
A. मोक्षेसु B. ममुक्ष
C. मुमुक्ष D. मुमुक्षु

49. 'वह स्त्री जिसका पति परदेस से आने वाला हो' के लिए एक शब्द है–
A. आगतपतिका B. प्रव्रत्स्यतपतिका
C. प्रेषितपतिका D. आगमिस्यतपतिका

50. 'जिसमें धैर्य न हो' के लिए एक शब्द है–
A. अधर B. धरातल
C. अधीर D. धीरता

51. 'जो पहले कभी न हुआ हो' के लिए एक शब्द है–
A. अद्भुत B. अभूतपूर्व
C. अपूर्व D. अनुपम

52. 'जिसे किसी से लगाव न हो' के लिए उपयुक्त एक शब्द है–
A. नश्वर B. लिप्सु
C. निर्लिप्त D. अलगाववादी

53. 'जो कुछ जानने की इच्छा रखता हो' के लिए एक शब्द है–
A. जिज्ञासु B. जननी
C. जानकी D. नीतिज्ञ

54. 'जो बात लोगों से सुनी गई हो' के लिए एक शब्द है–
A. अश्रुति B. सर्वप्रिय
C. लोकोक्ति D. किंवदन्ती

55. 'सबके समानाधिकार पर विश्वास' के लिए एक शब्द है–
A. अधिकारी B. समाजवाद
C. प्रगतिवाद D. अधिकारवाद

56. 'जिस बीमारी का ठीक होना सम्भव न हो' के लिए एक शब्द है–
A. असाध्य B. विकट
C. भयानक D. घातक

57. जिस पर विजय प्राप्त कर ली गई हो–
A. आक्रान्त B. अजेय
C. विजित D. पराजित

58. सूर्य के उदय होने का स्थान–
A. उदयाचल B. सूर्योदय
C. प्रभात स्थान D. गंधमादन

59. जो कहा न जा सके–
A. अकथित B. अकथनीय
C. अकथ्य D. नामुमकिन

60. जिसे बहुत बातें करनी आती हों–
A. वाचाल B. गम्भीर
C. समालोचक D. मुनि

61. जो स्त्री के वशीभूत हो–
A. स्त्रीदास B. गुलाम
C. स्त्रैण D. प्रेमी

62. जो समान न हो–
A. बराबर B. जटिल
C. अविषम D. विषम

63. जिसे पढ़ना-लिखना आता हो–
A. अल्पज्ञानी B. शिक्षित
C. बुद्धिजीवी D. साक्षर

64. जो खाना मुफ्त में मिलता हो–
A. भण्डार B. लंगर
C. खुराक D. राशन

65. जो अपने कर्त्तव्य को न जानता हो–
A. अनजान B. अज्ञानी
C. किंकर्त्तव्यविमूढ़ D. कर्त्तव्यहीन

66. 'युद्ध में स्थिर रहने वाला' के लिए एक शब्द है–
A. योद्धा B. साहसी
C. युधिष्ठिर D. वीर

67. 'जो ईश्वर में विश्वास रखता है' के लिए एक शब्द है–
A. आस्थावान B. धार्मिक
C. आध्यात्मिक D. आस्तिक

68. आयु में बड़ा व्यक्ति–
A. कनिष्ठ B. पूजनीय
C. ज्येष्ठ D. वरिष्ठ

69. नया उदित होने वाला–
A. नवोदित B. नवजात
C. नवागन्तुक D. इनमें से कोई नहीं

70. बहुत-सी भाषाओं को जानने वाला–
A. तत्वचिन्तक B. बहुज्ञ
C. बहुभाषाविद् D. भाषा-वैज्ञानिक

71. जो किसी की ओर मुँह किए हो–
A. अभिमुख B. अनमुख
C. सुमुख D. इनमें से कोई नहीं

72. 'सात सौ वाली' के लिए निम्नलिखित में से कौन-सा शब्द उपयुक्त है?
A. सतखड़ा B. सतनजा
C. सतमासा D. सतसई

73. 'तेज चलने वाला' के लिए एक शब्द है–
A. गतिशील B. चुस्त
C. कर्मठ D. द्रुतगामी

74. 'बिना स्वार्थ के कार्य करने वाला' के लिए एक शब्द होगा–
A. सहायक B. निस्वार्थी
C. पुण्यात्मा D. हितैषी

75. 'किसी की सहायता करने वाला' के लिए एक शब्द है–
A. सहकार B. सहायक
C. सहृदय D. सहचर

मुहावरा एवं लोकोक्तियाँ

1. 'सब्जबाग दिखाना' मुहावरा का अर्थ है–
A. बाग में घूमने जाना B. साग-सब्जी पैदा करना
C. प्रलोभन देना D. भयभीत करना

2. 'खुदा गंजे को नाखून न दे' लोकोक्ति का अभिप्राय है–
A. छोटे आदमी का प्रेम अस्थिर होता है
B. लज्जित होकर दूसरे पर क्रोध न निकाले
C. एक दोष पहले से था, दूसरा और आ गया
D. अत्याचारी को शक्ति नहीं मिलनी चाहिए

3. 'कभी नाव गाड़ी पर कभी गाड़ी नाव पर' लोकोक्ति का सही आशय है–
A. संघर्ष होना B. जीवन में उतार-चढ़ाव का क्रम
C. भलाई करना D. एक-से स्वभाव वाले होना

4. 'एक हाथ से ताली नहीं बजती' लोकोक्ति का अभिप्राय है–
A. शत्रुता दोनों पक्षों की गलती से होती है
B. संघर्ष बराबरी वाले दो पक्षों में होना चाहिए
C. एक आदमी से काम नहीं चलता
D. सराहना हेतु दोनों हाथ से ताली बजाएँ

5. 'उड़ती चिड़ियों के पंख गिनना' मुहावरा का सही अर्थ होगा–
A. अनुभवी होना B. वाक्चतुर होना
C. प्रतिभाशाली होना D. असंभव कार्य करना

6. 'नक्कारखाने में तूती की आवाज' मुहावरा का अर्थ है–
A. तूती की आवाज सबसे ऊँची होती है
B. नक्कारखाने में तूती नहीं बोलती
C. नकारे लोगों की सर्वत्र तूती बोलती रहती है
D. समर्थ व्यक्ति के सामने असमर्थ व्यक्ति का प्रभाव नहीं पड़ता

7. 'आँख के अंधे नाम नयनसुख' का सही अर्थ है–
A. गुणों के विरुद्ध नाम का होना
B. बुद्धिहीन, किन्तु पर्याप्त धनवान
C. अंधा आदमी प्रायः गुणवान होता है
D. एक आँख के अंधे को भी सभी सुखद आ सकते हैं

8. 'चिकना घड़ा होना' मुहावरा का सही अर्थ है–
A. चिकना चुपड़ा होना B. समृद्ध होना
C. निर्लज्ज होना D. मधुरभाषी होना

9. 'बेटा समय रहते न पढ़े, तो भविष्य में बुरी तरह पछताओगे' – वाक्य में 'बुरी तरह पछताओगे' के स्थान पर यह मुहावरा आ सकता है–
A. अंगारों पर लोटोगे B. आठ-आठ आँसू रोओगे
C. अंचरा पसारोगे D. कुएँ में गिरोगे

10. "मुहावरे का प्रयोग वाक्य के अन्तर्गत होता है और लोकोक्ति पूर्ण वाक्य में होती है।" यह कथन–
A. सही है
B. गलत है
C. कथन का प्रथम अंश सही है
D. कथन का अंतिम अंश सही है

11. 'समय के अनुसार काम करना चाहिए' अर्थ की बोधक लोकोक्ति है–
A. झूठ के पैर नहीं होते
B. जाके पांव न फटी बिवाई, सो क्या जाने पीर पराई
C. उँगली पकड़ कर पहुँचा पकड़ना
D. का बरसा जब कृषि सुखाने

12. 'भारत के अतुलित धन वैभव पर अंग्रजों ने दाँत गड़ा दिए'–वाक्य में प्रयुक्त 'दाँत गड़ा दिए' का अर्थ है–
A. किसी वस्तु को गलत ढंग से पाने की गहरी चाह
B. दूसरे की वस्तु देखकर ललचा जाना
C. दूसरे की वस्तु चुराने की चेष्टा करना
D. धोखे से दूसरे की वस्तु लेना

13. 'चाँद पर थूकना' मुहावरे का आशय है–
A. असम्भव काम करना
B. निरर्थक काम करना
C. सौंदर्य का अनादर करना
D. सम्माननीय का अनादर करना

14. 'नियम विरुद्ध कार्य करना' अर्थ के अनुकूल सही मुहावरा है–
A. सूरज को दिया दिखाना
B. उल्टी गंगा बहाना
C. दाई से पेट छिपाना
D. नौ दो ग्यारह हो जाना

15. 'खाला जी का घर' मुहावरे का क्या अर्थ है?
A. आसान कार्य B. मौसी का घर
C. भाई-भतीजावाद D. रिश्तेदार को लाभ पहुँचाना

16. 'सिर चढ़ाना' मुहावरे का अर्थ है–
A. मनमानी करने की छूट देना
B. सिर पर बैठाना
C. सिरदर्द का बहाना करना
D. सिर पर उठा लेना

17. किस लोकोक्ति का अर्थ "वैभव क्षणिक होता है" होगा?
A. साँच को आँच नहीं
B. अधजल गगरी छलकत जाए
C. पाँचों उँगलियाँ बराबर नहीं होतीं
D. चार दिन की चाँदनी फिर अँधेरी रात

18. 'आँधी के आम होना' मुहावरे का अर्थ है–
A. मुफ्त उपलब्ध होना
B. संयोगवश बहुत सस्ता उपलब्ध होना
C. वैभवशाली बनना
D. अत्यन्त प्रिय होना

19. 'पाँच सात की लकड़ी, एक जने का बोझ' लोकोक्ति का अर्थ है–
A. बहुत कठिन कार्य होना
B. असम्भव बड़ी शर्त रखना
C. छोटे या कमजोर व्यक्ति की बात को कोई नहीं मानता
D. मिलकर काम करने से कठिन कार्य भी सरल हो जाता है

20. इनमें से कौन एक लोकोक्ति है?
A. अंगूठा दिखाना B. अंधा होना
C. ऊँट के मुँह में जीरा D. इधर-उधर की हाँकना

21. 'कलम तोड़ना' मुहावरे का क्या अर्थ है?
A. सही लिखना
B. अच्छा लिखना
C. ज्यादा लिखना
D. बेकार लिखकर प्रायश्चित करना

22. 'ढाँक के तीन पात' का अर्थ है–
A. अपने स्थान पर अडिग रहना
B. साफ इनकार कर देना
C. बेकार घूमना
D. कभी किसी विशेषता से सम्पन्न न होना

23. 'घड़ों पानी पड़ जाना' मुहावरे का अर्थ है–
A. चिन्ता में डूब जाना B. बर्बाद हो जाना
C. पसीने से भीग जाना D. लज्जा से दब जाना

24. किस लोकोक्ति का अर्थ 'बिना परिश्रम के सफलता नहीं मिलती' होगा?
A. नौ दिन चले अढ़ाई कोस
B. जिन खोजा तिन पाइयाँ गहरे पानी पैठ
C. बालू से तेल निकालना
D. डूबते को तिनके का सहारा

25. 'हाथ कंगन को आरसी क्या' कहावत का अर्थ है–

A. समझदार के लिए उपदेश व्यर्थ है

B. प्रत्यक्ष के लिए प्रमाण की क्या आवश्यकता है

C. मूल्यवान वस्तु के सामने तुच्छ वस्तु का कोई महत्व नहीं

D. हाथ में कंगन ही चाहिए आरसी नहीं

26. 'दाँतों तले अंगुली दबाना' का अर्थ होगा–

A. मुसीबत में पड़ना B. बहुत हैरान होना

C. आश्चर्य करना D. दीनता प्रकट करना

27. 'अनिश्चितता' के भाव को प्रकट करने के लिए उपयुक्त मुहावरे का चयन कीजिए–

A. बंद मुट्ठी में क्या है

B. पर्दे के पीछे कौन है

C. न जाने भाग्य में क्या है

D. न जाने ऊँट किस करवट बैठेगा

28. 'कुपात्र की सहायता करना व्यर्थ है' इस उक्ति को चरितार्थ करने वाली कहावत है–

A. अंधे को न्यौता, दो जने आये

B. कुत्ते को खिलाई खीर, पाप में न पुण्य में

C. गधे की खाई खेती, न पाप में न पुण्य में

D. बन्दर क्या जाने अदरक का स्वाद

29. मूर्ख व्यक्ति के सामने ज्ञान की बातें करने के लिए उपयुक्त मुहावरा क्या होगा?

A. रेत से तेल निकालना B. अंधे के आगे रोना

C. भैंस के आगे बीन बजाना D. आकाश से बातें करना

30. निम्नलिखित मुहावरे का अर्थ बताइए–

'सिर से पानी गुजर जाना'

A. अच्छी चीज का और अच्छा हो जाना

B. अपमान सहन कर लेना

C. सहनशीलता की सीमा टूट जाना

D. बाढ़ आ जाना

31. 'बहती गंगा में हाथ धोना' इस मुहावरे का क्या अर्थ है?

A. अधिकाधिक उन्नति होना

B. अवसर का फायदा उठाना

C. असम्भव काम को सम्भव करना

D. बहुत परिश्रम करना

32. निम्नलिखित वाक्यों में मुहावरे का सही प्रयोग क्या है?

A. धोनी अच्छे क्रिकेट का प्रदर्शन करके राँची वापस पहुँचा तो लोगों ने मैदान मार लिया

B. धोनी अच्छे क्रिकेट का प्रदर्शन करके राँची वापस पहुँचा, तो लोगों के हाथ के तोते उड़ गए

C. धोनी अच्छे क्रिकेट का प्रदर्शन करके राँची वापस पहुँचा, तो लोगों ने तिल का ताड़ बना लिया

D. धोनी अच्छे क्रिकेट का प्रदर्शन करके राँची वापस पहुँचा, तो लोगों ने उसे सिर आँखों पर बिठा लिया

33. निम्नलिखित के लिए उपयुक्त मुहावरा क्या है?

'मुसीबत देखकर घबरा जाना'

A. नाक पर धब्बा लगना B. नौ दो ग्यारह होना

C. दाँतों तले अंगुली दबाना D. नानी याद आना

34. 'काठ की हांडी बार-बार नहीं चढ़ती' लोकोक्ति का अर्थ है–

A. बुरे लोग लाख प्रयत्न के बाद भी अपनी बुराई नहीं छोड़ते

B. कठिन काम अकेले आदमी के वश की बात नहीं है

C. छल कपट का काम एक बार ही होता है

D. दुष्ट व्यक्ति बात से नहीं, बल्कि दण्ड से ही मानता है

35. 'रंगा सियार' मुहावरे का अर्थ क्या है?

A. डरपोक व्यक्ति B. धोखेबाज व्यक्ति

C. झूठ बोलने वाला व्यक्ति D. वीर व्यक्ति

36. 'बेपेंदी का लोटा' मुहावरे का अर्थ क्या है?

A. निर्धन व्यक्ति

B. स्थिर विचारों का न होने वाला व्यक्ति

C. मूर्ख व्यक्ति

D. दुष्ट व्यक्ति

37. 'घी के दिए जलाना' मुहावरा का सही अर्थ है–

A. दीपावली मनाना B. खुशी मनाना

C. रईसी प्रकट करना D. अपने को विशिष्ट समझना

38. 'सोने में सुगन्ध' मुहावरा का सही अर्थ है–

A. सुन्दर वस्तु में और गुण होना

B. सुगन्ध से युक्त आभूषण

C. सुन्दर आभूषण होना

D. सुगन्धित सोना

39. 'आँख का अंधा गाँठ का पूरा' लोकोक्ति का सही अर्थ है–

A. अंधा परन्तु विवेकशील होना

B. मूर्ख धनी

C. अंधे के पास धन होना

D. आँखों का रोग

40. 'गोद में लड़का, शहर भर में ढिंढोरा' मुहावरा का सही अर्थ है–

A. छोटे शिशु को तलाशना

B. अत्यधिक शरारती बालक

C. पास में वस्तु रहते हुए चारों ओर खोजना

D. छोटे बालक की प्रशंसा करना

41. 'पानी का बुलबुला' मुहावरे का क्या अर्थ है?

A. शीघ्र नष्ट हो जाने वाला

B. स्वच्छंद हो जाना

C. हार कर भागना

D. कष्ट उठाना

42. 'चाँदी का जूता मारना' मुहावरे का सही अर्थ है–

A. लुभाना B. आदर करना

C. शोभा बढ़ाना D. रुपए के बल पर दबाना

43. 'आगे नाथ न पीछे पगहा' लोकोक्ति का क्या अर्थ है?
A. पूर्ण स्वतन्त्र B. अपने मन की करना
C. बन्धन रहित होना D. इधर-उधर भागना

44. 'अन्धे पीसे कुत्ते खाएं' लोकोक्ति का सही अर्थ क्या है?
A. बेहिसाब काम करना
B. असावधानी से अयोग्य को लाभ
C. लाचारी का अनुचित लाभ
D. अपना माल लुटाना

45. 'अधजल गगरी छलकत जाए' का क्या अर्थ है?
A. गगरी में छेद होना B. बेकायदे काम करना
C. व्यर्थ की बातें करना D. कम ज्ञान का अधिक प्रदर्शन

46. 'जस दूल्हा तसि बनी बराता' लोकोक्ति का क्या अर्थ है?
A. अच्छा दूल्हा और अच्छे साथी
B. अच्छा दूल्हा और खराब बराती
C. सभी लोगों का अच्छा होना
D. जैसा व्यक्ति वैसे साथी

47. 'तीन लोक से मथुरा न्यारी' लोकोक्ति का अर्थ है–
A. बहुत सुन्दर होना
B. दूर की वस्तु सुन्दर लगना
C. जरूरत से ज्यादा बड़ाई करना
D. कृष्ण भक्त होना

48. 'थोथा चना बाजे घना' लोकोक्ति का क्या अर्थ है?
A. बहुत अधिक बोलना
B. ओछे व्यक्ति अधिक दिखावा करते हैं
C. बढ़ा-चढ़ाकर बात करना
D. बहुत शोर करना

49. 'खग जाने खग ही की भाषा' का क्या अर्थ है?
A. पक्षियों की भाषा जानना
B. समान प्रवृत्ति वाले ही एक-दूसरे को समझते हैं
C. पक्षी अपनी भाषा स्वयं समझते हैं
D. पक्षियों की तरह बोलना

50. 'अदृश्य शत्रु' अर्थ के अनुरूप उपयुक्त मुहावरा है–
A. मीठी छुरी B. मुँह में राम बगल में छूरी
C. पेट में दाढ़ी D. आस्तीन का साँप

51. 'पापड़ बेलना' मुहावरे का क्या अर्थ है?
A. पापड़ बनाना B. मुसीबत उठाना
C. खाना बनाना D. पतली रोटी बेलना

52. 'पानी-पानी होना' मुहावरे का क्या अर्थ है?
A. घबड़ा जाना B. बहुत भीग जाना
C. बहुत लज्जित होना D. बाढ़ आ जाना

53. 'गूलर का फूल होना' मुहावरे का क्या अर्थ है?
A. सुगंधित होना B. फूल की तरह खिलना
C. दुर्लभ होना D. अति प्रसन्न होना

54. 'कान का कच्चा होना' मुहावरे का क्या अर्थ है?
A. कम सुनना B. सुनी बात पर विश्वास करना
C. दूसरे की बात न मानना D. कान का कमजोर होना

55. 'उन्नीस-बीस होना' मुहावरे का क्या अर्थ है?
A. बहुत कम अन्तर होना B. बहुत अन्तर होना
C. हिसाब जोड़ना D. भाग जाना

56. 'खून का घूँट पीना' मुहावरे का क्या अर्थ है?
A. गुस्सा करना B. खून की उल्टी करना
C. क्रोध दबाना D. दाँत से होठ कट जाना

57. 'पौ बारह होना' मुहावरे का सही अर्थ है–
A. सब तरह की सुख-सुविधाओं का होना
B. उपद्रव करना
C. पलायन कर जाना
D. प्रयासरत होना

58. 'कागजी घोड़े दौड़ाना' मुहावरे का सही अर्थ है–
A. प्रयास करना B. लिखा-पढ़ी करना
C. कागज काला करना D. व्यर्थ का काम करना

59. 'कान भरना' मुहावरे का अर्थ है–
A. धोखा देना B. चाणक होना
C. चुगली करना D. असर न होना

60. 'सिर उठाना' मुहावरे का सही अर्थ है–
A. रंग उतर जाना B. भेद प्रकट करना
C. बहुत पछताना D. विद्रोह करना

61. 'आडम्बर' बहुत, किन्तु वास्तविकता कुछ नहीं' के लिए सही लोकोक्ति है–
A. आँख का अंधा नाम नयनसुख
B. ऊँची दुकान, फीका पकवान
C. ऊँट के मुँह में जीरा
D. खोदा पहाड़, निकली चुहिया

62. 'चैन की वंशी बजाना' का अर्थ है–
A. साइकिल की चैन की बांसुरी बनाकर बजाना
B. मौज करना
C. फुर्सत में वंशी बजाना
D. बेरोजगार होना

63. 'आँख की किरकिरी होना' का अर्थ है–
A. अप्रिय लगना B. धोखा देना
C. कष्टदायक होना D. बहुत प्रिय होना

64. 'कीचड़ उछालना' मुहावरा का सही अर्थ है–
A. मल फेंकना
B. दूसरे के कपड़े गन्दे करना
C. बदनाम करना
D. दलदल में फँसना

65. 'अवांछित संवाद' अर्थ के लिए उपयुक्त मुहावरा है–
A. सिर खपाना B. सिर खाना
C. सिर नीचा होना D. सिर पड़ना

गद्यांश (अपठित-बोध)

गद्यांश 1

यदि हम निरन्तर प्रयत्न करेंगे तो निश्चय ही अपने सभी लक्ष्यों को प्राप्त कर लेंगे, किन्तु प्रायः देखा जाता है कि अधिक आशावादी लोग थोड़ा सा प्रयत्न करके अधिक फल की कामना करने लगते हैं और मनोवांछित फल प्राप्त न होने पर निराश हो जाते हैं। अतः जीवन में सफलता प्राप्त करने के लिए परिस्थितियों के समक्ष घुटने न टेकें, बल्कि दृढ़ता से उनका मुकाबला करें। याद रखें, जितना कठोर हमारा परिश्रम होगा उसका फल भी उतना ही मीठा होगा।

उपर्युक्त गद्यांश को ध्यानपूर्वक पढ़ें और निम्न प्रश्नों के उत्तर के लिए सही विकल्प को चुनें:

1. फल न मिलने पर कौन निराश हो जाते हैं?
A. आशावादी लोग　B. कम आशावादी लोग
C. अधिक आशावादी लोग　D. निराशावादी लोग

2. लक्ष्य प्राप्ति के लिए क्या किया जाना चाहिए?
A. फल की कामना　B. हिम्मत से मुकाबला
C. निरन्तर प्रयत्न　D. परिस्थितियों से मुकाबला

3. आशावादी शब्द का विलोम शब्द है:
A. निराश　B. निराशावादी
B. दुखी　D. अप्रसन्न

4. मनोवांछित शब्द का क्या अर्थ है?
A. इच्छित　B. परीक्षित
C. लाभदायक　D. मन को खुश करने वाले

5. परिश्रम शब्द का अर्थ है:
A. साहस　B. हिम्मत
C. काम　D. कठिन मेहनत

गद्यांश 2

पन्द्रह अगस्त 1947 को हमारा देश स्वतंत्र हुआ। स्वतन्त्रता प्राप्ति के बाद विश्व के दूसरे देशों के साथ भारत के राजनयिक एवं सांस्कृतिक सम्बन्ध जुड़े। पर्यटकों के साथ-साथ राजनीतिज्ञों और साहित्यकारों को भी विदेश यात्रा के पर्याप्त अवसर मिले। विभिन्न प्रकार की छात्रवृत्तियों के माध्यम से बहुत से लोग विदेशों में पढ़ने गए। बहुत से लोगों ने विदेशों में उपलब्ध आजीविका के अवसरों का लाभ उठाया। इन सबके परिणामस्वरूप प्रचुर मात्रा में यात्रावृत्तांत लिखे गए। विदेश-विषयक यात्रावृतांत्तों में रूस और स्वदेश-विषयक यात्रावृतांत्तों में लेखकों की दृष्टि कश्मीर से कन्याकुमारी तक व्याप्त हुई।

उपर्युक्त गद्यांश को ध्यानपूर्वक पढ़ें और निम्नलिखित प्रश्नों के उत्तर के लिए सही विकल्प को चुनें:

1. भारत कब स्वतंत्र हुआ?
A. 15 अगस्त 1947　B. 15 अगस्त 1946
C. 15 अगस्त 1948　D. 15 अगस्त 1949

2. स्वतंत्र भारत के अन्य देशों के साथ किस प्रकार के संबंध जुड़े?
A. राजनीतिक　B. राजनयिक
C. धार्मिक　D. राजनयिक एवं सांस्कृतिक

3. आजीविका का क्या अर्थ है?
A. उपार्जन　B. वेतन
C. मेहनत　D. रोजगार

4. यात्रा-वृत्तांत का क्या अर्थ है?
A. भ्रमण　B. पर्यटन
C. सफरनामा　D. विदेशभ्रमण

5. स्वतंत्र का विलोम शब्द है:
A. परतंत्र　B. आजाद
C. गुलामी　D. मुक्ति

गद्यांश 3

युवा वर्ग का मस्तिष्क नई-नई बातों की ओर ज्यादा तेज दौड़ता है। उसमें अन्य वर्ग के व्यक्तियों से अधिक आवेश और शक्ति होती है। इस अवस्था में यदि सही शिक्षा और उचित मार्ग-दर्शन न मिले तो यही शक्ति प्रेरणा और निर्माण के स्थान पर विनाश की ओर ले जाती है। बिगड़ने और बनने की यही आयु होती है। दुर्भाग्य से हमारे देश में शिक्षा पद्धति केवल उपाधि बाँटने का काम ही करती है। एक सम्पूर्ण व्यक्तित्वपूर्ण मनुष्य बनाना आज की शिक्षा पद्धति के लिए मुश्किल है।

उपर्युक्त गद्यांश को ध्यानपूर्वक पढ़ें और निम्नलिखित प्रश्नों के उत्तर के लिए सही विकल्प को चुनें।

1. निर्माण का विलोम शब्द क्या हैं?
A. रचना　B. बनावट
C. विनाश　D. सृजन

2. मार्ग-दर्शन का क्या अर्थ है?
A. उपाधि　B. रास्ता
C. उद्देश्य　D. रास्ता दिखलाना

3. शक्ति विनाश की ओर कब अग्रसर होती है?
A. अधिक आवेश और शक्ति के अभाव में
B. सही शिक्षा और उचित मार्ग दर्शन के अभाव में
C. दुर्भाग्यपूर्ण शिक्षा पद्धति के कारण
D. इनमें से कोई नहीं

4. हमारे देश की शिक्षा पद्धति क्या कार्य करती है?
A. मार्ग-दर्शन　B. शक्ति प्रेरणा
C. उपाधि देना　D. उपर्युक्त सभी

5. दुर्भाग्य का विपरीत शब्द है:
A. भाग्य　B. सौभाग्य
C. भाग्यशाली　D. भाग्यवान

गद्यांश 4

भिखारी की भाँति गिड़गिड़ाना प्रेम की भाषा नहीं है। यहाँ तक कि मुक्ति के लिए भगवान् की उपासना करना भी अधम उपासना में गिना जाता है। प्रेम कोई पुरस्कार नहीं चाहता। प्रेम सर्वथा प्रेम के लिए ही होता है। भक्त इसलिए प्रेम करता है कि बिना प्रेम किए वह रह ही नहीं सकता। जब तुम किसी मनोहर प्राकृतिक दृश्य को देखकर उस पर मोहित हो जाते हो तो तुम किसी फल की याचना नहीं करते और न वह दृश्य ही तुमसे कुछ माँगता है। फिर भी उस दृश्य का दर्शन तुम्हारे मन को आनंद से भर देता है।

उपर्युक्त गद्यांश को ध्यानपूर्वक पढ़ें और निम्नलिखित प्रश्नों के उत्तर के लिए सही विकल्प का चयन करें:

1. प्रेम का उद्देश्य क्या होता है?

A. मुक्ति B. उपासना
C. भक्ति D. प्रेम

2. मुक्ति का अर्थ है:

A. आजादी B. स्वतंत्रता
C. परतंत्र D. निर्वाण

3. कैसी उपासना अधम मानी गई है?

A. प्रेम की उपासना
B. भगवान की उपासना
C. मुक्ति की उपासना
D. भक्ति की उपासना

4. मनोहर शब्द हैं:

A. विशेषण B. संज्ञा
C. सर्वनाम D. अव्यय

5. प्राकृतिक शब्द का अर्थ है:

A. ईश्वरीय B. मानव संबंधी
C. प्रकृति संबंधी D. प्रेम संबंधी

गद्यांश 5

कुछ लोग भाग्यवादी होते हैं और सब-कुछ भाग्य के सहारे छोड़कर कर्म से विरत हो जाते हैं। ऐसे लोग समाज के लिए बोझ हैं। वे कभी कोई बड़ा काम नहीं कर पाते। बड़ी-बड़ी खोज, बड़े-बड़े आविष्कार और बड़े-बड़े निर्माण कार्य कर्मशील लोगों के द्वारा ही संभव हो सके हैं। हम अपनी बुद्धि और प्रतिभा तथा कार्य-क्षमता के बल पर सही मार्ग पर चल सकते हैं, किन्तु बिना कठिन श्रम के अपने लक्ष्य तक नहीं पहुँच सकते। कठिन परिश्रम करने के बाद पाई गई सफलता हमारे मन को अलौकिक आनंद से भर देती है। यदि हम अपने कार्य में अपेक्षित श्रम नहीं करते तो हमारा मन ग्लानि का अनुभव करता है।

उपर्युक्त गद्यांश को ध्यानपूर्वक पढ़ें और निम्नलिखित प्रश्नों के उत्तर के लिए सही विकल्प चुनें:

1. ''आविष्कार'' शब्द का अर्थ है :

A. अनुसंधान B. खोज
C. निर्माण D. विनाश

2. अलौकिक शब्द का क्या अर्थ है?

A. संसारिक B. भौतिक
C. अमानुषी D. प्राकृतिक

3. सफलता का विलोम क्या है?

A. सफल B. असफल
C. सफलतापूर्वक D. असफलता

4. परिश्रम करने और न करने से हमारे जीवन पर क्या प्रभाव पड़ता है?

A. लोग भाग्यवादी बन जाते हैं
B. कर्म से विरत हो जाते हैं
C. मन में ग्लानि का अनुभव होता है
D. इनमें से कोई नहीं

5. किस प्रकार के लोग समाज के लिए बोझ हैं?

A. भाग्यवादी B. कर्मठ
C. परिश्रमी D. प्रतिभाशाली

गद्यांश 6

वैदिक काल से हिमालय के पहाड़ बहुत पवित्र माने जाते हैं। इसमें कोई सन्देह नहीं कि हिमालय के पहाड़ों का दृश्य अति सुन्दर है। उसकी विशालता को देखकर मन में आनन्द और कृतज्ञता की लहर उठती है। ऐसा लगता है कि यह विशाल सृष्टि प्रभु की अनुपम देन है। सारी सृष्टि के प्रति समभाव जाग्रत होता है। वस्तुतः यह दृष्टि कोरी कल्पनात्मक या आध्यात्मिक नहीं है। देखा जाए तो सारे भारत की जलवायु का समतोल करने वाले यह हिमालय के पहाड़ हैं, विशेषकर उत्तरी भारत को वर्षा और पानी देने वाले ये ही हैं। गंगोत्री, यमुनोत्री, बद्री, केदार को तीर्थ माना जाता है, जो व्यर्थ कल्पना नहीं है। उन स्थानों से निकलने वाली पवित्र नदियाँ ही वास्तव में हमारी प्राणदात्री रही हैं।

उपर्युक्त गद्यांश को ध्यानपूर्वक पढ़ें और निम्नलिखित प्रश्नों के उत्तर के लिए सही विकल्प चुनें :

1. हिमालय के पर्वत बहुत पवित्र कब से माने जाते हैं?

A. पाषाण काल से
B. वैदिक काल से
C. प्राचीन काल से
D. आधुनिक काल से

2. विशालता शब्द है :

A. जातिवाचक B. भाववाचक
C. विशेषण D. सर्वनाम

3. भारत की जलवायु को समतोल कौन करता है?

A. गंगोत्री B. यमुनोत्री

C. केदार D. हिमालय

4. सृष्टि का समानार्थक शब्द है :

A. सृजन B. रचना

C. प्रकृति D. संसार

5. प्राणदात्री का क्या अर्थ है?

A. गंगोत्री

B. यमुनोत्री

C. प्राणसंचार करने वाली

D. समभाव जाग्रत करने वाली

गद्यांश 7

सच्चा मित्र एक शिक्षक की भाँति होता है। जिस प्रकार शिक्षक अपने छात्र को सन्मार्ग की ही ओर अग्रसर करता है, उसी प्रकार एक सच्चा मित्र अपने मित्र को पाप के गर्त में गिरने से बचाता है। मानव-जीवन अधिक रहस्यपूर्ण है। कभी-कभी जीवन में ऐसे अवसर उपस्थित हो जाते हैं, जब मनुष्य की धर्मबुद्धि नष्ट हो जाती है और उसका मन द्रुत गति से पाप की ओर दौड़ता है। ऐसे समय में मित्र का ही उपदेश अधिक कल्याणकारी सिद्ध होता है। मित्र के उपदेश का जितना प्रभाव हृदय पर पड़ता है, उतना और किसी का नहीं पड़ता है।

उपर्युक्त गद्यांश को ध्यानपूर्वक पढ़ें और निम्नलिखित प्रश्नों के उत्तर के लिए सही विकल्प चुनें :

1. सच्चा मित्र किस प्रकार का होता है?

A. विपत्ति में सहायता देने वाला

B. गलत मार्ग पर चलने से रोकने वाला

C. शिक्षक के भाँति

D. धार्मिक गुरु की तरह

2. सन्मार्ग शब्द का विपरीत शब्द है :

A. अग्रसर B. कुमार्ग

C. सुमार्ग D. मार्गदर्शक

3. व्यक्ति को पाप के गर्त्त में गिरने से कौन बचाता है?

A. शिक्षक B. भाई

C. पिता D. सच्चा मित्र

4. मानव पाप की ओर कब दौड़ता है?

A. जब स्वार्थी बन जाता है

B. जब धर्म-बुद्धि नष्ट हो जाती है

C. जब सच्चामित्र साथ छोड़ देता है

D. जब धनवान बन जाता है

5. उपदेश में कौन-सा उपसर्ग है?

A. उ B. उप

C. दे D. देश

गद्यांश 8

सब तरह के भावों को प्रकट करने की योग्यता रखने वाली और निर्दोष होने पर भी यदि कोई भाषा अपना निज का साहित्य नहीं रखती, तो वह रूपवती भिखारिन की तरह कदापि आदरणीय नहीं हो सकती। उनकी शोभा, उसकी बड़ी सम्पन्नता, उसकी मान-मर्यादा उसके साहित्य पर ही अवलम्बित रहती है। उसके विचारों और राजनैतिक स्थितियों का प्रतिबिम्ब देखने को यदि कहीं मिल सकता है, तो उसके ग्रन्थ साहित्य में मिल सकता है। सामाजिक शक्ति या सजीवता, सामाजिक अशक्ति या निर्जीवता और सामाजिक सभ्यता तथा असभ्यता का निर्णायक एकमात्र साहित्य है।

उपर्युक्त गद्यांश को ध्यानपूर्वक पढ़ें और निम्नलिखित प्रश्नों के उत्तर के लिए सही विकल्प चुनें :

1. साहित्य विहीन भाषा किस प्रकार की होती है?

A. आदरणीय B. भिखारिन

C. रूपवती D. रूपवती भिखारिन

2. रूपवती का पुल्लिंग रूप है:

A. रूपवान B. सुन्दर

C. सुन्दरी D. रूपवत

3. भाषा की मान मर्यादा किस पर निर्भर करती है?

A. लिपि पर B. साहित्यकार पर

C. भक्ति पर D. साहित्य पर

4. ''सम्पन्नता'' शब्द का विपरीत शब्द है:

A. गरीबी B. विपन्न

C. अमीर D. विपन्नता

5. राजनैतिक, सामाजिक शक्ति का दर्शन हमें किसमें मिलता है?

A. समाज B. राज्य

C. नेता D. साहित्य

गद्यांश 9

स्वतंत्र भारत का सम्पूर्ण दायित्व आज विद्यार्थियों के ही ऊपर है, क्योंकि आज जो विद्यार्थी हैं, वे ही कल स्वतंत्र भारत के नागरिक होंगे। भारत की उन्नति, उसका उत्थान उन्हीं की उन्नति और उत्थान पर निर्भर करता है। अतः विद्यार्थियों को चाहिए कि वे अपने भावी जीवन का निर्माण बड़ी सतर्कता और सावधानी के साथ करें। उन्हें प्रत्येक क्षण अपने राष्ट्र, अपने समाज, अपने धर्म, अपनी संस्कृति को अपनी आँखों के सामने रखना चाहिए, जिससे उनके जीवन से राष्ट्र को कुछ बल प्राप्त हो सके। जो विद्यार्थी राष्ट्रीय दृष्टिकोण से अपने जीवन का निर्माण नहीं करते, वे राष्ट्र और समाज के लिए भार-स्वरूप हैं।

उपर्युक्त गद्यांश को ध्यानपूर्वक पढ़ें और निम्नलिखित प्रश्नों के उत्तर के लिए सही विकल्प चुनें :

1. भारत की उन्नति किस पर निर्भर करती है?

A. युवाओं पर
B. नेताओं पर
C. साहित्यकारों पर
D. विद्यार्थियों पर

2. **उन्नति** का समानार्थक शब्द है :

A. पतन B. उत्थान
C. विकास D. उदय

3. **उत्थान** का विपरीत शब्द है :

A. उदय B. पतन
C. पराजय D. हार

4. किसे अपने जीवन का निर्माण सतर्कता और सावधानी से करना चाहिए?

A. युवाओं को B. नेताओं को
C. बच्चों को D. विद्यार्थियों को

5. धर्म, संस्कृति तथा समाज का रक्षक कौन है?

A. नागरिक B. ग्रामीण
C. विद्यार्थी D. युवा

गद्यांश 10

हास्य एक ऐसा माध्यम है, जो नीरस-जीवन को भी सुखद बना देता है। हास्य का जादू इतना प्रभावशाली होता है कि वह छूत के रोग की तरह चारों ओर फैल जाता है। जिसने कभी हँसना नहीं सीखा, सचमुच उसने जीना नहीं सीखा। सामान्यतः मनुष्य को जीवन में इतनी मुसीबतें झेलनी पड़ती हैं कि वह अपने जीवन को पहाड़ समझने लगता है। ऐसे दूभर जीवन को यदि जीने योग्य बनाना हो तो उसके लिए आवश्यक है कि जीवन में हँसने की गुंजाइश हो। हँसी के सहारे मनुष्य अपने कष्टों को भुलाने का प्रयत्न करता है। संघर्ष, तनाव, व्यस्तता, घुटन यदि आज के जीवन की सहज देन हैं, तो इनसे बचने के लिए यह आवश्यक है कि हम हँसना सीखें।

उपर्युक्त गद्यांश को ध्यानपूर्वक पढ़ें और निम्नलिखित प्रश्नों के उत्तर के लिए सही विकल्प चुनें :

1. नीरस जीवन को कौन सुखद बना देता है?

A. संगीत B. गीत
C. आमोद प्रमोद D. हास्य

2. **नीरस** का संधि विच्छेद है :

A. नी + रस
B. नि + रस
C. निः + रस
D. नीः + रस

3. किसका जीवन व्यर्थ है?

A. जिसने रोना नहीं सीखा
B. जिसने हँसना नहीं सीखा
C. जिसने गाना नहीं सीखा
D. इनमें से कोई नहीं

4. **हँसना** शब्द है :

A. संज्ञा B. विशेषण
C. क्रिया विशेषण D. क्रिया

5. तनाव और घुटन से बचने के लिए क्या करना चाहिए?

A. रोना चाहिए B. गाना चाहिए
C. हँसना चाहिए D. काम करना चाहिए

गद्यांश 11

किसी पुस्तक को पढ़ने में जल्दी नहीं करनी चाहिए, जो कुछ लेखक कहता है, उसे समझने की चेष्टा करनी चाहिए। प्रत्येक शब्द का अर्थ समझने की चेष्टा करनी चाहिए। यदि लेखक योग्य है, तो दूसरी बार वह पुस्तक और अधिक आनन्द देगी और तीसरी बार और अधिक। प्रत्येक बार अध्ययन करने पर आपको नवीन सुन्दर और नए विचार मिलेंगे और उसे आप जितना ही पढ़ेंगे, उतना ही स्नेह करने लगेंगे। सहस्रों व्यक्तियों ने गीता और रामायण तथा कुरान और बाइबिल को बार-बार पढ़ा है। उनका अनुभव है कि प्रत्येक बार उन्हें नई सूझ और नए विचार मिलते गए। कुछ लोग तो इस बात पर गर्व करते हैं कि उन्होंने अमुक पुस्तक को अनेक बार पढ़ा है, उन्हें कंठस्थ हो गई है।

उपर्युक्त गद्यांश को ध्यानपूर्वक पढ़ें और निम्नलिखित प्रश्नों के उत्तर के लिए सही विकल्प चुनें :

1. किसे समझने की चेष्टा करनी चाहिए?

A. पुस्तक B. रामायण
C. महाभारत D. गीता

2. पुस्तक की सजीवता किस पर निर्भर करती है?

A. लेखक B. प्रकाशक
C. पाठक D. चिन्तक

3. **आनन्द** का विपरीत शब्द है :

A. शोक B. दुख
C. संताप D. खुशी

4. नवीन, सुन्दर और नए विचार हमें कहाँ से प्राप्त होता हैं?

A. पुस्तक को बार-बार पढ़कर
B. सुनकर
C. भाषण से
D. अच्छे व्यक्तियों से मिलने पर

5. **कंठस्थ** शब्द का शब्दार्थ है :

A. कंठ में स्थित B. सुंदर कंठ
C. जबानी याद D. पंडित जी

गद्यांश 12

अहिंसा परम धर्म है और हिंसा आपद् धर्म। मनुष्य बराबर अहिंसा की ओर चलना चाहता है, किन्तु परिस्थितियाँ उससे हिंसा कराती है, अर्थात् परमधर्म की रक्षा के लिए आदमी बराबर आपद्धर्म से काम लेता रहा है। भारत अपनी सेनाओं को विघटित कर दे, तब भी उसका अपमान उससे अधिक होने वाला नहीं, जितना नेफा में हुआ। किन्तु परमधर्म पर टिकने की सामर्थ्य अगर भारत में नहीं है, तो आपद्धर्म पर उसे आना चाहिए। व्यवहारतः आपद्धर्म परमधर्म का विरोधी नहीं, उसका रक्षक है।

उपर्युक्त गद्यांश को ध्यानपूर्वक पढ़ें और निम्नलिखित प्रश्नों के उत्तर के लिए सही विकल्प चुनें :

1. **परमधर्म** का विपरीत शब्द है :

A. महान धर्म B. आपद्धर्म
C. सच्चाधर्म D. इनमें से कोई नहीं

2. आपद्धर्म किसे कहा जाता है?

A. अहिंसा B. सत्याग्रह
C. विपत्ति D. हिंसा

3. मानव से हिंसा कौन करवाती है?

A. लोभ B. स्वार्थ
C. द्वेष D. परिस्थितियाँ

4. **सामर्थ्य** का शब्दार्थ है :

A. संघर्ष B. परिश्रम
C. शक्ति D. पराक्रम

5. **परमधर्म** की रक्षा कौन करता है?

A. अहिंसा B. हिंसा
C. आपदधर्म D. युद्ध

गद्यांश 13

वर्तमान काल विज्ञापन का युग माना जाता है। समाचार-पत्रों के अतिरिक्त रेडियो और टेलीविजन भी विज्ञापन के सफल साधन हैं। विज्ञापन का मूल उद्देश्य उत्पादक और भोक्ता में सीधा सम्पर्क स्थापित करना होता है। जितना अधिक विज्ञापन किसी पदार्थ का होगा, उतनी ही उसकी लोकप्रियता बढ़ेगी। इन विज्ञापनों पर धन तो अधिक व्यय होता है, पर इनसे बिक्री बढ़ जाती है। ग्राहक जब इन आकर्षक विज्ञापनों को देखता है तो वह उस वस्तु-विशेष के प्रति आकृष्ट होकर उसे खरीदने को बाध्य हो जाता है।

उपर्युक्त गद्यांश को ध्यानपूर्वक पढ़ें और निम्नलिखित प्रश्नों के उत्तर के लिए सही विकल्प चुनें :

1. वर्तमान को किसका युग माना जाता है?

A. फैशन B. विज्ञापन
C. संगीत D. धन

2. उत्पादक तथा भोक्ता के बीच कौन संबंध स्थापित करता है?

A. टेलीविजन B. समाचार-पत्र
C. रेडियो D. विज्ञापन

3. **वर्तमान** शब्द का विपरीत शब्द है :

A. अर्वाचीन B. आधुनिक
C. आजकल D. प्राचीन

4. **आकर्षक** का शब्दार्थ है :

A. विकर्षक B. सुन्दर
C. मनमोहक D. आश्चर्यजनक

5. भोक्ता किस कारण वस्तुओं को खरीदने के लिए बाध्य हो जाता है?

A. विज्ञापन
B. आकर्षक विज्ञापन
C. लोकप्रियता के कारण
D. आसानी से उपलब्ध होना

गद्यांश 14

लगभग दो सौ वर्ष की गुलामी ने भारत के राष्ट्रीय स्वाभिमान को पैरों से रौंद डाला, हमारी संस्कृति को समाप्त कर दिया, हमारे विश्वासों को हिला दिया और हमारे आत्मविश्वास को चकनाचूर कर दिया, किन्तु अपने इस बूढ़े देश से प्यार करने वाले, इसके एक सामान्य संकेत पर प्राण न्यौछावर करने वाले दीवानों का अभाव न था। एक आवाज उठी और देखते ही देखते राष्ट्र का दबा हुआ आत्माभिमान उन्मत्त हो उठा। इतिहास साक्षी है जाने और अनजाने सहस्त्रों देशभक्त स्वतंत्रता की अनमोल निधि को पाने के लिए शहीद हो गए।

उपर्युक्त गद्यांश को ध्यानपूर्वक पढ़ें और निम्नलिखित प्रश्नों के उत्तर के लिए सही विकल्प चुनें :

1. **स्वाभिमान** का संधि विच्छेद है:

A. स्वा + भिमान B. स्वः + अभिमान
C. स्व + अभिमान D. स्वा + अभिमान

2. भारत का राष्ट्रीय स्वाभिमान किस कारण समाप्त हो गया था?

A. लम्बे गुलामी से
B. निरंकुश शासक से
C. स्वार्थी मानव से
D. धर्म के विनाश से

3. **आत्मविश्वास** का शब्दार्थ है

A. घमण्ड B. गर्व
C. अपने पर विश्वास D. अभिमान

4. भारत की अनमोल निधि को पाने के लिए कौन शहीद हो गए?

A. देशभक्त B. नेता
C. युवा D. युवती

5. **अनमोल निधि** का शब्दार्थ है:

A. अनन्त खजाना B. अमूल्य खजाना
C. बहुमूल्य D. स्वतंत्रता

गद्यांश 15

दुनिया के विभिन्न देशों के विकास पर विहंगम दृष्टि डालने से यह स्पष्ट हो जाता है कि आज जिस देश ने वैज्ञानिक उपलब्धियों के सहारे अपना औद्योगीकरण कर लिया, उसी को उन्नत देश कहा जाता है। जिस देश में औद्योगीकरण का स्तर नीचा है, वह पिछड़ा हुआ देश कहा जाता है। वैज्ञानिक आविष्कारों और औद्योगीकरण के आधार पर ही किसी देश की प्रगति को आँका जाता रहा है। विज्ञान ने मानव को पूरी तरह बदल दिया है।

उपर्युक्त गद्यांश को ध्यानपूर्वक पढ़ें और निम्नलिखित प्रश्नों के उत्तर के लिए सही विकल्प चुनें :

1. **विहंगम दृष्टि** का क्या अर्थ है?
   A. एक झलक　B. गहन दृष्टि
   C. गहन चिन्तन　D. इनमें से कोई नहीं

2. **विकास** का विपरीत शब्द है :
   A. उत्थान　B. उदय
   C. पतन　D. विनाश

3. **वैज्ञानिक** शब्द में कौन-सा प्रत्यय हैं?
   A. निक　B. वै
   C. ईक　D. इक

4. मानव जीवन को किसने बदल दिया है :
   A. विकास　B. वैज्ञानिक
   C. विज्ञान　D. उद्योग

5. किसी भी देश की स्तर को किससे नापा जाता है?
   A. उपलब्धियों पर　B. औद्योगीकरण से
   C. वैज्ञानिकों से　D. आविष्कारों से

गद्यांश 16

विश्व का वर्तमान उन्नत रूप मानव-श्रम की ही कहानी कह रहा है। गगन चुंबी अट्टालिकाएँ, लंबी-चौड़ी सड़कें, बड़े-बड़े विशाल नगर आकाश में उड़ते वायुयान तथा मानव-जीवन को सुखी और समृद्ध बनाने में योगदान करने वाले ज्ञान-विज्ञान के अनन्त रूप-ये सभी मनुष्य के श्रम का जयघोष करते हैं। स्पष्ट है कि मनुष्य और उसका शरीर विधाता की अनुपम रचना है जो निश्चय ही महान उद्देश्यों की संपूर्ति के लिए दिया गया है। इस दुर्लभ तन को यदि हम आलस्य, प्रसाद अथवा घटिया कामों में गँवा देते हैं तो उस विधाता के प्रति अन्याय करते हैं।

उपर्युक्त गद्यांश को ध्यानपूर्वक पढ़ें और निम्नलिखित प्रश्नों के उत्तर के लिए सही विकल्प चुनें :

1. विश्व का वर्तमान रूप किसका उद्योतक है?
   A. चिन्तक का　B. नेता का
   C. वैज्ञानिक का　D. मानव श्रम

2. **गगन चुंबी अट्टालिकाएँ** का अर्थ है :
   A. आकाश में उड़ने वाला　B. आकाश को छूने वाला
   C. बहुमंजिली इमारत　D. इनमें से कोई नहीं

3. आकाश का समानार्थक शब्द है :
   A. वसुन्धरा　B. धरा
   C. पयोद　D. गगन

4. **सुखी** का विपरीत शब्द है :
   A. प्रसन्न　B. अप्रसन्न
   C. दुखी　D. उदासी

5. विधाता की अनुपम रचना क्या है?
   A. मानव शरीर　B. समुद्र
   C. वन　D. पृथ्वी

गद्यांश 17

हमारे देश में एक ऐसा भी युग था जब नैतिक और आध्यात्मिक विकास ही जीवन का वास्तविक लक्ष्य माना जाता था। अहिंसा की भावना सर्वोपरि थी। आज पूरा जीवन दर्शन ही बदल गया है। सर्वत्र पैसे की हाय-हाय तथा धन का उपार्जन ही मुख्य ध्येय हो गया है, भले ही धन- उपार्जन के तरीके गलत ही क्यों न हों? इन सबका असर मनुष्य के प्रतिदिन के जीवन पर पड़ रहा है। समाज का वातावरण दूषित हो गया है–

बाह्य वातावरण तो दूषित है ही, आज सब जानते हैं पर्यावरण की समस्याएँ कितनी चिन्तनीय हो उठी है। इन सबके कारण मानसिक और शारीरिक तनाव-खिंचाव और व्याधियाँ पैदा हो रही हैं।

उपर्युक्त गद्यांश को ध्यानपूर्वक पढ़ें और निम्नलिखित प्रश्नों के उत्तर के लिए सही विकल्प चुनें :

1. भारत का प्राचीन आदर्श था :
   A. सत्य और अहिंसा
   B. नैतिक और आध्यात्मिक विकास
   C. धन उपार्जन
   D. इनमें से कोई नहीं

2. **अहिंसा** का विपरीत शब्द है :
   A. हिंसा　B. सत्याग्रह
   C. विनम्रता　D. नैतिकता

3. जीवन दर्शन क्यों बदल गया है?
   A. हिंसा के कारण
   B. अहिंसा के कारण
   C. धन लिप्सा के कारण
   D. आध्यात्मिक विकास के कारण

4. समाज का वातावरण दूषित क्यों हो गया है?
   A. शारीरिक तनाव
   B. मानसिक व्याधियाँ
   C. पर्यावरण की समस्याएँ
   D. धन उपार्जन के गलत तरीके

5. **पर्यावरण** का शब्दार्थ है:
   A. जलमंडल　B. स्थलमंडल
   C. वायुमंडल　D. वातावरण

उत्तरमाला

संधि

1	2	3	4	5	6	7	8	9	10
A	A	B	C	D	A	D	B	C	B
11	**12**	**13**	**14**	**15**	**16**	**17**	**18**	**19**	**20**
A	C	A	C	A	A	C	C	A	D
21	**22**	**23**	**24**	**25**	**26**	**27**	**28**	**29**	**30**
A	C	C	A	A	B	D	D	A	B
31	**32**	**33**	**34**	**35**	**36**	**37**	**38**	**39**	**40**
D	C	C	A	A	B	C	C	C	D
41	**42**	**43**	**44**	**45**	**46**	**47**	**48**	**49**	**50**
A	A	B	B	A	B	D	B	A	C
51	**52**	**53**	**54**	**55**	**56**	**57**	**58**	**59**	**60**
C	A	A	A	B	C	A	C	C	C
61	**62**	**63**	**64**	**65**	**66**	**67**	**68**	**69**	**70**
C	A	A	A	A	C	B	A	B	B
71	**72**	**73**	**74**	**75**					
B	A	A	B	D					

समास

1	2	3	4	5	6	7	8	9	10
C	B	C	A	C	B	A	A	B	A
11	**12**	**13**	**14**	**15**	**16**	**17**	**18**	**19**	**20**
D	A	B	D	B	C	C	D	A	B
21	**22**	**23**	**24**	**25**	**26**	**27**	**28**	**29**	**30**
A	A	C	A	A	C	A	A	A	A
31	**32**	**33**	**34**	**35**	**36**	**37**	**38**	**39**	**40**
B	A	C	C	A	D	B	B	C	A
41	**42**	**43**	**44**	**45**	**46**	**47**	**48**	**49**	**50**
A	A	A	C	A	A	A	D	B	D
51	**52**	**53**	**54**	**55**	**56**	**57**	**58**	**59**	**60**
C	A	A	C	C	A	C	C	B	B
61	**62**	**63**	**64**	**65**	**66**	**67**	**68**	**69**	**70**
B	C	A	C	B	D	A	B	C	A

वर्तनी

1	2	3	4	5	6	7	8	9	10
B	A	D	B	A	A	B	A	D	C
11	**12**	**13**	**14**	**15**	**16**	**17**	**18**	**19**	**20**
D	D	B	B	D	C	C	A	B	B
21	**22**	**23**	**24**	**25**	**26**	**27**	**28**	**29**	**30**
C	A	D	B	D	B	B	B	C	D
31	**32**	**33**	**34**	**35**	**36**	**37**	**38**	**39**	**40**
C	A	C	A	D	C	B	C	A	C
41	**42**	**43**	**44**	**45**	**46**	**47**	**48**	**49**	**50**
C	D	C	C	A	D	C	A	D	B

51	52	53	54	55	56	57	58	59	60
A	C	D	C	C	B	B	A	D	C
61	62	63	64	65	66	67	68	69.	70
B	B	B	B	A	C	A	A	D	B
71	72	73	74	75	76	77	78	79	80
B	B	A	C	B	B	A	B	D	A
81	82	83	84	85	86	87	88	89	90
B	C	A	A	D	D	E	B	A	C
91	92	93	94	95	96	97	98	99	100
A	B	D	C	C	A	A	C	A	B
101	102	103	104	105	106	107	108	109	110
E	D	C	B	A	B	A	C	D	E
111	112	113	114	115					
D	E	C	A	C					

पर्यायवाची

1	2	3	4	5	6	7	8	9	10
D	C	D	D	A	D	C	B	D	D
11	12	13	14	15	16	17	18	19	20
A	D	A	A	C	A	D	C	A	B
21	22	23	24	25	26	27	28	29	30
A	C	B	B	A	A	A	D	B	D
31	32	33	34	35	36	37	38	39	40
B	D	C	C	C	A	D	A	D	D
41	42	43	44	45	46	47	48	49	50
C	C	D	C	A	A	C	D	C	A
51	52	53	54	55	56	57	58	59	60
D	C	A	D	A	D	A	D	C	D
61	62	63	64	65	66				
D	D	B	C	B	A				

विलोमार्थी शब्द

1	2	3	4	5	6	7	8	9	10
C	B	A	B	D	A	D	A	A	A
11	12	13	14	15	16	17	18	19	20
C	D	B	A	C	D	C	A	B	C
21	22	23	24	25	26	27	28	29	30
D	B	B	B	D	C	C	C	A	C
31	32	33	34	35	36	37	38	39	40
D	A	C	B	A	D	B	A	B	A
41	42	43	44	45	46	47	48	49	50
C	A	A	C	B	D	B	A	D	C
51	52	53	54	55	56	57	58	59	60
B	C	A	B	D	A	C	C	C	A
61	62	63	64	65	66	67	68	69	70
D	D	A	A	C	B	D	C	B	B
71	72	73	74	75					
A	B	A	D	A					

वाक्यों की शुद्धता

1	2	3	4	5	6	7	8	9	10
A	A	B	C	C	B	D	A	B	A
11	12	13	14	15	16	17	18	19	20
A	B	C	B	C	D	C	C	B	A
21	22	23	24	25	26	27	28	29	30
B	A	C	C	D	A	A	A	C	C
31	32	33	34	35	36	37	38	39	40
D	D	B	B	C	B	C	D	A	C
41	42	43	44	45	46	47	48	49	50
A	E	A	D	A	D	C	B	A	D
51	52	53	54	55	56	57	58	59	60
C	B	C	A	B	D	A	C	C	D
61	62	63	64	65	66	67	68	69	70
C	A	C	C	B	D	D	D	C	B
71	72	73	74	75	76	77	78	79	80
C	C	C	B	A	A	B	D	C	A

वाक्यांश के लिए एक शब्द

1	2	3	4	5	6	7	8	9	10
D	C	D	A	B	B	D	D	C	A
11	12	13	14	15	16	17	18	19	20
D	D	D	C	D	B	D	A	A	D
21	22	23	24	25	26	27	28	29	30
C	B	B	D	C	A	B	D	C	D
31	32	33	34	35	36	37	38	39	40
D	B	D	A	C	A	D	D	A	A
41	42	43	44	45	46	47	48	49	50
C	D	B	C	D	C	C	D	D	C
51	52	53	54	55	56	57	58	59	60
B	C	A	D	B	A	C	A	B	A
61	62	63	64	65	66	67	68	69	70
C	D	D	B	C	C	D	C	A	C
71	72	73	74	75					
A	D	D	B	B					

मुहावरा एवं लोकोक्तियाँ

1	2	3	4	5	6	7	8	9	10
C	D	B	A	A	D	A	C	B	A
11	12	13	14	15	16	17	18	19	20
D	A	D	B	A	A	D	B	D	C
21	22	23	24	25	26	27	28	29	30
B	D	D	B	B	C	D	B	C	C

31	32	33	34	35	36	37	38	39	40
B	D	D	C	B	B	B	A	B	C
41	**42**	**43**	**44**	**45**	**46**	**47**	**48**	**49**	**50**
A	D	C	C	D	D	C	B	B	D
51	**52**	**53**	**54**	**55**	**56**	**57**	**58**	**59**	**60**
B	C	C	B	A	C	A	D	C	D
61	**62**	**63**	**64**	**65**					
B	B	A	C	B					

गद्यांश (अपठित-बोध)

गद्यांश 1

1. C **2.** D **3.** B **4.** A **5.** D

गद्यांश 2

1. A **2.** D **3.** D **4.** C **5.** A

गद्यांश 3

1. C **2.** D **3.** B **4.** C **5.** B

गद्यांश 4

1. D **2.** D **3.** C **4.** A **5.** C

गद्यांश 5

1. B **2.** D **3.** D **4.** C **5.** A

गद्यांश 6

1. B **2.** B **3.** D **4.** A **5.** C

गद्यांश 7

1. C **2.** B **3.** D **4.** B **5.** B

गद्यांश 8

1. D **2.** A **3.** D **4.** D **5.** D

गद्यांश 9

1. D **2.** B **3.** B **4.** D **5.** C

गद्यांश 10

1. D **2.** C **3.** B **4.** D **5.** C

गद्यांश 11

1. A **2.** A **3.** A **4.** A **5.** C

गद्यांश 12

1. B **2.** D **3.** D **4.** C **5.** C

गद्यांश 13

1. B **2.** D **3.** D **4.** C **5.** B

गद्यांश 14

1. C **2.** A **3.** C **4.** A **5.** B

गद्यांश 15

1. A **2.** D **3.** C **4.** C **5.** B

गद्यांश 16

1. D **2.** C **3.** D **4.** C **5.** A

गद्यांश 17

1. B **2.** A **3.** C **4.** D **5.** D

❑❑❑

साहित्य

आदिकाल

- हेमचन्द्र अपभ्रंश व्याकरण के रचयिता थे।
- आदिकाल को 'आदिकाल' का नाम हजारी प्रसाद द्विवेदी ने दिया था।
- खड़ी बोली/कौरवी बोली का सम्बन्ध पश्चिमी हिन्दी से है।
- बघेली बोली का सम्बन्ध पूर्वी हिन्दी से है।
- खड़ी बोली का उद्‌भव अपभ्रंश के शौरसेनी के उत्तरी रूप से हुआ है।
- श्रावकाचार को हिन्दी की प्रथम रचना माना जाता है।
- धीरेंद्र वर्मा ने आदिकाल को 'अपभ्रंश काल' कहा है।
- 'गाथा सप्तशती' की रचना प्राकृत भाषा में हुई है।
- ब्रजभाषा का उद्‌भव शौरसेनी के मध्यवर्ती रूप से हुआ है।
- चंदबरदायी कृत 'पृथ्वीराज रासो' में शृंगार और वीर रस का समावेश है।
- आदिकाल में धर्म से सम्बन्धित पुस्तकों का सृजन मुख्यतः अपभ्रंश भाषा में मिलता है।
- आदिकाल में खड़ी बोली को काव्य का आधार सर्वप्रथम 'अमीर खुसरो' ने बनाया था।
- अमर खुसरो की रचनाओं को देशी भाषा काव्य के अन्तर्गत माना जाता है।
- आदिकालीन हिन्दी साहित्य को मुख्यतः अपभ्रंश-हिन्दी के वर्ग में रखा जाता है।
- 'मैथिल कोकिल' के नाम से प्रसिद्ध विद्यापति का समय सम्वत् 1460 माना जाता है।
- आदिकाल में 'अवधूत संप्रदाय' का सम्बन्ध नाथों से है।
- आदिकाल में जैनों द्वारा रचित साहित्य को सर्वाधिक प्रमाणिक माना जाता है।
- रामायण में संस्कृत भाषा का प्रयोग किया गया है।
- अमीर खुसरो ने फारसी तथा खड़ी बोली दोनों में रचना की है।
- मैथिल कोकिल 'विद्यापति' संस्कृत, अपभ्रंश तथा मैथिली तीनों में रचना की है।
- वर्णरत्नाकर मैथिली की पहली गद्य रचना है। इसके लेखक ज्योतिरीश्वर ठाकुर हैं।
- 'ढ़ोला मारू रा दूहा' के रचयिता कल्लोल कवि हैं।
- 'कीर्तिलता' की भाषा मिश्रित अपभ्रंश है।
- 'पृथ्वीराज विजय' की रचना जयानक ने की थी।

आदिकाल के प्रमुख रचनाकार तथा उनकी रचनायें

क्र.सं	रचनाकार	रचनायें
1.	सहरपा	दोहाकोष
2.	ज्योतिरीश्वर ठाकुर	वर्णरत्नाकर
3.	शबरपा	चर्यापद
4.	श्रीधर	रणमल्ल छंद
5.	जगनिक	परमाल रासो
6.	हाल कवि	गाथा सप्तशती
7.	नल्ल सिंह	विजयपाल रासो
8.	विद्यापति	पदावली, कीर्तिपताका, कीर्तिलता, भूपरिक्रमा
9.	अमीर खुसरो	खालिकबारी, पहेलियां, दो सुखने, गजल
10.	राजशेखर	कर्पूर मंजरी
11.	चन्दबरदायी	पृथ्वीराज रासो
12.	नरपति नाल्ह	बीसलदेव रासो
13.	कल्लोल	ढोला मारू रा दूहा

भक्तिकाल

- 'हरडेवानी' दादू की रचनाओं का संग्रह है।
- 'चित्रावली' की रचना उस्मान ने की थी।
- भक्तिकालीन 'प्रेमाश्रयी शाखा' पर सूफी मत का प्रभाव सर्वाधिक है।
- 'मधुमालती' के रचयिता मंझन है।
- तुलसीदास जी के गुरु का नाम 'नरहरि दास' था।
- गोस्वामी तुलसीदास ने 'रामचरित मानस' की रचना दोहा-चौपाई पद्धति पर की है।
- तुलसीदास की रचना 'विनय पत्रिका' गीत पद्धति पर आधारित है।
- 'बीजक' ग्रंथ का प्रणयन सधुक्कड़ी भाषा में किया गया है।
- 'विनय-पत्रिका' की भाषा ब्रजभाषा है।
- चंदायन की रचना मुल्ला दाऊद ने की थी।
- चंदायन की रचना से हिन्दी में सूफी काव्य परम्परा का सूत्रपात होता है।
- पद्‌मावत की भाषा अवधी है।

- ✦ रामचरित मानस की भाषा अवधी है।
- ✦ ब्रज भक्तिकालीन हिन्दी काव्य की सर्वाधिक प्रमुख भाषा है।
- ✦ तुलसीदास की 'गीतावली' ब्रजभाषा में लिखी गयी है।
- ✦ मीराबाई पर सूफियों का प्रभाव था।
- ✦ 'गीत-गोविंद' के रचयिता जयदेव हैं।

भक्तिकाव्य के प्रमुख रचनाकार तथा उनकी रचनायें

क्र.सं	रचनाकार	रचनायें
1.	कबीर	बीजक
2.	नाभादास	भक्तमाल
3.	दादू	हरडेवानी
4.	मूल्ला दाउद	चंदायन
5.	मंझन	मधुमालती
6.	उसमान	चित्रावली
7.	जायसी	पद्मावत, चित्रलेखा, अखरावट, कहरनामा
8.	नरपति व्यास	नल दमयन्ती
9.	तुलसीदास	दोहावली, जानकी मंगल, रामचरितमानस
10.	जयदेव	गीत-गोविन्द
11.	सूरदास	सूरसागर, साहित्य लहरी
12.	रसखान	प्रेमवाटिका, सुजान खान

रीतिकाल

- ✦ आचार्य रामचंद्र शुक्ल के अनुसार रीतिकाल की समय सीमा 1643 ई. से 1843 ई. के बीच है।
- ✦ मतिराम की रचना 'छंदसार' पिंगल ग्रंथ का उदाहरण है।
- ✦ रीतिकाल के प्रसिद्ध कवि भूषण की रचना 'शिवराज भूषण' अलंकार ग्रंथ का प्रमुख उदाहरण है।
- ✦ केशवदास को अलंकारवादी आचार्य कहा जाता है।
- ✦ **'करणा भरण श्रुतिभरण'** नामक काव्य का सम्बन्ध अलंकार विद्या से है।
- ✦ रीतिकाल के अधिकांश कवियों की भाषा थी–ब्रजभाषा।
- ✦ रीतिकाल के कवि घनानंद को 'साक्षात् रस मूर्ति' माना जाता है।
- ✦ 'विज्ञान गीता' उपदेशात्मक है।
- ✦ रीतिकाल के कवि पद्माकर ने भक्ति, श्रृंगार और वीर तीनों में समान अधिकार से रचना की है।
- ✦ सिखों के दसवें गुरु 'गुरु गोविंद सिंह' को रीतिकाल के रीतिमुक्त काव्य धारा का माना गया है।

रीतिकाल के प्रमुख रचनाकार तथा उनकी रचनायें

क्र.सं	रचनाकार	रचनायें
1.	चिंतामणि	पिंगल, कविकुल-कल्पतरु, रसमंजरी, काव्य-प्रकाश
2.	केशवदास	कवि प्रिया, रसिक प्रिया
3.	कृपाराम	हिततरंगिणि, रस तरंगिणि
4.	करनेस	कर्णाभरण, श्रुतिभूषण, भूपभूषण
5.	रहीम	रहीम सतसई, मदनाष्टक, श्रृंगार सोरठा, नगरशोभा
6.	मतिराम	छन्दसार, रसराज, साहित्यसार, अलंकार पंचाशिका
7.	भूषण	शिवराज भूषण, शिवा बावनी, छत्रसाल दशक, भूषण उल्लास
8.	बिहारी	बिहारी सतसई
9.	कुलपति मिश्र	रस रहस्य
10.	सुखदेव मिश्र	वृत्त विचार, छन्द विचार, रसार्णव, श्रृंगार लता
11.	पद्माकर	जगत विनोद, पद्माभरण, गंगा लहरी, प्रबोध पचासा
12.	घनानंद	इश्कलता, विरहलीला, सुजानसागर, कृपाकांड
13.	जोधराण	हम्मीर रासो
14.	गुरु गोविंद सिंह	चण्डी चरित्र, सुनीति प्रकाश, बुद्धिसागर
15.	रसखान	प्रेमवाटिका, सुजान रसखान

रीतिकाल का नामकरण करने वाले विभिन्न विद्वान

क्र.सं	विद्वान	नामकरण
1.	आचार्य शुक्ल	रीतिकाल
2.	मिश्रबंधु	अलंकृत मध्यकाल
3.	ग्रियर्सन	रीतिकाव्य
4.	विश्वनाथ प्रसाद मिश्र	श्रृंगार काल

आधुनिक काल

- ✦ आधुनिक काल में सम्मिलित हैं–भारतेन्दु युग, द्विवेदी युग, छायावादी युग, प्रगतिवादी युग तथा प्रयोगवादी युग।
- ✦ भारतेन्दु युग के प्रमुख रचनाकार हैं–भारतेन्दु हरिश्चन्द्र, बालकृष्ण भट्ट, प्रताप नारायण मिश्र, बद्रीनारायण चौधरी
- ✦ द्विवेदी युग के प्रमुख रचनाकार हैं–आचार्य महावीर प्रसाद द्विवेदी, श्रीधर पाठक, रामनरेश त्रिपाठी, अयोध्या सिंह उपाध्याय 'हरिऔध', मैथिलीशरण गुप्त, श्यामसुन्दर दास।
- ✦ छायावादी युग के प्रमुख रचनाकार हैं–जयशंकर प्रसाद, सूर्यकान्त त्रिपाठी 'निराला', सुमित्रानन्दन पंत तथा महादेवी वर्मा।

हिन्दी साहित्य के गद्य एवं पद्य से सम्बन्धित कुछ महत्त्वपूर्ण रचनाकार

सूरदास

महाप्रभु वल्लभाचार्य के शिष्य सूरदास अष्टछाप के कवियों में सर्वाधिक प्रसिद्ध हैं। उनके तीन ग्रंथो सूरसागर, साहित्य लहरी और सूर सारावली में सूरसागर सर्वाधिक लोकप्रिय ग्रंथ है। सूर 'वात्सल्य' और 'श्रृंगार' के श्रेष्ठ कवि माने जाते हैं। उनकी कविता में ब्रजभाषा का निखरा हुआ रूप है।

तुलसीदास

तुलसीदास का जन्म उत्तर प्रदेश के बाँदा जिले के राजापुर गाँव में सन् 1532 में हुआ था। रामचरितमानस, कवितावली, गीतावली, दोहावली, कृष्णगीतावली तथा विनयपत्रिका उनकी प्रमुख रचनाएं हैं। तुलसीदास ने रामचरितमानस की रचना अवधी में और विनय पत्रिका तथा कवितावली की रचना ब्रजभाषा में की। विनय पत्रिका की रचना गेय पदों में हुई है।

देव

देव का जन्म इटावा में सन् 1673 में हुआ था। रसविलास, भावविलास, काव्यरसायन, भवानीविलास आदि देव के प्रमुख ग्रंथ माने जाते हैं। देव रीतिकाल के प्रमुख कवि हैं। रीतिकालीन कविता का सम्बन्ध दरबारों, आश्रयदाताओं से था। इस कारण उसमें दरबारी संस्कृति का चित्रण अधिक हुआ है। आलंकारिकता और श्रृंगारिकता उनके काव्य की प्रमुख विशेषताएं हैं।

जयशंकर प्रसाद

जयशंकर प्रसाद का जन्म सन् 1889 में वाराणसी में हुआ। छायावादी काव्य प्रवृत्ति के प्रमुख कवियों में एक जयशंकर प्रसाद का सन् 1937 में निधन हो गया। उनकी प्रमुख काव्य-कृतियाँ हैं–चित्राधार, कानन-कुसुम, झरना, आँसू, लहर और कामायनी। अजातशत्रु, चन्द्रगुप्त, स्कंदगुप्त और ध्रुवस्वामिनी उनके नाटक हैं तथा कंकाल, तितली और इरावती उनके उपन्यास हैं।

सूर्यकांत त्रिपाठी 'निराला'

सूर्यकांत त्रिपाठी 'निराला' का जन्म बंगाल के महिषादल में सन् 1899 में हुआ। उनकी प्रमुख काव्य रचनाएं हैं–अनामिका, परिमल, गीतिका, कुकुरमुत्ता और नए पत्ते। छायावादी रचनाकारों में उन्होंने सबसे पहले मुक्त छंद का प्रयोग किया।

नागार्जुन

नागार्जुन का जन्म बिहार के दरभंगा जिले के सतलखा गाँव में सन् 1911 में हुआ। उनका मूल नाम बैद्यनाथ मिश्र था। नागार्जुन की प्रमुख काव्य-कृतियां हैं–युगधारा, सतरंगे पंखों वाली, हजार-हजार बाँहों वाली, तुमने कहा था, पुरानी जुतियों का कोरस, मैं मिलटरी का बूढ़ा घोड़ा। उनको आधुनिक कबीर भी कहा जाता है। छायावादोत्तर दौर के वे ऐसे अकेले कवि हैं, जिनकी कविता गाँव की चौपालों और साहित्यिक दुनिया में समान रूप से लोकप्रिय रही। उन्होंने छंदों में काव्य-रचना की और मुक्त छंद में भी।

रामवृक्ष बेनीपुरी

रामवृक्ष बेनीपुरी का जन्म बिहार के मुजफ्फरपुर जिले के बेनीपुर गाँव मे सन् 1899 में हुआ। उन्होंने अनेक दैनिक, साप्ताहिक एवं मासिक पत्र-पत्रिकाओं का संपादन किया। उनकी रचना-यात्रा के महत्त्वपूर्ण पड़ाव हैं–पतितो के देश में (उपन्यास); चिंता के फूल (कहानी), आम्रपाली (नाटक); माटी की मूरतें (रेखाचित्र); पैरों में पंख बांध कर (यात्रा-वृत्तांत); जंजीरें और दीवारें (संस्मरण) आदि। विशिष्ट शैलीकार होने के कारण उन्हें 'कलम का जादूगर' कहा जाता है।

महावीर प्रसाद द्विवेदी

महावीर प्रसाद द्विवेदी का जन्म सन् 1864 में ग्राम दौलतपुर, जिला राय बरेली (उत्तर प्रदेश) में हुआ। वे हिन्दी के पहले व्यवस्थित संपादक, भाषावैज्ञानिक, इतिहासकार, पुरातत्ववेत्ता अर्थशास्त्री, समाजशास्त्री एवं लेखक थे। उनकी प्रमुख कृतियां हैं–रसज्ञ रंजन, साहित्य-सीकर, साहित्य-संदर्भ, अद्भुत आलाप (निबंध संग्रह)। संपत्तिशास्त्र उनकी अर्थशास्त्र से सम्बन्धित पुस्तक है। उन्होंने कविता की भाषा के रूप में ब्रजभाषा के बदले खड़ी बोली को प्रतिष्ठित किया। हिन्दी में पहली बार समालोचना को स्थापित करने का श्रेय भी उनको जाता है।

कबीर

कबीर का जन्म काशी में हुआ था। कबीर गुरु रामानंद के शिष्य थे। उन्होंने जनचेतना और जनभावनाओं को अपने सबद और साखियों के माध्यम से जन-जन तक पहुँचाया। कबीर की भाषा को सधुक्कड़ी कहा जाता है।

मीरा

मीराबाई का जन्म जोधपुर के चोकड़ी गाँव में 1503 में हुआ माना जाता है। 13 वर्ष की आयु में मेवाड़ के महाराणा सांगा के कुंवर भोजराज से उनका विवाह हुआ। विवाह के कुछ ही वर्ष पश्चात् पहले पति, फिर पिता और एक युद्ध के दौरान स्वसुर का भी देहांत हो गया। मध्यकालीन भक्ति आंदोलन की आध्यात्मिक प्रेरणा ने जिन कवियों को जन्म दिया उनमें मीराबाई का विशिष्ट स्थान है। मीरा हिन्दी और गुजराती दोनों की कवयित्री मानी जाती हैं। मीरा संत रैदास की शिष्या थीं। मीरा की भक्ति दैन्य और माधुर्यभाव की है।

बिहारी

बिहारी का जन्म 1595 में ग्वालियर में हुआ था। बिहारी ने आचार्य केशवदास से काव्य शिक्षा पायी थी। बिहारी सतसई बिहारी की

रचना है। रीति का उन्हें भरपूर ज्ञान था। इनकी कविता शृंगार रस की है। बिहारी की भाषा बहुत कुछ शुद्ध ब्रज है पर है वह साहित्यिक। ओरक्षा में बिहारी रहीम के संपर्क में आए।

मैथिलीशरण गुप्त

1886 में झाँसी के चिरगाँव में जन्मे मैथिलीशरण गुप्त अपने जीवनकाल में ही राष्ट्रकवि के रूप में विख्यात हुए। गुप्त जी रामभक्त कवि थे। गुप्त जी की कविता की भाषा विशुद्ध खड़ी बोली है। गुप्त जी की प्रमुख कृतियां हैं–साकेत, यशोधरा, जयद्रथ वध।

सुमित्रानंदन पंत

सुमित्रानंदन पंत का जन्म 1900 ई. में वर्तमान उत्तराखंड के कौसानी-अलमोड़ा में हुआ था। वे छायावाद के प्रमुख स्तंभ माने जाते हैं। इनकी प्रमुख कृतियां हैं–वीणा, पल्लव, युगवाणी, ग्राम्या, स्वर्ण किरण, कला और बूढ़ा चांद और लोकायतन।

महादेवी वर्मा

महादेवी वर्मा का जन्म 1907 ई. में उत्तर प्रदेश के फर्रुखाबाद में हुआ था। महादेवी ने छायावाद के चार प्रमुख रचनाकारों में औरों से भिन्न अपना एक विशिष्ट स्थान बनाया। महादेवी का समस्त काव्य वेदनामय है। महादेवी की प्रमुख काव्य कृतियां हैं–नीहार, रश्मि, नीरजा, सांध्य गीत, दीपशिखा, प्रथम आयाम और अग्निरेखा तथा गद्य रचनाएं हैं–अतीत के चलचित्र, शृंखला की कड़ियाँ, स्मृति की रेखाएं, पथ के साथी, मेरा परिवार और चिंतन के क्षण।

प्रेमचंद

31 जुलाई 1880 को बनारस के करीब लमही गाँव में जन्मे धनपत राय ने उर्दू में गुलाब राय और हिन्दी में प्रेमचंद नाम से लेखन कार्य किया। उनके प्रमुख उपन्यास हैं–गोदान, गबन, प्रेमाश्रम, सेवासदन, निर्मला, कर्मभूमि, रंगभूमि, कायाकल्प, प्रतिज्ञा और मंगल सूत्र।

प्रसिद्ध रचनाएँ एवं रचनाकार

रचनाएँ	रचनाकार	रचनाएँ	रचनाकार
राग गोविन्द	मीरा बाई	माटी हो गई सोना	कन्हैया लाल मिश्र प्रभाकर
दीपशिखा	महादेवी	साकेत	मैथिलीशरण गुप्त
आखिरी कलाम	जायसी	गीता-प्रवचन	विनोबा भावे
इन्द्र धनुष रौंदे हुए	अज्ञेय	चन्द्रकान्ता	देवकीनन्दन खत्री
साहित्य लहरी	सूरदास	अंधा युग	धर्मवीर भारती
द्वापर	मैथिली शरण गुप्त	कुकुरमुत्ता	निराला
रामचरित मानस	तुलसीदास	शेष स्मृतियाँ	डॉ. रघुवीर सिंह
कर्ण	केदारनाथ मिश्र 'प्रभात'	अतीत के चलचित्र	महादेवी
बिहारी सतसई	बिहारी लाल	तितली	प्रसाद
प्रेम पत्रिका	घनानन्द	जानकी मंगल	तुलसीदास
पद्मावत	जायसी	रास पंचाध्यायी	नन्ददास
रंगभूमि	प्रेमचन्द	लोकायतन	पंत
विनय पत्रिका	तुलसीदास	हिततरंगिणी	कृपाराम
सन् बयालिस के संस्मरण	श्रीराम शर्मा	बरवै नायिका भेद	रहीम
यामा	महादेवी वर्मा	रसिकप्रिया	केशव दास
शृंखला की कड़ियाँ	महादेवी	शृंगार शिला	वृन्द
उर्वशी	दिनकर	कर्णाभरण	करनेस बन्दीजन
बाबरा अहेरी	अज्ञेय	प्रिय प्रवास	हरिऔध
बलचनमा	नागार्जुन	रामचन्द्रिका	केशवदास
साधना के पथ पर	हरिभाऊ उपाध्याय	कला और बूढ़ा चाँद	पंत
भारत भारती	मैथिलीशरण गुप्त	चिंतामणि	आचार्य शुक्ल
पैरों में पंख बाँधकर	बेनीपुरी	शृंगार सतसई	रहीम
पृथ्वी राज रासो	चन्दवरदाई	ललित ललाम	मतिराम
लाल चीन	भगवत शरण उपाध्याय	वैदेही वनवास	हरिऔध
प्रेम वाटिका	रसखान	छत्रसाल दशक	भूषण
नवरस	बाबू गुलाबराय	कंकाल	प्रसाद
प्रेम माधुरी	भारतेन्दु हरिश्चन्द्र		

रचनाएँ	रचनाकार
भाव विलास	देव
अणिमा	निराला
काव्य निर्णय	भिखारीदास
रमैनी	कबीरदास
गंगा लहरी	पद्माकर
भरतेश्वर बाहुवली रास	शालिभद्र सूरि
रसकेलिवल्ली	घनानन्द
पउम चरिउ	स्वयं भू
मदनाष्टक	रहीम
प्राकृत व्याकरण	जैनाचार्य हेमचन्द्र
जगद्विनोद	पद्माकर
वीसलदेव रास	नरपति नाल्ह
प्रेम फुलवारी	भारतेन्दु हरिश्चन्द्र
संदेश रासक	अद्द हयाण
रस कलश	हरिऔध
सुकवि कीर्तन	महावीर प्रसाद द्विवेदी
उद्धव शतक	रत्नाकर
कश्मीर सुषमा	श्रीधर पाठक
कबीर का रहस्यवाद	डॉ. राम कुमार वर्मा
पथिक	रामनरेश त्रिपाठी
मधुशाला	बच्चन
कामायनी	प्रसाद
टेढ़े-मेढ़े रास्ते	भगवती चरण वर्मा
तुलसीदास	निराला
प्रभात फेरी	नरेन्द्र शर्मा
सांध्यगीत	महादेवी
हिम किरीटिनी	माखन लाल चतुर्वेदी
युगाधार	सोहन लाल द्विवेदी
हम विषपायी जनम के	बालकृष्ण शर्मा नवीन
मौर्य विजय	सियाराम शरण गुप्त
हुँकार	दिनकर
इत्यलम्	अज्ञेय
भस्मांकुर	नागार्जुन
मैला आँचल	फणीश्वर नाथ रेणु
सिन्दूर की होली	लक्ष्मी नारायण मिश्र
छठा बेटा	उपेन्द्रनाथ अश्क
नूतन ब्रह्मचारी	बाल कृष्ण भट्ट
मादा कैक्टस	लक्ष्मी नारायण लाल
कुसुम कुमारी	किशोरी लाल गोस्वामी
ठेठ हिन्दी का ठाठ	हरिऔध
आदर्श हिन्दू	लज्जाराम मेहता
चित्रलेखा	भगवती चरण वर्मा
दादा कामरेड	यशपाल
जहाज का पंछी	इलाचन्द्र जोशी
गिरती दीवारें	उपेन्द्रनाथ अश्क

रचनाएँ	रचनाकार
मानस का हंस	अमृत लाल नागर
ब्रह्मपुत्र	देवेन्द्र सत्यार्थी
वैशाली की नगर वधू	आचार्य चतुरसेन शास्त्री
नदी यशस्वी है	नरेश मेहता
गढ़कुण्डार	वृन्दावन लाल वर्मा
राग दरबारी	श्रीलाल शुक्ल
शेखर : एक जीवनी	अज्ञेय
एक पति के नोट्स	महेन्द्र भल्ला
झूठा सच	यशपाल
दिल्ली का दलाल	पाण्डेय बेचन शर्मा 'उग्र'
नदी के द्वीप	अज्ञेय
सेवासदन	प्रेमचन्द
चुटकी भर चाँदनी	केशनी प्रसाद चौरसिया
उत्तराधिकारी	यशपाल
जहाँ लक्ष्मी कैद है	राजेन्द्र यादव
माँस का दरिया	कमलेश्वर
शिव शम्भु का चिट्ठा	बाल मुकुन्द गुप्त
अशोक के फूल	आचार्य हजारी प्रसाद द्विवेदी
लिफाफा देखकर	शैलेन्द्र नाथ श्रीवास्तव
नई पौध	नागार्जुन
नई कविता के प्रतिमान	लक्ष्मीकान्त वर्मा
डूबते मस्तूल	प्रियंवदा
साये में धूप	दुष्यन्त कुमार
कलम का सिपाही	अमृत राय
बाबा बटेसर नाथ	नागार्जुन
रश्मिरथी	दिनकर
आवारा भीड़ के खतरे	हरिशंकर परसाई
डाक बंगला	कमलेश्वर
एक चिथड़ा सुख	निर्मल वर्मा
नेताजी कहिन	मनोहर श्याम जोशी
युगवाणी	पंत
नहुष	मैथिली शरण गुप्त
ठण्डा लोहा	धर्मवीर भारती
संस्कृति के चार अध्याय	दिनकर
लहरों का राजहंस	मोहन राकेश
सुखदा	जैनेन्द्र कुमार
परशुराम की प्रतीक्षा	दिनकर
शिवा बावनी	भूषण
भारत की खोज	पं. जवाहर लाल नेहरू
मृगनयनी	वृन्दावन लाल वर्मा
जहाँगीर जस चन्द्रिका	केशवदास
तमस	भीष्म साहनी
त्याग पत्र	जैनेन्द्र कुमार
रेणुका	दिनकर

वस्तुनिष्ठ प्रश्न

1. हिन्दी साहित्य में गद्य का विकास–
A. पद्य के साथ-साथ हुआ
B. पद्य से पहले हुआ
C. पद्य के बाद हुआ
D. उपरोक्त में से कोई नहीं

2. आधुनिक काल में कुल मिलाकर–
A. पद्य और गद्य बराबर लिखा गया
B. पद्य अधिक लिखा गया
C. गद्य अधिक लिखा गया
D. उपरोक्त में से कोई नहीं

3. हिन्दी में गद्य का प्राचीनतम रूप किस ग्रंथ में मिलता है?
A. चौरासी वैष्णवन की वार्ता B. चन्द छंद बरनन की महिमा
C. पद्मपुराण D. सुख सागर

4. 'चौरासी वैष्णवन की वार्ता' का रचयिता कौन था?
A. विट्ठलनाथ जी B. गोकुलनाथ जीं
C. नाभादास जी D. गंग कवि

5. 'अष्टयाग' किसकी रचना है?
A. गोकुलनाथ जी B. विट्ठलनाथ जी
C. नाभादास जी D. रामप्रसाद निरंजनी

6. प्रारम्भिक गद्य की भाषा क्या थी?
A. अपभ्रंश B. खड़ी बोली
C. अवधी D. ब्रजभाषा

7. जैन 'पद्म पुराण' का अनुवाद किसने किया था?
A. लक्ष्मण सिंह B. दौलत राम
C. श्रद्धाराम फिल्लौरी D. रामप्रसाद निरंजनी

8. 19वीं शताब्दी के आरम्भ में हिन्दी गद्य के चार मुख्य लेखक हुए। उनमें से एक ने 'सुखसागर' लिखा। उसका नाम क्या था?
A. सदल मिश्र B. लल्लू लाल
C. सदासुख लाल D. इंशाअल्ला खां

9. 'रानी केतकी की कहानी' किसने लिखी थी?
A. इंशाअल्ला खां B. लक्ष्मण सिंह
C. बालकृष्ण भट्ट D. प्रताप नारायण मिश्र

10. नीचे पुस्तकों और लेखकों के जोड़े दिये गए हैं। इनमें एक जोड़ा गलत है। बताइये कौन-सा जोड़ा गलत है?
A. भाषा योगवशिष्ट – नाभादास
B. नासिकेतोपाख्यान – सदल मिश्र
C. शृंगार रस मंडन – विट्ठल नाथ
D. प्रेमसागर – लल्लू लाल

11. ईसाई पादरियों ने किस प्रकार हिन्दी गद्य के प्रसार में योगदान किया?
A. उन्होंने गद्य लेखन पर पुरस्कार दिये
B. स्वयं हिन्दी गद्य में लिखा
C. बाइबिल का हिन्दी में अनुवाद कराया और उसे बांटा
D. उपरोक्त सभी

12. 'सितारे हिन्द' किसकी उपाधि थी?
A. राजा शिवप्रसाद B. राजा लक्ष्मण सिंह
C. देवकीनंदन खत्री D. श्रीनिवास दास

13. 'इतिहास तिमिर नाशक' ग्रंथ का रचयिता कौन है?
A. भारतेन्दु हरिश्चन्द्र
B. बालकृष्ण भट्ट
C. राजा शिवप्रसाद 'सितारे हिन्द'
D. राजा लक्ष्मण सिंह

14. भारतेन्दु हरिश्चन्द्र के समय में हिन्दी गद्य की बड़ी उन्नति हुई। इसमें इनके दो सहयोगियों की प्रमुख भूमिका थी, जिनमें एक का नाम था प्रतापनारायण मिश्र और दूसरे का नाम था–
A. देवकीनंदन खत्री B. श्यामसुंदर दास
C. श्रीनिवास दास D. बालकृष्ण भट्ट

15. भारतेन्दु हरिश्चन्द्र के काल में हिन्दी गद्य में–
A. नाटक लिखे गये B. निबंध लिखे गये
C. आलोचना लिखी गई D. उपरोक्त तीनों लिखे गये

16. द्विवेदी युग में हिन्दी गद्य–
A. का रूप पूर्णतः स्थिर हो गया
B. उर्दू मिश्रित हो गया
C. की उपेक्षा हुई
D. में केवल कुछ कहानियां लिखी गईं

17. द्विवेदी-युग में रामचन्द्र शुक्ल ने साहित्य के किस क्षेत्र में मूल्यवान योगदान किया?
A. उपन्यास के क्षेत्र में B. कहानी के क्षेत्र में
C. नाटक के क्षेत्र में D. आलोचना के क्षेत्र में

18. मिश्र बंधु का योगदान गद्य के किस क्षेत्र में रहा?
A. नाटक के क्षेत्र में B. कहानी के क्षेत्र में
C. आलोचना के क्षेत्र में D. उपन्यास के क्षेत्र में

19. द्विवेदी युग में ही हिन्दी के महान् उपन्यासकार की रचमायें प्रकाश में आईं। वह उपन्यासकार थे–
A. जैनेन्द्र कुमार B. यशपाल
C. प्रेमचन्द D. इलाचन्द जोशी

20. छायावादी कवियों में जयशंकर प्रसाद ने गद्य की किस विधा को समृद्ध बनाया?

A. नाटक B. उपन्यास
C. निबन्ध D. कहानी

21. छायावादी कवि निराला का प्रसिद्ध उपन्यास है–

A. अलका B. चन्द्रकला
C. सावित्री D. इन्द्रा

22. महादेवी वर्मा की रचना 'अतीत के चलचित्र'–

A. कहानी संग्रह है B. उपन्यास है
C. निबन्ध-संग्रह है D. संस्मरणों का संग्रह है

23. 'भारत दुर्दशा' नाटक का लेखक कौन है?

A. भारतेन्दु हरिश्चन्द्र B. देवकीनंदन खत्री
C. बालकृष्ण भट्ट D. प्रतापनारायण मिश्र

24. 'चन्द्रकान्ता संतति' उपन्यास के कितने खण्ड निकले थे?

A. 14 खण्ड B. 8 खण्ड
C. 3 खण्ड D. 24 खण्ड

25. तिलिस्म और ऐयारी से भरे 'चंद्रकान्ता संतति' उपन्यास का सबसे बड़ा योगदान यह रहा कि–

A. उपन्यास के नए क्षेत्र खुल गए
B. हिन्दी गद्य का रूप निखर गया
C. इसी किस्म के बहुत-से उपन्यास लिखे गये
D. असंख्य लोगों ने इस उपन्यास को पढ़ने के लिए हिन्दी भाषा सीखी

26. मुंशी प्रेमचंद के 'गोदान' उपन्यास में मुख्य पात्र (हीरो) का नाम क्या है?

A. मधुवा B. होरी
C. विशाल देव D. दिव्या

27. निराला के उपन्यास 'निरूपमा' में किस समस्या का वर्णन है?

A. ग्राम्य-जीवन की वास्तविकतायें
B. दहेज प्रथा
C. मध्यवर्गीय समाज की आर्थिक विपन्नता
D. प्रादेशिक भेदभाव और सामाजिक कुरीतियां

28. कुछ विद्वान 'परीक्षा गुरु' को हिन्दी का प्रथम उपन्यास मानते हैं। इसके लेखक हैं–

A. रामचन्द्र शुक्ल B. श्रीनिवास दास
C. बालकृष्ण भट्ट D. बाबू राधाकृष्ण दास

29. बालकृष्ण भट्ट का उपन्यास 'सौ अजान एक सुजान' कैसा उपन्यास है?

A. सांस्कृतिक B. ऐतिहासिक
C. तिलिस्मी D. उपदेशात्मक

30. निम्नलिखित उपन्यासों में से कौन-सा उपन्यास अम्बिकादत्त व्यास का है?

A. नूतन ब्रह्मचारी B. मरता क्या न करता
C. मृण्मयी D. आश्चर्य वृतान्त

31. उपन्यासों के विकास के प्रारम्भिक चरण के सम्बन्ध में कौन-सा कथन सही है?

A. कुछ उपन्यास मौलिक हैं
B. कुछ उपन्यास अनूदित हैं
C. इनका लाभ यह हुआ कि मौलिक उपन्यास लेखन की प्रवृति बढ़ी
D. उपरोक्त सभी

32. निम्नलिखित उपन्यासों में से कौन-सा उपन्यास अयोध्या सिंह उपाध्याय 'हरिऔध' का नहीं है?

A. वेनिस का बाँका B. ठेठ हिन्दी का ठाठ
C. अधलिखा फूल D. रसिक लाल

33. हिन्दी के प्रथम मौलिक उपन्यासकारों में देवकीनंदन खत्री विख्यात हैं। इनका सर्वाधिक लोकप्रिय उपन्यास 'चन्द्रकान्ता संतति' है। इसके अलावा भी इनका एक अन्य उपन्यास है, जिसका नाम है–

A. अंगूठी का नगीना B. भूतनाथ
C. दिल्ली के दलाल D. युगान्तर

34. 'संन्यासी' एक प्रसिद्ध उपन्यास है। इसके लेखक का नाम है–

A. वृन्दावनलाल वर्मा B. यशपाल
C. उपेन्द्रनाथ अश्क D. इलाचन्द्र जोशी

35. निम्नलिखित उपन्यासों में से कौन-सा उपन्यास यशपालजी का नहीं है?

A. दादा कामरेड B. दिव्या
C. देशद्रोही D. भिखारिणी

36. किसको 'उपन्यास सम्राट' माना जाता है?

A. जैनेन्द्र कुमार B. यशपाल
C. उपेन्द्रनाथ अश्क D. प्रेमचंद

37. 'चित्रलेखा' एक अति लोकप्रिय उपन्यास है। इसके लेखक का नाम है–

A. चतुरसेन शास्त्री B. पाण्डेय बेचन शर्मा 'उग्र'
C. वृन्दावनलाल वर्मा D. भगवतीचरण वर्मा

38. जयशंकर प्रसाद के दो उपन्यासों में एक का नाम 'कंकाल' है, और दूसरे का–

A. तीन वर्ष B. मां
C. तितली D. वैशाली की नगरवधू

39. मुंशी प्रेमचंद के उपन्यास–

A. ऐतिहासिक हैं B. सामाजिक हैं
C. रोमांटिक हैं D. मनोवैज्ञानिक हैं

40. निम्नलिखित उपन्यासों में से कौन-सा उपन्यास प्रेमचंदजी का नहीं है?

A. गबन B. निर्मला
C. गोदान D. विसर्जन

41. 'वैशाली की नगरवधू' किसका उपन्यास है?

A. जैनेन्द्र कुमार B. चतुरसेन शास्त्री
C. वृन्दावनलाल वर्मा D. इलाचन्द्र जोशी

42. ऐतिहासिक उपन्यासों के लिए कौन-सा नाम विख्यात है?

A. यशपाल B. अज्ञेय

C. उपेन्द्रनाथ अश्क D. वृन्दावनलाल वर्मा

43. 'शेखर-एक जीवनी' किसका बहुचर्चित उपन्यास है?

A. राहुल सांकृत्यायन B. धर्मवीर भारती

C. अमृतलाल नागर D. अज्ञेय

44. नीचे कुछ उपन्यासों और उनके लेखकों के नामों के जोड़े दिये गए हैं। इनमें से कौन-सा जोड़ा सही नहीं है?

A. जयशंकर प्रसाद – तितली

B. देवकीनंदन खत्री – भूतनाथ

C. जैनेन्द्र कुमार – सुनीता

D. अज्ञेय – दिव्या

45. 'मैला आँचल' उपन्यास का लेखक कौन है?

A. फणीश्वरनाथ रेणु B. धर्मवीर भारती

C. अज्ञेय D. नरेश मेहता

46. 'शेखर-एक जीवनी' अज्ञेय का लिखा हुआ उपन्यास है। यह–

A. अपनी ऐतिहासिक पृष्ठभूमि के लिए विख्यात है

B. अपने सांस्कृतिक मूल्यों के लिए विख्यात है

C. नवीन शैली व पैनी मनोवैज्ञानिक दृष्टि के लिए विख्यात है

D. सामाजिक कुरीतियों का पर्दाफाश करने के लिए विख्यात है

47. प्रेमचन्द जी के 'गोदान' में–

A. जीवन के जीते-जागते चित्र हैं

B. जीवन की कठोर वास्तविकता का सूक्ष्म विवेचन है

C. ग्राम-जीवन की रीतियों का सूक्ष्म विवेचन है

D. उपरोक्त सभी

48. प्रसादजी के 'कंकाल' उपन्यास में–

A. सामाजिक बंधनों की विषमता और व्यक्ति की सहज प्रवृत्तियों का संघर्ष अंकित है

B. समाज-व्यवस्था प[illegible]ीखा व्यंग्य है

C. आदर्श और यथार्थ के बीच खड़ी खाई का रूप है

D. उपरोक्त सभी

49. निम्नलिखित में कौन-सा एक उपन्यास वृन्दावनलाल वर्मा का नहीं है?

A. गढ़ कुण्डार B. झांसी की रानी

C. विराटा की पद्मिनी D. देशद्रोही

50. 'बूंद और समुद्र' किसका विख्यात उपन्यास है?

A. उदय शंकर भट्ट B. फणीश्वरनाथ रेणु

C. शैलेश मटियानी D. अमृतलाल नागर

51. निम्नलिखित आंचलिक उपन्यासों में से एक फणीश्वरनाथ रेणु का नहीं है। वह है–

A. मैला आँचल B. परती परिकथा

C. द्रामा D. पल्टू बाबू रोड

52. 'चिट्ठीरसैनी' किसका प्रसिद्ध उपन्यास है?

A. उपेन्द्रनाथ अश्क B. हरिकृष्ण प्रेमी

C. शैलेश मटियानी D. यशपाल

53. 'चित्रलेखा' और 'तीन वर्ष' के अतिरिक्त भगवतीचरण वर्मा के अन्य उपन्यास हैं–

A. टेढ़े-मेढ़े रास्ते B. भूले-बिसरे चित्र

C. सीधी-सच्ची बातें D. उपरोक्त सभी

54. 'गिरती दीवारें' किसका उत्तम उपन्यास है?

A. उपेन्द्रनाथ अश्क B. धर्मवीर भारती

C. अमृतलाल नागर D. नागार्जुन

55. 'मृगनयनी' किसका उपन्यास है?

A. जैनेन्द्र कुमार का B. वृन्दावनलाल वर्मा का

C. अमृतलाल नागर का D. उपरोक्त में से कोई नहीं

56. निम्नलिखित सूची-I का सूची-II से मिलान कीजिए तथा नीचे दिए गए कूट की सहायता से सही उत्तर का चयन कीजिए :

सूची-I	सूची-II
(*a*) अपने-अपने अजनबी	1. धर्मवीर भारती
(*b*) सूरज का सातवां घोड़ा	2. अज्ञेय
(*c*) खाली कुर्सी की आत्मा	3. इलाचंद जोशी
(*d*) प्रेत और छाया	4. लक्ष्मीकान्त वर्मा

कूट :

	(*a*)	(*b*)	(*c*)	(*d*)
A.	2	1	4	3
B.	1	2	4	3
C.	1	2	3	4
D.	3	4	2	1

57. हरिवंश राय बच्चन की रचना "क्या भूलूं क्या याद करूं" किस कोटि के अन्तर्गत आती है?

A. आत्मकथा B. यात्रा वृत्तान्त

C. इंटरव्यू D. रेखाचित्र

58. महादेवी वर्मा की रचना 'पथ के साथी' किस कोटि के अन्तर्गत आती है?

A. संस्मरण B. रेखाचित्र

C. यात्रा वृत्तान्त D. जीवनी

59. नीचे कुछ रचनायें दी हुई हैं और उनके सामने उनके लेखकों के नाम हैं। कौन-सा जोड़ा गलत है?

A. अरे यायावर याद रहेगा – अज्ञेय

B. मैं इनसे मिला – पद्मसिंह शर्मा कमलेश

C. जंजीरें और दीवार – रामवृक्ष बेनीपुरी

D. माटी हो गई सोना – महादेवी वर्मा

60. धर्मवीर भारती की रचना 'ठेले पर हिमालय' किस कोटि की है?

A. जीवनी B. यात्रा वृत्तान्त

C. संस्मरण D. इंटरव्यू

61. 'एक बूंद सहसा उछली' किसका विख्यात यात्रा संस्मरण है?

A. निर्मल वर्मा का B. रामवृक्ष बेनीपुरी का

C. अज्ञेय का D. डा. रघुवंश का

62. हिन्दी की सर्वप्रथम मौलिक कहानी किसे माना जाता है?

A. इन्दुमती B. आकाशदीप

C. ग्यारह वर्ष का समय D. उसने कहा था

63. हिन्दी की सर्वप्रथम मौलिक कहानी 'इन्दुमती' का लेखक कौन था?

A. गिरिजादत्त वाजपेयी B. किशोरी लाल गोस्वामी
C. रामचन्द्र शुक्ल D. प्रताप नारायण मिश्र

64. चन्द्रधर शर्मा 'गुलेरी' की सुविख्यात कहानी कौन-सी है?

A. छाया B. उसने कहा था
C. बड़े घर की बेटी D. शतरंज के खिलाड़ी

65. प्रेमचंद का सर्वोत्कृष्ट उपन्यास कौन-सा है?

A. निर्मला B. सेवासदन
C. रंगभूमि D. गोदान

66. मुंशी प्रेमचंद ने अपने उपन्यासों में किस समस्या को प्रस्तुत किया है?

A. विधवा विवाह B. अनमेल विवाह
C. दहेज प्रथा D. उपरोक्त तीनों

67. 'मधुआ' कहानी किसकी है?

A. प्रेमचन्द की B. प्रसादजी की
C. यशपाल की D. अज्ञेय की

68. 'जार्ज पंचम की नाक' कहानी का लेखक कौन है?

A. कमलेश्वर B. हरिकृष्ण प्रेमी
C. भीष्म साहनी D. अज्ञेय

69. प्रेमचंद की 'पूस की रात' कहानी–

A. भारतीय किसान की टूटन की कहानी है
B. भारतीय मध्यवर्ग के मिथ्याभिमान की कहानी है
C. वर्ग संघर्ष की कहानी है
D. अशिक्षा के अभिशाप की कहानी है

70. प्रसादजी की मधुआ कहानी एक–

A. शराबी के हृदय-परिवर्तन की कहानी है
B. रईस की हृदयहीनता की कहानी है
C. बालक के शोषण की कहानी है
D. उपरोक्त में से कोई नहीं

71. यशपाल ने अपनी कहानी 'खच्चर और आदमी' में क्या बताया है?

A. खच्चर आदमी से श्रेष्ठ है
B. आदमी खच्चर से श्रेष्ठ है
C. जों अपने को परिस्थितियों में ढाल ले वही बच पाता है
D. मनुष्य परिस्थितियों का दास है

72. अज्ञेय की 'शरणदाता' कहानी–

A. मानव संघर्ष की कहानी है
B. साम्प्रदायिकता-विरोधी कहानी है
C. नारी ममता की कहानी है
D. उपरोक्त तीनों

73. 'कानों में कंगना' नामक कहानी का लेखक कौन है?

A. विश्वम्भर नाथ शर्मा 'कौशिक'
B. राधिकारमण प्रसाद
C. पदुमलाल पुन्नालाल बख्शी
D. रायकृष्ण दास

74. 'ताई' कहानी का लेखक कौन है?

A. वृन्दावनलाल वर्मा B. राजेन्द्र यादव
C. मन्नू भंडारी D. विश्वम्भर नाथ शर्मा 'कौशिक'

75. निम्नलिखित कहानियों में से कौन-सी कहानी उषा देवी मित्रा की लिखी हुई है?

A. भाई-बहन B. लछमा
C. अधूरा चित्र D. सान्ध्य तारा

76. 'आत्माराम' और 'पंच परमेश्वर' किसकी कहानियां हैं?

A. सुदर्शन B. शिवपूजन सहाय
C. चंडी प्रसाद 'हृदयेश' D. प्रेमचंद

77. गिरिजादत्त वाजपेयी की एक उत्तम कहानी है–

A. रानी सारंधा B. प्रतिध्वनि
C. हार की जीत D. पंडित और पंडितानी

78. 'पुरस्कार' और 'आकाशदीप' कहानियां किसकी हैं?

A. रायकृष्ण दास B. सुदर्शन
C. चन्द्रकिरण सौनरिक्सा D. जयशंकर प्रसाद

79. 'हार की जीत' नामक अत्यन्त लोकप्रिय और महान् चरित्र वाली कहानी का लेखक कौन है?

A. सुदर्शन B. चतुरसेन शास्त्री
C. विष्णु प्रभाकर D. यशपाल

80. गुलेरीजी की 'उसने कहा था' कहानी का सार क्या है?

A. अमृतसर का जन-जीवन B. युद्ध की निस्सारता
C. निःस्वार्थ बलिदान D. अपराध का मनोविज्ञान

81. 'बैताल पचीसी' और 'सिंहासनबत्तीसी' कहानियों को हिन्दी में किसने अनूदित किया?

A. लल्लू लाल B. शिवप्रसाद 'सितारे हिन्द'
C. भारतेन्दु हरिश्चन्द्र D. उपरोक्त में से कोई नहीं

82. 'रानी केतकी की कहानी' कहानी के बारे में कौन-सा कथन सही नहीं है?

A. यह कहानी ठेठ हिन्दी में है
B. इसमें रानी केतकी और उदयभान की प्रेम-कथा का वर्णन है
C. इसके लेखक सदल मिश्र हैं
D. इसके लेखक इंशाअल्ला खां हैं

83. 'राजा भोज का सपना' किसकी कहानी है?

A. शिवप्रसाद 'सितारे हिन्द' B. चतुरसेन शास्त्री
C. उषा देवी मित्रा D. सुदर्शन

84. मनोवैज्ञानिक कहानीकारों में किसकी गणना नहीं की जाती?

A. राजेन्द्र यादव B. अज्ञेय
C. इलाचन्द्र जोशी D. पाण्डेय बेचन शर्मा 'उग्र'

85. जैनेन्द्रजी कहानी के सम्बन्ध में प्रेमचंद की परिपाटी में आते हैं; क्योंकि उन्होंने अपनी कहानियों के लिए

A. मनोवैज्ञानिक विषय चुने
B. सामाजिक और पारिवारिक विषय चुने
C. राष्ट्र निर्माण के विषयों को अपनाया
D. उपरोक्त तीनों

86. 'मिठाई वाला' कहानी का लेखक कौन है?
A. भगवतीचरण वर्मा B. भगवती प्रसाद वाजपेयी
C. यशपाल D. सुदर्शन

87. निम्नलिखित कहानियों में से कौन-सी कहानी रायकृष्ण दास की है?
A. रमणी का रहस्य B. अपना-अपना भाग्य
C. नन्दिनी D. कमल की बेटी

88. प्रसाद जी की प्रथम कहानी कौन-सी थी?
A. ग्राम B. मधुआ
C. आकाशदीप D. पुरस्कार

89. निम्नलिखित में से कौन-सा कहानी संग्रह प्रसाद जी का नहीं है?
A. छाया B. आकाशदीप
C. कोठरी की बात D. प्रतिध्वनि

90. 'रक्षा बन्धन' किसकी कहानी है?
A. शिवपूजन सहाय की B. जैनेन्द्र की
C. सुदर्शन की D. कौशिक की

91. निम्नलिखित में से कौन-सा कहानी संग्रह वृन्दावनलाल वर्मा का नहीं है?
A. हर सिंगार B. दबे पांव
C. कलाकार का दण्ड D. मानुषी

92. 'नई कहानी' वर्ग के कहानीकारों में निम्न में से किसका नाम नहीं आता?
A. मोहन राकेश का B. राजेन्द्र यादव का
C. कमलेश्वर का D. विष्णु प्रभाकर का

93. 'दुलाई वाली' कहानी किसकी थी?
A. रामचन्द्र शुक्ल की
B. विश्वम्भर नाथ शर्मा 'कौशिक' की
C. प्रेमचंद की
D. वंग महिला की

94. कहानी के विकास-क्रम में महत्वपूर्ण भूमिका निभाने वाली पत्रिका का नाम है–
A. सरस्वती B. इन्दु
C. उपरोक्त दोनों D. इन्दुमती

95. जैनेन्द्रजी का चिन्तन एवं दृष्टिकोण–
A. गांधीवादी B. प्रगतिशील
C. यथार्थवादी D. साम्यवादी

96. आंचलिक कहानी संग्रह 'ठुमरी' किसका है?
A. उपेन्द्र नाथ 'अश्क' B. शैलेश मटियानी
C. रघुवीर सहाय D. फणीश्वर नाथ 'रेणु'

97. विष्णु प्रभाकर की 'अधूरी कहानी' का उद्देश्य–
A. साम्प्रदायिक सद्भाव है B. नारी-उत्थान है
C. कुंठा-उन्मूलन है D. अहंकार का पतन है

98. 'काकी' कहानी किसकी है?
A. सुदर्शन B. कौशिक
C. सियारामशरण गुप्त D. प्रेमचन्द

99. 'परदा' कहानी में यशपालजी का उद्देश्य–
A. मध्यम वर्ग की निर्धनता का वर्णन करना है
B. उन्माद की निंदा करना है
C. झूठी प्रतिष्ठाप्रियता की पोल खोलना है
D. परदा-प्रथा की बुराइयां बताना है

100. 'दो बांके' किसका कहानी संग्रह है?
A. भगवती प्रसाद वाजपेयी B. भगवतीचरण वर्मा
C. मन्नू भंडारी D. होमवती देवी

101. कालिदास के 'शकुन्तला' नाटक का हिन्दी अनुवाद किसने किया?
A. भारतेन्दु हरिश्चन्द्र B. राजा लक्ष्मण सिंह
C. बाबू गोपाल चन्द्र D. प्रताप नारायण मिश्र

102. निम्नलिखित नाटकों में से कौन-सा नाटक भारतेन्दुजी द्वारा लिखित नहीं है?
A. भारत दुर्दशा B. भारत-सौभाग्य
C. नील देवी D. अन्धेर नगरी

103. भारतेन्दुजी के 'चन्द्रावली' नाटक में–
A. भारत की दयनीय दशा का चित्रण है
B. शासन-व्यवस्था पर व्यंग्य है
C. आदर्श प्रेम का चित्रण है
D. ऐतिहासिक खोज है

104. 'दुखिनी बाला' किसका नाटक है?
A. भारतेन्दु बाबू B. राधाकृष्ण दास
C. प्रतापनारायण मिश्र D. अम्बिकादत्त व्यास

105. द्विवेदी युग में–
A. मौलिक नाटक खूब लिखे गए
B. नाटकों के अनुवाद खूब हुए
C. नाटकों का मनुष्य के जीवन में निकट का सम्बन्ध रहा
D. उपरोक्त सभी

106. द्विजेन्द्र लाल राय के बंगला नाटकों का हिन्दी अनुवाद किसने किया?
A. श्रीनिवास दास B. बाबू सीताराम
C. सत्य नारायण D. रूप नारायण

107. प्रसाद युग से पूर्व मैथिलीशरण गुप्त का कौन-सा नाटक आया था?
A. चन्द्रगुप्त B. चन्द्रहास
C. चन्द्रकला D. चन्द्रोदय

108. प्रसादजी के नाटकों में–
A. साहित्यिक भाषा है
B. ऐतिहासिक पुट है
C. भारतीय सभ्यता और संस्कृति के गौरव का चित्रण है
D. उपरोक्त सभी

109. निम्नलिखित नाटकों में से कौन-सा नाटक प्रसादजी द्वारा लिखित नहीं है?
A. राज्यश्री B. स्कन्दगुप्त
C. अजातशत्रु D. विश्वामित्र

110. उदयशंकर भट्टजी के नाटक–
A. राष्ट्रीयता प्रधान हैं B. पौराणिक हैं
C. ऐतिहासिक हैं D. अन्तर्द्वन्द्व प्रधान हैं

111. 'अम्बा' और 'मतस्यगंधा' किसके नाटक हैं?
A. हरिकृष्ण प्रेमी B. विश्वम्भर नाथ शर्मा 'कौशिक'
C. सुदर्शन D. उदय शंकर भट्ट

112. 'सिन्दूर की होली' किसका विख्यात नाटक है?
A. लक्ष्मीनारायण मिश्र B. उपेन्द्रनाथ अश्क
C. सेठ गोविन्द दास D. माखनलाल चतुर्वेदी

113. मोहन राकेश की ख्याति किस नाटक से फैली?
A. शशिगुप्त B. कर्तव्य
C. आषाढ़ का एक दिन D. रेशमी टाई

114. निम्नलिखित में से कौन-सा नाटक लक्ष्मी नारायण लाल का नहीं है?
A. अंधा कुआं B. मादा कैक्टस
C. सूखा सरोवर D. लहरों का राजहंस

115. हिन्दी का प्रथम एकांकी नाटककार कौन था?
A. प्रसादजी B. रामकुमार वर्मा
C. भगवतीचरण वर्मा D. उपेन्द्र नाथ अश्क

116. हिन्दी का सर्वप्रथम एकांकी नाटक किसे माना जाता है?
A. बड़ा आदमी B. एक बूंद
C. कारवां D. दस मिनट

117. 'देवताओं की छाया में' किसका एकांकी-संग्रह है?
A. उपेन्द्रनाथ अश्क B. रामकुमार वर्मा
C. भुवनेश्वर मिश्र D. सेठ गोविन्द दास

118. 'सबसे बड़ा आदमी' किसका एकांकी है?
A. भगवतीचरण वर्मा B. विष्णु प्रभाकर
C. जगदीश चन्द्र माथुर D. उदय शंकर भट्ट

119. 'गरुड़ध्वज' और 'दशाश्वमेध' किसके विख्यात ऐतिहासिक नाटक हैं?
A. रामकुमार वर्मा B. हरिकृष्ण प्रेमी
C. उपेन्द्रनाथ अश्क D. लक्ष्मीनारायण मिश्र

120. 'युगे-युगे क्रान्ति' नाटक किसका है?
A. जगदीशचन्द्र माथुर B. सेठ गोविन्द दास
C. विष्णु प्रभाकर D. देवराज दिनेश

121. जगदीश चन्द्र माथुर का एकांकी संकलन है–
A. कुलीनता B. रंगमंच
C. भोर का तारा D. मां का बेटा

122. 'आधे-अधूरे' किसका नाटक है?
A. नरेश मेहता B. देवराज दिनेश
C. विपिन अग्रवाल D. मोहन राकेश

123. निम्नलिखित नाटकों में से कौन-सा लक्ष्मीकांत वर्मा का है?
A. आदमी का जहर B. तीन अपाहिज
C. नया-पुराना D. उपरोक्त में से कोई नहीं

124. 'पृथ्वीराज की आँखें' और 'कैलेण्डर का आखिरी पन्ना' किसके विख्यात एकांकी हैं?
A. सेठ गोविन्द दास B. विष्णु प्रभाकर
C. रामकुमार वर्मा D. उदय शंकर भट्ट

125. सेठ गोविन्द दास के एकांकियों में–
A. गांधीवादी विचारधारा है
B. राजनैतिक एवं सामाजिक समस्याओं का चित्रण है
C. ऐतिहासिक पृष्ठभूमि है
D. उपरोक्त A और B दोनों

126. सेठ गोविन्ददास के प्रसिद्ध कहानी संग्रह हैं–
A. नवरस B. एकादशी
C. स्पर्द्धा D. उपरोक्त तीनों

127. उदय शंकर भट्ट के एकांकियों में–
A. मनोविश्लेषणात्मक शैली है B. अन्तर्द्वन्द्व का चित्रण है
C. भाषा पात्रों के अनुकूल है D. उपरोक्त तीनों

128. 'एकला चलो रे' किसका विख्यात एकांकी है?
A. उदय शंकर भट्ट B. हरिकृष्ण प्रेमी
C. उपेन्द्र नाथ अश्क D. विष्णु प्रभाकर

129. 'अधिकार का रक्षक' और 'लक्ष्मी का स्वागत' किसके विख्यात एकांकी हैं?
A. हरिकृष्ण प्रेमी B. रेवती शरण शर्मा
C. धर्मवीर भारती D. उपेन्द्र नाथ अश्क

130. लोकप्रिय एकांकी 'रीढ़ की हड्डी' किसकी रचना है?
A. गिरजा कुमार माथुर B. लक्ष्मीकान्त वर्मा
C. भारत भूषण अग्रवाल D. जगदीश चन्द्र माथुर

131. 'मुझे जीने दो' किसका लोकप्रिय एकांकी है?
A. लक्ष्मीकान्त मिश्र B. जयनाथ नलिन
C. रेवती शरण शर्मा D. उपरोक्त में से कोई नहीं

132. 'लस्सी का गिलास' एकांकी का लेखक कौन है?
A. सद्गुरु शरण अवस्थी B. विष्णु प्रभाकर
C. जयनाथ नलिन D. विनोद रस्तोगी

133. निम्नलिखित में से कौन-सा एकांकी विमला लूथरा का नहीं है?
A. लाइन क्लीअर B. मुन्ने का नामकरण
C. प्रीतिभोज D. डाक्टर बीबी

134. 'रसोईघर में प्रजातंत्र' विष्णु प्रभाकर का एकांकी है, जिसमें–
A. व्यंग्य है B. क्षोभ है
C. उद्‌बोधन है D. निराशा है

135. निम्नलिखित में से किसे हिन्दी का सशक्त नाटककार माना जाता है?
A. मुंशी प्रेमचंद B. सेठ गोविन्द दास
C. जयशंकर प्रसाद D. भारतेन्दु हरिश्चन्द्र

136. 'विशाख' और 'एक घूंट' नाटकों का लेखक कौन है?
A. हरिकृष्ण प्रेमी B. लक्ष्मी नारायण लाल
C. जयशंकर प्रसाद D. उदय शंकर भट्ट

137. 'लहरों का राजहंस' किसका प्रसिद्ध नाटक है?
A. मोहन राकेश B. जगदीश चन्द्र माथुर
C. जयशंकर प्रसाद D. उदय शंकर भट्ट

138. 'आनरेरी मजिस्ट्रेट' का लेखक कौन है?
A. भगवती प्रसाद वाजपेयी B. रामकुमार वर्मा
C. देवकीनंदन खत्री D. हरिकृष्ण प्रेमी

139. 'अम्बपाली' किसकी रचना है?
A. श्रीनिवास दास B. उदय शंकर भट्ट
C. रामवृक्ष बेनीपुरी D. उपेन्द्र नाथ अश्क

140. ऐतिहासिक तथ्यों और काल्पनिक प्रसंगों के मिश्रण से जगदीश चन्द्र माथुर ने किस नाटक की रचना की?
A. क्षत्राणी B. शिवानी
C. कोणार्क D. सूर्यरथ

141. 'धूर्त रसिक लाल' का लेखक कौन है?
A. गोपालराम गहमरी B. भगवतीचरण वर्मा
C. शिवपूजन सहाय D. पं. लज्जा राम मेहता

142. प्रेमचंद रचित 'मान सरोवर' के कितने भाग हैं?
A. तीन भाग B. पांच भाग
C. सात भाग D. आठ भाग

143. 'वयं रक्षामः' किसका उपन्यास है?
A. गुरुदत्त का B. चतुरसेन शास्त्री का
C. भगवतीचरण वर्मा का D. इलाचन्द्र जोशी का

144. 'मुण्डमाल' किसकी रचना है?
A. कौशिक B. रामकुमार वर्मा
C. शिवपूजन सहाय D. उपरोक्त में से कोई नहीं

145. 'कोठरी की बात' कहानी-संग्रह किसका है?
A. यशपाल का B. जैनेन्द्र का
C. अज्ञेय का D. धर्मवीर भारती का

146. 'चारुमित्रा' और 'तैमूर की हार' किस लेखक के एकांकी हैं?
A. उपेन्द्र नाथ अश्क B. भुवनेश्वर प्रसाद
C. विष्णु प्रभाकर D. रामकुमार वर्मा

147. उपेन्द्रनाथ अश्क के अधिकांश एकांकी–
A. आदर्शवादी हैं B. राजनैतिक हैं
C. सामाजिक व पारिवारिक हैं D. मनोवैज्ञानिक हैं

148. 'यशस्वी भोज' किसका एकांकी है?
A. लक्ष्मी नारायण लाल B. देवराज दिनेश
C. उदय शंकर भट्ट D. सेठ गोविन्द दास

149. 'चिरंजीव' का विख्यात एकांकी है–
A. दो कलाकार B. माटी की मूरत
C. पंचकन्या D. दादी मां जागी

150. 'ध्रुवस्वामिनी' प्रसादजी का–
A. सामाजिक नाटक है B. ऐतिहासिक नाटक है
C. पारिवारिक नाटक है D. पौराणिक नाटक है

151. 'बादल की मृत्यु' एकांकी के रचनाकार हैं–
A. रामकुमार वर्मा B. आचार्य शुक्ल
C. प्रसाद D. विष्णु प्रभाकर

152. धर्मवीर भारती के एकांकी का नाम है–
A. निशानेबाज B. नदी प्यासी थी
C. उपर्युक्त दोनों D. इनमें से कोई नहीं

153. अमृतराय की एकांकी हैं–
A. राह चलते B. रूसी लोग
C. उपर्युक्त दोनों D. इनमें से कोई नहीं

154. 'एक साहित्यिक की डायरी' के लेखक हैं–
A. अज्ञेय B. मुक्तिबोध
C. धर्मवीर-भारती D. अमृतराय

155. उपन्यास और रचनाकारों को सुमेलित करें–

रचनाकार	उपन्यास
(*i*) राजेन्द्र यादव	(*a*) अंधेरे बंद कमरे
(*ii*) मोहन राकेश	(*b*) एक सड़क सत्तावन गलियाँ
(*iii*) कमलेश्वर	(*c*) आँचल में कोई
(*iv*) वृन्दावन लाल वर्मा	(*d*) कुलटा

कूट :

	(*i*)	(*ii*)	(*iii*)	(*iv*)
A.	(*a*)	(*d*)	(*c*)	(*b*)
B.	(*b*)	(*d*)	(*c*)	(*a*)
C.	(*d*)	(*a*)	(*b*)	(*c*)
D.	(*b*)	(*a*)	(*d*)	(*c*)

156. 'टेढ़े-मेढ़े रास्ते' उपन्यास के लेखक हैं–
A. रांगेय राघव B. अमृतराय
C. मन्नू भंडारी D. भगवती चरण वर्मा

157. 'निशिकान्त' उपन्यास के लेखक हैं–
A. विष्णु प्रभाकर B. प्रभाकर माचवे
C. नरेश मेहता D. राम नरेश त्रिपाठी

158. 'अपने-अपने अजनबी' उपन्यास लिखा है–
A. मुक्तिबोध B. अज्ञेय
C. चतुरसेन शास्त्री D. शमशेर

159. 'नागार्जुन' के उपन्यास का नाम है–
A. हीरक जयंती B. मशाल
C. जंजीरे D. उपर्युक्त सभी

160. 'दीर्घतपा' उपन्यास लिखा है–
A. नरेश मेहता B. रांगेय राघव
C. रेणु D. मन्नू भण्डारी

161. उषा प्रियंवदा के उपन्यास का नाम है–
A. हम तिनके B. पचपन खम्भे, लाल दीवारें
C. जंगल के फूल D. धूमकेतु

162. भीष्म साहनी का उपन्यास है–
A. सोनल का फूल B. वृषित
C. गंगामैया D. बसन्ती

163. अमृतराय के उपन्यास का नाम है :

A. धुँआ B. छोटे-छोटे पक्षी
C. कुरू-करू स्वाहा D. नई ईमारत

164. 'नवनिधी' किसका कहानी संग्रह है?

A. पंकज बिष्ट B. नागार्जुन
C. प्रेमचंद D. अज्ञेय

165. 'कोठरी की बात' कहानी संग्रह के रचयिता हैं–

A. मुक्तिबोध B. अज्ञेय
C. लाला श्रीनिवासदास D. प्रभाकर माचवे

166. यशपाल के कहानी संग्रह का नाम है–

A. फूलों का कुर्ता B. पिंजड़े की उड़ान
C. उपर्युक्त दोनों D. इनमें से कोई नहीं

167. 'संगीनों का साया' किसका काव्य संग्रह है?

A. प्रभाकर माचवे B. राहुल सांकृत्यायन
C. यशपाल D. अज्ञेय

168. कहानी संग्रह और लेखकों के नाम को सुमेलित करें–

लेखक	**कहानी संग्रह**
(*i*) मोहन राकेश	(*a*) फिर बसन्त आया
(*ii*) कमलेश्वर	(*b*) पहला पाठ
(*iii*) भीष्म साहनी	(*c*) नए बादल
(*iv*) उषा प्रियंवदा	(*d*) मांस का दरिया

कूट :

	(*i*)	(*ii*)	(*iii*)	(*iv*)
A.	(*d*)	(*a*)	(*c*)	(*b*)
B.	(*d*)	(*c*)	(*d*)	(*a*)
C.	(*c*)	(*d*)	(*b*)	(*a*)
D.	(*a*)	(*c*)	(*b*)	(*d*)

169. 'मेरी जीवन रेखा' आत्मकथा के रचयिता हैं–

A. हजारी प्रसाद द्विवेदी B. महावीर प्रसाद द्विवेदी
C. राहुल सांकृत्यायन D. प्रभाकर माचवे

170. 'मेरा जीवन साथी' किसकी आत्मकथा है?

A. नंद दुलारे वाजपेयी B. अज्ञेय
C. राम कुमार वर्मा D. प्रेमचंद

171. 'मेरी जीवन यात्रा' किसकी रचना है?

A. नागार्जुन B. राहुल सांकृत्यायन
C. महावीर प्रसाद द्विवेदी D. मुक्तिबोध

172. 'आत्मकथा' किसकी रचना है?

A. महात्मा गाँधी B. जवाहर लाल नेहरू
C. डॉ. राजेन्द्र प्रसाद D. लाल बहादुर शास्त्री

173. 'मेरी आत्म कहानी' आत्मकथा किसने लिखी है?

A. चतुरसेन शास्त्री B. महावीर प्रसाद द्विवेदी
C. राहुल सांकृत्यायन D. महात्मा गाँधी

174. 'सौष्ठववादी' किसकी समीक्षा पद्धति को कहा जाता है?

A. डॉ. नगेन्द्र B. हजारी प्रसाद द्विवेदी
C. आचार्य शुक्ल D. नंद दुलारे वाजपेयी

175. रामविलास शर्मा द्वारा लिखित है–

A. प्रगति और परम्परा B. भाषा, युगबोध और कविता
C. परम्परा का मूल्यांकन D. उपर्युक्त सभी

176. 'भारतीय साहित्य के इतिहास की समस्याएँ' लिखा है–

A. राम कुमार वर्मा B. राम विलास शर्मा
C. नंद दुलारे वाजपेयी D. हजारी प्रसाद द्विवेदी

177. 'पाप के पुजारी' नाटक के रचयिता हैं–

A. प्रभाकर माचवे B. दिनकर
C. रामविलास शर्मा D. नरेश मेहता

178. 'आचार्य रामचन्द्र शुक्ल और हिन्दी आलोचना' लिखा है–

A. डॉ. नगेन्द्र B. रामविलास शर्मा
C. हजारी प्रसाद द्विवेदी D. नामवर सिंह

179. 'मार्क्स, त्रात्सकी और एशियाई समाज' लिखा है–

A. रामकुमार वर्मा B. डॉ. नगेन्द्र
C. हजारी प्रसाद द्विवेदी D. राम विलास शर्मा

180. 'ऐन्दुई हिन्दुस्तानी' का प्रकाशन हुआ–

A. 1849 ई. B. 1839 ई.
C. 1832 ई. D. 1843 ई.

181. रीतिकाव्य की भूमिका किसने लिखी?

A. रामविलास शर्मा B. डॉ. राम कुमार वर्मा
C. आचार्य शुक्ल D. डॉ. नगेन्द्र

182. शुक्ल जी ने रासो शब्द की उत्पत्ति किसके द्वारा मानी है?

A. रास शब्द से B. रासक शब्द से
C. रसायण शब्द से D. रस शब्द से

183. रोमांस शब्द आया है–

A. अंग्रेजी भाषा में B. यूनानी भाषा में
C. जर्मन भाषा में D. फ्रांसीसी भाषा में

184. भारत में रोमांटिक कथाओं का उद्भव काल माना जाता है–

A. हड़प्पा काल से B. वेद काल से
C. महाभारत काल से D. आदि काल से

185. 'विकलांग श्रद्धा का दौर' के लेखक हैं–

A. प्रभाकर माचवे B. नरेश मेहता
C. बालकृष्ण भट्ट D. हरिशंकर परसाई

186. परसाई जी की कृति है–

A. निठल्ले की डायरी B. तुलसी भूषण
C. राम रत्नाकर D. रुक्मिणी परिणय

187. भारतेन्दु की भक्तिपरक रचना का नाम है–

A. भक्त सर्वस्त B. रुक्मिणी परिणय
C. उपर्युक्त दोनों D. इनमें से कोई नहीं

188. भारतेन्दु की प्रेम संबंधी रचना का नाम है–

A. प्रेम सरोवर B. प्रेम मालिका
C. उपर्युक्त दोनों D. इनमें से कोई नहीं

189. अम्बिका दत्त व्यास की प्रसिद्ध कृति का नाम है–
A. षटऋतु B. प्रेमतरंग
C. प्रेम माधुरी D. बिहारी बिहार

190. 'प्रेम पथिक' के रचनाकार हैं–
A. अम्बिकादत्त व्यास B. नरेश मेहता
C. ठाकुर जगमोहन सिंह D. वियोगी हरि

191. 'बैशाख माहात्म्य' रचना है–
A. बालकृष्ण भट्ट B. भारतेन्दु
C. वियोगी हरि D. ठाकुर जगमोहन सिंह

192. 'नये जमाने की मुकरी' के रचनाकार का नाम है–
A. अम्बिकादत्त व्यास B. प्रताप नारायण मिश्र
C. बद्रीनारायण चौधरी D. भारतेन्दु

193. 'हिन्दी हिन्दू, हिन्दुस्तान' के रचयिता हैं–
A. भारतेन्दु B. प्रतापनारायण मिश्र
C. वियोगी हरि D. अम्बिकादत्त व्यास

194. नीचे कुछ रचनाकारों और रचनाओं के नाम दिए जा रहे हैं, उन्हें सुमेलित करें।

रचनाकार	रचना
(*i*) प्रताप नारायण मिश्र	(*a*) युगल स्त्रोत
(*ii*) राधाचरण गोस्वामी	(*b*) शिवशम्भू के चिट्ठे
(*iii*) बालमुकुन्द गुप्त	(*c*) नव भक्त माल
(*iv*) बद्री नारायण चौधरी	(*d*) मन की लहर

कूट :

	(*i*)	(*ii*)	(*iii*)	(*iv*)
A.	(*d*)	(*b*)	(*a*)	(*c*)
B.	(*d*)	(*c*)	(*b*)	(*a*)
C.	(*b*)	(*c*)	(*a*)	(*d*)
D.	(*a*)	(*b*)	(*c*)	(*d*)

195. खड़ी बोली के लिए सशक्त आंदोलन चलाया–
A. आचार्य शुक्ल B. हजारी प्रसाद द्विवेदी
C. महावीर प्रसाद द्विवेदी D. नंद दुलारे वाजपेयी

196. 'विरहिणी ब्रजांगना' के रचयिता हैं–
A. माखनलाल चतुर्वेदी B. मैथिलीशरण गुप्त
C. दिनकर D. श्रीधर पाठक

197. 'मिलन' किसकी रचना है?
A. राम नरेश त्रिपाठी B. रामचरित उपाध्याय
C. श्रीधर पाठक D. मैथिलीशरण गुप्त

198. 'शाकुन्तलम्' के रचयिता हैं–
A. दिनकर B. केदारनाथ अग्रवाल
C. माखनलाल चतुर्वेदी D. मैथिलीशरण गुप्त

199. 'काव्य मंजूषा' और 'सुमन' किसकी पद्य रचनाएँ हैं?
A. महावीर प्रसाद द्विवेदी B. प्रसाद
C. मैथिलीशरण गुप्त D. अज्ञेय

200. मैथिलीशरण गुप्त की पद्य रचना है–
A. किसान B. स्वर्गीय पीपा
C. प्रेम प्रबंध D. रस कलश

201. 'पारिजात' महाकाव्य किसके द्वारा रचित है?
A. मैथिलीशरण गुप्त B. सियाराम शरण गुप्त
C. हरिऔध D. श्रीधर पाठक

202. प्रिय प्रवास आधारित है–
A. स्कंध पुराण पर B. उपनिषद पर
C. महाभारत पर D. भागवत पुराण पर

203. 'दिवस का अवसान समीप था' कहाँ से उद्धृत है?
A. प्रिय प्रवास से B. करुणालय से
C. झरना से D. युगांत से

204. सियाराम शरण गुप्त की रचना है–
A. मौर्य विजय B. रसिक रहस्य
C. विष्णुप्रिया D. स्वदेश संगीत

205. 'वीर क्षत्राणी' के रचनाकार हैं–
A. देवी प्रसाद पूर्ण B. सियाराम शरण गुप्त
C. लाला भगवानदीन D. रामचरित उपाध्याय

206. 'महामानव' प्रबंध काव्य किसने लिखा?
A. मोहन लाल महतो वियोगी B. गुरुभक्त सिंह
C. मैथिलीशरण गुप्त D. ठाकुर प्रसाद सिंह

207. 'छायावाद को स्थूल के प्रति सूक्ष्म का विद्रोह' किसने माना है–
A. आचार्य शुक्ल B. हजारी प्रसाद द्विवेदी
C. नंद दुलारे वाजपेयी D. डॉ॰ नगेन्द्र

208. छायावाद पर किसका प्रभाव है?
A. द्वैतवाद का B. अद्वैतवाद का
C. विशिष्ट द्वैतवाद का D. मार्क्सवाद का

209. किसे 'भारतीय आत्मा' कहा जाता है?
A. दिनकर B. मैथिलीशरण गुप्त
C. प्रसाद D. माखनलाल चतुर्वेदी

210. 'उच्छ्वास' किसका काव्य संग्रह है?
A. प्रसाद B. निराला
C. हरिऔध D. पंत

211. छायावाद की प्रथम कृति का नाम है–
A. आँसू B. गुंजन
C. झरना D. पल्लव

212. रजत शिखर और शिल्पी किसके द्वारा लिखे गए?
A. निराला द्वारा B. प्रसाद द्वारा
C. पंत द्वारा D. महादेवी वर्मा

213. 'ग्रंथि' काव्य संग्रह के रचयिता हैं–
A. निराला B. पंत
C. मैथिलीशरण गुप्त D. प्रसाद

214. 'चित्रलेखा' के रचयिता हैं–
A. चन्द्रधर शर्मा 'गुलेरी' B. भगवती चरण वर्मा
C. जैनेन्द्र D. प्रसाद

215. बच्चन जी की प्रमुख काव्य कृति है–
A. निशा निमंत्रण B. अभिशाप
C. चित्राधार D. महाराणा का महत्व

216. 'सृजन के क्षण' किसका प्रमुख काव्य है?
A. अज्ञेय B. मुक्तिबोध
C. भगवतीचरण वर्मा D. दिनकर

217. 'महाराणा का महत्व' किसकी रचना है?
A. निराला B. प्रसाद
C. पंत D. केदारनाथ अग्रवाल

218. 'हिमकिरीटिनी' किसका प्रसिद्ध काव्य संग्रह है?
A. धूमिल B. आरसी प्रसाद सिंह
C. माखनलाल चतुर्वेदी D. दिनकर

219. 'उर्मिला' किसका काव्य संग्रह है?
A. प्रेमचंद B. भारतेंदु
C. मैथिलीशरण गुप्त D. नवीन जी

220. द्वन्द्व गीत किसका काव्य संग्रह है?
A. जगन्नाथ प्रसाद मिलिन्द B. दिनकर
C. माखनलाल चतुर्वेदी D. देवराज दिनेश

221. 'इतिहास के आँसू' काव्य संग्रह के रचयिता हैं–
A. दिनकर B. माखनलाल चतुर्वेदी
C. मैथिलीशरण गुप्त D. हरिवंश राय बच्चन

222. 'स्वर्णोदय' और 'कर्ण' किसका काव्य संग्रह है?
A. हरिऔध B. श्रीधर पाठक
C. मुक्तिबोध D. केदारनाथ मिश्र

223. 'ऋतुम्भरा' किसका काव्य संग्रह है?
A. माखन लाल चतुर्वेदी B. प्रसाद
C. सुभद्रा कुमारी चौहान D. दिनकर

224. 'मेघगीत' व 'अवन्तिका' किसका काव्य संग्रह है?
A. देवकी नंदन विभव B. जानकी वल्लभ शास्त्री
C. महेश चंद प्रसाद D. सुभद्रा कुमारी चौहान

225. 'रूप रश्मि' किसका काव्य संग्रह है?
A. हरिकृष्ण B. शम्भूनाथ सिंह
C. देवकी नंदन विभव D. नवीन

226. कवि और उनके काव्य संग्रह को सुमेलित करें–

कवि	काव्य संग्रह
(*i*) नरेन्द्र शर्मा	(*a*) प्रवास के गीत
(*ii*) उपेन्द्रनाथ 'अश्क'	(*b*) उर्मियां
(*iii*) विद्यावती कोकिल	(*c*) कुसुमांजलि
(*iv*) देवकी नंदन विभव	(*d*) सुहागिन

कूट :

	(*i*)	(*ii*)	(*iii*)	(*iv*)
A.	(*a*)	(*b*)	(*c*)	(*d*)
B.	(*d*)	(*a*)	(*c*)	(*b*)
C.	(*a*)	(*b*)	(*d*)	(*c*)
D.	(*b*)	(*d*)	(*c*)	(*a*)

227. 'आधुनिक कवि' किसका काव्य संग्रह है?
A. दिनकर B. भारतेन्दु
C. हरिऔध D. उपेन्द्रनाथ 'अश्क'

228. पेरिस में प्रगतिशील लेखक संघ की स्थापना कब हुई?
A. 1931 ई॰ B. 1932 ई॰
C. 1934 ई॰ D. 1935 ई॰

229. निराला की भिक्षुक, विधवा और बादल कविताएँ संग्रहीत हैं–
A. अनामिका में B. परिमल में
C. गीतिका में D. तुलसीदास में

230. 'मधुकण' किसका काव्य संग्रह है?
A. दिनकर B. भगवती चरण वर्मा
C. पंत D. प्रसाद

231. कालक्रम से हिन्दी के प्रथम प्रगतिवादी कवि हैं–
A. केदारनाथ अग्रवाल B. रांगेय राघव
C. रामेश्वर करूण D. रामविलास शर्मा

232. कवि और उनके द्वारा रचित काव्य संग्रह को सुमेलित करें।

कवि	काव्य संग्रह
(*i*) केदारनाथ अग्रवाल	(*a*) युगधारा
(*ii*) नागार्जुन	(*b*) रूप तरंग
(*iii*) रामविलास शर्मा	(*c*) नींद के बादल
(*iv*) शिवमंगल सिंह	(*d*) कल्लोल

कूट :

	(*i*)	(*ii*)	(*iii*)	(*iv*)
A.	(*a*)	(*b*)	(*d*)	(*c*)
B.	(*a*)	(*c*)	(*b*)	(*d*)
C.	(*d*)	(*a*)	(*c*)	(*b*)
D.	(*b*)	(*c*)	(*a*)	(*d*)

233. 'अजेय खण्डहर' काव्य संग्रह है–
A. रांगेय राधव B. नागार्जुन
C. रामविलास शर्मा D. माखनलाल चतुर्वेदी

234. 'दूब के आंसू' किसका काव्य संग्रह है?
A. रणजीत B. सुदर्शन
C. कमलेश D. मुक्तिबोध

235. 'नई कविता' नाम का प्रचार किया–
A. कमलेश ने B. डॉ॰ जगदीश गुप्त ने
C. हरिनारायण विद्रोही D. अज्ञेय ने

236. 'नई कविता' पत्रिका का संपादन वर्ष है–
A. 1952 ई॰ B. 1953 ई॰
C. 1954 ई॰ D. 1955 ई॰

237. नकेनवादी परम्परा के प्रतिनिधि कवि हैं–
A. नलिन विलोचन शर्मा B. केसरी कुमार
C. नरेश मेहता D. उपर्युक्त सभी

238. प्रतीकवाद की स्थापना कहाँ हुई?
A. इटली B. फ्रांस
C. जर्मनी D. यूनान

239. बिम्बवाद की स्थापना हुई–
A. इंग्लैंड B. यूनान
C. जर्मनी D. फ्रांस

240. दादावाद के विकसित रूप को कहते हैं–
A. प्रयोगवाद B. यथार्थवाद
C. अतियथार्थवाद D. आदर्शवाद

241. 'भग्नदूत' किसका काव्य संग्रह है?
A. मुक्तिबोध B. अज्ञेय
C. माखन लाल चतुर्वेदी D. कमलेश

242. 'मंजीर' काव्य संग्रह के रचयिता हैं–
A. प्रयाग नारायण त्रिपाठी B. दिनकर
C. गिरिजा कुमार माथुर D. रामस्वरूप चतुर्वेदी

243. 'सात गीत वर्ष' किसका काव्य संग्रह है?
A. गिरिजा कुमार माथुर B. नलिन विलोचन
C. लक्ष्मीकांत वर्मा D. धर्मवीर भारती

244. 'जागते रहो' किसका काव्य-संग्रह है?
A. गिरिजा कुमार माथुर B. केदारनाथ अग्रवाल
C. भारतभूषण अग्रवाल D. दिनकर

245. नीचे कवि और उसके काव्य संग्रह को सुमेलित करें।

कवि	काव्य संग्रह
(*i*) शमशेर	(*a*) मेपल
(*ii*) डॉ. रघुवीर सहाय	(*b*) कुछ कविताएँ, कुछ और कविताएँ
(*iii*) दुष्यंत कुमार	(*c*) लोग भूल गए हैं
(*iv*) प्रभाकर माचवे	(*d*) सूर्य का स्वागत

कूट :

	(*i*)	(*ii*)	(*iii*)	(*iv*)
A.	(*a*)	(*b*)	(*d*)	(*c*)
B.	(*b*)	(*c*)	(*a*)	(*d*)
C.	(*d*)	(*b*)	(*c*)	(*a*)
D.	(*b*)	(*c*)	(*d*)	(*a*)

246. 'चन्द्रगुप्त मौर्य' रचना की–
A. बालकृष्ण शर्मा B. श्याम नारायण प्रसाद
C. नटवर लाल सनेही D. राम खेलावन

247. 'संशय की एक रात' के रचनाकार हैं–
A. नवीन B. नरेश मेहता
C. दिनकर D. मुक्तिबोध

248. 'दिग्विजय' के रचयिता हैं–
A. अरूण पोद्धार B. आचार्य तुलसी
C. कमलेश D. बलदेव प्रसाद मिश्र

249. नीचे रचनाकार और रचनाओं को सुमेलित करें–

रचनाकार	रचना
(*i*) नागार्जुन	(*a*) सुवर्णा
(*ii*) नरेन्द्र शर्मा	(*b*) भस्मांकुर
(*iii*) परमानंद	(*c*) उत्तरायण
(*iv*) रामकुमार वर्मा	(*d*) निष्कासिका

कूट :

	(*i*)	(*ii*)	(*iii*)	(*iv*)
A.	(*b*)	(*a*)	(*c*)	(*d*)
B.	(*b*)	(*a*)	(*d*)	(*c*)
C.	(*a*)	(*d*)	(*c*)	(*b*)
D.	(*c*)	(*a*)	(*d*)	(*b*)

250. नीचे रचनाकार और रचनाओं को सुमेलित करें–

रचनाकार	रचना
(*i*) नरेश मेहता	(*a*) सत्यकाम
(*ii*) सुमित्रानंदन पंत	(*b*) प्रणभंग
(*iii*) दिनकर	(*c*) महाप्रस्थान
(*iv*) भारतभूषण अग्रवाल	(*d*) अग्निलीक

कूट :

	(*i*)	(*ii*)	(*iii*)	(*iv*)
A.	(*a*)	(*b*)	(*c*)	(*d*)
B.	(*b*)	(*a*)	(*d*)	(*c*)
C.	(*a*)	(*d*)	(*c*)	(*b*)
D.	(*c*)	(*a*)	(*d*)	(*b*)

251. नीचे दिए गए रचनाकार और रचनाओं को सुमेलित करें–

रचनाकार	रचना
(*i*) भवानी प्रसाद मिश्र	(*a*) कालजयी
(*ii*) पंत	(*b*) पुरूषोत्तम राम
(*iii*) नरेंद्र शर्मा	(*c*) द्रौपदी
(*iv*) केदार नाथ मिश्र	(*d*) ऋतुम्भरा

कूट :

	(*i*)	(*ii*)	(*iii*)	(*iv*)
A.	(*a*)	(*d*)	(*c*)	(*b*)
B.	(*a*)	(*b*)	(*d*)	(*c*)
C.	(*c*)	(*a*)	(*d*)	(*b*)
D.	(*a*)	(*b*)	(*c*)	(*d*)

252. 'सारथी' के रचनाकार हैं–
A. अनूप शर्मा B. भारतभूषण अग्रवाल
C. राम गोपाल शर्मा D. नरेन्द्र शर्मा

253. नीचे रचनाकारों और रचनाओं को सुमेलित करें?

रचनाकार	रचना
(*i*) बालकृष्ण शर्मा नवीन	(*a*) कालजयी (प्रबंध काव्य)
(*ii*) देवेन्द्र शर्मा	(*b*) प्राण अपर्ण
(*iii*) उपेन्द्रनाथ 'अश्क'	(*c*) सुनंदा (प्रबंध काव्य)
(*iv*) सियाराम शरण गुप्त	(*d*) चांदनी रात

कूट :

	(i)	(ii)	(iii)	(iv)
A.	(a)	(b)	(d)	(c)
B.	(b)	(a)	(d)	(c)
C.	(c)	(a)	(d)	(b)
D.	(d)	(b)	(a)	(c)

254. 'नई कविता' के प्रमुख कवि हैं-
A. दिनकर B. प्रसाद
C. निराला D. अज्ञेय

255. नवगीत के प्रवर्तन का श्रेय किसे है?
A. राजेन्द्र प्रसाद सिंह B. अज्ञेय
C. डॉ॰ देवराज D. शमशेर

256. प्रज्ञा नामक साहित्यिक संस्था है–
A. कोलकाता में B. इलाहाबाद में
C. दिल्ली में D. मेरठ में

257. रंगायन संस्था है–
A. मुम्बई में B. कोलकाता में
C. दिल्ली में D. हैदराबाद में

258. साहित्यिक संस्था कहाँ है?
A. मुम्बई B. दिल्ली
C. बनारस D. कोलकाता

259. नवगीत परम्परा में सर्वाधिक प्रसिद्धि किसे मिली?
A. राजेन्द्र प्रसाद सिंह B. अज्ञेय
C. नीरज D. इनमें से कोई नहीं

260. नीचे दिए गए कवि और उनके काव्य संग्रह को सुमेलित करें।

कवि	काव्य संग्रह
(i) नीरज	(a) संघर्ष
(ii) रवीन्द्र भ्रमर	(b) सोन मछरी मन बसो
(iii) राजेन्द्र प्रसाद सिंह	(c) मिट्टी बोलती है
(iv) रमेश रंजक	(d) संजीवनी कहाँ

कूट :

	(i)	(ii)	(iii)	(iv)
A.	(a)	(b)	(c)	(d)
B.	(a)	(d)	(b)	(c)
C.	(b)	(c)	(a)	(d)
D.	(a)	(b)	(d)	(c)

261. भाषा किसका साधन है?
A. लिखने का B. बोलने का
C. अध्ययन का D. अभिव्यक्ति का

262. भाषा—
A. जड़ होती है B. विकासोन्मुख होती है
C. बोधगम्य होती है D. उपर्युक्त तीनों

263. भाषा में किन शब्दों का बाहुल्य होता है?
A. तत्सम B. तद्भव
C. विदेशी D. लोक व्यवहार के

264. हिन्दी के विकास के आदिकाल में इस पर किसका प्रभाव रहा?
A. संस्कृत का B. देशज शब्दों का
C. ब्रज भाषा का D. अपभ्रंश का

265. खड़ी बोली का विकास कब हुआ?
A. आधुनिक युग में B. मध्य युग में
C. आदिकाल में D. उपर्युक्त में से कोई भी नहीं

266. अपभ्रंश भाषा का व्याकरण किसने लिखा?
A. हेमचन्द्र B. चन्द्रनाथ
C. उमानाथ D. धर्मेन्द्र

267. निम्नलिखित में से कौन-सी बिहारी बोली है?
A. ब्रज B. मैथिली
C. बुन्देली D. अवधी

268. भाषा को बोलने में किसका प्रयोग किया जाता है?
A. लिपि का B. ध्वनियों का
C. दोनों का D. दोनों में से कोई भी नहीं

269. व्याकरण—
A. भाषा की लिपि निर्धारित करता है
B. भाषा को सुबोध बनाता है
C. भाषा का रूप निर्धारित करता है
D. भाषा के वर्णों का अध्ययन करता है

270. वर्ण—
A. स्वर हैं B. व्यंजन हैं
C. ध्वनियाँ हैं D. उच्चारण हैं

271. हिन्दी में कितने वर्ण हैं?
A. 56 B. 26
C. 44 D. 36

272. स्वर/स्वरों—
A. मूल ध्वनियाँ हैं
B. को किसी अन्य ध्वनि की सहायता के बिना उच्चरित किया जा सकता है
C. की संख्या 11 है
D. उपरोक्त सभी

273. जिन स्वरों के उच्चारण में 'अ' के उच्चारण के बराबर समय लगता है, उन्हें क्या कहते हैं?
A. दीर्घ स्वर B. ह्रस्व स्वर
C. प्लुत स्वर D. पूर्ण स्वर

274. संयुक्त स्वर का एक उदाहरण है—
A. आ B. अ
C. इ D. उ

275. क् + ष =
A. श B. क्ष
C. ष D. उपर्युक्त में से कोई नहीं

276. व्यंजन तीन प्रकार के होते हैं–
(i) स्पर्श, (ii) अन्तस्थ और (iii) ....
A. ऊष्म B. कन्ठ्य
C. दन्तोष्ठ D. नासिका

277. त, थ, द, ध, का उच्चारण—
A. दाँतों के साथ जिह्वा के मेल से होता है
B. कंठ और ओठों के मेल से होता है
C. केवल ओठों से होता है
D. जीभ के प्रयोग के बिना होता है

278. एक या एक से अधिक वर्णों के संयोग से बनी ध्वनियों को क्या कहते हैं?
A. स्वर B. व्यंजन
C. शब्द D. रूढ़ि

279. व्युत्पत्ति के आधार पर शब्दों के तीन भेद होते हैं—
(i) रूढ़ि, (ii) यौगिक और (iii) ....
A. मिश्र B. योगरूढ़ि
C. तद्भव D. उपर्युक्त में से कोई भी नहीं

280. 'पाठशाला' शब्द किस वर्ग का है?
A. यौगिक B. रूढ़ि
C. योगरूढ़ि D. उपर्युक्त में से कोई भी नहीं

281. 'नीलकंठ' शब्द किस वर्ग का है?
A. यौगिक B. रूढ़ि
C. योगरूढ़ि D. उपर्युक्त में से कोई भी नहीं

282. जो शब्द संस्कृत के हैं और जिन्हें हिन्दी में ज्यों-का-त्यों इस्तेमाल किया जाता है, क्या कहलाते हैं?
A. तत्सम B. तद्भव
C. देशज D. उपर्युक्त में से कोई भी नहीं

283. 'अग्नि' शब्द किस वर्ग का है?
A. तत्सम B. तद्भव
C. देशज D. उपरोक्त में से कोई नहीं

284. संस्कृत मूल वाले शब्दों को जब हिन्दी में कुछ परिवर्तन के साथ इस्तेमाल किया जाता है, तो उन्हें क्या नाम दिया जाता है?
A. अविकारी B. तद्भव
C. तत्सम D. देशज

285. 'खेत' शब्द किस वर्ग का है?
A. देशज B. तत्सम
C. तद्भव D. विदेशी

286. काव्य में कितने स्थायी भाव प्रधान माने गए हैं?
A. पाँच B. सात
C. नौ D. ग्यारह

287. मन में जिसके प्रति भाव (स्थायी भाव) प्रकट होता है, इसे कहते हैं–
A. आलम्बन B. आश्रय
C. उद्दीपन D. संचारी भाव

288. संचारी भाव कितने माने गए हैं?
A. ग्यारह B. बाईस
C. तैंतीस D. सात

289. शृंगार रस का स्थायी भाव क्या है?
A. उत्साह B. शोक
C. रति D. विनोद

290. संचारी भाव
A. स्थायी भाव को पुष्ट करता है
B. स्थायी भाव के सहयोगी का काम करता है
C. अपना काम करने के बाद स्थायी भाव में ही लुप्त हो जाता है
D. उपरोक्त तीनों

291. रौद्र रस का स्थायी भाव क्या है?
A. शोक B. जुगुप्सा
C. क्रोध D. भय

292. वात्सल्य रस का स्थायी भाव क्या है?
A. स्नेह B. उत्साह
C. प्रेम D. जुगुप्सा

293. जिसके कारण हृदय में भाव प्रवृत्त होता है, वह क्या कहलाता है?
A. विभाव B. आलम्बन
C. उद्दीपन D. आश्रय

294. हास्य रस के कितने भेद हैं?
A. दो B. तीन
C. छह D. आठ

295. करुण रस का स्थायी भाव क्या है?
A. क्रोध B. भय
C. जुगुप्सा D. शोक

296. रस का आधार क्या है?
A. अनुभूति B. काव्य
C. संचारी भाव D. अलंकार

297. एक ओर अजगरहिं लखि एक ओर मृग राय।
विकल बटोही बीच ही परयौ मूरछा खाय।
उक्त पद में रस कौन-सा है?
A. करुण रस B. रौद्र रस
C. वीभत्स रस D. भयानक रस

298. जशोदा हरि पालने झुलावै।
हलरावै दुलरावै जोई सोई कछु गावै।
उक्त पद में रस कौन-सा है?
A. शृंगार रस B. वात्सल्य रस
C. वीभत्स रस D. वीर रस

299. 'क्या भाग रहा है भार देख?
तू मेरी ओर निहार देख
मैं त्याग चला निस्सार देख
अटकेगा मेरा कौन काम?
उक्त पद में रस कौन-सा है?
A. शांत रस B. वात्सल्य रस
C. रौद्र रस D. करुण रस

300. 'अखिल भुवन चर-अचर सब, हरि मुख में लखि मातु।
चकित भई गद्‌गद् वचन, विकसित दृग पुलकातु।'
उक्त पद में रस कौन-सा है?
A. शांत रस B. वात्सल्य रस
C. अदभुत रस D. वीभत्स रस

301. इसमें रस कौन-सा है–
'बरतस लालच लाल की मुरली धरी लुकाय।
सौंह करै, भौंहन हँसै, दैन कहै, नटिं जाय।।'
A. करुण रस B. हास्य रस
C. शृंगार रस D. रौद्र रस

302. 'सभय बिलोके लोग सब जानि जानकी भीर।
हृदय न हरप विषाद कछु बोले श्रीरघुवीर।।
उक्त पद में रस कौन-सा है?
A. शांत रस B. शृंगार रस
C. वीर रस D. करुण रस

303. वीर रस कितने प्रकार के होते हैं?
A. तीन B. चार
C. पाँच D. छह

304. रस की भांति भाव के भी शुद्ध रूप में न होने और किसी विकार या दोष से युक्त होने के कारण उसे कहा जाता है–
A. रसाभाव B. भावाभाव
C. भाव-सन्धि D. भाव सबलता

305. जहाँ किसी भाव के शांत होते ही सहसा किसी दूसरे भाव के उदय होने का वर्णन होता है, वहां–
A. भावोदय होता है B. भाव-संधि होती है
C. भावसबलता होती है D. रसाभाव होता है

306. 'चेतक के पीछे दो काल, पड़े हुए ये ले असि ढाल।
उसके पथ में उनको मार, पावन की अपनी करवान।'
उक्त पंक्तियों में क्या है?
A. भाव-संधि B. भावोदय
C. भाव-शांति D. भावाभास

307. जहाँ दो भावों का संचार एक ही साथ वर्णन किया जाए, वहाँ क्या होता है?
A. भावाभास B. रसाभाव
C. भाव-शांति D. भाव-संधि

308. जहाँ दो से अधिक परस्पर विरोधी व उदासीन भावों के गड्डमड्ड होने अथवा एक साथ उदय होने का भाव हो, वहाँ क्या होता है–
A. भावाभास B. भाव-संधि
C. भाव-शांति D. भावसबलता

309. रस में विरोध कितने प्रकार का माना जाता है?
A. दो B. तीन
C. चार D. पाँच

310. जो स्वर द्रो स्वरों के योग से उच्चारित होते हैं, वे क्या कहलाते हैं?
A. ह्रस्व B. दीर्घ
C. व्यंजन D. गुरु

311. स्वर के उच्चारण में जो समय लगता है, उस अवधि को क्या कहते हैं?
A. मात्रा B. ह्रस्व
C. लघु D. वर्ण

312. लघु वर्ण की कितनी मात्रा होती है?
A. एक B. दो
C. चार D. पाँच

313. गुरु वर्ण की कितनी मात्रा होती है?
A. एक B. दो
C. चार D. तीन

314. 'मान्धाता' शब्द में तीनों मात्राएँ क्या हैं?
A. लघु B. गुरु
C. ह्रस्व D. दीर्घ

315. छंदों में प्रवाह होना चाहिए, जिससे पढ़ने में रुकावट न हो। इस प्रवाह को क्या कहते हैं?
A. क्रम B. यति
C. गण D. गति

316. चरणों में रुकावट, विराम, विश्राम को क्या कहते हैं?
A. गण B. क्रम
C. गति D. यति

317. छंद में गण शब्द का क्या तात्पर्य है?
A. दो अक्षरों का समूह B. तीन अक्षरों का समूह
C. पाँच अक्षरों का समूह D. छह अक्षरों का समूह

318. छंदों में त्रि-वर्ण के कितने समूह हैं?
A. तीन B. चार
C. सात D. आठ

319. छंद के दो या चार चरणों के अन्त में जब कोई एक स्वर आता है, तब उस अक्षर की एकता को क्या कहते हैं?
A. यति B. गति
C. क्रम D. तुक

320. छंदों के कितने भेद हैं?
A. दो B. तीन
C. चार D. आठ

321. चौपाई छंद के एक चरण में कितनी मात्राएँ होती हैं?

A. 16 B. 14
C. 17 D. 13

322. 'खंजन मंजु तिरीछे नयननि, निज पति कहेऊ तिन्हंहि सिय सयननि।'

प्रस्तुत छंद क्या है?

A. चौपाई B. सोरठा
C. दोहा D. रोला

323. वर्णों के अनुसार गणों का मिलान कीजिए तथा दिए गए कूट की सहायता से सही उत्तर का चयन कीजिए–

गण	वर्ण
(*a*) रगण	1. सावन
(*b*) तगण	2. सौतेला
(*c*) भगण	3. साधना
(*d*) मगण	4. साकार

कूट :

	(*a*)	(*b*)	(*c*)	(*d*)
A.	3	4	1	2
B.	1	2	4	3
C.	1	2	3	4
D.	3	4	2	1

324. वर्णों के अनुसार गणों का मिलान कीजिए तथा दिए गए कूट की सहायता से सही उत्तर का चयन कीजिए–

गण	वर्ण
(*a*) नगण	1. सुभाषा
(*b*) यगण	2. सुजाता
(*c*) जगण	3. सरिता
(*d*) सगण	4. सरल

कूट :

	(*a*)	(*b*)	(*c*)	(*d*)
A.	2	1	4	3
B.	4	2	1	3
C.	1	2	3	4
D.	3	4	2	1

325. मगण गण में गण का क्या लक्षण है?

A. पहला वर्ण गुरु B. बीच वर्ण गुरु
C. अन्त वर्ण गुरु D. तीनों वर्ण गुरु

326. तगण गण में गण का क्या लक्षण है?

A. अन्त का वर्ण लघु B. बीच का वर्ण लघु
C. तीनों वर्ण लघु D. पहला वर्ण लघु

327. जगण गण में गण का क्या लक्षण है?

A. बीच का वर्ण लघु B. बीच का वर्ण गुरु
C. अन्त का वर्ण लघु D. अन्त का वर्ण गुरु

328. निम्न में अर्द्धमात्रिक छंद कौन-सा है?

A. दोहा B. रोला
C. सोरठा D. चौपाई

329. निम्न में अर्द्धसममात्रिक छंद कौन-सा है?

A. दोहा B. रोला
C. सोरठा D. कुण्डलिया

330. छंदों में विषम चरणों से तात्पर्य है–

A. पहला और दूसरा चरण
B. दूसरा और तीसरा चरण
C. पहला और चौथा चरण
D. पहला और तीसरा चरण

उत्तरमाला

1	2	3	4	5	6	7	8	9	10
C	C	A	B	C	D	B	C	A	A
11	**12**	**13**	**14**	**15**	**16**	**17**	**18**	**19**	**20**
C	A	C	D	D	A	D	C	C	A
21	**22**	**23**	**24**	**25**	**26**	**27**	**28**	**29**	**30**
A	D	A	D	D	B	D	B	D	D
31	**32**	**33**	**34**	**35**	**36**	**37**	**38**	**39**	**40**
D	D	B	D	D	D	D	C	B	D
41	**42**	**43**	**44**	**45**	**46**	**47**	**48**	**49**	**50**
B	D	D	D	A	C	D	A	D	D
51	**52**	**53**	**54**	**55**	**56**	**57**	**58**	**59**	**60**
C	C	D	A	B	A	A	A	D	B
61	**62**	**63**	**64**	**65**	**66**	**67**	**68**	**69**	**70**
C	A	B	B	D	D	B	A	A	A
71	**72**	**73**	**74**	**75**	**76**	**77**	**78**	**79**	**80**
C	A	B	D	D	D	D	D	A	C
81	**82**	**83**	**84**	**85**	**86**	**87**	**88**	**89**	**90**
A	C	A	A	B	B	A	A	C	D

91	92	93	94	95	96	97	98	99	100
D	D	D	C	A	D	A	C	C	B
101	102	103	104	105	106	107	108	109	110
B	B	C	B	B	D	B	D	D	B
111	112	113	114	115	116	117	118	119	120
D	A	C	D	A	B	A	A	D	C
121	122	123	124	125	126	127	128	129	130
C	D	A	C	D	D	D	A	D	D
131	132	133	134	135	136	137	138	139	140
C	C	D	A	C	C	A	A	C	C
141	142	143	144	145	146	147	148	149	150
D	D	B	C	C	D	C	B	D	B
151	152	153	154	155	156	157	158	159	160
A	B	C	B	C	D	A	B	A	C
161	162	163	164	165	166	167	168	169	170
B	D	A	C	B	C	A	C	B	D
171	172	173	174	175	176	177	178	179	180
B	C	A	D	D	B	C	B	D	B
181	182	183	184	185	186	187	188	189	190
D	C	D	C	D	A	A	C	D	D
191	192	193	194	195	196	197	198	199	200
B	D	B	B	C	B	A	D	A	A
201	202	203	204	205	206	207	208	209	210
C	D	A	A	C	D	D	B	D	D
211	212	213	214	215	216	217	218	219	220
C	C	B	B	A	A	B	C	D	B
221	222	223	224	225	226	227	228	229	230
A	D	C	B	B	C	C	D	B	B
231	232	233	234	235	236	237	238	239	240
C	B	A	C	B	C	D	B	A	C
241	242	243	244	245	246	247	248	249	250
B	C	D	C	D	D	B	C	B	C
251	252	253	254	255	256	257	258	259	260
D	C	B	D	A	C	A	D	C	D
261	262	263	264	265	266	267	268	269	270
D	B	D	D	A	A	B	B	C	C
271	272	273	274	275	276	277	278	279	280
C	D	B	A	B	A	A	C	B	A
281	282	283	284	285	286	287	288	289	290
C	A	A	B	C	C	A	C	C	D
291	292	293	294	295	296	297	298	299	300
C	A	C	C	D	A	D	B	A	C
301	302	303	304	305	306	307	308	309	310
B	C	B	B	A	B	D	D	B	B
311	312	313	314	315	316	317	318	319	320
A	A	B	B	D	D	B	D	D	C
321	322	323	324	325	326	327	328	329	330
A	A	A	B	D	A	B	A	C	D

❑❑❑

ENGLISH

Section-I: Language
Section-II: Literature

SECTION-I

LANGUAGE

1 Unseen Passages for Comprehension

INTRODUCTION

Comprehension means the act of comprehending or the capacity of the mind to understand. In the examination papers, questions on comprehension test are included to judge the ability of the aspirants to understand the given passage.

In the English language paper, questions on comprehension test are very important for the aspirants appearing in the competitive examinations. Therefore, they should try to learn how to solve these questions. Practice of solving these questions will greatly help them in the examination.

Directions: *In this chapter few passages for comprehension test are given. Read the passages carefully and answer the questions given after each passage. Each question is provided with four alternative answers and they are marked as 'A', 'B', 'C', and 'D'. Out of the four alternatives, choose the correct answer according to the context of the passage.*

PASSAGE-1

This is the age of the Machine, Machines are everywhere, in the fields, in the factory, at home, in the street, in the city, in the country, every where. To fly, it is not necessary to have wings; there are machines. The swim under the sea, it is not necessary to have gills; there are machines. To kill our fellowmen in overwhelming numbers, there are machines. Petrol machines alone provide ten times more power than all human beings in the world. In the busiest countries, each individual has six hundred human slaves in his machines.

What are the consequences of this abnormal power? Before the War, it looked as though it might be possible, for the first time in history to provide food and clothing and shelter for the teeming population of the world—every man, woman and child. This would have been the greatest triumphs of science. And yet, if you remember, we saw the world crammed, full of food and people hungry. Today, the larders are bare and millions, starving. That's the war, you would say. When the machines of peace once more begin to ....

1. According to the passage, which of the following is not necessary to fly?
   A. Wings B. Arms
   C. Feet D. Machines
2. Petrol machinery is used to provide:
   A. ten times more power than human beings in the world
   B. less power than human beings in the world
   C. as much power as human beings in the world
   D. None of the above is correct
3. What could be one of the greatest triumphs of science?
   A. to provide food, clothing and shelter to everyone
   B. none would get food, clothing and shelter
   C. only rich people would get food, clothing and shelter
   D. people would get only clothing
4. This is the age of the:
   A. machine B. animal husbandry
   C. agriculture D. wars
5. The machine age produces:
   A. goods
   B. food
   C. goods but avoids the consequences
   D. None of the above

PASSAGE-2

What are the good parts of our civilization? First and foremost there are order and safety. If today I have a quarrel with another man, I do not get beaten merely because I am physically weaker and he can knock me down. I go to law and the law will decide as fairly as it can between the two of us. Thus in disputes between man and man. Right has taken the place of might. Moreover, the law protects me from robbery and violence. Nobody may come and break into my house, steal my books or run off with my children. Of course, there are burglars, but they are very rare and the law punishes them whenever, it catches them.

It is difficult for us to realize how much this safety means. Without safety those higher activities of mankind which make up civilization could not go on. The inventor could not invent, the scientist find out or the artist make beautiful things. Hence, order and safety, although they are not themselves civilization, are things without which civilization could be impossible. They are as necessary to our civilization as the air we breathe is to us; and we have grown so used to them that we do not notice them any more than we notice the air.

1. The first and foremost good parts of civilization are:
   A. order and insecurity
   B. only insecurity
   C. order and safety
   D. insecurity and lawlessness
2. In disputes between man and man:
   A. right has taken the place of might
   B. might has taken the place of right
   C. might is right
   D. None of the above
3. According to the passage, the burglars are:
   A. many B. rare
   C. found nowhere D. not punished
4. An artist can create beautiful things only if:
   A. there is disorder
   B. there is no safety
   C. there is safety
   D. there is neither safety nor order
5. According to the writer, man does not notice order and safety as:
   A. he does not notice the air he breathes
   B. he does not notice the food he eats
   C. he does not notice the shelter he needs
   D. None of the above is correct

PASSAGE-3

The purpose of education is to make the student an expert in his subject. This must be clearly understood, and mere muddling through lessons and lectures and books and passing examination are relegated to secondary importance as means to the end—which is excellence in the field choosen.

But there are so many fields, and no man can become an expert in all the fields. It is necessary to decide which fields are the important ones that a man should know well.

It is clear that one's own work is the most important. This has been realised and modern civilization has accordingly provided vocational education. It is now possible to acquire high professional skill in the various fields, medicine, engineering production, commerce and so on—but with good and bad mixed together, and no standard for guidance.

1. The purpose of education is to make the student:
   A. an expert in all fields
   B. an expert in his subject
   C. only capable of earning
   D. confident only
2. What, according to the writer, is the end?
   A. excellence in the field chosen
   B. passing the examination
   C. earning more and more money
   D. cramming lectures and books
3. According to the passage, can a man become an expert in all fields?
   A. Yes B. Partially yes
   C. Sometimes D. No
4. According to the writer, which of the following is the most important work?
   A. someone else's work B. one's own work
   C. nobody's work D. everyone's work
5. The modern civilization has provided
   A. vocational education B. art of conversation
   C. adult education D. higher education

PASSAGE-4

English education, which was introduced in India in the earlier part of the nineteenth century, established her cultural contact with the West. Priot to this, India had for centuries remaind in a state of isolation, although in very early times she had sent out cultural missions to the other Asiatic countries. India really began to borrow from the West and assimilate new ideas on an extensive scale only after the British had taken up the direction of her educational policy.

It is true that Western education at first exerted an unsettling influence on young men and led to errors in life and conduct. They hated everything Indian, aped western manners and modes of life, and forgot their glorious past. There were scholars who ignored modern Indian languages, avoided classical Indian literature, and made a fetish of speaking and writing English.

1. When was English education introduced in India?
   A. in the twentieth century
   B. in the later part of the nineteenth century
   C. in the earlier part of the nineteenth century
   D. in the eighteenth century
2. When did India begin to borrow from the West?
   A. after the British had taken up the direction of her educational policy
   B. before the British had taken up the direction of her educational policy
   C. in the twentieth century
   D. None of the above is correct

3. What did India send out to other Asiatic countries?
   A. economic mission B. military forces
   C. cultural missions D. None of these

4. Western education exerted an unsettling influence on:
   A. old men B. young men
   C. old women D. children

5. Young men forgot their:
   A. glorious past B. present
   C. future D. originality

PASSAGE-5

We all wish to change the structure of existing society, usher in a Sarvodaya society—one where there is equality and the fullest freedom—as early as possible. The problem is, how are we to build such a one in our country? Had Gandhiji been here, he would have shown us the way. Under his inspiration we worked and fought for our independence. When we achieved freedom his disciples became the Government of the country, and from that time I was considering whether it was possible to set up a society of Gandhiji's conception by legislation or through political power and leadership.

After independence the whole country looked at Delhi for action, I do not know, how many believe that the State Government is capable of establishing Sarvodaya society. For myself, as the years passed, I became more and more convinced that looking to Delhi was not Gandhiji's way. In Delhi we observe the normal processes of Parliamentary Democracy: there is a ruling party, there is an Opposition, there are elections, there is the rule of the majority, and all the rest. But the people have realised that through the administrative machinery and by legislative enactment we cannot create the society of our dreams. No doubt, state action can create a socialist society; it cannot make the real, the ideal of 'Sarvodya' on earth.

1. The writer wants to change the structure of existing society because:
   A. he wants to bring in a modern society
   B. he wants to westernise the structure of existing society
   C. he wants to usher in a 'Sarvodya society'
   D. he wants nothing new

2. The writer fought for independence under the inspiration of
   A. Pt. Nehru B. Lal Bahadur Shastri
   C. Indira Gandhi D. Gandhiji

3. According to the writer, is State Government able to establish the society of our dreams?
   A. No B. Yes
   C. Partially so D. Always

4. What do we observe in Delhi?
   A. 'Sarvodaya society'
   B. Normal processes of Parliamentary Democracy
   C. Monopoly of ruling party
   D. An ideal administration

5. What can state action do?
   A. It can create 'Sarvodaya society'
   B. It can create chaos
   C. It can create socialist society
   D. It can create an ideal world

PASSAGE-6

Each nation has its own peculiar character which distinguishes it from others. But the peoples of the world have, more points in which they are all like each other than points in which they are different. One type of person that is common in every country is the one who always tries to do as little as he possibly can and to get as much in return as he can. His opposite, the man who is in the habit of doing more than is strictly necessary and is ready to accept what is offered in return, is rare everywhere.

Both these types are usually unconscious of their character. The man who avoids effort is always talking about his 'rights'; he appears to think that society owes him a pleasant easy life. The man who is always doing more than his sheer talks of 'duties' feels that the individual is in debt to society, and not society to the individual. As a result of their view, neither of these men thinks that he behaves at all strangely.

1. What type of person is common in every nation?
   A. A person who wants to do little and get more
   B. A person who wants to do more and get little
   C. Each person is different
   D. There is no such type of person that is common in every country

2. A person doing more and getting little:
   A. is rare everywhere
   B. is found in our country
   C. is common in all countries
   D. is found nowhere

3. The man who talks about his 'rights':
   A. avoids meeting other people
   B. avoids hard work
   C. knows his duties well
   D. believes in hard work

4. The man who talks of 'duties':
   A. is always hard working
   B. avoids hard work
   C. does not know his duties well
   D. always thinks of his 'right' first

5. Which one of the following thinks that the individual is in debt to the society?
   A. a person who talks of his 'rights only'
   B. a person who is always doing more than his sheer talks of 'duties'
   C. every citizen of the country
   D. a person who talks of his 'duties' only

PASSAGE-7

But I do recommend some game as a part of recreation. As long as I could see to play and sufficient leisure, I enjoyed immensely the game of real or court tennis, a very ancient game, requiring activity as well as skill, a game in which Americans may take interest and some pride, becuase for the first time, at any rate in the recent history of the game, an amateur is champion of the world and that amateur is an American. The English are sometimes criticized for paying too much attention to games. Football is a national game in America as well as in England but I do not suppose that either you or we think that our soldier fought any worse in the war of having been fond of football. I put games definitely as a desirable part of recreation, and I would say: have one or more games of which you are fond, but let them at any rate in youth be games which test the stamina, the staying power and the activity of the whole body, as well as skill.

Sport shall be mentioned next. I have had a liking for more than one form of sport, but an actual passion for salmon and trout fishing. Salmon fishing, as I have enjoyed it, fishing not from a boat but from one's feet, either on the bank or wading deep in the stream, is a glorious and sustained exercise for the whole body, as well as being an exciting sport; but many of my friends do not care for it. To them, I say, as one who was fond of George Meredith's novels once said to a man who complained that he should not read them, 'why should you?' If you do not care for fishing, do not fish. Why should you? but if we are to be on equal terms and you are to be on the same happy level as I have been, then find something for yourself which you like as much as I like fishing.

1. According to the writer, games are a part of:
A. enjoyment B. leisure
C. recreation D. earning

2. Court tennis requires:
A. activity only
B. skill only
C. both activity and skill
D. less skill and more activity

3. Football is a national game in:
A. America only B. England only
C. America and England D. China

4. The writer recommends games for the youth which test the:
A. stamina
B. staying power and activity of the whole body
C. skill
D. All of the above

5. Salmon fishing is:
A. an exciting sport B. a dull sport
C. a terrible sport D. not worth enjoying

PASSAGE-8

The history of civilization shows how man always has to choose between making the right and wrong use of the discoveries of science. This has never been more true than in our own age. In a brief period amazing discoveries have been made and applied to practical purpose.

It would be ungrateful not to recognize how immense are the boons, which science has given to mankind. It has brought within the reach of multitudes benefits and advantages which only a short time ago were the privilege of the few. It has shown how malnutrition, hunger and disease can be overcome. It has not only lengthened life but it has deepened its quality. Fields of knowledge, experience and recration open in the past only a few, have been thrown open to millions. Through the work of science the ordinary man today has been given the opportunity of a longer and fuller life then was over possible to his grandparents.

1. Amazing discoveries of science have been made:
A. in a brief period B. in a long period
C. in our forefathers' age D. in centuries

2. The boons of science are:
A. few B. found nowhere
C. immense D. very few

3. Which of the following can be overcome with the help of science?
A. Malnutrition B. Disease
C. Hunger D. All of these

4. Science provides a chance of:
A. shorter and fuller life
B. longer and fuller life
C. longer and dull life
D. None of these

5. What on the whole, has science done to mankind?
A. It has reduced the quality of our life
B. It has shortened our life
C. It has deepened the quality of life
D. It has done a great harm to mankind

PASSAGE-9

'A man who has no sense of history', Hitler declared, 'is like a man who has no ears or eyes.' He himself claimed to have had a passionate interest in history since his school days and he displayed considerable familiarity with the course of European history. His conversation was studded with historical references and historical parallels. More than that, Hitler's whole gamut of thought was historical and his sense of mission was derived from his sense of history.

Like his contemporary Spengler, Hitler was fascinated by the rise and fall of civilizations. He was himself born at a critical moment in European history when the liberal bourgeois world of the nineteeth century was disintegrating.

What would take its place? The future lay with the 'Jew-Bolshevik' ideology of the masses unless Europe could be saved by the Nazi racist ideology of the elite.

1. Who has no ears or eyes?
   A. A man having sense of history
   B. A man who has no sense of history
   C. A man who has extra knowledge
   D. A man having passionate interest in history
2. Hitler displayed familiarity with:
   A. scientific facts B. Indian history
   C. European history D. None of these
3. Hitler's sense of mission was derived from:
   A. his love of mankind B. his sense of history
   C. nowhere D. contemporary society
4. The rise and fall of civilization fascinated:
   A. Scientists B. Hitler
   C. Alexander the Great D. Mahatma Gandhi
5. Hitler was born at a moment when:
   A. the bourgeois world of the 19th century was integrating
   B. everything was liberally treated
   C. the bourgeois world of the 19th century was disintegrating
   D. None of these is correct

PASSAGE-10

The chief limitation of natural science is that it is not human. But we have to live with human beings including ourselves—and nearly all the problems of life are human, whereas the problems and subject matter of physics, chemistry and biology are not. When we enter their laboratories, we find litle human there, except ourselves and our fellow-workers. We are in a world of cells, elements, atoms (or whatever substitute for them the latest analysis reveals). There are obvious dangers in living in such a world. It is too unlike the world of men to be a good preparation for it; the fundamental reality in that world is human personality; the ideal society is a community of such personalities, self-controlling, self-developing, self-respecting and respecting others. But natural science is not concerned with personality, at least in this sense and in these relations; and there is a risk that when we return to the human world, we may be inclined to ignore its difference from the laboratory, and even to treat men as if they were elements or cells. It is perhaps their training which explains why some scientists are sympathetic towards communism.

Some people turn to communism because it offers them a positive faith in an age of scepticism, makes their decision for them and, once accepted, relieves them of the painful task of thinking for themselves. Materialistic scientists are attracted to communism for a different reason. Its drastic methods resemble those inanimate material with atoms and cells, manipulating and controlling them in the interest of a great overriding end. It is this control and manipulation that makes the triumphs of science possible; and it seems natural to apply a similar technique to social and political problems, and so achieve more rapid and effective results than the tedious methods of persuasion allow. This technique appears to offer the quickest way to a better and more rational world, and in so good a cause it seems wrong to be too tender with individual personalities and consciences.

1. The chief limitation of natural science is that it is:
   A. immoral B. spiritual
   C. human D. not human
2. In the laboratories, we are in the world of:
   A. the cells
   B. the skeletons
   C. cells, elements and atoms
   D. None of the above is correct
3. Why do people turn to communism?
   A. It offers them a positive faith
   B. It makes their decision for them
   C. It relieves them of the painful task of thinking
   D. All of the above
4. The control and manipulation of atoms and cells make:
   A. the triumph of science possible
   B. the trimph of science impossible
   C. the solution of all problems
   D. Nonc of the above is correct
5. Political and social problems can also be solved with:
   A. the technique of control and manipulation
   B. tenderness
   C. rudeness
   D. All of the above

PASSAGE-11

Great thinkers, though universal in their teachings, can be properly understood only in relation to their times. Buddha has been widely misunderstood. He has been widely acclaimed by positivists, agnostics, atheists and ethical humanists, as preaching their philosophy. Buddha's teachings can be correctly appreciated by understanding India of the 6th century B.C. in which he lived and this is a difficult task.

In the 6th century India, there were different schools of thought but all the schools agreed on transmigration of souls, the philosophy of Karma and man's final goal of Nirvana. Buddha accepted these doctrines though he denied dogmatic theologies. But Buddha's contribution was the stress on the supremacy of the ethical. He laid stress on the need for pacifying the heart and following the moral law. Suffering could be ended by silencing the appetites of the body and exercising rigid control over our emotions.

Buddha was interested, not in God but in man and human effort Man could raise himself even to divinehood by his efforts. Even-though they lacked devotional elements, Buddha's teaching are essentially religious. Buddha combined in himself spiritual profundity, moral strength and discreet intellectual reserve. With the lapse of time his service to mankind is being increasingly appreciated. His message has a meaning for all time.

1. Great thinkers can be properly understood:
A. by understanding India of 6th century B.C.
B. by correctly appreciating Buddha's teachings
C. by understanding their philosophies
D. by understanding them in relation to their time

2. According to the writer:
A. Buddha did not believe in dogmatic theologies
B. Buddha's age did not believe in transmigration of souls
C. Buddha did not contribute anything to ethics
D. Buddha did not accept doctrines

3. Rigid control over emotions:
A. will make one supreme
B. will lead one nearer to God
C. and silencing the appetites of the body could end suffering
D. will make one dogmatic

4. Buddha was interested in:
A. men and not God B. God and not man
C. man and God D. neither man nor God

5. Can we call Buddha's teachings religious?
A. No, because he did not teach about God
B. No, because they lack devotional elements
C. We cannot say
D. Yes

PASSAGE-12

It is said that wars are fought for the sake of peace. Many a politician justifies wars as being the means of bringing about stability in the international relations. So far as the aim of those who are always busy in society is concerned, their motive is not always to achieve freedom from work. Their ultimate purpose is not to be idle. To be busy is a mode of life or habit. Those who are busy in society, say, businessmen, or people in authority, politicians or statesmen, officials or employees, are all part of the continuous machine which keeps the society going.

People are busy so that different activities of a society are carried out and the wherewithals which mankind badly needs are provided. No society, however, prosperous and endowed with bounties of nature, can afford to have the objective of being idle in the long run. No doubt, advanced countries ensured minimum facilities of living and amenities of work for their workmen; they even fix their working hours so that after their busy day's life they can have some leisure at their disposal for self development or peace of mind. Yet, with the passage of time a busy society has the tendency to become busier. Even with the best computers and automations at the disposal of the modern technocrats man power continues to remain busy, as one phase of achievement leads automatically to the second phase of work. War may have the intention of peace but business is undending so long as a society has the objective of progress and does not become stationary or stagnant or decadent.

1. According to the passage, busy people:
A. want freedom work
B. want to be idle
C. do not like rest
D. are part of a machine which runs society

2. Why are people busy?
A. to carry out different activities of society
B. to provide needs of mankind
C. Both 'A' and 'B'
D. None of the above

3. Author says that:
A. no society can be idle
B. developed countries can be idle
C. underdeveloped countries can be idle
D. All of the above

4. Computers and automations:
A. have made man idle
B. could not relieve man from busy life
C. Both of the above
D. None of the above

5. With the passage of time man is becoming busier because
A. he likes to be busy
B. he is born to be busy
C. to be busy is mode of life or habit
D. All of the above

PASSAGE-13

Every individual has his value. He has virtues and qualities which need appreciation by those who come in his contact. A true appreciation has to be impartial and unbiased but while evaluating a person, there is nothing wrong in offering just praise. Just praise is only a debt and it should be duly paid at the right moment. If it is not paid, the debt stands and the person not praised feels offended.

Flattery is, however, a different phenomenon. It is more on the plus side than just an equation of a personality. By its very definition it connotes something beyond deserving. It is, however, relished by the person to whom it is tendered. When a person is given a praise beyond what he deserves, he naturally relishes such an appreciation. This is called flattery. Since it is offered when it is not obligatory on the part of a person offering it, it is termed as present. In day-to-day human relations, flattery plays an important part. It wins new friends and deepens old friendships. One most beautiful thing about flattery is that it does not cost in financial terms, yet as a present it is as valuable as any precious gift of kind. Sweet words, appropriately used, go a long way in building friendly relations.

Thus our social behaviour when guided by the advice tendered in the statement of this paragraph is likely to make us popular. We are obliged to appreciate the good points of our friends and relations but if we present them with flattering words, even if they are beyond what they deserve, we are gainers in human relations.

1. According to the writer just praise is:
A. a debt which should be paid at every moment
B. a true appreciation which is impartial and unbiased
C. offered to offend someone
D. None of the above

2. Flattery is:
A. praising beyond what someone deserves
B. is better than appreciation
C. is same as appreciation
D. is a good quality

3. Every man has got virtues for which:
A. he needs appreciation
B. he doesn't need appreciation
C. he needs flattery
D. None of the above

4. According to the passage, praise is debt and flattery is:
A. love B. hatred
C. good D. gift

5. In building friendship, sweet words:
A. are helpful
B. are dangerous
C. are most essential
D. are not at all required

PASSAGE-14

Every genius that comes to the world, achieves greatness through the capacity of taking trouble. All great men of the world who have achieved impossible things in their life time have undergone hardships, sacrifices, trials and tribulations. There is no easy victory over failure. No hard achievement is smooth and easy. History of great men reminds us that with strong determination man can achieve any thing he may set his mind upon, however impossible it may seem apparently.

A man with determination and iron-will can defeat all hurdles in the way of his mission. Even the most intelligent people suffer in life if they cannot cope with their circumstances and labour hard to achieve the goal of their life. A genius who is fired with real zeal and determination to achieve his ideal comes to possess the necessary capacity to bear the hardships, cross the hurdles and achieve the final victory. Genius and hard work go together to bring the desired results. The stage of greatness comes after many stages of frustration and disappointment. The weaker man gives way to those frustrations but the genius perseveres and holds on to their mission until they achieve the object of their life.

1. The writer feels that victory over failure:
A. is not possible B. is not good
C. is absolute D. is not easy

2. According to the passage genius implies:
A. failing again and again
B. capacity of taking trouble and hardship
C. stages of frustration and disappointment
D. escape from hardship

3. Which of the following is correct?
A. Only dull people should work hard
B. Intelligent people need not labour hard
C. Even intelligent people have to cope with circumstances
D. None of the above

4. It can be inferred that:
A. genius and hard work go together
B. genius and hard work are opposed to each other
C. genius and hard work end in frustration
D. All of the above

5. A man can-defeat all hurdles by:
A. coping with all situations
B. strong determination and iron-will
C. becoming strong
D. becoming tall

PASSAGE-15

Life is a struggle. "We live in deeds and not in years." If we rest, we rust. If we work we shine like jewels. Adventures are the essence of life but action also entails contemplation. Proper action needs the proper initiative. Napoleon took the wrong initiative and brought the downfall of France. Proper action is always taken by the wise persons. The wise persons always foreshadow the hardships for executing a policy. They become passive when they forecast that their efforts are at stake. All great leaders and diplomats take the steps keeping in view their reputation.

We should strike when the iron is hot. Some persons take the steps haphazardly with the result that they lose the opportunity and thus they are treated as fools. Angels are wise people and very particular about their action. It has been the aim of all philosophers to understand the world. After understanding, they move very gradually and not like fools who plunge into the situation without contemplation. Mr. Ayub Khan under Bhutto's influence plunged into war with India inflicting destruction to humanity. Our ex-prime

Minister Lal Bahadur Shastri gauged the situation. He responded to the challenge of Pakistan and won the battle. Fools always meddle with the situation without bringing about any change but wise persons penetrate into the matter and take the appropriate action.

1. According to the writer:
   A. Napoleon acted wisely
   B. we may rust like iron
   C. we may shine like metals
   D. leaders and diplomats act keeping in view their reputation
2. Some people are treated as fools because
   A. they act haphazardly
   B. they strike when the iron is hot
   C. they act like philosophers
   D. All of the above
3. Mr. Ayub Khan was
   A. wise to decalre war against India
   B. foolish to disobey Bhutto
   C. not wise in declaring war against India
   D. None of the above
4. What is the aim of the philosopher?
   A. To act like angels
   B. To act like Ayub Khan
   C. To act like Bhutto
   D. To understand the world
5. The passage implies that
   A. one should act quickly
   B. understanding should precede action
   C. fools penetrate into the matter
   D. None of the above

PASSAGE-16

With human beings the world ever ensnared by the performance of mechanical tasks and the pursuit of equally mechanical distractions, the time is not distant when nothing but the most abominable entertainments will succeed in steering them. If it happens so, the present civilisation will emerge as a mere imitation of the Romans in which the Romans desired more gladiators, tightrope walking elephants and fantastically rare animals to be slaughtered. This is one danger which is likely to cut at the roots of the modern civilisation because it threatens the existence of mental activities.

I would prefer to be bored by an eight hour job in an office or writing streams of words of journalism rather than be amused by the monotony of modern pleasures. It is the lack of participation which is the most damaging aspect of modern pleasures. This organised distraction combines within itself the performance of movies, gramophones, radios and the press which go a long way in killing the residue of initiative or sense of participation. Even in the case of newspapers, no mental effort is required on the part of the readers as the contents are presented in such a cut and dried manner that one need not undergo the fatigue of a single thought. Consequently for years together men continue scanning newspapers and magazines by merely moving their eyes.

If idealists failed too stem the root, in future, pleasures will take on incredibly monstrous shape.

1. The writer feels that human activities and distractions are:
   A. logical B. interesting
   C. intellectual D. mechanical
2. According to the passage entertainments
   A. relieve a man
   B. are badly needed
   C. threaten the existence of mental activities
   D. are useless
3. The writer prefers
   A. modern pleasures to office work
   B. modern pleasures to journalism
   C. neither journalism not office work
   D. journalism and office work to modern pleasures
4. Modern pleasures, according to the writer
   A. are indispensable
   B. are useless because they don't amuse men
   C. cripple the sense of participation
   D. do not make men take the initiative
5. Which of the following is correct?
   A. The author says that reading newspapers is bad
   B. Mental effort is not required in reading newspapers
   C. We should imitate Romans
   D. We should slaughter animals

ANSWERS

PASSAGE-1

1	2	3	4	5
A	A	A	A	C

PASSAGE-2

1	2	3	4	5
C	A	B	C	A

PASSAGE-3

1	2	3	4	5
B	A	D	B	A

PASSAGE-4

1	2	3	4	5
C	A	C	B	A

PASSAGE-5

1	2	3	4	5
C	D	A	B	C

PASSAGE-6

1	2	3	4	5
A	A	B	A	C

PASSAGE-7

1	2	3	4	5
C	C	C	D	A

PASSAGE-8

1	2	3	4	5
A	C	D	B	C

PASSAGE-9

1	2	3	4	5
B	C	B	B	C

PASSAGE-10

1	2	3	4	5
D	C	D	A	A

PASSAGE-11

1	2	3	4	5
A	A	C	A	D

PASSAGE-12

1	2	3	4	5
D	C	A	B	C

PASSAGE-13

1	2	3	4	5
B	A	A	D	A

PASSAGE-14

1	2	3	4	5
D	B	C	A	B

PASSAGE-15

1	2	3	4	5
D	A	C	D	B

PASSAGE-16

1	2	3	4	5
D	C	D	C	B

2 Parts of Speech

Whatever we speak is called speech. Speech comprises sentences which are composed of words. We can divide words into different classes called parts of speech, according to their use. The parts of speech are eight in number as shown in the table given below along with their definitions and examples.

Part of speech	*Definition or Function*	*Examples*
Noun	Name of a person, place, animal, quality or thing	Ram, boy, dog, pen, sun, Delhi, truth, honesty
Pronoun	Used in place of a noun	I, you, he she, they
Articles & Determiners	Points out indefinite and definite nouns	a, an, the, few, some
Adjective	Describes a noun or pronoun	big, honest, wooden, valuable, quiet, deep, soft, narrow
Adverb	Describes a verb, an adjective or another adverb	silently, widely, softly, quietly, very, carefully
Verb	Tells about action or state of something or someone	is, am, was, have, do, like, walk, work, make, throw, tell
Conjuction	Joins words, clauses or sentences	and, but, when, yet, while, else
Preposition	Links a noun or pronoun to another word	at, to, after, on for, under, over, with
Interjection	Expresses sudden feelings or emotions	Ah!, Alas!, oh!, ouch!, hi!, well!, Hurrah!

NOUNS

A word which denotes a person, a thing, an animal or a place is said to be a noun.

There are two noun numbers in English — the *Singular* and the *Plural*.

Singular Numbers : A noun that denotes one person or one thing, is said to be in the Singular number. For example — book, pencil, bird, dog, hen etc. are in singular number.

Plural Number : A noun that denotes more than one person or one thing is said to be in plural number. For example — boys, pens, lions, girls, men etc. are in plural number.

REMEMBER

Singular	*Plural*
Cat	Cats
Pen	Pens
Tree	Trees

Singular	*Plural*
Bush	Bushes
Glass	Glasses
Judge	Judges
Watch	Watches
Thief	Thieves
Scarf	Scarves
Leaf	Leaves
Half	Halves
Roof	Roofs
Gulf	Gulfs
Radio	Radios
Folio	Folios
Volcano	Volcanoes
Potato	Potatoes
Piano	Pianos
Fly	Flies
Lady	Ladies

Singular	*Plural*
Lady	Ladies
Monkey	Monkeys
Child	Children
Woman	Women
Axis	Axes
Foot	Feet
Englishman	Englishmen
Vertex	Vertices
Book	Books
Room	Rooms
Bus	Buses
Box	Boxes
Dish	Dishes
Tax	Taxes
Calf	Calves
Knife	Knives
Wife	Wives
Wolf	Wolves
Monarch	Monarchs
Hoof	Hoofs
Staff	Staffs
Bamboo	Bamboos
Hero	Heroes
Mango	Mangoes
Photo	Photos
Baby	Babies
Country	Countries
Boy	Boys
Ox	Oxen
Man	Men
Tooth	Teeth
Basis	Bases
Goose	Geese
Radius	Radii
Stimulus	Stimuli

1. Note the change in plurals of the following nouns:

Singular	*Plural*
copy	copies
baby	babies
body	bodies
family	families
fly	flies
city	cities
army	armies
bay	bays
cry	cries
duty	duties
country	countries
diary	diaries
fairy	fairies
spy	spies
storey	storeys
monkey	monkeys

2. The following nouns do not undergo any change in plural form, in general:

Singular	*Plural*
deer	deer
thousand	thousand
hundred	hundred
dozen	dozen
sheep	sheep
pair	pair
score	score
gross	gross

☛ We can write—

(*a*) thousands of men; (*b*) two pairs of shoes; (*c*) dozens of mangoes; (*d*) scores of people etc.

But—

(*a*) two thousand rupees; (*b*) three hundred men; (*c*) five dozen eggs, etc.

3. The following nouns are usually used in plural forms. They take a plural verb after them:

eatables	fetters	surroundings
riches	alms	spectacles
trousers	pants	scissors
premises	thanks	annals
congratulations	goods	shorts
tongs	pains (for troubles)	arms

4. The following are the nouns which are plural in appearance but are usually used in singular number. They are followed by a singular verb:

news	politics	physics
mathematics	economics	ethics
politics	classics	gallows
statistics	athletics	innings
mechanics	summons	mumps

5. Collective nouns often used as plurals:

public	police	cattle
audience	clergy	folk
people	poultry	nation
elite	gentry	glitterati

6. The nouns that are usually used in singular forms:

advice	hair	rice
fuel	alphabet	machinery
offspring	issue	furniture
mischief	stationery	luggage
bedding	information	abuse

7. Material nouns are always used in singular number:

gold	copper	milk
water	silk	wool

☛ They may be used in plural with a different meaning. *e.g.*, copper coins (coppers), chains or fetters (irons), cans made of tin (tins).

GENDERS

The difference in sex is denoted by Gender in grammar. The various genders are as follows:

1. **Masculine Gender :** A noun that denotes a male is said to be of the masculine gender, as man, uncle, ox, boy etc.
2. **Feminine Gender :** A noun that denotes a female is said to be of feminine gender, as woman, aunt, princess, cow etc.
3. **Common Gender :** Nouns which denote both males and females are said to be of the common gender, as friend, cousin, person, parent, baby etc.
4. **Neuter Gender :** A noun that denotes the name of object without life is said to be of neuter gender, as file, table, pencil etc.

REMEMBER

Masculine	*Feminine*
Boy	Girl
Brother	Sister
Sorcerer	Sorceress
Father-in-law	Mother-in-law
Land-lord	Land-lady
Gentleman	Lady
Earl	Countess
Sir	Madam
Emperor	Empress
Pea-cock	Pea-hen
Hero	Heroine
Mr.	Mrs.
Master	Mistress
Heir	Heiress
Lion	Lioness
Actor	Actress
Colt	Filly
Horse	Mare
Hunter	Huntress
Abbot	Abbess
Author	Authoress
Widower	Widow
He-goat	She-goat
Bridegroom	Bride
Priest	Priestess
Shepherd	Shepherdess
Stag	Hind
Son	Daughter
Murderer	Murderess
Son-in-law	Daughter-in-law
Man-servant	Maid-servant
Bachelor	Spinster
Monk	Nun
Lad	Lass
Duke	Dutchess
Milk-man	Milk-maid
Step-father	Step-mother
Viceroy	Vicerine
Governor	Governess
Wizard	Witch
Host	Hostess
Mayor	Mayoress
Buck	Doe
Dog	Bitch
Count	Countess
Prince	Princess
God	Goddess
Ox	Cow
Grand-father	Grand-mother
Milk-man	Milk-woman
Tiger	Tigress
Poet	Poetess
Nephew	Niece
Fox	Vixen

PRONOUNS

The repetition of a noun in a sentence or a set of sentences is really boring. So, instead of repeating the noun, we can use a word (for that noun) called the pronoun.

"A pronoun is a word that we use instead of a noun".

Example:

This is *Sachin. He* plays cricket.

☛ *He* is the pronoun used in place of *Sachin.*

Kinds of Pronouns

1. **Personal pronouns :** A pronoun which is used instead of the name of a person is known as a 'Personal Pronoun'. A list of the 'Personal pronouns' is listed below :

   I, my, mine, me, we (First Person)
   You, your, yours (Second Person)
   He, his, him, she, her, hers, it, its, they, their, theirs, them (Third Person)

2. **Demonstrative, Indefinite and Distributive Pronouns :**

   (*a*) Demonstrative Pronouns : Pronouns used to point out the objects to which they refer are called Demonstrative Pronouns.

   Examples:

   (*i*) *This* is a present from my uncle.
   (*ii*) *These* are merely excuses.
   (*iii*) Bembay mangoes are better than *those* of Bangaluru.

   (*b*) Indefinite Pronouns : All pronouns which refer to persons or things in a general way and do not refer to any particular person or thing are called Indefinite Pronouns.

Examples:

(*i*) *Somebody* has stolen my watch.

(*ii*) *Few* escaped unhurt.

(*iii*) Did you ask *anybody* to come?

(*c*) **Distributive Pronouns :** Each, either, neither are called distributive pronouns because they refer to persons or things one at a time. For this reason they are always singular and followed by the verb in singular.

Examples:

(*i*) *Each* of the men received a reward.

(*ii*) *These* men received *each* a reward.

(*iii*) *Either* of you can go.

3. **Relative Pronouns :** A relative pronoun refers or relates to some noun going before, which is called its Antecedent.

Examples:

(*i*) I met Hari *who* used to live here.

(*ii*) I have found the pen *which* I had lost.

(*iii*) Here is the book *that* you lent me.

4. **Interrogative Pronouns :** These pronouns, are used for asking questions.

Examples:

(*i*) *Whose* book is this?

(*ii*) *What* will all the neighbours say?

(*iii*) *Which* do you prefer, tea or coffee?

☛ Interrogative pronouns can also be used in asking indirect questions. Consider the following examples:

(*i*) I asked *who* was speaking.

(*ii*) Tell me *what* you have done.

(*iii*) Say *which* you would like best.

Behaviour of the Pronouns

1. If three pronouns are used together in the same sentence they are arranged in the following order :

2	+	3	+	1
↓		↓		↓
Second Person		Third Person		First Person

Examples:

I, you and he must help *that* poor man. (Incorrect)

You, he and I must help *that* poor man. (Correct)

2. When two or more singular nouns are joined by and, the pronoun used for them should be plural.

Examples:

Mohan and Sohan are friends. *They* play football. *They* live at Lajpat Nagar.

3. But if these nouns joined by and refer to the same person or thing, the pronoun used should be singular.

Examples:

(*i*) Delhi, the beautiful city and the capital of India, is famous for *its* historical monuments.

(*ii*) The manager and owner of the firm expressed *his* views on the demands of the workers.

4. When two nouns are used with as well as, the pronoun agrees with the first subject.

Examples:

(*a*) Mohan as well as his friends is doing *his* work.

(*b*) The students as well as their teachers are doing *their* work.

5. When two singular nouns joined by 'and' are preceded by *each* or *every,* the pronoun used must be singular and should agree in gender with the second noun.

Examples:

(*a*) Every man and every woman will do *her* best for the nation.

(*b*) Each boy and each girl went to *her* house.

6. When two nouns are joined by using 'with', the pronoun agrees with the noun coming before 'with'.

Examples:

(*a*) The boy with *his* parents has gone to see a movie.

(*b*) The children with *their* parents have gone to picnic.

7 When two different nouns are joined by either.......... or; neither .... nor, the pronoun is used according to the number and gender of the second noun.

Examples:

(*a*) Either your sister or you have done *your* work.

(*b*) Neither the students nor the teacher was in *his* class.

8. The pronoun coming after '*than*' must be in the same case as that coming before '*than*'.

Examples:

(*a*) She plays better than *me.* (Incorrect)

She plays better than *I.* (Correct)

(*b*) His elder brother is more intelligent than *him.* (Incorrect)

His elder brother is more intelligent than *he.* (Correct)

9. 'Many a' always takes a singular pronoun and singular verb.

Example:

Many a soldier has met *his* death in the battle field.

10. 'Who', 'Whose', 'Whom' are used only for persons.

Examples:

(*a*) *Who* is knocking at the door?

(*b*) *Whose* pen is this?

(*c*) *What* do you want?

11. 'Which' is used for things.

Example:

Which game do you like?

MULTIPLE CHOICE QUESTIONS

Directions: *In the following questions choose the correct options to fill in the blanks.*

1. The place was so dirty that ..... wished to run away from there.
A. everybody B. anybody
C. few D. some

2. ..... was there to help me.
A. Somebody B. Anything
C. Anybody D. Nobody

3. Is there .... to eat?
A. some B. something
C. any D. few

4. ..... of the students were making a great noise.
A. Anyone B. Somebody
C. Many D. Nobody

5. ..... of the students can solve this sum.
A. Someone B. Anybody
C. Somebody D. None

6. ...... of us should try our best to make India a heaven.
A. Any B. Somebody
C. Anybody D. All

7. ...... of us do not know the real meaning of our lives.
A. Any B. Something
C. Several D. Many

8. My .... black.
A. hairs are B. hair is
C. hairs shall D. hair will

9. She saw two .... on the last Sunday.
A. thiefs B. theifs
C. thieves D. theives

10. My sister is a ....
A. bacheloress B. bachelor
C. unmaried D. spinster

11. One is supposed to do ....
A. our duty B. their duty
C. one's duty D. his duty

12. Take anything .... you want.
A. that B. which
C. than D. then

13. I cannot tolerate ....
A. separated you B. your separation
C. separation from you D. you separated

14. He is .... faithful partner.
A. Yours B. You
C. Your D. Your's

15. Ajay is more smart than ....
A. her B. hers
C. herself D. she

16. Vivek works harder than ....
A. me B. I
C. her D. his

17. They should help ....
A. the poor people B. the poor
C. the poor persons D. the poor peoples

18. .... are mad.
A. All his sons B. His all sons
C. Sons all his D. All sons his

19. The poor fellow .... to fate.
A. resigned B. resigned himself
C. resigned itself D. resigned themselves

20. Nobody will help you but ....
A. I B. me
C. ours D. his

21. It is a good chance, You must avail .... this opportunity.
A. of B. yourself of
C. for D. from

22. The person who is elected .... my relative.
A. is B. he is
C. his D. him

23. He made ....
A. yours mention
B. mention of you
C. mention for you
D. mention about you

24. ...., I know, he is quite faithful.
A. As far as B. So far as
C. So far this D. So far so

25. It is a duty of a person to take .... for his family.
A. pain B. pains
C. pain-killers D. pained

26. She does not love .... husband.
A. his B. her
C. its D. their

27. Let .... work together.
A. him and me B. he and I
C. he and him D. I and me

28. Copper, Silver and Gold ....
A. each will do B. either will do
C. any one will do D. any will do

29. Jessica and Roma are very irregular .... habits.
A. in her B. in their
C. in its D. in every

30. One likes to enjoy .... who was a great poet.
A. The sonnets of Shakespeare

B. Shakespeare's sonnets
C. Sonnets
D. Shakespeare

31. That is the boy .... everybody loves.
A. whom B. who
C. that D. whose

32. That is the girl .... won the first prize.
A. whom B. who
C. whose D. which

33. That is the man .... purse was lost.
A. who B. whom
C. whose D. their

ANSWERS

1	2	3	4	5	6	7	8	9	10
A	D	B	C	D	D	D	B	C	D
11	**12**	**13**	**14**	**15**	**16**	**17**	**18**	**19**	**20**
C	A	C	C	D	B	B	A	B	B
21	**22**	**23**	**24**	**25**	**26**	**27**	**28**	**29**	**30**
B	A	B	A	B	B	A	C	B	A
31	**32**	**33**							
A	B	C							

ARTICLES

The family of the articles has only three members. They are : A, An and The. However, they fall under two groups :

(*a*) Definite Article (*b*) Indefinite Article

'The' is known as definite article whereas 'a' and 'an' are known as indefinite articles.

Use of the Definite Article 'The'

'The' is used before:

1. The superlative degree :
   He is the ablest man of the town.
   (ablest is a superlative degree)
2. The name of states, countries etc. having a descriptive name :
   (*i*) The J & K is a small state. (J & K is a descriptive name)
   (*ii*) He lives in the U.S.A. (U.S.A. is a descriptive name)
   (But 'the Delhi' and 'the America' are wrong because neither Delhi nor America is a descriptive name)
3. The names of the scriptures :
   The Gita is a holy book. (Gita is a scripture)
4. Name of newspapers :
   The Tribune is published from Chandigarh.
5. Name of rivers, canals, seas, oceans, bays, gulfs, groups of islands etc. :
   (*i*) The Ganga is a holy river.
   (*ii*) The Indian Ocean is the deepest ocean.
   (*iii*) The Persian Gulf is a narrow gulf.
6. The name of famous buildings :
   The Taj is one of the best buildings in India.
7. The names of nationals, sects and communities:
   (*i*) The English defeated the Germans in the World War.
   (*ii*) The rich should help the poor.
   (*iii*) The Hindus believe in the caste system.
8. Proper nouns used as common nouns :
   (*i*) Kalidas is the Shakespeare of India.
   (*ii*) Delhi is the London of India.
9. Famous historical events :
   The Industrial Revolution changed the face of England.
10. The directions and the celestial bodies :
    The sun rises in the east.
11. Titles :
    Akbar, the Great was loved by his subjects.

Do not use 'the' :

1. Before languages :
   The English is an international language. (Incorrect)
   English is an international language. (Correct)
2. Before the names of games :
   The hockey is a popular game. (Incorrect)
   Hockey is a popular game. (Correct)

Use of the Indefinite Articles 'A' and 'An'

'A' is used before :

1. All singular common nouns beginning with a consonant:
   (*i*) A boy sings a song.
   (*ii*) A black and a white cow were grazing in the field.
2. If a word begins with a vowel but gives the sound of a consonant, 'a' should be used before it :
   (*i*) He was helped in his work by a European.

(ii) He is a one-eyed man.
(iii) It is a useful work.

'An' is used as follows:

1. All singular common nouns beginning with a vowel (*i.e.*, a, e, i, o, u) :
   (i) He is an artist.
   (ii) He is an old man.
   (iii) I intend to buy an umbrella.
2. If a word starts with a consonant but gives the sound of a vowel, "an" should be used before it :
   (i) Brutus is an honourable man.
   (ii) He is an honour to his profession.
   (iii) He is an L.L.B.
   (iv) He is an M.A.
   (v) You will reach there in an hour.

Demonstratives, that, these and those :

1. The demonstrative adjectives and pronouns are for objects nearby the speaker:
   (i) This (singular) those (plural)
   and for objects far away from the speaker:
   (ii) That (singular) those (plural)
2. Demonstratives are the only adjectives that agree in number with their nouns.
   (i) That hat is nice.
   (ii) Those hats are nice.
3. When there is the idea of selection, the pronoun "one" (or "ones") often follows the demonstrative.
   (i) I want a book. I'll get this (one).
   (ii) If the demonstrative is followed by an adjective, "one"(or "ones") must be used.
   (iii) I want a book. I'll get this big one.

MULTIPLE CHOICE QUESTIONS

Directions: *In the following questions choose the correct options to fill in the blanks.*

1. .... will have to be paid for this material.
A. Half rupee B. Half a rupee
C. A half rupee D. An half rupee

2. .... is taking keen interest in India.
A. The USA B. USA
C. An USA D. A USA

3. Only .... can save our country.
A. the Hitler B. a Hitler
C. Hitler D. an Hitler

4. I can run for ....
A. hundred miles B. the hundred miles
C. a hundred miles D. an hundred miles.

5. .... man-eater has been killed.
A. The B. A
C. An D. Either A or B

6. What .... fine idea!
A. the B. an
C. a D. No article

7. .... earth is moving around the sun.
A. An B. A
C. The D. No article

8. This is .... first example while I got.
A. the B. a
C. an D. No article

9. This is .... house which was built during earthquake.
A. a B. an
C. the D. No article

10. .... America is a rich country.
A. The B. An
C. A D. No article

11. .... U.S.A. is a developed country.
A. A B. An
C. The D. No article

12. .... Bible is a holy book.
A. A B. The
C. An D. No article

13. .... rich should help the poor.
A. The B. A
C. An D. No article

14. .... Gold is a costly metal.
A. The B. A
C. An D. No article

15. Kalidas is .... Shakespeare of India.
A. a B. an
C. the D. No article

16. I cannot do .... difficult work.
A. a such B. the such
C. such the D. such a

17. How foolish .... plan it is!
A. a B. an
C. the D. No article

18. An ink is .... useful article.
A. an B. a
C. the D. No article

19. There are .... husband and wife.
A. a B. an
C. the D. No article

20. He is learning .... French
A. the B. a
C. an D. No article

ANSWERS

1	2	3	4	5	6	7	8	9	10
B	A	B	C	D	C	C	A	C	D
11	**12**	**13**	**14**	**15**	**16**	**17**	**18**	**19**	**20**
C	B	A	D	C	D	A	B	D	D

ADJECTIVES & ADVERBS

An Adjective is a word which adds something to the meaning of a noun or a pronoun.

Mridula is an *intelligent* girl.
He has a *black* goat.
He is a *brilliant* student.
She is a *clever* girl.
It is a *beautiful* picture.

In the sentences given above, the words in italics are adjectives.

An Adverb is a word which qualifies the meaning of a Verb, an Adjective or another Adverb.

(*i*) He talks *slowly.*
(*ii*) He is a *very* good student.
(*iii*) He talks *very* slowly.

In sentence (*i*), *slowly* qualifies the verb *talks.*
In sentence (*ii*), *very* qualifies the adjective *good.*
In sentence (*iii*), *very* qualifies the adverb *slowly.*

Adjectives have three degrees of comparison :

1. **Positive Degree :** It expresses the common form of an adjective.

   Example:
   Ram is a *tall* boy.
   In the above sentence *tall* is an adjective and expresses the common form.

2. **Comparative Degree :** It expresses the more of the same form.

   Example:
   Ram is *taller* than Mahesh.
   In the above sentence *taller* is an adjective that expresses the more of the common form of the adjective *tall.*

"When and How to Use" Comparative Degree?

(*a*) Comparative Degree is used when two persons or two groups of persons or things are compared.

Examples :
(*a*) He is *wiser* than his younger brother.
(*b*) This glass is *cleaner* than the other.

(*b*) When two different qualities in the same person are compared, more is used instead of 'er' to form the comparative. The formula used in this case should be :

More + Positive Degree
She is *fairer* than polite. (Incorrect)
She is *more fair* than polite. (Correct)

(*c*) When selection of one out of two persons or things is meant, the degree of comparison is followed by of and *the* is used before it.

Example:
Zia is abler of *the* two sisters.

(*d*) If two comparatives are used in the same sentence to impress upon an idea, both should be preceded by the definite article.

Examples :
(*i*) The higher you go, the cooler it is.
(*ii*) The more we get, the more we desire.

(*e*) When one person or thing is compared with another of the same kind, other is used after the comparative degree. In such sentences other is normally preceded by any or all.

Examples:
(*i*) Kalidas is greater than any dramatist. (Incorrect)
Kalidas is greater than any other dramatist. (Correct)
(*ii*) Lead is heavier than all metals. (Incorrect)
Lead is heavier than all other metals. (Correct)

(*f*) Senior, junior, superior, inferior, prior, anterior (earlier than) and posterior (later than) are always followed by 'to'.

Examples:
(*i*) Ram is senior *to* Mohan by three years.
(*ii*) That pen is inferior *to* that.
(*iii*) He is junior *to* me in rank.
(*iv*) This event was posterior *to* that.

☛ Never use *than* after the above mentioned adjectives.

Important Information

(*a*) 'Preferable' is also used as an adjective of the comparative degree. As such, it is always followed by *to* and not *a*.
Death is preferable than dishonour. (Incorrect)
Death is preferable *to* dishonour. (Correct)

(*b*) To intensify the Degree of comparison, we use *far* or *much* before the comparative.

Examples:

(*i*) This book is *far* better than that.

(*ii*) His performance was *much* better than Mohan's.

Warning: Always avoid the use of double comparatives.

Don't say: Ram is more cleverer than his younger brother.

Say: Ram is cleverer than his younger brother.

3. **Superlative Degree :** It expresses the most of the common form of an adjective.

Example:

He is the ablest man of the town.

How and when to use the Superlative Degree?

(*a*) The Superlative Degree is used when more than two persons or things are compared.

(*b*) The Superlative Degree is generally preceded by 'the' and followed by 'of' in most of the cases or otherwise.

(*c*) When an adjective of the superlative degree is preceded by a Possessive Adjective or a Noun in the Possessive case, 'the' should not be used before it.

Example:

Which is Kalidas' best play?

It will be a blunder to use 'the' before the Superlative Degree in such cases.

Don't say : Which is Kalidas' the best play.

(*d*) To intensify the degree of comparison, *by far* is used before the superlative degree.

Example:

India is *by far* the most beautiful country of the world.

☛ Always avoid the use of double superlatives.

Don't say : He is the most strongest boy in the class.

Say : He is the strongest boy in the class.

Use of some Important Adjectives

1. (*a*) '**Some**' is used as follows :

(*i*) With countable nouns where it means— a little, a small quantity.

(*ii*) In a question which shows some request.

Examples:

(*i*) There is some water in the bottle.

(*ii*) Some of the students were absent yesterday.

(*iii*) Will you have some milk?

(*iv*) Will you buy some fruit for me?

(*b*) '**Any**' is used as follows :

(*i*) In negative sentences.

(*ii*) In interrogative sentences.

(*iii*) After 'Hardly', 'Scarcely' and 'Barely'.

(*iv*) After 'If'.

Examples:

(*i*) There is not any sugar in the pot.

(*ii*) We haven't any rice in the house.

(*iii*) I have hardly any money.

(*iv*) There are scarcely any plants in this field.

(*v*) If there is any danger, blow the whistle.

2. (*a*) **Older :** Older (and oldest) are used for persons animals and things. But 'Older' and 'Oldest' refer to the persons who do not belong to the same family.

Examples:

(*i*) Radha is older than Shyama.

(*ii*) John is the oldest member of the staff.

(*b*) **Elder** (and **eldest**) are used in respect of the members of the same family like sons, daughters, brothers, sisters.

Examples:

(*i*) My elder sister is a lecturer.

(*ii*) Meenakshi is the eldest of the three sisters.

☛ (*i*) 'Elder' is not followed by 'than'.

(*ii*) 'Elder' and 'Eldest' cannot be used for things.

3. (*a*) **'Few'** is negative and is the opposite of 'Many'. It means 'not many'.

(*b*) **'A few'** is positive and means 'some at least'. It is the opposite of 'None'.

(*c*) **'The few'** means 'minority' and suggests 'whether there is'.

Examples:

(*i*) We have few holidays in school.

(*ii*) Only a few boys will pass in the examination.

(*iii*) The few poems that he wrote are very popular.

4. (*a*) **Further** means 'something additional'.

(*b*) **Farther** means 'a greater distance'.

Examples:

(*i*) Further discussion will be held in the office of the principal.

(*ii*) Amritsar is farther from Delhi than Ambala.

5. (*a*) **Little** is negative. It means, 'not much', or 'hardly any'.

(*b*) **A little** is positive. It means 'some quantity'.

(*c*) **The little** denotes quantity. It means, 'not much but all that is, or whatever quantity there is'.

Examples:

(*i*) There is little hope of his success.

(*ii*) He knows a little of everything.

(*iii*) I have spent the little money I had.

(*iv*) The little knowledge of Urdu proved very useful to me.

6. (*a*) '**Much**' expresses 'quantity'.
(*b*) '**Many**' expresses 'number'.
(*c*) **'Many a'**—'Singular noun' and 'Singular verb' are used with 'many a'.

Examples:
(*i*) There is not *much* water in the jug.
(*ii*) *Many* boys are absent today.
(*iii*) *Many* a battle has been fought on the soil of India.

7. (*a*) '**Less**' denotes 'in a small degree'.
(*b*) '**Fewer**' denotes 'number'.

Examples:
(*i*) He devotes less time to his studies.
(*ii*) There are no fewer than ten chairs in this room.

8. (*a*) '**Each**' is used for a single number of 'two persons' or 'things'.
(*b*) '**Every**' is used for a single number of 'many persons' or 'things'.

Examples:
(*i*) Each boy must take part in games.
(*ii*) There were only two poets. Each poet recited his poem.
(*iii*) Every man dies in this world.
(*iv*) Every man is expected to do his duty.

9. (*a*) '**Either**' means one of the two or both.
(*b*) '**Neither**' is negative of the either.

Examples:
(*i*) You may buy either of these two chairs.
(*ii*) Neither of them could speak on the stage.

10. (*a*) '**Later**' expresses 'late in time'.
(*b*) '**Latter**' means 'second in position or order'.

Examples:
(*i*) My father reached later than I expected.
(*ii*) The latter position was better than the former.

Use of some Important Adverbs

1. (*a*) **Also, too, enough:**
(*i*) He taught English. Also, he edited the school magazine
(*ii*) He is a writer and also he is a painter.
(*iii*) He is too obstinate to listen to any reason.
(*iv*) This is too difficult a piece for the junior students.
(*v*) Sarla was kind enough to help the poor.
(*vi*) He is brave enough to face the truth.

☛ 'Too' is used in a negative sense, but enough is used in a positive sense.

(*b*) **Fairly and rather:** Both suggest the meaning 'moderately'. But, mainly 'fairly' is used with the words that denote a positive meaning and rather is used with the words that denote a negative meaning:
(*i*) Rita did fairly well in that competition, but her performance was rather poor in sports.
(*ii*) Mona is fairly rich, but she is rather stingy.

☛ 'Rather' can also be used in a positive sense.
(*i*) This is a rather interesting job.
(*ii*) That boy is rather smart.

(*c*) **Hardly, barely, scarcely:** These words mostly convey the negative suggestions and are almost similar.
(*i*) I have hardly any strength now.
(*ii*) There was barely any supply to the township,
(*iii*) There were scarcely a hundred guests present.

☛ With slight variance in the meaning, the words given above convey the idea of 'very little', 'not enough', 'lack of quantity and number'.

(*d*) **Yet, Still:** These adverbs can often be used to connect the sentence units:
(*i*) He has been defeated many times in the contest; still he wants to be a competitor.
(*ii*) Mona was sick; yet she went on doing her work.

(*e*) **Alone:**
(*i*) He alone (none else) is capable of handling that fire.
(*ii*) He hunted all alone in the forest. (not in any company)

Special Note:

(*a*) Apart from their conventional positions the adverbs might be used in different positions with different meanings and angles.
(*i*) He had only four books.
(*ii*) John only contacted his friend in need.
(*iii*) He greeted me only.
(*iv*) Only he greeted me there.

(*b*) **Inversion:** Some adverbs can be inverted *i.e.* placed in the beginning of the sentence and then be followed by an interrogative form. The most common of these adverb are: so, seldom, never, nowhere, under no circumstances, hardly, scarcely etc.
(*i*) So big was the bus that it could not enter the narrow lane.
(*ii*) Hardly had he reached the station when he received the message.

MULTIPLE CHOICE QUESTIONS

Directions: *In the following questions choose the correct options to fill in the blanks.*

1. The girl whom you met is the .... sister of Ravi.
A. eldest B. elder
C. older D. oldest

2. The historical place is ....
A. seeing worth B. worthy of seeing
C. worth seeing D. worthy seeing

3. These flowers smell ....
A. sweet B. sweetly
C. more sweetly D. sweetest

4. .... aspirant cannot pass the entrance examination.
A. Each B. Every
C. All D. No

5. Prem Chand .... second Shakespeare.
A. is a B. is
C. is the D. is an

6. .... student in the class got prizes.
A. Each and every B. Every and each
C. Every D. Never

7. It is .... picture than the one we saw last Monday.
A. interesting B. much interesting
C. more interesting D. most interesting

8. She is clever ....
A. that her mother is B. as her mother is
C. to her mother is D. than her mother is

9. They will get ....
A. Red, green and black paper
B. Red, green black paper
C. Red and green and black paper
D. Red green black paper

10. Health is .... wealth.
A. preferable to B. more preferable than
C. more preferable to D. most preferable then

11. .... water that was in the jug evaporated.
A. Little B. The little
C. Small D. A small

12. He has not sung .... songs.
A. much B. most
C. more D. many

13. Srishti has searched .... office.
A. whole the B. the whole
C. a whole D. some whole

14. Premchand was .... best and .... famous writer.
A. a, the most B. the, a most
C. the, more D. the, the most

15. William Shakespeare is famous as ....
A. a poet and a dramatist
B. a poet and dramatist
C. the poet and the dramatist
D. a poet and the dramatist

16. What does the .... leader suggest?
A. other B. another
C. others D. anothers

17. He .... money.
A. has few B. have few
C. has little D. have little

18. The .... boys are rewarded.
A. first two B. two first
C. firsts two D. two's first

19. He is .... brave.
A. stronger than B. stronger then
C. more strong then D. more strong than

20. No sooner said ....
A. so done B. and done
C. then done D. but done

21. She returned .... than I had thought.
A. quickly B. more quicker
C. more quickly D. quicker

22. He is .... foolish person.
A. rather the B. a rather
C. rather a D. rather

23. This pen .... rupees.
A. costs twenty B. twenty costs only
C. costs only twenty D. only costs twenty

24. It is .... pride.
A. nothing else but B. nothing else than
C. else nothing than D. but

25. This tea is .... to drink.
A. too hot B. very hot
C. enough hot D. much hot

ANSWERS

1	2	3	4	5	6	7	8	9	10
A	C	A	B	A	C	C	C	A	A
11	**12**	**13**	**14**	**15**	**16**	**17**	**18**	**19**	**20**
B	D	B	D	B	A	C	A	D	C
21	**22**	**23**	**24**	**25**					
C	C	C	A	A					

DETERMINERS

Determiners are actually Adjectives. They are always followed by nouns.

Determiners are of the following kinds:

1. **Demonstrative Determiners**
   this, that, these, those
2. **Possessive Determiners**
   my, our, your, his, her, its, their
3. **Quantitative Determiners**
   some, any, much, enough, sufficient, whole, a little, the little, little, all, both
4. **Numerical Determiners**
   a few, some, few, the few, any, several, many, no, etc.
   One, two, three ... (Cardinals)
   First, second, third ... (Ordinals)
5. **Distributive Determiners**
   either, neither
6. **Articles**
   Indefinite: a, an
   Definite: the

MULTIPLE CHOICE QUESTIONS

Directions: *In the following questions choose the correct options to fill in the blanks.*

1. Give me .... rice.
   A. some B. few
   C. a few D. any
2. .... sheep grazing on the slope of the hill had gone away.
   A. Any B. The few
   C. This D. Much
3. Have you got .... magazines to read?
   A. all B. much
   C. some D. little
4. I have .... money that I want to spend on shares.
   A. any B. much
   C. less D. some
5. There is .... owl on the branch of the tree.
   A. a B. the
   C. an D. some
6. My brother is .... MBA.
   A. a B. an
   C. the D. any
7. Have you got .... cheese?
   A. some B. many
   C. a few D. few
8. No, I have not got .... cheese.
   A. many B. few
   C. any D. some
9. There is only .... milk left in the bottle.
   A. enough B. few
   C. much D. a little
10. There is .... hope of his recovery.
    A. any B. little
    C. many D. few
11. .... dogs were barking at the strangers.
    A. Some B. Any
    C. Much D. Less
12. The girl bought her father .... juice.
    A. few B. some
    C. any D. many
13. You should take .... honey everyday.
    A. any B. many
    C. a little D. a few
14. .... boy was punished by the teacher.
    A. Either B. All
    C. Any D. Many
15. .... girl was asked to join the army.
    A. None B. Neither
    C. All D. Any
16. .... water in the jug has been drunk by Mohan.
    A. The little B. The few
    C. A few D. Few
17. I shall play .... piano at the party.
    A. some B. any
    C. the D. few
18. .... labourers were found dead in the mine.
    A. Any B. Fewer
    C. Many D. Less
19. Could I borrow .... umbrella?
    A. our B. your
    C. yours D. my
20. My brother is standing in the .... row.
    A. any B. many
    C. some D. first

ANSWERS

1	2	3	4	5	6	7	8	9	10
A	B	C	D	C	B	A	C	D	B
11	12	13	14	15	16	17	18	19	20
A	B	C	A	B	A	C	C	B	D

VERBS

A verb is a word that tells something about the action or state of or happenning to a person or thing.

A verb tells the following:

1. What a person or thing does.

Examples:

(*i*) Sachin goes to school daily.

(*ii*) The bell *rang* loudly.

(*iii*) Many birds fly in the sky.

(*iv*) She *sang* a song.

2. What a person or thing is.

Examples:

(*i*) India *is* the biggest democracy in the world.

(*ii*) Ram Mehar *is* very rich.

(*iii*) They *are* happy.

3. What is done to a person or thing.

Examples:

(*i*) You *are liked* by all.

(*ii*) Two thieves *were arrested.*

(*iii*) Four students *were punished* by the teacher.

4. What happens to a person or thing.

Examples:

(*i*) His maternal uncle *died* last week.

(*ii*) Two ships *sank* yesterday.

(*iii*) Leaves *turn* yellow in autumn.

5. What a person or thing has, had, and so on.

Examples:

(*i*) I *have* a new car.

(*ii*) He *had* a scooter last year.

(*iii*) He *has* several cows and goats.

It goes without saying that a verb is the most important part of a sentence. No sentence is complete without a Verb.

Important Information

1. If two or more singular nouns are joined by 'and' the verb used will be plural.

Example:

(*i*) He and I were going to the market.

(*ii*) Ram and Mohan are friends.

2. If two singular nouns joined by 'and' points out to the same thing or person, the verb used must be singular.

Example:

(*i*) Rice and curry is the favourite food of the Punjabis.

(*ii*) The Collector and District Magistrate is away.

3. In case two subjects are joined by 'as well as' the verb agrees with the first subject.

Example:

(*i*) Kanta as well as her children is playing.

(*ii*) Children as well as their mother are playing.

In the case of first sentence the verb (is) agrees with Kanta and in the case of second sentence the verb (are) agrees with the children.

4. 'Neither', 'Either', 'Every', 'Each', 'Everyone', and 'Many a' are followed by a singular verb.

Example:

(*i*) Either of the plans is to be adopted.

(*ii*) Neither of the two brothers is sure to pass.

(*iii*) Every student is expected to be obedient.

(*iv*) Everyone of them desires this.

(*v*) Many a person is drowned in the sea.

5. If two subjects are joined by 'Either .... or' / 'Neither .... nor', the verb agrees with the subject near to it.

Example:

(*i*) Either my brother or I am to do this work.

(*ii*) Neither he nor they are prepared to do this work.

6. 'A great many' is always followed by a 'plural noun' and a 'plural verb'. For example :

A great many students have been declared successful.

7. Similarly if two subjects are joined by 'with', 'together with', 'no less than', in addition to 'and not', etc. the verb agrees with the first subject.

Example:

(*i*) The boy with his parents has arrived.

(*ii*) He, no less than I, is to blame.

8. Nouns, plural in form, but singular in meaning, take a singular verb.

Example:

This news was broadcast from television yesterday.

MULTIPLE CHOICE QUESTIONS

Directions: *In the following questions choose the correct options to fill in the blanks.*

1. The bus with all its passengers .... lost.
A. were B. was
C. are D. would

2. You as well as I .... responsible for this work.
A. am B. are
C. was D. is

3. Raghava like all his companions .... a spoiled child.
A. are B. were
C. is D. will be

4. Pen and ink .... required for me.
A. are B. were
C. is D. has required

5. Every girl and every boy .... attended the seminar.
A. have B. has
C. is D. are

6. Not only she but all her sisters ...... been married.
A. has B. have
C. is D. are

7. There .... nothing but miseries in life.
A. is B. are
C. were D. will be

8. Neither prose nor poem .... given.
A. were B. was
C. has D. have

9. Either he or I .... wrong.
A. is B. are
C. am D. were

10. Either Sulekha or Rekha .... coming here.
A. are B. is
C. were D. have

11. .... the child or his parents to blame?
A. Is B. Are
C. Were D. Has

12. You and I .... neighbours.
A. am B. are
C. was D. has

13. The house with all its belongings ..... sold away.
A. were B. are
C. was D. must

14. Either water or juice .... required.
A. is B. are
C. were D. has

15. There were not as many tables as .... required.
A. was B. were
C. is D. are

16. They each .... a book.
A. have B. are
C. has D. is

17. He and I .... close friends.
A. is B. am
C. was D. are

18. She as well as I .... guilty.
A. is B. are
C. am D. must be

19. Purushottam .... not read more on this chapter.
A. needs B. has been need
C. need D. had been need

20. He came .... to his aunt.
A. run B. running
C. to run D. in run

21. She dislikes .... meat.
A. eat to B. to eat
C. eating D. to eating

22. He likes ....
A. sing to B. singing
C. to sing D. to singing

23. We are ready .... the match.
A. play to B. to playing
C. playing D. to play

24. .... is injurious to health.
A. Smoking B. To smoke
C. To smoking D. Smoke to

25. He loves .... raw vegetables.
A. eaten B. eating
C. to eating D. eat to

26. He seemed .... finished his homework.
A. have to B. to have
C. having D. to having

ANSWERS

1	2	3	4	5	6	7	8	9	10
B	B	C	C	B	B	A	B	C	B
11	**12**	**13**	**14**	**15**	**16**	**17**	**18**	**19**	**20**
A	B	C	A	B	A	D	A	C	B
21	**22**	**23**	**24**	**25**	**26**				
C	B	D	A	B	B				

CONJUNCTIONS

A conjunction is a word which connects words, clauses or sentences.

Look at the following sentences.

(*i*) He bought apples *and* mangoes.
(*ii*) God made the country *and* man made the town.
(*iii*) The door was open *but* there was no one in the house.
(*iv*) He knows that I am here *and* that I want to see him.

In the sentence (*i*), *and* connects two words—*apples* and *mangoes.*

In the sentence (*ii*), *and* connects two sentences—*God made the country* and *man made the town.*

In the sentence (*iii*), *but* connects two sentences— *The door was open* and *there was no one in the house.*

In the sentence (*iv*), *and* connects two clauses—*that I am here* and *that I want to see him.*

The main coordinating conjunctions are:

and, but, for, or, nor, also, either ..... or, neither ..... nor.

There are some conjunctions which are used in pairs. They are:

either .... or, ... neither .... nor, both .... and, though .... yet, whether .... or, not only .... but also.

Example: *Either* take it *or* leave it.

It is *neither* useful *nor* ornamental.

They *both* like *and* respect me.

Though he is suffering from high fever, *yet* he does not cry.

He does not care *whether* you go *or* stay.

He is *not only* doltish, *but also* obstinate.

The conjunctions which are used in pairs in this way, are called correlative conjunctions, or merely correlatives.

Use of Important Conjunctions

1. **As soon as:** As soon as denotes simultaneous time.

   Example: As soon as he saw his enemy, he took to his heels.

2. **No sooner .... than :**

   (*a*) 'No sooner' is always followed by 'than'.

   (*b*) Please remember that 'No sooner' is always followed by do/does/did. As such only first form of the verb should be used after the subject.

   Example:
   No sooner did he see his enemy than he took to his heels.

3. **Hardly:** 'Hardly' is followed by 'when'.

   Examples:
   (*i*) Hardly had I left the house when it started raining.
   (*ii*) We had hardly come into the room when his father began chastising him.

☛ A. 'Hardly' is never followed by 'than'.
B. 'Scarcely' can also be used in the sense and manner of 'Hardly'.

4. **Lest:** Lest is used in the sense of 'so that .... not'. It is always followed by 'should'. Lest is negative in sense. Hence 'not' should never be used with it.

   Example:
   Work hard lest you should fail.

☛ 'Lest' is always followed by 'should' and not 'may'.

5. **Unless:** Unless expresses condition. It is also used in the negative sense. Use of 'not' is not allowed with 'unless' because 'unless' is already in the negative sense.

   Example:
   Unless you labour hard you will not pass.

6. **Until:** 'Until' expresses time. It means 'till not'.

   Example:
   Wait here until I return.

☛ Until is in the negative sense. So 'not' should not be used with it.

Example :
Wait here until I do not return. (Incorrect)
Wait here until I return. (Correct)

7. **As well as:** When two subjects are joined by 'as well as', the verb always agrees with the first subject.

   Examples:
   (*i*) The teacher as well as students is playing.
   (*ii*) Students as well as the teacher are playing.

☛ 'Both' and 'as well as' cannot be used together in the same sentence.

Examples:
Both Sita as well as Kanta are beautiful. (Incorrect)
Sita as well as Kanta is beautiful. (Correct)
Both Sita and Kanta are beautiful. (Correct)

8. **As if:** 'As if' is used in the sense of pretension. While using 'as if' in a sentence, we should see that even the third person singular subject gets 'were'.

   Example:
   He talks as if he were mad.

9. **Till:** Till expresses time. Till is always used in the affirmative.

   Example:
   We did not come back till sunset.

10. **Rather than:** 'Rather than' is used in the sense of 'preference'. 'Rather' is always followed by 'than'.

Example:

I would rather die than submit.

11. As long as/so long as: Both express time during which an action or event takes place.

Example:

As long as there is life, there is hope.

12. However: It is both a subordinate and co-ordinate clause.

Examples:

(*a*) Mala worked hard, she however, failed.

(*b*) However hard he may work, he cannot pass.

13. Such as: 'Such as' gives us the sense of 'like'. Such is always followed by 'as'.

Example:

Life is such a puzzle as cannot be solved.

MULTIPLE CHOICE QUESTIONS

Directions: *In the following questions choose the correct options to fill in the blanks.*

1. Neither he .... his friend is good.
A. or B. and
C. but D. nor

2. The officer asked the peon .... why he was late.
A. that B. if
C. but D. No word needed

3. Both Ajay .... Vijay are intelligent.
A. or B. nor
C. and D. No word needed

4. No Sooner did the thief see the public .... he ran away.
A. then B. and
C. but D. than

5. Abhinav .... his brothers was going to Mumbai.
A. but B. yet
C. No word needed D. together with

6. He behaves .... he were the captain of the team.
A. as if B. as
C. No word needed D. that

7. Either Rupali .... Sonali is going to attend the meeting.
A. and B. but
C. nor D. or

8. Neither Nirmal .... Ashwinee is going to listen the speech.
A. and B. but
C. nor D. or

9. Ravi .... Prakash are going to Kolkata.
A. or B. nor
C. but D. and

10. Rice .... curry is my usual breakfast.
A. and B. but
C. then D. than

11. Hardly had he left .... his brother came.
A. then B. than
C. when D. that

12. I would rather have a copy .... a book.
A. then B. than
C. when D. that

13. He is no other .... my friend.
A. then B. than
C. when D. but

14. He saw a snake ....he awoke.
A. then B. when
C. than D. No word needed

15. Ten years have passed .... my grandmother died.
A. since B. when
C. then D. than

16. She is .... good .... bad.
A. either, not B. neither, or
C. neither, nor D. neither, than

17. The cellphone is both cheap .... best.
A. than B. and
C. then D. or

18. No sooner did the rogue see the police .... he disappeared.
A. then B. than
C. so D. because

19. Srishti will go .... Sanju goes.
A. if B. than
C. then D. although

20. She is wise .... timid.
A. and B. yet
C. but D. however

21. Make hay .... the sun shines.
A. though B. while
C. after D. before

22. He is so weak .... he cannot walk.
A. but B. that
C. then D. so

23. Although he is rich, ... he is unhappy.
A. but B. yet
C. so D. still

24. Wait here .... I come back.
A. till B. until
C. before D. after

25. He is my friend .... I shall help him.
A. so　　B. hence
C. that is why　　D. therefore

26. He must go away .... he will be beaten.
A. otherwise　　B. and
C. or　　D. else

27. God loves good men .... good men love God.
A. and　　B. or
C. that　　D. those

28. He was late .... he was not punished.
A. but　　B. yet
C. still　　D. therefore

29. Walk slowly ...., you may fall.
A. and　　B. or
C. so　　D. otherwise

30. Work hard, ... you will fail.
A. and　　B. or
C. otherwise　　D. else

ANSWERS

1	2	3	4	5	6	7	8	9	10
D	D	C	D	D	A	D	C	D	A
11	12	13	14	15	16	17	18	19	20
C	B	B	B	A	C	B	B	A	C
21	22	23	24	25	26	27	28	29	30
B	B	B	A	B	C	A	C	D	D

PREPOSITIONS

A *Preposition* is a word which is placed before a noun or a pronoun to show its relation to some other word in the sentence.

(*i*) I saw a goat *in* the field.
(*ii*) I am fond *of* hot coffee.

In sentence (*i*), the word *in* shows the relation between two things—*goat* and *field.*

In sentence (*ii*), the word *of* shows the relation between the attribute expressed by the adjective *found* and *tea.*

The words *in* and *of* are here used as prepositions.

The noun or pronoun which is used with a preposition is called its object. The noun or pronoun is in the objective case. It is governed by the preposition. Now it is absolutely clear that in sentence (*i*), the noun *field* is in the objective case. The word *field* is governed by the preposition *in.*

A preposition may have two or more objects.

The road runs over *hill* and *plain.*

Here, the words *hill* and *plain* are used as objects.

Use of Important Prepositions

1. Among, Between

'**Among**' is used for more than two persons or things; '**Between**' is used only for two.

Examples:

(*i*) Distribute these sweets *among* the poor students of the class.
(*ii*) Distribute these books *between* Ram and Shyam.

2. Among, In

'**Among**' is used before collective plural nouns. '**In**' is used before collective singular nouns.

Examples:

(*i*) I found him standing *among* the crowd.
(*ii*) I saw him in the crowd.

3. Beside, Besides

'**Beside**' means 'by the side of'. '**Besides**' means 'in addition to'.

Examples:

(*i*) The daughter was sitting *beside* her mother.
(*ii*) *Besides* his relatives, he invited his friends also.

4. In, Within

'**In**' means at the expiry of a period of time in future, '**Within**' means before the expiry of a period of time in any tense.

Examples:

(*i*) She will return *in* a week.
(*ii*) I shall finish my work *within* a weak.

5. On, Upon

'**On**' is used for things at rest; '**Upon**' is used for things in motion.

Examples:

(*i*) He is sitting *on* the floor.
(*ii*) The dog sprang *upon* the table.

6. By, With

'**By**' denotes the agent or doer, '**With**' denotes the instrument with which anything is done.

Examples:

(*i*) The bird was killed *by* the hunter with an arrow.
(*ii*) He beat the dog *with* a stick.
(*iii*) I shall reach here *by* five o'clock.

7. After, In

'**After**' means at the end of a period of time in the past.
'**In**' means at the end of a period of time in future.

Examples:

(*i*) I shall return your book *in* a week.
(*ii*) He returned the book *after* a week.

8. For, From, Since

'**For**' is used before a noun denoting a period of time with all the tenses. '**From**' is used before a noun or phrase denoting a point of time, it is used in all the tenses. '**Since**' is used before a noun or phrase denoting some point of time and is always produced by a verb in the perfect continuous tense or third form of a verb.

Examples:

(*i*) We have been playing cards *for* two hours.
(*ii*) She stayed with her uncle *from* the 15th of March to the 15th of May.
(*iii*) I have been reading this book *since* morning.

9. Above, Over

'**Above**' means 'higher from', **Over** is used in the following four senses:

(*i*) In the sense of 'above' :
At noon, the sun is *over* our heads.
(*ii*) In the sense of 'beyond' :
I cannot get *over* my disappointment.
(*iii*) In the sense of 'Superiority' :
God *over* all blesses for ever more.
(*iv*) In the sense of 'Conclusion' :
It is all *over* with me.

10. At, Towards

'**At**' denotes the idea of aim, '**Towards**' denotes the idea of destination.

Examples:

(*i*) He threw the stone *at* the cat.
(*ii*) He went *towards* the house.

11. At, In, On

'At' is used as follows :

(*i*) '**At**' is used with small towns and villages.

Examples :

(*a*) He was born *at* Sonepat.
(*b*) He lives *at* village Bangra. (Bangra is a village)

(*ii*) '**At**' is used before a noun denoting a definite point of time.

Example:

He called on me *at* 9 p.m. yesterday.

'In' is used as follows :

(*iii*) '**In**' is used with the names of big cities, provinces and countries.

Examples:

(*a*) His father lives *in* England.
(*b*) His younger brother lives *in* Lucknow.

(*iv*) '**In**' is used before the names of months and years.

Example:

His elder sister was born *in* 1972 *in* the month of May.

'**On**' is used with dates and names of days.

Examples :

(*a*) I joined college *on* the 26th April.
(*b*) He will leave for Kolkata *on* Wednesday next.

Important Information

1. '**In**' is also used in the following phrases :
In the morning; In the evening, In winter, In summer.
2. '**In**' also denotes a place inside anything.
He travelled *in* a crowded bus.
3. '**At**' is used in the following phrases :
At home, *At* the station, *At* work, *At* play.

12. Below, Beneath

Below means 'of lower level in position, dignity and expectation' etc. *Beneath* means 'under'.

Examples:

(*i*) It is *below* my dignity to talk to her.
(*ii*) They rested *beneath* the shade of a tree.

13. In, Into, To

'**In**' expresses Rest or Motion inside anything. '**Into**' expresses Motion towards the inside of anything or change from one medium to another. '**To**' denotes motion from one place to another.

Examples:

(*i*) The boys are *in* the room.
(*ii*) Translate this passage from English *into* Hindi.
(*iii*) Every morning he goes *to* the temple.

14. Till, By, Of, Off

- 'Till' means upto or not earlier than.
- 'By' means not later than.
- 'Of' shows cause, source, separation, quality, contents, possession, apposition, point of reference, space in time etc.
- 'Off' shows separation at a near distance, and detached condition.

Consider the following examples:

(*i*) I shall work *till* 5 a.m.
(*ii*) Asha died *of* cancer.
(*iii*) The nib *of* the pen is made *of* gold.
(*iv*) He presented me a bottle *of* perfume.
(*v*) Our principal is a man *of* principle.
(*vi*) He lived in the house *of* his friend.
(*vii*) *By* this time tomorrow, I'll have finished my job.
(*viii*) My house is *off* the road.
(*ix*) The book fell *off* the table.

MULTIPLE CHOICE QUESTIONS

Directions: *Tick the correct preposition for the blank in each of the following sentences.*

1. He applied ...... the manager.
A. for B. to
C. with D. by

2. Trust ...... God and do the right.
A. in B. for
C. to D. with

3. She is worthy ...... a prize.
A. with B. for
C. to D. of

4. Mr. Gomes has no taste ...... music.
A. of B. for
C. with D. to

5. You are hard ...... hearing.
A. at B. of
C. with D. for

6. He is sure ...... his success
A. for B. with
C. on D. of

7. Preeti was warned ...... the danger ahead.
A. for B. at
C. of D. about

8. I am thankful ...... you for a good advice.
A. for B. with
C. to D. of

9. Deepak would not surrender .... the police.
A. with B. to
C. for D. on

10. The small plant in your lawn is very sensitive ...... touch.
A. on B. with
C. to D. about

11. Divya was sure to succeed ..... the examination.
A. for B. in
C. to D. with

12. Geeta was jealous ...... Ravina's beauty.
A. to B. with
C. for D. of

13. He was ignorant ..... what was happening there.
A. for B. of
C. to D. with

14. Your pen is inferior ...... mine.
A. than B. with
C. from D. to

15. Reenu is no match ...... Meenu.
A. to B. for
C. with D. upon

16. It is necessary ...... you to apply for this job.
A. on B. with
C. for D. to

17. Be loyal ...... your country.
A. for B. to
C. on D. with

18. Mukesh is junior ...... me.
A. than B. to
C. from D. of

19. Deepika was innocent ...... the crime.
A. of B. with
C. from D. to

20. I am desirous.... joining the Indian cricket team.
A. for B. of
C. to D. on

ANSWERS

1	2	3	4	5	6	7	8	9	10
B	A	D	B	B	D	D	D	B	D
11	**12**	**13**	**14**	**15**	**16**	**17**	**18**	**19**	**20**
B	D	B	D	B	D	B	B	A	B

INTERJECTIONS

An *interjection* is a word which expresses a sudden feeling for emotion. It must be borne in mind that an interjection has no grammatical relation with any other word in a sentence.

It is a convention that an interjection is followed by the exclamation mark(!).

An interjection usually expresses *joy, grief, surprise, anger, contempt, alarm, attention,* approval, disapproval , etc.

Important interjections and the emotions they express are named below:

Joy : *Hurrah! Ha! Ha!*
Grief : *Alas! Ah!*

Surprise : *Oh! What!*
Approval : *Bravo! Hear! Hear! Well done!*
Calling : *Hello! Hi! Hey!*
Contempt : *Fie! Pooh!*

Observe the following sentences

Hurrah! We have won the match.

Alas! It is a sad day for us. We have lost the game.

Hush! Don't make a noise. The baby is sleeping.

Hello! What are you doing there? Who is there?

Oh! I got such a fright.

Ah! I should have been there. What a sorry plight.

Hark! Don't you hear a sound?

What! So early.

The following interjection phrases are in common use:

Ah me!	Good God!
For shame!	Hold on!
Well done!	Off with you!
Good Grace!	Dear me!
Good heavens!	

Other parts of speech are also sometimes used as interjections. Some examples are given below:

Noun : A horse! A horse! My kingdom for a horse!
Pronoun : What a lame excuse! What a beautiful sight it is!
Verb : Would that I were young again!
Adverb : How lovely the flowers are!
Conjunction : If I could only see her once again!
Infinitive : To think of him as a friend!

MULTIPLE CHOICE QUESTIONS

Directions: *Tick the correct interjection to be applied to the given sentences.*

1. .... The meeting is going on.
   A. What! B. Oh!
   C. Hurrah! D. Hush!
2. .... We have won the match.
   A. Chi-Chi! B. Fie! Fie
   C. Hurrah! D. Phew!
3. .... He is no more.
   A. Hush! B. Alas!
   C. Hark! D. Pooh!
4. .... How good of you.
   A. Oh! B. Hush!
   C. Good Heavens! D. Bravo!
5. .... You took so much trouble for us.
   A. What! B. Oh!
   C. Phew! D. Well!
6. .... A soldier and afraid of death.
   A. Hurrah! B. Bravo!
   C. Fie on you! D. Pshaw!
7. .... He didn't accept your proposal.
   A. Oh!
   B. What!
   C. Hark!
   D. Good Heavens!
8. .... The cuckoo is singing.
   A. Hark! B. What!
   C. Oh! D. Hurrah!
9. .... What do I see here?
   A. Good heavens B. What!
   C. Ha! Ha! D. Hush!
10. .... Well done.
   A. What! B. Oh!
   C. Bravo! D. Hurrah!
11. .... What do you talk of him?
   A. Chi! Chi! B. Alas!
   C. Well! D. Hark!
12. .... What next?
   A. Hush! B. Well!
   C. Hurrah! D. Hark!

ANSWERS

1	2	3	4	5	6	7	8	9	10
D	C	B	A	B	C	B	A	A	C
11	**12**								
A	B								

3 Spelling Test

The most common errors in English are of spellings of words. Even the most learned men are sometimes confused about the correct spellings of some words. One must keep and use a dictionary religiously. Never ignore and let pass a new word casually without checking its spelling and meaning.
A number of questions to test your knowledge of spellings are compiled here. Try to solve as many as you can.

MULTIPLE CHOICE QUESTIONS

Directions: *Find the correctly spelt words.*

1. A. Discriminate B. Discremineta C. Discrimenate D. Discriminat

2. A. Juddicious B. Judiceous C. Judicious D. Judiceus

3. A. Accompalish B. Ackmplesh C. Acomplush D. Accomplish

4. A. Damage B. Dammage C. Damaige D. Dammege

5. A. Lackdaisical B. Lackadaisical C. Lckadaisicle D. Lackadisical

6. A. Efficiant B. Effecient C. Efficient D. Eficient

7. A. Survellance B. Surveilance C. Surveillance D. Survaillance

8. A. Schedule B. Schdule C. Schedale D. Schedeule

9. A. Occurad B. Occurred C. Ocurred D. Occured

10. A. Licentious B. Licontious C. Licenttious D. Licientious

11. A. Chancelery B. Chancellery C. Chancellary D. Chancelary

12. A. Itenerary B. Itinarery C. Itinarary D. Itinerary

13. A. Grieff B. Grief C. Grieef D. Grrief

14. A. Indipenseble B. Indispansible C. Indispensable D. Indipensable

15. A. Guarantee B. Garuntee C. Guaruntee D. Gaurantee

16. A. Meddicine B. Medicine C. Medicene D. Medicinne

17. A. Benefeted B. Benefitted C. Benifited D. Benefited

18. A. Kleptomonia B. Kleptemonia C. Kleptomania D. Klaptomania

19. A. Sepalchrle B. Sepalchral C. Sepulchrle D. Sepulchral

20. A. Acommodation B. Acomodation C. Accomodation D. Accommodation

21. A. Teracherous B. Treacherous C. Treacheraus D. Treachereans

22. A. Querrelsome B. Quarrelsame C. Quarrelsome D. Querralsome

23. A. Farmament B. Farmement C. Fermament D. Fremament

24. A. Sympathetic B. Smypathetic C. Sympothetic D. Sympethetic

25. A. Pecification B. Pacification C. Pecifacation D. Pecefication

26. A. Meritricious B. Merefrecious C. Meretricious D. Merritricious

27. A. Hypocritical B. Hypocretical
C. Hypocriticel D. Hypocirticel

28. A. Vaingloriaus B. Vaniglorious
C. Vaniglerious D. Vaingloreus

29. A. Imprecticability B. Impracticebility
C. Impracticibility D. Impracticability

30. A. Prograssive B. Progressive
C. Progresive D. Prograsive

31. A. Incradulous B. Incredulous
C. Incridulous D. Incredalous

32. A. Uncivilized B. Uncevilized
C. Uncivillized D. Uncevelized

33. A. Osttentatious B. Ostentetious
C. Ostentatious D. Ostenttatious

34. A. Extravagant B. Extreragent
C. Extreregant D. Extravegent

35. A. Missunderstood B. Miesunderstood
C. Misunderstood D. Misunderstod

36. A. Belligerent B. Beligirent
C. Belligarant D. Belligerrent

37. A. Pasiveness B. Passiveness
C. Passeveniss D. Passivines

38. A. Astonished B. Astronished
C. Astoneshed D. Asstonished

39. A. Obnosious B. Obnoxeous
C. Obnoxious D. Obnoseous

40. A. Polyendry B. Poliendry
C. Pollyendry D. Polyandry

41. A. Sincerely B. Sencerely
C. Sincerelly D. Sincerrely

42. A. Efflorascence B. Eflorescene
C. Efflloreseence D. Efflorescence

43. A. Vulnarable B. Valnerable
C. Velnerable D. Vulnerable

44. A. Rigourous B. Rigerous
C. Rigorous D. Regerous

45. A. Omenous B. Ominous
C. Ommineous D. Omineous

46. A. Puerille B. Puerrile
C. Puerile D. Purrile

47. A. Satellite B. Sattellite
C. Satelite D. Sattelite

48. A. Pesanger B. Passenger
C. Pessenger D. Pasanger

49. A. Humurous B. Humorous
C. Humoreus D. Humorrous

50. A. Equinimity B. Equanimmity
C. Equannimity D. Equanimity

51. A. Exeggerate B. Exaggerate
C. Exadgerate D. Exagerate

52. A. Fariegn B. Forein
C. Foriegn D. Foreign

53. A. Rennaissance B. Rennaisance
C. Renaisance D. Renaissance

54. A. Excesive B. Excessive
C. Exccessive D. Exccesive

55. A. Forcaust B. Forcast
C. Forecast D. Forecaste

56. A. Valuptuous B. Volluptous
C. Voluptuous D. Volupttuous

57. A. Entrepraneur B. Entreprenuer
C. Entrapreneur D. Entrepreneur

58. A. Paralleted B. Paralelled
C. Parralleled D. Parallelled

59. A. Ocasion B. Occassion
C. Occasion D. Ocassion

60. A. Boquet B. Bouquet
C. Bouquete D. Bouquette

61. A. Loquacieous B. Lequacious
C. Loquacious D. Lequocious

62. A. Cataclysm B. Cataclism
C. Catacilysm D. Cataclesm

63. A. Chettering B. Chaterring
C. Chattering D. Chatering

64. A. Fulfilment B. Fulffilment
C. Fulfilmient D. Fullfilment

65. A. Conjectore B. Conjecture
C. Cenjecture D. Cenjectire

66. A. Endication B. Endicaltion
C. Indication D. Indicetion

67. A. Splendour B. Spllendour
C. Splandour D. Splendeur

68. A. Excllusion B. Exclussion
C. Exclusion D. Exclosion

69. A. Discourage B. Disscourage
C. Discourege D. Discaurage

70. A. Curageous B. Courageous
C. Courrageous D. Couregeous

71. A. Abandon B. Abanddon
C. Abendon D. Abbandon

72. A. Embarassment B. Emberrassement
C. Embarrassment D. Embbaresment

73. A. Veneration B. Venration
C. Venneration D. Venerration

74. A. Tacciturnity B. Taciturnity
C. Taciturrnity D. Tacitturnity

75. A. Despponding B. Despending C. Desponding D. Dessponding

76. A. Bueyant B. Buoyant C. Bueeyant D. Buoyent

77. A. Eccintric B. Eccentrie C. Eccentric D. Eccintrie

78. A. Corrigible B. Corigible C. Corregible D. Corrigiblle

79. A. Amandable B. Amendable C. Amenddable D. Amendablle

80. A. Occasional B. Occassional C. Occesional D. Occessional

81. A. Exttirpate B. Extirpete C. Extirpate D. Exterpate

82. A. Vorecious B. Varacious C. Voarcious D. Voracious

83. A. Insolvent B. Insolvant C. Insollvent D. Insolvvent

84. A. Querrel B. Querral C. Quarrel D. Quarel

85. A. Contrebution B. Contribution C. Contributtion D. Conterbution

86. A. Desgrace B. Disgrece C. Disgrice D. Disgrace

87. A. Harassment B. Herassment C. Harasment D. Harassmient

88. A. Tranquilitty B. Tranquility C. Trenquility D. Tranquillity

89. A. Imaginative B. Imeginative C. Imagenative D. Imaginetive

90. A. Suficient B. Suficiant C. Sufficient D. Sufficiant

91. A. Adequate B. Edequate C. Adaquete D. Edaquete

92. A. Exparienced B. Experianced C. Experienced D. Experrienced

93. A. Flatering B. Fletering C. Flattering D. Fletaring

94. A. Cuttiveted B. Culltrivated C. Cultivated D. Caltivated

95. A. Materialistic B. Materielistic C. Meterialistic D. Matterialistic

96. A. Praiceworthy B. Peiseworthy C. Praiseworthy D. Praisaworthy

97. A. Tranquil B. Trenquil C. Tranquel D. Trinquil

98. A. Neggardly B. Nigardly C. Niggerdly D. Niggardly

99. A. Magnanimity B. Megnanimity C. Magnenimity D. Magnanimety

100. A. Darogate B. Derogate C. Derogeta D. Deragate

101. A. Philanthropist B. Philenthropist C. Phelanthropist D. Philanthropest

102. A. Ephameral B. Ephimeral C. Ephemeral D. Ephemerel

103. A. Fanaticism B. Fenaticism C. Faneticism D. Fanatecism

104. A. Profesional B. Professionel C. Professional D. Profissional

105. A. Ameteur B. Amateur C. Amataur D. Amateor

106. A. Philenderer B. Philandarer C. Philanderer D. Philonderer

107. A. Honorary B. Henorary C. Honerary D. Honorery

108. A. Darmatologist B. Dermatologist C. Dermetologist D. Dermatologest

109. A. Compansation B. Compensetion C. Compensotion D. Compensation

110. A. Quadruplets B. Quedruplets C. Quadroplets D. Quadruplats

111. A. Econemist B. Economest C. Economist D. Econimist

112. A. Catholic B. Cetholic C. Cathelic D. Cathilic

113. A. Unfevourable B. Unfevaurable C. Unfavourable D. Unfivourable

114. A. Bombastic B. Bombestic C. Bombostic D. Bombastie

115. A. Posthumaus B. Posthomous C. Posthumous D. Pasthumous

116. A. Epitaph B. Epetaph C. Epiteph D. Epitoph

117. A. Falicitate B. Felicitate C. Falecitate D. Falecetate

118. A. Schezophrenia B. Schizaphrenia C. Schizophrenia D. Schizophrania

119. A. Claustrophobia B. Cloustrophobia C. Claustraphobia D. Claustrophabia

120. A. Connoiseur B. Connaisseur C. Connaissour D. Connoisseur

121. A. Transperency B. Transparency C. Transpirency D. Tranporency

122. A. Superanuation B. Superennuation C. Superannuation D. Superannuetion

123. A. Antiquated B. Antiqueted
C. Antequated D. Antiquatted

124. A. Adalescent B. Addescant
C. Adolescent D. Adolascent

125. A. Newrologist B. Neurologist
C. Neurologest D. Newrologest

126. A. Obstatricion B. Obstitricion
C. Obstetricion D. Obstetracion

127. A. Illiterate B. Iliterate
C. Illitarate D. Illiterete

128. A. Thioretical B. Theoretical
C. Theoratical D. Theoritical

129. A. Mersenary B. Marcenary
C. Marcenery D. Mercenary

130. A. Archeic B. Arcaic
C. Archeic D. Archaic

131. A. Dormetory B. Durmitory
C. Dormitori D. Dormitory

132. A. Aristocracy B. Arestocracy
C. Arestocracy D. Aristocrecy

133. A. Lagislature B. Legislature
C. Lageslature D. Legesleture

134. A. Dormetory B. Dormitery
C. Dormitory D. Dermitory

135. A. Garulous B. Garrulaus
C. Gorrulous D. Garrulous

136. A. Regecide B. Regicide
C. Rigecide D. Ragicide

137. A. Epicurean B. Epecurean
C. Epicurian D. Epicorean

138. A. Commetti B. Commitee
C. Committee D. Comitte

139. A. Inemitable B. Inimitable
C. Inimetable D. Inimitabli

140. A. Pletocray B. Plitocracy
C. Plotocracy D. Plutocracy

141. A. Immortal B. Emortal
C. Immortel D. Immortol

142. A. Perrhic B. Pyrrhic
C. Pyrrhec D. Porrhec

143. A. Chauvinism B. Chouvinism
C. Chevinism D. Cauvinism

144. A. Rumenate B. Ruminote
C. Rimunote D. Ruminate

145. A. Teciturn B. Tociturn
C. Tecitorn D. Taciturn

146. A. Verteran B. Viteran
C. Veterain D. Veteran

147. A. Antitode B. Antedote
C. Antidote D. Autitote

148. A. Audeble B. Audible
C. Audcble D. Audebli

149. A. Bellicose B. Billicose
C. Bellecose D. Belicose

150. A. Pilferage B. Peliferage
C. Pilfarege D. Poliferage

151. A. Ribut B. Rebit
C. Rebut D. Rebute

152. A. Sychologist B. Psycologist
C. Psychologist D. Psychogist

153. A. Neucteus B. Neucleus
C. Nucleus D. Neocleus

154. A. Negotcate B. Negociate
C. Negotiate D. Nagotiate

155. A. Skelled B. Skilled
C. Skiled D. Skillid

156. A. Logecal B. Logical
C. Lagical D. Logicle

157. A. Effeciency B. Efficiency
C. Eficiency D. Efficency

158. A. Cumpartment B. Compartment
C. Compartant D. Comportent

159. A. Continuous B. Cuntinuous
C. Continus D. Contineuous

160. A. Valuable B. Valueable
C. Valuabel D. Valoble

161. A. Courteous B. Curteous
C. Corteous D. Courtus

162. A. Prophecy B. Phropecy
C. Propecy D. Propheci

163. A. Lonesome B. Lonsome
C. Lonesum D. Lonsum

164. A. Formedable B. Formidable
C. Formidabul D. Formdable

165. A. Inibriated B. Enibrited
C. Inebriated D. Inubrited

166. A. Guellible B. Guiellible
C. Guillibel D. Guillible

167. A. Subsequent B. Subsiquent
C. Subsequint D. Subquent

168. A. Alein B. Alien
C. Abein D. Abien

169. A. Misogynesm B. Mesogynism
C. Misogynism D. Misosogesim

170. A. Sanguini B. Sangune
C. Sangiune D. Sanguine

171. A. Exemplary B. Eximplary
C. Exemplari D. Examplary

172. A. Sycophants B. Sicophants
C. Sycopants D. Sycophints

173. A. Petchy B. Patchy
C. Patchi D. Patche

174. A. Impassi B. Impasse
C. Impase D. Inpassi

175. A. Aceelerate B. Accilerate
C. Accelerate D. Accelerati

176. A. Vendictive B. Vindective
C. Vindictive D. Vindictivi

177. A. Prudint B. Prudient
C. Prudente D. Prudent

178. A. Superfluons B. Superfleos
C. Superflous D. Superfluous

179. A. Expidite B. Expedeti
C. Expedite D. Expedit

180. A. Livity B. Levity
C. Levety D. Levite

181. A. Reluctant B. Riluctant
C. Reluctent D. Relictunt

182. A. Desparge B. Disparage
C. Disperage D. Disparege

183. A. Maegre B. Meager
C. Meagre D. Megre

184. A. Accedental B. Aceedent
C. Accidantle D. Accidental

185. A. Cheapiness B. Chaepness
C. Chepness D. Cheapness

186. A. Febulous B. Fabulus
C. Fabulous D. Fibulous

187. A. Colusion B. Collision
C. Colision D. Collison

188. A. Eradicated B. Erradicated
C. Eradecated D. Eradiceted

189. A. Ageonise B. Agonise
C. Agonice D. Agonisee

190. A. Comit B. Commiet
C. Commit D. Commite

191. A. Tasiturn B. Taciturn
C. Taceturn D. Tacitorn

192. A. Omnevorous B. Omnivorous
C. Omniverous D. Omnivarous

193. A. Feud B. Fued
C. Fiud D. Feued

194. A. Pselm B. Slam
C. Psalm D. Salm

195. A. Haphazard B. Hapahazard
C. Haphzard D. Haphazrd

196. A. Peevishness B. Pievishness
C. Peivishness D. Peeveshness

197. A. Gelactic B. Galectic
C. Galactic D. Galactec

198. A. Imbibision B. Imbision
C. Embibition D. Imbibition

199. A. Zoparasite B. Zooparaset
C. Zooparasite D. Zoprasite

200. A. Neuralgia B. Nuraliga
C. Neurolgia D. Neuraltia

ANSWERS

1	2	3	4	5	6	7	8	9	10
A	C	D	A	B	C	C	A	B	A
11	**12**	**13**	**14**	**15**	**16**	**17**	**18**	**19**	**20**
C	D	B	C	A	B	B	C	D	D
21	**22**	**23**	**24**	**25**	**26**	**27**	**28**	**29**	**30**
B	C	C	A	B	C	A	B	D	B
31	**32**	**33**	**34**	**35**	**36**	**37**	**38**	**39**	**40**
B	A	C	A	C	A	B	A	C	D
41	**42**	**43**	**44**	**45**	**46**	**47**	**48**	**49**	**50**
A	D	D	C	B	C	A	B	B	D
51	**52**	**53**	**54**	**55**	**56**	**57**	**58**	**59**	**60**
B	D	D	B	C	C	D	A	C	B
61	**62**	**63**	**64**	**65**	**66**	**67**	**68**	**69**	**70**
C	A	C	A	B	C	A	C	A	B
71	**72**	**73**	**74**	**75**	**76**	**77**	**78**	**79**	**80**
A	C	A	B	C	B	C	A	B	A

81	82	83	84	85	86	87	88	89	90
C	D	A	C	B	D	A	B	A	C
91	**92**	**93**	**94**	**95**	**96**	**97**	**98**	**99**	**100**
A	C	C	C	A	C	A	D	A	B
101	**102**	**103**	**104**	**105**	**106**	**107**	**108**	**109**	**110**
A	C	A	C	B	C	A	B	D	A
111	**112**	**113**	**114**	**115**	**116**	**117**	**118**	**119**	**120**
C	A	C	A	C	A	B	C	A	D
121	**122**	**123**	**124**	**125**	**126**	**127**	**128**	**129**	**130**
B	C	A	C	B	C	A	B	D	D
131	**132**	**133**	**134**	**135**	**136**	**137**	**138**	**139**	**140**
D	A	B	C	D	B	A	C	B	D
141	**142**	**143**	**144**	**145**	**146**	**147**	**148**	**149**	**150**
A	B	A	D	D	D	C	B	A	A
151	**152**	**153**	**154**	**155**	**156**	**157**	**158**	**159**	**160**
C	C	C	C	B	B	B	B	A	A
161	**162**	**163**	**164**	**165**	**166**	**167**	**168**	**169**	**170**
A	A	A	B	C	D	A	B	C	D
171	**172**	**173**	**174**	**175**	**176**	**177**	**178**	**179**	**180**
A	A	B	B	C	C	D	D	C	B
181	**182**	**183**	**184**	**185**	**186**	**187**	**188**	**189**	**190**
A	B	C	D	D	C	B	A	B	C
191	**192**	**193**	**194**	**195**	**196**	**197**	**198**	**199**	**200**
B	B	A	C	A	A	D	D	C	A

4 Punctuation

Punctuation Marks help us to make grammatically correct sentences.

The following pairs of sentences will bring home to you the importance of punctuation marks:

(*i*) Jack, my neighbour, is going abroad.

(*ii*) Jack, my neighbour is going abroad.

The sentence no. (*i*) means 'Jack' is my neighbour and he is going abroad. The sentence no. (*ii*) means that I'm telling Jack that my neighbour is going abroad.

The following are some most commonly used punctuation marks:

1. Full Stop
2. Note of Interrogation
3. Note of Exclamation
4. Comma
5. Inverted commas
6. Apostrophe
7. Capital Letters
8. Colon
9. Semicolon
10. Dash
11. Oblique
12. Parentheses
13. Hyphen

1. Full Stop (.)

(A) At the end of a statement or an imperative sentences the full stop is applied.

(*i*) Mohan sings a song. (Positive Statement)

(*ii*) She does not tell a lie. (Negative Statement)

(*iii*) Open the door. (Imperative Sentence)

(B) To mark abbreviations:

(*i*) M.L.A. (*ii*) M.B.B.S.

(*iii*) B.A. (*iv*) Mr R.S. Gill

☛ Now a days after Mr, Mrs, Miss, a full stop is not applied.

2. Note of Interrogation (?)

It is used to make direct questions as well as tags.

(*i*) What are you doing?

(*ii*) Where is your friend?

(*iii*) You like eggs, don't you?

(*iv*) She doesn't obey her elder brother, does she?

☛ The note of interrogation is not used after indirect questions.

(*i*) She was sure whether her brother would come there to see her or not.

(*ii*) I asked him when he would start a confectionary shop.

3. Note of Exclamation (!)

(A) It is used after an optative sentence

(*i*) May you live long!

(*ii*) May God bless you!

(B) After an exclamatory sentence

(*i*) What a beautiful butterfly it is!

(*ii*) How wonderful the rainbow is!

(C) After an Interjection

(*i*) Hurrah! We have won the match.

(*ii*) Alas! I am done.

4. Comma (,)

It is used:

(A) To separate identical words.

(*i*) Mohit is tall, thin and handsome.

(*ii*) I bought apples, bananas and guava yesterday.

(*iii*) This shopkeeper sells cakes, pastries and biscuits.

(B) In sentences of direct speech.

(*i*) She said, "I wish to be a doctor."

(*ii*) "Don't move," the man shouted.

(C) To separate pairs of words when they are joined by 'and'.

(*i*) I like rice and curry, idli and dosa.

(*ii*) In the fair were present all kinds of persons rich and poor, weak and strong, foolish and wise.

(D) To join two coordinate clauses when the latter is the consequence of the former.

(*i*) He was rejected by his friends, and he decided never to meet any of them in future.

(*ii*) He was beaten by his opponent, and he decided to leave boxing.

(E) To separate a noun or phrase in apposition.

(*i*) The Mahabharata, the longest epic, was written by Ved Vyas.

(*ii*) Hari, the tallest boy in our class, is a good player of basketball.

(F) To separate an adverbial clause from the rest of the sentences.

(*i*) If you tell me the reality, you won't be punished.

(*ii*) As soon as the thief saw the policeman, he ran away.

(*iii*) When he laughs, the dog in his house will bark.

(G) To separate a nominative of address

(*i*) Where are you, Mr Smith?

(*ii*) How are you, Seema?

(H) To separate a noun clause from the rest of the sentence.

(*i*) When she will get up, nobody knows.

(*ii*) Why he is crying so loudly, is known to his parents only.

(*iii*) What he says, no one cares.

5. Inverted Commas (" ")

Inverted commas are used in sentences of direct speech.

(*i*) She says, "I can drive a car."

(*ii*) He said to me, "I'll convey your message to your uncle."

6. Apostrophe (')

It is used:

(A) To make Genitive Case when the noun is singular

(*i*) Mohan's shirt

(*ii*) James' shoes or James's shoes.

(B) To make Genitive Case when the noun is plural

(*i*) Boys' college (*ii*) Girls' hostel

(*iii*) Men's club (*iv*) Women's hostel

(C) To make plural form of letters and figures

(*i*) H's (*ii*) A's

(*iii*) 4's (*iv*) 8's

(D) To denote the omission of letter or letters from words

(*i*) can't (*ii*) don't

(*iii*) won't

(E) To express a possessive pertaining to a period of time

(*i*) a week's holiday. (*ii*) a year's programme.

7. Capital Letters (A, B, C,...)

Capital letters are used as under:

(A) The first word of a sentence should start with a capital letter.

(*i*) She does not know how to play the piano.

(*ii*) We are going to perform a dance in London.

(B) A proper name should be started with a capital letter.

(*i*) Mohan is my fast friend.

(*ii*) I like all students of my class but I like Ajay, Rajesh and Vinod in particular.

(*iii*) Delhi is the capital of India.

(C) The important words in the title of a book should start with a capital letter each:

(*i*) The Cat and the Mouse.

(*ii*) Love and Life.

(D) The first letter of the days of a week and the months of year should be written in capital.

(*i*) Sunday, Monday, Tuesday.

(*ii*) January, February, March.

(E) The names of all rivers, oceans, mountains, bays, channels, peaks, etc., should start with a capital letter.

(*i*) The Ganga

(*ii*) The Himalayas

(*iii*) The Bay of Bengal

(*iv*) Mount Everest

(*v*) The English Channel

(*vi*) The Indian Ocean

(F) The names of all holy books, magazines, newspapers, etc. should start with a capital letter.

(*i*) The Gita (*ii*) The Bible

(*iii*) The Tribune (*iv*) The Sun

8. Colon (:)

Colon represents a long pause. It is not used so frequently but in some cases it is applied.

(A) To quote the names of certain items both proper and common nouns:

(*i*) Some of Shakespeare's plays are: Macbeth, Tempest, Julius Caesar, etc.

(*ii*) The following items are required by our school urgently:

(*i*) Five Hockey Sticks

(*ii*) Ten Cricket Bats

(*iii*) Four Football

(*iv*) Eight Basketballs

(B) To introduce a quotation.

(*i*) Keats says: A thing of beauty is a joy forever.

(*ii*) Shakespeare says: All that glitters is not gold.

(C) Before some examples:

(*i*) I know several languages:
Hindi, Punjabi, French and English.

(*ii*) Mohan is: honest, wise, handsome, rich and kind.

9. Semicolon (;)

It represents a pause which is longer than a comma but is of less duration than a colon. A semicolon is used:

(A) To mark off a series of clauses:

(*i*) We love our young ones; they too in return love us.

(*ii*) This forest is a witness to good and bad days of mankind; this is here since ancient times.

(B) To break up long sentences:

My brother reads in 10th standard; he always goes to school late; he is almost everyday punished by the teacher.

10. Dash (—)

It is used:

(A) To mark a sudden change in our thoughts

(*i*) I think you like berries—but your brother told me that you spend no money on fruit.

(*ii*) You must read this book—but how can you read it when you're writing a letter to your friends?

(B) To mark a sudden interruption in a sentence.

I know him—I met him five years ago—where? I can't recall.

(C) To divulge a secret in a dramatic way.

(*i*) The most famous modern novelist is—Sydney Sheldon.

(*ii*) The best singer is—Mohammad Rafi.

11. Oblique (/)

(A) It is used to represent abbreviations

(*i*) D/o (Daughter of)

(*ii*) S/o (Son of)

(*iii*) W/o (Wife of)

(B) To represent masculine gender or feminine gender

(*i*) He/She can join the army.

(*ii*) I'll ask questions to him/her.

(C) To represent possibilities

(*i*) The girl/girls should work even harder.

(*ii*) The boy/boys cannot be given any special rights.

12. Parentheses (or Brackets) ( )

These are used:

(A) To explain something additional which is usually not of much significance.

(*i*) Manoj (a five year old boy) saved the life of his friend.

(*ii*) Meena (a girl of 5th standard) was called by the President for her remarkable paintings.

(B) To separate an after thought

(*i*) All his sons (including the eldest one, who is an addict to alcohol) are going abroad.

(*ii*) All the ingredients (excluding milk) should be put in a pan.

13. Hyphen (-)

It is shorter than a dash in length. It is most often used to make compound words or to break a word falling at the end of a line.

(*i*) maid-servant (*ii*) self-respect

MULTIPLE CHOICE QUESTIONS

Directions: *In the questions given below, which one alternative out of four has been applied with correct punctuation marks?*

1. Hurry up the train leaves at six o'clock
A. Hurry up; the train leaves at six o'clock.
B. Hurry up, the train leaves at six O'clock.
C. Hurry up! the train leaves at six o'clock.
D. Hurry up, the train leaves at six o'clock.

2. It is a sin to waste food said the father
A. It is a sin to waste food said the father.
B. 'It is a sin to waste food' said the father.
C. "It is a sin to waste food" said the father.
D. "It is a sin to waste food," said the father.

3. This is his fathers car
A. This is his fathers' car.
B. This is his father's car.
C. This is his father's car.
D. This is his fathers' car.

4. The man asked the taxi driver will you take me to the airport
A. The man asked the taxi driver, will you take me to the airport?
B. The man asked the taxi driver, "Will you take me to the airport?"
C. The man asked the taxi driver, "Will you take me to the airport."
D. The man asked the taxi driver, "will you take me to the airport!"

5. Bring me a glass of water said the teacher I am feeling very thirsty
A. "Bring me a glass of water," said the teacher, "I am feeling very thirsty."
B. "Bring me a glass of water" said the teacher, "I am feeling very thirsty."
C. "Bring me a glass of water" said the teacher "I am feeling very thirsty."
D. "Bring me a glass of water, said the teacher, "I am feeling very thirsty."

6. Ram said I am in a hurry I cannot spare tiine
A. Ram said, "I am in a hurry" "I cannot spare time."
B. Ram said "I am in a hurry I cannot spare time."
C. Ram said, "I am in a hurry, I cannot spare time."
D. Ram said, "I am in a hurry I cannot spare time."

7. How have you found so much wealth asked Anil's wife
A. "How have you found so much wealth!" asked Anil's wife.
B. "How have you found so much wealth?" asked Anil's wife.
C. "How have you found so much wealth." asked Anil's wife.
D. "How have you found so much wealth?", asked Anil's wife.

8. What is the matter why are you crying he asked the child

A. "What is the matter, why are you crying?" he asked the child.

B. "What is the matter? why are you crying?" he asked the child

C. "What is the matter" "why are you crying?" he asked the child.

D. "What is the matter? Why are you crying?" he asked the child.

9. I am going to marry and I want a house to live in said the young man

A. "I am going to marry and I want a house to live in", said the young man.

B. "I am going to marry" and "I want a house to live in" said the young man.

C. "I am going to marry and I want a house to live in" said the young man.

D. "I am going to marry and I want a house to live in." said the young man.

10. What harm is there if we admit the error the lawyer said

A. "What harm is there, if we admit the error?" the lawyer said.

B. "What harm is there if, we admit the error?" the lawyer said.

C. "What harm is there if we admit the error?" the lawyer said.

D. "What harm is there? if we admit the error". the lawyer said.

11. The more we hate one another the worse it will be for everybody

A. The more we hate one another the worse it will be for everybody.

B. The more we hate one another, the worse it will be for everybody.

C. The more we hate one another; the worse it will be for everybody.

D. The more we hate one another – the worse it will be for everybody.

12. Anita's father Mr Anil Kumar is a teacher

A. Anita's father Mr Anil Kumar is a teacher.

B. Anita's father, Mr Anil Kumar is a teacher.

C. Anita's father Mr Anil Kumar, is a teacher.

D. Anita's father, Mr Anil Kumar, is a teacher.

13. Considering all aspects of the matter they decided to give up the plan.

A. Considering all aspects of the matter, they decided to give up the plan.

B. Considering, all aspects of the matter, they decided to give up the plan.

C. Considering all aspects, of the matter, they decided to give up the plan.

D. Considering all aspects of the matter they decided to give up the plan.

14. The Narmada the Ganga and the Yamuna are three of the largest Indian rivers

A. The Narmada, the Ganga and the Yamuna are three of the largest Indian rivers

B. The Narmada, the Ganga, and the Yamuna are three of the largest Indian rivers

C. The Narmada, the Ganga and the Yamuna are three of the largest Indian rivers.

D. The Narmada, the Ganga and, the Yamuna are three of the largest Indian rivers.

15. What a remarkable victory

A. What, a remarkable victory.

B. What a remarkable victory.

C. What a remarkable victory?

D. What a remarkable victory!

16. The election many people said would spring a big surprise and they were proved right

A. The election, many people said, "would spring a big surprise and they were proved right."

B. "The election," many people said, "would spring a big surprise and they were proved right."

C. "The election" many people said, "Would spring a big surprise and they were proved right."

D. "The election" many people said "would spring a big surprise and they were proved right."

17. Are you going he asked we are not I replied

A. "Are you going?" he asked, "We are not." I replied.

B. "Are you going?" he asked, "we are not" I replied.

C. "Are you going?" he asked. "We are not," I replied.

D. "Are you going?" he asked, "we are not" I replied.

18. Here I am master I am ready to go wherever you want me to go he said

A. "Here I am, master, I am ready to go," wherever you want me to go he said.

B. "Here I am master, I am ready to go wherever you want me to go" he said.

C. "Here I am master, I am ready to go wherever you want me to go", he said.

D. "Here I am, master, I am ready to go wherever you want me to go", he said.

19. What is your reason for refusing to marry this girl asked his mother

A. "What is your reason for refusing to marry this girl?" asked his mother.

B. "What is your reason, for refusing to marry this girl?" asked his mother.

C. "What is your reason for refusing to marry this girl?" asked his mother

D. "What is your reason for refusing to marry this girl," asked his mother.

20. He said my brother had an accident on Sunday the 28th April 2013 and is still confined to bed

A. He said "my brother had an accident on Sunday the 28th April 2013 and is still confined to bed."
B. He said "My brother had an accident on Sunday the 28th April 2013 and is still confined to bed."
C. He said, "My brother had an accident on Sunday, the 28th April 2013, and is still confined to bed."
D. He said," My brother had an accident on Sunday, the 28th April 2013 and is still confined to bed."

21. How many r's are there in referred I asked

A. How many r's are there in referred? I asked.
B. "How many r's are there, in referred" I asked.
C. "How many r's are there in referred?" I asked.
D. "How many rs' are there in referred?" I asked.

22. Friends colleagues relatives none stood by him

A. Friends, colleagues, relatives none stood by him.
B. Friends, colleagues, relatives, none stood by him.
C. Friends, colleagues, relatives, none, stood by him
D. Friends, colleagues, relatives none, stood by him.

23. He said I am sorry I could not reach in time

A. He said, "I am sorry I could not reach in time."
B. He said "I am sorry. I could not reach in time."
C. He said, "I am sorry. I could not reach in time."
D. He said "I am sorry I could not reach in time."

24. Never listen to his stories don't believe what he says and always distrust him

A. Never listen to his stories, don't believe what he says? and always distrust him.
B. Never listen to his stories, don't believe, what he says? and always distrust him.
C. Never listen to his stories, do'nt believe what he says and always distrust him.
D. Never listen to his stories, don't believe what he says and always distrust him.

25. Man proposes God disposes

A. Man proposes God disposes.
B. Man proposes, God disposes.
C. Man proposes, God disposes!
D. Man proposes God disposes!

26. He asked me what I wanted

A. He asked me, what I wanted?
B. He asked me "what I wanted."
C. He asked me what I wanted.
D. He asked me "what I wanted!"

27. He said to me lets wait for him

A. He said to me, "Let's wait for him."
B. He said to me 'Lets wait for him.'
C. He said to me, "let's wait for him."
D. he said to me, "Let's wait for him."

28. In india the ganga and the yamuna are regarded as sacred rivers

A. In India, the Ganga and the Yamuna are regarded as sacred rivers.
B. In India, the ganga and the Yamuna are regarded as sacred rivers.
C. In India, the ganga and the yamuna are regarded as sacred rivers.
D. In India, the Ganga and the yamuna are regarded as sacred rivers.

29. To err is human to forgive divine

A. To err is human to forgive divine.
B. To err is human, to forgive divine.
C. To err, is human to forgive, divine.
D. To err is human; to forgive, divine.

30. He was born on August 16, 1944 in Howrah West Bengal

A. He was born on August 16, 1944 in Howrah West Bengal.
B. He was born on August 16, 1944, in Howrah West Bengal.
C. He was born on, August 16 1944 in Howrah West Bengal.
D. He was born on August, 16 1944, in Howrah West Bengal.

31. He is to tell you the truth is a fool

A. He is, to tell you the truth, is a fool.
B. He is to tell you, the truth is a fool.
C. He is to tell you the truth, is a fool.
D. He is to tell you the truth is a fool.

32. This in brief is what he said

A. This in brief is what he said.
B. This in brief, is what he said.
C. This, in brief, is what he said.
D. This, in brief is what, he said.

33. If you need my help write to me

A. If you need my help write to me.
B. If, you need my help, write to me.
C. If you need, my help, write to me.
D. If you need my help, write to me.

34. They started running for they were getting late

A. They started running, for they were getting late.
B. They started running for they were getting late.
C. They started running for, they were getting late.
D. They started, running for, they were getting late.

35. The sun having set it became pleasant

A. The sun having set it became pleasant.
B. The sun, having set, it became pleasant.
C. The sun having set, it became pleasant.
D. The sun, having set it, became pleasant.

36. Mr Sushil please listen to me

A. Mr Sushil please listen to me.
B. Mr Sushil, please listen to me.
C. Mr Sushil please, listen to me.
D. Mr Sushil, please, listen to me.

37. Wherever you go you face the same difficulties
A. Wherever you go you face the same difficulties.
B. Wherever, you go, you face the same difficulties.
C. Wherever you go, you face, the same difficulties.
D. Wherever you go, you face the same difficulties.

38. Tell me what I can do for you
A. Tell me what I can do for you.
B. Tell me what I can do for you!
C. Tell me what I can do for you?
D. Tell me, what I can do for you?

39. May you live long
A. May you live long.
B. May you live long?
C. May you live long!
D. May, you live long!

40. May God the Greatest bless you
A. May God the Greatest bless you.
B. May God, the Greatest bless you!
C. May God, the Greatest, bless you.
D. May God, the Greatest, bless you!

41. The sun having risen the fog disappeared
A. The sun having risen the fog disappeared.
B. The sun having risen, the fog disappeared.
C. The sun having risen; the fog disappeared.
D. The sun, having risen, the fog disappeared!

42. Having done his homework he went to bed
A. Having done his homework he went to bed.
B. Having done, his homework he went to bed.
C. Having done, his homework, he went to bed.
D. Having done his homework, he went to bed.

43. He is indeed a foolish boy
A. He is indeed, a foolish boy.
B. He is indeed a foolish boy.
C. He is, indeed, a foolish boy.
D. He, is indeed, a foolish boy.

44. Naresh my younger brother has gone to Patna
A. Naresh, my younger brother, has gone to Patna.
B. Naresh, my younger brother has gone to Patna.
C. Naresh my younger brother, has gone to Patna.
D. Naresh! my younger brother has gone to Patna.

45. Well I shall look into the matter
A. Well I shall look into the matter.
B. Well, I shall look into the matter.
C. Well I shall, look into the matter.
D. Well I shall, look into, the matter.

46. All right you can go
A. All right you can go.
B. All right you, can go.
C. All right, you can go.
D. All right! you can go.

47. Carry on your work I am watching you
A. Carry on your work I am watching you.
B. Carry on, your work, I am watching you.
C. Carry on, your work, I am watching you.
D. Carry on your work, I am watching you.

48. He was a kind bold man and we all praised him.
A. He was a kind bold man and we all praised him
B. He was a kind, bold man and we all praised him.
C. He was a kind bold, man and we all praised him.
D. He was, a kind bold man, and we all praised him.

49. He said honesty is the best policy
A. He said honesty is the best policy.
B. He said, honesty is the best policy.
C. He said "Honesty is the best policy."
D. He said, "Honesty is the best policy."

50. What a beautiful flower it is
A. What a beautiful flower it is.
B. What a beautiful flower it is?
C. What a beautiful flower it is!
D. What! a beautiful flower it is.

ANSWERS

1	2	3	4	5	6	7	8	9	10
D	D	C	B	A	C	B	D	A	C
11	**12**	**13**	**14**	**15**	**16**	**17**	**18**	**19**	**20**
B	D	A	C	D	B	C	D	A	D
21	**22**	**23**	**24**	**25**	**26**	**27**	**28**	**29**	**30**
C	B	A	D	B	C	A	A	D	B
31	**32**	**33**	**34**	**35**	**36**	**37**	**38**	**39**	**40**
A	C	D	A	C	B	D	A	C	D
41	**42**	**43**	**44**	**45**	**46**	**47**	**48**	**49**	**50**
B	D	C	A	B	C	D	B	D	C

VOCABULARY-I

5 Synonyms and Antonyms

English is the most popular language of the world. It comprises thousands of words. No one can remember all the words and their meanings but everyone must try to read and learn the maximum number of words and their meanings. Readers must keep and use a dictionary religiously. Several important words are listed below with their synonyms and antonyms. Learn as many as you can.

ABANDON
Syn.: discard, desert, discontinue, renounce, relinquish, abnegate, forsake, surrender, give up, quit.
Ant.: retain, maintain, uphold, stay, remain.

ABATE
Syn.: lessen, decrease, diminish, subside, slacken, subside, allay, reduce, curtail.
Ant.: increase, enlarge, heighten, intensify, raise.

ABBREVIATE
Syn.: shorten, abridge, compress, curtain, condense, contract, prune, truncate, reduce.
Ant.: enlarge, expand, lengthen, extend, elongate, prolong, protract.

ABILITY
Syn.: competence, aptitude, capability, talent, intelligence, cleverness, capacity.
Ant.: inability, incompetence, incapacity, incapability, inaptitude.

ABLE
Syn.: capable, competent, intelligent, talented, efficient, skilful.
Ant.: unable, incapable, inefficient, incompetent.

ABRUPT
Syn.: sudden, curt, steep, hasty, unexpected, disconnected, disjointed, brusque, rough.
Ant.: expected, anticipated, gradual, courteous, smooth.

ABSURD
Syn.: illogical, irrational, inconsistent, silly, inane, unreasonable, funny, ridiculous, laughable, ludicrous, nonsensical, fatuous.
Ant.: logical, reasonable, rational, consistent, sensible, sound, proper, sane.

ACCURATE
Syn.: exact, precise, correct, actual, just, right, correct.
Ant.: incorrect, inexact, improper, fallacious, inaccurate, misleading, erroneous.

ADEQUATE
Syn.: ample, abundant, enough, sufficient, plentiful, copious.
Ant.: inadequate, insufficient, meagre, scant, scantly, skimpy.

AFFABLE
Syn.: urbane, polite, friendly, courteous, amiable, suave, good-tempered.
Ant.: impolite, unfriendly, discourteous, haughty.

AKIN
Syn.: kindred, similar, allied, cognate, alike, related, analogous.
Ant.: dissimilar, unrelated, unallied, unconnected, different, unlike, separate.

ALERT
Syn.: wary, vigilant, watchful, attentive, heedful, cautious, lively, fully awake.
Ant.: unwatchful, sluggish, relaxed, quiet, restful.

ABNORMAL
Syn.: unusual, irregular, anomalous, unnatural, odd, strange, erratic.
Ant.: usual, regular, natural, normal, customary.

ACTIVE
Syn.: brisk, energetic, lively, nimble, agile.
Ant.: inactive, indolent, sluggish, lazy, passive, torpid.

ACTUAL
Syn.: real, genuine, authentic, true, concrete, factual, existing.
Ant.: unreal, implied, assumed, false, imaginary, fictitious.

AMBIGUOUS
Syn.: vague, uncertain, undecided, undefined, obscure, doubtful, indistinct, dubious, perplexing.

Ant.: lucid, plain, clear, obvious, unambiguous, unmistakable, indisputable.

APT

Syn.: appropriate, apposite, suitable, fitting, pertinent, germane, relevant, congruent, harmonious, congruous.

Ant.: inapt, inappropriate, incongruous, improper, unsuitable, inapposite, irrelevant.

ARDENT

Syn.: fervid, fervent, warm, impassioned, plowing, intense, eager, earnest, passionate, hearty, cordial, enthusiastic.

Ant.: cool, indifferent, apathetic, nonchalant, unimpassioned.

ATROCIOUS

Syn.: nefarious, heinous, cruel, outrageous, beastly, horrible, horrendous.

Ant.: noble, humane, honourable, laudable, admirable, moral.

AUDACIOUS

Syn.: bold, daring, fearless, impudent, brash, rash, reckless, impertinent, madcap, insolent, brave, disrespectful, intrepid.

Ant.: cowardly, timid, fearful, meek, humble, afraid, frightened, scared, different, panicky, apprehensive, shy, mousy, timorous, fidgety.

AUTHENTIC

Syn.: genuine, real, trustworthy, true, reliable, accurate, authoritative, sound, tangible, definite, actual, precise, exact, correct, factual, veritable, sterling.

Ant.: apocryphal, unreliable, spurious, false, fictitious, fake, sham, imaginary, counterfeit, baseless, untrue.

BEAUTIFUL

Syn.: catching, prepossessing, fetching, cute, enticing, engaging, attractive, charming, fascinating, captivating, alluring, tempting, lovely, bewitching, reductive, pretty, enchanting, winning, comely.

Ant.: ugly, unattractive, unprepossessing, repulsive, gaunt, haggard, unpleasing, revolting, hideous.

BITTER

Syn.: tart, harsh, pungent, unpalatable, acrid, spiteful, cutting, stinging, sour, unpleasant, sarcastic, resentful, biting, sardonic, caustic, severe, acrimonious, poignant, distasteful.

Ant.: tasty, toothsome, tasteful, palatable, pleasant, delicious, warm.

BRIGHT

Syn.: brilliant, shining, luminous, lustrous, radiant, sparkling, quick-witted, cheerful, clever, resplendent, flashing, lucid, limpid, sagacious, keen, astute, shrewd, brainy, intelligent.

Ant.: dull, ignorant, cheerless, imbecile, murky, dark, gloomy, sullen.

BRIEF

Syn.: compendious, concise, short, terse, laconic, curt, succinct, condensed, compact, pithy.

Ant.: long, lengthy, prolonged, protracted, elongated, lengthened, extended, detailed, prolix, verbose, wordy.

BRUTAL

Syn.: atrocious, savage, beastly, brutish, fiendish, devilish, barbarous, cruel, ruthless, merciless, crude, ferocious, bestial, heinous.

Ant.: humane, gentle, civilised, merciful, polished, sympathetic, tender, liberal, considerate, good-natured.

CANDID

Syn.: frank, outspoken, sincere, impartial, honest, artless, ingenuous, straightforward.

Ant.: sly, wily, insincere, reserved, unfair, evasive.

CAPRICIOUS

Syn.: unpredictable, impulsive, fickle, changeable, inconstant, whimsical.

Ant.: constant, firm, steadfast, unswerving.

CARELESS

Syn.: heedless, inattentive, indifferent, negligent, remiss, lax, unmindful.

Ant.: cautious, vigilant, careful, mindful, attentive.

CERTAIN

Syn.: indisputable, reliable, sure, definite, undisputed, unmistakable, positive, absolute.

Ant.: uncertain, disputable, doubtful, indefinite, ambiguous, dubious, questionable.

CHEEK

Syn.: impudence, impertinence, effrontery, gall, temerity, audacity, insolence, sauce, sass.

Ant.: politeness, courtesy, humility, gentleness, respect.

☛ *Cheek* also means either side of the face below the eye.

Examples: She has healthy rosy *cheeks*.
They are dancing *cheek* to *cheek*.

CHEERFUL

Syn.: genial, happy, jolly, merry, jovial, pleasant, lively, cheery, sunny, jocund, gay.

Ant.: cheerless, joyless, dejected, unhappy, doleful, sorrowful, mournful, glum, dreary, dismal.

CHARM (Verb)

Syn.: fascinate, attract, please, delight, influence, entice, enchant, entrance, enrapture, allure, captivate, bewitch, ravish, tempt, lure, seduce, beguile, enthral, thrill.

Ant.: repel, repulse, rebuff, snub, disgust, deter, disturb, irritate, annoy, alarm, frighten, terrify.

COMFORTABLE

Syn.: cosy, snug, pleasant, pleasing, pleasurable, satisfied.

Ant.: uncomfortable, disagreeable, dissatisfied, disturbed, displeasing, irritating, miserable, wretched, troubled, cheerless.

COMPLETE (Adj)

Syn.: whole, thorough, total, entire, full, perfect, exhausive, consummate.

Ant.: incomplete, imperfect, partial, unfinished, uncompleted, unaccomplished, deficient, skimpy, sketchy.

CORDIAL

Syn.: sincere, friendly, earnest, warm, hearty, ardent, heartfelt, amiable, affable.

Ant.: unfriendly, insincere, cold, distant, formal, reserved.

COURAGE

Syn.: bravery, boldness, valour, heroism, fearlessness, intrepidity, nerve, gallantry, pluck, fortitude, daring.

Ant.: cowardice, timidity, pusillanimity, fear, funk.

CURIOUS

Syn.: inquisitive, inquiring, prying, strange, unusual, nosey, meddlesome.

Ant.: incurious, uninquiring, uninquisitive, uninterested, unconcerned, indifferent, common, usual.

CORRECT (Adj)

Syn.: accurate, proper, exact, precise, right, true, regular, perfect.

Ant.: incorrect, improper, inexact, wrong, untrue, irregular, imperfect.

DAFT

Syn.: silly, crazy, irrational, foolish, unreasonable, reckless, insane, imbecile, lumpish.

Ant.: sane, sound, sensible, deft, rational, reasonable.

DAINTY

Syn.: pretty, neat, delicate, refined, tasty, delicious, fastidious, elegant, toothsome, exquisite, cute, tasteful, palatable.

Ant.: inelegant, coarse, vulgar, rough, crude, rude, nasty, dirty.

DEEP

Syn.: abstruse, profound, intense, learned, sagacious, extreme, devious, vivid, submerged, bottomless, unfathomable, abysmal, mysterious, knotty, astute, recondite, intricate.

Ant.: shallow, apparent, familiar, artless, commonplace, ordinary, trite, naive, superficial, cursory, simple, banal.

DELIGHT

Syn.: joy, pleasure, rapture, ecstasy, enjoyment, bliss, gratification, gusto, comfort.

Ant.: displeasure, discomfort, sorrow, distress, misery, anguish, suffering, agony, woe, despair, depression.

DETRIMENTAL

Syn.: harmful, injurious, hurtful, pernicious, damaging, noxious.

Ant.: good, beneficial, valuable, useful, profitable, harmless, inoffensive, unobnoxious.

DIFFICULT

Syn.: hard, troublesome, perplexing, tough, laborious, irksome, toilsome, arduous, knotty, burdensome, uphill, herculean, enigmatic.

Ant.: easy, uncomplicated, intelligible, lucid, plain, simple, facile, manageable, tractable, elementary, rudimentary.

DILIGENT

Syn.: industrious, laborious, hard-working, attentive, assiduous, observant, mindful, vigilant, watchful, wakeful, careful.

Ant.: careless, heedless, inattentive, indifferent, unobservant, unmindful.

DISHONEST

Syn.: untrustworthy, false, fraudulent, deceitful, crooked, tricky, deceptive, treacherous, unjust, unfair, unreliable.

Ant.: trustworthy, reliable, fair, just, candid, frank, sincere, upright, truthful, veracious, honest.

DOCILE

Syn.: pliant, tractable, amenable, teachable, yielding, compliant, tame, submissive, gentle, unresisting, dutiful, passive, acquiescent, unassertive, manageable, governable, obsequious.

Ant.: obstinate, stubborn, intractable, self-willed, dogged, defiant, insolent, resistant, resisting, obdurate, disobedient, wilful, uncompromising, unyielding, refractory, recalcitrant.

DOUBTFUL

Syn.: questionable, uncertain, unsure, unlikely, improbable, disputable, debatable, dubious, controversial, fishy, moot, ambiguous.

Ant.: certain, sure, probable, indisputable, unquestionable, positive, absolute, definite, clear, unmistakable, reliable, trustworthy, undoubted, undeniable, indubitable.

DROLL

Syn.: amusing, laughable, funny, comic, sarcastic, whimsical, comical, odd, queer, farcical, ludicrous, ridiculous, absurd, diverting, rompish.

Ant.: sad, lamentable, lugubrious, tragic, painful, dolorous, hurtful, distressing, grievous, woeful, rueful, mournful, deplorable, touching.

DULL

Syn.: stupid, boring, monotonous, foolish, unintelligent, cheerless, gloomy, uninteresting, spiritless, blunt, doltish, sad, stolid, dismal, dowdy, drab, unfashionable, insensible.

Ant.: sensible, cheerful, bright, intelligent, clever, lively, animated, brilliant, sharp, talented, jolly, merry, joyful, gay, jocund, energetic, keen, active, intense, brisk, lively, trenchant, rousing.

EAGER

Syn.: ardent, earnest, zealous, keen, fervent, fervid, vehement, intent, agog, avid, excited, impatient, curious, anxious, enthusiastic, wistful, hearty, cordial, desirous.

Ant.: indifferent, disinterested, cool, loath, unconcerned, apathetic, reluctant, unwilling, disinclined.

EFFICIENT

Syn.: capable, able, competent, gifted, effective, effectual, efficacious, skilful, proficient, talented, intelligent, adept.

Ant.: inefficient, incompetent, ineffectual, unskilled, inexpert.

ELIGIBLE

Syn.: fit, suitable, desirable, worthy, qualified, acceptable, right.

Ant.: unfit, unsuitable, unworthy, unacceptable, undesirable, unqualified.

EMPHEMERAL
Syn.: short-lived, transitory, transient, fleeting, momentary, fugitive, evanescent, fugacious, temporary.
Ant.: eternal, perpetual, perennial, permanent, intransient, lifelong, everlasting, long-lived, prolonged, protracted.

ENORMOUS
Syn.: immense, gigantic, colossal, huge, vast, gargantuan, monstrous, prodigious, stupendous, plentiful, plenteous, copious.
Ant.: trivial, insignificant, ordinary, average, small, little, tiny, diminutive.

ENOUGH
Syn.: plenty, ample, sufficient, abundant, adequate.
Ant.: insufficient, inadequate, meagre, scanty, deficient, scant, jejune, skimpy.

ENTHUSIASM
Syn.: verve, ardour, zeal, fervour, fanaticism.
Ant.: apathy, indifference, detachment, ennui, unconcern, lethargy, weariness, exhaustion, lassitude, languor.

EXPERT (Adj)
Syn.: adept, skilled, adroit, proficient, skilful, deft, dexterous, versed, accomplished.
Ant.: inexpert, unskilful, unskilled, maladroit, clumsy, lungling, unqualified, raw, inexperienced, green, incompetent.

FACE (V)
Syn.: confront, oppose, defy, meet, encounter, resist.
Ant.: avoid, shun, elude, avert, eschew.

FAITHFUL
Syn.: loyal, trustworthy, conscientious, true, accurate, devoted, exact, reliable, staunch, steadfast, constant, dependable, compliant.
Ant.: disloyal, untrustworthy, inaccurate, inexact, unreliable, unfaithful, treacherous, undependable, untrue, fickle.

FICKLE
Syn.: inconstant, disloyal, unfaithful, capricious, impulsive, unpredictable, changeable, unstable, variable, vacillating, wavering, fanciful, whimsical, mutable, irresolute, erratic, unreliable, fitful.
Ant.: steady, steadfast, unchangeable, unwavering, constant, loyal, faithful, reliable, dependable, stable, immutable, invariable.

FIT (Adj)
Ant.: suitable, appropriate, proper, advantageous, sound, well, meet, becoming, fitting, qualified, apt, apposite, decent, decorous, congruent, congruous, concordant, harmonious, eligible.
Ant.: unfit, unsuitable, unbecoming, disadvantageous, unwell, indecent, indecorous, improper, inappropriate, inapt, incongruent, ineligible.

FOOLISH
Syn.: silly, stupid, unwise, ridiculous, absurd, asinine, imbecile, indiscreet, irrational, idiotic, brainless, senseless, nonsensical, witless, preposterous, inane, fatuous, imprudent, inconsistent, illogical, laughable, paradoxical, dotty.
Ant.: wise, sane, prudent, discreet, sound, sensible, rational, sagacious, judicious, sage.

FRIENDLY
Syn.: kindly, pleasantly, amicable, cordial, hearty, warm-hearted, affable, genial, well-inclined, good-tempered, amiable, favourable, pleasing, sociable, companionable, nice, neighbourly, benevolent, well-disposed.
Ant.: hostile, unsociable, unfavourable, unfriendly, adverse, inimical, antagonistic, distant, reserved, cool, ill-inclined, ill-disposed, resistant, opposed.

FUNDAMENTAL
Syn.: basic, primary, essential, cardinal, indispensable, original, rudimentary, elementary, radical, most important, prime, chief.
Ant.: secondary, subordinate, minor, inferior, resultant, second-rate, subsidiary.

FUNNY
Syn.: amusing, jocular, jocose, laughable, eccentric, absurd, droll, comical, comic, playful, ludicrous, farcical, humorous, ridiculous, odd, queer, diverting, strange.
Ant.: sad, serious, solemn, sober, sedate, staid, grave, sorrowful, mournful.

GARRULOUS
Syn.: talkative, chatty, verbose, loquacious, communicative, glib, voluble, prolix, wordy, long-winded, diffuse, profuse, discussive, rambling, circumlocutory, maundering, periphrastic.
Ant.: laconic, reticent, silent, taciturn, uncommunicative, terse, reserved, short-spoken.

GENUINE
Syn.: authentic, sound, true, real, pure, veritable, unadulterated, unalloyed, unaffected, natural, factual, actual, legitimate, undistorted, tangible, valid, sterling.
Ant.: sham, spurious, fictitious, artificial, adulterated, alloyed, impure, apocryphal, untrue, fallacious, unsound, invalid.

GIFTED
Syn.: talented, intelligent, sagacious, competent, wise, able, proficient, efficient, capable, shrewd, inventive, skilful, ingenious, experienced.
Ant.: foolish, doltish, silly, stupid, idiotic.

GLORIOUS
Syn.: famous, beautiful, splendid, magnificent, enjoyable, pleasant, grand, exalted, lofty, majestic, sublime, noble, bright, radiant, renowned.
Ant.: base, ignoble, low, ordinary, ridiculous.

GOOD (N)
Syn.: benefit, profit, advantage, virtue, boon, weal, prosperity, blessing, gain, welfare, righteousness, merit.

Ant.: harm, injury, corruption, wickedness, depravity, detriment, disadvantage, ill, calamity, loss, evil, curse.

GRACEFUL

Syn.: elegant, pleasing in style and attitude, polite, considerate, comely, beautiful, attractive, lithe, lissom, svelte, sylphlike, willowy.

Ant.: ungainly, awkward, lumbering, uncouth, ill mannered, not refined.

GRAND

Syn.: august, exalted, stately, splendid, majestic, lofty, superb, imposing, dignified, noble, princely, magnificent, big, pompous, gorgeous, sublime, impressive.

Ant.: mean, common, insignificant, secondary, inferior, unimportant, little, undignified, unimposing, petty, paltry, beggarly, lowly.

GRIM

Syn.: fearful, stern, fierce, ruthless, horrible, determined, strong-willed, horrid, repellent, frightful, ghastly, gristly, gloomy, severe, unrelenting, unpleasant, depressing, determined, repulsive, dingy, drab, savage, appalling, ferocious, ugly, sullen, hideous.

Ant.: handsome, pretty, graceful, elegant, gentle, gracious, friendly, humane, benign, mild, docile, attractive.

GRUFF

Syn.: rough, surly, blunt, harsh, rude.

Ant.: affable, courteous, mild, smooth.

HARMFUL

Syn.: detrimental, pernicious, prejudicial, deleterious, injurious, noxious, hurtful, mischievous, obnoxious, inauspicious, oppressive, baneful, baleful, menacing, malignant, unhealthful, vitiated, damaging.

Ant.: helpful, profitable, beneficial, advantageous, harmless, useful, favourable, good, salutary, healthful, inoffensive, unobnoxious.

HARMONIOUS

Syn.: congruous, concordant, uniform, proportioned, consistent, tuneful, melodious, sweet-sounding, agreeable, friendly, amicable, cordial.

Ant.: unfriendly, hostile, unfavourable, adverse, opposing, opposed, antagonistic, contrary, discordant, conflicting, inconsistent.

HARSH

Syn.: rough, stern, cruel, severe, blunt, coarse, gruff, discordant, raucous, hoarse, rugged, severe, shrill, strident, austere, acrimonious, ungenial, sharp, sour, ungracious, brutal, heartless.

Ant.: gentle, mild, smooth, soft, melodious.

HEALTHY

Syn.: robust, strong, vigorous, lusty, hearty, sound, well, hygienic, salubrious, wholesome, salutary, bracing, invigorating, harmless, healthful, hale and hearty, inoffensive, laudable, moral.

Ant.: diseased, delicate, infirm, injurious, frail, noxious, sick, ailing, ill, sick.

HEARTY

Syn.: warm, earnest, sincere, heartfelt, cordial, sound, ardent, friendly, enthusiastic, cheerful, healthy, fervent, fervid.

Ant.: cool, reserved, taciturn, insincere.

HONEST

Syn.: frank, sincere, direct, fairly earned, truthful, upright, virtuous, right, sincere, genuine, trustworthy.

Ant.: dishonest, untrustworthy, tricky, deceitful, fraudulent, insincere.

HONOUR (N)

Syn.: privilege, probity, integrity, glory, distinction, great respect, glory, dignity, reverence, grandeur, high-mindedness, eminence, renown, fame.

Ant.: dishonour, disrespect, contempt, irreverence, disgrace, degradation, slight, infamy, perfidy, treachery, improbity, scorn, disdain.

HUMOROUS

Syn.: droll, amusing, ludicrous, funny, jocular, merry, comic, jocose, waggish, farcical.

Ant.: solemn, serious, sober, grave, composed, sedate, dignified.

IDLE

Syn.: indolent, lazy, inactive, unemployed, useless, unoccupied, slothful, futile.

Ant.: active, busy, occupied, working, industrious, employed.

INDUSTRIOUS

Syn.: diligent, hard-working, laborious, assiduous, sedulous.

Ant.: lethargic, inactive, apathetic, lazy, idle, indolent, slothful, torpid, sluggish, shiftless, slack, lax, supine.

IMPORTANT

Syn.: significant, valuable, weighty, influential, momentous, prominent, material, essential, remarkable, eventful.

Ant.: insignificant, unimportant, petty, trivial, mean, secondary, minor, uninfluential, worthless, valueless, immaterial, inferior.

INGENIOUS

Syn.: adroit, clever, dexterous, quick-witted, skilful, talented, smart, bright, sharp, adept, original, inventive, expert, intelligent.

Ant.: unskilled, dull, foolish, clumsy, awkward, stupid, unskilful, inexpert, maladroit, incompetent, inexperienced, unconversant, ungainly.

INGENUOUS

Syn.: innocent, open, candid, frank, sincere, straightforward, truthful, artless, honest, naive, simple, trusting, unaffected, outspoken.

Ant.: insincere, reserved, sly, wily, contrived, disingenuous, mean, pretentious, sham, affected, priggish.

INFINITE

Syn.: boundless, endless, unlimited, unbounded, limitless, immeasurable, interminable, stupendous, eternal, immense, vast, incalculable, numberless, countless, bottomless, unfathomable, inexhaustible, indefinite, perpetual.

Ant.: finite, limited, restricted, bounded, conditioned, confined, definite, determinate, circumscribed.

INTELLIGENT

Syn.: brainy, clever, bright, brilliant, keen, sagacious, quick-witted, discerning, sharp, shrewd, astute, canny, perspicacious, perceptive, nimble, well-informed, enlightened.

Ant.: foolish, doltish, dull, stupid, unintelligent, stolid, obtuse, silly, inane.

INTEGRITY

Syn.: honesty, probity, uprightness, rectitude, truthfulness, sincerity, trustworthiness, fairness, wholeness, completeness, oneness, totality, entirety, indivisibility.

Ant.: dishonesty, duplicity, unfairness, deceit, fraud, improbity.

IRRITABLE

Syn.: peevish, touchy, irascible, testy, short-tempered, fretful, splenetic, petulant, grumpy, pettish, snappish, choleric, peppery, churlish, cantankerous, fractious, crabbed.

Ant.: calm, composed, agreeable, gracious, cheerful, genial, good-natured, blithe, jaunty, buoyant, lively, animated.

JEALOUS

Syn.: envious, invidious, suspicious, resentful, covetous, jaundiced, distrustful, apprehensive, intolerant.

Ant.: unenvious, unjealous, tolerant, liberal, genial, indifferent, unsuspecting.

JOLLY

Syn.: genial, jovial, jubilant, lively, gay, joyful, merry, mirthful, cheerful, light-hearted, jocular, jocund, blithe.

Ant.: cheerless, joyless, sad, mournful, gloomy, morose, sullen, lugubrious, sorrowful, melancholy, dismal, unhappy.

JUST

Syn.: fair, honest, proper, right, reasonable, well-founded, deserved, impartial, true, upright, exact, precise, proportioned, normal.

Ant.: unfair, unjust, improper, unreasonable, partial, untrue, inexact, abnormal, ill-proportioned, prejudiced, biased.

KEEN

Syn.: acute, sharp, penetrating, astute, clever, cunning, quick, shrewd, wily, eager, enthusiastic, intense, deep, strong, cutting, ardent, nippy, avid, fervent.

Ant.: indifferent, blunt, dull, languid, indifferent, cool, careless, half-hearted, unconcerned, lukewarm, impervious, insouciant.

KIND (Adj)

Syn.: friendly, gentle, mild, obliging, benign, lenient, helpful, sympathetic, favourable, benevolent, amiable, good-natured, cordial, courteous, gracious, warm-hearted, humane, compassionate, generous, philanthropic.

Ant.: unfriendly, unfavourable, discourteous, unkind, harsh, severe, hard, callous, cruel, inhumane.

KNOWLEDGE

Syn.: understanding, learning, information, instruction, acquaintance, cognition, cognizance, awareness, comprehension, apprehension, consciousness, familiarity, ken, enlightenment, experience, attainments, scholarship, education.

Ant.: ignorance, nescience, illiteracy, incomprehension, inexperience, unawareness.

LABORIOUS

Syn.: diligent, hard-working, industrious, toilsome, tedious, tiresome, irksome, arduous, assiduous, wearisome, strenuous, painstaking, uphill.

Ant.: easy, light, feasible, indiligent, lazy, indolent, simple, idle.

LACONIC

Syn.: curt, terse, concise, pithy, short, brief, succinct, crisp, compendious, compact.

Ant.: lengthy, prolix, wordy, circumlocutory, verbose, discursive, long-winded, rambling, roundabout, copious, diffuse.

LAX

Syn.: negligent, careless, remiss, sluggish, inattentive, neglectful, heedless, vague, desultory, unmethodical, loose, slack, relaxed.

Ant.: careful, meticulous, attentive, methodical, severe, strict, heedful, regardful, cautious, prudent, discreet.

LESSEN

Syn.: shorten, abate, curtail, decrease, reduce, diminish, abridge, mitigate, contract, deduct, subtract, shrink, attenuate.

Ant.: increase, enlarge, augment, extend, expand, grow, amplify, enhance, magnify.

LIVELY

Syn.: high-spirited, vigorous, energetic, active, animated, brisk, bright, blithe, frolicsome, merry, playful, spirited, forceful, sprightly, vivacious, joyous, joyful, gay.

Ant.: dull, listless, insipid, vapid, inactive, uninteresting, depressed, languid, torpid, apathetic, indifferent, sluggish, dejected, joyless, cheerless, unlively, spiritless.

LOGICAL

Syn.: cogent, convincing, sound, valid, effective, reasonable, natural, rational, sane, relevant.

Ant.: illogical, invalid, ineffective, unreasonable, unnatural, irrational, insane, irrelevant, fallacious.

MADDEN

Syn.: infuriate, enrage, incense, derange, craze, anger, offend, displease, embitter, exasperate, rankle, affront, irritate, provoke, nettle, inflame, annoy.

Ant.: placate, pacify, soothe, calm, assuage, appease, mollify.

MALICIOUS

Syn.: spiteful, malignant, malevolent, evil-minded, hostile, rancorous, virulent, wicked, malign, pernicious, vicious, harmful, maleficent, ill-disposed, ill-intentioned.

Ant.: benign, kind, good-natured, benevolent, cordial, unselfish, sympathetic, gracious, well-intentioned, humane, warm-hearted, affectionate.

MASTERLY

Syn.: skilful, adept, deft, dexterous, expert, skilled, consummate, perfect, masterful, dominating.

Ant.: unskilled, maladroit, clumsy, inexpert.

METHODICAL

Syn.: orderly, logical, systematic, regular, procedural, planned, arranged, tidy.

Ant.: disorderly, illogical, irregular, unsystematic, unmethodical, untidy, desultory, unarranged, disarranged, sloppy, chaotic, anarchical.

MODEST

Syn.: moderate, inexpensive, not showy or splendid in appearance, not vain or boastful, shy, bashful, humble, meek, reserved, unassuming, unpretentious, diffident, unobtrusive, coy.

Ant.: immodest, showy or splendid in appearance, vain, boastful, ostentatious, pretentious, proud, arrogant, bold, conceited, haughty, disdainful, pert, imperious, domineering, priggish, smug, self-satisfied, egotistic, self-important.

MOMENTOUS

Syn.: important, prominent, significant, weighty, material, pressing, influential, grave, consequential, serious, notable, solemn, memorable, remarkable.

Ant.: unimportant, immaterial, inconsequential, insignificant, mean, petty, trivial, slight, niggling, trifling.

NATURAL

Syn.: innate, inherent, original, normal, spontaneous, unaffected, characteristic, typical, native, unstudied, inborn, naive, ingenuous, inbred, ingrained, usual, intrinsic.

Ant.: unnatural, abnormal, artificial, affected, forced, irregular, unusual, inconsistent, fictitious.

NECESSARY

Syn.: requisite, needful, essential, inevitable, unavoidable, indispensable.

Ant.: unnecessary, optional, unessential, dispensable, voluntary, discretional, casual.

NICE

Syn.: pleasant, agreeable, friendly, kind, fine, subtle, respectable, scrupulous, dainty, attractive, fastidious, tasteful, delicate, choosy, refined, palatable, delectable, pleasing, pleasurable.

Ant.: disagreeable, coarse, unscrupulous, rough, nasty, rueful, mournful, woeful, deplorable, distressing.

NIMBLE

Syn.: agile, sharp, active, brisk, lively, spry, quick.

Ant.: slow, sluggish, clumsy, inert, lazy, indolent, awkward, slothful.

NOVICE

Syn.: beginner, tyro, neophyte, apprentice, greenhorn, learner, acolyte, rookie.

Ant.: expert, adept, master, teacher, trainer, instructor.

OBEDIENT

Syn.: observant, dutiful, complying, compliant, loyal, faithful, devoted, fractable, docile, submissive, pliable, pliant, yielding.

Ant.: disloyal, unfaithful, intractable, uncomplying, uncompliant, unruly, unsubmissive, refractory, resisting, contumacious, recalcitrant.

OBSTINATE

Syn.: stubborn, obdurate, dogged, tenacious, persistent, insistent, headstrong, pertinacious, unyielding, determined, self-willed, wilful, resolute.

Ant.: irresolute, subservient, yielding, submissive, amenable, wavering.

OFFENSIVE (Adj)

Syn.: insulting, annoying, disgusting, repulsive, aggressive, distasteful, foul, aggressive, obnoxious, nasty.

Ant.: pleasant, defensive, inoffensive, harmless, blameless, unaggressive, innocuous.

OWN (V)

Syn.: possess, confess, admit, avow, acknowledge, have, hold, concede.

Ant.: deny, disclaim, disavow, renounce, disown, abjure, abandon.

PEEVISH

Syn.: irritable, touchy, testy, tetchy, irascible, fretful, bad-tempered, crabbed, pettish, petulant, snappish, waspish, fractious, hot-headed, crabby, churlish.

Ant.: affable, genial, good-natured, good-tempered, pleasant, cordial, hearty, jolly, soft-spoken, polite, urbane.

PERFECT (Adj)

Syn.: complete, excellent, ideal, exact, precise, total, absolute, thorough, faultless, indefective, indeficient, immaculate, impeccable, sound, spotless, entire, utter, consummate.

Ant.: imperfect, incomplete, inexact, deficient, faulty, unsound, deformed, impaired, blemished, crude.

PLEASANT

Syn.: enjoyable, polite and friendly, pleasurable, agreeable, pleasing, delectable, palatable, delightful, cheerful, delicious, jocular, merry.

Ant.: unpleasant, disagreeable, unlively, lugubrious, dismal, sad, mournful, offensive, unpleasing, disgusting, obnoxious, nasty.

PLENTIFUL

Syn.: ample, abundant, copious, profuse, plenteous, prolific, bounteous, bountiful, lavish.

Ant.: scanty, meagre, limited, skimpy, insufficient, sparing, scarce, deficient, rare.

POMPOUS

Syn.: self-important, ostentatious, high-flown, bombastic, grandiose, arrogant, haughty, grand, imposing, lofty, magnificent, majestic, stately, sublime, dignified, showy, pretentious, assuming, turgid, magniloquent.

Ant.: unassuming, plain-mannered, unpretending, modest, unobtrusive, humble-minded, unpreten-tious, bashful, coy.

PRECISE

Syn.: exact, accurate, definite, correct, punctilious, fastidious, particular, proper.

Ant.: inexact, inaccurate, indefinite, incorrect, improper, vague, ambiguous, rough, circumlocutory.

PREPOSSESSING

Syn.: attractive, charming, taking, alluring, engaging, winning, appealing, winsome.

Ant.: unattractive, repulsive, ugly, unprepossessing, ill-looking.

PREPOSTEROUS

Syn.: outrageous, absurd, unreasonable, ridiculous, foolish, silly, stupid, inconsistent, irrational, nonsensical, laughable, idiotic, illogical, ludicrous.

Ant.: consistent, reasonable, rational, logical, sensible, sound, just, fair, right, moderate.

PRINCIPAL (Adj)

Syn.: chief, main, foremost, prime, leading, most important, pre-eminent, outstanding, excellent, conspicuous, highest, first-rate, cardinal, fundamental, primary, paramount, supreme, predominant.

Ant.: minor, inferior, subordinate, secondary, auxiliary, subsidiary.

PUSHY

Syn.: aggressive, offensive, forceful, belligerent, bold, impudent, rude, disrespectful, insolent, self-assertive.

Ant.: cowardly, timid, defensive.

QUESTIONABLE

Syn.: doubtful, uncertain, suspicious, dubious, disputable, debatable, arguable, fishy, controversial.

Ant.: certain, indisputable, obvious, evident, unquestionable, sure.

QUICKEN

Syn.: hasten, hurry, speed, accelerate, refresh, animate, rush, expedite.

Ant.: retard, slacken, moderate, curb, shorten, slow, relax, delay, impede, hinder, obstruct.

QUIET (Adj)

Syn.: calm, peaceful, serene, hushed, silent, modest, restrained, subdued, gentle, unostentatious, restful, relaxed, leisurely, unhurried, reposeful, tranquil, quiescent, unobtrusive, passive, undisturbed, motionless, still, mild, modest.

Ant.: loud, agitated, disturbed, perturbed, noisy.

QUIET (N)

Syn.: calm, calmness, hush, peace, repose, rest, silence, stillness, tranquility, serenity, quiescence, quietude.

Ant.: agitation, disturbance, uproar, noise, din, noisiness, loudness, tumult, excitement, turmoil, commotion, unrest.

RAPID

Syn.: speedy, quick, swift, fast, prompt, expeditious, hasty, hurried.

Ant.: slow, sluggish, slack, tardy, leisurely, gradual, languid.

REASONABLE

Syn.: sensible, logical, moderate, tolerable, acceptable, average, sound, fair, rational, inexpensive, sober, temperate.

Ant.: unreasonable, absurd, unfair, illogical, irrational, intolerable, immoderate, expensive, senseless, preposterous, ridiculous, silly, excessive, obstinate.

REGULAR

Syn.: proper, systematic, symmetrical, normal, usual, habitual, constant, orderly, steady, methodical, consistent.

Ant.: irregular, improper, abnormal, unusual, disorderly, inconstant, desultory, unmethodical, changeable, erratic, sporadic.

REMARKABLE

Syn.: unusual, exceptional, august, impressive, extra-ordinary, uncommon, splendid, singular, notable, noteworthy, striking, distinguished, wonderful, famous, prominent, conspicuous, imposing.

Ant.: ordinary, average, inconspicuous, normal, usual, common, customary, undistinguished.

RESPONSIBLE

Syn.: answerable, trustworthy, dependable, accountable, liable, chargeable, reliable.

Ant.: irresponsible, untrustworthy, undependable, unreliable, unaccountable, unanswerable.

RICH

Syn.: wealthy, affluent, prosperous, opulent, nourishing, abundant, ample, fruitful, fertile, luxuriant, vivid, bountiful, sumptuous, gorgeous, sonorous, well-to-do, plentiful, fecund, well-heeled, productive, wholesome, nutritious.

Ant.: poor, needy, penniless, beggarly, indigent, destitute, barren, sterile, unfruitful, unproductive, impecunious, hard up, necessitous.

SCHOOL (V)

Syn.: train, teach, direct, lead, guide, educate, instruct, control, discipline, inform, enlighten, tutor.

Ant.: misdirect, mislead, misguide, deceive, delude.

SCRUPULOUS

Syn.: absolutely honest, extremely careful and tho-rough, paying great attention to details, exact, meticulous, punctilious, upright, moral, conscientious, veracious, truthful, right-minded, high-principled.

Ant.: dishonest, deceitful, tricky, fraudulent, unscrupulous, careless, unprincipled, conscienceless, knavish.

SILLY

Syn.: foolish, doltish, indiscreet, stupid, unwise, childish, inane, fatuous, senseless, absurd, ridiculous, idiotic, nonsensical, irrational, preposterous, outrageous, imprudent.

Ant.: wise, prudent, rational, sane, discreet, sound, intelligent, sensible, sapient, sagacious, discerning, perspicacious, brainy, brilliant, well-advised, judicious, astute, shrewd.

SLY

Syn.: foxy, wily, crafty, cunning, deceitful, secretive, furtive, roguish, mischievous, stealthy, underhand, surreptitious.

Ant.: open, frank, candid, ingenuous, sincere, artless.

SOFTEN

Syn.: mollify, soothe, ease, calm, comfort, quiet, temper, moderate, mitigate, abate, allay, alleviate, assuage, diminish, lessen, extenuate, relieve.

Ant.: harden, stiffen, augment, irritate, increase, aggravate, worsen, enhance, heighten, intensify, infuriate, indurate.

SUITABLE

Syn.: appropriate, proper, fitting, right, becoming, apposite, eligible, seemly, apt, meet, decorous, seasonable.

Ant.: unsuitable, improper, unbecoming, inapt, indecorous, unseemly, ineligible, inappropriate, inapposite.

TEDIOUS

Syn.: boring, tiresome, wearisome, irksome, monotonous, dreary, uninteresting, dull, humdrum, drab.

Ant.: interesting, amusing, entertaining, exciting, delightful, brisk.

TERRIBLE

Syn.: horrible, alarming, fearful, shocking, frightful, awesome, appalling, dreadful, terrifying, frightening, formidable, terrific, horrid, terrible, fearsome.

Ant.: pleasing, encouraging, safe, secure, joyous, informidable, unastounding.

TOLERABLE

Syn.: endurable, bearable, passable, sufferable, acceptable.

Ant.: intolerable, unbearable, unacceptable, unendurable.

TOTALLY

Syn.: fully, wholly, completely, entirely, absolutely, thoroughly, perfectly, utterly.

Ant.: partially, partly, incompletely, somewhat.

TRUE

Syn.: accurate, actual, unerring, correct, authentic, exact, real, veracious, constant, faithful, loyal, genuine, precise, veritable, reliable, rightful, sincere, factual, legitimate.

Ant.: untrue, inaccurate, incorrect, inexact, unreal, unfaithful, disloyal, unreliable, insincere, false, spurious, fictitious, erroneous, inconstant, fickle, fallacious, apocryphal.

UNASSUMING

Syn.: modest, reserved, retiring, humble, diffident, bashful, shy, coy, unpretentious, unostentatious.

Ant.: arrogant, boastful, haughty, proud, vain, immodest, pretentious, ostentatious, pert, vainglorious, imperious, smug, priggish, domineering.

URBANE

Syn.: suave, affable, polite, civil, courteous, refined, well-bred, well-mannered, accomplished, sophisticated, courtly, amiable.

Ant.: uncivil, uncouth, rude, ill-mannered, discourteous, impolite, boorish, impertinent.

UTTER (Adj)

Syn.: complete, entire, thorough, full, whole, perfect, absolute, sheer, total, downwright, consummate, arrant.

Ant.: incomplete, imperfect, partial, meagre, lacking, wanting, deficient, sketchy, skimpy.

VALID

Syn.: binding, sound, legal, logical, effective, cogent, operative, weighty, well-grounded, just.

Ant.: invalid, illegal, illogical, unjust, unsound, ineffective, null and void, inoperative.

VANITY

Syn.: pride, egotism, arrogance, conceit, immodesty, self-esteem, smugness, priggishness, vainglory, boasting, boast, bombast, bluster, brag, rodomontade.

Ant.: modesty, humility, meekness, simplicity, unostentatiousness.

VIGOROUS

Syn.: energetic, active, strong, potent, powerful, mighty, forceful, animated, lively, spirited, sprightly, brisk, vivacious, intense.

Ant.: powerless, ineffective, ineffectual, dull, feeble, unsound, impotent, flabby.

VITAL

Syn.: essential, indispensable, necessary, basic, cardinal, paramount, energetic, lively, dynamic.

Ant.: unessential, unimportant, dispensable, immaterial, insignificant.

WELCOME (Adj)

Syn.: pleasing, agreeable, acceptable, gratifying, pleasant, pleasurable.

Ant.: unwelcome, unacceptable, disagreeable, distasteful, unpleasant, offensive, repugnant, repulsive, unpalatable.

WISE

Syn.: prudent, sagacious, sage, learned, profound, well-advised, judicious, scholarly, well-informed, well-read, shrewd.

Ant.: unwise, foolish, shallow, silly, stupid, inane, fatuous, injudicious, imprudent, ill-advised, doltish, uneducated, unschooled.

WRONG (Adj)

Syn.: erroneous, incorrect, unjust, inaccurate, mistaken, faulty, untrue, unprecise, improper, bad, amiss, inappropriate, unsuitable, false, unfair, unfit.

Ant.: right, correct, true, proper, suitable, exact, just, precise, fair, accurate.

YEARLING

Syn.: youngling, colt, filly, cub, whelp, puppy.
Ant.: elder, doyen, old-timer, veteran.

YEARN

Syn.: desire, strongly, pine, long, hanker, grieve, mourn.
Ant.: hate, detest, despise, loathe, dislike, abominate.

YIELDING

Syn.: pliant, tractable, docile, submissive, compliant, flexible, soft, manageable.
Ant.: intractable, unmanageable, awkward, stubborn, obstinate, obdurate, unyielding, inflexible, hard, unruly, recalcitrant.

YOUNG

Syn.: youthful, new, fresh, inexperienced, immature, youngish, teen-age, juvenile, adolescent, green, puerile.
Ant.: old, elderly, experienced, aged, senior, mature, full-grown.

ZANY (Adj)

Syn.: ridiculous, eccentric, amusing, ludicrous, foolish, doltish, silly, inane, fatuous, stupid, droll, funny, whimsical, dull, drab.
Ant.: wise, intelligent, accomplished, well-informed, shrewd, brisk, active.

ZANY (N)

Syn.: merry-andrew, buffoon, clown, madcap, fool, comedian, jester, nitwit, dunce, dolt, nincompoop, ninny, simpleton, numbskull, oaf, loon, dullard, dunderhead, blockhead, goof, idiot, booby, bonehead, dunce, imbecile.
Ant.: sage, scholar, genius, wise person, intelligent person.

ZEAL

Syn.: enthusiasm, energy, verve, keenness, vim, vigour, heartiness, earnestness, spirit, eagerness, warmth, ardour, fervour, devotion, dash, briskness, alacrity, intensity, vehemence.
Ant.: apathy, indifference, unconcern, ennui, detachment, coldness, torpor, torpidity.

ZEALOUS

Syn.: eager, keen, enthusiastic, deep, strong, intense, earnest, passionate, spirited, ardent, warm, energetic, fervent, fervid, impassioned, vehement.
Ant.: cold, apathetic, indifferent, nonchalant, calm and casual, cool.

ZENITH

Syn.: acme, top, summit, apex, climax, vertex, culmination, peak, prime, highest point.
Ant.: nadir, lowest point or part, base, bottom, foot.

ZEST

Syn.: gusto, relish, enthusiasm, exhilaration, thrill, great enjoyment or excitement.
Ant.: distaste, disrelish, dislike, insipidity.

MULTIPLE CHOICE QUESTIONS

Directions (Qs.1 to 50): *Choose the words which are most nearly the SAME in meaning to the words given in capital letters.*

1. CARP
A. to find fault unreasonably
B. to hone
C. to twist a meaning unfairly
D. to jump to a conclusion

2. GIBE
A. sneering remark B. praise
C. expose D. measure

3. IMPALPABLE
A. bad taste B. bad odour
C. cannot be felt D. wholly false

4. DISQUISITION
A. uncomfortable B. formal discourse
C. deprived D. cross-examination

5. PROSCRIBE
A. to order B. to declare
C. to protect D. to prohibit

6. OSTRACIZE
A. to expand B. to describe
C. to exclude D. to curtail

7. INVEIGH
A. to encroach B. to murder
C. to hurt D. to rail

8. CONCOCT
A. to blame B. to falsify
C. to prepare or make up D. to make fool

9. BURGEON
A. to sprout B. to begin
C. to diminish D. to intrude

10. CAJOLE
A. to scold B. to ridicule
C. to wheedle D. to scorn

11. ARCHAIC
A. damaged
B. belonging to an earlier period
C. neophyte
D. lame

12. ATTENUATE
A. to support B. to pay attention
C. to brood D. to weaken

13. PERFUNCTORY
A. half-hearted B. orator
C. performer D. stern

14. INTERNECINE
A. insincere B. peaceful
C. deadly D. unreliable

15. PROLETARIAT
A. wealthy class B. trade agreement
C. intellectual class D. working class

16. PALLIDNESS
A. wanness B. obsess
C. egress D. transgress

17. IMPECUNIOUSNESS
A. habitual poverty B. aloofness
C. impulsiveness D. peerless

18. REPARTEE
A. irrelevant B. sarcasm
C. witty retort D. introvert

19. TENOR
A. timid B. topical
C. support D. purport

20. TERMAGANT
A. selfish B. shrewish woman
C. self-dependent D. brave

21. RELEGATE
A. retaliation B. banish
C. repeat D. bold

22. UBIQUITOUS
A. universal B. frenzied
C. omnipresent D. absent

23. UNTRAMMELLED
A. unfettered B. unwearied
C. indubitable D. unbroken

24. CHURLISH
A. sophisticated B. childish
C. rude D. polite

25. GUMPTION
A. common sense B. guilt
C. insidious D. idealistic

26. QUISLING
A. cheat B. partriot
C. traitor D. loyal

27. ARDUOUS
A. strange B. difficult
C. unique D. antique

28. DOUGHTY
A. coarse B. stupid
C. impudent D. strong and able

29. COGNIZANT
A. suitable B. aware
C. ignorant D. substitute

30. OVERTURE
A. tentative proposal B. declaration
C. exaggeration D. treaty

31. ABASH
A. lowered B. humiliate
C. embarass D. appreciate

32. ABSOLVE
A. solution B. resolve
C. confusion D. pardon

33. ACCOLADE
A. accomodation B. allotment
C. award of merit D. punishment

34. IMPUTATION
A. impending B. attribution
C. impression D. insistent

35. IMBUE
A. to force B. to attack
C. to charge D. to saturate

36. IMBROGLIO
A. complicated situation B. climax
C. beginning D. conclusion

37. OBFUSCATE
A. to surrender B. to confuse
C. to argue D. to punish

38. ENTHRALL
A. to exclude B. to idealize
C. to captivate D. to point out

39. EXCULPATE
A. murder B. to sentence to death
C. to involve in crime D. to free from blame

40. RIPOSTE
A. resignation B. re-appointment
C. commitment D. clever retort

41. RETRENCHMENT
A. forced withdrawal B. encroachment
C. official order D. reduction of expenses

42. SUPERCILIOUS
A. arrogant B. misbehaved
C. urbane D. sophisticated

43. MENDACITY
A. sincerity B. falsehood
C. gaiety D. consciousness

44. RETICENCE
A. cruelty B. simplicity
C. secretiveness D. honesty

45. RENDITION
A. artistic interpretation B. summarize
C. illustration D. elucidation

46. FEUD
A. conference B. debate
C. dual D. bitter quarrel

47. TRITE
A. unusual B. commonplace
C. widespread D. unique

48. SUPPLICATE
A. to entreat B. to provide
C. to intimate D. to affiliate

49. HIRSUTE
A. horrible B. hostile
C. humorous D. hairy

50. VICISSITUDE
A. unfortunate B. misfortune
C. change of fortune D. change of mind

Directions Directions (Qs. 51 to 100): *Choose the words which are most nearly the OPPOSITE in meaning to the words given in capital letters.*

51. ODIUM
A. affection B. hatred
C. fulfilment D. scarcity

52. COMPOSURE
A. wordiness B. tranquility
C. noisy D. perspicuity

53. INEQUITY
A. balance B. justice
C. justified D. unequal

54. PERVERSE
A. appropriate B. exact
C. similar D. reasonable

55. EXTRINSIC
A. inherent B. extraordinary
C. god-gifted D. appreciating

56. ASSENT
A. indifferent B. descent
C. disagreement D. consent

57. FICTITIOUS
A. artificial B. illusive
C. deceiving D. real

58. DISINGENUOUS
A. sincere B. genius
C. practical D. sensible

59. ABBREVIATE
A. epitomize B. abdicate
C. amplify D. abate

60. ABHORRENCE
A. detest B. abduct
C. respect D. sympathy

61. CALUMNY
A. vituperation B. eulogy
C. obloquy D. disturbed

62. CALEFACTION
A. separation B. calid
C. cooling D. warmth

63. CARIOUS
A. careful B. putrid
C. anxious D. fresh

64. DISENCUMBER
A. burden B. free
C. discharge D. able

65. HORTATIVE
A. disappointing B. hostile
C. pleasant D. deterring

66. OBLITERATE
A. restore B. refractory
C. highly qualified D. rural

67. RETICENT
A. resonant B. relinquish
C. taciturn D. garrulous

68. VENGEANCE
A. subdued B. submissive
C. forgiveness D. forgetfulness

69. FLAUNT
A. covered B. hide
C. curtailed D. apparent

70. EXPURGATE
A. insert B. stain
C. scrutinize D. exterminate

71. DAWDLE
A. fiddle B. dally
C. hurry D. dauby

72. DISCOUNTENANCE
A. credit B. encourage
C. appreciate D. entertain

73. INSURRECTION
A. exhume B. sedition
C. surrender D. subjection

74. PERMUTATION
A. refusal B. rejection
C. transference D. sequence

75. SAUNTER
A. shelter B. linger
C. wander D. hasten

76. MOURNFUL
A. cheerful B. humorous
C. jolly D. joyous

77. DESSICATE
A. exonerate B. concenterate
C. saturate D. propagate

78. SPUNK
A. strong B. timidity
C. bold D. miser

79. PREVARICATE
A. exaggerate B. state truthfully
C. irrelevant D. illustrate

80. FLEDGLING
A. childish B. energetic
C. old man D. experienced person

81. BILK
A. small in size B. balance to pay
C. pay in full D. credit

82. CHARY
A. brash B. slow
C. lethargic D. exhausted

83. CRASS
A. refined B. garrulous
C. boastful D. introvert

84. SPLENETIC
A. distant B. cordial
C. strange D. unfamiliar

85. ADHERENT
A. oppose B. revengeful
C. rival D. opponent

86. UNASSUAGED
A. harmful B. satisfied
C. soothed D. kind

87. PULCHRITUDE
A. tranquility B. unknown
C. unsightliness D. pleasant

88. VOUCHSAFE
A. scholarship B. admit
C. permit D. prohibit

89. TESTY
A. even-tempered B. difficult
C. puzzled D. cheerful

90. JETTISON
A. burden B. overloaded
C. submerge D. salvage

91. GADFLY
A. joyous B. thoughtful
C. nuisance D. tranquility

92. FURORE
A. sensitive B. discomposure
C. calmness D. excitement

93. FRUGALITY
A. economy B. extravagance
C. futility D. furitive

94. GERMANE
A. apposite B. pertinent
C. irrelevant D. ovum

95. GRANDILOQUENT
A. simplicity B. turgidity
C. bombastic D. dumbness

96. GULLIBLE
A. incredulous B. shrewdness
C. circumvent D. beguile

97. HALCYON
A. serene B. stormy
C. robust D. delusion

98. HARANGUE
A. annoy B. oration
C. mumble D. blissful

99. INCONGRUITY
A. constant B. convenient
C. consequent D. consistent

100. PIQUANT
A. irritating B. sarcastic
C. soothing D. enviable

ANSWERS

1	2	3	4	5	6	7	8	9	10
A	A	C	B	D	C	D	C	A	C
11	**12**	**13**	**14**	**15**	**16**	**17**	**18**	**19**	**20**
B	D	A	C	D	A	A	C	D	B
21	**22**	**23**	**24**	**25**	**26**	**27**	**28**	**29**	**30**
B	C	A	C	A	C	B	D	B	A
31	**32**	**33**	**34**	**35**	**36**	**37**	**38**	**39**	**40**
C	D	C	B	D	A	B	C	D	D
41	**42**	**43**	**44**	**45**	**46**	**47**	**48**	**49**	**50**
D	A	B	C	A	D	B	A	D	C
51	**52**	**53**	**54**	**55**	**56**	**57**	**58**	**59**	**60**
A	C	B	D	D	C	D	A	C	D
61	**62**	**63**	**64**	**65**	**66**	**67**	**68**	**69**	**70**
B	C	D	A	D	A	D	C	B	B
71	**72**	**73**	**74**	**75**	**76**	**77**	**78**	**79**	**80**
C	B	A	D	A	D	C	B	B	D
81	**82**	**83**	**84**	**85**	**86**	**87**	**88**	**89**	**90**
C	A	A	B	D	C	C	D	A	D
91	**92**	**93**	**94**	**95**	**96**	**97**	**98**	**99**	**100**
D	C	B	C	A	A	B	C	D	C

VOCABULARY-II

6 One Word Substitution

There are many words in English language which can be perfectly used for a number of words. These words help in expressing ideas in a short and correct manner for the right occasion. Such words not only enhance the vocabulary but also enable you to economise in the use of words to a great extent. Here is a categorywise list of many such words.

Pertaining to Government

To give up a throne or other office of dignity	*abdicate*
Absence of government	*anarchy*
Government by Sovereign of uncontrolled authority	*autocracy, despotism*
Government by departments of states	*bureaucracy*
Government of the people, for the people and by the people	*democracy*
Government by the nobility	*aristocracy*
The right of self-government	*autonomy*
Government by a few	*oligarchy*
Government by the wealthy	*plutocracy*
Government by divine guidance	*theocracy*
To decide a political question by the direct vote of the whole electorate	*referendum*
Sweeping governmental change	*revolution*
The science of government	*politics*

Pertaining to Religion

One who believes that man can have no knowledge of God but only of natural phenomena	*agnostic*
One who renounces his religious vows or forsakes his religious principles	*apostate*
One who does not believe in existence of God	*atheist*
One intolerantly devoted to a particular creed	*bigot*
To utter profane language against God or anything holy	*blaspheme*
A breaker of church images	*iconoclast*
Worship of images or idols	*idiolatory*
One who believes in one God	*monotheist*
One who believes in many Gods	*polytheist*

Pertaining to Marriage and Children

One who marries a second wife or husband while the legal spouse is alive	*bigamist*
One vowed to a single or unmarried life	*celibate*

One engaged to be married	*fiancé, fiancee*
A child whose parents are dead	*orphan*
A hater of marriage	*misogamist*
One who has more than two wives at a time	*polygamist*

Pertaining to Death

Dead and decaying flesh (esp. of animals)	*carrion*
A monument set up for persons who are buried elsewhere	*cenotaph*
To preserve a dead body from putrefaction	*embalm*
Words inscribed on a tomb	*epitaph*
An examination of dead body	*postmortem, autopsy*
An account in the newspaper of the funeral of one deceased	*obituary*
The property left to someone by a will	*legacy*
Occurring after death	*posthumous*
The act of killing a human being	*homicide*
Murder of a new born child	*infanticide*
Murder of a brother	*fratricide*
Murder of a sister	*sororicide*
Murder of a mother	*matricide*
Murder of a father	*patricide*
Murder of a parent	*parricide*
Murder of a king	*regicide*

Pertaining to the Literary Sphere

A work whose writer is unknown	*anonymous*
A record of one's life written by oneself	*autobiography*
The history of the life of a person	*biography*
The heading or short description of a newspaper article, chapter of a book etc.	*caption*
A humorous play, having a happy ending	*comedy*
A list of books in a library	*catalogue, bibliography*
A book in which the events of each day are recorded	*diary*
A books containing the words of a language with their definitions, in alphabetical order	*dictionary*
A book of names and addresses	*directory*
A short speech by a player at the end of a play	*epilogue*
A brief summary of a book	*epitome*
A book containing information on all branches of knowledge	*encyclopaedia*
To remove the offensive portions of a book	*expurgate*
A speech delivered without earlier preparation	*extempore*
A noisy or vehement speech intended to excite passions	*harangue*
A written account, usually in book form of the interesting and memorable experiences of one's life	*memoirs*
A note to help the memory	*memorandum*
A declaration of plans and promises put forward by a candidate for election, political party or a sovereign	*manifesto*
A short speech by a player at the beginning of a play	*prologue*
Literary theft, or passing off an author's original work as one's own	*plagiarism*
Speaking aloud to oneself	*soliloquy*
A play with a sad or tragic end	*tragedy*

Pertaining to Sciences and Arts

The study of all heavenly bodies and the earth in relation to them	*astronomy*
The science of land management	*agronomics*
The study of mankind	*anthropology*
The study of physical life or living matter	*biology*
The study of plants	*botany*
The art of beautiful hand-writing	*calligraphy*
The science which deals with the varieties of human race	*ethnology*
The study of the origin and history of words	*etymology*
The study of coins	*numismatics*
The study of human face	*physiognomy*
The art of making fireworks	*pyrotechnics*
The study of birds	*ornithology*
The study of languages	*philology*
At home equally on land or in water	*amphibious*
The inside of a nut	*kernel*
The central or innermost part of fruit	*core*
The animals of a certain region	*fauna*
The plants and vegetation of a certain region	*flora*
Absence of rain for a long time	*drought*
To supply land with water by artificial means	*irrigate*
One who studies plant and animal life	*naturalist*
A cud-chewing animal, *e.g.* the cow	*ruminant*
A gnawing animal, *e.g.* the rat	*rodent*
A four-footed animal	*quadruped*
Animals which carry their young in a pouch, *e.g.* kangaroo	*marsupials*
Soil composed largely of decayed vegetable matter	*humus*
A preparation for killing insects	*insecticide*
A plant or animal growing on another	*parasite*
Living for many years	*perennial*

Pertaining to Medicine

A substance which destroys or weakens germs	*antiseptic*
Any medicine which produces insensibility	*anaesthetic*
A medicine to counteract poison	*antidote*
Want or poorness of blood	*anaemia*
A medicine which alleviates pain	*anodyne*
To cut off a person's body a part which is infected	*amputate*
One who is recovering from illness	*convalescent*
To be able to tell the nature of disease by its symptoms	*diagnose*
A disease affecting many persons at the same place and time	*epidemic*
A disease confined to a particular district or place	*endemic*
To disinfect by smoke	*fumigate*
Free or exempt from infection	*immune*
A person who is sick	*invalid*
A cure for all diseases	*panacea*

A disease widely epidemic	*pandemic*
Confinement to one place to avoid spread of infection	*quarantine*

Pertaining to War

An unprovoked attack by an enemy	*aggression*
Shells, bombs, military stores	*ammunition*
A place where naval or military weapons are made or stored	*ordnance*
An agreement between belligerents to stop fighting	*armistice*
A general pardon of offenders	*amnesty*
To reduce to nothing	*annihilate*
Nations carrying on warfare	*belligerents*
To surround a place with the intention of capturing	*besiege*
To camp in the open air without tents or covering	*bivouac*
To seize for military use	*commandeer*
A person who is forced by law to become a soldier	*conscript*
An order prohibiting ships to leave the ports	*embargo*
A number of firearms being discharged continuously	*fusillade*
To make an examination or preliminary survey of enemy territory or military objectives	*reconnoitre*

Pertaining to Professions

One who attends to the diseases of the eye	*oculist*
One who tests eyesight and sells spectacles	*optician*
One who attends to the teeth	*dentist*
One skilled in the care of hands and feet	*chiropodist*
A physician who assists women at child-birth	*obstetrician*
One who drives a motor-car	*chauffeur*
One who makes or sells candles	*chandler*
One who preserves the skins of animals and mounts them so as to resemble the living animals	*taxidermist*
One who compiles a dictionary	*lexicographer*
One who writes books	*author*
One skilled in the treatment of diseases of animals	*veterinarian*
A tradesman who manages funerals	*undertaker*
One who draws up contracts and lends money on interest	*scrivener*
One who lends money and keeps goods as security	*pawnbroker*
A teacher who travels from place to place to give instruction	*peripatetic*
One who travels from place to place selling miscellaneous articles	*hawker, pedlar*
One who collects postage stamps	*philatelist*
One who lends money at exorbitant interest	*usurer*
One who takes care of a building	*janitor*
One who sells sweets and pastries	*confectioner*
One who works in a coal-mine	*collier*
One who flies an aeroplane	*pilot, aviator*
One who studies rocks and soils	*geologist*
One who shoes horses	*farrier*
A professional rider in horses races	*jockey*
One who deals in silks, cotton, woollen, and linen goods	*mercer*
One who deals in wines	*vintner*

One who deals in fish	*fishmonger*
One who deals in iron and hardware	*ironmonger*
One who sells fruits, vegetables, etc. from a barrow	*costermonger*
One who sets type (in a printing office)	*compositor*

Pertaining to Characteristics and Actions

One who devotes his life to the welfare and interests of other people	*altruist*
One who can use both hands with equal case	*ambidexterous*
One who fishes with a rod	*angler*
One who kills secretly or by surprise	*assassin*
A person who collects things belonging to ancient times	*antiquary*
One who is always finding faults	*censorious*
One living at the same time as another	*contemporary*
One who sneers at the aims and beliefs of his fellowmen	*cynic*
One who delights in speaking about oneself	*egotist*
One who exalts his own opinion	*egoist*
One who dies for a noble cause	*martyr*
One who retires from society to live a solitary life	*recluse, hermit*
One who maliciously sets fire to buildings	*incendiary*
One who is banished from his home or his country	*exile*
One who takes refuge in a foreign country	*refugee, alien*
One who runs away from justice or the law	*fugitive*
One who walks in his sleep	*somnambulist*
One who looks on the bright side of things	*optimist*
One who looks on the dark side of things	*pessimist*
A hater of mankind	*misanthropist*
One who knows everything	*omniscient*
One who is all powerful	*omnipotent*
One who is present everywhere	*omnipresent*
One who devotes his service or wealth for the love of mankind	*philanthropist*
One new to anything	*novice, tyro, neophyte*
One who engages in any pursuit for the love of it, and not for gain	*amateur*
One who journeys to a holy place	*pilgrim*
A leader of the people who can sway his followers by his oratory	*demagogue*
One who has special skill in judging art, music, tastes, etc.	*connoisseur*
One whose reasoning is clever yet false	*sophist*
One who makes a display of his learning	*pedant*
One who is indifferent to pain or pleasure	*stoic*
One who loves his country and serves it devotedly	*patriot*
One devoted to the pleasures of eating and drinking	*epicure*
One who poses to be what he is not	*hypocrite, impostor*
One who foretells events	*prophet*
One who pretends to know a great deal about everything	*mountebank, charlatan, quack*
One versed in many languages	*linguist*
One who cannot pay one's debts	*insolvent*
One who takes over after another in office or employment	*successor*
One who has been before another in office or employment	*predecessor*

One who is opposed to intellectual progress	*obscurant*
One who abstains from alcoholic drinks	*teetotaller*
One who hides away on a ship to obtain a free passage	*stowaway*
One who spends very little	*miser*
One who spends too much	*spendthrift*

Denoting Numbers

A collection of poems	*anthology*
A number of merchant ships protected by warships (in war-time)	*convoy*
A number of stars grouped together	*constellation*
A number of hired applauders, *i.e.* persons paid to clap	*claque*
A number of people at church	*congregation*
A number of people gathered together for some common purpose	*gathering, assembly, society*
A group of people who get together to work for some cause of common interest	*coterie*
A number of workmen, prisoners, thieves	*gang*
A number of sheep	*flock*
A number of geese	*gaggle*
A number of leopards	*leap*
A number of lions, monkeys	*pride, troop*
A number of herrings, mackerel	*shoal*
A number of fish taken in a net	*catch, haul*
A number of whales, porpoises	*school, gam*
A number of oxen or horses (two or more) harnessed together	*team*
A number of ships	*fleet*

Denoting Places

A place where bees are kept	*apiary*
A place where birds are kept	*aviary*
A place where fishes are kept	*aquarium*
A dwelling-place of an animal underground	*burrow*
A squirrel's home	*drey*
A nest of a bird of prey	*eyrie, aerie*
A place where spirituous liquors are produced	*distillery*
A place where clothes are washed and ironed	*laundry*
A place where Government records are kept	*archives*
A place where treasures of art, curiosities, etc. are preserved or exhibited	*museum*
A place where fruit trees are grown	*orchard*

Miscellaneous

Loud enough to be heard	*audible*
Not distinct enough to be heard	*inaudible*
Fit for food	*edible*
Unfit for human consumption	*inedible*
Fit to be chosen or selected	*eligible*
Not having the qualities for being chosen	*ineligible*
(Writing) that is easy to read	*legible*
Writing that is difficult to decipher	*illegible*

Able to read	*literate*
Unable to read	*illiterate*
Born of married parents	*legitimate*
Born of unmarried parents	*illegitimate*
To send back a person to his own country	*repatriate*
To banish from one's country	*expatriate*
To move from one country to another	*migrate*
One who leaves his country to settle in another	*emigrant*
One who comes into a foreign country to settle there	*immigrant*
Incapable of being redeemed from evil, *i.e.* beyond correction	*incorrigible*
That which cannot be rubbed out or blotted out	*ineffaceable, indelible*
That which cannot be conquered	*invincible*
Incapable of making errors	*infallible*
That which cannot be avoided or prevented	*inevitable*
Incapable of being burnt	*incombustible*
That which easily catches fire	*inflammable, flammable*
That which cannot be seen	*invisible*
Living for ever	*immortal*
Increase the gravity of an offence	*aggravate*
Ordinary or commonplace remark	*platitude*
That which cannot be satisfied	*insatiable*
That which cannot be repaired	*irreparable*
That which cannot be imitated	*inimitable*
Persons (or efforts) that cannot be wearied	*indefatigable*
One who eats too much	*glutton*
To destroy completely	*annihilate*
A statement open to more than one interpretation	*ambiguous*
A round about way of speaking	*circumlocution*
Cautious observation of events, etc.	*circumspection*
That which cannot be hurt	*invulnerable*

MULTIPLE CHOICE QUESTIONS

Directions: *Below are given some statements each of which is capable of being expressed by one word only. Each statement is followed by four such words of which only one is correct. Out of the given alternatives A, B, C and D choose the correct word which very closely fits each definition.*

1. One who does not believe in the existence of God:
A. atheist B. altruist
C. agnostic D. flippant

2. The large money paid for an early retirement:
A. gold mine B. golden handshake
C. gratuity D. lion's share

3. A hater of learning and knowledge:
A. misologist B. misogynist
C. philologist D. philanthropist

4. One who lives and acts for the welfare of others:
A. misanthrope B. credulous
C. altruist D. gregarious

5. Mental weariness for want of occupation:
A. desperate B. depression
C. fatigue D. ennui

6. That which makes it difficult to recognise the presence of real of somebody or something:
A. cover B. mask
C. make-up D. camouflage

7. To *bear a hand* in one's new business.
A. partnership B. interfere
C. assist D. join

8. One who renounces the world and practices self-discipline in order to attain salvation:
A. devotee B. ascetic
C. theist D. parsimonious

9. A place where gambling is practiced:
A. hotel B. motel
C. casino D. stadium

10. A sad song is a:
A. dirge B. elegy
C. ditty D. knell

11. A set of papers giving information about a person or event:
A. editorial B. agenda
C. dossier D. clippings

12. List and explanations of technical, difficult, etc. terms:
A. preface B. glossary
C. bibliography D. appendix

13. One who pays too much care to his clothes and personal appearance:
A. conscious B. dandy
C. cynosure D. leer

14. A child born after death of father:
A. effeminate B. immature
C. fatherless D. posthumous

15. A person who is hard to please:
A. insensible B. hypocrite
C. egoist D. fastidious

16. Complete failure in something attempted:
A. fiasco B. vain
C. falsies D. flop

17. A word which can be interpreted in any way:
A. confusing B. misnomer
C. ambiguous D. precise

18. A group of persons united by common interests:
A. society B. class
C. clique D. coterie

19. A person who is inexperienced and easily deceived:
A. fool B. immature
C. blackhorn D. greenhorn

20. Instruction by question and answer:
A. interrogatory B. catechism
C. bulletin D. alibi

21. Record of events by someone with first hand knowledge:
A. novice B. report
C. memoir D. itinerary

22. A mode of talk familiar to a particular group or profession:
A. jargon B. colloquial
C. slang D. abuses

23. Person who is crazy:
A. lackadaisical B. tarter
C. scrupulous D. loony

24. A person who readily believes others:
A. hasty B. immature
C. credulous D. credible

25. One who eats human flesh:
A. beast B. cannibal
C. maneater D. carnivorous

26. Intentional destruction of racial groups:
A. genocide B. homicide
C. fratricide D. communal riot

27. One with weakness of mind caused by old age:
A. dastard B. dotard
C. fop D. philanderer

28. Study of insects:
A. zoology B. philology
C. entomology D. etymology

29. A critical judge of any art particularly fine arts:
A. connoisseur B. veteran
C. philistine D. dilettante

30. One who introduces items of an entertainment:
A. consort B. compere
C. director D. introducer

31. A combination of business firms:
A. enterprise B. franchise
C. cartel D. autonomous

32. Freeing of suppressed emotions:
A. catastrophe B. catharsis
C. epilogue D. chagrin

33. One who believes in the power of fate:
A. optimist B. pessimist
C. fearful D. fatalist

34. The murder of brother:
A. genocide B. homicide
C. salvage D. fratricide

35. Additional to proper payment:
A. premium B. overtime
C. ex-gratia D. fringe

36. A person or thing used to tempt somebody into a position of danger:
A. decoy B. provocateur
C. jinx D. scapegoat

37. Custom of having more than one husband at the same time:
A. polygamy B. polyandry
C. bigamy D. sexagenary

38. A person of refined taste in food and drink:
A. emeritus B. epicure
C. glutton D. gourmand

39. A tombstone inscription:
A. epithet B. encomium
C. epistle D. epitaph

40. An office which has no work but high salary:
A. fortuitous B. gratuitous
C. sinecure D. ceremonial

41. One who is indifferent to pains and pleasure of life:
A. stoic B. metaphysical
C. pessimist D. sceptic

42. List of names of persons showing duties to be performed by each in turn:
A. notice B. bulletin
C. roster D. agenda

43. Long angry speech of criticism or accusation:
A. track record B. tirade
C. taut D. outburst

44. One who is in favour of never drinking alcoholic drinks:
A. idealist B. uxorious
C. teetotaller D. unalcoholic

45. Trying to win favour by flattery and charm:
A. smarmy B. shrewish
C. toady D. loquacious

46. A decision on which one cannot go back:
A. incorrigible B. irrevocable
C. rigid D. invulnerable

47. The science that studies the varieties of human race:
A. phrenology B. physiology
C. sociology D. ethnology

48. A person who hates women:
A. philogynist B. philatelist
C. misogamist D. misogynist

49. A group of people in a particular grade in an organisation:
A. colleague B. staff
C. echelon D. commission

50. Honourably discharged from service:
A. emeritus B. latitudinarian
C. infallible D. meritorious

51. Incapable of being wounded:
A. inevitable B. invulnerable
C. indomitable D. indefatigable

52. A short description of a picturesque scene or event of rural life:
A. narration B. panorama
C. idyll D. passage

53. The act of violating the sanctity of church:
A. sacrilege B. dissenter
C. immorality D. desecration

54. A dishonest dealing:
A. hanky-panky B. hocus-pocus
C. hoity-toity D. hilly-billy

55. A short and stout person:
A. lilliput B. hussy
C. humpty-dumpty D. paragon

56. Word that reads the same backwards as forwards (like did, dad, noon):
A. paradox B. palindrome
C. kowtow D. ragtag

57. Walking in sleep:
A. delusion B. somniloquism
C. somnabulism D. lethargic

58. Glamour and excitement:
A. razzle-dazzle B. razzmatazz
C. kudos D. winsome

59. Violent and bad tempered woman:
A. virago B. moll
C. concubine D. profane

60. One who pays excessive attention to preserving his health:
A. pagan B. bellicose
C. sycophant D. fop

61. Talking to one's own self:
A. pessimism B. introvert
C. soliloquy D. brooding

62. One who pretends to have more knowledge than he really has:
A. hypocrite B. charlaton
C. paragon D. lackadaisical

63. Brief biography of a person:
A. profile B. bibliography
C. synopsis D. resume

64. Very small allowance or wage:
A. lumpsum B. consolidated
C. pittance D. paltry

65. Purely spiritual love:
A. devotion B. platonic
C. passionate D. divine

66. Place where people often meet:
A. common room B. discotheque
C. roster D. rendezvous

67. A completely perfect person:
A. upright B. straightforward
C. paragon D. intellectual

68. Commencement of words with the same alphabet:
A. symmetry B. pun
C. phonetic D. alliteration

69. A person who loves everybody:
A. ascetic B. philander
C. philistine D. cosmopolitan

70. A government where the powers are concentrated in the hands of one person:
A. dictatorship B. autocracy
C. plutocracy D. anarchy

71. That which is outdated or out of use or fashion:
A. discarded B. obsolete
C. classic D. antic

72. Calendar giving information about sun, moon, stars and sometimes also the future:
A. almanac B. appendix
C. horoscope D. chronology

73. Collection in one volume of works by various authors:
A. panorama B. anthology
C. autobiography D. bibliography

74. One who takes part in a study, game, etc. for the love of it and not for professional gain:
A. apologist B. august
C. amateur D. avant-garde

75. A thing that causes annoyance:
A. bugbear B. arduous
C. anathema D. shrill

76. An allowance for support made to a wife by her husband after their legal separation:
A. alimony B. compensation
C. settlement D. ex-gratia

77. Place for hiding treasure, food, weapons, etc.:
A. store B. cache
C. stock D. armoury

78. A person who is stubborn in resisting change:
A. irresistible B. die-hard
C. dead beat D. terse

79. Able to use the left hand or the right hand equally well:
A. ambidextrous B. epicurean
C. apostle D. arbiter

80. A man who rarely speaks the truth:
A. liar B. unreliable
C. hypocrite D. bellicose

81. Partial or total loss of memory:
A. alexia B. anorexia
C. anexia D. amnesia

82. A word made by rearranging the letters of another word like eat–tea:
A. acronym B. anagram
C. byword D. dossier

83. A mass of snow and ice sliding down from a mountain:
A. avalanche B. glacier
C. icebery D. azure

84. To speak irreverently of God:
A. impious B. irreligious
C. immoral D. blasphemy

85. Sudden increase in business:
A. bonanza B. boom
C. bounce D. booze

86. Object of laughter or ridicule:
A. butt B. but
C. divert D. hurtle

87. A pioneer of a reform movement:
A. sinecure B. sycophant
C. gallant D. apostle

88. Art of handwriting:
A. cartography B. choreography
C. calligraphy D. graph

89. One who takes a low view of human nature:
A. coquette B. cynic
C. crony D. coy

90. Document that is handwritten by the author:
A. autograph B. holograph
C. editorial D. preface

91. A person who forsakes religion:
A. irreligious B. non-religious
C. fatalist D. apostle

92. Speaker or agitator who can stir the emotions of the masses:
A. demagogue B. dexterous
C. diligent D. reformist

93. Uncontrollable craving for alcohol:
A. dyspepsia B. delirium
C. edict D. dipsomania

94. A lady who remains unmarried:
A. concubine B. alien
C. spinster D. damsel

95. State payment to an unemployed person:
A. pension B. dole
C. increment D. grant in aid

96. Person slow at learning:
A. adroit B. dubious
C. dunce D. agile

97. One who has a good taste for food and enjoys it:
A. gourmet B. sensitive
C. deleterious D. debonair

98. One who is fond of gossip:
A. flippant B. flibbertigibbet
C. fuddy-duddy D. gregarious

99. A long, loud and angry speech:
A. incongruous B. hyperbole
C. hullabaloo D. harangue

100. A person chosen by the opposing parties to settle their differences:
A. mediator B. prude
C. paramour D. arbitrator

ANSWERS

1	2	3	4	5	6	7	8	9	10
A	B	A	C	D	D	C	B	C	A
11	**12**	**13**	**14**	**15**	**16**	**17**	**18**	**19**	**20**
C	B	B	D	D	A	C	C	D	B
21	**22**	**23**	**24**	**25**	**26**	**27**	**28**	**29**	**30**
C	A	D	C	B	A	B	C	A	B
31	**32**	**33**	**34**	**35**	**36**	**37**	**38**	**39**	**40**
C	B	D	D	D	A	B	B	D	C
41	**42**	**43**	**44**	**45**	**46**	**47**	**48**	**49**	**50**
A	C	B	C	A	B	D	D	C	A
51	**52**	**53**	**54**	**55**	**56**	**57**	**58**	**59**	**60**
B	C	D	A	C	B	C	B	A	A
61	**62**	**63**	**64**	**65**	**66**	**67**	**68**	**69**	**70**
C	B	A	C	B	D	C	D	D	B
71	**72**	**73**	**74**	**75**	**76**	**77**	**78**	**79**	**80**
B	A	B	C	A	A	B	B	A	C
81	**82**	**83**	**84**	**85**	**86**	**87**	**88**	**89**	**90**
D	B	A	D	B	A	D	C	B	B
91	**92**	**93**	**94**	**95**	**96**	**97**	**98**	**99**	**100**
D	A	D	C	B	C	A	B	D	D

VOCABULARY-III

7 Idioms & Phrases

An idiom is a group of words established by usage as having a meaning different from the individual words.

A phrase is a small group of words standing together as an idiomatic expression.

The use of idioms and phrases makes your expression more effective and powerful.

Learn and practise as many as you can.

An angel: A person who is gentle and kind to others

A devil: A particularly wicked or mischievous person

A giant: A person who is very large

A wizard: A clever and skillful person

An Adonis: A very handsome man

An Apollo: A man with a perfect physique or body shape

A Hercules: A very strong man

A Goliath: An extremely large man

A Judas: A mean traitor

A Samson: A very strong man

A Solomon: A very wise man

A dog: A worthless person; someone who is despised

A cat: A malicious, person. usually referring to females

A bear: A clumsy, rough person

A fox: A crafty, cunning person

A goose: A silly person

A lamb: An innocent harmless person

A monkey: A child who is lively and full of mischievous tricks

A mule: A very stubborn person

A wolf: A greedy and cunning person

A snake/serpent: A treacherous, dangerous person

A parrot: A person who learns things off by heart without understanding the real meaning

A pest: A troublesome person; one who annoys and pesters others

A pig: A greedy and dirty person

A shark: A greedy and cunning person; one who swindles others

A parasite: A person who lives off others and gives nothing in return

An ape: A person who foolishly imitates others

An ass/donkey: A stupid person

An elephant: A huge, clumsy, ungainly person

A wet blanket: A person who discourages others or prevents them from enjoying what they are doing

A stag party: A party where only men are allowed to be present

A hen party: A party where only women are allowed to be present

A working lunch/dinner: A meal at which the people who attend, discuss business

A working knowledge: Enough practical knowledge to do something

A willing horse: A helpful person who often gets all the work to do

A wild goose chase: A search for something which has no chance of being successful

A trend-setter: A person who starts a new fashion which becomes popular

A thick-skinned person: A person who is not easily offended

Teething troubles: Troubles and difficulties which occur during the early stages of an activity or enterprise, but which will lessen with time

A sweeping statement: A statement which is not careful or correct in its details; a generalisation

A spending spree: An outing during which one spends a lot of money

A tall order: A request which is unreasonably difficult to grant or carry out

A soft spot: A feeling of special fondness for something or someone

A sore point: A matter which irritates or hurts when it is mentioned

The small hours: The early morning hours just after midnight

A sleeping partner: A business partner who provides a share of the capital for a venture but does not take an active part in its operation

Small talk: Trivial, light conversation on unimportant topics

Second nature: Some acquired habit or skill which seems perfectly natural to someone; a very firmly fixed habit

A shady character: A person of very doubtful honesty or character

Second thoughts: A change of mind, attitude or decision after thinking about the matter

A security risk: A person who is a risk to a country's security because of his political activities; one whose loyalty is doubted

A jail bird: A man who has spent a lot of time in prison

A ladies' man: A man who likes to be with women or who likes to please them

A last fling: The last opportunity for pleasure or amusement before having to stop

An inside job: A theft committed by someone inside a building, i.e., by an employee, not a stranger

A knowing look: A look which suggests that, the person is well-informed of a matter

A hushed-up affair: An affair or matter that is kept secret by forcing silence about it

Hush money: A bribe paid to keep a matter secret from the public

A hot line: A direct telephone line between heads of governments, to be used at times of great difficulty

Hot news: Very recent, important or sensational news

High time: At the most important point of time

Fast living: A person who spends too much money in enjoying life

A fishy story: An untrue tale; an unlikely story

Half-hearted: Having no enthusiasm for a particular task

An iron will: A very strong will

Hot water: Trouble

A laughing stock: A person who is unkindly laughed at by everyone

A light-fingered person: A person who is in the habit of stealing small things

Pin money: A wife's allowance for her personal needs

Plain sailing: A plan or action that is simple and free from trouble

A pep talk: A friendly talk to give encouragement to win a game, etc. or to complete something well

A package tour: A completely planned holiday at a fixed price arranged by a company

A passing fancy: A temporary liking for something or someone

An open secret: Something supposed to be a secret but which in fact is known to everyone

A package deal: An offer or agreement which includes a number of things all of which must be taken

Plain dealing: Truthfulness and honesty, especially in business

A pet aversion: Something or someone much disliked

A sideline: Work one does apart from one's regular job

Second sight: An ability to foresee future events

A rolling stone: Person who travels around a lot without staying in any one place or job for long

A raw deal: An unjust or cruel treatment

In a rash moment: Doing something hastily without thinking of the results

A practical joke: A trick played on a person to make him look silly and to give amusement to others

A sugar daddy: An older man who has a relationship, especially sexual, with a younger woman, providing her with money and presents

Take-home pay/wages: The amount a person receives after taxes have been deducted

backstairs influence: Secret and usually unfair influence

Bad blood: Bad feelings or unfriendliness between two persons

A bad egg/a bad penny: A bad character

A false alarm: A warning of something bad, which does not happen

Elbow room: Space, in which to move and act freely

A double agent: A person who works secretly for two opposing sides without either of the sides knowing

A dead-end job: A job without prospects; a job that leads to nothing further

A dark horse: A person who competes successfully against another although little is known about him

A confirmed bachelor: A man who has no desire to marry

A burning question: A matter having to be dealt with at once; an urgent important matter

A big shot: An important person, usually someone who is wealthy and influential

A blind date: A social meeting of two persons, usually a boy and a girl who have not met before

Broken English: Imperfect, ungrammatical English

A chicken-hearted person: A timid, cowardly person

A close-fisted person : Someone who is stingy; a miser

A country cousin: A person who is simple and inexperienced and not used to city life

A close shave: A narrow escape from danger, an accident, etc.

A light sleeper: A person who is easi_ awakened from sleep

A cock-and-bull story: An invented story

A cold war: A serious political struggle between countries which does not actually result in fighting

A dog-eared book: A book where the corners of the pages have been turned down with use

An easy victim/mark: Somebody who can easily be cheated or treated badly

A bosom friend: A very close, trusted friend

Crocodile tears: Pretended sorrow; insincere tears

A fast colour: A colour which does not run out of the material when washed or dried

A fair copy: A neat, legible copy

An armchair critic: A person who critically judges others' work and gives advice, but who has not himself experienced doing the work

Apple-pie order: In perfect order

An absent-minded person: A forgetful, inattentive person

A flying visit: A very short visit

Forty winks: A short nap or sleep

Hard labour: Hard, manual work usually done as a punishment

Hard cash: Actual money, not a cheque, etc.

A hard drinker: A person who drinks large quantities of alcohol

A golden opportunity: A very good opportunity

A going concern: A successful, thriving business

A foregone conclusion: A result that is certain, sure

The naked eye: The eye unaided by any instrument

An odd-job man: A man who does various types of work, usually manual, for pay

Old hat: No longer fashionable

A grass widow: A wife who is alone because her husband is away temporarily

A good samaritan: A person who helps a stranger in difficulties

French leave: Absence from work that is taken without permission

The generation gap: The difficulties arising when younger and elder people do not understand each other's way of life

The happy medium: The middle course of doing something when opposite ways are suggested

A henpecked husband: A husband who is dominated and nagged by his wife

A hard and fast rule: A rule that cannot be changed; fixed, unchangeable rule

One-track mind: A person's mind that is limited and thinks of only one thing at a time

A short cut: An easier method of doing something or getting somewhere; a quicker, more direct way

A smal:-time business: A business limited in activity and profits

A splitting headache: A very severe and painful headache

A square deal: A fair bargain or fair treatment

A square meal: A meal with adequate good; a satisfying meal

Strong language: Angry language consisting of many swear words

Tall talk: Boastful talk

A tight spot/corner: A difficult situation

Tough luck: Bad luck; hard luck

Ready money: Money which is immediately available in coins or notes

Second best: Next to the best; second in value or importance

The writing on the wall: An indication that something bad or difficult is about to happen

A storm in a teacup: A big fuss made over a small, trivial event

The talk of the town: A person or event that is causing great excitement and is the subject of much discussion

A snake in the grass: A cunning, harmful person who pretends to be a friend; a false friend

A shot in the dark: A guess which is not supported by arguments; a wild guess

The tricks of the trade: The best and most successful ways of doing good business

The bottom of the ladder: In the least important position

A shot in the arm: Something which acts to bring back a happy state or condition

The man in the street: The ordinary, average man

The gift of the gab: A person fluent in speech; a persuasive speaker

A man about town: A man who is used to living in the city and associating with well-known fashionable people

The life and soul: The person who is the centre of attaction because he is amusing and lively

The lion's share: The greater part; an unfairly large share

The long arm of the law: The police

A bear hug: A rough, tight hug

A brain wave: A clever idea; sudden inspiration

A bone of contention: Something that causes argument

Birds of a feather: People of the same kind (often bad) who like each other's company

A feather in one's cap: A deserved honour that one is proud of

Castles in the air: Plans which cannot be carried out or which will probably not succeed

A fish out of water: A person who feels uncomfortable because he is in a strange place, or among people who are very different from himself

The ups and downs: The good and bad times, the happy and sad times

A stone's thorw: A short distance

A slip of the tongue: Something said unintentionally

A slap in the face: A rebuff

The rank and file: Ordinary people without special positions; the masses

A man of means: A rich man

A man of iron: A cruel, hard person

A jack of all trades: A person who can do many different kinds of work but who may not be good at any of them

By hook or by crook: By any means possible

By fits and starts: At irregular intervals

A pack of lies: A whole lot of untruths

A clean bill of health: A certificate or announcement that someone is healthy

A happy-go-lucky person: Someone who does not think or plan carefully

A stay-at-home person: A person who is in the habit of staying at home, and not liking to travel

A smash-and-grab robbery: A robbery done quickly, usually by breaking windows or showcases taking away valuables, and running away

A hit-and-run driver: A driver who drives away after an accident without stopping to find out about damage or injuries

A run-of the-mill job: An ordinary unexciting job

A round the-clock service: A twenty-four hour service

An out-of the way place: A place that is distant and far away from people and places

A much-talked-of affair: Something which is the subject of much discussion

A nine to six job: A job in which the working hours are from nine in the morning to six in evening

An open and shut case: A case which is easy to settle or solve

Bumper-to-bumper traffic: Cars that are very close together one after another

A hand-me-down dress: A dress used by someone after belonging to another

A well-to-do man/wom++an: A rich person

Again and again: Repeatedly; continually; very often

Back and forth/backward: Moving first in one direction and then in the opposite direction and forwards

By and by: Soon; before long

By and large: On the whole; in general; all things considered

Far and away: Very much

Far and near/far and wide: Everywhere

First and foremost: In the first place; firstly

Here and there: In various places; firstly

Here, there and everywhere: In all possible places; everywhere

In and out: Sometimes inside and sometimes outside

Up and about: On one's feet; up again after an illness

To-and fro: Backwards and forwards; from side to side

Through and through: Completely; entirely; in every way

Out and out: Complete, thorough; total

Out and away: By far

Over and over again: Again and again; repeatedly

Round and round: Repeatedly moving round

Once and for all: Finally; for the last time

On and on: Without stopping

Off and on: From time to time; occasionally

Every now and then/again: From time to time; at times

Now and again: Sometimes; occasionally; not very often

Nowadays: In these times

To backbite a person: To speak ill of someone

To back chat: To be cheeky; to talk back to someone

To be a bag of bones: To be extremely thin

To be a blockhead: To be an idiot

To be a great hand at: To be an expert

To be a sight for sore eyes: Something or someone who appears before another and is very welcome

To be all ears: To be eager to listen

To be armed to the teeth: Fully armed or protected

To be at one's wits' end: Completely puzzled

To be close-fisted: To be mean; miserly

To be double-faced: Insincere

To be down in the mouth: To feel depressed and unhappy

To be head and shoulders above someone else: To be very much better or superior

To be out of one's mind: To be mad; crazy

To be someone's blue-eyed boy: To be someone's favourite

To be the apple of someone's eye: To be someone's favourite

To bite someone's head off: To speak abruptly or sharply to another

To burn one's fingers: To get into trouble

To catch someone's eye: To suddenly exchange glances with another

To change hands: To pass from one owner to another

To dig someone in the ribs: To make unkind remarks or insinuations about another

To eat one's heart out for another: To long for someone who is unattentive

To foot the bill: To pay the bill, especially for some social outing

To get on someone's nerves: To irritate someone very greatly

To get something off one's chest: To confess to something

To get the upper hand: To gain mastery over an opponent

To give someone the cold shoulder: To ignore someone; to slight another

To give someone the sharp: To thoroughly scold another person edge of one's tongue

To go on all hands: To crawl on hands and knees

To have a chip on one's shoulder: To bear a grudge against the world/society

To have a finger in every pie: To have many business interests

To have a head like a sieve: To have a very poor memory

To have a skeleton in the cupboard: To have a guilty secret, especially a family scandal

To have at one's fingertips: To know thoroughly

To have cold feet: To be afraid

To have no backbone: To be a weak, spineless person

To have one's head screwed on: To be very sensible

To have someone under one's thumb: To dominate another

To have the upper hand: To be in command/charge; to be someone in power

To have two left hands: Someone who is clumsy

To hold one's tongue: To keep silent even though there is an urge to talk

To hold up one's head: To be able to look people in the face

To jump out of one's skin: To get a sudden fright

To keep a cool head: To keep calm, especially in an emergency

To keep a stiff upper lip: To remain calm and courageous

To keep one's fingers crossed: To hope for luck

To keep one's hair on: To keep cool and patient

To keep one's head above water: To avoid getting into debt or trouble

To keep someone at arm's length: Not too friendly with another

To knock something on the head: To suddenly stop an idea/project

To know something by heart: To be able to say something from memory

To lay hands on someone: To handle someone roughly

To lend a hand: To help

To let the grass grow under one's feet: To be inactive and uninvolved

To live from hand to mouth: To live in hardship with the barest essentials

To lose face: To lose one's reputation/honour

To lose heart: To be discouraged

To lose one's head: To be very angry; to lose control of oneself

To make a clean breast of something: To confess to something; to reveal all

To make neither head nor tail of something: To understand nothing of a particular issue

To pat someone on the back: To give praise and encouragement to another

To pay through the nose for something: To pay an excessively high price for something

To poison someone's mind: To turn someone against another person

To pull one's weight: To do one's share of work

To pull someone's leg: To play a joke on someone

To pull the wool over someone's eyes: To deceive another

To put one's back into it: To work hard

To put one's foot down: To be firm about an issue

To put one's shoulder to the wheel: To work hard and earnestly

To put someone's nose out of joint: To make someone jealous by taking his place as the centre of attraction

To rack one's brains: To try to recall or remember something

To receive with open arms: To welcome warmly

To save face: To save one's honour/reputation/name

To show a clean pair of heels: To escape by running

To snap someone's head off: To speak abruptly

To stand on one's own feet: To do things without help; to be independent

To sweep someone off his/her feet: To flatter and woo someone, usually a girl

To take matters into one's own hands: To do something independently without help

To take something to heart: To take something seriously

To take to one's heels: To run away

To throw dust in someone's eyes: To try to deceive someone

To tread in someone's foot steps: To follow the example of another, usually of talent/occupation

To tread on someone's toes: To offend another person

To try one's hand at: To try doing something for the first time

To turn a blind eye: To refuse to see

To turn a deaf ear: To refuse to hear

To turn up one's nose at something: To treat with contempt

To twist someone's arm: To force someone into doing something for you

To wash one's hands of something: To have nothing to do with a particular matter

The green-eyed monster: Jealousy

To scream blue murder: To complain loudly

Out of the blue: Suddenly; without warning

Once in a blue moon: Very rarely

To feel blue/have the blues: To be sad or depressed

A bolt from the blue: A complete surprise

Blue blood: Royal or noble blood

To blackmail someone: To threaten to reveal someone's misdeeds unless he pays money

In someone's black books: Out of favour with someone

A black sheep: A bad character who disgraces his family

A blacklist: A list of people groups, etc. who have done something wrong

Black and blue: Badly bruised after a beating/a fall

In black and white: In writing or print

A greengrocer: A person who sells fruit and vegetables

A greenhorn: An inexperienced person

The green light: The signal to proceed

Green with envy: Tilled with jealousy

Grey matter: Common sense; brains

In the pink of health: In excellent health

Purple with rage: So angry that the face becomes purple

To be caught red-handed: To be caught in the act of committing a crime

A red carpet welcome: A special ceremonial welcome to guest

The red flag: A flag used as a danger signal

A red-letter day: A notable, fortunate day that will be remembered

The red light: A signal to stop; a danger signal

Red tape: Official rules which cause delay in settling one's problems

To jump out of the frying-pan into the fire: To get out of one bad situation and fall into another worse situation

To see red: To lose control of oneself in anger

A white-collar job: An office job

A white elephant: A worthless possession which the owner wants to get rid of

The white flag: A sign that one accepts defeat or surrenders

To show the white feather: To show signs of cowardice

Yellow at heart: Cowardly

To be/feel off colour: To be unwell or rather ill

To come off with flying colours: To achieve great success

To have a high colour: To appear very red in the face

To show one's true colours: To show what one is really like; to show one's true character

A blue-collar job: A factory job

To act the goat: To behave foolishly

To air one's opinion: To express one's feelings in public

To be a chip off the old block: A son who is very much like his father in appearance, character, habits, etc

To be as fit as a fiddle: To be in excellent health

To be at a loose end: To have nothing to do

To be at a loss for words: Not knowing what to say; to be speechless

To be at death's door: To be so ill as to be near death

To be at sixes and sevens: To be in confusion and discord

To be at the end of one's teeter: To be at a loss as to what to do

To be born under a lucky star: To have considerable luck in whatever one does

To be born with a silver spoon in one's mouth: To be born into a rich family

To be dead beat: To be worn out by fatigue

To be in hot water: To be in serious trouble

To be in someone's bad/good books: To be out of/in favour with someone

To be in the doldrums: To be in low spirits

To be in the same boat: To have the same troubles/ circumstances

To be mad about someone: To like someone very much

To be made of money: To have plenty of money; to be well-off

To be on tenterhooks: To be in a state of suspense and anxiety

To be on the ball: To be alert, up-to-date, prepared

To be on the horns of a dilemma: Not knowing what to do from several courses of action

To be on the rocks: To be in danger of failing, collapse, especially a business, a marriage, etc

To be on top of the world: To be very happy; to be in high spirits

To be out of the woods: To be out of danger, especially a serious illness

To be quick on the uptake: To be alert and quick to do or say something

To be rolling in money: To be rich; to have plenty of money

To be scared to death: To be extremely frightened of something

To be slow on the uptake: Slow to do or say something

To be too big for one's boots: To think very highly of oneself

To bear the brunt of: To bear the main force or strain of some action

To beat about the bush: To be indecisive; not coming to the point

To blow hot and cold: To do one thing at one time and the opposite soon after

To blow one's own trumpet: To boast about one's abilities, achievements etc.

To break the ice: To take the first step; to be the first to begin, especially a conversation

To bring down the house: To cause loud and long applause through one's skill

To bring to light: To disclose, reveal

To build castles in the air: To think of things impossible to realize

To burn the candle at both ends: To use one's energy in two directions at the same time

To burn the midnight oil: To work till late at night

To call a spade a spade: To speak out bluntly and frankly

To clip one's wings: To deprive one of power and/or freedom

To cook an account: To tamper with/falsify an account

To come down on someone like a: To harshly criticise another ton of bricks

To come of age: To reach adulthood

To come to grief: To meet with danger

To come to light: To become known

To count-sheep: To try various methods to get to sleep

To cry over spilt milk: To be unhappy about something that can no longer be remedied

To curry favour: To seek/win favour by flattery or gifts

To cut off in its prime: To destroy something when it is at its best

To cut one's coat according to: To live within one's income one's cloth

To cut someone down to size: To put someone in his place especially a person who thinks too highly of himself

To do a city/the sights: To visit a city and see its well-known places

To do a thing by fits and starts: To work intermittently on something

To do a thing by hook or by crook: To do something by any means, fair or foul, direct or indirect

To do something on the spur of the moment: To suddenly decide to do something

To drop a brick: To say or do something very tactless and unexpected

To drop a hint: To make veiled and subtle suggestions

To eat like a horse: To eat a lot

To eat one's words: To take back what one has said; to apologise

To egg on: To spur on to further action

To face the music: To meet the worst; to face punishment for doing something wrong

To fall out with someone: To quarrel with someone

To fall through: To fail, especially a plan, project, etc.

To fancy someone/something: To take a great liking to someone/something

To fight shy of: To avoid

To fire someone: To dismiss someone from employment

To flog a dead horse: To try fruitlessly to revive interest in something

To follow the crowd: To follow unthinkingly; to believe or act as most people do

To follow suit : To do the same thing as another person

To gain ground: To make progress in an undertaking

To get away with something: To escape detection despite doing something wrong

To get blood out of stone: To get more than is fair out of someone

To get down to work: To start on the task in hand

To get even with someone: To take revenge of someone

To get hitched: To get married

To get into a flap: To get worried and nervous

To get into hot water: To be in/to get into trouble

To get off scot-free: To escape punishment; to be let off payment

To get out of bed on the wrong side: To start the day in a bad temper

To get the sack: To be dismissed from employment

To get wind of: To hear a rumour of

To get the wind up: To get worried and nervous; to get a fright

To give someone a telling-off: To scold someone

To give someone the slip: To manage to avoid someone who is looking for you

To give the game away: To let out a secret

To give up the ghost: To die; to cease trying

To go a long way: To excel; to go far, especially in a career

To go off at a tangent: To change suddenly to a different course of thought or action

To go like a bomb: To go fast; to function well, especially a vehicle

To go to rack and ruin: To fall into a ruined or disorganised state

To grin and bear it: To make the best of a bad job; to put up with something

To haul someone over the coals: To reprimand someone

To have a bee in one's bonnet: To be strong-minded over certain issues

To have a soft spot for: To be very fond of someone or something

To have an axe to grind: To have a selflsh motive for doing something

To have one's knife in someone: To be always finding fault with another person

To hit below the belt: To attack an opponent unfairly

To hit the nail on the head: To do or say exactly the right thing

To jog someone's memory: To remind someone of something

To keep a person in the dark: To keep something hidden from someone

To keep open house: To encourage visitors to come at any time

To keep one's pecker up: To keep one's courage up

To keep one's shirt on: To keep cool and calm in a dispute

To keep the ball rolling: To keep a conversation going

To keep up appearances: To pretend to be well-off and to live in a certain style

To kick the bucket: To die

To kid someone: To tease

To kill two birds with one stone: To accomplish two things with one action

To knock off work: To stop working

To know the ropes: To be thoroughly familiar with a particular situation

To knock someone down with a feather: To surprise someone very much

To kowtow to someone: To act in a very servile manner hoping for favour

To lay down the law: To speak in an authoritative way

To lead someone up the garden path: To deceive someone by hiding the real intention

To leave someone in the lurch: To desert someone in time of difficulties

To let bygones be bygones: To let things that are past and gone remain untouched and forgotten

To let the cat out of the bag: To reveal a secret; to expose a trick

To look like a wet week: To look miserable and depressed

To make a go of something: To try one's best to succeed in something

To make a hash/a mess of something: To fail at a task

To make believe: To pretend

To make both ends meet: To be able to manage on one's income

To make hay while sun shines: To take advantage of an opportunity

To make much ado about nothing: To make a great fuss about something unimportant

To make oneself scarce: To disappear

To nip something in the bud: To stop something before it can develop into something serious

To pass the buck: To pass on the responsibility

To pick holes in something: To find fault with

To pick to pieces: To analyse critically

To pick and choose: To make a careful selection

To play a double game: To do one thing openly and a different thing in secret

To play fast and loose: To disregard one's promises

To play second fiddle: To take a subordinate position

To pooh-pooh an idea: To express contempt for an idea

To pull strings: To use friends in influential positions, or to use one's own influence, to secure favours

To put the cart before the horse: To do the wrong thing first

To put two and two together: To arrive at a conclusion

To put a spoke in one's wheel: To hinder; to obstruct progress

To rain cats and dogs: To rain very heavily

To read between the lines: To detect the hidden meaning

To rule the roost: To domineer over others

To run in the blood: Inherited qualities

To see something through coloured spectacles: To see only the best points about a thing

To see the light: To begin to understand

To sit on the fence: To take neither side in a dispute; to remain neutral

To smell a rat: To become suspicious about something

To steer clear of: To avoid

To take French leave: To be absent from work without permission

To take someone for a ride: To deceive someone

To take the bull by the horns: To meet a difficulty with courage

To take the law into one's own hands: To punish a person, usually by force, witnout his being tried in a law court

To take with a pinch of salt: To accept what someone has said with doubt and misgiving

To talk nineteen to the dozen: To speak a lot

To talk the hind legs of a donkey: To talk a great deal at great length

To tear a strip off someone: To scold harshly

To throw cold water upon: To discourage effort

To turn over a new leaf: To give up one's bad ways, and lead a better life

To turn the tables on someone: To defeat someone who has previously defeated you

To upset the apple cart: To disturb the routine of something

MULTIPLE CHOICE QUESTIONS

Directions: *Select the options which express the correct meaning of the given Idioms/Phrases.*

1. Cats' paw
A. a person who is used as a tool by another person
B. very slowly and quietly
C. very cleverly
D. to share a responsibility

2. To catch a tartar
A. to overcome a serious problem
B. to attack one who turns out to be stronger than is expected
C. to achieve the goal
D. to struggle hard

3. Cheek of jowl
A. very soft
B. close together
C. intimate relationship
D. low in status

4. A chip of the old block
A. a symptom of a serious disease
B. a child of a parent
C. a part of a whole
D. offsprings who display characteristics of their parents

5. To cool one's heels
A. to be kept waiting
B. to give a cold response to somebody
C. to follow somebody
D. to answer all the queries of somebody

6. To cleanse the Augean stables
A. to clean something which has not been cleaned for a long time
B. to wind up a joint business
C. to remove the stains of blood
D. to remove the traces of murder

7. A cry in wilderness
A. The cry of the poors
B. a warning that goes unheeded
C. A speech made by a less important leader
D. A cry out of deep sorrow

8. To cut one's coat according to one's cloth
A. to work according to one's capacity
B. to allot portfolio according to one's capability
C. to live within one's means
D. to live as one desires

9. Chicken hearted
A. coward B. brave
C. kind D. mortal

10. To clip one's wings
A. to lessen one's power B. to defame
C. to dismiss D. to punish

11. To come round
A. to agree with another's point of view
B. to come back to the point of origin
C. a circular movement
D. to wander

12. To call to order
A. a command
B. to rebuke for improper or incorrect behaviour
C. to obey an order
D. to show superiority

13. To cover one's tracks
A. to maintain the secrecy
B. to hide one's weaknesses
C. to carefully hide all traces of one's actions
D. to conceal the falsity

14. To throw up one's cards
A. To make a last effort B. to cease to struggle
C. to end up the game D. to come out victorious

15. To let the cat out of the bag
A. to disclose a secret
B. to set free
C. a person without a shelter
D. to permit the thief to run away

16. To cave in
A. to interfere B. to prohibit
C. to find a way D. to give way

17. To chuck up
A. to abandon B. to decorate
C. to summarize D. to cut into pieces

18. A dead letter
A. a delayed report
B. a false report
C. something exaggerated
D. something which is null and void

19. To die in harness
A. to die in office B. to die with great pain
C. a premature death D. a cruel murder

20. At the drop of a hat
A. without fail
B. without delay
C. against the self-respect
D. against the will

21. Day in and day out
A. always
B. forever
C. to break a promise done earlier
D. to remain busy always

22. Champ at
A. to pounce at B. be impassioned
C. be composed D. be eager or impatient

23. Burn one's fingers
A. to get oneself into trouble
B. to commit a blunder
C. a heavy monetory loss
D. to be in great rage

24. Down in the dumps
A. in a solitary mood
B. in a bad mood
C. to be in an unfavourable situation
D. to decline

25. To beg the question
A. to beg the pardon
B. to request for some extra-time to finish the work
C. unanswerable
D. to assume in the premises somethign which is to be proved

26. To carry the day
A. to be victorious B. an on-going discussion
C. a memorable day D. a miserable phase of life

27. At death's door
A. on the point of expiring
B. on the point of gun
C. to show bravery
D. a gradual deterior

28. To pay the debt of nature
A. to die
B. to give birth
C. to safeguard the natural things
D. to avoid environmental pollution

29. To do up
A. to finish off B. to mend
C. to improve D. to make tidy

30. To do away with
A. to break B. to destroy
C. to get rid of D. to forget

31. To have to do with
A. to be interested in
B. to do something under compulsion
C. work done unenthusiastically
D. to complete

32. To egg on
A. just a beginning
B. to urge on
C. to develop something
D. an initial stage

33. To face the music
A. to face the consequences
B. to get filled with ecstasy
C. to be lucky
D. to lead a happy life

34. To end in smoke
A. all efforts in vain B. the end of life
C. to come to nothing D. to end the enmity

35. Eye to eye with
A. agree completely
B. a confrontation
C. full of anger
D. a quarrel between the two persons

36. To eat humble pie
A. to harass a humble person
B. a celebration or a treat without any cause
C. to confess that one is in the wrong
D. food provided to the needy or poor

37. Easy come easy go
A. what is gained without difficulty is spent without much thought
B. anything which is surplus
C. without any difficulty
D. to achieve something without any struggle

38. To eat out one's heart
A. to break one's heart B. to deceive someone
C. to get deceived D. to suffer intensely

39. To see with half an eye
A. to see with great ease
B. to dislike
C. to see stealthily
D. to feel jealous

40. A fair-weathered friend
A. A friend always eager to help
B. A friend who deserts one in times of adversity
C. a selfish friend
D. a true friend

41. A far cry
A. an unfulfilled desire B. a very low voice
C. rĕmote from D. a distant place

42. To feather one's nest
A. to provide for one's own comfort
B. to be proud
C. to succeed again
D. to decorate one's house

43. To fish in troubled waters
A. to be in trouble
B. to make capital out of other's troubles
C. to be in trouble because of other's fault
D. to laugh at other's trouble

44. To follow suit
A. to follow the command
B. to obey the rules
C. to work in accordance with
D. to behave in the same manner

45. To get the hang of a thing
A. to understand the implications of something
B. to get a trace of theft
C. to find a new resource
D. to have some indications

46. To get wind of
A. to get news about something much before the event actually takes place
B. to forget the event that had taken place
C. to spread a rumour
D. to have some idea of a conspiration

47. French leave
A. a long leave
B. a small leave
C. absence from one's place of work without prior information
D. to leave the place forever

48. To steal a march upon
A. to outshine somebody
B. to rob
C. to move forward
D. to crush the enemy

49. A long face
A. a sad or mournful countenance
B. a very shameful defeat
C. a shameful act
D. an ugly face

50. To set one's face against
A. to criticise openly
B. to oppose with determination
C. a biased disapproval
D. to show disappointment

51. To fall away from
A. to decline B. to desert
C. to avoid D. to leave

52. To fall flat
A. to cause no amusement or interest
B. to lie down
C. to defeat the opponent
D. to plead

53. To have a finger in the pie
A. to be mixed up in any affair
B. to interfere in other's work
C. to have a share in the profit
D. to be a member of an organisation

54. In full cry
A. in full volume B. in hot pursuit
C. a verbosity D. manifestation of grief

55. To give a piece of one's mind
A. to rebuke
B. to give an idea
C. to present one's view
D. to judge one's intelligence on the basis of his work or contributions

56. Gift of the gab
A. the ability of verbosity
B. the ability of writing creatively
C. the ability to speak in an impressive manner
D. a man of versatile genius

57. To give the cold shoulder
A. to give support
B. to be indifferent
C. to express anger silently
D. to behave in a cold manner with someone

58. To give devil his due
A. to give an evil person credit for whatever good he has done
B. to punish one who has committed sin
C. an evil person meeting a tragic end
D. to give devil his share

59. To give up the ghost
A. to die
B. to sacrifice
C. to murder
D. to convert from vicious to virtuous

60. To give wide berth to
A. to give more space
B. to keep far away from

C. to appreciate more than what one deserves
D. to maintain a distance

61. To go to pieces
A. to tear
B. to feel disheartened
C. to be wrecked completely
D. to dismantle

62. To have too many irons in the fire
A. to be engaged in too many things
B. to handle more than one work at the same time
C. to have lot of energy
D. to have various plans in the mind

63. To put a spoke in one's wheel
A. to obstruct one in his work
B. to assist one in his work
C. to interfere one in his work
D. to increase the strength of a team

64. On the rack
A. in a dilemma
B. tortured by anxiety
C. highly curious
D. to be in a disadvantageous position

65. To get into hot water
A. an acute pain
B. to be in trouble
C. to face a short-tempered person
D. to be in hypertension

66. Fish and blood
A. by extreme means
B. by unlawful ways
C. human nature
D. life-like

67. From hand to mouth
A. to harm and humiliate
B. to be a bankrupt
C. to spend all that is earned
D. to feed someone

68. Hit the nail on the head
A. to take revenge openly
B. to insult on the face
C. to do a wrong thing
D. to do exactly the right thing

69. Put the cart before the horse
A. to reverse the natural order
B. to put obstruction
C. to cause problem for others
D. to stop one's advancement

70. Pay back in one's own coin
A. to save money
B. to treat in the same way as one has been treated
C. to get the return of the investment
D. to give a befitting reply

ANSWERS

1	2	3	4	5	6	7	8	9	10
A	B	B	D	A	A	B	C	A	A
11	**12**	**13**	**14**	**15**	**16**	**17**	**18**	**19**	**20**
A	B	C	B	A	D	A	D	A	B
21	**22**	**23**	**24**	**25**	**26**	**27**	**28**	**29**	**30**
A	D	A	B	D	A	A	A	D	C
31	**32**	**33**	**34**	**35**	**36**	**37**	**38**	**39**	**40**
A	B	A	C	A	C	A	D	A	B
41	**42**	**43**	**44**	**45**	**46**	**47**	**48**	**49**	**50**
C	A	B	D	A	A	C	A	A	B
51	**52**	**53**	**54**	**55**	**56**	**57**	**58**	**59**	**60**
B	A	A	B	A	C	D	A	A	B
61	**62**	**63**	**64**	**65**	**66**	**67**	**68**	**69**	**70**
C	A	A	B	B	C	C	D	A	B

8 Tenses

1. Tense indicates a point in time or period of time in the past, present, or future tense.
2. Tense is related to the form of verb. The verb may consist of a single word, or a main verb and one or more auxiliary words. There are normally three forms of the verb, say, V_1, V_2, V_3 and for convenience a fourth form V_4 as verb+ing may be assumed.

A Comparative Chart Regarding Tenses and Verbs

Simple Present	**Simple Past**	**Simple Future**
V_1	V_2	shall/will + V_1
Present Continuous	**Past Continuous**	**Future Continuous**
is/am/are + V_4	was/were + V_4	shall/will + be + V_4
Present Perfect	**Past Perfect**	**Future Perfect**
has/have + V_3	had + V_3	shall/will + have + V_3
Present Perfect Cont.	**Past Perfect Cont.**	**Future Perfect Cont.**
has/have + been + V_4	had + been + V_4	shall/will + have been + V_4

Tenses tell us the time of actions.

There are three kinds of Tenses.

1. Present Tense
2. Past Tense
3. Future Tense

1. Present Tense

The tense which shows action in the present time is known as the present tense. It is of the following kinds :

(A) Present Indefinite Tense or Simple Present Tense
(B) Present Continuous Tense
(C) Present Perfect Tense.
(D) Present Perfect Continuous Tense.

(A) *Present Indefinite Tense or Simple Present Tense*

This tense is used:

1. To show an action in the present time without referring to its finishing time
   (*i*) I write a letter to my friend.
   (*ii*) She helps the old man lift the bag.

☛ With I, we, you, they or Plural Noun the first form of the Verb is used. But with He, She, It, or Singular Noun, first form of the verb + s/es is used.

2. To show a habit or liking or disliking in the present time
   (*i*) She hates meat.
   (*ii*) We like singing and dancing.
   (*iii*) I daily go out for a walk.
   (*iv*) My uncle daily drinks a cup of tea after dinner.
3. To refer to a universal truth
   (*i*) The sun rises in the east.
   (*ii*) A bat flies better when it is dark around.
   (*iii*) The stars twinkle at night.

Negative and Interrogative Sentences

With I, we, you, they or Plural Nouns: do not + 1st form of the verb is used.

In case of interrogative sentences Do + subject + 1st form of the verb + object is used.

With He, She, It, or a Singular Noun does not + 1st form of the verb is used.

In case of interrogative sentences Does + Subject + 1st form of the verb + object is used.

(*i*) He does not borrow anything from anybody.

(*ii*) I do not advise you to do this job.

(*iii*) Do they know how to write business letters?

(*iv*) Does she understand French?

(B) *Present Continuous Tense*

It is used to show the continuity of an action in the present time.

Affirmative Sentences

(*i*) I am sending a telegram to Jack.

(*ii*) You are admiring my opponent.

(*iii*) She is speaking for the manager.

☛ When 'I' is the subject of the sentence use am + present participle.

When 'we, you, they or a Plural Noun is the Subject of sentence 'are + present participle' is used. But if 'he, she, it or a Singular Noun' is the Subject of the sentence 'is + present participle' is used.

Negative and Interrogative Sentences

(*i*) I am not trying to find out errors in your essay.

(*ii*) Am I trying to find out errors in your essay?

(*iii*) He is not creating any problem to the children.

(*iv*) Is he creating any problem to the children?

(*v*) They are not decorating the room.

(*vi*) Are they decorating the room?

(C) *Present Perfect Tense*

The tense which shows the completion of an action in the present tense is known as the Present Perfect Tense

Affirmative Sentence

(*i*) I have eaten/taken breakfast.

(*ii*) She has mixed up the ingredients to bake a cake.

When the subject of the sentence is I, we, you, they or a plural noun use have + past participle.

When the subject of the sentence is 'he, she, it or a singular noun, use has + past participle.

Negative and Interrogative Sentences

(*i*) The officer has not granted leave to the clerk.

(*ii*) Has the officer granted leave to the clerk?

(*iii*) They have not shovelled snow on to the truck yet.

(*iv*) Have they shovelled snow on to the truck?

(D) *Present Perfect Continuous Tense*

The tense shows a part of an action having been completed and another part of it still being done in the Present Tense.

(*i*) He has been mending the shoes since morning.

(*ii*) We have been flying kites for three hours.

☛ Preposition 'since' is used when the point of time is given *i.e.* since 2001, since 5 o'clock, since morning, since evening, etc.

Preposition 'for' is used when the period of time is given, e.g., for two weeks, for three days, for five years, etc.

Negative and Interrogative Sentences

(*i*) The peon has not been ringing the bell for two hours.

(*ii*) Have the firemen been trying to extinguish fire since morning?

2. Past Tense

The tense which shows action in the past time is known as Past Tense. It is of the following kinds.

(A) Past Indefinite Tense or Simple Past Tense

(B) Past Continuous Tense

(C) Past Perfect Tense

(D) Past Perfect Continuous Tense

(A) *Past Indefinite or Simple Past Tense*

It is used in:

Affirmative Sentences

1. To show an action in the past time without referring to its finishing time

   (*i*) The scientist found the food contaminated with bacteria.

   (*ii*) The calves frisked in the courtyard.

   (*iii*) He typed three letters this morning.

☛ Subject + IInd form of verb + Object is used.

2. To show a habit in the past time

   (*i*) She used to go to temple daily.

   (*ii*) He daily prayed to God before going to office.

   (*iii*) They most often took a long walk in the morning.

3. To show historical truth

   (*i*) India got its freedom on 15 August, 1947.

   (*ii*) Mr. J.L. Nehru was elected the first Prime Minister of India.

Negative and Interrogative Sentences

(*i*) She did not attend the meeting.

(*ii*) We did not allow the children to play in the lawn.

(*iii*) Did he complain to the officer against you?

With 'did' first form of the verb is used.

With some Adverbs e.g. yesterday, ago, etc. Past Indefinite Tense is used.

(*i*) My father bought me a new bicycle five days ago.
(*ii*) A thief broke into my neighbour's last night.
(*iii*) We saw a movie yesterday.

(B) *Past Continuous Tense*

This tense shows the continuity of an action in the past.

Affirmative Sentences

(*i*) He was driving a car.
(*ii*) I was memorizing the lesson.
(*iii*) The workers were building the flyover.

Subject + was/were + Present Participle + object (if any)

Negative and Interrogative Sentences

(*i*) They were not planning to go to Sweden in Summer.
(*ii*) Was he advising his friends to help the poor?
(*iii*) Were the mechanics repairing the machines?
(*iv*) She was not taking any interest in houshold chores.

(C) *Past Perfect Tense*

This tense shows the completion of an action in the past time.

Affirmative Sentences

(*i*) She had finished painting the pictures.
(*ii*) We had planted the saplings of mango plants.
(*iii*) The doctor had operated upon the patient.

Subject + had + Past Participle + Object.

Negative and Interrogative Sentences

(*i*) Had she applied for the post of a clerk?
(*ii*) He had not reserved a berth in the Rajdhani Express.

(D) *Past Perfect Continuous Tense*

This tense shows the part completion of an action/work when the other part of the action/work is still continuing in the Past Tense.

Affirmative Sentences

(*i*) She had been working in that office for five years.
(*ii*) They had been living in that house since 2001.

Negative and Interrogative Sentences

(*i*) Had the gardener been watering the plants since morning?
(*ii*) The birds had not been chirping on the branches of the tree for three hours.

3. Future Tense

The tense which used to express the actions in future time is known as the future tense. It is of the following kinds:

(A) Future Indefinite Tense or Simple Future Tense
(B) Future Continuous Tense.
(C) Future Perfect Tense.
(D) Future Perfect Continuous Tense.

(A) *Future Indefinite Tense*

It is used to indicate the actions planned for future.

Affirmative Sentences

(*i*) I shall write a letter to my mother.
(*ii*) The maid will wash the clothes after the sunrise.
(*iii*) They will varnish the chairs.

Subject + Will/Shall + 1st form of the verb + Object

Negative and Interrogative Sentences

(*i*) He will not associate with those boys.
(*ii*) We shall not walk over the slippery snowy path.

(B) *Future Continuous Tense*

It is used to show a continuous action in the future time.

Affirmative Sentences

(*i*) She will be planning to meet the P.M.

The policeman will be standing on guard at the check post.

Negative and Interrogative Sentences

(*i*) They will not be carrying coal to the city from the mine.
(*ii*) Will you be singing on radio the next month?

(C) *Future Perfect Tense*

It is used to show the completion of an action in the future.

Affirmative Sentences

(*i*) You will have got admission in the new school by then.
(*ii*) He will have joined the army by then.

Negative and Interrogative Sentences

(*i*) She will not have told you the story of a lion and a mouse.
(*ii*) Shall we have reserved two berths in the Janata Express by then?

(D) *Future Perfect Continuous Tense*

It is used to show the part completion of a work/action and the continuity of the other part in the Future Tense.

Affirmative Sentences

(*i*) He will have been working in the office for five years.
(*ii*) They will have been painting the pictures since morning.

Negative and Interrogative Sentences

(*i*) She will not have been discussing the matter with her friends for two hours.
(*ii*) Will they have been begging for food since morning?

MULTIPLE CHOICE QUESTIONS

Directions: *Choose the correct tense form of each sentence from the options given below.*

1. I speak.
   A. Simple past tense
   B. Simple present tense
   C. Present continuous tense
   D. Simple future tense
2. He is speaking.
   A. Present continuous tense
   B. Simple future tense
   C. Future continuous tense
   D. Present perfect tense
3. You are speaking.
   A. Present perfect continuous tense
   B. Present continuous tense
   C. Past perfect continuous tense
   D. Past continuous tense
4. He spoke.
   A. Past perfect tense B. Simple future tense
   C. Present perfect tense D. Simple past tense
5. You will have spoken.
   A. Simple future tense B. Future perfect tense
   C. Simple past tense D. Past perfect tense
6. He will speak.
   A. Simple present tense B. Future perfect tense
   C. Simple past tense D. Simple future tense
7. We speak.
   A. Simple present tense B. Simple past tense
   C. Simple future tense D. Present perfect tense
8. You will have been speaking.
   A. Future continuous tense
   B. Simple future tense
   C. Future perfect continuous tense
   D. Future perfect tense
9. They will have spoken.
   A. Past perfect tense B. Future perfect tense
   C. Present perfect tense D. Simple past tense
10. He has spoken.
    A. Simple present tense B. Present perfect tense
    C. Simple past tense D. Past perfect tense
11. You will be speaking.
    A. Future continuous tense
    B. Past continuous tense
    C. Present perfect continuous
    D. Present continuous tense
12. I spoke.
    A. Simple present tense B. Present perfect tense
    C. Past perfect tense D. Simple past tense
13. They were speaking.
    A. Present continuous tense
    B. Past continuous tense
    C. Future continuous tense
    D. Past perfect tense
14. I had spoken.
    A. Past perfect tense B. Future perfect tense
    C. Simple present tense D. Present perfect tense
15. They have spoken.
    A. Past perfect tense B. Future perfect tense
    C. Simple present tense D. Present perfect tense
16. They have been speaking.
    A. Present continuous tense
    B. Past continuous tense
    C. Future continuous tense
    D. Present perfect continuous tense
17. He shall/will have been speaking.
    A. Future continuous tense
    B. Simple future tense
    C. Future perfect continuous tense
    D. Future perfect tense
18. We had been speaking.
    A. Past perfect tense
    B. Past perfect continuous tense
    C. Future perfect continuous tense
    D. Simple past tense
19. You have been speaking.
    A. Present perfect continuous tense
    B. Present continuous tense
    C. Past perfect continuous tense
    D. Past continuous tense
20. We had spoken.
    A. Simple past tense B. Past perfect tense
    C. Present perfect tense D. Future perfect tense
21. They will speak.
    A. Simple present tense
    B. Past perfect tense
    C. Simple future tense
    D. Future perfect tense
22. I had been speaking.
    A. Present perfect continuous tense
    B. Present continuous tense
    C. Past perfect continuous tense
    D. Past continuous tense
23. We shall/will be speaking.
    A. Past perfect tense
    B. Present perfect tense
    C. Past continuous tense
    D. Future continuous tense

24. You were speaking.
A. Past continuous
B. Present continuous
C. Past perfect tense
D. Past perfect continuous tense

25. I shall/will have been speaking.
A. Past perfect tense
B. Present perfect continuous tense
C. Present continuous tense
D. Future perfect continuous tense

26. I have spoken.
A. Simple past tense B. Simple present tense
C. Present perfect tense D. Simple future tense

27. I was speaking.
A. Past continuous tense
B. Simple future tense
C. Future continuous tense
D. Present perfect tense

28. I shall/will be speaking.
A. Future continuous tense
B. Present continuous tense
C. Past perfect continuous tense
D. Past continuous tense

29. I shall/will speak.
A. Past perfect tense B. Simple future tense
C. Present perfect tense D. Simple past tense

30. You speak.
A. Simple present tense B. Future perfect tense
C. Simple past tense D. Past perfect tense

31. We speak.
A. Simple past tense
B. Simple present tense
C. Present continuous tense
D. Simple future tense

32. I shall/will have spoken.
A. Present continuous tense
B. Simple future tense
C. Future continuous tense
D. Future perfect tense

33. You had spoken.
A. Past perfect tense
B. Present continuous tense
C. Past perfect continuous tense
D. Past continuous tense

34. He has been speaking.
A. Past perfect contintuous tense
B. Simple future tense
C. Present perfect continuous tense
D. Simple past tense

35. You spoke.
A. Present perfect continuous tense
B. Past perfect contintuous tense
C. Simple past tense
D. Past perfect tense

36. They speak.
A. Simple past tense
B. Simple present tense
C. Present continuous tense
D. Simple future tense

37. I have been speaking.
A. Present continuous tense
B. Present perfect continuous tense
C. Future continuous tense
D. Past perfect continuous tense

38. He will have spoken.
A. Present perfect continuous tense
B. Present continuous tense
C. Future perfect tense
D. Past continuous tense

39. We shall/will have spoken.
A. Past perfect tense
B. Future perfect tense
C. Past perfect continuous tense
D. Future perfect continuous tense

40. He had been speaking.
A. Past perfect tense
B. Future perfect tense
C. Past perfect continuous tense
D. Future perfect continuous tense

41. They spoke.
A. Simple past tense
B. Simple present tense
C. Present continuous tense
D. Simple future tense

42. You have spoken.
A. Present continuous tense
B. Simple future tense
C. Future continuous tense
D. Present perfect tense

43. He had spoken.
A. Past perfect tense
B. Present continuous tense
C. Past perfect continuous tense
D. Past continuous tense

44. He was speaking.
A. Past perfect tense
B. Past continuous tense
C. Present continuous tense
D. Simple past tense

45. They are speaking.
A. Past perfect continuous tense
B. Past continuous tense
C. Present continuous tense
D. Simple past tense

46. I am speaking.
A. Past continuous tense
B. Simple present tense
C. Present continuous tense
D. Simple future tense

47. We have spoken.
A. Present continuous tense
B. Simple future tense
C. Future continuous tense
D. Present perfect tense

48. He will have spoken.
A. Present perfect continuous tense
B. Present continuous tense
C. Future perfect tense
D. Past continuous tense

49. You will speak.
A. Past perfect tense
B. Simple future tense
C. Present perfect tense
D. Simple past tense

50. They will be speaking.
A. Future continuous tense
B. Future perfect tense
C. Past continuous tense
D. Present continuous tense

ANSWERS

1	2	3	4	5	6	7	8	9	10
B	A	B	D	B	D	A	C	B	B
11	**12**	**13**	**14**	**15**	**16**	**17**	**18**	**19**	**20**
A	D	B	A	D	D	C	B	A	B
21	**22**	**23**	**24**	**25**	**26**	**27**	**28**	**29**	**30**
C	C	D	A	D	C	A	A	B	A
31	**32**	**33**	**34**	**35**	**36**	**37**	**38**	**39**	**40**
B	D	A	C	C	B	B	C	B	C
41	**42**	**43**	**44**	**45**	**46**	**47**	**48**	**49**	**50**
A	D	A	B	C	C	D	C	B	A

9 Narration

Direct Speech and Indirect Speech

The words spoken by a speaker are in Direct Speech.

The words spoken by somebody and expressed by someone else with some modification are known as Indirect Speech.

(*a*) Rohit says to me, "You do not understand me."

(*b*) Rohit tells me that I do not understand him.

The sentence (*a*) shows the words spoken by Rohit. So, it is a sentence of direct speech.

The sentence (*b*) shows the words spoken by Rohit and they have been reported with certain modification. So, it is a sentence of Indirect Speech.

Important Rules Regarding the change of Direct Speech into Indirect Speech

1. In a sentence of direct speech the verb outside the inverted commas is known as the Reporting Verb.
2. The words inside the inverted commas are known as Direct Speech.
3. When the sentence is indirect speech, it won't take a sign of exclamation or a sign of interrogation.
4. The Reporting Verb can be given in Present, Past or Future Tense.
5. When the Reporting Verb is in Present or Future Tense, there will be no change in the tense of direct speech while converting it into indirect speech.
6. When the Reporting Verb is in Past Tense the tense of direct speech will be changed while converting it into Indirect Speech.
7. The following adverbs and possessives should be changed as given:
   (*i*) This into that
   (*ii*) These into those
   (*iii*) Here into there
   (*iv*) Now into then
   (*v*) Today into that day
   (*vi*) Last night into the previous night
   (*vii*) Tomorrow into the next day
   (*viii*) The next day/week into the following day/week
   (*ix*) Hence into thence.

Change of Tense

Reporting Verb	*Reporting Speech*	*Change of Tense*
Present Tense	Any Tense	No change
Future Tense	Any Tense	No change
Past Tense	Present/Future Tense	Change into corresponding Past Tense
Past Tense	Past Indefinite Tense	Change into Past Perfect Tense
Past Tense	Past Continuous Tense	Change into Past Perfect Continuous Tense
Past Tense	Past Pefect/Perfect Continuous Tense	No change
Past Tense	Universal Truth	No change
Past Tense	Proverb	No change

Transformation Based on Special Rules

1. Rule Related to Interrogative Sentence

- If the answer of an interrogative sentence is possible in yes-no manner.

Illustration.

M.S. Dhoni told Rahul Dravid, "Will you help me?"

M.S. Dhoni asked Rahul Dravid whether he would help him.

☛ The answer of Reporting Verb is possible in yes-no manner.

Rule of Transformation from Direct to Indirect speech

Step I : Change R.V. into ask.

Step II : In place of comma use 'if/whether'.

Step III : Change interrogative sentence into assertive sentence.

- If the answer of an interrogative sentence is not possible in yes-no manner.

Illustration:

Rahul Dravid told Dhoni, "What do you want?"

Rahul Dravid asked Dhoni what he wanted.

☛ Only in Step II, you have to avoid comma and inverted comma and rest will be same as mentioned above.

2. Rule related to Imperative Sentence

- Imperative sentence is a sentence which shows Order/ Advice/Request

Illustration:

My father said to me, "Go there".

My father ordered me to go there.

Rule of Transformation from Direct to Indirect Speech

Step I : Change R.V. as per meaning/sense of R.S. into order/request/advise.

Step II : In place of comma, use 'to'.

Step III : Rest portion will be same.

3. Rule related to Optative Sentence

- Optative sentence is a sentence which exposes the feeling of bless/curse/pray/wish.

Illustration:

Mother said to me, "May you live long!"

Mother blessed me that I might live long.

Rule of Transformation from Direct to Indirect Speech

Step I : Change R.V. as per meaning/sense of R.S. into bless/curse/pray/wish.

Step II : In place of comma, use 'that'.

Step III : Change optative sentence into assertive sentence.

4. Rule related to Exclamatory Sentence

- Exclamatory sentence is a sentence which takes note of exclamatory (!) mark in that sentence showing inner feeling.

Illustration:

She said, "Alas! I am ruined".

She exclaimed with sorrow that she was ruined.

Rule of Transformation from Direct to Indirect Speech

Step I : Change R.V. as per meaning/sense of R.S. into exclaim/exclaims/exclaimed/will or shall exclaim + joy/sorrow/anger/surprise/applause/ contempt.

Step II : Change comma into that.

Step III : Change note of exclamation (!) into full (.)

Step IV : Change exclamatory sentence into assertive sentence.

MULTIPLE CHOICE QUESTIONS

Directions: *Each sentence in direct speech is followed by four options in indirect speech, only one is correct. Spot the correct answer.*

1. She said, ''Shall I thread the needle?''

A. She asked if she should thread the needle.
B. She asked if she shall thread the needle.
C. She requested if she should thread the needle.
D. She says that if she would thread the needle.

2. We said, ''What a place it is!''

A. We said that it was a very fine place.
B. We said that is a very fine place.
C. We said that the place is fine.
D. We exclaimed with joy that the place was very fine.

3. My father said, ''The earth is round''.

A. My father said that the earth was round.
B. My father says that the earth is round.
C. My father said that the earth is round
D. My father ordered that the earth is round.

4. The teacher said, ''Don't make a noise''.

A. The teacher says to us not to make a noise.
B. The teacher asked us not to make a noise.
C. The teacher requested us not to make a noise.
D. The teacher asked us not to made a noise.

5. He said, ''Bring a chair at once''.

A. He ordered to bring a chair at once.
B. He requested to bring a chair at once.
C. He told to bring a chair at once.
D. He says to bring a chair at once.

6. I said to my sister, "Please, give me more money".

A. I requested my sister to give me more money.
B. I ordered my sister to give me more money.
C. I advised my sister to gave me more money.
D. I requested my sister to give her more money.

7. Baby said, "I will go".

A. Baby said that she will go.
B. Baby said that she could go.
C. Baby say that she will go.
D. Baby said that she would go.

8. The teacher says, "Two and two makes four".

A. The teacher says that two and two made four.
B. The teacher wishes that two and two makes four.

C. The teacher advises that two and two makes four.
D. The teacher says that two and two makes four.

9. He told me, "Shall I go to the picture?"
A. He asked that he should go to the picture.
B. He asked me if he shall go to the picture.
C. He asked me if he should go to the picture.
D. He requested me to go to the picture.

10. I told Ravi, "Do have a cup of tea".
A. I ordered Ravi to have a cup of tea.
B. I advised Ravi to had a cup of tea.
C. I requested Ravi to have a cup of tea.
D. I said Ravi to have a cup of cold tea.

11. She said, "I am an early-riser".
A. She regretted that she was an early-riser.
B. She said that she is an early-riser.
C. She said that she was an early-riser.
D. She regretted that she is an early-riser.

12. The police officer said to the criminal, "Speak as I tell you".
A. The police officer directed the criminal to speak as he told him.
B. The police officer told the criminal to speak as he told him.
C. The police officer advised the criminal to speak as he told him.
D. The police officer requested the criminal to speak as he told him.

13. The preacher said to me, "May God help you!"
A. The preacher prayed that God might help me.
B. The preacher prayed that God might help him.
C. The preacher requested that God might help me.
D. The preacher requested the God might help them.

14. She said to me, "Happy Diwali!"
A. She blessed me a happy Diwali.
B. She wished me a happy Diwali.
C. She prayed a happy Diwali.
D. She said to me a very happy Diwali.

15. He said, "Shall I open the gate?"
A. He asked that he should open the gate.
B. He asked if he should open the gate.
C. He ordered that he should open the gate.
D. He requested that he should open the gate.

16. She said to me, "Keep quite and listen to my words".
A. She requested me to keep quite and listen to her words.
B. She ordered me to keep quite and listen to her words.
C. She entreated me to keep quite and listen to her words.
D. She told me to keep quite and listen to her words.

17. My brother said to me, "What are you doing here?"
A. My brother asked me that what I was doing there.
B. My brother asked me what I was doing there.
C. My brother asked me that what was I doing there.
D. My brother asked me what I was doing here.

18. Ravi said, "My father lived in this city two years ago."
A. Ravi said that his father had lived in that city two years before.
B. Ravi said that his father had lived in that city two years ago.
C. Ravi told that his father had lived in that city ago two years.
D. Ravi asked that his father had lived in that city before two years.

19. My brother said to me, "When I was young, I used to play cricket".
A. My brother told me that when I was young, I used to play cricket.
B. My brother told me that when I was young, I used to play cricket.
C. My brother told me that when he was young, I used to play cricket.
D. My brother told me that when he was young, he used to play cricket.

20. The student said, "Sir, I am not guilty".
A. The student said with respect that he was not guilty.
B. The student pleaded that he was not guilty.
C. The student pleaded with respect that he was not guilty.
D. The student said respectfully that he was not guilty.

21. Mohini said to me, "Trust in God."
Mohini advised me:
A. that I should trust in God.
B. should trust in God.
C. trusted in God.
D. to trust in God.

22. I said to him, "Let us go to school."
I told him:
A. we would go to school.
B. we shall go to school.
C. that we would go to school.
D. that we should go to school.

23. Rajni said, "May God bless you?"
Rajni:
A. exclaimed with wish that God might bless me.
B. expressed a wish that God might bless me.
C. asked God to bless me.
D. shouted with joy to bless me.

24. My mother said to me, "Do not have so many friends."
My mother forbade me:
A. to have so many friends.
B. not to have so many friends.
C. to have been so many friends.
D. to possess so many friends.

25. Ram said, "Pay attention to me."
Ram asked:
A. pay attention to him.
B. paid attention to him.
C. having paid attention to him.
D. to pay attention to him.

Directions (Qs. 26 to 30): *A sentence correctly changed into indirect narration is followed by four sentencs in the direct narration. Pick out from the alternative one which, when changed into indirect narration will be the same as the indirect sentence preceding the alternatives.*

26. The driver asked the mechanic if he would repair his car.
A. "Repair the car," the driver ordered the mechanic.
B. "Please repair the car," the driver asked the mechanic.
C. "O, please repair the car," the driver asked the mechanic.
D. "Will you repair my car?" the driver asked the mechanic.

27. She thanked me and asked me not to disturb her.
A. "Thank you. Do not disturb me," she said.
B. "Dear friend than you, do not disturb," she said.
C. "Disturb not, thank you," she said.
D. "Thank you, please ask not to disturb," she said.

28. In a tone of anger she asked her boy-friend why he had come.
A. "You fool, why have you come," she said.
B. "Oh, why have you come," said she.
C. "You damned! Why have you come?" she said.
D. "You, you, O you why have you come," she said.

29. Calling him a coward, the girl asked him to come out.
A. "Come out, you coward!" said the girl.
B. "Come out," said the girl to the coward.
C. The girl said, "Alas coward come."
D. The girl said, "Come out".

30. He called her a naughty girl.
A. "Oh! naughty girl," said he.
B. "You naughty girl!" said he.
C. He said, "naughty girl."
D. "Naughty," boy said to her.

ANSWERS

1	2	3	4	5	6	7	8	9	10
A	D	C	B	A	A	D	D	C	C
11	**12**	**13**	**14**	**15**	**16**	**17**	**18**	**19**	**20**
C	A	A	B	B	B	B	A	D	C
21	**22**	**23**	**24**	**25**	**26**	**27**	**28**	**29**	**30**
A	D	B	A	D	D	A	C	A	B

10 Preposition Usage

A preposition is a word placed before a noun or a pronoun to show the relationship between things, people or events. It expresses relationship in space, position, direction, time, place, method, purpose or result.

Usage:

(*i*) A preposition is usually placed before a noun or noun-equivalent it governs.

e.g. She died of AIDS.

(*ii*) The preposition is always placed at the end when the object is the Relative pronoun 'that';

e.g. Here is the book that you asked for.

He snatched the paper that I was writing on.

(*iii*) For the sake of emphasis the object governed by the preposition is placed first/before the preposition;

e.g. This I aimed at.

His acheivement is known all the world over.

ERRORS IN USE OF PREPOSITIONS

Preposition of Time:

1. At is used (*a*) with a definite point of time (*b*) with festivals.

   e.g. I go to my office at 9.30 a.m.

   He will come at Christmas.

2. **In** is used: (*a*) with a specific time, period, month, year, season,

   e.g. I talk in the morning.

   In winter the weather is cold.

☛ 'At' is used with noon.

e.g. He comes at noon for lunch.

(*b*) With the future tense referring to the period in which action may take place:

e.g. Inflation will rise in future.

3. **On** is used with days and dates.

   e.g. The Annual function is on Saturday.

   My Birthday is on twenty-seventh July.

4. **By** determines the time by which anything is to be done; done before not later;

   e.g. Application should reach this office by 5th June.

   Work will be completed by Monday.

5. **Before** This implies 'earlier than';

   e.g. Children must reach school before the bell rings.

6. **From** It indicates the time of beginning.

   e.g. I am on leave from 10th April.

   She is dumb from birth.

7. **Since** expresses a specified time in the past up to the present.

   e.g. He has taken up this job last year and has been here ever since.

   I am waiting for him since yesterday.

8. **For** has three implications:

   (*a*) Firstly it expresses a period of time or say duration

   e.g. He worked in this office for eight years.

   (*b*) Secondly it refers to the specified time when something is intended to happen;

   e.g. The appointment is for 7.30 p.m.

   (*c*) Thirdly it indicates the occasion when something happens.

   e.g. I am going college for the first time.

Prepositions of Position

1. **At** refers to an exact point.

   e.g. He is going to meet him at Mcdonald Restaurant.

   She is at a meeting.

2. **In** implies inside; within the shape or area of.

   e.g. We live in India.

   He was hit in the chest.

3. **Between** is used for two persons or two things.

   e.g. Equator lies between the Tropic of Cancer and Tropic of Capricorn.

4. **Beside** shows a position next to.
   e.g. Whenever I travel, I keep my costly luggage beside me.
5. **Besides** means in addition to.
   e.g. Besides these flowers, we need some decoration materials too.
6. **Below** shows the position at a lower level.
   e.g. The temperature in Delhi remained below 5°C all day.
7. **Beneath** means in a lower position
   e.g. Several dead bodies are still lying beneath the debris caused by earthquake.
8. **Among** is used with more than two persons or things but before the word which starts with a consonant letter.
   e.g. He loves to sit among the children and narrate stories.
9. **Amongst** is used with more than two persons or things but before the word which starts with a vowel letter.
   e.g. Divide the chocolates amongst us.
10. **Over** is used for vertically above.
    e.g. A white cloth was spread over the dead body. There is a fan over the bed.
11. **Within** shows the position near by or approachable.
    e.g. Within the school campus, there is a swimming pool.
12. **Onto** means upon the surface.
    e.g. The child enjoyed jumping onto the sofa.

Preposition of Direction

1. **To** is used to express motion from one place to another.
   e.g. We walked to the hills and back.
2. **Towards** refers to direction in which the progress is being made.
   e.g. While performing on the stage one should face towards the audience.
3. **Into** denotes motion towards the inside of something.
   e.g. He immediately dived into the water and saved the child.
4. **At** refers to aim.
   e.g. He aimed at the bird on window.
5. **For** denotes direction.
   e.g. I will leave for Bombay tomorrow.
6. **Against** shows pressure.
   e.g. Place the ladder against the wall.
7. **Off** refers to separation.
   e.g. He slipped off the scooter.
8. **From** refers to the point of departure.
   e.g. He borrowed the money from his sister.

Other Uses of Prepositions

1. **About** shows nearness.
   e.g. His father is about to retire.
2. **Along** is used to express the position from one end to or towards the other end; or parallel with the length of something.
   e.g. We walked along the river bank.
3. **Across** is used in three different meaning
   Firstly, it refers to something extending from one side to the other.
   e.g. The railway bridge is to be constructed across the river.
   Secondly, to express from one side to the other side of something.
   e.g. He rowed across the Chilka lake.
   Thirdly, to express something that intersects or cross.
   e.g. On the death of her only son the mother cried with her arms across the chest.

MULTIPLE CHOICE QUESTIONS

Direction: *Fill in the blanks with suitable prepositions.*

1. Children should be able to adapt ..... harsh weather conditions.
   A. to B. with
   C. in D. onto
2. The boat which was rowed with only one oar went ..... in circles, only when it was rowed with both the oars, it moved.
   A. around B. round
   C. away D. about
3. The Sergeant was returning from a New Year eve dinner with friends when he chanced ..... five drunken passengers ..... a taxi harassing girl.
   A. upon, in B. against, in
   C. at, inside D. on, inside
4. In most parts of the city there were huge traffic jams with vehicles backed up ..... miles.
   A. to B. at
   C. through D. for
5. The huge surge in foreign exchange reserves ..... the current financial year should be a cause ..... concern to the policymakers.
   A. of, for B. of, of
   C. in, for D. in, of
6. Celebrations transform our life of routine and boredom ..... rejuvenation and rejoicing.
   A. towards B. unto
   C. into D. to
7. Miserly people are incapable of trusting life and that's why life does not open its treasures ..... them.

A. to B. for
C. within D. towards

8. There are so many people of Indian origin settled ..... the globe, from different professions.
A. throughout B. across
C. round D. wide

9. Fluctuations in business fortunes is another reason for companies going in .... a floating workforce.
A. to B. towards
C. through D. for

10. She hopes to be a teacher but her real talent lies in wielding the brush .... aplomb.
A. in B. with
C. beyond D. into

11. Thousands of young patriotic Indians responded to Vivekananda's clarion call and jumped whole-heartedly ...... the freedom struggle.
A. for B. to
C. in D. into

12. Today, the youth are so self-centered, they are not bothered ..... the poverty around them.
A. about B. with
C. to D. for

13. Many NRIs are looking ..... investing in India like buying homes.
A. for B. to
C. into D. at

14. The new Science and Technology Policy rightly reeks to put in place simplified administrative and financial procedures that will hopefully breathe fresh life .... Indian science.
A. within B. in
C. into D. for

15. She is not the only artist to have faced threats from underworld but she is the only one brave to talk ..... them.
A. about B. on
C. relating D. upon

16. Life would be fun without any restraint imposed ..... belonging to one religion.
A. for B. by
C. at D. on

17. There has been a large accession of books .... the library.
A. at B. to
C. for D. in

18. His aggressive way of dealing ..... people will make many misconotrue his actions.
A. of B. at
C. with D. in

19. He felt it to be an insult .... his pride when I did not believe his words.
A. in B. at
C. on D. to

20. The new hospital provides ample amenities ..... the patients.
A. for B. to
C. through D. towards

21. Literature cannot close its eyes ..... the ambient society.
A. upon B. on
C. against D. to

22. The monetary help that he rendered .... the most appropriate moment was really appreciable.
A. in B. at
C. to D. into

23. He had no option but to resign from the office after the defamation heaped ..... him.
A. against B. on
C. upon D. around

24. His habit of interfering made him extremely unpopular ..... his colleagues.
A. in B. against
C. on D. at

25. His ignoble tastes are ..... variance with his elevated social status.
A. in B. against
C. on D. at

26. It is difficult for an over-scrupulous person to live ..... coarse people.
A. in B. amongst
C. around D. between

27. After the earthquake, the whole city appeared to be .... a shambles.
A. at B. in
C. on D. upon

28. ...... circumstances compelled him, the lazy refused to work for his living.
A. Till B. Until
C. Since D. After

29. A shocked nation was trying to come to terms ..... the sudden death of the Prime Minister.
A. on B. at
C. with D. after

30. ...... his passing away, the nation has lost a great patriot who made an outstanding contribution to public life.
A. With B. On
C. In D. After

31. He never deviated ..... his commitment to serve the people of India with exceptional devotion.
A. from B. in
C. against D. at

32. .... this park was much bigger but recently a swimming pool has been built making it shrunk.
A. Previously B. Formerly
C. Earlier D. In early days

33. Indian farmers might hope ..... the forecast of rain and thunder to come true as their fields are dried of drought.

A. for B. in
C. with D. None of the above

34. She exuded confidence as she walked ..... the board-room for the interview.

A. to B. in
C. into D. at

35. It is imperative for the Indian economy to sustain high rates of growth ..... many years.

A. for B. over
C. through D. around

36. The use of narcotics is very much ..... the increase now especially among young people.

A. at B. on
C. to D. with

37. He is too much of an idealist to be concerned ..... worldly matters.

A. with B. of
C. to D. for

38. He carried on working late ..... the night.

A. till B. at
C. into D. in

39. Driving ...... the sun, we had to shade our eyes.

A. through B. into
C. in D. with

40. There's something strange .... the whole affair.

A. in B. into
C. around D. about

41. I could hardly hear the song .... the music in the background.

A. against B. for
C. since D. above

42. The standard of your work is well ..... the average of your class.

A. behind B. low
C. below D. beneath

43. His dead body was found ..... the debris caused by earthquake.

A. below B. beneath
C. under D. within

44. You could put it ...... to nostalgia when he talks about the old days in Delhi.

A. law B. beneath
C. down D. under

45. He is ...... the generation that headed West in search of fame and stayed back.

A. of B. from
C. in D. with

46. There are so many mistakes in these books, sometimes I feel like trying my hand ..... it.

A. on B. upon
C. with D. at

47. I do not remember why the curfew had been imposed but I still recollect that I was very afraid ..... it.

A. of B. to
C. about D. against

48. We all possess a reserve of strength and fortitude ..... which we are rarely conscious.

A. of B. about
C. to D. at

49. We never know life ..... we have borne its trials and hardships.

A. till B. until
C. since D. before

50. Delinquency is rampant .... the youth of today.

A. in B. around
C. amongst D. with

ANSWERS

1	2	3	4	5	6	7	8	9	10
A	D	A	D	C	C	A	B	D	B
11	**12**	**13**	**14**	**15**	**16**	**17**	**18**	**19**	**20**
D	A	D	C	A	B	B	C	D	B
21	**22**	**23**	**24**	**25**	**26**	**27**	**28**	**29**	**30**
A	B	C	D	D	B	B	B	C	C
31	**32**	**33**	**34**	**35**	**36**	**37**	**38**	**39**	**40**
B	C	A	C	B	B	A	C	B	D
41	**42**	**43**	**44**	**45**	**46**	**47**	**48**	**49**	**50**
D	C	B	C	B	D	A	A	B	C

11 Transformation of Sentences

A sentence may be written in many different ways conveying the same meaning. This is called transformation of sentences. Practise various methods of transformation given below:

REMOVING 'TOO'

By replacing 'too' with 'so that'

1. He is too weak to walk.
   He is so weak that he cannot walk.
2. The book was too tough to comprehend.
   The book was so tough that it could not be comprehended.

☛ Sentence No. 1 is in the Present Tense so in it 'cannot' has been used; Sentence No. 2 is in the Past Tense, so, in it 'could not' has been used.

INTERCHANGE OF DEGREE OF COMPARISON

Degree of Comparison of Adjectives

Read the following sentences:

1. She is as clever as a fox. (Positive)
   A fox is not cleverer than her. (Comparative)

☛ In Positive Degree as is used but in Comparative Degree a Negative sentence is used. If the negative has been used with the Positive Degree, it will be removed from the comparative degree.

2. He is not so weak as his brother. (Positive)
   He is stronger than his brother. (Comparative)
3. Shimla is the coldest tourist spot in India. (Superlative)
   Shimla is colder than any other tourist spot in India. (Comparative)
   No other tourist spot is as cold as Shimla. (Positive)
4. Rohit is one of the most intelligent boys in our class. (Superlative)
   Rohit is more intelligent than most other boys in our class. (Comparative)
   Very few boys in our class are so intelligent as Rohit. (Positive)
5. Gold is not the most expensive metal. (Superlative)
   A few metals are more expensive than gold. (Comparative)
   Some metals are at least as expensive as gold. (Positive)
6. Lead is the heaviest of all metals. (Superlative)
   Lead is heavier than any other metal. (Comparative)
   No other metal is so heavy as lead. (Positive)

CHANGING IMPERATIVE SENTENCES INTO ASSERTIVE

Read the following sentences:

1. Walk fast. (Imperative)
   You are ordered to walk fast. (Affirmative)
2. Let us take a cup of tea. (Imperative)
   It is proposed that we should take a cup of tea. (Affirmative)
3. Please bring me a glass of wate.. (Imperative)
   You are requested to bring me a glass of water. (Affirmative)
4. Work hard. (Imperative)
   You are advised to work hard. (Affirmative)
5. Don't smoke. (Negative imperative)
   You are forbidden to smoke. (Assertive)

INTERCHANGE OF AFFIRMATIVE AND NEGATIVE SENTENCES

Read the following sentences:

1. He runs slow. (Affirmative)
   He does not run fast. (Negative)
2. He loves himself the most. (Affirmative)
   He does not love anybody more than himself. (Negative)
3. Mr Sharma is a busy man. (Affirmative)
   Mr Sharma is not an idle man. (Negative)
4. She is as brilliant as you. (Affirmative)
   You are not more brilliant than her. (Negative)
5. He spoke angrily. (Affirmative)
   He did not speak calmly. (Negative)

INTERCHANGE OF INTERROGATIVE AND ASSERTIVE SENTENCES

Read the following sentences:

1. Why to speak ill of anybody? (Interrogative)
   We should not speak ill of anybody. (Assertive)
2. Who can win his fate? (Interrogative)
   No one can win his fate. (Assertive)
3. Where will you find such beautiful shoes? (Interrogative)
   You will not find such beautiful shoes anywhere. (Assertive)
4. How can he die without paying my debt? (Interrogative)
   He cannot die without paying my debt. (Assertive)
5. When will he learn manners? (Interrogative)
   He will never learn manners. (Assertive)
6. What can be done now? (Interrogative)
   Nothing can be done now. (Assertive)

INTERCHANGE OF EXCLAMATORY AND ASSERTIVE SENTENCES

Read the following sentences:

1. What a beautiful flower it is! (Exclamatory)
   It is a very beautiful flower. (Assertive)
2. How beautiful the Taj is! (Exclamatory)
   I am surprised that the Taj is very beautiful. (Assertive)

3. O for a one-rupee coin! (Exclamatory)
   A one-rupee coin is urgently desired. (Assertive)
4. Would that I were rich! (Exclamatory)
   I wish that I were rich. (Assertive)
5. O that I were rich! (Exclamatory)
   I wish that I were rich! (Assertive)

INTERCHANGE OF PARTS OF SPEECH

Read the following sentences:

1. This way you will **minimize** the risk. (Verb)
   This way you will bring the risk to the minimum level. (Adjective)
2. She fought **courageously**. (Adverb)
   She showed a great **courage** in the fight. (Noun)
3. She does not speak the **truth**. (Noun)
   She is not **truthful**. (Adjective)
4. He fought **bravely**. (Adverb)
   He fought with **bravery**. (Noun)
5. He **ran** fast. (Verb)
   He ran a fast **race**. (Noun)
6. He showed **generosity** towards his opponent. (Noun)
   He was **generous** towards his opponent. (Adjective)

CHANGING OF SIMPLE SENTENCES INTO COMPOUND ONES

Read the following sentences:

1. Besides being abused he was charged with misbehaving with others. (Simple)
   He was not only abused but also charged with misbehaving with others. (Compound)
2. You must run fast to catch the bus. (Simple)
   Run fast or you may miss the bus. (Compound)
3. Having finished her kitchen work, Mrs Sharma sat against the T.V. set. (Simple)
   Mrs Sharma finished her kitchen work and sat against the T.V. set. (Compound)
4. In spite of bitter cold, they managed to climb the hill. (Simple)
   It was bitter cold, yet they managed to climb the hill. (Compound)
5. In spite of being strong, he dare not oppose his opponents. (Simple)
   He is strong but still he dare not oppose his opponents. (Compound)

CHANGING OF SIMPLE SENTENCES INTO COMPLEX ONES

Read the following sentences:

1. In spite of being on crutches, he managed to catch the thief. (Simple)
   Though he was on crutches, he caught the thief. (Complex)
2. She is too weak in mathematics to solve even a simple sum. (Simple)
   She is so weak in mathematics that she cannot solve even a simple sum. (Complex)
3. The girl in all black is my classmate. (Simple)
   The girl, who is in all black, is my classmate. (Complex)
4. Because of/Owing to his negligence he lost his credibility. (Simple)
   He lost his credibility because he was negligent. (Complex)
5. He was happy at having been able to make an impressive speech. (Simple)
   He was happy that he was able to make an impressive speech. (Complex)
6. Put the ring at the place of your finding. (Simple)
   Put the ring where you found it. (Complex)

CHANGING OF COMPOUND SENTENCES INTO COMPLEX SENTENCES

Read the following sentences:

1. He is intelligent, but he is unkind. (Compound)
   Although he is intelligent, he is unkind. (Complex)
2. Buy a ticket or you cannot go inside the hall. (Compound)
   You cannot go inside the hall unless you buy a ticket. (Complex)
3. He could not attend the meeting, for he was ill. (Compound)
   He could not attend the meeting because he was ill. (Complex)
4. Work hard or you won't be able to earn a lot. (Compound)
   If you don't work hard, you cannot earn a lot. (Complex)
5. It was fog all around, yet he managed to cross the uneven stretch of land. (Compound)
   Although it was fog all around, he managed to cross the uneven stretch of land. (Complex)

ACTIVE & PASSIVE VOICE

Sentences containing a transitive verb can usually be written in Active as well as Passive voice. When the subject acts upon the object the sentence is written in Active voice. When the subject is acted upon, the sentence is written in Passive voice.

1. Do you read a book? (Active)
   Is a book read by you? (Passive)
2. He flies an aeroplane. (Active)
   An aeroplane is flown by him. (Passive)
3. She is unfolding the bed sheet. (Active)
   The bed sheet is being unfolded by her. (Passive)
4. Are the boys singing songs? (Active)
   Are songs being sung by the boys? (Passive)
5. Mohit has forwarded your request. (Active)
   Your request has been forwarded by Mohit. (Passive)
6. Have you ever seen the Taj? (Active)
   Has the Taj ever been seen by you? (Passive)
7. He freed all the slaves. (Active)
   All the slaves were freed by him. (Passive)
8. Did the dog bite the stranger? (Active)
   Was the stranger bitten by the dog? (Passive)
9. Ajeet was helping his relatives. (Active)
   His relatives were being helped by Ajeet. (Passive)
10. Was Karan grazing the horses? (Active)
    Were the horses being grazed by Karan? (Passive)
11. She had gained great flesh. (Active)
    Great flesh had been gained by her. (Passive)
12. Had you gripped the knob on the door? (Active)
    Had the knob on the door been gripped by you? (Passive)
13. I'll hit him hard. (Active)
    He will be hit hard by me. (Passive)
14. Will you imitate your brother? (Active)
    Will your brother be imitated by you? (Passive)
15. You will have opened the envelope? (Active)
    The envelope will have been opened by you. (Passive)
16. Will she have printed her name on the title page? (Active)
    Will her name have been printed on the title page by her? (Passive)

USE OF TIME-CLAUSES

As soon as
No sooner did .... than
Hardly had .... when
Scarcely had .... when or before

These sentences are used to express two actions taking place immediately one after the other.

1. As soon as the cat saw the dog, it started to run.
2. No sooner did the cat see the dog than it started to run.
3. Hardly had the cat seen the dog when it started to run.
4. Scarcely had the cat seen the dog when it started to run.

MULTIPLE CHOICE QUESTIONS

Directions: *In the following questions, one out of the given four alternatives is the correct transformation of the given statement, pick that one.*

1. You must be present in the meeting.
This statement can be converted into Negative as—
A. Nobody should be absent from the meeting.
B. You must not be absent from the meeting.
C. Anybody cannot be absent from the meeting.
D. You must not walk out of the meeting.

2. It is a beautiful bird.
This statement can be converted into Exclamatory as—
A. Is it a beautiful bird?
B. How is it a beautiful bird?
C. Who says it is not a beautiful bird?
D. What a beautiful bird it is!

3. It does not matter if we lose the match.
This statement can be converted into Interrogative as—
A. What does it matter if we lose the match?
B. Does it not matter if we lose the match?
C. Who says it does not matter if we lose the match?
D. How can we lose the match?

4. How happy I am!
This statement can be converted into Assertive as—
A. Am I happy?
B. I cannot say I am happy.
C. I am very happy.
D. How is it that I am happy?

5. There is none who cannot buy a bicycle.
This statement can be converted into Affirmative as—
A. Nobody can buy a bicycle.
B. Any one can buy a bicycle.
C. Some people cannot buy a bicycle.
D. It is useless to buy a bicycle.

6. You are forbidden to pluck flowers.
This statement can be converted into negative as—
A. You should not pluck flowers.
B. You are allowed to pluck flowers.
C. You are not allowed to pluck all the flowers.
D. You should give up the habit of plucking flowers.

7. He will definitely come here.
This statement can be converted into interrogative as—
A. When will he come here?
B. With whom will he come here?
C. How will he come here?
D. Will he not come here?

8. What a comfortable life he leads!
This sentence can be converted into an assertive sentence as—
A. I do not understand why he leads a comfortable life.
B. He leads a very comfortable life.
C. How does he lead a comfortable life.
D. Nobody knows how his life has become comfortable.

9. You should not absent yourself from the class any day.
This negative sentence can be converted into an affirmative one as—
A. You should be present in the class every day.
B. You should absent yourself from the class only rarely.
C. It is improper for you to be absent from the class.
D. You can come to the class any day you like.

10. What is the cause for worry?
This interrogative sentence can be converted into an assertive sentence as—
A. There is some cause for worry.
B. There is not much cause for worry.
C. There is no cause for worry.
D. Never think of a cause for worry.

11. You should give full information.
This statement can be converted into negative as—
A. Everybody should not give full information.
B. Nobody is allowed to give full information.
C. You should not hide anything.
D. You should not give full information only.

12. You dare not speak against me in public.
This statement can be converted into Interrogative as—
A. Dare you speak against me in public?
B. Is it proper for you to speak against me in public?

C. Can anybody speak against somebody in public?
D. Speaking against anybody in public is nobody's business.

13. A sailor should not be afraid of water.
This statement can be converted into Exclamatory as—
A. Should a sailor be afraid of water?
B. A sailor and afraid of water!
C. How afraid of water a sailor is!
D. A sailor cannot be afraid of water.

14. Oh! What an interesting book that was.
This statement can be converted into assertive as—
A. What an interesting book it was!
B. It was a very interesting book.
C. A very interesting book was read by me.
D. It was not an interesting book at all.

15. What can be done now?
This interrogative sentence can be converted into an assertive one as—
A. Nothing can be done now.
B. You can do everything now.
C. They can do something now.
D. Something can be done now.

16. It is useless to give any advice to an obstinate person.
This statement can be converted into negative as—
A. It is useless to ask an obstinate peson not to seek advice.
B. It is of no use giving advice to an obstinate person.
C. An obstinate person does not like the person who gives him any advice.
D. Some people do not make any use of advice given to obstinate persons.

17. Good people do not hate others.
This statement can be converted into interrogative as—
A. Do good people never hate others?
B. Why do not good people hate others?
C. When do good people say that they hate others.
D. Do good people hate others?

18. Isolation is very horrible for a child.
This statement can be converted into exclamatory as—
A. How horrible for a child isolation is !
B. How for a child isolation is horrible !
C. How horrible is for a child isolation !
D. How isolation is horrible for a child !

19. What a lame excuse !
This statement can be converted into assertive as—
A. A lame excuse it is.
B. How lame this excuse is.
C. Why do you make a lame excuse?
D. It is a very lame excuse.

20. True friends help each other not just once or twice.
This statement can be converted into affirmative as—
A. True friends help each other several times.
B. True friends help each other even unasked.
C. True friends help each other if they can.
D. True friends are helpful to each other.

Directions: *Select the correct transformation of the given sentences.*

21. She is too proud to listen to you.
A. She is very proud to listen to you.
B. She feels too proud to listen to you.
C. She is so proud listening to you.
D. She is so proud that she will not listen to you.

22. He ran so slowly that he could not catch the train.
A. He ran so slowly to catch the train.
B. He ran very slowly to catch the train.
C. He ran too slowly to catch the train.
D. He ran too slow to catch the train.

23. I like him because he is good person.
A. He is a good person. I like him.
B. He is a good person for which I like him.
C. He is a good person as I like him.
D. He is a good person for I like him.

24. In spite of working hard, he failed.
A. He worked hard but he failed.
B. He worked hard as he failed.
C. He worked hard so he failed.
D. He worked hard for which he failed.

25. Unless you work hard, you cannot pass.
A. If you work hard, you cannot pass.
B. Work hard if you cannot pass.
C. You cannot pass without working hard.
D. You should work hard, you can pass.

26. As soon as the thief saw the policeman, he started to run fast.
A. No sooner did the thief see the policeman when he started to run fast.
B. No sooner did the thief see the policeman than he started to run fast.
C. No sooner did the thief saw the policeman when he started to run fast.
D. No sooner did the thief saw the policeman than he started to run fast.

27. No sooner did I walk out of the house than it began to rain.
A. Hardly did I walked out of the house when it began to rain.
B. Hardly had I walked out of the house than it began to rain.
C. Hardly had I walked out of the house then it began to rain.
D. Hardly had I walked out of the house when it began to rain.

28. Hardly had the passenger boarded the bus when it punctured.
A. Scarcely had the passenger boarded the bus than it punctured.

B. Scarcely had the passenger boarded the bus then it punctured.
C. Scarcely had the passenger boarded the bus when it punctured.
D. Scarcely had the passenger boarded the bus but it punctured

29. Scarcely had the ship berthed in America when it began to blow hard.
A. No sooner did the ship berth in America than it began to blow hard.
B. As soon as the ship berthed in America then it began to blow hard.
C. Hardly had the ship berthed in America then it began to blow hard.
D. Scarcely had the ship berthed in America then it began to blow hard.

30. No sooner did she alight from the train than the guard whistled.
A. Scarcely had she alighted from the train then the guard whistled.
B. Scarcely had she alighted from the train than the guard whistled.
C. Scarcely had she alighted from the train when the guard whistled.
D. Scarcely did she alight from the train when the guard whistled.

Directions: *In these questions, the sentences have been given in Active/Passive voice. From the given options, choose the one which best expresses the given sentence in Passive/Active voice.*

31. We chose him our leader.
A. He was chosen our leader.
B. He has been chosen our leader.
C. He had chosen our leader.
D. He have been chosen our leader.

32. Who made a maiden century?
A. By whose was a maiden century made?
B. By whom was a maiden century make?
C. By whom was a maiden century made?
D. By whom had a maiden century made?

33. I may help her in her project.
A. She might be helped by me in her project.
B. She may be helped by me in her project.
C. She might be helped in her project by me.
D. In her project, she may be help by me.

34. Take medicine in time.
A. Medicine should be taken in time.
B. Medicine will be taken in time.
C. Medicine will be took in time.
D. Medicine shall take in time.

35. I am solving the questions.
A. The questions are being solved by me.
B. The questions have been solved by me.
C. The questions are to be solved by me.
D. The question are solved by me.

36. May I take this pen?
A. May this pen will be taken by me?
B. May this pen shall be taken by me?
C. May this pen should be taken by me?
D. May this pen be taken by me?

37. Can we send it by air?
A. Can this be sent by air?
B. Can it be sent by air?
C. Can it go by air?
D. Can it be send by air?

38. Who wrote this book?
A. By whom was this book written?
B. By whom is this book written?
C. By whom was this book being written?
D. By whom is this book being written?

39. What did you buy?
A. What is bought by you?
B. What is being bought by you?
C. What was bought by you?
D. What was being bought by you?

40. Whom do you want?
A. Who is wanted by you?
B. Who is being wanted by you?
C. You are wanted by whom?
D. You are being wanted by whom?

ANSWERS

1	2	3	4	5	6	7	8	9	10
B	D	A	C	B	A	D	B	A	C
11	**12**	**13**	**14**	**15**	**16**	**17**	**18**	**19**	**20**
C	A	B	B	A	B	D	A	D	A
21	**22**	**23**	**24**	**25**	**26**	**27**	**28**	**29**	**30**
D	C	B	A	C	B	D	C	A	C
31	**32**	**33**	**34**	**35**	**36**	**37**	**38**	**39**	**40**
A	C	B	A	A	D	B	A	C	A

12 Agreement of Subjects & Verbs

It is very important that the verb in a sentence should obey the subject, otherwise the sentence will be considered wrong.

1. **When the Subject is a Singular Noun**

   A singular noun takes a singular verb.

   (*i*) Mohit **makes** a noise in the class.

   (*ii*) The child is **crying** for a cake.

2. **When two singular nouns are joined with 'and'**

   When two singular nouns are joined with 'and' and they refer to two different persons, the plural verb should be used, *e.g.*,

   (*i*) The novelist and the poet **were** honoured by the government.

   (*ii*) The black and the white dogs **bark** at the strangers.

☛ Article 'the' is used with both the subjects.

   If article is used only once, the singular verb should be used.

   (*i*) The painter and singer is going abroad.

   (*ii*) The white and black dog has a bushy tail.

3. When the subjects together give a single idea, singular verb is used.

   (*i*) Slow and steady wins the race.

   (*ii*) Rice and curry is my favourite dish.

4. A collective noun takes a singular verb when it acts as a whole, but it takes a plural verb when the individual, of which it is composed are considered separately.

   (*i*) The committee was unanimous on imposing the new law.

   (*ii*) The committee have given their separate opinions in the matter.

5. When the subjects are joined by neither . . . nor, either . . . or, and 'or', the verb should obey the last subject.

   (*i*) Rakesh or his friends have been selected for the match.

   (*ii*) His friends or Rakesh has been selected for the match.

   (*iii*) Neither Rohit nor his brothers are going abroad.

   (*iv*) Neither his brothers nor Rohit is going abroad.

   (*v*) Either Sohan or his sisters were dancing at the function.

   (*vi*) Either his sisters or Sohan was dancing at the function.

6. Either, neither, either of, neither of, take singular verb.

   (*i*) Either boy was honest.

   (*ii*) Neither girl was allowed to leave the premises.

   (*iii*) Either of the boys was ready to help the old man.

   (*iv*) Neither of the girls was asked to join the extra classes.

7. Some nouns are always used as plurals so, they take plural verbs.

   (*i*) Where are your glasses?

   (*ii*) His pants are attractive.

   (*iii*) Cattle are grazing in the field.

   (*iv*) Whose scissors are these?

8. Some nouns are always used as singulars, so, they take singular verbs.

   (*i*) What is the latest news?

   (*ii*) The furniture in the house is of a poor quality.

   (*iii*) Mumps is not a fatal disease.

   (*iv*) Physics is a tough subject.

9. Nouns formed by alongwith, as well as, together with, accompanied by, etc., take verb according to the first subject.

   (*i*) I as well as you am to blame.

   (*ii*) You as well as I are going to see a movie.

   (*iii*) John accompanied by his parents is going to visit the Taj.

   (*iv*) His parents accompanied by John are going to visit the Taj.

   (*v*) His brothers together with Vivek are ready to whitewash the fence.

10. To indicate something hypothetical or not factually true, plural verb 'were' with *as if* is used.

    (*i*) He talks as if he were a king.

    (*ii*) She dresses herself as if she were a princess.

MULTIPLE CHOICE QUESTIONS

Directions: *In the following questions, a sentence is given followed by four options. Select the option that replaces the given sentence or its part correctly.*

1. Slow and steady win the race.
A. Slowly and steady wins the race.
B. Slow and steadily wins the race.
C. Slow and steady wins the race.
D. None of these.

2. These news were broadcasted on Radio BBC.
A. These news were broadcast on Radio BBC.
B. This news was broadcast on Radio BBC.
C. This news was broadcasted on Radio BBC.
D. None of these.

3. Every boy and girl were given a prize.
A. Every boy and girl were given prizes.
B. Every boy and girl was given prizes.
C. Every boy and girl was given a prize.
D. None of these.

4. Everyone of them were clapping at the performance of the clown.
A. Everyone of them were clapping at the performance of the clowns.
B. Everyone of them was clapping at the performance of the clowns.
C. Everyone of them was clapping at the performances about the clowns.
D. None of these.

5. Law and order are to be maintained at all costs.
A. Law and orders are to be maintained at all costs.
B. Law and order is to be maintained at all costs.
C. Laws and orders are to be maintained at all costs.
D. None of these.

6. Five hundred rupees are a long sum.
A. Five hundred rupee is a long sum.
B. Five hundred rupee is a big sum.
C. Five hundred rupees is a big sum.
D. None of these.

7. Mohit, not his friends are to blame.
A. Mohit, not his friends is to blame.
B. Mohit, not his friend are to blame.
C. Mohit, not his friends is on to blame.
D. None of these.

8. I as well as you are to blame.
A. I as well as you, is to blame.
B. I as well as you are to blames.
C. I as well as you, am to blame.
D. None of these.

9. The patient died before the doctor came.
A. The patient died before the doctor had come.
B. The patient had died before the doctor came.
C. The patient had died before the doctor had come.
D. None of these.

10. I knew that he will not respect his elders.
A. I knew that he would not respect his elders.
B. I knew that he shall not respect his elders.
C. I knew that he will not be respect his elders.
D. None of these.

11. He is one of the greatest player who has participated in one day cricket matches.
A. He is one of the greatest players who has ....
B. He is one of the greatest players who have ....
C. He is one of the greatest player who have ....
D. None of these.

12. He behaves as if he is king.
A. He behaves as if he are a king.
B. He behaves as if he are kings.
C. He behaves as if he were a king.
D. None of these.

13. He laughed as if he were mad.
A. He laughed as if he was mad.
B. He laughed as if he had been mad.
C. He laughed as if he are mad.
D. None of these.

14. The white and the black dog is dead.
A. The white and black dog are dead.
B. The white and the black dog are dead.
C. The white and black dogs are dead.
D. None of these.

15. The painter and poet are dead.
A. The painter and the poet is dead.
B. The painter and poets are dead.
C. The painter and poet is dead.
D. None of these.

16. The committee has announced their decision.
A. The committees has announced their decision.
B. The committee has announced its decision.
C. The committee have announced its decision.
D. None of these.

17. I wish I am a millionaire.
A. I wish I was a millionaire.
B. I wish I are a millionaire.
C. I wish I were a millionaire.
D. None of these.

18. A large number of students is absent.
A. A large numbers of students is absent.
B. A large number of students are absent.
C. A large number of student is absent.
D. None of these.

19. Walking on the road, I met one of my old friends.
A. When I was walking on the road, I met one of my old friend.
B. When I was walking on the road, I met one of my old friends.
C. Walking on the road, I met one of my friend.
D. None of these.

20. Our only guide were the stars.
A. Our only guide were the star.
B. Our only guides was the star.
C. Our only guide was the stars.
D. None of these.

21. Renu is living in this house since 2012.
A. Renu is living in this house for 2012.
B. Renu has been living in this house for 2012.
C. Renu has been living in this house since 2012.
D. None of these.

22. Better you had not to gone there.
A. Better you had not went there.
B. Better you had not gone there.
C. Better had you not to go there.
D. None of these.

23. You did not do so, nor he did.
A. You did not do so, he nor did.
B. You did not do so, nor did he.
C. You did not do so, he did nor.
D. None of these.

24. Hardly I had opened the window when a stream of cool breeze started rushing in.
A. Hardly I had opened the window then.........
B. Hardly had I opened the window when.........
C. Hardly had I opened the window then.........
D. None of these.

25. No sooner he did open the window, when the cool breeze started rushing in.
A. No sooner did he open the window then ....
B. No sooner did he open the window when ....
C. No sooner he did open the window than ....
D. None of these.

26. Neither she laughed nor I did.
A. Neither she laughed nor did I.
B. Neither she laughed did nor I.
C. Neither she laughed I did nor.
D. None of these.

27. Deepak alongwith his aunts were present in the party.
A. Deepak alongwith his aunts were present in the parties.
B. Deepak alongwith his aunts was present in the party.
C. Deepak alongwith his aunt were present in the party.
D. None of these.

28. Many a girls have gone to see the movie.
A. Many a girl have gone to see the movie.
B. Many a girls has went to see the movies.
C. Many a girl has gone to see the movie.
D. None of these.

29. Sohan, like Mohan, are good singers.
A. Sohan, like Mohan, is a good singer.
B. Sohan, like Mohan, is a good singers.
C. Sohan, like Mohan, are a good singer.
D. None of these.

30. The train arrived before I reached the station.
A. The train arrived before I had reached the station.
B. The train arrived before I have reached the station.
C. The train had arrived before I reached the station.
D. None of these.

31. Either he or she has done his work.
A. Either he or she has done their work.
B. Either he or she has done her work.
C. Either he or she has done their work.
D. None of these.

32. A hundred miles are a high distance.
A. A hundred miles are a big distance.
B. A hundred miles are a long distance.
C. A hundred miles is a long distance.
D. None of these.

33. 'A Tale of Two Cities' were written by Charles Dickens.
A. 'A Tale of Two Cities' was written by Charles Dickens.
B. 'A Tale of Two Cities' is wrote by Charles Dickens.
C. 'A Tale of Two Cities' are wrote by Charles Dickens.
D. None of these.

34. Many a boys were playing in the garden.
A. Many a boy were playing in the garden.
B. Many a boys was playing in the garden.
C. Many a boy was playing in the garden.
D. None of these.

35. A bandit besides his gangsters were nabbed by the police.
A. A bandit besides his gangster were nabbed by the police.
B. A bandit besides his gangsters was nabbed by the police.
C. A bandits besides his gangsters was nabbed by the police.
D. None of these.

36. The bell went when I reached the school.
A. The bell went when I had reached the school.
B. The bell had gone when I have reached the school.
C. The bell had gone when I reached the school.
D. None of these.

37. My teacher told me that the earth revolved round the sun.
A. My teacher told me that the earth was revolving round the sun.

B. My teacher told me that the earth revolves round the sun.
C. My teacher told me that the earth had revolved round the sun.
D. None of these.

38. Rice and curry are the favourite food of my brother.
A. Rice and curry is the favourite food...
B. Rice and curry are the favourite foods...
C. Rice and curry is the favourite foods...
D. None of these.

39. The Principal together with his staff were on a tour to the Himalayas.
A. The Principal together with his staffs were...
B. The Principal together with his staffs was...
C. The Principal together with his staff was...
D. None of these.

40. Neither Ravi nor his friends was present in the class.
A. Neither Ravi nor his friend were present in the class.
B. Neither Ravi nor his friends was present in the classes.
C. Neither Ravi nor his friends were present in the class.
D. None of these.

41. None of the ten pens are yours.
A. None of the ten pen are yours.
B. None of the ten pens is yours.
C. None of the ten pens are your.
D. None of these.

42. The captain with all his players are in the playground.
A. The captain with all his player are in the playgrounds.
B. The captain with all his player is in the playgrounds.
C. The captain with all his players is in the playground.
D. None of these.

ANSWERS

1	2	3	4	5	6	7	8	9	10
C	B	C	B	B	C	A	C	B	A
11	**12**	**13**	**14**	**15**	**16**	**17**	**18**	**19**	**20**
B	C	B	B	C	B	C	B	B	C
21	**22**	**23**	**24**	**25**	**26**	**27**	**28**	**29**	**30**
C	B	B	B	A	A	B	C	A	C
31	**32**	**33**	**34**	**35**	**36**	**37**	**38**	**39**	**40**
B	C	A	C	B	C	B	A	C	C
41	**42**								
B	C								

EXPLANATORY ANSWERS

1. When two different nouns combine to convey one idea or are treated as a unit, a singular verb is used.

2. The forms of broadcast are broadcast, broadcast; and 'news' word is always treated as singular.

3. 'Everyboy' is treated as a singular. So, it takes a singular verb.

4. 'Everyone' is treated as a singular, so it takes a singular verb.

5. When two different nouns combine to form one idea or are treated as a unit, the verb is singular.

6. In this case the plural noun has been used as a collective noun, so it takes singular verb. The word 'long' is mostly used to express the length, not a sum.

7. In this case, when two nouns or pronouns are connected by a comma + not the verb should be used according to the first noun or pronoun used.

8. When 'as well as' is used the verb should be applied according to the first noun or pronoun used.

9. When two events or actions take place in the past tense, the event taking place first, should be shown in Past Perfect Tense.

10. If the Principal Clause, is in the Past Tense, the Subordinate Clause must also be in the Past Tense unless there is a universal truth, habitual truth.

11. We have used the sentence in the sense, "Greatest among the other greatest players", so it should take a plural verb *i.e.,* 'have'. The plural antecedent of a relative pronoun should have a plural verb.

12. 'As if' is used to express a wish. A wish should be in the past tense and in the plural form. But if the main clause *i.e.,* the Principal Clause is in the Past Indefinite Tense, it should be followed by the Past Perfect Tense.

13. When the Principal Clause is in the Past Indefinite Tense, and 'as if' has been used there, the Subordinate Clause should be in the Past Perfect Tense.

14. The term 'The White and the Black' represents two dogs *i.e.,* one of the black colour and the other of the white colour. So, it needs a plural verb.

15. The term 'painter and poet' represents a single person who has two qualities. So, it needs a singular verb.

16. The word 'committee' can be used a singular as well as plural. When it is used as a singular, the verb must agree with it, and the pronoun should also be used accordingly.

17. When one expresses a wish and the Principal Clause is in the Present Indefinite Tense, the Subordinate Clause should be in the Past Tense and should be in Plural form.

18. 'Number' is singular in structure, but mostly it is used as a plural.

19. The participle must be attached with a noun or pronoun to which it refers. In this, we have used 'One of my old friends' *i.e.,* 'One among many'.

20. A verb must agree with its subject.

21. When time has been given, use Perfect Continuous Tenses. For the point of time use 'since'.

22. After phrases like 'had better' or 'better had' etc., infinite (to) is not used.

23. The verb comes before its subject when the sentence has been introduced by 'nor'.

24. The verb comes before its subject when the sentence has been introduced by 'hardly'. Apply 'when' with hardly.

25. The verb comes before its subject when the sentence has been introduced by 'No sooner'. Apply 'than' with 'No sooner'.

26. The verb comes before its subject when the sentence has been introduced by 'neither' or 'nor'.

27. Two nouns or pronouns connected by 'alongwith' take a singular verb, if the first subject is singular.

28. 'Many' should be followed by a singular noun and a singular verb, if the first subject is singular.

29. When two nouns or pronouns are connected by the word 'like' they need a singular verb, if the first subject is singular.

30. When two events or actions take place in the past, the action or event taking place first should be shown in the Past Perfect Tense and the other one should be shown in the Past Indefinite Tense.

31. In case of 'either or' the verb agrees with the last subject and in the case that is 'she'. So, the pronoun should also agree with the word 'she'.

32. When a plural noun is considered collectively, the verb should be singular. The word 'big' is mostly used with a sum *i.e.,* 'a big sum', 'a big amount' etc. 'high' is mostly used to express height a thing which has its basis above from the earth in the sky *i.e.,* 'a high star' etc. 'Tall' is mostly used to express the height of a thing which has its basis on the earth 'a tall building', 'a tall tower'.

33. When a plural noun is used as a proper name for some collective unit or when it denotes some specific quality, the verb should be in singular form.

34. 'Many a' needs a singular noun and a singular verb.

35. Two nouns or pronouns connected by 'besides' should take verb according to the first subject used.

36. When two actions or events take place in the past, the action or event which is taking place first should be shown in the Past Perfect Tense and the other should be in the Past Indefinite Tense.

37. In indirect speech the verb of the universal truth cannot be changed.

38. When two different nouns combine to give one idea or are treated as a unit they need a single verb.

39. When two nouns or pronouns are joined together by the word 'together' the verb should obey the first subject used.

40. In this case of 'Neither ...nor' the verb should agree with the last subject used.

41. 'None' takes a singular verb.

42. When two nouns or pronouns are joined with the word 'with' they take a verb in accordance with the first subject.

13 Spot the Error

The most common errors in English are of spellings, grammar and usage of words. By regular practice, the errors can be easily spotted and minimised.

COMMON ERRORS WITH NOUNS AND NOUN-PHRASES

Incorrect	Correct
1. I have bought new *furnitures.*	I have bought new *furniture.*
2. The wages of sin *are* death.	The wages of sin *is* death.
3. She told these *news* to her mother.	She told her mother this *news.*
4. He took *troubles* to do his work.	He took *trouble* (or pains) over his work.
5. The *cattles* were grazing.	The *cattle* were grazing.
6. He showered *many abuses* on me.	He showered *much abuse* on me.
7. I spent the holidays with my *family members.*	I spent the holidays with my *family.*
8. There is no *place* in this compartment.	There is no *room* in this compartment.
9. Write this new *poetry* in your *copy.*	Write this new *poem* in your *note-book.*
10. He took *insult* at this.	He took *offence* at this.
11. Put your *sign* here.	Put your *signatures* here.
12. She is my *cousin sister.*	She is my *cousin.*
13. *Sunil's* my *neighbour's* house was burgled.	*Sunil* my *neighbour's* house was burgled.
14. I lost a *ten-rupees* note.	I lost *a ten-rupee* note.
15. Road closed for *repair.*	Road closed for *repairs.*
16. His house is out of *repairs.*	His house is out of *repair.*
17. What is the *reason* of an earthquake?	What is the *cause* of an earthquake?
18. This building is made of *stones.*	This building is made of *stone.*
19. I disapprove of *these kinds* of games.	I disapprove of *this kind* of games.
20. Veena's and Sheela's father is ill.	Veena and Sheela's father is ill.
21. His *son-in-laws* are doctors.	His *sons-in-law* are doctors.
22. *Alms* is given to the *poor.*	*Alms* are given to the poor.
23. He always keeps his words.	He always keeps his *word.*
24. I carried the *luggages.*	I carried the *luggage.*
25. *Two-third* of the work is left.	*Two-thirds* of the work is left.

COMMON ERRORS WITH PRONOUNS

	Incorrect	Correct
1.	Both did not go.	Neither went.
2.	We all did not go.	None of us went.
3.	Each of these boys play.	Each of these boys plays.
4.	Whoever does best he will get a prize.	Whoever does best will get a prize.
5.	One should not waste his time.	A man should not waste his time.
6.	I and she are sisters.	She and I are sisters.
7.	He is wiser than me.	He is wiser than I.
8.	Between you and I, Anil is not to be trusted.	Between you and me, Anil is not to be trusted.
9.	Nobody was there but I.	Nobody was there but me.
10.	Who is there ? It is me.	Who is there ? It is I.
11.	Only he and me can use this card.	Only he and I can use this card.
12.	Let you and I go now.	Let you and me go now.
13.	Everyone got one's pay.	Everyone got his pay.
14.	Everyone is frightened when they see a tiger.	Everyone is frightened when he sees a tiger.
15.	These two friends are fond of one another.	These two friends are fond of each other.
16.	I did not like him coming at that hour.	I did not like his coming at that hour.
17.	Who do you think I met?	Whom do you think I met?
18.	You should avail this opportunity.	You should avail yourself this opportunity.
19.	When you have read these books, please return the same to me.	When you have read the books, please return them to me.
20.	They that are humble need fear no fall.	Those that are humble need fear no fall.

COMMON ERRORS WITH ADJECTIVES

	Incorrect	Correct
1.	These all oranges are good.	All these oranges are good.
2.	He held the book in the both hands.	He held the book in both hands.
3.	Both men have not come.	Neither man has come.
4.	That man should do some or other work.	That man should do some work or other.
5.	He is elder than I.	He is older than I.
6.	Shakespeare is greater than any other poets.	Shakespeare is greater than any other poet.
7.	He is a coward man.	He is a cowardly man.
8.	Many villagers cannot write his own name.	Many villagers cannot write their own name.
9.	Each of us loves our home.	Each of us loves his home.
10.	Much efforts bring their reward.	Much effort brings its reward.
11.	He found hundred rupees.	He found a hundred rupees.
12.	He had leave of four days.	He had four days leave.
13.	This is a worth seeing sight.	This is a sight worth seeing.
14.	He will spend his future life here.	He will spend the rest of his life here.
15.	There is a best teacher in that class.	There is a very good teacher in that class.
16.	Of the two plans this is the best.	Of the two plans this is the better.
17.	He is becoming strong every day.	He is becoming stronger every day.
18.	He is worst than I.	He is worse than I.
19.	Jaipur is hot than Delhi.	Jaipur is hotter than Delhi.

Incorrect	Correct
20. In our library the number of books is less.	In our library the number of books is small.
21. From the three he is more clever.	He is the cleverest of the three.
22. India is the first peace-loving country in the world.	India is the foremost peace-loving country in the world.
23. Verbal instruction will not do.	Oral instruction will not do.
24. Her command over French is most excellent.	Her command over French is excellent.
25. He has not some money with him.	He has not any money with him.
26. I have visited Bombay many a times.	I have visited Bombay many a time.
27. Death is more preferable to dishonour.	Death is preferable to dishonour.
28. I gave him a few books I had.	I gave him the few books I had.
29. If he wants farther help send him to me.	If he wants further help, send him to me.
30. She is so cunning as a fox.	She is as cunning as a fox.

COMMON ERRORS WITH VERBS

Incorrect	Correct
1. He asked had we taken our luggage.	He asked if we had taken our luggage.
2. She asked what are you doing.	She asked what we were doing.
3. Rama asked to Anil why he is angry.	Rama asked Anil why he was angry.
4. He does not care for his money.	He does not take care of his money.
5. He does not care for his work.	He takes no care over his work.
6. No one cared for him after his mother died.	No one took care of him after his mother died.
7. He got angry before I said a word.	He got angry before I had said a word.
8. I met a man who was my tutor 20 years ago.	I met a man who had been my tutor twenty years ago.
9. I had been for walking yesterday.	I went for a walk yesterday.
10. If I shall do this I shall be wrong.	If I do this I shall be wrong.
11. I have left trekking.	I have given up trekking.
12. I came to know as to how he did this.	I learnt how he did this.
13. I came to know why he was sad.	I found out why he was sad.
14. He knows to swim.	He knows how to swim.
15. The criminal's head was cut.	The criminal's head was cut off.
16. I said to him to go.	I told him to go.
17. I told the teacher to excuse me.	I asked the teacher to excuse me.
18. He is troubling me.	He is giving me trouble.
19. I have got a hurt on my leg.	I have hurt my leg.
20. She gave a speech.	She made a speech.
21. He has given his examination.	He has sat for his examination.
22. He took out his shoes.	He took off his shoes.
23. I have ordered for a new car.	I have ordered a new car.
24. He would not hear me.	He would not listen to me.
25. I struck a blow on his face.	I struck him in the face.
26. He denied to come.	He refused to come.
27. He lived there for a day.	He stayed there for a day.
28. The book is not found.	The book is lost.
29. Shut the light.	Turn off the light.
30. I must revenge my brother.	I must avenge my brother.

COMMON ERRORS IN SUBJECT-VERB AGREEMENT

	Incorrect	Correct
1.	The owners of this factory *is* very rich.	The owners of this factory *are* very rich.
2.	The pleasures of nature that one can experience at Shimla *is* beyond description.	The pleasures of nature that one can experience at Shimla *are* beyond description.
3.	There *is* no street lights in our colony.	There *are* no street lights in our colony.
4.	He and I *am* entrusted with the job.	He and I *are* entrusted with the job.
5.	Rice and curry *are* his favourite dish.	Rice and curry *is* his favourite dish.
6.	The honour and glory of our country *are* at stake.	The honour and glory of our country *is* at stake.
7.	Time and tide *waits* for none.	Time and tide *wait* for none.
8.	All the passengers with the driver *was* killed.	All the passengers, with the driver, *were* killed.
9.	The teacher, with her students, *were* going out.	The teacher, with her students, *was* going out.
10.	I as well as they *am* tired.	I as well as they *are* tired.
11.	Not only the soldiers but their captain also *were* captured.	Not only the soldiers but their captain also *was* captured.
12.	Neither you nor I *were* selected.	Neither you nor I *was* selected.
13.	Either of these two applicants *are* fit for the job but neither want to accept it.	Either of these two applicants *is* fit for the job but neither wants to accept it.
14.	One of these students are sure to stand first.	One of these students *is* sure to stand first.
15.	Everyone of these workers want a raise.	Everyone of these workers wants a raise.
16.	None of these letters has been answered so far.	None of these letters *have* been answered so far.
17.	None of the girls were present at the party.	None of the girls *was* present at the party.
18.	Many a battle were fought on Indian soil.	Many a battle *was* fought on Indian soil.
19.	A lot of work remain to be done.	A lot of work *remains* to be done.
20.	The majority of these girls likes music.	The majority of these girls *like* music.
21.	The number of admissions are encouraging.	The number of admissions *is* encouraging.
22.	A large number of boys was present.	A large number of boys *were* present.
23.	A variety of books was on display.	A variety of books *were* on display.
24.	Variety are the spice of life.	Variety *is* the spice of life.
25.	If my estimates are correct. I will need another hundred rupees.	If my estimate is correct, I will need another hundred rupees.
26.	Mathematics *are* my favourite subject.	Mathematics *is* my favourite subject.
27.	'Gulliver's Travels' *are* written by Swift.	'Gulliver's Travels' *is* written by Swift.
28.	Ten miles *are* a long distance to cover on foot.	Ten miles *is* a long distance to cover on foot.
29.	A new pair of shoes *are* to be purchased.	A new pair of shoes *is* to be purchased.
30.	The Committee *have* issued its report.	The Committee *has* issued its report.
31.	I, who am your friend, *has* always been on your side.	I, who am your friend, *have* always been on your side.
32.	I am the person who *have* always stood by you.	I am the person who *has* always stood by you.
33.	This is one of the best novels that *has* been published this year.	This is one of the best novels that *have* been published this year.
34.	Less than half the amount *have* been wasted.	Less than half the amount *has* been wasted.
35.	A lot of people *has* turned up for the show.	A lot of people *have* turned up for the show.
36.	Much of their honour *are* un-deserved.	Much of their honour *is* un-deserved.
37.	More than a decade *have* passed since this house was built.	More than a decade *has* passed since this house was built.
38.	Either she or he *are* mistaken.	Either she or he *is* mistaken.
39.	Plenty of information *are* available on the subject.	Plenty of information *is* available on the subject.
40.	Plenty of pamphlets *is* available on the subject.	Plenty of pamphlets *are* available on the subject.

COMMON ERRORS IN USE OF WILL, SHALL, WOULD, SHOULD, MAY, MIGHT, MUST

	Incorrect	Correct
1.	When I shall see him I shall tell him this.	When I *see* him, I shall tell him this.
2.	If I should do wrong, he would punish me.	If I *did* wrong, he would punish me.
3.	Until he will have confessed his fault, he will be kept in prison.	Until he *has* confessed his fault, he will be kept in prison.
4.	She will obey me.	She *shall* obey me.
5.	You would work hard.	You *should* work hard.
6.	You shall find him in the garden.	You *will* find him in the garden.
7.	He must have died of exposure, but we cannot be certain.	He *might* have died of exposure, but we cannot be certain.
8.	You might not show disrespect to your elders.	You *must* not show disrespect to your elders.
9.	You may take exercise in order to maintain good health.	You *must* take exercise in order to maintain good health.
10.	He must be a crook for all we know.	He *may* be a crook for all we know.

COMMON ERORRS IN THE USE OF ADVERBS

(Very, Much, Too, Enough, Quite, Hardly, Scarcely, Before, Ago, Since, Yet, Still, etc.)

	Incorrect	Correct
1.	He is very much angry.	He is *very* angry.
2.	She was very good enough to help me.	She was *good enough* to help me.
3.	She runs much fast.	She runs *very* fast.
4.	She runs very faster than Seema.	She runs *much* faster than Seema.
5.	It is bitter cold today.	It is *bitterly* cold today.
6.	He is a much learned man.	He is a very learned man.
7.	She is thinking very hardly.	She is thinking very hard.
8.	To tell in brief the film was boring.	*In short* the film was boring.
9.	He told the story in details.	He told the story *in detail.*
10.	I did it anyhow.	I *managed to do* it somehow.
11.	Aeroplanes reach Europe soon.	Aeroplanes reach Europe quickly.
12.	Before long there were dinosaurs on the earth.	*Long ago,* there were dinosaurs on the earth.
13.	This book is too interesting.	This book is *very* interesting.
14.	He lives miserly.	He lives in *a miserly* way.
15.	Just I had gone when she came.	I had just gone when she came.
16.	He sings good.	He sings *well.*
17.	He sings good than I.	He sings *better* than I.
18.	Really speaking it is cold.	*As a matter of fact* it is cold.
19.	He is enough tall to reach the ceiling.	He is *tall enough* to reach the ceiling.
20.	He went directly to his college.	He went *direct* to his college.
21.	He is presently at Delhi	He is at Delhi *at present.*
22.	Last night she returned lately.	Last night she *returned late.*
23.	He was even blamed by his friends.	He was *blamed even* by his friends.
24.	I only employed him for a week.	I employed him for a week only.

	Incorrect	Correct
25.	I met him four months before.	I met him four *months ago.*
26.	Anil seldom ever goes to school.	Anil *seldom goes* to school.
27.	I will wait here until you do not go.	I will wait here until *you go.*
28.	I never remember having met her before.	I *do not remember* having met her before.
29.	She has not been here too long to have many friends.	She has not *been here long* enough to have many friends.
30.	Hardly I have had any rest since one week.	Hardly have *I had* any rest for a week.
31.	Scarcely the water crossed the danger level, the warning signals were sounded.	Scarcely *had the* water *crossed the* danger level, when the warning signals were sounded.
32.	She is neat but fairly slow.	She is *neat* but rather slow.
33.	It is a rather good film.	It is a *fairly good* film.
34.	We yet have time to catch the bus.	We *still have* time to catch the bus.
35.	She has not still spent all her money.	She has *not yet* spent all her money.

COMMON ERRORS IN THE USE OF CONJUNCTIONS

	Incorrect	Correct
1.	As he is fat so he runs slowly.	As he is fat *he* runs slowly.
2.	If he is fat then he will run slowly.	If he is fat, he will run slowly.
3.	Though he is fat still he runs fast.	Though he is fat, *he runs* fast.
4.	*As* I pulled the trigger at the sametime he shook my arm.	As I pulled the trigger, he shook my arm.
5.	No sooner I had spoken than he left.	No sooner *had* I spoken than he left.
6.	Not only he will go, but also he will stay there.	Not only *will he* go, but he *will also* stay there.
7.	Neither he comes nor he writes.	Neither *does he* come nor *does he* write.
8.	Scarcely he entered the room than the telephone rang.	Scarcely *had* he entered the room *when the* telephone rang.
9.	Hardly she had left the house than it began to rain.	Hardly *had she* left the house *when* it began to rain.
10.	He is the fastest runner and he comes last.	He is the fastest runner *but* he comes last.
11.	She is as innocent as if she looks.	She is as innocent as she looks.
12.	Until he does not try he must be punished.	He must be punished unless he tries.
13.	I want to know as to why you are late.	I want to know why you are late.
14.	I am fond of Chinese food as for example sweet and sour prawns.	I am fond of Chinese food, for example, sweet and sour prawns.
15.	He was angry therefore I ran away.	He was angry so I ran away.
16.	I was trying to work, at that time he was disturbing me.	While I was trying to work, he was disturbing me.
17.	Supposing if he is late, what will happen?	Supposing he is late (or if he is late) what will happen?
18.	He asked me that why I was late.	He asked me why I was late.
19.	Let us catch a taxi lest we should not get late.	Let us catch a taxi lest we should get late.
20.	She dresses herself like the teacher does.	She dresses herself as the teacher does.
21.	Wait while I come.	Wait *until* (or *till*) I come.
22.	Until, there is corruption in India, there can be little progress.	*As long* as there is corruption in India there can be little progress.
23.	I have never told a lie nor cheated anybody.	I have never told a lie *nor have I* cheated anybody.
24.	Both Mohan as well as Arun are responsible for this action.	Both Mohan *and* Arun are responsible for this action.
25.	Hindus and Muslims both are to blame for the riots.	*Both Hindus* and Muslims are to blame for the riots.

	Incorrect	Correct
26.	I have bought paintings, books, records, and etc.	I have bought paintings, books *and records etc.*
27.	He as well as you is a fool.	He as well as you *are* a fool.
28.	He is so poor and he cannot save anything.	He is so *poor that* he cannot save anything.
29.	Such a book that you want is not available.	Such a book *as* you want is not available.
30.	Such was her condition as everyone was moved to pity.	Such was her condition that everyone was moved to pity.

COMMON ERRORS IN THE USE OF PREPOSITIONS

	Incorrect	Correct
1.	I will not listen him.	I will not listen *to* him.
2.	Copy this word by word.	Copy this word *for* word.
3.	He enquired from her where she lived.	He enquired *of* her where she lived.
4.	Sign here with ink.	Sign here *in* ink.
5.	Has she come in train or by foot?	Has she come *by* train or *on* foot?
6.	She said this at his face.	She said this *to* his face.
7.	Open the book on page one.	Open the book *at* page one.
8.	I was invited for lunch.	I was *invited to* lunch.
9.	I am ill since three months.	I have been *ill for* three months.
10.	This paper is inferior than that.	This paper is inferior *to* that.
11.	This resembles to that.	This *resembles* that.
12.	My brother is superior than you in strength.	My brother is superior *to* you in strength.
13.	He wrote me.	He wrote *to* me.
14.	I shall explain them this.	I shall explain this *to* them.
15.	Send this letter on my address.	Send this letter *to* my address.
16.	He suggested me this.	He suggested this *to* me.
17.	He goes *on his* work.	He goes *to his* work.
18.	He *reached to* Nagpur.	He *reached* Nagpur.
19.	He told *to me* to go.	He told *me* to go.
20.	The term begins *from* July 1st.	The term begins *on* July 1st.
21.	There are many advantages *from* this.	The advantages *of* this are many.
22.	We waste much time *in* trifles.	We waste much time *on* (or *over)* trifles.
23.	He sat *on* a tree.	He sat *in* a tree.
24.	This is a comfortable house to *live*.	This is a comfortable house to *live in*.
25.	This is the road to *go*.	This is the road to *go by*.
26.	He married *with* an Indian lady.	He *married an Indian* lady.
27.	He accompanied *with* his friend.	He *accompanied his* friend.
28.	He went *for doing some* business.	He went away *on* business.
29.	He went for *riding*.	He went *for a ride*.
30.	I *pitied on* him.	I *pitied* him.
31.	When this was searched it was found.	When this was searched *for* it was found.
32.	I shall inform them *this*.	I shall inform them *of* this.
33.	*Due to illness* I cannot go to school.	*Owing* to illness I cannot go to school.
34.	He went *to the back side* of the house.	He went *behind* (or to the back of) the house.
35.	I must go; there is no *help*.	I must go; there is no help *for it*.
36.	I *met with your* friend there.	I *met your* friend there.

Incorrect	Correct
37. The First World War was fought *during* 1914-1918.	The First World War was fought *between* 1914-1918.
38. England grew prosperous *between* Queen Victoria's reign.	England grew prosperous *during* Queen Victoria's reign.
39. He asked a holiday.	He asked *for* a holiday.
40. I am obliged of you for this good turn.	I am obliged *to* you for this good turn.
41. There is no harm to try.	There is no harm *in trying.*

MISCELLANEOUS ERRORS

(Including Ambiguities and Indianisms)

Incorrect	Correct
1. Many *homes* are lying vacant.	Many *houses* are lying vacant.
2. It is cool in the *shadow* of the tree.	It is cool in the *shade* of the tree.
3. She *keeps* good health.	She *enjoys* good health.
4. My leg is *paining.*	*I am feeling pain* in my leg.
5. *See* this word in the dictionary.	*Look up* this word in the dictionary.
6. The train will arrive *just now.*	The train will arrive *shortly.*
7. They are *pulling* on well.	They are *getting* on well.
8. The river has *over flown* its bank.	The river has *over flown* its banks.
9. He was appointed *on* the post.	He was appointed *to* the post.
10. Last but not *the least,* we have to discuss the problem of over population.	Last but not *least,* we have to discuss the problem of over population.
11. *Cities* after *cities* fell.	*City* after *city* fell.
12. What is the use Munir going there?	What is the use of Munir going there?
13. He *did many mischief.*	He *made much mischief.*
14. It is exact five *in* my watch.	It is exact five *by* my watch.
15. I will dine with them on *next Sunday.*	I will dine with them *Sunday next.*
16. Misfortunes when faced bravely and *manly* become less troublesome.	Misfortunes when faced bravely and *manfully* become less troublesome.
17. I am *laid down* with fever.	I am *laid up* with fever.
18. He is habituated to smoking.	He is *addicted* to smoking.
19. *According to my opinion* he is right.	*In my opinion* (or according *to me)* he is right.
20. Could you please *open* this knot?	Could you please *untie* this knot?

MULTIPLE CHOICE QUESTIONS

Directions: *In this section, each sentence has three parts, indicated by (A), (B) and (C). Read each sentence to find out whether there is an error. If you find an error in any one of the parts (A, B, C), indicate your response by marking the letter related to that part. If a sentence has no error, indicate this by marking '(D)' which stands for "No error". Errors may belong to grammar, usage or idiom. Ignore errors of punctuation, if any.*

1. (A) We are meeting today afternoon/(B) to discuss the matter/(C) and reach a compromise./(D) No error.

2. (A) Either Ram or/(B) you is responsible/(C) for this action./(D) No error.

3. (A) The student flatly denied/(B) that he had copied/(C) in the examination hall./(D) No error.

4. (A) By the time you arrive tomorrow/(B) I have finished/(C) my work./(D) No error.

5. (A) The speaker stressed repeatedly on/(B) the importance of improving/(C) the condition of the slums./(D) No error.

6. (A) The captain with the members of his team/(B) are returning/(C) after a fortnight./(D) No error.

7. (A) After returning from/(B) an all-India tour/(C) I had to describe about it/(D) No error.

8. (A) The teacher asked his students/(B) if they had gone through/(C) either of the three chapters included in the prescribed text./(D) No error.

9. (A) Although they are living in the country/(B) since they were married/(C) they are now moving to the town./(D) No error.

10. (A) Do you know/(B) how old were you/(C) when you came here?/(D) No error.

11. (A) Beware of/(B) a fair-weather friend/(C) who is neither a friend in need nor a friend indeed/(D) No error.

12. (A) Copernicus proved/(B) that Earth/(C) moves round the Sun./(D) No error.

13. (A) Seldom we have been treated/(B) in such a rude manner/(C) by the police personnel./(D) No error.

14. (A) Some men are born great,/(B) some achieve greatness/(C) and some had greatness thrust on them./(D) No error.

15. (A) The property/(B) was divided/(C) among the two brothers./(D) No error.

16. (A) I am quite certain/(B) that the lady is not only greedy/(C) but miserly./(D) No error.

17. (A) The aircraft overloaded/(B) there was something wrong of the battery/(C) and the engine was making a queer noise/(D) No error.

18. (A) A thorough inquiry of the misappropriation of funds/(B) is now imperative/(C) to bring the guilty to book/(D) No error.

19. (A) The brilliant success in the examination/(B) as well as his record in sports/(C) deserves high praise/(D) No error.

20. (A) While travelling by a train/(B) on a cold winter night/(C) an argument rose between two passengers in our compartment/(D) No error.

21. (A) I cannot find/(B) where has he gone/(C) though I have tried may best/(D) No error.

22. (A) If I was/(B) the Prime Minister of India/(C) I would work wonders/(D) No error.

23. Amit's severe bout of flu/(B) debilitated him so much/(C) that he was too tired to do for work for a week./(D) No error.

24. (A) This is the crux of the entire problem;/(B) everything centres on/(C) it being resolved./(D) No error.

25. (A) One of the major aims of the Air Force/(B) was the complete demolition of all means of transportation/(C) by the bombing of rail lines and terminals./(D) No error.

26. (A) His strong voice cut over/(B) the hum of conversation/(C) like a knife through butter./(D) No error.

27. (A) Even though they weren't expecting us/(B) they managed to knock up/(C) a marvellous meal./(D) No error.

28. (A) The celebrated singer was/(B) surrounded by the usual crowd/(C) of lackeys and hanger-ons./(D) No error.

29. (A) If it weren't/(B) for you,/(C) I wouldn't be alive today./(D) No error.

30. (A) He looked like a lion/(B) baulked from/(C) its prey./(D) No error.

31. (A) Widespread flooding/(B) is effecting/(C) large areas of the villages./(D) No error.

32. (A) She regards/(B) negotiating prices with customers/(C) as her special preserve./(D) No error.

33. (A) Often in political campaigns, a point is reached at which/(B) the candidates take out their gloves./(C) and start slugging with bare fists./(D) No error.

34. (A) If we really set to/(B) we can get the whole house/(C) cleaned in an afternoon./(D) No error.

35. (A) Pieces of rock plummeted/(B) down the mountainside/(C) in the ground below./(D) No error.

36. (A) Since the two parties each won/(B) the same number of seats,/(C) the minority party holds the balance of power./(D) No error.

37. (A) It's arrogant for you/(B) to assume you'll/(C)win every time./(D) No error.

38. (A) We've paid for our travel and accommod-ation,/(B) so we need only to take/(C) some pocket-money with us./(D) No error.

39. (A) There's no evidence to show/(B) that information technology secrets are more/(C) vulnerable in India than Britain or the US./(D) No error.

40. (A) It is shameful that hunting/(B) is still considered sport/(C) by some unscrupulous people in the civilized world./(D) No error.

41. (A) The Prime Minister's good looks won him/(B)the election but he has still to prove/(C) that he's not a just pretty face./(D) No error.

42. (A) The two books are the same/(B) except for the fact that this/(C) has an answer in the back./(D) No error.

43. (A) He estimated his income tax bill/(B) by extrapolation over figures/(C) submitted in previous years./(D) No error.

44. (A) The modern office block/(B) sticks out like a sore thumb/(C) among the old buildings in the area./(D) No error.

45. (A) I will try to put over/(B) some feelers to gauge/(C) people's reactions to our proposal./(D) No error.

46. (A) A major contribution of Mathura sculptors/(B)of that period were the creation and popularization/(C) of the Buddha's image in human form./(D) No error.

47. (A) Amit has been deceiving Mona/(B) for many years but she/(C) has not still tumbled to it. (C)/No error. (D)

48. (A) Mahavira was an advocate of nonviolence and vegetarianism,/(B) who revived and reorganized the Jain doctrine/(C) and established rules for their monastic order. (D) No error.

49. (A) Microwaves are the principle carriers/(B) of television, telephone and data transmissions/(C)between stations on earth and between the earth and satellites./ (D) No error.

50. (A) An unit is an abstract idea,/(B) defined either by reference to/(C) a randomly chosen material standard or to a natural phenomenon./(D) No error.

51. (A) With the crisis deepening,/(B) the critics sense an opportunity/(C) about putting in place a more radical strategy./(D) No error.

52. (A) The salesman gave us/(B) a big spiel about why/ (C) we should buy his product./(D) No error.

53. (A) I will need several weeks/(B) to invent the lie of the land before/(C) I can make any decision about the future of the business./(D) No error.

54. (A) You should be cautious/(B) and make a few discrete enquiries about/(C) the firm before you sign anything./ (D) No error.

55. (A) Your husband doesn't/(B) believe that you are older/(C) than I./(D) No error.

56. (A) There is a beautiful moon out tonight/(B) and Neeta and I are going for a stroll/(C) —would you like to come along with she and I?/ (D) No error.

57. (A) The data on/(B) the divorce case is/(C) on the judge's desk./(D) No error.

58. (A) The stood off/(B) from the crowd/(C) because of her height and flaming red hair./(D) No error.

59. (A) It's stupid to go/(B) to the expense of taking/(C) music lessons if you never practise/(D) No error.

60. (A) You will find it difficult/(B) to explain of your use/ (C) of such offensive language/(D) No error.

61. (A) Because of the/(B) extenuating circumstances/(C) the court acquitted him out of the crime/(D) No error.

62. (A) The carpet was badly stained/(B) to such an extent that/(C) you couldn't tell its original colour/(D) No error.

63. (A) It is greatly to Amit's credit/(B) that he gave back the money he found/(C) his honesty does for him credit/ (D) No error.

64. (A) A terrific hue and cry/(B) was raised/(C) at the new tax proposals/(D) No error.

65. (A) The former General was/(B) exiled of his country because of/(C) his part in the plot against the government/(D) No error.

66. (A) The company has/(B) set off itself some stiff production/(C) goals for this year/(D) No error.

67. (A) The music was so loud/(B) that we had to bellow over each/(C) other to be heard./(D) No error.

68. (A) When this beautiful girl arrived, (A) all the men in the room/(C) gravitated over her./(D) No error.

69. (A) The children are/(B) really in their element/(C) playing on the beach./(D) No error.

70. (A) The refugees are/(B) badly off for blankets,/(C) and even worse for food./(D) No error.

71. (A) From their vintage-point on the cliff,/(B) the children could watch/(C) the ships coming and going./(D) No error.

72. (A) A cogent remark/(B) compels acceptance because/ (C) of their sense and logic./(D) No error.

73. (A) Credit cards have/(B) brought about a revolution/ (C) in people's spending habits./(D) No error.

74. (A) In financial matters/(B) it is important to/(C) get disinterested advice./(D) No error.

75. (A) Some women admit that/(B) their principle goal in life/(C) is to marry a wealthy man./(D) No error.

76. (A) Take two spoonsful/(B) of this medicine/(C) every three hours./(D) No error.

77. (A) The film was so disjointed/(B) that I could not tell you/(C) what the story was about./(D) No error.

78. (A) He had been/(B) saved of death as if/(C) by divine intervention./(D) No error.

79. (A) I informed the principal/(B) that I was running temperature/(C) and, therefore, could not attend the meeting./(D) No error.

80. (A) The lady was broken with grief/(B) when she heard the sad news of the train disaster/(C) in which her brother was killed./(D) No error.

81. (A) The farmer is irrigating/(B) his fields/(C) since morning./(D) No error.

82. (A) I could not/(B) answer to/(C) the question./(D) No error.

83. (A) Two years passed/(B) since/(C) my cousin died./(D) No error.

84. (A) He hesitated to accept the post/(B) as he did not think/(C) that the salary would be enough for a man with a family of three (C)/ No error (D)

85. (A) Have you gone through/(B) either of these three chapters/(C) that have been included in this volume?/ (D) No error.

86. (A) I am learning English/(B) for ten years/(C) without much effect/(D) No error.

87. (A) Ramesh has agreed/(B) to marry with the girl/(C) of his parent's choice (D) No error.

88. (A) The pity is that/(B) no sooner he had left the place/ (C) than the fire broke out/(D) No error.

89. (A) When he was arriving/(B) the party was/(C) in full swing/(D) No error.

90. (A) The Dean wrote he constituted a committee of experts/(B) comprising of five members/(C) before the next meeting took place/(D) No error.

91. (A) Inflation and shortages/(B) have made it very difficult for him/(C) to make his both ends meet./(D) No error.

92. (A) The most studious boy/(B) in the class/(C) was made as the captain./(D) No error.

93. (A) I am participating/(B) in the two-miles race/(C) tomorrow morning./(D) No error.

94. (A) The sum and substance/(B) of his speech/(C) were essentially anti-establishment./(D) No error.

95. (A) It has been such a wonderful evening/(B) I look forward to meet you again/(C) after the vacations./(D) No error.

96. (A) When the boy committed a mistake/(B) the teacher made him to do/(C) the sum again./(D) No error.

97. (A) Unless the government does not revise its policy of liberalization/(B) the growth of the indigenous technology/(C) will be adversely affected./(D) No error.

98. (A) Supposing if you get/(B) a seat in the plane/(C) you will not take more than two hours to reach Mumbai./(D) No error.

99. (A) Whenever a person lost anything/(B) the poor folk around/(C) are suspected./(D) No error.

100. (A) Still impressive is that/(B) we achieve this selective attention/(C) through our latent ability to lip-read./(D) No error.

101. (A) The brakes and steering failed/(B) and the bus ran down the hill/(C) without anyone being able to control it./(D) No error.

102. (A) The polling was marred/(B) at many a place/(C) by attempts at rigging./(D) No error.

103. (A) He wanted to work all right/(B) but we saw that he was completely worn/(C) and so we persuaded him to stop./(D) No error.

104. (A) When a whale is washed ashore by the tide,/(B) the people flock together to see it./(C) wondering how so huge an animal can swim about in the water./(D) No error.

105. (A) Few scientists changed/(B) people's ideas as much as/(C) Darwin with his Theory of Evolution./(D) No error.

106. (A) Were he/(B) to see you,/(C) he would have been surprised./(D) No error.

107. (A) The number of marks carried by each question/(B) are indicated/(C) at the end of the question./(D) No error.

108. (A) An animal/(B) can be just as unhappy in a vast area/(C) or in a small one/(D) No error.

109. (A) It is time/(B) we did something/(C) to stop road accidents./(D) No error.

110. (A) A free press is not a privilege/(B) but the organic necessity/(C) in a free society./(D) No error.

111. (A) The Indian radio./(B) which was previously controlled by the British rulers./(C) is free now from the narrow vested interests./(D) No error.

112. (A) Because of the emergency help/(B) that the patient received./(C) he would have died/(D) No error.

113. (A) At present juncture,/(B) however, the super-computer/(C) would be a costly toy./(D) No error.

114. (A) Students should not take part/(B) in party politics and political demonstrations/(C) as they interfere in serious study./(D) No error.

115. (A) Wherever they go/(B) Indians easily adapt to/(C) local circumstances./(D) No error.

116. (A) According to the Bible/(B) it is meek and humble/(C) who shall inherit the earth./(D) No error.

117. (A) I was there/(B) many a time/(C) in the past./(D) No error.

118. (A) As much as I admire him for his sterling qualities./(B) I cannot excuse him for/(C) being unfair to his friends./(D) No error.

119. (A) Were you/(B) given a choice/(C) or you had to do it?/(D) No error.

120. (A) When he was asked what is wrong with him,/(B) he said that he was not well,/(C) and asked for leave of absence for one day./(D) No error.

121. (A) At the end of the year/(B) every student who had done adequate work/(C) was automatically promoted./(D) No error.

122. (A) Many times the news has been published/(B) in the papers that the end of the world will be certain/(C) if a nuclear war breaks out./(D) No error.

123. (A) Happily, zoos were/(B) unwilling to cooperate/(C) in a scheme that was potentially harmful to animal welfare./(D) No error.

124. (A) We discussed about the problem so thoroughly/(B) on the eve of the examination/(C) that I found it very easy to work it out./(D) No error.

125. (A) She reluctantly said that/(B) if nobody else was doing it/(C) she will do it./(D) No error.

126. (A) He will end up his work/(B) in the city/(C) by the end of the year./(D) No error.

127. (A) Though child marriage/(B) has been banned,/(C) the custom still prevailed among some groups in India./(D) No error.

128. (A) Supposing if/(B) there is no bus,/(C) how will you get there?(D) No error.

129. (A) At the moment the house/(B) was burgled the family/(C) attended a night party in the neighbourhood./(D) No error.

130. (A) On a holiday/(B) Sudha prefers reading/(C) than going out visiting friends/(D) No error.

131. (A) Neither he/(B) nor his father is interested/(C) in joining the party./(D) No error.

132. (A) A group of friends/(B) want to visit/(C) the new plant as early as possible./(D) No error.

133. (A) May I/(B) know who you want/(C) to see please/(D) No error.

134. (A) Myself and Gopal/(B) will take care of/(C) the function on Sunday./(D) No error.

135. (A) I could not put up in a hotel/(B) because the boarding and lodging charges/(C) were exorbitant./(D) No error.

136. (A) He is not coming tomorrow/(B) as he is having a pain in the chest/(C) and has to see a doctor./(D) No error.

137. (A) They have been/(B) very close friends/(C) until they quarrelled./(D) No error.

138. (A) Since India has gained Independence/(B) 49 years ago,/(C) much progress has been made in almost every field./(D) No error.

139. (A) The party chief made it a point to state that/(B) the Prime Minister and the Union Home Minister should also come/(C) and they see what his party men had seen./(D) No error.

140. (A) Due to me being a newcomer/(B) I was unable to get a house/(C) suitable for my wife and me./(D) No error.

141. (A) The reason why/(B) he was rejected/(C) was because he was too young./(D) No error.

142. (A) The scientist must follow/(B) his hunches and his data/(C) wherever it may lead./(D) No error.

143. (A) Firstly you should/(B) think over the meaning of the words/(C) and then use them./(D) No error.

144. (A) Scarcely had/(B) I arrived than/(C) the train left./(D) No error.

145. (A) Unless you stop to make noise at once/(B) I will have no option but to/(C) bring the matter to the attention of the police./(D) No error.

146. (A) He couldn't but help/(B) shedding tears at the plight of the villagers/(C) rendered homeless by a devastating cyclone./(D) No error.

147. (A) Since it was his first election campaign, the candidate was confused;/(B) none could clearly understand/(C) either the principles he stood for or the benefits he promised./(D) No error.

148. (A) It is an established fact that the transcendental American poets and philosophers,/(B) who lived in the latter half of the nineteenth century,/(C) were more influenced by Indian philosophy, in particular by Upanishadic Philosophy./(D) No error.

149. (A) The crew were on board/(B) and they soon busied themselves/(C) in preparing to meet the storm./(D) No error.

150. (A) One of the members/(B) expressed doubt if/(C) the Minister was an athiest./ (D) No error.

151. (A) A body of volunteers/(B) have been organised/(C) to spread the message of the saint./(D) No error.

152. (A) If I will have the time/(B) I shall try and make it/(C) to the zoo this afternoon./(D) No error.

153. (A) To facilitate exports and improve sales in the domestic market/(B) some of the improvised fabrics and garments fabricated out from them/(C) are displayed in the main pavilion./(D) No error.

154. (A) He gave them no money/(B) nor did help them/(C) in any way./(D) No error.

155. (A) Azharuddin is one of the finest batsmen/(B) that India have produced/(C) over the decades./(D) No error.

156. (A) An Indian ship/(B) laden with merchandise/ (C) got drowned in the Pacific./(D) No error.

157. (A) Though senior in age,/(B) his father is junior than/(C) my father in service./(D) No error.

158. (A) If I am you/(B) I would have seen to it/(C) that I won the prize./(D) No error.

159. (A) His father died of cholera/(B) but his mother also,/(C) though very weak, is out of danger./(D) No error.

160. (A) He asked me/(B) why did I call/(C) him a rogue./(D) No error.

161. (A) I have got/(B) my M.Sc. degree/(C) in 1988./(D) No error.

162. (A) They/(B) enjoyed thoroughly/(C) at the party./(D) No error.

163. (A) After the humiliating exposure/(B) he hanged his head/(C) in shame./(D) No error.

164. (A) Kamala's fountain-pen/(B) is as expensive/(C) as Shyama./(D) No error.

165. (A) I shall certainly/(B) write you/(C) when I shall reach New Delhi./(D) No error.

166. (A) The criminal was/(B) caught, convicted the hung/(C) in a short period of time./(D) No error.

167. (A) You will get/(B) all the information/(C) if you read this booklet carefully./(D) No error.

168. (A) She sang/(B) very well/(C) isn't it?/(D) No error.

169. (A) He is working in/(B) a bank is New Delhi/(C) for the past several months./(D) No error.

170. (A) There is no question/(B) of my failing/(C) in the examination./(D) No error.

ANSWERS

1	2	3	4	5	6	7	8	9	10
A	B	D	B	A	B	C	C	B	D
11	12	13	14	15	16	17	18	19	20
D	B	A	C	C	C	B	A	D	C
21	22	23	24	25	26	27	28	29	30
B	A	C	C	B	A	A	C	C	C
31	32	33	34	35	36	37	38	39	40
C	A	A	A	C	A	A	B	D	B
41	42	43	44	45	46	47	48	49	50
C	C	C	D	A	B	C	C	A	A
51	52	53	54	55	56	57	58	59	60
C	D	D	D	C	C	D	A	B	B
61	62	63	64	65	66	67	68	69	70
C	A	C	A	B	B	B	C	B	D
71	72	73	74	75	76	77	78	79	80
A	C	D	D	D	A	B	B	B	A
81	82	83	84	85	86	87	88	89	90
A	B	A	D	B	A	B	B	A	B
91	92	93	94	95	96	97	98	99	100
C	C	B	C	B	B	A	A	A	C
101	102	103	104	105	106	107	108	109	110
C	D	B	D	A	A	B	C	D	B
111	112	113	114	115	116	117	118	119	120
C	A	A	C	B	B	A	A	A	A
121	122	123	124	125	126	127	128	129	130
D	D	C	A	C	A	C	A	A	C
131	132	133	134	135	136	137	138	139	140
D	B	B	A	A	C	A	A	C	A
141	142	143	144	145	146	147	148	149	150
C	C	A	B	A	A	D	C	C	B
151	152	153	154	155	156	157	158	159	160
B	A	B	B	B	C	B	A	B	B
161	162	163	164	165	166	167	168	169	170
A	B	B	C	C	C	A	C	A	B

14 Correct Sentence Selection

One may use the same words in many ways but the best way is only one that makes the perfect usage of the words and conveys the proper meaning of the expression. Try it yourself in the following questions.

MULTIPLE CHOICE QUESTIONS

Directions: *There are four sentences in each of the following questions. One of the sentences is correct, and the rest are incorrect. You are to select the correct sentence in each question.*

1. A. She is either right nor wrong.
B. She is nor right or wrong.
C. She is neither right or wrong.
D. She is neither right nor wrong.

2. A. He went to Nepal five years ago.
B. He went to Nepal five years back.
C. He went to Nepal five years before.
D. He went to Nepal five years past.

3. A. Before leaving home, it began to rain.
B. As since I was leaving home, it began to rain.
C. As I was leaving home, it began to rain.
D. When leaving home, it began to rain.

4. A. I have given up alcoholic drinks two years before.
B. I have given up alcoholic drinks two years since.
C. I have given up alcoholic drinks two years ago.
D. I had given up alcoholic drinks two years ago.

5. A. I told to her to give me that book.
B. I said her to give me this book.
C. I said to her that to give me that book.
D. I asked her to give me that book.

6. A. My maternal grandmother said to me not go without having a cup of tea.
B. My material grandmother asked me not go without having a cup of tea.
C. My material grandmother asked me to go not without having a cup of tea.
D. My material grandmother asked me not to go without having a cup of tea.

7. A. His sister told me that he likes my new car.
B. His sister said me that she likes my new car.
C. His sister told me I like your new car.
D. His sister told me that she liked my new car.

8. A. The teacher asked me where was I going?
B. The teacher asked me where I am going.
C. The teacher asked me where I go.
D. The teacher asked me where I was going.

9. A. Your conduct admits no excuses.
B. Your conduct admit no excuse.
C. Your conduct is inexcusable.
D. Your conduct admit of no excuses.

10. A. The young woman tried on two coats and finally decided to buy the most expensive one.
B. The young woman tried on two coats and finally decided to buy the more expensive one.
C. The young woman tried on two coats and finally decided to buy the expensive one.
D. The young woman tried on coats two and finally decided to buy the very expensive one.

11. A. She is anxious about my health.
B. She is anxious of my health.
C. She is anxious for my health.
D. She is anxious with my health.

12. A. My youngest son had no difficulty with solving the problem.
B. My youngest son had no difficulty to solve the problem.

C. My youngest son had no difficulty in solving the problem.
D. My youngest son had no difficulty for solving the problem.

13. A. The plane had left before I reached the airport.
B. The plane left before I reached the airport.
C. The plane was leaving before I reached the airport.
D. The plane will leave before I reached the airport.

14. A. The four dacoits distributed the loot with themselves.
B. The four dacoits distributed the loot between themselves.
C. The four dacoits distributed the loot among themselves.
D. The four dacoits distributed the loot upon themselves.

15. A. What out country needs today is a number of selfless and competent leaders.
B. What our country need today is a number of unscrupulous leaders.
C. What our country needs today are a number of selfish leaders.
D. What our country needs today is a number of motivated leaders.

16. A. I am very sorry to learn that you lose the match yesterday.
B. I am very sorry to learn that you loosed the match yesterday.
C. I am very sorry to learn that you lost the match yesterday
D. I am very sorry to learn that you have lost the match yesterday.

17. A. It is our bounden duty to instil a sense of responsibility into people of the country.
B. It is our bounden duty to instigate a sense of responsibility into the people of the country.
C. It is our bounden duty to excite a sense of responsibility into the people of the country.
D. It is our bounden duty to incite a sense of responsibility into the people of the country.

18. A. He is over seventy years of age and are still alert and strong.
B. He is over seventy years of age but who is still alert and strong.
C. He is a man over seventy years of age but who is still alert and strong.
D. He is over seventy years of age, but is still alert and strong.

19. A. She told me that it is better to fail than pass by unfair means.
B. She told me it was better to fail than passing by unfair means.
C. She told whether it was better to fail than pass by unfair means.
D. She told me that it was better to fail than to pass by unfair means.

20. A. She asked me to name the capital of Nepal.
B. She asked me which is the capital of Nepal.
C. She asked me what is the capital of Nepal.
D. She told me in the capital of Nepal.

21. A. She heartily congratulated me about my splendid success in the examination.
B. She heartily congratulated me on my splendid success in the examination.
C. She heartily congratulated me for my splendid success in the examination.
D. She heartily congratulated me at my splendid success in the examination.

22. A. He replied that he will call on me tomorrow.
B. He replied that he would call on me tomorrow.
C. He had replied that he would have called on me tomorrow.
D. He replied that he will have called on me tomorrow.

23. A. I am sorry to say that she made me do the dirty job.
B. I am sorry to say that she made me to do the dirty job.
C. I am sorry to say that she would make me to do the dirty job.
D. I am sorry to say that she did me to do the dirty job.

24. A. Will you please excuse my dropping in at this untimely hour?
B. Will you please excuse me dropping at this untimely hour?
C. Will you please excuse my dropping at this untimely hour?
D. Will you please excuse my dropping by this untimely hour?

25. A. Now I must beg of your leave.
B. Now I must beg off your leave.
C. Now I must beg your leave.
D. Now I must beg leave of you.

26. A. When narrating the road accident, she was in tears.
B. As narrating the road accident, she was in tears.
C. In narrating the road accident, she was in tears.
D. When she was narrating the road accident, she was in tears.

27. A. A long period of ten years have passed since he has passed away.
B. A long period of ten years has passed since he passed away.
C. A long period of ten years passed since he has passed away.
D. A long period of ten years have passed since he had passed away.

28. A. Can you do it more quick than I?
B. Can you do it more quicker than I?
C. Can you do it more quickly than I?
D. Can you do it more quick than I can?

29. A. This coat is too small for her.
B. This coat is to small for her.
C. This coat is too much small for her.
D. This coat is much too small for her.

30. A. My boss was kind enough to grant me leave of absence for ten days.
B. My boss was enough kind to grant me leave of absence for ten days.
C. My boss was kindly enough to grant me leave of absence for ten days.
D. My boss was enough kind for granting me leave of absence for ten days.

31. A. You should work had lest you may fail in the examination.
B. You should work hard lest you should fail in the examination.
C. You should work hard lest you might fail in the examination.
D. You should work had lest you fail in the examination.

32. A. When entering the class-room, each of the boys kept quiet.
B. Entering the class-room, each of the boys kept quiet.
C. On entering the class-room, each of the boys kept quiet.
D. Since entering the class-room, each of the boys kept quiet.

33. A. She asked that why her son shall be punished.
B. She asked that why her son should be punished.
C. She asked why her son should be punished.
D. She asked on why her son shall be punished.

34. A. She gives me such troubles which I cannot endure them.
B. She gives me such troubles as I cannot endure them.
C. She gives on me such troubles that I cannot endure them.
D. She gives at me such troubles which I cannot endure.

35. A. I have not seen her long since.
B. I have not seen her since long.
C. I have not seen her since a long.
D. I have not seen her from a long time.

36. A. This is the same book which I lost a few weeks ago.
B. This is the same book that I lost a few weeks ago.
C. This is the same books that I lost a few weeks before.
D. This is the same book which I lost a few weeks past.

37. A. This cloth is more preferable than that.
B. This cloth is more preferable than that.
C. This cloth is more preferable to that.
D. This cloth is preferable to that.

38. A. I seldom or ever make a mistake.
B. I seldom and never make a mistake.
C. I seldom or never make a mistake.
D. I seldom that never make a mistake.

39. A. His command in the English language is very unique.
B. His command of the English language is unique.
C. His command of the English language is perfectly unique.
D. His command of the English language is totally unique.

40. A. Her speech was so halting that the stopped between each word.
B. Her speech was so halting that she stopped after each word.
C. Her speech was so halting that she has stopped each word.
D. Her speech was so halting that she was stopping between each word.

41. A. I do not know who you consider the best man of the two.
B. I do not know whom you consider to be the man of the two.
C. I do not know whom you consider better of the two.
D. I do not know who you consider as the best of the two.

42. A. Do you bathe yourself daily?
B. Do you bathe daily?
C. Do you bathe daily?
D. Do you daily bath?

43. A. Being a cold day, I did not go out to the house.
B. It being a cold day, I did not go out of the house.
C. Being a cold day, I have not gone out of the house.
D. It being a cold day, I had not gone out of the house.

44. A. One should do his duty honestly and efficiently.
B. One should do one's duty honestly and efficiently.
C. One should do his responsibility honestly and efficiently.
D. One should act his responsibility honestly and efficiently.

45. A. She is one of those girls who cannot control her anger.
B. She is one of those girls which cannot control her anger.
C. She is one of those girls that cannot control her anger.
D. She is one of those girls who cannot control their anger.

46. A. You should attentively listen what he says.
B. You should attentively listen to what he says..
C. You should attentively listen to what he say.
D. You should attentively listen to what he says.

47. A. If she will come, I shall certainly give her five hundred rupees.
B. If she will come, I shall certainly give with her five hundred rupees.
C. If she comes, I shall certainly give five hundred rupees upon her.
D. If she comes, I shall certainly give her five hundred rupees.

48. A. She asked me if I broke the mirror.
B. She asked me if I have broken the mirror.
C. She asked of me if I have broken the mirror.
D. She asked if I had broken the mirror.

49. A. Workers are prohibited to bring their cycles inside the factory premises.
B. Workers are prohibited from bringing their cycles inside the factory premises.
C. Workers are prohibited to bringing their cycles inside the factory premises.
D. Workers are prohibited from to bring their cycles inside the factory premises.

50. A. Do you remember the date of him leaving India for Japan?
B. Do you remember the date of his leaving India for Japan?
C. Do you remember the date from his leaving India for Japan?
D. Do you remember the date by his leaving India for Japan?

51. A. She expected to have passed in the examination.
B. She expected to have pass in the examination.
C. She expected in passing the examination.
D. She expected to pass the examination.

52. A. I have visited him four hours ago.
B. I have visited him four hours before.
C. I have visited him four hours since.
D. I visited him four hours ago.

53. A. I did not go out of the house after I wrote the letter.
B. I did not go out of the house since I wrote the letter.
C. I did not go out of the house after I had written the letter.
D. I did not go out of the house after I have written the letter.

54. A. The murderer was tried, convicted and hung.
B. The murderer was tried, convicted and was hung.
C. The murderer was tried, convicted and hunged.
D. The murderer was tried, convicted and hanged.

55. A. The sceneries of Kashmir are very beautiful.
B. The sceneries of Kashmir is very beautiful.
C. The scenery of Kashmir is very beautiful.
D. The scenery of Kashmir are very beautiful.

56. A. Unless you do not work hard, you will not achieve success in life.
B. Unless you work hard, you will not achieve success in life.
C. Unless you do not work hard, you will achieve success in life.
D. Unless you work hardly, you will not achieve success in life.

57. A. Every one of my children are intelligent and healthy.
B. Every one of my children is intelligent and healthy.
C. Every one of my childs are intelligent and healthy.
D. Every one of my childs is intelligent and healthy.

58. A. Neither of the two candidates are suitable for the job.
B. Neither of the two candidate is suitable for the job.
C. Neither of the two candidates is suitable for the job.
D. Neither of the two candidates is suit for the job.

59. A. As I am ill, so I shall not be able to attend the meeting.
B. As I am ill, so I shall not to be able to attend the meeting.
C. As I am ill, so I shall not be able for attending the meeting.
D. As I am ill, I shall not be able to attend the meeting.

60. A. She never has and never will disobey me.
B. She never have and never will disobey me.
C. She never has disobeyed, and never will disobey me.
D. She never have disobeyed and never will disobey me.

61. A. This is the third time he broke a cup.
B. This is the third time when he broke a cup.
C. This is the third time he had broken a cup.
D. This is the third time he has broken a cup.

62. A. Let you and I be friends again.
B. Let you and myself be friend again.
C. Let you and I become friends again.
D. Let you and me be friends again.

63. A. I have come for seeing you.
B. I have come on seeing you.
C. I have came to seeing you.
D. I have come to see you

64. A. I am true to my words.
B. I am true with my words.

C. I am true at my words.
D. I am true to my word.

65. A. She is very anxious with my health.
B. She is very anxious at my health.
C. She is very anxious about my health.
D. She is very anxious after my health.

66. A. This is one of the best books that has been published so far.
B. This is one of the best books which has been published so far.
C. This is one of the best books that have been published so far.
D. This is one of the best books which had been published so far.

67. A. She is taller than all the girls in the college.
B. She is taller then all the girls in the college.
C. She is taller than other girls in the college.
D. She is taller than all other girls in the college.

68. A. As far I am concerned, you are free to go anywhere you like.
B. As far I am concerned, you are to free go anywhere you like.
C. As far as I am concerned, you are free to go anywhere you like.
D. As far as I concerned, you are free to going anywhere you like.

69. A. He is confined to bed for about a week.
B. He was confined to bed for about a week.
C. He has been confine to bed for about a weak.
D. He has been confined to bed for about a week.

70. A. Subhash Bose was one of the greatest patriot of India.
B. Subhash Bose has been one of the greatest patriot of India.
C. Subhash Bose has been one of the greatest patriot of India.
D. Subhash Bose was one of the greatest patriots of India.

71. A. She is as good and even better than you.
B. She is as good as, or even better than, you.
C. She is as good as or even batter than you.
D. She is as good as and better than you

72. A. They said to me that the General English paper is difficult.
B. They said me that the General English paper is difficult.
C. They said to me that the General English paper was difficult.
D. They said to me that the General English paper has been difficult.

73. A. May I have some words with you?
B. May I have a few words with you?
C. Can I have words with you?
D. May I have a word with you?

74. A. Our General Manager asked me as to why I am late.
B. Our General Manager asked me as to why am I late.
C. Our General Manager asked me why I am late.
D. Our General Manager asked me why I was late.

75. A. The story should not exceed more than five hundred words.
B. The story should not exceed than five hundred words.
C. The story should not exceed five hundred words.
D. The story should not accede five hundred words.

76. A. What is the good of him trying to do that work?
B. What is the good of his trying to do that work?
C. What the good is of him trying to do that work?
D. What is the good at his trying to do that work?

77. A. He does his best to find faults with my work.
B. He does his best in finding faults with my work.
C. He does his best to find fault with my work.
D. He does his best to find faults of my work.

78. A. This is a most unique opportunity for you to go abroad.
B. This is the most unique opportunity for you to go abroad.
C. This is a unique opportunity for you to go abroad.
D. This is a unique opportunity with you to go abroad.

79. A. Will you please say my compliments to your father?
B. Will you please say my complements to your father?
C. Will you please tell my compliments to your father?
D. Will you please pay my compliments to your father?

80. A. I always have and shall be your fast friend.
B. I always have been and shall be your fast friend.
C. I always was and shall be your fast friend.
D. I always had been and shall be your fast friend.

81. A. Tell me whether she loves you or not.
B. Tell me whether she loves you or knot.
C. Tell me whether or not she loves you.
D. Tell me whether she love you or not.

82. A. Tagore was greater than any poet.
B. Tagore was great than any poet.
C. Tagore was greater then any poet.
D. Tagore was greater than any other poet.

83. A. Going up the hill, an old temple was seen.
B. Going up to the hill, an old temple was seen.
C. On our going up the hill, an old temple was seen.
D. By going up to the hill, an old temple was seen.

84. A. The reason of her failure last time was due to her negligence.
B. The reason of her failure last time is due to her negligence.
C. Her failure last time was due to her negligence.
D. Her failure last time is on account of her negligence.

85. A. Nothing is more deplorable as dishonesty of this kind.
B. Nothing is so deplorable as dishonesty of this kind.
C. Nothing is such deplorable like dishonesty of this kind.
D. Nothing is more deplorable than dishonesty of this kind.

86. A. My cousin asked me that why did I not write to him?
B. My cousin asked me why did I not write to him?
C. My cousin asked me as to why did I not write to him?
D. My cousin asked me why I did not write to him.

87. A. She has no other ambition but only to pass the examination.
B. She has no ambition but only to pass the examination.
C. She has no ambition other than to pass the examination.
D. She has no other ambition other then to pass the examination.

88. A. If I could have worked hard, I would have passed the examination.
B. If I could work hard, I would have passed the examination.
C. If I might have worked hard, I would have passed the examination.
D. If I had worked hard, I would have passed the examination.

89. A. Four men were suspected of the crime but none of them confessed their guilt.
B. Four men were suspected of the crime but none of them accepted their guilt.
C. Four men were suspected of the crime but none of them admitted their guilt.
D. Four men were suspected of the crime, but none of them confessed his guilt.

90. A. Sita is younger to Rita but senior than her (Rita) in service.
B. Sita is younger to Rita but more senior to her (Rita) in service.
C. Sita is younger than Rita, but senior to her (Rita) in service.
D. Sita is more younger than Rita but senior to her (Rita) in service.

91. A. Tell me how are you?
B. Say me how are you?
C. Tell to me how are you?
D. Tell me how you are?

92. A. He denied that he was not a dacoit.
B. He denied that he not was a dacoit.
C. He denied he was not a dacoit.
D. He denied that he was a dacoit.

93. A. She insisted to go to Kuala Lumpur.
B. She insisted for going to Kuala Lumpur.
C. She insisted on going to Kuala Lumpur.
D. She insisted at going to Kuala Lumpur.

94. A. She gave me a chair to sit.
B. She gave me a chair for sitting.
C. She gave me a chair to be seated.
D. She gave me a chair to sit on.

95. A. He is one of the wisest persons who has ever lived.
B. He is one of the wisest persons who have ever lived.
C. He is one of the wisest persons which has ever lived.
D. He is one of the wisest persons which have ever lived.

96. A. Nobody in their senses could do such a nasty work.
B. Nobody in their senses could do such a good work.
C. Nobody in his senses could do such a nasty work.
D. Nobody in their senses could do such a nasty work.

97. A. Please tell me where is the Birla Temple?
B. Please say me where is the Birla Temple?
C. Please tell to me where is the Birla Temple?
D. Please tell me where the Birla Temple is?

98. A. They have and are still doing excellent work.
B. They have and have still doing excellent work.
C. They have and have still been doing excellent work.
D. They have done and are still doing excellent work.

99. A. All our family member have gone to Calcutta.
B. All our family member has gone to Calcutta.
C. All our family member have gone to Calcutta.
D. All the members of our family have gone to Calcutta.

100. A. Although we are living in Delhi for fifty years, we have not seen the Red Fort.
B. Although we are living in Delhi for fifty years, we had not seen the Red Fort.
C. Although we have been living in Delhi for fifty years, we have not seen the Red Fort.
D. Although we live in Delhi for fifty years, we had not seen the Red Fort.

ANSWERS

1	2	3	4	5	6	7	8	9	10
D	A	C	D	D	D	D	D	C	B
11	**12**	**13**	**14**	**15**	**16**	**17**	**18**	**19**	**20**
A	C	A	C	A	C	A	D	D	A
21	**22**	**23**	**24**	**25**	**26**	**27**	**28**	**29**	**30**
B	B	A	A	D	D	B	C	D	A
31	**32**	**33**	**34**	**35**	**36**	**37**	**38**	**39**	**40**
B	C	C	B	B	B	D	C	B	B
41	**42**	**43**	**44**	**45**	**46**	**47**	**48**	**49**	**50**
C	C	B	B	D	D	D	D	B	B
51	**52**	**53**	**54**	**55**	**56**	**57**	**58**	**59**	**60**
D	D	C	D	C	B	B	C	D	C
61	**62**	**63**	**64**	**65**	**66**	**67**	**68**	**69**	**70**
D	D	D	D	C	C	D	C	D	D
71	**72**	**73**	**74**	**75**	**76**	**77**	**78**	**79**	**80**
B	C	D	D	C	B	D	C	D	B
81	**82**	**83**	**84**	**85**	**86**	**87**	**88**	**89**	**90**
C	D	C	C	D	D	C	D	D	C
91	**92**	**93**	**94**	**95**	**96**	**97**	**98**	**99**	**100**
D	D	C	D	B	C	D	D	D	C

15 Figures of Speech

It is a common saying that a picture is worth a thousand words. Same goes with the figures of speech as they elaborate the meaning of words.

FIGURATIVE LANGUAGE

One meaning of "figure" is "drawing" or "image" or "picture". Figurative language creates figures (pictures) in the mind of the reader or listener. These pictures help convey the meaning faster and more vividly than words alone.

We use figures of speech in "figurative language" to add colour and interest, and to awaken the imagination. Figurative language is everywhere, from classical works like Shakespeare or the Bible, to every day speech, pop music and television commercials. It makes the reader or listener use their imagination and understand much more than the plain words.

Figurative language is the opposite of literal language. Literal language means exactly what it says. Figurative language means something different to (and usually more than) what it says on the surface. *e.g.,*

- He ran fast. (literal)
- He ran like the wind. (figurative)

In the above example "like the wind" is a figure of speech (in this case, simile). It is important to recognize the difference between literal and figurative language. There are many figures of speech that are commonly used and which you can learn by heart. At other times, writers and speakers may invent their own figures of speech. If you do not recognize them as figures of speech and think that they are literal, you will find it difficult to understand the language.

In this chapter we will discuss four common types of figures of speech :

- Simile
- Metaphor
- Hyperbole
- Oxymoron

Simile

A simile is a figure of speech that says that one thing is like another different thing. We can use similes to make descriptions more emphatic or vivid.

We often use the words *as....as* and *like* with similes.

Common patterns for similes, with example sentences, are :

- Something AS *adjective* AS *something*
  His skin was as cold as ice.
  It felt as hard as rock.
  She looked as gentle as a lamb.
- Something LIKE something
  My love is like a red, red rose.
  These cookies taste like garbage.
  He had a temper (that was) like a volcano.
- Something LIKE something
  He eats like a pig.
  He smokes like a chimney.
  They fought like cats and dogs.

Here are some more examples of well known similes :

AS *adjective* AS *something*	**Meaning**
as blind as a bat	completely blind
as cold as ice	very cold
as flat as a pancake	completely flat
as gentle as a lamb	very gentle
as light as a feather	very light
as old as the hills	very old
as sharp as a knife	very sharp
as strong as a bull	very strong
as white as snow	pure white
as wise as an owl	very wise

LIKE something	Possible meaning (depending on context)
like a rose	beautiful
like a volcano	explosive
like garbage	disgusting
like an animal	inhuman
like spaghetti	entangled
like dewdrops	sweet and pure
like golddust	precious
like a tip	very untidy (tip = garbage dump)
like a dream	wonderful, incredible
like stars	bright and beautiful

LIKE something	Meaning
to drink like a fish	to drink a lot
to eat like a bird	to eat very little
to eat like a horse	to eat a lot
to eat like a pig	to eat impolitely
to fight like cats and dogs	to fight fiercely
to sing like an angel	to sing beautifully
to sleep like a log	to sleep well and soundly
to smoke like a chimney	to smoke heavily, all the time
to soar like an eagle	to fly high and free
to work like a dog	to work very hard

Note that with the AS...AS pattern, the first AS is sometimes suppressed, for example :

His skin was cold as ice.

The above patterns of simile are the most common, but there are others made with adverbs or words such as than and as if, for example :

- He ran as fast as the wind.
- He is larger than life.
- They ran as if for their lives.

Similes can include other figures of speech. For example. "He ran like greased lightning" is a simile that includes hyperbole (greased lightning).

Similes often make use of irony or sarcasm. In such cases they may even mean the opposite of the adjective used. Look at these examples :

- His explanation was as clear as mud. (not clear at all since mud is opaque)
- The film was about as interesting watching a copy of Windows download. (long and boring)
- Watching the show was like watching paint dry. (very boring)

Similes are often found (and they sometimes originate) in poetry and other literature. Here are a few examples :

- A woman without a man is like a fish without a bicycle—Irina Dunn
- Dawn breaks open like a wound that bleeds afresh—Wilfred Owen
- Death has many times invited me : it was like the salt invisible in the waves—Pablo Neruda
- Guiltless forever, like a tree—Robert Browning
- Happy as pigs in mud—David Eddings
- How like the winter hath my absence been—William Shakespeare
- As idle as a painted ship upon a painted ocean—Samuel Taylor Coleridge
- Jubilant as a flag unfurled—Dorothy Parker
- So are you to my thoughts as food to life—William Shakespeare
- Yellow butterflies flickered along the shade like flecks of sun—William Faulkner

Metaphor

A metaphor is a figure of speech that says that one thing is another different thing. This allows us to use fewer words and forces the reader or listener to find the similarities.

The word metaphor comes from the Greek word *metapherin* (meaning "transfer").

The simplest form of metaphor is : "The [first thing] is a [second thing]."

Look at this example :

Her home was a prison.

In the above sentence, we understand immediately that her home had some of the characteristics of a prison. Mainly, we imagine, she could not leave her home. She was trapped inside. Why it was a prison we do not know, but that would be clear from the context—perhaps her husband forced her to stay at home, perhaps she was afraid of the outside. We don't know, but the rest of the story would tell us. What is important here is that in five simple words we understand a lot about her environment, how she felt and how she behaved. In this sentence, "prison" is a metaphor.

Look at another example :

George is a sheep.

What is one characteristic of sheep? They follow each other. So we can imagine that George is a follower, not a leader. In this sentence "sheep" is a metaphor.

Metaphors are very common in everyday language. But poets also like to use metaphors.

Look at these examples of metaphors with sample sentences and meanings :

Metaphor example	Metaphorical sense	Original sense
I'm not an angel, but I wouldn't behave like that.	exemplary person	a spiritual being believed to be a messenger of God
America is a melting pot.	place where different peoples, styles and cultures are mixed together	a container in which metals or other materials are melted and mixed
John is a real pig when he eats.	greedy person	a four-legged animal kept for meat (pork)
My father is a rock.	very strong or reliable person	a hard, mineral material made of stone
How could she marry a snake like that!	traitor	a long, limbless reptile (e.g., cobra, python, viper)
The policeman let him off with a yellow card.	warning	(in soccer) a yellow card that the referee shows to players when cautioning them

All the above metaphors (the simplest form) are nouns. But there are other ways of making metaphors, for example with verbs or adjectives. Here are some examples :

Metaphor example	Original sense of the word (example)
The committee **shot** ideas **down** one by one.	Anti-aircraft guns that shoot down planes.
The private detective **dug** up enough evidence to convince the police to act.	Dugs like to bury bones and dig them up later.
He **broke into** her conversation	Burglars break into buildings.
The new movie was very popular. People **flocked** to see it.	Birds flock together before they migrate.
His head was **spinning** with ideas.	Some computer hard drives spin at over 10,000 revolutions per minute.
Reading that book **kindled** my interest in branches when you kindle a camp fire.	You need to start with twigs and small politics.
Tim lost his job after a **heated** argument with his boss.	We have a heated swimming pool.
The new car's **sexy** design increased sales for the company.	Some women think that lipstick makes them look sexy.
He was dressed rather vulgarly in a **loud** checked suit.	I can't hear you because the radio is too loud.
It wasn't long before their relationship turned **sour**.	Sour food has an acid taste like lemon or vinegar.

Difference Between Metaphor and Simile

Both similes and metaphors link one thing to another. A simile usually uses "as" or "like". A metaphor is a condensed simile, a shortcut to meaning, which omits "as" or "like". A metaphor creates a relationship directly and leaves more to the imagination. With simile, A is like B. With metaphor, *A* is *B*.

Simile	Metaphor
Your eyes are like the sun.	You are my sunshine.
He eats like a pig.	He is a pig.
He lives like a pig.	He is a pig.

Dead Metaphors

In the phrase "to grasp the concept" the physical action "to grasp" is used as a metaphor for "to understand" (which is non-physical). But this phrase has been used so often that most English speakers do not have an image of the physical action in their mind. This metaphor is a "dead metaphor".

Mixed Metaphors

The awkward use of two or more different metaphors at the same time is normally best avoided. It creates conflicting images in the reader or listener's mind, reduces each metaphor's impact, and generally causes confusion. Look at this example :

America is a **melting pot** where new ideas are **kindled**.

Hyperbole

Hyperbole is a figure of speech that uses an exaggerated or extravagant to create a strong emotional response. As a figure of speech it is not intended to be taken literally. Hyperbole is frequently used for humour. Examples of hyperbole are :

- They ran like greased lightning.
- He's got tons of money.
- Her brain is the size of a pea.
- He is older than the hills.
- I will die if she asks me to dance.
- She is as big as an elephant!
- I'm so hungry I could eat a horse.
- I have told you a million times not to lie!

The media and the advertising industry often use hyperbole (which may then be described as hyper or media hype).

Oxymoron

An oxymoron is a figure of speech that deliberately uses two contradictory ideas. This contradiction creates a paradoxical image in the reader or listener's mind that generates a new concept or meaning for the whole. Some typical oxymorons are :

- a living death
- sometimes you have to be cruel to be kind
- a deafening silence
- bitter-sweet
- The Sounds of Silence (song title)
- make haste slowly
- he was conspicuous by his absence

Pseudo Oxymorons

In the standard meaning of oxymoron the contradiction is deliberate. However, in popular usage oxymoron is sometimes used to mean "contradiction in terms", where the contradiction is unintentional. Such expressions, unlike real oxymorons, are commonly used without any sense of paradox in everyday language, for example :

- anecdotal evidence
- friendly fire
- pretty ugly

A common attempt at humour is to describe a certain phrase as an oxymoron, implying that the two parts of the phrase are mutually exclusive and that consequently the phrase as a whole must be nonsensical :

- airline food
- American culture
- eco-tourism
- Microsoft security
- military intelligence

The following are the other major Figures of Speech :

1. **Personification**—In Personification inanimate objects and abstract notions are spoken of as having life or intelligence.
2. **Onomatopoeia**—Onomatopoeia is that artifice of language by which the sound of words is made to suggest or echo the sense.
3. **Apostrophe**—An Apostrophe is a direct address to the dead, to the absent, or to a personified object or idea.
4. **Alliteration**—Alliteration consists in the repetition of the same sound or syllable at the beginning of two or more words.
5. **Irony**—Irony is a mode of speech in which the real meaning is exactly the opposite of that which is literally conveyed.
6. **Pun**—This consists in a play on the various meanings of a word, and is seldom used except as a joke.
7. **Metonymy**—In Metonymy an object is designated by the name of something which is generally associated with it.
8. **Synecdoche**—In Synecdoche a part is used to designate the whole, or the whole to designate a part.
9. **Antithesis**—In Antithesis a striking opposition or contrast of words or sentiments is made in the same sentence. It is employed to secure emphasis.
10. **Transferred Epithet**—In this figure an epithet is tranferred from its proper word to another that is closely associated with it in the sentence.

MULTIPLE CHOICE QUESTIONS

Directions (Qs. 1 to 20) : *Select the correct option for each of the following questions.*

1. Recognize the figure of speech in the following statement.
   He is the Newton of our class.
   A. Simile B. Hyperbole
   C. Metaphor D. Climax

2. Which of the following statements shows oxymoron:
   A. He is leading a busy life.
   B. He is leading a highly busy-idle life.
   C. He is leading an idle life.
   D. How happy I am!

3. Recognize the figure of speech in the following:
   The Child is father of the Man.
   A. alliteration B. hyperbole
   C. paradox D. metaphor

4. Which of the following shows Metonymy:
   A. Have you read the whole of George Eliot?
   B. Which building in Delhi do you like most?

C. Whose acting do you like most among the Bollywood actors?
D. Why are day and night equal on 21 March?

5. Recognize the figure of speech in the following statement.
I wandered lonely as a cloud.
A. Simile B. Metaphor
C. Alliteration D. Hyperbole

6. Which of the following phrases shows onomatopoeia:
A. living like a king.
B. looking beyond the horizon.
C. burning the candle at both ends.
D. murmuring of innumerable bees.

7. Recognize the figure of speech in the following:
Five miles meandering in mazy motion.
A. oxymoron B. climax
C. anticlimax D. alliteration

8. Which of the following shows 'climax':
A. I walk, I jump, I dance.
B. I run, I walk, I sit.
C. He lies, runs and sits.
D. She thinks, writes and observes.

9. Recognize the figure of speech in the following:
Lightly, O lightly, they bear her along.
A. Hyperbole B. Onomatopoeia
C. Climax D. Repetition

10. Which of the following shows 'Hyperbole':
A. You will have to speak for a hundred thousand years to describe her beauty.
B. Love begets love.
C. Better alone than in bad company.
D. Nothing can be decided by war.

11. What Figure of Speech is used when a statement is made emphatic by over statement?
A. Apostrophe B. Hyperbole
C. Personification D. Antithesis

12. What Figure of Speech is used when two contradictory qualities are predicted at once of the same thing?
A. Antithesis B. Onomatopoeia
C. Oxymoron D. Hyperbole

13. In which Figure of Speech the sense is conveyed by the sound of words?
A. Metonymy B. Synecdoche
C. Alliteration D. Onomatopoeia

14. In which Figure of Speech is there a play on the various meanings of a word?
A. Pun B. Metaphor
C. Transferred Epithet D. Irony

15. Which Figure of Speech is produced when the same sound is repeated more than twice at the beginning of a word?
A. Onomatopoeia B. Alliteration
C. Metonymy D. Synecdoche

16. Which of the following is an example of Onomatopoeia?
A. Sweet-bitter tears flowed from her eyes
B. The beetle wheels his droning flight
C. A load of learning lumbering in his head
D. Fair is that fair does

17. Which of the following is an example of Oxymoron?
A. There is kind cruelty in the surgeon's knife
B. Ruin seize thee, ruthless king!
C. And Brutus is an honourable man!
D. Kalidas is the Shakespeare of India

18. Which of the following is an example of Antithesis?
A. Who is to blame but you!
B. Fair is foul, and foul is fair!
C. As you sow, so will you reap
D. Forget me not!

19. Which of the following is an example of Apostrophe?
A. Barking dogs seldom bite
B. My misfortune is your fortune
C. O Solitude! Where are thy charms?
D. I am the monarch of all I survey

20. Which of the following is an example of Alliteration?
A. Sweet are the uses of adversity!
B. Thus idly busy rolls their world away
C. He is the heir apparent
D. With beaded bubbles winking at the brim

Directions (Qs. 21 to 50) : *In each of the following sentences or verses a Figure of Speech has been used. You have to choose the correct Figure of Speech out of the four choices given under each :*

21. Rivers of blood flowed on the battlefield :
A. Simile B. Metaphor
C. Hyperbole D. Alliteration

22. Camel is the ship of the desert :
A. Metaphor B. Simile
C. Pun D. Personification

23. 'O my love's like a red, red rose, that's newly sprung in June':
A. Alliteration B. Metaphor
C. Simile D. Hyperbole

24. "Opportunity knocks at the door but once."
A. Hyperbole B. Metaphor
C. Antithesis D. Personification

25. "Death lays his icy hand on Kings" :
A. Personification B. Antithesis
C. Metaphor D. Oxymoron

26. "The murmurous haunt of flies on summer eves."
A. Hyperbole B. Alliteration
C. Onomatopoeia D. Personification

27. "Milton! thou should'st be living at this hour. "
A. Personification B. Apostrophe
C. Alliteration D. Irony

28. How high his honour holds his haughty head!
A. Oxymoron B. Personification
C. Alliteration D. Irony

29. "Yet Brutus says he was ambitious. And Brutus is an honourable man."
A. Irony B. Oxymoron
C. Apostrophe D. Pun

30. Is life worth living? That depends upon the liver.
A. Pun B. Alliteration
C. Irony D. Metaphor

31. The pen is mightier than the sword.
A. Simile B. Metaphor
C. Metonymy D. Irony

32. A reeling road, a rolling road, that rambles round the shire.
A. Alliteration B. Metonymy
C. Personification D. Apostrophe

33. "The ploughman homeward plods his weary way."
A. Oxymoron B. Synecdoche
C. Transferred Epithet D. Pun

34. To err is human, to forgive divine :
A. Oxymoron B. Antithesis
C. Transferred Epithet D. Pun

35. He passed a sleepless night :
A. Transferred Epithet B. Antithesis
C. Synecdoche D. Oxymoron

36. The best brains assembled there :
A. Oxymoron B. Synecdoche
C. Irony D. Pun

37. I have many mouths to feed :
A. Synecdoche B. Irony
C. Pun D. Oxymoron

38. Man proposes, God disposes :
A. Synecdoche B. Antithesis
C. Pun D. Irony

39. O Death! Where is thy sting?
A. Metaphor B. Oxymoron
C. Personification D. Apostrophe

40. "Life is a tale told by an idiot,
Full of sound and fury ...."
A. Simile B. Personification
C. Metaphor D. Apostrophe

41. "Thy soul was like a star, and dwelt apart."
A. Metaphor B. Personification
C. Simile D. Onomatopoeia

42. He can devour mountains of food, and drink rivers of whisky.
A. Onomatopoeia B. Hyperbole
C. Metaphor D. Personification

43. "There Honour comes a pilgrim grey" :
A. Metaphor B. Apostrophe
C. Personification D. Onomatopoeia

44. An ambassador is a man who lies abroad for the good of his country :
A. Metonymy B. Personification
C. Pun D. Irony

45. "Husbands had she five on the holy altar" :
A. Hyperbole B. Metaphor
C. Irony D. Pun

46. His honour rooted in dishonour stood :
A. Antithesis B. Oxymoron
C. Irony D. Personification

47. "Sceptre and crown must tumble down."
A. Metonymy B. Antithesis
C. Irony D. Oxymoron

48. A lie has no legs :
A. Apostrophe B. Pun
C. Personification D. Irony

49. Youth is full of pleasure; Age is full of care :
A. Antithesis B. Pun
C. Metaphor D. Personification

50. The righteous shall flourish as the palm trees :
A. Simile
B. Transferred Epithet
C. Antithesis
D. Synecdoche

ANSWERS

1	2	3	4	5	6	7	8	9	10
C	B	C	A	A	D	D	A	D	A
11	**12**	**13**	**14**	**15**	**16**	**17**	**18**	**19**	**20**
B	C	D	A	B	B	A	B	C	D
21	**22**	**23**	**24**	**25**	**26**	**27**	**28**	**29**	**30**
C	A	C	D	A	C	B	C	A	A
31	**32**	**33**	**34**	**35**	**36**	**37**	**38**	**39**	**40**
C	A	C	B	A	B	A	B	D	C
41	**42**	**43**	**44**	**45**	**46**	**47**	**48**	**49**	**50**
C	B	C	C	C	B	A	C	A	A

SECTION-II

LITERATURE

1 Forms of Literature

Literature plays a very significant role in human life. It is considered to be the mirror of the society which reflects the image of the time in which it was created. It is a medium of expressing thoughts and ideas for the writer. It is one of the most ancient forms of entertainment in the history of mankind. At the beginning when there was no written form of language, literature was composed in the form of poetry and preserved through the words of mouth. In the history of literature, poetry is the most ancient form of literature. Then it developed into various other forms like drama, novel, and short story.

The major forms of literature are:

1. Drama
2. Non-fiction or prose
3. Poetry
4. Novel

Drama

The following are the Major Forms of Drama :

1. Miracles & Mystery Plays, Morality Plays and Interludes
2. Heroic, Revenge, Shakespearean, Sentimental, Tragedies & Melodramas
3. Comedies
   - Classical Comedies
   - Tragi-Comedies
   - Romantic Comedies
   - Comedy of Humour
   - Comedy of Manners
   - The Farce
   - The Masque
4. The Poetic Play
5. The Dramatic Monologue
6. The Problem Play
7. The One-Act Play

Non-Fiction or Prose

The following are the Major Forms of Prose :

1. Long Prose-Works
2. The Essay
3. The Periodical Journals
4. The Biography
5. The Autobiography
6. The Memoirs

Poetry

Poetry and its Major Forms are these :

1. The Epic
2. The Mock Epic
3. The Sonnet
4. The Ode
5. The Lyric
6. The Idyll
7. The Pastoral
8. The Elegy
9. The Pastoral Elegy
10. The Ballad
11. The Satire

Novel

The following are the Major Forms of the Novel :

1. The Prose Romances
2. The Travelogues
3. The Gothic Novel
4. The Picaresque Novel
5. The Epistolary Novel
6. The Domestic Novel
7. The Historical Novel
8. The Regional Novel
9. The Prophetic Novel
10. The Psychological Novel
11. The Short Story

DRAMA

The term 'drama' originates from Greek language, which means 'to do'. In a drama, we come across objective representation of the conflicts, actions, events and crisis from the lives of the concerned characters. Drama is the specific mode of fiction represented in performance. It is primarily a performing art. It is the most powerful literary expression as action is presented on the stage, engaging the audio-visual faculties of the audience.

Drama is an ancient form of literature having a long history of more than 2500 years. Historically speaking following are the stages in the development of drama:

STAGES IN THE DEVELOPMENT OF DRAMA

Greek Drama

History of literature shows the origin of drama in Greece in 6th century B.C. In ancient Greece dramatic competitions were held to celebrate the festival of God Dionysus. The dramatists participating in this competition were required to present a tetralogy of plays consisting of three tragedies and a satyr play. The plays performed in this period were tragedy, comedy and the satyr play. Aeschylus, Sophocles, Euripides, Aristophanes and Menander are the best-known dramatists of Ancient times.

Roman Drama

Greek drama came in contact with the Romans after the Roman Empire expanded into Greece territories in the 3rd century B.C. Roman dramatists of this period like Andronicus and Naevius took drama all over Europe. During the 2nd century B.C. it had become one of the chief means of entertainment with many men of letters practicing it. The comedies written by Plautus and Terence became very popular, many of which have survived. The Roman tragedian, Seneca popularized tragedy so much so that it is called Senecan tragedy.

Medieval Drama

The drama of the Middle Ages dealt with Bible stories and allegorical mysteries. It was being written in the regional languages of the times. To help the laymen understand the teachings of the religion, the clergymen used to perform the incidents from Bible in dramatic form. The plays of this period are called Mystery and Miracle plays.

Elizabethan Drama

With the construction of Globe Theatre in London, drama as a major form of literature flourished in England. The main practitioners of this form in 16th and 17th century are Ben Jonson, Shakespeare and Christopher Marlowe. The plays of this period were written on the themes like ancient history and Greek and Roman mythology, and contemporary socio-political issues.

Modern Drama

Henrik Ibsen and Bertolt Brecht dominate the modern drama of 19th and 20th Century respectively. Ibsen started a new kind of drama by making an ordinary housewife as the heroine of his play, 'A Doll's House'. Anton Chekhov, Eugene O'Neill, Luigi Pirandello, Samuel Beckett, Harold Pinter, John Osborne and George Bernard Shaw are the important dramatists of this period.

Indian Classical Drama

Indian Classical drama originated from the Rig-Veda. The plots of these plays were based on the stories taken from the great Sanskrit epics, *The Ramayana* and *The Mahabharata*. Our ancient writer, Bharata penned the theory of writing a play in his book '*Natya Shastra*'. Bhasa, Kalidasa, Sudraka, Asvaghosa and Harsha are the famous Sanskrit playwrights.

ELEMENTS OF DRAMA

Aristotle, in his book entitled 'The Poetics' has discussed theoretical aspects of drama. Here he has given emphasis on tragedy and its elements. These elements are plot, theme, character, diction, music and spectacle.

Plot

According to Aristotle's theory of drama in 'Poetics', plot is the most important element of drama. He equals the plot of a play with the soul in human body. The plot can be either simple or complex. Simple plot is straight-forward, with continuous movements, whereas the complex plot has peripeity and Anagnorisis. Peripeteia means the opposite results produced by the human actions. In such a plot the character goes on acting naively in certain way without realizing the effects of his actions. But these actions ultimately lead it to its doom. Anagnorisis means the realization of truth. The simple plot has only one story in it whereas the complex plot can have more than one story or episodes in it. The skill of the dramatist lies in knitting all these episodes in a single whole to create a singular effect on the audience.

An ideal plot can be divided into three parts—beginning, middle and an end. A good beginning is that which is not dependent on some previous incident or knowledge. A good middle is the outcome of the events which have taken place in the beginning and leads those events to their satisfactory conclusion. A good ending is the result of whatever has happened before the end. It is the natural conclusion of the events gone before.

Character

Drama is the representation of the conflicts of human life. And so it requires some characters in the happenings of life. As the dramatist represents a story, it is but natural that there should be some characters on whose life the story is based. The characters in a play are selected from the host of people according to the need of the plot. As the play has a limited canvas, he does not make his play over crowded with too many characters. There is no scope for a full length character study in a drama. So the writer selects only those incidents from the life of his protagonist that are necessary for the action of the play.

The characters are of two types—flat characters and round characters. A flat character does not grow with the development of the plot. It remains static from the beginning to the end of the play. On the other hand, round character grows with the action of the play. Another type of character is the stock character, a character that reappears again and again in various plays with the same attributes each time. Such characters are also called stereotypes or the stock characters.

While developing his characters, the dramatist uses the following methods: one method is to develop his characters by the help of the dialogues which the character speaks; the other method is to expose the character by through the speeches of the other characters; and the third method is the combination of the earlier two methods, i.e. developing the character partly through his/her own speeches and partly by what others say about him/her. Actually the last method is more convincing and so used by the greater number of writers.

One more aspect of the characters in a play is the selection of the hero or the heroine. The dramatist has to be very careful regarding this aspect because the success of the play is dependent on the proper selection of the characters. So the dramatist follows certain well-defined principles for this purpose. The Greek philosopher, Aristotle has laid down some rules for the proper choice of characters. According to Aristotelian canon the hero of a tragedy should be a 'good' person. It means the hero of a play should be of an intermediate type of person. He should neither be 'too good' nor 'too bad'. Similarly, the heroine of a play should also be selected as per the demands of the plot. The hero and the heroine should belong to the royal families or to the upper strata of the society because the fall of such a person from happiness to misery would create the cathartic effect on the minds of the audience.

Diction

As is mentioned earlier that there should be a proper selection of the characters, similarly there should be a proper choice of the language to be used in a play. Language or the diction is *'the choice of words made by the playwright and enunciation of the actors delivering these words'*. The dramatist represents only the selected incidents and events from the lives of the characters in the form of dialogue and action. Therefore the language used in the play should be decorative, stylistic and becoming to the specific class to which the character belongs. It means a king should speak like a king and a clown should speak like a clown. Otherwise the audience will not believe in whatever is happening on the stage. Shakespeare has closely followed this principle in his plays. The characters belonging to the upper strata of the society in his plays mostly speak in verse and the characters from lower classes use prose. As every word in a play helps the playwright to further the action so the diction is very important substance of the play.

Subject or the Theme

The various events of the plot are held together by some central idea. This central idea is called the 'subject' or 'theme' of the play. If the theme of a play is noble and dignified, it will make the play great and successful. A great work of art comes into existence if the theme is noble and worthy of artistic treatment. And so the dramatist must deal with noble and dignified action. It is possible that some plays with a good plot may be having a little or no theme in them. Such plays may become temporarily successful with the audience. This success is short-lived as the audiences forget about the play after coming out of the theatre. Therefore along with a well-constructed plot, there should be a good theme in a play to make it universal.

Music

The dramatist is relied on music to create a specific effect on the audiences. Music means the sound, rhythm and melody of the speeches. The history of dramaturgy shows that the performances of the plays were accompanied by music produced by the musicians. But with the development in the field of science and technology, modern theatre has introduced the use of recorded sounds. The dramatist is now able to make the play more realistic by the use of a variety of recorded sounds like the sounds of animals, wind, storm, rain and lightning.

Spectacle

The element of spectacle is also enriched in the modern times. Spectacle means the visual elements of the production of a play. It includes the stage, furniture, scenery, costumes and curtains.

A costume means the different things which the actors use on their body. A costume includes clothing, wigs, and masks and make up. Costumes help the audience to understand about the time and the place of the action. A mask is a special element of costume. Though mask is rarely used in modern theatre, it was indispensable in ancient India. Makeup is sometimes used to exaggerate and distort facial features. It also helps to conceal the signs of age or the colour of face. The scenery is a special element of stage properties. Its elements are balcony, trapdoors, elevators, and gallery. In modern theatre, lighting is used very effectively. It helps the dramatist to control the focus of the audience and create specific mood.

MAJOR FORMS OF DRAMA

1. Miracles & Mystery Plays, Morality Plays and Interludes
2. Heroic, Revenge, Shakespearean & Sentimental Tragedies & Melodramas
3. Comedies
   - Classical Comedies
   - Tragi-Comedies
   - Romantic Comedies
   - Comedy of Humour
   - Comedy of Manners
   - The Farce
   - The Masque
4. The Poetic Play
5. The Dramatic Monologue
6. The Problem Play
7. The One-Act Play

MIRACLE & MYSTERY PLAYS, MORALITY PLAYS AND INTERLUDES

These are all types of late-medieval drama, written in a variety of verse forms.

Miracle & Mystery Plays

The miracle play had as its subject either a story from the Bible, or else the life and martyrdom of a saint. In the usage of some historians, however, "miracle play" denotes only dramas based on saints' lives, and the term mystery play is applied to dramas based on the Bible.

"Mystery" is used in the archaic sense (probably derived from the Latin *ministerium*, "work," "occupation") of the "trade" conducted by each of the medieval guilds which sponsored these plays.

The plays representing biblical narratives originated within the church in about the tenth century, in dramatizations of brief parts of the Latin liturgical service, called tropes, especially the "*Quem quaeritis*" ("Whom are you seeking") trope portraying the visit of the three Marys to the tomb of Christ. Gradually these evolved into complete plays which were written in English instead of in Latin, produced under the auspices of the various trade guilds, and acted on stages set outside the church. The miracle plays written in England are unknown authorship. In the fourteenth century there developed in cities such as York and Chester the practice, on the feast of Corpus Christi (sixty days after Easter), of putting on great "cycles" of such plays, representing crucial events in the biblical history of mankind from the Creation and Fall of man, through the Nativity, Crucifixion, and Resurrection of Christ, to the Last Judgement. The precise way that the plays were staged is a matter of scholarly debate, but it is widely agreed that each scene was played on a separate "pageant wagon" which was drawn, in sequence, to one after another fixed station in a city, at each of which some parts of the cycle were enacted. The biblical texts were greatly expanded in these plays, and the unknown authors added scenes, comic as well as serious, of their own invention. For examples of the variety, vitality, and power of these dramas, see the Wakefield "Noah" and "Second Shepherd's Play," and the Brome "Abraham and Isaac."

Morality Plays

Morality plays were dramatized *allegories* of a representative Christian life in the plot form of a quest for salvation, in which the crucial events are temptations, sinning, and the climactic confrontation with death. The usual protagonist represents Mankind, or Everyman; among the other characters are personifications of virtues, vices, and Death, as well as angles and demons who contest for the prize of the soul of Mankind. A character known as the Vice often played the role of the tempter in a fashion both sinister and comic; he is regarded by some literary historians as a precursor both of the cynical, ironic villain and of some of the comic figures in Elizabethan drama, including Shakespeare's *Falstaff*. The best-known morality play is the fifteenth-century *Everyman*, which is still given an occasional performance; other notable examples, written in the same century, are *The Castle of Perseverance and Mankind*.

Interludes

Interlude (Latin, "between the play") is a term applied to a variety of short stage entertainments, such as secular farces and witty dialogues with a religious or political point. In the late fifteenth and early sixteenth centuries, these little dramas were performed by bands of professional actors; it is believed that they were often put on between the courses of a feast or between the acts of a longer play. Among the better-known interludes are John Heywood's farces of the first half of the sixteenth century, especially The Four PP (that is, the Palmer, the Pardoner, the 'Pothecary, and the Peddler, who engage in a lying contest), and *Johan the Husband, Tyb His Wife, and Sir John the Priest*.

Until the middle of the twentieth century, concern with medieval drama was scholarly rather than critical. Since that time a number of studies have dealt with the relationships of the texts to the religious and secular culture of medieval Europe, and have stressed the artistic excellence and power of the plays themselves.

THE TRAGEDY

The history of drama shows that tragedy originated in religious festival of the Greek God, Dionysus in 6th century B.C. Etymologically the word 'tragedy' is derived from Greek word 'tragodi' meaning 'a goat song' It came to be used for plays probably because of the practice of sacrificing a goat during the festival of Dionysus. The other reason may be that the winner of the dramatic contest was given a goat as the award. To participate in the dramatic contest, the contestants were required to present a tetralogy of plays consisting of three tragedies and a satyr play. In ancient Greek literature the concept of tragedy is different from the modern concept. The modern tragedy is usually considered to as a play with unhappy ending. However, many of the Greek tragedies end on a happy note.

Tragedy is defined as "the imitation of an action, serious, complete and of a certain magnitude, in a language beautified in different parts with different kinds of embellishment, through action and not narration, and through scenes of pity and fear bringing about the catharsis of these or such like emotions".

Plato considers 'imitation' to be an act of mimicry. But Aristotle has given a new meaning to this term. For him imitation does not mean servile copying but an imaginative recreation. Aristotle says that imitation is the basic principle of all fine arts. Tragedy is distinguished from other fine arts according to the object, medium and manner of imitation. On the basis of objects of imitation, tragedy is distinguished from comedy. Tragedy imitates serious actions whereas comedy imitates the non-serious. So far as the medium of imitation is concerned, tragedy is distinguished from the lyric, as tragedy uses several kinds of embellishments. Tragedy is differentiated from epic on the basis of its manner of imitation, as tragedy represents through action whereas epic narrates.

Aristotle has used the term 'magnitude' for the length of the action of a tragedy. In this respect, usually the tragedy is compared with the human body. As too short or too tall human body does not look beautiful, similarly, too short or too long tragedy is not good. As a tragedy is performed on the stage within two or three hours, the dramatic action should not be too long as the audience will forget about the beginning before the dramatic action reaches to its end. It should not also be too short as it would not allow the writer to develop the essential aspects of the plot and characters.

Any dramatic action must have a beginning, middle and an end. A good beginning is the one which is not dependent on any of the previous situation and from which further action flows out. A good middle arises out of the events which have gone before and leads the action towards its logical and convincing conclusion. A good end is the natural outcome of whatever has gone before without leading the action any further.

The function of tragedy, like any other work of literature, is to 'delight' or to 'please'. While speaking about the function of a tragedy, Aristotle has used the term 'catharses'. But Aristotle has not defined 'catharsis' and so there are endless debates on the exact meaning of the term. Some scholars consider that 'catharsis' means purgation. According to the theory of purgation, the spectators in the theatre are relieved or cleansed or purged of the harmful emotions of pity and fear. According to the other group of scholars Catharsis is the resolution of dramatic tension, within the plot. It means in his play, the dramatist represents the incidents which arouse the emotions of pity and fear for the fate of the protagonist. During the course of the action, the dramatist resolves the conflicts which help him to take the action to its logical conclusion along with creating the emotions of pity and fear.

TYPES OF TRAGEDY

1. Heroic Tragedy
2. Revenge Tragedy
3. Shakespearean Tragedy
4. Sentimental Tragedy
5. Melodrama

Heroic Tragedy

The Heroic Tragedy is also known as the Restoration Tragedy. The influence of French romance and drama produced its first important result in the form of the heroic play.

The Heroic Tragedy is artificial. Its emotions are unreal. It mainly deals with conflict between love and honour.

John Dryden was the principal writer of the Heroic Tragedy. His famous tragedies are *Tyannic Love, Conquest of Granada* and *All for Love.* In Dryden's heroic plays we find a hero of superhuman powers and with superhuman ideals; there is a heroine of unsurpassed beauty and constancy; there is an inner conflict in the minds of several characters between love and honour; and there is a striving story of fighting and martial enthusiasm, filled with intense dramatic interest. *All For Love* is the finest tragedy of this period.

Another playwright was Thomas Otway. He wrote *Alcibiades, Don Carlos, The Orphan* and *Venice Preserved.*

Revenge Tragedy

The Revenge Tragedy genre of English literature generally refers to a body of dramatic works written from the mid-1580s to the early 1640s, from the Elizabethan to the Caroline period. Typically, these works feature such themes and devices as a wronged revenge-seeker, ghosts, madness, delay, sinister intrigue, a play-within-the-play, torture, multiple murders, and the realistic depiction of bloody violence on stage. Nearly all of the major playwrights of the time contributed to this class of drama, including Thomas Kyd, William Shakespeare, John Marston, George Chapman, Cyril Tourneur, Thomas Middleton, John Webster, James Shirley, and John Ford. Most literary scholars have credited Kyd with initiating the dramatic archetype with his *The Spanish Tragedy* (1585–90) and the so-called *Ur-Hamlet*—a drama no longer extant but which is believed to have been written before 1589, and upon which Shakespeare likely based his great tragedy—and have credited Shakespeare with bringing the genre to its artistic maturity with *Hamlet* (c. 1600-01). Critics have maintained that revenge tragedy was a markedly dynamic genre, observing that while Kyd invented the basic formula, his successors added ingenious new layers of dramatic suspense, characterization, symbolism, and ideological representation to the theatrical form.

Shakespearean Tragedy

Shakespeare wrote tragedies from the beginning of his career. One of his earliest plays was the Roman tragedy *Titus Andronicus*, which he followed a few years later with *Romeo and Juliet*. However, his most admired tragedies were written in a seven-year period between 1601 and 1608. These includes his four major tragedies *Hamlet, Othello, King Lear* and *Macbeth*, along with *Antony* & *Cleopatra, Coriolanus, Cymbeline, Julius Caesar* and the lesser-known *Timon of Athens* and *Troilus* and *Cressida*.

Shakespearean Tragedy is fundamentally serious, involving the downfall of a heroic figure. The themes are lofty: passion *(Romeo and Juliet),* revenge *(Hamlet),* ambition *(Macbeth)* and jealousy *(Othello)*.

Unique elements of tragedy are the tragic hero who is an articulate, social authority, someone who is "important" within his society, this hero has at least one weakness or fault—a tragic flaw—which during the course of the drama grows until it overcomes his virtues and leads to his downfall and the destruction of his world; and chorus borrowed from Greek tragedy in which dancers/singers appear at intervals within the play to comment on the action—express objective judgement on the proceedings.

Sentimental Tragedy

While sentiment, in its modern sense, may be found in all forms of drama and theatre, Sentimental Drama was a specifically 18th century European form in which, as Oliver Goldsmith put it, "the virtues of private life are exhibited, rather than the vices exposed". "Sentiment" at this period meant "feeling" or "sensibility". While many of the plays were nominally comic, the characters tended to be dull and priggish, the plots bathetic and the language stilted. Despite this, it was popular with the rising middle-class audience, especially in Germany, France and Britain, because it tended to treat them seriously in ways which neither comedy nor tragedy did. For all its dramatic ineptness (at least from today's perspective) it is important in theatre-historical terms, as it marks an important stage in the development of serious prose drama.

In the English language, the most famous and most successful tragedies are those by William Shakespeare and his Elizabethan contemporaries.

A contemporary of Shakespeare, Christopher Marlowe, also wrote examples of tragedy in English, notably:

The Tragical History of Doctor Faustus; and *Tamburlaine*

John Webster also wrote famous plays of the genre: *The Duchess of Malfi* and *The White Devil*.

The Melodrama

Though the term "melodrama" is sometimes applied to the dramatic productions of a certain period, it also often designates a certain kind of literary structure.

Melodrama is the fantasy of a world that operates according to our heart's desires in contrast to the other formula types that are fantasies of particular actions or states of being that counter some of our deepest fears or concentrate on particular wishes for victory or love or knowledge. Therefore, melodrama can contain all the other fantasies and often does. In fact, its chief characteristic is the combination of a number of actions and settings in order to build up the sense of a whole world bearing out the audience's traditional patterns of right and wrong, good and evil.

One thing possessed in common by these otherwise very different sorts of stories is the quality that has traditionally been understood as the hallmark of melodrama: the drama of intensified effects (i.e., music, "melos") added to the play to increase its emotional power and intensify its hold on the audience. Therefore, the idea of melodrama has come to be associated with violence and sensationalism—"the plot revolves around malevolent intrigue and violent action, while credibility both of character and plot is sacrificed for violent effect and emotional opportunism." This is undoubtedly one major characteristic of melodrama, but the quest for intensified narrative or dramatic effects is characteristic of the entire range of formulaic types. Particular formulas come into existence and flourish at least in part because they invent heightened narrative or dramatic patterns. In this sense all formulaic stories are melodramatic, and we might look at the various formulaic types— adventure, romance, and mystery—as simply specialized forms of melodrama. Indeed, many of the modern specialized formulas such as the classical detective story, the spy story, the hard-boiled detective story, and the gothic romance did evolve historically from the broader melodramatic forms of the early nineteenth century.

The specific formulas that depend on the basic moral fantasy of melodrama are many and various. Some of the more important contemporary examples are the best-selling panoramic social novel such as those written by Irving Wallace, Harold Robbins, and Jacqueline Susann, the historical spectacle such as *Gone with the Wind,* the soap opera, the gangster saga, the professional drama such as the doctor, lawyer, or teacher story, and many others. Though extremely various in the cultural materials they employ, all these formulas are shaped by the basic qualities of melodrama: the heightening of feeling and moral conflict and multiple lines of action that work together to create a sense of the rightness of the world order.

Some important examples of melodramas are:

John Fletcher's *The Maid's Tragedy;* John Webster's *The White Devil;* John Ford's *The Broken Heart;* Thomas Heywood's *A Woman Killed with Kindness;* Francis Beaumont's *A King and No King*.

THE COMEDY

Comedy may be considered to be a representation of the character of a lower type. Here 'lower' means 'ridiculous.'

By presenting the character in a ridiculous manner, the writer of a comedy aims at producing laughter. Though the genre of comedy is practiced since the ancient times with the practitioners like Aristophanes and Plautus, the scholars have not paid enough attention towards the serious study of its nature and function. While speaking about the function of comedy, George Meredith says that comedy appeals to the intelligence pure and simple and aims not at our ribs or armpits but at our heads. It means, it is the business of a comedy writer to look on what ails the world. He observes his environment minutely and fids out its follies and exposes them. But while exposing those follies, the purpose of the writer is to 'correct' or 'reform' those follies. Some scholars are of the opinion that the function of a comedy is not 'to reform' or 'to correct' the follies of the world bur to provide light-hearted mirth. But while creating mirth, the comedian encourages the audience to laugh with not laugh at the follies of the world. Such kind of play is purely meant for the entertainment of the audience.

Comedies are of following types:

1. Classical Comedies
2. Tragi-Comedies
3. Romantic Comedies
4. Comedy of Humour
5. Comedy of Manners
6. The Farce
7. The Masque

The Classical Comedy

This type of comedy is written as per the rules laid down by the ancient Greek and Roman masters. The function of such a comedy is 'corrective' or 'reformative'. In this comedy some human folly is exposed and ridiculed. It follows the rules of three unities—unity of time, place and action. The writer of this comedy strictly avoids the mingling of comic with tragic.

The Tragi-Comedy

In understanding about tragi-comedy, one finds oneself in the position of the proverbial blind philosophers attempting to identify an elephant. The individual who gets hold of its trunk thinks it is a snake, he who grasps its tail supposes it a rope, while she who clasps one of its legs believes it to be a tree. A.E. Housman commented in the essay "the legitimate meanings of the word poetry were themselves so many as to embarrass the discussion of its nature." The same is true to a lesser degree of the word *tragi-comedy*. The nature of tragicomedy is difficult to define because its name has been used so variously since Plautus first coined the term as a joke in his *Amphitryon* and because the dramatic genre tragi-comedy can comprise so many different modes (romantic, satiric, pastoral, melodramatic, and so on, as well as, indispensably, tragic and comic).

This play is a combination of the elements of both the comedy and the tragedy. Naturally, the play ends on a happy note for some characters and on a sad note for the others. Shakespeare is a famous practitioner of this kind of play. Though Aristotle had opposed the mingling of the tragic with the comic, scholars like John Dryden and Dr. Samuel Johnson have defended this type of play by saying that it is nearer to the human life. These critics argue that as the life itself is a combination of happy and sad events there is no harm in combining them in plays. Shakespeare's well-known tragi-comedies are *The Winter's Tale, The Merchant of Venice* and *The Tempest*.

The study of genre, despite recurring critical objections, continues to be indispensable to the study of drama in particular. Genre is not simply a matter of definition or classification. Rather, genre communicates; genre enables comprehension and conditions response. As Tzvetan Todorov explains, "It is because genres exist as an institution that they function as 'horizons of expectation' for readers and as 'models of writing' for authors." And Marco De Marinis, writing of performance, similarly observes, "By supplying the receiver with intertextual schemas and systems of expectation, *genre* (in its widely accepted analytical and descriptive meaning as a 'class of texts with specific co-textual and/or contextual traits in common') plays a crucial role in the process of textual comprehension and interpretation."

Dramatic genres in particular are modes of perception, conveying attitudes to human experience, as much as they are formal categories.

Although tragi-comedy is an especially slippery genre, there is actually a good deal of critical agreement (among those critics who recognize it as a genre at all) as to which plays constitute its major achievements. Differences of opinion arise inevitably and properly at the edges of the genre. The familiar central examples of the genre range from *II Pastor Fido, The Malcontent, Measure for Measure, The Winter's Tale, A King and No King,* and *A Wife for a Month* to *The Wild Duck, The Cherry Orchard, The Playboy of the Western World, The Killer, Waiting for Godot, and No Man's Land*. Within each of these two groups, however, the plays seem in many respects quite unlike one another, and the modern tragi-comedies appear superficially to have little in common with those written in the sixteenth and early seventeenth centuries.

The Romantic Comedy

Romantic comedy is a popular genre that depicts burgeoning romance in human terms, and focuses on the foibles of those who are falling in love.

Comedy as a whole has rarely been seen as being as critically respectable as other genres; perhaps it is rather a self-defeating paradox to ask for it to be taken seriously. Even Shakespeare's comedies seem to be critically overshadowed by the tragedies, perhaps diminished by the foregrounding of characters who are not heroic or noble, and themes that concern issues that can be found in everyday life, such as love and relationships, rather than elemental issues of life, death, good and evil. The most respected romcoms are those associated with artistic figures that are respected as auteurs.

Romantic comedy has proved to be one of the most enduring genres. It has certainly undergone some ebbs and flows in its popularity, but, as with all the major genres, it proves perennially resilient. Audiences still enjoy the blueprint of the romantic comedy, with all its traditional ingredients. Every year sees the release of new romantic comedies, which are strongly in the mould of the earliest examples in history. We want to see the same characters, the same situations, the same narrative trajectory, the same settings and dialogue, with new stars that speak to new generations, yet tell the same story.

Romantic comedy does not follow the rules of writing a comedy laid down by the ancient classical writers. The writer freely mingles the comic with the tragic. The unities of time, place and action are modified as per the requirements of the plot. The aim of such a comedy is 'to produce innocent, good-natured laughter, thereby entertaining the audience without trying to teach anything.

Shakespearean Comedy

Shakespeare is a great writer of comedies. His comedies are called romantic or sunny comedies. With the help of his creative imagination, Shakespeare creates a brilliant world of romance which is far away from the drab realities of the everyday life. These comedies are usually set in some distant, far-off places, where the inhabitants have no other business but that of love-making. The lovers of a Shakespearean comedy fall in love at first sight and get married at the end. But the course of their love is always full of difficulties. There are made a lot of misunderstandings, family feuds, tears and sighs. Shakespeare forces his lovers to face these difficulties in order to test their love for each other. But ultimately, these lovers are helped to overcome these difficulties but the intervention of Goddess Fortune. Then comes the Goddess Marriage who unites the lovers in the bond of marriage followed by music, dance and merry-making.

The Comedy of Humours

A type of comedy developed by Ben Jonson, the Elizabethan playwright, based on the ancient physiological theory of the "four humours" that was still current in Jonson's time. The humours were held to be the four primary fluids—blood, phlegm, choler (or yellow bile), and melancholy (or black bile)—whose "temperament" (mixture) was held to determine a person's both physical condition and type of character. An imbalance of one or another humour in a temperament was said to produce four kinds of disposition, whose names have survived the underlying theory: sanguine (from the Latin "sanguis," blood), phlegmatic, choleric, and melancholic. In Jonshon's comedy of humours each of the major characters has a preponderant humour that gives him a characteristic distortion or eccentricity of disposition. Jonson expounds his theory in the "induction" to his play *Every Man in His Humour* (1598) and exemplifies the mode in his later comedies; often he identifies the ruling disposition of a humours character by his or her name: "Zeal-of-the-land Busy," "Dame Purecraft," "Wellbred." The Jonsonian type of humours character appears in plays by other Elizabethans, and remained influential in the *comedies of manners* by William Wycherley, Sir George Etheredge, William Congreve, and other dramatists of the English Restoration, 1660–1700.

The characters in a Comedy of Humour represent some 'humour'. The actions and behaviour of the characters are governed by some kind of passion. As the characters represent some typical trait, there is a lack of individuality in them. Rather they become stereotypes. Generally, these characters are taken from low life. The purpose of the writer of such a comedy is to satirize the follies of the characters and correct them.

The Comedy of Manners

A kind of comedy representing the complex and sophisticated code of behaviour current in fashionable circles of society, where appearances count for more than true moral character. Its plot usually revolves around intrigues of lust and greed, the self-interested cynicism of the characters being masked by decorous pretence. Unlike satire, the comedy of manners tends to reward its cleverly unscrupulous characters rather than punish their immorality. Its humour relies chiefly upon elegant verbal wit and repartee. In England, the comedy of manners flourished as the dominant form of Restoration comedy in the works of Sir George Etherege, William Wycherley (notably *The Country Wife*, 1675), and William Congreve; it was revived in a more subdued form in the 1770s by Goldsmith and Sheridan, and later by Oscar Wilde. Modern examples of the comedy of manners include Noël Coward's Design for living (1932) and Joe Orton's *Loot* (1965).

The Comedy of Manners is also called Restoration Comedy. It focuses upon the mannerism of the upper classes of the society. The characters of this comedy belong to the upper class. Here the dramatist represents a fashionable men and women, with their manners, love-intrigues, scandals and affectations. These comedies attempt to imitate everything refined. So anything coarse or low is strictly avoided.

The language of such a comedy is very witty and refined. The focus of the dramatist is not on the 'individuality' of the character but on its manners, so the characters become lifeless. This type of comedy was very famous during the

Restoration period with the writers like William Congreve, William Wycherley and Oliver Goldsmith practicing it.

The Farce

This was another popular form of theatre in France (and England) in the 19th century. Farce consists of unsubtle physical and verbal comedy. It flourishes in a moral community because it is anarchical, relying on overturning widely accepted values. The chief characteristics of farce are sexual misadventure, flirtation, verbal abuse and comic despair, which frequently lead to instant decisions and spontaneous action.

The most prolific and famous French farce writers were Feydeau (1862–1921) and Labiche (1815–1888). Labiche wrote nearly sixty plays and helped write about 100 others. Not surprisingly, the plays lack originality and concentrate on reworking old jokes. His most famous is *An Italian Straw Hat* (1851).

Feydeau was the originator of bedroom farces, the descendants of which can still be seen occasionally in London today.

Feydeau's middle period plays are the archetype of French farce. The principal characters are Parisian bourgeois, their major driving force is extra-connubial lust, and the basic source of the humour is their ever more desperate attempts to avoid being found out. Although no respectable married woman is ever seduced by her husband's best friend, it is not for want of trying on either side. The plots seem to have been constructed by a mad watchmaker, but the status quo is always restored at the end.

A farce is a comedy that focuses on physical humour. The dramatist aims at creating hilarious laughter by representing absurd characters and situations on the stage. To create his characters and situations, the dramatist makes use of exaggeration and extravagance. Exaggerated characters and situations, improbable coincidences, mistaken identities and miscommunication are the common techniques used by the writers to make his plot more complicated. All these instruments enable the dramatist to entertain his audience in the most direct way.

The Masque

Form of dramatic entertainment popular with the French and English aristocracy of the sixteenth and seventeenth centuries. Developed in Renaissance Italy, the masque was probably an evolution of primitive folk rituals. When adopted by court circles, it became a lavish spectacle, usually based on a mythological theme and involving elaborate costumes and stage machinery. Essentially it was a theatrical performance by a group of disguised guests (hence the name) who, arriving at a banquet, offered the host an entertainment of dances, poetry and music.

The characters in a masque wear some masks on their faces. Initially, a masque was a series of dances, illustrating some story, but afterwards it developed into a play. The writer of a masque chooses his characters and story from mythology. These masques were written to be performed on some private occasions by a limited number of characters. There is abundant use of music, dance, costly costumes and elaborate scenery.

The masque first appeared in the fifteenth century when Lorenzo de' Medici adapted the seasonal revels of the Florentines into sophisticated displays of art and poetry for the delight of his guests. In the French court these displays evolved into the *ballet de cour* and *the mascarade*. A form of the masque was brought to England in 1512 by Henry VIII, who liked to disguise himself as a player and pretend to be an uninvited guest at his own parties. Henry's daughter Elizabeth added the spoken introduction, which, with the inclusion of speeches and elements of court drama, was developed into a unified dramatic performance in the hands of Ben Jonson, who became court poet of the Stuarts in 1603. Until his time the main feature of the masque was the dance and revel, which the audience was invited to join. Under Jonson's influence the masque became a literary form, a dramatic poem of classical scholarship. Jonson also introduced the antimasque, so called because it preceded the main masque and because it included grotesque or comic elements in contrast, yet relevant, to the serious main masque. Jonson's influence was eventually eclipsed by his sometime collaborator and rival Inigo Jones, the architect and scenic designer, to whom theatrical spectacle was more important than literary content. It was Jones who thought of placing the layers on a raised stage and who eventually, by his attentions to spectacle rather than content, effected the deterioration of the masque as a dramatic form.

A courtly rather than a popular entertainment, the masque disappeared with the Puritan revolution of the 1640s. When the theatres reopened in 1660, however, scenic designers, playwrights, and actors took their principal inspiration not from the Elizabethan stage but from the masques of the court festivals.

THE POETIC PLAY

Poetic drama is not merely a drama which is written in verse, because prose may also be its effective medium. It is, in fact, a blending of the poetic and dramatic elements in a fruitful union. Here poetry is an integral part of the play, twined with plot, character and their interplay, not an element of isolated beauty or lyricism for its own sake, as is the case with splendid lyricism in some parts of Marlowe's *Dr. Faustus*, for example. At the same time the dramatic elements must be capable of sustaining the poetic grace and intensity. It means its themes and characters should be poetically convinced and should be larger than the average humanity and humdrum monotony of daily life, the passions and emotions permeating them should be naturally productive of the poetic expression, calculated to lift the mind of the spectator above the sphere of our ordinary joys and sorrows and send the penetrating gaze of his inner vision far down below the surface of life to the very springs of human action and human drives. Moreover, drama being so intimately bound up with the stage condition and the historic skill its practitioner must combine mastery over the poetic resources, with a real understanding of the peculiar needs and modes of the dramatic representation in the theatre. The history of the poetic drama in England is littered with the frozen anatomies of poetic plays written by the distinguished poets of the nineteenth century who failed to subordinate poetry to the general dramatic spirit and adapt the plays to the conditions and requirements of the stage.

Poetic drama reached its glorious peak in Elizabethan England when the general conditions of society and richness of language combined with the whole nation's insatiable craving for amusement and edification and the writer's intimacy with the theater to make the stage a national institution. But the glory did not last long and its decline was precipitated by the victory of the puritan fanaticism which sounded its death-knell. When it was revived again in the Restoration era, the conditions had changed and the heroic tragedy in rhyming couplet was simply the fury and the violence of its ghost. A sort of artificial respiration was given to it is the blank-verse tragedies which followed. They, however, failed to sustain its life and with one flash of life in Otway's *Venice Preserved* it gave up the ghost.

The nineteenth century efforts by the great poets were splendid failures on the big commercial stage, for which the writers themselves were partly to blame because they could not rise above the slavish imitation and adaptation of the Elizabethan blank-verse tragedy to re-orient the poetic drama to changed conditions of society and the taste and sensibility of the spectators. This was the condition when the present century opened with the prospect of a great dramatic Renaissance.

THE DRAMATIC MONOLOGUE

In theatre, a monologue (or monolog) is a speech presented by a single character, most often to express their thoughts aloud, though sometimes also to directly address another character or the audience. Monologues are common across the range of dramatic media (plays, films, etc.) as well as in non-dramatic media such as poetry. Monologues share much in common with several other literary devices including soliloquies, apostrophes, and asides. There are, however, distinctions between each of these devices.

One of the most important influences on the development of the dramatic monologue is the Romantic poets. The long, personal lyrics typical of the Romantic period are not dramatic monologues, in the sense that they do not, for the most part, imply a concentrated narrative. However, poems such as William Wordsworth's *Tintern Abbey* and Percy Bysshe Shelley's Mont Blanc, to name two famous examples, offered a model of close psychological observation and philosophical or pseudo-philosophical inquiry described in a specific setting.

The novel and plays have also been important influences on the dramatic monologue, particularly as a means of characterization. Dramatic monologues are a way of expressing the views of a character and offering the audience greater insight into that character's feelings. Dramatic monologues can also be used in novels to tell stories, as in Mary Shelley's Frankenstein, and to implicate the audience in moral judgments, as in Albert Camus' *The Fall* and Mohsin Hamid's *The Reluctant Fundamentalist*.

Monologues are also linked with soliliquys—such as in *Macbeth,* when Lady Macbeth reads a letter to herself and then speaks her thoughts as though she is thinking.

The Victorian Period

The Victorian period represented the high point of the dramatic monologue in English poetry.

Alfred, Lord Tennyson's *Ulysses,* published in 1842, has been called the first true dramatic monologue. After *Ulysses,* Tennyson's most famous efforts in this vein are Tithonus, *The Lotos-Eaters*, and St. Simon Stylites, all from the 1842 poems; later monologues appear in other volumes, notably *Idylls of the King*.

Matthew Arnold's *Dover Beach* and Stanzas from the *Grand Chartreuse* are famous, semi-autobiographical monologues. The former, usually regarded as the supreme expression of the growing skepticism of the mid-Victorian period, was published along with the later in 1867's New Poems.

Robert Browning is usually credited with perfecting the form; certainly, Browning is the poet who, above all, produced his finest and most famous work in this form. While *My Last Duchess* is the most famous of his monologues, the form dominated his writing career. Fra Lippo Lippi, Caliban upon Setebos, Soliloquy of the Spanish Cloister and Porphyria's Lover, as well as the other poems in *Men and Women* are just a handful of Browning's monologues.

Other Victorian poets also used the form. Dante Gabriel Rossetti wrote several, including *Jenny* and *The Blessed Damozel;* Christina Rossetti wrote a number, including *The Convent Threshold*. Algernon Charles Swinburne's *Hymn to Proserpine* has been called a dramatic monologue vaguely reminiscent of Browning's work.

THE PROBLEM PLAY

The "problem play" idea has sometimes helpfully, sometimes dubiously informed discussion of Shakespeare's plays, and though, along with much genre criticism, it has gone out of fashion now, it has figured periodically in the scholarship that helps us understand how the plays work technically. Problem play as a term has aroused debate because in some ways it may seem to solve nothing: it leaves us with only a question about a play's genre, not with even a tentative guideline for reading such as we get from calling a work comedy or tragedy.

As Harold Goddard wrote, we can find "nothing to indicate that Shakespeare's imagination ever allowed itself to be shackled by such prescriptions or definitions"; one of the few points that caused audiences of his own time to question his skills, his freedom with respect to Classical "rules" or transgressing genre expectations, allowed him to create plays that beg irresolution and thus continued meditation from his audiences.

The term problem play comes from F.S. Boas in Shakespeare and His Predecessors in 1896 (printed in the U.S. in New York by Charles Scribner's Sons, 1900): Boas used it to label those plays (such as *Measure for Measure, All's Well That Ends Well,* and *The Merchant of Venice*) that foreground perhaps unsolvable moral problems. More recently critics have used the term to indicate plays that defy easy categorization by genre, or literary type. Genre, a term that applies largely to the form and partly to the content of an artistic work (as in comedy, tragedy, epic, or novel), has much to do with how we read or view a work: if we attend a comedy or tragedy, we go with expectations about how we will find the work presented and how it will end. So criticism had already problematized problem play itself, since different critics have used it with different notions in mind. But it remains useful, because it directs our attention to an immediate interpretive difficulty that we experience as soon as we study particular plays. The idea of the problem play applies to nearly all of Shakespeare's plays: what we call them does make a difference in how we read and interpret and play them, since labels (like titles) guide audience expectations and invoke interpretive strategies.

THE ONE-ACT PLAY

In October 1909, when Strindberg wrote a brief preface to then unpublished *Författaren* (The Author), the fourth volume of his autobiography *Tjänstekvinnans son* (1886), he listed among his most important (viktigaste) works the one-act plays of the early 1890s as "one-actors out of cynical life." The item included The First Warning, Debit and Credit, Facing Death, Mother Love, Playing with Fire, and The Bond. He might just as well have included three one-act plays from the late 1880s: *The Stronger, Pariah,* and *Simoon.* All nine are short, stageworthy one-act plays; all were designed for production in experimental theaters; and all are interpretations of human situations from a cynical point of view.

Strindberg's hope of having a theater in which his plays wou'd be produced seemed to have a chance of realization in the late 1880s in Copenhagen but did not materialize until the Intimate Theater opened in Stockholm in 1907. He had written his great plays—*The Father* (1887), *Lady Julie* (1888), and *Creditors* (1888)—deliberately as what might very well be segments of actual life with increasing emphasis on universal themes, avoidance of distracting factors such as intermissions, and simplification of staging. The one-act plays listed above are essentially further extensions of his "attempts to transform drama into a form suitable for the time". They deal, moreover, with universal and timeless themes. The very brevity of these plays precludes examination in appreciable depth as in the longer plays of 1887 and 1888, but they have enough detail to provide audience and reader with material for creative participation and involvement. In each there is enough irritating matter to arouse reaction and to stimulate discussion.

The human situations presented are surely typical: people's willingness to claim credit for a fellow human being's success, a mother's manipulation of her daughter's life, a wife's indifference to her mate except when others obviously want him, denigration of a mate for one's own purposes, indifference to and rationalization of one's sins, playing with one's own and other's emotions, and the unhesitating destruction of a fellow human being at least partly in the name of religion.

NON-FICTION OR PROSE

Non-Fiction is prose writing that presents and explains ideas or that tells about real people, places, objects, or events. It is an account or representation of a subject which is presented as fact. This presentation may be accurate or not; that is, it can give either a true or a false account of the subject in question. However, it is generally assumed that the authors of such accounts believe them to be truthful at the time of their composition. Autobiographies biographies, essays, reports, letters, memos, and newspaper articles are all types of non-fiction.

Characteristics of Non-Fiction (Prose)

Works of non-fiction differ from works of fiction in several ways.

- The people, events, places, and ideas presented in nonfiction are real, not invented.
- Non-fiction is narrated by an author who is a real person.
- It presents facts, describes true-life experience, or discusses ideas.
- Non-fiction is written for a specific audience, or group of readers. In addition, it addresses a clear purpose, or reason for writing. The audience and purpose influence the type of information a writer includes.
- Tone, the author's attitude toward the subject or reader, is displayed through the writer's word choice and style.

The writer contributes more than informal to non-fiction.

- Style is the particular way in which a writer uses language. Style reflects an author's personality. Factors that contribute to an author's style include level of formality, use of figurative language, diction or word choice, sentence patterns, and methods of organization.

- Tone is the author's attitude toward both the subject and readers or listeners. In conversations, you can hear a speaker's tone in the way words and phrases are spoken. When reading, you can "hear" tone in an author's choice of words and details. The tone of a literary work can often be described with a single word such as: pompous, playful, serious, personal, sarcastic, or friendly.
- Perspective is the viewpoint or opinion an author expresses about the subject, either directly or indirectly. Bias occurs when a writer makes a one-sided presentation (for example, by ignoring relevant facts or by using emotional language that unfairly sways readers' or listeners' feelings).
- Purpose is the author's reason for writing. Common purposes are to inform, to persuade, to honour, to entertain, to explain, and to warn.

Types of Non-Fiction (Prose)

There are four main types, or modes, of non-fiction that are defined by their purposes.

- Narrative non-fiction tells stories of real-life events. Examples include autobiographies and memoirs. Some narrative non-fiction is reflective writing, which shares the writer's thoughts and feelings about a personal experience, an idea, or a concern. Examples include reflective essays, personal essays, and journals.
- Expository non-fiction informs or explains. Examples include analytical essays and research reports.
- Persuasive non-fiction presents reasons and evidence to convince the reader to act or think in a certain way. Examples include editorials and political speeches.
- Descriptive non-fiction uses details related to the senses to create mental images for the reader. Examples include character sketches and scientific observations.

NON-FICTION OR PROSE AND ITS MAJOR FORMS

The following are the Major Forms of Prose :

1. Long Prose-Works
2. The Essay
3. The Periodical Journals
4. The Biography
5. The Autobiography
6. The Memoirs

LONG PROSE-WORKS

In its ordinary and practical sense, Prose is the sustained use of language as we ordinary speak it. Prose is different from verse in the sense that it is not split up into meter or stanza forms like the verse. However, the lack of meter does not mean that prose has no art or aesthetic sense. The writing of distinguished prose has as much art as the writing of distinguished verse. In all literatures, written prose developed much later than written verse. Good prose has high aesthetic value, and it can fully make use of all figures of speech. Good prose can also have high poetic cadence too, as the prose of the Bible.

Many forms of literature are normally written in prose only. They include long social, religious, scientific, or metaphysical treatises, essays, prose romances, novels, short stories, biographies, autobiographies, memoirs, travelogues, adventures and literary criticism.

Many great authors wrote long prose-works even before the Age of Chaucer. They included long religious, metaphysical, political, and biographical treatises and prose-romances. The trend has come down ever since to the present day.

Some Examples of the great prose-works are:

Chaucer's : *The Treatise on the Astrolabe,*

Wyclif's : *The Bible,*

and Walter Pater's : *Renaissance*

THE ESSAY

An essay is generally a short piece of writing written from an author's personal point of view, but the definition is vague, overlapping with those of an article, a pamphlet and a short story.

Essays can consist of a number of elements, including: literary criticism, political manifestos, learned arguments, observations of daily life, recollections, and reflections of the author. Almost all modern essays are written in prose, but works in verse have been dubbed essays (e.g. Alexander Pope's *An Essay on Criticism* and *An Essay on Man*). While brevity usually defines an essay, voluminous works like John Locke's *An Essay Concerning Human Understanding* and Thomas Malthus's *An Essay on the Principle of Population* are counter examples.

THE PERIODICAL JOURNALS

A journal has several related meanings: a daily record of events or business; a private journal is usually referred to as a diary, a newspaper or other periodical, in the literal sense of one published each day many publications issued at stated intervals, such as magazines, or scholarly journals, academic journals, or the record of the transactions of a society, are often called journals. Although journal is sometimes used as a synonym for "magazine" in academic use, a journal refers to a serious, scholarly publication that is peer-reviewed. A non-scholarly magazine written for an educated audience about an industry or an area of professional activity is usually called a professional magazine.

The word "journalist", for one whose business is writing for the public press and nowadays also other media, has been in use since the end of the 17th century.

THE BIOGRAPHY

A biography or simply bio is a detailed description or account of a person's life. It entails more than basic facts like education, work, relationships, and death—a biography also portrays a subject's experience of these events. Unlike a profile or curriculum vitae (résumé), a biography presents a subject's life story, highlighting various aspects of his or her life, including intimate details of experience, and may include an analysis of the subject's personality.

Biographical works are usually non-fiction, but fiction can also be used to portray a person's life. One in-depth form of biographical coverage is called legacy writing. Works in diverse media—from literature to film—form the genre known as biography.

An authorized biography is written with the permission, cooperation, and at times, participation of a subject or a subject's heirs.

THE AUTOBIOGRAPHY

An autobiography is a written account of the life of a person written by that person. An autobiography is written by the person themselves or sometimes with the assistance of a collaborator or ghostwriter.

THE MEMOIRS

Memoir (from French: *mémoire: memoria*, meaning memory or reminiscence), is a literary non-fiction genre. More specifically, it is a collection of memories that an individual writes about moments or events, both public or private that took place in the author's life. The assertions made in the work are understood to be factual. While memoir has historically been defined as a subcategory of autobiography since the late 20th century, the genre is differentiated in form, presenting a narrowed focus. Like most autobiographies, memoirs are written from the first-person point of view. An autobiography tells the story of a life, while memoir tells a story from a life, such as touchstone events and turning points from the author's life. The author of a memoir may be referred to as a memoirist.

POETRY

A poem is a literary composition that is given intensity by particular attention to diction (sometimes involving rhyme), rhythm, and imagery. Poems, collectively are called poetry.

As writing poetry is an art, reading poetry also is an art. We cannot enjoy reading anything without understanding it. And understanding poetry requires a special taste and aesthetic sense. Poetry is the language of heart. It flows from heart to heart.

POETRY AND ITS MAJOR FORMS

Poetry and its Major Forms are these :

1. The Epic
2. The Mock Epic
3. The Sonnet
4. The Ode
5. The Lyric
6. The Idyll
7. The Pastoral
8. The Elegy
9. The Pastoral Elegy
10. The Ballad
11. The Satire

THE EPIC

An epic (from the Ancient Greek adjective "word, story, poem" is a lengthy narrative poem, ordinarily concerning a serious subject containing details of heroic deeds and events significant to a culture or nation. Oral poetry may qualify as an epic, and Albert Lord and Milman Parry have argued that classical epics were fundamentally an oral poetic form. Nonetheless, epics have been written down at least since the works of Virgil, Dante Alighieri, and John Milton. Many probably would not have survived if not written down. The first epics are known as primary, or original, epics. One such epic is the Old English story Beowulf. Epics that attempt to imitate these like Milton's *Paradise Lost* are known as literary, or secondary, epics. Another type of epic poetry is epyllion (plural: epyllia), which is a brief narrative poem with a romantic or mythological theme. The term, which means 'little epic', came into use in the nineteenth century. It refers primarily to the erudite, shorter hexameter poems of the Hellenistic period and the similar works composed at Rome from the age of the neoterics; to a lesser degree, the term includes some poems of the English Renaissance, particularly those influenced by Ovid. The most famous example of classical epyllion is perhaps *Catullus 64*.

In the East, the most famous works of epic poetry are the *Ramayana* and *Mahabharata*, with the *Iliad* and the *Odyssey*, which form part of the Western canon, fulfilling the same function in the Western world.

Oral epics or world folk epics

The first epics were products of preliterate societies and oral poetic traditions. In these traditions, poetry is transmitted to the audience and from performer to performer by purely oral means.

Early twentieth-century study of living oral epic traditions in the Balkans by Milman Parry and Albert Lord demonstrated the paratactic model used for composing these poems. What they demonstrated was that oral epics tend to be constructed in short episodes, each of equal status, interest and importance. This facilitates memorization, as the poet is recalling each episode in turn and using the completed episodes to recreate the entire epic as he performs it.

THE MOCK EPIC

A poem which deals with slight and trivial subjects but employs the elevated and dignified conventions of epic poetry. Thus, such a poem becomes a satire, a mockery, a burlesque at the inconsistency of the subject to its representation. The characteristic conventions of the epic poetry, such as invocations, epic similes, grand and elevated language, battles and supernatural machinery, are comically used in mock-epic, which make the trivial subject ridiculous. A few well-known examples are Alexander Pope's *Rape of the Lock*, Jonathan Swift's *Battle of the Books*, Pope's *The Dunciad*, Chaucer's *The Nun's Priest's Tale* and Boileau's" *Le Lutrin* (French).

THE SONNET

A sonnet is a form of poetry that originated in Europe, mainly Italy: the Sicilian poet Giacomo da Lentini is credited with its invention. They commonly contain 14 lines. The term "sonnet" derives only from the Occitan word *sonet* and the Italian word *sonetto*, both meaning "little song" or "little sound". By the thirteenth century, it signified a poem of fourteen lines that follows a strict rhyme scheme and specific structure. Conventions associated with the sonnet have evolved over its history. Writers of sonnets are sometimes called "sonneteers," although the term can be used derisively. One of the best-known sonnet writers is William Shakespeare, who wrote 154 of them (not including those that appear in his plays). A Shakespearean, or English sonnet consists of 14 lines, each line containing ten syllables and written in iambic pentameter, in which a pattern of an unstressed syllable followed by a stressed syllable is repeated five times. The rhyme scheme in a Shakespearean sonnet is a-b-a-b, c-d-c-d, e-f-e-f, g-g; the last two lines are a rhyming couplet.

Traditionally, English poets employ iambic pentameter when writing sonnets, but not all English sonnets have the same metrical structure: the first sonnet in Sir Philip Sidney's sequence *Astrophel and Stella*, for example, has 12 syllables: it is iambic hexameters, albeit with a turned first foot in several lines. In the Romance languages, the hendecasyllable and Alexandrine are the most widely used metres.

THE ODE

Ode (from the Ancient Greek is a type of lyrical verse. A classic ode is structured in three major parts: the strophe, the antistrophe, and the epode. Different forms such as the homostrophic ode and the irregular ode also exist. It is an elaborately structured poem praising or glorifying an event or individual, describing nature intellectually as well as emotionally.

Greek odes were originally poetic pieces accompanied by symphonic orchestras. As time passed on, they gradually became known as personal lyrical compositions whether sung (with or without musical instruments) or merely recited (always with accompaniment). For some, the primary instrument of choice was either the aulos or the lyre (the latter of which was the most revered instrument to the Ancient Greeks). The written ode, as it was practiced by the Romans, returned to the lyrical form of the Lesbian lyricists.

There are three typical forms of odes: the Pindaric, Horatian, and irregular. Pindaric odes follow the form and style of Pindar. Horatian odes follow conventions of Horace; the odes of Horace deliberately imitated the Greek lyricists such as Alcaeus and Anacreon. Odes by Catullus, as well as other poetry of Catullus, was particularly inspired by Sappho. Irregular odes are rhyming, but they do not employ the three-part form of the Pindaric ode nor the two- or four-line stanza of the Horatian ode.

English ode

An ode is typically a lyrical verse written in praise of, or dedicated to someone or something which captures the poet's interest or serves as an inspiration for the ode.

The initial model for English odes was Horace, who used the form to write meditative lyrics on various themes. The earliest odes in the English language, using the word in its strict form, were the Epithalamium and Prothalamium of Edmund Spenser.

In the 17th century the most important original odes in English are those of Abraham Cowley and Andrew Marvell. Marvell, in his Horatian Ode upon Cromwell's Return from Ireland uses a regular form (two four-foot lines followed by two three-foot lines) modelled on Horace, while Cowley wrote *"Pindarique"* odes which had irregular patterns of line lengths and rhyme schemes, though they were iambic. The principle of Cowley's *Pindariques* was based on a misunderstanding of Pindar's metrical practice but was widely imitated nonetheless, with notable success by John Dryden. With Pindar's metre being better understood in the 18th century, the fashion for Pindaric odes faded, though there are notable actual Pindaric odes by Thomas Gray, *The Progress of Poesy* and *The Bard*.

The Pindarick of Cowley was revived around 1800 by William Wordsworth for one of his very finest poems, the Intimations of Immortality ode; irregular odes were also written by Samuel Taylor Coleridge, John Keats, and Percy Bysshe Shelley who wrote odes with regular stanza patterns. Shelley's *Ode to the West Wind*, written in fourteen line terza rima stanzas, is a major poem in the form, but perhaps the greatest odes of the 19th century were Keats's *Five Great Odes* of 1819 which included *Ode to a Nightingale, Ode on Melancholy, Ode on a Grecian Urn, Ode to Psyche*, and *To Autumn*. After Keats, there have been comparatively few major odes in English. One major exception is the fourth verse of the poem *For the Fallen* by Laurence Binyon which is often known as *"The Ode to the Fallen"* or more simply as *"The Ode"*.

W.H. Auden also wrote *'Ode'*, one of his most popular poems from his earlier career when based in London, in opposition to people's ignorance over the reality of war. In interview Auden once stated that he had intended to title the poem *My Silver Age* in mockery of the supposedly imperial Golden age, however chose *'Ode'* as it seemed to provide a more sensitive exploration of warfare.

The English ode's most common rhyme scheme is ABABCDECDE.

THE LYRIC

Is a genre of poetry that expresses personal and emotional feelings. In the ancient world, lyric poems were sung, accompanied by a lyre a musical instrument. Lyric poems do not have to rhyme, and today do not need to be set to music or a beat. Aristotle, in *Poetics*, mentions lyric poetry (kitharistike played to the cithara, a type of lyre) along with drama, epic poetry, dancing, painting and other forms of mimesis. The lyric poem, dating from the Romantic era, does have some thematic antecedents in ancient Greek and Roman verse, but the ancient definition was based on metrical criteria, and in archaic and classical Greek culture presupposed live performance accompanied by a stringed instrument.

Although arguably the most popular form of lyric poetry in the Western tradition is the 14-line sonnet, either in its Petrarchan or its Shakespearean form, lyric poetry appears in a variety of forms. Other forms of the lyric include ballades, villanelles, odes, pastourelle and canzone.

Ancient Hebrew poetry relied on repetition, alliteration, and chiasmus for many of its effects. Ancient Greek and Roman lyric poetry was composed in strophes. Pindar's epinician odes, where strophe and antistrophe are followed by an epode, represent an expansion of the same basic principle. The Greeks distinguished, however, between lyric monody (e.g. Sappho, Anacreon) and choral lyric (e.g. Pindar, Bacchylides). In all such poetry the fundamental formal feature is the repetition of a metrical pattern larger than a verse or distich. In some cases (although not in antiquity), form and theme are wed in the conception of a genre, as in the medieval alva or aubade, a dawn song in which lovers must part after a night of love, often with the watchman's refrain telling them it is time to go. A common feature of some lyric forms is the refrain of one or more verses that end each strophe. The refrain is repeated throughout the poem, either exactly or with variation. In the medieval Galician-Portuguese *cantigas de amigo*, thought to reflect an old oral tradition, 90% of the texts have a refrain.

Lyric in European literature of the medieval or Renaissance period means a poem written so that it could be set to music—whether or not it is. A poem's particular structure, function or theme is not specified by the term. The lyric poetry of Europe in this period was created largely without reference to the classical past, by the pioneers of courtly poetry and courtly love. The troubadours, travelling composers and performers of songs, began to flourish towards the end of the 11th century and were often imitated in successive centuries. Trouveres were poet-composers who were roughly contemporary with and influenced by the troubadours but who composed their works in the northern dialects of France. The first known trouvere was Chretien de Troyes (1160s-80s). The dominant form of German lyric poetry in the period was the Minnesang, "a love lyric based essentially on a fictitious relationship between a knight and his high-born lady". Initially imitating the lyrics of the French troubadours and trouveres, Minnesang soon established a distinctive tradition. There is also a large body of medieval Galician-Portuguese lyric. Hebrew singer-poets of the Middle Ages include: Yehuda Halevi, Solomon ibn Gabirol and Abraham ibn Ezra.

In Italy, Petrarch developed the sonnet form pioneered by Giacomo da Lentini, which Dante used in his Vita Nuova. In 1327, according to the poet, the sight of a woman called Laura in the church of Sainte-Claire d'Avignon awoke in him a lasting passion, celebrated in the Rime sparse ("Scattered rhymes"). Later, Renaissance poets who copied Petrarch's style named this collection of 366 poems Il Canzoniere ("Song Book"). Laura is in many ways both the culmination of medieval courtly love poetry and the beginning of Renaissance love lyric.

The eighteenth and early nineteenth centuries constitute the period of the rise of Russian lyric poetry, exemplified by Aleksandr Pushkin. The Swedish "Phosphorists" were influenced by the Romantic movement and their chief poet, Per Daniel Amadeus Atterbom produced many lyric poems. Italian lyric poets of the period include Ugo Foscolo, Giacomo Leopardi, Giovanni Pascoli and Gabriele D'Annunzio. Japanese lyric poets include Taneda Santoka, Masaoka Shiki and Ishikawa Takuboku. Spanish lyric poets include Gustavo Adolfo Becquer, Rosalia de Castro and Jose de Espronceda.

THE IDYLL

A composition in verse or prose which describes scenes and incidents of country life which are simple, charming and appealing due to their idealised innocence and contentment. An idyll is a pastoral poem, and an ancient example is *Theocritus's Idylls* (in 3rd century B.C.) which describes the country life, and the charming rustic life of the Sicilians. John G. Whittler's *Maud Muller* is yet another example of an idyll.

THE PASTORAL

The originator of the pastoral was the Greek poet Theocritus, who in the third century BC wrote poems representing the life of Sicilian shepherds. ("Pastor" is Latin for "shepherd.") Virgil later imitated Theocritus in his Latin *Edogues*, and in doing so established the enduring model for the traditional pastoral a deliberately conventional poem expressing an urban poet's nostalgic image of the supposed peace and simplicity of the life of shepherds and other rural folk in an idealized natural setting. The conventions that hundreds of later poets imitated from Virgil's imitations of Theocritus include a shepherd reclining under a spreading beech tree and meditating on the rural muse, or piping as though he would ne'er grow old, or engaging in a friendly singing contest, or expressing his good or bad fortune in a love affair, or grieving over the death of a fellow shepherd. From this last type developed the pastoral elegy, which persisted long after the other traditional types had lost their popularity. Other terms often used synonymously with pastoral are idyll, from the title of Theocritus' pastorals; eclogue (literally, "a selection"), from the title of Virgil's pastorals; and bucolic poetry, from the Greek word for "herdsman."

Classical poets often described the pastoral life as possessing features of the mythical golden age. Christian pastoralists conjoined the golden age of pagan fable with the Garden of Eden in the Bible, and also exploited the religious symbolism of "shepherd" (applied to the ecclesiastical or parish "pastor," and to the figure of Christ as the Good Shepherd) to give many pastoral poems a Christian range of reference. In the Renaissance the traditional pastoral was also adapted to diverse satirical and allegorical uses. Edmund Spenser's *Shepherd's Calendar* (1579), which popularized the mode in English poetry, included most of the varieties of pastoral poems current in that period.

Such was the attraction of the pastoral dream that Renaissance writers incorporated it into various other literary forms. Sir Philip Sidney's *Arcadia* (1581 84) was a long pastoral romance written in an elaborately artful prose. (*Arcadia* was a mountainous region of Greece which Virgil substituted for Theocritus' Sicily as his idealized pastoral milieu.) There was also the pastoral lyric (Christopher Marlowe's *"The Passionate Shepherd to His Love"*), and the pastoral drama. John Fletcher's *The Faithful Shepherdess* is an example of this last type, and Shakespeare's *As You Like It*, based on the contemporary pastoral romance *Rosalynde* by Thomas Lodge, is set in the forest of Arden, a green refuge from the troubles and complications of ordinary life where enmities are reconciled, problems resolved, and the course of true love made to run smooth.

The last important series of traditional pastorals, and an extreme instance of their calculated and graceful display of high artifice, was Alexander Pope's *Pastorals* (1709). Five years later John Gay, in his Shepherd's Week, wrote a parody of the type by applying its elegant formulas to the crudity of actual rustic manners and language; by doing so, he inadvertently showed later poets the way to the seriously realistic treatment of rural life. In 1783 George Crabbe published *The Village* specifically in order to paint the cot. *As Truth* will paint it and as bards will not.

How far the term then lost its traditional application to a poetry of aristocratic artifice is indicated by Wordsworth's title for his realistic rendering of a rural tragedy in 1800: *"Michael, A Pastoral Poem"*.

THE ELEGY

A lament or a meditative poem, often written on the occasion of a death or other solemn event or theme. Although an elegy may appear as a discrete section in a larger work (as in the oration at the funeral of Beowulf), it is usually a complete poem in a formal style. A famous example is Thomas Gray's *"Elegy Written in a Country Churchyard"* (1751), whose thirty-two stanzas ruminate upon the passing of time and souls:

Can storied urn or animated bust
    Back to its mansion call the fleeting breath?
Can Honor's voice provoke the silent dust,
    Or Flattery soothe the dull cold ear of Death?

Perhaps in this neglected spot is laid
    Some heart once pregnant with celestial fire;
Hands that the rod of empire might have swayed,
    Or waked to ecstasy the living lyre.

THE PASTORAL ELEGY

One kind of elegy that is especially important in English literary history is the pastoral elegy, whose highlights include John Milton's *"Lycidas"* (1637) and Percy Bysshe Shelley's *"Adonais"* (an elegy for the dead John Keats, 1821). Pastoral elegies combine pastoral themes and images—nature deities, seasonal vegetation—with a memorialization of a deceased friend or comrade.

THE BALLAD

A ballad is a form of verse, often a narrative set to music. Ballads were particularly characteristic of the popular poetry and song of the British Isles from the later medieval period until the 19th century and used extensively across Europe and later the Americas, Australia and North Africa. Many ballads were written and sold as single sheet broadsides. The form was often used by poets and composers from the 18th century onwards to produce lyrical ballads. In the later 19th century it took on the meaning of a slow form of popular love song and the term is now often used as synonymous with any love song, particularly the pop or rock power ballad.

Most northern and west European ballads are written in ballad stanzas or quatrains (four-line stanzas) of alternating lines of iambic (an unstressed followed by a stressed syllable) tetrameter (eight syllables) and iambic trimeter (six syllables), known as ballad meter. Usually, only the second and fourth line of a quatrain are rhymed (in the scheme a, b, c, b), which has been taken to suggest that, originally, ballads consisted of couplets (two lines) of rhymed verse, each of 14 syllables. As can be seen in this stanza from *'Lord Thomas and Fair Annet'*:

The horse| fair Ann|et rode| upon|
He amb|led like| the wind|,
With sil|ver he| was shod| before,
With burn|ing gold| behind|.

However, there is considerable variation on this pattern in almost every respect, including length, number of lines and rhyming scheme, making the strict definition of a ballad extremely difficult. In southern and eastern Europe, and in countries that derive their tradition from them, ballad structure differs significantly, like Spanish romances, which are octosyllabic and use consonance rather than rhyme.

In all traditions most ballads are narrative in nature, with a self-contained story, often concise and relying on imagery, rather than description, which can be tragic, historical, romantic or comic. Another common feature of ballads is repetition, sometimes of fourth lines in succeeding stanzas, as a refrain, sometimes of third and fourth lines of a stanza and sometimes of entire stanzas.

THE SATIRE

Satire can be described as the literary art of diminishing or derogating a subject by making it ridiculous and evoking toward it attitudes of amusement, contempt, scorn, or indignation. It differs from the *comic* in that comedy evokes laughter mainly as an end in itself, while satire derides; that is, it uses laughter as a weapon, and against a butt that exists outside the work itself. That butt may be an individual (in "personal satire"), or a type of person, a class, an institution, a nation, or even (as in the Earl of Rochester's *"A Satyr against Mankind,"* 1675, and much of Jonathan Swift's *Gulliver's Travels*, 1726, especially Book IV) the entire human race. The distinction between the comic and the satiric, however, is sharp only at its extremes. Shakespeare's *Falstaff* is mainly a comic creation, presented primarily for our enjoyment; the puritanical Malvolio in Shakespeare's *Twelfth Night* is for the most part comic but has aspects of satire directed against the type of the fatuous and hypocritical Puritan; Ben Jonson's *Volpone* (1607) clearly satirizes the type of person whose cleverness—or stupidity—is put at the service of his cupidity; and John Dryden's *MacFlecknoe* (1682), while representing a permanent type of the pretentious poetaster, satirized specifically the living author Thomas Shadwell.

Satire has usually been justified, by those who practice it, as a corrective of human vice and folly; Alexander Pope, for example, remarked that "those who are ashamed of nothing else are so of being ridiculous." Its frequent claim (not always borne out in the practice) has been to ridicule the failing rather than the individual, and to limit its ridicule to corrigible faults, excluding those for which a person is not responsible. As Swift said, speaking of himself in his ironic *"Verses on the Death of Dr. Swift"* (1739):

Yet malice never was his aim;
He lashed the vice, but spared the name....
His satire points at no defect,
But what all mortals may correct....
He spared a hump, or crooked nose,
Whose owners set not up for beaux.

Satire occurs as an incidental element within many works whose overall mode is not satiric—in a certain character or situation, or in an interpolated passage of ironic commentary on some aspect of the human condition or of contemporary society. But for some literary writings, verse or prose, the attempt to diminish a subject by ridicule is the organizing principle of the whole, and these works constitute the formal genre labeled.

NOVEL

A novel is a book of long narrative in literary prose. The genre has historical roots both in the fields of the medieval and early modern romance and in the tradition of the novella. The latter supplied the present generic term in the late 18th century.

Further definition of the genre is historically difficult. The construction of the narrative, the plot, the way reality is created in the works of fiction, the fascination of the character study, and the use of language are usually discussed to show a novel's artistic merits. Most of these requirements were introduced in the 16th and 17th centuries, in order to give fiction a justification outside the field of factual history. The individualism of the presentation makes the personal memoir and the autobiography the two closest relatives among the genres of modern histories.

NOVEL AND ITS MAJOR FORMS

The following are the Major Forms of the Novel :

1. The Prose Romances
2. The Travelogues
3. The Gothic Novel
4. The Picaresque Novel
5. The Epistolary Novel
6. The Domestic Novel
7. The Historical Novel
8. The Regional Novel
9. The Prophetic Novel
10. The Psychological Novel
11. The Short Story

THE PROSE ROMANCES

Romances in verse were written much earlier than the Romances in prose. Prose Romances are the earliest form of the novel. They are simply fantasies in which the authors make the fullest use of their imagination and fancy and create an ideal world which bears little or no semblance with real life. The earliest of them is the famous *Morte d' Arthur*, the legends retold by Sir Thomas Malory in prose. This takes us back to the legendary world of knighthood and chivalry. The other sixteenth century prose romances are Lyly's *Euphues* in two parts and Sidney's *Arcadia*, a pastoral romance, conceiving a dream-land of pre fancy. Lodge's *Rosalynde* is a love-romance, so is also Robert Greene's *Pandosto*, Bacon's *The New Atlantis* is also a prose romance.

THE TRAVELOGUES

The novel proper started in a limited sense with Travelogues. The travelogues are travel-stories relating the adventures of the travelers or voyagers in unknown and unchartered seas. They often land on uninhabited islands or some islands inhabited by strange creatures. The earliest of them is Daniel Defoe's *Robinson Crusoe*. Robinson Crusoe lands on an uninhabited island and somehow managers to live there for several years, until he is rescued from there by a lucky chance by a passing ship of his own country. Another famous travelogue is Jonathan Swift's *Gulliver's Travels*. In this romance Gulliver lands on several islands inhabited by such strange creatures as the Lilliputians, Houynhnms, Brobdingnags, and Yahoos. However, Swift's episodes in these adventures have very pungent satire on contemporary political situations.

THE GOTHIC NOVEL

Derived from the word 'Goths' used for a Germanic tribe, the Gothic novel has supernatural elements like ghosts, haunted houses, etc. which induces horror, apprehension and insecurity. Examples – Horace Walpole's *Castle of Otranto, a Gothic Story*, Ann Radcliff's *The Mysteries of Udolpho*, etc.

THE PICARESQUE NOVEL

The picaresque novel (Spanish: "picaresca," from "picaro," for "rogue" or "rascal") is a popular sub-genre of prose fiction which is usually satirical and depicts, in realistic and often humorous detail, the adventures of a roguish hero of low social class who lives by his wits in a corrupt society. This style of novel originated in sixteenth century Spain and flourished throughout Europe in the seventeenth and eighteenth centuries. It continues to influence modern literature.

The word picaro starts to first appear in Spain with the current meaning in 1545. The word picaro does not appear in *Lazarillo de Tormes* (1554), the novella credited with founding the genre. The expression picaresque novel was coined in 1810.

The character type of Lazarillo, which determines the story and the so-called picaresque novel genre, has been shaped from characterization elements already present in Roman literature. With Petronius' *Satyricon*, Lazarillo takes some of the traits of the central figure of Encolpius, a former gladiator. but it is unlikely that the author had access to Petronius' work; from the comedies of Plautus, it borrows from the figure of the parasite and the supple slave; other traits are taken from Apuleius's *The Golden Ass*. *The Golden Ass* and *Satyricon* were particularly revived and widely read in renaissance Europe, and are rare surviving samples of a mostly lost genre, which was highly popular in the classical world, known as *"Milesian tales"*.

Arabic literature, which was read widely in Spain in the time of Al-Andalus and possessed a literary tradition with similar themes, is another possible formative influence on the picaresque style. *Al-Hamadhani* (d.1008) of Hamadhan (Iran) is credited with inventing the literary genre of maqamat in which a wandering vagabond makes his living on the gifts his listeners give him following his extemporaneous displays of rhetoric, erudition, or verse, often done with a trickster's touch *Ibn al-Astarkuwi* or *al-Ashtarkuni* (d.1134) also wrote in the genre maqamat, comparable to later European picaresque novels. While elements of Chaucer and Boccaccio have a picaresque feel and are likely to have contributed to the style, the modern picaresque begins with Lazarillo de Tormes, which was published anonymously in Antwerp and Spain in 1554. It is variously considered either the first picaresque novel or at least the antecedent of the genre. The title character, Lazarillo, is a picaro who must live by his wits in an impoverished country full of hypocrisy.

The autobiography of Benvenuto Cellini, written in Florence beginning in 1558, also has much in common with the picaresque. Another early example is Mateo Aleman's *Guzman de Alfarache* (1599), characterized by religiosity.

Francisco de Quevedo's *El buscon* (1604 according to Francisco Rico; the exact date is uncertain, yet it was certainly a very early work) is considered the masterpiece of the subgenre by A.A. Parker, because of his baroque style and the study of the delinquent psychology. However, a more recent school of thought, led by Francisco Rico, rejects Parker's view, contending instead that the protagonist, Pablos, is a highly unrealistic character, simply a means for Quevedo to launch classist, racist and sexist attacks. Moreover, argues Rico, the structure of the novel is radically different from previous works of the picaresque genre: Quevedo uses the conventions of the picaresque as a mere vehicle to show off his abilities with conceit and rhetoric, rather than to construct a satirical critique of Spanish Golden Age society.

Indeed, in order to understand the historical context that led to the development of these paradigmatic picaresque novels in Spain during the sixteenth and seventeenth centuries, it is essential to take into consideration the circumstances surrounding the lives of conversos, whose ancestors had been Jewish, and whose New Christian faith was subjected to close scrutiny and mistrust. In other European countries, these Spanish novels were read and imitated. In Germany, Grimmelshausen wrote *Simplicius Simplicissimus* (1669), the most important of non-Spanish picaresque novels. It describes the devastation caused by the Thirty Years' War. In Le Sage's *Gil Blas* (1715) is a classic example of the genre, which in France had declined into an aristocratic adventure. In Britain, the body of Tobias Smollett's work, and Daniel Defoe's *Moll Flanders* (1722) are considered picaresque, but they lack the sense of religious redemption of delinquency that was very important in Spanish and German novels. The triumph of *Moll Flanders* is more economic than moral.

The classic Chinese novel *Journey to the West* is considered to have considerable picaresque elements. Having been written in 1590, it is contemporary with much of the above - but is unlikely to have been directly influenced by the European genre.

THE EPISTOLARY NOVEL

An epistolary novel is a novel written as a series of documents. The usual form is letters, although diary entries, newspaper clippings and other documents are sometimes used. Recently, electronic "documents" such as recordings and radio, blogs, and e-mails have also come into use. The word epistolary is derived through Latin from the Greek word *epistole*, meaning a letter.

The epistolary form can add greater realism to a story, because it mimics the workings of real life. It is thus able to demonstrate differing points of view without recourse to the device of an omniscient narrator.

There are two theories on the genesis of the epistolary novel. The first claims that the genre originated from novels with inserted letters, in which the portion containing the third person narrative in between the letters was gradually reduced. The other theory claims that the epistolary novel arose from miscellanies of letters and poetry: some of the letters were tied together into a (mostly amorous) plot. Both claims have some validity. The first truly epistolary novel, the Spanish *"Prison of Love" (Carcel de amor)* (c.1485) by Diego de San Pedro, belongs to a tradition of novels in which a large number of inserted letters already dominated the narrative. Other well-known examples of early epistolary novels are closely related to the tradition of letter-books and miscellanies of letters. Within the successive editions of Edme Boursault's *Letters of Respect, Gratitude and Love (Lettres de respect, d'obligation et d 'amour)* (1669), a group of letters written to a girl named Babet was expanded and became more and more distinct from the other letters, until it formed a small epistolary novel entitled *Letters to Babet (Lettres a Babet)*. The immensely famous Letters of a Portuguese Nun *(Lettres portugaises)* (1669) generally attributed to Gabriel-Joseph de La Vergne, comte de Guilleragues, though a small minority still regard Marianna Alcoforado as the author, is claimed to be intended to be part of a miscellany of Guilleragues prose and poetry. The founder of the epistolary novel in English is said by many to be James Howell (1594–1666) with *"Familiar Letters"*, who writes of prison, foreign adventure, and the love of women.

The first novel to expose the complex play that the genre allows was Aphra Behn's *Love-Letters Between a Nobleman and His Sister* (1684), which appeared in three successive volumes in 1684, 1685, and 1687. The novel shows the genre's results of changing perspectives: individual points were presented by the individual characters, and the central voice of the author and moral evaluation disappeared (at least in the first volume; her further volumes introduced a narrator). Behn furthermore explored a realm of intrigue with letters that fall into the wrong hands, with faked letters, with letters withheld by protagonists, and even more complex interaction.

The epistolary novel as a genre became popular in the 18th century in the works of such authors as Samuel Richardson, with his immensely successful novels *Pamela* (1740) and *Clarissa* (1749). In France, there was *Lettres persanes* (1721) by Montesquieu, followed by *Julie, ou la nouvelle Heloise* (1761) by Jean-Jacques Rousseau, and Laclos' *Les Liaisons dangereuses* (1782), which used the epistolary form to great dramatic effect, because the sequence of events was not always related directly or explicitly. In Germany, there was Johann Wolfgang von Goethe's *Die Leiden des jungen Werthers* (1774) *(The Sorrows of Young Werther)* and Friedrich Holderlin's *Hyperion*. The first North American novel, *The History of Emily Montague* (1769) by Frances Brooke was written in epistolary form.

Starting in the 18th century, the epistolary form was subject to much ridicule, resulting in a number of savage burlesques. The most notable example of these was Henry Fielding's *Shamela* (1741), written as a parody of Pamela. In it, the female narrator can be found wielding a pen and scribbling her diary entries under the most dramatic and unlikely of circumstances.

The epistolary novel slowly fell out of use in the late 18th century. Although Jane Austen tried her hand at the epistolary in juvenile writings and her novella *Lady Susan*, she abandoned this structure for her later work. It is thought that her lost novel *"First Impressions"*, which was redrafted to become *Pride and Prejudice*, may have been epistolary: *Pride and Prejudice* contains an unusual number of letters quoted in full and some play a critical role in the plot.

The epistolary form nonetheless saw continued use, surviving in exceptions or in fragments in nineteenth-century novels. In Honore de Balzac's novel *Letters of Two Brides*, two women who became friends during their education at a convent correspond over a 17 year period, exchanging letters describing their lives. Mary Shelley employs the epistolary form in her novel *Frankenstein* (1818). Shelley uses the letters as one of a variety of framing devices, as the story is presented through the letters of a sea captain and scientific explorer attempting to reach the north pole who encounters Victor Frankenstein and records the dying man's narrative and confessions. In the late 19th century, Bram Stoker released one of the most widely recognized and successful novels in the epistolary form to date, *Dracula*. Printed in 1897, the novel is compiled entirely of letters, diary entries, newspaper clippings, telegrams, doctor's notes, ship's logs, and the like, which Stoker adroitly employs to balance believability and dramatic tension.

There are three types of epistolary novels: monologic (giving the letters of only one character, like *Letters of a Portuguese Nun*), dialogic (giving the letters of two characters, like *Mme Marie Jeanne Riccoboni's Letters of Fanni Butlerd* (1757), and polylogic (with three or more letter-writing characters). In addition, a crucial element in polylogic epistolary novels like *Clarissa*, and *Dangerous Liaisons* is the dramatic device of 'discrepant awareness': the simultaneous but separate correspondences of the heroines and the villains creating dramatic tension.

THE DOMESTIC NOVEL

The Domestic Novels as their title suggests, present the day-to-day life of the average of middle-class families. The life-patterns of the members of a family and their relations with their friends and neighbours are artistically presented in these novels. The festivals and festivities, functions and celebrations, birthdays, nuptials, and marriages are graphically described in these novels. Jane Austen is the most important writer of the domestic novels. Her *Pride and Prejudice, Sense and Sensibility* and *Emma* are the best examples of domestic novels.

THE HISTORICAL NOVEL

A novel that has as its setting a usually significant period of history and that attempts to convey the spirit, manners, and social conditions of a past age with realistic detail and fidelity (which is in some cases only apparent fidelity) to historical fact. The work may deal with actual historical personages...or it may contain a mixture of fictional and historical characters.

An early example of historical prose fiction is Luo Guanzhong's *14th century Romance of the Three Kingdoms*, which covers one of the most important periods of Chinese history and left a lasting impact on Chinese culture.

The historical novel was further popularized in the 19th century by writers classified as Romantics. Many regard Sir Walter Scott as the first to write historical novels. Gyorgy Lukacs, in his *The Historical Novel*, argues that Scott is the first fiction writer who saw history not just as a convenient frame in which to stage a contemporary narrative, but rather as a distinct social and cultural setting. His novels of Scottish history such as *Waverley* (1814) and *Rob Roy* (1817) focus upon a middling character who sits at the intersection of various social groups in order to explore the development of society through conflict. His *Ivanhoe* (1820) gains credit for renewing interest in the Middle Ages. Victor Hugo's *The Hunchback of Notre Dame* (1831) furnishes another 19th century example of the romantic-historical novel as does Leo Tolstoy's *War and Peace*. In the United States, James Fenimore Cooper was a prominent author of historical novels. In French literature, the most prominent inheritor of Scott's style of the historical novel was *Balzac*.

Though the genre has evolved since its inception, the historical novel remains popular with authors and readers to this day; bestsellers include Patrick O'Brian's *Aubrey–Maturin* series, Ken Follett's *Pillars of the Earth*, and Neal Stephenson's *Baroque Cycle*. A striking development in British/Irish writing in the past 25 years has been the renewed interest in the First World War. Works include William Boyd's *An Ice-Cream War*; Sebastian Faulks' *Birdsong* and *The Girl at the Lion d'Or* (concerned with the War's consequences); Pat Barker's *Regeneration Trilogy* and Sebastian Barry's *A Long Long Way*.

Many early historical novels played an important role in the rise of European popular interest in the history of the Middle Ages. Hugo's *Hunchback* often receives credit for fueling the movement to preserve the Gothic architecture of France, leading to the establishment of the Monuments historiques, the French governmental authority for historic preservation.

The genre of the historical novel has also permitted some authors, such as the Polish novelist Boleslaw Prus in his sole historical novel, *Pharaoh*, to distance themselves from their own time and place to gain perspective on society and on the human condition, or to escape the depredations of the censor.

In some historical novels, major historic events take place mostly off-stage, while the fictional characters inhabit the world where those events occur. Robert Louis Stevenson's *Kidnapped* recounts mostly private adventures set against the backdrop of the Jacobite troubles in Scotland. Charles Dickens's *Barnaby Rudge* is set amid the Gordon Riots, and *A Tale of Two Cities* in the French Revolution.

In some works, the accuracy of the historical elements has been questioned, as in Alexandre Dumas' *Queen Margot*. Postmodern novelists such as John Barth and Thomas Pynchon operate with even more freedom, mixing historical characters and settings with invented history and fantasy, as in the novels *The Sot-Weed Factor* and *Mason & Dixon* respectively. A few writers create historical fiction without fictional characters. One example is *I, Claudius*, by 20th century writer Robert Graves; another is the *Masters of Rome* series by Colleen McCullough.

THE REGIONAL NOVEL

This type of novel is set in a particular geographical section and deals with the living and culture of that area. Examples are: Thomas Hardy's *Wessex*, R.K.Narayan's *Malgudi*, etc.

These are the common types of novel. Apart from these there are many more varieties that excel in creating the literature of the time and making the essence of novel more dedicated and authentic in the present scenario.

THE PROPHETIC NOVEL

The Prophetic novels try to forecast what the future would be like. These novels do not claim to be absolutely correct or authentic. They only give us a tentative picture of the future on the basis of the tendencies prevailing in the present. Aidous Huxley in the Brave New World envisaged in 1932 a future in which the entire populace would be mentally conditioned by the totalitarian despots.

THE PSYCHOLOGICAL NOVEL

A Psychological fiction is a specific sub-genre of the wide ranging thriller genre. This genre often incorporates elements from the mystery genre in addition to the typical traits of the thriller genre. Usually thrillers focus on plot over fictional characters, emphasizing on intense physical action over the character's psyche. Psychological thrillers tend to reverse this formula to a certain degree, emphasizing the characters just as much if not more so than the plot. psychological novel, also called psychological realism, is a work of prose fiction which places more than the usual amount of emphasis on interior characterization, and on the motives, circumstances, and internal action which springs from, and develops, external action. The psychological novel is not content to state what happens but goes on to explain the motivation of this action. In this type of writing character and characterization are more than usually important, and they often delve deeper into the mind of a character than novels of other genres. The psychological novel can be called a novel of the "inner man," so to say. In some cases, the stream of consciousness technique, as well as interior monologues, may be employed to better illustrate the inner workings of the human mind at work. Flashbacks may also be featured. While these three textual techniques are also prevalent in "modernism," there is no deliberate effort to fragment the prose or compel the reader to interpret the text.

The Tale of Genji, written in 11th century Japan, has often been considered the first psychological novel. In the west, the origins of the psychological novel can be traced as far back as Giovanni Boccaccio's 1344 *Elegia di Madonna Fiammetta;* that is before the term psychology was coined.

THE SHORT STORY

A short story is a work of fiction that is usually written in prose, often in narrative format. A short story usually deals with a few characters and often concentrates on the creation of the mood rather than the plot.

The short story format tends to be more pointed than longer works of fiction, such as novellas (in the 20th and 21st century sense) and novels. Short story definitions based on length differ somewhat, even among professional writers, in part because of the fragmentation of the medium into genres. Since the short story format includes a wide range of genres and styles, the actual length is determined by the individual author's preference (or the story's actual needs in terms of creative trajectory or story arc) and the submission guidelines relevant to the story's actual market. Guidelines vary greatly among publishers.

Many short story writers define their work through a combination of creative, personal expression, and artistic integrity. They attempt to resist categorization by genre as well as definition by numbers, finding such approaches limiting and counter-intuitive to artistic form and reasoning. As a result, definitions of the short story based on length splinter even more when the writing process is taken into consideration.

A short story is often judged by its ability to provide a complete or satisfying treatment of its characters and subject. Fiction, such as novellas (in the 20th and 21st century sense) and novels. Short story definitions based on length differ somewhat, even among professional writers, in part because of the fragmentation of the medium into genres. Since the short story format includes a wide range of genres and styles, the actual length is determined by the individual author's preference (or the story's actual needs in terms of creative trajectory or story arc) and the submission guidelines relevant to the story's actual market. Guidelines vary greatly among publishers.

Many short story writers define their work through a combination of creative, personal expression, and artistic integrity. They attempt to resist categorization by genre as well as definition by numbers, finding such approaches limiting and counter-intuitive to artistic form and reasoning. As a result, definitions of the short story based on length splinter even more when the writing process is taken into consideration.

MULTIPLE CHOICE QUESTIONS

1. Which of the following is the oldest form of literature?
A. Drama B. Novel
C. Poetry D. Prose

2. The term 'drama' originates from which language?
A. English B. Arabic
C. Sanskrit D. Greek

3. 'Drama' originated in ______.
A. Greece B. Rome
C. London D. India

4. Which one of these is not a type of drama?
A. The Tragedy B. The Farce
C. The Masque D. The Ballad

5. Which one of these is a type of drama?
A. The Epic B. The Ode
C. The Farce D. The Satire

6. Which one is a prose work?
A. The Epic B. The Memoirs
C. The Idyll D. The Elegy

7. Which one of the following is not a prose work?
A. The Farce B. The Essay
C. The Biography D. The Memoirs

8. Which one is a major poetry form?
A. The Farce B. The Gothic
C. The Pastoral D. The Masque

9. Which one of the following is not a poetic form?
A. The Epic B. The Lyric
C. The Idyll D. The Farce

10. Which one is a major novel form?
A. The Melodrama B. The Tragedy
C. The Pastoral D. The Travelogues

11. Which one is not a major form of novel?
A. The Travelogue B. Gothic
C. Picaresque D. The Tragedy

12. Interlude is a type of ______.
A. Novel B. Poetry form
C. Prose form D. Drama

13. A sonnet is a form of ______.
A. Poetry B. Drama
C. Novel D. Prose

14. Shakespearan sonnet contains ______ lines.
A. four B. six
C. twelve D. fourteen

15. An ode is a ______.
A. Drama B. Novel
C. Poetry D. Prose

16. A ballad is a form of ______.
A. Prose B. Poetry
C. Novel D. Drama

17. A satire is a form of ______.
A. Poetry B. Prose
C. Drama D. Novel

18. Which one is a form of novel?
A. The Prophetic B. The Farce
C. The Masque D. The Elegy

19. Which one is not a form of novel?
A. Epistolary B. Regional
C. Pastoral D. Psychological

20. The elegy is a form of ______.
A. Drama B. Prose
C. Poetry D. Novel

21. Why were the *Interludes* introduced?
A. They pleased the common class of the spectators
B. They provided comic relief
C. They had better theatrical effect
D. They dealt with the real problems of life

22. The *Mystery Plays* deal with—
A. Heaven and Hell
B. Moral values
C. Biblical Themes
D. The life and deeds of the saints

23. Who is the author of *The Spanish Tragedy*?
A. Christopher Marlowe B. Thomas Kyd
C. Robert Greene D. George Peele

24. Which of the following plays is written by George Peele?
A. *Titus Andronicus*
B. *Jocasta*
C. *The Spanish Tragedy*
D. *The Wounds of Civil War*

25. What is the function of the *Chorus* in a play?
A. The Chorus is a band of singers who sing
B. The Chorus comes to declare the ending of an Act
C. The Chorus explains the past and the future events in the play
D. The Chorus represents the views of the dramatist

26. John Heywood's *Interlude* entitled 4PP (or 4P's) caricatures four professionals whose professions begins with P. In the four professionals listed below, which one is wrong?
A. The Piper B. The Palmer
C. The Pedlar D. The Pardoner

27. How many Dramatic Unities were recommended by the Greeks?
A. One central unity
B. No number fixed
C. Three dramatic unities
D. Two dramatic unities

28. In which one of the following plays the *Epilogue* appears?
A. *Dr. Faustus*
B. *Midsummer Night's Dream*
C. *Hamlet*
D. *As You Like it*

29. The *Miracle Plays* principally deal with the miracles performed by—
A. Supernatural powers
B. Personified Vices and Virtues
C. Saints and Sages
D. Magic

30. Virtues and Vices are personified in—
A. The Moralities B. The Miracles
C. The Interludes D. The Mysteries

31. Which is supposed to be the first regular tragedy in English?
A. *Morte de Arthur*
B. *Gorboduc*
C. *Troylus and Cryseyde*
D. *Roister Doister*

32. The first tragedy *Gorboduc* was later given the title—
A. *Corpus Christi*
B. *Ferrex and Porrex*
C. *Gammer Gurton's Needle*
D. *Endymion*

33. What is meant by 'Catastrophe'?
A. The ending of a tragi-comedy
B. The ending of a tragedy
C. The ending of a farce
D. The ending of a comedy

34. Which one of the following types of the plays is not meant for acting?
A. A Closet play B. A Chronicle play
C. A Masque D. A Romance

35. The *Resurrection of Lazarus* was a very popular play in the fifteenth century. It was a—
A. Morality Play B. Mystery Play
C. Miracle Play D. An Interlude

36. One of the following dramatists has written only tragedies. He is—
A. Ben Jonson B. John Webster
C. Marlowe D. John Ford

37. How many constituent parts are there in a Tragedy according to Aristotle?
A. Five B. Six
C. Four D. Three

38. At what stage of the plot in a play does the Epilogue appear?
A. At the end of the play
B. At any stage where its presence is felt necessary
C. In the beginning of the play
D. At the end of the third act

39. There were four famous theatrical Cycles enacting the Morality Plays. Which one of the following four names given below is wrong?
A. Towneley Cycle
B. Chester Cycle
C. York Cycle
D. Charles Cycle

40. Biblical themes were enacted in—
A. The Miracle plays
B. The Mystery plays
C. The Interludes
D. The Morality plays

41. In which year was the *Globe Theatre* built?
A. 1588 B. 1594
C. 1598 D. 1599

42. Who is the author of *The Spanish Tragedy*?
A. Thomas Lodge B. Thomas Kyd
C. George Peele D. Robert Greene

43. A *'Soliloquy'* is defined as the 'loud thinking' of a character. Who can hear this 'loud thinking'?
A. The heroine of the play
B. The whole audience
C. The character himself
D. The characters present on the stage

44. What is meant by *'Denouement'*?
A. The ending of a comedy
B. The ending of a romance
C. The ending of a tragedy
D. The ending of a historical play

45. What is the most significant feature of the *Morality Plays*?
A. They present biblical figures
B. They symbolise Christian moral values
C. They present saints and sages
D. They present Vices and Virtues as personified figures

46. *Everyman* was the most famous play of the 15th Century. It was a—
A. Miracle Play B. Morality Play
C. An Interlude D. Mystery Play

47. Which one of the following plays has a *Chorus* in it?
A. *Macbeth* B. *As You Like it*
C. *Doctor Faustus* D. *King Lear*

48. What type of play is *Christ's Nativity*?
A. A Mystery Play B. A Morality Play
C. A Miracle Play D. An Interlude

49. Which one of the following dramatists does not belong to the group of University Wits?
A. John Webster B. George Peele
C. Marlowe D. Thomas Kyd

50. *Gorboduc* is written in collaboration by—
A. Thomas Norton and John Skelton
B. Nicholas Uddal and Thomas Norton
C. Thomas Sackville and Thomas Norton
D. Sackville and Heywood

ANSWERS

1	2	3	4	5	6	7	8	9	10
C	D	A	D	C	B	A	C	D	D
11	**12**	**13**	**14**	**15**	**16**	**17**	**18**	**19**	**20**
D	D	A	D	C	B	A	A	C	C
21	**22**	**23**	**24**	**25**	**26**	**27**	**28**	**29**	**30**
B	C	B	A	C	A	C	D	C	A
31	**32**	**33**	**34**	**35**	**36**	**37**	**38**	**39**	**40**
B	B	B	A	C	C	B	A	D	B
41	**42**	**43**	**44**	**45**	**46**	**47**	**48**	**49**	**50**
D	B	B	A	D	B	C	A	A	C

2 Glossary of Literary Terms

Abridged edition

Condensed or shortened version of a work.

Absence

It is a modern term which is used to explain a work of art on the basis of aspects which are absent rather than those which are manifestly present in the work.

Acronym

1. A word formed from the initial letters of other words, *e.g.*
   NOIDA for New Okhla Industrial Development Authority.
2. The word may be considered synonymous to 'acrostic'.

Acrostic

1. It is a form of literary exercise in which the first letters of each line in a poem form a word as we read downwards.
2. Here are two Acrostics :
   (*i*) "Wait, O little child, wait!
   In the wind lies thy message,
   Not in the hubbub of the worldly;
   Else you may repent, says the sage."
   (The word formed is "WINE")

Act

Major division in a dramatic work.

Adage

Maxim or proverb.

Addendum

Addition or appendix to a book.

Aesthetic Realism

(*i*) According to Hudson, "Esther Waters" by George Moore was a landmark in this movement toward aesthetic realism.

(*ii*) This movement was the vehicle of the new realists of which Moore and Gossing were representatives.

(*iii*) According to Hudson, "they mistook mere ugliness for frankness and "seeing life steadily and seeing it whole."

Alexandrine

1. It is a line of six iambic feet instead of five.
2. It is not known for certain how this line originated.
3. It appears that it was evolved by Spenser by adding the Alexandrine to the eight-line stave (a b a b b c b c) of Chaucer that he used in the Monkeys Tale.

Alienation Effect

It was a term devised by the famous German playwright, Bartolt Brecht, who wanted to bring home the need, for realization of a kind of 'alienation' of the audience and the actors from the stage during the performance of a play, as the play being a play and not a part of real life.

Allegory

When the abstract or spiritual ideas are presented through living images, the result is the allegory.

Examples of Allegorical Works

(*i*) The Pilgrim Progress
(*ii*) The Scarlet Letter
(*iii*) The Faery Queene
(*iv*) Morality Plays, such as "Everyman".
(*v*) Seven Deadly Sins in Dr. Faustus, etc.

Alliteration

It signifies the repetition of initial consonant sounds, *e.g.* The furrow followed free.

Almanac

Book or table comprising a calendar of days, weeks and months indicating special occasions or events.

Anagnorisis

It means Discovery or Reversal in a Tragedy.

Anagram

Letters or word or phrase which, when re-arranged, form a new word.

Anapaest

It comprises two unaccented syllables followed by an accented one:

(*i*) Redeploy
(*ii*) Introduce
(*iii*) Camouflage

Androcentrism

The term implies the predominance of man in all social and intellectual activities.

Anecdote

Brief account or story about an individual.

'Angry Young Men'

It was a movement which came into existence in the second half of the twentieth century, mainly as a result of Osborn's play: "Look Back In Anger."

Annotation

Textual comment on a book.

Anthology

Collection of poetry or prose from diverse sources.

Anticipated Future

See 'Prosopopaeia'

Antithesis

1. It signifies the setting of one thing against another, often of opposite sense *e.g.*
   'A *friend never* betrays, an *enemy always* does.
2. 'Antithesis' can be expressed in literature also by presenting two aspects (of life) side by side, *e.g.* the real and the marvellous.

Aphorism

Short statement of a truth or dogma couched in memorable terms.

Apostrophe

It implies an exclamatory address to a person. (usually a dead one), some inanimate object or an abstract idea, *e.g.*

"Milton! thou shouldst be living with us at this hour..."

Archaism

It is a word or phrase which is no longer in use, *e.g.* loon, quoth, yclept, eftsoon(s), etc.

Archetypal Approach to Criticism

1. This Approach is also called Mythological, Ritualistic or Totemic Approach.
2. It endeavours to study literature on the basis of myth.

Areopagitica

This is the name of Milton's famous prose pamphlet, pleading for freedom, freedom of the press, in particular.

Argot

Slang or coarse vernacular language.

Aside

1. It is a kind of device similar to "soliloquy" (being probably comparatively brief) when a character speaks to himself.
2. The best example of an "aside" may be Shylock's words : "How like a fawning publican he looks" in Act, I sc. 3 of The Merchant of Venice.

Assonance

Unlike the alliteration (which signifies the repetition of consonant sounds), it signifies the repetition of vowel sounds, *e.g.*

I *hear* him *bear* the mark of a *seer* on his head.

Autobiography

An account of a person's life by himself or herself.

Avant-garde

Without going into historical aspects of the word, one can say that it implies those (persons) who support or create the newest ideas, fashions (generally literary or artistic), techniques, styles, etc. in an art, piece of literature, etc.

Ballad

Broadly-speaking, there are two kinds of ballads:

(*i*) Traditional Ballads such as those pertaining to Robin Hood, Chevy Chase, etc.
(*ii*) Modern Ballads, such as The Rime of Ancient Mariner, etc.

Bathos

1. It is a term to denote anticlimax.
2. It is generally used when there is sudden descent or fall from the sublime to the trite or ridiculous, *e.g.*
   Delay not thine departure hence,
   For thou mightst have a hot pudding, Awaiting thee.

Belles lettres

Essays on literary studies and the aesthetics of literature.

Bibliography

List of works on a particular subject or author.

Biography

An account of a person's life.

Blank verse

Poetry with unrhymed line endings (usually written in iambic pentameters).

Blurb

These are the words of praise or description of a book in a nutshell, inserted usually by the publisher on the cover page or jacket of the book, to attract the reader's eye.

Bound verse

Verse based on metrical pattern.

Burlesque

It is a way of writing which generates irony, humour and satire, *e.g.* Cervantes' Don Quixote, Samuel Butler's Hudibras, etc.

Bowdlerize

To 'cleanse' a work by omitting or cutting out indecent passages, phrases or words.

Cacophony

When the excessive use of high sounding words is made such that the meaning is lost or diminished in value in the sound, the result is cacophony instead of euphony.

Cadence

Rhythm and phrasing of language.

Caesura

1. In classical prosody, 'Caesura' means "break between words within a metrical foot." (Concise Oxford).
2. In English prosody, it means "pause about middle of line." (ibid.).
3. A Caesura "which does not immediately follow the ictus" is known as 'Feminine Caesura" (Chambers 20th century).

☛ In modern connotation, Caesura implies natural pause in a line of verse and not an unnatural or forced one.

Canon

Collection of works established as genuine.

Canto

Division of an epic or narrative poem.

Caption

Short description accompany-ing an illustration.

Caricature

The chief characteristics of characters are sometimes so exaggerated by the author that the characters look like some humorous or even funny creatures. The result is the creation of caricatures. This is what Dickens (more than any other author) has done.

Catalogue

List of books or works.

Catastrophe

It signifies the complete (often sudden) devastation of the fortunes of a character (often the hero and/or the heroine) in a play or piece of fiction.

Catharsis

This is the term used for the ousting of the emotions of pity and fear in the tragedy.

Chronicle Plays

1. These are the plays based on (English) History.
2. Such plays became very popular among the people in the sixteenth century.
3. These plays contain almost every important character, real or legendary, in the period of the times concerned.

Cipher

Writing that employs sub-stitution or transposition of letters.

Classic

(*i*) A classic (in reality, any book) is "the expression of man" as an individual.

(*ii*) It is also the expression of his mindset and the stance taken by him.

Cliche

Any word, phrase or expression that has lost its real effect for having been too frequently used by authors or laymen is called a cliche which may otherwise be quite lovable, *e.g.*

(*i*) The news is too good to be true.

(*ii*) The sorrow was too deep for tears.

(*iii*) Thanking you in anticipation, etc.

Climax

1. It is the main point of interest in a play or novel which is reached usually in the third act (or sometimes 4th of a 5 act of a play) or towards the end.
2. The resolution often takes place after the Climax or the forces for it start working or increase their intensity after it.

Colloquial

1. In speech, we sometimes make use of certain words and phrases which are not acceptable in standard speech
2. Such colloquial expressions should be avoided in all formal speech or writing.

Colonialism

The term differs from 'colonization' as the term may imply political or economic control of policies in a political unit without real annexation of land.

Colonisation

Literarily, the most significant modernist theories in the matter of

(*i*) colonisation

(*ii*) post colonisation

(*iii*) decolonisation, and

(*iv*) neo-colonisation have been provided and practised by—

(*a*) Ngugiwa Thiong'o

(*b*) Soyinka

(*c*) Achebe Chinua, etc.

Comedy

Humorous dramatic piece; *high comedy* has welldrawn characterization and witty dialogue; *low comedy*, or *slapstick* has absurd situations and boisterous action; *farce* is exaggerated comedy; *tragi-comedy* is a blend of the tragic and comic; *satire* uses sarcasm and wit to ridicule people's follies and vices (originally in verse).

Comic Relief

It is the name given to the brief light or comic dramatic action within the performance of a regular serious play to bring about a relief to the spectators to regain their real selves, for a short while to relax their strained nerves and prepare for further action, often more serious and culminating into breath-taking, gasping climax before denouement.

Conceit

1. A conceit is a far-fetched or highly complex and even obscure or unintelligible comparison between two, often dissimilar, persons or objects.
2. It was commonly used by the Elizabethans particularly the Metaphysical poets, especially Donne.

Concordance

Alphabetical index of words in a work, or works by a single author.

Confidant/Confidante

1. In a play when a character takes upon himself/herself the task of some secret or information characteristic about a character to another, the character indulging in such an activity is known as a "confidant" (mas.) or "confidante" (fem.)
2. Such information or secret is generally in the matter of love.
3. A good example of a 'confidante' is Nerissa in the Merchant of Venice.

Connotation

1. It signifies the suggested or implied meaning of word as against the transparent or literary meaning.
2. Connotative devices are brought into play by the artists, poets in particular to enhance pleasure and acceptability conveyed by words and other expressions.
3. Poets like Keats and T.S. Eliot frequently resort to the device of suggestiveness which is akin to connotation.

Consummation

1. When a work achieves complete satisfaction on all counts-literary as well as artistic, it is consummation that results.
2. An artist who has the knack, calibre or skill to make this achievement, is a consummate artist.

Copyright

Protective law to prevent pirating or plagiarism of an author's work.

Couplet

Two successive rhyming lines in poetry.

Court Comedy

1. It is opposed to the Domestic Comedy in the sense that instead of domestic scenes it contains other elements which attract a different kind of audience, *e.g.*

(*i*) endless play of words

(*ii*) elaborate dialogues

(*iii*) repartees, jests, retorts, etc.

Cycle

Group of works united by an overall theme.

Dactyl

Dactyl means one accented syllable followed by two unaccented ones, e.g.

(*i*) Lazily

(*ii*) Separate

(*iii*) Unspoken.

Decayed (or Constant) Metaphor

See Metaphor

Deism

A "deist" is a theist who believes in the existence of God but rejects the idea of a revealed religion.

Denouement

1. It is the final resolution of the problem in a piece of dramatic performance.
2. The best document comes about when it arises naturally out of the action of the play and not through the 'Deus ex machina'.

Detonation

When a word refers to its literal meaning independent of the meaning which the author may intend to convey, it is the device of "Detonation" which is at play.

Diabolus Ex Machina

1. The term literally means "devil out of the machine".
2. When all of a sudden a person or an event spoils the whole good game, causing unmitigated misery, it is the work of "Diabolus Ex Machina".
3. Thus, the term signifies sudden, unexpected turn of events for a plightful situation.

Dialect

Manner of speaking pertaining to a particular class or geographical region.

Dialectic

1. It was used originally to refer to the nature of a logical argument.
2. Later, it began to be linked to Kant, Hegel and Marx in varying forms.
3. The three generally accepted aspects of 'dialectic' are:
   (*i*) *Thesis:* It is akin to the (original) idea.
   (*ii*) *Antithesis:* It implies the inherent opposition in the thesis, which may operate after some time.
   (*iii*) *Synthesis:* It implies the resolution of the conflict to evolve a higher (or final) truth.

Dialogue

1. Dialogue is something very important in any poetic or prose play or a piece of prose fictions.
2. (*i*) The nature of the dialogue, including its language depends upon the kind of the play—a tragedy, comedy, romance, etc. or the kind of the scene prevailing there at the time and place of the dialogue.
   (*ii*) Much also depends upon the taste of the spectators or audience which again is related to the spirit of the age :

A Dialogical Novel

It is a kind of novel in which a number of voices, interactive in the scheme, operate in work, resulting in a kind of dialogue (or series of dialogues) as against the Monologic Presentation.

Diary

Sequential private record of personal and other events kept by an individual.

Diction

1. It refers to the selection, arrangement and order of words.
2. The term which has become more popular in literary world is "Poetic Diction" to which a lot of space has been devoted by Wordsworth in his "Preface to Lyrical Ballads."

Dictionary

Book containing the words of a language, and their definitions, alphabetically; two-language dictionaries contain the corresponding words of both languages and their meanings, also alphabetically; any book that gives words and phrases about a particular subject, arranged alphabetically.

Didactic

A work is didactic in nature when it undertakes to teach a moral, *e.g.* much of Wordsworth's poetry.

Digest

Publication where works are abridged.

Digression

1. When a writer, instead of carrying on the main plot or incident, starts indulging in a side story, dialogue or descriptive narration, it is digression that results.
2. Digression gives extraneous pleasure which is not inherent in or indispensable to the main story.
3. Digression can sometimes enhance the value of a work but more often it mars its spirit.

Documentary

Form of fiction or drama based on documentary evidence provided by newspapers, recent historical reports or other contemporary or recent factual evidence.

Doggerel

Rough, ill-constructed verse.

Domestic Comedy

1. One of the earliest examples of the Domestic Comedies is "Gammer Gurton's Needle" (Cir. 1562)
2. It presents realistic life of the peasant class of its times.
3. It is full of fun and coarse humour.

Double entendre

Ambiguity in a word or expression, one of whose meanings is usually bawdy or frivolous.

Drama

Work to be performed on a stage by actors.

Dramatic Irony

It is a device occurring in a drama when a character on the stage is unaware of a fact which the audience know and understand.

Dramatic Monologue

It is a kind of drama or piece of dramatic poetry in which only one character speaks out throughout the performance and script.

Dramatis Personae

Characters in a play.

Duologue

Conversation between two characters in a play, story or poem.

Edition

Total number of copies of a book printed from unchanged set of type.

Electicism

The term implies the gleaning of facts or ideas from different sources instead of depending on just one source (or a few sources).

Elegy

Serious meditative poem; often lamenting death.

Empathy

In a play or novel, when the reader or spectator begins to feel like the hero/heroine or some particular character as if he/she were that character, it is "empathy" which is at play.

Empiricism

Empiricism implies the importance of experiment and experience in the matter of gaining knowledge,

Encyclopedia

Comprehensive work encompassing and describing many aspects of knowledge; specialist work covering comprehensively a subject or discipline.

Epic

Long narrative poem incorporating myth, legend, folklore and history, about the deeds of heroes, warriors, important people; a grandiose treatment of an individual's or nation's story.

Epic Style

1. It is a style which is dignified and exalted (as grand style is), as:
   (*i*) Paradise Lost by Milton
   (*ii*) Aeneid by Virgil
   (*iii*) Iliad by Homer
   (*iv*) Hyperion by Keats, etc.
2. Sometimes, it is, also referred to as 'heroic' style.'

Epigram

1. It signifies some brief, witty word, saying or piece of writing.
2. Pope's work, for instance, is a model of "Epigrammatic" style.
3. Bacon's essays are a bundle of Epigrams.

Epilogue

It is the last item in a work of art (as in a drama) which often declares or comments upon the conclusion of the work.

Epistle

Direct address to another person, a 'letter' in the form of verse.

Epitaph

Valediction to dead person or persons; inscription on a tomb or grave.

Epithet

It comprises a word or group of words to describe the chief characteristics of a person, *e.g.*
(*i*) Alexander the Great
(*ii*) The Holy Bible.

Eponymous

Person whose name becomes the title of the work.

Erastianism

1. It implies the doctrine that the state should have supremacy over the church in ecclesiastical matters.
2. Erastianism was one of the doctrines which was vehemently opposed by the followers of the Oxford Movement
3. The doctrine is probably wrongly ascribed to Erastus.

Essay

Short composition, usually in prose, discussing a topic or variety of topics.

Euphemism

When an unpleasant expression has to be made in a comparatively pleasant or less harsh way, the mellowed or toned down words which are used express euphemism, *e.g.*
(*i*) Instead of saying about a person "He acted foolishly, we can say, "He should have acted more wisely."
(*ii*) Instead of saying about a person that he has died, we sometimes say, "God Almighty has called him" or "He has left for his heavenly abode."

Euphony

1. It signifies the pleasant combination of words which create desirable rhythms and tonal effects without interfering with the intended meaning.
2. An excessive use of such devices can lead to tautology or bombasticism and sound superficial or facile.
3. The generally accepted antonym of euphony is "Cacophony".

Euphuism

An ornate, floral style of writing popularized by Lyly.

Exposition

It signifies a way of writing where explanations are not withheld or suppressed but manifestly made clear to the reader for immediate response based on clarity.

Fable

A short narrative in prose or verse, often with animals, that points a moral.

Fiction

General term for an imaginative work, usually in prose.

Figure of Speech (or of Rhetoric)

It signifies the unusual use of words to heighten their effect.

First person

Style of novel, etc., in which narrator is a character.

Flashback

1. When a writer while presenting a situation suddenly refers to a past situation or event, it is the device of "flashback" that he exploits.
2. Browning, T.S, Eliot and Stream of consciousness novelists, in particular, take advantage of this device.

Folk tale

Story handed down by word of mouth from generation to generation.

Foot

In poetry, rhythmic unit of two or three syllables.

Foreshadowing

1. It is a device in which the author himself prepares the spectators (or readers) for the catastrophe or some important event which may be on the cards.
2. Such a device checks the readers, etc. from suffering from the malady of disbelief.
3. Shakespeare is probably one of the greatest masters of this device, and it is sometimes believed that one of the main reasons of Shakespeare's grand success was his convincing mastery over the technique of foreshadowing.

Foreword

Short introduction to a work.

Free verse (vers libre)

Poetry free from mechanical restrictions such as metre and rhyme, cadenced according to meaningful stress.

Fustian

It means the use of pompous, ornate, Euphuist or bombastic language.

Gazetteer

Geographical dictionary or index.

Ghost writer

Person who undertakes literary work for another who takes the credit.

Glossary

Alphabetical list of unfamiliar or uncommon words, usually appended to work in which they appear.

Haiku

According to Oxford Dictionary, "A Haiku is a Japanese poem of seventeen syllables, in three lines of five, seven and fine traditionally evoking images of the natural world."

Haplology

"Omission in utterance of a sound resembling a neighbouring sounds (as 'idolatry' for 'idololątry') (ibid.)

Haplography

"The inadvertent writing once of what should have been written twice." (Chambers 20th Century Dictionary)

Heroic Couplet

A couplet written in iambic pentametre is known as a 'heroic couplet'.

Heroic verse

A poem written in heroic couplets is known as 'heroic verse,' *e.g.* Pope's poems such as:

(*i*) Essay Man
(*ii*) Essay in Criticism
(*iii*) The Rape of the Lock, etc.

Homily

1. It is a term pertaining to a work which instead of laying stress on artistic or aesthetic standards, undertakes to urge the readers on to a high moral life.
2. It is just like a sermon in a church.
3. Such are the most of the poems of Longfellow.

Homograph

It implies a word which has the same spelling and pronunciation as another, but is different in meaning and origin from the other, *e.g.* :

(*i*) bear (*n*) an animal
(*ii*) bear (*v*) (to) tolerate
(*iii*) bear (*v*) (to) carry

Homonym

(*i*) It is "a word having the same sound and perhaps the same spelling as another, but a different meaning and origin" (Chambers.....)

(*ii*) Hence, *Homonymous* means: " having the same name : having different *significations* and origin but the same sound." (ibid.)

Hyperbole

It is a figure of speech which expresses an exaggerated statement to heighten the effect of a rhetorical statement, *e.g.*

(*i*) O child, may you never die!
(*ii*) Child is Father of the Man

Idiom

Form of expression of phrase peculiar to its language and possessing a meaning other than its literal one.

Idolatry

It means the worship of an image which is believed to be the abode of a superhuman being.

Idyll

Short pastoral poem conveying mood of happy innocence.

Imagism

School of poetry (early 1900s) concerned with precise language, direct treatment, and freedom of form.

Imperialism

It means the state policy for a country (as of England and certain other European countries, in particular during certain periods of history) to expands its area by annexing foreign lands and sub-during the natives.

Impersonality

It means that the author himself should not be palpably visible in a piece of literature, in other words, the work should be done on highly objective lines.

Indianism

When an expression is commonly used in India but is not used by the English, it is called an "Indianism," *e.g.*

(*i*) 'demise' instead of 'death'

(*ii*) 'bearer' instead of 'waiter'

(*iii*) 'left for his heavenly abode' instead of 'died,' etc.

Interior Monologue

1. It is a device, as used by James Joyce in Ulysses, to express the thoughts, feelings and emotions of a character on usually more than one levels of consciousness.
2. It is a sort of inner debate which may or may not be conflict in essence.

Interludes

Just as Miracles passed into Moralities, the latter gradually passed into Interludes, as the people wanted entertainment along with instruction.

Introduction

Essay stating author's intention to reader.

Inversion

It is the figure of speech (much used by Milton but ridiculed by many modern critics) in which words are presented in their unnatural order, *e.g.*

O God's glory I sing,
And to His Mercy I pray.

Irony

It is a device used to convey a meaning which is the opposite of the apparent meaning, *e.g.* What a brave son of India Jai Chand was!

Jingle

Verse or verses with strong rhyme and rhythm.

Journal

Paper, periodical or magazine.

Judicial Criticism

1. It is the kind of criticism which is a sort of judgement on a writer or his work of art.
2. Such kind of best example is Pope's "Essay on Criticism".

Legend

Story about a particular person containing myth and historical fact; explanation of symbols on a map or chart.

Lexicon

Dictionary, especially for Classical and Middle Eastern languages.

Limerick

1. It is a kind of humorous verse written in five jingling lines.
2. The form seems to have derived "from a refrain formerly used, referring to 'Limerick' in Ireland." (Chambers 20th Century Dictionary)

Linguistics

The scientific study of language.

Litotes

1. It is akin to "understatement" which is sometimes used by writers to emphasise the desired meaning, *e.g.* India is not lagging in Information Technology.
2. However, more often it is an "understatement used ironically, especially using a negative to express the category as :

   'I shan't be sorry when it's over' meaning 'I shall be very glad', or 'It was no easy matter' for 'It was very difficult.'"

   (Advanced Learner's Dictionary)

Lyric

Usually short, song-like poem in which the poet expresses personal feelings.

Manuscript

Book or work written by hand.

Maxim

Short statement or even sentence containing a general truth about human conduct and human nature.

Melodrama

1. It was a crude form of drama which appealed to the groundings who were not much interested in the artistic minuteness such as the plot, characterization, etc.

2. They wanted only entertainment through striking scenes and absorbing movement of incidents and situations.

Metaphor

It is a kind of simile when a comparison is suggested rather than explicitly stated, such that 'as' or 'like' is not used in such a case, *e.g.*

(*i*) Lala Lajpat Rai was the Lion of Punjab.
(*ii*) I see a lily on thy face.

Meter

Patterns of stressed and unstressed syllables in verse.

Metonymy

1. It implies the use of the name of some person or thing for another person or thing, *e.g.*
   (*i*) Have you studied 'Milton'?
   (Milton here means Milton's works).
   (*ii*) In the 'light' of these remarks:
   ('light' here means in view of....)
   (*iii*) Sceptre and Crown (i.e. monarchy)
   Must tumble down.

Metre

It may not be possible or even necessary to describe it here in full detail, but we can have a cursory look at the following:

1. *Monometre :* It means a line (or verse) with a single iamb (foot)
2. *Dimetre:* It means a line with two iambs.
3. *Trimetre:* It means a line with three iambs.
4. *Tetrametre:* It means a line with four iambs.
5. *Penta metre:* It means a line with five iambs.
6. *Hexta metre:* It means a line with six iambs.
7. *Hepta metre:* It means a line with seven iambs.

Miracle and Mystery Plays

1. These plays were sponsored by the church and were originally held within the premises of the church, but later, as the number of audience swelled, the boundaries of the church seemed too limited and the plays began of be held outside the church.
2. (*i*) The Miracle plays represented the lives of saints, and later for any biblical theme.
   (*ii*) The Mystery plays represented scenes from the life of Jesus Christ.

Mock Heroic

When an apparent epic is presented in a light vein, it is known as a "mock heroic" poem piece of fiction, etc., *e.g.* The Rape of the Lock

Modernism

Towards the close of the 20th century, a movement against such modes as realism and naturalism started in all forms of literature and art such as poetry, drama, novel, music, painting, architecture, sculpture, etc. which continued unabated during the first world war period and partly upto the middle of the century.

Modulation

1. Of necessity poetry is musical.
2. As in music, to avoid poetry from falling into "monotony," there is the system of "modulation" which here means, changing the key or tone, to introduce the element of variety to give or enhance pleasure.

Monologue

Single person addressing an audience alone, in drama, verse or prose. *Interior monologue*: unspoken but thought speech in verse or prose.

Moralities or Morality Play

1. They were basically allegories on the same lines as Miracles, or Mysteries but without direct represent of scriptural or Christ-concerned events or personages.
2. In Moralities abstract virtues and vices like Wisdom, Goodness, Justice, Evil, Vice, Greed, Lethargy, Lust, etc. were personified and presented on stage as persons.

Myth

Non-factual story that embodies explanation of how something comes to exist, usually involving supernatural or superhuman creatures.

Narrative

Story or tale in prose or verse.

Narratology

It means the study of different forms and structures of a narrative work in the matter of its various syntactical, literary and grammatical frameworks.

Neoclassicism

Movement of late 17th and 18th century reviving classical values in English literature, emphasizing discipline, reason and clarity.

Neologism

Newly-coined word.

New Wave (la Nouvelle Vague)

Movement in literature and cinema originating in France in late 1950s that attempted to eschew fixed values, revealing a character by the way he experienced objects and events, which were often meticulously described.

Nom de plume

Term used to indicate a fictitious name used by a writer to represent his work.

Novel

Extended piece of prose fiction.

Novelette

Long short story of some 15,000 words.

Novella

Prose fiction longer than a short story, shorter than a novel (about 30,000 words), concentrating upon a single event.

Obscurity

When a writer's language is not (or not easily) intelligible to the reader, the work concerned is termed as obscure.

Ode

Lyric poem describing an event or feelings about a person, object or event. *Pindaric Ode* (Greece) written for choral recitation in units of three stanzas; *Horatian Ode* (Rome) consisted of succession of stanzas following pattern of first one.

Omniscient Author

It is a device used by some outstanding modern novelists to move freely from the objective narrative to the internal or subjective psyche of a character or characters and then comment freely and apparently unattached on the significance, possibility or outcome of any or some events.

Onomatopoeia

When the very sound (pronunciation) of a word conveys the sense of the object producing such sound, the use of onomatopoeia becomes clear *e.g.*,

(*i*) The *lashing* of waves on the sea-shore
(*ii*) The *rustle* of leaves
(*iii*) The *hissing* of the snake
(*iv*) The *jungle* of coins
(*v*) The *clanging* of arms.

Oxymoron

It is a figure of speech in which two apparently contradictory words or terms are used to convey, a paradoxical sense, e.g.

(*i*) 'busy-idle days' (Lamb in Dream children)
(*ii*) Life in Death (Coleridge in 'Rime.....').

Pantomime

1. Pantomimes became popular in England particularly in the first quarter of the 18th century.
2. A Pantomime is a dramatic representation pertaining to some myth, legend or traditional tale (or it may have some fairy element in it).

Parable

A story which conveys a moral lesson is known as a parable, as for instance, the biblical parables.

Paradox

It is a figure of speech in which a truth is brought home through the use of self-contradictory statement, *e.g.*

(*i*) Cowards die many a time before their death.
(*ii*) Discretion is the better part of valour.
(*iii*) After death, we awake into an eternal life.

Parallelism

1. It is a rhetorical device where balancing sentences, phrases or words are used to enhance effect, e.g.

   What is important is not what you say, but what is important is what you mean.
2. Excessive use of this device leads to monotony and superficiality.

Parody

Comic imitation of serious words, style, sense, subject of a writer to make them appear ridiculous.

Pastoral

Literature depicting idealized rural life.

Pathetic Fallacy

When nature is shown as sympathising with human lot, the device used is called "pathetic fallacy," *e.g.*

(*i*) Byron's description of the battle of Waterloo in Childe Harold's Pilgrimage.
(*ii*) The behaviour of slow-moving nature in Tennyson's "Lotos-eaters".

Pedantry

The term refers to the excessive display of knowledge such as:

(*i*) Foreign words and phrases
(*ii*) Allusions
(*iii*) Archaic words
(*iv*) high sounding and sesquipedalian words
(*v*) cataloguing, etc.

when these are not strictly needed within the context of the work.

Periodic Sentence

A sentence in which the Principal clause occurs at the end when it is preceded by one or more subordinate clauses, such that the sense is clear only when the whole sentence is read, is known as a 'periodic sentence'.

Periodical

Magazine or journal published regularly.

Periphrasis

1. It means a round about way of saying a thing, *e.g.* An idle singer of an empty day, etc.
2. The term is close to circumlocution and euphemism in sense and effect.

Personification

It is a device where inanimate objects are shown as those having life and behaving likewise, *e.g.*

"But yonder comes the powerful *king* of day."

—***Thomson***

Pessimists

Although in English literature, we have a number of pessimist poets or a good number of poets expressing at times pessimistic ideas or writing sometimes in a pessimistic mood, yet two of the poets are known in particular, as "Pessimists." They are:

(*i*) Thomas Hardy

(*ii*) A.E. Housman

Philology

Study of literature, language and linguistics.

Picaresque

Chronicle of adventures of a rogue; originated in 16-century Spain.

Plagiarism

Wrongful appropriation and publication of another's work as one's own.

Platitude

It means a truth or generalization which is too well-known mainly because of its overuse, *e.g.*

Truth is evergreen.

Pleonasm

1. It means the use of words more than those which are absolutely necessary, *e.g.*
   (*i*) He sat *down* on the ground.
   (*ii*) He looked up *high* towards the sky.
   (*iii*) He has got *sole* monopoly over such kind of business.
2. In essence, it is akin to Tautology or circumlocution.

Plot

Plan or organization of events and characters in a play, work of fiction or poem as to induce curiosity and suspense in the audience or reader.

Poem

Literary work which may be in rhyme, blank verse or a combination of the two.

Poetic Diction

1. Diction stands chiefly for choice of words.
2. In poetry, poetic diction is unavoidable as mere metre is not enough to make a poem a literary piece of work.
3. In other words, mere versification or combination of words in rhyme or any other verse form does not make poetry.
4. The poets resort to several devices in this regard, some of which are :
   (*i*) Use of similes, metaphors, symbols, inversions, and other figures of speech as such as hyperbole, irony, antithesis, personification, etc.
   (*ii*) Omission of some parts of speech or grammatical rules.
   (*iii*) Use of archaic or uncommon words.
   (*iv*) Change in order of words, etc.
   (*v*) Use of picturesque phrases and expressions
   (*vi*) Use of other ornamental devices such as epithets
   (*vii*) Use of highly musical lies, fanciful flights etc.

Poetic Justice

1. It means the reward or punishment handed down to the characters at the end of a work of art according to their deeds.

Poetry

Any kind of metrical composition in a literary work.

Pornography

Work in which there is a deliberate emphasis on the sexual behaviour of characters, in order to arouse sexual excitement.

Potboiler

Work written essentially to gain the author a livelihood.

Precis

Concise statement; short summary of a work.

Preface

Introduction to a work.

Prologue

It is often the original statement by the writer (as in a drama) which highlights the chief aim of the work which is going to be unfolded or staged.

Propaganda

Work devoted to the dissemination of an idea or belief, usually biased.

Prose

Writings not in verse.

(Modern) Prose Style

1. The English prose style started by Bacon, flourished in the hands of Addison and Steele and numerous essayists and prose stylists that followed.

2. As a fine example of the latest modern prose style, Naipaul who won the Nobel Prize for Literature in 2001 deserves to be mentioned.

Prosody

Study of the handling of language in poetry.

Prosopopaeia

This figure of speech is used when:

(*i*) The past (called the Historic Present) is written in the present tense:
Sohrab and Rustam clash with their full might.

(*ii*) The (anticipated) future is written in the present tense:
Here, we go to our new house tomorrow with all our belongings carried in a lorry and then tucked in elegant mahogany almirahs.

Pseudonym

Name other than the true one used by an author to represent his work.

Psychological Process

It is the process applied to the study of a piece of literature to penetrate another's mind and to study the activities, utterances, etc. of various characters, as, for instance, to arrive at the exact nature of Hamlet's madness whether there was "method" in it or not.

Pun

1. When a word gives several meanings (often for fun) as in a play, it is the "pun" that is used.
2. Shakespeare is a great master of this device.
3. **Example :**
   (*i*) This is the *book*.
   (*ii*) It means
   (*a*) any book
   (*b*) a holy book, often the Bible.

Realism

Literature that attempts to depict life objectively and faithfully.

Refrain

Phrase, line or lines repeated at intervals or at the end of a stanza in poetry.

Review

Notice or critical article on musical, artistic or literary work.

Revue

Theatrical entertainment made up of sketches, dances, songs, recitals and improvised pieces, usually humorous, satirical or topical.

Rhetoric

Art of using language, in speaking or writing, to persuade. The persuasive style (rather than the content) of a work.

Rhythm

1. It signifies the measured regular beat or movement of sounded words in language.
2. Rhythm is a must in poetry as well as prose, as it introduces or enhances the element of pleasure, interest and curiosity.

Rhyme

Echoing sound or audible similarity in two or more words, especially at endings. Device used to construct much poetry.

Riddle

Puzzle, question or enigma; conundrum.

Roman a clef

Novel based upon actual people under disguised names.

Romance

Tale of chivalry, originally written in verse (Medieval times); term applied now to any wonderful or mysterious tale far removed from reality.

Romance Languages

Languages which have emerged straightaway from Latin and/or Greek, are called Romance Languages.

Romanticism

Movement originating in late 18th century as revolt against neoclassicism, emphasizing imaginative style.

Saga

Lengthy prose work, sometimes in several parts, describing the history and events surrounding medieval kings, warrriors and, recently, fictitious families.

Satire

Any work in which wickedness, folly, vice and corruption in individuals and society is exposed by ridicule and scorn.

Science fiction

Literature based on scientific fact or fantasy, on earth or on other worlds in space, often set in periods in the distant future.

Semantics

Branch of linguistics dealing with meaning, and the change of meaning, in words.

Semiology

General study or science of signs with which humans communicate with each other (including words and their use in every context).

Sermon

Verbal instruction of some length, usually religious.

Short story

Work of fiction usually revolving around single event.

Sic

Included in brackets after a printed word or quoted passage to indicate that it is quoted accurately, however actually incorrect.

Simile

1. When we draw comparison between two persons by using (usually 'like', as-so or as) it is the 'simile' that we make use of, *e.g.*
   (*i*) As red as a rose
   (*ii*) As happy as a lark
   (*iii*) She looked like a violet, half-hidden behind the rock.
2. *An Exaggerated Simile:* It is a simile in which the sense is clearly exaggerated, *e.g.*
   (*i*) He ran as fast as lightning
   (*ii*) He has in himself the force as much as there is in ten horses.

Slang

Colourful and vernacular language of the street, marketplace, barrackroom, workplace, sportsplace and playground.

Soliloquy

Kind of monologue in which a stage character expresses his thoughts and feelings.

Song

Poem or verse set to music.

Sonnet

14-line poem of set rhyme-scheme; Elizabethan (Shakespearean) *ababcdcdefefgg*, Italian *abbaabba cdcdcd* (or *cdecde*).

Stanza

Group of lines of verse in definite pattern, usually repeated in a poem.

Strophe and Anti Strophe

1. Strophe is "the song sung by the chorus (in a Greek play) as it moved towards one side, answered by an exact counterpart." (Chambers 20th Century Dictionary)
2. Anti-Strophe is the term for the Strophe, "as it returned : part of any ode thus answered..." (*ibid.*)

Style

Characteristic manner of expression in prose or verse; the way in which a thing is written by an author.

Stock Material

Material necessary for a writer to write.

Stock Characters

Characters that are commonly found in most of pieces of dramas or fiction.

Stock Situations

Situations which are frequently presented by authors in their works.

Synthesis, Poetry of

The term "Poetry of Synthesis" is referred to by I.A. Richards, and it has been thus explained by Cleanth Brooks—

"... a poetry which does not leave out what is apparently hostile to its dominant tone, and which, because it is able to fuse the irrelevant and disordant, has come to terms with itself and invulnerable to irony."

Structure

"The structure meant is a structure of meaning, evaluations and interpretations : and the principle of unity which informs it seems to one of balancing and harmonizing connotations, attitudes and meanings."

Tragedy of Blood (And Thunder)

1. It was basically a melodramatic presentation of horrible, gory scenes.
2. The first famous tragedy of this kind is Kyd's "Spanish Tragedy".

Sublimity

It is a term which is used to describe inexplicable beauty which is beyond any rules to describe or measure.

Symbolism

French poetic movement of late 19th century that developed as revolt against realism, concentrating on evoking emotions by use of indirect suggestion (symbol and metaphor); flourished in Russia at turn of century as literary movement, and later in British novel.

Synecdoche

1. This figure of speech is used when the understanding of one thing by means of another is employed.
2. This can be done in several ways, some of which are mentioned below :
   (*i*) When a part stands for a whole or genus, e.g. We have fifty *hands* in our factory. (hands = workers)
   (*ii*) When a whole or genus stands for a part, e.g. He belongs to a different *world* from yors (world = category, social set-up, economic status, etc.)
   (*iii*) When an individual represents a class, *e.g.* He is the *Nestor* of our village. (Nestor = the oldest man)

Syntax

It means :

(*i*) The way a sentence is constructed
(*ii*) Arrangement of words in writing (or in speech) according to the rules of grammar
(*iii*) Rules pertaining to this system or arrangement.

Synonym

A word similar in meaning to another.

Synopsis

Outline of the main points of a work; a summary.

Tale

Spoken or written narrative.

Tautology

Overuse of synonyms or repetition of ideas in sentence.

Theme

Central idea of a work, rather than its subject.

Thesis

Long essay or treatise on a subject, usually expository; work presented to examiners for academic qualification.

Third person

Style of novel, etc., in which narrator is outside action.

Tract

Short printed treatise on religious or political subject.

Tragedy

It is "a drama in which the principal characters are involved in desperate circumstances or led by overwhelming passions. It is invariably serious and dignified. The movement is always stately, but grows more and more rapid as it approaches the climax; and the end is always calamitous, resulting in death or dire misfortune of the principals."

Tragic Flaw

In Shakespeare's tragedies, in particular, we often find a particular flaw in the character of the hero which ultimately leads to the fall of his destiny, along with the fall of his state or estate.

Transferred Epithet

When an epithet is transferred from a person to a thing, it is known as a 'transferred epithet', *e.g.*

(*i*) It is a *foolish* idea

(*ii*) Let *happy* days come.

Translation

Rendering of a work into another language.

Treatise

Formal work examining a subject and the principles underlying it.

Trochaic Line Metre

1. A line in verse is known as a *"trochaic" line* when the first, third and other odd syllables in it are accented (as in the 'Iambic metre') irrespective of the length of the line.
2. A poem comprising such lines is known as having been written in the "Trochaic" metre.

Understatement

It is practically the opposite of hyperbole and is sometimes used by the writers to emphasise indirectly the desired meaning.

Vade mecum

Manual or handbook carried for frequent reference.

Verisimilitude

It is the likeness of truth presented in a work of art that makes it similar to the characteristics or situation in real life and that enables the readers to accept it ungrudgingly as truth (and may be, sometimes, more than real happening in life).

Vernacular

Domestic or native language.

Versification

Study of how traditional verse is constructed.

Wit

Dryden defines (in "Annus Mirabilis") wit as "delightful imagining of persons, actions, passions or things."

Yarn

Story or tale, sometimes improbable and far-fetched.

3 Authors & Their Works

WILLIAM SHAKESPEARE (1564–1616)

Life

William Shakespeare was born on 23rd April 1564 at Stratford-on-Avon. His father was a grain-dealer. His business deteriorated when William was yet a child and so William could not study more than a few years in the local grammar school and left it at the age of about 13 to help out in his family's business. He married at the age of 18 to Anne Hathaway, who was eight years his senior. They had three children, but the marriage was not happy. According to tradition, William was caught poaching deer and rabbits in Thomas Lucy's park at Charlecote. He was lynched and ran away from home, gradually reaching London. There he got a job as a holder of visitors' horses at a theatre. He later on got a job as an actor and is supposed to have done the roles of the type of Ghost in *Hamlet* and Adam in *As You Like it.* Shakespeare very soon got the hang of the theatre and began revising plays or writing plays based on English translations of Greek and Latin stories. These plays were very successful with audiences and provoked the jealousy of rivals like Greene who denounces Shakespeare in a pamphlet entitled *A Groatsworth of Wit* (1592). Greene describes him as "an upstart crow beautified with our feathers, that with his Tyger's heart wrapped in a player's hide ....".

From then on there was no stopping of Shakespeare's upward rise in career. He was attached to and wrote his plays for the Earl of Leicester's Players. In 1595, his name appears on the Payroll of the Lord Chamberlain's and finally of the King's Servants. These companies performed at The Rose, The Curtain and The Theatre. The company finally bought the Globe and Shakespeare, growing prosperous, became a partner of the Globe Theatre and later of the Blackfriars.

Shakespeare wrote and published for twenty years from 1591 to 1611. During this period he wrote 37 plays and more than 154 sonnets. The first 126 of the sonnets are addressed to a man Mr. W.H., the Earl of Southampton, who introduced him to the important courtiers, and the remainder to a "dark lady". He grew prosperous day by day, acquired estate, got his father to apply for a coat of arms and became a gentleman by inheritance. He bought New Place, the largest house at Stratford and retired there after 1611. After a drinking bout in 1616, he fell sick and died untimely.

Works

Shakespeare wrote the famous love poems, *Venus and Adonis* (1593) and *The Rape of Lucrece* (1594) dedicated to the Earl of Southampton. These poems in themselves entitle him to a place among the immortals. But he was destined to become famous and known to posterity as England's greatest dramatist. He began, as was the custom of the times, by collaborating with Marlowe and Kyd in revising and touching up old plays like *Titus Andronicus, Henry VI* and *Richard III.* The exact sequence of dates in which his plays came out is not known, but only sixteen were published in quarto form during his life-time. There were copyright laws at the time and unscrupulous writer 'pirates' took down bits of the plays as they were enacted and published them in different editions. In 1623, seven years after his death, two of Shakespeare's friends and fellow-actors, Heminge and Condell, published all his plays as the first folio in memory of their worthy friend. This folio contains all the plays except *Pericles.* There are references to Shakespeare's plays in *Palladis Tamia, Wit's Treasury* (1593) by Francis Meres. The date of composition is guessed by topical and contemporary allusions in the plays and the tone and metre used.

In the earlier plays there is in general a youthful exuberance, a lot of verbal wit, strange conceits and light-heartedness. The blank verse used is end-stopped (the sense ends with each line) and rhyming couplets are used. As the plays grow in maturity and Shakespeare's art advances he uses run-on lines in which the sense of one line carries on to the next. This allows the verse to express a greater range of emotions. Still later on, feminine endings are used, that is, a number of unstressed syllables are added at the ends of lines. In the last plays, rhyme completely disappears.

Shakespeare's plays were written in three periods. Although their date of writing is based on conjecture, the periods give a clue to the gradual development of his art.

Early Period (1590-1596)

Henry VI (three plays), *Richard III, Richard II, Love's Labour Lost, A Midsummer Night's Dream, Romeo and Juliet.*

Middle Period (1596-1608)

Herry IV (two plays), *The Merchant of Venice, As You Like It, Julius Caesar, Hamlet, Othello, Macbeth, Tweifth Night King Lear, Antony and Cleopatra,* etc.

Late Period (1608-1613)

Cymbeline, The Tempest, Pericles, The Winter's Tale, etc.

The above are some of the 37 plays he wrote. An analysis of the plays reveals some common characteristics of the different categories like comedies and tragedies. The comedies are boisterous and farcical. They show Shakespeare's immature period. *The Merchant of Venice* (1596) is one of his most popular comedies with several episodes woven together. In those days when the Christians hated the Jews, Shakespeare's portrayal of Shylock in sympathetic tones caused a stir. *A Midsummer Night's Dream* (1595), the one play for which Shakespeare did not borrow the story, takes us to a wonderland of fairies, the impish Puck Goodfellow and Bottom whose scenes are the most hilarious in all Shakespeare. In this play, Theseus says *"The lunatic, the lover, and the poet/Are of imagination all compact."* This line refers to Shakespeare's own weird fancies as he creates them in his plays. *The Merry Wives of Windsor* (1600) was written on the behest of Queen Elizabeth. The character Falstaff is one of Shakespeare's best creations. According to the critic Hazlitt, Falstaff is all laughter and merriment, "laughing 3 inches below the skin". *Much Ado about Nothing* (1598) contains bracing wit-combats between Benedick and Beatrice. *As You Like It* (1600) provides glimpses of an emotionally rich life in the forest of Arden. *Twelfth Night* (1601) is a hilarious comedy. Through Malvolio, Shakespeare satirizes Puritanism.

Histories like *Richard III* (1593) and *Richard II* (1596) show the influence of Marlowe on Shakespeare. He wrote the three parts of *Henry VI* (1591-92) in collaboration with Marlowe. Most of these histories show the patriotic victory of kings.

The tragedies show Shakespeare's maturity in character delineation. *Titus Andronicus* (1594) is a horror play. *Romeo and Juliet* (1594) is a romantic tragedy which has become immortal. The four great tragedies of Shakespeare are psychological plays which show how a man of high rank falls from grace, becomes a plaything of destiny and ends up wretchedly all because of a "fatal flaw" in his character. In Greek tragedy, man was a complete puppet whose destiny was in the hands of the gods. Shakespeare often alludes to this: *"As flies to wanton boys are we to the gods/They kill us for their sport"*. But he gives his tragic characters "will-power". The tragic flaw in their characters, however, becomes the cause of their undoing. Thus with *Julius Caesar* (1599), it is his inordinate ambition; with *King Lear* (1605) it is dotedness and bad temper; with *Hamlet* (1601), it is over-refinement of thought leading to indecision; and with *Othello* (1604), it is simplicity causing suspicion. *Timon of Athens* (1607) is the tragedy of a misanthrope. *Coriolanus* (1606) depicts how pride leads to downfall. The last plays — *Pericles* (1608), *Cymbeline* (1609), *The Winter's Tale* (1610) and *The Tempest* (1611) have happy endings. With *The tempest* Shakespeare bid farewell to the theatre just as Prospero in the play puts away his wand and magic books.

To estimate the complete contribution of Shakespeare to English literature and the literature of the world is a difficult task. Thousands of books have been written on Shakespeare by scholars from all over the world and his plays have been translated into all the major languages. They are enacted everywhere and the Russians even claim he was a Slav! Even after 400 years his fame is on the rise. In *Julius Caesar,* Brutus says, *"How many times will this scene of ours be acted over/In states unborn and accents yet unknown".* This indeed was a prophetic statement about his own plays.

Dryden stated that Shakespeare had 'a universal mind' and Ben Jonson said, "Shakespeare was not of an age but for all times." Indeed Shakespeare's characters — a gallery of 800 — are types of characters that have inhabited this planet throughout the human history. Shakespeare could enter into his characters and present them so vividly that they are more real than life itself. Master of the whole keyboard of emotions and expressions, the subtlest feelings are expressed in his plays. No wonder we quote him the most after the Bible.

Another aspect of his genius is that he excelled many of his contemporaries in whatever they invented. Thus he took Marlowe's 'mighty line' or the blank verse and made it a supple instrument for expressing many intense feelings. Ben Jonson described the 'humours' or human moods in his plays; Shakespeare bettered him in the description of greed, vice, folly and virtue.

Many have expressed doubt about his claim to the authorship of 37 plays in just 20 years. Yet there is no cause for doubt here. After all, he borrowed the stories from Latin and Greek translations and enlivened them with his genius. One of the sources of his Roman histories like *Julius Caesar,* for example, was Plutarch's *Lives of the Noble Romans* translated by North.

Shakespeare undoubtedly had many demerits, but these are overwhelmed and eclipsed by his outstanding gifts. Shakespeare, not being educated more than a few years in grammar school, was thrown upon his own resources. He observed Nature and human behaviour very keenly and had rare intuition and imagination. So he was trained in the school of life. His faults of grammar so prevalent in his plays are glossed off as poetic licence. In fact, he created his own grammar, using nouns as adjectives and inventing syntax. These have become expressions so apt, it is impossible to change or correct them without reducing the impact.

What was Shakespeare's philosophy? Was he a Christian? Shakespeare's ideas as expressed through his noble characters show universal virtue free from dogma and any religious denomination. They are virtues in the human spirit. He was capable of seeing good in all people.

"There is a soul of goodness
In things evil
Distil it if we may".

His advocacy of the cause of Shylock, the Jew, in the days when rank hatred existed for them among the Christians, shows the truth of the above lines. It reinforces the view that Shylock was a man *"more sinned against than sinning"*. Portia's speech on mercy and forgiveness in *The Merchant of Venice* is one of the most beautiful passages of his plays: *"The quality of mercy is not strained/It droppeth like the gentle rain from above/This mightiest in the mightiests"*.

The great range and variety of human behaviour treated by Shakespeare gives his plays an everlasting interest. We may ascribe to the Bard what he himself makes Enobarbus say of Cleopatra:

"Age cannot wither her
Nor custom state her infinite variety".

SUMMARY AND MAIN POINTS

Life

1. He was born on or about 23 April, 1564 at Stratford-on-Avon, Warwickshire.
2. His father was a prosperous tradesman.
3. He was sent to a Grammar school where he learnt "small Latin and less Greek."
4. Later misfortunes overtook the family.
5. In his 19th year, he married Anne Hathaway, who was eight years his senior.
6. His marriage seems to have been an unhappy one.
7. (*i*) There are several anecdotes why he left for London, but we need not study them here.
   (*ii*) It is almost certain that he went to London in or about 1587 to seek fortunes there.
8. It was the time when drama was being popularized by the University Wits.
9. (*i*) There are again several stories how he came on the stage, but what we are concerned here is that soon he gained popularity and appeared on the stage as an actor.
   For example, he acted in Ben Jonson's "Everyman in His Humour."
   (*ii*) Soon alongwith being an actor, he became a playwright also.
10. It is certain from the deathbed words of Greene who called him an "upstart" that by 1592, Shakespeare had quite established himself as a playwright.
11. Soon he became a shareholder in prestigious theatres such as the Globe and the Blackfriars.
12. (*i*) He also purchased property in London and Stratford.
    (*ii*) It is clear that he had become sufficiently prosperous.
13. However, misfortunes were not late in visiting him :
    (*i*) His only son died in 1596.
    (*ii*) His father died in 1601.
    (*iii*) His mother died in 1608.
14. Still, financially he was sound.
15. Between 1610 and 1612 he retired to his hometown, Stratford, where he bought the largest house in the town named the New Place.
16. As his health broke down, he died on 23rd April, 1616.

Works

In all, he wrote :

(*i*) 37 plays
(*ii*) Two narrative poems:
  (*a*) Venus and Adonis
  (*b*) Lucrece
(*iii*) 154 sonnets:
  (*a*) 126 addressed to a man—a patron or friend.
  (*b*) the rest 28 addressed to a dark lady.

His dramatic work is generally divided in four periods:

1. **The First Period (1588-93) :** It was the period of apprenticeship and experiment. It included:
   (*i*) Revision of old plays such as:
     (*a*) Henry VI
     (*b*) Titus Andronicus,
   (*ii*) the first comedies such as :
     (*a*) Love's Labour's Lost
     (*b*) Two Gentlemen of Verona
     (*c*) The Comedy of Errors, and
     (*d*) A Midsummer Night's Dream, and
   (*iii*) the first attempt at writing a tragedy—Romeo and Juliet.
2. **The Second Period (1594-1600) :** It was the period of the great Comedies and Chronicle Plays, such as
   (*a*) Richard II
   (*b*) King John
   (*c*) The Merchant of Venice

(*d*) Henry IV Part I
(*e*) Henry IV Part II
(*f*) Henry V
(*g*) The Taming of the Shrew
(*h*) The Merry Wives of Windsor
(*i*) Much Ado About Nothing
(*j*) As You Like It, and
(*k*) Twelfth Night

3. **The Third Period (1601-08):** This was the period of his great tragedies and sombre comedies, such as
   (*i*) Julius Caesar
   (*ii*) Hamlet
   (*iii*) All's Well That Ends Well
   (*iv*) Measure for Measure
   (*v*) Troilus and Cressida
   (*vi*) Othello
   (*vii*) King Lear
   (*viii*) Macbeth
   (*ix*) Antony and Cleopatra
   (*x*) Coriolanus
   (*xi*) Timon of Athens
4. **The Fourth Period (1608-12):** This was the period of later comedies or what are known as "Dramatic Romances"—
   (*a*) (*i*) Cymbeline
   (*ii*) The Tempest
   (*iii*) Winter's Tale
   (*b*) There are two other plays of this period which are only partly written by Shakespeare
   (*i*) Pericles
   (*ii*) Henry VIII

☛ Henry VIII was completed by his friend, Fletcher (1579-1625) after his death.

Characteristics

1. No single writer has contributed to literature as much literary work as Shakespeare has done.
2. There is "infinite variety" in his work.
3. He was indisputably a versatile genius—a deft master both at prose and verse of all kinds:
   (*i*) blank verse
   (*ii*) rhyme
   (*iii*) dramatic verse
   (*iv*) narrative verse, etc.
4. He is the most often quoted among all the English writers.
5. He is one of the greatest poets and dramatists of the world, probably the greatest.
6. It is said that he is the only man in the history of mankind who has said all that is worth-saying.
7. He himself might not be a great thinker, but he could reproduce the borrowed matter in an original form such as none else perhaps could do.
8. No other writer, not even Dickens, has been able to produce so many living and throbbing characters as he has done.
9. It is estimated that he coined more than 15000 (some say, about 18000) words which he contributed to the English language.
10. He is the single writer who has given such a solid footing to the English language that its undying endurance over the centuries can hardly ever be doubted.
11. Needless to say his command over the language he uses is unrivalled.
12. Though a romantic writer, he is all the same the master of realism.
13. He steered the drama clear of stiff classical rules based on ancient masters, and made it a national movement.
14. With all the brutalities as shown by him like other dramatists, unlike them, he upheld the moral law such that truth triumphs in the long run, though poetic justice is not essentially done.
15. Thus his dramas are true to life and human nature.
16. There is a mixture of tragedy and comedy in his dramas as in life.
17. He is the master of true humour and has genuine sympathy with mankind.

Shakespeare's Faults

Like everyone he too is not without faults. Here are listed some of his faults:

1. The feeling of hastiness is evident at places in his works.
2. At places, he uses claptrap methods and means to cater to the 'groundlings', thus sacrificing some of the essential elements of genuine drama, consistency of character and propriety.
3. At places his psychology is hopelessly crude and unconvincing; his style vicious; his wit forced and poor; his tragic language bombastic.
4. At some places there are factual errors in his dramas such that the story, plot, scenes and characters start seeing unreal, *e.g.*
   (*i*) The modern Switzerland in 'Winter's Tale' is shown as having a sea-coast.
   (*ii*) There are trees of coconut and palm-dates side by side in 'As You Like It'.
   (*iii*) Sometimes, the "mistaken identity" scenes as in 'The Merchant of Venice' and 'Twelfth Night' seem unreal.

JOHN MILTON (1608–1674)

Life

John Milton was born on December 9, 1608 in London. His father was a lawyer-cum-banker. Although a Puritan, he loved art and literature and was known as a musician. Milton was trained in music and inherited a love for music. He was charming and aloof. After his education at St. Paul's School he joined Christs' College, Cambridge. But he was rusticated from college for protesting against the curriculum.

Even while he was at Cambridge, he wrote Latin and Italian poems. The best one was *Ode on the Morning of Christ's Nativity* written at the age of twenty-one. In this poem he celebrates the end of paganism and "the death of Pan". The style is rich with Elizabethan devices.

He refused ordination as minister or taking holy orders under the Church of England because this would have fettered his liberated conscience. He settled at Horton near London and devoted himself to writing poems. *L' Allegro* and *Il Penseroso* and two masques *Arcades* and *Comus* and the famous elegy, *Lycidas,* are the works of this period.

In 1638 he left for a tour of the Continent. He won many friends in Italy because of his interest in and mastery of Latin and Italian. But before he could go to Greece, he heard of the conflict between the King and the Parliament and hurried back to England to support the latter. He also taught for a time at a school and wrote a tract on education.

Between 1640 and 1660 he wrote prose pamphlets and some sonnets. When the Commonwealth was established, he was appointed Latin Secretary to the department of foreign affairs. He married Mary Powell in 1643. The marriage was an unhappy one. The daughter of a Cavalier Royalist, she could not tolerate Milton's puritanical ways and left him after marriage. He was much aggrieved and wrote tract pleading for a change in divorce laws. Mary returned to him after two years and he had three daughters by her.

Milton turned fully blind in 1653. Andrew Marvell and others assisted him in his work of writing. He accepted his blindness as the will of God in his beautiful sonnet *On His Blindness: "They also serve who only stand and wait".*

He married Catherine Woodcock after his first wife died. But Catherine also expired within fifteen months. When monarchy was restored, Milton lost his post and was arrested. He was soon released. He lost some of his property. Now Milton set himself to writing the work that was to make him immortal. In 1667, he completed the *Paradise Lost.* During this period he married for the third time. He finished *Paradise Regained* and *Samson Agonistes* in 1671. He died on November 8, 1674.

Milton was a tolerant Puritan. That is why he got along well with a Royalist father-in-law and a Catholic brother. In later life he became an Arian and did not accept Christ as the divine son. He kept away from wine and women in order to concentrate on higher goals. An unshakeable idealist, he could not understand man completely. His desire to reform mankind was too ambitious and failed. His poetry is remembered today for its magnificent grandeur rather than for any message.

Works

There are four clear-cut periods in Milton's career as a poet: (1) At Cambridge till 1632, (2) At Horton from 1632 to 1638, (3) The period of journalism from 1640 to 1660, (4) The final period of his masterpieces.

The period of his youth produced the famous *Ode on the Morning of Christ's Nativity* (1629). The poem is marred by exaggeration and metaphysical conceits in describing his devotion to the infant Jesus. He also wrote a number of Latin and Italian poems which have been translated into English.

In 1632, he wrote the exquisite *"L' Allegro"* and *Il Penseroso.* The titles only are in Italian. The poems and their spirit are quite English. The first one describes the poet's thoughts in a gay mood and *Il Penseroso* describes the gloomy side of his thinking. The poems are written in octosyllabic couplets and have a haunting music. *L'Allegro* means *'the cheerful man'* and describes his revels, his delight in a castle or a theatre and *Il Penseroso,* his pensive thoughts. Dr. Johnson is said to have admired these poems very much. The poems depict not so much natural scenes as moods of the mind. Milton seeks pure pleasure. In *L'Allegro*, it is Mirth, fresh, rosy and vigorous, dancing on tiptoe. In *Il Penseroso,* divine Melancholy is presented as a pensive nun *"devout and pure .... with even step and musing gait".*

Milton's inner conflict, the moral problem before him, is the theme in the masques *Arcades* and *Comus.* Although these are Renaissance in form, the spirit is grave, austere and Miltonic. *Comus* (1634) is a paean to chastity. It is obviously didactic and lacks any dramatic power to thrill. A young, immaculate heroine is confronted by the magician, Comus, who is drunk and sensual. He tries to have her beautiful virginity, but she is successful in warding him off. The poem is full of discourses and learned reminiscences of the classics and lyrical grace. The morality is high and only the select few could appreciate it.

In *Lycidas* (1637) Milton laments the death of a friend by drowning. The elegy asks the question that if a young man full of promise is carried away in the prime of youth then what avails in this life? Pleasure, therefore, calls him to *"sport with Amaryllis in the shade, Or with the tangles of Neaera's hair".* But another voice, that of fame, calls him away to a life of virtue.

Milton wrote in prose for twenty years. He also composed some exquisite sonnets including the one *On His Blindness* where he regrets he might be incapable of performing God's wish on earth because of his impairment, but consoles himself that even through poetry he can fulfill his life:

"And that one talent which is death to hide
Lodged with me useless
But Patience to prevent that murmur soon replies
They also serve who only stand and wait".

The Restoration of 1660 deprived him of his post for sometime. Poverty, blindness and leisure brought forth his best works: *Paradise Lost* (1667), *Paradise Regained* and *Samson Agonistes* (1671). Here we read in magniloquent lines through great biblical allegories of his personal unhappiness and a nation's agony. He is Beelzebub Satan and Samson in rebellion. Thrown out of Heaven by God, Satan exhorts:

"What though the field be lost
All is not lost
The unconquerable will to survive".

He wrote in blank verse only and used choruses in *Samson Agonistes. Paradise Lost* is his magnum opus, a Puritan's meditation of the Bible or his interpretation of it. The story of Adam and Eve becomes the drama of conscience, the exposure to temptation. The Bible has the ingredients of his own life. *Paradise Regained* is a reply to *Paradise Lost.* This poem is an allegory based on the story of Christ's fast for forty days where he resists the three temptations of Satan and destroys the latter's reign on earth. Christ is seen not as divine incarnation, but as a superman. In fact, Milton himself is Christ, like in that he resists the great temptation for worldly fame by mastering Greek culture and becoming a poet. Literature, philosophy and art are all vain compared to the true wisdom of the Bible.

In *Samson Agonistes,* we again see Milton. He is Samson betrayed by Delilah. He is alone and isolated, blind and helpless, the last of the Republicans among the triumphant Royalists. He lashes out against woman, as the inferior of the human race, deceitful and untrustworthy. The poem is like a Hellenic drama, but lacks movement. There is unending dialectics and reasoning.

SUMMARY AND MAIN POINTS

Life

1. Milton got a very good education and this, combined with his matchless genius, enabled him to achieve things never attempted, much less achieved, by any poet so far.
2. (*i*) His father became a puritan and Milton inherited all the qualities of virtue, purity, discipline and austerity from him.
   (*ii*) However, Milton by natural bent of mind was a great lover of art, music and literature. Hence the qualities of Hebraism and Hellenism blended in him in equal measure.
3. Thus Milton was :
   (*i*) a religious man
   (*ii*) a great scholar
   (*iii*) a lover of music, if not a musician
   (*iv*) a great epic poet
   (*v*) a politician
   (*vi*) a radical in thought
   (*vii*) a lover and crusader of liberty and freedom, particularly that of the press and the soul.
   (*viii*) a reformer
   (*ix*) a lover of beauty in man and nature
   (*x*) He had spirit of devotion and dedication to cause and duty.
4. Milton imbibed the love of religion, art, music and literature and even politics from his father and those of generosity and charity from his mother.
5. From 1632 onwards, Milton withdrew to the country home of his father in Horton where he led an almost solitary life studying deeply the classics in various languages such as :
   (*i*) Greek (*ii*) Latin (*iii*) Hebrew
   (*iv*) French (*v*) Italian (*vi*) Spanish
   (*vii*) English, etc.
6. Not only this, Milton also got a mastery over such disparate subjects as:
   (*i*) music (*ii*) science (*iii*) mathematics
   (*iv*) theology, etc.
7. (*i*) Thereafter, Milton went on a continental tour. He visited France, Switzerland and Italy.
   (*ii*) He met Grotius, the Dutch scholar in Paris, and Galileo in Florence where he was serving a jail term.
8. As Civil War broke out in England, Milton hurried back to England.
9. In His "Tenure of Kings and Magistrates," Milton asserted the divine right of the people to take the action necessary for their self-defence and protection, as against the Divine Right of the King asserted earlier by James I and now by Charles I.
10. (*i*) Milton was married in 1643 to Mary Powell.
    (*ii*) She was not a woman of high calibre and, moreover, she was fond of a luxurious life.
    (*iii*) To cap it all, she belonged to a Royalist family.
11. (*i*) Just a month after their marriage, the girl deserted Milton.
    (*ii*) It was then that Milton wrote :
    (*a*) "Doctrine and Discipline of Divorce," and
    (*b*) "Tetrachordon"
    (*iii*) This he did to justify the repudiation of marriage from his side.
    (*iv*) Milton's arguments were not taken with pleasant approval by the people of England.
12. (*i*) After the death of his wife he married the second time.

(*ii*) After her death he wrote his famous sonnet: "Methought I saw my late espoused saint."

(*iii*) He married the third time in 1663.

(*iv*) Now, Milton had been stone blind since 1652 and his third wife was like a nurse to him.

13. (*i*) He wrote "Defensio pro Populo Anglicano"—a controversial work but containing powerful prose.

(*ii*) However, his best prose work is "Areopagitica" in which he fights the cause of freedom of press like a true crusader.

Works

Early works : Among his early works, we have :

1. On the Morning of Christ's Nativity
2. L'Allegro
3. Il Penseroso
4. The Masque of Comus (1634)
5. Lycidas
6. Sonnets

Characteristics

1. **On the Morning of Christ's Nativity:** Long points out, "In his early work Milton appears as the inheritor of all that was best in Elizabethan literature, and his first work, the ode "On the Morning of Christ's Nativity" approaches the high-water mark of lyric poetry in England."

2. **L'Allegro and Il Penseroso:**

(*i*) These poems belong to Milton's Horton period.

(*ii*) The former is about the happy man, and the latter about the sad man.

(*iii*) Long writes on **L'Allegro:**

"The air is sweet; birds are singing; multitude of sights, sounds, fragrances, fill all the senses; and to this appeal of nature the soul of man responds by being happy, seeing in every flower and hearing in every harmony some exquisite symbol of human life."

(*iv*) **In Il Penseroso,** we have inter alia:

(*a*) a scene of twilight and the appearance of the moon.

(*b*) "a quiet thoughtfulness.... which is not sad, though like all quiet moods, it is akin to sadness, and which sounds the deeps of human emotion in the presence of nature." (Long)

3. **Comus**

(*i*) According to Long, it "is in many respects the most perfect of Milton's poems".

(*ii*) In Comus, we have inter alia:

(*a*) dance and music

(*b*) gorgeous visual scenery

(*c*) the hoary past moral purpose but so consummately delineated by Milton—
The Triumph of Virtue over vice.

4. **Lycidas**

(*i*) It is an elegy written by Milton on the death of his college friend, Edward King.

(*ii*) It is a blend of "high moral purpose with the noblest poetry." (Long)

(*iii*) There is abundance of supernatural element in the poem in the form of nymphs, fauns, satyrs, etc.

(*iv*) So, the poem is an unrivalled example of "Pagan Renaissance."

5. **Sonnets**

(*i*) Milton made use of the form which is known as Miltonic, Italian or Petrarchan in his sonnets instead of the Shakespearean form.

(*ii*) Instead of love, Milton directed his sonnets towards such subjects as:

(*a*) fulfilment of duty

(*b*) unflinching patriotism

(*c*) music and harmony

(*d*) undying love for political struggle

(*e*) undeterrable faith in God and His creation.

(*f*) justification of ways of God to man which he later endeavoured most vehemently, elaborately and consummately in Paradise Lost.

(*iii*) That is why Wordsworth says of him:

"Thy soul was like a star and dwelt apart;
Thou hadst a voice whose sound was like the sea—
Pure as the naked heavens, majestic, free."

(*iv*) Some of his famous sonnets are:

(*a*) On Arriving at the Age of Twenty Three

(*b*) On His Deceased Wife

(*c*) The Massacre in Piedmont

(*d*) On His Blindness

(*v*) Unlike Wordsworth who wrote 500 or more sonnets, Milton did not write many sonnets.

6. **Paradise Lost**

(*i*) Its theme is the Fall of Man.

(*ii*) In it Milton wanted to justify the ways of God to man.

(*iii*) No doubt, it is Milton's greatest and best work which has made him immortal.

(*iv*) According to Lamartine, it is "the dream of a Puritan fallen asleep over his Bible."

(*v*) It was composed by Milton when he had fully lost his eye-sight.

(*vi*) Paradise Lost has 12 books like any true epic.

Book I: It contains *inter alia*:

(*i*) A noble invocation

(*ii*) A description of Satan and his legions,

(*iii*) The description of the rebel angels' plot to wife out the state of innocence of Adam and Eve, our first parents, as created by God.

Book II: It contains *inter alia*:

(*i*) The great meeting of the devils

(*ii*) The start of Satan's journey to cause temptation of Adam and Eve.

Book III: It contains *inter alia*:

(*i*) God's despatch of Raphael to undertake the warning of Adam and Eve about the impending danger.

(*ii*) The Son of God's offer of personal sacrifice to take upon himself the punishment to man for disobedience to God.

(*iii*) Satan is also seen again.

Book IV: It contains *inter alia*:

(*i*) The scene of Paradise

(*ii*) Satan is caught while tempting Eve in a dream, but is not punished.

Book V, VI: It contains *inter alia*:

(*i*) Eve's narration of her dream to Adam.

(*ii*) Scenes of their daily routine

(*iii*) Arrival of Raphael, etc.

Book VII: It contains the story of creation as told by Raphael.

Book VIII: It contains Adam's narration of his own story, etc.

Book IX: It describes Satan's temptation of Eve, etc.

Book X: It contains *inter alia*:

(*i*) God's judgement upon Adam and Eve.

(*ii*) Their repentance

(*iii*) Satan and his followers' changing into hissing serpents.

Book XI: It describes :

(*i*) God's acceptance of Adam's repentance, but His ordering of his banishment from Eden.

(*ii*) Michael's departure to execute God's orders.

Book XII: It describes *inter alia* :

(*i*) Adam and Eve's having the assurance regarding their future redemption.

(*ii*) Man's first ancestors' being turned out of paradise "hand in hand."

Comments: The poem is :

(*i*) a triumph of Milton's most artistic blank verse.

(*ii*) a triumph of the Epic art.

(*iii*) an assertion of the Puritan view-point.

(*iv*) a perfect expression of Milton's own love of music, liberty, justice, etc.

(*v*) a triumph of sublimity and what is called "the grand style."

(*vi*) a justification of man's ways to God, instead of God's ways to man, as Milton claimed to assert.

(*vii*) the unrivalled character of Satan which resembles Milton's own in many respects.

(*viii*) a triumph of Hebraism.

(*ix*) a triumph of the subjective art.

(*x*) a triumph of the Elizabethan wonder, which earned Milton the title : "A belated Elizabethan".

7. **Paradise Regained**

(*i*) It is a bare poem as compared to Paradise Lost in the matter of style, as is shorn of ornate prosody.

(*ii*) It has wonderful lines and passages showing Milton's :

(*a*) purity and loftiness of mind

(*b*) most exquisite scenery and imagery

(*iii*) Here, Christ, who spurns the tempter, is, in fact, Milton himself as 'In Paradise Lost' Milton is often identified with Satan, who loves liberty above anything else, at least in the first two books.

(*iv*) The theme of the poem is "Christ's temptation in the wilderness."

8. **Samson Agonistes**

(*i*) Samson was an Israeli wrestler who was blind and much maligned.

(*ii*) He was a champion of liberty.

(*iii*) Milton can indisputably be identified with him.

(*iv*) The poem is "a pure tragedy, with all the passion and restraint which marked the old Greek dramas." (Long)

(*v*) The climax is reached when Samson chained with the central pillar of a dome where his tormentors are making merry, brings down the whole structure which destroys all.

WILLIAM WORDSWORTH (1770–1850)

Life

William Wordsworth was born on April 7, 1770 at Cockermouth in the cumberland highlands. His father was a lawyer and land agent. He lost both the parents by the age of fourteen. His school days at Hawkeshead was full of joy, spent in games and reading. He joined St John's College, Cambridge when he was seventeen and went on a walking tour of France during one of his vacations. Taking his degree in 1791 he went to France to stay. The cause of the French Revolution — liberty and equality — attracted him much. He spent 1797-98 mostly with Coleridge and published *Lyrical Ballads* in collaboration with him. After this he visited Germany with his sister Dorothy. Finally he returned to Grasmere in the Lake district of England. Here he published the second volume of the *Lyrical Ballads* and married his cousin Mary Hutchinson.

Wordsworth's life was spent in quiet contempiation and meditation in the beautiful Lake district. Here nature inspired him to write his poetry. He also visited Wales, Scotland and Ireland. He was left a legacy of money by a kind man and got a job as sinecure — distributor of stamps. A man of simple living and high thinking, he could lead a comfortable life and devote himself to poetry. In 1842, the Government provided him a pension of £ 300 a year.

Earlier Wordsworth's poetry received no recognition. In fact, there was adverse criticism of it. But during the last two decades of his life, recognition came to him. He received an honorary degree from the Universities of Durham and Oxford. In 1843 he was appointed poet-laureate. He died in 1850.

Wordsworth was of hardy north-country stock. In austerity he reminds us of Milton. Wordsworth's egotism came in the way of appreciation of the poetry of others.

Works

Most of Wordsworth's voluminous work is dull and prosaic. Only a few works like *The Prelude* and *The Excursion* make him worthy of the recognition he received as poet-laureate. First and foremost, Wordsworth was the High Priest of Nature. While Cowper, Burns, Blake, Byron, Shelley and Keats all loved Nature 'it was only the external forms'. To Wordsworth Nature was where the Spirit of the Supreme Being dwelt Nature revealed God's peace and mystery. He had a mystic understanding of Nature. Nature showed the bonds that united all forms of life together — birds, animals and humans. To love all was the message of Nature, Nature was a great teacher. In his own words:

"One impulse from a vernal wood
May teach you more of man,
Of moral evil and of good,
Than all the sages can".

To be able to learn such lessons, Wordsworth advocated a receptive heart. If one bared oneself to the influence of Nature one received wisdom, health, beauty, grace and peace of mind. In one of his *Lucy* poems he says:

"And beauty born of murmuring sound
Shall pass into her face".

When England went to war with France, his mind was in conflict between patriotic loyalty and his love and admiration for the Revolution. War shattered all hopes. He returned to Nature to restore his faith in divine providence and found Nature a great healer.

Nature was a teacher of morals. *"Stern Daughter of the voice of God,"* he called her. His attitude to Nature developed in stages. First, he saw the visionary gleams of childhood in the *Ode on the Intimations of Childhood.*

"There was a time when valley, rock and hill
Seem'd apparelled in celestial light".

Later he developed a passion for Nature which gave him *"aching joys."* Finally, Nature in all its manifestations gave him a lesson in living: *"the meanest flower that blows"* gave him *"thoughts that do often lie too deep for tears".*

Once when Wordsworth was returning home from Cambridge, he passed through a very beautiful landscape of mountains and the sea and that moment of enchantment with Nature was a flash of illumination. He realized that his mission of life was to teach mankind. He wished to bring mankind back to Nature for healing and morals. He set out to write the long poem *The Recluse,* consisting of two parts *The Prelude* (1850) and *The Excursion* (1814). He could not finish the work. Wordsworth claimed that his work as a poet was to teach and this is what he does. The poem is marred by too much moralizing.

Wordsworth felt that the real characters for his poetry must be common, noble men, not Lords and Ladies. He, therefore, wrote a number of poems like *The Idiot Boy, Harry Gill* and *Peter Bell* (1819) in which metre is ignored and common everyday speech is used. The effect is prosaic poetry — dull and ineffective. The real great poetry of Wordsworth is that which springs from his genius, not his poetic beliefs. Wordsworth's great poetry shows spiritual depths of calm reflection. As he writes in *Laodamia,* his classical poem, *"For the Gods approve / The depth and not the tumult of the soul".*

Wordsworth wrote a great variety of poems — odes, lyrics and almost 400 sonnets of which *Upon Westminster Bridge, On Milton* and *The World is too much with Us* are famous.

According to Wordsworth, poetry was "emotion recollected in transquillity". *The Solitary Reaper, To a Highland Girl, The Daffodils, Tintern Abbey* and the *Immortality Ode* were written after sometime had elapsed from the event described. These events were moments of perception and when the time had passed the emotions stirred by those moments surfaced clearly. These emotions are then put into words.

SUMMARY AND MAIN POINTS

Life

1. He was born at Cockermouth, Cumberland. (A poet/critic has called him "the gander of Cockermouth").
2. He got education at Hawkeshead School, Lancashire, and Cambridge.
3. He paid two visits to France :
   (*i*) The first time in 1790
   (*ii*) The second time in 1791-92.

   Long divides his life into four periods :
   (*i*) *1770-87:* It belongs to his childhood and youth-Cumberland.
   (*ii*) *1787-97:* This period covers :
   (*a*) his life at Cambridge
   (*b*) his travels abroad which enabled him to be influenced by the revolutionary ideas.

☛ We know that his revolutionary enthusiasm died soon with :
 (*i*) the excesses of the Revolution including what is called "The Reign of Terror,"
 (*ii*) the rise of tyrannical Napoleon
 (*iii*) 1797-99: This period was very significant as it enabled him to understand his own abilities and take full advantage of them.
 (*iv*) 1799-1850: It was practically a period of retirement in the lake region of his birth and childhood and to remain in direct touch with nature.

Works

1. His "Lyrical Ballads"—a book which is often considered the start of the Revival of Romanticism in England appeared in 1798.
2. His Preface to the Lyrical Ballads is considered important in the history of Criticism of English literature.
3. (*i*) He intended to write a single great poem under the caption "The Recluse."
 (*ii*) The poem was intended to give a comprehensive treatment of: (*a*) nature, (*b*) man and (c) society.
 (*iii*) His intention was that his "The Prelude"—the Growth of a Poet's Mind—should introduce the Recluse.
 (*iv*) (*a*) The first book of The Recluse "The Home at Grasmere" was published posthumously in 1888.
 (*b*) The name of the second book was 'The Excursion.'
 (*c*) The third was never completed by the poet.

His most famous poems are :

1. The Prelude
2. Tintern Abbey
3. Ode on Intimations of Immortality.
4. Ode to Duty or Education of Nature
5. The Rainbow
6. The Solitary Reaper
7. Michael
8. To a Skylark
9. Yarrow Revisited
10. Lucy Gray
11. She Dwelt Among the Untrodden Ways
12. Daffodils

He also wrote a large number of sonnets such as :

1. On Milton
2. On Westminster Bridge
3. The World is Too Much With Us, etc.

Characteristics

1. He was a great lover of nature.
2. He felt the presence of a spirit in nature, that is, the spirit of nature.
3. He believed in pantheism.
4. He believed that nature could bestow peace, sympathy, love, joy and other virtues on man.
5. He did not like to depict nature "red in tooth and claw."
6. He believed that nature gave purity to man and ennobled his heart.
7. He was a great lover of the common man and the rustic and rural life.
8. He loved the child and thought that because of its innocence, purity of thought and nearness to God, childhood was the golden period of human life.
9. He loved all creation and all kinds of creatures, including the smallest and most insignificant animals and insects.
10. He believed that "nature never did betray the heart that loved her."
11. He himself practised what he preached and spent most of his time in the company of nature.
12. His poetry is full of :
 (*i*) vivid descriptions of scenes of nature.
 (*ii*) simple human affections.
 (*iii*) fervent adulations of childhood and love of animals.
 (*iv*) depictions of country and village life.
 (*v*) sweet and haunting music.
 (*vi*) personal reminiscences and memories
 (*vii*) autobiographical tones
 (*viii*) adulation of simplicity and homeliness.
 (*ix*) tones of true theism and fervent faith in greatness, goodness and benignity of nature.
13. Although much of his later poetry is dull and interesting, yet it contains flashes of imaginative lines and good poetry.

JOHN GALSWORTHY (1867–1933)

John Galsworthy was an English novelist and playwright. His notable works include *The Forsyte Saga* (1906–1921) and its sequels, *A Modern Comedy* and *End of the Chapter*. He won the Nobel Prize in Literature in 1932.

Life

John Galsworthy was born on 14 August 1867 at Kingston Hill in Surrey, England, the son of John and Blanche Bailey (nee Bartleet) Galsworthy. His family was wealthy and well established, with a large estate in Kingston upon Thames that is now the site of three schools: Marymount International School, Rokeby Preparatory School, and Holy Cross. He attended Harrow and New College, Oxford, training as a barrister, and was called to the bar in 1890. However, he was not keen to begin practising law and instead travelled abroad to look after the family's shipping business. During these travels he met Joseph Conrad, then the first mate of a sailing-ship moored in the harbour of Adelaide, Australia, and the two future novelists became close friends. In 1895 Galsworthy began an affair with Ada Nemesis Pearson Cooper (1864–1956), the wife of his cousin Major Arthur Galsworthy. After her divorce ten years later, they married 23 September 1905 and stayed together until his death in 1933. Before their marriage, they often stayed clandestinely in a farmhouse called Wingstone in the village of Manaton on Dartmoor, Devon. From 1908 he took out a long lease on part of the building and made it their regular second home until 1923.

From the Four Winds, a collection of short stories, was Galsworthy's first published work in 1897. These and several subsequent works were published under the pen name John Sinjohn, and it would not be until *The Island Pharisees* (1904) that he would begin publishing under his own name, probably owing to the death of his father. His first full-length novel, *Jocelyn* was published in an edition of 750 under the name of *John Sinjohn* – he later refused to have it republished. His first play, *The Silver Box* (1906), – in which the theft of a prostitute's purse by a rich 'young man of good family' is placed beside the theft of a silver cigarette case from the rich man's father's house by 'a poor devil', with very different repercussions – became a success, and he followed it up with *The Man of Property* (1906), the first in the Forsyte trilogy. Although he continued writing both plays and novels, it was as a playwright that he was mainly appreciated at the time. Along with those of other writers of the time, such as George Bernard Shaw, his plays addressed the class system and social issues, two of the best known being *Strife* (1909) and *The Skin Game* (1920).

He is now far better known for his novels, particularly *The Forsyte Saga,* his trilogy about the eponymous family and connected lives. These books, as with many of his other works, deal with social class, upper-middle class lives in particular. Although sympathetic to his characters, he highlights their insular, snobbish, and acquisitive attitudes and their suffocating moral codes. He is viewed as one of the first writers of the Edwardian era who challenged some of the ideals of society depicted in the preceding literature of Victorian England. The depiction of a woman in an unhappy marriage furnishes another recurring theme in his work. The character of Irene in *The Forsyte Saga* is drawn from Ada Pearson, though her previous marriage was not as miserable as that of the character.

Through his writings he campaigned for a variety of causes, including prison reform, women's rights, animal welfare, and the opposition of censorship. During World War I he worked in a hospital in France as an orderly after being passed over for military service. He was elected as the first president of the PEN International literary club in 1921, was appointed to the Order of Merit in 1929 — after earlier turning down a knighthood — and was awarded the Nobel Prize in 1932. He was too ill to attend the Nobel awards ceremony, and died six weeks later on 31 January 1933 of a stroke at his London home.

John Galsworthy lived for the final seven years of his life at Bury in West Sussex. In accordance with his will he was cremated at Woking with his ashes then being scattered over the South Downs from an aeroplane, but there are also memorials in High gate 'New' Cemetery and in the cloisters of New College, Oxford (the latter cut and placed in the cloisters by Eric Gill). The popularity of his fiction waned quickly after his death but the hugely successful adaptation of *The Forsyte Saga* in 1967 renewed interest in his work.

A number of John Galsworthy's letters and papers are held at the University of Birmingham Special Collections.

In 2007, Kingston University, London opened a new building named in recognition of his local birth. Galsworthy Road in Kingston, location of Kingston Hospital, is also named for him.

Works

- *From the Four Winds,* 1897 (as John Sinjohn)
- *Jocelyn,* 1898 (as John Sinjohn)
- *Villa Rubein,* 1900 (as John Sinjohn)
- *A Man of Devon,* 1901 (as John Sinjohn)
- *The Island Pharisees,* 1904
- *The Silver Box,* 1906 (his first play
- *The Man of Property,* 1906 – first book of *The Forsyte Saga* (1922)
- *The Country House,* 1907
- *A Commentary,* 1908
- *Fraternity,* 1909
- *A Justification for the Censorship of Plays,* 1909
- *Strife,* 1909
- *Fraternity,* 1909
- *Joy,* 1909
- *Justice,* 1910
- *A Motley,* 1910
- *The Spirit of Punishment,* 1910
- *Horses in Mines,* 1910
- *The Patrician,* 1911
- *The Pigeon,* 1912
- *The Eidest Son,* 1912
- *Quality,* 1912
- *Moods, Songs, and Doggerels,* 1912
- *For Love of Beasts,* 1912
- *The Inn of Tranquillity,* 1912

- *The Dark Flower,* 1913
- *The Fugitive,* 1913
- *The Mob,* 1914
- *The Freelands,* 1915
- *The Little Man,* 1915
- *A Bit's Love,* 1915
- *A Sheaf,* 1916
- *The Apple Tree,* 1916
- *Beyond,* 1917
- *Five Tales,* 1918
- *Indian Summer of a Forsyte,* 1918 – first interlude of *The Forsyte Saga*
- *Saint's Progress,* 1919
- *Addresses in America,* 1912
- *The Foundations,* 1920
- *In Chancery,* 1920 – second book of *The Forsyte Saga*
- *Awakening,* 1920 – second interlude of *The Forsyte Saga*
- *Awakening,* 1920 – second interlude of *The Forsyte Saga*
- *The Skin Game,* 1920
- *To Let,* 1921 – third book of *The Forsyte Saga*
- *A Family Man,* 1922
- *The Little Man,* 1922
- *Loyalties,* 1922
- *Windows,* 1922
- *Captures,* 1923
- *Abracadabra,* 1924
- *The Forest,* 1924
- *Old English,* 1924
- *The White Monkey,* 1924 – first book of *A Modern Comedy* (1929)
- *The Show,* (1925
- *Escape,* 1926
- *The Silver Spoon,* 1926 – second book of *A Modern Comedy*
- *Verses New and Old,* 1926
- *Castles in Spain,* 1927
- *A Silent Wooing,* 1927 – first Interlude of *A Modern Comedy*
- *Passers By,* 1927 – second Interlude of *A Modern Comedy*
- *Swan Song,* 1928 – third book of *A Modern Comedy*
- *The Manaton Edition,* 1923–26 (collection, 30 vols.)
- *Exiled,* 1929
- *The Roof,* 1929
- *On Forsyte Change,* 1930
- *Two Essays on Conrad,* 1930
- *Soames and the Flag,* 1930
- *The Creation of Character in Literature,* 1931 (The Romanes Lecture for (1931).
- *Maid in Waiting,* 1931 – first book of *End of the Chapter* (1934)
- *Forty Poems,* 1932
- *Flowering Wilderness,* 1932
- *Over the River,* 1933
- *Autobiographical Letters of Galsworthy: A Correspondence with Frank Harris,* 1933
- *The Grove Edition,* 1927–34 (collection, 27 Vols.)
- *Collected Poems,* 1934
- *Flowering Wilderness,* 1932 – second book of *End of the Chapter*
- *One More River* (originally *Over the River*), 1933 – third book of *End of the Chapter*
- *Punch and Go,* 1935
- *The Life and Letters,* 1935
- *The Winter Garden,* 1935
- *Forsytes, Pendyces and Others,* 1935
- *Selected Short Stories,* 1935
- *Glimpses and Reflections,* 1937
- *Galsworthy's Letters to Leon Lion,* 1968
- *Letters from John Galsworthy* 1900–1932, 1970

SUMMARY AND MAIN POINTS

1. Galsworthy's early works which were written over the pseudonym "John Sinjohn" were all rejected by the publishers.
2. (*i*) His first work which made him widely known was 'The Man of Property' (a novel).
   (*ii*) It deals with middle-class Victorian society.
3. In 1904 he published his play "Island Pharisees", which reappeared as "The Pigeon" in 1922.
4. The same year (1922) was published "The Forsyte Saga.
5. In all, he wrote about thirty works of fiction. According to Long, the best among them all is "Indian Summer of a Forsyte."
6. Galsworthy is better known as a play-wright than a fiction writer.
7. His plays are what now we know as "Problem Plays."
8. His most famous plays among his thirty plays are :
   (*i*) Strife (For this work he received the Nobel Prize for Literature)
   (*ii*) Justice (1910)
   (*iii*) Loyalties (1922)
   (*iv*) The Silver Box (1909)
   (*v*) Escape (1926)

The Skin Game was adapted and directed by Alfred Hitchocock in 1931. It starred C.V. France, Helen Haye, Jill Esmond, Edmoud Gwenn, and John Longden.

Escape was filmed in 1930 and 1948. The latter was directed by Joseph L. Mankiewicz, starring Rex Harrison, Peggy Cummins, and William Hartnell. The screenplay was by Philip Dunne.

One More River (a film version of Galsworthy's *Over the River*) was filmed by James Whale in 1934. The film starred Frank Lawton, Colin Clive (one of Whale's most frequently used actors), Diana Wynyard, and featured Mrs. Patrick Campbell in a rare sound film appearance.

The First and the Last, as short play, was adapted as *21 Days*, starring Vivien Leigh and Laurence Olivier.

Galsworthy's short story *The Apple Tree* was adapted into a radio play for Orson Welles's *Lady Esther Almanac* radio series on CBS, first broadcast on 12 January 1942; the play was again produced by Welles for CBS on *The Mercury Summer Theatre* of 6 September 1946. The 1988 film *A Summer Story* was also based on *The Apple Tree.*

The Patrician was broadcast on NBC University Theater of the Air radio show on 24 February 1950.

Characteristics

In the works of **John Galsworthy (1867-1933)** we find an artistic conscience. Like Wells, he also attacked the concept of property and commercialism in his novels. He too exposed and criticized national prejudices, especially those existing among his own class, the landed gentry. He was widely read in Continental Literature and was especially influenced by France and Russia. Turgenev with his noble realism was his ideal. He is a detached and impartial observer of his country's decadent values. He advocates a fearless search for truth. *In The Island Pharisees* (1904) he exposes the stagnation of thought among English privileged classes. A similar theme is touched in other novels like *The Country House* (1907), *The Patrician* (1911) and *The Dark Flower* (1913) where country squires, aristocracy and artists are critically studied. *The Forsyte Saga* (1922) is his masterpiece. It is a natural history of the rich upper-middle class family. He describes their attitude to events like the Great War, the growth of socialism, unemployment and the coal strike.

MULTIPLE CHOICE QUESTIONS

1. Shakespeare was born at:
A. London B. Stratford-on-Avon
C. Leicester D. Edinburgh

2. Shakespeare married:
A. Portia B. Imogen
C. Anne Hathaway D. Lucy

3. Shakespeare's first job in a London theatre was:
A. acting as a ghost
B. translating plays
C. to write plays
D. holding visitor's horses

4. Shakespeare first wrote his plays for:
A. Earl of Leicester's Players
B. The Globe
C. The King's Players
D. The Shakespeare Society

5. Shakespeare wrote:
A. 20 plays B. 35 plays
C. 24 plays D. 37 plays

6. His sonnets are mostly addressed to:
A. Queen Elizabeth
B. Ben Jonson
C. The Earl of Southampton
D. The Duke of Edinburgh

7. *Venus* and *Adonis* is a poem of:
A. Two Sisters B. Victory
C. Love D. Greek art

8. The play written in collaboration with Marlowe was:
A. Winter's Tale B. Merchant of Venice
C. Titus Andronicus D. Hamlet

9. Portia is a character in the Shakespearean play:
A. Merchant of Venice
B. Twelfth Night
C. The Tempest
D. Romeo and Juliet

10. The Shakespearean play which describes the assassination of a Roman general is:
A. Macbeth B. Julius Caesar
C. Othello D. Richard II

11. The first folio of all of Shakespeare's plays were published in:
A. 1616 B. 1638
C. 1640 D. 1623

12. The only play missing from the first folio is:
A. The Winter's Tale
B. The Merry Wives of Windsor
C. Pericles
D. A Midsummer Night's Dream

13. Shakespeare wrote his plays in:
A. Rhyming couplets B. Blank verse
C. Quatrains D. Iambic metre

14. The Jew with whom Shakespeare showed sympathy in one of his plays is:
A. Morose B. Barabbas
C. Nicodemus D. Shylock

15. Puck Goodfellow in *A Midsummer Night's Dream* is a/an:
A. impish fairy B. courtier
C. moneylender D. soldier

16. The downfall of Shakespeare's tragic characters is owing to:
A. the Will of God B. a fatal flaw in character
C. destiny D. evil advisers

17. Shakespeare got the plot of most of his plays from:
A. Existing plays
B. Ben Jonson
C. The original classics
D. Translations of Greek, Roman and other European stories.

18. Although Macbeth is a murderer, he is still the hero because:
A. he wants to become the king
B. his life ends tragically
C. he shows uncommon intelligence and vitality
D. he refuses to surrender

19. The part of a play where all the major themes and characters are introduced is known as:
A. Revelation B. Exposition
C. Chorus D. Introduction

20. Among Shakespeare's 37 plays, *Macbeth* was .... in order of being published.
A. 28th B. 26th
C. 30th D. 35th

21. In tragedy, human beings are shown coming to terms with forces larger and greater than themselves. These forces are:
A. Devils B. Fate or Death
C. Circumstances D. Natural calamities

22. The cause of the downfall of a Shakespearean hero is:
A. *hubris* or pride B. God's will
C. a bad woman D. some wrong decision

23. The book which influenced Shakespeare the most in introducing witches in *Macbeth* was:
A. Demonology
B. Chronicles of Scotland
C. Discovery of Witchcraft
D. Written by King James I

24. Shakespeare's Macbeth is an important source of information about the history of:
A. Scotland
B. England of his own times
C. Ireland
D. The world

25. The belief in Elizabethan times that the King was God's representative or image on earth led to the theory of the:
A. Divine Right of Kings
B. Great Chain of Being
C. Natural Order
D. Witchcraft

26. According to the Elizabethans anything that went contrary to the natural order was:
A. good B. strange
C. revolutionary D. evil

27. In Tudor England, women's role in society was:
A. more important than men
B. that of a slave
C. equal to men
D. secondary to men

28. Widows could not protect their property, and if they showed bold ideas, they were accused of being:
A. thieves B. wrongful owners
C. witches D. greedy

29. In the beginning of *Macbeth*, the three witches meet:
A. in a health B. in a ruined building
C. in a forest D. in a barn

30. What title do the witches use to hail Macbeth?
A. General B. Victor
C. Glamis D. King

31. The fourth witch is the name usually given to:
A. One of Duncan's royal maids
B. An invisible spirit
C. Macduff's wife
D. Lady Macbeth

32. The witches prophesy that Macbeth cannot be killed till a forest comes moving down towards him. This forest is:
A. Dunsinane B. The Black Forest
C. Brinam Wood D. The Scottish Forest

33. Duncan wants to make which one of these his successor to the throne?
A. Malcolm, his own son
B. Macbeth
C. Banquo
D. Fleance

34. In the beginning of the play, Macbeth is shown returning from:
A. a tour B. a holiday
C. battle D. an expedition

35. Lady Macbeth is described as:
A. masculine B. frail as any woman
C. kind-hearted D. dull and powerless

36. Lady Macbeth does not wish to kill the sleeping Duncan because:
A. he resembles her father
B. it is not proper for a woman
C. her husband is the one who will succeed him
D. it is not proper to kill the enemy in sleep

37. Duncan is a guest of the Macbeths at:
A. Edinburgh Castle B. Dunsinane
C. Buckingham D. Inverness Castle

38. A speech in which an actor reveals his innermost thoughts is called a:

A. Soliloquy B. Aside
C. Chorus D. Loud thinking

39. The dagger that Macbeth sees in the air is:

A. his own dagger held by a spirit
B. a projection of his imagination signifying the murder of his conscience and peace
C. some other object resembling a dagger
D. suspended from a thread

40. Who says "I have supped too much with horrors/And know the taste of blood"?

A. Banquo B. Duncan
C. Macbeth D. Lady Macbeth

41. Who says that all the sweet scents of Arabia cannot remove the stench of blood and all the seven seas cannot wash off the blood of Duncan from the hands?

A. Lady Macbeth B. Malcolm
C. The Witches D. Macbeth

42. No man of woman born will be able to kill Macbeth. So the witches prophesied. But Macduff succeeds in killing him because he was born from:

A. a goddess B. a miracle
C. a Caesarean operation D. a test-tube

43. Lady Macbeth's sleep-walking is a result of her:

A. deep sense of guilt B. overactive brain
C. dreams D. pretence

44. Which of these plays by Shakespeare does *not* use 'cross-dressing' as a device?

A. *As You Like It*
B. *Julius Caeser*
C. *Cymbeline*
D. *Two Gentlemen of Verona*

45. The etymological meaning of the word "trope" is

A. gesture B. turning
C. mirror D. desire

46. In the late seventeenth century a "Battle of Books" erupted between which two groups?

A. Cavaliers and Roundheads
B. Abolitionists and Enthusiasts for slaves
C. Champions of Ancient and Modern Learning
D. The Welsh and the Scots

47. Shakespeare's sonnets:

A. do not carry a dedication.
B. are dedicated to James I of England.
C. are dedicated to Mary Arden.
D. are dedicated to an unknown "Mr. W.H."

48. Which of the following poems uses *terza rima*?

A. John Keats's "Ode to a Nightingale"
B. P.B. Shelley's "Ode to the West Wind"
C. William Wordsworth's "The Solitary Reaper"
D. Alfred Tennyson's "Ulysses"

49. When one says that "someone is no more" or that "someone has breathed his/ her last", the speaker is resorting to

A. euphism B. euphony
C. understatement D. euphemism

50. Which of the following are "companion poems"?

A. "Gypsy songs" and "Songs and Sonnets"
B. "L'Allegro" and "Il Penseroso"
C. "The Good Morrow" and "The Sun Rising"
D. "Full Fathom Five" and "Hark, Hark! the Lark"

51. '*Fluency*' in language is the same as:

A. the ability to put oneself across comfortably in speech and/or writing
B. the ability to command language rather than language commanding the user
C. glibness
D. accuracy

52. What is a mock-heroic poem? A mock-heroic poem

A. mocks at heroic pretensions in poets and critics
B. mocks heroism, an exaggerated virtue in all epics
C. uses a heroic style to deride airs and affectations
D. uses a mocking style to deride heroes and hero-worship

53. In drama, an aside is addressed…

A. to an audience by an actor; the words so spoken are not meant to be heard by other actors on the stage.
B. to other actors on the stage; the words so spoken are not meant to be heard by the audience.
C. by the playwright to the audience.
D. by the protagonist to his/her antagonist

54. Which of the following is not a revenge tragedy?

A. *Hamlet*
B. *The Duchess of Malfi*
C. *Volpone*
D. *Gorboduc*

55. "The pen is mightier than the sword" is an example of

A. simile B. image
C. conceit D. metonymy

56. An epilogue is

A. prefixed to a text which it introduces.
B. suffixed to a text which it sums up or extends.
C. a piece of writing or speech that formally begins a book.
D. a piece of writing or speech that bears no relation to the text at hand.

57. Items in a published book appear in the following order:

A. Index, Copyright Page, Bibliography, Footnotes
B. Copyright Page, Bibliography, Index, Footnotes
C. Copyright Page, Footnotes, Bibliography, Index
D. Bibliography, Copyright Page, Index, Footnotes

58. Which of the following statements on The Prelude by William Wordsworth is/are not true?

1. *The Prelude* was published posthumously.
2. In this poem, Wordsworth records his development as a poet.
3. The poem runs to 14 books; at crucial stages the poet celebrates the sublime natural scenery in developing his spiritual, moral and imaginative nature.
4. Poems like "Michael", "The Old Cumberland Beggar", "She dwelt among the untrodden ways", "Nutting" etc. are the highlights of this volume.

A. 1 to 4 are true B. 1 is not true
C. 4 is not true D. Only 3 is true

59. One of the following *Canterbury Tales* is in prose, identify.

A. *The Pardoner's Tale*
B. *The Parson's Tale*
C. *The Monk's Tale*
D. *The Knight's Tale*

60. A 'curtal sonnet' consists of

A. 11 lines B. 12 lines
C. 13 lines D. 14 lines

61. The expression "murderous innocence" is an example of

A. Oxymoron B. Zeugma
C. Chiasmus D. Pun

62. Which of the following works of John Milton is an elegy?

A. *Lycidas* B. *L'Allegro*
C. *Camus* D. *Paradise Lost*

63. The rhyme scheme of the Spenserian sonnet is

A. abab bcbc cdcd ee B. abab cdcd efef gg
C. abba cddc effe gg D. abba abba cde cde

64. A monosyllabic rhyme on the final stressed syllable of two lines of verse is called

A. monorhyme B. feminine rhyme
C. masculine rhyme D. eye rhyme

65. A sequence of repeated consonantal sounds in a stretch of language is

A. alliteration B. acrostic
C. assent D. syllable

66. English Iambic Pentameter was brought to its first maturity in

A. sonnet B. dramatic verse
C. lyric D. elegy

67. The Restoration comedy has been criticized mainly for its

A. excessive wit and humour
B. bitter satire and cynicism
C. indecency and permissiveness
D. superficial reflection of society

68. Sexual possessiveness is a theme of Shakespeare's

A. *Coriolanus*
B. *Julius Caesar*
C. *Henry IV Part–I*
D. *A Midsummer Night's Dream*

69. Johnson's *Dictionary of the English Language* was published in the year

A. 1710 B. 1755
C. 1739 D. 1759

70. The first complete printed English Bible was produced by

A. William Tyndale B. William Caxton
C. Miles Coverdale D. Roger Ascham

71. Arrange the following in ascending order in terms of size:

1. epic 2. epigram
3. stanza 4. sonnet

A. 1 2 3 4 B. 2 1 3 4
C. 2 3 4 1 D. 1 3 4 2

72. Hyperbole is

1. an extravagant exaggeration
2. a racist slur
3. a metrical skill
4. a figure of speech

A. 1 is correct
B. 1 and 4 are correct
C. 1 and 3 are correct
D. 3 is correct

73. The poetry of Wordsworth and Coleridge was notably influenced by...

A. The Napoleonic Wars
B. The Glorious Revolution
C. The French Revolution
D. Poor Laws

74. "He's not the brightest man in the world" is an example of :

A. Chiasmus B. Hyperbole
C. Litotes D. Simile

75. *Prosody studies*:

A. Line endings B. Meanings of words
C. Patterns of prose D. Metrics

76. *"Formal Criticism"* relates to the structure of:

A. Literary devices B. Myths
C. Content D. Form

77. A *"Foot"* in prosody is a basic unit of :

A. rhyme
B. length
C. rhythmic measurement
D. height

78. "Iambus" is a metrical foot consisting of :

A. two syllables B. three syllables
C. four syllables D. one syllable

79. An "Idyll" is usually a poem about a :
A. picturesque city life
B. panoramic view of nature
C. picture of industrial society
D. picturesque country life

80. The rhyme scheme of the Shakespearean sonnet is :
A. abab, cdcd, efef, gg B. abba, cddc, effe, gg
C. abab, cdcd, efef, gh D. aabb, ccdd, eeff, gg

81. A poem that captures the essence of a moment in a simple image is:
A. Lyric B. Ballad
C. Ode D. Haiku

82. The word 'nature' in the eighteenth century literature stands for :
A. Nature of writing B. External nature
C. Human nature D. The Universe

83. Who is given credit for first using the term "romantic"?
A. Friedrich Schlegel B. Kant
C. Coleridge D. Schiller

84. Heroic Couplet is a pair of :
A. Rhyming iambic pentameter lines
B. Unrhyming iambic pentameter lines
C. Rhyming iambic hexameter
D. Unrhyming iambic hexameter

85. Heroic quatrain is :
A. a stanza in blank verse
B. eight line stanza in iambic hexameter
C. four line stanza in iambic pentameter
D. six line stanza in iambic pentameter

86. Victorian Age witnessed a clash between:
A. faith and reason
B. tradition and modernity
C. oriental and occidental civilization
D. romanticism and neo romanticism

87. The historical novel began in:
A. Restoration Period B. Augustan Age
C. Victorian Period D. Romantic Period

88. Internal rhyme is :
A. the basic rhythmic structure of a poem
B. rhyming of two words in alternative lines
C. rhyming of two or more words in the same line of poetry
D. all the lines of a poem ending with the same line pattern

89. "Fancy" deals with:
A. "Fixities and definities"
B. "Imagination and Reason"
C. "Judgement and Memory"
D. "Structure and Superstructure"

90. The early religious drama is associated with:
A. Superstitions and beliefs
B. Mysteries and histories
C. Interludes and mysteries
D. Miracles and morality

91. Feminine ending refers to :
A. a stressed final syllable in a line of verse
B. the ending of a poem in a stressed syllable
C. the ending of a poem in an unstressed syllable
D. an unstressed final syllable in a line of verse

92. Johnson's edition of Shakespeare appeared in:
A. 1752 B. 1765
C. 1791 D. 1760

93. After Shakespeare made his debut as a London playwright, he was described as an 'upstart crow' by :
A. Robert Greene B. Thomas Lodge
C. Christopher Marlowe D. John Lyly

94. The term 'metaphysical poets', was first used by:
A. Ben Jonson B. Dr. Johnson
C. Helen Gardner D. Dryden

95. Which are the figures of speech used in the following lines by Blake?
"Tyger, tyger, burning bright
In the forest of the night,
What immortal hand or eye
Could frame thy fearful symmetry?"
A. simile and personification
B. irony and synecdoche
C. apostrophe and synecdoche
D. metonymy and apostrophe

96. More's Latin Masterpiece *Utopia* was translated into English in :
A. 1551 B. 1498
C. 1516 D. 1532

97. The Gutenberg Bible was first published in:
A. 1456 B. 1516
C. 1449 D. 1498

98. Restoration Comedy marks the restoration of :
A. women's rights B. democracy
C. monarchy D. human rights

99. "Hamartia" means :
A. reversal of fortunes B. purgation of emotions
C. depravity D. error of judgement

100. The term "gothic", a category of fiction, also applies to:
A. architecture B. painting
C. music D. theater

101. Miracle plays are based on the lives of :
A. Knights B. Crusaders
C. Pilgrims D. Saints

102. A metrical foot consisting of an unstressed syllable followed by a stressed syllable is:
A. dactyl B. trochee
C. iamb D. anapaest

103. Using "the Bench" for the judiciary is an example of :
A. metaphor B. irony
C. synecdoche D. metonymy

104. Four feet, comprising a monosyllable, trochee, dactyl and first paeon is often called:
A. running rhythm B. sprung rhythm
C. blank verse D. rhymed verse

105. "Essays of Elia" are:
A. political ideology B. economic disparity
C. literary criticism D. personal impressions

106. "Peripetia" means :
A. purgation of emotion B. tragic flaw
C. reversal of fortune D. recognition of error

107. "Gynocriticism" focuses on :
A. Criticism on women
B. Criticism by women
C. Criticism of male writers by women writers
D. Women as writers

108. Pre-Raphaelite poetry is mainly concerned with:
A. narrative and style B. narrative and nature
C. form and design D. form and value

109. Who among the Victorians is called "the prophet of modern society"?
A. Ruskin B. Carlyle
C. Macaulay D. Arnold

110. The mystery plays deal with:
A. the life of Christ B. the New Testament
C. Psalms D. Apocrypha

111. Pope's "Essay on Criticism" sums up the art of poetry as taught first by:
A. Aristotle B. Horace
C. Longinus D. Plato

112. A particle is:
A. a patchwork of words, sentences, passages
B. a satirical poem
C. a love song
D. a collection of lines from different poems

113. "Careless she is with artful Care/Affecting to seem unaffected" is an example of:
A. irony B. paradox
C. simile D. metaphor

114. A metrical foot containing a stressed, followed by an unstressed, syllable is:
A. anapaest B. iamb
C. trochee D. dactyl

115. The rhyme scheme of a Spenserian sonnet is:
A. abba, cbcb, cdcd, ee
B. abab, bccb, ccdd, ee
C. aabb, bcbc, ccdd, ee
D. abab, bcbc, cdcd, ee

116. Using the expression "Crown" for the monarchy is an example of:
A. Metonymy B. Synecdoche
C. Irony D. Metaphor

117. Dr. Johnson's *A Dictionary of the English Language* was published in:
A. 1755 B. 1756
C. 1757 D. 1758

118. A figure of speech in which two terms opposite in meaning are placed side-by-side in one phrase is known as:
A. paradox B. oxymoron
C. sarcasm D. antithesis

119. A stanza of eight iambic pentametres on the pattern of ab, ab, ab, cc is known as:
A. Rhyme royal B. Ottava rima
C. Tennysonian stanza D. Spenserian stanza

120. In the assertion "Four out of five people suffer from *dreaded* pyorrhoea", the writer wants to arouse the feeling of:
A. Sympathy B. Fear
C. Hatred D. Ill-will

121. "John is six feet tall and 240 lb" is an assertion of:
A. a fact B. a judgement
C. an opinion D. an inference

122. What is the pseudonym of John Galsworthy?
A. John Gals B. Elia
C. John Sinjohn D. Boz

123. "I wandered lonely as a cloud" makes an assertion that:
A. The poet travelled with the cloud
B. The poet moved aimlessly with the cloud
C. Both the poet and the cloud were lonely
D. The poet moved as aimlessly as the cloud

124. Which was Galsworthy's first published novel?
A. Jocelyn
B. A Man of Devon
C. Villa Rubcin
D. The Science

125. The First Folio of Shakespeare's plays appeared in:
A. 1664 B. 1631
C. 1623 D. 1650

126. Restoration comedy begins with:
A. Congreve B. Sheridan
C. Dryden D. Etherege

127. The soul of tragedy, according to Aristotle is:
A. Thought B. Character
C. Plot D. Spectacle

128. "United we stand, divided we fall" is an example of:
A. Antithesis B. Bathos
C. Tautology D. Litotes

129. A metre in which an unaccented syllable precedes the accented is called:
A. anapaestic B. dactylic
C. catalectic D. iambic

130. Which play analyses the impact of modern publicity on private domestic tragedy?
A. The Show B. Escape
C. Jocelyn D. None of these

131. According to Galsworthy, which play made a great sensation, especially in Parliamentary and official circles?
A. The Mob B. Justice
C. The Skin Game D. The Eldest Son

132. John Galsworthy was awarded the Nobel Prize for literature in
A. 1942 B. 1932
C. 1922 D. 1912

133. The masterpiece of Galsworthy is
A. The Forsyte Saga B. The Freelands
C. Fraternity D. The Patrician

134. Galsworthy deals with the inadequacy of the administration of justice and the attitude of different types of people towards and escaped prisoner in the play
A. Escape B. The Show
C. Jocelyn D. None of these

135. Which universities awarded D. Litt to Galsworthy?
A. Oxford and Princeton University
B. Cambridge and Sheffiled University
C. Oxford and Cambridge
D. None of the above

136. Which novel of Galsworthy illustrates the breaking down of inhibitions and barriers as the result of war?
A. Saint's Progress B. Fraternity
C. Jocelyn D. None of these

137. What is "The White Monkey"?
A. A pet B. A book
C. A poem D. A painting

138. D. Litt was conferred upon Galsworthy in the year
A. 1929 B. 1930
C. 1940 D. None of these

139. The Forsyte Saga includes two interludes. Name the interludes.
A. Indian Autumn of Forsyte Tales and Awakening
B. Indian Winter of Forstye Tales and Awakening
C. Indian Summer of Forsyte Tales and Awakening
D. None of these

140. Galsworthy's Forsyte Saga is said to be an English parallel to
A. Milton's Paradise Lost
B. Thomas Mann's Buddenbrooks
C. Seth's A Suitable Boy
D. Shakespeare's Hamlet

141. Which novel earned Galsworthy the reputation of a novelist?
A. Jocelyn B. Country Mouse
C. The Island Pharisees D. Fraternity

142. In 1929, which honour was conferred upon Galsworthy?
A. Order of merit B. Order of demerit
C. Booker Prize D. All of the above

143. Which play of Galsworthy is a study in social pride and social convention?
A. The Mob B. The Skin Game
C. The Loyalties D. The Silver Box

144. Which play made Galsworthy famous as a dramatist?
A. Justice B. The Silver Box
C. Loyalties D. None of these

145. What is the title of Galsworthy's collection of essays?
A. The Inn of Tranquility
B. The River of Tranquility
C. The Ocean of Tranquility
D. None of the above

146. Which play of Galsworthy dramatizes strike?
A. Mob B. Justice
C. Strife D. None of these

147. What is the name of Galsworthy's first play?
A. Loyalties B. Joy
C. Justice D. Silver Box

148. The Essays and Stories—The White Monkey, The Silver Spark, Swan Song, A Slient Wooing and Passers by were collected together as
A. awakening B. a modern tragedy
C. a modern comedy D. None of these

149. In 1931, Oxford University and Princeton University conferred upon Galsworthy
A. Knighthood B. Honorary Doctorate
C. Both A and B D. None of these

150. Galsworthy is the chief exponent of
A. romantic tales B. adventures tales
C. problem plays D. None of these

ANSWERS

1	2	3	4	5	6	7	8	9	10
B	C	D	A	D	C	C	C	A	B
11	12	13	14	15	16	17	18	19	20
D	C	B	D	A	B	D	C	B	A

21	22	23	24	25	26	27	28	29	30
B	A	D	B	A	D	D	C	A	C
31	32	33	34	35	36	37	38	39	40
D	C	A	A	C	A	A	A	B	C
41	42	43	44	45	46	47	48	49	50
A	C	A	B	B	C	D	B	D	B
51	52	53	54	55	56	57	58	59	60
A	C	A	C	D	B	C	C	B	A
61	62	63	64	65	66	67	68	69	70
A	A	A	C	A	A	C	D	B	C
71	72	73	74	75	76	77	78	79	80
C	B	C	C	D	A	C	A	D	A
81	82	83	84	85	86	87	88	89	90
D	C	A	A	C	A	B	C	B	A
91	92	93	94	95	96	97	98	99	100
C	B	A	B	D	A	A	C	D	A
101	102	103	104	105	106	107	108	109	110
D	C	C	B	D	C	D	B	A	B
111	112	113	114	115	116	117	118	119	120
A	A	B	C	D	B	A	B	B	B
121	122	123	124	125	126	127	128	129	130
A	C	D	A	C	A	C	A	B	A
131	132	133	134	135	136	137	138	139	140
B	B	A	A	B	A	B	B	C	B
141	142	143	144	145	146	147	148	149	150
C	A	C	B	A	C	D	C	B	C

4 English Literature At A Glance

THE OLD ENGLISH PERIOD

ANGLO-SAXON PERIOD (450-1050)

Beowulf is probably the oldest epic of the Teutonic world. It is believed to be belonging to the first half of the sixth century.

Some important works of the Anglo-Saxon period (Pre-Christian Era).

Some important works of the Anglo-Saxon period are: *The Ruined Burg, The Lover's Message. The Maiden's Complaint, The Wanderer* and *the Seafarer.*

'*The Wanderer* is also known as *'Widsith'*. The work is based on the wandering life of the gleeman.

Belonging to this period, we also have *"Deor's Lament"*, which, according to Long is, "much more poetic than *'Widsith,'* and is the one perfect lyric of the Anglo-Saxon period."

In the *Seafarer*, we have glimpses of hard sea life along with the call of the sea, which we, in our times, find more pronouncedly, but perhaps less picturesquely, in Masefield's *"Sea-Fever"*.

Some Christian writers of the Anglo-Saxon period.

Whereas the pagan literature of the Anglo-Saxon period was chiefly in the form of oral legends which they had brought with them from the foreign lands which they previously inhabited, the Christian writing mainly came into existence as a result of the teachings of the monks who had come under the influence of two schools—the Augustinian School (from Rome) and Northumbrian School (from Ireland).

While the former, did not produce much lasting works, the latter produced a number of good and great writers, *e.g.*, **The Venerable Bede (673-735), Caedmon (seventh century)** and **Cynewulf (eighth century)**.

Besides the poets mentioned above, we have **Alfred (848-90)** who is chiefly known as a translator.

ANGLO-NORMAN PERIOD (1066-1350)

Some important works of the Anglo-Norman period.

One important work of this period is *Geoffrey's "Historic Regum Britanniae"* (1137) commonly known as *"History"*. Geoffrey is believed to have died in 1154.

Geoffrey's work which became immensely popular in his own life, is a mixture of pagan and Christian legends and is based more on lies than on real historical events.

However, the said work has its literary value for its poetry and romance pertaining to king Arthur and his Knights, and hence, it became a source of inspiration and scintillating subject matter for such illustrious authors as Malory, Shakespeare and Tennyson.

Geoffrey's work was in Latin verse. Thereafter appeared *"Layman's Brut"* (c. 1200) which has its main interest in giving Arthur's legends in (Anglo-Saxon) English itself.

Then there appeared what are known as *"Metrical Romances"* which were based on the "matter" of France, Rome and Britain.

While in the *Matter of France,* **Charlemagne's** exploits dominated and in the *Matter of Rome* Alexander's adventures and the war of Troy were the main subjects, in the *Matter of Britain*, exploits of Arthur and his knights of the Round Table were chief subject matter. There were a number of cycles pertaining to the knights of Arthur, among them being **Sir Gawain (1350)** *Quest of the Holy Grail, Death of Arthur, Merlin, etc.*

Besides the above, other works of the period included ballads, lyrics and such poems as the *Owl and the Nightingale, Ormulum, Cursor Mundi (1320), The Pearl, Patience, Cleanness, etc.* Also **Roger Bacon's** *"Opus Majus"* appeared in 1267.

THE AGE OF CHAUCER (1340-1400)

The Hundred years war between England and France had already started in 1338 when **Chaucer** was born in **1340**.

In the earlier years of the war, England was all-powerful and under Edward III it won victories over France at Sluys in 1340 and Crecy in 1346, culminating in the capture of Calais in 1347.

Another thumping victory was won by the Black Prince, Edward III's son in 1356 by defeating the French at Poitiers.

As a result of the English victories, the English foreign trade began to flourish, particularly in the export of wool to Flanders, which filled the coffers of the English king and the people also became richer, as we notice conspicuously in **Chaucer's** *Canterbury Tales* when we consider the lot of so many acters, particularly those belonging to landed aristocracy.

This picture is also graphically depicted in **Trevelyan's** *British History of Six Centuries*.

It was unfortunate for England that in the moment of its glory it was overtaken by plague, the Black Death which took a heavy toll of life all over Europe in 1348-49.

As a result of the Black Death, most of the labourers who escaped death, left the country, and this caused an intense scarcity of the availability of essential commodities at cheap rates. To meet this menace, the Parliament tried to force the labourers to accept the same wages as they were getting before the Black Death, and it all finally precipitated into the well-known Peasants' Revolt during the reign of Richard II.

In spite of the passage of certain statutes purported to safeguard the English clergy against the undue domination of the Pope, the low simmering of wrath among the clergymen for several reasons, there emerged in the "Lollards Movement" under the leadership of the redoubtable Wyclif.

Another prominent feature, this one in the literary world, was the slow advent of the spirit of New Learning from Italy and drastic changes in the structure of the English language which had already been continuing as the inevitable outcome of the Norman conquest at Hastings in 1066.

These were the general conditions in which the most significant writers of the age—**Chaucer, Langland, Dunbar,** etc. lived and flourished, thus heralding a new age slowly, but boldly and surely.

MAJOR AUTHORS AND THEIR WORKS OF CHAUCER'S AGE

Sir Thomas More (1478-1535)
Utopia (English Version)

William Tyndale (1485-1536)
New Testament

Geoffrey Chaucer (1340-1400)
The Boke of the Duchesse
The Romaunt of the Rose
The House of Fame
Troylus Cryseyde
The Canterbury Tales
Legends of Good Women
The Parliament of Fouls

Wyclif (1320-1384)
The Bible

John Heywood (1564-1627)
Four P's

Thomas Sackville and Thomas Norton : (1536-1608) (1532-1584)
Gorboduc

THE SEVENTEENTH CENTURY

THE RENAISSANCE (1578-1625)

The Renaissance of English Literature coincides with the Age of Queen Elizabeth I. Hence, in the history of English literature, this period is also called as the *Elizabethan Age*. The inspiration for the great works of this period came from the prolific translations into English of works of ancient Rome and Greece. Thus, **Plutarch's** *Lives* was translated by **Sir Thomas North (1579)** from the French version. Montaigne's Essays was translated by **John Florio (1603)**. In verse, **Ovid's** *Metamorphoses* was translated by **Arthur Golding (1565, 1567)**. Among other works of foreign origin translated into English were Ariosto's *Orlando Furioso* by **Harrington (1591)**, and Homer's *Iliad* by **George Chapman (1598)**.

The rising English stage and the English novel borrowed from Boccaccio, Cinthio, Bandello and Straparola — the Italians. Attracted though England was to Italian art, it resisted the evil influences of debauchery, crime and passions that the Italian spirit represented. Yet, the time was ripe in England for the full development of every art and literary form. Renaissance means *a flowering again of art and culture*. It inculcated a sense of wonder in things. England also wanted to rival Spain, France and Portugal in her navigational triumphs. Thus in 1578, Sir Francis Drake circumnavigated the world, and in 1588, the English navy destroyed the Armada. The same spirit of adventure moved literature. In *Apologie for Poetrie*, Sidney described the poet — of all sciences 'the monarch'. Poets were encouraged to innovate new styles and rhythms.

Poetry

Three great men of letters led the Renaissance in England — Spenser, Sidney and Lyly.

Edmund Spenser (1552-1599) wrote the *Shepheardes Calendar* (1579)—an allegory. The union of line and metre is varied and rich. In *Hymnes In honour of Love and Beautie*, he sets forth his philosophy, the conflict in his mind between paganism and Christianity. He also wrote a satire named, *Mother Hubberd's Tale* to denounce the neglect of arts and letters. His pastoral, *Colin Clout's Come Home Again* describes his stay in London in 1589. His *Amoretti* (1595) are sonnets on love and his *Epithalamion* is an ode, but his masterpiece is the *Faerie Queene* (1589, 1595), an allegory in which characters represent virtues and vices. In it his lyrical quality and colour-effects are at their best. The *Faerie Queene* is Queen Elizabeth. The nine-line stanza he used is now called the *Spenserian stanza*.

Sir Philip Sidney (1554-1586) was a scholar, knight and courtier. In 1580 he wrote *Arcadia* which has a blend of pastoral and heroic elements. It is a romance of chivalry and love. The language is characterized by *pathetic fallacy* — endowing inanimate objects with feelings and sensations. William Shakespeare borrowed from this style. His other poem, *Astrophel and Stella* (1591) describes his lost love for the daughter of an Earl. His *Apologie for Poetrie* (1595) written in an unaffected prose, is a plea for poetry.

John Lyly (1554-1606) invented an artistic, flowery style called *euphuism* through his famous romance, *Euphues, the Anatomy of Wit* (1579). This style was adopted by the refined people of the Court. The style is characterized by the use of alliteration and antithesis, fantastic metaphors and similes based on mythology, and natural history of flora and fauna.

The works of these three trail-blazed many poets and sonneteers like Samuel Daniel, Michael Drayton, Thomas Watson, Henry Constable and Thomas Lodge. Notable works from 1590 to 1603 were **Samuel Daniel's (1562-1619)** *The Civil Wars* (1595) describing the *War of the Roses*, **Michael Drayton's (1563-1631)** *Idea, the Shepherd's Garland*, *The Baron's Wars, England's Heroicall Epistles* (1603) and *Poly-Olbion*, a long description of England in 15,000 alexandrines or lines of twelve syllables. England came to be known as *"a nest of singing birds"* because of the great number of lyrics and poems written in this period. **Thomas Campion (1567-1620)** published an anthology called *Two Books of Ayres* (1612). Many of the best poems are found in plays by Ben Jonson, Thomas Dekker, Beaumont and Fletcher, and Webster. But those of William Shakespeare are probably the most beautiful. In his *Sonnets*, he describes his love for a married woman who betrays him. Other poems of this period are Marlowe's Hero and Leander (1598), Shakespeare's *Venus and Adonis* (1593) and *The Rape of Lucrece* (1594).

After Elizabeth's reign, in James I rule, poetry became religious and didactic. The Protestant spirit dominated the literary works. The poems of George Wither, William Browne, the Fletcher brothers and William Drummond show the influence of Spenser still.

Ben Jonson (1573-1637) was the greatest humanist of the time. He was mainly a playwright but wrote poems also. His poetry is found in collections like *Epigrams* and *The Forest* (1616) and *The Underwoods* (1640). He was a satirist and neo-classicist being influenced by the Latin classics.

John Donne's (1573-1631) poetry is revolutionary. He disobeys the laws of rhythm and uses a device called the metaphysical conceit in which strangely opposite ideas are juxtaposed.

Prose

Much of the prose of the period is poetical, influenced by euphuism. Robert Greene, Thomas Lodge, Thomas Nashe, Thomas Deloney, and Thomas Dekker are the major writers. **Robert Greene's (1558-1592)** works include *Mamilia* and *Menaphon* and **Thomas Lodge's (1558-1625)** include *Rosalynde: Euphues Golden Legacie* (1590). **Thomas Nashe (1567-1601)** wrote pamphlets like The *Anatomie of Absurdities* and *The Terrors of the Night*. **Thomas Dekker's (1572-1632)** *The Gils Horne booke* is famous for its picturesque prose. Most of the poets and prose writers of this period were also dramatists. Shakespeare used prose for homely and humorous scenes and verse for tragic ones.

Many writers of the English Renaissance were inspired by the literary criticism of the Continent to write some themselves. Stephen Gosson's *The Schoole of Abuse* (1579) and *Sidney's Apologie for Poetrie* are good examples. Sidney eulogizes the poet as a law-giver. The period also saw works of religious prose. **Richard Hooker's (1554-1600)** pamphlet on the Marlin Marprelate controversy is a famous one. Hooker's *Of the Laws of Ecclesiastical Polity* (1594) is a masterpiece of English prose. The most seminal work of the period is the authorized version of the Bible published in 1611. The work was commissioned by James I. A beautiful prose minus archaism is used by the revisers. The diction was to influence the English language very deeply. It is the language of daily speech, yet fresh and lofty.

Side by side with religious literature, secular and philosophical literature, mostly written by **Francis Bacon (1561-1626)**, came out. He had taken all knowledge as his province and elaborated his doctrines in his *Novum Organum* (1620). His ideas influenced the formation of *The Royal Society for Improving Natural Knowledge* in 1645. His most popular work is his *Essays* written on diverse topics in a terse, epigrammatic style. The English writers quote copiously from Bacon today. His sentences are household terms. Take for example, *"He that hath wife and children hath given hostages to fortune"*. *"Some books are to be tasted, others to be swallowed and some few to be chewed and digested"*.

Another great prose-writer of the period was **Robert Burton (1577-1640)** whose *The Anatomy of Melancholy* (1621) is full of pedantry. He borrowed from numerous sources and is full of melancholy and jests; his style abounds in synonyms and epithets.

Drama

Drama thrived in the Renaissance. Foreign influence, especially of Italy, predominated. Plays were written so that the public would enjoy them and applaud the stage. There was a great variety of plays written — pure tragedy, tragi-comedy, historical drama, romantic comedy, comedy of errors, farce, pastoral, etc. The stage was a simple structure, circular in form with a courtyard open to the sky. A platform projected into the courtyard. Boys played the female roles. The public consisted of groundlings and courtiers on galleries. The unities of time, place and action were disregarded. Farce and tragedy were found in succession.

Several mythological allegories were acted before the court. **John Lyly's** euphuistic romances like *Campaspe* (1584), *Sapho and Phao, Endymion* (1592), *Midas* were praises of the queen. **George Peele (1558-1598)** wrote *The Araygnement of Paris* (1584) and *The Old Wives' Tale.* There were violent plays like **Thomas Kyd's (1558-1594)** The *Spanish Tragedie* (1585) and **Christopher Marlowe's (1564-1593)** *Tamburlaine, the Great* (1587) and *Doctor Faustus* (1592). *Doctor Faustus* is an allegory on the Renaissance love of power. It shows how Doctor Faustus, the scientist, sells his soul to the devil for twenty-four years of full power to satisfy every desire. In the end his agony increases as the devil approaches to claim his soul. Marlowe also wrote *The Jew of Malta*, which shows the unbridled love for wealth, and the historical play Edward II. Marlowe crafted the blank verse (mighty line as Shakespeare called it and used). This was suited to the fiery speeches of his characters.

The towering genius of the age was certainly **William Shakespeare (1564-1616)**. He was versatile and wrote about 36 plays and 144 sonnets. "Shakespeare was not of an age but for all times" and "Poets are born not made", wrote Ben Jonson about him. He created a gallery of nearly 800 characters who typify personalities found through human history. Julius Caesar's pride and ambition, Macbeth's unbridled ambition, King Lear's dotedness, and Othello's susceptibility to suspicion against his wife — are tragic flaws that govern men even today.

Shakespeare was not educated except for a few years at a grammar school. He had 'little Latin and less Greek' and read books in translation from Latin and Greek. He adapted the stories into a World entirely his own, instinct with life and vibrancy. Shakespeare began his career by acting for the stage. Then he wrote plays and staged them, mainly to seek court patronage. His great success made him the envy of his contemporaries like Robert Greene. In his tragedies he depicts the fall of great men owing to a tragic flaw in their character. Although they had the will to change their destiny, a fate controlled them. He used the beliefs of his time like the supernatural powers and phenomena to capture the interest of his audience. Some of his historical plays are *Richard II* (1596) and *King John* (1595). Among the romantic comedies *As You Like It* (1600), *The Merchant of Venice* (1596) and *Twelfth Night* (1601) are popular. *A Midsummer Night's Dream* (1595) is a fairy play. *Romeo and Juliet* (1594) is a tragicomedy. He used prose and blank verse.

His *Henry IV* (I & 2) (1597, 1598) contain much more blank verse than his other plays. In depth of psychological insight, and power of style *Hamlet* (1601), one of Shakespeare's great tragedies, stands supreme. *The Tempest* (161I) is one of his last plays which shows the dramatist's mellowed maturity.

Even after 400 years, Shakespeare's plays are very popular, being translated into almost every important language. *"Age cannot wither her nor custom stale her infinite variety"*; Shakespeare described Cleopatra in these words. The same may be said about his plays also.

Ben Jonson was Shakespeare's antithesis. He borrowed the style of the classics and was very erudite. He carefully studied society and wrote about it. He took the different 'humours' or dominating characteristics of men and satirized them in *Every Man in his Humour* (1598) and *Every Man out of his Humour* (1599), *Volpone, or the Fox* (1605) and *The Alchemist* (1605). He also wrote the historical tragedies, *Sejanus His Fall* (1603) and *Catiline His Conspiracy* (1611). The plays are very true to history. John Marston, Thomas Dekker, Thomas Heywood and Middleton were other playwrights of the age. John Webster (1580-1625) is famous for horror plays like *The White Devil* (1609-1612) and *The Duchess of Malfi* (1613-1614).

MAJOR AUTHORS AND THEIR WORKS

Edmund Spenser (1552-1599)

The Faerie Queene
The Shepheardes Calendar
Amoretti
Epithalamion
Prothalamion
Mother Hubberd's Tale
The Ruins of Time
The Tears of the Muses
Astrophel

Phillip Sidney (1554-1586)

Arcadia
Astrophel and Stella
An Apologie for Poetrie

Ben Jonson (1573-1637)

Every Man in His Humour
Every Man Out of His Humour
Volpone Or the Fox
Cynthia's Revels

The Alchemist
Bartholomew Fayre
Epicaene or the Silent Women
Sejanus His Fall
Catline His Conspiracy
The Poetaster
The Devil as an Ass
The Masque of Beauty

Samuel Daniel (1562-1619)
Delia
Civil Wars between the Two Houses of Lancaster and York

Michael Drayton (1563-1631)
The Battle of Agincourt
England's heroic Epistles
The Barons' Wars
Polyolbion

William Shakespeare (1564-1616)
The Two Gentlement of Verona
The Merry Wives of Windsor
Measure for Measure
The Comedy of Errors
Love's Labour's Lost
The Taming of the Shrew
All's Well that Ends Well
A Midsummer Night's Dream
The Merchant of Venice
Much Ado About Nothing
As You Like it
Twelfth Night
Romeo and Juliet
Macbeth
Hamlet
King Lear
Othello
Antony and Cleopatra
Julius Caesar
Timon of Athens
Coriolanus
Titus Andronicus
Troilus and Cressida
King John
King Richard the Second
King Henry the Fourth-Part First
King Henry the Fourth-Second Part
King Henry the Fifth
King Henry the Sixth-First Part
King Henry the Sixth-Second Part
King Henry the Sixth-Third Part
King Richard the Third
King Henry the Eighth
Cymbeline
Pericles
The Winter's Tale
The Tempest
Venus and Adonis and Rape of Lucrece
(Narrative Poems)
Sonnets (154 in number).

Christopher Marlowe (1564-1593)
Tamburlaine the Great
Edward II
Doctor Faustus
The Jew of Malta
The Tragedy of Dido, Queen of Carthage.

George Peele (1558-1597)
The Araygnement of Paris
The Famous Chronicle of King Edward I

Robert Greene (1560-1592)
Frier Bacon and Frier Bungey
Orlando Furioso
Pandosto

Thomas Nashe (1567-1601)
The Unfortunate Traveller Or The Life of Jack Wilton

Thomas Lodge (1558-1625)
The Wounds of Civil War
Rosalynde

Thomas Kyd (1557-1595)
The Spanish Tragedy

John Lyly (1554-1606)
Euphues, The Anatomy of Wit
Euphues and His England
Endymion

Francis Bacon (1561-1626)
Essays
The Advancement of Learning
The New Atlantis
Novum Organum

John Webster (1580-1625)
The White Devil
The Duchess of Malfi
The Devil's Law Case.

Thomas Heywood (1575-1650)
A Woman Killed with Kindness
The English Traveller
The Captives

Robert Burton (1577-1640)
The Anatomy of Melancholy

Sir Thomas Browne (1605-1682)
Religio Medici
Vulgar Errors
Hydrotaphia or Urne Burriale
Christian Morals

Thomas Hobbes (1588-1679)
Leviathan

Jeremy Taylor (1613-1667)
The Liberty of Prophesying
Holy Living
Holy Dying

END OF THE RENAISSANCE (1625-1660)

Prose

Puritanism set the trend for the literature during the reign of Charles I. The Bible was the guiding spirit which may be best seen in Milton's works. The zealous Calvinists enforced Presbyterianism. The passionate curiosity for life which characterized the Renaissance gave place to a search for salvation. **Sir Thomas Browne (1605-1682)** was a scientist, but in his *Pseudodoxia Epidemica or Vulgar Errors* (1646), we see his belief in miracles. His *Religio Medici* (1642) speaks of the vanity of earthly life. **George Herbert's (1596-1633)** *The Country Parson* and **Jeremy Taylor's (1613-1667)** *Holy Living* (1650) and *Holy Dying* (1651) are sermons championing religious freedom. **John Milton (1608-1674)**, who is famous as a poet, wrote numerous pamphlets in favour of divorce which are models of beautiful prose. His *Areopagitica* (1644) is a speech for the liberty of unlicensed writing.

Another great prose-writer was **Thomas Hobbes (1588-1679)** whose *Leviathan* (1651) is a famous work. He was an empiricist and realist and believed that sensations and ideas are caused by physical reasons. Numerous works of ethics, sociology and history were written. *The History of the Rebellion and Civil Wars in England* was written by **Edward Hyde (1609-1674). Izaac Walton (1593-1683)** wrote the biographies of John Donne and George Herbert. *The Compleat Angler* (1653) is his famous work on the post-Civil War scene and contains descriptions of the English countryside.

Poetry

Two types of poets existed then — the Cavaliers, who were the Royalists, and the religious or Metaphysical poets. Thomas Carew, Sir John Suckling, John Cleveland, Robert Herrick were Cavalier poets who displayed epicurean tastes. Imagination and sensuous imagery predominate their poems. Among the religious poets, Herbert, Crashaw, Vaughan and Marvell stand out. They were mystics. **George Herbert's (1593-1633)** style is simple and expresses Christian piety in his anthology The Temple (1633). His poems *The Pulley and Love* are very popular. **Richard Crashaw (1613-1649)** used fantastic conceits; e.g. he describes the maudlin St Mary Magdalene's eyes as "walking baths, compedious oceans", **Henry Vaughan (1622-1695)** was a mystic and his poem The Retreat is a nostalgic longing for the blissful heavenly state of childhood.

John Milton's greatest achievement was his *Paradise Lost* (1667). In theme it deals with the fall of man. In form, it follows the strict unity of the classical epic. His other poems are *L'Allegro* (1632), *II Penseroso* (1632), *Comus* (1634), *Lycidas* (1637), *Samson Agonistes* (1671), etc.

RESTORATION LITERATURE (1620-1734)

Prose

In 1660, Charles II returned to the throne and the Puritan republic ended. The year is also marked as the beginning of the modern literature. **John Bunyan's (1628-1688)** works, *Grace Abounding* (1666) and *The Pilgrim's Progress* (1678) are the last surviving works of Puritan faith. The Pilgrim's Progress is an allegory describing the trials and tribulations on the way to salvation as faced by a Christian. Bunyan's prose is a blend of common speech and the grandeur of the revised Bible.

The scientific spirit took over the reign. The Royal Society of London for the Improvement of Natural Knowledge, to which Bacon and William Harvey (who discovered the circulation of blood) had contributed, now had many learned men. **Sir Isaac Newton** published Principia in 1687. He discovered the laws of gravity, of the diffraction of white light and the theory of fluxions.

John Locke (1632-1704) propounded a new philosophy of commonsense and intelligent reasoning in his *An Essay Concerning Human Understanding* (1690). It lays stress on development of character. It was to influence the English thought. Voltaire was one of his French disciples.

Poetry

Restoration literature was derived from pre-Commonwealth national literature and was a reaction against Puritan oppression. It rejected severe moral codes of conduct and was chiefly satiric in nature. **Samuel Butler's (1612-1680)** poem, *Hudibras* published in three parts (1663, 1664 & 1678), is a typical work of this period. It is inspired by *Don Quixote*. He satirizes Sir Hudibras as a grotesque Presbyterian with a squire called Ralpho.. It lays bare all the human follies in octosyllabic couplets. Many court poets like **Andrew Marvell (1621-1678)** and **John Oldham (1653-1683)** were veterans of the Republican era and satirize the follies of the new age.

The great poet of the period was **John Dryden (1631-1700)**. He excelled in almost every kind of composition. He wrote a series of heroic stanzas in honour of Cromwell on his death. He was a disciple of the metaphysical poets displaying their far-fetched images and conceits. In *Astraea Redux* (1660), he celebrated the return of Charles II and in *Annus Mirabilis* (1667) he commemorated the Great Fire of London and the war with Holland. He was a staunch Tory and his famous satires are *Absalom and Achitophel* (1681), *The Medal and Mac-Flecknoe*. In this last work he satirizes Shadwell, the Whig poet. *The Hind and the Panther* (1687) is an allegory on Catholicism and Anglicanism. Dryden also translated the classics, chiefly Persuis and Juvenal. He turned Virgil's *Aeneid* into brilliant couplets. His *Alexander's Feast* is an ode in honour of St. Cecilia.

Drama

The dramatic works of the Restoration were licentious and full of cynicism. They regarded the moral code of the Puritans as a matter of ridicule. Scenery now played an important part on the stage and actresses, not boys, played the female roles. The theatre was regarded as a place of vice and evil. Shakespeare's plays were rewritten and his tragedies like *Romeo and Juliet* given happy endings. French influence dominated and extraordinary superhuman feats were described. Heroes were presented as ideals and were made to give pompous speeches.

Dryden wrote many plays like *Aureng-zebe* or *The Great Mogul* (1675) and The Conquest of Granada (1669, 1670) which abound in rhetoric.

The tragedians were **Thomas Otway (1651-1685)**, Nathaniel Lee (1653-1692) and **Nicholas Rowe (1674-1718)**. The comedy of this period reflects the gay intrigues of the society. Caricature and farce were used and obscenity also touched it. The main aim was to amuse. **Sir George Etheredge (1635-1691)** was an innovator and **William Wycherley (1640-1715)** was a moralist playwright. **William Congreve (1670-1729)** wrote a series of masterpieces including *The Way of the World* (1700). **John Vanbrugh** (1664-1726) and **George Farquhar (1678-1707)** were other comedy writers of the period.

Criticism

Dryden was the first English critic. *The Essay of Dramatick Poesie* (1668) is his longest single prose work and a major piece of English literary criticism. It is in the form of a discussion between four characters, one of whom is Dryden himself. It deals with topics related to theatre and evaluates the works of the Elizabethan dramatists, especially of Shakespeare.

The Diarists of the Restoration Period

One of the sources of information and genres of prose writing during the Restoration were diaries. The important names are those of John Evelyn, Samuel Pepys and Roger North. **John Evelyn (1620-1706)** was a rich man who had cultured tastes. He was a member of the Royal Society and had wide interests in diverse fields like gardening, forestry, navigation and architecture. His *Diary* which was written almost throughout his lifetime throws a floodlight on the major social and national events of the time like the Galley Slaves and the Great Fire. It is written in a plain, graphic style. **Samuel Pepys (1633-1703)** had a chequered career. Coming from the middle classes, he joined the civil services and rose to be the secretary of the Admiralty. He also became the President of the Royal Society and a member of Parliament. His famous *Diary*, covering a period of ten years, is in the form of confessions. It was written in laconic sentences like the messages of a telegram and was in a sort of code which was deciphered only in 1825. The diary shows him to be a man of versatile interests like music, science and literature. But the most controversial aspect is the detailed confessions of his life. Nobody seemed to guess he was a libertine, a morally debauched character who could stoop to low means. When we read the diary, it seems he is writing of another person. **Roger North** belonged to an elite family. He was a Tory gentleman and was engaged in the politics of the times. His famous work is *North's Lives of the Norths* containing biographies of three relatives and an autobiography. His pen pictures and anecdotes are in colloquial style.

MAJOR AUTHORS AND THEIR WORKS

Robert Herrick (1591-1574)
Noble Numbers
Hesperides

Thomas Carew (1598-1639)
Poems
'He that loves a rosy cheek'

Sir John Suckling (1660-1642)
'Ballad upon a Wedding'
'Why so pale and wan, Fond Lover'?

Andrew Marvell (1621-1678)
'To His Coy Mistress'
'The Rehearsal Transprosed'
'Ode upon Cromwell's Return from Ireland'
New Letters (a Prose Work)

George Herbert (1593-1633)
The Temple
Affliction
Easter Wings
The Collar
Man

Richard Crashaw (1613-1649)
Carmen Deo Nostro
The Infant Morturs
Steps to the Temple

John Milton (1608-1674)

Paradise Lost (*in twelve Books*)
Paradise Regained
Comus
Lycidas
Samson Agonistes
L'Allegro
Ill Penseroso
Areopagitica (*Prose Work*)
Ode on the Morning of Christ's Nativity
Sonnets (*including*) :
'On His Blindness'
'On the Late Massacre in Piedmont'
'When the Assault was Intended to the City'
'On His Having Arrived at the Age of Twenty-three'
A large number of Tracts and Pamphlets in support of the Parliament

John Donne (1573-1631)

Songs and Sonnets
Aires and Angels
A Nocturnall upon Lucies Day
A Valediction : Forbidding Mourning
The Extasie
Devotions (*Sermon in Prose*)
Ignatius His Enclave (*a Prose Work*)
Of the Progress of the Soul
Death's Duell

Abraham Cowley (1618-1667)

Pyramus and Thisbe
The Mistress
The Davideis
Pindarique Odes
Constantia and Philetus
Discourse by Way of Vision
Concerning the Government of Cromwell (a Prose Work)

Henry Vaughan (1622-1695)

Poems
Regeneration
The Retreat
Olor Iscanus
Thalia Redivia
Silex Scintillans

John Dryden (1631-1700)

(*i*) *Heroic Stanzas on the Death of Oliver Cromwell*
Astraea Redux (on the Restoration of Charles II)
Absalom and Achitophel
Religio Laici
The Hind and the Panther
The Fables
Annus Mirabilis
The Medal
Mac Flecknoe
Alexander's Feast
Prefaces to His Plays (in Prose)
An Essay of Dramatic Poesy
(*ii*) *Dryden's Plays*
Tyrannic Love
Conquest of Granada
All for love
The Rival Ladies
The Indian Emperor
Aureng-Zeb
Don Sebastian
Cleomenes
Love Triumphant

John Vanbrugh (1664-1726)

The Relapse
The Provoked Wife
The Confederacy

George Farquhar (1678-1707)

The Recruiting Officer
The Beaux Stratagem

Thomas Otway (1652-1685)

Orphan
Venice Preserved
Don Carlos
Alcibiades

Nathaniel Lee (1653-1692)

Nero
The Rival Queens
Sophonisba

John Bunyan (1628-1688)

The Pilgrim's Progress
Grace Abounding
The Life and Death of Mr. Badman
The Holy War

John Locke (1632-1704)

Essay on the Human Understanding
Treatise on Government
Thoughts on Education

John Evelyn (1620-1706)

Diary

Samuel Pepys (1633-1703)

Diary

MULTIPLE CHOICE QUESTIONS

1. Who wrote the *Faerie Queene?*
A. John Lyly B. Edmund Spenser
C. Ben Jonson D. Shakespeare

2. What is the nine-line stanza used in the *Faerie Queene* called?
A. Alexandrine B. Shakespearean
C. Spenserian D. Petrarchan

3. *The Anatomy of Melancholy* is written by:
A. Robert Burton B. John Dryden
C. Thomas Dekker D. Milton

4. *Doctor Faustus* is a story of:
A. a scientist
B. revenge
C. the Renaissance love of power
D. a greedy Jew

5. Marlowe invented:
A. sprung rhythm B. sonnet
C. allegory D. blank verse

6. *Romeo and Juliet* is a:
A. tragedy B. comedy
C. tragi-comedy D. history

7. *Every Man in His Humour* is written by:
A. Ben Jonson B. Dryden
C. John Donne D. Marston

8. Dryden wrote:
A. *Sejanus*
B. *The Compleat Angler*
C. *Aureng-zebe*
D. *Principia*

9. The song *Drink to me only with thine eyes* is written by:
A. Lyly B. Ben Jonson
C. Shakespeare D. Spenser

10. The Puritan Parliament closed the theatres in:
A. 1638 B. 1632
B. 1606 D. 1642

11. *The Shoemaker's Holiday* is a play written by:
A. Shakespeare B. Marlowe
C. Thomas Dekker D. Marston

12. Ben Jonson's *The Poetaster* is a satire on:
A. Marston and Dekker
B. Marlowe
C. Kyd
D. Greene

13. The main theme of Webster's plays is his:
A. humour
B. satire
C. preoccupation with death
D. social life

14. Marlowe, Kyd, Lyly and Greene were known as:
A. Humorists
B. University Wits
C. The Rivals of Shakespeare
D. The Decadents

15. The person who collaborated with Beaumont for many plays was:
A. Fletcher B. Shakespeare
C. Marston D. Greene

16. Herrick, Carew, Suckling and Lovelace were collectively called:
A. Metaphysical Poets
B. Religious Poets
C. Puritans
D. Cavalier Poets

17. The *Horatian Ode* by Andrew Marvel is addressed to:
A. Cromwell B. Charles II
C. Queen Elizabeth D. Shakespeare

18. *Comus* by Milton is a/an:
A. masque B. ode
C. epic D. lyric

19. *Lycidas* is an elegy by Milton on:
A. Arthur Hallam B. Edward King
C. Cromwell D. Ben Jonson

20. *The Compleat Angler* is written by:
A. Milton B. Robert Burton
C. Izaak Walton D. Thomas Fuller

21. *Leviathan* is written by:
A. Milton B. Marvel
C. Thomas Hobbes D. Farquhar

22. *The Pilgrim's Progress* by John Bunyan is a/an:
A. book of philosophy
B. treatise on education
C. masque
D. allegory

23. Samuel Butler's satire on Puritanism is:
A. *Hudibras*
B. *Way of the World*
C. *Utopia*
D. *Paradise Lost*

24. John Evelyn's *Diary* is famous for:
A. describing major social events of his times
B. describing personal experiences
C. scholarly research
D. noting facts and figures

25. Samuel Pepys' *Diary* is mainly:
A. social B. confessional
C. descriptive D. argumentative

ANSWERS

1	2	3	4	5	6	7	8	9	10
B	C	A	C	D	C	A	C	B	D
11	**12**	**13**	**14**	**15**	**16**	**17**	**18**	**19**	**20**
C	A	C	B	A	D	A	A	B	C
21	**22**	**23**	**24**	**25**					
C	D	A	A	B					

THE EIGHTEENTH CENTURY

THE AUGUSTAN AGE (1700-1740)

In general, the eighteenth century was the age of understanding and enlightenment. The emphasis was on the advancement of the human mind. Sensibility was the guiding principle. This age borrowed the humour and poetic technique of the previous century.

This age is generally called *The Augustan Age* or *The Age of Queen Anne* because the queen patronized the men of letters. The period is also known as the Classical Age. It was an age of tolerance and harmony and was guided by reason. Dryden still wrote and was a contemporary of French authors Corneille, Racine and Moliere. Many English works were translated by the French. Poetry was still for aristocrats and the courts, but prose spread among the common public. People demanded instructions and information and practical hints for living. This led writers to use a simple style to be comprehensible to all.

Poetry

Matthew Prior (1664-1721) began by writing a parody of The Hind and the Panther in which he expounded his opinions on politics. **Sir Samuel Garth (1661-1791)** and **Joseph Addison (1672-1719)** used the heroic couplet of Dryden. Addison described Marlborough's victory at Blenheim in his poem *The Campaign* (1704). But the poetical luminary of the period was **Alexander Pope (1688-1744)**. He polished Dryden's couplet and used it as a weapon of satire, like in the famous *An Essay on Man* (1732-1734). His *An Essay on Criticism* (1711) and *The Rape of the Lock* (1712, 1714) are other great works. The latter is in mock-heroic style and describes the anger of a lady whose lock of hair had been cut off. Pope also translated the Iliad. He wrote *The Dunciad* (1728) to castigate bad poets. His *Imitations of Horace* (1733-1737) is highly admired even today.

Jonathan Swift, usually known as a prose writer, also showed a gift or versification like in his poem *On the Death of Dr. Swift*. **John Gay (1685-1732)** was popular for his fables like *The Hare with Many Friends* and his songs in *The Beggar's Opera*. **Edward Young's (1683-1765)** *The Commaint, or Night Thoughts on Life, Death, and Immortality* (1742), is a poet's delight in meditation underlining the vanity of all earthly glory.

Prose

This period saw an increasing demand for the circulation of facts and ideas among the public. **Daniel Defoe (1659-1731)** was a trail-blazer as a Journalist and his popular works are *The True-Born Englishman* (1701) and *The Shortest Way with the Dissenters* (1702). Defoe wrote the first English novel *Robinson Crusoe* (1719), which is a children's classic or collection of adventure stories. He cultivated the art of reporting and presented his stories as historical narratives which are precise and practical.

Steele, Addison, Swift, Arbuthnot were the other great prose-writers of the time. They introduced a style adorned by figures of speech. The periodicals of Steele and Addison contain essays which deal with practical moral questions and reflect the morals of the time.

Richard Steele (1672-1729) led a dissipated life and was full of remorse for it. He extols the Bible as a guide in life in his work *The Christian Hero*. He launched the journal *The Tatler* in 1709. **Joseph Addison** propagated rational and moderate ideas. He collaborated with Steele on *The Tatler*. Steele then founded *The Spectator* in 1711 and Addison again collaborated. Here they were merely the spectators of the society and its foibles. It epitomizes the whole nation. The character of Sir Roger de Coverley is a masterpiece, a comic personality with eccentricities. Other characters, Sir Andrew Freeport. Will Honeycomb, Captain Sentry capture the imagination of the readers.

Jonathan Swift (1667-1745) enjoyed ridicule rather than correction. He lays bare all the vices of man as something that are beyond correction. He ridiculed the modern authors in his The *Battle of the Books* (1704) and attacked the Papists and Presbyterians in *The Tale of a Tub* (1704). His most popular work is a children's classic, *Gulliver's Travels* (1726), which is also a satire on politics, religions, science and nature of man.

John Arbuthnot (1667-1735) was another humanist and man of wit and is known for his *The History of John Bull* (1712), an amusing allegory on the politics of the time.

During this period a number of deists like Locke, Collins and Tindal propounded a philosophy advocating reasoning rather than superstitious beliefs as advocated by orthodox Christians. Earl of Shaftesbury (1671-1713), Lord Bolingbroke (1678-1751) and Mandeville were other rationalists of the time who wrote many prose works.

THE AGE OF TRANSITION (1740-1800)

Like all other periods of transition, this age was also disturbed and confused. Two movements can be clearly observed in the writings of the time: (*i*) the allegiance to the old order of classicism, and (*ii*) the search after the new order of Romanticism. The period was marked by new learning, new philosophy, growth of historical research and new realism.

This period is also known as the *Age of Johnson* because **Samuel Johnson (1709-1784)**, the greatest English man of letters, flourished during this period. Samuel Johnson was a versatile man of letters translator, journalist, commentator, critic, novelist, biographer and poet. He created two satirical poems, *London* (1738) and *The Vanity of Human Wishes* (1749). He had a supple style and describes his personal reflections in his essays *The Rambler* (1750-1752) and *The Idler* (1758-1760). His *Dictionary of English Language* (1747-1755) shows remarkable precision in definition and a feeling for the correct use of words. Besides the novel *Rasselas, Prince of Abyssinia* (1759) his best works are biographical and literary studies and his edition of *Shakespeare* (1765). His *Lives of the Poets* (1777-1781) is a biographical work. His admirer James Boswell's famous biography of Johnson has made him immortal. He is described here in candid details. His prejudices, excellences and demerits are all laid bare.

Poetry

Poetry showed the influence of Dryden and Pope. It was mainly didactic and satirical and the couplet still was the major form.

Oliver Goldsmith's (1728-1774) *Deserted Village* (1770) is a masterpiece of the period. **James Thomson's (1700-1748)** *The Seasons* (1730) is a praise of the beauties of Nature in all her diversity. Other noteworthy poems of the period are **William Collins' (1721-1759)** *Ode to Evening*, a delightful lyric, and **Thomas Gray's (1716-1771)** *Elegy Written in a Country Churchyard* (1751).

A general belief in human liberty was seen as the French Revolution proceeded. **William Cowper** (1731-1800) who wrote *The Ballad of John Gilpin,* **George Crabbe (1754-1832)**, the Scotsman **Robert Burns (1759-1796)** and the mystic **William Blake (1757-1827)** echoed the sentiments of the period. Burns was a farmer and wrote in original racy dialect thus causing a break from convention. Blake was a visionary and his poems are collected in *Songs of Innocence* (1789) and *Songs of Experience* (1794). In *The Tyger,* he uses the Lamb as a symbol of innocence and of Jesus, and the Tiger as the symbol of evil in the world, of the evil seen in the French Revolution where thousands were sent to the guillotine.

Novel

The period saw the development of the novel. A series of masterpieces came out. In the novel, the author could describe events in detail. Defoe's novels so far were based on strange subjects. Now they concentrated on commonplace events of family life and society. Adventure of earlier novels gave place to character portrayal. The novels were very long and filled with minute details. **Samuel Richardson (1689-1761)** wrote *Pamela, or Virtue Rewarded* (1740) and *Clarissa Harlowe* (1747-1748). **Henry Fielding (1707-1754)** is famous for *Joseph Andrews* (1742) and *Tom Jones* (1749), **Tobias Smollet (1721-1771)** wrote *The Adventures of Roderick Random* (1748) and *The Expedition of Humphry Clinker* (1771), **Laurence Sterne (1713-1768)** wrote *Tristram Shandy* (1760), and **Oliver Goldsmith** *The Vicar of Wakefield* (1766).

Letter

There were famous letter writers also, like **Lord Chesterfield (1694-1773). Horace Walpole (1719-1797), Thomas Gray and Richardson**. Frequently, a series of letters was bound into book-form. Collections of this kind were the letters of **Lady Mary Wortley Montagu (1689-1762)**, written to Pope from Constantinople, and of Thomas Gray, from the Lake District. Chesterfield's letters to his son contain comments on political and social matters. Richardson's *Pamela* is entirely in letter-form.

Drama

The century was the age of the great novels. Drama lost originality and talent. People saw Shakespeare's plays enacted, but what attracted them was the genius of the actors. However, there were a few good plays written. For instance, Johnson's *Irene* (1749), Fielding's *The Miser*, Goldsmith's anti-sentimental comedy *She Stoops to Conquer* (1773), and Sheridan's *The School for Scandal* (1777) and *The Rivals* (1775).

Historical Work

Towards the last part of the century the history of England was rocked by many revolutionary changes the impact of which were felt in English literature. Till the mid-18th century Victorian England reigned supreme. She was mistress of the seas and her imperial rule covered many colonies. In 1776, America declared her independence and the British Parliament was divided on the issue. Many Britishers favoured the American claims. In 1789, the French Revolution broke out and here too the Britishers were divided into two camps. Inspired by the writings of Rousseau, many believed the Revolution was being fought for the right causes. The Parliament resounded with the speeches of the famous. Some even accused Warren Hastings for his extortion policies in India and some others were against slave-trade.

Treatises on philosophy by **David Hume (1711-1776)** and histories by **William Robertson (1721-1793)** and political economy (*Wealth of Nations*) by **Adam Smith (1723-1790)** came out.

Edmund Burke (1729-1797) read law and began writing to propound his views on human feelings and emotions. His language is as oratorical in Parliament at the trial of Warren Hastings as in his famous writing *A Philosophical Inquiry into the Origin of our Ideas of the Sublime and the Beautiful* (1756).

Other orators who expressed themselves in writing were Tom Paine, Godwin and Jeremy Bentham. **William Godwin (1756-1836)** advocated the elimination of government in *Enquiry Concerning Political Justice* (1793). He proscribed law, marriage, gratitude, everything that limited liberty. His monumental work is *The Decline and Fall of the Roman Empire* (1776-1788) in which he describes the growth of Christianity and his belief in reason rather than the divine. At the same time **William Paley (1743-1805)** wrote *A View of the Evidences of Christianity* (1794) to prove the existence of miracles by logic.

MAJOR AUTHORS AND THEIR WORKS

Alexander Pope (1688-1744)
Pastorals
An Essay on Criticism
Windsor Forest
The Rape of the Lock
Dunciad
Translation of Iliad and Odyssey
To Lord Bathrust
On the Use of the Riches
An Essay on Man
Epistle to Dr. Arbuthnot
Of the Knowledge and Characters of Men
Of the Characters of Women
The Messiah
Satires and Epistles of Horace Imitated

Matthew Prior (1664-1721)
Solomon on the Vanity of the World
Alma : or the Progress of the Mind
The Town and Country Mouse

John Gay (1685-1732)
Fables
The Shepherd's Week
The Rural Sports
Trivia
The Beggar's Opera
The Streets of London

Edward Young (1683-1765)
Night Thoughts

Dr. Samuel Johnson (1709-1784)
The Vanity of Human Wishes
London
The Lives of the Poets
Preface to Shakespeare
Dictionary of the English Language
A Journey to the Western Islands of Scotland
The Rambler
Rasselas
Prince of Abyssinia
The Life of Savage
The Adventurer
The Idler

Daniel Defoe (1661-1731)
Robinson Crusoe
Mall Flanders
Colonel Jack
The Memoirs of a Cavalier
Captain Singleton
Journal of the Plague Year
Roxana

Jonathan Swift (1667-1745)
The Battle of the Books
A Tale of a Tub
Gulliver's Travels
Journal to Stella
The Drapier's Letters
Cadenus and Vanessa

Joseph Addison (1672-1719)
The Spectator
The Campaign
Public Credit
The Vision of Mirza
Cato
Rosamond
The Drummer

Richard Steele (1672-1729)
The Tatler
The Guardian
The Funeral
The Lying Lover
The Tender Husband
The Conscious Lover

Thomas Gray (1716-1771)
Elegy Written in a Country Churchyard
On a Distant Prospect of Eton College
On the Death of a Favourite Cat
The Bard
The Progress of Poesy
The Fatal Sisters
The Descent of Odin

MULTIPLE CHOICE QUESTIONS

1. *The Hind and the Panther* is a parody about:
   A. religion
   B. society
   C. politics
   D. human beings in general
2. Which poem is in mock-heroic style?
   A. *The Rape of the Lock*
   B. *The Christian Hero*
   C. *On the Death of Dr. Swift*
   D. *The Hare with Many Friends*
3. Who was the first journalist of the age?
   A. Dryden B. Daniel Defoe
   C. Swift D. Arbuthnot
4. Who wrote the first English dictionary?
   A. Goldsmith B. Boswell
   C. Webster D. Samuel Johnson
5. Lord Chesterfield is famous as a:
   A. Novelist B. Letter-writer
   C. Playwright D. Poet
6. The novel written in epistolary or letter form is:
   A. *Joseph Andrews* B. *Pamela*
   C. *Vicar of Wakefield* D. *Tom Jones*
7. Johnson's biographer was:
   A. Boswell B. Irene
   C. Swift D. Edmund Burke
8. A play which describes heroes as virtues personified and is full of pompous speeches is:
   A. Heroic play
   B. Sentimental Comedy
   C. Anti-Sentimental Comedy
   D. Tragi-Comedy
9. Edmund Burke was:
   A. poet and scholar B. playwright
   C. orator and writer D. lexicographer
10. *The Decline and Pall of the Roman Empire* is written by:
    A. Paley B. Smith
    C. Johnson D. Godwin
11. The main reason why papers came out in Queen Anne's time was:
    A. People were hungry for information about current events
    B. People wanted to contact businessmen
    C. People wanted to improve their writing style
    D. People liked sensational fiction stories
12. The characters Sir Andrew Freeport, Captain Sentry and Sir Roger are featured in:
    A. *The Tatler* B. *The London Gazette*
    C. *The Spectator* D. *The Review*
13. The countries that influenced British literature and art in the 18th century were:
    A. Germany and Holland
    B. Sweden and Norway
    C. Austria and France
    D. France and Italy
14. The religious revival of the 18th century started by John and Charles Weslay was known as:
    A. Methodism B. Deism
    C. Presbyterianism D. Evangelism
15. *The Hind and the Panther Transvers'd to the Story of the Country and City Mouse* is a poem by:
    A. Dryden B. Matthew Prior
    C. Pope D. John Gay
16. John Gay is famous for a musical drama named:
    A. *The Beggar's Opera* B. *Polly*
    C. *The Secretary* D. *Fables*
17. *The Ballad of John Gilpin* is written by:
    A. Thomas Gray B. William Cowper
    C. William Blake D. Robert Burns
18. The son of a British Prime Minister is famous for his letters and *The Castle of Otranto*, a gruesome play. His (the son's) name was:
    A. Robert Walpole B. Horace Walpole
    C. William Pitt D. Churchill
19. *Wealth of Nations* is written by:
    A. Joshua Reynolds B. Adam Smith
    C. Godwin D. David Hume
20. Sheridan was a:
    A. poet B. dramatist
    C. novelist D. musician
21. *The Rivals* is a play by:
    A. Sheridan B. Goldsmith
    C. Johnson D. David Garrick
22. *Origin of our Ideas of the Sublime and the Beautiful* is an essay by:
    A. Edmund Burke B. Godwin
    C. Thomas Paine D. Hume
23. The greatest Scottish poet of the 18th century is:
    A. Robert Burns B. Waltor Scott
    C. William Cowper D. John Gay
24. The lines, *"O My luve's like a red, red rose,/That's newly sprung in June;...."* are attributed to:
    A. William Blake B. Fergusson
    C. Robert Burns D. Macpherson
25. Who was known as the "Man of Feeling" after his sentimental novel *The Man of Feeling*?
    A. Francis Burney B. Ann Rediliffe
    C. Matthew Lewis D. Henry Mackenzie

ANSWERS

1	2	3	4	5	6	7	8	9	10
C	A	B	D	B	B	A	B	C	D
11	12	13	14	15	16	17	18	19	20
A	C	D	A	B	A	B	B	B	B
21	22	23	24	25					
A	A	A	C	D					

THE NINETEENTH CENTURY

THE ROMANTIC AGE (1798-1830)

The eighteenth century literature of England was inspired by reason, but the nineteenth century was the age of imagination. The Preface to the *Lyrical Ballads* by William Wordsworth and Samuel Taylor Coleridge in 1798, heralds the period of English Romanticism. The authors of this work were disgusted with the excesses of the French Revolution, they condemned the Rationalist Movement. England turned away from the literature of France and transferred her sympathies to Germany. The philosophical doctrine of Romanticism was inspired by Germany. Romanticism was essentially poetic. Although poles apart in their political beliefs, Wordsworth and Shelley both considered the poet as the guide, prophet and seer of mankind.

Poetry

For the great Romantics — Wordsworth, Shelley, Keats, Byron — the study of the wondrous world of feelings, senses, instincts, of Man' relation to Nature, were of prime importance. Romanticism is shot with *metaphysics*. As M. Lanson puts it, *tout traverse de frissons metaphysique* Alexander Pope had used poetry to depict the thoughts of the philosophers in his *Essay on Man*. The Romantics, dedicated to Romantic imagination — *the esemplastic imagination* as Coleridge called it — were convinced that what was revealed to their poetic intuitions, was right, the Truth. Mysterious forces divine in origin moved the earth, not cold rationalist cause and effect. Pope's couplet was dull and too precise governed by convention. The Romantics sought a lyrical form using unusual images and association of words. They found models for these in the Renaissance and the old popular poetry.

William Wordsworth (1770-1850) is aptly called the "High Priest of Nature". He saw Nature as the *'Stern Daughter of the voice of God'*, man's conscience whose balmy presence never disappointed. He was born in 1770 in the picturesque Lake District of England. Here he spent happy years of his childhood in communion with God and Nature. After study at Cambridge, he went to France in 1791 and was enthused by the cause of the Revolution. But when the Reign of Terror came and thousands died at the guillotine, his fine sensibilities, his search for human equality and peace received a rude shock. He engaged himself in the philosophy of William Godwin for sometime. Finding no solution to the problem of human pain, he finally turned to the study of Nature. In the poems of the Lyrical Ballads he describes the mundane happenings of country life, the activities of humble people. He used their common dialect with its flawed grammar as his style. He decries the coming of the industrial era which mechanized English life. With no ornament, his poetry draws its power from the intensity of his feelings and imagination, In The Prelude (1805), a long poem, Wordsworth set out to look back and retrospect on his life. He follows the growth, the turnings of his poetic genius since childhood, ruminates on his errors and recalls the corrective lessons of Nature. In his great moral poem, The Excursion (1814), he uses a philosophy to refute the pessimism that the Revolution had brought.

Samuel Taylor Coleridge (1772-1834) was Wordsworth's "Spirits Brother". He was guided by the same philosophy of the imagination. While Wordsworth's imagination gave him a special vision of the common things of rustic life, Coleridge stirred up the supernatural. To appreciate his poetry peopled with strange, translunary beings like *The Ancient Mariner,* one needs *'that willing suspension of disbelief that constitutes poetic faith'*. In *The Rime of the Ancient Mariner*, Coleridge describes the strange adventures of a sailor in a ship. Having killed an albatross, the mariner suffers from hallucinations. The poem, with strange rhythm and cadences, creates a wondrous world. Coleridge was a master of lyrical style. His other famous poems are *Christabel* (1816), and *Kubla Khan* (1816). *Kubla Khan* was written as a result of an opium dream and described the wonderful, strange palace of the Chinese king, Kubla Khan. Coleridge certainly fulfils the meaning of *'Renaissance'* as *'a renascence of wonder'*.

Robert Southey (1774-1843) wrote poetry based on outlandish settings and myths like *Thalaba, the Destroyer* (1801), *The Curse of Kehama* (1810), and *Roderick, the Last of the Goths* (1814). His descriptions are rich and graphic and he uses a great variety of verse forms. He wrote a number of poems in ballad form.

Walter Scott (1771-1832) also had an interest in ballad poetry. He translated the *Lenore* from German (1796). His

The Minstrelsy of the Scottish Border (1802) shows a great romantic interest in the Middle Ages and the days of chivalry.

The second generation of great Romantic poets include Shelley, Keats and Byron.

Percy Bysshe Shelley (1792-1822) gave up his title and wealth to write poetry. His aim was to awaken mankind to the millenium, the coming future, which would remove human anguish and sorrow. His famous ode, *Ode to the West Wind* is an impassioned exhortation — *Make me thy lyre eu'n as the forest is ...... If Winter comes, can Spring be far behind?* He came under the influence of William Godwin, the philosopher. He proclaimed himself an atheist at the age of 21. His works include *Queen Mab* (1813), *Prometheus Unbound* (1818-1819), which shows human revolt against false gods, *To a Skylark, Adonais* (1821), which is an elegy to Keats, and The Cenci (1819). Shelley's style is a mixture of abstractions and visual images.

John Keats (1795-1821) was the most sensuous of the great Romantic poets. As we read his poems, richly laden with imagery and associations, all the senses are stirred up the visual, olfactory, auditory and tactile. It is said he tasted pepper in wine to describe certain lines. His famous odes are *To a Nightingale, To Autumn* and *On a Grecian Urn.*

Lord George Gordon Byron (1788-1824) was a wealthy nobleman who shunned the popular beliefs of his times. He was notorious as a dilletante. At the age of 19, he wrote Hours of Idleness (1807). With the publication of *Childe Harold's Pilgrimage* (1812) he became famous. Childe Harold was Byron himself, the figure of the disillusioned man, the hero fed up of pleasures and debauches. He lives an outlawed life and is rebellious in spirit. He took on more incarnations in his poems, *The Giaour* (1813), *The Corsair* (1814), *The Siege of Corinth* (1815). In these he displayed his own passions and eccentricities. In 1816, divorced from his wife, he retired to Switzerland and then to Italy. He wrote a number of plays — *Manfred* (1817), *Cain* (1821) and *The Deformed Transformed* (1824). The crowning work was his lyrical, satirical *Don Juan* (1819-1823). He went to Greece to fight for its independence, but died of illness. His satire is political, against England and also against English hypocrisy and cant. His licentious descriptions caused scandals. Don Juan, his magnum opus, is written in ottava rima or eight-line stanzas and is full of wit and mockery.

Thomas Moore (1779-1852), Thomas Campbell (1777-1844), Samuel Rogers (1763-1855), James Hogg (1770-1835), Walter Savage Landor (1775-1864) and **Leigh Hunt (1784-1859)** were other poets of the time.

Novel

Novels of terror and mystery prospered from 1800 to 1830. **Matthew Gregory Lewis** (1775-1818) wrote *Tales of Terror* (1800) and *Tales of Wonder* (1801). **Charles Lamb's (1775-1834)** *Tales from Shakespeare* (1807) is very popular even today. *Mrs Shelley,* the poet's wife, wrote the classic *Frankenstein* in which a scientist creates a monster that turns on its creator and destroys his most beloved ones. It is a novel of prophetic fear. **Miss Mary Mitford** wrote on country life and **Maria Edgeworth (1767-1849)** brought out educational novels like Belinda (1801) and *Tales of Fashionable Life* — novels for children.

Jane Austen (1775-1817) produced half a dozen novels which are drawing-room comedies of life. They study the passion and distress of young ladies and the life of country-folk. The novels — *Pride and Prejudice* (1813), *Sense and Sensibility* (1811), *Emma* (1816), *Persuasion* (1818), *Mansfield Park* (1814), *Northanger Abbey* (1818) — are realistic and witty, full of bracing dialogue.

Walter Scott was Scotland's greatest novelist recreating the past of his country's myths and ballads with rich humour. *Waverly* (1814), *Guy Mannering* (1815), *The Heart of Midlothian* (1818) contain history and direct observation. In *Ivanhoe* (1820), he describes the history of England in the days of the legendary Richard, the Lion Heart. *Kenilworth* (1821), *Quentin Dunward* (1823) were his other famous historical novels. He imbued the Romantic era with a love for the Middle Ages.

Prose/Criticism

The Romantic Age saw a number of reviewers and critics like **Jeremy Bentham (1748-1832)**, who expounded utilitarian doctrines, **Sydney Smith (1771-1845)**, and **William Cobbett (1762-1835)**. Coleridge, the poet, interpreted the doctrines of Kant and Schelling which show the distinction between pure reason and practical reason.

Lamb, Hazlitt, De Quincey and Leigh Hunt were Romantic critics of literature. **Charles Lamb's** essays on Shakespeare's tragedies state that we cannot do justice to them by staging them since the passions which are to be felt in their intensity are torn to tatters by the gimmickry of the actors. **William Hazlitt's (1778-1830)** criticism of some of Shakespeare's characters like Falstaff — *he laughs three inches below the flesh* — is a masterpiece. Coleridge's famous work of criticism, *Biographia Literaria* (1817), marvellously analyses Wordsworth's poetry. The Romantics believed that Shakespeare's art was organic like a work of Nature and *"esemplastic"* — able to blend different elements by imagination. **Thomas De Quincey's (1785-1859)** style is penetrating and incisive when criticizing the poets in *The Confessions of an English Opium Eater* (1821).

MAJOR AUTHORS AND THEIR WORKS

William Wordsworth (1770-1850)

The Lyrical Ballads
The Prelude
The Excursion
Tintern Abbey

Ode on Intimations of Immortality
Michaei
The Solitary Reaper
Loadamia
Ode to Duty
To Milton
The Leech-Gatherer
Upon Westminster Abbey
The Rainbow
We Are Seven
The World Is Too Much with Us
To the Cuckoo
The Daffodils
Lucy Gray
Simon Lee
Early Spring
Strange Fits of Passion Have I Known

Walter Scott (1771-1832)
The Bride of Lammermoor
Ivanhoe
Quentin Durward
The Heart of midlothian
Old Mortality
The Antiquity
Guy Mannering
Waverly
Rob Roy
Kenilworth
Red Gauntlet
The Black Dwarf
The Monastery
The Abbot
The Pirate
The Fortunes of Night
The Betrothed
The Talisman
Woodstock
Lives of the Novelists
Life of Napoleon
Tales of Grandfather
The Lay of the Last Minstrel
The Minstrelsy of the Scottish Border
Marmion
The Lady of the Lake
Rockeby

Robert Southey (1774-1843)
Joan of Arc
Wat Tyler
After Blenheim
The Holly Tree
The Scholar
A Vision of Judgement
Madoc
Life of Nelson
Thalaba the Destroyer
Roderick
The Curse of Kehama

S.T. Coleridge (1772-1834)
Biographia Literaria
Table Talk
Aids to Reflection
Christabel
Kubla Khan
The Rime of the Ancient Mariner
France : An Ode
Destiny of Nations
Frost at Midnight
Dejection : An Ode
Youth and Age
Religious Musings

Lord Byron (1788-1824)
Childe Harold's Pilgrimage
Don Juan
The Bride of Abydos
Manfred
The Giaour
Hours of Idleness
The Vision of Judgement
The Prisoner of Chillon
Lara
Marino Faliero
English Bards and Scotch Reviewers
The Siege of Corinth
The Corsair
Cain

P.B. Shelley (1792-1822)
On the Necessity of Atheism
The Revolt of Islam
Prometheus Unbound
The Mask of Anarchy
Hellas
The Cenci
The Witch of Atlas
The Indian Serenade
Ozymandias of Egypt
Epipsychidion
Alaster
Queen Mab

Adonais
Ode to the West Wind
The Cloud
Ode to a Skylark
O World! O Life! O Time!
Defence of Poetry (a Prose Work)
To Night
The Sensitive Plant
A Lament

John Keats (1795-1821)

Endymion
Lamia
Hyperion
The Eve of St. Agnes
Isabella
The Eve of St. Mark
La Belle Dame Sans Merci
Ode to a Nightingale
Ode to Autumn
Ode On a Grecian Urn
Ode to Psyche
On Melancholy
On First Looking into Chapman's Homer
Bright Star

Jane Austen (1775-1871)

Sense and Sensibility
Pride and Prejudice
Mansfield Park
Emma
Persuasion
Northanger Abbey

Charles Lamb (1775-1834)

Essays of Elia
The Last Essays of Elia
John Woodvil
Tales from Shakespeare
Specimens of English Dramatic Poets
The English Comic Writers
The Old Familiar Faces

William Hazlitt (1778-1830)

Characters of Shakespeare's Plays
The English Poets
The English Comic Writers
The Dramatic Literature of the Age of Elizabeth
The Round Table : A Collection of Essays
Table Talk on Men and Manners
The Spirit of the Age

Thomas De Quincey (1785-1859)

Confessions of an English Opium Eater
Joan of Arc
English Mail Coach
Dream Fugue
Murder Considered as One of the Fine Arts
Suspiria de Profundis

Samuel Rogers (1763-1855)

Pleasures of Memory
Italy

James Hogg (1770-1835)

Kilmeny
The Queen's Wake

Thomas Campbell

Pleasures of Hope
Theodoric
Gertrude of Wyoming
Lachiel
Lord Ullin's Daughter
The Last Man
Ye Mariners of England
Hohenlinden
The Battle of Baltic

Thomas Moore (1779-1852)

Lalla Rookh
Irish Melodies

Leigh Hunt (1784-1859)

Story of Rimini
Autobiography

Walter Savage Landor (1775-1864)

Gebir
Hellenics
Imaginary Conversations
The Citations of William Shakespeare
Pericles and Aspasia

THE VICTORIAN ERA (1830-1880)

During this era, the conflict between religion and science, mysticism and rationalism, became intense. There were those who, influenced by Darwin's theory of evolution as expounded in his *On the Origin of Species,* lost their faith in the biblical explanation of man's descent from Adam and Eve. They wanted to shun dogma and accept the scientific spirit. Others lamented the loss of faith and the rising consumer values. Mathew Arnold in his poem *Dover Beach* writes:

"The Sea of Faith was once too at the full.....

But now I only hear its long withdrawing melancholy roar......"

Prose

Carlyle and Ruskin echoed the prophecies of the Romantic era in their prose works. **Thomas Carlyle (1795-1881)**, the Scotsman, abandoned orthodoxy and came under the influence of the German writers Schiller, Novalis, Richter and Goethe. His work *Sartor Resartus* (1833-1834) is a sort of allegory based on a German professor who has written a treatise on clothes. He penetrates through the clothes to the essence of the man's being. Carlyle was also a historian. His historical works are *The French Revolution* (1837) and *The History of Frederich II of Prussia, called frederik the Great* (1858-1865). These are satirical and prophetic, expounding how man and society are organized. He was against materialism and praised the Magi and prophets of the past. He advocates strength and power.

John Ruskin (1819-1900) was indignant about the ugliness of existence brought in by industrialism and the machine. *Unto This Last* (1860), which influenced Gandhiji's economic theories, describes his disgust for soulless labour. He was a student of arts. *Modern Painters* (1843, 1860) is about landscape painters like Turner. He also wrote *The Seven Lamps of Architecture* (1849) and *The Stones of Venice* (1851-1853), praising Gothic art.

Matthew Arnold (1822-1888), the poet, wanted his countrymen to inculcate classical qualities to become harmonious in morals and in creative works. The English must break away from their insular moorings by imbibing the teachings of Greece and the French. He is *the detector-general of the intellectual failings of his own nation*. Poetry, according to him, is important in character formation, and culture is *"the minister of the sweetness and light essential to the perfect character"*. His works include *On translating Homer, The Study of Celtic Literature and Essays in Criticism* (1865, 1889). He wrote St. Paul and Protestantism advocating that dogma should be removed from Christianity and it should adjust itself to the findings of science.

A number of philosophers, historians and scholars wrote in this period. Charles Darwin's theory of evolution dramatically affected human thought. **John Stuart Mill (1806-1873)** expounded the processes of logic and political economy. **Herbert Spencer (1820-1903)** and **Thomas Henry Huxley (1825-1895)** were scientists. **Thomas Babington Macaulay (1800-1859)** was a poet, essayist and historian who advocated English education in India. The Oxford Movement gave rise to religious writers like **John Keble (1792-1866)** and **John Henry Newman (1801-1890)**. Newman's famous work is *Apologia pro Vita Sua* (1864) in which he explains why he had converted to the Roman Church.

Novel

The transition from Walter Scott's novels to Charles Dicken's first novel in 1836 is a great one. When Queen Victoria ascended the throne, **Frederick Marryat (1792-1848)** produced sea-stories; **Edward Bulwer Lytton (1803-1873)** wrote about Byronic heroes, attractive criminals and historical novels like *The Last Days of Pompeii* (1834); **Benjamin Disraeli** (1804-1881), the Prime Minister of England, wrote *Coningsby: or The New Generation* (1844) and *Sybil: or The Two Nations* (1845) to show that the aristocrats of the society had a duty towards the unfortunate ones. In Disraeli's novels, one finds the politics of Queen Victoria's reign.

Perhaps the greatest Victorian novelist is **Charles Dickens (1812-1870)**, whose identification with the underdog in society was unmatched by any writer. One reason for this is his own troubled childhood led in penury under the shadow of a father who was in debtor's prison. The part of his life comes through vividly in his novel *David Copperfield* (1849-1850) which is also an indictment of the cruel, unimaginative schools of his times. He was a master craftsman in character delineation. A host of characters and their dialogues have become household in the English-speaking world. Thus the incorrigible optimist Micawber, Geakle, Pickwick, Fagin and others are types of characters that may be seen all around us anywhere. Dickens had a forgiving sense of humour. He never let bitterness creep into his recreations of painful events of the past. Among his famous novels are: *Pickwick Papers* (1836; in the picaresque style), *Barnaby Rudge* (1841) and *A Tale of Two Cities* (1859; based on the French Revolution), *Oliver Twist* (1837) and *Hard Times* (1854); novels exposing social conditions. He has a picturesque style and concrete imagination.

William Makepeace Thackeray (1811-1863) made a penetrating analysis of upper middle class and aristocratic society. He was a master of irony. In *The Book of Snobs* (1849), he ridicules the tendency to fawn on nobility and to imitate their manners. *Vanity Fair* (1847-1848), *History of Pendennis* (1848-1850), *The Newcomes* (1853-1855), *The History of Henry Esmond* (1852) and *The Virginians* (1857-1859) are pictures of contemporary life in which he depicts human eccentricities and follies. He was adept at reproducing jargon and idiolects.

The Romantic spirit was still alive in the works of the Bronte sisters. **Charlotte Bronte (1816-1855)** wrote *Jane Eyre* (1847), the story of a governess in a terrifying house. Her sister **Emily Bronte (1818-1848)** wrote *The Wuthering Heights* (1847), set in a wild landscape. Powerful passions and characters have made this one of the greatest novels of all times.

George Eliot (1819-1880), a pen-name for Mary Ann Evans, wrote Adam Bede (1859), the story of a girl who was forced to murder her own baby. *The Mill on the Floss* (1860) and *Romola* (1863) are other novels by her. In *Middlemarch, a Study of Provincial Life* (1871-1872), the novelist builds up, from the lives of a great number of deeply studied characters, the complex picture of the life of a small town.

Poetry

The poetry of this period still shows the influence of the Romantic Era. **Alfred, Lord Tennyson (1809-1892)** was an eclectic, selecting the best of his forerunners. He was first interested in style and metre, but later on ideas started interesting him. A great many poems by him are flawlessly beautiful. If *The Lotus Eaters* is softly languorous, *Ulysses* has a striking severity. Tennyson also experienced the intellectual crisis of his times and shared its anxieties. For instance, *The Princess* (1847) is occupied with the question of feminism. *In Memoriam* (1850) is one of his most beautiful poems. It is an elegy on the premature death of his friend Arthur Hallam. It concerns itself with the belief in immortality, the conflict between the hopes of Christianity and the rationalism of science. It is composed of octosyllabic quatrains. He shows a type of Byronic revolt in Locksley Hall (1886) and Maud (1855). In *Idylls of the King* (1859, 1869, 1889) he took Arthurian legends as his theme.

Robert Browning (1812-1889) was famous for using the technique of dramatic monologue in his poems. Through the protagonists of his poems he gives vent to his feelings, passions and aspirations. Thus in *Paracelsus* (1835), he describes the highly ambitious hero who wanted to transform man's life. We find here Browning's views on truth and philosophy. His other poems include *Sordello* (1840), *Pippa Passes* (1841), *My Last Duchess, Porphyria's Lover* and his masterpiece, *The Ring and the Book* (1868-1869). In his works we find an excess of thought and a rare vocabulary. He uses blank verse dexterously. His brusque speech, broken syntax and uneven rhythm are in contrast to Tennyson's. As Pound and Eliot have said, Browning brought verse nearer to modern colloquial speech. Browning's characters are remote in time and culture. Some of these are Rabbi Ben Ezra, Fra Lippo Lippi and Andrea del Sarto. In *The Ring and the Book* he takes as his subject an Italian crime and explores the minds of all his characters. He strikes a note of hope in his poems. The lines *"God's in his heaven/And all's well with the world"* lay bare his beliefs. But in general, Browning is considered a difficult poet.

Matthew Arnold (1822-1888) was a reflective poet with a melancholic bent. A deep brooding pensiveness informs his poetry. Dover Beach shows his concern with the loss of faith in a world of science. His epic poem *Sohrab and Rustum, Tristram and Iseult, The Scholar Gypsy* are other famous works.

Dante Gabriel Rossetti, William Morris and Algernon Charles Swinburne together are known as the Pre-Raphaelite poets. They affected Raphael, the Renaissance painter, in their desire to paint sonorous wordpictures which may not have much content to conveyor any philosophy to reveal. It was in accordance with the aestheticism of Ruskin. In fact Rossetti and Morris were painters as well as poets. They worshipped beauty like John Keats did. Robert Buchanan attacked these poets as belonging to *the fleshly school of poetry*.

Dante Gabriel Rossetti (1828-1882) translated the Italian poet Dante's *Vita Nuova*. His *The Blessed Damozel* is an exquisite poem and his best sonnets are contained in *The House of Life* in which he extols his young and beautiful wife. They are full of rich sounds and images and mystic symbols. Rossetti was inspired by the ballads of the Middle Ages. Like the primitive Italian painters, he uses rich colours and depicts warm sensuous feelings.

William Morris (1834-1896) was enchanted by Gothic art of the Middle Ages. His poems drew inspiration from those of Froissart, Chaucer and Malory. He borrowed stories from Scandinavia and Iceland. His poems are like frescoes and are very lyrical in quality. The famous ones are *The Earthly Paradise* (1868-1870) and *The Life and Death of Jason* (1867). These works show rhythm and use of archaism. He strove to bring civilization back to art from the utilitarian industrialization.

Algernon Charles Swinburne (1837-1909) was a prodigy. He was a musician, and a sonority of rhymes filled his poetry. He took romantic themes like revolt against society, hatred of monarchy and struggle against traditional morality. His *Atalanta in Calydon* (1865) is his masterpiece and is known for its choral passages.

To these poets of the Victorian Age must be added the name of **Edward Fitzgerald (1809-1883)** whose **The Rubaiyat of Omar Khayyam (1859)** is a classic.

MAJOR AUTHORS AND THEIR WORKS

Alfred Lord Tennyson (1809-1892)

The Princess
In Memoriam
Maud
Enoch Arden
Idylls of the King
Queen Mary
Harold
Backet
Akbar's Tomb
Crossing the Bar
Locksley Hall
Locksley Hall Sixty Years After
Dora
Poems by Two Brothers
The Falcon
The Cup
Poems Chiefly Lyrical
Ulysses
Poems Chiefly Lyrical
Ulysses
The Lotos-Eaters
The Death of Oenone and Other Poems

Robert Browning (1812-1889)
Pauline
Paracelsus
Strafford
Sordello
Bells and Pomegranates
Christmas Eve and Easter Day
Men and Women
Dramatis Personae
The King and the Book
Asolando
Pippa Passes
Fra Lippo Lippi
Andrea del Sarto
King Victor and King Charles
Dramatic Lyrics
Dramatic Romances and Lyrics

Matthew Arnold (1822-1888)
Sohrab and Rustum
Tristram and Iseult
Balder Dead
Empedocles on Etna
Stanzas from the Grande Chartreuse
The Strayed Reveller and Other Poems
Dover Beach
Thyrsis
Scholar Gypsy
On Translating Homer
New Poems
On the Study of Celtic Literature
Essays in Criticism
Culture and Anarchy
Literature and Dogma
Mixed Essays
Friendship's Garland
God and the Bible

D.G. Rossetti (1828-1882)
The Blessed Damozel
World's Worth
Ave
The White Ship
Sister Helen
Eden Bower
The House of Life
Ballads and Sonnets

Christina Georgina Rossetti (1830-1894)
The Goblin Market
The Prince's Market
A Pageant and Other Poems

William Morris (1834-1896)
The Defence of Guenevere
The Life and Death of Jason
The Earthly Paradise
A Dream of John Bull
News from Nowhere
A Tale of the House of the Wolfings
The Roots of the Mountains
The Story of the Glittering Plain
The Sundering Flood
Hope and Fears for Art
Signs of Change

A.C. Swinburne (1837-1909)
Atalanta in Calydon
Erechtheus
Tristram of Lyonesse
Chasteland
Bathwell
Mary Stuart
William Blake : A Critique
A Study of Shakespeare
A Study of Ben Jonson
Songs Before Sunrise

Edward Fitzgerald (1809-1883)
Euphranor : A Dialogue on Youth
Translation of Rubaiat

Thomas Carlyle (1795-1881)
Sartor Resartus
The French Revolution
Heroes and Hero-Worship
Past and Present
The Letters and Speeches of Oliver Cromwell
Latter-day Pamphlets
Life of John Sterling
History of Frederick the Great
Chartism

John Ruskin (1819-1900)
The Modern Painters
Salsette and Elephanta
The Seven Lamps of Architecture
The Stones of Venice
The Two Paths
Unto This Last
Munera Pulveris
Time and Tide by Wear and Tyne
Fors Clavigera
Sesame and Lilies
The Crown of Wild Olive

T.B. Macaulay (1800-1859)

History of England from the Accession of James II

Lays of Ancient Rome

Charles Dickens (1812-1870)

Pickwick Papers

Nicholas Nickleby

Martin Chuzzlewit

Dombey and Son

David Copperfield

Bleak House

A Tale of Two Cities

Great Expectations

Our Mutual Friend

Edwin Drood

Oliver Twist

Little Dorrit

Baraby Rudge

The Uncommercial Traveller

A Christmas Carol

Hard Times

Old Curiosity Shop

William Makepeace Thackeray (1811-1863)

Vanity Fair

Barry Lyndon

Pendennis

Henry Esmond

The New Comes

The Virginians

Adventures of Philip

The Book of Snobs

The History of Pendennis

Lovel the Widower

The Round about Papers

The English Humorists of the Eighteenth Century

The Four Georges

Rebecca and Rowena

The Rose and The Ring

Ivanhoe—the Legend of the Rhine

George Meredith (1828-1909)

The Ordeal of Richard Feveral

Evan Harrington

Emilia in England

Rhoda Fleming

Vittoria

The Adventures of Harry Richmond

Diana of the Crossways

One of Our Conquerous

The Amazing Marriage

The Egoist

Beauchamp's Career

The Tragic Comedians

Charlotte Bronte (1816-1855)

Jane Eyre

Shirley

The Professor

Villette

Emily Bronte (1818-1848)

Wuthering Heights

George Eliot (1810-1880)
(Mary Ann Evans)

Adam Bede

The Mill on the Floss

Silas Marner

Scenes of Clerical Life

Life of Jesus

Romola

Fleix Holt the Radical

Daniel Deronda

Middlemarch

Benjamin Disraeli (1804-1881)

Vivian Gray

Sybil : Or the Two Nations

The Voyage of Captain Popavilla

Henrietta Temple

Coningsby : or the New Generation

Tancred : or the New Crusade

The Wondrous Tale of Alroy and the Rise of Iskander

Contarini Fleming : A Psychological Auto-biography

R.L. Stevenson (1850-1894)

Travels with a Donkey in the Cevennes

An Inland Voyage

Virginibus Pueresque

New Arabian Nights

Treasure Island

The Strange Case of Dr. Jackyll and Mr. Hyde

Kidnapped

The Black Arrow

The Master of Ballantrae

Catriona

Underwords

A Child's Garden of Verses

Thomas Hardy (1840-1828)

Under the Greenwood Tree

Desperate Remedies

A Pair of Blue Eyes

Two on a Tower

Far From the Madding Crowd

The Return of the Native
The Mayor of Casterbridge
Tess of the D'Urbervilles
Jude the Obscure
The Hand of Ethelberta
The Trumpet Major
The Woodlanders
The Well-beloved
A Laodicean
A Group of Noble Dames
Life's Little Ironies
Wessex Poems
The Dynasts
A Changed Man
Winter Words
The Waiting Supper and Other Tales

MULTIPLE CHOICE QUESTIONS

1. *"Bliss was it in that dawn to be alive, But to be young was very heaven!"* These lines have been attributed to:
A. Wordsworth B. Shelley
C. Keats D. Byron

2. *The Essays of Elia* is written by
A. De Quincey B. Charles Lambs
C. Hazlitt D. Cobbett

3. The publication of Wordsworth's Lyrical Ballads coincides with the
A. French Revolution
B. War for American Independence
C. Industrial Revolution
D. Invention of the steam engine

4. The poem Coleridge wrote as a result of an opium-induced dream was:
A. *The Solitary Reaper*
B. *Christabel*
C. *Rime of the Ancient Mariner*
D. *Kubla Khan*

5. Byron's poem, *The Vision of Judgment,* is an attack on the works of:
A. Coleridge B. Keats
C. Shelley D. Southey

6. *Childe Harold* is a poem by:
A. Coleridge C. Southey
B. Byron D. Shelley

7. *Prometheus Unbound* is written by:
A. Browning B. Tennyson
C. Shelley D. Spenser

8. *Adonais* is an elegy on:
A. Keats B. Arthur Hallam
C. Byron D. Shakespeare

9. John Keats is famous for his:
A. odes B. plays
C. blank verse D. masques

10. *Tales from Shakespeare* was written by:
A. Coleridge
B. Lamb and his sister Mary
C. Wordsworth
D. Byron

11. *Confessions of an English Opium Eater* is written by:
A. De Quincey B. Coleridge
C. Byron D. Leigh Hunt

12. William Godwin was a:
A. Psychologist B. Statesman
C. Scotsman D. Philosopher

13. *Don Juan* by Byron is written in:
A. blank verse B. rhyming couplets
C. ottava rima D. quatrains

14. The educational novel written by Maria Edgeworth is:
A. *Waverly* B. *Belinda*
C. *Ivanhoe* D. *Northanger Abbey*

15. Coleridge's *Biographia Literaria* critically analyzes the works of:
A. Byron B. Wordsworth
C. Keats D. Shelley

16. *The Stones of Venice* is a book about:
A. History of Venice B. Landscapes
C. Romantic Literature D. Gothic Art

17. Hopkins and Patmore were:
A. religious poets B. nature poets
C. war poets D. critics

18. Swinburne, Rossetti and Morris together were known as the:
A. Decadent poets B. Pre-Raphaelite poets
C. War poets D. Absurd poets

19. Christina Rossetti's work containing poems for children is:
A. *The Earthly Paradise*
B. *Scholar Gypsy*
C. *Goblin Market*
D. *The House of Life*

20. Swinburne's masterpiece known for its choral passages is:
A. *Atalanta in Calydon*
B. *Cain*
C. *Sohrab and Rustam*
D. *Queen Mab*

ANSWERS

1	2	3	4	5	6	7	8	9	10
A	B	C	D	D	B	C	A	A	B
11	**12**	**13**	**14**	**15**	**16**	**17**	**18**	**19**	**20**
A	D	C	B	B	D	A	B	C	A

THE MODERN AGE (1880-ONWARDS)

As the 20th century dawned, new values replaced the old ones and shaped the literature of Great Britain. England fast lost its imperial image as her colonies revolted and fought for independence. Industrialization progressed by leaps and bounds and the two World Wars brought economic depression. All this affected the content of literature. Writers sought new vehicles of expression. The findings of **Sigmund Freud** in the realms of psychology took novelists to the subconscious mind. A great number of writers who became famous men of letters in English came from Ireland **(G.B. Shaw, W.B. Yeats, James Joyce and Samuel Beckett)** and from America **(T.S. Eliot and Ezra Pound)**. Socialism became a practising creed and feminism raised her head. Dogmatic Christianity was more or less ignored. Although great strides were made in scientific inventions, science could not provide suitable answers to the deep questioning of the human mind resulting in ethical philosophy. The age saw the end of feudalism. Victorian reticence and prudery gave way to decadence in literature. English writers came under the influence of the French Parnassians and Symbolists. Scandinavia and Russia represented by **Ibsen** and **Tolstoy** also influenced the British men of letters. Many a poet wished to fight free from the fixed rules of versification and wrote in free verse. Many imitated the American poet **Walt Whitman**. English literature became more expansive in its concerns. The life and culture of foreign lands were depicted. Although **Kipling** was an imperialist, his works go beyond England. Being born in India, his works give a graphic view of the country. The great Celtic Revival under Yeats brought a new strain to English literature. Finally, the theatre, lying dormant for a century, now woke up with renewed vigour.

Criticism

The Age began with scholarly works in literary history. **Leslie Stephen (1832-1904)** wrote biographical and critical essays. He produced *The English Utilitarians and the Dictionary of National Biography*. He was an agnostic and rationalist. **A.C. Bradley (1851-1935), H.J.C. Grierson (1866-1960)** and **Edward Dowden (1843-1913)** were other famous critics. Bradley is famous for his critical work on Shakespeare's tragedies.

Walter Horatio Pater (1839-1894) propounded the literary doctrine *Art for Art's Sake* which was a quest for the most refined pleasure. The exquisite in art came from a reflection of the past. He eulogized the accomplishments of the Renaissance. His prose style was rich, musical and classical. His works include *Studies in the History of the Renaissance* (1873) and *Marius the Epicurean* (1885).

John Addington Symonds (1840-1893) was another admirer of the Renaissance. **Oscar Wilde (1856-1900)**, more known as a novelist and dramatist, gave a wider dimension to the theory of Art for Art's Sake by spicing it with wit and paradox. **George Saintsbury (1845-1933)** and **Sir Walter Raleigh (1861-1922)** were other famous critics.

Poetry

Most of the poetry written in this period are the works of those more renowned as novelists: Robert Louis Stevenson, Rudyard Kipling and Thomas Hardy. William Butler Yeats, who pioneered the Celtic Revival, Thomas Steams Eliot, whose *Wasteland* is a watershed leading to modern poetry, Gerard Manley Hopkins, the Catholic poet, are the famous poets of this period.

Rudyard Kipling (1865-1936) wrote on imperialist themes in *Barrack Room Ballads* (1892), *The Seven Seas* (1896) and *Five Nations* (1903). These poems were aimed by their rugged music to rouse people to protest. He combined folk-music with music-hall chorus. It had the sound of drum beats and bugle-calls and even the refinements of chamber music. The poetry of imperialism, heroism of national policy, contained slang and even biblical allusions. In fact, his popularity was that of Walt Whitman, the national poet of America. Many of his subjects were from India, like the poem *Gunga Din*.

W.E. Henley (1849-1903) also wrote poetry which praised Britain's colonial power. *The Song of the Sword, For England's Sake* and *London Voluntaries* are some of his better-known poems.

There were also a group of poets called the Decadents. They were aesthetes and their doctrine was *'Art for Art's Sake'*. **Oscar Wilde** was the leading poet of the group. *The Ballad of Reading Gaol* (1898) is his famous work inspired by his crime and imprisonment.

A group of poets had a pessimistic view of life. **John Davidson (1857-1909), Ernest Dawson (1867-1900)** and **A.E. Housman (1859-1936)** are some of these poets. But the leading pessimist of the age was **Thomas Hardy (1840-1928)**, better known as a novelist. He published *Wessex Poems* (1898) after the novel *Jude the Obscure* failed to receive public acclaim. His poetry was musical and highly individual. He had a disillusioned view of life. From 1903 to 1908, he produced the vast poetical work *The Dynasts*, written under the background of Napoleon's struggle against Europe combining real history with symbolic flashes. His poem, *To an Unborn Pauper Child,* reveals his utter dejection with life: *'Breathe : hid heart'*, it begins.

Francis Thompson (1859-1907) and **Gerard Manley Hopkins (1844-1889)** were religious poets of the beginning of the twentieth century. Thompson's poem, *The Hound of Heaven* is a masterpiece. It describes God as a Heavenly Hound chasing man to capture his soul and man fleeing Him in the pleasures of life. The Jesuit, Hopkins invented a new type of verse called *'sprung rhythm'*. It was filled with strange word coinages and is difficult for the ordinary reader to understand. His poetry reflects the conflict within him between his attraction to Roman Catholicism and his joy for the beautiful creation. He wrote a number of religious poems of which *The Wreck of the "Deutschland"* is one of the best. It describes the death of five Franciscan nuns on board the ship, *Deutschland*.

Irish, English and Continental influences met in **W.B. Yeats (1865-1939)**. He was born in Ireland but came to live in London. He was influenced by the strange mystical visions of William Blake, by pre-Raphaelite refinement and even the mysticism and occultism of the Orient, especially of India. His poetry is an attempt to revive Celtic mysticism and Irish mythology. Apparently it was Yeats who introduced Rabindra Nath Tagore to the West. He also came under the influence of Verlaine, a French symbolist poet. His best poetry is in *The Wild Swans at Coole* (1919), *The Tower* (1928) and *The Winding Stair* (1933). Some of his well-known poems are: *Easter* (1916), *The Second Coming, Byzantium, A Prayer for my Daughter, Leda and Swan, Sailing to Byzantium, Meru, Lapis Lazudili, Among School Children,* etc. His progress as a poet can be assessed by comparing the beautiful but simple *Lake Isle of Innisfree* with the beautiful and profound *Byzantium*.

The towering poet of the 20th century is **Thomas Steams Eliot (1888-1965)**. Eliot came on to the scene when the West was passing through tremendous upheavals — belief in religion, especially of the Church was fading, democracy was the new experiment in politics, and many modernist trends were noticeable in literature. Eliot proclaimed himself "a royalist in politics, an Anglo-Catholic in religion and a classicist in literature". Tradition, according to him, was not the dead past but the past living in the present. In his essay *Tradition and the Individual Talent*, he states that "the talent of an artist shows itself not where he differs from the ancients but where, in his work, they assert their immortality". Eliot's poetry shows metaphysical, symbolist and imagist strains, but his individual talent shines forth unmistakeably. An eclectic philosophy, borrowed from his own Christianity and Buddhism and the Upanishads informs his poetry. His poetry, especially *The Wasteland* (1922) is a poem that describes the zeitgeist (spirit of the times) and the *angoisse metaphysique* (metaphysical anguish) of life in post-World War Europe. It begins with the sentence *"April is a cruel month"* and this sets the strain for the whole poem. A brooding sense of futility and human inanity pervades modern life. Eliot achieves this effect by a combination of literary allusions to the past which stirs associations, and by what is called as the *objective correlative*. This last technique means that images are described which call up an emotion or a feeling. His other poems are *The Lave Song of J. Alfred Prufrock* and *Four Quartets* (1944). These lines from the *Four Quartets* may sum up the disillusionment of the times: *"Footfalls echo in the memory/Down the passage one could not take / To the door one could not open"*. Eliot was a poet of spiritual regeneration.

As the century proceeds, a host of poets make their mark **Stephen Spender (1909-1995), W.H. Auden (1907-1973), C. Day Lewis (1904-1972), Louis MacNeice (1907-1963)** — all of them wrote with a Social awareness, exposing the horror of the bourgeois culture and capitalist exploitation and the terror of totalitarianism.

We cannot end this section of the early modern twentieth century without a reference to **Rupert Brooke (1887-1915), Wilfred Owen (1893-1918)** and **Siegfried Sassoon (1886-1967)** popularly known as the "War poets". They had served the Armed Forces in the First World War, and after 1918, disillusioned by the horrors they had witnessed took their pens to write against the war. The poem *The Soldier* is one of the finest lyrics in the English language. It describes the poet's sense of impending death in battle and his love for his country: *"If I should die/Think only this of me/That there is a part of England/Buried in some foreign land"*. Another poem is Sassoon's *Everyone Sang,* which describes the exultation felt by the soldiers returning home after the General Armistice was signed. They are described as *freed birds*.

Novel

Just like poetry, the novel of this century reflects the great passions and strivings of the age. The discoveries of **Sigmund Freud (1856-1939)** revealed the relationship of man's behaviour to his subconscious mind. The subconscious contains impressions of past experiences which influence a person's attitudes and behaviour. These discoveries led not only to new methods of psychiatric treatment but also to new dramatic techniques in the art of the novel. The stream-of-consciousness method used by James Joyce and Virginia Woolf spring from these discoveries. The modern novel is more and more concerned with an analysis of human behaviour. The focus shifts from a description of the external atmosphere to the thoughts of the characters.

Thomas Hardy's works are tinged with a gloomy pessimism reminiscent of Schopenhauer, and an analogy may be found in his works to Flaubert and Zola from France.

Hardy's country Dorsetshire and the surroundings become the 'Wessex' of his novels. His work is full of realistic descriptions of the countryside. The places, full of pre-historic and Roman remains, heaths, have a character, and influence the people living there. The pre-historic past presses on the life of today. He is adept at delineating rustic characters. Man is a puppet of fate and an uncontrollable destiny drives him along life. A bitter helplessness pervades his novels *Far from the Madding Crowd* (1874), *The Return of the Native* (1878), *The Mayor of Casterbridge* (1886), and *Jude the Obscure* (1895). His success reached a climax with *Tess of the d'Urbervilles* (1891). His *Tess of the D'UrberviUes* and *Jude the Obscure,* because of their frank handling of sex and religion, aroused the hostility of the reading public. These two books, however, present Hardy's most moving indictments of the human situation.

The works of George Robert Gissing (1857-1903) produce a sense of absolute dejection. He worked as an ill-paid hack in the poor districts of London and described these places vividly in his books. Although impressed by Charles Dickens, his writings show none of Dickens' humour. One bitter, wretched world, a miserable London, exists in his works. Thus *Demos, a Story of English Socialism* (1886) describes the futility of socialist agitation, *The Nether World* (1889), the wretchedness of the London slums, *New Grub Street* (1891), the hopeless lot of a penniless writer, and *The Odd Women* (1893), the plight of unmarried women. His style is as bare and unaffected as his ideas.

Robert Louis Stevenson (1850-1894) stands in contrast to Hardy and Gissing in his recreation of the life of action and adventure. Although he suffered from an incurable malady, he did not lose faith in himself. He brought out *An Inland Voyage* (1878), *Travels with a Donkey in the Cevennes* (1879), *The Silverado Squatters, Treasure Island* (1833), *Kidnapped* and *The Master of Ballantrae* (1889) among others. The last three are very popular among children the world over. He also wrote children's adventure classics like *The Treasure Island* (1883), *Dr Jekyll and Mr. Hyde* (1886) and *Kidnapped* (1886). In *Dr. Jekyll and Mr Hyde* he touches upon the dual nature of man his good and evil aspects. His style is vivid and full of interesting details.

Another great novelist was the Pole, **Joseph Conrad (1857-1924)**, who perfected his knowledge of English and wrote in a vivid style with a strong foreign accent. His experience of sailing life and work in the English merchant service gave him the ideas to write masterpieces like *The Nigger of the Narcissus* (1897), and *Lord Jim: A Tale* (1900). Like the Slavs he was preoccupied with the problem of human misery. *Lord Jim* and *The Heart of Darkness* (1902) show his anger at what the white man had done to exploit Africa and other nations. A trait of his narrative technique is the gradual picture of his character formed from fragmentary descriptions of witnesses. He has a rich, sensuous prose style full of striking imagery.

Rudyard Kipling wrote stories about Indian life: *Plain Tales from the Hills* (1888) and *Soldiers Three* (1888). *Plain Tales from the Hills* depicts an Englishman's encounter with the strange East. Kipling was born in Bombay and spent his early life in India. He knew the land and its customs, its people and languages. His best book is *Kim* (1901), the story of a half-Irish boy, who speaks the language of the rustics of India and accompanies a Buddhist Lama on his search for "Nirvana" or Salvation. Kipling is adept at describing the sights and smells of India and its colourful people with their racy dialects. He also wrote two animal epics entitled, *The Jungle Book* (1894) and a series of short stories for children like *Captains Courageous* (1897), *Just So Stories* (1902) and *Puck of Pook's Hill* (1906). Kipling was influenced by Carlyle's doctrine of energy. As a spokesman of the Imperialist theme he believed that it was ideal for a person to sacrifice himself for his tribe. He believed that especially the white man was ordained to rule and lead nations. His works praise Britain's hegemony over her colonies.

Shortly after Kipling, came H. G. Wells and John Galsworthy who were Socialists and criticized the English society. **H.G. Wells** (1866-1946) began by writing stories with a semi-scientific flavour like *The Time Machine* (1895), *The Island of Dr Moreau* (1896), *The Invisible Man* (1897) and *The War of the Worlds* (1898). The stories are ingenuously plotted and thrill and disturb the readers. Later on Wells' interest shifted to social problems. He became a member of the Fabian Society. He wrote *Mankind in the Making* (1903) describing how society would look like when reformed by socialism. He also satirized the society in *Love and Mr Lewisham* (1900), *Kipps* (1905). *Tono-Bungay* (1909) and *Marriage* (1912). He does not glorify Britain's past and he scorns the existing institutions of his country. He wrote a number of remarkable books after the outbreak of World War I in 1914. These show his restless self-examining spirit. Some of these are *Mr Britling Sees it through* (1916) and *The Undying Fire* (1919).

In the works of **John Galsworthy (1867-1933)** we find an artistic conscience. Like Wells, he also attacked the concept of property and commercialism in his novels. He too exposed and criticized national prejudices, especially those existing among his own class, the landed gentry. He was widely read in Continental Literature and was especially influenced by France and Russia. Turgenev with his noble realism was his ideal. He is a detached and impartial observer of his country's decadent values. He advocates a fearless search for truth. *In The Island Pharisees* (1904) he exposes the stagnation of thought among English privileged classes. A similar theme is touched in other novels like *The Country House* (1907), *The Patrician* (1911) and *The Dark Flower* (1913) where country squires, aristocracy and artists are critically studied. *The Forsyte Saga* (1922) is his masterpiece. It is a natural history of the rich upper-middle class family.

He describes their attitude to events like the Great War, the growth of socialism, unemployment and the coal strike.

Enoch Arnold Bennett (1867-1931) wrote a number of different types of novels presenting a detailed picture of an industrial district in the provinces. He is a realist like the French nationalists. His masterpiece is *The Old Wives' Tale* (1908).

G.K. Chesterton (1874-1936) was a champion of tradition and he refuted and opposed the attacks of his contemporaries against English society in *Orthodoxy* (1908), *The Napoleon of Notting Hill* (1904). He believed in tradition sanctified by ages of experience and even in the religious bond between men. His style is effective with the use of imagery and comparison and he spices it with plenty of humour.

James Joyce (1882-1941) pioneered a new type of novel with the *stream-of-consciousness* technique. Characters in *Ulysses* (1922) unreel themselves by a sort of interior monologue. Speech is mimicked and styles are parodied. *Ulysses* is modelled on the *Odyssey* of Homer and set in the slums of Dublin. The thousand pages of this novel cover just one day in the life of Leopold Bloom and Stephen Dedalus. Joyce coined words from several languages and was a master craftsman with wit and conceits. His other famous work is the autobiographical *A Portrait of the Artist as a Young Man* (1916) which describes his adolescence and sensuous tendencies.

Virginia Woolf (1882-1941) continued the stream-of-consciousness technique. Her works *To the Lighthouse* (1927) and *Mrs Dallaway* (1925) reveal the hidden inner life of her characters.

E.M. Forster (1879-1970) was the novelist of cultural relations. In **A Passage to India** (1924) he studies the conflict between the west and the east and takes a favourable stand for the latter. *Where Angels Fear to Tread* (1905) studies how the cultural divide between an Italian girl and her English husband leads to the ruination of their marriage and life.

D.H. Lawrence (1885-1930) was a prolific writer. His outspoken views on sexual relations raised much hue and cry. He considered sex the religion of the blood. His novels were dubbed pornographic. He believed in the free expression of human personality, in being guided by unrestrained primitive instincts. In *Sons and Lovers* (1913) he studies the relationship of son and mother and the social disparity of a father, a coalminer and a mother, a teacher. The novel is autobiographical. Other works by him are *The Rainbow* (1915), *Women in Love* (1921), and *The Plumed Serpent* (1926). *The Rainbow,* suppressed as obscene, treats the conflict between man and woman. *Lady Chatterley's Lover* (1928) was canned for being obscene.

George Orwell (1903-1950) wrote novels which were an indictment of totalitarian government: *Animal Farm* (1945) and *Nineteen Eighty-Four* (1949). **Aldous Huxley's** *Brave New World* (1932) is a prophetic book about the future of civilization in the context of scientific advancement.

Drama

After Shakespeare, **George Bernard Shaw (1856-1950)** is the great playwright whose works enlivened the British stage. Shaw, like Ibsen, believed in drama as a vehicle for ideas. He had a rich Irish sense of humour and his plays are satires on various social and philosophical themes. His general technique was to discuss the problem of his play first in its preface. Often this preface is longer than the play itself. *Widowers' Houses* (1892) was his first play. In this he discusses the problem of Housing. In *Mrs Warren's Profession* (1894) he lays bare the profession of a prostitute. In *Arms and the Man* (1894) the theme is the chocolate-cream soldier. Shaw was an iconoclast breaking well-established idols or myths. Thus this play disillusions us of the romantic image of a soldier. He is not one who is willing to die for his country, but one who loves his life. When the enemy is weak, he attacks, but withdraws and takes to his heels if the enemy is strong. George Bernard Shaw had a keen interest in the English language and formulated a standard pronunciation for it. He studies the theme of how language can influence one's rise in the social ladder. Professor Higgins succeeds in teaching a flower-girl to rid herself of a cockney accent and to speak well enough to pass for royalty! In *Man and Superman* we see Shaw as a master conversationalist. Ideas are discussed without much action taking place in the play. *The Apple Cart* (1929) shows the weaknesses of democracy. Although an Irish man, Shaw did not write on Irish themes as such.

Oscar Wilde reminds one of the Restoration playwrights Sheridan and Congreve in his comedy of manners. His style is full of paradox and verbal wit. Some of his famous plays are *Lady Windermere's Fan* (1892), *A Woman of No Importance* (1893) and *The Importance of Being Ernest* (1895).

John Galsworthy's plays *Strife* (1909), *Justice* (1910) and *Loyalties* (1922) were based on the theme of class exploitation.

W.B. Yeats contributed to the Irish drama. His Celtic theme comes through in *The Countess Cathleen* (1892) and *The Land of Heart's Desire* (1894). **Sean O'Casey** (1884-1964) and **J. M. Synge** (1871-1909) were other noted Irish playwrights. The latter's plays, *The Playboy of the Western World* (1907) and *Riders to the Sea* (1904) are famous.

T.S. Eliot's contribution to the modern theatre were religious and moral plays. He uses the Greek "chorus" style in *Murder in the Cathedral* (1935) to heighten the dramatic effect of the murder of Thomas Becket by the Archbishop of Canterbury's men. *The Family Reunion* (1939) is a play about sin and expiation. Eliot pruned verse to sound like prose. This is done dexterously in *The Cocktail Party* (1949) and *The Confidential Clerk* (1953) where characters speak verse which sounds like prose.

A group of playwrights came to be known as the "Angry Young Men". **John Osborne (1929-1994)** was the most prominent of them. His play *Look Back in Anger* (1956) catches the mood of the frustrated youth in post-War England. In his plays, he exposes the wretchedness of the working class.

Harold Pinter (1930-2008) mixes comedy and horror in his plays like *The Birthday Party* (1958).

Another group of dramatists drew their inspiration from France. *The Absurd Theatre*, as it was called, began in France with Albert Camus, Jean Genet and Ionesco as its pioneers. In England, **Samuel Beckett (1906-1989)** was the Irish dramatist of this school. His plays *Endgame* (1955), *Krapp's Last Tape* (1958) and *Waiting For Godot* (1906) show the meaninglessness of human action and the unrelieved gloom of existence.

MAJOR AUTHORS AND THEIR WORKS

George Bernard Shaw (1856-1950)

Widowers' Houses
Candida
You Never Can Tell
Man and Superman
Back to Methuselah
Saint Joan
Heartbreak House
The Philanderer
Mrs. Warren's Profession
Caesar and Cleopatra
John Bull's Other Island
Major Barbara
The Doctor's Dilemma
Getting Married
The Apple Cart
Pygmalion
The Dark Lady of the Sonnets
Plays Pleasant and Unpleasant
The Millionaire
The Intelligent Woman's Guide to Socialism
Everybody's Political What is What
Cashel Byron's Profession
Love Among the Artists
Androcles and the Lion
The Devil's Disciple
The Man of Destiny

W.B. Yeats (1865-1939)

The Land of Heart's Desire
The Countess Cathleen
The Shadowy Waters
The Hour-glass
The Resurrection
The King's Threshold
On Baile's Strand
The Cat and the Moon
Ideas of Good and Evil
Discoveries
The Wind among the Reeds
The Wanderings of Oisin
The Tower
The Winding Stair and Other Poems
Lake Isle of Innisfree
Byzantium

John Galsworthy (1867-1933)

The Silver Box
Strife
The Skin Game
The Man of Property
Justice
Loyalties
Escape
The Inn of Tranquility
The Forsyte Saga
The Country House
Fraternity
The Patrician
The Dark Flower
Saint's Progress
Maid in Waiting
Flower Wilderness

Rudyard Kipling (1865-1936)

Kim
The Jungle Book
Barrack-room Ballads
Departmental Ditties
The Seven Seas
The Five Nations
Tales from the Hills
Soldiers Three
Life's Handicap
The Phantom Rickshaw
Many Inventions
The Day's Work
Just-so Stories for Little Children
Rewards and Fairies
Debits and Credits

H.G. Wells (1866-1946)

The Time Machine
Love and Mr. Levisham
Kipps

The History of Mr. Polly
Mr. Britling Sees It Through
Christina Albertas Father
The Wonderful Visit
The Island of Dr. Moreau
The Invisible Man
The War of the Worlds
The First Men in the Moon
The Food of the Gods
Marriage
Experiment in Autobiography
The Contemporary Novel

Joseph Conrad (1857-1924)
The Nigger of the 'Narcissus'
Typhoon
Lord Jim
Victory
Almayer's Folly
An Outcast of the Islands
Youth
Heart of Darkness
The Secret Agent
The Shadow of Line
Suspense-A Napoleonic Novel

Arnold Bennett (1867-1931)
The Old Wives' Tale
Clayhanger
Riceyman Steps
Buried Alive
Hilda Lessways
These Twain
Sacred and Profane Love
The Pretty Lady
The Love Match
The Author's Craft

Walter de la Mare (1873-1956)
Peacock Pie
Memoirs of a Midget
Songs of Childhood
Bells and Grass
The Traveller
Early the Morning
Love

T.S. Eliot (1888-1965)
The Waste Land
Prufrock and Other Observations
Gerontion
The Hollow Men
Ash Wednesday
Four Quartets
Sweeney Agonistes
Murder in the Cathedral
The Rock
The Family Reunion
The Cocktail Party
The Confidential Clerk
The Sacred Wood
After Strange Gods
The Elder Statesman
The Idea of a Christian Society
What is a Classic?
For Lancelot Andrews
The Use of Poetry and the Use of Criticism
Elizabethan Essays
Points of View

Virginia Woolf (1882-1941)
The Voyage Out
Jacob's Room
Mrs. Dalloway
To The Light House
The Waves
Flush
Orlando : A Biography
The Common Reader
Roger Fry
The Death of the Moth
Mr. Bennett and Mrs. Brown
A Room of One's Own
Between the Acts (Unfinished)

E.M. Forster (1879-1970)
Abinger Harvest
Two Cheers for Democracy
A Passage to India
Howard's End
The Hill of Devi
The Celestial Omnibus
Collected Short Stories
Where Angels Fear to Tread
The Longest Journey
The Story of the Siren
A Room with a View
The Eternal Moment

James Joyce (1882-1941)
Ulysses
Portrait of the Artist as a Young Man
Finnegans Wake
Dubliners

D.H. Lawrence (1885-1930)
Sons and Lovers
Woman in Love
Lady Chatterly's Lover
The Rainbow
The White Peacock
Kangaroo
The Plumed Serpent

Aldous Huxley (1894-1963)
Point Counter Point
The Burning Wheel
Those Barren Leaves
Brave New World
After Many a Summer
Eyeless in Gaza
Antic Hay
Time Must Have a Stop
Crome Yellow
The Defeat of Youth
The Perennial Philosophy
The Devils of Loudun

George Orwell (1903-1950)
The Animal Farm
The Road to Wigan Pier
Nineteen Eighty-Four
Burmese Days
Keep the Aspidistra Flying

Oscar Wilde (1854-1900)
The Sphinx
The Ballad of Reeding Gaol
The Canterville Ghost
De Profundis
The Duchess of Padua
The Importance of Being Earnest
An Ideal Husband
Lady Windermere's Fan
Salome
The Picture of Dorian Gray
The Happy Prince and the Other Tales

Harold Pinter (1930-2008)
The Birthday Party
The Dumb Waiter
The Care Taker
A Night Out
The Home Coming
Old Times
Silence

MULTIPLE CHOICE QUESTIONS

1. The Celtic Revival was begun by:
A. George Bernard Shaw
B. W.B. Yeats
C. J.M. Synge
D. James Joyce

2. *The Wasteland* is written by:
A. T.S. Eliot B. John Galsworthy
C. Thomas Hardy D. Virginia Woolf

3. Hardy is famous for his poem:
A. *The Hound of Heaven*
B. *The Dynasts*
C. *Four Quartets*
D. *Wild Swans of Coole*

4. The Irish dramatist, who wrote absurd plays, was
A. W.B. Yeats B. Samuel Beckett
C. Sean O'Casey D. J.M. Synge

5. *Everyone Sang* is a poem about:
A. socialism B. music
C. war D. death

6. *The Old Wives'* Tale is written by:
A. Robert Gissing B. Galsworthy
C. H.G. Wells D. Arnold Bennet

7. Robert Louis Stevenson wrote stories about:
A. adventure B. human nature
C. war D. nature and man

8. *The Invisible Man* is written by:
A. D.H. Lawrence B. H.G. Wells
C. Kipling D. Dickens

9. *Nigger of the Narcissus* is written by:
A. Hardy B. Eliot
C. Lawrence D. Conrad

10. Sex was considered the religion of the blood by:
A. D.H. Lawrence B. Ibsen
C. G.B. Shaw D. Oscar Wilde

11. The British novelist and poet who described India best was:
A. Virginia Woolf B. Graham Greene
C. Rudyard Kipling D. Aldous Huxley

12. Rupert Brooke, Wilfred Owen and Siegfried Sassoon are together known as:
A. Flower Poets B. War Poets
C. Poets of Revolt D. Patriotic Poets

13. Walt Whitman was the national poet of:
A. England B. Poland
C. America D. France

14. *The Wreck of the Deutschland* is a:
A. war poem B. historical poem
C. romantic poem D. religious poem

15. *Sprung rhythm* was invented by:
A. Gerard Manley Hopkins
B. T.S. Eliot
C. Auden
D. Yeats

16. *The Family Reunion* — a play, is written by:
A. W.B. Yeats B. T.S. Eliot
C. Cecil Day Lewis D. Louis MacNiece

17. Gissing's *The Odd Women* is a work on:
A. plight of unmarried women
B. poverty of slum-dwellers
C. war and love
D. the life force

18. *Ulysses* is written by:
A. Virginia Woolf B. George Orwell
C. Arnold Bennett D. James Joyce

19. *The Patrician* is written by:
A. Kipling B. H.G. Wells
C. Henry James D. Galsworthy

20. *Look Back in Anger* is written by:
A. A. J. Cronin B. Aldous Huxley
C. D. H. Lawrence D. John Osborne

ANSWERS

1	2	3	4	5	6	7	8	9	10
B	A	B	B	B	D	A	B	D	A
11	**12**	**13**	**14**	**15**	**16**	**17**	**18**	**19**	**20**
C	B	C	D	A	B	A	D	D	D

INDIAN WRITING IN ENGLISH

ANAND, MULKRAJ (1905-2004)

He was greatly influenced by Premchand on the one hand and Tagore on the other.

Some of his famous novels are :

1. The Village (1939)
2. Across the Black Waters (1940)
3. The Sword and the Sickle (1942)
4. Untouchable (1933) (his first novel)
5. Seven Summers (1951)
6. Private Life of an Indian Prince (1953)
7. The Big Heart (1945)
8. Coolie (1936) (It was recast in seventies)
9. Two Leaves and a Bud (1937)
10. The Old Woman and the Cow (1960)
11. The Road (1961)
12. Death of a Hero (1963)
13. Confession of a Lover (1976)
14. Morning Face (1968)

AUROBINDO, GHOSE (1872-1950)

- He was known as the "firebrand" of India.
- He was a poet, a saint, a philosopher, statesman, yogi and a prophet.
- He is one of the pre-Independence Titanic trio of Indian poets—Tagore, Aurobindo and Sarojini Naidu.
- He is chiefly known for his
  - (*i*) Savitri (1953) a poetic epic on a grand scale.
  - (*ii*) The Life Divine (1939-40)
  - (*iii*) Essays on Gita
- He is a great exponent and proponent of ancient Indian thought.
- According to R. K. Singh, "Aurobindo is sympathetic to the modernist trends in writing and study of poetry and, in fact, himself adopts some of the methods followed by the modern poets."
- To quote Mr. Singh again, "In Aurobindo's literary order, poetry is a means of spiritual expression that helps to open the consciousness..."

CHATTERJEE, BANKIM CHANDRA (1838-94)

- He is generally called 'The Father of Bengali fiction.'
- Today he is most known for his patriotic bent of mind.
- In all he wrote 14 novels.
  - (*i*) Some of them are historical.
  - (*ii*) Others are social.
  - (*iii*) Still others are philosophical with stress on renunciation and non-attachment.
- Some of his novels are :
  - (*i*) *The Poison Tree* (*1884*): It is a story of Hindu life in Bengal of the period
  - (*ii*) Kapalkundala (1885)

(*iii*) Durgeshnandini (1890)
(*iv*) Krishnakanta's Will (1895)
(*v*) The Two Rings (1897)
(*vi*) Rajmohan's Wife (1904) (published posthumously)
(*vii*) Anand Math (1884)

CHAUDHURI, NIRAD, C. (1897-1999)

- He came into limelight with the publication of his "The Autobiography of an Unknown Indian." (1951).
- His other important works are:
  (*i*) A Passage to India (1959)
  (*ii*) Continent of Circe (1966)
  (He received the Duff Cooper Memorial Prize).
  (*iii*) The Intellectual in India (1967)
  (*iv*) To Live or Not to Live (1970)
- He is known for his most correct and chaste prose for which he has earned much acclaim from the scholars and critics, including Khushwant Singh.

DESAI, ANITA (Born-1937)

- She is a renowned novelist and short story writer.
- Some of her famous novels are :
  (*i*) Cry, the Peacock (1963)
  (*ii*) Voices in the City (1965)
  (*iii*) Bye-Bye, Blackbird (1971)
  (*iv*) Fire on the Mountain (1977)
  (*v*) Clear Light of Day (1980)
- Her collection of short stories is captioned "Games at Twilight" (1978)

GANDHI, M.K. (1869-1948)

1. His famous work in English is "My Experiments with Truth."
2. The work is an important autobiographical writing which is held in high esteem for its truthfulness, frankness, simplicity and directness of expression in non-ornamental effective English.

MARKANDAYA, KAMALA (1924-2004)

1. She is one of the modern novelists and is known for her:
   (*i*) Nectar in a Sieve (her first novel) (It is a novel on miserable rural life).
   (*ii*) Some Inner Fury (1955)
   (It is a novel of violence and destruction)
   (*iii*) A Silence of Desire (1960)
   (It is a novel urging the readers to speak out frankly to unburden their hearts).
   (*iv*) Possession (1963)
   (The problem of possession is discussed in this novel).
   (*v*) A Handful of Rice (1966)
   (It depicts the life of the poor classes in Madras).
   (*vi*) The Coffer Danus (1969)
   (*vii*) The Nowhere Man (1972)
   (*viii*) Two Virgins (1973)
   (*ix*) The Golden Honeycomb (1977)
   (*x*) Pleasure City (1982).

KHUSHWANT SINGH (Born-1915)

- He is known for his novels :
  (*i*) Train to Pakistan (his masterpiece)
  (*ii*) I Shall Not Hear the Nightingale (1959). (It describes the social life of a Sikh family during the pre-Independence period).
- "The Mark of Vishnu" is another of his well-known works.
- Some of his known stories
  (*a*) Karma
  (*b*) When Sikh Meets Sikh
  (*c*) The Rape, etc.
- He is also known for his:
  (*i*) A History of the Sikhs
  (*ii*) Translation of Japji Sahib, etc.
- His regular columns appear weekly in some dailies, *e.g.* :
  (*i*) 'With Malice Towards One And All'—The Hindustan Times.
  (*ii*) 'This Above All'—The Tribune.
- Mulk Raj Anand is stated to have said that Khushwant Singh's "Train to Pakistan" is likely to last, while about his other creative literary work, one may have some doubts.
- Among his latest work is "Truth, Love and Little Malice."

MULLER, MAX (1823-1900)

- He was a famous Indologist, German orientalist and linguist, who unearthed a lot of ancient Indian history and Sanskrit scriptures, the Rig Veda, in particular, of which he published six colossal volumes, for which he had got an assignment from the East India Company in 1847.
- Actually he was a student of Sanskrit, who started comparative study of languages and "Avesta" (in 1845) which is the renowned sacred book of the Zoroastrians.
- He gave seven lectures on Indian and ancient Indian philosophy at Cambridge University, which have now been published by Rupa & Co. under the caption: "India : What Can it Teach Us?"
- He distnguishes the highest wisdom of Greece and India by using the terms "to know ourselves" and "to know our self", respectively.
- Muller makes very appreciative comments on the Rig Veda and the Vedic Religion.

NAIDU, SAROJINI (1879-1946)

- She is a well-known Indian English poet who started writing poetry at a very early age and she was inspired by Edmund Gosse to choose Indian themes and scenery rather than imitating the English classics.
- She is now known as 'The Nightingale of India.'
- She took a keen interest in India's struggle for freedom.

Some of her works are :

1. The Golden Threshold (1905)
2. The Bird of Time (1912)
3. The Broken Wing (1917)
4. The Sceptred Flute (1946)
5. The Feather of the Dawn (1961) (It appeared posthumously)

Some of her famous poems are :

1. The Queen's Rival
2. Palanquin Bearers
3. To My Fairy Fancies
4. The Pardah Nashin
5. Awake
6. Village Song
7. The Soul's Prayer
8. Fishermen of Coromondel
9. It You Call Me
10. Caprice
11. Summer Woods
12. Songs of Radha
13. The Bird Sanctuary, etc.

NANDY, PRITISH (Born-1947)

- He was the editor of the 'Illustrated Weekly of India' and has now Telecast a T.V. serial over the Doordarshan: "Hungama Unlimited."
- (*i*) He is a prolific poet, though he is still not considered one of the best.
  (*ii*) Most of his poetry has been dismissed by critics as mere experimental gimmickry. Such was Saleem Peeradina.
  (*iii*) Even Nissim Ezekiel dubbed him to be a poetaster.
- Some of his works are :
  (*i*) Gods and Olives (1967)
  (*ii*) On Either Side of Arrogance (1968)
  (*iii*) From the Outer Bank of the Brahmputra (1969)
  (*iv*) Riding the Midnight River (1975)
  (*v*) In secret Anarchy (1979), etc.
- He has written a number of anthologies and translated a number of poets including Agyeya, Amrita Pritam, Kaifi Azmi etc.
- He has also written some short stories and a verse play.

NARAYAN, R.K. (1906-2001)

- Of the three great novelists, Narayan, Anand and Rao, it is Narayan who has won the maximum accolade both in India and abroad.
- One of his great achievements is his creation of the famous town of Malgudi like Hardy's Wessex.
- Narayan is the true master of humour, irony, realism, romance and artistry.
- Most of his novels and stories depict the life of people of South India.
- It is sometimes held that Narayan lacks true pathos, genuine depth of feeling, realistic description of poverty and misery, the elements which go in for making a novelist a great one.
- However, he has earned much popularity as a novelist, and within the range of his own art, he cannot be taken except with due regard and attention.

Some of his famous novels are :

1. Swami and Friends (1935)
2. Bachelor of Arts
3. The English Teacher
4. The Financial Expert
5. Mr. Sampath (1949)
6. The Guide (1958)
7. The Man-eater of Malgudi
8. The Dark Room (1939)
9. Waiting for the Mahatma
10. The Vendor of Sweets
11. The Painter of Signs (1976)

(He won the Sahitya Akademi Award for 'Guide' in 1961)

R.K. NARAYAN (as a short story writer)

- Some of his stories have appeared in the following collections:
  (*i*) Malgudi Days
  (*ii*) Dodu and Other Stories
  (*iii*) Cyclone and Other Stories
  (*iv*) Gods, Demons and Others

Narayan has written a few hundred stories, most of them quite interesting and highly readable:

Some of his famous short stories are :

1. The Golden
2. A Career
3. The Snake Song
4. Man Hunt
5. A Willing Slave
6. An Astrologer's Day
7. The Doctor's word
8. God of Troubles, etc.

NEHRU, JAWAHARLAL (1889-1964)

- He needs no introduction as a freedom fighter, statesman and first Prime Minister of India.
- Some of his literary works are :
  (*i*) An Autobiography (1936)
  (*ii*) Glimpses of World History (1939)
  (*iii*) Discovery of India (1946)
- Children enjoy reading his "Letters from Father to His Daughter."
- He is known for his simple, chaste, poetic English which is a model of natural style.

PRITAM, AMRITA (1919-2005)

- She is the most famous Punjabi Author.
- She won the Jnanpith Award for her "Kagaj Te Kenvas" in 1981.
- Her best known autobiographical work which appeared in the seventies is "Rasidi Ticket."
- (*i*) Her "Shadows of words : An Auto-biography" (a transcreation of the Hindi original by Jyoti Sabharwal) has been published by Macmillan in 2002.
  (*ii*) The book presents "an inner journey down the memory lane" presented by the author, who considers old age the best part of her life, like the last sips of tea, which are "usually the sweetest."

RADHAKRISHAN, SARVAPALLI (1888-1975)

- He is known as an outstanding educationist and a philosopher who presented the Hindu/Indian viewpoint to the world.
- His works include
  (*i*) An Idealist View of Life (Lectures)
  (*ii*) Indian Philosophy (1923, 1927)
  (*iii*) The Hindu View of Life (1932)
  (*iv*) An Idealist View of Life (1932)
  (*v*) Eastern Religious and Western Thought (1939)
- He wrote in a very simple, intelligible prose-style.

RAO, RAJA (1908-2006)

- His famous works are:
  (*i*) The Serpent and the Rope (1960)
  (*ii*) Kanthapura (1938)
  (*iii*) The Cat and Shakespeare (1965-66)
- (*i*) He was awarded the Sahitya Akademi Award for his 'The Serpent and the Rope' in 1964.
  (*ii*) He was also decorated with Padma Bhushan in 1969.

Raja Rao as a short story writer

- He is also a well-known short story writer.
- His first collection of short stories was "Jauni" which was published in France in 1930.
- The collection: "The Cow of the Barricades" was published in 1947

Some of his famous short stories are :

1. Akkayya
2. The Little Gram-shop
3. Kanaka Pal
4. Narsiga

ROY, ARUNDHATI (Born-1961)

She made her debut with her novel: "The God of Small Things" which won her the Booker Prize in 1997, besides a handful amount running into crores as royalty for less than four hundred pages which comprise the said novel.

DE, SHOBHA (Born-1948)

- She is a renowned contemporary Indian English novelist and T.V. serial script writer.
- Some of her novels are prescribed in universities in England and Australias.
- Her T.V. serial "Swabhiman" which ran into numerous episodes was telecast over the Doordarshan.
- (*i*) She has become even more popular with her serial "Kittie Party" telecast over the Zee T.V.
  (*ii*) According to the Tribune, it "is a clever insight into the mind of today's urban Indian women poised at the crossroads of modernity and tradition."

TAGORE, RABINDRANATH (1861-1941)

Tagore was a versatile genius. He was a :

(*i*) poet
(*ii*) novelist
(*iii*) short story writer
(*iv*) dramatist
(*v*) musician
(*vi*) actor (in dramas)
(*vii*) painter
(*viii*) statesman and a host of other things.

Some of his famous novels are :

1. The House and the World (1919)
2. The Wreck (1921)
3. Gora (1923)

VIVEKANANDA, SWAMI (1863-1902)

He is a well-known Indian seer, prophet, recluse preacher, lecturer and poet, who:

(*i*) made the ancient Indian philosophy known to the whole world at the Parliament of Religious in Chicago, USA.

(*ii*) Brought about a wave of resurgence among the Indian masses through his stirring spiritually inspired speeches which were also full of:

(*a*) patriotic fervour
(*b*) love for universal brotherhood.
(*c*) spirit of social uplight, etc.

SOME LITERARY MASTERPIECES

CANTERBURY TALES

by Chaucer

'Canterbury Tales' is a collection of stories in verse by Chaucer. These tales are told by twenty-nine pilgrims who are going on a visit to the shrine of St. Thomas-a-Becket at Canterbury.

Each tale is a complete unit in itself without being intended to be linked with other tales. But, in the narration which is fictional in essence, we have head-links which are actually connecting passages. The headlinks are descriptions of the pilgrims as well as the events that take place in the course of the journey besides valuable digressions.

In those days, the people were very fond of pilgrimages for the sake of religious devotion and fun and they generally travelled in groups to face the dangers of the journey. The tales are written and descriptions of pilgrims given as if Chaucer himself had met such characters and had some experiences like those given.

The pilgrims meet at the Tabard Inn in Southwark on the eve of their departure and there they plan the journey. Chaucer himself is one of the pilgrims and the host of the Inn, Harry Bailly, not only gives a hearty welcome to the pilgrims but also accompanies them to the shrine.

Since the journey is quite tedious, each pilgrim is required to tell two tales on the journey towards the shrine and two during the return journey. But, Chaucer could complete only twenty four tales during his life time and in this sense, the Canterbury Tales is only a fragment.

An important aspect of the tales which brings Chaucer near to a dramatist and a novelist is that the tales differ in character as widely as do those by whom they are told.

The Knight tells, a chivalrous tale, the Clerk a devotional tale while the Miller's and the Reeve's tales are coarse and farcical in complete harmony with their own characters.

UTOPIA

by Thomas More

The period when Renaissance was in full bloom, Utopia was written by Sir Thomas More who lived from 1478-1535. He was imbued with the spirit of humanism.

The Greek word "Utopia" means "nowhere". Hence, it is in this light that Sir More tried to present an imaginary ideal republic of his dreams, which was of course, impossible to be achieved on this earth.

Utopia was originally written in Latin and was published in 1516. Later, it was translated into Italian and French. It was much later, after death of More, that its English translation appeared.

The Important characters in the book are :

1. The writer himself.
2. Peter Giles—writers's friend
3. Raphael Hythloday—a Portuguese traveller.

The book comprises two parts. In part one the protagonist (Hythloday) describes his voyaging with the explorer, Amerigo Vespucci.

In part two Hythloday describes the country of Utopia.

COMMENTS :

Utopia Glorifies

1. A democratic society.
2. A socialistic society with public control over wealth.
3. Religious tolerance
4. Economic equality
5. Peace and prosperity (upto a limit)
6. Love of this world.
7. Love of nature and natural way of living.
8. Love of beauty.
9. Love of the common man.
10. Love of human dignity.

Utopia Condemns

1. Aristocracy
2. Elitism
3. Asceticism and stoicism
4. Other worldliness
5. Fanaticism and bigotry.
6. False Chivalry
7. A Luxurious way of life
8. Scholasticism
9. Narrow-mindedness
10. War, Jingoism and Chauvinism.

GORBODUC

by Thomas Norton & Thomas Sackville

The other name of Gorboduc is Ferrex and Porrex. It is known for being the first regular English tragedy. It was written by Thomas Norton and Thomas Sackville and was first staged in 1562, that is, two years before the birth of Shakespeare. The work became a model for the Renaissance dramatists. It is, in essence, a Senecan tragedy of revenge.

The important characters in this tragedy are :

1. Gorboduc, The king of England
2. Ferrex—Gorboduc's elder son
3. Porrex—Gorboduc's younger son
4. Videna—The Queen

5. The murderers of the king and the queen
6. The nobles
7. The common people, etc.

The story in a nutshell: After the king divides his kingdom between his two sons, the latter begin to quarrel as a result of which Porrex kills Ferrex. The latter is so much loved by the queen that she kills Porrex. The people rise in revolt and kill the king and the queen. The nobles thereafter kill the murderers of the royal couple. This leads to a bloody civil war. There is chaos and anarchy as the question of success remains unsolved.

Senecan Features

1. Division into five acts.
2. Revenge as the chief motive.
3. A chain of murders—one murder leading to the other.
4. A ghost as one of the characters.
5. Lack of humour and any comic relief.
6. All-pervading seriousness and blood and thunder.
7. Avoidance of bloodshed on the stage, as it is reported by the characters through dialogues and monologues.
8. A plethora of rhetorical speeches by the characters.
9. Appearance of the chorus at the end of each act.

The use of blank verse in a drama was for the first time made in Gorboduc.

ASTROPHEL AND STELLA

by Philip Sidney

Astrophel and Stella is a sonnet series written by Sir Philip Sidney, Sidney is known more as a critic for his 'Apologie for Poetry' than as a poet, though his poetic claim is not altogether rejectable. His chief position as a poet rests on Astrophel and Stella.

Significance

1. The work is significant in the sense that it is perhaps the first work in English literature written in the white heat of passion, arising out of a personal and intimate experience.
2. In spite of artificiality of certain sonnets and general Petrarchan extravagance in the series, the work, having arisen out of real experience and genuine feelings, does not altogether look unreal.
3. It sounds real in several respects as in the apostrophe to the moon, in minute, vivid details and descriptions, etc.
4. Though the excessive use of conceits, hyperboles and embellishments mars the series in certain respects, yet its overall significance for the English literature cannot be underestimated.
5. Sidney was, no doubt, influenced by Petrarch. Yet he tries to assert himself every now and then by following a rhyme scheme other than the Petrarchan.
6. His most frequently used rhyme scheme is abba, abba, cdcd, ee. In other words, his sonnets end with a couplet in the Shakespearean style.

DOCTOR FAUSTUS

by Christopher Marlowe

The play opens with the chorus which announces the theme of the play i.e., the story of a scholarly doctor who has his end because of excessive lust for knowledge in the fields of magic and necromancy.

At the start Faustus looks at several fields of study such as Logic, Medicine, Law, Divinity, etc. But he finally settles at Magic. Then appear the Good Angel and the Evil Angel. The former warns Faustus against studying Magic book. He asks him to study the holy books. But the latter encourages him to study the Magic book.

The End of Faustus: His end is as tragic as it can be. He has not indulged or little indulged in sensual pleasures. What makes his sin more serious in theological circles in his association with Satan and the Satanic forces-demons, ghosts, devils etc. So, he gets no forgiveness and relief of any kind despite all his wailings and is taken away to hell by the Devils.

THE WINTER'S TALE

by Robert Green

Robert Greene's prose novel 'Pandosto' or 'The Triumph of Time' was published in 1588 and reprinted in 1607. This became the source for Shakespeare's *The Winter's Tale* which seems to have been composed in 1610 or 1611.

The title signifies an old wives' tale told to the curious children before they go to bed. Hence, such a tale can contain fairy-tale, exaggerative or legendary elements which may be far from reality because of some romantic, imaginary, unreal, absurd persons, incidents and situations.

Characters

Polixenes—the King of Bohemia, Leontes—the King of Sicilia, Hermione—Leontes's wife, Mamillus—Son of Leontes, Camillo—a Gicilian Lord, Cleomenes & Dion—courtiers, Paulina—Antigonus's wife, Emilia—the queen's lady, Florizel—the son of the king of Bohemia, Florizel—known as Doricles, Paulina.

BARTHOLOMEW FAIR

by Johnson

It is one of the most famous of Jonson's comedies which pleases all but hurts none. It is an authentic picture of the London of Queen Elizabeth's times. It was first staged in 1624, in manuscript form. It was published later in 1631.

There is a broad spectrum of humanity in the work at all levels, chiefly low level. Thus we have in the play gallants, gulls, cutpurses and bawds, lovers, squires, servants and justices of peace, etc.

Important Characters

1. **Bartholomew Cokes:** He is a foolish young squire.
2. **Waspe:** He is servant to Cokes who accompanies him to the fair.
3. **Grace Wellborn:** She is the fiancee of Waspe.
4. **Edgeworth:** He is a cutpurse.
5. **Nightingale:** A ballad singer and companion and accomplice of Edgeworth.
6. **Adam Overdo:** A justice of peace.
7. **Zeal-of-the Land Busy:** He is a Puritan who becomes an object of mockery.
8. **Dame Purecraft:** She is a rich widow.
9. **Winwife:** He is a London gallant who is Busy's rival in wooing Purecraft.
10. **Quarlous:** He is a gamester but he is guised as a madman. He is Busy's friend, with whom he finds himself in a quarrel. He at last wins the hand of Purecraft.

Plot: There is virtually no plot in the play but only a presentation of a plethora of incidents and episodes which are mostly left undeveloped. Jonson's chief aim is to hold a mirror to the London life of his times.

The main incidents are

1. Cokes being relieved of purse, sword, cloak and marriage licence at the hands of Edgeworth.
2. Overdo being taken for a pickpocket and put in the stocks.
3. Waspe and Busy being put in the stocks for fighting and creating nuisance.
4. Overdo's escape from the stocks.
5. Quarlous's disclosing to Overdo the real face of Edgeworth.
6. Overdo's invitation to all to dinner.
7. Quarlous's winning of the hand of Purecraft.

Thus, the play proves Jonson to be a gentle satirist who has an ocean of sympathy with his characters of all kinds.

PARADISE LOST

by John Milton

Needless to say that the said Epic is the greatest heroic poem in English literature and one of the greatest of its kind in world literature.

A true epic on classical lines though with several diversional elements, as it is, it has twelve books.

A bookwise "Argument of Paradise Lost" is given by W.J. Long, which may be summarised as under :

Book I

It contains *inter alia*,

(*i*) a statement of the subject, the Fall of Man, and

(*ii*) a noble invocation for light and divine guidance.

Thereafter, in it, we have—

(*i*) description of Satan and the rebel agents. Satan's physical size, his gigantic shield, etc. are on supernatural lines, as can be visualised for a devil of his kind, as in a true epic in particular.
Satan's great power of oratory is also there before us.

(*ii*) the ouster of the rebel angels from heaven by the Almighty.

(*iii*) the diabolical plot of the rebel angels to wreak their vengeance on God by beguiling Adam and Eve, God's children and first parents of mankind, from their state of innocence by bringing about their fall by eating the forbidden fruit in the Eden.

(*iv*) a description of the sulphurous hell-fire and the eternal agonies undergone by the damned spirits there.

(*v*) the raising of Satan's palace, Pandemonium.

Book II

It contains, *inter alia*,

(*i*) a description of the council of devils in the Pandemonium.

(*ii*) Satan's desire to take up the task of beguiling Adam and Eve upon himself.

(*iii*) his journey to the gates of hell, guarded by Sin and Death.

Book III

It contains *inter alia*—

(*i*) God's behest to Raphael to warn Adam and Eve of the imminent danger of disobedience to them.

(*ii*) Son of God's offer to take upon himself the sin of the impending disobedience of man.

(*iii*) Satan's meeting with Uriel, the Angel of the sun, for the purpose of learning the way to earth, the abode of God's new creation.

(*iv*) Satan's journey to the earth in the guise of an angel of light.

Book IV

It contains, *inter alia*—

(*i*) The scenes of Paradise and of Adam and Eve being in the state of innocence.

(*ii*) Eden being guarded by an angel.

(*iii*) The arrest of Satan when he is trying to tempt Eve in a dream.

(*iv*) the setting free of Satan in an unconvincing way.

Book V

It contains, *inter alia*—

(*i*) the description by Eve of her dream to Adam.

(*ii*) Adam and Eve's routine life.

(*iii*) Raphael's visit to Eden.

(*iv*) Raphael's description of the revolt of the fallen angels.

Book VI

It contains, *inter alia*—

a continuation of Raphael's description of the revolt of the fallen angels.

Book VII

It contains a description of the story of creation by Raphael.

Book VIII

It contains Adam's description to Raphael of himself and his meeting with Eve.

Book IX

It contains an account of Satan's temptation of Eve.

Book X

It contains, *inter alia*—

(*i*) God's judgement on Adam and Eve.
(*ii*) Sin and Death's construction of a highway through chaos to the earth.
(*iii*) Satan's return to Pandemonium.
(*iv*) Adam and Eve's repentance.
(*v*) the turning of fallen angels into serpents.

Book XI

(*i*) Acceptance of Adam's repentance by God.
(*ii*) Michael's departure to bring into effect Adam and Eve's banishment from Eden.
(*iii*) Michael's prophecy regarding the destiny of man.

Book XII

It contains *inter alia*—

(*i*) Continuation of Michael's prophecy.
(*ii*) Learning by Adam and Eve of future redemption of mankind.
(*iii*) Adam and Eve's departure out of Eden.

Given below are some extracts from Book I:

The lines given below state the theme: The Fall of Man and present an Invocation to the Muse and the Holy spirit (*i.e.* the spirit of God):

THE WAY OF THE WORLD

by Congreve

As the play opens, we find two men Mirabell and Fainall talking to each other in a Chocolate House.

We learn that Fainall is married to Lady Wishfort's daughter, Arabella who is referred to as Mrs Fainall in the play. We also learn, that Mirabell loves Lady Wishfort's niece, Millament. Lady Wishfort is not only Millament's aunt but also her guardian.

It is learnt that Mirabell often went to Wishfort's house ostensibly to court her but actually to meet Millament. This pretence of Mirabell is at last exposed by Mrs. Marwood.

An enigmatic situation is now created for Millament. Since Lady Wishfort has learnt about Mirabell's sham, she forbids any meeting between him and Millament, Further, in order to inherit the lady's wealth, she has to marry according to her wish. This means that if she marries Mirabell against her wishes, she is likely to be deprived of the fortune of the lady who is fifty-five.

Mirabell has his own plot. He arranges marriage between his servant, Waitwell and Lady Wishfort's maid servant, Foible. The purpose of this marriage is that Waitwell is presented by Mirabell as his (imaginary) uncle, named Sir Rowland.

As Foible has been taken into confidence, she would impress upon Lady Wishfort that Sir Rowland, a wealthy man, has in his heart a deep love and wants to marry her. Through this plan Mirabell wanted to cause embarrassment to Lady Wishfort by revealing the identify of Sir Rowland later and thus compelling her to allow Millament to marry him.

A hindrance is created in the execution of the plot when Mrs. Marwood, Fainall's mistress comes to know about the plan, and she makes her lover aware of it. Besides, not only Millament but also Mrs. Fainall know about this plot.

Mrs. Fainall had once been Mirabell's mistress and in her heart of hearts, she still loves him. Hence, she also does not want that Mirabell should marry Millament, as her heart is burning with the fire of jealousy.

Mr. Fainall is a mean fellow, and he finds it an easy opportunity to blackmail Lady Wishfort. For this, he threatens to divorce Mrs. Fainall. It is further another proof of his avaricious nature that in a deed which is in his possession, he has already arranged the settlement of major part of Mrs. Fainall's estate in his own favour.

It is at the most critical moment when Sir Rowland and Lady Wishfort are busy in constructive prospects and Mirabell and Millament have agreed to marry each other, that Fainall makes his appearance.

Thus Mirabell's apple-cart is disturbed. However, Foible reveals the secret of Fainall's love affair with Mrs. Marwood. However, Fainall, rising on the crest of the situation sets forth certain conditions to remain silent. The conditions concern the fortunes of Mrs. Fainall and Millament and the marriage of Lady Wishfort.

Just then Waitwell presents a deed which is executed by Mrs. Fainall before her marriage with Fainall. In it, she has conferred her then estate on Mirabell. Thus the deed with Fainall becomes infructuous.

The net result of this *deus ex machina* is that Mirabell and Millament now have no obstacle in tying the nuptial knot to each other.

SENSE AND SENSIBILITY AND PRIDE AND PREJUDICE

by Jane Austen

In essence, the novel *Sense and Sensibility* is a satire on sentimentalism. Elinor represents sense, while sensibility is represented by her sister Marianne. The story, like all stories of Jane Austen, is very simple, but interesting.

Mrs. Henry Dashwood with her three daughters Elinor, Marianne and Margaret, is left in a very straitened situation on the death of her husband. They have to retire to Devonshire where they begin to live in a very humble cottage.

Edward Ferrars is the brother of Mr. John Dashwood. John is the step son of Mr. Henry Dashwood. He had been entrusted by the latter to take care of his wife and daughter after his death. But he does not discharge his responsibilities in this respect.

Edward and Elinor fall in love with each other. Marianne falls in love with a poor, unscrupulous young man, John Willoughby.

Willoughby suddenly leaves for London. Marianne and Elinor go after him. But Willoughby says that he is going to be married to a rich heiress. Elinor also learns that even her lover, Edward, has been untrue to her, as he is already engaged to Lucy Steel who is the niece of Edward.

Edward's mother is not happy with his engagement to Lucy, and settles her property on his younger brother, Robert, who is a fool of the first water. Then Robert and Lucy are married, while Edward stands rejected. Then Edward marries Elinor. Marianna who has been wooed by Colonel Brandon, marries him.

Immature style of Jane Austen is evident in this novel, but her future greatness and maturity is also visible here in seed form. The novel was completed in 1797, though it was published in 1813.

The story of Pride and Prejudice which is regarded as her best work and was published in 1813 is well-known to all scholars and need not be given here. It is in this novel that all the plot and stylistic perfection of Jane Austen comes into play. It is here that the dialogues are most lively, characters life like and her humour at its best.

Whereas in Sense and Sensibility, her characters such as Mrs. Jennings, her stupid daughter, her uncouth son-in-law and Mr. Palmer are some of the humorous characters they are no match for Mr. Collins, Mrs. Bennet, Catherina de Borough and others of Pride and Prejudice.

DAVID COPPERFIELD (1849-50)

by Charles Dickens (1812-70)

David Copperfield is perhaps the most popular novel of Dickens. It is an autobiographical novel in which Dickens's power of characterization, depicting humorous and pathetic situations and characters is perhaps the best brought out. The novel is told in the first person.

THE MAYOR OF CASTERBRIDGE

by Thomas Hardy

It was published serially in 1886. It is the story of a man who brings doom upon himself.

THE MILL ON THE FLOSS (1860)

by George Eliot (1819-80)

The Mill on the Floss is the most popular novel of George Eliot. It is also perhaps her most autobiographical novel. The story represents the typical Victorian problem of morality and a moral order which spares nobody.

The Mill mentioned in the title of the novel is the imaginary mill 'Dorlcote Mill' owned by Mr. Tulliver. The mill is situated on the river Floss.

The two main characters in the novel are:

(*i*) Tom Tulliver, and

(*ii*) Maggie Tulliver.

THE WASTELAND

by T.S. Eliot

When the Wasteland was published in book form in 1922, it was soon realized to be the beginning of the emergence of the Modernist Poetry.

Earlier the Georgians and the Imagists had appeared and disappeared but their effect, particularly that of the latter, had been retained in the inner recesses of the minds of the writers, poets included, even though superficially the movement of Imagism had all but spent itself.

It was because Ezra Pound who had occupied a pivotal position in the movement which had such protagonists as Hilda Doolittle and Aldington, also was instrumental in giving the final shape, as were now have, to Eliot's poem.

The Wasteland depicts the collapsing civilization of Europe and, connotatively, the fall of values in the modern world. The poem is highly realistic in this sense, but it promises vaguely some possibility of redemption through some everlasting philosophies such as that of the Buddha and the Upanishadas.

It cannot be disputed that the overwhelming picture of pessimism, death and desolation in the poem is to a great extent the result of the annihilation and mayhem which was witnessed in the First World War that ended in 1917. Then there emerged a particularly distressing mood in the twenties and this mood of depression of the entire period all over the world is very deftly brought about in the poem.

The poem's merit does not lie just in depicting a particular mood, but in its employment of complex symbolism and references to mythology, history, culture, religion and literature from varied sources in modern and medieval world and even the remote ancient times.

SAINT JOAN

by G.B. Shaw

It is one of the most famous plays of G.B. Shaw. It is this play which won him the Nobel Prize. The play was first produced in 1923.

Historical Background to Saint Joan: Saint Joan is a historical play which is based on the life and career of a real character, Joan of Arc. She was a common country girl, who was born in 1412. As a girl, she heard divine voices and had divine visions. But she was sent to the stake on the charges of heresy in 1431.

Social, political and religious conditions of the period are closely related to the story of Joan of Arc.

It was in 1415 that the English forces under the leadership of their young king, Henry V defeated Charles VI, the French King at Agincourt—a decisive battle which aroused waves of nationalism in England.

As a result of this humiliating defeat, the French king had to accept certain most unpleasant terms such as :

1. He had to sign a treaty with the English King in 1420.
2. According to it, he had to :
   (*i*) disown his own son, the Dauphin, declaring him as illegitimate.
   (*ii*) marry his infant daughter to the English king.
   (*iii*) allow the English to keep with them large area of France which they had conquered.

It is to be noted that at that time, France was not one united country. It consisted of a number of estates which were under the control of different feudal lords or barons.

TO THE LIGHT HOUSE

by Virginia Woolf

Virginia Woolf's most famous novel, Mrs. Dalloway was published in 1925. Two years later, another masterpiece of hers was published in 1927.

It is the only novel of Mrs. Woolf which has a Three Part Structure :

(*i*) Part I: The Window
(*ii*) Part II: Time Passes
(*iii*) Part III: The Lighthouse.

The main characters in the novel are:

1. **Mrs. Ramsay:** She is a middle-aged charming woman, a mother of eight children. She is the central figure in the novel.
2. **Mr. Ramsay:** He a scholar and philosopher of great repute and has won several academic honours.
3. **Charles Tansley:** He is an intelligent young student of Mr. Ramsay.
4. **Minta Doyle:** He is a young man who loves Paul Rayley.
5. **Paul Rayley:** She loves Doyle.
6. **Augustus Carmichael:** He is an old man and poet.
7. **Lily Briscoe:** She is a painter.
8. **William Bankes:** He is an old friend of Mr. Ramsay's.
9. **James Ramsay:** He is six year old child of Ramsays.
10. **Cam** : Janes's sister.

The scene is laid in the island of Skye in the Hebrides.

The story is autobiographical in nature in the sense that:

(*i*) Mr. and Mrs. Ramsay resemble Mrs. Woolf's parents.
(*ii*) Lily Briscoe greatly resembles Mrs. Woolf herself.

The novel whether more artistic than Mrs. Dalloway or not, has earned as much if not more popularity than Mrs. Woolf's other masterpiece.

The novel is written on the stream-of-consciousness technique:

(*i*) In the *Window,* not only the personality of Mrs. Ramsay is revealed, but also we have the personality of Mr. Ramsay before us which is laid bare through the eyes of Lily Briscoe, Charles Tansley, William Bankes, etc.
(*ii*) In *Time Passes*, we learn more about Mrs. Ramsay and others through the memory of the Charwoman, Mrs. Mc Nab.
(*iii*) In *Lighthouse* we have another focus on Mrs. Ramsay through the memory of Lily Briscoe.

The novel is poetic, as usually all of Mrs. Woolf's novels are

ADVENTURES OF HUCKLEBERRY FINN

by Mark Twain

The novel opens with a warning to the reader:

"Persons attempting to find a moral in it will be banished; persons attempting to find a plot in it will be shot."

Although Mark Twain wrote this novel as a companion to Tom Sawyer, yet it is much more than that. However, a link with the earlier novel is established in the first chapter.

Huck is adopted by the widow Douglas to "civilize" him. The money which is found at the end of Tom Sawyer is put by Judge Thatcher on interest and it fetches a dollar to each boy 'all the year round.'

Huck is not much interested in Douglas' prescriptions of a strict disciplined moral life. Twain attains a technical tour de force by shifting narrative to the first person. This enables Twain to establish *point of view*. Huck is the model of *radical innocence* and *instinctive knowledge*.

SONS AND LOVERS

by D. H. Lawrence

The family of Morels lived in the mining village of Betswood. Mrs. Morel who has had a puritan nourishment, still upholds the values of refinement and nobility. She gets enamoured of Morel's rich ruddy face and merry laughter as well as wavy black hair. Mr. Morel is also captivated by her. The two get married.

The two have an antithetical nature and temperament. Whereas Mrs. Morel is a puritan lady, Mr. Morel is fond of a sensuous, luxurious life. He tries to domineer over his wife. But she rebels against this and the result is that even the children dislike Mr. Morel.

The estrangement between the couple becomes intense when one day, out of jealousy, Mr. Morel clips off the curls of the young William, whom his mother loves so such.

Mrs. Morel does not give up her efforts to reform her husband. But he rather goes more and more astray in his fondness for drinking, etc.

The couple had two more children. Morel tries to entertain the children, but often, the more Mrs. Morel instigates them against him, the more he teases them.

Mrs. Morel is frightened of her estranged relationship with her husband and focuses all her attention on her sons. She wants to possess her first child William whose love affair with Lily she condemns. But the boy dies of pneumonia.

Then Paul Morel, the third child, and the hero of the novel, falls ill. He is suffering from bronchitis. She nurses him tenderly and virtually treats him as her lover. This is how the famous Oedipus complex gets manifested in the novel.

Paul has relationship with three women, that is, his mother, Miriam and Clara. Among these, Miriam is his beloved.

The relationship between Paul and Miriam develops as Paul goes to the Willey Farm with his mother. He offers to teach her French and algebra and thus a friendship develops between the two. But, as Lawrence himself points out, their friendship is "chaste" and purely spiritual.

This relationship between Paul and Miriam cannot become an everlasting one since Mrs. Morel is afraid that Miriam is going to suck Paul's soul and she herself can ill-afford to lose her son. Paul too realises that as long as his mother is alive, his relationship with any woman cannot be permanent.

Paul is interested not only in a spiritual relationship with Miriam. He wants to have with her a physical contact also, but this she denies to him.

Since Paul cannot get physical satisfaction from Miriam, he enters into physical union with a married woman, Clara, who lives separately from her husband. But, the problem is that the woman is unable to satisfy Paul spiritually. The result is that Paul is thrashed by Clara's husband to his complete discomfiture.

Since Paul feels that his failure with both the women, Miriam and Clara, has been because of his mother's possessive nature towards his soul, he begins to hate her. But, when she falls ill with cancer, he tries to arrange the best medical treatment for her.

Being no longer able to witness the agonising misery of his mother, he ends the story of her life by administering morphia to her.

Now, it was impossible for Paul to establish relationship with any woman. He had to be lonely, and there was no escape for him from this state of affairs.

HAMLET

by Shakespeare

Introduction: The king of Denmark has recently died. On his death, his son, Hamlet, the Prince of Denmark, who is a student at the University of Wittenberg, is summoned to the Danish Court.

Hamlet feels miserable that his father's throne has been seized by his uncle, Claudius and his mother has married him.

Ophelia: Another shock comes to Hamlet when his beloved, Ophelia, rejects his suit on the advice of his father, Polonius.

The Ghost: Hamlet learns from his friend, Horatio, and two officers that they have sighted his father's ghost. As Hamlet himself encounters the ghost, the latter tells him the reality that his father had been poisoned by his uncle. The ghost also burdens Hamlet with the responsibility of avenging his death.

The spies: Claudius appoints two spies, Rosencrantz and Guildenstern to keep a watch on Hamlet. The latter arranges the staging of a play "The Murder of Gonzago" to which the king is also invited. The king's abnormal behaviour while watching the play (in which the murder of a king in a manner similar to that in which Hamlet's father is killed is staged) convinces Hamlet of Claudius's guilt.

Having been convinced of Claudius's and his mother's collusion in the murder of his father, Hamlet scolds his mother in a closed room. But as he hears an echo from behind the curtain, he thrusts his rapier at the person hidden. This is how Polonius who was eavesdropping gets killed.

Cause of Hamlet's Madness: Claudius tries his best to know the real cause of Hamlet's "madness," "ecstasy" or distraction, but having failed in his effort, he decides to send him out to England.

In the Ship: In the ship with the two spies, Rosencrantz and Guildenstern, Hamlet opens the sealed letter which contains the orders for his execution on his reaching England. He cleverly replaces these orders for the execution of the spies who lose their life in the venture.

Ophelia's Madness and Death: On learning about the death of her father, Ophelia goes mad, while her brother Laertes burns with the desire for revenge which is sharpened by Claudius.

The Duel: As Ophelia's dead body is being lowered in the grave, Hamlet grapples with Laertes. The two have a bloody duel in which both of them are badly wounded.

Claudius's end: When the two fighters are dying the villainy of Claudius is divulged by Laertes and Gertrude, the Queen. Hamlet kills Claudius with his poisoned rapier and soon Fortinbras arrives to be the next ruler of Denmark.

A Dialogue between the ghost and Hamlet

There are several extremely interesting scenes in Hamlet. Hamlet's dialogue with the ghost of his father is one of them. Here are the following lines which need no explanation.

MACBETH

by Shakespeare

Macbeth was the Lord of Glamis. He was related to Duncan, the king of Scotland. As the play begins, he returns with another general, Banquo, after crushing the rebellion of the Lord of Cawdor.

The Three Witches: When the two generals were returning, they met three witches, one of whom addressed Macbeth as the Lord of Cawdor. Macbeth felt greatly excited as he heard the witches' prophecies that he would soon be king and Banquo's descendants would also be kings. Thereafter, they disappeared.

Macbeth's Promotion: Soon thereafter, Macbeth was informed by two nobles that he had been made Lord of Cawdor by the king. This further thrilled Macbeth as he realized that the prophecy of the witches had come out true. He was so curious and enthusiastic that he wanted that the second prophecy of the witches that he would become the king should also turn true as early as possible.

Duncan's visit to Macbeth's Castle: The king Duncan wanted to visit Macbeth's castle to honour him. Meanwhile, Macbeth informed his wife through a letter regarding the witches' prophecies.

Lady Macbeth's Ambition: Lady Macbeth was even more ambitious than Macbeth and wanted to see him king. As Macbeth reached home, at the earliest, she incited her husband to murder Duncan to make the prophecy come out true. Macbeth was hesitant in accepting this advice.

Duncan was warmly welcomed by the Macbeth couple. He loved the peaceful atmosphere of the castle and went to sleep peacefully and without an iota of suspicion in his mind.

Lady Macbeth continued inciting her husband and even called him a coward when he expressed hesitation and his feeling of non-propriety in killing a guest who was also one of their kins.

The couple drugged the guards and they went into a sound sleep. Then Lady Macbeth herself went to kill Duncan, but now the king's face seemed to her as that of her father. So, she could not execute her plan.

The Bloody Dagger: Thereafter, Macbeth went into the king's room, but as he saw the vision of a bloody dagger, he changed his mind. Yet again, he took courage and struck a dagger into Duncan's heart and killed him.

The Voice: As Macbeth told his wife about the deed, he heard a voice: "Macbeth shall sleep no more." As Macbeth was now terribly overtaken by fear and madness, Lady Macbeth, showing greater courage, put the blood-covered dagger by the side of the guards and stained their clothes with blood to put the blame on them.

The Porter: Soon, the gate knocked. As the porter opened the gate, two of Duncan's nobles entered and went into the king's room where they found him dead.

Duncan's sons: As the news of the king's murder was conveyed to Macbeth, he killed the two guards. Meanwhile, as the news reached Scotland, the king's sons began to run for safety. The elder one, Malcom fled to England. Macbeth was then proclaimed king of Scotland.

Banquo: Macbeth was satisfied that the witches' second prophecy had also turned out to be true, but he feared Banquo. It was because the witches had also prophesied that Banquo's descendants would be kings. Hence, to perpetuate his kingdom Macbeth made up his mind to kill not only Banquo but also his son, Fleance.

The Banquet: Macbeth hit upon a plan. He invited all the nobles to a banquet. As Banquo and his son were on their way to Macbeth's castle, two assassins hired by Macbeth waylaid Banquo and his son. In the attempt, Banquo was killed but his son escaped.

Banquo's Ghost: Macbeth saw Banquo's ghost seated in a chair at the banquet. He even heard the ghost's whispers. Those present there were surprised to note Macbeth's strange behaviour.

For a brief period, the ghost disappeared, but soon it appeared again. Macbeth began to tremble and cry wildly. His such behaviour made him a suspect in the eyes of the guests.

The Witches Again: Macbeth went to consult the witches again. As he saw them, they called three ghosts. Macbeth was told the following three prophecies in turn :

(*i*) Macbeth should beware of Macduff.

(*ii*) No man born of woman could harm Macbeth.

(*iii*) Macbeth could never be defeated until Birnam Wood came to Dunsinane hill.

Lady Macbeth's mental state: Lady Macbeth was in an extremely depressed mood. As such she committed suicide. Macduff had run away to England. It was reported to Macbeth that the Birnam wood was marching towards Dunsinane hill. Macbeth felt puzzled. Soon, it was known that the green branches of the wood were being carried by Malcom's soldiers who were marching towards Macbeth.

Macbeth and Macduff: A fight started between Macbeth and Macduff face to face besides their soldiers fighting with their opposites. As Macduff told Macbeth that he was taken from his mother's womb, Macbeth felt so much discouraged that he got killed without a fight. The witches' prophecies had come full circle on Macbeth, as all his ambition was finally dashed to the ground with true poetic justice meeting out to him, which is perhaps not present in any other of Shakespeare's plays.

Macbeth is a great poet and *inter alia,* Macbeth is a wonderful piece of lyrical and dramatic poetry.

ARMS AND THE MAN

• ***by G. B. Shaw***

The young, romantic Raina is standing in her balcony to enjoy the beauty of the night in that month of November in 1885. She has all the romantic ideas of heroism of her lover Major Sergius Saranoff who is out taking part in the war between the Bulgarians and the Serbs.

Suddenly, there comes an intruder. He is a Swiss officer, Captain Bluntschli. He threatens Raina with his pistol and orders her to keep quiet.

Soon, a Russian army officer enters Raina's room to search for the fugitive. Raina hides Bluntschli behind the curtain. She tells the officer that nobody has entered her room.

As the officer goes away, Raina offers some chocolate cream to the fugitive. He tells her that he always carries chocolates to the war in place of cartridges. Then he goes to sleep.

It is the 6th of March, 1886. As Major Petkoff, Raina's father returns from the war, he is welcomed by Raina and her mother, Catherine. Major Sergius also comes. He has resigned from the army as he has not been given promotion.

The two family servants, Nicola, the man-servant and Louka, the maid-servent are already engaged. But when Sergius and Louka are alone, Sergius embraces Louka. She tells him that Raina loves a Swiss officer and would marry him.

Bluntschli comes to return the coat lent to him by Raina and Catherine. Major Petkoff instructs Bluntschli to prepare papers for sending three regiments. The papers are then delivered to the messengers.

Raina has already learnt from Bluntschli about non-heroic part of Sergius in the army. Sergius thinks that she is no longer loyal to him.

At last Raina is married to Bluntschli to which both Petkoff and his wife agree. Louka gets married to Serguis.

In this way, the myth of both the heroism of a soldier and the romance of love is exploded by Shaw in his own inimitable, interesting and simple way.

THE PORTRAIT OF A LADY

by Henry James

It is perhaps Henry James' most important novel which was written in 1881. James believed in images rather than in a story. Yet, if the novel is to be studied as a story, it can be said to be the psychological study of Isabel Archer a young American girl who leaves America with her aunt Mrs. Touchett and goes to Europe in a sort of what may be called her spiritual odyssey.

☛ 1. While portraying Isabel, Henry James had the model of his cousin Mary Temple called "Minny" in his mind. The young girl died in 1870 when she was only 24.
2. The European tour is arranged as once dreamed by Minny, though she got no opportunity to fulfil her dream.
3. Minny had died of T.B.; here we find Ralph dying of the same disease.
4. Gardencourt is a 16th Century English mansion– the kind of architecture Henry cherished.
5. Henry was particularly fond of painting and architecture.
6. Isabel's European odyssey comprises a visit to several countries, *e.g.* England, Italy, France, Greece, Turkey and Egypt.
7. It is to be noted that Henry James had a high regard for the European culture with its vast history, but he had no fondness for his native, American culture which had no history except that worth the name.
8. Isabel is shown as having fondness for Browning and George Eliot, as Minny also had. Besides she is also interested in the German philosophy.

THE GUIDE

by R.K. Narayan

Written in 1958, The Guide which won R.K. Narayan the Sahitya Akademi Award is one of his best novels and a masterpiece giving ample proof of his *tour de force* in the matter of artistic technique.

There are two distinct aspects of the story of The Guide. One half of it is supposed to be told by Raju, the hero, to one of his followers (as he turns from a tourist guide to a saint). The entire life story of Raju is however put in a flashback and told as such by the author. This technical achievement is a rare triumph in the modern artistic style.

Again, to understand more clearly, the story of Raju as saint forms the objective aspect and that of Raju as a tourist guide the autobiographical aspect. This artistic pattern is woven in the entire novel and this is what makes it artistically unique.

Simply speaking, it is the story of Raju's life and death. Raju has to indulge in several vocations and avocations, such as:

(*i*) as a food vendor at the railway station.
(*ii*) as a tourist guide.
(*iii*) as a sentimental adulterer.
(*iv*) as a manager to a dancing girl, Rosy.
(*v*) as a prisoner.
(*vi*) as a reluctantly holy martyred saint.

The setting is, as usual with Narayan, Malgudi town. It is at the newly set up railway station that Raj becomes a vendor. As a tourist guide also, he is quite successful.

One day Rosy, the dancer, and Marco, her husband, an archaeologist, engaged Raju as their guide. There were often quarrels between the husband and the wife.

Raju fell in love with Rosy and spent most of his time with her. He wanted to make her a famous dancer. Rosy's husband at last left her and she now lived with Raju. She was his 'snake-girl'.

Raju who was too ambitious, crossed the limit of propriety. He got addicted to habits such as gambling, drinking, etc. But when he forged the signature of Rosy on an important document, he was caught by Rosy's husband. He had to spend two years in jail. Then Rosy parted ways with him.

After completing his jail term, Raju went to a village, Mangal. There the people mistook him for a saint. Raju, depending on the art of simulation and dissimulation, found it a golden opportunity to be something, and if still dilly-dallying, he willy-nilly took it upon himself to be a holy man.

It was Raju's misfortune that his test was too near and too hard and it was beyond his imagination and comprehension. As usual, the villages were a superstitious lot, and as the famine hit the village, they expected of Raju to do some miracle to appease the rain God.

Raju had no grounding in such machinations of the so-called holy men and he had to go on a fast into death to cause the rain god to show his mercy. Once started, it was now impossible to give up the fast, as the whole area had been converted into a hubbub of pilgrims, tourists, visitors and mediamen who were reporting every now and then on Raju's determination and condition.

The days passed by and yet there was no sign of a cloud. It was the twelfth day of his fast. Raju was too weak to walk or even talk. Somehow he managed to reach the bank of the river, the venue of his prayer for rain. He collapsed uttering the words, "Velan, it's raining in the hills. I can feel it coming up under my feet, up my legs."

GORA

by R.N. Tagore

Written in 1923, it is perhaps the most famous novel of Tagore. It is a patriotic novel which expresses the voice of Resurgent India which is arousing to shake up the shackles of slavery. The novel expresses true secularism and a fusion of the oriental and the occidental. Even Gourmohan, the hero, the son of an English lady is brought up in a Hindu household and stands for that universal blend of ideologies and cultures which is so characteristic of Tagore.

MULTIPLE CHOICE QUESTIONS

1. Who wrote *Don Juan*?
A. Shakespeare B. Tennyson
C. Byron D. T.S. Eliot

2. Who wrote *The Life of Johnson*?
A. Boswell B. Macaulay
C. Churchill D. Sir Walter Raleigh

3. *Priest's Nun's Tale* was written by
A. Spenser B. Charles Lamb
C. Tennyson D. Chaucer

4. Who is said to have first used the term "Metaphysics"?
A. Matthew Arnold B. Sidney
C. Donne D. Dr. Johnson

5. The writer of *Volpone* is
A. Johnson B. Milton
C. Jonson D. Shelley

6. Which is the correct chronological sequence?
A. Spenser—Chaucer—Milton—Donne
B. Spenser—Wordsworth—Tennyson—T.S. Eliot
C. Milton—Shakespeare—Philip Larkin—Keats
D. Auden—Eliot—Shelley—Keats

7. *Pilgrim's Progress* was written by
A. Milton B. Shelley
C. Swinburne D. John Bunyan

8. The writer of the line : *"Stone walls do not a prison make"* is
A. Lovelace B. Milton
C. W.B. Yeats D. T.S. Eliot

9. *"Monkey's Paw"* is a
A. Poem B. Drama
C. Short story D. Novel

10. Lyrical Ballads appeared in
A. 1690 B. 1798
C. 1802 D. 1800

11. The writer of *'A Pair of Blue Eyes'* is
A. Thackeray B. Dickens
C. George Eliot D. Thomas Hardy

12. *Hard Times* was written by
A. Thackeray B. Dickens
C. Trollope D. Marquese

13. Which of the following poets was most impressed by the German philosophy?
A. Chaucer B. Wordsworth
C. Coleridge D. Southey

14. The two cities referred to in *"A Tale of Two Cities"* are
A. London and Paris B. London and Rome
C. Rome and Paris D. Moscow and Rome

15. *The Peasant's Bread* is a story by
A. Maupassant B. Tagore
C. R.K. Narayan D. Tolstoy

16. *The Financial Express* was written by
A. Raja Rao B. R.K. Narayan
C. Tagore D. Mulk Raj Anand

17. *"Negative Capability"* is a term associated with
A. Tagore B. Shelley
C. Keats D. Coleridge

18. The most impressive treatment of "imagination" has been given by
A. Coleridge B. Shelley
C. Eliot D. Yeats

19. *Lady Chatterley's Lover* was banned because it was considered
A. obscene B. revolutionary
C. obscurantist D. None of these

20. *For Whom The Bell Tolls* was written by
A. Marquese B. Hemingway
C. Hawthorne D. None of these

21. The writer of : *"A Pair of Mustachios"* is
A. Anand B. Tagore
C. Raja Rao D. Anita Desai

22. The writer of *Scarlet Letter* is
A. Henry James B. James Joyce
C. Hawthorne D. None of these

23. Rousseau is associated with
A. French Revolution
B. American War of Independence
C. Russian (Bolshevik) Revolution
D. None of these

24. Who wrote *'Train to Pakistan'*?
A. Narayan B. Manohar Malgaon
C. Khushwant Singh D. Anand

25. Who is the writer of *Azadi*?
A. R.K. Narayan B. Khushwant Singh
C. Tagore D. Chaman Nahal

26. *"The God of Small Things"* is written by
A. R.K. Narayan B. Hemingway
C. Graham Greene D. Arundhati Roy

27. Who wrote the poem *"Listeners"*?
A. Tennyson B. Thomas Hood
C. Goldsmith D. Walter de la Mare

28. In writing *"Canterbury Tales"* Chaucer was influenced by
A. Decameron B. The Divine Comedy
C. The Holy Bible D. None of these

29. *'Animal Farm'* was written by
A. James Joyce B. Virginia Woolf
C. George Orwell D. Hemingway

30. Shobha De is a
A. poet B. dramatist
C. novelist D. an actress

31. Dunciad was written by
A. Dryden B. Pope
C. Tennyson D. Shelley

32. Bernard Shaw got the Nobel Prize for
A. Pygmalion B. Man and Superman
C. Saint Joan D. None of these

33. The Victorian Period is marked by
A. Great political upheavals
B. Great social security
C. Great wars
D. Economic deprivation

34. Swift is known mainly as
A. an essayist B. a poet
C. a satirist D. a short story writer

35. Who is the writer of the novel *"The Village"*?
A. Khushwant Singh B. Anita Desai
C. Mulk Raj Anand D. R.K. Narayan

36. The most famous writer of the heroic couplet is
A. Dryden B. Chaucer
C. Spenser D. Pope

37. *Macflecknoe* is a poem written by
A. Dryden B. Pope
C. Tennyson D. Yeats

38. Who wrote *'Everyman in His Humour'*?
A. Shakespeare B. Jonson
C. Milton D. Keats

39. *'Indian Jugglers'* is an essay by
A. De Quincey B. Gardiner
C. Hazlitt D. Lamb

40. Who wrote *'The Gropes of Wrath'*?
A. Pearl Buck B. Hemingway
C. Virginia Woolf D. John Steinbeck

41. Who rendered into English the ancient Greek tragedy *"Atlanta in Calydon"*?
A. Swinburne B. Shelley
C. Tennyson D. Arthur Hugh Clough

42. *The Deserted Village* was written by
A. Cowper B. Goldsmith
C. Keats D. Johnson

43. *'Savitri'* is an epic written by
A. Tagore
B. Prem Chand
C. Aurobindo
D. Bankim Chandra Chatterjee

44. The anthem *"Vande Mataram"* occurs in
A. Godan B. Anand Math
C. Gora D. Train to Pakistan

45. *'All Fool's Day'* is an essay written by
A. Charles Lamb B. Hazlitt
C. A.G. Gardiner D. R.C. Stevenson

46. The drama *Tamburlaine* is written by
A. Shakespeare B. Marlowe
C. Lyly D. Green

47. The book *"Appreciations"* was written by
A. Morris B. Arnold
C. Walter Pater D. Christina Rossetti

48. *"The Admirable Crichton"* was written by
A. Steinbeck B. T.S. Eliot
C. Trollope D. James Barrie

49. *"The Death of a Salesman"* was written by
A. James Barrie B. Eugene O'Neill
C. Arthur Miller D. None of these

50. The Restoration period is said to have started from
A. 1660 B. 1676
C. 1625 D. 1645

51. Who wrote *"The Lady's Not for Burning"*?
A. Barrie B. Christopher Fry
C. Robert Bridges D. T.S. Eliot

52. Who wrote the poem *"Brahma"*?
A. T.S Eliot B. Emerson
C. Whitman D. Frost

53. The writer of *Walden* is
A. Tennyson B. Whitman
C. Thoreau D. Frost

54. In *'Sons and Lovers'* Lawrence has depicted the life of
A. factory workers B. miners
C. farmers D. animals

55. Who wrote *Kim*?
A. Kipling B. Tagore
C. Lawrence D. Narayan

56. *'The Hairy Ape'* is a famous play by
A. Barrie B. Eugene O'Neill
C. Christopher Fry D. T.S. Eliot

57. Who is the writer of *Frankenstein*?
A. George Eliot B. Jane Austen
C. Mary Shelley D. Emile Bronte

58. Who wrote the *'Cries of Children'*?
A. Robert Browning B. Elizabeth Barrett
C. Thomas Hood D. Cowper

59. Which poet is known as poet's poet?
A. Shakespeare B. Milton
C. Spenser D. Shelley

60. Who wrote the maximum number of sonnets?
A. Shakespeare B. Milton
C. Sidney D. Wordsworth

61. *Adonais* is the eulogy written on the death of
A. Coleridge B. Byron
C. Keats D. Wordsworth

62. Who wrote *Mother*?
A. Tolstoy B. Maxim Gorky
C. Chekhov D. Hardy

63. Who is associated with *Malgudi*?
A. Narayan B. Anand
C. Manohar Malgonkar D. Anita Desai

64. The author of *Beowulf* is
A. Bede B. Cynewulf
C. Chaucer D. Unknown

65. The Anglo-Saxon period is often said to be from 450 to ......
A. 900 B. 1000
C. 1050 D. 1100

66. *"To a Mountain Daisy"* is a poem by
A. Wordsworth B. Shelley
C. Keats D. Burns

67. Who wrote: *"The Devil's Disciple"*?
A. Galsworthy B. Barrie
C. Shaw D. Fry

68. Who wrote *"The Decline and Fall of the Roman Empire"*?
A. Walter Raleigh B. Trollope
C. Smollett D. Edward Gibbon

69. Richard Hooker was a prose writer of the
A. Victorian period B. Romantic period
C. Elizabethan period D. Chaucerian age

70. Alexander Dumas was
A. an English writer B. an American writer
C. a French writer D. a German writer

71. Which one was not one of the Lake poets?
A. Shelley B. Wordsworth
C. Southey D. Coleridge

72. *The Theory of Catharsis* is associated with
A. Plato B. Dryden
C. Aristotle D. Sidney

73. Who wrote *'In Defence of Poetry'*?
A. T.S. Eliot B. Yeats
C. Keats D. Shelley

74. *'The Playboy of the Western World'* is a play by
A. Barrie B. Synge
C. Fry D. Eliot

75. *'Silent Woman'* is a play by
A. Marlowe B. Shakespeare
C. Ben Jonson D. Lyly

76. The Scene of *Beowulf* is laid in
A. England B. France
C. Spain D. None of these

77. *"Kidnapped"* was written by
A. Dickens B. Thackeray
C. Hardy D. R.L. Stevenson

78. *'The Prisoner of Zenda'* was written by
A. Sterne B. Trollope
C. Anthony Hope D. George Eliot

79. What was the full name of Cervantes?
A. Jim Cervantes B. John Cervantes
C. Miguel de Cervantes D. Sir Roger Cervantes

80. Besides being a poet, Chaucer was
A. a trader B. a manufacturer
C. a teacher D. a diplomat

81. The name of William Golding's first novel is
A. The Inheritors B. Lord of the Flies
C. Pincher Martin D. The Pyramid

82. The author of *Erewhon* is
A. Hardy B. Marquese
C. Samuel Butler D. Cervantes

83. Which of the following is a *Comedy of Manners*?
A. The Way of the World
B. The Duchess of Malfi
C. The Lady's Not for Burning
D. The Hairy Ape

84. Which one among the following is not a pessimist?
A. Gissing B. Browning
C. Hardy D. Thomson

85. Charles Reade's drama *"Drink"* was adapted from a work of
A. Goethe B. Zola
C. Mallarwe D. Tennyson

86. Which one among the following was not a utilitarian?
A. Rousseau B. James Mill
C. Ricardo D. Bentham

87. *'The Praise of Folly'* was written by
A. Walter Raleigh B. Thomas Moore
C. Charles Lamb D. Ruskin

88. Who wrote: *"In Praise of Idleness"*?
A. Bertrand Russell B. Thomas More
C. Charles Lamb D. Hazlitt

89. The real name of Saki is
A. H.H. Munro B. Samuel Butler
C. George Orwell D. The Duke

90. Who started: *"The Tatler"*?
A. Addison B. Swift
C. Steele D. Stevenson

91. The poem *'The Song of the Shirt'* was written by
A. Mrs. Browning B. Pope
C. Shelley D. Thomas Hood

92. *Sir Roger* was originally the creation of
A. Addison B. Dryden
C. Steele D. Milton

93. Who wrote: *"Areopagitica"*?
A. Charles Lamb B. Hazlitt
C. De Quincey D. Milton

94. *'The Selfish Giant'* is a story written by
A. Tagore B. Oscar Wilde
C. Maupassant D. Tolstoy

95. Who wrote : *"Four Quartets"*?
A. T.S. Eliot B. W.B. Yeats
C. W.H. Auden D. Philip Larkins

96. Who wrote : *"Look Back in Anger"*?
A. Steinbeck B. Christopher Fry
C. John Osborne D. Barrie

97. Who wrote : *"The Devils of Loundun"*?
A. Bertrand Russell B. Aldous Huxley
C. J.B. Priestley D. Hazlitt

98. Who wrote : *"Principles of Human Knowledge"*?
A. Milton B. John Bunyan
C. Nash D. George Berkeley

99. Who wrote : *"Liber Amoris"*?
A. Lamb B. Hazlitt
C. Byron D. Wordsworth

100. *"A Railway Clerk"* is a poem by
A. Keki N. Daruwallah B. Nissim Ezekiel
C. Shiv K. Kumar D. Jayanta Mahapatra

101. Who won The Booker of Bookers?
A. Arundhati Roy B. Khushwant Singh
C. Mulk Raj Anand D. Salman Rushdie

102. Who wrote: *"The Battle of Books"*?
A. Bacon B. Hazlitt
C. Swift D. None of these

103. Who wrote: *"Nectar in a Sieve"*?
A. Mulk Raj Anand B. Manohar Malgonkar
C. Kamala Markandaya D. Pearl S. Buck

104. *'The Good Earth'* was written by
A. Raja Rao B. R.K. Narayan
C. Pearl S. Buck D. Kamala Markandaya

105. The writer of *'The Dove Found No Rest'* is
A. Pearl S Buck B. Hemingway
C. Raja Rao D. Dennis Stoll

106. Who wrote: *"So Many Hungers"*?
A. Bhabani Bhattacharya
B. Kamala Markandaya
C. Manohar Malgonkar
D. Chaman Nahal

107. Who is the writer of *"The Middleman and Other Stories"*?
A. Mulk Raj Anand B. Bharati Mukherjee
C. Tagore D. Prem Chand

108. Cicero was a Roman
A. philologist B. physician
C. orator D. None of these

109. Who is the writer of *"Gita Rahasya"*?
A. Tulsi Das B. Vivekananda
C. Shivananda D. B.G. Tilak

110. *'The Rubaiyat of Omar Khayyam'* was translated into English by
A. Robert Browning B. Tennyson
C. Fitz Gerald D. Hopkins

111. Mayakovsky was the famous poet of
A. France B. Italy
C. Austria D. Russia

112. Marquese originally wrote his *"One Hundred Years of Solitude"* in
A. French B. German
C. Spanish D. Italian

113. Identify Emile Bronte's novel in the following
A. Persuasion B. Wuthering Heights
C. Jane Eyre D. Middlemarch

114. Which one is believed to be the first English tragedy?
A. Gorboduc B. The Spanish Tragedy
C. Dr. Faustus D. The Jew of Malta

115. Which of the following works is not by Milton?
A. Paradise Lost B. Il Penseroso
C. Lycidas D. Maud

116. *'Music At Night'* is a book of essays by
A. A.G. Gardiner B. Bertrand Russell
C. Aldous Huxley D. Chesterton

117. The character of Sherlock Holmes was created by
A. Arthur Conan Doyle B. Hazlitt
C. I.A. Richards D. Agatha Christie

118. Who wrote the Preface to the *Gitanjali*?
A. W.B. Yeats B. T.S. Eliot
C. Auden D. Phiiip Larkin

119. What can be said to be the tragic flaw in *Hamlet*?
A. Revenge B. Indecisiveness
C. Hastiness D. Suspicion

120. Who wrote *'The Spanish Tragedy'*?
A. Shakespeare B. Thomas Kyd
C. Marlowe D. Lyly

121. Name the author of *"1984"*
A. George Orwell B. Graham Greene
C. Naipaul D. James Joyce

122. Who is the creator of *Wessex*?
A. Dickens B. Smollett
C. Meredith D. Hardy

123. Whose novel *"The Foundation Pit?"* was discovered only a few years ago?
A. Andrey Platanov B. Cherneshevysky
C. Jane Austen D. George Eliot

124. The novel *"We"* was written by
A. Andrey Platanov B. Tolstoy
C. Maxim Gorky D. Zamayatin

125. Name the writer of *"What Is To Be Done"*
A. Zamayatin B. Gorky
C. Cherneshevysky D. Chekhov

126. Name the writer of the novel *"Les Miserables"*
A. Virginia Woolf B. Mrs. Radcliffe
C. Victor Hugo D. James Joyce

127. Which of the following novels is not by Salman Rushdie?
A. Midnight's Children B. Grimus
C. The Moor's Last Sigh D. The Lighthouse

128. A sonnet comprises
A. 16 lines B. 14 lines
C. 12 lines D. 20 lines

129. Who is renowned for his outstanding work *"Holy Sonnets"*?
A. Donne B. Herrick
C. Milton D. Pope

130. Which of the following is not written by Hugo Charteris?
A. Pictures in the Wall B. A Piece of String
C. The Old Boys D. The Boarding House

131. Which of the following works is by H.G. Wells?
A. All in a Garden Fair B. The Invisible Man
C. A Child of the Jago D. Point Counter Point

132. Who wrote : *"The Ideal of a Christian Church"*?
A. John Keble B. Newman
C. Nash D. William George Ward

133. Which of the following odes is not by Keats?
A. Ode on Intimations of Immortality
B. Ode to a Nightingale
C. Ode on a Grecian Urn
D. Ode to Autumn

134. Which of the following works is not that of David Hume?
A. Treatise of Human Nature
B. The Rise and Fall of the Roman Empire
C. Political Discourses
D. History of Great Britain

135. Who is the writer of *'The School for Scandal'*?
A. Ben Jonson B. R.B. Sheridan
C. Congreve D. Webster

136. Who is the writer of the poem *"The Canonization"*?
A. Milton B. Dryden
C. Donne D. Chaucer

137. Name the writer of the poem *"Wind Hour"*?
A. Hopkins B. Eliot
C. Dryden D. Yeats

138. Who is the writer of the poem *"Adam's Course"*?
A. Eliot B. Tagore
C. Yeats D. Shelley

139. Who wrote the poem: *"Lay Your Sleeping Head"*?
A. Auden B. Yeats
C. Stephen Spender D. Ted Hughes

140. The play *"The Birthday Party"* is written by
A. G.B. Shaw B. Galsworthy
C. Harold Pinter D. Osborne

141. Who is believed to be the writer of *"On the Sublime"*?
A. Aristotle B. Longinus
C. Plato D. M. Arnold

142. Name the author of *"An Essay on Dramatic Poesie"*
A. Dryden B. Sidney
C. Shelley D. Arnold

143. Who is the writer of *"Culture and Society"*?
A. Cleanth Brooks B. Eliot
C. Bertrand Russell D. Raymond Williams

144. The writer of the *'Mirror and the Lamp'* is
A. Hume B. Lionel Trilling
C. M.H. Abrams D. Sean Lucy

145. The writer of *"Provide Provide"* is
A. Whitman B. Frost
C. Yeats D. Auden

146. Who wrote *"Desire Under the Elms"*?
A. Arthur Miller B. Osborne
C. Eugene O'Neill D. Shaw

147. Who is the writer of *"A Severed Head"*?
A. Iris Murdoch B. Paul Scott
C. Goldwing D. Huxley

148. *'Das Kapital'* is written by
A. Engel B. Freud
C. Marx D. Lawrence

149. *"Waiting for Godot"* is written by
A. Samuel Beckett B. Ibsen
C. Brecht D. Chekhov

150. Who is the writer of *"A House for Mr. Biswas"*?
A. Salman Rushdie B. V.S. Naipaul
C. Vikram Seth D. R.K. Narayan

151. Name which is not the work of Marlowe
A. Richard I B. Tambarlaine
C. The Jew of Malta D. Dr. Faustus

152. Name the writer of the poem *"The Weary Blues"*
A. Longfellow B. Whitman
C. Frost D. Langston Hughes

153. Which of the following poems is not written by Robert Lowell?
A. In the Cage B. Dolphin
C. Good Morning D. The Old Flame

154. Which of the following poems is written by Wallace Stevens?
A. Red Sun Blues B. Sunday Morning
C. From Survivor D. "Going"

155. Which of the following poems is not written by Philip Larkin?
A. Art Grass B. Sad Steps
C. Traveller D. Church going

156. *Oedipus Rex* was written by
A. Sophocles B. Homer
C. Seneca D. Aeschylus

157. Flaubert's famous work is
A. Odysseus B. Madame Bovary
C. The Trial D. The Outsider

158. Northrop Fry is basically a
A. Dramatist B. Novelist
C. Poet D. Critic

159. The writer of *"The Beauty in a State"* is
A. Raja Rao B. Tagore
C. Shelley D. Ananda Coomaraswami

160. The most important work of K.R. Srinivas Iyengar is
A. Indian Way of Writing
B. Indians Under the Foreign Rule
C. Indian Writing in English
D. Indian Literary Scene

161. The writer of *"The Swan and the Eagle"* is
A. M.K. Naik B. C.D. Narasimhaiah
C. Bruce King D. V.K. Gokak

162. Who wrote the poem: *"The Lake Isle of Innisfree"*?
A. Yeats B. Eliot
C. Spender D. Auden

163. Who wrote : *"The Lives of the Poets"*?
A. Boswell B. Hazlitt
C. Macaulay D. Dr. Johnson

164. Who wrote: *"The Interpretation of Dreams"*?
A. Marx B. Jung
C. Freud D. Darwin

165. Who wrote : *"Principles of Literary Criticism"* (in 1924)?
A. T.R. Leavis B. Kenneth Brooke
C. I.A. Richards D. A.G. Gardiner

166. Whose book "Language" (1933) is considered *"The Bible of American Linguistics"*?
A. Robert A. Hall B. Bloomfield
C. Bernard Bloch D. Edward Sapir

167. Which of the following poems is not by Frost?
A. Design B. Birches
C. Reluctance D. Michael

168. The famous soliloquy *"To be or not to be"* occurs in
A. Macbeth B. King Lear
C. Hamlet D. Othello

169. Which is the *'Odd man out'* in the following?
A. Paradise Lost B. The Ramayana
C. Essay on Man D. Iliad

170. Which Italian poet is most famous for his sonnets?
A. Petrarch B. Dante
C. Ovid D. None of these

171. What figure of speech has been used in the following line?
"Milton! thou shouldn't be living with us at this hour."
—*Wordsworth*
A. Hyperbole B. Simile
C. Metaphor D. Apostrophe

172. Which figure of speech has been used in the term : *"immemorial elms"*?
A. Allegory B. Rhyme
C. Alliteration D. Oxymoron

173. Which play of Shaw is also sometimes called *"The Chocolate Soldier"*?
A. Arms and the Man B. Candida
C. Pygmalion D. Saint Joan

174. Which one among the following cannot be deemed to be a writer of the *"Problem Play"*?
A. G.B. Shaw
B. Galsworthy
C. Harley Granville-Barker
D. Eliot

175. Who is the writer of *"Metamorphoses"*?
A. Ovid B. Dante
C. Petrarch D. Virgil

176. The book *"Euphues"* was written by
A. Greene B. Jonson
C. Dryden D. John Lyly

177. Who can be said to be the greatest writer of the *Comedy of Humours*?
A. Dryden B. Ben Jonson
C. Congreve D. Etherege

178. Which one among the following is not a play by Ben Johnson?
A. Volpone
B. Alchemist
C. Every man out of His Honour
D. The Way of the World

179. Who is the writer of the book *"Prince"*?
A. Ovid B. Boccaccio
C. Machiavelli D. Montaigne

180. Who is the writer of the essay *"Simulation and Dissimulation"*?
A. Montaigne B. Lamb
C. De Quincey D. Bacon

181. Name the figure of speech for which Lyly is chiefly remembered
A. Malapropism B. Euphuism
C. Melodramaticism D. None of these

182. *Utopia* was written by
A. Walter Raleigh B. Sir Thomas Moore
C. Daniel Defoe D. None of these

183. The other name for *Euphues* is
A. The Anatomy of Melancholy
B. The Anatomy of Joy
C. The Anatomy of Wit
D. None of these

184. *Ferrex and Porrex* is the other name for
A. The Spanish Tragedy
B. Dr. Faustus
C. Goboduc
D. None of these

185. Which one among the following belongs to the group known as University Wits?
A. Shakespeare B. Congreve
C. Dryden D. Marlowe

186. *Astrophel and Stella* is a
A. play B. novel
C. sonnet sequence D. short story

187. What is the Greek meaning of *'Utopia'*?
A. An ideal place
B. A healthy place
C. A lovely place
D. Not a place (=*ou*=not; *topos*=a place)

188. The word "Volksgeist" means
A. The spirit of the age
B. (As per) tradition, custom and consensus
C. The essence of something
D. None of these

189. Which one of the following was a contemporary of Chaucer?
A. Spenser B. Herrick
C. Robert Graves D. John Gower

190. The famous work of Boccaccio is
A. Decameron B. Divine Comedy
C. Essays D. A collection of sonnets

191. What is meant by *"Grub Street"*?
A. The literary scene of hacks' crowds during Pope's period.
B. Unhygienic streets of London
C. Streets full of worms
D. Plague-infested streets

192. Who wrote: *"Idylls of the King"*?
A. Tennyson B. Browning
C. Spenser D. Keats

193. What could be another name for Renais[illegible]nce?
A. The New Learning B. The Reformation
C. The Prostantism D. Humanism

194. Who wrote: *'Hudibras'*?
A. Butler B. Addison
C. Steele D. Goldsmith

195. *"London"* by Dr. Johnson is
A. An epic B. A verse satire
C. A prose satire D. A critical work

196. Who wrote *Moll Flanders*?
A. Richardson B. Fielding
C. Smollett D. Defoe

197. *The Gothic novel* was primarily a novel of
A. Pity B. Terror
C. Love D. Description of nature

198. *'Unto This Last'* is a work by
A. Carlyle B. Pater
C. Oscar Wilde D. John Ruskin

199. Who is the writer of *"The Blessed Damozel"*?
A. Christina Rossetti B. Emile Bronte
C. D.G. Rossetti D. W.B. Yeats

200. Who among the following was not a critic?
A. M. Arnold B. Ruskin
C. Dryden D. Tennyson

201. Which one among the following was not a contemporary or predecessor of Shakespeare?
A. Marlowe B. Kyd
C. Fry D. Greene

202. Who among the following was not a prose writer?
A. Ascham B. Coleridge
C. Hooker D. Raleigh

203. Who among the following was not a character writer?
A. Wordsworth B. Joseph Hall
C. John Earle D. Sir Thomas Overbury

204. Who among the following was not an essayist of the seventeenth century?
A. Halifax B. Sir Thomas Browne
C. Hazlitt D. Sir William Temple

205. About whom has it been said :
"He knew small Latin and less Greek"
A. Ben Jonson B. Shakespeare
C. Milton D. Aristotle

206. Who said about Shakespeare:
"He was not of age but of ages"?
A. Jonson B. Johnson
C. Dryden D. Arnold

207. Who wrote: *'Modern Painters'*?
A. Rossetti B. Reynolds
C. Hazlitt D. Ruskin

208. Which one of the following is not the work of Lamb?
A. Of Style B. All Fools' Day
C. Dream Children D. Grace Before Meat

209. Who is stated to have said :
"veni, vidi, vici"?
A. Julius Caesar B. Alexander
C. Napoleon D. Homer

210. Who wrote : *"The Advancement of Learning"*?
A. Pope B. Tennyson
C. Bacon D. Eliot

211. Who wrote: *"We are hollow men"*?
A. Eliot B. Yeats
C. Tagore D. Ezekiel

212. By which character is the following line in Shakespeare's Julius Caesar spoken?
"I'm well-armed in honesty"?
A. Caesar B. Cassius
C. Brutus D. Cicero

213. *'The Way of All Flesh'* was written by
A. Swift B. Congreve
C. Butler D. Addison

214. Who is the writer of *"The Good Companions"*?
A. A.G. Gardiner B. Chatterton
C. Hazlitt D. J.B. Priestley

215. Who is the writer of the poem *'Vagabond'*?
A. MacNeice B. Masefield
C. Sir Henry Newbolt D. Rupert Brooke

216. *"Gallathea"* in written by
A. Spenser B. Herbert
C. Lyly D. Shelley

217. Who wrote: *"The Harp of India"*?
A. Govind Chunder Dutt
B. Michael Madhusudan Dutt
C. Henry L.V. Derozio
D. V.K. Gokak

218. *"King Porus—A Legend of Old"* is written by
A. Henry Derozio B. Toru Dutt
C. Sarojini Naidu D. Michael Madhusudan

219. Who is the writer of the poem *"The Dance of the Eunuchs"*?
A. Nissim Ezekiel B. Kamala Das
C. Daruwallah D. A.K. Ramanujan

220. Which Indian poet wrote the poem *"The Trojan War"*?
A. Vikram Seth B. Keki N. Daruwalla
C. Sri Aurbindo D. Tagore

221. Who wrote: *"Jonathan Wild"*?
A. Richardson B. Smollett
C. Defoe D. Fielding

222. *"Of Revenge"* is one of the essays of
A. Lamb B. Hazlitt
C. Gardiner D. Bacon

223. Who wrote: *"The Confessions of An English Opium-Eater"*?
A. Coleridge B. Shelley
C. De Quincey D. James Joyce

224. Who wrote the poem *"Rhapsody on a Windy Day"*?
A. Yeats B. Spenser
C. Eliot D. Housman

ANSWERS

1	2	3	4	5	6	7	8	9	10
C	A	D	D	C	B	D	A	C	B
11	**12**	**13**	**14**	**15**	**16**	**17**	**18**	**19**	**20**
D	B	C	A	D	B	C	A	A	B
21	**22**	**23**	**24**	**25**	**26**	**27**	**28**	**29**	**30**
A	C	A	C	D	D	D	A	C	C
31	**32**	**33**	**34**	**35**	**36**	**37**	**38**	**39**	**40**
B	C	A	C	C	D	A	B	C	D
41	**42**	**43**	**44**	**45**	**46**	**47**	**48**	**49**	**50**
A	B	C	B	A	B	C	D	C	A

51	52	53	54	55	56	57	58	59	60
B	B	C	B	A	B	C	B	C	D
61	**62**	**63**	**64**	**65**	**66**	**67**	**68**	**69**	**70**
C	B	A	D	C	D	C	D	C	C
71	**72**	**73**	**74**	**75**	**76**	**77**	**78**	**79**	**80**
A	C	D	B	C	D	D	C	C	D
81	**82**	**83**	**84**	**85**	**86**	**87**	**88**	**89**	**90**
B	C	A	B	B	A	B	A	A	C
91	**92**	**93**	**94**	**95**	**96**	**97**	**98**	**99**	**100**
D	C	D	B	A	C	B	D	B	B
101	**102**	**103**	**104**	**105**	**106**	**107**	**108**	**109**	**110**
D	C	C	C	D	A	B	C	D	C
111	**112**	**113**	**114**	**115**	**116**	**117**	**118**	**119**	**120**
D	C	B	A	D	C	A	A	B	B
121	**122**	**123**	**124**	**125**	**126**	**127**	**128**	**129**	**130**
A	D	A	D	C	C	D	B	A	B
131	**132**	**133**	**134**	**135**	**136**	**137**	**138**	**139**	**140**
B	D	A	B	B	C	A	C	A	C
141	**142**	**143**	**144**	**145**	**146**	**147**	**148**	**149**	**150**
B	A	D	C	B	C	A	C	A	B
151	**152**	**153**	**154**	**155**	**156**	**157**	**158**	**159**	**160**
A	D	C	B	C	A	B	D	D	C
161	**162**	**163**	**164**	**165**	**166**	**167**	**168**	**169**	**170**
B	A	D	C	C	B	D	C	C	A
171	**172**	**173**	**174**	**175**	**176**	**177**	**178**	**179**	**180**
D	C	A	D	A	D	B	D	C	D
181	**182**	**183**	**184**	**185**	**186**	**187**	**188**	**189**	**190**
B	B	C	C	D	C	D	B	D	A
191	**192**	**193**	**194**	**195**	**196**	**197**	**198**	**199**	**200**
A	A	A	A	B	D	B	D	C	D
201	**202**	**203**	**204**	**205**	**206**	**207**	**208**	**209**	**210**
C	B	A	C	B	A	D	A	A	C
211	**212**	**213**	**214**	**215**	**216**	**217**	**218**	**219**	**220**
A	C	C	D	B	C	C	D	B	C
221	**222**	**223**	**224**						
D	D	C	C						

5

Literary General Knowledge

NOBEL PRIZE FOR LITERATURE 2010–2022

Year	*Laureate*	*Country*	*Language*	*Genre(s)*
2010	Mario Vargas Llosa	Peru Spain	Spanish drama	novel, short story, essay
2011	Tomas Transtromer	Sweden	Swedish	poetry, translation
2012	Mo Yan	China	Chinese	novel, short story
2013	Alice Munro	Canada	English	short story
2014	Patrick Modiano	France	French	novel, screenplay
2015	Svetlana Alexievich	Belarus	Russian	history, essay
2016	Bob Dylan	United States	English	poetry, song lyrics
2017	Kazuo Ishiguro	United Kingdom	English	novel, screenplay, short story
2018	Olga Tokarczuk	Poland	Polish	novel, short story, poetry, essay, screenplay
2019	Peter Handke	Austria	German	novel, short story, drama, essay, translation, screenplay
2020	Louise Glück	United States	English	poetry, essay
2021	Abdulrazak Gurnah	Tanzania (UK)	English	novel, short story, essay
2022	Annie Ernaux	France	French	autobiography, novel

MAN BOOKER PRIZE (2010-2022)

Year	*Winner*	*Book*	*Genre*	*Country*
2010	Howard Jacobson	The Finkler Question	Novel	United Kingdom
2011	Julian Barnes	The Sense of an Ending	Novel	United Kingdom
2012	Hilary Mantel	Bring Up the Bodies	Historical novel	United Kingdom
2013	Eleanor Catton	The Luminaries	Historical novel	New Zealand
2014	Richard Flanagan	The Narrow Road to the Deep North	Historical novel	Australia
2015	Marlon James	A Brief History of Seven Killings	Historical/ experimental novel	Jamaica
2016	Paul Beatty	The Sellout	Satirical novel	United States
2017	George Saunders	Lincoln in the Bardo	Historical/ experimental novel	United States
2018	Anna Burns	Milkman	Novel	United Kingdom
2019	Margaret Atwood	The Testaments	Novel	Canada
	Bernardine Evaristo	Girl, Woman, Other	Experimental novel	United Kingdom

Year	Winner	Book	Genre	Country
2020	Douglas Stuart	Shuggie Bain	Novel	United Kingdom United States
2021	Damon Galgut	The Promise	Novel	South Africa
2022	Shehan Karunatilaka	The Seven Moons of Maali Almeida	Novel	Sri Lanka

FAMOUS BOOKS AND AUTHORS

Book	Author
A Secular Agenda	Arun Shourie
A Suitable Boy	Vikram Seth
Accession of Extinction	D.R. Mankekar
Adam Beda	George Eliot
Adhe Adhure	Mohan Rakesh
Adonis	P.B. Shelley
Adventures of Huckleberry Finn	Mark Twain
Adventures of Sherlock Holmes	Arthur Conan Doyle
Adventures of Tom Sawyer	Mark Twain
Advise and Consent	Allen Drury
Affluent Society	J.K. Galbraith
After the Dark Night	S.M. Ali
Age of Reason	Jean Paul Sartre
Agni Pariksha	Acharya Tulsi
Agni Veena	Kazi Nazrul Islam
The Agony and the Ecstasy	Irving Stone
Ain-i-Akbari	Abul Fazal
Airport	Arthur Hailey
Ajat Shatru	Jai Shankar Prasad
Akbarnama	Abul Fazal
Alchemist, The	Ben Jonson
Alice in Wonderland	Lewis Carroll
All is Well that Ends Well	William Shakespeare
All Quite on the Western Front	Erich Maria Remarque
All the President's Men	Carl Bernestin and Bob Woodward
All the Prime Minister's Men	Janardhan Thakur
All things Bright and Beautiful	James Herroit
Amar Kosh	Amar Singh
Ambassador's Journal	J.K. Galbraith
Ambassador's Report	Chester Bowles
An American Tragedy	Theodore Drieser
An Autobiography	Jawaharlal Nehru
An Eye to China	David Selbourne
An Idealist View of Life	Dr. S. Radhakrishnan
An Unknown Indian	Nirad C. Choudhury
Anandmath	Bankim Chandra Chatterjee
Ancient Mariner	Samuel Taylor Coleridge
And Quiet Flows the Don	Mikhail Sholokhov
Androcles and the Lion	George Bernard Shaw
Animal Farm, The	George Orwell
Anna Karenina	Count Leo Tolstoy
Another Life	Derek Walcott
Answer of History	Mohammed Raza Pahlavi
Antony and Cleopatra	William Shakespeare
Ape and Essence	A. Huxley
Apple Cart	George Bernard Shaw
Arabian Nights	Sir Richard Burton
Area of Darkness	V.S. Naipaul
Arms and the Man	George Bernard Shaw
Around the World in Eighty days	Jules Verne
Arrangement, The	Elia Kazan
Arrival and Departure	Arthur Koestler
Arrowsmith	Sinclair Lewis
Arthashastra	Kautilya
As You Like It	William Shakespeare
Ascent of the Everest	Sir John Hunt
Ashtadhyayi	Panini
Asian Drama	Gunnar Myrdal
Asia and Western Dominance	K.M. Panikkar
Atoms of Hope	Mohan Sundara Rajan
August 1914	Alexander Solzhenitsyn
August Coup, The	Mikhail S. Gorbachev
Autumn Leaves	O. Pulla Reddi
Avanti Sundari	Dandi
Babur Nama	Zaheeruddin Mohammed Babur

Book	Author
Babbit	Sinclair Lewis
Back of Methuselah	George Bernard Shaw
Backward Place, A	Ruth P. Jhabwala
Bandicoot Run	Manohar Malgonkar
Bang-i-Dara	Mohammed Iqbal
Bangla Desh The Unfinished Revolution	Lawrence Liftschultz
Banyan Tree, The	Hugh Tinker
Beast and Man	Murry Midgely
Beginning of the Beginning	Acharya Rajneesh
Betrayal of Pearl Harbour	James Rusbridge and Eric Nave
Bend in the Ganges, A	Manohar Malgonkar
Ben Hur	Lewis Wallace
Bermuda Triangle	Charles Berlitz
Berry Patches	Yevgeny Yevtushenko
Best and the Brightest, The	David Halberstan
Between the Lines	Kuldip Nayar
Beyond Modernisation, Beyond Self	Sisir Kumar Ghose
Bharat Bharati	Maithili Sharan Gupta
Bharatiya Parampara Ke Mool Swar	Govind Chandra Pande
Big Breach, The	Richard Tomlinson
Big Fisherman, The	Lloyd C. Douglas
Biographia Literaria	Samuel Taylor Coleridge
Bisarjan	Rabindra Nath Tagore
Birth and Death of Sun	George Gamow
Bitter Sweet	Noel Coward
Black Arrow, The	Robert Louis Stevenson
Blind Ambitions	John Dean
Blind Beauty	Boris Pasternak
Blind Men of Hindustan ! Indo-Pak Nuclear War	General K.S. Sundarji
Bliss was it in that Dawn	Minoo Masani
Bloodline	Sidney Sheldon
Blue Bird	Maurice Macterlink
Bone People, The	Kerl Hulme
Born Free	Joy Adamson
Bread, Beauty and Revolution	Khwaja Ahmed Abbas
Breakthrough	Gen. Moshe Dayan
Bride for the Sahib and other Stories, A	Khushwant Singh
Bride's Book of Beauty, The	Mulk Raj Anand

Book	Author
Broken Wings	Sarojini Naidu
Brothers Karamazhov	Fyodor Dostoevsky
Bubble, The	Mulk Raj Anand
Bhudha Charitam	Ashvaghosha
Bunch of Old Letters, A	Jawaharlal Nehru
Butterfield-8	John O' Hara
By Love Possessed	James Cozzens
Caesar and Cleopatra	George Bernard Shaw
Cancer Ward	Alexander Solzhenitsyn
Candida	George Bernard Shaw
Candide	Voltaire
Canterbury Tales	Geoffery Chaucer
Cardinal, The	Henry M. Robinson
Centennial	James Michener
Chandalika	Rabindra Nath Tagore
Chemmeen	Thakazhi Sivasankar Pillai
Cherry Orchard	Anton Chekov
Chesaplake	James A. Michener
Chidambara	Sumitra Nandan Pant
Chikaveera Rajendra	Masti Venkatesh Iyengar
Children of Gebelawi	Naguib Mahfouz
Childe Herolds Pilgrimage	Lord Byron
China Passage, A	J.K. Galbraith
China's Watergate	Leo Goodstadt
Chinese Betrayal	B.N. Mullick
Chitra	Rabindra Nath Tagore
Chittirappaval	P.V. Akilandam
Chomas Drum	K. Shivaram Karnath
Chronicle of a Death Foretold	Gabrel Garcia Marquez
Class, The	Eric Segal
Climate of Treason	Andrew Boyle
Comedy of Errors	William Shakespeare
Common Sense	Thomas Paine
Comus	John Milton
Communist Manifesto	Karl Marx
Confessions	J.J. Rousseau
Confessions of a Lover	Mulk Raj Anand
Confessions of an Opium Eater, The	Thomas Dequicey
Confidential Clerk	T.S. Eliot
Conquest of Self	M.K. Gandhi
Conservationist, The	Ms. Nadine Gordimer
Continent of Circle	Nirad C. Choudhury

Book	Author
Coolie	Mulk Raj Anand
Coup, The	John Updike
Count of Monte Cristo	Alexander Dumas
Court Dancer	Rabindra Nath Tagore
Covertly Papers	Joseph Addison
Cresent Moon	Rabindra Nath Tagore
Crescent over Kashmir	Anil Maheshwari
Crime and Punishment	Fyodor Dostoevsky
Crisis into Chaos	E.M.S. Namboodiripad
Crisis in India, The	Ronald Segal
Critique of Pure Reason, A	Immanuel Kant
Crown and the Loincloth, The	Chaman Nahal
Crown of Wild Olive, The	John Ruskin
Cry My Beloved Country	Alan Patan
Culture in the Vanity Bag	Nirad C. Choudhury
Curtain Raisers	K. Natwar Singh
Dangerous Summer, The	Ernest Hemingway
Darkness at Noon	Arthur Keostler
Dark Room, The	R.K. Narayan
Dashkumar Charitam	Dandi
Das Kapital	Karl Marx
Daughter of the East	Benazir Bhutto
David Copperfield	Charles Dickens
Day in Shadow, The	Nayantara Sehgal
Days of His Grace	Eyvind Johnson
Dean's December	Saul Below
Death of a City	Amrita Pritam
Death of a Patriot	R.E. Harrington
Death of a President	William Manchester
Death, The Supreme Friend	Kakasaheb Kalelkar
Debacle	Emile Zola
Decameron	Giovanni Boccaccio
Decline and Fall of the Roman Empire	Edward Gibbon
Decline and Fall of Indira Gandhi	D.R. Mankekar and Kamala Mankekar
Decline of the West	O Spengier
Deewan-i-Ghalib	Mirza Ghalib
Delhi	Khushwant Singh
Democracy Means Bread and Freedom	Piloo Mody
Democracy Redeemed	V.K. Narsimhan
Descent of Man	Charles Darwin
Deserted Village	Oliver Goldsmith

Book	Author
Devdas	Sharat Chandra Chatterjee
Die Blendung	Elias Canetti
Dilemma of our Time	Harold Joseph Laski
Diplomacy in Peace and War	J.N. Kaul
Discovery of India	Jawaharlal Nehru
Distant Drums	Manohar Malgonkar
Distant Neighbours	Kuldip Nayar
Divine Comedy	A. Dante
Divine Life	Swami Sivananda
Doctor's Dilemma	George Bernard Shaw
Dolls's House, A	Ibsen
Don Juan	Lord Byron
Don Quixote	Saavedra Miguel de Cervantes
Double Helix, The	J.D. Watson
Dragon's Teeth	U.B. Sinclair
Dream in Hawaii, A	Bhabani Bhattacharya
Dream of Fair to Middling Women	Samuel Beckett
Dreams Roses and Fire	Eyvind Johnson
Dr. Jekyll and Mr. Hyde	Robert Louis Stevenson
Durgesh Nandini	Bankim Chandra Chatterjee
Dynamics of Social Change	Chandra Shekhar
Earth	Emile Zola
Earth Mother, The	Pupul Jayakar
Economic Planning of India	Ashok Mehta
Economics of the Third World	S.K. Ray
Education of Public Man	Hubert Humphery
Eight Lives	Raj Mohan Gandhi
Elegy Written in a Country Church Yard	Thomas Grey
Emile	J.J. Rousseau
Emma	Jane Austen
End of Era	C.S. Pandit
Ends and Means	Aldous Huxley
Envoy to Nehru	Escott Reid
Essays for Poor to the Rich	John Kenneth Galbraith
Essays of Elia	Charles Lamb
Essays on Gita	Sri Aurobindo Ghosh
Eternal Himalayas	Major H.P.S. Ahluwalia
Eternal India	Indira Gandhi
Executioner's Song	Norman Mailer
Expanding Universe	Arthur Stanley Eddington

Book	Author
Eye of the Storm, The	Patric White
Face to Face	Lasse & Mrs. Lisa Berg
Faces of Everest	Maj. H.P.S. Ahluwalia
Facts are Facts	Khan Abdul Wali Khan
Fall of a Sparrow, The	Salim Ali
Family Reunion	T.S. Eliot
Far From the Madding Crowd	Thomas Hardy
Far Pavilions, The	M.M. Kaye
Faraway Music, The	Svetlana Allilueva
Farewell the Trumpets	James Morris
Farewell to Arms, A	Ernest Hemingway
Farm House	George Orwell
Father and Sons	Ivan Turgenev
Faust	J.W. Von Goethe
Fidelio	L. Beethoven
Fifth Horseman, The	Larry Collins and Dominique Lapierre
Final Days, The	Bob Woodward and Carl Bernstein
Finding a Voice-Asian Women in Britain	Amrit Wilson
Fire Next Time, The	James Balbwin
First Circle	Alexander Solzhenitsyn
Flames form the Ashes	P.D. Tandon
Flounder, The	Gunter Grass
Food Nutrition and Poverty in India	V.K.R.V. Rao
For Whom the Bell Tolls	Ernest Hemingway
Forbidden Sea, The	Tar Ali Baig
Forsyte Saga	John Galsworthy
Forty Nine Days	Amrita Pritam
Freedom At Midnight	Larry Collins and Dominique Lapierre
French Revolution	Thomas Carlyle
Friends and Foes	Sheikh Mujibur Rehman
Friends not Masters	Ayyub Khan
From Here to Eternity	James Jones
From India to America	L. S. Chandrashekhar
From Raj to Rajiv	Mark Tully & Zaheer Masani
Ganadevata	Tara Shanker Bandopadhyay
Gandhi and Stalin	Louis Fisher
Gardener	Rabindra Nath Tagore
Gathering Storm	Winston Churchill

Book	Author
Geeta Govinda	Jaya Dev
Ghasiram Kotwal	Vijay Tendulkar
Gita Rahasya	Bal Gangadhar Tilak
Glimpses of World History	Jawaharlal Nehru
Godan	Munshi Prem Chand
Godfather, The	Mario Puzzo
God of Small Things, The	Arundhati Roy
Gold Bat, The	P.G. Wodehouse
Golden Gate	Vikram Seth
Golden Threshold, The	Sarojini Naidu
Gone with the Wind	Margaret Mitchel
Good Earth	Pearl S. Buck
Gora	Rabindra Nath Tagore
Grammar of Politics	Harold Joseph Laski
Grapes of Wrath	John Steinbeck
Great Challenge, The	Louis Fishcer
Great Depression of 1990, The	Ravi Batra
Great Expectations	Charles Dickens
Great Gatsby	F. Scott Fitzgerald
Great Illusion	Norman Angel
Great Tragedy	Z.A. Bhutto
Guide, The	R.K. Narayan
Gulag Archipelago	Alexander Solzhenitsyn
Gul-i-Naghma	Raghupati Sahai (Firaq) Gorakhpuri
Gulistan and Bostan	Sheikh Saadi
Gulliver's Travels	Jonathan Swift
Gurusagaram	O.P. Vijayan
Hamlet	William Shakespeare
Handful of Dust, A	Evelyn Waugh
Harry Potter*	J.K. Rowling
Harsha Charita	Ban Bhatt
Heat and Dust	Ruth P. Jhabwala
Heir Apparent	Dr. Karan Singh
Henderson, the Rain King	Saul Below
Henry Esmond	William Thackeray
Hero of our Times	Richard Hough
Heroes and Hero Worship	Thomas Carlyle
Higher than Hope	Fatima Meer
Himalayan Blunder	Brigadier J.P. Dalvi
Hindu Civilization	J.M. Barrier
Hinduism	Nirad C. Choudhury
Hindu View of Life	Dr. S. Radhakrishnan

Book	Author	Book	Author
Hounds of Baskervilles, The	Arthur Conan Doyle	**India's Priceless Heritage**	N.A. Palkhivala
House Divided	Pearl S. Buck	**India**	Magasthenes
House for Mr. Biswas, A	V.S. Naipaul	**Indira's India**	S. Nihal Singh
Huckieberry Finn	Mark Twain	**Indira Gandhi's Emergence and Style**	Nayantara Sehgal
Human Factor	Graham Greene	**Inheritance of Loss, The**	Kiran Desai
Humboldt's Gift, The	Saul Bellow	**Inner Circle, The**	Jonathan Frost
Humour	Ben Johnson	**Inside Asia (also, Inside Europe and Inside Africa)**	John Gunter
Hunchback of Notre Dame	Victor Hugo	**Inside Third Reich**	Albert Spencer
Hungary Stones	Rabindra Nath Tagore	**Intimacy**	Jean Paul Sartre
I Am Not an Island	K.A. Abbas	**Invisible Man**	H.G. Wells
I Follow the Mahatma	K.M. Munshi	**Iron in the Soul**	Jean Paul Sartre
Idiot, The	Fyodor Dostoevsky	**Isabella**	John Keats
Idols	Sunil Gavaskar	**Islamic Bomb**	Stev Weissman and Herbert Krounsney
Idylls of the King	Alfred Tennyson	**Island in the Steams**	Ernest Hemingway
If I am Assassinated	Z.A. Bhutto	**Is Paris Burning**	Larry Collins and Dominique Lapierre
Illiad	Homer	**Ivanhoe**	Sir Walter Scott
Importance of Being Earnest	Oscar Wilde	**Jane Eyre**	Charlotte Bronte
In Afghanistan's Shadow	Salig S. Harrison	**Jazz**	Toni Morison
In Evil Hour	Gabriel Garcia Marquez	**Jean Christopher**	Roman Rolland
In a Free State	V.S. Naipaul	**Jinnah-India-Partition Independence**	Jaswant Singh
In Memorium	Alfred Lord Tennyson	**Jobs for Millions**	V.V. Giri
In Search of Gandhi	Richard Attenbrough	**Judgement, The**	Kuldip Nayar
In Search of Identity	Anwar-al-Sadat	**Judge's Miscellany, A**	M. Hidayatullah
India A Wounded Civilization	V.S. Naipaul	**Jullius Caesar**	William Shakespeare
India Changes	Taya Zinkin	**Jungle Book**	Rudyard Kipling
India Discovered	John Keay	**Justice of Peace Ke Aansu**	Janardan Prasad Singh
India Divided	Rajendra Prasad	**Kadambari**	Bana Bhatt
India from Curzon to Nehru and After	Durga Das	**Kagaz te Kanwas**	Amrita Pritam
India Remembered	Percival and Margaret Spear	**Kali Aandhi**	Kamleshwar
India of Our Dreams	M.V. Kamath	**Kamayani**	Jai Shanker Prasad
India, The Critical Years	Kuldip Nayar	**Kamasutra**	S.J. Vatsyayan
India Today	Rajni Palme Dutt	**Kanthapura**	Raja Rao
India We Left	Humphry Trevelyan	**Kapal Kundala**	Bankim Chandra Chatterjee
India Wins Freedom	Maulana Abul Kalam Azad	**Kashmir-Behind the Vale**	M.J. Akbar
Indian Home Rule	M.K. Gandhi	**Kaya Kalp**	Munshi Prem Chand
Indian Muslims	Mohammed Mujeeb	**Kayar**	Thakazhi Sivasankara Pillai
Indian Muslims The Need For a Positive Outlook	Wahiduddin Khan	**Ken Attendant Godot**	Samuel Backett
Indian Philosophy	Dr. S. Radhakrishnan	**Kenilworth**	Sir Walter Scott
Indian War of Independence	V.D. Savarkar		
India's China War	Neville Maxwell		

Book	Author
Khak-i-Dil	Jan Nissar Akhtar
Kidnapped	Robert Louis Stevenson
Killer Angels	Michael Shaara
Kim	Rudyard Kipling
King of Dark Chamber	Rabindra Nath Tagore
King Lear	William Shakespeare
Kipps	H. G. Wells
Kissinger Years, The	T.N. Kaul
Kitni Navon Main Kitni Bar	S.H. Vatsyayan
Kore Kagaz	Amrita Pritam
Kublai Khan	Samuel Taylor Coleridge
Kulliyat-i-Iqbal	M. Iqbal
Kumar Sambhava	Kalidas
L'Allegro	John Milton
La Divine Comedia	A. Dante
Lady Chatterley's Lover	D.H. Lawrence
Lady of the Lake	Sir Walter Scott
Lajja	Ms. Taslima Nasreen
Last Days of Pompeii	Edward George Lytton
Last Maharaja, The	Jean Louis Nou and Jacques Pouchepadass
Last Thing	C.P. Snow
Laws Versus Justice	V.R. Krishna Iyer
Lead Kindly Light	Vincent Shean
Le Contract Social (The Social Contract)	J.J. Rousseau
Leaders	Richard Nixon
Leaves of Grass	Walt Whiteman
Letters from the Field	Margaret Mead
Les Miserables	Victor Hugo
Leviathan	Thomas Hobbes
Life Divine	Aurbindo Ghosh
Life of Dr. Johnson	James Boswell
Light that Failed	Rudyard Kipling
Lines of Fate	Marek Kharitonov
Lipika	Rabindra Nath Tagore
Living Room	Graham Greene
Lolita	V. Nabokov
Long Walk to Freedom	Nelson Mandela
Look Back in Anger	John Osborne
Lord of the Files	William Golding
Lost Child	Mulk Raj Anand
Lost Honour	John Dena
Lotus Eaters	A Tennyson

Book	Author
Love Story	Eric Segal
Lycidas	John Milton
Macbeth	William Shakespeare
Magic Mountain	Maharishi Ved Vyas
Main Street	Sinclair Lewis
Major Barbara	George Bernard Shaw
Making of a Midsummer Night's Dream, The	David Selbourne
Malgudi Days	R.K. Narayan
Malti Madhav	Bhavabhuti
Malavikagnimitra	Kalidas
Man and Superman	George Bernard Shaw
Man Eaters of Kumaon	Jim Corbett
Man of Destiny	George Bernard Shaw
Mankind and Mother Earth	Arnold Toynbee
Man, The Unknown	Lewis Carroll
Man for All Seasons, A	Robert Bolt
Man for Moscow	G. Wynne
Many Worlds	K.P.S. Menon
Marriage and Morals	Bertrand Russel
Masters, The	C.P. Snow
Mati Matal	Gopinath Mohanty
Maurice	E.M. Forster
Mayor of Casterbridge	Thomas Hardy
Meghdoot	Kalidas
Mein Kampf	Adolf Hitler
Memories of Hope	Charles de Gaulle
Memories of Malgudi	R.K. Narayan
Men who Kept the Secrets	Thomas Powers
Men who Killed Gandhi, The	Manohar Malgonkar
Merchant of Venice	William Shakespeare
Middle Ground, The	Margaret Drabble
Middle March	George Eliot
Midnight's Children*	Salman Rushdie
Midsummer Night's Dream, A	William Shakespeare
Mill on the Floss	George Eliot
Miser, The	Moliere
Mistaken Identify	Nayantara Sehgal
Moby Dick	Hermann Melville
Modern Painters	John Ruskin
Moon and Six Pence	W. Somerset Maugham
Moonlight Sonata	L Beethoven
Mookhajiva Kanasugalu	K. Shivram Karnath

Book	Author	Book	Author
Mother	Maxim Gorky	**O'Jerusalem**	Larry Collins and Dominique Lapierre
Mother India	Katherine Mayo	**Occasion for Loving**	Nadine Gordimer
Mountbatten and Independent India	Larry Collins & Dominique Lapierre	**Oddakkuzal**	G. Shankara Kurup
Mountbatten and The Partition of India	Larry Collins & Dominique Lapierre	**Odyssey**	Homer
Mrinalini	Bankim Chandra Chatterjee	**Of Human Bondage**	W. Somerset Maugham
Mrs. Gandhi's Second Reign	Arun Shourie	**Old Man and the Sea**	Ernest Hemingway
Much Ado About Nothing	William Shakespeare	**Oliver Twist**	Charles Dickens
Mudra Rakshasa	Vishakhadatta	**Omeros**	Derek Walcott
Murder in the Cathedral	V.S. Eliot	**One Day on the Life of Ivan Denisovich**	Alexander Solzhenitsyn
Muslim Dilemma in India	M. K. A. Baig	**One Hundred Years of Solitude**	Gabriel Marquez
My Days	R.K. Narayana	**One World**	Wendell Wilkie
My Early Life	M.K. Gandhi	**One World to Share**	Sridath Ramphal
My Experiments with Truth	M.K. Gandhi	**Origin of Species**	Charles Darwin
My India	S. Nihal Singh	**Oru Desattinte Katha**	S.K. Pottekkatt
My Life and Times	V.V. Giri	**Oscar and Lucinda**	Peter Carey
My Music, My Love	Ravi Shankar	**Othello**	William Shakespeare
My Own Boswell	M. Hidayatullah	**Other Side of Midnight, The**	Sidney Sheldon
My Presidential Years	R.Venkata Raman	**Our Films, Their Films**	Satyajit Ray
My Struggles	E.K. Nayanar	**Paddy Clarke Ha Ha Ha**	Roddy Doyle
My Truth	Indira Gandhi	**Pakistan Papers**	Mani Shankar Aiyer
Mysterious Universe	James Jens	**Painted Veil**	W. Somerset Maugham
Naked Came the Stranger	Penelope Ashe	**Painter of Signs**	R.K. Narayan
Naked Face, The	Sidney Sheldon	**Pair of Blue Eyes, A**	Thomas Hardy
Naked Triangle, The	Balwant Gargi	**Pakistan Crisis**	David Loshak
Naku Thanthi	D.R. Bendre	**Pakistan Cut to Size**	D.R. Mankekar
Nana	Emile Zola	**Pakistan, The Gathering Storm**	Benazir Bhutto
Nature of Mass Poverty, The	J.K. Galbraith	**Panchatantra**	Vishnu Sharma
Natya Shastra	Bharat Muni	**Paradise Lost**	John Milton
Neela Chand	Shiv Prasad Singh	**Paradise Regained**	John Milton
Nehru Family and Sikhs	Harbans Singh	**Passage to England, A**	Nirad C. Choudhury
Netaji Dead or Alive	Samar Guha	**Passage to India, A**	E.M. Forster
New Dimensions of India's Foreign Policy	Atal Behari Vajpayee	**Past and Present**	Thomas Carlyle
Nine Days' Wonder	John Mansfield	**Pather Panchali**	Bibhuti Bhushan Bandhopadhayaya
Nineteen Eighty-four	George Orwell	**Patriot, The**	Pearl S. Buck
1999-Victory Without War	Richard Nixon	**Personal Adventure, A**	Theodore H. White
Nisheeth	Uma Shanker Joshi	**Peter Pan**	J. M. Berrie
Niti-Sataka	Bharatrihari	**Pickwick Papers**	Charles Dickens
Nixon in White House	Seymour M. Hersh	**Pilgrim's Progress**	John Bunyan
Non-Violence in Peace and War	M.K. Gandhi	**Pinjar**	Amrita Pritam
Nuclear India	G.G. Mirchandani and P.K.S. Namboodari	**Plans for Departure**	Nayantara Sehgal
		Portrait of India	Ved Mehta

Book	Author	Book	Author
Post Office	Rabindra Nath Tagore	**Reminiscences of the Nehru Age**	M.O. Mathai
Power and Glory	Graham Greene	**Reprieve**	Jean Paul Sartre
Power That Be	David Halberstan	**Republic**	Plato
Pratham Pratishruti	Ashapurna Devi	**Resurrection**	Count Leo Tolstoy
Prelude	William Wordsworth	**Return of the Native, The**	Thomas Hardy
Prem Pachisi	Munshi Prem Chand	**Returning to the Source**	Acharya Shree Rajneesh
Premonitions	P.N. Haksar	**Revenue Stamps, The**	Amrita Pritam
Price of Power	Kissinger	**Rich Like Us**	Nayantara Sehgal
Pride and Prejudice	Jane Austen	**Riding the Storm**	Harold MacMillan
Prince	Nicolo Machiaveli	**Rights of Man**	Thomas Paine
Principla	Issac Newton	**Rise and Fall of the Great Powers**	Paul Kennedy
Prison and Chocolate Cake	Nayantara Sehgal	**Ritu Samhara**	Kalidas
Prison Diary	Jaya Prakash Narayan	**Rivals, The**	R.B. Shridan
Prisoner of Zenda	Anthony Hope	**Road to Folly**	Leslie Ford
Prisoner's Scrapbook, A	L.K. Advani	**Robe, The**	Lloyd C. Douglas
Prithviraj Raso	Chanda Bardai	**Robinson Crusoe**	Daniel Defoe
Professor, The	Charlotte Bronte	**Romeo and Julliet**	William Shakespeare
Promises to Keep	Chester Bowels	**Rubaiyat**	Omar Khayyam
Pygmalion	George Bernard Shaw	**Rubaiyat-i-Omar Khayyam**	Edward Fitzgerald
Pyramids of Sacrifice	Peter L. Berger	**Sadar-i-Riyasat**	Karan Singh
Radharani	Bankim Chandra Chatterjee	**Saket**	Maithili Sharan Gupta
Rage of Angels	Sidney Sheldon	**Sakha Ram Binder**	Vijay Tendulkar
Raghuvansha	Kalidas	**Samler's Planet**	Saul Bellow
Ragtime	E.L. Doctorow	**Sands of Time**	Sidney Sheldon
Rainbow, The	Pearl S. Buck	**Satanic Verses**	Salman Rushdie
Rains Came	Louis Bromefield	**Sanctuary**	William Faulkner
Rajtarangini	Kalhana	**Satyartha Prakash**	Swami Dayanand
Ram Charita Manas	Tulsidas	**Savitri**	Sri Aurobindo Ghosh
Ramayana	Maharishi Valmiki	**Scarlet Letter**	Nathaniel Hawthorne
Rangbhoomi	Munshi Prem Chand	**Scarlet Pimpernal**	Baroness Orczy
Rang-i-Shairi	Raghupati Sahai (Firaq Gorakhpuri)	**Sceptred Flute**	Sarojini Naidu
Rape of Bangladesh	Anthony Mascarenhas	**Scholar Extraordinary**	Nirad C. Choudhury
Rape of the Lock	Alexander Pope	**School for Scandal, The**	R.B. Sheridan
Ratnavali	Harsh Vardhan	**Scope of Happiness, The**	Vijayalakshmi Pandit
Razor's Edge	W. Somerset Maugham	**Search for Home, A**	Sasthi Brata
Rebel, The	Albert Camus	**Sense and Sensibility**	Jane Austen
Rebirth	Leonid Brezhnev	**Sense of Time, A**	H.S. Vatsyayan
Red and Black, The	Stendhal	**Sesame and Lilies**	John Ruskin
Red Badge of Courage	Stephan Crane	**Seven Lamps of Architecture**	John Ruskin
Red Star over China	Edgar Snow	**Seven Summers**	Mulk Raj Anand
Reflections of the French Revolution	Edmund Burke	**Shadow from Ladakh**	Bhabani Bhattacharya
		Shahnama	Firdausi

Book	Author
Shakuntala	Kalidas
Shalimar	Manohar Malgonkar
Shall We Tell the President	Jeffrey Archer
Shape of Things to Come	H.G Wells
Shame	Salman Rushdie
She Stoops to Conquer	Oliver Goldsmith
Ship of Fools	Katherine Anne Porter
Shivaji, The Great Patriot	Lala Lajpat Rai
Shoes of the Fisherman, The	Morris West
Silas Marner	George Eliot
Six Characters in Search of an Author	Lugi Pirandello
Slave, The	Issac Bashevis Singer
Small Land	Leonid Brezhnev
Sohrab and Rustam	Matthew Arnold
Song of India, The	Sarojini Naidu
Sonnets, The	William Shakespeare
Sons and Lovers	D.H. Lawrence
Sound and the Fury, The	William Faulkner
Soz-i-Watan	Munshi Prem Chand
Spaniard in the Works, A	John Lennon
Spirit of the Age	William Hazlitt
Spy Catcher	Peter Wright
St. John	George Bernard Shaw
Story of My Life	Moshe Dayan
Story of Real Man	Nikolayev Polevol
Strangers and Brothers Omnibus	C.P. Snow
Sunny Days	Sunil Gavaskar
Study of History, A	Arnold Toynbee
Swami and Friends	R.K. Narayan
Swapnavasvadatta	Bhasa
Sword and the Sickle	Mulk Raj Anand
Tale of a Tub, A	Jonathan Swift
Tale of Two Cities, A	Charles Dickens
Tales from Shakespeare	Charles Lamb
Talisman	Sir Walter Scott
Tamas	Bhisham Sahni
Tarzan of the Apes	Edger Rice Burroughs
Tears of D'Urbervilles	Thoms Huardy
Tempest, The	William Shakespeare
Thank You, Jeeves	P.G. Wodehouse
The Garden of Life	Naveen Patnaik
The White Tiger*	Arvind Adiga

Book	Author
Thieves in the Night	Arthur Koestler
Thirteenth Sun	Amrita Pritam
Three Musketeers	Alexander Dumas
Thorn Birds	Colleen McCollough
Thousand Days, A	Arthur M. Shlesinger
Through the Indian Looking Glass	David Selbourne
Through the Looking Glass	Lewis Carroll
Times Machine	H.G. Wells
Time to be Happy	Nayantara Sehgal
To Live or not to Live	Nirad C. Choudhury
Tom Jones	Henry Fielding
Train to Pakistan	Khushwant Singh
Traveller, The	Olive Goldsmith
Treasure Island	Robert Louis Stevenson
Trial, The	Franz Kafka
Trinity	Leon Uris
Triumph	John Kenneth Galbraith
Tropic of Cancer	Henry Miller
Tryst with Destiny	L. S. Gopalan
Twelfth Night	William Shakespeare
Twenty Years After	Alexander Dumas
Two Leaves and a Bud	Mulk Raj Anand
Two Women	Alberto Moravia
Ulysses	James Joyce
Uncle Tom's Cabin	H.B. Stowe
Unhappy India	Lala Lajpat Rai
Universe Around Us	James Jeans
Unto this Last	John Ruskin
Untold Story	General B.M. Kaul
Upturned Soil, The	Mikhail Sholokhov
Urvashi	Ramdhari Singh Dinkar
Utopia	Thomas More
Uttar Ramcharita	Bhava Bhuti
Valley of Dolls	Jacqueline Susann
Vanity Fair	William Thackeray
Vendor of Sweets, The	R.K. Narayan
Vicar of Wakefield	Oliver Goldsmith
Victim, The	Saul Bellow
View From Delhi, A	Chester Bowles
View From the UN	U. Thant
Village by the Sea, A	Anita Desai
Village, The	Mulk Raj Anand

Book	Author	Book	Author
Vinay Patrika	Tulsidas	**Where the Grass is Greener**	David M. Smith
Virangana	Maithili Sharan Gupta	**White House Years**	Henry Kissinger
Virginians, The	William Thackeray	**Wings of Fire**	A.P.J. Abdul Kalam*
Vish Vriksha	Bankim Chandra Chatterjee	**Willhelm Meister**	J.W. Von Goethe
		Without Fear or Favour	Neelam Sanjiva Reddy
Voice of Conscience	V.V. Giri	**Witness to an Era**	Frank Moraes
Voice of Freedom , A	Nayantara Sehgal	**Woman's Life, A**	Guy de Maupassant
Voice of the Voiceless	Ruth Harring	**Wonder That Was India, The**	A.L. Basham
Waiting for Godot	Thomas Becket	**Worthy it is**	Odysseus Elytis
Wake up India	Annie Besant	**Wreck , The**	Rabindra Nath Tagore
Walls of Glass, The	K.A. Abbas	**Wuthering Heights**	Emile Bronte
War and Peace	Count Leo Tolstoy	**Yajnaseni**	Pratibha Roy
War of the Worlds, The	H.G. Wells	**Yama**	Mahadevi Verma
Waste Land	T.S. Eliot	**Yashodhara**	Maithili Sharan Gupta
Way to all Flesh	Samuel Butler	**Yayati**	V.S. Khandekar
Way of the World, The	William Congreve	**Year of the Upheaval**	Henry Kissinger
Wealth of Nations	Adam Smith	**Year of the Vulture, The**	Amita Malik
Week with Gandhi, A	Louis Fisher	**Yesterday and Today**	K.P.S. Menon
We Indians	Khushwant Singh	**Zhivago, Dr.**	Boris Pasternak
We, the People	N.A. Palkivala	**Zulfi, My Friend**	Piloo Mody

FAMOUS AUTHORS IN DIFFERENT LANGUAGES

English	William Shakespeare, John Milton, Chaucer, Spenser, Lord Byron, P.B. Shelley, John Keats, Francis Bacon, T.S. Eliot, Cecil Dlay Lewis, Alduous Huxley, W.B. Yeats Bunyan, Dryden, Dr. Johnson, Alexander Pope, Robert Browning, Charles Lamb, Charles Dickens, Thomas Hardy, W.M. Thackeray, George Eliot, Alfred Tennyson, Robert Bridges, George Bernard Shaw, D.H. Lawrence, Oliver Goldsmith, Sheridan, Walter Scott, William Wordsworth, S.T. Coleridge, Henry Fielding, Somerset Maugham, J.K. Rowling.
French	Imile Zola, Gustave Flaubert, Moliere, Proudhon, Jean Paul Sartre, Le Sage, Victor Hugo, Alexander Dumas, Balzac.
German	Goethe, Hoffman, Lessing, Schelling, Schaupenhuer, Heinrich Heine, Guenter Grass
Russian	Tolstoy, Mikhail Solokhov, Turgenev, Dostoevsky, Maxim Gorky, Techov, Alexander Salzhenitsyn, Boris Pasternak
Greek	Homer, Aesop, Aristophanes, Euripedes, Herodotus, Hesoid, Theocritus, Xenophon, Aeschylus, Sophocles
Latin	Dante, Boccacio, Terence, Virgil, Ovid, Horace, Seneca
Norwegian	John Bojer, Ibsen
Persian	Ghalib, Umar Khyyam, Abul Fazal, Amir Khusro, Faiz, Firdausi, Mohd. Iqbal Saddi
Spanish	Juan Valera, Lope De Vega, Cervantes

FAMOUS CHARACTERS AND THEIR CREATORS

Character	Creator	Character	Creator
Adam	Milton	Ariel	William Shakespeare
Alice	Lewis Carroll	Antonio	William Shakespeare
Ancient Mariner	Coleridge	Anna Karenina	Leo Tolstoy

Character	Creator
Bassomio	William Shakespeare
Bertie Wooster	P.G. Wodehouse
Brutus	William Shakespeare
Beatrix	Thackery
Beatrice	William Shakespeare
Christian	John Bunyan
Cordelia	William Shakespeare
Cleopatra	William Shakespeare
Clare	Thomas Hardy
Claudius	William Shakespeare
David Copperfield	Charles Dickens
Dushyanta	Kalidas
Don Quixote	Cervantes
Eliza Doolittle	George Bernard Shaw
Estella	Charles Dickens
Faust	J.W. Von Goethe
Gora	Rabindranath Tagore
Hamlet	William Shakespeare
Harry Potter	J.K. Rowling
Hyde	R.L. Stevenson
Hercule Poirot	Agatha Christie
Hawkins	R.L. Stevenson
Hector	Homer
Ivanhoe	Sir Walter Scott
Iago	William Shakespeare
James Bond	Ian Fleming
Juliet	William Shakespeare
Jessica	William Shakespeare

Character	Creator
Jean Valjin	Victor Hugo
Jacques	William Shakespeare
Jeeves	P.G. Wodehouse
King Arthur	Tennyson
Kim	Rudyard Kipling
Long John Silver	R.L. Stevenson
Macbeth	William Shakespeare
Micawber	Charles Dickens
Miranda	William Shakespeare
Mephistopheles	J.W. Von Goethe
Mellors	D.H. Lawrence
Malaprop	Sheridian
Oliver Twist	Charles Dickens
Peggotty	Charles Dickens
Priyangbada	Kalidas
Portia	William Shakespeare
Pip	Charles Dickens
Perry Mason	Erle Stanley Gardner
Pickwick	Charles Dickens
Rip Van Winkle	Washington Irving
Sam Weller	Charles Dickens
Surpanakha	Valmiki
Shylock	William Shakespeare
Sherlock Halmes	Arthur Conan Doyle
Shakuntala	Kalidas
Sancho Panza	Cervantes Saavedra
Tess	Thomas Hardy
Watson	Arthur Conan Doyle
Zhivago	Boris Pasternak

GREAT POETS

Language	Poet
Hindi	Surdas, Tulsidas, Keshav
Sanskrit	Valmiki, Vedvyas, Kalidas
Bengali	Rabindra Nath Tagore
Urdu	Mirza Ghalib
Persian	Sheikh Saadi
Latin	Virgil
Greek	Homer
English	Shakespeare
German	Goethe
Italian	Dante
French	Sully Proudhone
Punjabi	Waris Shah

GREAT INDIAN AUTHORS AND POETS IN ENGLISH

Kamala Das; Manohar Malgonkar; R.K. Narayan; Raja Rao; Mulk Raj Anand; Bhabani Bhatacharya; Sasthi Brata; Arun Joshi; Chaman Nahal; K.A. Abbas; Anita Desai; R. Prawer Jhabwala; Kamla Markandaya; Khushwant Singh; Manoj Dass.

WELL KNOWN QUOTATIONS

1. A thing of beauty is a joy for ever; Its loveliness increases; It will never pass into nothingness.
— Keats: Endymion
2. A little knowledge is a dangerous thing *— Pope*
3. Beauty is truth, truth beauty that is all. Ye know on earth, all all ye need to know
— Keats: Ode on a Grecian urn

4. All the world is a stage and all the man and women merely players — *Shakespeare: As you like it*
5. Some books are to be tested, others to be swallowed and some few to be chewed and digested — *Bacon*
6. Better to reign in hell than serve in heaven — *Milton: Paradise lost*
7. The child is father of the man — *Wordsworth: My heart leaps up*
8. A single step for man — a giant leap for mankind — *Neil Armstrong*
9. Dilli Chalo — *Netaji Subhash Chandra Bose*
10. To be or not to be — that is the question. — *Shakespeare: Hamlet*
11. Only free men negotiate. I shall never negotiate while I am still a prisoner — *Nelson Mandela*
12. Truth and non-violence are my God — *Mahatma Gandhi*
13. Let a hundred flowers bloom and let a thousand schools of thought contend — *Mao Tse-tung*
14. Jai Jawan, Jai Kisan — *Lal Bahadur Shastri*
15. Eureka! Eureka! — *Archimedes*
16. Some are born great, some achieve greatness and some have greatness thrust upon them — *Shakespeare*
17. Where wealth accumulates, men decay — *Goldsmith*
18. Power tends to corrupt and absolute power corrupts absolutely — *Lord Acton*
19. Man is by nature a political animal — *Aristotle*
20. I have nothing to offer but blood, toil, tears and sweat — *Winston Churchill*
21. I came, I saw, I conquered — *Julius Ceaser*
22. For fools rush in where angels fear to tread — *Pope*
23. Generations to come, it may, will scarce believe that such a one as this ever in flesh and blood walked upon this earth — *Einstein*
24. Government of the people, by the people, for the people — *Lincoln*
25. East is east and west is west and never the twain shall meet — *Kipling*
26. Swaraj is my birth right — *Bal Gangadhar Tilak*
27. Cowards die many times before their death: The valiant never taste of death but once — *Shakespeare: Julius Ceaser*
28. Where ignorance is bliss, It is folly to be wise — *Grey*
29. I know nothing except the fact of my ignorance — *Socrates*
30. We are such stuff as dreams are made of and our little life is rounded with a sleep — *Shakespeare: The Tempest*
31. What's in a name? That which we call a rose By any other name would smell as sweet — *Shakespeare: Merchant of Venice*
32. Patriotism is the best refuge of a scoundrel — *Samuel Johnson*
33. Reading maketh a full man; conference a ready man; and writing an exact man — *Francis Bacon*
34. It is excellent to love a giant's strength but it is tyrannous to use it like a giant — *Shakespeare: Measure to Measure*
35. Water, water everywhere
Not any drop to drink — *S.T. Coleridge: The Ancient Mainer*
36. It is strange but true, for truth is always strange — *Byron: Don Juan*
37. Virtue is its own reward — *Cicero: De Fintibus*
38. Frailty, thy name is woman — *Shakespeare: Hamlet*
39. We don't fear to negotiate, but we do not negotiate out of fear — *J.F. Kennedy*
40. Give us good mothers and I shall give you good nation — *Napoleon*
41. The woods are lovely, dark and deep
But I have promises to keep
And miles to go before I sleep — *Robert Frost*
42. We have made a tryst with destiny — *Pt. Nehru*
43. Eli, Eli, Lamma Sabcathani (My God, my God, why last thou forsaken me) — *Jesus Christ at the Cross*
44. If winter comes can spring be for behind — *Shelley*
45. Man does not live by bread alone — *Bible*
46. Nothing is good or bad, thinking makes it so — *Shakespeare: Hamlet*
47. Garibi hatao — *Indira Gandhi*
48. Aram haram hai — *Jawaharlal Nehru*
49. Quit India — *Mahatma Gandhi*
50. Jai Jawan, Jai Kisan, Jai Vigyan — *Atal Behari Vajpayee*

MULTIPLE TYPE QUESTIONS

1. Who are the authors of following works?
A. *Hidden Love*
B. *My Book of Human Rights*
C. *Devil May Care*
D. *A Prisoner of Birth*

2. Who was the first English writer to win Nobel Prize for Literature?

3. Whose autobiography is titled *Freedom in Exile*?

4. Who wrote *The Dream of the Red Chamber,* China's greatest novel?

5. Name the author of following Books—
A. *Reconciliation, Islam, Democracy and the West;*
B. *My Country: My Life* (Autobiography);
C. *Good-bye Shahzadi: A Political Biography of Benazir Bhutto.*

6. Which Indian freedom-fighter and staunch nationalist's work is *India Wins Freedom*?

7. Who has written the *Tales Of The Future*?

8. Which American historian wrote the 10-volume *History of the United States*?

9. *Songs of Innocence* is the work of which English poet, philosopher and artist?

10. Who is the author of *'The Enchantress of Florence'*?

11. Name the sister of forceful novelist Charlotte Bronte who wrote *Wuthering Heights.*

12. Which Libyan leader and military dictator wrote *The Green Book*?

13. Which former British Prime Minister's autobiography is titled *Full circle*?

14. Which is the longest biography in publishing history?

15. Who is the author of best sold series of Harry Potter?

16. What is the pen name of K.K. Nair, who wrote a 10 volume *History of Literature*?

17. Who is the author of *'The Kalam Effect – My Years with the President'*?

18. Which is the longest single-volume novel of the 20th century?

19. Which Pakistani Prime Minister's autobiography is titled *Daughter of the East?*

20. Name the Russian-American novelist, poet, and an authority on butterflies, whose *Lolita* is world famous.

21. Which Indian diplomat and author's work is *The Flying Troika*?

22. Name the Indian author and journalist, settled in New York, who became blind at the age of 3, and is a writer for *New Yorker.*

23. Who is credited to have authored the first modern Indian novel in English, *Rajmohan's Wife*?

24. Which British Prime Minister (1951-55), won Nobel Prize for literature?

25. Name the Indian writer and social critic, whose work includes *Autobiography of an Unknown Indian.*

26. Which English satirist's work is *Gulliver's Travels?*

27. Which India-born British writer's controversial book *The Satanic Verses* made Iran's spiritual leader Ayatollah Khomeini sentence him to death?

28. Which French novelist and dramatist's works include *Jean-Christophe* (a ten-volume novel), biographies of Mahatma Gandhi and Vivekananda?

29. Which Indian president authored the *Hindu View of Life?*

30. Which Hindi writer's real name was Dhanpat Rai?

31. Which Greek Philosopher and educator's work, *Dialogues,* includes the *Republic,* the longest and one of the most celebrated works?

32. What do you call the art of compiling dictionaries?

33. What was the pseudonym of Lewis Carroll?

34. Give the title of the book Jim Corbett wrote on animals.

35. Who is called the Father of English poetry?

36. What is the term for 'the fear of books'?

37. Which former Indian Prime Minister's autobiography is titled *The Insider*?

38. What is the title of famous Musician Pt. Ravi Shankar's autobiography?

39. A. Which book is considered China's greatest novel?
B. Who wrote it?

40. A. Who wrote *Mahatma Gandhi and his Apostles*?
B. What was the title of the book on Mahatma Gandhi by Romain Rolland?

41. Name the German poet who wrote a poem appreciating Kalidasa's *Shakuntala.*

42. Who created the character 'Tarzon'?

43. In Arthur Conan Doyle's novels, who narrates the Sherlock Holmes stories?

44. Which English novelist and playwright wrote detective thrillers including *The Four Just Men* and *The Ringer*?

45. This 19th century Irish author and dramatist authored *An Ideal Husband.* Who was he?

46. Who wrote the following books:
A. Confessions
B. Confessions of a Lover
C. Confessions of an English Opium Eater

47. Who wrote the following two books :
A. *A Passage to England*
B. *A Passage to India*

48. Which famous character, created by Jonathan Swift, found himself lying on the island of Laputa?

49. Name the British jounalist and author of best-sellers like *Day of the jackal, The Odessa File* and *The Dogs of War.*

50. Which German philosopher wrote *Critique of Pure Reason*?

51. Name the Hungarian author of *Darkness at Noon.*

52. Name the ghost who narrates the stories to king Vikramaditya.

53. Who wrote the famous sea-story *The Cruel Sea*?

54. Which country is the setting for the famous story of *Alibaba and the Forty Thieves*?

55. Name the authors of the following books:
A. *Making Peace with Partition*
B. *The Grapes of Wrath*

56. Who wrote the book *Pather Panchali*?

57. Which staunch socialist leader of India wrote *Prison Diary*?

58. Who wrote *Small is Beautiful: A study of Economics as if people Mattered*?

59. Who is considered the Father of comedy?

60. Who wrote the book *Somnium*, regarded by some people as the first science fiction to be written?

61. Who wrote the book *The Great Indian Novel*?

62. Who wrote the famous sea-story *The Rover*?

63. Dr. Samuel Johnson's biography was written by ....

64. Name the Sanskrit writer who wrote the famous *Kamasutra.*

65. Which English author is known for his works like *The Time Machine, Kipps* and *The Outline of History*?

66. Which English writer developed the stream-of-consciousness technique and is known for works like *To the Lighthouse, Mrs. Dalloway* and *Orlando*?

67. Which Indian authored *Bread, Beauty and Revolution*?

68. A business tycoon of world fame, authored *Business @ the Speed of Thought.* Name him.

69. Who wrote the following books:
A. *Conquest of Self*
B. *Devdas*

70. Give the names of the authors of following books:
A. *The Book of Negroes* B. *The God of Small Things*
C. *Hungary Stones* D. *The Water Babies*

71. Name the British historian who authored the adage "power tends to corrupt and absolute power corrupts absolutely".

72. Which Indian Sanskrit scholar and poet wrote *Kadambari* and *Harsha Charita*?

73. Which Italian author and humanist, also called the Father of the Novel, wrote *Life of Dante*?

74. Who said it— "All the world is a stage And all the man and women merely players"?

75. Name the French educationist, who as a (blind) teacher of the blind, devised the touch system of reading and writing for blind.
(**Clue:** She died in the year 2000.)

76. Name the authentic book on statecraft by Chanakya (Kautilya) (4th century B.C.).

77. Which English poet wrote *The Canterbury Tales*?

78. Who wrote the following books:
A. Secrets of the World's Inspirational Women (Westland);
B. Gandhi : A Political and Spiritual Life
C. *Brushes with History : Autobiography of Dr. K.K. Birla*

79. Which football player's autobiography, released in 2007, is titled 'Moments'?

80. Along which famous road is Rudyard Kipling's novel *Kim* set?

81. In *Alice in Wonderland,* a fictional work of Lewis Caroll, to which animal does Alice first speak in French?

82. In which book of the Old Testament were the Ten Commandments first listed?

83. Name the musical maestro whose work is '*The Secret of My Life*'.

84. Name the author of the following works.
A. My Truth B. India Divided

85. Name the Indian aristocrat whose work is 'India– *From Midnight to the Mellenium*'.

86. Who is the author of '*The Post American World*'?

87. Name the Indian-born American who authored the prize winner book 'The Namesake'?

88. Who is the author of the prize winner book 'The White Tiger'?

ANSWERS

1. A. Angshumita Deka.
B. Jaya-shree Gupta.
C. Sebastian Faulks.
D. Jeffrey Archer.

2. Rudyard Kipling, in 1907.

3. Dalai Lama.

4. Cao Chan (he wrote 80 of the 120 chapters). Following his death in 1763, Kao Eh finished it.

5. A. Mrs. Benazir Bhutto;
B. Lal Krishna Advani;
C. Shyam Bhatia.

6. Abul Kalam Azad (1888-1958).

7. Jayant Narlikar.

8. George Bancroft (1800-1891).

9. William Blake (1757-1827).

10. Salman Rushdie.

11. Emily Bronte (1818-48).

12. Col. Muammar al Gaddafi (1924-2011). (He took power in a coup in 1969 and became President in 1977).

13. Sir Anthony Eden.

14. The ongoing biography of Sir Winston Churchill, coauthored by his son Randolph and the historian Martin Gilbert (both UK).

15. J.K. Rowling.

16. Krishna Chaitanya.

17. P.M. Nair.

18. *A Suitable Boy* (p. 1349) by Vikram Seth.

19. Benazir Bhutto.

20. Vladimir Nabokov (1899-1977).

21. Kumara Padmanabha Shivashankar Menon (1898-1982).

22. Ved Mehta (b. 1934).

23. Bankim Chandra Chattopadhyaya (1834-94). He is often called the 'Father of the Indian novel'.

24. Sir Winston Churchill (1874-1965).

25. Nirad C. Chaudhary (1897-1999).

26. Jonathan Swift (1667-1745).

27. Salman Rushdie (b. 1946).

28. Romain Rolland (1866-1944).

29. Dr. Sarvepalli Radhakrishnan (1888-1975).

30. Munshi Premchand (1880-1936).

31. Plato (427-347 B.C.). He was a pupil of legendary Socrates and teacher of Aristotle.

32. Lexicography.

33. Charles Lutwidge Dodgson.

34. *Man-eaters of Kumaon*.

35. Geoffery Chaucer.

36. Bibliophobia.

37. P.V. Narasimha Rao.

38. *My Music and My Life*.

39. A. *The Dream of the Red Chamber*.
B. Cao Chan wrote 80 of the 120 chapters of the book. Following his death in 1763, Kao Eh finished it.

40. A. Ved Mehta.
B. *Mahatma Gandhi*.

41. J.W. Von Goethe.

42. Edgar Rice Burroughs.

43. Dr. Watson.

44. Edgar Wallace (1875-1932).

45. Oscar Wilde (1854-1900).

46. A. J.J. Rousseau.
B. Mulk Raj Anand.
C. Thomas De Quincey.

47. A. Nirad C. Choudhuri.
B. E.M. Forster.

48. Gulliver.

49. Fredrick Forsyth (b.1939).

50. Immanuel Kant (1724-1804).

51. Arthur Koestler (1905-83).

52. Betaal.

53. Nicholas Monsarrat.

54. Persia.

55. A. Radha Kumar.
B. John Steinbeck.

56. Bibhuti Bhushan.

57. Jayaprakash Narayan.

58. Ernst Schumacher.

59. Aristophanes.

60. Johannes Kepler.

61. Shashi Tharoor.

62. Joseph Conrad.

63. James Boswell.

64. Vatsyayana (5th century A.D.).

65. Herbert George Wells (1866-1946).

66. Virginia Woolf (1882-1941).

67. Khwaja Ahmad Abbas.

68. Bill Gates.

69. A. Mahatma Gandhi.
B. Sarat Chandra.

70. A. Lawrence Hill.
B. Arundhati Roy.
C. Rabindranath Tagore.
D. Charles Kingsley.

71. John Acton (1834-1902).

72. Banabhatta (7th Century).

73. Giovanni Boccaccio.

74. Shakespeare.

75. Louis Braille (1809-52).

76. *Artha Shastra*.

77. Geoffrey Chaucer.

78. A. Zerbanoo Gifford.
B. Kathryn Tidrick.
C. Sonia Gandhi.

79. Christiano Ronaldo.

80. Grand Trunk Road.

81. The Mouse.

82. Exodus.

83. Zubin Mehta.

84. A. Smt. Indira Gandhi.
B. Dr. Rajendra Prasad.

85. Shashi Tharoor.

86. Farid Zakaria.

87. Jhumpa Lahiri.

88. Arvind Adiga.

Mathematics

1

Rational Numbers

Rational Numbers

A rational number is defined as a rational number of the form $\frac{p}{q}$, where p and q are integers and $q \neq 0$.

The set of rational numbers encloses the set of integers and fractions. The rules given above for addition, subtraction, multiplication and division also apply on rational numbers.

Rational numbers that are not integral will have decimal values. These values can be of two types:

(a) Terminating (or Finite) Decimal Fractions:

For example : $\frac{17}{4} = 4.25$, $\frac{21}{5} = 4.2$ and so forth

(b) Non terminating Decimal Fractions: Amongst non-terminating decimal fractions there are two types of decimal values:

(i) Non-terminating Periodic Fractions: These are non-terminating decimal fractions of the type $x.a_1a_2a_3...a_n\ a_1a_2a_3...a_n\ a_1a_2a_3...a_n$ written as $x.\overline{a_1\,a_2\,a_3...a_n}$

For example : $\frac{1}{3} = 0.3333\ ... = 0.\bar{3}$

$\frac{16}{3} = 5.333\ .... = 5.\bar{3}$ and so on.

(c) Non-terminating Non-periodic Fractions: These are the form $x.\ b_1b_2b_3...b_n\ \ c_1c_2c_3...\ c_n$

For example : 5.2731687143...

Pure Recurring Decimal : A decimal in which all the digits after the decimal point are repeated. For Example : $0.\bar{6}$, $0.\overline{16}$, ...$0.\overline{123}$.

Mixed Recurring Decimal : A decimal in which at least one of the digits after the decimal points is not repeated and then same digit and digits are repeated.

For example : $2.1\bar{6}$, $0.3\bar{5}$, $0.78\bar{5}$

Conversion of Pure Recurring of the form $\frac{p}{q}$:

Example 1: (*i*) $0.\bar{3}$, (*ii*) $0.\overline{35}$, (*iii*) $0.\overline{585}$

(*i*) Let $x = 0.\bar{3}$ Then,

$x = 0.3333...$ ...(*i*)

$10x = 3.3333...$ ...(*ii*)

On subtracting (*i*) from (*ii*), we get

$9x = 3$

$x = \frac{3}{9} = \frac{1}{3}$

$\Rightarrow 0.\bar{3} = \frac{1}{3}$ *i.e.,* $0.333... = \frac{1}{3}$

(*ii*) Let $x = 0.\overline{35}$ Then,

$x = 0.353535...$ ...(*i*)

$100x = 35.3535...$ ...(*ii*)

On subtracting (*i*) from (*ii*), we get

$99x = 35$

$x = \frac{35}{99}$

$\therefore 0.\overline{35} = \frac{35}{99}$

(*iii*) Let $x = 0.\overline{585}$, Then

$x = 0.585\ 585\ 585$ ...(*i*)

$1000x = 585.585\ 585...$ ...(*ii*)

On subtracting (*i*) from (*ii*)

$999x = 585$

$x = \frac{585}{999}$

$\therefore 0.\overline{585} = \frac{585}{999}$

Shortcut : Write down the bar digit in numerator of a fraction and write down the same number of digit 9 in denominator of the fraction. For example:

$0.\bar{3} = \frac{3}{9}$, $0.\overline{35} = \frac{35}{99}$, $0.\overline{585} = \frac{585}{999}$,

$2.\bar{3} = 2 + 0.\bar{3} = 2 + \frac{3}{9} = 2 + \frac{1}{3} = 2\frac{1}{3} = \frac{7}{3}$

$15.\overline{32} = 15 + 0.\overline{32} = 15 + \frac{32}{99} = 15\frac{32}{99}$

Conversion of Mixed Recurring Fraction into $\frac{p}{q}$ form :

$0.235\ 35\ 35\ ... = 0.2\overline{35}$

Let $x = 0.2\overline{35}$

Then, $10x = 2.\overline{35}$

$10x = 2 + 0.\overline{35}$

$10x = 2 + \frac{35}{99}$

$10x = \frac{2 \times 99 + 35}{99} = \frac{198 + 35}{99}$

$10x = \frac{233}{99} \Rightarrow x = \frac{233}{990}$

(*ii*) $15.7\overline{12}$

Let $x = 15.7\overline{12}$

Then, $10x = 157.\overline{12}$

$10x = 157 + 0.\overline{12}$

$10x = 157 + \frac{12}{99}$

$10x = 157 + \frac{4}{33}$

$10x = \frac{157 \times 33 + 4}{33}$

$10x = \frac{5185}{33}$

$x = \frac{5185}{330}$

Irrational Numbers: A number is an irrational number, if it has a non-terminating and non-repeating decimal representation *i.e.*, irrational number can not be written in the form of $\frac{p}{q}$, where p and q are both integers and $q \neq 0$.

For example : $\sqrt{2}, \sqrt{3}$.

If a and b are two positive rational numbers such that ab is not a perfect square of a rational number then, $\sqrt{ab}$ is an irrational number lying between a and b. Also if a, b are rational numbers, then $\frac{a+b}{2}$ is a rational number between them.

Example 1 : Insert a rational and an irrational number between 2 and 3.

Sol. A rational Number between 2 and 3

$= \frac{2+3}{2} = 2.5$

An irrational Number between 2 and 3

$= \sqrt{2 \times 3} = \sqrt{6}$

Some useful results on Rational/Irrational Number

(*i*) $\sqrt{n}$ is rational number if n is a perfect square. For example, $\sqrt{4}, \sqrt{9}, \sqrt{16}$

(*ii*) Negative of an irrational number is an irrational number.

(*iii*) The sum of a rational number and an irrational number is an irrational number.

(*iv*) The product of a non-zero rational number and an irrational number is an irrational number.

(*v*) The sum, difference, product and quotient of two irrational number need not be an irrational number.

(*vi*) π is an irrational number.

(*vii*) Decimal expansion of a rational number is either terminating or non-terminating (recurring).

(*viii*) Decimal expansion of an irrational number is non-terminating non-recurring.

(*ix*) A real number is either rational or irrational number.

Comparison of Fraction

1. If the denominator of the fractions are same, the largest is one whose numerator is the largest.

Example : Which is the largest fraction among $\frac{3}{8}, \frac{7}{8}$ and $\frac{5}{8}$?

Solution: $\frac{7}{8}$

2. If the numerators of the fractions are same, the largest is one whose denominator is the smallest.

Example : Which is the largest fraction among $\frac{5}{2}, \frac{5}{7}$ and $\frac{5}{9}$?

Solution : $\frac{5}{2}$

3. If neither the numerators nor denominators of the fraction are same then they are converted into equivalent fractions of the same, denominator by taking the L.C.M. of the denominators of the given fractions. Then the fractions are compared according to (1).

Example : Which is the largest fraction among $\frac{1}{2}, \frac{2}{3}, \frac{4}{5}$ and $\frac{5}{8}$.

Solution : LCM of 2, 3, 5 and 8 = 120

Then, $\frac{1}{2} = \frac{1 \times 60}{2 \times 60} = \frac{60}{120}$

$\frac{2}{3} = \frac{2 \times 40}{3 \times 40} = \frac{80}{120}$

$$\frac{4}{5} = \frac{4 \times 24}{5 \times 24} = \frac{96}{120}$$

$$\frac{5}{8} = \frac{5 \times 15}{8 \times 15} = \frac{75}{120}$$

Largest fraction = $\frac{96}{120}$, that is $\frac{4}{5}$

4. Two fractions can also be compared by cross multiplication method.

Example : Which is greater $\frac{6}{13}$ or $\frac{5}{7}$?

Solution: Step 1 : Cross multiplying the two given fractions

$$\frac{6}{13} \times \frac{5}{7}$$

We get 6 × 7 = 42 and 13 × 5 = 65

Step 2 : Since 65 is greater than 42 and in 65, the numerator of $\frac{5}{7}$ is included.

$\therefore$ $\frac{5}{7}$ is greater than $\frac{6}{13}$.

5. If the difference of the numerator and denominator of each of the given fractions be same, then the fraction of the largest numerator is the largest.

Example : Which one of the following fractions is the largest $\frac{2}{3}, \frac{3}{4}, \frac{5}{6}$ and $\frac{9}{10}$?

Solution : Since in each of the given fractions the difference between the numerator and denominator is same and the largest numerator is 9. Therefore, the largest fraction is $\frac{9}{10}$.

Multiple Choice Questions

1. The decimal form of an irrational number is neither .... nor ....

A. terminating, repeating
B. terminating, non-repeating
C. non-terminating, non-repeating
D. non-terminating, repeating

2. π is a/an :

A. rational number
B. irrational number
C. neither rational nor irrational number
D. None of these

3. The decimal representation of a rational number is either .... or ....

A. terminating, recurring
B. non-terminating, non-recurring
C. terminating, non-terminating, recurring
D. None of these

4. Which one of the following statements is true?

A. The sum of two irrational numbers is always an irrational number.
B. The sum of two irrational numbers is always a rational number.
C. The sum of two irrational numbers may be a rational number or an irrational number.
D. The sum of two irrational numbers is always an integer.

5. Which of the following is a correct statement?

A. Sum of two irrational numbers is always irrational.
B. Sum of a rational and irrational number is always an irrational number.
C. Square of an irrational number is always a rational number.
D. Sum of two rational numbers can never be an integer.

6. Which of the following statements is true?

A. Product of two irrational numbers is always irrational.
B. Product of a rational and an irrational number is always irrational.
C. Sum of two irrational numbers can never be irrational.
D. Sum of an integer and a rational number can never be an integer.

7. Which of the following is irrational?

A. $\sqrt{\frac{4}{9}}$ B. $\frac{4}{5}$
C. $\sqrt{7}$ D. $\sqrt{81}$

8. Which of the following is irrational?

A. 0.14
B. $0.14\overline{16}$
C. $0.\overline{1416}$
D. 0.1014001400014

9. Which of the following is rational?

A. $\sqrt{3}$ B. π
C. $\frac{4}{0}$ D. $\frac{0}{4}$

10. The number 0.318564318564318564.... is:

A. a natural number B. an integer

C. a rational number D. an irrational number

11. $23.\overline{43}$ when expressed in the form $\frac{p}{q}$ (p, q are integers, $q \neq 0$), is:

A. $\frac{2320}{99}$ B. $\frac{2343}{100}$

C. $\frac{2343}{999}$ D. $\frac{2320}{199}$

12. $0.\overline{001}$ when expressed in the form $\frac{p}{q}$ (p, q are integers, $q \neq 0$), is:

A. $\frac{1}{1000}$ B. $\frac{1}{100}$

C. $\frac{1}{1999}$ D. $\frac{1}{999}$

13. The value of $0.\overline{23}+0.\overline{22}$ is:

A. $0.\overline{45}$ B. $0.\overline{43}$

C. $0.\overline{42}$ D. 45

14. $5.\overline{23}+6.\overline{33}-3.\overline{11} = ?$

A. $8.\overline{55}$ B. $7.\overline{45}$

C. $8.\overline{45}$ D. $9.\overline{25}$

15. If $\sqrt{12} = 3.464$, value of $\sqrt{\frac{3}{4}}+2\sqrt{\frac{4}{3}}$ is:

A. 3.17 B. 3.464

C. 3.1753 D. None of these

ANSWERS

1	2	3	4	5	6	7	8	9	10
A	B	C	C	B	B	C	D	D	C
11	**12**	**13**	**14**	**15**					
A	D	A	C	C					

EXPLANATORY ANSWERS

7. $\sqrt{\frac{4}{9}} = \frac{2}{3}$, $\frac{p}{q}$ form $q \neq 0$ rational number

$\frac{4}{5}$, $\frac{p}{q}$ form, $q \neq 0$ rational number

$\sqrt{7}$, $\sqrt{7}$ is not an integer ∴ Irrational number

$\sqrt{81} = \frac{9}{1}$, $\frac{p}{q}$ form, $q \neq 0$, rational number

10. 0.318564318564318 ....

$0.\overline{31854}$ (Recurring form)

∴ This is a rational number

11. $23.\overline{43} = 23+0.\overline{43} = 23 + \frac{43}{99}$

$$= \frac{23\times99+43}{99} = \frac{2277+43}{99} = \frac{2320}{99}$$

13. $0.\overline{23}+0.\overline{22} = \frac{23}{99}+\frac{22}{99}$

$$= \frac{23+22}{99} = \frac{45}{99} = 0.\overline{45}$$

14. $5+0.\overline{23}+6+0.\overline{33}-3-0.\overline{11}$

$$= 8+0.\overline{56}-0.\overline{11} = 8+0.\overline{45} = 8.\overline{45}$$

15. $\sqrt{\frac{3}{4}}+2\sqrt{\frac{4}{3}} = \sqrt{\frac{9}{12}}+2\times\sqrt{\frac{12}{9}}$

$$= \frac{3}{\sqrt{12}}+2\times\frac{\sqrt{12}}{3}$$

$$= \frac{3}{3.464}+2\times\frac{3.464}{3}$$

$$= 0.8660 + 2.3093 = 3.1753$$

□□□□□

2

Square and Square Root

☛ Points To Remember

- A number n is a perfect square number, if $n = m^2$
- A perfect square number is never negative.
- A square number never ends in 2, 3, 7 or 8.
- The number of zeros at the end of a perfect square is even.
- The square of an even number is even.
- The square of an odd number is odd.
- There are no natural number p and q such that $p^2 = 2q^2$.
- A number m is a square root of n, if $n = m \times m = m^2$. Positive square root of n is written as $\sqrt{n}$.
- If p and q are perfect squares ($q \neq 0$), then
  (*i*) $\sqrt{p \times q} = \sqrt{p} \times \sqrt{q}$
  (*ii*) $\sqrt{\dfrac{p}{q}} = \dfrac{\sqrt{p}}{\sqrt{q}}$
- A perfect squares leaves remainder 0 or 1 on division by 3.
  The following table gives the possible remainders for some other prime divisors.

Divisor	Possible Remainders
3	0, 1
5	0, 1, 4
7	0, 1, 2, 4
11	0, 1, 3, 4, 5, 9
13	0, 1, 3, 4, 9, 10, 12

- The unit's digit of the square of a natural number is the unit's digit of the square of the digit at unit's place of the given natural number.

Unit's digit of the number	Unit's digit of the square of the number
0	0
1 or 9	1
2 or 8	4
3 or 7	9
4 or 6	6
5	5

- For every natural number n,
  $$(n + 1)^2 - n^2 = (n + 1) + n$$
  e.g.; $9^2 - 8^2 = 9 + 8 = 17$
  $19^2 - 18^2 = 19 + 18 = 37$
- The square of a natural number n is equal to the sum of first n odd natural numbers.
  e.g.; $2^2 = 1 + 3$
  $4^2 = 1 + 3 + 5 + 7 = 16$
  n^2 = Sum of first n odd natural numbers.
- A triplet (m, n, p) of three natural numbers m, n and p is called a pythagorean triplet if $m^2 + n^2 = p^2$
- The square root of a perfect square number can be obtained by :
  (*i*) the prime factorization.
  (*ii*) the division method.
- If n is not a perfect square, then $\sqrt{n}$ is not a rational number.
- Squares of natural numbers having all digits 1 have a following pattern:

$1^2 = 1$
$11^2 = 1\ \mathbf{2}\ 1$
$111^2 = 1\ 2\ \mathbf{3}\ 2\ 1$
$1111^2 = 1\ 2\ 3\ \mathbf{4}\ 3\ 2\ 1$
$11111^2 = 1\ 2\ 3\ 4\ \mathbf{5}\ 4\ 3\ 2\ 1$
$111111^2 = 1\ 2\ 3\ 4\ 5\ \mathbf{6}\ 5\ 4\ 3\ 2\ 1$
⋮
$111111111^2 = 1\ 2\ 3\ 4\ 5\ 6\ 7\ 8\ \mathbf{9}\ 8\ 7\ 6\ 5\ 4\ 3\ 2\ 1$

In this pattern the sum of the digits of every number on the right hand side is a perfect square at given below:

$1 + 2 + 1 = 4 = 2^2$
$1 + 2 + 3 + 2 + 1 = 9 = 3^2$
$1 + 2 + 3 + 4 + 3 + 2 + 1 = 16 = 4^2$
. . . .
$1 + 2 + 3 + 4 + 5 + 6 + 7 + 8 + 9 + 8 + 7 + 6 + 5 + 4 + 3 + 2 + 1 = 81 = 9^2$.

- Observe the following pattern

$11^2 = 121$
$101^2 = 10201$
$1001^2 = 1002001$
$10001^2 = 100020001$

- Observe the following pattern

$$11^2 = 121$$
$$101^2 = 10201$$
$$10101^2 = 102030201$$
$$1010101^2 = 1020304030201$$
$$101010101^2 = 10203040504030201$$

- **Short Cut Method to find Squares Column Method**

Using $(a + b)^2 = a^2 + 2ab + b^2$.

Make three columns: What is square of 86

$a = 8, b = 6$

Step	Column I (a^2)	Column II $2ab$	Column III b^2
I	$(8)^2 = 64$	$2 \times 8 \times 6 = 96$	$(6)^2 = 36$
II	64	96 + 3 = 99	**36**
III	64 + 9 = **73**	96 + 3 = **99**	**36**

The bold digits give the required square $86^2 = 7396$.

Square Root

Square root of a given number is that number which is multiplied by itself is equal to the given number.

For example, square root of 81 is 9 because $92 = 9 \times 9 = 81$.

Methods of Finding the square root

(a) Prime Factorization Method

(i) Prime Factorization Method

(ii) Group the Factors in Paris

(iii) Take one number from each pair of factors and then multiply them together.

Example: Find the square root of 4761?

Solution: $4761 = \underbrace{23 \times 23} \times \underbrace{3 \times 3}$

$\therefore \sqrt{4761} = 23 \times 3 = 69.$

(b) Method of Division: This method is used when the number is large and the factors cannot be easily determined.

Example: Find the square root of 226576?

Solution:

```
        476
   4 | 226516
     | 16
  87 |  665
   7 |  609
 946 |   5676
   6 |   5676
     |     ×
```

$\sqrt[2]{226576} = 476.$

Multiple Choice Questions

1. $\sqrt{53824} = ?$

A. 202 B. 232

C. 242 D. 332

2. The value of $\sqrt{10+\sqrt{25+\sqrt{108+\sqrt{154+\sqrt{255}}}}}$ is:

A. 4 B. 6

C. 8 D. 10

3. Evaluate : $\sqrt{41-\sqrt{21+\sqrt{19-\sqrt{9}}}}$.

A. 3 B. 5

C. 6 D. 6.4

4. $\left(\frac{\sqrt{625}}{11} \times \frac{14}{\sqrt{25}} \times \frac{11}{\sqrt{196}}\right)$ is equal to:

A. 5 B. 6

C. 8 D. 11

5. If $x * y = x + y + \sqrt{xy}$, the value of 6*24 is:

A. 41 B. 42

C. 43 D. 44

6. $\sqrt{\frac{25}{81} - \frac{1}{9}} = ?$

A. $\frac{2}{3}$ B. $\frac{4}{9}$

C. $\frac{16}{81}$ D. $\frac{25}{81}$

7. The value of $\sqrt{0.01} + \sqrt{0.81} + \sqrt{1.21} + \sqrt{0.0009}$ is:

A. 2.03 B. 2.1

C. 2.11 D. 2.13

8. If $\sqrt{18225} = 135$, then the value of $\left(\sqrt{182.25} + \sqrt{1.8225} + \sqrt{0.018225} + \sqrt{0.00018225}\right)$ is:

A. 1.49985 B. 14.9985

C. 149.985 D. 1499.85

9. If $\sqrt{3^n} = 729$, then the value of n is:

A. 6 B. 8

C. 10 D. 12

10. If $\sqrt{1+\frac{x}{169}} = \frac{14}{13}$, then x is equal to:

A. 1 B. 13
C. 27 D. None of these

11. What is the least number which should be subtracted from 549162 in order to make it a perfect square?
A. 28 B. 36
C. 62 D. 81

12. If $\sqrt{\left(1+\frac{27}{169}\right)}=1+\frac{x}{13}$, then x equals:
A. 1 B. 3
C. 5 D. 7

13. $\sqrt{3\sqrt{3\sqrt{3\sqrt{3\sqrt{3\sqrt{3}}}}}}=?$
A. $3^{\frac{31}{64}}$ B. $3^{\frac{31}{32}}$
C. $3^{\frac{1}{64}}$ D. None of these

14. $\sqrt{248+\sqrt{52+\sqrt{144}}}=?$
A. 14 B. 16
C. 16.6 D. 18.8

15. Given that $\sqrt{4096}=64$, the value of $\sqrt{4096}+\sqrt{40.96}+\sqrt{.004096}$ is:
A. 70.4 B. 70.464
C. 71.104 D. 71.4

16. If $\sqrt{0.03\times0.3\times a}=0.03\times0.3\times\sqrt{b}$, then the value of $\frac{a}{b}$ is:
A. 0.009 B. 0.03
C. 0.09 D. None of these

17. If $\sqrt{1+\sqrt{1-\frac{2176}{2401}}}=1+\frac{x}{7}$, then the value of x is:
A. 3 B. 1
C. 5 D. 7

18. If $a=\frac{\sqrt{5}+1}{\sqrt{5}-1}$ and $b=\frac{\sqrt{5}-1}{\sqrt{5}+1}$; then the value of $\frac{a^2+ab+b^2}{a^2-ab+b^2}$ is:
A. $\frac{3}{4}$ B. $\frac{4}{3}$
C. $\frac{3}{5}$ D. $\frac{5}{3}$

19. The smallest number by which 3600 must be multiplied to make if perfect cube, is:
A. 40 B. 60
C. 20 D. 15

20. If $\sqrt{12}=3.464$, then the value of $\sqrt{\frac{3}{4}}+2\sqrt{\frac{4}{3}}$ is:
A. 3.17 B. 3.464
C. 3.1753 D. None of these

ANSWERS

1	2	3	4	5	6	7	8	9	10
B	A	C	A	B	B	D	B	D	C
11	**12**	**13**	**14**	**15**	**16**	**17**	**18**	**19**	**20**
D	A	B	B	B	A	B	B	B	C

EXPLANATORY ANSWERS

1.

```
  2 | 53824 (232
    | 4
 43 | 138
    | 129
462 |  924
    |  924
    |   ×
```

$\therefore\ \sqrt{53824}=232.$

2. Given exp. $=\sqrt{10+\sqrt{25+\sqrt{108+\sqrt{154+15}}}}$

$=\sqrt{10+\sqrt{25+\sqrt{108+\sqrt{169}}}}$

$=\sqrt{10+\sqrt{25+\sqrt{108+13}}}=\sqrt{10+\sqrt{25+\sqrt{121}}}$

$=\sqrt{10+\sqrt{25+11}}=\sqrt{10+\sqrt{36}}$

$=\sqrt{10+6}=\sqrt{16}=4$

3. Given exp. $=\sqrt{41-\sqrt{21+\sqrt{19-3}}}$

$=\sqrt{41-\sqrt{21+\sqrt{16}}}=\sqrt{41-\sqrt{21+4}}$

$=\sqrt{41-\sqrt{25}}=\sqrt{41-5}=\sqrt{36}=6$

4. Given exp. $=\frac{25}{11}\times\frac{14}{5}\times\frac{11}{14}=5$

5. $6*24 = 6 + 24 + \sqrt{6\times 24} = 30+\sqrt{144} = 30+12 = 42$

6. $\sqrt{\frac{25}{81}-\frac{1}{9}} = \sqrt{\frac{25-9}{81}} = \sqrt{\frac{16}{81}} = \frac{\sqrt{16}}{\sqrt{81}} = \frac{4}{9}$

7. Given exp. $= \sqrt{\frac{1}{100}}+\sqrt{\frac{81}{100}}+\sqrt{\frac{121}{100}}+\sqrt{\frac{9}{10000}}$

$= \frac{1}{10}+\frac{9}{10}+\frac{11}{10}+\frac{3}{100}$

$= 0.1 + 0.9 + 1.1 + 0.03 = 2.13$

8. Given exp. $= \sqrt{\frac{18225}{10^2}}+\sqrt{\frac{18225}{10^4}}+\sqrt{\frac{18225}{10^6}}+\sqrt{\frac{18225}{10^8}}$

$= \frac{\sqrt{18225}}{10}+\frac{\sqrt{18225}}{10^2}+\frac{\sqrt{18225}}{10^3}+\frac{\sqrt{18225}}{10^4}$

$= \frac{135}{10}+\frac{135}{100}+\frac{135}{1000}+\frac{135}{10000}$

$= 13.5 + 1.35 + 0.135 + 0.0135 = 14.9985$

9. $\sqrt{3^n} = 729 = 3^6 \Leftrightarrow \left(\sqrt{3^n}\right)^2 = (3^6)^2$

$\Leftrightarrow 3^n = 3^{12} \Leftrightarrow n = 12$

10. $\sqrt{1+\frac{x}{169}}=\frac{14}{13} \Rightarrow 1+\frac{x}{169}=\frac{196}{169}$

$\Rightarrow \frac{x}{169}=\left(\frac{196}{169}-1\right)=\frac{27}{169} \Rightarrow x = 27.$

11.

7	$\overline{54}\,\overline{91}\,\overline{62}$ (741
	49
144	591
	576
1481	1562
	1481
	81

$\therefore$ Required number to be subtracted = 81.

12. $\sqrt{1+\frac{27}{169}} = 1+\frac{x}{13} \Rightarrow \sqrt{\frac{196}{169}} = \frac{13+x}{13}$

$\frac{14}{13} = \frac{13+x}{13} \Rightarrow 14 = 13 + x$

$\therefore \quad x = 1$

13. $\sqrt{3\sqrt{3\sqrt{3\sqrt{3.3^{\frac{1}{2}}}}}} = \sqrt{3\sqrt{3\sqrt{3.3^{\frac{3}{4}}}}} = \sqrt{3\sqrt{3.3^{\frac{7}{8}}}}$

$= \sqrt{3.3^{\frac{15}{16}}} = 3^{\frac{31}{32}}$

14. $\sqrt{248+\sqrt{52+12}} = \sqrt{248+\sqrt{64}}$

$= \sqrt{248+8} = \sqrt{256} = 16$

15. $\sqrt{4096}+\sqrt{\frac{4096}{100}}+\sqrt{\frac{4096}{1000000}} = 64 = \frac{64}{10}+\frac{64}{1000}$

$= 64 + 6.4 + 0.064 = 70.464$

16. $\sqrt{0.03\times 0.3\times a} = 0.03\times 0.3\times\sqrt{b}$

Taking square of both sides, we get

$0.03 \times 0.3 \times a = 0.03 \times 0.3 \times 0.03 \times 0.3 \times b$

$\frac{a}{b} = \frac{0.03\times 0.3}{1} = 0.009$

17. We have,

$\sqrt{1+\sqrt{\frac{225}{2401}}} = 1+\frac{x}{7} \Rightarrow \sqrt{1+\frac{15}{49}} = 1+\frac{x}{7}$

$\sqrt{\frac{64}{49}} = 1+\frac{x}{7} \Rightarrow \frac{8}{7} = 1+\frac{x}{7}$

$1+\frac{1}{7} = 1+\frac{x}{7}$

$\therefore \quad x = 1$

18. $a + b = \frac{\sqrt{5}+1}{\sqrt{5}-1}+\frac{\sqrt{5}-1}{\sqrt{5}+1} = \frac{(\sqrt{5}+1)^2+(\sqrt{5}-1)^2}{(\sqrt{5})^2-(1)^2}$

$\therefore \quad = \frac{2(\sqrt{5})^2+(1)^2}{5-1} = \frac{6}{2} = 3$

$ab = \frac{\sqrt{5}+1}{\sqrt{5}-1}\times\frac{\sqrt{5}-1}{\sqrt{5}+1} = 1$

$\frac{a^2+ab+b^2}{a^2-ab+b^2} = \frac{(a+b)^2-2ab+ab}{(a+b)^2-2ab-ab}$

$= \frac{(a+b)^2-ab}{(a+b)^2-3ab}$

$= \frac{(3)^2-1}{(3)^2-3\times 1} = \frac{9-1}{9-3} = \frac{8}{6} = \frac{4}{3}$

19.

3	3600
3	1200
2	400
2	200
2	100
2	50
5	25
5	5
5	1

$3600 = 3 \times 3 \times 2 \times 2 \times 2 \times 2 \times 5 \times 5$

$= 3 \times 2 \times 2 \times 5 = 60$

20. $\sqrt{\frac{3}{4}}+2\sqrt{\frac{4}{3}} = \sqrt{\frac{12}{16}}+2\sqrt{\frac{12}{9}} = \frac{\sqrt{12}}{4}+2\times\frac{\sqrt{12}}{3}$

$= \frac{3.464}{4}+2\times\frac{3.464}{3}$

$= 0.866 + 2.3093 = 3.1753$

□□□□□

3

Cubes and Cube Roots

Points To Remember

- If n is a perfect cube and $n = m^3$, then m is a cube root of n. A cube root of n is written as $\sqrt[3]{n}$ or $(n)^{1/3}$.
- The cube root of a perfect cube can be obtained by prime factorization of the number.
- The cube root of a product of two perfect cubes is the product of the cube roots of the perfect cubes *i.e.*, $\sqrt[3]{ab} = \sqrt[3]{a} . \sqrt[3]{b}$
- The cube root of a Quotient of two perfect cubes is the quotient of their cube roots *i.e.*, $\sqrt[3]{\frac{a}{b}} = \frac{\sqrt[3]{a}}{\sqrt[3]{b}}$, $b \neq 0$, where a and b are perfect cubes.
- The cube root of a negative perfect cube is negative.

Number m	Perfect cubes m^3	Cube roots $\sqrt[3]{m^3}$
1	1	1
2	8	2
3	27	3
4	64	4
5	125	5
6	216	6
7	343	7
8	512	8
9	729	9
10	1000	10

Cube Root

The cube root of a given number is that number which when raised to the third power produces the given number, that is the cube root of a number x is the number whose cube is x.

The cube root of x is written as $\sqrt[3]{x}$

For example, cube root of 64 is 4 as $4 \times 4 \times 4 = 64$.

Method to find Cube Root

Method of Factorisation

(1) Write a given number as product of prime factors.
(2) Take the product of prime numbers; choosing one out of three of each type.

This product gives the cube root of the given number.

Example: Find the cube root of 42875.

Solution: Resolving 42875 into prime factors, we get

$$42875 = \underbrace{5 \times 5 \times 5}\times\underbrace{7 \times 7 \times 7}$$

$$\therefore \quad \sqrt[3]{4287} = 5 \times 7 = 35.$$

Multiple Choice Questions

1. What is the cube root of 2197?
A. 13 B. 15
C. 17 D. 19

2. What is the cube root of 117649?
A. 39 B. 49
C. 59 D. 65

3. What is the cube root of $\frac{343}{125}$?
A. $\frac{5}{7}$ B. $\frac{9}{11}$
C. $\frac{7}{5}$ D. $\frac{9}{5}$

4. What is the cube root of $-\frac{2197}{1331}$?
A. $-\frac{13}{11}$ B. $-\frac{13}{9}$
C. $-\frac{11}{13}$ D. $-\frac{13}{17}$

5. What is the unit digits of the cube root of 226981?
A. 1 B. 9
C. 6 D. 8

6. By what least number 675 be multiplied to obtain a number which is a perfect cube?
A. 5 B. 6
C. 7 D. 8

22. What is the smallest number by which 3600 be divided to make it a perfect cube?

A. 9 B. 50
C. 300 D. 450

23. $\sqrt[3]{0.000216}$ is equal to:

A. 0.0006 B. 0.006
C. 0.06 D. 0.6

24. If $1^3 + 2^3 + 3^3 + ... + 10^3 = 3025$, then the value of $2^3 + 4^3 + 6^3 + ... + 20^3$ is equal to:

A. 6050 B. 9075
C. 12100 D. 24200

25. $\sqrt[3]{333+\sqrt[3]{987+\sqrt[3]{2197}}}$

A. 21 B. 18
C. 7 D. 3

ANSWERS

1	2	3	4	5	6	7	8	9	10
A	B	C	A	A	A	D	C	A	C

EXPLANATORY ANSWERS

1. $(2197)^{1/3} = (13 \times 13 \times 13)^{1/3}$
$= [(13)^3]^{1/3}$
$= (13)^{3 \times 1/3}$

13	2197
13	169
13	13
	1

$= 13.$

Other Method: 2197, here unit digit is 7. Unit digit is cube root of 3, after striking out the last three digit from the right, the number is 2. 1 is the largest number whose cube is less than 2. The required cube root is 13.

2. $(117649)^{1/3} = 49$

3. $\sqrt[3]{\frac{343}{125}} = \sqrt[3]{\frac{7 \times 7 \times 7}{5 \times 5 \times 5}} = \frac{7}{5}$

4. $-\sqrt[3]{\frac{2197}{1331}} = -\sqrt[3]{\frac{13 \times 13 \times 13}{11 \times 11 \times 11}} = -\frac{13}{11}$

13	2197
13	169
13	13
	1

11	1331
11	121
11	11
	1

5. Unit digit of 226981 is

$(1)^3 = 1$

6. $675 = 5 \times 5 \times 3 \times 3 \times 3.$

To make it a perfect cube, it must be multiplied by 5.

7. $3600 = 2^3 \times 5^2 \times 3^2 \times 2.$

To make it a perfect cube, it must be divided by $5^2 \times 3^2 \times 2$ *i.e.*, 450.

8. $\sqrt[3]{\frac{216}{1000000}} = \frac{6}{100} = 0.06$

9. $2^3 + 4^3 + 6^3 + ... + 20^3$
$= 2(1^3 + 2^3 + 3^3 + ... + 10^3$
$= 2 \times 3025$
$= 6050$

10. $\sqrt[3]{333+\sqrt[3]{987+\sqrt[3]{(13)^3}}}$
$= \sqrt[3]{333+\sqrt[3]{987+13}}$
$= \sqrt[3]{333+\sqrt[3]{1000}}$
$= \sqrt[3]{333+10}$
$= \sqrt[3]{343} = 7$

□□□□□

4

Exponents and Powers

Points To Remember

- If n is a positive integer and a is a rational number, then $a^n = a \times a \times a \times ... \times a$ (n times)

  a^n is called the nth power of a. The rational number a is called **base** and n is called **Index** or **exponent** of the nth power of a.
- If $a^n = x$ then

  $a = (x)^{1/n}$.

  $(x)^{1/n}$ is also written in the form as $\sqrt[n]{x}$ and it is read as nth root of x. $\sqrt[n]{x}$ is called **Surd** and n is known as the **index of the Surd.**
- **Laws of indices :** If a and b be any two rational numbers and m, n are integer, then:

  (i) $a^m \times a^n = a^{m+n}$

  (ii) $a^m \div a^n = a^{m-n}$

  (iii) $a^m \div a^m = a^{m-m} = a^0 = 1$

  (iv) $(a \times b)^m = a^m \times b^m$

  (v) $(a^m)^n = a^{mn}$

  (vi) $(-a)^m = (-1)^m a^m$

  (vii) $\left(\frac{p}{q}\right)^m = \frac{p^m}{q^m}$, where p, q are integers and $q \neq 0$.

  (viii) $\left(\frac{p}{q}\right)^{-m} = \left(\frac{q}{p}\right)^m$

  (ix) $\left(\frac{p}{q}\right)^m \times \left(\frac{p}{q}\right)^n = \left(\frac{p}{q}\right)^{m+n}$

  (x) $\left(\frac{p}{q}\right)^m \div \left(\frac{p}{q}\right)^n = \left(\frac{p}{q}\right)^{m-n}$

  (xi) $\left[\left(\frac{p}{q}\right)^m\right]^n = \left(\frac{p}{q}\right)^{mn}$
- If a is a negative rational number and n is an odd positive integer, then the nth root of a is minus of the nth root of $|a|$.
- If a is a negative rational number and n is an even positive integer, then the nth root of a is not defined.
- Let a be any positive rational number and $\frac{m}{n}$ be a positive rational number in the lowest form. Then $a^{\frac{m}{n}}$ is defined as the nth root of a^m. *i.e.,* $a^{m/n} = (a^m)^{1/n}$.

  $$a^{-m/n} = \frac{1}{a^{m/n}}.$$
- If a is a rational number and n is a positive integer such that nth root of a *i.e.*, $(a)^{1/n}$ or $\sqrt[n]{a}$ is an irrational number, then $a^{1/n}$ is called a radical or a Surd of index n and a is called the radical.
- A radical that contains no rational factor other than 1, is called a pure radical.
- A radical which has a rational factor other than unity, the other factor being irrational, is called a mixed radical.
- A square root radical is said to be in simplest form, if

  (i) there is no fraction in the radicand

  (ii) no perfect square is a factor of radicand.

  (iii) there is no radical in the denominator.

Rationalisation

Some Identities : Let a and b be positive real numbers, then

(i) $\left(\sqrt{a}\right)^2 = a$

(ii) $\sqrt{a}\,\sqrt{b} = \sqrt{ab}$

(iii) $\frac{\sqrt{a}}{\sqrt{b}} = \sqrt{\frac{a}{b}}$

(iv) $\left(\sqrt{a}+\sqrt{b}\right)\left(\sqrt{a}-\sqrt{b}\right) = a - b$

(v) $\left(a+\sqrt{b}\right)\left(a-\sqrt{b}\right) = a^2 - b$

(vi) $\left(\sqrt{a} \pm \sqrt{b}\right)^2 = a \pm 2\sqrt{ab} + b$

(vii) $\left(\sqrt{a}+\sqrt{b}\right)\left(\sqrt{c}+\sqrt{d}\right) = \sqrt{ac}+\sqrt{ad}+\sqrt{bc}+\sqrt{bd}$

Rationalisation factor for $\frac{1}{\sqrt{a}}$ is $\sqrt{a}$ and for $\frac{1}{a \pm \sqrt{b}}$, the rationalisation factor is $a \mp \sqrt{b}$ [if $a^2 - b^2 = 1$]

Rationalisation factor for $\frac{1}{\sqrt{a} \pm \sqrt{b}}$ is $\sqrt{a} \mp \sqrt{b}$ [if $a^2 - b^2 = 1$)

Comparison of Surd

(*i*) If two surds are of the same order, then the one whose radicand is larger, is the larger of the two.

Ex: $\sqrt[3]{19} > \sqrt[3]{15}, \sqrt{7} > \sqrt{5}$ etc.

(*ii*) If two surds are distinct order, we change them into the surds of the same order.

This order is the L.C.M. of the orders of the given surds.

Ex. Which is the greatest out of $\sqrt[3]{5}, \sqrt[4]{3}, \sqrt[5]{4}$?

$$\sqrt[3]{5} = (5)^{\frac{1}{3}}$$

$$\sqrt[4]{3} = (3)^{\frac{1}{4}}$$

$$\sqrt[5]{4} = (4)^{\frac{1}{5}}$$

$\therefore$ LCM of (3, 4, 5) = 60

$$\sqrt[3]{5} = (5)^{\frac{1}{3}} = (5)^{\frac{20}{60}} = \sqrt[60]{(5)^{20}}$$

$$\sqrt[4]{3} = (3)^{\frac{1}{4}} = (3)^{\frac{15}{60}} = \sqrt[60]{(3)^{15}}$$

$$\sqrt[5]{4} = (4)^{\frac{1}{5}} = (4)^{\frac{12}{60}} = \sqrt[60]{(4)^{12}}$$

$\therefore$ $\sqrt[3]{5}$ is the greates.

Multiple Choice Questions

1. The value of $\{2 - 3\ (2 - 3)^3\}^3$ is:
A. 5 B. 125
C. 1/5 D. –125

2. $(256)^{0.16} \times (256)^{0.09}$:
A. 4 B. 16
C. 64 D. 256.25

3. If $10^{2y} = 25$, then 10^{-y} equals:
A. $-\frac{1}{5}$ B. $\frac{1}{50}$
C. $\frac{1}{625}$ D. $\frac{1}{5}$

4. The value of $x - y^{x-y}$ when $x = 2$ and $y = -2$ is:
A. 18 B. –18
C. 14 D. –14

5. If $9^{x+2} = 240 + 9^x$, then $x =$
A. 0.5 B. 0.2
C. 0.4 D. 0.1

6. If $8^{x+1} = 64$, what is the value of 3^{2x+1}?
A. 1 B. 3
C. 9 D. 27

7. If $4^x - 4^{x-1} = 24$, then $(2x)^x$ equals:
A. $5\sqrt{5}$ B. $\sqrt{5}$
C. $25\sqrt{5}$ D. 125

8. $\dfrac{5^{n+2} - 6 + 5^{n+1}}{13 \times 5^n - 2 \times 5^{n+1}}$ is equal to:
A. $\frac{5}{3}$ B. $-\frac{5}{3}$
C. $\frac{3}{5}$ D. $-\frac{3}{5}$

9. If $\left(\frac{2}{3}\right)^x \left(\frac{3}{2}\right)^{2x} = \frac{81}{16}$, then $x =$
A. 2 B. 3
C. 4 D. 1

10. If $(16)^{2x+3} = (64)^{x+3}$, then $4^{2x-2} =$
A. 64 B. 256
C. 32 D. 512

11. $\left(999\frac{1}{7} + 999\frac{2}{7} + 999\frac{3}{7} + 999\frac{4}{7} + 999 + \frac{5}{7} + 999\frac{6}{7}\right)$ is simplified to:
A. 2997 B. 5979
C. 5994 D. 5997

12. The value of $1 + \frac{1}{4 \times 3} + \frac{1}{4 \times 3^2} + \frac{1}{4 \times 3^3}$ is:
A. $\frac{121}{108}$ B. $\frac{3}{2}$
C. $\frac{31}{2}$ D. None of these

13. $\left(\dfrac{785 \times 785 \times 785 + 435 \times 435 \times 435}{785 \times 785 + 435 \times 435 - 785 \times 435}\right)$ simplifies to:
A. 350 B. 785
C. 1220 D. 1320

14. $\frac{1}{5} + 999\frac{494}{495} \times 99 = ?$
A. 90000 B. 90900
C. 99000 D. 99990

15. $\left(1 + \frac{1}{x+1}\right)\left(1 + \frac{1}{x+2}\right)\left(1 + \frac{1}{x+3}\right)\left(1 + \frac{1}{x+4}\right) = ?$
A. $\frac{x+5}{x+1}$ B. $\left(x + \frac{1}{x+5}\right)$
C. $\frac{1}{(x+5)}$ D. $\left(1 + \frac{1}{x+5}\right)$

ANSWERS

1	2	3	4	5	6	7	8	9	10
B	A	D	D	A	D	C	B	C	B
11	**12**	**13**	**14**	**15**					
D	A	C	C	A					

EXPLANATORY ANSWERS

2. $(256)^{0.16+0.09} = (256)^{0.25} = (256)^{\frac{1}{4}} = 4$

3. We have, $10^{2y} = 25$

$$(10^y)^2 = 25$$
$$10^y = \sqrt{25} = 5$$
$$10^{-y} = \frac{1}{5}$$

4. $2 - (-2)^{2-(-2)} = 2 - (-2)^4$

$$= 2 - 16 = -14$$

5. $9^x \times 9^2 = 240 + 9^x$

$$81 \times 9^x = 240 + 9^x$$
$$80 \times 9^x = 240$$
$$9^x = 3$$
$$3^{2x} = 3^1$$
$$2x = 1$$
$$x = \frac{1}{2} = 0.5$$

6. $8^{x+1} = 8^2$

$$x + 1 = 2$$
$$x = 1$$
$$3^{2x+1} = 3^{2\times 1+1} = 3^3 = 27$$

7. $4^x - 4^{x-1} = 24$

$$4^x - \frac{4^x}{4} = 24$$
$$4 \times 4^x - 4^x = 96$$
$$3 \times 4^x = 96$$
$$4^x = 32$$
$$2^{2x} = 2^5$$
$$2x = 5$$
$$x = \frac{5}{2}$$
$$(2x)^x = \left(2\frac{5}{2}\right)^{5/2} = (5^5)^{\frac{1}{2}} = 25\sqrt{5}$$

8. $\dfrac{5^{n+1}(5-6)}{5^{n+1}(13\times 5^{-1})-2} = \dfrac{-1}{\frac{13}{5}-2} = -\dfrac{5}{3}$

9. $\left(\frac{3}{2}\right)^{-x}\left(\frac{3}{2}\right)^{2x} = \left(\frac{3}{2}\right)^4$

$$-x + 2x = 4$$
$$x = 4$$

10. $(4)^{2\,(2x+3)} = (4)^{3(x+3)}$

$$4x + 6 = 3x + 9$$
$$x = 3$$
$$4^{2x-2} = 4^{2\times 3-2} = 4^4 = 256$$

11. Given exp. $= \left(1000-\frac{6}{7}\right)+\left(1000-\frac{5}{7}\right)+\left(1000-\frac{4}{7}\right)+$

$$\left(1000-\frac{3}{7}\right)+\left(1000-\frac{2}{7}\right)+\left(1000-\frac{1}{7}\right)$$
$$= 6000-\left(\frac{6}{7}+\frac{5}{7}+\frac{4}{7}+\frac{3}{7}+\frac{2}{7}+\frac{1}{7}\right)$$
$$= 6000-\frac{21}{7} = 6000-3 = 5997$$

12. Given exp. $= \dfrac{4\times 3^3+3^2+3+1}{4\times 3^3}$

$$= \frac{108+9+3+1}{108} = \frac{121}{108}$$

13. Given exp. $= \left(\dfrac{a^3+b^3}{a^2+b^2-ab}\right) = (a+b),$

where $a = 785,\ b = 435$

$$= (785 + 435) = 1220$$

14. $\frac{1}{5}+\left(999+\frac{494}{495}\right)\times 99$

$$= \frac{1}{5}+(999\times 99)+\frac{494}{495}\times 99$$
$$= \frac{1}{5}+\frac{494}{5}+999\times 99$$
$$= \frac{495}{5}+(1000-1)\times 99$$
$$= 99 + 99000 - 99 = 99000$$

15. $\left(\dfrac{x+2}{x+1}\right)\left(\dfrac{x+3}{x+2}\right)\left(\dfrac{x+4}{x+3}\right)\left(\dfrac{x+5}{x+4}\right) = \dfrac{x+5}{x+1}$

❑❑❑❑❑

5

Direct and Inverse Proportions

Important Facts and Formulae

1. **Direct Proportion:** Two quantities are said to be directly proportional, if on the increase (or decrease) of the one, the other increases (or decreases) to the same extent.

   Ex. 1. Cost is directly proportional to the number of articles.
   (*More Articles, More Cost*)

   Ex. 2. Work done is directly proportional to the number of men working on it.
   (*More Men, More Work*)

2. **Indirect Proportion :** Two quantities are said to be indirectly proportional, if on the increase of the one, the other decreases to the same extent and vice-versa.

   Ex. 1. The time taken by a car in covering a certain distance is inversely proportional to the speed of the car.
   (*More speed, Less is the time taken to cover a distance*)

   Ex. 2. Time taken to finish a work is inversely proportional to the number of persons working at it.
   (*More persons, Less is the time taken to finish a job.*)

Remark : In solving questions by chain rule, we compare every item with the term to be found out.

Formulae:

(*i*) If $W_1 = W_2$

$$M_1 \times D_1 \times T_1 \times E_1 = M_2 \times D_2 \times T_2 \times E_2$$

(*ii*) If $W_1 \neq W_2$

$$\frac{M_1 \times D_1 \times T_1 \times E_1}{W_1} = \frac{M_2 \times D_2 \times T_2 \times E_2}{W_2}$$

where M → Number of Men
D → Number of Days
T → Time
E → Efficiency
W → Work

Multiple Choice Questions

1. If the cost of x metres of wire is d rupees, then what is the cost of y metres of wire at the same rate?

A. ₹ $\left(\frac{xy}{d}\right)$ B. ₹ (xd)
C. ₹ (yd) D. ₹ $\left(\frac{yd}{x}\right)$

2. If the price of 6 toys is ₹ 264.37, what will be the approximate price of 5 toys?

A. ₹ 140 B. ₹ 100
C. ₹ 200 D. ₹ 220

3. The price of 357 mangoes is ₹ 1517.25. What will be the approximate price of 9 dozens of such mangoes?

A. ₹ 3000 B. ₹ 3500
C. ₹ 4000 D. ₹ 2500

4. If a quarter kg of potato costs 60 paise, how many paise will 200 gm cost?

A. 48 paise B. 54 paise
C. 56 paise D. 72 paise

5. If 11.25 m of uniform iron rod weighs 42.75 kg, what will be the weight of 6 m of the same rod?

A. 22.8 kg B. 25.6 kg
C. 28 kg D. 26.5 kg

6. On a scale of map, 0.6 cm represents 6.6 km. If the distance between the points on the map is 80.5 cm, the actual distance between these points is:

A. 9 km B. 72.5 km
C. 190.75 km D. 885.5 km

7. An industrial loom weaves 0.128 metres of cloth every second. Approximately, how many seconds will it take for the loom to weave 25 metres of cloth?

A. 178 B. 195
C. 204 D. 488

8. A flagstaff 17.5 m high casts a shadow of length 40.25 m. The height of the building, which casts a shadow of length 28.75 m under similar conditions will be:

A. 10 m B. 12.5 m
C. 17.5 m D. 21.25 m

9. A man completes $\frac{5}{8}$ of a job in 10 days. At this rate, how many more days will it take him to finish the job?

A. 5 B. 6

C. 7 D. $7\frac{1}{2}$

10. 36 men can complete a piece of work in 18 days. In how many days will 27 men complete the same work?

A. 12 B. 18

C. 22 D. 24

11. If 7 spiders make 7 webs in 7 days, then 1 spider will make 1 web in how many days?

A. 1 B. $\frac{7}{2}$

C. 7 D. 49

12. If 18 binders bind 900 books in 10 days, how many binders will be required to bind 660 books is 12 days?

A. 22 B. 14

C. 13 D. 11

13. If 18 pumps can raise 2170 tonnes of water in 10 days, working 7 hours a day, in how many days will 16 pumps raise 1736 tonnes, working 9 hours a day?

A. 9 days B. 8 days

C. 7 days D. 6 days

14. 120 men had provisions for 200 days. After 5 days, 30 men died due to an epidemic. The remaining food will last for:

A. 150 days B. $146\frac{1}{4}$ days

C. 245 days D. 260 days

15. A garrison of 500 men had provisions for 24 days. However, a reinforcement of 300 men arrived. The food will now last for:

A. 18 days B. $17\frac{1}{2}$ days

C. 16 days D. 15 days

ANSWERS

1	2	3	4	5	6	7	8	9	10
D	D	D	A	A	D	B	B	B	D
11	**12**	**13**	**14**	**15**	**16**	**17**	**18**	**19**	**20**
C	D	C	D	D					

EXPLANATORY ANSWERS

1. Cost of x metres = ₹ d. Cost of 1 metre

$$= ₹\left(\frac{d}{x}\right)$$

Cost of y meters = $₹\left(\frac{d}{x} \times y\right) = ₹\left(\frac{dy}{x}\right)$.

2. Let the required price be ₹ x. Then,

Less toys, Less cost (Direct proportion)

$\therefore$ 6 : 5 : : 264.37 : $x \Leftrightarrow 6x = (5 \times 264.37)$

$\Leftrightarrow \quad x = \frac{(5 \times 264.37)}{6}$

$\Leftrightarrow \quad x = 220.308$

$\therefore$ Approximate price of 5 toys = ₹ 220.

3. Let the required price be ₹ x. Then, *More mangoes, More price (Direct Proportion)*

$\therefore$ 357 : (49 × 12) : : 1517.25 : x

$\Leftrightarrow \quad 357x = (49 \times 12 \times 1517.25)$

$\Leftrightarrow \quad x = \frac{(49 \times 12 \times 1517.25)}{357}$

$\Leftrightarrow \quad x = 2499.$

Hence, the approximate price is ₹ 2500.

4. Let the required cost be x paise. *Less weight, Less cost (Direct Proportion)*

$\therefore$ 250 : 200 : : 60 : x

$\Leftrightarrow \quad 250 \times x = (200 \times 60)$

$x = \frac{(200 \times 60)}{250}$

$\Leftrightarrow \quad x = 48.$

5. Let the required weight be x kg. Then, *Less length, Less weight (Direct Proportion)*

$\therefore$ 11.25 : 6 : : 42.75 : x

$\Leftrightarrow \quad 11.25 \times x = 6 \times 42.75$

$\Leftrightarrow \quad x = \frac{(6 \times 42.75)}{11.25}$

$\Leftrightarrow \quad x = 22.8.$

6. Let the actual distance be x km. Then,

More distance on the map. *More is the actual distance (Direct Proportion)*

$\therefore$ 0.6 : 80.5 : : 6.6 : x

$\Leftrightarrow \quad 0.6x = 80.5 \times 6.6$

$\Leftrightarrow \quad x = \frac{80.5 \times 6.6}{0.6}$

$\Leftrightarrow \quad x = 885.5.$

7. Let the required time be x seconds. *Then, More metres, more time (Direct Proportion)*

$\therefore$ 0.128 : 25 : : 1 : x

$\Leftrightarrow \quad 0.128 \times x = 25 \times 1$

$\Leftrightarrow \quad x = \frac{25}{0.128} = \frac{25 \times 1000}{128}$

$\Leftrightarrow \quad x = 195.31$

$\therefore$ Required time = 195 sec (approximately).

8. Let the height of the building be x metres.

Less lengthy shadow, *Less is the height (Direct Proportion)*

$\therefore$ 40.25 : 28.75 : : 17.5 : x

$\Leftrightarrow \quad 40.25 \times x = 28.75 \times 17.5$

$\Leftrightarrow \quad x = \frac{(28.75 \times 17.5)}{40.25} \Leftrightarrow x = 12.5$

9. Work done $= \frac{5}{8}$. Balance work $= \left(1 - \frac{5}{8}\right) = \frac{3}{8}$.

Less work, Less days (Direct Proportion)

Let the required number of days be x

Then $\frac{5}{8} : \frac{3}{8} :: 10 : x \Leftrightarrow \frac{5}{8} \times x = \frac{3}{8} \times 10$

$\Leftrightarrow \quad x = \left(\frac{3}{8} \times 10 \times \frac{8}{5}\right) = 6.$

10. Let the required number of days be x.

Then, *Less men, More days (Indirect Proportion)*

$\therefore$ 27 : 36 : : 18 : x

$\Leftrightarrow \quad 27 \times x = 36 \times 18$

$\Leftrightarrow \quad x = \frac{36 \times 18}{27} \Leftrightarrow x = 24.$

11. Let the required number of days be x. Then,

Less spiders, More days *(Indirect Proportion)*

Less webs, Less days *(Direct Proportion)*

$\therefore \begin{array}{ll} \text{Spiders} & 1:7 \\ \text{Webs} & 7:1 \end{array} \Bigg\} :: 7 : x$

$\therefore \quad 1 \times 7 \times x = 7 \times 1 \times 7 \Leftrightarrow x = 7.$

12. Let the required number of binders be x.

Less books, Less binders *(Direct Proportion)*

More days, Less binders *(Indirect Proportion)*

$\begin{array}{ll} \text{Books} & 900 : 600 \\ \text{Days} & 12 : 10 \end{array} \Bigg\} :: 18 : x$

$\therefore \quad (900 \times 20 \times x) = (600 \times 10 \times 18)$

$\Leftrightarrow \quad x = \frac{600 \times 10 \times 18}{900 \times 12} = 11.$

13. *Less pumps, more days* *(Indirect)*

Less Water, less days *(Direct)*

More working hrs., less days *(Indirect)*

$\begin{array}{ll} \text{Pumps} & 16 : 18 \\ \text{Water} & 2170 : 1736 \\ \text{Working hours} & 9 : 7 \end{array} \Bigg\} : : 10 : x$

$\therefore \quad x = \left(\frac{18 \times 1736 \times 7 \times 10}{16 \times 2170 \times 9}\right) = 7 \text{ days.}$

14. The remaining food is sufficient for 120 men for 195 days.

But, now remaining men = 90.

Less men, more days (Indirect)

$\therefore$ 90 : 120 :: 195 : x

or $\quad x = \left(\frac{120 \times 195}{90}\right) = 260 \text{ days.}$

15. More men, less number of days (Indirect)

800 : 500 : : 24 : x

or $\quad x = \left(\frac{500 \times 24}{800}\right) = 15 \text{ days.}$

❑❑❑❑❑

6

Comparing Quantities

Percentage

I. Concept of Percentage : By a certain percent, we mean that many hundredths. Thus, x percent means x hundredths, written as $x\%$.

To express $x\%$ as a fraction : We have, $x\% = \frac{x}{100}$.

Thus, $20\% = \frac{20}{100} = \frac{1}{5}$; $48\% = \frac{48}{100} = \frac{12}{25}$, etc.

To express $\frac{a}{b}$ as a percent : We have, $\frac{a}{b} = \left(\frac{a}{b} \times 100\right)\%$.

Thus, $\frac{1}{4} = \left(\frac{1}{4} \times 100\right)\% = 25\%$;

$0.6 = \frac{6}{10} = \frac{3}{5} = \left(\frac{3}{5} \times 100\right)\% = 60\%$.

II. If the price of a commodity increases by R%, then the reduction in consumption so as not to increase the expenditure is

$$\left[\frac{R}{(100+R)} \times 100\right]\%$$

If the price of a commodity decreases by R%, then the increase in consumption so as not to decrease the expenditure is

$$\left[\frac{R}{(100-R)} \times 100\right]\%$$

III. Results on Population : Let the population of a town be P now and suppose it increases at the rate of R% per annum, then :

1. Population after n years $= P\left(1+\frac{R}{100}\right)^n$.

2. Population n years ago $= \frac{P}{\left(1+\frac{R}{100}\right)^n}$.

IV. Results on Depreciation : Let the present value of a machine be P. Suppose it depreciates at the rate of R% per annum. Then :

1. Value of the machine after n years $= P\left(1-\frac{R}{100}\right)^n$.

2. Value of the machine n years ago $= \frac{P}{\left(1-\frac{R}{100}\right)^n}$.

V. If A is R% more than B, then B is less than A by

$$\left[\frac{R}{(100+R)} \times 100\right]\%$$

If A is R% less than B, then B is more than A by

$$\left[\frac{R}{(100-R)} \times 100\right]\%.$$

Profit & Loss

Cost Price : The price at which an article is purchased, is called its cost price, abbreviated as C.P.

Selling Price : The price at which an article is sold, is called its selling price, abbreviated as S.P.

Profit or Gain : If S.P. is greater than C.P., the seller is said to have a profit or gain.

Loss : If S.P. is less than C.P., the seller is said to have incurred a loss.

Formulae :

1. Gain = (S.P.) – (C.P.)
2. Loss = (C.P.) – (S.P.)
3. Loss or gain is always reckoned on C.P.
4. Gain % $= \left(\frac{\text{Gain} \times 100}{\text{C.P.}}\right)$
5. Loss % $= \left(\frac{\text{Loss} \times 100}{\text{C.P.}}\right)$
6. S.P. $= \frac{(100 + \text{Gain\%})}{100} \times$ C.P.
7. S.P. $= \frac{(100 - \text{Loss\%})}{100} \times$ C.P.

8. $\text{C.P.} = \dfrac{100}{(100 + \text{Gain\%})} \times \text{S.P.}$

9. $\text{C.P.} = \dfrac{100}{(100 - \text{Loss\%})} \times \text{S.P.}$

10. If an article is sold at a gain of say, 35%, then S.P. = 135% of C.P.

11. If an article is sold at a loss of say, 35%, then S.P. = 65% of C.P.

12. When a person sells two similar items, one at a gain of say, x%, and the other at a loss of x%, then the seller always incurs a loss given by:

$$\text{Loss \%} = \left(\frac{\text{Common Loss and Gain\%}}{10}\right)^2 = \left(\frac{x}{10}\right)^2.$$

13. If a trader professes to sell his goods at cost price, but uses false weights, then

$$\text{Gain\%} = \left[\frac{\text{Error}}{(\text{True Value}) - (\text{Error})} \times 100\right]\%.$$

Discount

Market Price (M.P.)—The attached price is called the market price (M.P.) or list price (L.P.) of the article and the reduction allowed in the price is called the **discount**.

(*i*) Discount = M.P. – S.P.

(*ii*) $\text{Discount \%} = \dfrac{\text{Discount} \times 100}{\text{M.P.}}$

(*iii*) $\text{S.P.} = \text{M.P.} - \dfrac{\text{Discount\%} \times \text{M.P.}}{100}$

(*iv*) $\text{S.P.} = \text{M.P.} \times \left(1 - \dfrac{\text{Discount\%}}{100}\right)$

(*v*) $\text{M.P.} = \dfrac{100 \times \text{S.P.}}{100 - \text{Discount\%}}$,

$\text{S.P.} = \text{M.P.} \left(\dfrac{100 - \text{Discount\%}}{100}\right)$

$\text{M.P.} - \text{S.P.} = \dfrac{\text{M.P.} \times \text{Discount\%}}{100}$

$\text{Discount\%} = \left(\dfrac{\text{M.P.} - \text{S.P.}}{\text{M.P.}}\right) \times 100$

Simple Interest

Important Facts and Formulae

1. **Principal :** The money borrowed or lent out for a certain period is called the **principal** or the sum.
2. **Interest :** Extra money paid for using other's money is called **interest**.
3. **Simple Interest (S.I.) :** If the interest on a sum borrowed for a certain period is reckoned uniformly, then it is called **simple interest**.

Let Principal = P, Rate = R% per annum (p.a.) and Time = T years. Then,

(*i*) $\text{S.I.} = \left(\dfrac{\text{P} \times \text{R} \times \text{T}}{100}\right)$

(*ii*) $\text{P} = \left(\dfrac{100 \times \text{S.I.}}{\text{R} \times \text{T}}\right)$; $\text{R} = \left(\dfrac{100 \times \text{S.I.}}{\text{P} \times \text{T}}\right)$

and $\text{T} = \left(\dfrac{100 \times \text{S.I.}}{\text{P} \times \text{R}}\right)$

Compound Interest

Compound Interest : Sometimes it so happens that the borrower and the lender agree to fix up a certain unit of time, say yearly or half-yearly or quarterly to settle the previous account.

In such cases, the amount after first unit of time becomes the principal for the second unit, the amount after second unit becomes the principal for the third unit and so on.

After a specified period, the difference between the amount and the money borrowed is called the Compound Interest (*abbreviated* as C.I.) for that period.

Important Facts and Formulae

Let Principal = P, Rate = R% per annum, Time = n years.

I. When interest is compound Annually:

$$\text{Amount} = \text{P}\left(1 + \frac{\text{R}}{100}\right)^n$$

II. When interest is compounded Half-yearly :

$$\text{Amount} = \text{P}\left[1 + \frac{(\text{R}/2)}{100}\right]^{2n}$$

III. When interest is compounded Quarterly :

$$\text{Amount} = \text{P}\left[1 + \frac{(\text{R}/4)}{100}\right]^{4n}$$

IV. When interest is compounded Annually but time is in fraction, say $3\frac{2}{5}$ years.

$$\text{Amount} = \text{P}\left(1 + \frac{\text{R}}{100}\right)^3 \times \left(1 + \frac{\frac{2}{5}\text{R}}{100}\right)$$

V. When Rates are different for different years, say R_1%, R_2%, R_3% for 1st, 2nd, 3rd year respectively.

Then, $$\text{Amount} = \text{P}\left(1 + \frac{R_1}{100}\right)\left(1 + \frac{R_2}{100}\right)\left(1 + \frac{R_3}{100}\right).$$

VI. Present worth of Rs. x due n years hence is given by :

$$\text{Present Worth} = \frac{x}{\left(1 + \frac{\text{R}}{100}\right)^n}.$$

Multiple Choice Questions

1. If the cost of a book worth ₹ 50 is increased by ₹ 25. What is the rate of increase?
A. 50% B. 60%
C. 70% D. 80%

2. A number decreases by $72\frac{1}{2}\%$ gives 87. What is the number?
A. 90 B. 100
C. 120 D. 140

3. 25% of a number is less than 18% of 650 by 19. What is the number?
A. 193 B. 392
C. 396 D. 492

4. Two candidates fought an election, one get 65% of the votes and won by 300 votes. What is the total number of votes polled?
A. 1000 B. 1200
C. 1400 D. 1500

5. 96% of the population of a town is 23040. What is the total number of population?
A. 21000 B. 24000
C. 26000 D. 24000

6. If 75% of students in a school are boys and the number of girls is 420. What is the number of boys?
A. 1160 B. 1170
C. 1260 D. 1420

7. The population of a village is 5000; and it increase at the rate of 2% every year. What will be the population after 2 years?
A. 5200 B. 5400
C. 5202 D. 6300

8. The population of a town increases by 5% annually. If it is 15435 now, what was the population 2 years ago?
A. 8400 B. 9300
C. 9700 D. 9850

9. The population of a town is 8000. It increases by 10% during first year and by 20% during second year. What will be the population after 2 years.
A. 10,120 B. 10,560
C. 11,420 D. 12,460

10. Kavita went to school for 216 days in a year. If her attendance was 90%, then find out the number of days the school was open in that year?
A. 100 days B. 140 days
C. 240 days D. 280 days

11. A farmer sold two bullocks for ₹ 18000 each. On one bullock he gained 20% and on the other he lost 20%. What is his total loss or gain?
A. ₹ 1500 B. ₹ 1600
C. ₹ 1750 D. ₹ 1520

12. By selling 144 hens, Mukesh lost the S.P. of 6 hens. What is the loss per cent?
A. 2% B. 4%
C. 6% D. 8%

13. A shopkeeper purchased 100 blankets at ₹ 2000 each. He found that 10 blankets were defective and he sold these at ₹ 1200 each. At what rate should he sell the remaining blankets so as to gain 14% on the whole?
A. ₹ 2400 B. ₹ 2600
C. ₹ 2800 D. ₹ 3200

Directions (14 and 15) : *A goldsmith bought 100g of gold for ₹ 54000 from a wholesaler. He then sold it at a gain of 10%.*

14. S.P. of 10g of gold for the goldsmith.
A. ₹ 5820 B. ₹ 5460
C. ₹ 5370 D. ₹ 5940

15. C.P. of 10g of gold for the wholesaler, if his profit is 8%.
A. ₹ 2000 B. ₹ 4000
C. ₹ 5000 D. ₹ 5500

Directions (16 to 18) : *William sells a quintal of wheat for ₹ 924 and earns a profit of 12%. By selling a quintal of rice for the same amount he loses 12%. Find,*

16. C.P. of wheat :
A. ₹ 825 B. ₹ 935
C. ₹ 945 D. ₹ 1025

17. C.P. of rice :
A. ₹ 920 B. ₹ 980
C. ₹ 1050 D. ₹ 1120

18. Gain or loss per cent on the whole transaction.
A. ₹ 23 B. ₹ 25
C. ₹ 27 D. ₹ 29

19. A tricycle is sold at a gain of 16%. Had it been sold for ₹ 100 more, the gain would have been 20%. What is the C.P. of the tricycle?
A. ₹ 2500 B. ₹ 2210
C. ₹ 2350 D. ₹ 2400

20. Manish bought 20 dining tables for ₹ 1,20,000 and sold these at a profit equal to the selling price of 4 dining tables. What is the S.P. of one dining table?
A. ₹ 5500 B. ₹ 7500
C. ₹ 8500 D. ₹ 9000

21. A cloth merchant offers 15% festival discount on every saree sold. If a certain saree is sold for ₹ 680, what is its marked price?

A. ₹ 800 B. ₹ 900
C. ₹ 1250 D. ₹ 1300

22. A shopkeeper offers 10% discount on an article and still makes a profit of 20%. What is the C.P. of the article if the marked price is ₹ 350?
A. ₹ 259.20 B. ₹ 262.50
C. ₹ 265.75 D. ₹ 272.5

23. A manufactures marks his goods in such a way that after allowing 20% discount, he makes a profit of 18%. What is the marked price of an item which costs him ₹ 200?
A. ₹ 295 B. ₹ 310
C. ₹ 315 D. ₹ 375

24. The marked price of a brand of coffee is ₹ 35 for 100g. But the shopkeeper gives a cup costing ₹ 7.50 free with it. Even then he gets a gain of 10%. What is the cost price of 100g of coffee?
A. ₹ 15 B. ₹ 25
C. ₹ 35 D. ₹ 65

25. A car is marked at ₹ 2,25,000. The manufacturer gives a discount of 10%. The dealer also gives a discount of 5%. What is the S.P. of the car?
A. ₹ 1,72,369 B. ₹ 1,64,370
C. ₹ 1,52,393 D. ₹ 1,92,375

26. What is the interest on ₹ 2000 for 3 years at 8% per annum?
A. 480 B. 490
C. 510 D. 420

27. What is the simple interest on ₹ 4000 for 3 years at the rate of 10% p.a.?
A. ₹ 1200 B. ₹ 1300
C. ₹ 2200 D. ₹ 1424

28. What is the simple interest on ₹ 9280 at the rate of $4\frac{1}{2}$% per annum for 5 months?
A. ₹ 374 B. ₹ 174
C. ₹ 184 D. ₹ 192

29. Pawan borrowed ₹ 3000 from a friend at simple interest. After 5 years he paid ₹ 4500; and cleared his debt. What is the rate of interest?
A. 12% B. 15%
C. 10% D. 20%

30. In what time will a sum amount to 5 times of itself at the rate of $7\frac{1}{2}$% per annum?
A. 2 years B. $5\frac{1}{2}$ years
C. $13\frac{1}{3}$ years D. $53\frac{1}{3}$ years

31. A sum was put at simple interest at a certain rate for 2 years. Had it been put at 3% higher rate, it would have fetched ₹ 300 more. What is the sum?
A. ₹ 6000 B. ₹ 5000
C. ₹ 5500 D. ₹ 6500

32. What simple interest will discharge a debt of ₹ 2210 due in 4 years at 7% per annum?
A. ₹ 628.2 B. ₹ 638.4
C. ₹ 618.8 D. ₹ 698.2

33. ₹ 800 amount to ₹ 920 in 3 years at simple interest. If the interest rate is increased by 3%. What is the amount?
A. ₹ 892 B. ₹ 992
C. ₹ 1002 D. ₹ 782

34. Kamal lent ₹ 600 to Meena for 2 years and ₹ 150 to Anil for 4 years and received altogether from both ₹ 90 as simple interest. What is the rate of interest?
A. 6% p.a. B. 5% p.a.
C. $8\frac{1}{2}$% p.a. D. 10% p.a.

35. The difference between the interest received from two different banks on ₹ 500 for 2 years is ₹ 2.50. What is the difference between their rates?
A. 0.35% B. 0.55%
C. 0.25% D. 0.65%

36. What is the amount of ₹ 6000 lent at 5% per annum for 2 years if the interest is compounded annually?
A. ₹ 6615 B. ₹ 6720
C. ₹ 6625 D. ₹ 6612

37. What is the compound interest on ₹ 25600 for 2 years at 6.25% per annum?
A. ₹ 3300 B. ₹ 3500
C. ₹ 4000 D. ₹ 3350

38. What is the amount and compound interest on ₹ 16000 for 3 years, if the rate of interest is 2% per annum?
A. ₹ 989.2 B. ₹ 987.43
C. ₹ 979.33 D. ₹ 991.24

39. Simple interest on a sum of money for 3 years at $6\frac{1}{4}$% per annum is ₹ 2400. What will be the compound interest on that sum at the same rate for the same period?
A. ₹ 2430.43 B. ₹ 2553.13
C. ₹ 2522.17 D. ₹ 2532.19

40. The difference between the compound interest and the simple interest on a certain sum for 2 years at 10% per annum is ₹ 300. What is the sum?
A. ₹ 20,000 B. ₹ 25,000
C. ₹ 30,000 D. ₹ 35,000

ANSWERS

1	2	3	4	5	6	7	8	9	10
A	C	B	A	B	C	C	A	B	C
11	**12**	**13**	**14**	**15**	**16**	**17**	**18**	**19**	**20**
A	B	A	D	C	A	C	C	A	B
21	**22**	**23**	**24**	**25**	**26**	**27**	**28**	**29**	**30**
A	B	A	B	D	A	A	B	C	D
31	**32**	**33**	**34**	**35**	**36**	**37**	**38**	**39**	**40**
B	C	B	B	C	A	A	C	B	C

EXPLANATORY ANSWERS

1. Cost price = ₹ 50
Increase = ₹ 25

$$\text{Rate of increase} = \frac{25\times100}{50} = 50\%$$

2. Let Number = x

$$72\frac{1}{2}\% \text{ of } x = 87$$

$$\frac{145}{2\times100}\times x = 87$$

$$x = \frac{87\times2\times100}{145} = 120$$

3. Let number = x

18% of 650 – x × 25% = 19

$$\frac{18}{100}\times650 - 19 = \frac{25x}{100}$$

$$117 - 19 = \frac{x}{4}$$

$$98\times4 = x$$

$$x = 392$$

4. Let total number of votes = x

65% of x – 35% of x = 300

30% x = 300

$$\frac{30}{100}\times x = 300 \Rightarrow x = \frac{300\times100}{30}$$

$$x = 1000$$

5. Let total population = x

96% of x = 23040

$$\frac{96}{100}\times x = 23040$$

$$x = \frac{23040\times100}{96} = 960\times25 = 24000$$

6. Per cent of girls = 25%

Let total number of students = x

25% of x = 420

$$\frac{25}{100}\times x = 420$$

$$x = 420\times4 = 1680$$

Total number of students = 1680.

No. of boys = 75% of 1680

$$= \frac{75}{100}\times1680 = 1260$$

7. Population = 5000

$$\text{Increase in 1st year} = 5000\times\frac{2}{100} = 100$$

Population after 1 year = 5000 + 100 = 5100

Increase in population in 2nd year

$$= 5100\times\frac{2}{100} = 102$$

Population of 2 years

= 5100 + 102 = 5202

8. Population = 15435
Time = 2 yrs.
Rate = 5% p.a.

Population after 2 years

$$= \frac{P}{\left(1+\frac{r}{100}\right)^n} = \frac{15435}{\left(1+\frac{5}{100}\right)^2}$$

$$= \frac{15435}{\left(\frac{21}{20}\right)^2} = \frac{15435\times20\times20}{21\times21}$$

$$= 21\times400 = 8400$$

9. P = 8000
r_1 = 10%
r_2 = 20%
Time = 2 years

Population after two years

$$= P\left(1+\frac{r_1}{100}\right)\left(1+\frac{r_2}{100}\right)$$

$$= 8000\left(1+\frac{10}{100}\right)\left(1+\frac{20}{100}\right)$$

$= 8000 \times \frac{11}{10} \times \frac{6}{5}$

$= 10560$

10. Let total no. of days = x

90% of $x = 216$

$\frac{90}{100} x = 216$

$x = \frac{216 \times 10}{9} = 240$ days

11. S.P. = 18000

Profit = 20%

Let C.P. = x

$x + x \times 20\% = 18000$

$\frac{120}{100} x = 18000$

$x = \frac{18000 \times 5}{6} = 15000$

C.P. of 1st bullock = 15000

Again,

S.P. = 18000

Loss = 20%

Let C.P. = x

$x - x \times \frac{20}{100} = 18000$

$\frac{80}{100} x = 18000$

$x = \frac{18000 \times 5}{4}$

$x = 22500$

Total C.P. = 22500 + 15000

= 37500

Total S.P. = 18000 + 18000 = 36000

Loss = 37500 – 36000

= ₹ 1500

12. Let S.P. of 1 hen = ₹ 1

S.P. of 144 hens = ₹ 144

Loss = S.P. of 6 hens = 6 × 1 = ₹ 6

C.P. of 144 hens = 144 + 6 = ₹ 150

$\text{Loss\%} = \frac{\text{loss} \times 100}{\text{C.P}} = \frac{6 \times 100}{150} = 4\%$

13. C.P. of 100 blankets = 100 × 2000

= ₹ 200000

Profit = 14%

S.P. $= 200000 + 200000 \times \frac{14}{100}$

= 228000

S.P. of 10 blankets = 1200 × 10

= 12000

Remaining S.P. = 228000 – 12000

S.P. of 90 blankets = 216000

S.P. of 1 blanket $= \frac{216000}{90}$

= ₹ 2400

Direction (14 and 15): C.P. of 100g. gold = ₹ 54000

Profit = 10%

S.P. of 100g. gold $= 54000 + 54000 \times \frac{10}{100}$

= 54000 + 5400

= 59400

14. S.P. of 100g. gold $= \frac{59400}{100} \times 10$ = ₹ 5940

15. S.P. of wholesaler (10 gm.) $= \frac{54000}{100} \times 10$

= 5400.

C.P. of wholesaler for 10g. = x

$x + x \times 8\% = 5400$

$\frac{108}{100} \times x = 5400$

$x = \frac{5400 \times 100}{108}$

= ₹ 5000

Directions (16 to 18) : Let C.P. of Wheat = ₹ x

16. $x + x \times 12\% = 924$

$\frac{112}{100} x = 924$

$x = \frac{924 \times 100}{112}$

x = ₹ 825

17. Let C.P. of Rice = ₹ x

$x - x \times \frac{12}{100} = 924$

$\frac{88}{100} x = 924$

$x = \frac{924 \times 100}{88}$ = ₹ 1050

18. Total S.P. = 924 + 924 = 1848

Total C.P. = 825 + 1050

= 1875

Profit = 1875 – 1848 = ₹ 27

19. Let C.P. of tricycle = ₹ x

116% of $x + 100 = 120\% \, x$

$\frac{116}{100} \times x + 100 = \frac{120}{100} x$

$\frac{6}{5} x - \frac{29}{25} x = 100$

$\frac{30x - 29x}{25} = 100$

$\Rightarrow \quad x = 100 \times 25$

$\Rightarrow \quad x$ = ₹ 2500

20. C.P. of 20 dining tables = ₹ 120000

C.P. of 1 dining table $= \frac{120000}{20}$

= ₹ 6000.

Let his profit = ₹ x per dining table

S.P. of 1 dining table = 6000 + x

Total profit = 4 (6000 + x)

= 24000 + 4x

S.P. price of 20 dining table

= 120000 + 24000 + 4x

= 144000 + 4x.

S.P. price of 1 dining table

$$\frac{6000+x}{1} = \frac{144000+4x}{20}$$

$$120000 + 20x = 144000 + 4x$$

$$16x = 144000 - 120000$$

$$16x = 24000$$

$$x = \frac{24000}{16}$$

Profit = 1500

S.P. of 1 dining table

= 6000 + 1500 = ₹ 7500

21. S.P. = ₹ 680

Discount = 15%

$$\text{M.P.} = \frac{100 \times \text{S.P.}}{100 - \text{Discount\%}}$$

$$= \frac{100 \times 680}{100 - 15} = \frac{100 \times 680}{85} = ₹\ 800$$

22. C.P. = ₹ x

120% of x = 350 − 350 × 10%

$$\frac{120}{100} \times x = 350 - 35 = 315.$$

$$x = \frac{315 \times 5}{6} = \frac{525}{2}$$

C.P. = ₹ 262.50

23. Let M.P. = ₹ x

80% x = 118% of 200

$$\frac{80}{100} \times x = \frac{118}{100} \times 200$$

$$x = \frac{236 \times 5}{4} = ₹\ 295$$

24. Let C.P. of 100 gm coffee = ₹ x

110% of x = 35 − 7.50 = 27.50

$$\frac{110}{100} \times x = 27.50$$

$$x = \frac{27.50 \times 100}{110 \times 100}$$

C.P. = ₹ 25.

25. M.P. = ₹ 225000

$$\text{1st S.P.} = 225000 - 225000 \times \frac{10}{100}$$

= 225000 − 22500 = 202500

$$\text{2nd S.P.} = 202500 - 202500 \times \frac{5}{100}$$

= 202500 − 10125 = ₹ 192375

26. P = ₹ 2000

T = 3 yrs

R = 8% p.a.

$$\text{Interest} = \frac{\text{PRT}}{100} = \frac{2000 \times 8 \times 3}{100}$$

= ₹ 480

27. P = ₹ 4000

T = 3 yrs.

R = 10% p.a.

$$\text{S.I.} = \frac{\text{PRT}}{100} = \frac{4000 \times 10 \times 3}{100}$$

= ₹ 1200

28. P = 9280

$$R = \frac{9}{2}\%\ \text{p.a.}$$

$$T = \frac{5}{12}\ \text{yr.}$$

$$\text{S.I.} = \frac{\text{PRT}}{100} = \frac{9280 \times 9 \times 5}{100 \times 2 \times 12}$$

= 58 × 3 = ₹ 174

29. P = ₹ 3000

A = ₹ 4500

S.I. = A − P = 4500 − 3000 = 1500

T = 5 yrs.

$$R = \frac{\text{S.I.} \times 100}{\text{P} \times \text{T}} = \frac{1500 \times 100}{3000 \times 5} = 10\%$$

30. P = ₹ 100

A = ₹ 500

S.I. = 500 − 100 = ₹ 400

$$R = \frac{15}{2}\%\ \text{p.a.}$$

$$T = \frac{\text{S.I.} \times 100}{\text{P} \times \text{R}}$$

$$= \frac{400 \times 100 \times 2}{100 \times 15} = \frac{160}{3} = 53\frac{1}{3}\ \text{yrs.}$$

31. Let Rate = x%

$$\frac{\text{P} \times (x+3) \times 2}{100} - \frac{\text{P} \times x \times 2}{100} = 300$$

$$\frac{2\text{P}(x+3)}{100} - \frac{2\text{P}x}{100} = 300$$

$$2Px + 6P - 2Px = 30000$$

$$P = \frac{30000}{6}$$

$$\text{Principle} = ₹\ 5000$$

32. P = 2210
R = 7
T = 4

$$S.I. = \frac{PRT}{100} = \frac{2210 \times 7 \times 4}{100} = ₹\ 618.80$$

33. P = 800
A = 920
T = 3 yrs.
S.I. = 920 – 800 = 120

$$R = \frac{S.I. \times 100}{P \times T}$$

$$= \frac{120 \times 100}{800 \times 3} = 5\%\ p.a.$$

New rate = 5 + 3 = 8%

$$S.I. = \frac{PRT}{100} = \frac{800 \times 8 \times 3}{100} = ₹\ 192$$

A = P + S.I. = 800 + 192 = ₹ 992

34. $\frac{600 \times 2 \times R}{100} + \frac{2150 \times 4 \times R}{100} = 90$

12 R + 6 R = 90
18 R = 90

$$R = \frac{90}{18}$$

R = 5% p.a.

35. $\frac{500 \times r_1 \times 2}{100} - \frac{500 \times r_2 \times 2}{100} = 2.50$

$10\ (r_1 - r_2) = 2.50$

$$r_1 - r_2 = \frac{2.50}{10}$$

$r_1 - r_2 = 0.25\%$

36. P = ₹ 6000
R = 5% p.a.
T = 2 years

$$A = P\left(1+\frac{r}{100}\right)^n = 6000\left(1+\frac{5}{100}\right)^2$$

$$= 6000 \times \frac{21}{20} \times \frac{21}{20}$$

= 15 × 21 × 21 = ₹ 6615

37. P = ₹ 25600
R = 6.25 p.a.
T = 2 years

$$A = P\left(1+\frac{r}{100}\right)^n = 25600\left(1+\frac{6.25}{100}\right)^2$$

$$= 25600\left(\frac{17}{16}\right)^2$$

$$= 25600\ \frac{17}{16} \times \frac{17}{16} = 28900$$

C.I. = A – P = 28900 – 25600
= ₹ 3300

38. P = ₹ 16000
n = 3 years
R = 2% p.a.

$$A = P\left(1+\frac{R}{100}\right)^n = 16000\left(1+\frac{2}{100}\right)^3$$

$$= 16000 \times \frac{51}{50} \times \frac{51}{50} \times \frac{51}{50}$$

$$= \frac{16 \times 51 \times 51 \times 51}{125} = \frac{2122416}{125}$$

= ₹ 16979. 33
C.I. = A – P
= 16979.33 – 16000
= ₹ 979.33

39. S.I. = ₹ 24000

$$R = \frac{25}{4}\%\ p.a.$$

T = 3 years

$$P = \frac{S.I. \times 100}{R \times T} = \frac{2400 \times 100 \times 4}{25 \times 3}$$

= ₹ 12800.

$$A = P\left(1+\frac{r}{100}\right)^n = 12800\left(1+\frac{25}{400}\right)^3$$

$$= ₹\ 12800 \times \frac{17}{16} \times \frac{17}{16} \times \frac{17}{16} = \frac{245650}{16}$$

= 15353.13
C.I. = A – P
= 15353.13 – 12800 = ₹ 2553.13

40. $P\left[\left(1+\frac{r}{100}\right)^n - 1\right] - \frac{PRT}{100} = 300$

$$P\left[\left(1+\frac{10}{100}\right)^2 - 1\right] - \frac{P \times 10 \times 2}{100} = 300$$

$$P\left(\frac{121}{100} - 1\right) - \frac{P}{5} = 300$$

$$P \times \frac{21}{100} - \frac{P}{5} = 300$$

$$\frac{21P - 20P}{100} = 300$$

P = 300 × 100
= ₹ 30,000

❒❒❒❒❒

7

Simplification

Algebric Identies

Some Important Formula

(*i*) $(a + b)^2 = a^2 + 2ab + b^2$

(*ii*) $(a - b)^2 = a^2 - 2ab + b^2$

(*iii*) $a^2 - b^2 = (a - b)(a + b)$

(*iv*) $(a + b + c)^2 = a^2 + b^2 + c^2 + 2ab + 2bc + 2ca$

(*v*) $(a + b - c)^2 = a^2 + b^2 + c^2 + 2ab - 2bc - 2ca$

(*vi*) $(a - b + c)^2 = a^2 + b^2 + c^2 - 2ab - 2bc + 2ca$

(*vii*) $(-a + b + c)^2 = a^2 + b^2 + c^2 - 2ab + 2bc - 2ca$

(*viii*) $(a + b)^3 = a^3 + b^3 + 3ab(a + b)$ or
$= a^3 + b^3 + 3a^2b + 3ab^2$

(*ix*) $(a - b)^3 = a^3 - b^3 - 3ab\,(a - b)$ or
$= a^3 - b^3 - 3a^2b + 3ab^2$

(*x*) $a^3 + b^3 = (a + b)\,(a^2 + b^2 - ab)$ or
$= (a + b)^3 - 3ab(a + b)$

(*xi*) $a^3 - b^3 = (a - b)\,(a^2 + b^2 + ab)$ or
$= (a - b)^3 + 3ab\,(a - b)$

(*xii*) $a^3 + b^3 + c^3 \quad 3abc = (a + b + c)(a^2 + b^2 + c^2 - ab - bc - ca)$

If $a + b + c = 0$
$a^3 + b^3 + c^3 = 3abc$

(*xiii*) $(x + a)\,(x + b) = x^2 + (a + b)x + ab$

(*xiv*) $(a + b)^2 + (a - b)^2 = 2(a^2 + b^2)$

(*xv*) $(a + b)^2 - (a - b)^2 = 4ab$

(*xvi*) $(a + b)^3 + (a - b)^3 = 2(a^3 + 3ab^2)$

(*xvii*) $(a + b)^3 - (a - b)^3 = (2(b^3 + 3a^2b)$

(*xviii*) If $x + \frac{1}{x} = t$

Then, $x^2 + \frac{1}{x^2} = t^2 - 2$

(*xix*) If $x - \frac{1}{x} = t$

Then, $x^2 + \frac{1}{x^2} = t^2 + 2$

(*xx*) $x^3 + \frac{1}{x^3} = \left(x + \frac{1}{x}\right)^3 - 3\left(x + \frac{1}{x}\right)$

(*xxi*) $x^2 - \frac{1}{x^3} = \left(x - \frac{1}{x}\right)^3 + 3\left(x - \frac{1}{x}\right)$

(*xxii*) $x + \frac{1}{x} = \sqrt{x^2 + \frac{1}{x^2} + 2}$

(*xxiii*) $x - \frac{1}{x} = \sqrt{x^2 + \frac{1}{x^2} - 2}$

Factorization of Algebraic Expressions

Factorization : The process of writing an algebraic expression as the product of two or more algebraic expressions is called factorization.

Factors : The algebraic expressions that may be multiplied to obtain the given algebraic expressions are called factors of the given expression.

Factor Theorem : If $f(x)$ is completely divisible by $(x - a)$ then $f(a) = 0$, $(x - a)$ is called factor of $f(x)$, if and only if $f(a) = 0$

Remainder Theorem : If an expression $f(x)$ is divided by $(x - a)$ then the remainder is $f(a)$.

e.g., $f(x) = ax^3 + bx + cx + d$

$f(a) = a \cdot a^3 + b \cdot a + c \cdot a + d$ is known as remainder of the given polynomials.

Multiple Choice Questions

1. $(28)^3 + (-15)^3 + (-13)^3 = ?$

A. 16380 B. 16250
C. 16420 D. 16280

2. If $x + \frac{1}{x} = 5$, What is the value of $x^3 + \frac{1}{x^3}$:

A. 120 B. 210
C. 110 D. 105

3. If $x^2 + \frac{1}{x^2} = 83$, what is the value of $x^3 - \frac{1}{x^3} = ?$

A. 756 B. 754
C. 856 D. 932

4. $23^3 - 17^3 = ?$

A. 7254 B. 7153
C. 7271 D. 7154

5. If $x + \frac{1}{x} = 15$, then the value of $x^2 + \frac{1}{x^2}$ will be:

A. 228 B. 230
C. 323 D. 223

6. If $x = 12$ and $y = 4$, the value of $(x+y)^{x/y}$ will be:

A. 4096 B. 3896
C. 4196 D. 5086

7. If $x + y = 2z$, then the value of $\left(\frac{x}{x-z} + \frac{z}{y-z}\right)$ will be:

A. 1 B. 4
C. 3/2 D. 2

8. If $x + y + z = 0$, then the value of $\frac{(x+y)(y+z)(z+x)}{xyz}$ will be:

A. –3 B. –2
C. 0 D. –1

9. If $x + \frac{1}{x} = 3$, the value of $x^4 + \frac{1}{x^4}$ will be:

A. 49 B. 47
C. 37 D. 42

10. If $\left(x + \frac{1}{x}\right)^2 = 0$, then the value of $\left(x^2 + \frac{1}{x^2}\right)$ will be:

A. 1 B. –1
C. 2 D. –2

ANSWERS

1	2	3	4	5	6	7	8	9	10
A	C	A	A	D	A	A	D	B	D

EXPLANATORY ANSWERS

1. Let $a = 28$, $b = -15$ and $c = -13$. Then

$$a + b + c = 28 - 15 - 13 = 0$$
$$a^3 + b^3 + c^3 = 3abc$$
$$(28)^3 + (-15)^3 + (-13)^3 = 3 \times 28 \times (-15) \times (-13) = 16380$$

2. $$x^3 + \frac{1}{x^3} = \left(x + \frac{1}{x}\right)^3 - 3\left(x + \frac{1}{x}\right)$$
$$= (5)^3 - 3 \times 5 = 125 - 15 = 110$$

3. If $x^2 + \frac{1}{x^2} = 83$, what is the value of $x^3 - \frac{1}{x^3} = ?$

$$\left(x - \frac{1}{x}\right)^2 = x^2 + \frac{1}{x^2} - 2$$
$$x - \frac{1}{x} = \sqrt{83 - 2} = \sqrt{81}$$
$$x - \frac{1}{x} = 9$$
$$\therefore \left(x^3 - \frac{1}{x^3}\right) = \left(x - \frac{1}{x}\right)^3 + 3\left(x - \frac{1}{x}\right)$$
$$= (9)^3 + 3 \times 9$$
$$= 729 + 27 = 756$$

4. $$23^3 - 17^3 = (20 + 3)^3 - (20 - 3)^3$$
$$= 2(3^3 + 3 \times 20^2 \times 3)$$
$$[\because (a + b)^3 - (a - b)^3 = 2(b^3 + 3a^2b)]$$
$$= 2\,(27 + 3600)$$
$$= 54 + 7200 = 7254$$

5. $\because x + \frac{1}{x} = 15$

$$\Rightarrow \left(x + \frac{1}{x}\right)^2 = (15)^2 \Rightarrow x^2 + \frac{1}{x^2} + 2.x\frac{1}{x} = 225$$
$$\therefore x^2 + \frac{1}{x^2} = 225 - 2 = 223.$$

6. $(x+y)^{x/y} = (12+4)^{12/4} = (16)^3 = 4096.\ [\because x = 12, y = 4]$

7. $\because x + y = 2z \Rightarrow x - z = z - y = -(y - z)$

$$\therefore \frac{x}{x-z} + \frac{z}{y-z} = \frac{x}{-(y-z)} + \frac{z}{y-z} = \frac{z-x}{y-z} = 1.$$
$$[\because x - z = z - y]$$

8. $\because$
$$x + y + z = 0 \Rightarrow x + y = -z$$
$$x + y + z = 0 \Rightarrow y + z = -x$$
and
$$x + y + z = 0 \Rightarrow z + x = -y$$
$$\therefore \frac{(x+y)(y+z)(z+x)}{xyz} = \frac{(-z)(-x)(-y)}{xyz} = -1.$$

9. $\because x + \frac{1}{x} = 3 \Rightarrow \left(x + \frac{1}{x}\right)^2 = (3)^2$

$$\Rightarrow x^2 + \frac{1}{x^2} + 2.x.\frac{1}{x} = 9 \Rightarrow x^2 + \frac{1}{x^2} = 9 - 2 = 7$$
$$\because x^2 + \frac{1}{x^2} = 7 \Rightarrow \left(x^2 + \frac{1}{x^2}\right)^2 = (7)^2$$
$$\Rightarrow x^4 + \frac{1}{x^4} + 2.x^2.\frac{1}{x^2} = 49$$
$$\therefore x^4 + \frac{1}{x^4} = 49 - 2 = 47.$$

□□□□□

8

Mensuration

PART–A
AREA OF PLANE FIGURES

AREA OF RECTILINEAR FIGURES

Points to Remember

Rectilinear Figure : A figure made up of some line segment is called a rectilinear figure and the line segments forming the figure are known as its sides.

Closed Rectilinear Figure : A rectilinear figure is said to be a closed rectilinear figure if it has no free ends.

Simple Rectilinear Figure : A rectilinear figure is said to be simple if no two sides of it intersect except at a common end-point.

Region : The part of the plane enclosed by a simple closed rectilinear figure is called the region enclosed by it.

Area : The magnitude of the plane region enclosed by a simple closed figure is called its area.

Various units of Measurement of Area

1 dm^2 = 10×10 cm^2 = 100 cm^2
1 m^2 = 10×10 dm^2 = 100 dm^2
1 m^2 = 100×100 cm^2 = 10000 cm^2
1 dam^2 = 10×10 m^2 = 100 m^2
1 arc = 1 dam^2 = 100 m^2
1 hm^2 = 100×100 m^2 = 10000 m^2
1 hectare = 10000 m^2
1 hectare = 100 acres
1 km^2 = $(1000 \times 1000)m^2$ = $10^6 m^2$
1 km^2 = 100 hectares.

Some Important Formula

(*i*) Area of rectangle $= l \times b$

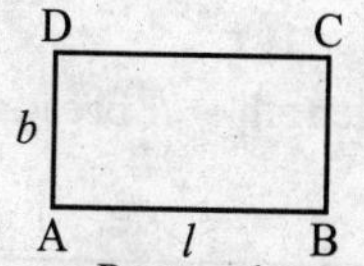

Rectangle

(*ii*) Length $= \dfrac{\text{Area}}{\text{Breadth}}$ (*iii*) Diagonal $= \sqrt{l^2 + b^2}$

(*iv*) Perimeter $= 2\,(l + b)$

(*v*) Area of the square $= a^2$ sq units

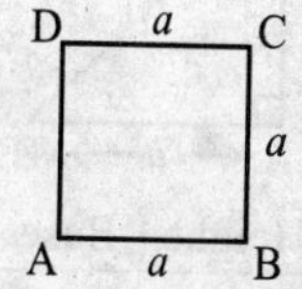

(*vi*) Diagonal of the square $= \sqrt{2}\, a$ units

(*vii*) Perimeter of the square $= 4a$ units

(*viii*) Side of the square $= \dfrac{1}{\sqrt{2}}$ (diagonal)

(*ix*) Side of the square $= \sqrt{\text{Area}}$ units

(*x*) Area of parallelogram = Base × height $= a \times h$

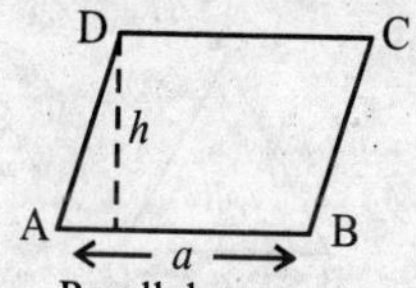

Parallelogram

(*xi*) Base of a parallelogram $= \dfrac{\text{Area}}{\text{Height}}$

(*xii*) Side of parallelogram $= \dfrac{\text{Area}}{\text{Corresponding altitude}}$

(*xiii*) Area of rhombus

$$= \frac{1}{2} \text{(product of diagonals)} = \frac{1}{2}\,(d_1 \times d_2)$$

(*xiv*) $d_1{}^2 + d_2{}^2 = 4a^2$

or $a = \dfrac{1}{2}\sqrt{d_1^2 + d_2^2}$

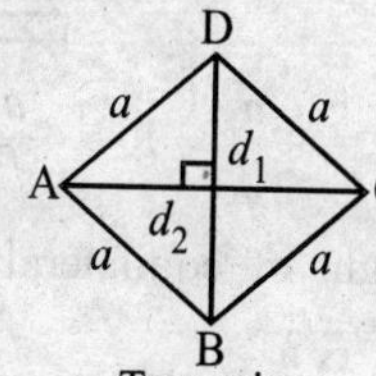

Trapeziun

(*xv*) Area of Trapezium

$$= \frac{1}{2} \times \text{(Sum of parallel sides)} \times \text{height}$$

(*xvi*) Area of quadrilateral

$$\text{ABCD} = \frac{1}{2} \times d\,(h_1 + h_2)$$

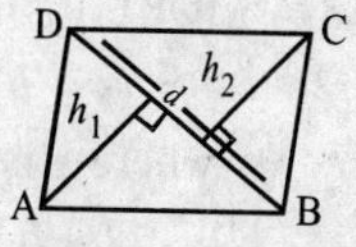

(*xvii*) Area of four walls = 2 (Length + Breadth) × Height

Triangle

(*i*) Area of right angle triangle.

$$= \frac{1}{2} \times \text{base} \times \text{height} = \frac{1}{2} \times a \times h$$

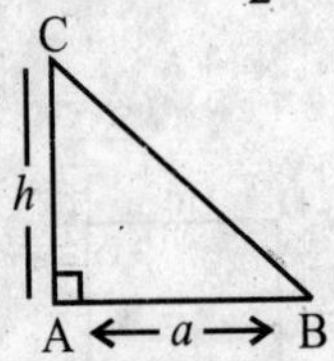

$$\text{inradius, } r = \frac{\text{Height} + \text{Base} - \text{Hypotenuse}}{2}$$

$$\text{Circum radius, R} = \frac{\text{Hypotenuse}}{2}$$

(*ii*) Area of triangle whose three sides are given.

$$s = \frac{a+b+c}{2}$$

$$\text{Area of } \Delta\,\text{ABC} = \sqrt{s(s-a)(s-b)(s-c)}$$

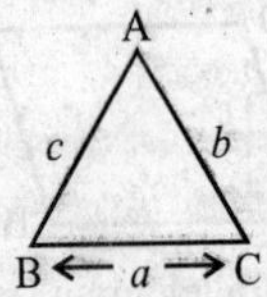

$$r = \frac{\Delta}{s},\ \text{R} = \frac{abc}{4\Delta}$$

(*iii*) Area of an equilateral triangle

$$\text{ABC} = \frac{\sqrt{3}}{4}(\text{side})^2 = \frac{\sqrt{3}}{4}(a)^2$$

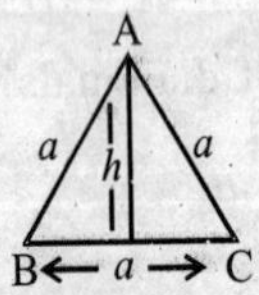

$$r = \frac{a}{2\sqrt{3}},\ \text{R} = \frac{a}{\sqrt{3}},\ \text{R} : r = 2 : 1$$

(*iv*) Height of equilateral triangle

$$= \frac{\sqrt{3}}{2} \times \text{side} = \frac{\sqrt{3}}{2} \times a$$

(*v*) Area of an isosceles triangle

$$\text{ABC} = \frac{1}{2} \times \text{base} \times \sqrt{(\text{equal side})^2 - \frac{1}{4}(\text{base})^2}$$

$$= \frac{1}{2}a \times \sqrt{b^2 - \frac{1}{4}a^2}$$

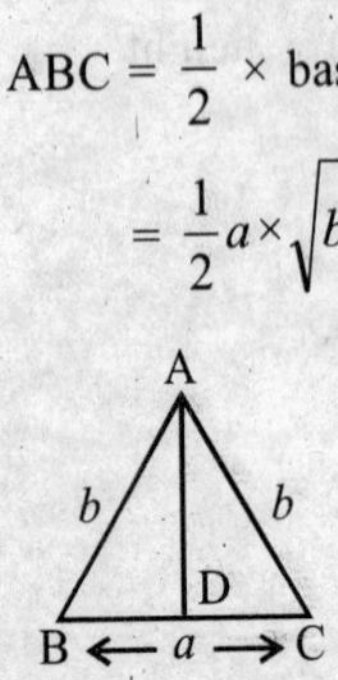

(OR)

$$= (s-b)\sqrt{s(s-a)}$$

where s is semi-perimeter

$$s = \frac{b+b+a}{2} = \frac{2b+a}{2}$$

Circumference and Area of A Circle

Points To Remember:

- The perimeter of a circle is called its circumference.
- The ratio of the circumference of a circle to its diameter is the same for all circles. The constant ratio is denoted by π.

$$\pi = \frac{22}{7} \text{ or } 3.14 \qquad \frac{\text{Circumference}}{\text{Diameter}} = \pi$$

- Circumference of a circle = $2\pi r$
- Area of a circle of radius r is given by $A = \pi r^2$
- Radius of a circle = $\frac{\sqrt{A}}{\pi}$
- Length of arc $\widehat{AB}$
- $(l) = \frac{\pi r \theta}{180°}$

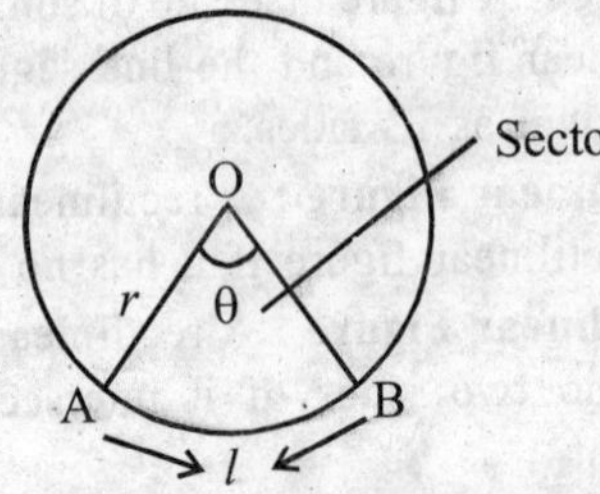

- Area of Sector AOB = $\frac{\pi r^2 \theta}{360°} = \frac{1}{2} rl.$
- Area of segment = $\frac{\pi r^2 \theta}{360°} - \frac{1}{2} r^2 \sin\theta$

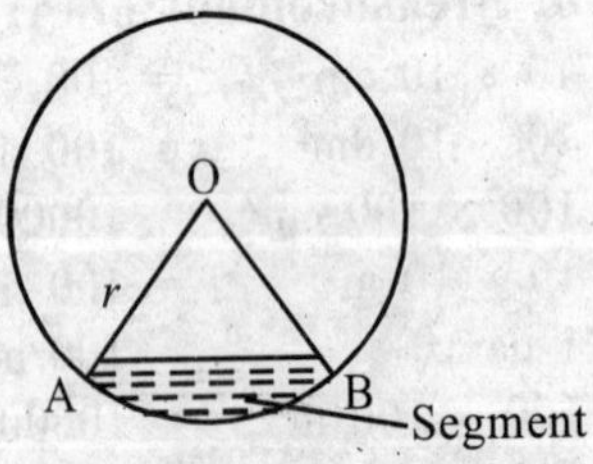

PART–B

SURFACE AREA AND VOLUME OF CUBE, CUBOIDS AND CYLINDER

Surface Area and Volume

(A) Cube and Cuboid

1. **Cuboid :** Let length = l, breadth = b and height = h units. Then,

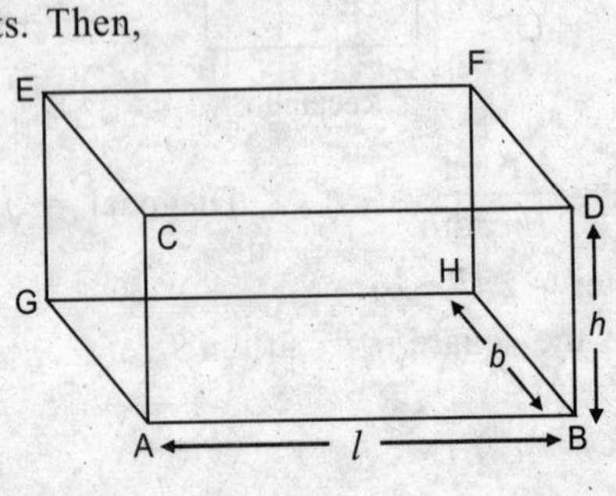

(1) Volume = $(l \times b \times h)$ cubic units
(2) Curved surface area = $2(l + b)h$ sq. units (area of four walls of a room)
(3) Total surface area = $2(lb + bh + hl)$ sq. units
(4) Diagonal = $\sqrt{l^2 + b^2 + h^2}$ units.

2. Cube : Let each edge of a cube be of length a. Then,

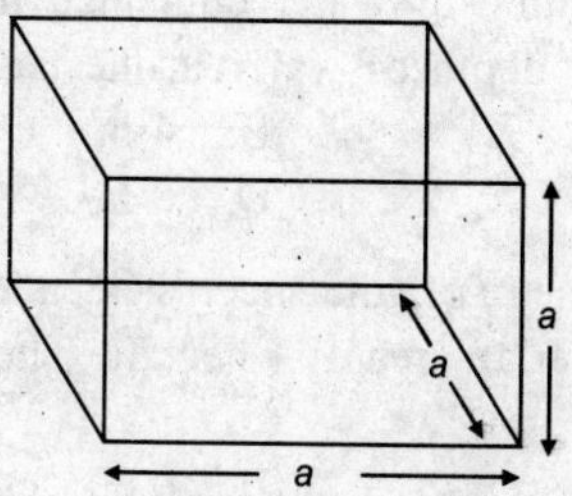

(1) Volume = a^3 cubic units
(2) Curved surface Area = $4a^2$ sq. units
(3) Total surface Area = $6a^2$ sq. units
(4) Diagonal = $\sqrt{3}a$ units

Right Circular Cylinder

A solid generated by the revolution of a rectangle about one of its sides is called a right circular cylinder.

(*i*) Lateral (curved) surface area of cylinder = $2\pi rh$
(*ii*) Total surface area of a cylinder = $2\pi rh + 2\pi r^2$
$- 2\pi r\,(h + r)$
(*iii*) Volume of a cylinder = $\pi r^2 h$

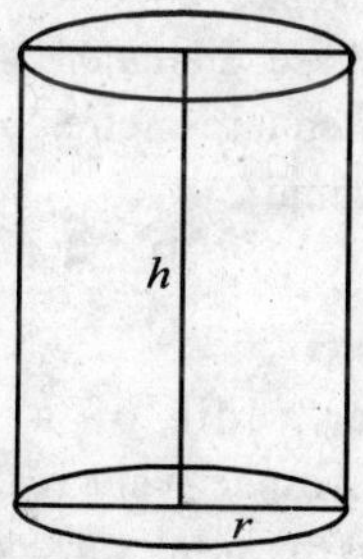

Hallow Cylinder

(*i*) Each base surface area = $\pi\,(R^2 - r^2)$
(*ii*) Curved surface area = External surface area + Internal surface area = $2\pi Rh + 2\pi rh = 2\pi h\,(R + r)$

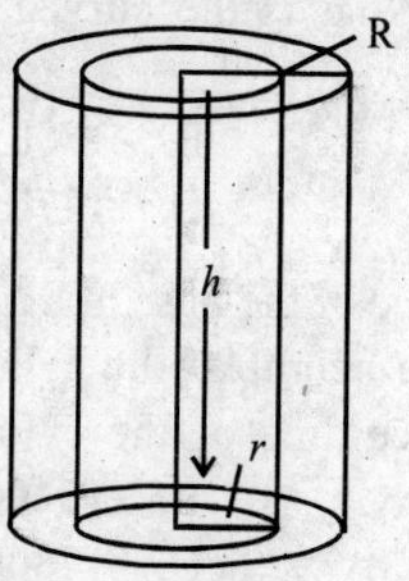

(*iii*) Total surface area
$= 2\pi Rh + 2\pi rh + 2\pi\,(R^2 - r^2)$
$= 2\pi h\,(R + r) + 2\pi\,(R + r)\,(R - r)$
$= (R + r)\,[2\pi h + 2\pi\,(R - r)]$
$= (R + r)\,[2\pi\,(h + R - r)]$
$= 2\pi\,(R + r)\,(h + R - r)$.

(*iv*) Volume of the material
= Exterior volume − Interior volume
$= \pi R^2 h - \pi r^2 h = \pi h(R^2 - r^2)$

Right Circular Cone

A right circular cone is a solid generated by revolving a line segment which passes through a fixed point and which makes a constant angle with a fixed line.

(*i*) Curved surface area of a cone = πrl

Where $l = \sqrt{h^2 + r^2}$

(*ii*) Total surface area of a cone
$= \pi rl + \pi r^2 = \pi r\,(l + r)$

(*iii*) Volume of the cone = $\frac{1}{3}\pi r^2 h$

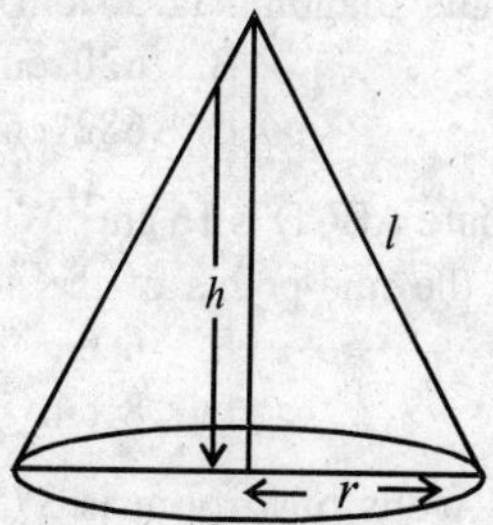

Cone

Sphere/Hemisphere

- **Sphere:** The set of all points in space which are equidistant from a fixed point, is called a *sphere*. The fixed point is called the *centre* of the sphere and constant distance is called its *radius*.

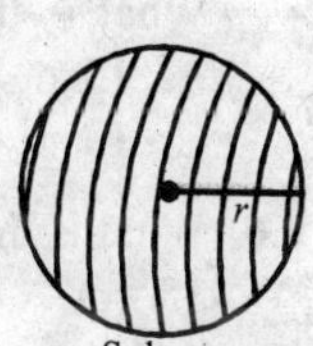

Sphere

- **Hemisphere :** A plane through the centre of a sphere divides the sphere into two equal parts, each of which is called a hemisphere.
- **Spherical shell :** The difference of two solid concentric spheres is called a spherical shell.

Important formula

(*i*) Surface area of the sphere = $4\pi r^2$
(*ii*) Volume of the sphere = $\frac{4}{3}\pi r^3$
(*iii*) Curved surface area of a hemisphere = $2\pi r^2$
(*iv*) Total surface area of a hemisphere = $3\pi r^2$
(*v*) Volume of a hemisphere = $\frac{2}{3}\pi r^3$

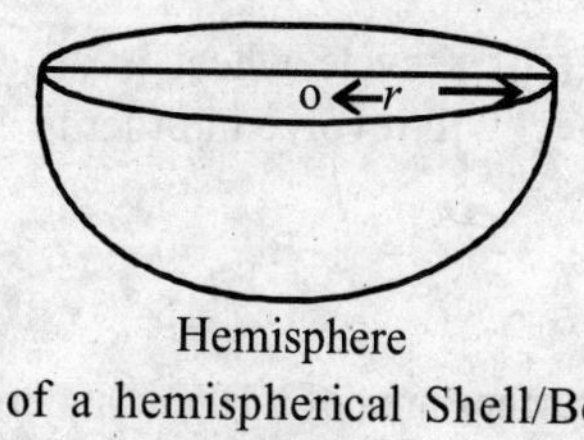

Hemisphere

(*vi*) Volume of a hemispherical Shell/Bowl

Volume = $\frac{2}{3}\pi(r_1^3 - r_2^3)$

Curved surface area
$= 3\pi r_1^2 + 3\pi r_2^2 = 3\pi(r_1^2 + r_2^2)$

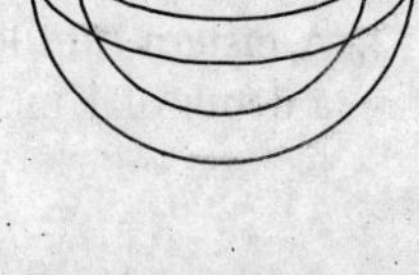

Multiple Choice Questions

1. The length of a rectangle is twice its breadth. What is the dimensions of the rectangle if its area is 288 cm^2?
A. 24 cm, 12 cm B. 16 cm, 10 cm
C. 20 cm, 16 cm D. 28 cm, 10 cm

2. The length and breadth of a rectangular field are in the ratio 3 : 2. If the area of the field is 3456 m^2. What is its dimensions?
A. 48 m, 60 m B. 72 m, 48 m
C. 40 m, 70 m D. 64 m, 52 m

3. What is the area of a rectangular plot if one side of it is 48 cm and its diagonal is 50 cm?
A. 560 cm^2 B. 620 cm^2
C. 672 cm^2 D. 682 cm^2

4. The area of square ABCD is 16 cm^2. What is the area of the square joining the mid-points of the sides?
A. 4 cm^2 B. 6 cm^2
C. 10 cm^2 D. 8 cm^2

5. The area of 4 walls of a room is 375 m^2. The breadth and height of the room are 10 m and 7.5 m respectively. What is the length of the room?
A. 15 m B. 16 m
C. 17 m D. 18 m

6. What is the circumference of a circle whose diameter is 35 cm?
A. 110 cm B. 112 cm
C. 115 cm D. 120 cm

7. What is the circumference of a cycle wheel whose radius is 3.7 dm?
A. 20.35 cm B. 23.24 cm
C. 22.34 cm D. 24.24 cm

8. The diameter of a coin is 2 cm. What is its circumference?
A. 5.28 cm B. 6.28 cm
C. 7.28 cm D. 5.25 cm

9. Two circles having the same centre have radii 350 m and 490 m. What is the difference in their circumferences?
A. 820 m B. 840 m
C. 880 m D. 860 m

10. The diameter of a cycle wheel is 70 cm. How many times the wheel will revolve in order to cover a distance of 110 m?
A. 50 B. 60
C. 40 D. 45

11. What is the surface area of a 10 cm × 4 cm × 3 cm brick?
A. 84 sq. cm B. 124 sq. cm
C. 164 sq. cm D. 180 sq. cm

12. A cistern 6 m long and 4 m wide contains water up to a depth of 1 m 25 cm. The total area of the wet surface is:
A. 49 m^2 B. 50 m^2
C. 53.5 m^2 D. 55 m^2

13. The area of the base of a rectangular tank is 6500 cm^2 and the volume of water contained in it is 2.6 cubic metres. The depth of water in the tank is:
A. 3.5 m B. 4 m
C. 5 m D. 6 m

14. Half cubic metre of gold sheet is extended by hammering so as to cover an area of 1 hectare. The thickness of the sheet is:
A. 0.0005 cm B. 0.005 cm
C. 0.05 cm D. 0.5 cm

15. In a shower, 5 cm of rain falls. The volume of water that falls on 1.5 hectares of ground is:
A. 75 cu. m B. 750 cu. m
C. 7500 cu. m D. 75000 cu. m

16. The curved surface area of a right circular cylinder of height 14 cm is 88 cm^2. What is the radius of the base of the cylinder?
A. 2 cm B. 3 cm
C. 1 cm D. 4 cm

17. It is required to make a closed cylinderical tank of height 1 m and base diameter 140 cm from a metal sheet. How many square metres of the metal sheet are required for the same?
A. 3.4 m^2 B. 4.4 m^2
C. 2.4 m^2 D. 5.4 m^2

18. Inner and outer radii of a metallic pipe are 3 cm and 3.5 cm respectively if the length of the pipe is 56 cm. What is its total surface area?
A. 2225 cm^2 B. 2244 cm^2
C. 2264 cm^2 D. 2288 cm^2

19. A right circular cylinder has base radius 8 cm and height 35 cm. What is the curved surface area of the cylinder?
A. 1760 cm^2 B. 1780 cm^2
C. 1750 cm^2 D. 1770 cm^2

20. The circumference of the base of a right circular cylinder is 176 cm. If the height of the cylinder is 1 m, what is the lateral surface area of the cylinder?
A. 17500 cm^2 B. 17400 cm^2
C. 17600 cm^2 D. 17800 cm^2

21. Diameter of the base of a cone is 10.5 cm and its slant height is 10 cm. What is the curved surface area of the cone?
A. 154 cm^2 B. 165 cm^2
C. 175 cm^2 D. 185 cm^2

22. The height of a cone is 16 cm and the radius of its base is 12 cm. What is the curved surface area and the total surface area of the cone?
A. 753.6 cm^2, 1205.76 cm^2
B. 853.6 cm^2, 1208.76 cm^2
C. 953.5 cm^2, 1212.76 cm^2
D. 764.6 cm^2, 1185.76 cm^2

23. Curved surface area of a cone is 308 cm^2 and its slant height is 14 cm. What is the radius of the base and total surface area of the cone?
A. 7 cm, 462 cm B. 5 cm, 460 cm^2
C. 6 cm, 452 cm^2 D. 4 cm, 475 cm^2

24. The radius of the base of a conical tent is 12 m. The tent is 9 m high. What is the cost of the canvas required to make the tent, if one square metre of canvas costs ₹ 120?
A. ₹ 67885.20 B. ₹ 68885.20
C. ₹ 66985.20 D. ₹ 68675.20

25. What is the curved surface area of a right circular cone whose slant height is 10 cm and base radius is 7 cm?
A. 210 cm^2 B. 220 cm^2
C. 230 cm^2 D. 215 cm^2

26. Diameter of a sphere is 10 cm. What is its surface area?
A. 314.28 cm^2 B. 318.24 cm^2
C. 312.28 cm^2 D. 310.28 cm^2

27. The surface of a solid hemisphere with its circular base is to be painted. If the radius of the hemisphere is 28 cm, find the cost of painting the surface at the rate of ₹ 3 per 100 cm^2.
A. ₹ 220.76 B. ₹ 218.76
C. ₹ 221.76 D. ₹ 230.5

28. Assuming the earth to be a sphere of radius 6370 km. What is surface area of the earth?
A. 510109600 km^2 B. 410109600 km^2
C. 520109600 km^2 D. 490109600 km^2

29. What is the surface area of a sphere whose diameter is 14 cm?
A. 616 cm^2 B. 612 cm^2
C. 624 cm^2 D. 620 cm^2

30. The radius of a spherical balloon increases from 7 cm to 14 cm as air is being pumped into it. What is the ratio of surface areas of the balloon in the two cases?
A. 2 : 3 B. 1 : 4
C. 3 : 4 D. 4 : 5

ANSWERS

1	2	3	4	5	6	7	8	9	10
A	B	C	D	A	A	B	B	C	A
11	**12**	**13**	**14**	**15**	**16**	**17**	**18**	**19**	**20**
C	A	B	B	B	C	B	D	A	C
21	**22**	**23**	**24**	**25**	**26**	**27**	**28**	**29**	**30**
B	A	A	A	B	A	C	A	A	B

EXPLANATORY ANSWERS

1. Let length of rectangle = x cm.

$$\text{Breadth} = \frac{x}{2} \text{ cm.}$$

$$\text{Area of rectangle} = 288$$
$$l \times b = 288$$
$$x \times \frac{x}{2} = 288$$
$$x^2 = 288 \times 2 = 576$$
$$x = \sqrt{576} = \sqrt{24 \times 24} = 24 \text{ cm.}$$
$$\text{Length} = 24 \text{ cm.}$$
$$\text{Breadth} = \frac{24}{2} = 12 \text{ cm.}$$

2. Let length = $3x$ and breadth = $2x$

$$\text{Area of rectangular field} = 3456\ m^2$$
$$l \times b = 3456$$
$$3x \times 2x = 3456$$
$$x^2 = \frac{3456}{6}$$
$$x = \sqrt{576} = 24.$$
$$\text{Length} = 3x = 3 \times 24 = 72 \text{ m.}$$
$$\text{Breadth} = 2x = 2 \times 24 = 48 \text{ m.}$$

3. Area of rectangular plot = length × breadth

$$AD^2 = BD^2 - AB^2 = 50^2 - 48^2$$
$$= (50 + 48)(50 - 48)$$
$$= 98 \times 2 = 14 \times 7 \times 2$$
$$= 7 \times 2 \times 7 \times 2$$
$$AD = \sqrt{7 \times 2 \times 7 \times 2} = 7 \times 2 = 14 \text{ cm.}$$
$$\text{Area} = 48 \times 14 = 672 \text{ cm}^2.$$

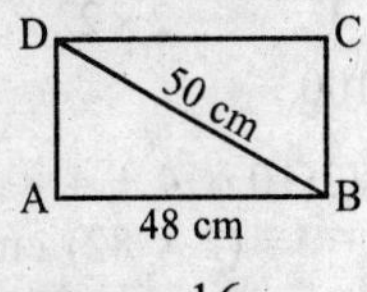

4. Area of square = 16

$$\text{side}^2 = 16$$
$$\text{side} = \sqrt{16}$$
$$AB = 4$$

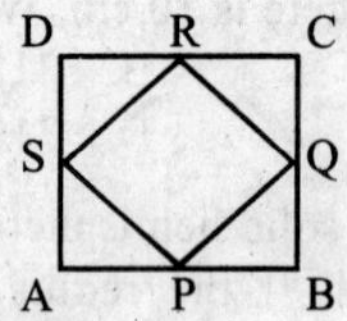

Diagonal of PQRS = 4 cm.

$\sqrt{2}$ side = 4

2 side^2 = 16

$$\text{Area} = \text{side}^2 = \frac{16}{2} = 8 \text{ cm}^2.$$

5. Area of four walls = $2(l+b) \times h$

$2(l+b) \times h = 375$

$2(l+10) \times 7.5 = 375$

$$l + 10 = \frac{375}{15}$$

$l = 25 - 10 = 15$ m.

6. $d = 35$ cm.,

$$r = \frac{d}{2} = \frac{35}{2} \text{ cm.}$$

$$\text{Circumference} = 2\pi r = 2 \times \frac{22}{7} \times \frac{35}{2}$$

$= 22 \times 5 = 110$ cm.

7. $r = 3.7$ dm

Circumference = $2\pi r$

$$= 2 \times \frac{22}{7} \times 3.7 = 2 \times 3.14 \times 3.7$$

$= 23.236$ cm $= 23.24$ cm.

8. $d = 2$ cm.

$$r = \frac{2}{2} = 1 \text{ cm}$$

$$\text{Circumference} = 2\pi r = 2 \times \frac{22}{7} \times 1$$

$= 2 \times 3.14 = 6.28$ cm.

9. Difference in circumference = $2\pi R - 2\pi r$

$= 2\pi(R - r)$ $\qquad R = 490$ m

$$= 2 \times \frac{22}{7}(490 - 350) \qquad r = 350 \text{ m}$$

$$= 2 \times \frac{22}{7} \times 140 = 44 \times 20 = 880 \text{ m.}$$

10. Nos. of revolution

$$= \frac{110}{2 \times \pi \times \frac{70}{2} \times \frac{1}{100}} = \frac{110 \times 100 \times 2 \times 7}{2 \times 22 \times 70} = 50.$$

11. Surface area = $[2(10 \times 4 + 4 \times 3 + 10 \times 3)]$ cm^2

$= (2 \times 82)$ cm^2 $= 164$ cm^2.

12. Area of the wet surface = $[2(lb + bh + lh) - lb]$

$= 2(bh + lh) + lb$

$= [2(4 \times 1.25 + 6 \times 1.25) + 6 \times 4]$ m^2

$= 49$ m^2.

13. Volume = $(2.6 \times 100 \times 100 \times 100)$ cu. cm.

$$\text{Depth} = \frac{\text{Volume}}{\text{Area of the base}} = \left(\frac{2.6 \times 100 \times 100 \times 100}{6500}\right) \text{cm}$$

$= 400$ cm $= 4$ m.

14. $$\text{Volume of gold} = \left(\frac{1}{2} \times 100 \times 100 \times 100\right) \text{cm}^3.$$

Area of sheet = 10000 m^2 = $(10000 \times 100 \times 100)$ cm^2

$$\therefore \text{Thickness of the sheet} = \left(\frac{1 \times 100 \times 100 \times 100}{2 \times 10000 \times 100 \times 100}\right) \text{cm}$$

$= 0.005$ cm.

15. Area = (1.5×10000) m^2 = 15000 m^2.

$$\text{Depth} = \frac{5}{100} \text{m} = \frac{1}{20} \text{m}.$$

$\therefore$ Volume = (Area × Depth)

$$= \left(15000 \times \frac{1}{20}\right) \text{m}^3 = 750 \text{ m}^3.$$

16. Curved surface of right circular cylinder = 88 cm^2

$2\pi rh = 88$

$$2 \times \frac{22}{7} \times r \times 14 = 88$$

$$r = \frac{88}{88} = 1 \text{ cm.}$$

17. Area of cylinder = $2\pi rh$

$$= 2 \times \frac{22}{7} \times 100 \times 70$$

$$= \frac{44 \times 1000}{100 \times 100} \text{m}^2 = 4.4 \text{ m}^2.$$

18. $h = 56$ cm

$r = 3$ cm

$R = 3.5$ cm

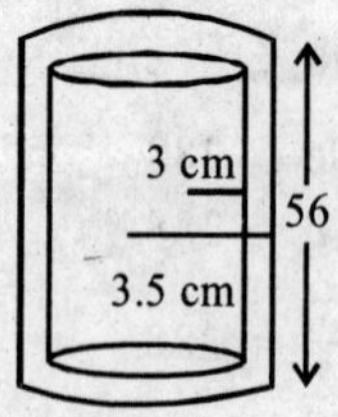

$$2\pi rh = 2 \times \frac{22}{7} \times 3 \times 56$$

$= 44 \times 24 = 1056$ cm^2

$$2\pi Rh = 2 \times \frac{22}{7} \times 3.5 \times 56$$

$= 44 \times 28 = 1232$ cm^2

Surface area = 1056 + 1232 cm^2

= 2288 cm^2.

19. Curved surface of the cylinder

$= 2\pi rh$

$$= 2\times\frac{22}{7}\times 8\times 35$$
$$= 44 \times 40 = 1760 \text{ cm}^2.$$

20. $2\pi r = 176 = 2\times\frac{22}{7}\times r = 176$

$$\Rightarrow \quad r = \frac{176\times 7}{2\times 22} = 28 \text{ cm}$$

$$h = 1 \text{ m} = 100 \text{ cm}$$

Lateral surface of the cylinder

$$= 2\pi rh$$
$$= 2\times\frac{22}{7}\times 28\times 100$$
$$= 17600 \text{ cm}^2.$$

21. Curved surface of the cone $= \pi rl$

$$= \frac{22}{7}\times\frac{10.5}{2}\times 10$$
$$= 22 \times 7.5 = 165 \text{ cm}^2.$$

22. Curved surface of the cone

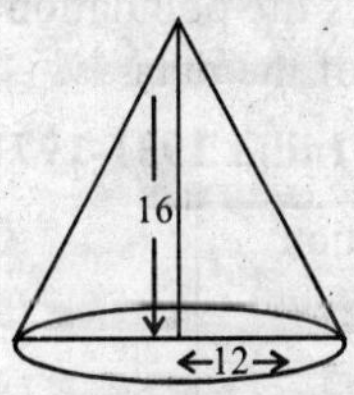

$$l^2 = 16^2 + 12^2$$
$$= 256 + 144$$
$$= 400$$
$$l = \sqrt{400}$$
$$= 20$$

$$= \pi rl$$
$$= \frac{22}{7}\times 12\times 20$$
$$= 3.14 \times 240 = 753.6 \text{ cm}^2.$$

Total surface area

$$= \pi rl + \pi r^2$$
$$= 753.6 + \frac{22}{7}\times 12\times 12$$
$$= 753.6 + 3.14 \times 144$$
$$= 753.6 + 452.16 = 1205.76 \text{ cm}^2.$$

23. Curved surface area of cone, $\pi rl = 308$

$$\frac{22}{7}\times r\times 14 = 308 \Rightarrow r = \frac{308\times 7}{22\times 14}$$
$$r = 7 \text{ cm}.$$

Total surface area of the cone $= \pi rl + \pi r^2$

$$= 308 + \frac{22}{7}\times 7\times 7$$
$$= 308 + 154 = 462 \text{ cm}^2.$$

24. Curved surface area of the tent $= \pi rl$

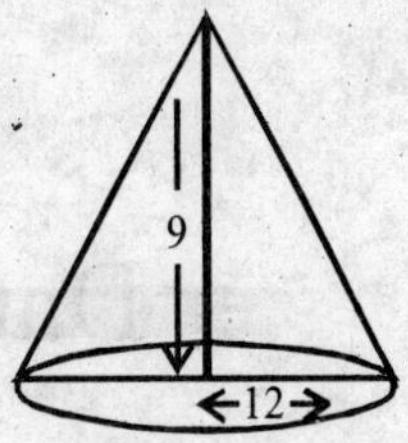

$$l^2 = 12^2 + 9^2$$
$$= 144 + 81$$
$$= 225$$
$$l = \sqrt{225} = 15$$
$$= \frac{22}{7}\times 12\times 15 = \frac{3960}{7}$$
$$= 565.71 \text{ m}^2$$

The cost of canvas $= 565.71 \times 120$

$$= ₹\ 67885.20.$$

25. Curved surface of the cone $= \pi rl$

$$= \frac{22}{7}\times 7\times 10 = 220 \text{ cm}^2.$$

26. $r = \frac{10}{2} = 5$ cm

Surface area of the sphere $= 4\pi r^2$

$$= 4\times\frac{22}{7}\times 5\times 5$$
$$= \frac{88\times 25}{7} = \frac{2200}{7} = 314.28 \text{ cm}^2.$$

27. The cost of painting

$$= 3\pi r^2 \times \frac{3}{100}$$
$$= 3\times\frac{22}{7}\times 28\times 28\times\frac{3}{100}$$
$$= \frac{66\times 84}{25} = \frac{5544}{25}$$
$$= ₹\ 221.76.$$

28. Surface area of the earth $= 4\pi r^2$

$$= 4\times\frac{22}{7}\times 6370\times 6370$$
$$= 88 \times 910 \times 6370 \text{ km}^2$$
$$= 510109600 \text{ km}^2.$$

29. Surface area of sphere $= 4\pi r^2$

$$= 4\pi \times 7 \times 7$$
$$= 4\times\frac{22}{7}\times 7\times 7 = 4\times 154 = 616 \text{ cm}^2.$$

30. The ratio of Areas

$$= \frac{4\pi\times 7\times 7}{4\pi\times 14\times 14} = \frac{1}{4} = 1 : 4.$$

9

Data Handling

Graphical Representation of Statistical Data

One of the most convincing and appearing ways in which statistical result may be presented is through diagrams and graphs. The impressions created by diagrams last much longer than those created by the figures presented in a tabular form.

> *Rather than present data numerically in the form of a table it can sometimes be better to illustrate the information through the use of graphs, charts, diagrams and so on.*

The frequency distribution of a discrete value is best represented by a bar diagram. The height of the bars is proportional to the frequency of each variate-value. The bars must be kept distinct to show that the variate-values are distinct.

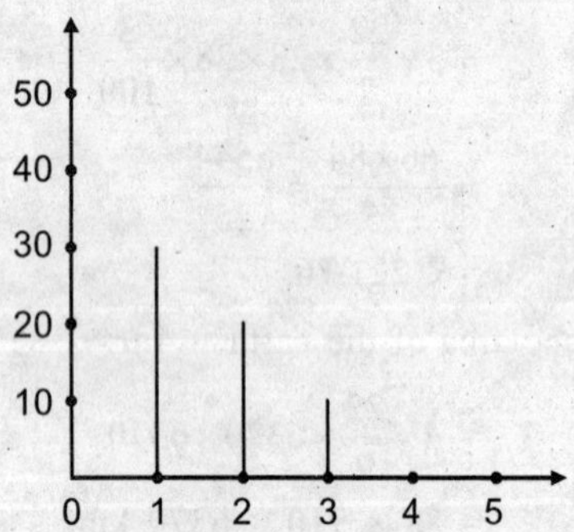

A simple bar chart is used to illustrate a frequency distribution. The lengths of the bars are proportional to the frequency and the bars are of equal width.

Some Important Types of Diagrams and Graphs

The different types of Diagrams and Graphs

(1) Bar diagram
(2) Histogram
(3) Frequency circle
(4) Cumulative frequency curve of the ogive
(5) Pie diagram.

Bar Diagram

Bar diagram is the easiest and most adaptable general purpose chart. In this, bars or rectangles of uniform width are drawn with equal spaces in between on the axis. Along the y-axis is shown, the scale of the height of the rectangles. Thickness of bars is not taken into account, they should be so constructed that they look attractive and beautiful. This can be done by colouring them or by preparing designs in them. However, the colour or designs of all bars representing one type of data should be identical. The bars may be vertical or horizontal. Some of the main bar diagrams are:

(*i*) Simple Bar-Diagram
(*ii*) Sub-divided Bar-Diagram
(*iii*) Multiple Bar-Diagram

The following Examples of Illustrate :

Example: The following table gives the population of India (in millions). Draw a bar diagram of the data:

Population (in million) of India 1931-1971

Year	Population (*in millions*)
1931	275.5
1941	312.1
1951	356.9
1961	439.9
1971	546.9

Solution: The above data is represented by a simple bar diagram as follows :

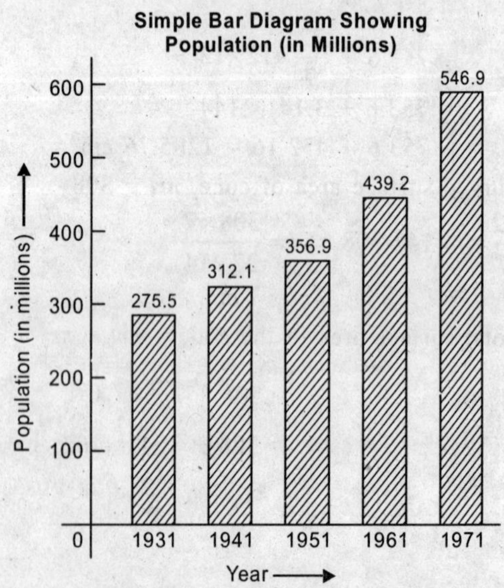

Here years are denoted on the x-axis and population (in millions) on the y-axis. The length of each bar corresponds to the number representing population on the y-axis.

Solution:

1 (*c*): The total of the central angles corresponding to the three crops which cover 50% of the total area, should be 180°. Now, the total of the central angles for the given combinations are:

(*a*) Wheat, Barley and Jowar
$= (72° + 36° + 18°) = 126°$

(*b*) Rice, Wheat and Jowar
$= (72° + 72° + 18°) = 162°$

(*c*) Rice, Wheat and Barley
$= (72° + 72° + 36°) = 180°$

(*d*) Bajra, Maize and Rice
$= (18° + 45° + 72°) = 135°$

Clearly, (*c*) is the required combination.

2 (*a*): The area under any of the food crops is proportional to the central angle corresponding to that crop.

Let, the area under rice production be x million acres.

Then, $18 : 72 = 1.5 : x \Rightarrow x = \left(\frac{72 \times 1.5}{18}\right) = 6.$

Thus, the area under rice production = 6 million acress

3 (*b*): Let, the total production of barley be T tonnes and let Z acres of land be put under barley production.

Then, the total production of wheat = (6T) tonnes.

Also, area under wheat production = (2Z) areas.

$$\left[\because \frac{\text{Area under Wheat production}}{\text{Area under Barley production}} = \frac{72°}{36°} = 2 \text{ and therefore, Area under wheat} = 2 \times \text{Area under barley} = (2Z) \text{ acres}\right]$$

Now, yield per acre for wheat $= \left(\frac{6T}{2Z}\right)$ tonnes/acre $= \left(\frac{3T}{Z}\right)$ tonnes/acre and yield per acre for barley $= \left(\frac{T}{Z}\right)$ tonnes/acre.

$\therefore$ Required Ratio $= \left(\frac{3T/Z}{T/Z}\right) = 3:1.$

Multiple Choice Questions

1. Which one of the following is not the graphical representation of statistical data?
A. Bar graph
B. Histogram
C. Frequency polygon
D. Cumulative frequency distribution

2. In a frequency distribution, ogives are graphical representation of:
A. Frequency
B. Relative frequency
C. Cumulative frequency
D. Raw data

3. A frequency polygon is constructed by plotting frequency of the class interval and the:
A. upper limit of the class
B. lower limit of the class
C. mid value of the class
D. any values of the class

4. In a histogram the area of each rectangle is proportional to:
A. the class mark of the corresponding class interval
B. the class size of the corresponding class interval
C. frequency of the corresponding class interval
D. cumulative frequency of the corresponding class interval

5. In a histogram, each class rectangle is constructed with base as:
A. frequency
B. class-intervals
C. range
D. size of the class

6. Read the bar graph shown in figure and answer the following question:
In which year is the increase of students maximum?

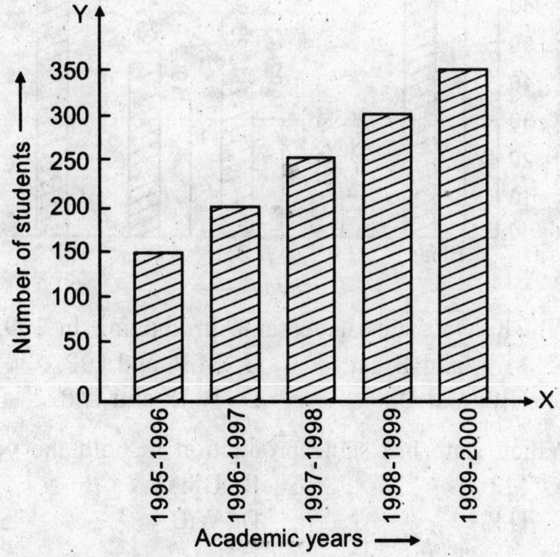

A. 1996-1997 B. 1997-1998
C. 1999-2000 D. None of these

Directions (Qs. 7 to 9) : *Read the following bar graph shown in figure and answer the following questions:*

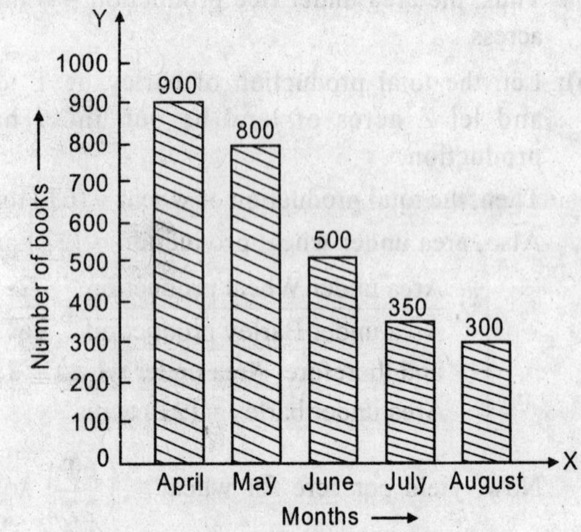

7. In which month was the sale of the books maximum?

A. April B. May
C. June D. August

8. In which month was the sale of the books minimum?

A. April B. May
C. July D. August

9. What is the total sale during these five months?

A. 3800 copies B. 2850 copies
C. 2800 copies D. 2950 copies

Directions (Qs. 10 to 12) : *Read the following bar graph given in figure and answer the following questions:*

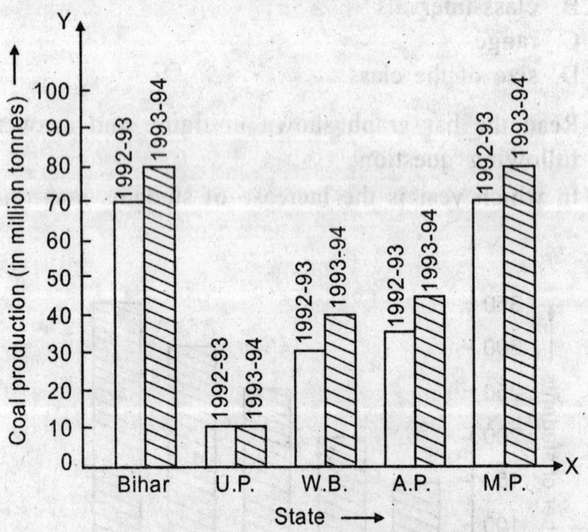

10. Which two states have same production in 1993-94?

A. M.P. and Bihar B. M.P. and U.P.
C. U.P. and Bihar D. W.B. and U.P.

11. Which state has same production in both the years?

A. M.P. B. Bihar
C. U.P. D. W.B.

12. Which state has minimum production?

A. M.P. B. A.P.
C. W.B D. U.P.

Directions (Qs. 13 to 15) : *The following bar graph shows the results of an annual examination in a secondary school.*

Read the bar graph and choose the correct alternative in each of the following.

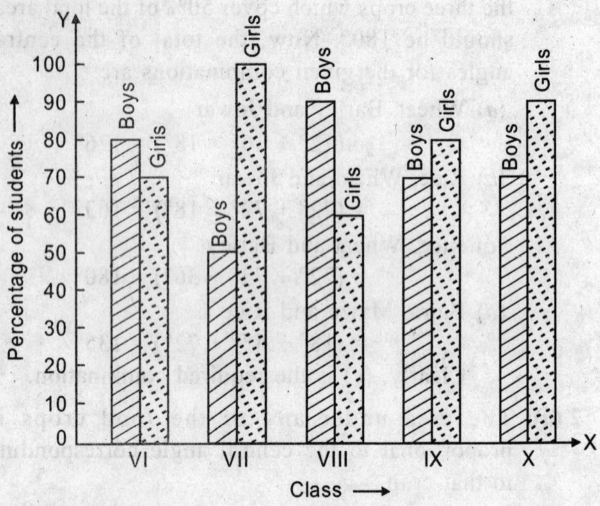

13. The pair of classes in which the results of boys and girls are inversely proportional are:

A. VI, VIII B. VI, IX
C. VIII, IX D. VIII, X

14. The class having the lowest failure rate of girls is:

A. VII B. X
C. IX D. VIII

15. The class having the lowest pass rate of boys is:

A. VI B. VII
C. VIII D. IX

Directions (Qs. 16 to 20) : *Study the following bar-graph and answer the questions given below.*

Production of Fertilizers by a Company (in 10000 tonnes) over the Years

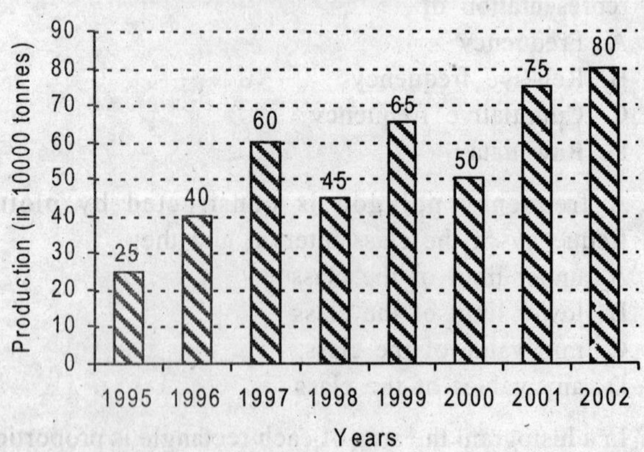

16. In how many of the given years was the production of fertilizers more than the average production of the given years?

A. 1 B. 2
C. 3 D. 4

17. The average production of 1996 and 1997 was exactly equal to the average production of which of the following pairs of years?

A. 2000 and 2001 B. 1999 and 2000
C. 1995 and 1999 D. 1995 and 2001

18. What was the percentage decline in the production of fertilizers from 1997 to 1998?
A. 30% B. 25%
C. 21% D. 20%

19. In which year was the percentage increase in production as compared to the previous year the maximum?
A. 2002 B. 1999
C. 1997 D. 1996

20. What was the percentage increase in production of fertilizers in 2002 compared to that in 1995?
A. 320% B. 220%
C. 200% D. 150%

Directions (Qs. 21 to 25) : *The circle-graph given here shows the spendings of a country on various sports during a particular year. Study the graph carefully and answer the questions given below it.*

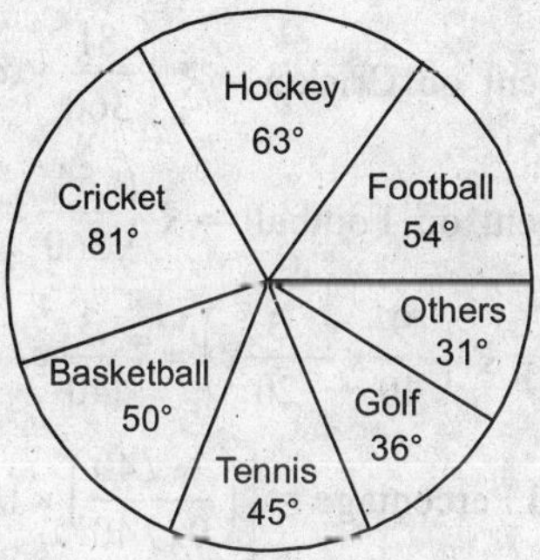

21. What per cent of the total spendings is spent on Tennis?
A. $12\frac{1}{2}\%$ B. $22\frac{1}{2}\%$
C. 25% D. 45%

22. How much per cent more is spent on Hockey than that on Golf?
A. 27% B. 35%
C. 37.5% D. 75%

23. How much per cent less is spent on Football than that on Cricket?
A. $22\frac{2}{9}\%$ B. 27%
C. $33\frac{1}{3}\%$ D. $37\frac{1}{2}\%$

24. If the total amount spent on sports during the year was ₹ 2 crores, the amount spent on Cricket and Hockey together was:
A. ₹ 8,00,000
B. ₹ 80,00,000
C. ₹ 1,20,00,000
D. ₹ 1,60,00,000

25. If the total amount spent on sports during the years be ₹ 1,80,00,000, the amount spent on Basketball exceeds that on Tennis by:
A. ₹ 2,50,000 B. ₹ 3,60,000
C. ₹ 3,75,000 D. ₹ 4,10,000

ANSWERS

1	2	3	4	5	6	7	8	9	10
D	C	C	C	B	D	A	D	B	A
11	**12**	**13**	**14**	**15**	**16**	**17**	**18**	**19**	**20**
C	D	B	A	B	D	D	B	D	B
21	**22**	**23**	**24**	**25**					
A	D	C	B	A					

EXPLANATORY ANSWERS

6. The increase in the number of students is uniform as the increase in the heights of bars is uniform. Hence, in this case the increase is not maximum in any of the year.

7. The sale of the books was maximum in the month of April as the height of the rectangle corresponding to April month is maximum.

8. The sale of the books was minimum in the month of August as the height of the corresponding rectangle is minimum.

9. Total sale of the books during 5 months.
(900 + 800 + 500 + 350 + 300) = 2850 copies.

10. M.P. and Bihar have same production in 1993-1994.

11. U.P. has the same production in both the years.

12. U.P.

16. Average production (in 10000 tonnes) over the given years

$$= \frac{1}{8} \times (25 + 40 + 60 + 45 + 65 + 50 + 75 + 80) = 55$$

$\therefore$ The productions during the years 1997, 1999, 2001 and 2002 are more than the average production.

17. Average production (in 10000 tonnes) of 1996 and 1997 $= \frac{40+60}{2} = 50.$

We shall find the average production (in 10000 tonnes) for each of the given alternative

(*a*) 2000 and 2001 $= \frac{50+75}{2} = 62.5$

(*b*) 1999 and 2000 $= \frac{65+50}{2} = 57.5$

(*c*) 1995 and 1999 $= \frac{25+65}{2} = 45$

(*d*) 1995 and 2001 $= \frac{25+75}{2} = 50$

$\therefore$ The average production of 1996 and 1997 is equal to the average production of 1995 and 2001.

18. Required percentage $= \left[\frac{(45-60)}{60} \times 100\right]\% = -25\%.$

$\therefore$ There is a decline of 25% in production from 1997 to 1998.

19. The percentage increase in production compared to previous year for different years are :

In 1996 $= \left[\frac{(40-25)}{25} \times 100\right]\% = 60\%$

In 1997 $= \left[\frac{(60-40)}{40} \times 100\right]\% = 50\%$

In 1999 $= \left[\frac{(65-45)}{45} \times 100\right]\% = 44.44\%$

In 2002 $= \left[\frac{(80-75)}{75} \times 100\right]\% = 6.67\%$

Clearly, there is maximum percentage increase in production in 1996.

20. Required percentage $= \left[\frac{(80-25)}{25} \times 100\right]\% = 220\%$

21. Percentage of money spent on Tennis

$$= \left(\frac{45}{360} \times 100\right)\% = 12\frac{1}{2}\%$$

22. Let the total spendings on sports be ₹ x. Then,

Amount spent on Golf = ₹ $\left(\frac{36}{360} \times x\right) = ₹\frac{x}{10}$

Amount spent on Hockey = ₹ $\left(\frac{63}{360} \times x\right) = ₹\frac{7}{40}x.$

Difference = ₹ $\left(\frac{7}{40}x - \frac{x}{10}\right) = ₹\frac{3x}{40}$

$\therefore$ Required Percentage $= \left[\left(\frac{3x/40}{x/10}\right) \times 100\right]\% = 75\%$

23. Let the total spendings on sports be ₹ x. Then,

Amount spent on Cricket = ₹ $\left(\frac{81}{360} \times x\right) = ₹\left(\frac{9}{40}x\right)$

Amount spent on Football = ₹ $\left(\frac{54}{360} \times x\right) = ₹\left(\frac{3}{20}x\right)$

Difference = ₹ $\left(\frac{9}{40}x - \frac{3}{20}x\right) = ₹\frac{3}{40}x$

$\therefore$ Required Percentage $= \left[\left(\frac{3x/40}{9x/40}\right) \times 100\right]\% = 33\frac{1}{3}\%$

24. Amount spent on Cricket and Hockey together

$= ₹\left[\frac{(81+63)}{360} \times 2\right]$ crores = ₹ 0.8 crores = ₹ 8000000.

25. Amount spent on Basketball exceeds that on Tennis by :

₹ $\left[\frac{(50-45)}{360} \times 18000000\right]$ = ₹ 250000.

❑❑❑❑❑

10

Statistics

Statistics is defined as the mathematics of the collection, organisation and interpretation of numerical data, especially the analysis of population characteristics by inference from the sampling.

Points To Remember

- Observations gathered initially are called **Raw data**.
- The difference between the highest and the lowest values of the observations in given data is called the range.
- Mean of given data

$$= \frac{\text{Sum of all observations}}{\text{Total number of observation}}$$

- In given data, the number of times a particular observation occurs is called its **frequency**.
- A table showing the frequencies of various observations of data is called a frequency distribution table or simply a frequency table.
- When the number of observations is large, we make use of tally marks to count the frequencies.
- Tallies are usually marked in bunches of five for ease of counting.
- When the list of observations is very large, we organise the data into groups called classes or class interval. The data so obtained is called grouped data or a grouped frequency distribution.
- The lower value of a class interval called its lower class limit and the upper value of a class interval is called its upper class limit.
- The difference between the upper and lower values of a class interval is called its **width** or **size**.
- The mid-value of a class interval is called its class mark.
- The frequency of a class interval is called its class frequency.
- A histogram is a graphical representation of grouped data in which class intervals are taken along the horizontal axis and frequencies along the vertical axis.

Measures of Central Tendency

Generally, average value of a distribution in the middle part of the distribution, such type of values are known as measures of central tendency.

The following are the five measures of central tendency:

1. Arithmetic Mean
2. Geometric Mean
3. Harmonic Mean
4. Median
5. Mode

1. **Arithmetic Mean :** The arithmetic (or simple mean) of a set of observations is obtained by dividing the sum of the value of observations by the number of observations.

   ***(i)* Arithmetic Mean for Unclassified (Ungrouped) Data:** If n observations, $x_1, x_2, x_3, ..., x_n$, then their arithmetic mean

$$\text{A or } \bar{x} = \frac{x_1 + x_2 + ... + x_n}{n} = \frac{\sum_{i=1}^{n} x_i}{n}$$

   ***(ii)* Arithmetic Mean for Frequency Distribution :** Let $f_1, f_2, ... f_n$ be corresponding frequencies of $x_1, x_2, ..., x_n$. Then, arithmetic mean

$$A = \frac{x_1 f_1 + x_2 f_2 + ... + x_n f_n}{f_1 + f_2 + ... + f_n} = \frac{\sum_{i=1}^{n} x_i f_i}{\sum_{i=1}^{n} f_i}$$

   ***(iii)* Arithmetic Mean for Classified (Grouped) Data :** For a classified data, we take the class marks $x_1, x_2, ..., x_n$ of the classes as variables, then arithmetic mean by

$$\text{Direct method is } A = \frac{\sum_{i=1}^{n} x_i f_i}{\sum_{i=1}^{n} f_i}$$

   ***(iv)* Combined Mean :** If $A_1, A_2, ..., A_n$ are the n arithmetic mean having number of corresponding observations $n_1, n_2, ..., n_r$, then arithmetic mean of the combined group x is called the combined mean of the observation

$$A = \frac{n_1 A_1 + n_2 A_2 + ... + n_r A_r}{n_1 + n_2 + ... + n_r} = \frac{\sum_{i=1}^{r} n_i A_i}{\sum_{i=1}^{r} n_i}$$

   ***(v)* Weighted Arithmetic Mean :** If $w_1, w_2, ..., w_n$ are the weights assigned to the values $x_1, x_2, ...,$

x_n respectively, then the weighted arithmetic mean is:

$$A_w = \frac{\sum_{i=1}^{n} w_i x_i}{\sum_{i=1}^{n} w_i}$$

Properties of Arithmetic Mean

(*i*) Mean is dependent of change of origin and change of scale.

(*ii*) Algebraic sum of the deviations of a set of values from their arithmetic mean is zero.

(*iii*) The sum of the squares of the deviations of a set of values is minimum when taken about mean.

2. Geometric Mean

(*i*) If $x_1, x_2, ..., x_n$ be n non-zero observations, then their geometric mean is defined as:

$$G = \sqrt[n]{x_1 x_2, ... x_n}$$

3. Harmonic Mean : The harmonic mean of n non-zero observations $x_1, x_2, ..., x_n$ is defined as

$$HM = \frac{n}{\frac{1}{x_1} + \frac{1}{x_2} + ... + \frac{1}{x_n}} = \frac{n}{\sum_{i=1}^{n} \frac{1}{x_i}}$$

4. Median : The median of a distribution is the value of the middle variable, when the variables are arranged in ascending or descending order.

Median (M_d) is an average of position of the numbes.

(*i*) Median for Simple Distribution : Firstly, arrange the data in ascending or descending order and then find the number of observations *n*.

(*a*) If *n* is odd, then $\left(\frac{n+1}{2}\right)$ th term is the median.

(*b*) If *n* is even, then there are two middle terms namely $\left(\frac{n}{2}\right)$ th and $\left(\frac{n}{2}+1\right)$ th terms. Hence,

Median = Mean of $\left(\frac{n}{2}\right)$ th and $\left(\frac{n}{2}+1\right)$ th observations

$$= \frac{1}{2}\left[\left(\frac{n}{2}\right)\text{th} + \left(\frac{n}{2}+1\right)\text{th}\right] \text{ of observations}$$

Properties

(*i*) The median can be calculated graphically, while mean cannot be.

(*ii*) The sum of the absolute deviations taken from the median is less than the sum of the absolute deviations taken from any other observation in the data.

(*iii*) Median is not affected by extreme values.

5. Mode : The mode (M_0) of a distribution is the value at the point about which the observations tend to be most heavily concentrated. It is generally the value of the variable which appears to occur most frequently in the distribution.

The value which is repeated maximum number of times, is the required mode.

e.g. Mode of the data 70, 80, 90, 96, 70, 96, 90 is 96 as 96 occurs maximum number of times.

Propperties

(*i*) It can be calculated graphically.

(*ii*) It is not affected by extreme values.

(*iii*) It can be used for open-ended distribution and qualitative data.

In a moderately symmetric distribution mean, median and mode are connected by the following formula

Mode = 3 Median – 2 Mean

Relation between Mean, Median and Mode

(*i*) Mean – Mode = 3(Mean – Median)

(*i*) Mode = 3 Median – 2 Mean

Effects of Average and Dispersion on Change of Origin and Scale

	Change of Origin	Change of Scale
Mean	Dependent	Dependent
Median	Not Dependent	Dependent
Mode	Not Dependent	Dependent

Note : (*i*) Change of origin means either subtract of add in observation

(*ii*) Change of scale means either multiply or divide in observations.

Multiple Choice Questions

1. The mean of *n* observations is $\overline{X}$. If *k* is added to each observation, then the new mean is:

A. $\overline{X}$ B. $\overline{X}+k$
C. $\overline{X}-k$ D. $k\overline{X}$

2. The mean of a set of seven numbers is 81. If one of the numbers is discarded, the mean of the remaining numbers is 78. The value of discarded number is:

A. 98 B. 99
C. 100 D. 101

3. For which set of numbers do the mean, median and mode all have the same value?

A. 2, 2, 2, 2, 4 B. 1, 3, 3, 3, 5
C. 1, 1, 2, 5, 6 D. 1, 1, 1, 2, 5

4. For the set of numbers 2, 2, 4, 5 and 12, which of the following statements is true?
A. Mean = Median B. Mean > Mode
C. Mean < Mode D. Mode = Median

5. The empirical relation between mean, mode and median is:
A. Mode = 3 Median – 2 Mean
B. Mode = 2 Median – 3 Mean
C. Median = 3 Mode – 2 Mean
D. Mean = 3 Median – 2 Mode

6. The mean of a, b, c, d and e is 28. If the mean of a, c, and e is 24, what is the mean of b and d?
A. 31 B. 32
C. 33 D. 34

7. Which of the following is dependent of the change of origin?
A. Mean B. Median
C. Mode D. Variance

8. What is the mean of first nine even natural numbers?
A. 10 B. 12
C. 11 D. 13

9. What is the median of first 15 odd numbers?
A. 15 B. 17
C. 19 D. 21

10. If the mean of a given data is 51 kg and its median is 50 kg. What is the mode of that data?
A. 52 kg B. 51 kg
C. 53 kg D. 54 kg

11. What is the mode of the given data :
16, 20, 8, 17, 27 34, 28, 32, 27, 15, 27, 54, 42.
A. 8 B. 27
C. 54 D. None of these

12. What is the mean of the following data?

Marks obtained	45	27	20	56	82	75	17
No. of students	5	3	8	7	2	4	12

A. 34.22 B. 36.22
C. 37.22 D. None of these

13. What is the median of the following data?

Marks obtained	72	47	62	57	42	52	67
No. of students	9	8	11	8	3	6	5

A. 56.5 B. 57.5
C. 58.5 D. 59.5

ANSWERS

1	2	3	4	5	6	7	8	9	10
B	B	B	B	A	D	A	A	B	C
11	12	13							
B	C	D							

EXPLANATORY ANSWERS

8. $\text{Mean} = \dfrac{2+4+6+8+10+12+14+16+18}{9} = \dfrac{90}{9} = 10$

9. First 15 odd numbers are 3, 5, 7, 9, 11, 13, 15, 17, 19, 21, 23, 25, 27, 29, 31
$n = 15$, which is odd
$\text{Median} = \left(\dfrac{15+1}{2}\right)\text{th term} = 8\text{th term} = 17$

10. Mode = 3 × median – 2 × Mean
= 3(51) – 2(50) = 153 – 100 = 53 kg

11. Mode = 27, as it occurs 3 times.

12.

Marks obtained (x_i)	No. of Students (f_i)	$x_i f_i$
45	5	225
27	3	81
20	8	160
56	7	392
82	2	164
75	4	300
17	12	204
	$\Sigma f_i = 41$	$\Sigma f_i x_i = 1526$

$\text{Mean} = \dfrac{\Sigma f_i x_i}{\Sigma f_i} = \dfrac{1526}{41} = 37.219 \approx 37.22$

13.

Marks obtained	No. of Students	Cumulative frequency
42	3	3
47	8	3 + 8 = 11
52	6	11 + 6 = 17
57	8	17 + 8 = 25
62	11	25 + 11 = 36
67	5	36 + 5 = 41
72	9	41 + 9 = 50

N = 50 (even)

$$\text{Median} = \dfrac{\left(\dfrac{50}{2}\right)\text{th term} + \left(\dfrac{50}{2}+1\right)\text{th term}}{2}$$

$$= \dfrac{25\text{th term} + 26\text{th term}}{2}$$

$$= \dfrac{57+62}{2} = \dfrac{119}{2} = 59.5$$

□□□□□

11

Probability

Important Facts and Formulae

1. **Experiment :** An operation which can produce some well-defined outcomes is called an experiment.

2. **Random Experiment :** An experiment in which all possible outcomes are known and the exact output cannot be predicted in advance, is called a random experiment.

Examples of Performing a Random Experiment:

(*i*) Rolling an unbiased dice.

(*ii*) Tossing a fair coin.

(*iii*) Drawing a card from a pack of well-suffled cards.

(*iv*) Picking up a ball of certain colour from a bag containing balls of different colours.

Details:

(*i*) When we throw a coin. Then either a Head (H) or a Tail (T) appears

(*ii*) A dice is a solid cube, having 6 faces, marked, 1, 2, 3, 4, 5, 6 respectively. When we throw a die, the outcome is the number that appears on its upper face.

(*iii*) A pack of cards has 52 cards.
It has 13 cards of each suit, namely Spades, Clubs, Hearts and Diamonds.
Cards of spades and clubs are black cards.
Cards of hearts and diamonds are red cards.
There are 4 honours of each suit.
These are Aces, Kings, Queens and Jacks.
These are called face cards.

3. **Sample Space :** When we perform an experiment, then the set S of all possible outcomes is called the sample space.

Examples of Sample Spaces:

(*i*) In tossing a coin, S = {H, T}.

(*ii*) If two coins are tossed, then S = {HH, HT, TH, TT}.

(*iii*) In rolling a dice, we have, S = {1, 2, 3, 4, 5, 6}.

4. **Event :** Any subset of a sample space is called an event.

5. **Probability of Occurrence of an Event:**
Let S be the sample space and let E be an event. Then, $E \subseteq S$.

$$\therefore \quad P(E) = \frac{n(E)}{n(S)}$$

6. **Results on Probability:**

(*i*) $P(S) = 1$

(*ii*) $0 \le P(E) \le 1$

(*iii*) $P(\phi) = 0$

(*iv*) For any events A and B, we have:
$P(A \cup B) = P(A) + P(B) - P(A \cap B)$

(*v*) If $\bar{A}$ denotes (not-A), then $P(\bar{A}) = 1 - P(A)$.

Example 1 : Two unbiased coins are tossed. What is the probability of getting at most one head?

Solution: Here S = {HH, HT, TH, TT}.

Let E = event of getting at most one head.

$\therefore$ E = {T T, HT, TH}

$$\therefore \quad P(E) = \frac{n(E)}{n(S)} = \frac{3}{4}.$$

Example 2 : An unbiased die is tossed. Find the probability of getting a multiple of 3.

Solution : Here S = {1, 2, 3, 4, 5, 6}

Let E be the event of getting a multiple of 3.

Then, E = {3, 6}

$$\therefore \quad P(E) = \frac{n(E)}{n(S)} = \frac{2}{6} = \frac{1}{3}$$

Example 3 : A bag contains 6 white and 4 black balls. Two balls are drawn at random. Find the probability that they are of the same colour.

Solution : Let S be the sample space. Then,

$n(S)$ = Number of ways of drawing 2 balls out of (6 + 4)

$$= {}^{10}C_2 = \frac{(10 \times 9)}{(2 \times 1)} = 45.$$

Let E = Event of getting both balls of the same colur. Then,

$n(E) =$ Number of ways of drawing (2 balls out of 6) or (2 balls out of 4)

$= ({}^6C_2 + {}^4C_2) = \frac{(6\times5)}{(2\times1)} + \frac{(4\times3)}{(2\times1)} = (15+6) = 21$

$\therefore \quad P(E) = \frac{n(E)}{n(S)} = \frac{21}{45} = \frac{7}{15}.$

Example 4 : Two dice are thrown together. What is the probability that the sum of the numbers on the two faces is divisible by 4 or 6?

Solution : Clearly, $n(S) = 6 \times 6 = 36$.

Let E be the event that the sum of the numbers on the two faces is divisible by 4 or 6. Then

$E = \{(1, 3), (1, 5), (2, 2), (2, 4), (2, 6), (3, 1), (3, 3), (3, 5), (4, 2), (4, 4), (5, 1), (5, 3), (6, 2), (6, 6)\}$

$\therefore n(E) = 14.$

Hence, $P(E) = \frac{n(E)}{n(S)} = \frac{14}{36} = \frac{7}{18}.$

Multiple Choice Questions

1. Following table shows the marks scored by a group of 90 students in a mathematics test of 100 marks.

Marks	0-20	20-30	30-40	40-50	50-60	60-70	70-100
No. of students	7	10	10	20	20	15	8

What is the probability that a student obtained less then 20% marks?

A. $\frac{5}{90}$ B. $\frac{7}{90}$

C. $\frac{1}{10}$ D. None of these

2. A dice is rolled 600 times and the occurrence of the outcomes 1, 2, 3, 4, 5 and 6 are given below:

Outcome	1	2	3	4	5	6
Frequency	200	30	120	100	50	100

The probability of getting a prime numbers is:

A. $\frac{1}{3}$ B. $\frac{2}{3}$

C. $\frac{49}{60}$ D. $\frac{39}{125}$

3. A bag contains 50 coins and each coin is marked from 51 to 100. One coin is picked at random. The probability that the number on the coin is not a prime number, is

A. $\frac{1}{5}$ B. $\frac{3}{5}$

C. $\frac{2}{5}$ D. $\frac{4}{5}$

4. In a football match, a player makes 4 goals from 10 penalty kicks. The probability of converting a penalty kick into a goal by the player, is:

A. $\frac{1}{4}$ B. $\frac{1}{6}$

C. $\frac{1}{3}$ D. $\frac{2}{5}$

5. Three coins are tossed simultaneously 200 times with the following frequencies of different outcomes:

Outcome	3 heads	2 heads	1 head	No head
Frequency	23	72	77	28

What is the probability of getting at most two heads?

A. $\frac{177}{200}$ B. $\frac{172}{200}$

C. $\frac{19}{40}$ D. None of these

Directions (Qs. 6 to 9) : *1000 families with 2 children were selected randomly, and the following data were recorded:*

Number of boys in a family:	0	1	2
Number of families :	140	560	300

If a family is chosen at random, find the probability that it has:

6. No boy

A. 0.14 B. 0.56

C. 0.3 D. None of these

7. One boy

A. 0.56 B. 0.3

C. 0.14 D. None of these

8. At least one boy

A. 0.14 B. 0.56

C. 0.86 D. 0.7

9. At most one boy

A. 0.7 B. 0.56

C. 0.14 D. 0.86

10. In a simultaneous throw of two coins, the probability of getting at least one head is:

A. $\frac{1}{2}$ B. $\frac{1}{3}$

C. $\frac{2}{3}$ D. $\frac{3}{4}$

11. Three unbiased coins are tossed. What is the probability of getting at least 2 heads?

A. $\frac{3}{4}$ B. $\frac{1}{4}$

C. $\frac{3}{8}$ D. $\frac{7}{8}$

12. In a single throw of a die, what is the probability of getting a number greater than 4?

A. $\frac{1}{2}$ B. $\frac{1}{3}$

C. $\frac{2}{3}$ D. $\frac{1}{4}$

ANSWERS

1	2	3	4	5	6	7	8	9	10
B	A	D	D	A	A	A	C	A	D
11	**12**								
D	B								

EXPLANATORY ANSWERS

1. Total No. of students = 90

No. of students scoring less than 20 marks = 7

Required probability = $\frac{7}{90}$

2. Total outcomes = 600

Total outcomes of getting prime numbers,

(2, 3, 5) = 30 + 120 + 50 = 200

$\therefore$ Required probability = $\frac{200}{600} = \frac{1}{3}$

3. Total prime no. between 51 to 100 (53, 59, 61, 67, 71, 73, 79, 83. 89, 97) = 10

$\therefore$ Total Non-prime No = 50 − 10 = 40

$\therefore$ Required probability = $\frac{40}{50} = \frac{4}{5}$

4. Required probability = $\frac{4}{10} = \frac{2}{5}$

5. No. of coins getting at most two heads

= 28 + 77 + 72 = 177

Required probability = $\frac{177}{200}$

6. Total number of families = 1000

Number of families having no boy child = 140.

$\therefore$ Probability that a family chosen at random does not have a boy child

$= \frac{140}{1000} = 0.14$

7. Total number of families = 1000

Number of families having one boy child = 560

$\therefore$ Probability that a family chosen at random has one boy child

$= \frac{560}{1000} = 0.56$

8. Total number of families = 1000

Number of families having at least one boy child

= 560 + 300 = 860

$= \frac{860}{1000} = 0.86$

9. Total number of families = 1000

Number of families having at most one boy child

= 140 + 560 = 700

$\therefore$ Probability that a family chosen at random has at most one boy child

$= \frac{700}{1000} = 0.7$

10. Here S = {HH, HT, TH, T T},

Let E = event of getting at least one head

= {HT, TH, HH}

$\therefore$ $P(E) = \frac{n(E)}{n(S)} = \frac{3}{4}$.

11. Here S = {TTT, TTH, THT, HTT, THH, HTH, HHT, HHH}.

Let E = event of getting at most two heads

Then, E = {TTT, TTH, THT, HTT, THH, HTH, HHT}

$\therefore$ $P(E) = \frac{n(E)}{n(S)} = \frac{7}{8}$.

12. When a die is thrown, we have S = {1, 2, 3, 4, 5, 6}

Let E = event of getting a number greater than 4

= {5, 6}

$\therefore$ $P(E) = \frac{n(E)}{n(S)} = \frac{2}{6} = \frac{1}{3}$.

SCIENCE

Various Sciences

- **Acoustics:** The study of sound and sound waves.
- **Aerodynamics:** The study of forces acting upon bodies in motion in the air (*e.g.*, aircraft, missiles, etc.).
- **Aeronautics:** Concerned with all activities of aerial locomotion (art of flying).
- **Agronomy:** The science of soil management and the production of field crops.
- **Agrostology:** The study of grasses.
- **Anatomy:** The science of the structure of the animal/ human body learnt by dissection.
- **Anaesthesiology:** A branch of medicine concerned with administration of anaesthetics and the condition of the patient while under anaesthesia.
- **Anthropology:** The study of the origin and physical and cultural development of mankind.
- **Archaeology:** A scientific study of the material remains of the past as evidence of man's life, culture and history.
- **Astronautics:** A science dealing with space travel and space vehicles.
- **Astrophysics:** A branch of astronomy dealing with the physical nature of heavenly bodies.
- **Astronomy:** The science of heavenly bodies (planets).
- **Astrogeology:** The study of structures and formation of rocks and minerals on other planets.
- **Bacteriology:** A branch of microbiology dealing with bacteria.
- **Biology:** The science of living organisms; subdivided into Botany and Zoology.
- **Biophysics:** The physics of the vital processes of living organisms.
- **Botany:** The science of the plant kingdom.
- **Bryology:** The study of mosses.
- **Cardiology:** A branch of medicine dealing with heart.
- **Carpology:** The study of fruits and seeds.
- **Ceramics:** The art of making objects from clay.
- **Cetology:** The study of acquatic mammals, especially whales.
- **Chemistry:** The study of elements, their behaviour and laws of their combination etc.
- **Chorology:** The study of geographical areas; plants and animal distribution.
- **Cosmetology:** The study of cosmetics and their use.
- **Cosmology:** The study of the universe—its origin, nature, structure and evolution.
- **Craniology:** The study of skulls (not to be confused with phrenology which is not a science).
- **Cryogenics:** Concerned with the production, control and application of extremely low temperatures.
- **Cytology:** A branch of biology dealing with structure and function of cells.
- **Cytopathology:** The study of diseased cells.
- **Dactylogy:** The study of fingerprints.
- **Dermatology:** A branch of medicine dealing with skin.
- **Dietetics:** The science of diet and nutrition.
- **Ecology:** The study of relationship between organisms and their environment.
- **Entomology:** Deals with study of insects.
- **Endocrinology:** The study of glands.
- **Etymology:** A study of the origin and history of words.
- **Genetics:** A branch of biology dealing with heredity and the laws that govern it.
- **Geology:** A study of the chemical composition of the earth's crust.
- **Gerontology:** A branch of medicine studying the ageing process, problems and diseases.
- **Gynaecology:** A branch of medicine dealing with female diseases of the reproduction system.
- **Haematology:** A branch of medicine studying blood and its disorders.
- **Hepatology:** A branch of medicine dealing with the liver.
- **Histology:** The study of tissues.
- **Horticulture:** A branch of agricultural science dealing with flowers, fruits, vegetables, etc.
- **Hydrology:** The science of water with reference to its occurrence and properties in the hydrosphere and atmosphere.
- **Hygiene:** A branch of medicine dealing with health and its preservation.

- **Immunology:** A branch of medicine dealing with the immune system of the body.
- **Lithology:** The study of the characteristics of rocks.
- **Morphology:** A biological study of external form and structure of living organisms and their parts.
- **Mycology:** Concerned with fungi and fungal diseases.
- **Nephrology:** A branch of medicine dealing with kidney diseases.
- **Neuropathology:** A branch of medicine dealing with changes produced by diseases in the nervous system.
- **Obstetrics:** A branch of medicine dealing with pregnancy, labour and child birth.
- **Oncology:** A branch of medicine dealing with tumours.
- **Ophthalmology:** A branch of medicine dealing with eyes and related diseases.
- **Orology:** The study of mountains.
- **Ornithology:** The science of birds.
- **Orthopaedics:** A branch of medicine dealing with diagnosis and treatment of diseases of the skeletal system (bones).
- **Osteology:** A study of bones.
- **Paediatrics:** A branch of medicine dealing with child disease (infants).
- **Palaeontology:** The study of fossils and ancient life-forms.
- **Parasitology:** The science of parasites, especially those connected with diseases.
- **Pathology:** A branch of medicine that deals with etiologies, mechanisms and manifestation of diseases.
- **Pharmacology:** A branch of medicine dealing with drugs, their chemistry, effects on body, etc.
- **Physiology:** A study of the life processes of various organs of living organisms.
- **Psychiatry:** The study and treatment of mental and emotional disorders.
- **Radiology:** A branch of medical science dealing with the use of x-rays for diagnosis and treatment.
- **Semiology:** The science dealing with signs, sign language or system of signalling.
- **Seismology:** The study of earthquakes and related phenomena.
- **Theology:** The study of religions.
- **Toxicology:** A branch of pharmacology dealing with poisons and other toxic substances.
- **Urology:** The study of the physiology and pathology of the urogenital tract.
- **Virology:** The science that deals with viruses.
- **Zoology:** A branch of biology that deals with animal life.
- **Zymology:** A study that deals with the process of fermentation.

Scientific Instruments

Name of Instrument	Use
Altimeter	Measures altitude (used in aircraft)
Ammeter	Measures strength of electric current
Anemometer	Measures force and velocity of wind and determines its direction
Audiometer	Measures intensity of sound
Barometer	Measures atmospheric pressure
Balometer	Measures heat radiation
Callipers	Measures inner and outer diameters of solids
Calorimeter	Measures quantities of heat
Cardiogram (ECG)	Traces movements of the heat; recorded on a cardiograph
Chronometer	Determines longitude of a vessel at sea
Cryometer	Measures very low temperatures, usually below 0°C
Dynamo	Converts mechanical energy into electrical energy
Dynamometer	Measures electrical power
Electroencephalograph (EEC)	Records and interprets the electrical waves of the brain recorded on electroencephalograms
Electrometer	Measures very small, potential difference in electric current
Electroscope	Detects presence of an electric current
Endoscope	Examines internal organs of the body
Fathometer	Measures depth of the ocean
Fluxmeter	Measures magnetic flux
Galvanometer	Measures the electric current
Hydrometer	Measures the relative density of liquids
Hygrometer	Measures level of humidity
Hydrophone	Measures sound under water
Kymograph	Graphically records physiological movement (*e.g.*, blood pressure/heartbeat)
Lactometer	Measures the relative density of milk to determine purity (fat content)

Name of Instrument	Use
Manometer	Measures the pressure of gases
Microphone	Converts sound waves into electrical vibrations
Microscope	To obtain a magnified view of small objects
Nephetometer	Measures the scattering of light by particles suspended in a liquid
Ohmmeter	Measures electrical resistance in ohms
Ondometer	Measures the frequency of electromagnetic waves
Periscope	To view objects above sea level (used in submarines)
Polygraph	Instrument that simultaneously records changes a physiological process such as heartbeat, blood pressure and respiration—used as a lie detector
Pyknometer	Determines the density and coefficient of expansion of liquids
Pyrheliometer	Measures components of solar radiation
Pyrometer	Measures very high temperature
Quadrant	Measures altitudes and angles in navigation and astronomy.
	Detects the direction and range of an approaching aeroplane by means of radiowaves (Radio, Angle, Detection and Range)
Refractometer	Measures refractive indices
Resistance Thermometer	An accurate type of thermometer in which temperature is measured by determining the electrical resistance of a coil of thin wire

Name of Instrument	Use
Salinometer	Determines salinity of solutions
Sextant	Used by navigators to find the latitude of a place by measuring the elevation above the horizon of the sun or another star—also measures the height of distant objects
Sphygmomanometer	Measures blood pressure
Stereoscope	To view two-dimensional pictures
Stethoscope	Used by doctors to hear and analyze heart and lung sounds
Stroboscope	To view rapidly moving objects
Tachometer	To determine speed, especially the rotational speed of a shaft (used in aeroplanes and motor-boats)
Tacheometer	Used to measure distances, elevations and bearings during survey
Tangent	Galvanometer measures the strength of direct current
Telescope	To view distant objects in space
Theodolite	Measures horizontal and vertical angles
Tonometer	Measures the pitch of sound
Transponder	Used to receive a signal and transmit a reply immediately
Udometer	Rain gauge
Venturimeter	Measures rate of flow of liquids
Viscometer	Measures the viscosity of liquids
Voltmeter	Used to measure potential difference between two points
Wattmeter	Measures the power of an electric circuit
Wavemeter	Measures the wavelength of a radiowave

Scientific Inventions and Discoveries

Invention	Inventor(s)
Adding Machine	Pascal
Aeroplane	Wright brothers
Ballpoint Pen	C. Biro
Barometer	E. Torricelli
Bicycle	K. Macmillan
Bicyle Tyre	J. B. Dunlop
Centigrade Scale	A. Celsius
Cinematograph	Thomas Alva Edison
Computer	Charles Babbage
Cine Camera	Friese-Greene
Cinema	A.L. and J. L. Lumiere

Invention	Inventor(s)
Clock (Mechanical)	Hsing and Ling-Tsan
Clock (Pendulum)	C. Hugyens
Diesel Engine	Rudolf Diesel
Dynamite	Alfred Nobel
Dynamo	Michael Faraday
Electric Iron	H.W. Seeley
Electric Lamp	Thomas Alva Edison
Electromagnet	W. Sturgeon
Film (with sound)	Dr Lee de Forest
Fountain Pen	L.E. Waterman
Gas Lighting	William Murdoch

Invention	Inventor(s)
Gramophone	Thomas Alva Edison
Jet Engine	Sir Frank Whittle
Lift	E.G. Otis
Locomotive	Richard Trevithick
Machine Gun	Richard Gatling
Match (safety)	J.E. Lundstrom
Microphone	David Hughes
Microscope	Z. Janssen
Motor Car (petrol)	Karl Benz
Motorcycle	Edward Butler
Neon-Lemp	G. Claude
Nylon	Dr W. H. Carothers
Parachute	Louis Lenormand
Photography (paper)	W.H. Fox Talbot
Printing Press	J. Gutenberg
Radar	Dr A.H. Taylor and L.C. Young
Radium	Marie and Pierre Curie
Rayon	Viscos Co.
Razor (safety)	K. C. Gillette
Razor (electric)	Col. J. Schick
Refrigerator	J. Harrison and A. Catlin
Revolver	Samuel Colt
Rubber (vulcanised)	Charles Goodyear
Rubber (waterproof)	Charles Macintosh
Safety Lamp	Sir Humphry Davy
Safety Pin	William Hurst
Sewing Machine	B. Thimmonnier
Scooter	G. Bradshaw
Ship (stream)	J.C. Perier
Ship (turbine)	Sir Charles Parsons
Shorthand (modern)	Sir Isaac Pitman
Spinning Frame	Sir Richard Arkwright
Stream Engine (piston)	Thomas Newcombe
Stream Engine	James Watt
Stainless Steel	Harry Brearley
Submarine	D. Bushnell
Tank	Sir Ernest Swington
Telegraph Code	Samuel F. B. Morse
Telephone	Alexander Graham Bell
Telescope	Hans Lippershey
Television	John Logie Baird
Terylene	J. Whinfield and H. Dickson
Thermometer	Galileo Galilei
Tractor	J. Froelich
Transistor	Bardeen, Shockley and Brattain
Typewriter	C. Sholes
Radio Valve	Sir J. A. Fleming
Watch	A. L. Brequet
X-ray	Wilhelm Roentgen
Zip Fastener	W. L. Judson

Medical Discoveries

Discovery	Made by
Antibiotic (Penicillin)	Alexander Fleming
Antiseptic	Joseph Lister
Aspirin	Felix Hoffmann
Blood Circulation	William harvey
Blood Group	K. Landsteiner
Blood Transfusion	James Blundell
Cholera and TB Germs	Robert Koch
Diphtheria Germs	Klebs & Loffler
Electro cardiogram (ECG)	William Einthoven
Heart-Lung Machine	John Heynsham Gibbon
Hypodermic Syringe	Charles Gabriel Pravaz
Heart Transplant	Christian Barnard
Kidney Machine	W. J. Kolff
Malaria Germs	A. Laveran
Organ Transplant	John P. Merril
Scan (CAT)	Godrey Hounsfield
Stethoscope	Rene Laennec
Thermometer (Clinical)	Sir Thomas
Ultrasound	Ian Donald
X-ray	W. Roentgen

Important Vaccines

Vaccine	Discovered by
Small Pox	Edward Jenner
Cholera	Louis Pasteur
Diphtheria and Tetanus	Emil Adolf Von Belming and Shibasaburo Kitasato
Polio Vaccine	Jonas E. Salk
TB Vaccine	Leon Calmette and Camille Guerin
Measles Vaccine	John F. Enders
Rabies Vaccine	Louis Pasteur
Typhus Vaccine	J. Niccolle

Classification of Blood Groups

Blood Group	Can donate blood to	Can receive blood from
A	A, AB	A and O
B	B, AB	B and O
AB	Only AB	AB, A, B and O
O	AB, A, B and O	Only O

Diseases Affecting Different Parts of Body

Disease	Part of the Human Body Affected
AIDS	Immune system of the body (resistance)
Arthritis	Joints
Asthma	Bronchial muscles (lungs)
Cataract	Eyes
Conjunctivitis	Eyes
Glaucoma	Eyes
Trachoma	Eyes
Diabetes	Pancreas, blood
Dermatitis	Skin
Diphtheria	Throat
Eczema	Skin
Hypokalemia	Rise in heart beat, kidney damage
Goitre	Joints
Hepatitis, Jaundice	Liver
Malaria	Spleen
Meningitis	Spinal cord and brain
Polio	Legs
Pyrrhoea	Teeth and gums
Pleurisy	Lungs
Rheumatism	Joints
Pneumonia	Lungs
Sinusitis	Facial bones
Typhoid	Intestines, whole body
Tuberculosis	Lungs
Tonsillitis	Glands in throat (tonsils)

Chemical names and formulae of some commonly known compounds

Chemical Name	Formulae
Alum	Potassium aluminium sulphate $K_2SO_4Al_2(SO_4)_3$, $24H_2O$
Edible soda	Sodium bicarbonate $NaHCO_3$
Bleaching powder	Calcium hypochloride $Ca(OCl)Cl_2$
Caustic Soda	Sodium hydroxide NaOH
Blue vitriol	Copper sulphate $CuSO_4$, $5H_2O$
Chalk	Calcium Carbonate $CaCO_3$
Borax	Sodium borate $Na_2B_4O_7$, $10H_2O$
Galena	Lead sulphide PbS
Gypsum	Calcium sulphate $2CaSO_4$, H_2O
Formalin	Formaldehyde HCHO
Green vitriol	Ferrous sulphate $FeSO_4$
Dry ice	Solid carbon dioxide CO_2
Grape juice	Glucose $C_2H_{12}O_6$
Common salt	Sodium chloride NaCl
Caustic potash	Potassium hydroxide KOH
Chile salt peter	Sodium Nitrate or Soda nitre $NaNO_3$
Carbolic acid	Fenol C_6H_5OH
Alcohol	Ethyl alcohol C_2H_5OH
Bauxite	Hydrated aluminium oxide Al_2O_3, $2H_2O$
Washing soda	Sodium carbonate Na_2CO_3, $10H_2O$
Acid salt	Hydrogen chloride HCl
Salt peter	Potassium nitrate KNO_3
Litharge	Lead oxide PbO_2
Lime water	Calcium hydroxide $Ca(OH)_2$
Laughing gas	Nitrous oxide N_2O
Red solution	Potassium permanganate $KMNO_4$
Lime (unhydrated)	Calcium oxide CaO
Red sindoor	Lead peroxide Pb_3O_4
Acid of saltpeter	Nitric acid HNO_3
Muratic acid	Hydrochloric acid HCl

Chemical Name	Formulae
Limestone	Calcium carbonate $CaCO_3$
Sal ammoniac (Nausadar)	Ammonium chloride NH_4Cl
Soda ash	Anhydrous sodium carbonate Na_2CO_3
Silica	Silicon oxide SiO_2
T.N.T.	Trinitrotoluene $C_6H_2CH_3(NO_2)_3$
Calomel	Mercurous Chloride Hg_2Cl_2
Vinegar	Solution of dilute acetic acid CH_3COOH
White lead	Basic lead carbonate $2Pb_2CO_3.Pb(OH)_2$
Starch	Polysaccharide $C_6H_{10}O_5$
Plaster of Paris	Calcium sulphate hemihydrate $(CaSO_4)_2H_2O$
Hypo	Sodium Thiosulphate $Na_2S_2O_3.5H_2O$

Chemical Name	Formulae
Butanal	Butyraldehyde C_3H_9CHO
Butanone	Methyl ethyl ketone $CH_3COC_2H_5$
Aniline	Phenylamine, Amino benzene $C_6H_5NH_2$
Alum stone	Alunite $KAl_3[SO_4(OH)_2]_3$
Aspirin	Acetyl salicylic acid $CH_3COOC_6H_4COOH$
Arsine	Arsenic hydride AsH_3
Epsom salt	Magnesium sulphate $MgSO_4.7H_2O$
Furan	Furfuran C_4H_4O
Fruit Sugar	Fructose $C_5H_{12}O_6$
Pyrite	Ferrous Sulphate (FeS_2)
Urea	$CO(NH_2)_2$
Zinc Sulphate	Hepta hydrate $ZnSO_4.7H_2O$ and Monohydrate $ZnSO_4.H_2O$

Important Alloys

Alloy	Components quantity	Percent
Brass	Copper	60-80
	Zinc	40-20
Bronze	Copper	80
	Zinc	10
	Tin	10
Gun metal	Copper	88
	Zinc	01
	Tin	10
	Lead	01
German Silver	Copper	30-60
	Zinc	25-35
	Nickel	15-35
Solder	Tin	50
	Lead	50

Alloy	Components quantity	Percent
Duralumin	Aluminium	95.0
	Copper	04.0
	Magnesium	0.5
	Manganese	0.5
Magnelium	Aluminium	90-95
	Magnesium	05-10
Nickel Steel	Iron	96-98
	Nickel	02-04
Stainless Steel	Iron	74
	Chromium	18
	Nickel	08
Electrum	Silver	55-88
	Gold	22-45

MULTIPLE CHOICE QUESTIONS

1. Which of the following is an antibiotic?
A. Aspirin B. Paracetamol
C. Penicillin D. Sulphadizine

2. Digestion of food starts in:
A. mouth B. liver
C. stomach D. intestines

3. By taking the pulse rate of the human body, a doctor determines:
A. heartbeat
B. functioning of heart valves
C. the amount of blood in body
D. the condition of liver

4. A thermostat is used to:
A. purify air B. regulate humidity
C. regulate temperature D. regulate air pressure

5. Heat from the sun reaches the earth by:
A. reflection B. conduction
C. convection D. radiations

6. Dew forms most readily on nights that are:
A. calm and clear B. stormy
C. windy D. cloudy

7. The full moon rises in the:
A. South B. North
C. East D. West

8. An aeroplane is able to fly because:
A. it is lighter than air
B. it is heavier than air
C. it is made of very light materials
D. moving air can lift objects

9. The souring of milk is caused by the action of:
A. a protozoa B. bacteria
C. viruses D. None of these

10. The smallest living thing that can cause disease in the human body is:
A. flea B. bacteria
C. a protozoa D. viruses

11. The most abundant gas in the air is:
A. oxygen B. carbon dioxide
C. nitrogen D. hydrogen

12. Which is the element common to brass and bronze?
A. Copper B. Iron
C. Zinc D. Aluminium

13. The densest element known so far is:
A. iron B. mercury
C. osmium D. tungsten

14. The most ductile element is:
A. gold B. silver
C. iron D. aluminium

15. The metal having highest melting point is:
A. chromium B. tungsten
C. diamond D. silver

16. The gas which constitutes most of Venus's atmosphere is:
A. oxygen B. nitrogen
C. hydrogen D. carbon dioxide

17. The most common acid found in the nature is:
A. acetic acid B. citric acid
C. lactic acid D. hydrochloric acid

18. The bomb that cannot destroy the property but can damage the life only is:
A. atom bomb B. hydrogen bomb
C. fission bomb D. neutron bomb

19. The waves received by our Television sets are:
A. light waves B. radio waves
C. cosmic waves D. micro waves

20. Which of the following machines will fail to give satisfactory result in vacuum?
A. Bicycle B. Sewing machine
C. Fan D. Washing machine

21. Which of the following is the best conductor of electric current?
A. Aluminium B. Copper
C. Silver D. Gold

22. Tungsten is mainly used for making filament of electric bulbs because of its:
A. low cost
B. high melting point
C. high electrical conductivity
D. low thermal conductivity

23. The element common to bone and cement is:
A. silicon B. calcium
C. nitrogen D. phosphorus

24. The raw material common to cement and glass is:
A. soda B. rock
C. gypsum D. sand

25. What is essentially required to digest the food in stomach?
A. Air B. Water
C. Enzymes D. Minerals

26. Domestic electric meters record the consumption of electricity in:
A. Volts B. Amperes
C. Watts D. Ohms

27. Which of the following gases does not pollute air?
A. Carbon dioxide B. Carbon monoxide
C. Nitrogen dioxide D. Sulphur dioxide

28. Polio is a disease caused due to:
A. bacterial infection B. virus infection
C. protozoal infection D. food poisoning

29. Which form of gold is the softest?
A. 16 Carat B. 18 Carat
C. 20 Carat D. 22 Carat

30. Filtration of wastes from the blood in human body is done by:
A. heart B. lungs
C. kidney D. intestines

31. Speed of sound waves is maximum in:
A. vacuum B. gases
C. liquids D. solids

32. How many colours are there in the rainbow?
A. 7 B. 10
C. 12 D. 5

33. Barometer measures:
A. wind velocity B. atmospheric pressure
C. amount of rainfall D. atmospheric moisture

34. Anemometer measures:
A. amount of rainfall
B. atmospheric pressure
C. wind velocity
D. amperage of an electrical current

35. Sphygmomanometer measures:
A. specific heat, latent heat, heat of chemical combination and other thermal properties
B. intensity of light
C. distance covered, or steps taken, by a person walking
D. blood pressure

36. Meteorology is the study of:
A. meteors and meteorites
B. the climate
C. the weather
D. the measurement of length

37. Oil, water and gas can be present in a well in the ascending order of:
A. water, oil, gas B. gas, water, oil
C. water, gas, oil D. oil, water, gas

38. Vegetables can be cooked quickly in a pressure cooker because:
A. steam can boil vegetables faster than water
B. boiling point increases with the increase in pressure
C. high pressure lowers the boiling point
D. All the above

39. A person suffering from which of the following cannot see with clarity the horizontal and vertical lines simultaneously?
A. Myopia B. Hypermitropia
C. Astigmatism D. Squint

40. When a flake of ice melts in a water bowl, the level of water inside the bowl:
A. remains unchanged
B. goes down
C. increases
D. nothing can be said definitely

41. To an astronaut in a satellite the colour of the sky would appear to be:
A. black B. blue
C. grey D. white

42. A fuse wire is used for:
A. allowing high currents to flow harmlessly
B. breaking the electrical circuit
C. saving a man from receiving electric shocks
D. All the above

43. Excessive intake of alcohol damages a person's:
A. kidneys
B. liver
C. stomach
D. All the above to a certain degree

44. Which of the following is common in all acids?
A. Hydrogen
B. Oxygen
C. Nitrogen
D. None of the above

45. After boiling, rice grains grow in volume and weight because:
A. starch swells in water and heat
B. heat enlarges solid
C. rice is a fatty grain
D. All the above

46. Hygrometer is used for measuring:
A. temperature B. relative humidity
C. rainfall D. density of water

47. Phobos and Deimos are the satellites of:
A. Uranus B. Mars
C. Venus D. Saturn

48. Plants are grown along river banks in order to check:
A. siltage and floods B. pollution
C. rainfall D. All the above

49. Which one of the following signifies the optical technique of recording waves and amplitude?
A. Holography B. Bibliography
C. Audiography D. None of the above

50. People use iron ploughs now, instead of the old wooden ploughs. This change signifies:
A. advance technology B. appropriate technology
C. obsolete technology D. ultimate technology

51. Acetyl salicylic acid is used commonly as:
A. pain-reliever B. tear gas
C. chemical fertilizer D. preservative

52. In a village where fuel is not available and people are poor, which of the following measures is the most suitable to prevent disease through contaminated water from the wells?
A. Using chemicals to purify water
B. Boiling the water
C. Use of micro-organisms to purify water
D. None of the above

53. One of the main constituents of Gobar gas is:
A. thyamine B. methane
C. phosphate D. carbon monoxide

54. Quartz is softer than:
A. Diamond B. Corundum
C. Topaz D. All the above

55. Emerald and diamond are made of:
A. Beryllium and Carbon
B. Carbon
C. Silica
D. Silica and Beryllium

56. Human brain receives and sends signals as:
A. chemical impulses B. physical impulses
C. electrical impulses D. mechanical impulses

57. The ductless glands secreting hormones directly into human blood are known as:
A. exocrine glands B. endocrine glands
C. metabolic glands D. ductlands

58. Arrange the three forms of iron in descending order of carbon contents and other impurities in them:

I. wrought iron

II. cast iron

III. pig iron

A. III, II, I B. III, I, II

C. I, II, III D. II, I, III

59. Foot and mouth diseases attack:

A. cattle, sheep and pigs

B. cattle only

C. cattle and pigs only

D. cattle and sheep only

60. Which one of the following has maximum nitrogen content?

A. Sodium nitrate

B. Urea

C. Ammoniam sulphate

D. None of the above has enough nitrogen

61. Radio carbon dating is used for determining the age of:

A. fossils B. buildings

C. babies D. rocks

62. Pasteurization of milk means:

A. heating of milk upto 100°C

B. heating of milk at 65°C

C. cooling of milk at 100°C

D. cooling of milk upto 0°C

63. Ranikhet disease affects:

A. dogs B. cows

C. poultry D. sheep

64. Wisdom teeth appear in a human being between:

A. 17 and 20 years of age

B. 30 and 40 years of age

C. 10 and 17 years of age

D. 4 and 8 years of age

65. Decomposition of matter takes place due to the effect of:

A. bacteria B. virus

C. fungi D. algae

66. Bile is secreted by:

A. pancreas B. small intestine

C. stomach D. liver

67. Polio myelitis which causes polio is spread by:

A. mosquito B. virus

C. water D. adulterated food

68. Which of the following is a genetically transmitted disease?

A. Myopia B. Long sightedess

C. Colour blindness D. Night blindness

69. Which of the following is a metal?

A. Arsenic B. Sulphur

C. Potassium D. Carbon

70. How does weedicide remove weeds?

A. It removes the water required for growth

B. It destroys the roots of the weeds

C. It destroys the nutrients required for the growth of weeds

D. All of the above

71. A diamond is a:

A. form of fossilised mammal of ancient times

B. crystalline form of pure carbon

C. hard rolled under sea stone made into a diamond by the saliva of huge sea monsters and thereafter dug out from the mines

D. natural crystallized glass

72. High heel and/or pointed shoes are harmful because:

A. they injure the feet

B. they weaken the eyesight

C. they cause polio

D. they cause backache and sleeplessness

73. When returning to the earth, spacecrafts have a communication blackout, the reason is:

A. the returning spacecraft is doing so against the force of gravity which interferes with the radio waves

B. during the re-entry period the density of the plasma generated by the intense frictional heat is so high that the operational frequencies used for communication becomes very much less than the plasma cut-off frequency resulting in a total blackout

C. stellar X-rays attract and absorb the sound waves

D. the sounds created by the whirring of the mechanism of the spacecraft renders the sounds inaudible

74. Respiration is:

A. to change the food into energy

B. the process during which food is oxidized and its chemical energy is transformed into useful form

C. a sort of exercise

D. interconversion of food and energy

75. Dialysis is:

A. the same process as osmosis

B. the diffusion of sugar molecules through water

C. the process involved in the diffusion of toxic substance through a membrane

D. the evaporation of surplus sugar

76. Mycology is the study of:

A. Mica

B. Ants

C. Changes of a structure as a result of environment

D. Fungi

77. In human body, quantity of water is about:

A. 10% B. 20%

C. 65% D. 80%

78. What does the urine of a man contain mainly?

A. Urea B. Sugar

C. Salt D. None of the above

79. The filament of electric bulb is made of:
A. iron B. tungsten
C. nichrome D. silver

80. The lightning rod used for protecting building from lightning is made of:
A. glass B. cement
C. wood D. copper

81. When a body becomes positively charged, it:
A. loses electrons
B. gains electrons
C. loses protons
D. None of the above is correct

82. During which season our body needs more fats?
A. Summer season B. Rainy season
C. Winter season D. Spring season

83. Deficiency of insulin causes:
A. Beri-Beri B. Fever
C. Cancer D. Diabetes

84. Iron is heavier than water, still the ship floats on the sea because:
A. weight of the ship is less than the weight of water in the sea
B. weight of the ship is more than sea water
C. weight of the ship is less than the weight of water that the ship displaces
D. weight of ship is equal to the weight of water that ship displaces

85. Photosynthesis results in:
1. release of oxygen
2. release of carbon dioxide
3. formation of carbohydrates
4. intake of carbon dioxide

A. 1, 2, 3 are correct B. 1,3,4 are correct
C. 2,3,4 are correct D. only 1 is correct

86. The Pythagorean Theorem states that:
A. in any triangle the square of the longest side equals the sum of the squares of the other sides
B. in any triangle the square of the longest side equals the square of the sum of the other sides
C. in a right-angled triangle the square of the hypotenuse equals the sum of the squares of the other two sides
D. in an isosceles triangle the third side equals the sum of the two equal sides

87. The formula for inter conversion of Centigrade, Fahrenheit and Reaumur scales is:

A. $\frac{F-32}{9}=\frac{C}{5}=\frac{R}{4}$ B. $\frac{F+32}{9}=\frac{C}{5}=\frac{R}{4}$

C. $\frac{F-32}{9}=\frac{C}{9}=\frac{R}{4}$ D. $\frac{F-32}{4}=\frac{C}{9}=\frac{R}{5}$

88. Which one of the following statements is incorrect?
A. The length of the days and nights is not the same all the year round
B. The axis of the earth is inclined at an angle of 66-1/2 to the plane of its orbit
C. Water pipes are apt to burst in very cold weather
D. Evaporation produces heat

89. Which of the following statements is correct?
A. Boiling of an egg is a chemical change
B. Freezing of ice cream is a chemical change
C. Burning of a candle is a physical change
D. Extracting the juice from an orange is a chemical change

90. When a bullet is fired why does the gun kick back?
A. Because the man firing the gun is light in weight
B. Because the gun is heavier than the firing soldier
C. Because the bullet goes out very fast
D. Because to every action there is an equal and opposite reaction

91. Which one of the following definitions is wrong?
A. *Amino Acids:* Large chemical substances containing carbon and oxygen
B. *Proteins:* Giant molecules of carbon, nitrogen and oxygen which are broken into small molecules during digestion
C. *Carbohydrates:* Big molecules used for getting energy
D. *Lipids:* A group of organic compounds found in living cells

92. The depth to which a floating body sinks in pure water is a measure of its
A. Density B. Weight
C. Inertia D. Viscosity

93. Which one of the following is a contagious disease?
A. Malaria B. Small pox
C. Cholera D. Tuberculosis

94. A pure (sun) spectrum is that in which:
A. only ultra violet and infra red rays are not seen
B. all the seven colours which combine to make up the sun light are clearly, distinctly and separately visible
C. all the seven colours are found
D. where the rainbow is found

95. What do fertilisers contain?
A. Calcium B. Sodium
C. Phosphorus D. Nitrogen

96. In which the purest form of carbon is found?
A. Coke B. Diamond
C. Graphite D. Coal

97. What is Tritium?
A. Compound of hydrogen
B. Isobar of hydrogen
C. Isotope of hydrogen
D. Oxide of hydrogen

98. How do the centripetal forces pull a body?
A. Upward B. Downward
C. Inwards D. Outwards

99. What does Mycology study?
A. Minerals B. Sound
C. Insects D. Fungus

100. DNA is concentrated in the:
A. Microsome B. Nucleus
C. Chromatin D. Cell wall

101. Vinegar is obtained by the fermentation process; what does it contain?
A. Acetic acid B. Formic acid
C. Nitric acid D. Oxalic acid

102. When the leaves of a plant show chlorosis, the possible cause can be:
A. increase in nitrate content in the soil
B. increase in chloride content in the soil
C. decrease in phosphorus content in the soil
D. deficiency of trace elements in the soil

103. Which of the properties of elements is a whole number?
A. Atomic number B. Atomic weight
C. Molecular weight D. Equivalent weight

104. What does the process in which a heavy nucleus breaks to give two or more small nuclei and large amount of energy is called:
A. electrolysis B. fission
C. fusion D. ionization

105. What is the process in which two or more small nuclei join to form a large nucleus with evolution of energy is called:
A. electrolysis B. fission
C. ionization D. diffusion

106. The main endocrine gland present in the human body is:
A. Adrenal gland B. Pituitary gland
C. Thyroid gland D. Pancreas gland

107. Which one is wrongly matched?
A. Phosphorus – Match
B. Potassium Sulphate – Fertilizer
C. Methyl Isocynate – Tyre
D. Silicon – Glass

108. Which one of the following pairs is incorrect?
A. Malaria – Mosquitoes
B. Small Pox – Virus
C. Typhoid – Fungi
D. Cholera – Water

109. Which one group of the following belongs to 'lichens'?
A. Algae and bacteria
B. Virus and bacteria
C. Algae and fungi
D. All the above

110. Arrange the following elements, present in human body, in the descending order of their percentage:
1. Oxygen 2. Nitrogen
3. Carbon
A. 1 and 2 only B. 1 and 3 only
C. 1, 3, 2 D. 2 and 3 only

111. Which one of the following is given to a typhoid patient?
A. Chloroquin B. Vitamin A
C. Chloromycetin D. Sulphur

112. Which one of the following is called a growth gland?
A. Adrenal B. Thyroid
C. Pituitary D. None of the above

113. Which one of the following is a rich source of vitamin A?
A. Potato tuber B. Carrot root
C. Onion bulb D. Maize grains

114. Of the following the best way to put out a petrol fire is to use:
A. water
B. rugs
C. soda water fire extinguisher
D. carbon tetrachloride extinguisher

115. Which type of nerves carry impulses from the sense organs in response to stimulus?
A. Motor B. Sensory
C. Secretory D. All the above

116. The gas which helps in burning is:
A. Carbon Monoxide B. Hydrogen
C. Oxygen D. Nitrogen

117. Which one of the following best defines IQ?
A. $\frac{\text{Actual Age}}{\text{Mental Age}} \times 100$ B. $\frac{\text{Mental Age}}{\text{Actual Age}} \times 100^2$
C. $\frac{\text{Actual Age}}{\text{Mental Age}} \times 10$ D. $\frac{\text{Mental Age}}{\text{Actual Age}} \times 1000$

118. Which one of the following is called 'red planet'?
A. Mercury B. Jupiter
C. Venus D. Mars

119. The instrument used to measure radio activity is called:
A. Gyroscope B. Nephoscope
C. Machmeter D. Geiger Counter

120. Which one is the most popular fodder for poultry?
A. Barley B. Maize
C. Wheat D. Bajra

121. Hygrometer is used to measure:
A. humidity of the atmosphere
B. density of milk
C. speed of sound in water
D. None of the above

122. The process of making an object white, by destroying its colour is known as:
A. corrosion B. bleaching
C. dehydration D. pyrolysis

123. Pencillin is given to a patient in order to:
A. cure hereditary diseases
B. cure all diseases
C. prevent any rise in bodily temperature
D. prevent the growth of several types of disease-causing bacteria

124. A lectometer is used for checking the purity of:
A. milk B. oil
C. sugar D. gold

125. What are Picoplanktons?
A. Animals that are extinct now
B. Micro organisms
C. A platform in the Arabian sea off Mumbai, used for drilling
D. None of the above

126. For getting instant energy an athlete should take:
A. Carbohydrate B. Protein
C. Vitamin D. Chewing Gum

127. The amoeba type organisms in the human body, causing malaria and amoebic dysentery are known as:
A. bacteria B. virus
C. fungi D. protozoa

128. Seeds are best preserved in:
A. hot and dry condition B. cool but dry condition
C. dry condition D. wet and cool condition

129. When a ship enters sea from a river, its level:
A. remains same
B. rises
C. may or may not change
D. decreases

130. Kilowatt is the measuring unit of:
A. power B. current
C. work D. energy

131. Solar energy is the result of:
A. fusion of Helium
B. fusion of Hydrogen atoms
C. fission of Uranium atoms
D. fission of Hydrogen atom

132. Which among the following is least likely to catch fire?
A. Terycot B. Rayon
C. Nylon D. Cotton

133. The energy released on account of the motion of a body is termed as the:
A. potential energy B. kinetic energy
C. relative velocity D. None of these

134. The propounder of the Law of Gravitation was:
A. Faraday B. Edison
C. Newton D. Archimedes

135. Which originates from a plant?
A. Chloromycetin B. Quinine
C. Insulin D. Aspirin

136. Shortage of Vitamin A results in:
A. Beri Beri B. Rickets
C. Scurvy D. Night blindness

137. What percentage of oxygen does the atmospheric air contain?
A. 25% B. 35%
C. 21% D. 10%

138. Which metal is used for galvanising iron to immunize it against rusting?
A. Tin B. Nickel
C. Zinc D. Copper

139. The process by which plants make food is called:
A. Phototropism B. Photosynthesis
C. Transpiration D. Hydrotropism

140. The normal temperature of the human body is:
A. 32°C B. 27°C
C. 37°C D. 40°C

141. Which of the following is a gas?
A. Carbon dioxide B. Alcohol
C. Mercury D. Latex

142. The change of ice into water is a/an:
A. chemical change B. physical change
C. atomic change D. electrical change

143. The function of calcium in our body is:
A. to increase the supply of blood to the heart
B. to provide strength to the bones and teeth
C. to provide oxygen to the blood
D. to provide more sugar in our blood
E. to help digestion

144. Primary gold has a purity of .... carats
A. 14 B. 22
C. 23 D. 24

145. What is a fracture?
A. Bleeding B. Swelling
C. A broken bone D. Bruising

146. What colour does copper turn a flame?
A. Red B. Green
C. Yellow D. Mauve

147. Which of the following can build dams?
A. Otters B. Beavers
C. Water rats D. Racoons

148. Which animal fights snakes?
A. Monkey B. Mongoose
C. Tiger D. Jackal

149. In what units are light waves measured?
A. Curies B. Ohms
C. Ergs D. Angstrom

150. In a human body, the basic building block is:
A. Muscle B. Cell
C. Bones D. Nerves

151. Which trays should be used to form ice balls quickly in a freezer?
A. Rubber B. Wood
C. Ebonite D. Aluminium

152. Which disease does virus cause?
A. Typhoid fever B. Conjunctivitis
C. Malarial fever D. Cholera

153. What causes decomposition of animal remains?
A. Bacteria B. Hormones
C. Enzymes D. Insects

154. How would a stick held vertically in a beaker full of water look when glanced from the sides?
A. Unchanged B. Bent
C. Thinner D. Thicker

155. In which unit can we measure food energy?
A. Calorie B. Keloin
C. Joule D. Erg

156. The radio does not receive/catch the audio waves in a running train properly since:
A. the coach is metallic
B. running train makes deafening noise
C. friction between wheels and railway lines interferes the radio waves
D. None of the above

157. The drug most widely used to relieve pain is:
A. opium B. aspirin
C. morphine D. baralgan

158. A car has a speedometer to measure the:
A. time B. distance
C. speed D. pressure

159. Heat from the sun reaches the earth by:
A. convection B. radiation
C. conduction D. friction

160. Shadows are caused by things which are:
A. transparent B. heavy
C. light D. opaque

161. Vanadium is:
A. an element used in nuclear fission
B. a metal used as a substitute of gold
C. a metal used to make steel strong
D. a metal found without any alloy

162. A vitamin that has vital influence on organs of reproduction and is found in germinating wheat is:
A. A B. B
C. E D. D

163. We are asked to wear white clothes in summer because:
A. they look more graceful
B. they are visible from long distance
C. white clothes absorb less heat
D. it is a convention

164. We can always see only one side of the moon because:
A. it is a stationary satellite of the earth
B. of the rotation of the earth
C. it takes equal times to rotate round its axis and to revolve round the earth
D. of the revolution of the earth

165. Diptheria and influenza are caused by:
A. bacteria and virus respectively
B. bacteria
C. virus and bacteria respectively
D. None of the above

166. Vitamin A deficiency causes:
A. sexual disorders B. night blindness
C. falling of hair D. weakness

167. Which of the following should be avoided by a heart patient?
A. Bread B. Cream
C. Apple D. Rice

168. Which of the following is indispensable for the growth of teenagers?
A. Carbohydrate B. Protein
C. Vitamin D. Fat

169. Which of the following is available in the sea in plenty and is given to patients suffering from a deficiency disease?
A. Planktons B. Iodine
C. Vitamin A D. None of the above

170. The most likely period when a woman can conceive is:
A. on the 12th day of the menstrual cycle
B. 5th to 10th day of the menstrual cycle
C. 15th to 19th day of the menstrual cycle
D. at any time during menstrual cycle

171. Which one of the following blood groups is universal recipient?
A. AB B. A
C. O D. B

172. The possibility of the birth of fraternal twins arises during/after:
A. fertilization
B. fertilization stage
C. 3rd to 5th month of pregnancy
D. 5th to 7th month of pregnancy

173. Which one of the following groups is closely related from the point of view of taxonomy?
A. housefly, dragonfly, butterfly
B. earthworm, seahorse, hookworm
C. silverfish, cuttlefish, starfish
D. None of the above

174. Arrange in right order from childhood onwards the growth of the following teeth:
1. incisors 2. canines
3. pre-molars 4. molars
A. 1, 2, 3, 4 B. 1, 2, 4, 3
C. 2, 3, 1, 4 D. 4, 1, 3, 2

175. Assertion (A) : Eclipses cannot occur on all full moon and new moon days.
Reason (R) : The moon revolves in an elliptical orbit round the earth.
A. A and R are true but R does not explain A
B. Both A and R are false
C. A and R are true and R correctly explains A
D. A is true but R is false

176. Name the appropriate technology which should be adopted for rural electrification and cooking?
A. nuclear energy B. biogas
C. solar power D. None of the above

177. Einstein discovered:
1. jet propulsion 2. television
3. photo electric effect 4. theory of relativity
5. radioactivity
A. 1, 5 B. 3, 4
C. 4, 2, 1 D. 3, 4, 5

178. What are the tapes in tape-recorders coated with?
A. Magnesium oxide B. Silver bromide
C. Iron oxide D. Zinc oxide

179. Identify which one of the following is not a parasite?
A. Housefly B. Louse
C. Mosquito D. Tick

180. Which one of the following determines the sex of a child?
A. Rh factor of the parents
B. Chromosomes of the father
C. Blood group of the mother
D. Chromosomes of the mother

181. Triple Antigen prevents:
A. whooping cough, tetanus, diphtheria
B. polio tetanus, small pox
C. small pox, typhoid, malaria
D. tetanus, diptheria, malaria

182. What is the normal range of the adult human heart-beat per minute?
A. 50 to 59 B. 60 to 80
C. 81 to 90 D. 91 to 110

183. What would be the effect of breathing air without oxygen?
A. One would collapse within 30 seconds and be dead within 5 minutes
B. One would become unconscious but be living for few days
C. One would start vomiting and be dead in 2 hours
D. One would be alive for few days

184. The Isotope of Uranium which is very much radioactive is:
A. U 235 B. U 238
C. U 233 D. All the above

185. A tube light works on the principle of:
A. chemical effect of current
B. heating effect of current
C. magnetic effect of current
D. discharge of electricity through gases

186. A cut diamond sparkles because of its:
A. hardness
B. emission of light
C. high polish
D. high refractive index

187. A person in normal health requires per day:
A. 1,000 — 1,800 calories
B. 4,000 — 5,000 calories
C. 2,500 — 3,000 calories
D. 3,000 — 4,000 calories

188. Absolute Zero is equivalent to:
A. 73.16° Centigrade B. 70.02° Fahrenheit
C. 137.02° Fahrenheit D. –273.15° Centigrade

189. By the term high speed steels we understand:
A. extra soft steels
B. very light steels
C. extra hard steels
D. steels with much of carbon in them

190. The best known and most commonly used artificial fibre is:
A. Rayon B. Terryfibre
C. Cellulose D. Protein based fibres

191. Brass is an:
A. alloy of copper and tin
B. alloy of copper and zinc
C. alloy of zinc and tin
D. amalgam of zinc and tin

192. 'ELISA' test is done for detection of:
A. AIDS B. Kalazar
C. Cancer D. Diabetes

193. Which one of the following is credited for developing blood grouping method?
A. Karl Landsteiner B. Robert Koch
C. William Harvey D. Louis Pasteur

194. Which of the following is a conventional source of energy?
A. Hydro B. Solar
C. Geothermal D. Wind

195. Acceleration due to gravity on the surface of the moon is 0.166 g. A man weighing 60 kg on the earth would weigh ...... on the moon.
A. 16.6 kg B. 60 kg
C. 30 kg D. 10 kg

196. Plants take nitrogen in the form of:
A. nitrate B. element N
C. nitrite D. ammonia

197. When the reading of barometer goes up, it is an indication of:
A. storm B. fair weather
C. rainfall D. snowy condition

198. Main constituent of pearl is:
A. calcium carbonate and magnesium carbonate
B. calcium carbonate
C. calcium sulphate and calcium carbonate
D. calcium oxide and ammonium chloride

199. Which of the following metals has the lowest melting point?
A. Silver B. Zinc
C. Gold D. Tin

200. Astronaut can jump higher on the moon's surface than on the earth because:
A. he is weightless on the moon
B. there is no atmosphere on the moon
C. the force of gravity on the lunar surface is less than that on the earth
D. the moon is smaller than the earth

201. When metal is heated, the density of metal:
A. increases
B. decreases
C. remains the same
D. first increases afterwards decreases

202. A piece of red cloth is kept in blue light, its colour will appear:
A. blue B. red
C. green D. black

203. An important metal used with iron to produce stainless steel is:
A. aluminium B. tin
C. chromium D. carbon

204. Small rain-drops are spherical in shape because of:
A. surface-tension
B. gravity
C. atmospheric pressure
D. evaporation

205. The weight of a body at the centre of the earth is:
A. increased B. neutralised
C. decreased D. the same

206. The conservation of energy principle refers to the fact that:
A. it is essential not to waste natural gas and oil, for these are limited in supply
B. solar heating makes use of the sun's energy, which would otherwise be wasted
C. energy can neither be created nor destroyed
D. nuclear-power plants recycle spent fuel

207. The American scientists have discovered new secrets about the milky way, we call galaxy. The secrets are:
A. the entire galaxy is revolving in the reverse order—East to west at a very fast speed
B. there are about 5000 enormous gas clouds in the milky way and that these clouds are most massive objects in the galaxy
C. the galaxy is the only one of its kind in the universe
D. the galaxy is perfectly spherical

208. Lode stone is:
A. a very hard stone B. a blue variety of stone
C. a natural magnet D. an artificial magnet

209. The instrument which measures the movement of clouds by casting their images through a peephole onto a black mirrored surface is called:
A. Nephoscope B. Periscope
C. Stethoscope D. Gyroscope

210. The meteorologist uses only his eyes to measure which of the following?
A. Snow B. Ceiling
C. Rain D. Visibility

211. Red blood corpuscles are produced in:
A. spleen B. liver
C. bone marrow D. kidneys

212. Conjuctivitis is a disease of the:
A. lever B. eyes
C. kidney D. heart

213. Bile is stored in:
A. lungs B. kidney
C. heart D. lever

214. Insulin is used in the treatment of:
A. diabetes B. cancer
C. small pox D. plague

215. Which of these, famous scientists thought of the Theory of Relativity?
A. Newton B. Einstein
C. Galileo D. Copernicus

216. Which do you not find in the nucleus of an atom?
A. A proton B. A neutron
C. An electron D. None of these

217. What element has the lightest atom of all?
A. Oxygen B. Copper
C. Carbon D. Hydrogen

218. How would you make dry ice from carbon-dioxide?
A. By heating it B. By baking it
C. By freezing it D. By drying it

219. Radium is used to cure which disease?
A. Cancer B. Bright's disease
C. Haemophilia D. Typhoid fever

220. The "fizz" in soda water is caused by:
A. oxygen B. hydrogen
C. carbon dioxide D. nitrogen

ANSWERS

1	2	3	4	5	6	7	8	9	10
C	A	A	C	D	A	C	D	B	D
11	12	13	14	15	16	17	18	19	20
C	A	C	A	B	D	A	D	D	C
21	22	23	24	25	26	27	28	29	30
C	B	B	C	C	C	A	B	D	C
31	32	33	34	35	36	37	38	39	40
D	A	B	C	D	C	A	B	C	A
41	42	43	44	45	46	47	48	49	50
A	B	D	C	A	B	B	A	A	A
51	52	53	54	55	56	57	58	59	60
A	A	B	D	A	A	B	A	A	B
61	62	63	64	65	66	67	68	69	70
A	B	C	A	A	D	B	C	C	D
71	72	73	74	75	76	77	78	79	80
B	D	B	B	C	D	C	A	B	D
81	82	83	84	85	86	87	88	89	90
A	C	D	C	B	C	A	D	A	D
91	92	93	94	95	96	97	98	99	100
A	A	B	B	D	B	C	C	D	C
101	102	103	104	105	106	107	108	109	110
A	D	A	B	D	B	C	C	C	C
111	112	113	114	115	116	117	118	119	120
C	B	B	C	B	C	A	D	D	B
121	122	123	124	125	126	127	128	129	130
A	B	D	A	B	A	D	B	B	A
131	132	133	134	135	136	137	138	139	140
B	D	B	C	B	D	C	C	B	C
141	142	143	144	145	146	147	148	149	150
A	B	B	D	B	B	B	B	D	B
151	152	153	154	155	156	157	158	159	160
D	B	A	D	A	D	B	C	B	D
161	162	163	164	165	166	167	168	169	170
C	C	C	C	A	B	B	B	B	C
171	172	173	174	175	176	177	178	179	180
A	B	A	A	D	B	B	C	A	B
181	182	183	184	185	186	187	188	189	190
A	B	A	B	D	D	C	D	C	A
191	192	193	194	195	196	197	198	199	200
B	A	A	A	D	A	B	B	D	C
201	202	203	204	205	206	207	208	209	210
C	D	C	A	B	C	B	C	A	D
211	212	213	214	215	216	217	218	219	220
C	B	D	A	B	C	D	C	A	C

GENERAL STUDIES

1

Neighbouring Countries of India

(History, Geography, Polity, Economy & Culture)

NEPAL

NEPAL–AT A GLANCE

- **Location:** Nepal is a landlocked country in Central Asia. Located in the central Himalayas, Tibet (Chinese autonomous region) is to the north and India to the east and south.
- **Area:** 147,181 sq. km.
- **Capital:** Kathmandu.
- **Largest Cities:** Kathmandu, Biratnagar, Lalitpur.
- **Principal Rivers:** Karnali, Narayani, Kosi.
- **Monetary Unit:** Nepalese rupee.
- **Languages:** Nepali (official), Newari, Bhutia, Maithili.
- **Type of Government:** Republic.

ECONOMIC SUMMARY

Principal agricultural products: Rice, Maize, Wheat, Millet, Jute, Sugarcane, Oilseed, Potatoes. **Labour force in Industry:** 7%. **Major Products:** Cigarettes, Sugar, Lumber, Jute, Hydroelectric power, Cement. **Natural Resources:** Water, Timber, Hydroelectric potential. **Exports:** Clothing, carpets, Leather goods. **Imports:** Petroleum products, fertiliser, machinery. **Major Trading Partners:** India, Japan, US, Europe.

The history of Nepal is intertwined with the history of the broader Indian subcontinent and the surrounding regions, comprising the areas of South Asia and East Asia.

Nepal is a multi-ethnic, multiracial, multicultural, multi-religious, and multilingual country. The most spoken language is Nepali followed by several other ethnic languages.

The Kingdom of Nepal was established in 1768 and started a campaign of unifying all of Nepal that would form modern territories of Nepal. Some former territories had been lost due to the kingdom having participated in the Sino-Nepalese War which ended in both victory and loses, ultimately accepting as a tribute state of Qing dynasty of China from 1792 to 1865. The Anglo-Nepalese War ended in British victory and ceded some Nepalese territory. In a historical vote for the election of the constituent assembly, the Nepalese parliament voted to abolish the monarchy in June 2006. Nepal became a federal republic on 28 May 2008 and was formally renamed the 'Federal Democratic Republic of Nepal' ending the 200-year-old reign of the Shah monarchs.

BANGLADESH

BANGLADESH–AT A GLANCE

- **Location:** Located in South Asia, Bangladesh has a coastline on the Bay of Bengal. It mainly comprises the delta of the Ganges river. India borders the country to the west, north and east. Myanmar is located to its south-cast.
- **Area:** 143,998 sq. km.
- **Capital:** Dhaka
- **Largest Cities:** Chittagong, Khulna, Rajshahi, Nerayanganj, Rangpur, Mymensingh, Comilla, Sylhet, Barisal.
- **Principal Rivers:** Ganges, Brahmaputra.
- **Flag:** Bottle green with a red disc in the centre.
- **Monetary Unit:** Taka.
- **Type of Government:** Parliamentary Democracy.

ECONOMIC SUMMARY

Principal Agricultural Products: Rice, Jute, Potatoes, Tea, Sugar, Wheat. **Major Industrial Products:** Jute goods, Textiles, Leather, Sugar, Fertiliser, Paper, Pharmaceuticals. **Natural Resources:** Natural gas, Uranium, Timber. **Exports:** Jute goods, Jute, Tea, Leather, Seafood. **Imports:** Foodgrains, Fuels, Raw cotton, Yarn, Manufactured goods. **Major Trading Partners:** US., Japan, India, China, South Korea, Germany.

Bangladesh officially the People's Republic of Bangladesh, is a country in South Asia. Bangladesh shares land borders with India to the west, north, and east, and Myanmar to the southeast; to the south it has a coastline along the Bay of Bengal. It is narrowly separated from Nepal and Bhutan by the Siliguri Corridor; and from China by 100 km of the Indian state of Sikkim in the north. Dhaka, the capital and largest city, is the nation's economic, political, and cultural hub. Chittagong, the largest seaport, is the second-largest city. The official language is Bengali, one of the most eastern branches of the Indo-European language family.

Bangladesh forms the sovereign part of the historic and ethnolinguistic region of Bengal, which was divided during the Partition of British India in 1947. The country has a Bengali Muslim majority. Ancient Bengal was an important cultural center in the Indian subcontinent as the home of the states of Vanga, Pundra, Gangaridai, Gauda, Samatata, and Harikela.

In 1947, East Bengal became the most populous province in the Dominion of Pakistan. It was renamed as East Pakistan with Dhaka becoming the country's legislative capital. The Bengali Language Movement in 1952; the East Bengali legislative election, 1954; the Six point movement of 1966; and the 1970 Pakistani general election resulted in the rise of Bengali nationalism and pro-democracy movements in East Pakistan. The refusal of the Pakistani military junta to transfer power to the Awami League led by Sheikh Mujibur Rahman led to the Bangladesh Liberation War in 1971, in which the Mukti Bahini aided by India waged a successful armed revolution. The conflict saw the 1971 Bangladesh genocide and the massacre of pro-independence Bengali civilians, including intellectuals. The new state of Bangladesh became the first constitutionally secular state in South Asia in 1972. Islam was declared the state religion in 1988. In 2010, the Bangladesh Supreme Court reaffirmed secular principles in the constitution.

Bangladesh is a unitary parliamentary constitutional republic based on the Westminster system. Bengalis make up 98% of the total population of Bangladesh, and the large Muslim population of Bangladesh makes it the third-largest Muslim-majority country. It maintains the third-largest military in South Asia after India and Pakistan; and has been a major contributor to UN peacekeeping operations. A middle power in the Indo-Pacific, Bangladesh is an emerging economy.

It hosts one of the largest refugee populations in the world due to the Rohingya genocide. Bangladesh faces many challenges, including the adverse effects of climate change, poverty, illiteracy, corruption, authoritarianism and human rights abuses. However, the poverty rate has halved since 2011 and the country is expected to become a middle income country in this decade. Once a historic center of the muslin cloth trade, Bangladesh is now one of the world's largest modern garment exporters.

CHINA

CHINA–AT A GLANCE

- **Location:** China comprises the main centre of the continent of Asia, with a coastline on the Yellow Sea, East China Sea and South China Sea. North Korea has a border in the north-east, Russia and Mongolia are to the north, Tajikistan, Kyrgyzstan and Kazakhstan to the west, and to the south are Afghanistan, Pakistan, India, Nepal, Bhutan, Myanmar, Laos and Vietnam.
- **Area:** 9,596,961 sq. km.
- **Capital:** Beijing
- **Largest Cities:** Beijing (Peking), Shanghai, Tianjin (Tientsin), Canton, Wuhan, Shenyang (Mukden), Nanjing (Nanking), Chongqing (Chungking), Harbin, Chengdu, Xian, Dalian (Darian), Jinan, Changchun, Qingdao (Tsingtao), Shenzen, Taiyan, Zengzhou, Kunming.
- **Principal Rivers:** Yongtze (Chang Jang), Huang He (Yellow River), Xijiang (Sinkiang or Pearl River), Heilongjiang (Amur).
- **Flag:** Red with a large star and four smaller stars, all in yellow in the canton.
- **Monetary Unit:** Yuan Renminbi.
- **Type of Government:** Communist party-led State.
- **Languages:** Standard Chinese or Mandarin; Yue or Cantonese; also local dialects.

ECONOMIC SUMMARY

Principal Products: Rice, Wheat, Grains, Cotton. **Major Industrial Products:** Iron and steel, Textiles, Armaments, Petroleum. **Natural Resources:** Coal, Natural Gas, Limestone, Marble, Metals, Hydropower potential. **Exports:** Agricultural products, petroleum, minerals, Metals, Textiles, Garments, Telecommunications and recording equipment, Illicit drugs. China is illicit producer of opium (bulk production in Yunnan Province). **Imports:** Grains, Chemical fertiliser, Steel, Industrial raw material, Machinery and equipment. **Major Trading Partners:** Japan, US, Germany, India, Taiwan, Singapore, Canada, C.I.S. countries, Italy.

China officially the People's Republic of China is a country in East Asia. It is the world's most populous country, with a population of more than 1.4 billion. China spans five geographical time zones and borders 14 countries, the second most of any country in the world after Russia. The country consists of 23 provinces, five autonomous regions, four municipalities, and two Special Administrative Regions (Hong Kong and Macau). The national capital is Beijing.

China emerged as one of the world's first civilizations in the fertile basin of the Yellow River in the North China Plain. China was one of the world's foremost economic powers for most of the two millennia from the 1st until the 19th century. For millennia, China's political system was based on absolute hereditary monarchies, or dynasties, beginning with the semi-legendary Xia dynasty in the 21st century BCE. Since then, China has expanded, fractured, and re-unified numerous times. In the 3rd century BCE, the Qin reunited core China and established the first Chinese empire. The succeeding Han dynasty (206 BCE - 220 CE) saw some of the most advanced technology at that time, including papermaking and the compass, along with agricultural and medical improvements. The invention of gunpowder and movable type in the Tang dynasty (618-907) and Northern Song Dynasty (960-1127) completed the Four Great Inventions. Tang culture spread widely in Asia, as the new Silk Road brought traders to as far as Mesopotamia and the Horn of Africa. The Qing dynasty, China's last dynasty, which formed the territorial basis for modern China, suffered heavy losses to foreign imperialism in the 19th century.

The Chinese monarchy collapsed in 1912 with the Xinhai Revolution, when the Republic of China (ROC) replaced the Qing dynasty. China was invaded by the Empire of Japan during World War II. The Civil War resulted in a division of territory in 1949 when the Chinese Communist Party (CCP) established the People's Republic of China on the mainland while the Kuomintang-led ROC government retreated to the island of Taiwan. Both claim to be the sole legitimate government of China, although the United Nations has recognized the PRC as the sole representation since 1971. China conducted a series of economic reforms since 1978, and entered into the World Trade Organization in 2001.

China is currently governed as a unitary one-party socialist republic by the CCP. China is a permanent member of the United Nations Security Council and a founding member of several multilateral and regional cooperation organizations such as the Asian Infrastructure Investment Bank, the Silk Road Fund, the New Development Bank, the Shanghai Cooperation Organization, and the RCEP, and is a member of the BRICS, the G8+5, the G20, the APEC, and the East Asia Summit.

China is the world's largest economy by GDP at purchasing power parity, second-largest economy by nominal GDP, and the world's second wealthiest country by total wealth. The country has the fastest growing major economy and is the world's largest manufacturer and exporter. China is a recognized nuclear-weapon state with the world's largest standing army by military personnel and second-largest defense budget.

BHUTAN

BHUTAN–AT A GLANCE

- **Location:** A landlocked country, Bhutan is located in Central Asia, in the eastern Himalayas, with India to the south and Tibet to the north.
- **Area:** 38,394 sq. km.
- **Capital and Largest City:** Thimphu.
- **Principal Rivers:** Amo-chu, Wang-chu, Machu.
- **Flag:** Diagonally yellow over orange, overall in the centre a white dragon.
- **Monetary Unit:** Ngultrum.
- **Type of Government:** Monarchy.

ECONOMIC SUMMARY

Per Capita GDP: $8,700. **Principal Products:** Oil palms, Peanuts, Cotton, Coffee, Tobacco, Corn, Rice Livestock, Fish. **Major Industrial Products:** Processed palm oil, Palm kernel oil. **Natural Resources:** Low grade iron ore, Limestone, Some off-shore oil. **Exports:** Palm and agricultural products. **Imports:** Clothing, consumer goods, Lumber, Fuels, Foodstuffs, Machinery, Transportation equipment. **Major Trading Partners:** France and other Western European countries, US, Japan, Thailand, China, Brazil.

Bhutan, country of south-central Asia, located on the eastern ridges of the Himalayas. Historically a remote kingdom, Bhutan became less isolated in the second half of the 20th century, and consequently the pace of change began to accelerate. With improvements in transportation, by the early 21st century a trip from the Indian border to the Bhutanese capital, Thimphu, that once took six days by mule could be made in just a few hours by car along a winding mountain road from the border town of Phuntsholing. The governmental structure also changed radically. Reforms initiated by King Jigme Dorji Wangchuk (reigned 1952-72) in the 1950s and '60s led to a shift away from absolute monarchy in the 1990s and toward the institution of multiparty parliamentary democracy in 2008.

The economic core of Bhutan lies in the fertile valleys of the Lesser Himalayas, which are separated from one another by a series of high and complex interconnecting ridges extending across the country from north to south. The political nucleus of Bhutan is centred in the Paro and Thimphu valleys in the Lesser Himalayan region. Its location between the Assam-Bengal Plain of India to the south and the Plateau of Tibet of southwestern China to the north gives the country considerable geopolitical significance.

Bhutan's northern and western boundary with the Tibet Autonomous Region (part of China), although undefined, generally follows the crest of the Great Himalayas. In the Duars Plain to the south of the Himalayan range lies Bhutan's boundary with the Indian states of West Bengal and Assam. Bhutan borders the Indian states of Arunachal Pradesh to the east and Sikkim to the southwest.

MYANMAR

MYANMAR–AT A GLANCE

- **Location:** Located in East Asia, Myanmar has a coastline on the Bay of Bengal. Bangladesh and India are to its west, China to its north and Laos and Thailand to its east.
- **Area:** 676,578 sq. km.
- **Capital:** Nay Pyi Taw.
- **Largest Cities:** Nay Pyi Taw, Mandalay, Moulmein, Bassein, Pegu, Yangon (Rangoon).
- **Principal Rivers:** Irrawaddy, Sittang, Mekong.
- **Flag:** Three horizontal stripes of yellow, green and red with a five-pointed white star in the middle.
- **Monetary Unit:** Kyat.
- **Type of Government:** Presidential republic dominated by the military.
- **Languages:** Burmese; minority languages.

ECONOMIC SUMMARY

Principal Products: Sugarcane, Corn, Rice, Peanuts. **Major Products:** Textiles, Footwear, Processed agricultural products, Wood and wood products, Refined petroleum. **Natural Resources:** Timber, Tin, Antimony, Zinc, Copper, Precious stones, Crude oil, Natural gas. **Exports:** Rice, Teak, Oil seeds, Metals, Rubber, Gems. **Imports:** Machinery, Construction and transportation equipment, Manufactured goods. **Major Trading Partners:** Japan, EU, China, South-east Asia. Before Afghanistan overtook it in recent years, Myanmar was the world's largest illicit producer of opium poppy.

Myanmar, also called Burma, country, located in the western portion of mainland Southeast Asia. In 1989 the country's official English name, which it had held since 1885, was changed from the Union of Burma to the Union of Myanmar; in the Burmese language the country has been known as Myanma (or, more precisely, Mranma Prañ) since the 13th century. The English name of the city that served as the country's capital from 1948 to 2006, Rangoon, also was dropped in 1989 in favour of the common Burmese name, Yangon.

In 2005 the government began to shift its administrative centre, first to the city of Pyinmana (some 200 miles north of Yangon) and then to Nay Pyi Taw (Naypyidaw), a newly constructed city near Pyinmana. Nay Pyi Taw was proclaimed the capital of Myanmar in 2006.

People of Myanmar are made up of a striking array of different ethnic groups, which include Bamar/Burmese (by some distance the largest in number), Shan, Karen, Kachin, Chin, Mon, Han Chinese and Indian, to name but a few.

This variety of ethnicities also means massive language diversity, although Burmese is the official language, and English is widely used - to varying degrees of proficiency.

Since 2005, the capital has been located in Nay Pyi Taw, but the former capital, Yangon (Rangoon), remains the biggest city, commercial centre, and arrival point for most visitors. The moving of capitals is in fact in line with the tradition of upheaval and renewal in Myanmar - the country has had many capitals over the years, including Mandalay, Inwa and Mrauk U, to name just a few.

Stretching from latitude 10° N to about 28° 30′ N, Myanmar is the northernmost country of Southeast Asia; it is shaped like a kite with a long tail that runs south along the Malay Peninsula. The country is bordered by China to the north and northeast, Laos to the east, Thailand to the southeast, the Andaman Sea and Bay of Bengal to the south and southwest, Bangladesh to the west, and India to the northwest. Its total length from north to south is about 1,275 miles (2,050 km), and its width at the widest part, across the centre of the country at about the latitude of the city of Mandalay, is approximately 580 miles (930 km) from east to west.

PAKISTAN

PAKISTAN–AT A GLANCE

- **Location:** Pakistan has a coastline on the Arabian Sea to the South. Iran is located to its west, Afghanistan to its north-west, China to its north-east and India to the east.
- **Area:** 796,095 sq. km.
- **Capital:** Islamabad.
- **Largest Cities:** Islamabad, Karachi, Lahore, Faisalabad (Lyallpur), Rawalpindi, Hyderabad, Multan, Gujranwala, Peshawar, Sialkot.
- **Principal Rivers:** Indus, Sutlej, Chenab, Ravi, Jhelum.
- **Flag:** Green charged at the centre, with a white crescent and white five-pointed star. A white vertical stripe at the mast to one-quarter of the flag.
- **Monetary Unit:** Pakistan Rupee.
- **Type of Government:** Parliamentary democracy in a federal setting.
- **Languages:** Urdu (official), English (official), Punjabi, Sindhi, Pashtu and Baluchi.

ECONOMIC SUMMARY

Principal Agricultural Products: Wheat, Rice, Cotton. **Major Products:** Cotton textiles, Processed foods, petroleum products, construction material. **Natural Resources:** Natural gas, Limited petroleum, Iron ore. **Exports:** Cotton, Rice, Carpets, Textiles, Clothings. **Imports:** Foodgrains, Edible oil, Crude oil, Machinery, Chemicals, Transport equipment. **Major Trading Partners:** US, EU, Japan, China.

Pakistan, officially the Islamic Republic of Pakistan, is a country in South Asia. It is the world's fifth-most populous country, with a population of almost 227 million, and has the world's second-largest Muslim population. It has a 1,046-kilometre (650-mile) coastline along the Arabian Sea and Gulf of Oman in the south, and is bordered by India to the east, Afghanistan to the west, Iran to the southwest, and China to the northeast. It is separated narrowly from Tajikistan by Afghanistan's Wakhan Corridor in the north, and also shares a maritime border with Oman.

Pakistan is the site of several ancient cultures, including the 8,500-year-old Neolithic site of Mehrgarh in Balochistan, and the Indus Valley Civilisation of the Bronze Age, the most extensive of the civilisations of the Old World. The region that comprises the modern state of Pakistan was the realm of multiple empires and dynasties, including the Achaemenid; briefly that of Alexander the Great; the Seleucid, the Maurya, the Kushan, the Gupta; the Umayyad Caliphate in its southern regions, the Hindu Shahi, the Ghaznavids, the Delhi Sultanate, the Mughals, the Durranis, the Sikh Empire, British East India Company rule, and most recently, the British Indian Empire from 1858 to 1947.

Spurred by the Pakistan Movement, which sought a homeland for the Muslims of British India, and election victories in 1946 by the All-India Muslim League, Pakistan gained independence in 1947 after the Partition of the British Indian Empire, which awarded separate statehood to its Muslim-majority regions and was accompanied by an unparalleled mass migration and loss of life. Initially a Dominion of the British Commonwealth, Pakistan officially drafted its constitution in 1956, and emerged as a declared Islamic republic. In 1971, the exclave of East Pakistan seceded as the new country of Bangladesh after a nine-month-long civil war. In the following four decades, Pakistan has been ruled by governments whose descriptions, although complex, commonly alternated between civilian and military, democratic and authoritarian, relatively secular and Islamist. Pakistan elected a civilian government in 2008, and in 2010 adopted a parliamentary system with periodic elections.

Pakistan is a regional and middle power nation, and has the world's sixth-largest standing armed forces. It is a declared nuclear-weapons state, and is ranked amongst the emerging and growth-leading economies, with a large and rapidly-growing middle class.

MALDIVES

MALDIVES–AT A GLANCE

- **Location:** Maldives is a group of about 2,000 islands grouped into 12 clusters, situated about 700 km south-west of Sri Lanka in northern Indian Ocean.
- **Area:** 298 sq. km.
- **Capital:** Male.
- **Principal Rivers:** There are no significant rivers.
- **Flag:** Red with a green panel bearing a white crescent.
- **Monetary Unit:** Maldivian Rufiyaa.
- **Type of Government:** Republic.
- **Languages:** Divehi.

ECONOMIC SUMMARY

Principal Agricultural Products: Coconuts, Millet. **Major Products:** Fish, Processed coconuts. **Natural Resources:** Fish, Coconuts. Tourism is also an important sector of the economy. **Exports:** Fish, Clothing, Ambergris. **Imports:** Rice, Wheat, Flour, Sugar, Drugs, Textile, Petroleum Products. **Major Trading Partners:** US, UK, Singapore, Thailand, Germany, India.

Maldives officially the Republic of Maldives, is an archipelagic country in the Indian subcontinent of Asia, situated in the Indian Ocean. It lies southwest of Sri Lanka and India, about 750 kilometres (470 miles; 400 nautical miles) from the Asian continent's mainland. The chain of 26 atolls stretches from Ihavandhippolhu Atoll in the north to Addu Atoll in the south (across the Equator).

Malé is the capital and the most populated city, traditionally called the "King's Island" where the ancient royal dynasties ruled for its central location.

The Maldivian Archipelago is located on the Chagos-Laccadive Ridge, a vast submarine mountain range in the Indian Ocean; this also forms a terrestrial ecoregion, together with the Chagos Archipelago and Lakshadweep. With an average ground-level elevation of 1.5 metres (4 ft 11 in) above sea level, and a highest natural point of only 5.1 metres (17 ft), it is the world's lowest-lying country.

In the 12th century Islam reached the Maldivian Archipelago, which was consolidated as a sultanate, developing strong commercial and cultural ties with Asia and Africa. From the mid-16th century, the region came under the increasing influence of European colonial powers, with Maldives becoming a British protectorate in 1887. Independence from the United Kingdom came in 1965, and a presidential republic was established in 1968 with an elected People's Majlis. The ensuing decades have seen political instability, efforts at democratic reform, and environmental challenges posed by climate change.

Maldives became a founding member of the South Asian Association for Regional Cooperation (SAARC). It is also a member of the United Nations, the Commonwealth of Nations, the Organisation of Islamic Cooperation, and the Non-Aligned Movement. The World Bank classifies the Maldives as having an upper-middle income economy. Fishing has historically been the dominant economic activity, and remains the largest sector by far, followed by the rapidly growing tourism industry. The Maldives rates "high" on the Human Development Index, with per capita income significantly higher than other SAARC nations.

SRI LANKA

SRI LANKA–AT A GLANCE

- **Location:** Located in South Asia, the island of Sri Lanka is off the south-east coast of India, separated by the Palk Strait.
- **Area:** 65,610 sq. km.
- **Capital:** Sri Jayewardenepura Kotte (Colombo).
- **Largest Cities:** Sri Jayewardenepura Kotte (Colombo), Kandy, Jaffna, Galle.
- **Principal Rivers:** Mahaweli Ganga, Kelani Ganga.
- **Flag:** A Yellow field bearing two panels : in the hoist two vertical strips of green and orange; in the fly, dark red with a gold lion holding a sword and in each corner a gold 'bo' leaf.
- **Monetary Unit:** Sri Lanka Rupee.
- **Type of Government:** Republic.
- **Languages:** Sinhala (official and national), Tamil (national), English commonly used.

ECONOMIC SUMMARY

Principal Agricultural Products: Tea, Coconuts, Rubber, Rice, Spices, Cotton, Oil seeds, Wheat, Millet, Sheep. **Major Products:** Processed Rubber, Tea, Coconuts, Textiles, Cement, Refined petroleum. **Natural Resources:** Limestone, Graphite, Gems. **Exports:** Petroleum products, Gems and Jewellery, Tea, Rubber. **Imports:** Petroleum, Machinery, Transport equipment, Sugar, Fertiliser. **Major Trading Partners:** Saudi Arabia, US, UK, Germany, Japan, Singapore, India, Iran, Taiwan, Belgium, Hong Kong, China.

Sri Lanka formerly known as Ceylon, and officially the Democratic Socialist Republic of Sri Lanka, is an island country in South Asia. It lies in the Indian Ocean, southwest of the Bay of Bengal, and southeast of the Arabian Sea; it is separated from the Indian subcontinent by the Gulf of Mannar and the Palk Strait. Sri Lanka shares a maritime border with India and the Maldives. Sri Jayawardenepura Kotte is its legislative capital, and Colombo is its largest city and financial centre.

Sri Lanka's documented history goes back 3,000 years, with evidence of prehistoric human settlements that dates to at least 125,000 years ago. It has a rich cultural heritage. The earliest known Buddhist writings of Sri Lanka, known collectively as the Pali canon, date to the fourth Buddhist council, which took place in 29 BCE. Sri Lanka's geographic location and deep harbours have made it of great strategic importance, from the earliest days of the ancient Silk Road trade route to today's so-called maritime Silk Road. Because its location made it a major trading hub, it was already known to both Far Easterners and Europeans as long ago as the Anuradhapura period. The country's trade in luxury goods and spices attracted traders of many nations, which helped to create Sri Lanka's diverse population. During a period of great political crisis in the Sinhalese kingdom of Kotte, the Portuguese arrived in Sri Lanka (largely by accident) and then sought to control the island's maritime regions and its lucrative external trade. Part of Sri Lanka became a Portuguese possession. After the Sinhalese-Portuguese war, the Dutch and the Kingdom of Kandy took control of those areas. The Dutch possessions were then taken by the British, who later extended their control over the whole island, colonising it from 1815 to 1948. A national movement for political independence arose in the early 20th century, and in 1948, Ceylon became a dominion. The dominion was succeeded by the republic named Sri Lanka in 1972. Sri Lanka's more recent history was marred by a 26-year civil war, which began in 1983 and ended decisively in 2009, when the Sri Lanka Armed Forces defeated the Liberation Tigers of Tamil Eelam.

Today, Sri Lanka is a multinational state, home to diverse cultures, languages, and ethnicities. The Sinhalese are the majority of the nation's population. The Tamils, who are a large minority group, have also played an influential role in the island's history. Other long established groups include the Moors, the Burghers, the Malays, the Chinese, and the indigenous Vedda.

AFGHANISTAN

AFGHANISTAN–AT A GLANCE

- **Location:** A landlocked country, Afghanistan is located in Central Asia. Pakistan is to its east and south, Iran and Turkmenistan to its west, Uzbekistan and Kyrgyzstan to its north. The country has a small border with China to the north-east.
- **Area:** 652,230 sq. km.
- **Capital:** Kabul.
- **Largest Cities:** Kabul, Kandahar, Herat, Mazar-i-Sharif, Qonduz, Charikar, Jalalabad.
- **Principal Rivers:** Helmand, Amu Darya (Oxus).
- **Flag:** Black, white and green, inscribed 'God is Great' and 'There is no other God but Allah and Mohamed is his Prophet'.
- **Monetary Unit:** Afghani.
- **Type of Government:** Islamic republic.
- **Languages:** Pashto, Dari Persian, other Turkic and minor languages.

ECONOMIC SUMMARY

Principal Products: Opium, Wheat, Cotton, Fruits, Wool, Nuts. **Major Products:** Soap, Furniture, Shoes, Carpets, Textiles, Cement, Coal. **Natural Resources:** Natural gas, Oil, Coal, Copper, Sulphur, Lead, Zinc, Iron, Salt, Precious and semi-precious stones. **Exports:** Frish and dried fruits, Raw cotton, Natural gas, Carpets. **Imports:** Petroleum products, machinery and other capital goods, Yarns and textiles, and food supplies. **Major Trading Partners:** Eastern European and CIS countries, Japan and China, Pakistan, Iran, Germany, etc.

Afghanistan officially the Islamic Emirate of Afghanistan, is a landlocked country located at the crossroads of Central and South Asia. Referred to as the "Heart of Asia", it is bordered by Pakistan to the east and south, Iran to the west, Turkmenistan to the northwest, Uzbekistan to the north, Tajikistan to the northeast, and China to the northeast and east. The country is predominately mountainous with plains in the north and the southwest, which are separated by the Hindu Kush mountain range. Kabul is the country's largest city and serves as its capital.

The modern state of Afghanistan began with the Durrani dynasty in the 18th century, with the Durrani Afghan Empire being formed by Ahmad Shah Durrani. The Durrani Empire at its peak having spanned from eastern Iran to northern India. Following its decline and the death of Ahmad Shah Durrani, and Timur Shah, it was divided into multiple smaller independent kingdoms now undergoing civil war, including but not limited to: Herat, Kandahar and Kabul. Afghanistan would be reunited in the 19th century after wars of unification led by Dost Mohammad Khan, where he conquered the independent principalities in Afghanistan. Dost Mohammad died in 1863, weeks after his last campaign to unite Afghanistan, and as a result throwing Afghanistan back into civil war with his successors. During this time, Afghanistan became a buffer state in the Great Game between the British Empire (in British-ruled India) and the Russian Empire; from India, the British attempted to subjugate Afghanistan but were repelled in the First Anglo-Afghan War; however, the Second Anglo-Afghan War saw a British victory and the successful establishment of British political influence over Afghanistan. Following the Third Anglo-Afghan War in 1919, Afghanistan became free of foreign dominance, and eventually emerged as the independent Kingdom of Afghanistan in June 1926 under Amanullah Khan. This monarchy lasted almost 50 years, until Zahir Shah was overthrown in 1973, following which the Republic of Afghanistan was established. Since the late 1970s, Afghanistan's history has been dominated by extensive warfare, including coups, revolutions, invasions, insurgencies, and civil wars. The country is currently under the control of the Taliban, an Islamist political movement that returned to power in 2021 after a 20-year-long war with the United States and its allies.

❑❑❑

2

Indian History

ANCIENT INDIA

INDUS VALLEY CIVILISATION (2500-1750 BC)

- The earliest excavations in the Indus valley were done at Harappa in the West Punjab and Mohenjodaro in Sindh. Both places are now in Pakistan.

Important Sites

- The most important sites are Kot Diji in Sindh, Kalibangan in Rajasthan, Ropar in the Punjab, Banawali in Haryana, Lothal, Surkotada and Dhaulavira, all the three in Gujarat.
- Mohenjodaro is the largest of all the Indus cities and it is estimated to have spread over an area of 200 hectares.

Indus Valley Civilisation : An Objective Study

Major Sites	*Excavators*	*Year*	*River*	*Location*	*Important Findings*
1. Harappa	D.R. Sahni	1921	Ravi	West Punjab (Pakistan)	Granaries, Virgin Goddess, Cemetery, Stone symbol of Lingam and Yoni
2. Mohenjodaro	R.D. Banerjee	1922	Indus	Sindh (Pakistan)	Great Bath, Great Granary, Assembly Hall, Proto-Shiva, Brick Kilns, Mesopotamian seals
3. Chanhudaro	N.G. Mazumdar	1931	Indus	Sindh (Pakistan)	Bronze toy cart, Ink-pot, Lipstick, City without a citadel
4. Kalibangan	B.B. Lal & B.K. Thapar	1953	Ghaggar	Ganganagar (Rajasthan)	Decorated bricks, ploughed field surface, Firealtars
5. Lothal	S.R. Rao	1957	Bhogwa	Ahmedabad (Gujarat)	Dockyard, Rice husk, Fire altars, Double burial
6. Banawali	R.S. Bist	1973	Ghaggar	Hissar (Haryana)	Toy plough, Gridiron pattern of Town planning.
7. Dholavira	R.S. Bist	1990	Luni	Kutchh (Gujarat)	A Large well & a bath, A stadium
8. Surkotada	J. Joshi	1964	—	Gujarat	Bones of Horse, Pot burials

Salient Features of the Harappan Culture

- The Harappan Civilization was primarily Urban.
- Mohenjodaro and Harappa were the planned cities.
- The large-scale use of burnt bricks in almost all kinds of constructions are the important characteristics of the Harappan culture.
- Another remarkable feature was the underground drainage system connecting all houses to the street drains which were covered by stone slabs or bricks.
- The most important public place of Mohenjodaro is the Great Bath measuring 39 feet length, 23 feet breadth and 8 feet depth.
- Agriculture was the most important occupation. In the fertile soils, farmers cultivated two crops a year. They were the first who had grown paddy.
- Wheat and barley were the main crops grown besides sesame, mustard and cotton.
- Animals like sheep, goats and buffalo were domesticated. The use of horse is not yet firmly established.
- Bronze and copper vessels are the outstanding examples of the Harappan metal craft.
- A large number of seals numbering more than 2000 have been discovered.

Social Life

- Jewelleries such as bangles, bracelets, fillets, girdles, anklets, ear-rings and finger rings were worn by women. These ornaments were made of gold, silver, copper, bronze and semi precious stones.
- Fishing was a regular occupation while hunting and bull fighting were other pastimes.

- Manufacture of terracotta (burnt clay) was a major industry of the people.
- Figures of animals such as sacred bull and dove were discovered. The figures of Mother Goddesses were used for religious purposes.
- Most of the inscriptions were engraved on seals. It is interesting to note that the Indus script has not yet been deciphered.
- The Pipal tree was used as a religious symbol.
- The origin of the '*Swastika*' symbol can be traced to the Harrapan Civilization.
- The chief male deity was Pasupati, (proto-Siva) represented in seals as sitting in a yogic posture with three faces and two horns.

THE VEDIC PERIOD

RIG VEDIC AGE (1500 - 1000 B.C.)

- The Early Vedic period is known from the *Rig Veda*.
- The *Rig Veda* refers to Saptasindhu or the land of seven rivers. This includes the five rivers of the Punjab, namely, Jhelum, Chenab, Ravi, Beas and Sutlej along with the Indus and Saraswati.
- Historians view that the Aryans came from Central Asia. They entered India through the Khyber pass between 2000 B.C. and 1500 B.C. They first settled in seven places in the Punjab region which they called Sapta Sindhu. Slowly, they moved towards the Gangetic Valley.
- The Aryan Civilisation was a rural civilisation.

Vedic Literature

- The word 'Veda' is derived from the root 'vid', which means to know and signifies 'superior knowledge'.
- The Vedic literature consists of the four Vedas – Rig, Yajur, Sama and Atharva.
- The *Rig Veda* is the earliest of the four Vedas divided into 10 mandalas and it consists of 1028 hymns. The hymns were sung by *Hotri* in praise of various gods.
- The *Yajur Veda* consists of various details of rules to be observed at the time of sacrifice. Its hymns were recited by *Adharvayus*.
- The *Sama Veda* is set to tune for the purpose of chanting during sacrifice. It is called the book of chants and the origins of Indian music are traced in it. Its hymns were recited by *Udgatri*.
- The *Atharva Veda* contains details of rituals.
- Besides the Vedas, there are other sacred works like the Brahmanas, the Aranyakas, the Upanishads, and the epics Ramayana and Mahabharata.

Political Organisation

- During this period, the kingdom was tribal in character. Each tribe formed a separate kingdom.
- The basic unit of political organisation was *kula* or family.
- The highest political unit was called *jana* or tribe.
- There were several tribal kingdoms during the Rig Vedic period such as Bharatas, Matsyas, Yadus and Purus. The head of the kingdom was called as *rajan* or king.
- There were two popular bodies called the *Sabha* and *Samiti*. The former seems to have been a council of elders and the latter, a general assembly of the entire people.

Social Life

- Family was the basis of the society.
- The head of the family was known as *grihapathi*.

Economic Condition

- The Rig Vedic Aryans were pastoral people and their main occupation was cattle rearing. Their wealth was estimated in terms of their cattle.
- Carpentry was another important profession.

RELIGION

- The important Rig Vedic gods were Prithvi (Earth), Agni (Fire), Vayu (Wind), Varuna (Rain) and Indra (Thunder).
- Indra was the most popular among them during the early Vedic period.
- There were also female gods like Aditi and Ushas. There were no temples and no idol worship during the early Vedic period.

Rigvedic Rivers

River	Name in Rigveda
Indus	Sindhu
Jhelum	Vitasta
Chenab	Asikni
Ravi	Parushini
Beas	Vipasa
Sutlej	Sutudri
Gomati	Gomal
Saraswati	Sarasvati
Ghaggar	Prishadavati

LATER VEDIC PERIOD (1000–600 B.C.)

- This age is also called as the Epic Age because the two great epics the Ramayana and Mahabharata were written during this period.
- The Sama, Yajur, Atharva Vedas, Brahmanas, Aranyakas, Upanishads and the two epics are the sources of information for this period.

Political Organisation

- Larger kingdoms were formed during the later Vedic period.
- The king performed various rituals and sacrifices to strengthen his position.

- They include Rajasuya (consecration ceremony), Asvamedha (horse sacrifice) and Vajpeya (chariot race).
- Kingship became hereditary.
- Kings assumed titles like Ekrat, Samrat and Sarvabhauma.

Economic Condition

- Iron was used extensively in this period and this enabled the people to clear forests and to bring more land under cultivation. Agriculture became the chief occupation.
- Taxes like Bali, Sulk and Bhaga were collected from the people.
- Wealth was calculated in terms of cows.

Social Life

- The four divisions of society (Brahmins, Kshatriyas, Vaisyas and Sudras) or the Varna system was thoroughly established during the Later Vedic period.
- The Ashrama system was formed to attain 4 purusharthas. They were *Dharma*, *Artha*, *Kama* and *Moksha*.

Religion

- Gods of the Early Vedic period like Indra and Agni lost their importance. Prajapathi (the creator), Vishnu (the protector) and Rudra (the destroyer) became prominent during the Later Vedic period.

JAINISM AND BUDDHISM

JAINISM

- Jainism originated in the 6th century B.C. It rejected Vedic religion and avoided its rituals.
- Founded by Rishabha Deva. Rishabha Deva was succeeded by 23 Thirthankaras (prophets). Mahavira was the 24th Thirthankara.

Vardhamana Mahavira (540-468 B.C.)

- Vardhamana was born in a village called Kundagrama near Vaishali in Bihar.
- His father was *Siddhartha*. He was the head of a famous Kshatriya clan.
- His mother was *Trisala*. She was a princess of the Lichchhavi clan. She was the sister of the ruler of Vaishali.
- Vardhamana was married to *Yasoda*, a princess. They had a daughter.
- At the age of 30, he left his home and family. He became an ascetic (monk). He wandered from place-to-place in search of truth for 12 years.
- In the 13th year of his penance, he attained the highest spiritual knowledge called Kevalya or Jnana. Thereafter, he was called Mahavira and Jina. His followers were called Jains and his religion Jainism.
- He died at the age of 72 in 468 B.C. at a place called Pavapuri near modern Rajgir in Bihar.

Teachings of Jainism

- The three principles of Jainism, also known as Triratnas (three gems), are:
  1. right faith.
  2. right knowledge.
  3. right conduct.
- Mahavira preached his disciples to follow the five principles. They are:
  1. Ahimsa—not to injure any living beings
  2. Satya—to speak the truth
  3. Asteya—not to steal
  4. Tyag—not to own property
  5. Brahmacharia—to lead a virtuous life.

Spread of Jainism

- Mahavira preached his religion in Prakrit language which was the language of the masses.
- Chandragupta Maurya, Kharavela of Kalinga and the royal dynasties of south India such as the Gangas, the Kadambas, the Chalukyas and the Rashtrakutas patronised Jainism.
- Jainism was divided into two sects after Vallabhi Council, namely *Svetambaras* (wearing white dresses) under Sthulbhadra and *Digambaras* (naked) under Bhadrabahu.
- The first Jain Council was convened at Pataliputra by Sthulabahu, the leader of the *Digambaras*, in the beginning of the 3rd century B.C.
- The second Jain Council was held at Vallabhi in 5th century A.D. The final compilation of Jain literature called *Twelve Angas* was completed in this council.

BUDDHISM

Gautama Buddha (563-483 B.C.)

- Buddha's original name was *Siddhartha*.
- Siddhartha was born in the Lumbini Garden near Kapilavastu in Nepal. His father was Suddhodana. He was a Sakya chief of Kapilavastu. His mother, Mayadevi, died when Siddhartha was only seven days old. He was brought up by his step mother Mahaprajapati Gauthami.
- At the age of sixteen Siddhartha, married Yasodhara and gave birth to a son, Rahul.
- The sight of an old man, a diseased man, a corpse and an ascetic turned him away from worldly life. He left home at the age of twenty-nine in search of Truth.
- He wandered for seven years and at last, he sat under a bodhi tree at Bodh Gaya in Bihar and did intense penance, after which he got Enlightenment (Nirvana) at the age of thirty-five. Since then, he became known as the Buddha or 'the Enlightened One'.
- Buddha delivered his first sermon at Sarnath near Banaras (now Varanasi).
- He died at the age of 80 in 483 B.C. at Kushinagar in Uttar Pradesh.

Teachings of Buddha

- The Four Noble Truths of Buddha are:
  1. The world is full of suffering.
  2. The cause of suffering is desire.
  3. If desires are get rid off, suffering can be removed.
  4. This can be done by following the Eightfold Path.
- The Eightfold Path consists of:
  1. Right Thought.
  2. Right Belief.
  3. Right Speech.
  4. Right Action.
  5. Right Living.
  6. Right Efforts.
  7. Right Knowledge.
  8. Right Meditation.

Buddhist Literature

- In Pali language.
- Buddhist scriptures in Pali are commonly referred to as *Tripitakas, i.e.*, 'Three Baskets'.
- ***Vinaya Pitaka:*** Rules of discipline in Buddhist monasteries.
- ***Sutta Pitaka:*** Largest, contains collection of Buddha's sermons.
- ***Abidhamma Pitaka:*** Explanation of the philosophical principles of the Buddhist religion.

Main Buddhist Councils

Buddhist Council	Time	Place	Chairman	Patron
First	483 BC	Rajagriha	Mahakashyapa	Ajatasatru
Second	383 BC	Vaishali	Sabakamuni	Kalashoka
Third	250 BC	Patliputra	Moggaliputta Tissa	Ashoka
Fourth	AD 72	Kundalvana	Vasumitra, Ashwaghosa	Kanishka

The Mahajanapadas

Mahajanapadas	Capital
1. Kashi	Varanasi
2. Kosala	Shravasti
3. Anga	Champanagri
4. Magadh	Girivraj or Rajgriha
5. Vajji	Vaishali
6. Malla	Kushinagar and Pavapuri
7. Chedi	Shuktimati
8. Vatsa	Kaushambi
9. Kuru	Hastinapur, Indraprastha and Isukara
10. Panchal	Ahichhatra and Kampilya
11. Matsya	Viratnagar
12. Surasen	Mathura
13. Asmaka	Paudanya
14. Avanti	Ujjaini
15. Gandhara	Taxila
16. Kamboj	Rajpur (Hatak)

DYNASTIES OF ANCIENT INDIA

HARYANKA DYNASTY

- Bimbisara was the founder of Haryanka Dynasty.
- He was a contemporary of both Vardhamana Mahavira and Gautama Buddha.
- During his rule, Darius I, the Achaemenian emperor, conquered the Indus Valley area.
- Ajatasatru imprisoned his father Bimbisara.
- The first Buddhist Council was convened by Ajatasatru at Rajgir.
- The immediate successor of Ajatasatru was Udayin.
- Udayin laid the foundation of the new capital at Pataliputra situated at the confluence of the two rivers, the Ganges and the Sone.
- Shishunaga was the founder of Shishunaga dynasty.
- After Shishunaga, the mighty empire began to collapse. His successor was Kakavarman or Kalasoka. During his reign, the second Buddhist Council was held at Vaishali.
- Kalasoka was killed by the founder of the Nanda dynasty.

NANDAS

- The fame of Magadha scaled new heights under the Nanda dynasty.
- Mahapadmananda was the founder of Nanda rule in Magadha.
- The last Nanda ruler was Dhana Nanda. Alexander invaded India during his rule.

MAURYAN EMPIRE

CHANDRAGUPTA MAURYA (322–298 B.C.)

- Chandragupta Maurya was the founder of the Mauryan Empire. He overthrew Nanda dynasty with the help of Chanakya.
- Chandragupta defeated Seleukos Nikator, the Greek general of Alexander, in a battle in 305 B.C.
- Seleukos sent Megasthenes as Greek Ambassador to the Court of Chandragupta. Megasthenes wrote *Indica*.

- Chandragupta was a follower of Jainism.
- He came to Sravana Belgola, near Mysore with a Jain monk called Bhadrabahu. The hill in which he lived until his death is called Chandragiri.
- Chanakya served as prime minister during the reigns of Chandragupta and Bindusara.

BINDUSARA (298–273 B.C.)

- Chandragupta Maurya was succeeded by his son Bindusara.
- Bindusara was called by the Greeks as "*Amitraghatha*" meaning, slayer of enemies.

ASHOKA (273–232 B.C.)

- Ashoka was the most famous ruler of the Mauryan dynasty.
- The most important event of Ashoka's reign was his victorious war with Kalinga in 261 B.C.
- Ashoka convened the Third Buddhist Council at Pataliputra around 250 B.C. in order to strengthen the *Sangha*. It was presided over by Moggaliputta Tissa.
- Ashoka's edicts and inscriptions were deciphered by James Prinsep in 1837.
- The last Mauryan king, Brahadratha was killed by his minister Pushyamitra Sunga. It put an end to the Mauryan Empire.

SUNGAS

- The founder of the Sunga dynasty was *Pushyamitra Sunga*, who was the commander-in-chief under the Mauryas.
- He ascended the throne of Magadha in 185 B.C.
- Pushyamitra was a staunch follower of Brahmanism. He performed two asvamedha sacrifices.
- After the death of Pushyamitra, his son Agnimitra became the ruler.
- Agnimitra was a great conqueror. He was also the hero of the play *Malavikagnimitram* written by Kalidasa.

KANVA

- The last Sunga ruler was Devabhuti, who was murdered by his minister Vasudeva Kanva, the founder of the *Kanva dynasty*.
- The Kanva dynasty ruled for 45 years. After the fall of the Kanvas, the history of Magadha was a blank until the establishment of the Gupta dynasty.

SATAVAHANAS

- The founder of the Satavahana dynasty was Simuka.
- The greatest ruler of the Satavahana dynasty was *Gautamiputra Satakarni*.
- The greatest port of the Satavahanas was Kalyani on the west Deccan. Gandakasela and Ganjam on the east coast were the other important seaports.
- The fine painting at Amaravathi and Nagarjunakonda caves belong to this period.

SANGAM AGE (300 B.C. TO A.D. 300)

- The Sangam Age constitutes an important chapter in the history of South India.
- According to Tamil legends, there existed three Sangams (Academy of Tamil poets) in ancient Tamil Nadu popularly called Muchchangam. These Sangams flourished under the royal patronage of the Pandyas.
- *The first Sangam*, held at then Madurai, chaired by Agastya.
- *The second Sangam* was held at Kapadapuram, chaired by Tolkappiyar.
- *The third Sangam* at Madurai was founded by Mudathirumaran.

Political History

- The Tamil country was ruled by three dynasties namely the Chera, Chola and Pandyas during the Sangam Age.

CHERAS

- The Cheras ruled over parts of modern Kerala. Their capital was Vanji and their important seaports were Tondi and Musiris.
- The greatest Chera King was *Senguttuvan*.

CHOLAS

- The Chola kingdom of the Sangam period extended from modern Tiruchi district to southern Andhra Pradesh.
- Their capital was first located at Uraiyur and then shifted to Puhar. Kaveripattinam served as their port.

GUPTA PERIOD

- The Gupta period is considered as the *Golden Age* in the history of India because this period witnessed all round developments in Religion, Literature, Science, Art and Architecture.

CHANDRAGUPTA I (320-334 A.D.)

- In the beginning of the 4th Century A.D., Sri Gupta established a small Kingdom at Pataliputra. He is considered as the founder of the Gupta dynasty.
- The first notable ruler of the Gupta dynasty was Chandragupta I. He assumed the title *Maharajadhiraja*. The Meherauli Iron Pillar inscription mentions his extensive conquests.
- Chandragupta I is considered to be the founder of the Gupta era which starts with his accession in A.D. 320.

SAMUDRAGUPTA (335-380 A.D.)

- Samudragupta was the greatest of the rulers of the Gupta dynasty. The Allahabad Pillar inscription provides a detailed account of his reign.

- Because of his military achievements, Samudragupta was hailed as '*Indian Napoleon*'.

CHANDRAGUPTA II (380-414 A.D.)

- Samudragupta was succeeded by his son Chandragupta II Vikramaditya.
- The greatest of the military achievements of Chandragupta II was his war against the Saka *satraps* of western India.
- The famous Chinese pilgrim, Fahien visited India (A.D. 399 - A.D. 414) during the reign of Chandragupta II.

SUCCESSORS OF CHANDRAGUPTA II

- Kumaragupta (415-455) was the son and successor of Chandragupta II. His reign was marked by general peace and prosperity.
- Kumaragupta was the founder of the Nalanda University.
- Kumaragupta was followed by *Skandagupta* who ruled from A.D. 456 to A.D. 468.
- After Skandagupta's death, many of his successors like Purugupta, Narasimhagupta, Buddhagupta and Baladitya could not save the Gupta empire from the Huns. Ultimately, the Gupta power totally disappeared due to the Hun invasions and later by the rise of Yasodharman in Malwa.

PUSHYABHUTI DYNASTY (600 - 647 A.D.)

- The greatest king was *Harshavardhana*, son of Prabhakar Vardhana of Thaneshwar. He shifted the capital to *Kannauj*.
- *Hieun Tsang* visited during his reign.
- He established a large monastery at Nalanda. Banabhata adorned his court, wrote Harshacharita and Kadambari. Harsha himself wrote three plays–Priyadarshika, Ratnawali and Nagananda.

PALLAVAS

- The Pallavas established their kingdom in Tondaimandalam by Simhavishnu with its capital at Kanchipuram.
- Other great Pallava rulers were Mahendravarman I, Narasimhavarman I, and Narasimhavarman II.
- The *Kailasanatha temple* at Kanchipuram is the greatest architectural masterpiece of the Pallava art.

CHALUKYAS (543-755 A.D.)

- Pulakesin I was the founder of the Chalukya dynasty. He established a small kingdom with Vatapi or Badami as its capital.
- The structural temples of the Chalukyas exist at Aihole, Badami and Pattadakal (Virupaksha temple). Cave temple architecture was also famous under the Chalukyas. Their cave temples are found in Ajanta, Ellora and Nasik.

RASHTRAKUTAS (755-975 A.D.)

- The art and architecture of the Rashtrakutas were found at Ellora and Elephanta.

CHOLAS

- Cholas became prominent in the ninth century and established an empire comprising the major portion of South India. Their capital was Tanjore.
- The founder of the Chola kingdom was Vijayalaya.
- Rajaraja Chola built the famous Brihadeeswara temple at Tanjore.
- *Dancing Figure of Shiva* (Nataraja) belong to Chola period.

MEDIEVAL INDIA

ARAB CONQUEST OF SIND

- In 712 A.D., Muhammad bin Quasim invaded Sind. Quasim defeated Dahir, the ruler of Sind and killed him in a well-contested battle.

Mahmud of Ghazni

- In 1024, Mahmud marched from Multan across Rajaputana, defeated the Solanki King Bhimadeva I, plundered Anhilwada and sacked the famous temple of Somanatha. This was his last campaign in India. Mahmud died in 1030 A.D.
- Mahmud patronized art and literature. *Firdausi* was the poet-laureate in the court of Mahmud.

Muhammad Ghori

- Prithviraj Chauhan defeated Ghori in the first battle of Tarain near Delhi in 1191 A.D.
- In the Second Battle of Tarain in 1192, Muhammad Ghori thoroughly routed the army of Prithiviraj, who was captured and killed.
- After his brilliant victory over Prithviraj at Tarain, Muhammad Ghori returned to Ghazni leaving behind his favourite general Qutb-ud-din Aibak to make further conquests in India.

SULTANATE PERIOD

SLAVE DYNASTY (1206-1290)

- The Slave dynasty was also called Mamluk dynasty. Mamluk was the Quranic term for slave.

Qutb-ud-din Aibak

- Qutb-ud-din Aibak was a slave of Muhammad Ghori, who made him the Governor of his Indian possessions.

- After the death of Ghori in 1206, Aibak declared his independence. He assumed the title Sultan and made Lahore his capital.
- Muslim writers call Aibak Lakh Baksh or giver of lakhs because he gave liberal donations to them.
- He built the famous Quwat-Ul-Islam mosque at Delhi. He began the construction of the famous Qutb Minar at Delhi but did not live long to complete it. It was later completed by Iltutmish.

Iltutmish (1210-1236 A.D.)

- Iltutmish belonged to the Ilbari tribe and hence his dynasty was named as Ilbari dynasty.
- He shifted his capital from Lahore to Delhi.
- He organised the *Iqta system* and introduced reforms in civil administration and army.

Raziya (1236-1240 A.D.)

- She appointed an Abyssinian slave Yakuth as Master of the Royal Horses.
- In 1240, Altunia, the governor of Bhatinda revolted against her. She went in personally to suppress the revolt but Altunia killed Yakuth and took Raziya prisoner.
- Bahram Shah, son of Iltutmish killed her.

Balban (1266-1286 A.D.)

- Balban introduced rigorous court discipline and new customs such as prostration and kissing the Sultan's feet to prove his superiority over the nobles.
- He also introduced the Persian festival of *Nauroz* to impress the nobles and people with his wealth and power.
- He established a separate military department - *diwan-i-arz* – and reorganized the army.

KHILJI DYNASTY (1290-1320 A.D.)

- The founder of the Khilji dynasty was Jalaluddin Khilji.
- Ala-ud-din Khilji was the greatest ruler of the Khilji Dynasty.
- He was the first Muslim ruler to extend his empire right upto Rameshwaram in the South.
- The Sultan had built a new city called Siri near Delhi.
- Amir Khusrau the great Persian poet, patronised by Balban, continued to live in Ala-ud-din Khilji's court also.
- He introduced the system of *dagh* (branding of horses) and prepared *huliya* (descriptive list of soldiers).
- Ala-ud-din Khilji maintained a large permanent standing army and paid them in cash from the royal treasury.

TUGHLAQ DYNASTY

- Ghiyas-ud-din Tughlaq was the founder of the Tughlaq dynasty.
- To have the capital at the centre of the empire and safe from the Mongol raids, Tughlaq chose Devagiri as his new capital in A.D. 1327. The Sultan renamed the new capital Daulatabad.
- In 1329-30, Muhammad-bin-Tughlaq introduced a token currency.
- Firoz Shah Tughlaq became Sultan after the death of Muhammad-bin-Tughlaq in A.D. 1351.
- He was the first Sultan to impose irrigation tax.
- He had built new towns of Firozabad, Jaunpur, Hissar and Firozpur.
- Timur—Mongol leader of Central Asia, ordered general massacre in Delhi (AD 1398) at the time of Nasiruddin Mahmud (later Tughlaq king).

SAYYID DYNASTY

- Before his departure from India, Timur appointed Khizr Khan as governor of Multan. He captured Delhi and founded the Sayyid dynasty in 1414.
- Mubarak Shah, Mohammed Shah and Alam Shah were some of the other important noteworthy rulers of Sayyid Dynasty.

LODHI DYNASTY

- The Lodhis were Afghans.
- Bahlol Lodhi was the first Afghan ruler while his predecessors were all Turks. He died in 1489 and was succeeded by his son, Sikandar Lodhi.
- In 1504, Sikandar Lodhi founded the city of Agra and transferred his capital from Delhi to Agra.
- Babar marched against Delhi and defeated and killed Ibrahim Lodhi in the first battle of Panipat (1526).

BAHMANI AND VIJAYANAGAR KINGDOMS

- The break up of the Delhi Sultanate provided an opportunity for the rise of a number of kingdoms in the Deccan.
- After the decline of the Tughlaqs, there arose two important kingdoms in the Deccan. They were the Bahmani and Vijayanagar kingdoms.

VIJAYANAGAR EMPIRE

- The Vijayanagar Kingdom was set up in A.D. 1336. Its aim was to check the spread of Muslim power and protect Hindu Dharma in South India.
- Four dynasties – Sangama, Saluva, Tuluva and Aravidu – ruled Vijayanagar from A.D. 1336 to 1672.
- Vijayanagar was founded in 1336 by Harihara and Bukka of the Sangama dynasty.
- The Moroccan traveller, Ibn Batuta, Venetian traveller Nicolo de Conti, Persian traveller Abdur Razzak and the Portuguese traveller Domingo Paes were among them who left valuable accounts on the socio-economic conditions of the Vijayanagar Empire.

- The Hampi ruins and other monuments of Vijayanagar provide information on the cultural contributions of the Vijayanagar rulers.

KRISHNA DEVA RAYA (1509-1530)

- The Tuluva dynasty was founded by Vira Narasimha.
- The greatest of the Vijayanagar rulers, Krishna Deva Raya belonged to the Tuluva dynasty.
- Krishna Deva Raya himself authored a Telugu work, *Amukthamalyadha* and Sanskrit works, *Jambavati Kalyanam* and *Ushaparinayam*.
- He built the famous *Vittalaswamy* and *Hazara Ramaswamy* temples at Vijayanagar.
- Krishna Deva Raya renovated Virupaksha temple in A.D. 1510.
- After his death the enemies of Vijayanagar joined together and defeated the Vijayanagar ruler in the battle of Talaikota.

BAHMANI KINGDOM

- The founder of the Bahmani kingdom was Alauddin Bahman Shah also known as Hasan Gangu in 1347. Its capital was Gulbarga.
- Ahmad Wali Shah shifted the capital from Gulbarga to Bidar.
- *Gol Gumbaj* was built by *Muhammad Adil Shah*; it is famous for the so called '*Whispering Gallery*'.
- *Quli Qutub Shah* built the famous *Golcunda Fort*.

MUGHAL EMPIRE (1526-1707 AD)

BABAR (1526-1530 AD)

- Babar was the founder of the Mughal Empire in India.
- On 21st April, 1526 the first Battle of Panipat took place between Babar and Ibrahim Lodhi, who was killed in the battle.
- Babar was the first one to use guns or artillery in a battle on the Indian soil.
- Babar defeated Rana Sanga of Mewar in the battle of Kanwah in A.D. 1527.
- Babar was a soldier-scholar and wrote his own autobiography called Babar Nama in Turkish language.

HUMAYUN (1530-1556 AD)

- Sher Shah defeated Humayun at Chausa in A.D. 1539 and again at Kannauj in A.D. 1540.
- After losing his kingdom, Humayun became an exile for the next fifteen years.
- In 1555, Humayun defeated the Afghans and recovered the Mughal throne.
- After six months, he died in 1556 due to his fall from the staircase of his library.
- *Gulbadan Begum*, Humayun's half-sister wrote *Humayun-nama*.

SHER SHAH SURI

- The founder of the Sur dynasty was Sher Shah, whose original name was Farid.
- Sher Shah became the ruler of Delhi in 1540.
- Sher Shah organized a brilliant administrative system. The central government consisted of several departments.
- He built a new city on the banks of the river Yamuna near Delhi.
- Now the old fort called Purana Quila and its mosque is alone surviving.
- He built a Mausoleum at Sasaram, which is considered as one of the master pieces of Indian architecture.

AKBAR (1556-1605 AD)

- When Akbar ascended the throne in A.D. 1556 he was only 14 years old. His guardian Bairam Khan served him as a faithful minister and tutor.
- Bairam Khan, along with Akbar met Hemu in the second Battle of Panipat in 1556. Hemu was initially successful, but lost his consciousness after an arrow hit him. Akbar killed him.
- The Battle of Haldighati was fought between Rana Pratap of Mewar and Mughal army led by Man Singh and Asif Khan. Some historian say that this battle was indecisive but some say that Rana Pratap was defeated.
- Akbar abolished the pilgrim tax and in 1562, he abolished Jaziya.
- Akbar evolved a new faith called Din-i-Illahi or Divine Faith.

JAHANGIR (1605-1627 AD)

- When Akbar died, Prince Salim succeeded with the title Jahangir (Conqueror of World) in 1605.
- Jahangir's eldest son, Khusrau, rebelled against him. He was arrested and put into prison.
- *Guru Arjun Dev, the fifth Sikh Guru* was executed by Jahangir.
- In 1611, Jahangir married Mehrunnisa who was known as Nurjahan (Light of World).
- Jahangir died in A.D. 1627.

SHAHJAHAN (1628-1658 AD)

- The reign of Shahjahan is generally considered as the *Golden Age* of the Mughal period.
- Shahjahan is called as the *Prince of Builders*. He had built the Jama Masjid and Red Fort in Delhi and Taj Mahal in Agra.
- Fine arts like painting, music and literature reached high level of development during Shahjahan's time.

AURANGAZEB (1658-1707 AD)

- Aurangazeb was the last great Mughal ruler. He ascended the throne after killing his three brothers Dara, Shuja and Murad in a fratricidal war.
- Aurangazeb defeated Sikandar Shah of Bijapur and annexed his kingdom.
- Aurangazeb was against the Sikhs and he executed the ninth Sikh Guru Tegh Bahadur.
- He was called *Darvesh* or a *Zinda Pir*. He forbade *Sati*. Conquered Bijapur (AD 1686) and Golconda (AD 1687) and reimposed Jaziya and Pilgrim tax in AD 1679.
- He built *Biwi ka Makbara* on the tomb of his queen *Rabaud-Durani* at Aurangabad; *Moti Masjid* within Red Fort, Delhi; and the Jami or Badshahi Mosque at Lahore.
- Aurangazeb died in A.D. 1707.

LATER MUGHALS / FALL OF THE MUGHALS

Bahadur Shah (1707-1712)

- Assumed the title of *Shah Alam I*.

Jahandar Shah (1712-1713)

- First puppet Mughal emperor. He abolished *jaziya*.

Farrukhsiyar (1713-1719)

Mohammad Shah (1719-1748)

- Nadir Shah (*of Iran*) defeated him in the Battle of Karnal (1739) and took away *Peacock throne* and *Kohinoor diamond*.

Ahmad Shah (1748-1754)

Alamgir II (1754-1759),

Shah Alam II (1759-1806)

Akbar II (1806-1837)

- He gave Ram Mohan Roy the title '*Raja*'. He sent Raja Ram Mohan Roy to London to seek a raise in his allowance.

Bahadur Shah II (1837-1857)

- He was confined by the British to the Red Fort. During the revolt of 1857, he was proclaimed the Emperor by the rebels. He was deported to Rangoon after that.

Literature of Mughal Period

Author	Work
Babar	Tuzuk-i-Babari
Abul Fazal	Ain-i-Akbari, Akbarnamah
Jahangir	Tuzuk-i-Jahangiri
Hamid	Padshahnama
Darashikoh	Majm-ul-Bahrain
Mirza Md Qasim	Alamgirnama

THE MARATHAS

SHIVAJI (1627-1680 AD)

- Shivaji was born at Shivner in 1627. His father was Shahji Bhonsle and mother Jija Bai.
- His religious teacher was Samarth Ramdas and guardian was Dadaji Kondadev.
- In 1674, Shivaji crowned himself at Raigarh and assumed the title Chatrapathi.
- *Ashtapradhan* (eight ministers) helped in administration. These were Peshwas, Sar-i-Naubat (Military), Mazumdar or Amatya (Accounts); Waqenavis (Intelligence); Surnavis (Corres-pondence); *Dabir* or *Sumanta* (Ceremonies); *Nyayadhish* (Justice); and *Panditrao* (Charity).
- Successors of Shivaji were Shambhaji, Rajaram and *Shahu* (fought at Battle of Khed in AD 1708).

THE PESHWAS

- Balaji Vishwanath was the first Peshwa. He began his career as a small revenue official and became Peshwa in 1713. Baji Rao I was the eldest son of Balaji Vishwanath. He was considered as the "greatest exponent of guerilla tactics after Shivaji".
- It was during reign of Balaji Baji Rao (Nanasaheb) when the Marathas lost the Third Battle of Panipat.
- Baji Rao II (last Peshwa) was the first Maratha to have fled from the British attacks instead of fighting with them. Baji Rao II surrendered to Sir John Malcom.

THE SIKH

- Guru Nanak Dev was the founder of Sikhism, the religion that draws its elements from both Hinduism and Islam.
- Name of the ten Sikh Gurus and their works are given below:
  1. **Guru Nanak Dev (1469-1539AD):** The founder of Sikhism.
  2. **Guru Angad Dev (1504-1552AD):** Developed Gurmukhi.
  3. **Guru Amar Das (1479-1574AD):** Struggled against Sati system and Purdah system.
  4. **Guru Ram Das (1534-1581AD):** Founded Amritsar, the holy city of Sikhism.
  5. **Guru Arjun Dev (1563-1606AD):** He built the *Swarn Mandir* (Golden Temple).
  6. **Guru Hargobind (1595-1644 AD):** Established Akal Takht.
  7. **Guru Har Rai (1630-1661 AD)**
  8. **Guru Har Krishan (1656-1664 AD)**
  9. **Guru Tegh Bahadur (1621-1675 AD)**
  10. **Guru Gobind Singh (1666-1708 AD):** Founded the Khalsa and Sikh baptism, composed many poems, and nominated the Sikh sacred text as the final and enduring Guru.

MODERN INDIA

THE ADVENT OF THE EUROPEANS

THE PORTUGUESE

- Vasco-da-Gama, a Portuguese explorer, sailed through the route of Cape of Good Hope and reached near Calicut on 20th May 1498 A.D. during the reign of King Zamorin (Hindu King of Calicut).
- Vasco-da-Gama founded a factory at Cannanore on his second visit to India in 1501. In due course, Calicut, Cochin and Cannanore became the Portuguese trading centres.
- Francisco Almeida came to India in 1505. He was the first Governor of Portuguese possessions in India.
- The real founder of Portuguese power in India was *Alfonso de Albuquerque*. He captured Goa from the rulers of Bijapur in 1510. It was made their headquarters.

THE DUTCH

- The United East India Company of the Netherlands founded a factory at Masulipatnam in 1605.
- They built their first fort on the main land of India at Pulicut in 1609, near Madras (Chennai). They captured Nagapattinam from the Portuguese.
- They made Agra, Surat, Masulipatnam and Chinsura in Bengal as their trading centres.

THE DANES

- The Danish East India Company was established in 1616 in Denmark.
- They came to South India and founded a factory at Tranquebar (Tharangambadi) in 1620. They also made settlements at Serampore near Calcutta (Kolkata).

THE ENGLISH

- The English East India Company was formed in 1599 under a charter granted by Queen Elizabeth in 1600.
- The East India Company sent Sir William Hawkins to the court of the Mughal Emperor Jahangir in 1609 to obtain permission to erect a factory at Surat.
- In 1615, Sir Thomas Roe, another British merchant, came to Jahangir's court.
- He stayed for three years and succeeded in getting permission to set up their trading centres at Agra, Surat, Ahmedabad and Broach.
- In 1690, the British got permission from Aurangazeb to build a factory on the site of Calcutta. In 1696 a fort was built at that place. It was called Fort William.

THE FRENCH

- The French East India Company was established in 1664 under the inspiring and energetic leadership of Colbert, the economic adviser of the French King Louis XIV.
- In 1667, the first French factory was established at Surat by Francis Caron who was nominated as Director-General.
- French were defeated by English in the *Battle of Wandiwash* (1760).

EAST INDIA COMPANY

- After the Battle of Plassey in 1757 and the Battle of Buxar in 1764, the East India Company became a political power.
- India was under the East India Company's rule till 1858 when it came under the direct administration of the British Crown. Robert Clive was the first Governor of Fort William under the Company's rule.

GOVERNOR-GENERALS OF BENGAL

Warren Hastings (1772-85 AD)

- In 1772, the Company appointed Warren Hastings as the Governor of Fort William. The Dual System introduced by Robert Clive was abolished by Warren Hastings.
- Warren Hastings was known for his expansionist policy. His administration witnessed the Rohilla War, the First Anglo-Maratha War and the Second Anglo-Mysore War.
- Pitt's India Act (1784) was passed.

Lord Cornwallis (1786-93 AD)

- Cornwallis inaugurated the policy of making appointments mainly on the basis of merit thereby laying the foundation of the Indian Civil Service.
- Lord Cornwallis introduced Permanent Revenue Settlement.
- Tipu Sultan signed the Treaty of Srirangapatnam in 1792 with the British.

Sir John Shore (1793-98 AD)

- Played an important role in the introduction of Permanent Settlement.
- *Battle of Kharda* between the Nizams and the Marathas (1795).

Wellesley (1798-1805)

- Wellesley came to India with a determination to launch a forward policy that he adopted to achieve his object is known as the 'Subsidiary Alliance'.
- The Fourth Anglo-Mysore War started in 1799. The war was short and decisive. Tipu fought till his capital Srirangapatnam was captured and he himself was shot dead.
- Peshwa Baji Rao II signed the *Treaty* of *Bassein* with the British in 1802. It was a subsidiary treaty and the Peshwa was recognized as the head of the Maratha kingdom.
- The Treaty of Deogaon(1803) was signed between Bhonsle and Wellesley.

Lord Minto (1807-1813)

- Lord Minto concluded the Treaty of Amritsar with Ranjit Singh of Punjab in 1809.
- The Charter Act of 1813 was passed during this period.

Lord Hastings (1813-1823)

- Anglo Nepal War (1814-1816) and Treaty of Sugauli (1816).
- Third Maratha War (1817-18), dissolution of Maratha confederacy and creation of Bombay Presidency.
- He encouraged the freedom of the Press and abolished the censorship introduced in 1799.

GOVERNOR-GENERALS OF INDIA

Lord William Bentinck (1828-1835)

- Charter Act of 1833 was passed and he was made the first Governor-General of India. Before him, the designation was Governor-General of Bengal.
- The social reforms of William Bentinck made his name immortal in the history of British India. These include the abolition of *Sati*, the suppression of Thugs and the prevention of female infanticide.
- The Government Resolution in 1835 made English the official and literary language of India.

Lord Metcalfe (1835-36 AD)

- Known as liberator of press in India.

Lord Auckland (1836-42 AD)

- First Afghan War (1838-42), a disaster for the English.

Lord Ellenborough (1842-44 AD)

- Brought an end to Afghan war. War with Gwalior (1843), *Annexation of Sind* by Charles Napier (1843).

Lord Hardinge (1844-48 AD)

- First Anglo-Sikh War (1845-46) and Treaty of Lahore (1846). Gave preference to English educated persons in employment.

Lord Dalhousie (1848-1856)

- The Doctrine of Lapse was applied by Dalhousie.
- The first railway line connecting Bombay with Thane was opened in 1853.

VICEROYS OF INDIA

Lord Canning (1856-62 AD)

- Lord Canning became the first Viceroy of India in 1858.
- Revolt of 1857, Mutiny took place. Indian Penal Code 1860 was passed.

Lord Elgin (1862 AD)

- Wahabi Movement.

Lord John Lawrence (1864-69 AD)

- Established the *High Courts* at Calcutta, Bombay and Madras in 1865.
- Telegraphic communication was opened with Europe. Created the Indian Forest Department.

Lord Northbrooke (1872-76 AD)

- Kuka Rebellion in Punjab, Famine in Bihar.

Lord Lytton (1876-80)

- In 1878, the Vernacular Press Act was passed. This Act empowered a Magistrate to secure an undertaking from the editor, publisher and printer of a vernacular newspaper that nothing would be published against the English Government. This Act crushed the freedom of the Indian press. In 1878, the Arms Act was passed. This Act prevented the Indians to keep arms without appropriate license.
- Lord Lytton also held a Darbar at Delhi in 1877 in which Queen Victoria was declared as the Empress of India. This extravagant Darbar cost millions of ruppes.
- In 1878, the Statutory Civil Service was established exclusively for Indians.

Lord Ripon (1880-84 AD)

- Lord Ripon repealed the Vernacular Press Act and earned much popularity among Indians.
- Ripon appointed a Commission in 1882 under the chairmanship of Sir William Hunter.
- The Commission came to be known as the Hunter Commission. The Commission recommended for the expansion and improvement of the elementary education of the masses.
- Ripon was founder of local self-government in modern India.

Lord Dufferin (1884-88 AD)

- *Third Burmese War* (1885-86 AD). Establishment of the Indian National Congress in 1885.

Lord Lansdowne (1888-94 AD)

- Factory Act of 1891 granted weekly holiday and stipulated working hours for women and children.

Lord Elgin II (1894-99 AD)

- Southern uprisings of 1899. Great famine of 1896-1897 and Lyall Commission on famine was established.

Lord Curzon (1899-1905 AD)

- Curzon instituted in 1902, a Universities Commission to go into the entire question of university education in the country.
- On the basis of the findings and recommendations of the Commission, Curzon brought in the Indian Universities Act of 1904, which brought all the universities in India under the control of the government.

Lord Minto (1905-10 AD)

- Swadeshi Movement (1905-08); foundation of Muslim League (1906); Surat Session and split in the Congress (1907). Morley-Minto Reforms (1909).

Lord Hardinge (1910-16 AD)

- Capital shifted from Calcutta to Delhi (1911); Delhi Durbar; Partition of Bengal was cancelled.
- The Hindu Mahasabha was founded in 1915 by Pandit Madan Mohan Malaviya.

Lord Chelmsford (1916-21 AD)

- Gandhi returned to India (1915) and founded the Sabarmati Ashram (1916), Champaran Satyagraha, Satyagraha at Ahmedabad (1981), Kheda Satyagraha (1918).
- Rowlatt Act (March, 1919) and the Jallianwala Bagh Massacre (13th April, 1919).
- Khilafat Committee was formed and Khilafat Movement started (1919-20).
- Non-Cooperation Movement started (1920-22).

Lord Reading (1921-26)

- Moplah Rebellion (1921) took place. *Kakori Train* Robbery on 1st August, 1925.
- *Communal Riots* of 1923-25 in Multan, Amritsar, Delhi etc.

Lord Irwin (1926-31 AD)

- Lahore Session of Congress and *Poorna Swaraj* Declaration (1929).
- Simon Commission visited India in 1927.
- Dandi March (12th March, 1930). Civil Disobedience Movement (1930).
- First Round Table Conference was held in England in 1930. Gandhi-Irwin Pact.

Lord Willingdon (1931-36 AD)

- *Second Round Table Conference* in London in 1931 and *third* in 1932.

Lord Linlithgow (1936-43 AD)

- Congress Ministries resignation celebrated as '*Deliverance Day*' by the Muslim League (1939), the Lahore Resolution (23rd March, 1940) of the Muslim League demanding separate state for the Muslims. (It was at this session that Jinnah propounded his Two-Nation Theory). Outbreak of World War II in 1939. Cripps Mission in 1942. Quit India Movement (8th August, 1942).

Lord Wavell (1943-47 AD)

- Cabinet Mission Plan (16th May, 1946).
- First meeting of the Constituent Assembly was held on 9th December, 1946.
- Arranged the Shimla Conference on 25th June, 1945 with Indian National Congress and Muslim League but failed.

Lord Mountbatten (March to Aug, 1947)

- Last viceroy of British India and the first Governor-General of free India.
- Partition of India decided by the 3rd June Plan or Mountbatten Plan.

NATIONAL MOVEMENT (1885-1947)

INDIAN NATIONAL CONGRESS (1885)

- Allan Octavian Hume, a retired civil servant in the British Government took the initiative to form an all-India organization. Thus, the Indian National Congress was founded and its first session was held at Bombay in 1885. W.C. Banerjee was its first president. It was attended by 72 delegates from all over India.
- The second session was held in Calcutta in 1886 and the third in Madras in 1887. Between 1885 and 1905, the Congress leaders were moderates. The Moderates had faith in the British justice and goodwill. They were called moderates because they adopted peaceful and constitutional means to achieve their demands.
- In 1905, Gopal Krishna Gokhale founded the Servants of India Society to train Indians to dedicate their lives to the cause of the country.

Partition of Bengal (1905)

- By Lord Curzon on 16th October, 1905 through a royal proclamation, reducing the old province of Bengal in size by creating East Bengal and Assam out of the rest of Bengal.
- The partition of Bengal in 1905 provided a spark for the rise of extremism in the Indian National Movement.
- Curzon's real motives behind this partition were:
  - To break the growing strength of Bengali nationalism since Bengal was the base of Indian nationalism.
  - To divide the Hindus and Muslims in Bengal.
  - To show the enormous power of the British Government in doing whatever it liked.

Swadeshi Movement (1905)

- The Swadeshi Movement involved programmes like the boycott of government service, courts, schools and colleges and of foreign goods. It was both a political and economic movement.
- Lal, Bal, Pal and Aurobindo Ghosh played an important role.

Muslim League (1906)

- In December 1906, Muslim delegates from all over India met at Dacca for the Muslim Educational Conference.
- Taking advantage of this occasion, Nawab Salimullah of Dacca proposed the setting up of an organisation to look after the Muslim interests. The proposal was accepted.
- The All-India Muslim League was finally set up on December 30, 1906.

Minto Morley Reforms (1909)

- Minto, the Viceroy and Morley, the Secretary of State for India jointly proposed reforms to the Indian Councils. An Act, called the Indian Councils Act or the Minto-Morley Reforms Act was passed in 1909.
- A separate communal electorate was introduced for the Muslims.

The Lucknow Pact (1916)

- During the 1916 Congress session at Lucknow two major events occurred.
- The divided Congress became united. An understanding for joint action against the British was reached between the Congress and the Muslim League and it was called the Lucknow Pact.
- The signing of the Lucknow Pact by the Congress and the Muslim League in 1916 marked an important step in the Hindu-Muslim unity.

The Home Rule Movement (1916)

- Two Home Rule Leagues were established, one by B.G. Tilak at Poona in April 1916 and the other by Mrs. Annie Besant at Madras in September 1916.
- While Tilak's Movement concentrated on Maharashtra, Annie Besant's Movement covered the rest of the country.

August Declaration

- On 20 August, 1917, Montague, the Secretary of State in England, promised the gradual development of self-governing institutions in India.
- This August Declaration led to the end of the Home Rule Movement.

Rowlatt Act (1919)

- In 1917, a committee was set up under the presidentship of Sir Sydney Rowlatt to look into the militant Nationalist activities.
- On the basis of its report the Rowlatt Act was passed in March 1919 by the Central Legislative Council. As per this Act, any person could be arrested on the basis of suspicion. No appeal or petition could be filed against such arrests.
- This Act was called the Black Act and it was widely opposed. An all-India hartal was organized on 6 April, 1919.

Jallianwala Bagh Massacre (13 April, 1919)

- On 13th April, the Baisakhi day (harvest festival), a public meeting was organized at the Jallianwala Bagh (garden). Gen. Dyer marched in and without any warning opened fire on the crowd. The firing continued for about 10 to 15 minutes and it stopped only after the ammunition exhausted.
- According to official report 379 people were killed and 1137 wounded in the incident. There was a nationwide protest against this massacre and Rabindranath Tagore renounced his knighthood as a protest.

Khilafat Movement (1920)

- The chief cause of the Khilafat Movement was the defeat of Turkey in the First World War.
- The Muslims in India were upset over the British attitude against Turkey and launched the Khilafat Movement.
- Ali brothers, *Mohd Ali* and *Shaukat Ali* started this movement. It was jointly led by the Khilafat leaders and the Congress.

Non-Co-operation Movement (1920-22)

- Mahatma Gandhi announced his plan to begin Non-Cooperation with the government as a sequel to the Rowlatt Act, Jallianwala Bagh massacre and the Khilafat Movement.
- It was approved by the Indian National Congress at the Nagpur session in December, 1920.
- The Congress observed the Non-Co-operation movement in 1920. The main aim of this movement was to attain Swaraj through non-violent and peaceful means.
- The whole movement was abruptly called off on 11th February, 1922 by Gandhi following the Chauri-Chaura incident in the Gorakhpur district of U.P. Many top leaders of the country were stunned at this sudden suspension of the Non-Co-operation Movement.
- On 5th February an angry mob set fire to the police station at *Chauri-Chaura* and twenty two police men were burnt to death.

Swaraj Party

- Leaders like Motilal Nehru and Chittranjan Das formed a separate group within the Congress known as the Swaraj Party on 1 January, 1923.
- The Swarajists wanted to contest the council elections and wreck the government from within.

Simon Commission (1927)

- The Act of 1919 included a provision for its review after a lapse of ten years. However, the review commission under the chairmanship of Sir John Simon was appointed by the British Government two years earlier of its schedule in 1927.
- Indian leaders opposed the commission, as there were no Indians in it, they cried *Simon Go Back*.
- The government used brutal repression and at Lahore, *Lala Lajpat Rai* was severely beaten in lathi-charge.

Nehru Report (1928)

- The Secretary of State, Lord Birkenhead, challenged the Indians to produce a Constitution that would be acceptable to all. The challenge was accepted by the Congress, which convened an all party meeting on 28 February, 1928.
- A committee consisting of eight was constituted to draw up a blueprint for the future Constitution of India. It was headed by Motilal Nehru. The Report published by this Committee came to be known as the Nehru Report.

Lahore Session (1929)

- On Dec. 19, 1929, under the Presidentship of J.L. Nehru, the INC, as its Lahore session, declared Poorna Swaraj (Complete Independence) as its ultimate goal.
- On Dec. 31, 1929, the newly adopted tricolour flag was unfurled and Jan. 26, 1930 was fixed as the First Independence Day, which was to be celebrated every year.

Dandi March (1930)

- On 12th March, 1930, Gandhi began his famous March to Dandi with his chosen 79 followers to break the salt laws. He reached the coast of Dandi on 5 April, 1930 after marching a distance of 200 miles and on 6 April formally launched the Civil Disobedience Movement by breaking the salt laws.

Civil Disobedience Movement

- Countrywide mass participation by women.
- The Garhwal soldiers refused to fire on the people at Peshawar.

Round Table Conference

- The first Round Table Conference was held in November 1930 at London and it was boycotted by the Congress.
- On 8th March, 1931 the Gandhi-Irwin Pact was signed. As per this pact, Mahatma Gandhi agreed to suspend the Civil-Disobedience Movement and participate in the Second-Round Table Conference.
- In September 1931, the Second Round Table Conference was held at London. Mahatma Gandhi participated in the Conference but returned to India disappointed. In January 1932, the Civil-Disobedience Movement was resumed.

Poona Pact (1932)

- The idea of separate electorate for the depressed classes was abandoned, but seats reserved for them in the provincial legislature were increased.
- Thus, Poona Pact agreed upon a joint electorate for upper and lower castes.

Demand for Pakistan

- *Chaudhary Rehmat Ali* gave the term *Pakistan* in 1933.
- In March 1940, the Muslim League demanded the creation of Pakistan.

Cripps Mission (1942)

- The British Government in its effort to secure Indian co-operation in the Second World War sent Sir Stafford Cripps to India on 23 March, 1942. This is known as Cripps Mission. The main recommendations of Cripps was the promise of Dominion Status to India.
- Congress rejected it. Gandhi called Cripp's proposals as a "Post-dated Cheque".

Quit India Movement (1942-1944)

- The All India Congress Committee met at Bombay on 8th August, 1942 and passed the famous Quit India Resolution. On the same day, Gandhi gave his call of 'do or die'.
- On 8th and 9th August, 1942, the government arrested all the prominent leaders of the Congress. Mahatma Gandhi was kept in prison at Poona.
- Pandit Jawaharlal Nehru, Abul Kalam Azad, and other leaders were imprisoned in the Ahamednagar Fort. Quit India Movement was the final attempt for country's freedom.

Indian National Army (INA)

- On July 2, 1943, Subhash Chandra Bose reached Singapore and gave the rousing war cry of *'Dilli Chalo'*. He was made the President of Indian Independence League and soon became the supreme commander of the Indian National Army. He gave the country the slogan of *Jai Hind.*
- INA had three fighting brigades named after Gandhi, Azad and Nehru. Rani of Jhansi Brigade was an exclusive women force. INA headquarters were at Rangoon and Singapore.

Cabinet Mission (1946)

- The Cabinet Mission put forward a plan for solution of the constitutional problem. A proposal was envisaged for setting up an Interim Government, which would remain in office till a new government was elected on the basis of the new Constitution framed by the Constituent Assembly. Elections were held in July 1946 for the formation of a Constituent Assembly. Muslim league observed the *Direct Action Day* on 16 August, 1946.
- An Interim Government was formed under the leadership of Jawaharlal Nehru on 2 September, 1946.

Mountbatten Plan (1947)

- On 20 February 1947, Prime Minister Atlee announced in the House of Commons the definite intention of the British Government to transfer power to responsible Indian hands by a date not later than June 1948.
- Lord Mountbatten armed with vast powers became India's Viceroy on 24 March, 1947. The partition of India and the creation of Pakistan appeared inevitable to him.
- After extensive consultation Lord Mountbatten put forth the plan of partition of India on 3 June, 1947.
- The Congress and the Muslim League ultimately approved the Mountbatten Plan.

Indian Independence Act, 1947

- The salient features of this Act was the partition of the country into India and Pakistan would come into effect from 15 August, 1947.
- On 15th August, 1947 India, and on the 14th August Pakistan came into existence as two independent states.
- Lord Mountbatten was made the first Governor General of Independent India, whereas Mohammad Ali Jinnah became the first Governor General of Pakistan.
- C. Rajagopalachari became the first and last Indian Governor-General of India. When India became a Republic on 26 January, 1950 Dr. Rajendra Prasad became the first President of our country.

Socio-Religious Movements and Organisation

Name of the Organisation	*Founder*	*Year*	*Place*
Atmiya Sabha	Ram Mohan Roy	1815	Calcutta
Brahmo Samaj	Ram Mohan Roy	1828	Calcutta
Dharma Sabha	Radhakanta Dev	1829	Calcutta
Tattvabodhini Sabha	Debendranath Tagore	1839	Calcutta
Nirankaris	Dayal Das, Darbara Singh, Rattan Chand etc.	1840	Punjab
Manav Dharma Sabha	Durgaram Manchharam	1844	Surat
Paramhansa Mandli	Dadoba Pandurung	1849	Bombay
Namdharis	Ram Singh	1857	Punjab
Radha Swami Satsang	Tulsi Ram	1861	Agra
Brahmo Samaj of India	Keshab Chandra Sen	1866	Calcutta
Dar-ul-Ulum	Maulana Hussain Ahmed	1866	Deoband
Prarthna Samaj	Atmaram Pandurung	1867	Bombay
Arya Samaj	Swami Dayanand Saraswati	1875	Bombay
Theosophical Society	Madam H.P. Blavatsky and Col. H.S. Olcott	1875	New York (USA)
Sadharan Brahmo Samaj	Anand Mohan Bose	1878	Calcutta
Deccan Education Society	G.G. Agarkar	1884	Pune (Poona)
Muhammadan Educational Conference	Syed Ahmad Khan	1886	Aligarh
Indian National Conference	M.G. Ranade	1887	Bombay
Deva Samaj	Shivnarayan Agnihotri	1887	Lahore
Nadwah-ul-Ulama	Maulana Shibli Numani	1894	Lucknow
Ramakrishna Mission	Swami Vivekananda	1897	Belur
Servents of Indian Society	Gopal Krishna Gokhale	1905	Bombay
Poona Seva Sadan	Mrs. Ramabai Ranade and G.K. Devadhar	1909	Pune (Poona)
Social Service League	N.M. Joshi	1911	Bombay
Seva Samiti	H.N. Kunzru	1914	Allahabad

Newspapers and Journals

- *Bengal Gazette* (1780) (India's first newspaper)—James Augustus Hikky
- *Kesari*—B.G. Tilak
- *Maratha*—B.G. Tilak
- *Sudharak*—G.K. Gokhale
- *Amrit Bazar Patrika*—Shishir Kumar Ghosh and Motilal Ghosh
- *Yugantar*—Bhupendranath Datta and Birender Kumar Ghosh
- *Bombay Chronicle*—Firoze Shah Mehta
- *New India (Daily)*—Annie Besant

Books and Authors

- *Causes of the Indian Mutiny*—Sir Syed Ahmed Khan
- *Ghulam Giri*—Jyotiba Phule
- *Anandmath*—Bankim Chand Chatterjee
- *Satyarth Prakash*—Swami Dayanand
- *Unhappy India*—Lala Lajpat Rai
- *India Divided*—Dr. Rajendra Prasad
- *The Discovery of India*—J.L. Nehru
- *Neel Darpan*—Dinbandhu Mitra
- *Hind Swaraj*—M.K. Gandhi
- *What Congress and Gandhi have done to the untouchablos*—Dr. B.R. Ambodkar

Important Sayings

- *'Back to Vedas'*—Dayanand Saraswati
- *'Dilli Chalo!'*—Subhash Chandra Bose's battle cry of *Azad Hind Fauj*
- *'Do or Die'*—Mahatma Gandhi (while launching Quit India movement in 1942)
- *'Give me blood and I will give you freedom'*—Subhash Chandra Bose (in his address to soldiers of *Azad Hind Fauj*)
- *'My ultimate aim is to wipe every tear from every eye'*—Jawaharlal Nehru
- *'Swaraj is my birthright and I will have it'*—Bal Gangadhar Tilak
- *'Inqualab Zindabad'*—Bhagat Singh
- *'Jai Jawan, Jai Kisan'*—Lal Bahadur Shastri
- *'Sarfaroshi ki tamanna Ab Hamare Dil mein Hai'*—Ram Prasad Bismill
- *'Saare Jahan Se Achcha,* Hindustan Hamara'—Dr. Mohammed Iqbal
- *'Hindi, Hindu, Hindustan'*—Bhartendu Harishchandra
- *'Vande Mataram'*—Bankim Chandra Chatterjee

❒❒❒

3

Geography

WORLD GEOGRAPHY

THE UNIVERSE

- Existing matter and energy are together known as **Universe.**

GALAXY

- A galaxy is a huge system of billions of stars and clouds of dust and gases.
- Our solar system is a part of *Milky Way* galaxy.
- There are millions of galaxies that make the Universe.

STARS

- Stars account for 98 per cent of the matter in a galaxy. The stars nearest to the earth are *Proxima Centauri, Alpha Centauri, Barnard's Star, Sirius* and so on. Of these, *Sirius* is the brightest.

LIGHT YEAR

- Light year is the distance travelled by light in one year at a speed of 2,99,792.5 km. per second.

SOLAR SYSTEM

- The Sun, eight planets, satellites and some other celestial bodies known as asteroids and meteoroids form the solar system.

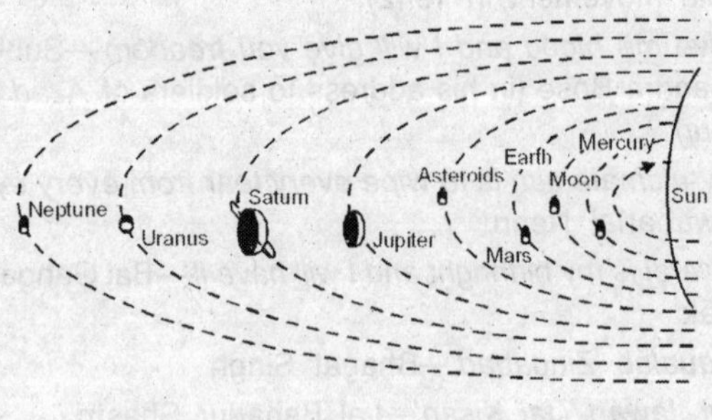

SUN

- The Sun is in the centre of the solar system.
- The Sun is a mixture of gases. It consists of 92% hydrogen, 7.8% helium and 0.2% other gases.
- The Sun is about 150 million km away from the earth.
- The sun is an ultimate source of energy for life on Earth.
- Sunlight takes 8 min 16.6 sec to reach earth.

Facts about Sun

Diameter	— 1.392×10^6 km
Volume	— 1.304 × 106 times the volume of earth
Temperature	— 6000°C at surface and 15 million degree C at the centre
Relative density	— 1.4
Gravitational Pull	— 28 times the gravitational pull of the earth

Facts about Planets

Closest to Sun	*Mercury*
Farthest from Sun	*Neptune*
Heaviest	*Jupiter*
Hottest	*Venus*
Inner	*Mercury, Venus, Earth, Mars*
Largest	*Jupiter*
Smallest	*Mercury*
Moons, None	*Mercury, Venus*
Moon; Largest	*Ganymede (Jupiter), larger than Mercury*
Nearest to Earth	*Venus*
Orbits; Order	*Mercury (closest to Sun), Venus, Earth, Mars, Jupiter, Saturn, Uranus, Neptune.*
Rings/largest number	*Saturn*
Spin; Backwards	*Venus (East to West)*

COMETS

- It has a head and a tail. Its tail originates only when it gets closer to the sun. The tail can be 20-30 million km long. It always point away from the sun because of the force exerted by solar wind and radiation on the cometory material.

THE EARTH

- The earth is the third nearest planet to the Sun.
- From the outer space, the earth appears blue because its two-thirds surface is covered by water. It is, therefore, called a blue planet. It is the densest of all planets.
- Rotation is the movement of the earth on its axis. Due to this rotation, day and night occur.
- The earth takes about 23 hours 56 minutes and 4 seconds to complete one rotation around its axis.
- Earth takes 365¼ days (one year) to revolve around the sun.

THE EARTH: FACTS AND FIGURES

- *Mass of Earth*—5.880 × 10^{21} tonnes
- *Density of Earth*—5.517 times that of water
- *Volume of Earth*—1.083 × 10^{11} cubic km
- *Equatorial circumference*—4.007 × 104 km
- *Polar Diameter*—12,714 km
- *Equatorial Diameter*—12756 km
- *Polar or Meridional circumference*—4.0 × 10^{4} km
- *Estimated Age*—At least 4600 million years
- *Land Surface*—148,951,000 sq km
- *Water Surface*—361,150,000 sq km (71 per cent of total area)
- *Highest Point of the land surface*—Mt. Everest (8,848 metres)
- *Lowest point of the land surface*—Shores of the Dead Sea (396 metres below the sea level)
- *Greatest Ocean depth*—Mariana Trench, East of Philippines (11,033 metres below the sea level)

THE MOON

- Earth has only one satellite, that is, the moon.
- Its diameter is only one-quarter that of the earth. It is about 3,84,400 km away from us.
- The moon moves around the earth in about 27 days. It takes exactly the same time to complete one spin. As a result, only one side of the moon (only 59% of its surface) is visible to us on the earth.
- Moonlight takes 1.3 sec. to reach earth.

LATITUDE

- Imaginary lines drawn parallel to the equator. Measured as an angle whose apex is at the centre of the earth.
- The equator represents 0° latitude, while the North Pole is 90°N and the South Pole 90°S.
- 23½°N represents Tropic of Cancer while 23½°S represents Tropic of Capricorn.

LONGITUDE

- It is the angular distance measured from the centre of the earth. On the globe the lines of longitude are drawn as a series of semicircles that extend from the North Pole to the South Pole through the equator. They are also called meridians.
- The distance between any two meridians is not equal. At the equator, 1 degree = 111 km. At 30°N or S, it is 96.5 km. It goes on decreasing this way until it is zero at the poles.

INTERNATIONAL DATE LINE

- It is the 180° meridian running over the Pacific Ocean, deviating at Aleutian Islands, Fiji, Samoa and Gilbert Islands.
- Travellers crossing the Date Line from west to east repeat a day and travellers crossing it from east to west lose a day.

INDIAN STANDARD TIME (IST)

- Indian Standard Time is calculated on the basis of 82.5°E longitude which passes through Uttar Pradesh, Madhya Pradesh, Odisha, Chattisgarh and Andhra Pradesh.

ECLIPSES

- Sun is the only source of light for both the Earth and Moon. Eclipses occur when the light thus received is either blocked by the earth or by the Moon.
- Eclipses occur when either the Earth moves behind the Moon's shadow or the Moon moves behind the Earth's shadow.

LUNAR ECLIPSE

- Lunar eclipse occur only when the following conditions are met.
  1. The Sun, Earth and Moon must be aligned in a straight line.
  2. The Earth must be positioned between the Sun and the Moon.
  3. The Moon must be in its full phase (Full Moon).

SOLAR ECLIPSE

- Solar eclipses occur only when the following conditions are met.
  1. The Sun, Earth and Moon must be aligned in a straight line.
  2. The Moon must be positioned between the Sun and the Earth.
  3. Must be a New Moon day.

ROCKS

- Rocks are composed of many minerals such as silica, aluminium, iron and magnesium.
- The nature of the rock is determined by the presence of its minerals.
- Rocks can be classified into three types:

1. ***Igneous rocks*** are formed by magma that reaches the earth's surface along deep cracks and at volcanic vents. e.g., Mica, Granite etc.

2. ***Sedimentary rocks*** are formed by the accumulation and cementation of mud, silt, or sand derived from weathered igneous rock frag-ments. e.g., Gravel, Peat, Gypsum etc.

3. ***Metamorphic rocks*** are igneous or sedimentary rocks that have been altered by heat and/or pressure, either because they have been buried and folded deep in the crust, or because they have come into contact with molten igneous rock, e.g., Gneiss, Marble, Quartzite etc.

VOLCANOES

Sudden eruption of hot magma (molten rock), gases, ash and other material from inside the Earth to its surface.

- ***Active*** which erupts frequently, e.g., Mauna Loa (Hawaii), Etna (Sicily), Vesuvius (Italy), Stromboli (Mediterranean Sea).
- ***Dormant*** Not erupted for quite sometime, e.g., Fujiyama (Japan), Krakatoa (Indonesia), Barren Island (Andamans).
- ***Extinct*** Not erupted for several centuries, e.g., Arthur's Seat, Edinburgh, Scotland.

EARTHQUAKES

- Earthquakes are a form of wave energy that is transferred through bedrock. It is transmitted from the point of the earthquake focus, as spherical seismic waves. They travel in all directions outward.
- The intensity of earthquake waves is recorded by *Seismograph*.

LANDFORMS

- There are three major landforms: mountains, plateaus and plains.

MOUNTAINS

- A mountain can be defined as an area of land that rises abruptly from the surrounding region.
- There are three types of mountains- *Fold Mountains, Block Mountains* and the ***Volcanic Mountains***.
- Himalayas, Alps, Andes, Rockies, Atlas, etc are examples of Fold Mountains. The Aravali range in India is one of the oldest **fold mountain** systems in the world.
- The Rhine valley and the Vosges mountain in Europe are examples of such mountain systems.
- Volcanic mountains are formed due to volcanic activity.
- Mt. Kilimanjaro in Africa and Mt. Fujiyama in Japan are examples of such mountains.

Major Mountain Ranges of the World

Range	Location	Highest Peak (m)	Length (km)
Andes	South America	6,960	7,200
Himalayas-Karakoram-Hindukush	South Central Asia	8,848	4,800
Rockies	North America	4,401	4,800
Great Dividing Range	East Australia	2,228	3,600
Western Ghat	Western India	2,637	1,610
Caucasus	Europe	5,642	1,200
Alaska	USA	6,194	1,130
Alps	Europe	4,808	1,050
Apennines	Europe	2,912	—
Ural	Asia	1,895	—
Atlas	North West Africa	—	1,930

PLATEAUS

- A plateau is an elevated flat land. It is a flat-topped table land standing above the surrounding area.

Principal Mountain Peaks of the World

Mountains	Height in Metres
1. Mount Everest	8,848
2. K-2 (Godwin Austen)	8,611
3. Kanchenjunga	8,597
4. Lhotse	8,511
5. Makalu I	8,481
6. Dhaulagiri I	8,167
7. Mansalu I	8,156
8. Chollyo	8,153
9. Nanga Parbat	8,124
10. Annapurna I	8,091
11. Gasherbrum I	8,068
12. Broad Peak I	8,047
13. Gasherbrum II	8,034
14. Shisha Pangma (Gosainthan)	8,014
15. Gasherbrum III	7,952

PLAINS

- A relatively low-lying and flat land surface with least difference between its highest and lowest points is called a Plain.

OCEANS

- Oceans of the world is classified into four groups: the Pacific, the Atlantic, the Arctic and the Indian.
- The Pacific is the largest ocean, being twice the size of the Atlantic. It covers about a third of the Earth's surface, and contains more than half the water on the planet.

Oceans of the World

Names	Area (Sq. Km.)	Greatest Depth
Pacific	166,240000	Mariana Trench
Atlantic	86,560000	Puerto Rico Trench
Indian	73430000	Java Trench
Arctic	13230000	—

Major Rivers of the World

River	Origin	Falls in	Length (Km.)
Nile	Victoria lake	Mediterranean Sea	6,650
Amazon	Andes (Peru)	Atlantic Ocean	6,428
Yangtze	Tibetan Kiang Plateau	China Sea	6,300
Mississippi Missouri	Itaska lake (USA)	Gulf of Mexico (USA)	6,275
Yenisei	Tannu-Ola Mts.	Arctic Ocean	5,539
Hoang Ho	Kunlun Mts.	Gulf of Chibli	5,464
Ob	Altai Mts., Russia	Gulf of Ob	5,410

River	Origin	Falls in	Length (Km.)
Congo	Lualaba & Luapula rivers	Atlantic Ocean	4,700
Amur	Northeast China	Sea of Okhotsk	4,444
Lena	Baikal Mts	Laptev Sea	4,400
Mekong	Tibetan Highlands	South China Sea	4,350
Mackenzie	Great Slave Lake	Beaufort Sea	4,241
Niger	Guinea	Gulf of Guinea	4,200

Major Gulfs of the World

Names	Area (Sq. Km.)	Names	Areas (Sq. Km.)
Gulf of Mexico	15,44,000	Gulf of St. Lawrence	2,37,000
Gulf of Hudson	12,33,000	Gulf of California	1,62,000
Arabian Gulf	2,38,000	English Channel	89,900

Important Straits of the World

Straits	Water Bodies joined	Area
Bab-al-Mandeb	Red Sea & Arabian Sea	Arabia & Africa
Bering	Arctic Ocean & Bering Sea	Alaska & Asia
Bosphorus	Black Sea & Marmara Sea	Turkey
Dover	North Sea & Atlantic Ocean	England & Europe
Florida	Gulf of Mexico & Atlantic Ocean	Florida & Bahamas Islands
Gibralter	Mediterranean Sea & Atlantic Ocean	Spain & Africa
Malacca	Java Sea & Bay of Bengal	India & Indonesia
Palk	Bay of Bengal & Indian Ocean	India & Sri Lanka
Magellan	South Pacific & South Atlantic Ocean	Chile
Sunda	Java Sea & Indian Ocean	Indonesia

Important Lakes of the World

Lake	Location	Area (Sq. Km.)
Caspian	Russia and CIS	371000
Superior	Canada and USA	82414
Victoria	Tanzania (Africa)	69485
Huron	Canada and USA	59596
Michigan	USA	58016
Tanganyika	Africa	32892
Baikal	Russia (CIS)	31502
Great Bear	Canada	31080
Malawi	Malawi (Tanzania)	30044
Great Slave	Canada	28438

Highest Waterfalls of the World

Name(s) (Foreign)	Location
Angel (Salto Angel)	Canaima Nat'l Park, Venezuela
Tugela	Natal Nat'l Park, South Africa
Utigord (Utigordsfoss)	Norway
Monge (Mongefoss)	Marstein, Norway
Gocta Cataracts	Chachapoyas, Peru
Mutarazi (Mtarazi)	Nyanga Nat'l Park, Zimbabwe
Yosemite	Yosemite Nat'l Park, California, U.S.
Espelands (Espelandsfoss)	Hardanger Fjord, Norway
Lower Mar Valley (Ostra Mardolafoss)	Eikesdal, Norway
Tyssestrengene	Odda, Norway

Important Cities on River Banks (World)

City	Country	River
Adelaide	Australia	Torrens
Amsterdam	Netherlands	Amsel
Alexandria	Egypt	Nile
Ankara	Turkey	Kazil
Bangkok	Thailand	Chao Praya
Basra	Iraq	Eupharates and Tigris
Baghdad	Iraq	Tigris
Berlin	Germany	Spree
Bonn	Germany	Rhine
Budapest	Hungary	Danube
Bristol	UK	Avon
Buenos Aires	Argentina	Laplata
Chittagong	Bangladesh	Majyani
Canton	China	Si-Kiang
Cairo	Egypt	Nile
Chung King	China	Yang-tse-kiang
Cologne	Germany	Rhine
Dandzing	Germany	Vistula
Dresden	Germany	Elbe
Dublin	Ireland	Liffy
Hamburg	Germany	Elbe
Kabul	Afghanistan	Kabul
Karachi	Pakistan	Indus
Lahore	Pakistan	Ravi
Leningrad	Russia	Neva
Lisbon	Portugal	Tagus
Liverpool	England	Messey
London	England	Thames
Moscow	Russia	Moskva
Montreal	Canada	St. Lawrence
Nanking	China	Yang-tse-kiang
New Orleans	U.S.A.	Mississipi
New York	U.S.A.	Hudson
Ottawa	Canada	Ottawa
Paris	France	Seine
Philadelphia	U.S.A	Delaware
Perth	Australia	Swan
Prague	Czech Republic	Vitava
Quebec	Canada	St. Lawrence
Rome	Italy	Tiber
Rotterdam	The Netherlands	New Moss
Stalingrad	Russia	Volga
Shanghai	China	Yang-tse-kiang
Sidney	Australia	Darling
Saint Louis	U.S.A	Mississippi
Tokyo	Japan	Arakava
Vienna	Austria	Danube
Warsaw	Poland	Vistula
Washington D.C.	U.S.A.	Potomac
Yangoon	Myanmar	Irawaddy

World's Geographical Surnames

City of Sky-scrapers—New York
City of Seven Hills—Rome
City of Dreaming Spires—Oxford
City of Golden Gate—San Francisco
City of Magnificent Buildings—Washington D.C.
City of Eternal Springs—Quito (S. America)
China's Sorrow—Hwang Ho; *Cockpit of Europe*—Belgium
Dark Continent—Africa
Emerald Isle—Ireland; *Eternal City*—Rome
Empire City—New York; *Forbidden City*—Lhasa (Tibet)
Garden City—Chicago; *Gate of Tears*—Strait of Bab-el-Mandeb
Gift of the Nile—Egypt; *Granite City*—Aberdeen (Scotland)
Hermit Kingdom—Korea; *Herring Pond*—Atlantic Ocean
Holy Land—Jerusalem; *Island Continent*—Australia
Islands of Cloves—Zanzibar
Isle of Pearls—Bahrein (Persian Gulf)
Key to the Mediterranean—Gibralter
Land of Cakes—Scotland
Land of Golden Fleece—Australia
Land of Maple Leaf—Canada
Land of Morning Calm—Korea
Land of Midnight Sun—Norway
Land of the Thousand Lakes—Finland
Land of the Thunderbolt—Bhutan
Land of White Elephant—Thailand
Land of Thousand Elephants—Laos
Land of Rising Sun—Japan
Loneliest Island—Tristan De Gunha (Mid-Atlantic)
Manchester of Japan—Osaka
Pillars of Hercules—Strait of Gibraltar
Pearl of the Antilles—Cuba
Playground of Europe—Switzerland
Quaker City—Philadelphia; *Queen of the Adriatic*—Venice
Roof of the World—The Pamirs, Central Asia
Sugar bowl of the world—Cuba
Venice of the North—Stockholm; *Windy City*—Chicago
Whiteman's grave—Guinea Coast of Africa
Yellow River—Huang Ho (China)
Sickman of Europe—Turkey

Important Boundaries

Durand Line	Pakistan & Afghanistan
MacMohan Line	India & China
Radcliff Line	India & Pakistan
Maginot Line	France & Germany
Oder Niesse Line	Germany & Poland
Hindenberg Line	Poland & Germany (at the time of First World War)
38th Parallel	North & South Korea
49th Parallel	USA & Canada

Continents: Some Facts

Continent	Biggest Counrty	Highest Peak	Longest River
Asia	China	Mt. Everest (8848 m)	Yangtze Kiang
Africa	Algeria	Mt. Kilimanjaro (5895 m)	Nile
North America	Canada	Mt. Mckinley (6194 m)	Mississippi Missouri
South America	Brazil	Mt. Acancagua (6960 m)	Amazon
Europe	Russia	Mt. Elbrus (5642 m)	Ob
Australia	Australia	Mt. Coscuisco (2228 m)	Darling
Antarctica	—	Vinson Massif (5140 m)	—

INDIAN GEOGRAPHY

AREA AND LOCATION

- India is in the southern parts of the Asian continent. In the west of India lies the Arabian Peninsula while in the east lies the Indo-China Peninsula.
- India extends between 8°4' N and 37°6' N latitudes and between 68°7' E and 97°2' E longitudes.
- India, has a total geographic area of 32,87,263 sq. km. This is only 2.42 % of the total geographic area of the world but holds 17.5 per cent of the world's population.
- The 23½°N, which is the Tropic of Cancer, runs across the country.
- India has a length of 3214 km from north to south and 2933 km from east to west. It has a land frontier of 15200 km.
- The total length of the coastline of the mainland, Lakshadweep Islands and Andaman and Nicobar Islands is 7,516.6 km.
- India ranks seventh among the countries of the world, in terms of the geographical extent.
- India is bordered on three sides by water and on one by land, it is also a peninsula.
- India shares its common border with Afghanistan and Pakistan in the north-west, China and Bhutan in the north, and Bangladesh in the east. In the south, Sri Lanka is separated from India by a strait, known as the Palk Strait.
- There are 28 States, and 8 Union Territories (Delhi is National Capital Territory).
- 82°30' E longitude is considered as the Indian Standard Meridian. The local time of this longitude is taken as the Indian Standard Time (IST). This is 5½ hours ahead of the Greenwich Mean Time.

THE INDIAN STATES/UTs ON INTERNATIONAL BOUNDARIES ARE:

- ***Bordering Pakistan:*** Jammu and Kashmir, Punjab, Rajasthan, Gujarat.
- ***Bordering China:*** Jammu and Kashmir, Ladakh, Himachal Pradesh, Uttarakhand, Sikkim, Arunachal Pradesh.
- ***Bordering Nepal:*** Bihar, Uttarakhand, UP, Sikkim, West Bengal.
- ***Bordering Bangladesh:*** West Bengal, Mizoram, Meghalaya, Tripura, Assam.
- ***Bordering Bhutan:*** West Bengal, Sikkim, Arunachal Pradesh, Assam.
- ***Bordering Myanmar:*** Arunachal Pradesh, Nagaland, Manipur, Mizoram.
- ***Bordering Afghanistan:*** Jammu and Kashmir (Pakistan-occupied area).

Important Passes

Jammu & Kashmir	Burzi-La
Himachal Pradesh	Bara La, Cha-La, Shipki-La
Uttarakhand	Niti-La, Lipu-Lekh-La
Sikkim	Jelep-La, Nathu-La
Arunachal Pradesh	Bomdi-La
Ladakh	Joji-La

Heighest Mountain Peaks of India

Peaks	Elevation• (in mts.)
Godwin Austin (K2)	8611*
Kanchenjunga	8598
Nanga Parvat	8126
Gasherbrum	8068*
Broad Peak	8047*
Dastegil	7885*
Masherbrum (East)	7821
Nanda Devi	7817
Masherbrum (West)	7806*
Rakoposhi	7788*
Kamet	7756
Saser Kangdi	7672

• Above mean sea level in metres.

** Situated in Pak occupied Kashmir (PoK).*

Towns at River Banks

Town	River	Town	River
Agra	Yamuna	Varanasi	The Ganges
Ayodhya	Saryu	Kolkata	Hooghly
Cuttuck	Mahanadi	Delhi	Yamuna
Dibrugarh	Brahmaputra	Ferozepur	Satluj
Guwahati	Brahmaputra	Hardwar	The Ganges
Hyderabad	Musi	Jabalpur	Narmada
Kanpur	The Ganges	Kota	Chambal
Kurnool	Tungbhadra	Lucknow	Gomti
Ludhiana	Sutlej	Nasik	Godavari
Pandharpur	Bhima	Patna	The Ganges
Sambalpur	Mahanadi	Srinagar	Jhelum
Srirangapattam	Cauveri	Prayagraj	Confluence of the Ganges and the Yamuna
Surat	Tapti		
Vijaywada	Krishna		
Ahmedabad	Sabarmati		
Ferozpur	Sutlej	Raurkela	Brahmani
Jabaplpur	Narmada	Vadodara	Vishwamitri

Waterfalls of India

Waterfall	Hgt (Mt.)	River	State
Kunchikal	455	Varahi	Karnataka
Jog/Gersoppa	260	Sharavati	Karnataka
Rakim Kund	168	Gaighat	Bihar
Chachai	127	Bihad	Madhya Pradesh
Kevti	98	Mahanadi	Madhya Pradesh
Sivasamudram	90	Cauveri	Karnataka

Important Lakes of India

Name of lake	State/UT
Pulicat Lake	Tamil Nadu & Andhra Pradesh Border
Sambhar Lake	Rajasthan
Tso Moriri Lake	Jammu & Kashmir
Vembanad Lake	Kerala
Wular & Dal Lakes	Jammu and Kashmir
Chilka Lake	Odisha
Kolleru Lake	Andhra Pradesh
Loktak Lake	Manipur
Lonar Lake	Maharashtra
Pangong Lake	Ladakh

Rivers of India

Name	Originates From	Falls Into
Yamuna	Yamunotri	Ganga
Chambal	Singar Chouri Peak, Vindhyan escarpment	Yamuna
Ghaghara	Matsatung Glacier	Ganga
Kosi	Near Gosain Dham Peak	Ganga
Sabarmati	Aravalis	Gulf of Khambat
Krishna	Western Ghats	Bay of Bengal
Godavari	Nasik district in Maharashtra	Bay of Bengal
Caurey	Brahmagir Range of Western Ghats	Bay of Bengal
Tungabharda	Western Ghats	Krishna
Ganges	Combines Sources	Bay of Bengal
Sutlej	Mansarovar Rakas lakes	Chenab
Indus	Near Mansarovar Lake	Arabian Sea
Ravi	Kullu Hills near Rohtang Pass	Chenab
Beas	Near Rohtang Pass	Sutlej
Jhelum	Verinag in Kashmir	Chenab
Son	Amarkantak	Ganga
Brahmaputra	Near Mansarovar Lake	Bay of Bengal
Narmada	Amarkantak	Gulf of Khambat
Tapti	Betul District in Madhya Pradesh	Gulf of Khambat
Mahanadi	Raipur District in Chhattisgarh	Bay of Bengal
Luni	Aravallis	Rann of Kuchchh
Ghaggar	Himalayas	Near Fatehabad
Betwa	Vindhyanchal	Yamuna

Geographical Surnames

Bengal's Sorrow	Damodar River	City of Lakes	Srinagar
City of Palaces	Kolkata	Twin City	Hyderabad-Secunderabad
Gateway of India	Mumbai	City of Seven Islands	Mumbai
Pink City	Jaipur	Diamond Harbour	Kolkata
Paris of India	Jaipur	Switzerland of India	Kashmir
Manchester of India	Ahmedabad	Rice Bowl	Chhattisgarh
Kashmir of South	Kerala	Fruit Bowl	Himachal Pradesh
Son of Sea	Lakshadweep	Ganga of South	Cauvery
Queen of Mountains	Mussourie	Pitsburg of India	Jamshedpur
Iron City	Jamshedpur	City of Bridges	Srinagar
Hollywood of India	Mumbai	Residence of God	Allahabad
Scotland of East	Meghalaya	A Cross-road (Quadrivial) of National Highways	Kanpur
City of Nababs	Lucknow	Heart of India	Delhi
City of Temples & Ghats	Varanasi	Black River	Sharda
Land of Five Rivers	Punjab	City of Festivals	Madurai
City of Golden Temple	Amritsar	Queen of Deccan	Pune
Garden of India	Bangaluru	Sorrow of Bihar	Kosi River
Spice Garden of India	Kerala		

Some Major Irrigational and Multipurpose Projects

S.No.	Name of Project	Related State	River
1.	Bargi Project	Madhya Pradesh	Bargi
2.	Beas	Joint Venture of Haryana, Punjab and Rajasthan	Beas
3.	Bhadra	Karnakata	Bhadra
4.	Bhakra Nangal	Haryana, Punjab and Rajasthan	Sutluj
5.	Bhima I	Maharashtra	Pawana
6.	Bhima II	Maharashtra	Krishna
7.	Chambal	Joint Project of M.P. and Rajasthan	Chambal
8.	Damodar Valley Project	West Bengal and Bihar	Damodar
9.	Dulhasti Power Project	Jammu and Kashmir	Chenab
10.	Farakka	West Bengal	Hooghly
11.	Gandak	Bihar and U.P.	Gandak
12.	Ghataprabha	Karnataka	Ghataprabha
13.	Hasdeo Bango Project	Madhya Pradesh, Chhattisgarh	Hasdeo
14.	Hirakud	Odisha	Mahanadi
15.	Jayakwadi	Maharashtra	Godavari
16.	Kakrapara	Gujarat	Tapti
17.	Kangsbati	West Bengal	Kangsbati and Kumari
18.	Karjan	Gujarat	Karjan
19.	Kosi	Bihar	Kosi
20.	Koyana	Maharashtra	Koyana
21.	Krishna Project	Maharashtra	Krishna
22.	Kukadi	Maharashtra	Kukadi
23.	Left Bank Ghagra Canal	Uttar Pradesh	Ghagra
24.	Madhya Ganga Canal	Uttar Pradesh	Ganga
25.	Mahanadi Delta Scheme	Odisha	(The irrigation scheme will utilise releases from Hirakund Reservoir)
26.	Mahi	Gujarat	Mahi

S.No.	Name of Project	Related State	River
27.	Malaprabha	Karnataka	Malaprabha
28.	Mayurakshi	West Bengal	Mayurakshi
29.	Nagarjunasagar	Andhra Pradesh	Krishna
30.	Panam	Gujarat	Panam
31.	Parambikulam Aliyar	Tamil Nadu and Kerala	Perimbikulam
32.	Pochampad	Andhra Pradesh	Godavari
33.	Pong Dam	Punjab	Beas
34.	Ramganga	Uttarakhand	Ramganga
35.	Ranjit Sagar Dam (Thein Dam)	Punjab	Ravi
36.	Rihand	Uttar Pradesh	Rihand
37.	Sabarmati	Gujarat	Sabarmati
38.	Sharda Sahayak	U.P.	Ghagra
39.	Sone High Level Canal	Bihar	Sone
40.	Tawa	Madhya Pradesh	Tawa
41.	Tehri Dam	Uttarakhand	Bhagirathi
42.	Tungabhadra	Andhra Pradesh and Karnataka	Tungabhadra
43.	Ukai	Gujarat	Tapti
44.	Upper Krishna	Karnataka	Krishna
45.	Upper Penganga	Maharashtra	Penganga
46.	Uri Power Project	Jammu and Kashmir	Jhelum

Major Indian Crops

Crops	Temp(°c)	Water(cm)	States where Produced
Wheat	15°-25°	60-90	Uttar Pradesh, Punjab, Haryana.
Rice	24°-26°	80-200	West Bengal, Uttar Pradesh, Andhra Pradesh, Bihar, Punjab
Maize	18°-21°	50-60	Karnataka, Uttar Pradesh, Maharashtra
Jowar	20°-35°	40-60	Maharashtra, Madhya Pradesh, Karnataka
Soyabean	25°-27°	50-120	Madhya Pradesh
Cotton	20°-30°	80-150	Maharashtra, Gujarat, Karnataka, Madhya Pradesh
Tobacco	20°-25°	75-80	Andhra Pradesh, Madhya Pradesh, Gujarat, Karnataka, Maharashtra, Uttar Pradesh
Tea	24°-30°	100-200	Assam, West Bengal, Kerala, Tamil Nadu, Uttar Pradesh
Ground Nut	15°-25°	60-130	Gujarat, Maharashtra

Mineral Wealth at a Glance (Metallic Minerals)

Mineral	Chief Producers
Bauxite	Odisha, Gujarat, Jharkhand
Chromite	Odisha, Karnataka
Coal	Jharkhand, West Bengal
Copper	Madhya Pradesh, Rajasthan
Diaspore	Uttar Pradesh, Madhya Pradesh
Gold	Karnataka
Iron	Odisha, Karnataka, Goa
Lead	Rajasthan, Andhra Pradesh
Lignite	Tamil Nadu, Jammu & Kashmir
Manganese	Odisha, Karnataka
Natural Gas	Gujarat, Assam
Petroleum	Gujarat, Assam, Andhra Pradesh
Silver	Andhra Pradesh, Rajasthan, Jharkhand
Tungsten	Rajasthan
Zinc	Rajasthan, W. Bengal

Zones and Headquarters of Indian Railways

S.No.	Zone	Headquarters
1.	Central	Mumbai (Victoria Terminus)
2.	Eastern	Kolkata
3.	Northern	New Delhi
4.	North-Eastern	Gorakhpur
5.	North-East Frontier	Maligaon, Guwahati
6.	Southern	Chennai
7.	South-Central	Secunderabad
8.	South-Eastern	Kolkata
9.	Western	Mumbai, Churchgate
10.	East Coast	Bhubaneswar
11.	East Central	Hajipur
12.	North Central	Prayagraj
13.	North Western	Jaipur
14.	South Western	Hubballi
15.	West Central	Jabalpur
16.	South East Central	Bilaspur
17.	Metro Railway	Kolkata
18.	South Coast Railway	Vishakhapatnam (Proposed)

Major National Highways

N H	Connects
NH 1	New Delhi-Ambala-Jalandhar-Amritsar
NH 2	Delhi-Mathura-Agra-Kanpur-Prayagraj-Varanasi-Kolkata
NH 3	Agra-Gwalior-Nasik-Mumbai
NH 4	Thane and Chennai *via* Pune and Belgaum
NH 5	Kolkata-Chennai
NH 6	Kolkata-Dhule
NH 7	Varanasi-Kanyakumari (2369 km)
NH 8	Delhi-Mumbai (*via* Jaipur, Baroda and Ahmedabad)
NH 9	Mumbai-Vijaywada
NH 10	Delhi-Fazilka
NH 24	Delhi-Lucknow
NH 26	Lucknow-Varanasi

Major Ports of Country

1. Shyama Prasad Mukherjee (Kolkata)
2. Mumbai
3. J.L. Nehru Port (Nhava Sheva)
4. V.O. Chidambaranar (Tuticorin)
5. Chennai
6. Mormugao
7. New Mangalore
8. Paradeep
9. Deendayal (Kandla)
10. Vishakhapatnam
11. Cochin
12. Kamarajar (Ennore).

Major International Airports in India

International Airports	City
Indira Gandhi International Airport	Delhi
Anna International Airport	Chennai
Sri Guru Ram Dass Jee International Airport	Amritsar
Rajiv Gandhi International Airport	Hyderabad
Calicut International Airport	Kozhikode
Chhatrapati Shivaji International Airport	Mumbai
Kempegowda International Airport	Bengaluru
Dabolim Internation Airport	Goa
Netaji Subash Chandra Bose International Airport	Kolkata
Trivendrum International Airport	Thiruvananthapuram
Lokpriya Gopinath Bordoloi International Airport	Guwahati
Sardar Vallabhbhai Patel International Airport	Ahmedabad

❑ ❑ ❑

4

Indian Polity

INDIAN CONSTITUTION

- Demand for a Constituent Assembly composed of the people of India officially asserted by the Congress for the first time in 1935.
- The election for Indian Constitution Assembly held in 1946 according to the *Cabinet Mission Plan.*
- The first session of the Assembly was held in New Delhi on December 9, 1946. *Sachidanand Sinha* was elected provisional chairman of the session.
- On December 11, 1946, Dr. Rajendra Prasad was elected as the Permanent Chairman of the Constituent Assembly.
- The Constitution was framed by the Constituent Assembly of India, set-up in December 1946, in accordance with the Cabinet Mission Plan, under the Chairmanship of Sachidanand Sinha, initially.
- The total membership of Constituent Assembly after partition was 299, among them 70 were representatives from the Indian states and others from British India.
- The Chairman of the Drafting Committee was **Dr. BR Ambedkar**, also called the Father of the Constitution.
- The Constituent Assembly took 2 years, 11 months and 18 days to complete the Constitution.
- The Constitution, adopted on 8th November, 1949, contained 395 Articles and Schedules.
- The Constitution was delayed till 26th January because, in 1929, on this day Indian National Congress demanded Poorna Swaraj in Lahore Session under JL Nehru.
- Indian Constitution is a comprehensive document and it is the lengthiest written Constitution in the World.

THE PREAMBLE

- ***The Preamble of the Constitution:*** "We the people of India, having solemnly resolved to Constitute India into a Sovereign, Socialist, Secular Democratic Republic and to secure to all its citizen:

  Justice, Social, economic and political;

  Liberty of thought, expression, belief, faith and worship;

  Equality of status and of opportunity; and to promote among them all;

  Fraternity assuring the dignity of the individual and the unity and integrity of the nation;

  In our Constituent Assembly, this twenty-sixth day of November, 1949, do hereby adopt, enact and give to ourselves this constitution."

Foreign Sources of Indian Constitution

Foreign Sources	*Subject*
Britain	Parliamentary system, collective responsibilities of Cabinet
America	Fundamental right, Independent Judiciary, Judicial review
Canada	Division of powers
Ireland	Directive principles
Germany	Emergency provisions
Russia	Fundamental duties
Australia	Concurrent list

IMPORTANT ARTICLES

PART - I

UNION AND ITS TERRITORIES (ARTICLE 1 - 4)

- The Constitution says, "India, that is Bharat, shall be a Union of States".
- Parliament has the power to create any State, reduce it, change the name of boundaries of any State.

PART - II

CITIZENSHIP (ARTICLE 5 - 11)

- The Constitution provides for a single Citizenship.
- ***Indian Citizenship can be acquire:***
  1. by birth
  2. by descent
  3. by registration
  4. by naturalisation
  5. by incorporation of territory
- ***Indian Citizenship can be lost by:***
  1. renunciation;
  2. termination — it takes place if a citizen of India voluntary acquires the citizenship of another country; and
  3. deprivation — if the Government terminates the citizenship.

PART - III

FUNDAMENTAL RIGHTS (ARTICLE 12 - 35)

- Following fundamental rights are enjoyed by every Indian citizen, irrespective of caste, colour, creed and sex:
  1. ***Right to Equality:*** No special privileges, no distinction on grounds of religion, caste, creed and sex.
  2. ***Right to Freedom:*** The right to freedom of expression and speech, the right to choose one's own profession, the right to reside in any part of the Indian Union.
  3. ***Right to Freedom to Religion:*** Except when it is in the interest of public order, morality, health or other conditions, everybody has the right to profess, practice and propagate his religion freely.
  4. ***Cultural and Educational Rights:*** The Constitution provides that every community can run its own institutions to preserve its own culture and language.
  5. ***Right against Exploitation:*** Traffic in human beings and forced labour and the employment of children under 14 years in factories or mines, are punishable offences.
  6. ***Rights to Constitutional Remedies:*** When a citizen finds that any of his fundamental rights has been encroached upon, he can move the Supreme Court, which has been empowered to safeguard the fundamental rights of a citizen (Article 32).

PART - IV

DIRECTIVE PRINCIPLES OF STATE POLICY (ARTICLE 36 - 51)

- Directive principles are not enforceable through courts. Main aim of Directive principles is to provide social and economic base of a genuine democracy.

Some Important Directive Principles:

- Provisions for adequate means of livelihood for all citizens (Art. 39).
- Right to work (Art. 41).
- Right to human condition of work and maternity relief (Art. 42).
- Right to a living wage and condition of work ensuring decent standard of life of worker (Art. 43).
- Common Civil Code (Art. 44).
- Prohibit consumption of liquor (Art. 47).
- Prevent slaughter of useful cattle (Art. 48).
- Organise Panchayati Raj (Art. 40).
- Separate the judiciary from the executive (Art. 50).
- Protect and maintain places of historic monuments (Art. 49).
- International peace (Art. 51).

PART - IV A

FUNDAMENTAL DUTIES (ARTICLE 51A)

- The fundamental duties for the Indian citizens have been incorporated in the Constitution through the Constitution (42nd) Amendment Act, 1976. These duties are:
  1. to abide by the Constitution and respect its ideals and institutions, the National Flag and the National Anthem;
  2. to cherish and follow the noble deeds which inspired our national struggle for freedom;
  3. to uphold and protect the sovereignty, unity and integrity of India;
  4. to defend the country and render national service when called upon to do so;
  5. to promote harmony and the spirit of common brotherhood amongst all the people transcending religious, regional or sectional diversities and to renounce practices derogatory to the dignity of women;
  6. to value and preserve the rich heritage of our composite culture;
  7. to protect and improve natural environment including forests, lakes, rivers and wildlife, and to have compassion for living creatures;
  8. to develop the scientific temper, humanism and the spirit of inquiry and reform;
  9. to safeguard public property and to abjure violence;
  10. to strive towards excellence in all spheres of individual and collective activity so that the nation constantly rises to higher levels of endeavour and achievement.
  11. who is parent or guardian to provide opportunities for education to his child or, as the case may be, ward between age of six and fourteen years.

PART - V

UNION (ARTICLE 52 - 151)

THE PRESIDENT

- The President is the Constitutional head of the Republic of India. He is more or less the titular head of the executive.
- He is the constitutional head but not the real executive. The real power is vested in the hands of the Council of Ministers.
- President is the first citizen of India.
- ***Qualifications:*** (i) Indian citizen, (ii) age not less than 35 years, (iii) should have qualification for election to Lok Sabha, (iv) should not hold any office of profit, (v) should not be a Member of Parliament or State Legislature.
- ***Election:*** Indirectly elected through Electoral College consisting of elected members of both the Houses of the

Parliament and elected members of the Legislative Assemblies of the States.

- According to the 70th Amendment Act, 1992, the expression 'States' include the National Capital Territory of Delhi and the Union Territory of Puducherry. Members of the Legislative Councils have no right to vote in the Presidential election.
- ***Powers:*** He makes appointments to all the constitutional posts.
- He can address either House of Parliament and dissolve Lok Sabha.
- All Bills passed by Parliament must receive his assent to become an Act.
- He issues ordinances when Parliament is not in session. No Money Bill can be introduced in Lok Sabha without his recommendation.
- He appoints 12 members of special repute in the Rajya Sabha.
- He has the power of *Pardon* to a criminal in special cases.
- The President holds the office for a period of five years. He is eligible for re-election.
- He is also entitled to rent free official residence called Rashtrapati Bhawan.

Vice-President

- ***Article 63*** of the Constitution stipulates a Vice-President for India.
- The Vice-President acts as the ex-officio Chairman of the Council of States (Rajya Sabha).
- He is elected by an electoral college consisting of the members of both Houses of Parliament in accordance with the system of proportional represen-tation by means of the single transferable vote. He must be a citizen of India, not less than 35 years of age, and should be eligible for election as a member of the Council of States.
- Disputes in connection with election of a president or a vice-president are to be a dealt with in accordance with Article-71. Such disputes shall be decided by the Supreme Court.

Council of Ministers

- The Constitution of India provides for a parliament system of government under which the President is only Constitutional ruler and the real power is exercised by the Council of Ministers, headed by the Prime Minister.
- Council of Ministers is composed of all Union Ministers—the Prime Minister, Cabinet Ministers, Ministers of State and Deputy Ministers.
- The Council of Ministers is Collectively responsible to the Lok Sabha.
- The Prime Minister is a link between the President and the Council of Ministers.

Prime Minister

- The Prime Minister is the leader of the majority party in the Parliament.
- He is appointed by the President. Other Ministers are appointed by the president on his advice.
- The Prime Minister is the head of the Government and the head of the Council of Ministers.
- Jawaharlal Nehru was the first Prime Minister and the longest serving so far.

Union Legislature

- The Legislature of the Union, which is called 'Parliament' consists of the President and the two Houses of Parliament known as the Council of states (Rajya Sabha) and the House of the People (Lok Sabha).

RAJYA SABHA

- The Rajya Sabha is the Upper House of the Parliament and it is constituted of representatives from the States or the Constituent units of the Indian Union.
- It is a permanent body, one third of its members retiring after every two years.
- Its maximum strength is 250. Out of these, twelve members are nominated by the President from well-known personalities in the realm of Science, Art, Literature and Social Service. Rest of 238 representatives of the States and Union Territories are elected.
- Currently, the strength of the Rajya Sabha is 245.

LOK SABHA

- The Lok Sabha whose life is five years, is the Lower House of Parliament and comprises of members directly elected by the people.
- The House of the people (Lok Sabha) at present consists, 543 members directly elected from the states and Union Territories. By the 104th Constitutional amendment Act, 2019 the 2 Anglo-Indian reserved seats nominated by President in Lok Sabha are abolished.
- The House of the People shall continue for five years (unless sooner dissolved) from the date of its meeting and no longer and the expiry of the said period of 5 years shall operate as dissolution of the House.

Parliamentary Committees

- There are several Parliamentary Committees to assist the Parliament in its deliberations.
- These are appointed or elected by the respective Houses of Lok Sabha and Rajya Sabha on a motion made or are nominated by their presiding officers.
- Among the Standing Committees, three are financial Committees: (i) Public Account Committee; (ii) Estimate Committee; (iii) Public undertaking Committee.

Speaker of Lok Sabha

- Speaker is elected by the Lok Sabha from among its members.
- The Speaker will have the final power to maintain order within the House of the People and to interpret its rules of procedure.
- A Deputy-Speaker is also elected to officiate in absence of the Speaker.
- *G.V. Mavlankar* was the first Speaker of the Lok Sabha (1952-1956).

Supreme Court

- The Constitution provides for the Supreme Court, which consists of Chief Justice and 33 judges. They are appointed by the President of India.

QUALIFICATION AND TENURE

- Eligibility conditions for a judge of the Supreme Court are that he must be : (i) a citizen of India; (ii) a judge of a high court for a minimum period of 5 years; or (iii) an advocate of a high court for at least ten years or a distinguished jurist.
- Judges hold office till the age of 65.
- They can resign earlier or can be removed by the President on the recommendation of the two Houses of the Parliament by 2/3rd majority of the members present and voting.

Powers

- *Original jurisdiction:* Cases involving Government of India and the states or cases involving the enforcement of Fundamental Rights fall under original jurisdiction.
- *Appellate Jurisdiction:* In cases which are brought to it in the form of appeals against the judgement of the lower courts—It hears appeals in civil and criminal cases.
- *Advisory functions:* the Supreme Court advises the President on the constitutionality of a particular legal matter. However, its advice is not binding on the President.

Other Powers:

1. it is a court of record and can punish for contempt of itself;
2. it can make rules for regulating the practice and procedure of courts with the approval of the President; and
3. it can recommend to the President the removal of chairman and members of the UPSC. Supreme Court enjoys the power of judicial review (right of the court which declares as unconstitutional, the laws passed by the legislature and orders issued by executive) though it is not specifically mentioned in the Constitution.

- The first Chief Justice of India was H.J. Kania (1950-51).

COMPTROLLER AND AUDITOR GENERAL (CAG) (ARTICLE 148-151)

- The Comptroller and Auditor General of India is guardian of the public purse.
- It is his duty to see that not a *paisa* is spent out of consolidated fund of India or of a state without the authority of the appropriate legislature.
- He is appointed by President of India.
- A person with long administrative experience and knowledge of accounts is appointed.
- Holds office for 6 yrs or till 65 yrs of age.
- The President can remove him only on the recommendation of the 2 houses of Parliament (as in case of judge of Supreme Court).
- The CAG submits its reports to the President (in case of accounts relating to the Union Government) or to the State Governors (for State Government Accounts).
- The first CAG of India was *V Narahari Rao* (1948-1954).
- The CAG is not eligible for further office under the Union or State Governments. The expenses of the office of the CAG is charged to the Consolidated Fund of India.

ATTORNEY GENERAL OF INDIA

- The Attorney General of India is the first law officer of the Government of India.
- Though he is not a member of cabinet he has the right to speak in the House of Parliament, but he has no right to vote.
- The Attorney General of India shall be appointed by the President and shall hold office during his pleasure.
- His duty shall be to give advice on such legal matter from time-to-time as may be referred to him by the President.
- To be appointed as Attorney General, a candidate must be qualified to be appointed as a Judge of the Supreme Court.
- The Attorney General can participate in proceedings of the Parliament without the Right to Vote (Article 88).
- The first Attorney General of Independent India was MC Setalvad (1950-1963).

PART - VI

THE STATES (ARTICLE 152 - 237)

The Governor

- The Governor is appointed by the President and holds office during the pleasure of the President.
- Apart from the power to appoint the council of ministers, if the governor finds that the government of state cannot be carried on in accordance with the provisions of the

constitution (Art. 356), he may send his report to the President who may assume to himself the functions of the government of the state. (This is popularly known as 'President's Rule').

- Article 161 gives the Governor the power to grant pardons, reprieves, remission of punishment to persons convicted under the state law.
- Article 171 states that the States where Legislative Councils exists, the Governor can nominate some members from amongst those distinguished in literature, science, arts, cooperative movement and social service.

STATES LEGISLATURE (ARTICLE 168 - 212)

- The state legislature consists of Governor and legislative assembly.
- In some state like *Bihar, Maharashtra, Andhra Pradesh, Karnataka, Uttar Pradesh and Telangana* have a legislative council.
- The membership of the council should not be more than *one-third* of the legislative assembly but not less than 40.
- The legislative assembly of each state shall be composed of members chosen by direct election on the basis of adult suffrage and the number of members shall not be more than 500 or less than 60.
- The assembly of Sikkim, Goa, Puducherry and Mizoram have less than 60 members.

HIGH COURTS (ARTICLE 214-232)

- The High Court stands at the apex of the State Judiciary.
- As per the Constitution, there shall be a High Court in each State. But there may be a common High Court for two or more States and Union Territory, if it is provided by a law of the Parliament. For example, the Chennai High Court has its Jurisdiction over the State of Tamil Nadu and the Union Territory of Puducherry.
- The State Government has no control over it.
- There are 25 High Courts in India.
- The Calcutta High Court, established in 1862, is the oldest High Court in India.

THE PANCHAYATS (ARTICLE 243-243 O)

- Panchayati Raj was introduced in India with a view to associate the people with administration at grass-root level.
- It is a three-tier system as recommended by Balwant Rai Mehta Committee.
- Introduced by the 73rd Amendment Act, 1992 which envisaged a three tier system of local governance.

These are:

1. Gram Panchayat at the village level
2. Panchayat Samiti at the block level
3. Zila Parishad at the district level.

Jurisdiction and Seat of High Courts

Name	Year	Territorial Jurisdiction	Seat
Allahabad	1866	Uttar Pradesh	Prayagraj (Bench at Lucknow)
Andhra Pradesh	2019	Andhra Pradesh	Amaravati
Bombay	1862	Maharashtra, Goa, Dadar and Nagar Haveli and Daman and Diu	Mumbai (Benches at Nagpur, Panaji and Aurangabad)
Calcutta	1862	West Bengal and Andaman & Nicobar	Kolkata (Circuit Benches at Port Blair and Jalpaiguri)
Chhattisgarh	2000	Chhattisgarh	Bilaspur
Delhi	1966	Delhi	Delhi
Guwahati	1948	Assam, Nagaland, Mizoram and Arunachal Pradesh	Guwahati (Benches at Kohima, Aizawl and Itanagar)
Gujarat	1960	Gujarat	Ahmedabad
Himachal Pradesh	1971	Himachal Pradesh	Shimla
Jammu and Kashmir and Ladakh	1928	Jammu & Kashmir, Ladakh	Srinagar and Jammu
Jharkhand	2000	Jharkhand	Ranchi
Karnataka	1884	Karnataka	Bengaluru (Circuit Benches at Dharwar and Gulbarga)
Kerala	1958	Kerala & Lakshadweep	Ernakulam
Madhya Pradesh	1956	Madhya Pradesh	Jabalpur (Benches at Gwalior and Indore)
Madras	1862	Tamil Nadu & Puducherry	Chennai (Bench at Madurai)
Orissa	1948	Odisha	Cuttack
Patna	1916	Bihar	Patna
Punjab and Haryana	1966	Punjab, Haryana and Chandigarh	Chandigarh
Rajasthan	1949	Rajasthan	Jodhpur (Bench at Jaipur)
Sikkim	1975	Sikkim	Gangtok
Uttarakhand	2000	Uttarakhand	Nainital
Tripura	2013	Tripura	Agartala
Meghalaya	2013	Meghalaya	Shillong
Manipur	2013	Manipur	Imphal
Telangana	2019	Telangana	Hyderabad

THE MUNICIPALITIES (ARTICLE 243 P-243 ZG)

- Big cities have municipal corporations headed by the elected Mayor.
- For small towns there are elected boards or councils, in turn, elect their Presidents.
- Introduced by the 74th Amendment Act, 1993 which envisages three types of urban local bodies, namely, municipality (nagar palika), city council (nagar panchayat).
- Municipal governance in India was first introduced in Madras in 1688.

PART - XIII

(ARTICLE 301 - 307)

- In this part from Article 301-307 trade, commerce and intercourse within the territory of India are given.

PART - XIV

(ARTICLE 308 - 323)

- In this part services under the union and the states are given.
- ***Article 312:*** *All India Services* and ***Article 315:*** Public Service Commissions for the Union and for the States.
- The first Public Service Commission was set up in 1926, on the recommendations of the Lee Commission.

UNION PUBLIC SERVICE COMMISSION (UPSC)

- This Commission is responsible for:

1. recruitment to all civil services and posts, under the Union Government by written examinations, interviews and promotions, and
2. advising the Government on all matters relating to methods of recruitment, principles to be followed in making promotions and transfers. Its Chairman is appointed by the President.

STAFF SELECTION COMMISSION (SSC)

- The Union Government has constituted a Staff Selection Commission for recruitment to non-technical Class-III posts in the central government and in subordinate offices.
- The Administrative Reforms Commission had recommended the setting up of such a Commission.
- The Commission has also been entrusted with the responsibility of making recruitment to Group 'B' services like Assistants' and Stenographers Grade 'C'.
- The Commission has a chairman and two members.

ELECTIONS (ARTICLE 324-329)

- The Constitution provides for an independent election commission to ensure free and fair election to the Parliament, the State legislature and the offices of President and Vice-President.
- Consists of Chief Election Commissioner +2 Election Commissioners. They all enjoy equal powers.
- The Chief Election Commissioner and other Election Commissioners are appointed by the President.
- Election Commissioners are appointed for a term of 5 yrs.
- They are not eligible for re-appointment. Also, they cannot hold any office of profit after their retirement.
- The Election Commission was established on 25th January, 1950 under Article 324 of the Constitution.
- The first Chief Election Commissioner was *Sukumar Sen.*

Functions

- Preparation of electoral rolls and keeping voters list updated.
- Recognition of various political parties and allotment of election symbols.

NITI AAYOG

- The Indian government has replaced Planing Commission with a new institution named **NITI Aayog (National Institution for Transforming India).**
- The Niti Aayog will comprise the following:

1. Prime Minister of India as the Chairperson.
2. Governing Council comprising the Chief Ministers of all the States and Lt. Governors of Territories.
3. Regional Councils will be formed to address specific issues and contingencies impacting more than one state or a region. These will be formed for a specified tenure. The Regional Councils will be convened by the Prime Minister and will comprise of the Chief Ministers of States and Lt. Governors of Territories in the region. These will be chaired by the Chairperson of the NITI Aayog or his nominee.
4. Experts, specialists and practitioners with relevant domain knowledge as special invitees nominated by the Prime Minister.

- The full-time organizational framework will comprise of, in addition to the Prime Minister as the Chairperson:

1. Vice-Chairperson : To be appointed by the Prime Minister.
2. Members : Full-time.
3. Part-time members : Maximum of 2 from leading universities research organizations and other relevant institutions in an ex-officio capacity. Part time members will be on a rotational basis.
4. Ex Officio members : Maximum of 4 members of the Council of Ministers to be nominated by the Prime Minister.
5. Chief Executive Officer : To be appointed by the Prime Minister for a fixed tenure, in the rank of Secretary to the Government of India.
6. Secretariat as deemed necessary.

FINANCE COMMISSION

- The constitution of the Finance Commission is laid down in Art. 280. The chairman must be a person having experience in public affairs; and the other four members also having wide experience in financial matters.
- It consists of Chairman and 4 other members.
- It shall be the duty of the Finance Commission to advice the President on matters such as the distribution between the Union and States of the net proceeds of taxes that is required to be shared.
- The Finance Commission is not a permanent body. It is dissolved after it has submitted its recommendations.

Important Amendments to the Constitution

First Amendment, 1951	:	Added Ninth Schedule.
Twenty-sixth Amendment, 1971	:	The privy and privileges of the former rulers of Indian States were abolished.
Thirty-first Amendment, 1973	:	The upper limit of representation of states was raised from 500 to 525. The upper limit for representation of the UTs was reduced from 25 to 20.
Thirty-sixth Amendment, 1975	:	Sikkim was made a full-fledged state of Indian Union and it was included in the First Schedule.
Thirty-eight Amendment, 1975	:	This act led to the amendment of Article 123, Article 213 and Article 352 which stated that the satisfaction of President or of Governor contained in these Articles would be called in question in any court of law.
Forty-second Amendment, 1976	:	This amendment was done in accordance with the recommendations of Swaran Singh Committee and included a number of amendments.
Forty-third Amendment, 1977	:	It provided for the restoration of the Jurisdiction of the Supreme Court and High Courts, curtailed by the enactment of the Constitution (Forty-Second Amendment) Act, 1976.
Forty-fourth Amendment, 1978	:	The right to property was deleted as Fundamental Right and was made a legal right.
Fifty-third Amendment, 1986	:	The Act grants statehood to the Union Territory of Mizoram, thus making it the 23rd State of the Indian Unions.
Fifty-sixth Amendment, 1987	:	The UT of Goa converted into Goa state through this amendment whereas Daman and Diu were organised under a new UT.
Seventy-third Amendment, 1992	:	It is concerning Panchayati Raj.
Seventy-fourth Amendment, 1992	:	It is regarding Municipal Boards and Corporations.
Eighty-ninth Amendment, 2003	:	It provides for constitution of a separate National Commission for Scheduled Tribes. (Earlier, there was a combined National Commission for both SC/STs).
Ninety-first Amendment, 2003	:	It is regarding restricting the total number of Ministers including Prime Minister/ Chief Minister in Lok Sabha and State Legislatures to 15% of the total number of the Union or State Legislatures.
Ninety-sixth Amendment, 2011	:	Amendment of 8th Schedule, it replaces 'Orissa' with 'Odisha'.
Ninety-eight Amendment, 2013	:	(Insert Article 371 J) To empower the Governor of Karnataka to take steps to develop Hydrabad Karnataka Region.
Ninety-ninth Amendment, 2015	:	The amendment is in toto quashed by Supreme Court on 16 October, 2015.
One hundredth Amendment, 2015	:	Exchange of certain enclave territories with Bangladesh and conferment of citizenship rights to residents of enclaves consequent to signing of Land Boundary Agreement (LBA) Treaty between India and Bangladesh.
One hundred and First Amendment, 2016	:	The act amends the constitution to introduce "The Goods and Services Tax (GST).
One hundred and Third Amendment, 2019	:	Provides 10 per cent reservation to Economically Weaker Sections of General Community.
One hundred and Fourth Amendment, 2019	:	The One Hundred and Fourth Amendment of the Constitution of India, extends the deadline for the cessation for the reservation of seats for members from Scheduled Castes and Scheduled Tribes in the Lok Sabha and State Legislative Assemblies by a period of 10 years. It shall come into force on the 25th day of January, 2020.
One hundred and Fifth Amendment Act, 2021	:	This Act restores the power of State Governments to identify and specify Socially and Economically Backward Classes (SEBCs).

NATIONAL SYMBOLS

STATE EMBLEM

- State Emblem of India is an adaptation from the Sarnath Lion Capital of Ashoka. It was adopted by the Government of India on January 26, 1950.
- In the adapted form, only three lions are visible, the fourth being hidden from the view.
- The wheel (Dharma Chakra) appears in relief in the centre of the abacus with a bull on the right and a horse on the left.
- The bell-shaped lotus has been omitted. The words ''Satyameva Jayate'' meaning ''Truth alone triumphs'' are inscribed below the Emblem in Devanagari script.

NATIONAL FLAG

- The National Flag of India is a horizontal tricolour of deep saffron (Kesari), white and dark green in equal proportion.
- In the centre of the white band there is a wheel in navy blue colour. It has 24 spokes.
- The ratio of the length and the breadth of the flag is 3 : 2. Its design was adopted by the Constituent Assembly of India on July 22, 1947.

NATIONAL ANTHEM

- Rabindranath Tagore's song 'Jana-gana-mana' was adopted by the Constituent Assembly as the National Anthem of India on January 24, 1950.

Jana-gana-mana-adhinayaka jaya he,
Bharata-bhagya-vidhata
Punjab-Sindh-Gujarat-Maratha-
Dravida-Utkala-Banga
Vindhya-Himachala-Yamuna-Ganga
Uchhala-jaladhi-taranga.
Tava subha name jage,
Tava subha asisa mange,
Gahe tava jaya gatha,
Jana-gana-mangala-dayak,
jaya he Bharata bhagya vidhata,
Jaya he, jaya he, jaya he,
Jaya jaya jaya, jaya he.

NATIONAL SONG

- Bankim Chandra Chatterji's 'Vande Mataram' which was a source of inspiration to the people in their struggle for freedom, has been adopted as National Song. It has an equal status with the National Anthem.

Vande Mataram
Sujalam, suphalam, malayaja-shitalam,
Shasya shyamalam, Mataram
Shubhrajyotsna, pulkita yaminim,
Phulla kusumita drumadalashobhinim,
Subhasinim sumadhura—bhashinim,
Sukhadam, Varadam, Mataram.

- **National Bird and Animal of India:** Peacock and Tiger.
- **National Aquatic Animal:** Dolphin
- **National Flower:** Lotus
- **National Calendar:** It was adopted on March 22, 1957. It has 365 days in the year and the first month of the year is Chaitra.

❒❒❒

5

Indian Economy

NATIONAL INCOME

- According to the National Income Committee (1949), "A national income estimate measures the volume of commodities and service turned out during a given period counted without duplication". Thus, national income measures the net value of goods and services produced in a country during a year and it also includes net earned foreign income. In other words, a total of national income measures the flow of goods and services in an economy.
- National income is a flow concept not a stock concept.
- In India, National income estimates are related with the financial year (April 1 to 31st March).
- The various concepts of national income are as follows:
  - *(i)* **GNP (Gross National Product):** GNP refers to the money value of total output or production of final goods and services produced by the nationals of a country during a given period of time, generally a year.
  - *(ii)* **NNP (Net National Product):** NNP is obtained by subtracting depreciation value from GNP. NNP can be calculated in two ways: *(a)* at market prices of goods and services and *(b)* at factor cost.
  - *(iii)* **National Income:** When NNP is obtained at factor cost, it is known as National Income. National Income is calculated by subtracting net indirect taxes from NNP at market prices. The obtained value is known as NNP at factor cost or National income.
  - *(iv)* **Personal Income:** Personal income is that income which is actually obtained by nationals. Personal income is obtained by subtracting corporate taxes and payments made for social securities provisions from national income and adding to it govern-ment transfer payments, business transfer payments and net interest paid by the government.

Methods of Measuring National Income

- According to Simon Kuznets, national income of a country is calculated by following mentioned three methods:
  - *(i)* **Product Method:** S. Kuznets gave a new name to this method, *i.e.*, product service method. In this method, net value of final goods and services produced in a country during a year is obtained and the total obtained value is called total final product.
  - *(ii)* **Income Method:** In this method, a total of net incomes earned by working people in different sectors and commercial enterprises is obtained.
  - *(iii)* **Consumption Method:** It is also called expenditure method. Income is either spent on consumption or saved. Hence, national income is the addition of total consumption and total savings.
- In India, a combination of production method and income method is used for measuring estimating national income.
- For measuring national income in India, in 1868, the first attempt was made by *Dada Bhai Nauroji*. He, in his book, *"Poverty and Un-British Rule in India"*, estimated Indian per capita annual income at a level of ₹ 20.
- After independence, the Government of India appointed the National Income Committee in August, 1949, under the Chairmanship of Prof. P.C. Mahalanobies, to compile authoritative estimates of national income.
- Estimation and publishing of National Income data by CSO (Central Statistical Organization) is done every year.
- National income includes the contribution of three sectors--primary sector, secondary sector, Tertiary sector.
- Under Primary Sector—Agriculture, Forest, Fisheries and allied sector are included.
- Under Secondary Sector—Manufacturing, Construction, Electricity, Gas and Water Supply are included.
- Under Teritiary Sector—Trade, Transport, Communication, Banking, Insurance, Real Estate, Community and Personal Services are included.
- The contribution of primary sector in GDP was 55.4% in 1950-1951. But now the share of primary sector in national income has come down. In 2020-21, the contribution of primary sector in GDP was 19.9%.
- The contribution of secondary sector has shown a steady increase from 15% in 1950-51 to 25.8% in 2020-21.
- The contribution of tertiary sector indicated a sharp improvement from 29.6% in 1950-51 to about 54.3% in 2020-21.
- At present estimation of national income is based on the base year of 2011-2012.

POPULATION

Census-2011: Population, Density, Decadal Growth Rate

S.N.	State/UTs	Population		Density		Decadal G. (%)
		2001	2011	2001	2011	2001–2011
1.	J&K	10,143,700	1,25,41,302	100	124	23.6
2.	Himachal Pradesh	6,077,900	68,64,602	109	123	12.9
3.	Punjab	24,358,999	2,77,43,338	484	551	13.9
4.	Chandigarh	900,635	10,55,450	7,900	9258	17.2
5.	Uttarakhand	8,489,349	1,00,86,292	159	189	18.8
6.	Haryana	21,144,564	2,53,51,462	478	573	19.9
7.	Delhi	13,850,507	1,67,87,941	9,340	11320	21.2
8.	Rajasthan	56,507,188	6,85,48,437	165	200	21.3
9.	Uttar Pradesh	166,197,921	19,98,12,341	690	829	20.2
10.	Bihar	82,998,509	10,40,99,452	881	1106	25.4
11.	Sikkim	540,851	6,10,577	76	86	12.9
12.	Arunachal Pradesh	1,097,968	13,83,727	13	17	26.0
13.	Nagaland	1,990,036	19,78,502	120	119	–0.6
14.	Manipur	2,293,896	28,55,794	103	128	31.79
15.	Mizoram	888,573	10,97,206	42	52	23.5
16.	Tripura	3,199,203	36,73,917	305	350	14.8
17.	Meghalaya	2,318,822	29,66,889	103	132	27.9
18.	Assam	26,655,528	3,12,05,576	340	398	17.1
19.	West Bengal	80,176,197	9,12,76,115	903	1028	13.8
20.	Jharkhand	26,945,829	3,29,88,134	338	414	22.4
21.	Odisha	36,804,660	4,19,74,218	236	270	14.0
22.	Chhattisgarh	20,833,803	2,55,45,198	154	189	22.6
23.	Madhya Pradesh	60,348,023	7,26,26,809	196	236	20.3
24.	Gujarat	50,671,017	6,04,39,692	258	308	19.3
25.	Daman & Diu	158,204	2,43,247	1,413	2191	53.8
26.	Dadra & N. Haveli	220,490	3,43,709	449	700	55.9
27.	Maharashtra	96,878,627	11,23,74,333	315	365	16.0
28.	Andhra Pradesh	76,210,007	4,93,86,799	277	308	11.0
29.	Karnataka	52,850,562	6,10,95,297	276	319	15.6
30.	Goa	1,347,668	14,58,545	364	394	8.2
31.	Lakshadweep	60,650	64,473	1,895	2149	6.3
32.	Kerala	31,841,374	3,34,06,061	819	860	4.9
33.	Tamil Nadu	62,405,679	7,21,47,030	480	555	15.6
34.	Puducherry	974,345	12,47,953	2,030	2546	28.1
35.	Andaman & Nicobar Islands	356,152	3,80,581	43	46	6.9
36.	Telangana	—	3,51,93,978	—	307	13.58
	India	**1,028,737,436**	**1,21,08,54,977**	**325**	**382**	**17.7**

POVERTY

- There are two types of common standards in economic literature for the measurement of poverty:
    1. **Absolute Poverty:** In the absolute standard, minimum physical quantities of cereals, pulses, milk, butter, etc. are determined for a subsistence level and then the price quotations converted into monetary terms the physical quantities. Aggregating all of the quantities included, a figure expressing per capita consumer expenditure is determined. The population whose level of income or expenditure below the figure, is considered to be below the poverty line.
    2. **Relative Standard:** According to the relative standard, income distribution of the population in different fractile groups is estimated and a comparison of the levels of living of the top 5 to 10 per cent with the bottom 5 to 10 per cent of the population reflects the relative standards of poverty.
- The defect of the relative standard approach is that it indicates the relative position of different segments of the population in the income hierarchy. Even in affluent societies, such pockets of poverty exist. But for underdeveloped countries, it is the existence of mass poverty that is the cause for concern.
- The NITI Aayog, the nodal agency for estimating the number and proportion of people living below the poverty line at national and state levels, separately for rural and urban areas, makes poverty estimates based on a large sample survey of household consumption expenditure carried out by the National Sample Survey Office (NSSO) approximately every five years.
- For estimation and review of poverty, the Planning Commission constituted an expert group under the chairmanship of Prof. Suresh D. Tendulkar in December 2005, which submitted its report in December 2009.
- The recomputed poverty estimates for the years 1993-94 and 2004-05 as recommended by the Tendulkar Committee have been accepted by the Planning Commission.
- As per the Tendulkar Committee Report, the national poverty line at 2004-05 prices was a monthly per capita consumption expenditure of ₹ 446.68 in rural and ₹ 578.80 in urban areas in 2004-05.

Poverty Line

Committee	Year	Per capita Expenditure per day (₹)		Per capita Average Montly Expenditure (₹)		All India Poverty Line (Average Monthly Expenditure per Family of 5)	
		Rural	Urban	Rural	Urban	Rural	Urban
Rangarajan	2011-12	32.4	46.9	972	1407	4760	7035
	2009-10	26.7	39.9	801	1198	4005	5990
Tendulkar	2011-12	27.2	33.3	816	1000	4080	5000
	2009-10	22.4	28.7	673	860	3365	4300

Various Employment Generations Programmes

S.N.	Programme	Year of beginning	Objective
1.	Community Development Programme (CDP)	1952	Overall development of rural areas with people's participation.
2.	Green Revolution	1966-67	To increase the foodgrains, specially wheat production.
3.	Drought-Prone Area Programme (DPAP)	1973	To try an expedient for protection from drought by achieving environmental balance and by developing the ground water.
4.	Command Area Development Programme (CADP)	1974-75	To ensure better and rapid utilisation of irrigation capacities of medium and large projects.
5.	Twenty Point Programme (TPP)	1975	Poverty eradication and raising the standard of living.
6.	Antyodaya Yojana	1977-78	To make the poorest families of the village economically independent (only in Rajasthan State).

S.N.	Programme	Year of beginning	Objective
7.	Training Rural Youth for Self-Employment (TRYSEM)	Aug., 15, 1979	Programme of training rural youth for self-employment.
8.	Integrated Rural Development Programme (IRDP)	Oct., 2, 1980	All-round development of the rural poor through a programme of asset endowment for self-employment.
9.	National Rural Employment Programme (NREP)	1980	To provide profitable employment opportunities to the rural poor.
10.	Development of Women and Children in Rural Areas (DWCRA)	Sept. 1982	To provide suitable opportunities of self-employment to the women belonging to the rural families who are living below the poverty line.
11.	Comprehensive Crop Insurance Scheme	April 1, 1985	For insurance of agricultural crops.
12.	Council for Advancement of People's Action and Rural Technology (CAPART)	Sept. 1, 1986	To provide assistance for rural prosperity.
13.	Jawahar Rozgar Yojana	April 1989	For providing employment to rural unemployed.
14.	Nehru Rozgar Yojana	Oct. 1989	For providing employment to urban unemployed.
15.	Supply of Improved Toolkits to Rural Artisans	July 1992	To supply modern toolkits to the rural craftsmen except the weavers, tailors, embroiders and tobacco labourers who are living below the poverty line.
16.	Employment Assurance Scheme (EAS)	Oct., 2, 1993	To provide employment of at least 100 days in a year in villages.
17.	District Rural Development Agency (DRDA)	1993	To provide financial assistance for rural development.
18.	Mahila Samridhi Yojana	2 Oct., 1993	To encourage the rural women to deposit in Post-office Saving Account.
19.	Ganga Kalyan Yojana	1997-98	To provide financial assistance to farmers for exploring and developing ground and surface water resources.
20.	Kasturba Gandhi Education Scheme	Aug., 15, 1997	To establish girls schools in districts having low female literacy rate.
21.	Swarna Jayanti Shahari Rozgar Yojana (SJSRY)	Dec., 1997	To provide gainful employment to urban unemployed and under-employed poor through self-employment or wage-employment.
22.	Bhagya Shree Bal Kalyan Policy	Oct., 19, 1998	To uplift the girls conditions.
23.	Rajrajeshwari Mahila Kalyan Yojana	Oct., 19, 1998	To provide insurance protection to women.
24.	Swarna Jayanti Gram Swarozgar Yojana	April 1999	For eliminating Rural poverty and unemployment and promoting self-employment.
25.	Jan Shree Bima Yojana	Aug., 10, 2000	Providing Insurance Security to people living below poverty line.
26.	Antyodaya Anna Yojana	Dec., 25, 2000	To provide food security to poor.
27.	Ashraya Bima Yojana	June 2001	To provide compensation to labourers who have lost their employment.
28.	Pradhan Mantri Gram Sadak Yojana (PMGSY)	Dec., 25, 2000	To line all villages with Pacca Road.
29.	Mahatma Gandhi National Rural Employment Guarantee Act (MNREGA)	Feb., 2, 2006	To provide at least 100 days wage-employment in rural areas.
30.	Pradhan Mantri Kaushal Vikas Yojana	March 2015	To Provide skill training to youth.
31.	Pradhan Mantri Jeevan Jyoti Bima Yojana	2015-16	Renewable one year life cover of ₹ 2 lakh to all savings bank account holders in the age group of 18-50 years covering death due to any reason for a premium of ₹ 330 per annum per sub-scriber.

S.N.	Programme	Year of beginning	Objective
32.	Pradhan Mantri Suraksha Bima Yojana	2015-16	Renewable one year accidental death cum disability to all savings bank account holders in the age group of 18-70 years for a premium of ₹ 12 per annum per subscriber.
33.	Atal Pension Yojana	2015-16	Pension to the labourers of unorganized sector
34.	Deen Dayal Upadhyay Grameen Kaushlya Yojana	Sep. 24, 2015	Skill development of rural youth.
35.	Atal Innovation Mission	2015-16	Atal Innovation Mission and Self Employement and Talent Utilisation.
36.	Swachh Bharat Mission	Oct. 2, 2014	Providing access to clean toilet to all rural households and initiating solid and liquid waste management activities in all gram panchayats.
37.	Pandit Deen Dayal Upadhyay Shramev Jayate Scheme	Oct. 16, 2014	To improve employability, skill development and other conveniences for labour.
38.	Shyama Prasad Mukherjee Rurban Mission	Sept. 16, 2015	Setting up 300 village clusters by 2019-20 across the country with all possible urban amenities.
39.	HriDay	2015-16	Heritage City Development and Augmentation Yojana to preserve and rejuvenate the rich cultural heritage of the country through the identified 12 cities.
40.	PRASAD	2015-16	National Mission on Pilgrimage Rejuvenation and Spiritual Augmentation Drive (PRASAD).
41.	'Housing for all by 2022'	June 18, 2015	Providing affordable housing in Urban Areas.
42.	Pradhan Mantri Awas Yojana	June 25, 2015	Providing housing facilities in rural areas.
43.	Startup India, Standup India	16 Jan., 2016	To provide Support to all start-up businesses in all aspects of doing business in India.
44.	Pradhan Mantri Ujjwala Yojana	May 1, 2016	Launched to Provide free LPG connection to women from below poverty line families.
45.	Urja Ganga Yojana (UGY)	Oct. 24, 2016	To provide the accessibility of approx, 5 Lakh LPG gas cylinders within next 5 years.
46.	Pradhan Mantri Surakshit Matritva Abhiyan	June 9, 2016	To improve the quality and coverage of Antenatal care with Diagnostics and counselling Services as part of Reproductive Maternal Neonatal Child and Adolescent Health.
47.	Pradhan Mantri Vittiya Saksharta Abhiyan (PMVSA)	Dec. 1, 2016	To go for cashless transaction and payment modes like using credit or debit cards or the payment wallets to reduce the malpractice in the country.
48.	Digi Dhan Vyapar Yojana (DDVY)	Dec. 15, 2016	To increase the "Cashless Transactions".
49.	Pradhan Mantri Garib Kalyan Yojana (PMGKY)	Dec. 2016	To improve the financial position of the poor people.
50.	Atal Amrit Abhiyan (AAA)	Dec. 25, 2016	To provide health insurance against 437 illnesses including 5 critical diseases.
51.	Ayushman Bharat Programme	Sept. 23, 2018	To provide health facility to poor family.
52.	Atmanirbhar Bharat Abhiyan	May, 2020	Economic stimulus relief package announced for the poor to overcome difficulties caused by Coronavirus.
53.	SMILE	Feb. 12, 2022	Support for marginalised Individuals for Livelihood & Enterprieses.

AGRICULTURE

- Agriculture is an important sector of the economy. Though the share of agriculture in national income has come down since the inception of planning era in the economy but still it has substantial share in GDP.
- In terms of composition, out of the total share of 14.65 per cent that agriculture and allied sector had in GDP in 2019-20.
- Agriculture in our country provides livelihood to about 49% of the population.
- Gross Capital Formation (GCF) in Agriculture and Allied sector relative to GVA in this sector has been snowing a fluctuating trent from 18.3 per cent in 2011-12 to 18.8 per cent in 2021-22.
- Agriculture provides raw materials to various industries

and other agro-based industries. Cotton and Jute textile industries, Sugar, Vanaspati industry etc. are directly dependent on agriculture.

- India's foreign trade is deeply associated with Agriculture Sector. Value of agriculture exports to total exports of the country was 13.8 per cent in 2013. But the share of agriculture has come down in foreign trade at present. Share of agriculture in foreign trade was 11.76 per cent in 2018-19.

Various Crops and their producing states

Crops/Groups of Crops	Producing State (In Descending Order)
I. Foodgrains	
Rice	West Bengal, Uttar Pradesh, Punjab
Wheat	Uttar Pradesh, Madhya Pradesh, Punjab
Maize	Karnataka, Madhya Pradesh, Maharashtra
Total Nutri/ Coarse Cereals	Karnataka, Rajasthan, Maharashtra
Gram	Maharashtra, Madhya Pradesh, Rajasthan
Tur	Maharashtra, Karnataka, Uttar Pradesh
Total Pulses	Madhya Pradesh, Maharashtra, Rajasthan
Total Food-grains	Uttar Pradesh, Madhya Pradesh, Punjab
II. Oilseeds	
Groundnut	Gujarat, Rajasthan, Tamil Nadu
Rapeseed & Mustard	Rajasthan, Madhya Pradesh, Haryana
Soyabean	Maharashtra, Madhya Pradesh, Rajasthan
Sunflower	Karnataka, Telangana, Odisha
Total Oilseeds	Rajasthan, Madhya Pradesh, Gujarat
III. Other Cash Crops	
Sugarcane	Uttar Pradesh, Maharashtra, Karnataka
Cotton	Gujarat, Maharashtra, Telangana
Jute & Mesta	West Bengal, Assam, Bihar,

Source: Economic Survey 2022-23

ECONOMIC PLANNING

- Economic Planning refers to any directing or planning of economic activity outside the mechanisms of the market. Planning is an economic mechanism for resources allocation and decision-making held in contrast with the market mechanism. Economic Planning can be applied to production, investment, distribution or all three of these functions.
- In the year 1934, Sir M. Visheshvraya wrote a book named 'Planned Economy for India', which was the first attempt in this direction.
- In 1938, the Indian National Congress, under the leadership of Pt. Jawaharlal Nehru, made a National Planning Committee.
- In 1944, eight industrialists of Bombay (Now Mumbai) presented a well-organised plan called 'The Bombay Plan'.
- Inspired by the economic views of Mahatma Gandhi, Shri Sriman Narayan Constructed a plan in 1944 which is known as 'Gandhian Plan'.
- Mr. M.N. Rao, chairman of post-war Reconstruction Committee of Indian Trade Union, introduced a 'People's Plan' in April 1945.
- In January 1950, Shri Jaiprakash Narayan published a plan called 'Sarvodaya Plan'.
- The Planning Commission was constituted on 15th March, 1950, by the Government of India.
- There is no account of Planning Commission in the Indian Constitution. Therefore, it was constituted in the form of an advisory and specialised institution by means of a document of the Government. Consequently, the Government has been changing its nature and organisation from time to time.
- Pt. Jawaharlal Nehru was appointed as the first Chairman of Planning Commission.
- The Prime Minister is the ex-officio chairman of Planning Commission.
- National Development Council (NDC) is a non-statutory body which was constituted to build co-operation between the States and the Planning Commission for economic planning.
- The National Development Council (NDC) was constituted on 6th August, 1952. The Prime Minister is the chairman and the secretary of the Planning Commission remains its secretary.

Niti Aayog

- The National Institution for Transforming India, also called NITI Aayog, was formed via a resolution of the Union Cabinet on January 1, 2015. NITI Aayog is the premier policy 'Think Tank' of the Government of India, providing both directional and policy inputs. While designing strategic and long term policies and programmes for the Government of India, NITI Aayog also provides relevant technical advice to the Centre and States.
- The Government of India, in keeping with its reform agenda, constituted the NITI Aayog to replace the Planning Commission instituted in 1950. This was done in order to

better serve the needs and aspirations of the people of India. An important evolutionary change from the past, NITI Aayog acts as the quintessential platform of the Government of India to bring States to act together in national interest, and thereby fosters Cooperative Federalism.

- At the core of NITI Aayog's creation are two hubs - **Team India Hub** and the **Knowledge and Innovation Hub**. The Team India Hub leads the engagement of states with the Central government, while the Knowledge and Innovation Hub builds NITI's think-tank capabilities. These hubs reflect the two key tasks of the Aayog. NITI Aayog is also developing itself as a State of the Art Resource Centre, with the necessary resources, knowledge and skills, that will enable it to act with speed, promote research and innovation, provide strategic policy vision for the government, and deal with contingent issues.

First Five Year Plan (1951-1956)

- The First Five Year Plan began on April 1, 1951 and ended on March 31, 1956.
- The plan was based on the model of Harrod-Domer.
- The plan has given highest priority to agriculture, irrigation and power projects.
- The achievements of this plan were more than its targets. The annual compound growth rate of national income was 3.6% (target 2.1%) during the planning period.
- The per capita income growth rate was 1.8% and ICOR was 2.95 during this plan.

Second Five Year Plan (1956-1961)

- Based on the model prepared by Prof. P.C. Mahalnobis, the Second Five Year Plan was started on April 1, 1956 and ended on March 31, 1961.
- The fundamental objective of this plan was to initiate and accelerate the process of industrial- isation so that the development of Indian economy takes a firm base.
- The Industrial policy, 1956 (During Second Five Year Plan), was based on the objective of establishing the socialistic pattern of society.
- Large industries including steel plants (Durgapur, Bhilai and Rourkela) were set up. The Locomotive factory at Chittaranjan and Coach factory at Perambur were other major projects of this period.

Third Five Year Plan (1961-1966)

- This plan started on April 1, 1961 and ended on March 31, 1966.
- The basic aim of this plan was to push the economy upto the take-off stage development.
- This plan set as its goal the establishment of a self-reliant and self-generating economy.
- In this plan top priority was given to agriculture but it also laid adequate emphasis on the development of basic industries, which were vitally necessary for rapid economic development of the country.

Annual Plans (1966-1969)

- The Fourth Plan was scheduled to begin from April 1, 1966, but due to the unfortunate failure of third plan, the production in various sector of the economy became stagnant.
- In 1966, the Government of India declared the devaluation of rupee, with a view to increase the exports of the country. However, favourable results couldnot be obtained. Under these circumstances the fourth plan was postponed for sometime and Three Annual Plans were implemented during this period.
- Some of the economists called this period, *i.e.* from 1966 to 1969 as 'Plan Holiday' because no regular planning was done during this period.

Fourth Five Year Plan (1969-1974)

- The Fourth Plan started on April 1, 1969 and ended on March 31, 1974.
- Growth with stability and progress towards self-reliance were the prime objective of the plan.
- The plan aimed at 5.5 per cent average rate of growth in the national income.

Fifth Five Year Plan (1974-1979)

- The Fifth Five Year Plan began on April 1, 1974 which was scheduled to end on March 31, 1979.
- The final draft of the Fifth Plan was prepared and launched by D.P. Dhar proposed to achieve the two main objectives— removal of poverty and attainment of self-reliance.
- The plan objective, 'removal of poverty is also known as the slogan 'Garibi Hatao'.
- This plan also gave high priority to bring inflation under control and to achieve stability in economic situation.

Sixth Five Year Plan (1980-1985)

- The Janta Government ended the Fifth Five Year Plan, one year to its term, *i.e.,* only within four years span (1974-78) and introduced a new plan since April 1, 1978. This plan was named as the "Rolling Plan".
- In 1980, the Sixth Plan (Rolling Plan) prepared by Janta Government was abandoned by the Congress Government and a new Sixth Plan was introduced for the period 1980-85.

- The focus of Janta Government's Sixth Plan (Rolling Plan) was enlargement of the employment potential in agriculture and allied activities, whereas the focus of Congress Sixth Plan was to solve the problem of poverty by creating conditions of an expanding economy.

Seventh Five Year Plan (1985-1990)

- The 7th plan began on April 1, 1985 and ended on March 31, 1990.
- This plan emphasised policies and programmes which aimed at rapid growth in foodgrains production, increased employment opportunities and productivity within the framework of basic tenents of planning, *i.e.*, growth, modernisation, self-reliance and social justice.

Eighth Five Year Plan (1992-1997)

- The 8th Five Year Plan which was supposed to start from April 1, 1990 could not be started on scheduled time because of some political changes at the Centre during 1990-92.
- NDC ratified the format of the Plan in one of its meeting held on May 23, 1992. This Plan began on April 1, 1992 which ended on March 31, 1997.
- The Plan has initiated the process of fiscal reforms as also of economic reforms with a view to provide a new dynamism to economy.
- Fundamental objective of this Plan was human development.
- Pradhanmantri Rojgar Yojana (1993) was started during this Plan.

Ninth Five Year Plan (1997-2002)

- The 9th Plan began on April 1, 1997 and ended on March 31, 2007.
- 'Growth with Equity and Distributive Justice' was determined as the main focus of the Ninth Plan. In order to achieve this focus, four fields were identified which are as follows:
  (*i*) Quality of life
  (*ii*) Employment promotion
  (*iii*) Regional imbalance
  (*iv*) Self-dependence

Tenth Five Year Plan (2002-2007)

- The 10th Plan began on April 1, 2002 and ended on March 31, 2007.
- The Plan has not been able to achieve its target of 8 per cent growth of GDP, but has taken the economy to a higher trajectory of growth rate at 7.8 per cent as against 5.5 per cent in the 9th Plan.
- Gross domestic savings averaged 28.2 per cent in 10th Plan as against 23.1 per cent in the 9th plan.
- The economy has been able to reduce its ICOR from a level of 4.3 during the 9th Plan to a level of 4.2 during the 10th Plan.
- Our foreign exchange reserve reached a level of US $ 185 billion in February 2007. This is another indication of the strength of the economy.

Eleventh Five Year Plan (2007-12)

- The 11th Plan began on April 1, 2007 and ended on March 31, 2012.
- The 11th Plan visualises "Faster and more inclusive growth" as its objective.
- 11th Plan has fixed a target of pushing up overall GDP growth to an average rate of 9.0 per cent.

Twelfth Five Year Plan (2012-17)

- The 12th Plan began on April 1, 2012 and ended on March 31, 2017.
- Real GDP Growth Rate of 8.0 per cent.
- Agriculture Growth Rate of 4.0 per cent.
- Manufacturing Growth Rate of 7.1 per cent.
- Industrial Sector Growth Rate of 7.6 per cent.
- Service Sector Growth Rate of 9.0 per cent.
- Generate 50 million new work opportunities.
- Eliminate gender and social gap in school enrolment.
- Reduce Total Fertility Rate to 2.1 by the end of Twelfth Five Year Plan.

15-Year Vision Plan

With the end of the Twelfth Plan in March 2017 the era of five year plans came to an end. NITI Aayog has come forward with a draft 15-year vision plan to catapult the country's economy to more than three times as compared to the present day. The new plan is set to replace the centralised five-year plans the country has been following for decades. The new plan is accompanied by shorter sub-plans—a seven-year strategy for 2017-24, and a three-year 'Action Agenda' from 2017-18 to 2019-20. No less than 300 specific action points covering a wide range of sectors have been drawn up as part of the 15-year vision. The 15-year vision document has a seven-year strategy document for 2017-24 as the 'National Development Agenda'. Separately, a three-year 'Action Agenda' from 2017-18 to 2019-20 is also under works to assess funding requirements. The three-year agenda is further divided into seven parts, with a number of specific action points for each part to boost economic growth. India's urban population is expected to increase by 22 crores by 2031. The plan is likely to lay emphasis on urban development, taking a note from China's elaborate long-term development agenda.

COMMUNITY DEVELOPMENT

Community development is a continuous process of social action by which the people of a community:

- Define their common and group needs;
- Organize themselves formally and informally for democratic planning and action;
- Make group and individual plans to meet their needs and solve their problems;
- Execute their plans with maximum reliance upon their own resources; and
- Supplement their resources from outside the community, when necessary with services and material.

According to Carl Tylor, "community development is a method by which people in villages are involved in helping to improve their own economic and social conditions and thereby they became effective working groups in the programme of their national development". This carries the assumption that people became dynamic if they are permitted to make their own decisions end are helped to carry on the programme.

Community Development Programme

The community development programme was started in India, just after independence (1952). It was a multi project programme with the aim of an overall development of rural people. This programme consisted of agriculture, animal husbandry, irrigation, cooperation, public wealth, education, social education, communication, village industries etc. There are officials for each activity at district level to plan execute and evaluate the programme up to the village level.

Essential Elements of Community Development

The Successful Community Development programme stresses the following basic elements:

- Activities undertaken must correspond to the basic needs of the community. The first projects should be initiated in response to the expressed needs of people.
- There should be concerted action and the establishment of multi-purpose programme.
- Change in the attitudes of the people is as important as the material achievement through Community Development during the initial stages of development.
- Community Development aims at increased and better participation of the people in community affairs, revitalization of existing forms of local government and transition towards effective local administration where it is not yet functioning.
- The identification, encouragement and training of local leadership should be a basic objective in any programme.
- Greater reliance on the participation of women and youth in community projects invigorates development programmes, establishes them on a wide bases and success long-range expansion.
- To be fully effective, community self help projects require both internal and external assistance from the government.

Objectives of the Community Development Programme

In India, the objective behind the community development programme is to develop the resources of the people numbering about 640 millions who form the rural population. The elements of development are:

- General: Farm, home, public service and village community.
- Specific: To bring improvement in the production of crops and animals, living conditions, health and education of the people.
- Elements which need change are: People-men, women and youth.
- Change agents: The change agents are:
  - ❑ Voluntary local leaders-members of Panchayats, village and Block Advisory Committees etc.
  - ❑ Professional community development workers-Village Level Workers, extension officers, block development officers etc.

Causes of failure

The causes of the failure of the community development programme are as follows:

- Uneven distribution of the benefits of the programme
- Absence of clearly defined priorities in the programme.
- Failure to evoke popular response.
- Unqualified personnel
- Lack of functional responsibility.

❑❑❑

6

General Science

IMPORTANT INVENTIONS

Name of Invention	Inventor	Nationality	Year
Aeroplane	Orville & Wilbur Wright	U.S.A.	1903
Ball-Point Pen	John J. Loud	U.S.A.	1888
Barometer	Evangelista Torricelli	Italy	1644
Bicycle	Kirkpatrick Macmillan	Britain	1839-40
Bifocal Lens	Benjamin Franklin	U.S.A.	1780
Car (Petrol)	Karl Benz	Germany	1888
Celluloid	Alexander Parkes	Britain	1861
Cinema	Nicolas & Jean Lumiere	France	1895
Clock (mechanical)	I-Hsing & Liang Ling-Tsan	China	1725
Diesel Engine	Rudolf Diesel	Germany	1895
Dynamo	Hypolite Pixii	France	1832
Electric Lamp	Thomas Alva Edison	U.S.A.	1879
Electric Motor (DC)	Zenobe Gramme	Belgium	1873
Electric Motor (AC)	Nikola Tesla	U.S.A.	1888
Electro-magnet	William Sturgeon	Britain	1824
Electronic Computer	Dr. Alan M. Turing	Britain	1943
Film (moving outlines)	Louis Prince	France	1885
Film (musical sound)	Dr. Le de Forest	U.S.A.	1923
Fountain Pen	Lewis E. Waterman	U.S.A.	1884
Gramophone	Thomas Alva Edison	U.S.A.	1878
Helicopter	Etienne Oehmichen	France	1924
Jet Engine	Sir Frank Whittle	Britain	1937
Laser	Charles H. Townes	U.S.A.	1960
Lift (Mechanical)	Elisha G. Otis	U.S.A.	1852
Locomotive	Richard Trevithick	Britain	1804
Machine Gun	James Puckle	Britain	1718
Microphone	Alexander Graham Bell	U.S.A.	1876
Microscope	Z. Janssen	Netherlands	1590
Motor Cycle	G. Daimler	Germany	1885
Photography (on film)	John Carbutt	U.S.A.	1888
Printing Press	Johann Gutenberg	Germany	c.1455
Razor (safety)	King C. Gillette	U.S.A.	1895
Refrigerator	James Harrison & Alexander Catlin	U.S.A.	1850
Safety Pin	Walter Hunt	U.S.A.	1849
Sewing machine	Barthelemy Thimmonnier	France	1829
Ship (steam)	J.C. Perier	France	1775
Ship (turbine)	Hon. Sir C. Parsons	Britain	1894
Skyscraper	W. Le Baron Jenny	U.S.A.	1882
Slide Rule	William Oughtred	Britain	1621
Steam Engine (condenser)	James Watt	Britain	1765
Steel Production	Henry Bessemer	Britain	1855
Steel (stainless)	Harry Brearley	Britain	1913
Submarine	David Bushnell	U.S.A.	1776

Name of Invention	Inventor	Nationality	Year
Tank	Sir Ernest Swinton	Britain	1914
Telegraph	M. Lammond	France	1787
Telegraph Code	Samuel F.B. Morse	U.S.A.	1837
Telephone (perfected)	Alexander Graham Bell	U.S.A.	1876
Television (mechanical)	John Logie Baird	Britain	1926
Television (electronic)	P.T. Farnsworth	U.S.A.	1927
Thermometer	Galileo Galilei	Italy	1593
Transformer	Michael Faraday	Britain	1831
Transistor	Bardeen, Shockley & Brattain	U.S.A.	1948
Washing Machine (elec.)	Hurley Machine Co.	U.S.A.	1907
Zip-Fastener	W.L. Judson	U.S.A.	1891

IMPORTANT DISCOVERIES

Discovery	Discoverer	Nationality	Year
Aluminium	Hans Christian Oerstedt	Denmark	1827
Atomic number	Henry Moseley	England	1913
Atomic structure of matter	John Dalton	England	1803
Chlorine	C.W. Scheele	Sweden	1774
Electromagnetic induction	Michael Faraday	England	1831
Electromagnetic waves	Heinrich Hertz	Germany	1886
Electromagnetism	Hans Christian Oersted	Denmark	1920
Electron	Sir Joseph Thomson	England	1897
General theory of relativity	Albert Einstein	Switzerland	1915
Hydrogen	Henry Cavendish	England	1766
Law of electric conduction	Georg Ohm	Germany	1827
Law of electromagnetism	Andre Ampere	France	1826
Law of falling bodies	Galileo	Italy	1590
Laws of gravitation & motion	Isaac Newton	England	1687
Laws of planetary motion	Johannes Kepler	Germany	1609-10
Magnesium	Sir Humphry Davy	England	1808
Neptune (Planet)	Johann Galle	Germany	1846
Neutron	James Chadwick	England	1932
Nickel	Axel Cronstedt	Sweden	1751
Nitrogen	Daniel Rutherford	England	1772
Oxygen	Joseph Priestly; C.W. Scheele	England; Sweden	1772
Ozone	Christian Schonbein	Germany	1839
Pluto (Planet)	Clyde Tombaugh	U.S.A	1930
Plutonium	G.T. Seaborg	U.S.A	1940
Proton	Ernest Rutherford	England	1919
Quantum Theory	Max Planck	Germany	1900
Radioactivity	Antoine Bacquerel	France	1896
Radium	Pierre & Marie Curie	France	1898
Silicon	Jons Berzelius	Sweden	1824
Special theory of relativity	Albert Einstein	Switzerland	1905
Sun as centre of solar system	Copernicus	Poland	1543
Uranium	Martin Klaproth	Germany	1789
Uranus (Planet)	William Herschel	England	1781
X-rays	Wilhelm Roentgen	Germany	1895

GEOGRAPHICAL EXPLORATIONS/DISCOVERIES

Place	Explorer/Discoverer	Nationality	Year
America	Christopher Columbus	Italy	1492
Hawaii Islands (Sandwich Islands)	Captain James Cook	England	1778
Newfoundland	John Cabot	England	1497
New Zealand	Abel Janszoon Tasman	Holland	1642
North Pole	Robert Peary	USA	1909
Sea Route to India (via Cape of Good Hope)	Vasco da Gama	Portugal	1498
South Pole	Roald Amundsen	Norway	1911

SCIENTIFIC INSTRUMENTS

Name of Instrument	*Used for*
Altimeter	measuring altitude
Ammeter	measuring strength of an electric current
Anemometer	measuring the velocity of wind
Audiometer	measuring level of hearing
Barometer	measuring atmospheric pressure
Callipers	measuring the internal and external diameters of tubes
Calorimeter	measuring quantity of heat
Compass	finding out direction
Dynamo	converting mechanical energy into electrical energy
Eudiometer	measuring volume changes during chemical reactions between gases
Galvanometer	detecting and determining the strength of small electric currents
Hydrometer	measuring specific gravity of a liquid
Hygrometer	measuring the humidity in the atmosphere
Lactometer	measuring the purity of milk
Manometer	measuring the gaseous pressure
Micrometer	measuring minute distances, angles, etc.
Microscope	seeing magnified view of very small objects
Photometer	measuring intensity of light from distant stars
Pyrometer	measuring high temperatures
Radar	detecting and finding the presence and location of moving objects like aircraft, missile, etc.
Radiometer	measuring the emission of radiant energy
Rain Gauge	measuring the amount of rainfall
Seismograph	measuring and recording the intensity and origin of earthquake shocks
Sextant	measuring altitude and angular distances between two objects or heavenly bodies
Spectrometer	measuring the refractive indices
Spherometer	measuring the curvature of spherical objects/surface
Sphygmomanometer	measuring blood pressure
Stethoscope	ascertaining the condition of heart and lungs by listening to their function
Stroboscope	viewing objects that are moving rapidly with a periodic motion as if they were at rest
Tachometer	measuring the rate of revolution or angular speed of a revolving shaft
Telescope	viewing magnified images of distant objects
Theodolite	measuring the horizontal and vertical angles
Thermocouple	measuring the temperature inside furnaces and jet engines
Thermometer	measuring human body temperature
Thermostat	regulating constant temperature
Ultrasonoscope	measuring utrasonic sounds
Viscometer	measuring the viscosity of a fluid
Voltmeter	measuring potential difference between two points.

DISEASES AND THE PARTS OF BODY THEY AFFECT

Disease	*Part of body affected*	*Disease*	*Part of body affected*
AIDS	Immune system of body	Jaundice	Liver
Arthritis	Inflammation of joints	Meningitis	Brain or spinal cord
Asthma	Lungs	Pleurisy	Pleura (inflammation of)
Cataract	Eyes	Polio	motor neurons
Conjunctivitis	Eyes	Pneumonia	Lungs
Diabetes	Pancreas	Pyorrhoea	Sockets of teeth
Diphtheria	Throat	Tuberculosis	Lungs
Glaucoma	Eyes	Typhoid	Intestine
Eczema	Skin	Malaria	Spleen
Goitre	Front of the neck (due to enlargement of thyroid gland)	Leukaemia	Blood
Gout	Joints of bone	Rickets	Bones

❐ ❐ ❐

7

Miscellaneous

FIRST IN THE WORLD

- First Chinese visitor to India : *Fahien*
- First foreign invader of India : *Alexander, the Great (Greek)*
- First person to climb Mt. Everest : *Tenzing Norgay (India) and Edmund Hillary (New Zealand) (1953)*
- First atom bomb dropped at : *Hiroshima (Japan)*
- First man in the space : *Yuri Gagarin (former USSR)*
- First woman in the space : *Valentina Tereshkova (former USSR)*
- First person to walk in the space : *Alexei Leonov (former USSR)*
- First person to land on the moon : *Neil Armstrong (USA)*
- First and the only woman to have climbed Mt. Everest twice : *Santosh Yadav (Indian; May 12, 1992; May 10, 1993)*
- First person on Mt. Everest without oxygen : *Phu Dorjee (Indian; May 9, 1984)*
- First person to climb Mt. Everest twice : *Nawang Gombu*
- First person to climb Mt. Everest maximum times : *Chhewang Nima Sherpa (19 times)*
- First President of the USA : *George Washington*
- First woman Prime Minister : *Sirimavo Bandaranaike (Sri Lanka)*
- First person to swim across English Channel : *Mathew Webb*
- First woman to swim across English Channel : *Gertrude Caroline Ederle*
- First woman to climb Mt. Everest : *Junko Tabei (Japan)*
- First woman to climb Mt. Everest alone and without oxygen supplies : *Alison Hargreaves (Briton: May 13, 1995)*
- First Aeroplane to fly around the world without refuelling : *Voyager (Dec. 1986)*
- First test-tube Baby : *Louise Brown (UK; 1978)*
- First all-talking Film : *Jaz Singer (1927)*
- First Secretary-General of the UN : *Trygve Lie (Norway: 1946-53)*
- First woman President of the UN General Assembly : *Vijayalakshmi Pandit (India: 1953)*
- First woman to reach North Pole : *Ann Bancroft (1986)*
- First person to reach North Pole : *Robert Peary*
- First person to reach South Pole : *Amundsen (1911)*
- First woman to command Spacecraft in Space : *Ellin Collins*

CAPITAL & CURRENCIES

Country	Capital	Currency
* Afghanistan	Kabul	Afghani
* Albania	Tirana	Lek
* Algeria	Algiers	Dinar
* Angola	Luanda	New Kwanza
* Argentina	Buenos Aires	Peso
* Armenia	Yeravan	Dram
* Australia	Canberra	Dollar
* Austria	Vienna	Euro
* Azerbaijan	Baku	Manat
* Bahrain	Manama	Dinar
* Bangladesh	Dhaka	Taka
* Barbados	Bridgetown	Dollar
* Belarus	Minsk	Ruble
* Belgium	Brussels	Euro
* Benin	Porto Novo	Franc
* Bhutan	Thimphu	Ngultrum[1]
* Bolivia	La paz	Dollar
* Botswana	Gaborone	Pula
* Brazil	Brasilia	Real
* Bosnia Herzegovina	Sarajevo	Dinar
* Bulgaria	Sofia	Lev
* Cambodia	Phnom-Penh	Riel
* Canada	Ottawa	Dollar
* Chile	Santiago	Peso
* China	Beijing	Yuan
* Colombia	Bogota	Peso
* Congo	Brazzaville	Franc
* Croatia	Zagreb	Kuna
* Cuba	Havana	Peso

Country	Capital	Currency
✶ Cyprus	Nicosia	Euro
✶ Czech Republic	Prague	Koruna
✶ Denmark	Copenhagen	Krone
✶ Ecuador	Quito	Sucre
✶ Egypt	Cairo	Pound
✶ Estonia	Tallinn	Euro
✶ Ethiopia	Addis Ababa	Birr
✶ Fiji	Suva	Dollar
✶ Finland	Helsinki	Euro
✶ France	Paris	Euro
✶ Georgia	Tbilisi	Lari
✶ Germany	Berlin	Euro
✶ Ghana	Accra	Cedi
✶ Greece	Athens	Euro
✶ Guatemala	Guatemala City	Quetzal
✶ Guyana	George Town	Dollar
✶ Hungary	Budapest	Forint
✶ Iceland	Reykjavik	Krona
✶ India	New Delhi	Rupee
✶ Indonesia	Jakarta	Rupiah
✶ Iran	Teheran	Rial
✶ Iraq	Baghdad	Dinar
✶ Ireland	Dublin	Euro
✶ Israel	Jerusalem	Shekel
✶ Italy	Rome	Euro
✶ Jamaica	Kingston	Dollar
✶ Japan	Tokyo	Yen
✶ Jordan	Amman	Dinar
✶ Kazakhstan	Akmola	Tenge
✶ Kenya	Nairobi	Shilling
✶ Korea (S)	Seoul	Won
✶ Korea (N)	Pyongyang	Won
✶ Kyrgyzstan	Bishkek	Som
✶ Kuwait	Kuwait City	Dinar
✶ Laos	Vientiane	Kip
✶ Latvia	Riga	Euro
✶ Lebanon	Beirut	Pound
✶ Liberia	Monrovia	Dollar
✶ Libya	Tripoli	Dinar
✶ Lithuania	Vilnius	Litas
✶ Luxembourg	Luxembourg	Euro
✶ Macedonia	Skopje	Dinar
✶ Malawi	Lilongwe	Kwacha
✶ Malaysia	Kuala Lumpur	Ringgit
✶ Maldives	Male	Rufiyaa
✶ Mali	Bamako	Franc
✶ Mauritius	Port Louis	Rupee
✶ Mexico	Mexico City	Peso
✶ Moldavia	Chisinau	Leu
✶ Mongolia	Ulan Bator	Tugrik
✶ Morocco	Rabat	Dirham
✶ Mozambique	Maputo	Metical

Country	Capital	Currency
✶ Myanmar (Burma)	Nay Pyi Taw	Kyat
✶ Namibia	Winohoek	Dollar
✶ Nepal	Kathmandu	Rupee
✶ Netherlands	Amsterdam	Euro
✶ New Zealand	Wellington	Dollar
✶ Nigeria	Abuja	Naira
✶ Norway	Oslo	Krone
✶ Oman	Muscat	Rial
✶ Pakistan	Islamabad	Rupee
✶ Panama	Panama City	Balboa
✶ Peru	Lima	New Sole
✶ Philippines	Manila	Peso
✶ Poland	Warsaw	Zloty
✶ Portugal	Lisbon	Euro
✶ Qatar	Doha	Riyal
✶ Romania	Bucharest	Leu
✶ Russia	Moscow	Ruble
✶ Saudi Arabia	Riyadh	Rial
✶ Senegal	Dakar	Franc
✶ Slovakia	Bratislava	Euro
✶ Spain	Madrid	Euro
✶ Sri Lanka	Colombo	Rupee
✶ Sudan	Khartoum	Dinar
✶ Suriname	Paramaribo	Guilder
✶ Sweden	Stockholm	Krona
✶ Switzerland	Berne	Swiss Francs
✶ Syria	Damascus	Pound
✶ South Africa	Capetown (Legislative) Pretoria *(Administrative)*	Rand
✶ Tadzhikistan	Dushanbe	Ruble
✶ Taiwan	Taipei	Dollar
✶ Tanzania	Dodoma	Shilling
✶ Thailand	Bangkok	Baht
✶ Tunisia	Tunis	Dinar
✶ Turkey	Ankara	Lira
✶ Turkmania	Ashikabad	Manat
✶ Uganda	Kampala	Shilling
✶ Ukraine	Kiev	Hyrvnia
✶ United Arab Emirates	Abu Dhabi	Dirham
✶ U.K.	London	Pound Sterling
✶ U.S.A.	Washington	Dollar
✶ Uruguay	Montevideo	Peso
✶ Uzbekistan	Tashkent	Som
✶ Venezuela	Caracas	Bolivar
✶ Vietnam	Hanoi	Dong
✶ Yemen	Sana'a	Rial
✶ Zimbabwe	Harare	Dollar
✶ Congo (Zaire)	Kinshasa	Zaire
✶ Zambia	Lusaka	Kwacha

GEOGRAPHICAL EXPLORATIONS/DISCOVERIES

Place	Explorer/Discoverer	Nationality	Year
America	Christopher Columbus	Italy	1492
Hawaii Islands (Sandwich Islands)	Captain James Cook	England	1778
Newfoundland	John Cabot	England	1497
New Zealand	Abel Janszoon Tasman	Holland	1642
North Pole	Robert Peary	USA	1909
Sea Route to India (via Cape of Good Hope)	Vasco da Gama	Portugal	1498
South Pole	Roald Amundsen	Norway	1911

NATIONAL MONUMENTS OF SOME FAMOUS COUNTRIES

Monument	Country	Monument	Country
Great Wall of China	China	Pyramid (Giza)	Egypt
Taj Mahal (Agra)	India	Kinder Disk	Denmark
Emperial Palace (Tokyo)	Japan	Leaning Tower of Pisa	Italy
Opera House (Sydney)	Australia	Statue of Liberty (New York)	USA
Eiffel Tower (Paris)	France	Kremlin (Moscow)	Russia

INTELLIGENCE AGENCIES OF SOME PROMINENT COUNTRIES

Country	Intelligence Agency
* India	*Research & Analysis Wing (RAW), Intelligence Bureau (I.B.), Central Bureau of Investigation (C.B.I.)*
* Pakistan	*Inter Service Intelligence (I.S.I.)*
* U.S.A.	*Central Intelligence Agency (CIA), Federal Bureau of Investigation (FBI)*
* Britain	*Military Intelligence (M.I.)-5 and 6, Special Branch, Ultra, Joint Intelligence Organisation*
* Israel	*Mosad*
* Egypt	*Mukhabarat*
* Japan	*Nicho*
* Russia	*K.G.B. (Komitel Gosudarstvennoy Bezopasnosty) (Committee for State Security)*
* Canada	*Security Intelligence Service (SIS)*
* S. Africa	*Bureau of State Security (BSS)*
* Iran	*Sabak*
* Iraq	*Al-Mukhabarat*
* Australia	*Australian Security and Intelligence Organisation (ASIO)*
* France	*S.D.E.C.E.*
* Spain	*C.E.S.I.D.*

IMPORTANT NEWS AGENCIES OF THE WORLD

Agency	Country
PTI, UNI, UNIVARTA	India
Antara	Indonesia
Tanjug	Serbia
Associated Press (AP)	America
Reuters, NAFEN	United Kingdom
Angence France Press (AFP)	France
TASS	Russia

MAJOR LANGUAGES OF THE WORLD AND THEIR SPEAKERS

Listing the languages spoken by approximately 1% of humankind (those spoken by more than 60,000,000 people), this table enumerates speakers of each tongue as a primary language.

Language	Speakers (millions)
* Chinese	1,298.6
* Spanish	442.4
* English	378.3
* Hindi	260
* Arabic	315.3
* Portuguese	222.7
* Bengali	242
* Russian	153
* Japanese	128
* Javanese	84
* Lahnda	118
* German	76.8
* Korean	77.2
* French	76.8
* Telugu	74
* Marathi	71.8
* Turkish	71
* Tamil	68
* Vietnamese	68
* Urdu	69.2
* Italian	64.8
* Malay	60
* Persian	61.5

***(Source:** The World Almanac-2019)*

NAME OF PARLIAMENTS OF SOME COUNTRIES

Country	Name of Parliament	Country	Name of Parliament
Afghanistan	Shora	Norway	Storting
Argentina	National Congress	Poland	Sejm
Australia	Federal Parliament	Russia	Federal Assembly (Council of the Federation and State Duma
Austria	National Assembly	South Africa	National Assembly and Senate
Bangladesh	Jatiya Sansad	Spain	Cortes Generales
India	Lok Sabha and Rajya Sabha	Sweden	Riksdag
Bhutan	Tshogdu (National Assembly)	Switzerland	Federal Assembly (Nationalrat and Standerat)
Britain	House of Commons and House of Lords	North Korea	Supreme People's Assembly
Canada	House of Commons and Senate	South Korea	National Assembly
China	National People Congress	U.S.A.	Congress (Senate and House of Representatives)
Denmark	Folketing	Ethiopia	Federal Council and House of Representatives
Iran	Majlis (Islamic Consultative Assembly)	Iceland	Alpingi
Israel	Knesset	Bulgaria	National Assembly
Japan	Diet	Cuba	National Assembly of People's Power
Myanmar	Pyithu Hluttaw (People's Assembly)		
Nepal	Rashtriya Panchayat		
The Netherlands	States-General		

LARGEST AND SMALLEST COUNTRIES (Top 5)

Largest Country (Area-wise)	Largest Country (Population-wise)	Smallest Country (Area-wise)	Smallest Country (Population-wise)
Russia	China	Vatican City	Vatican City
Canada	India	Monaco	Nauru
China	USA	Nauru	Tuvalu
United States	Indonesia	Tuvalu	Palau
Brazil	Brazil	San Marino	Monaco

RELIGIONS OF THE WORLD

Religion	Member	Percentage	Religion	Member	Percentage
Christianity	2.4 billion	32.9%	Buddhism	521 million	7%
Islam	1.7 billion	23.6%	Sikhism	25 million	0.3%
Hinduism	1.01 billion	13.7%			

NATIONAL EMBLEMS OF IMPORTANT COUNTRIES

Country	National Emblem	Country	National Emblem
America	Golden Rod	Australia	Kangaroo
Ireland	Shamrock	Italy	White Lily
Israel	Candelabrum	Iran	Rose
Canada	White Lily	Great Britain	Rose
Chile	Candor and Huemul	Germany	Corn Flower
Japan	Chrysanthemum	Zimbabwe	Zimbabwe Bird
Denmark	Beach	Turkey	Crescent and Star
The Netherlands	Lion	New Zealand	Kiwi, Fern Southern Cross
Norway	Lion	Nepal	Kukri
Pakistan	Crescent	Poland	Eagle

Country	National Emblem	Country	National Emblem
France	Lily	Belgium	Lion
Bangladesh	Water Lily	Mongolia	The Soyombo
Russia	Double headed eagle	Lebanon	Cedar Tree
Sudan	Secretary Bird	Syria	Eagle
India	Lioned Capital		

FIRST IN INDIA

* The first Indian to get the Nobel Prize for Literature : *Rabindra Nath Tagore*
* The first Indian to get the Nobel Prize for Physics : *C.V. Raman*
* The first Indian to get the Nobel Prize for Peace : *Mother Teresa*
* The first Indian to get the Nobel Prize for Economics : *Amartya Sen*
* The first Indian to get Special Oscar award (1992) : *Satyajit Ray*
* The first and the last Indian Governor-General of free India : *C. Rajagopalachari*
* The first woman to become the Governor of a State : *Smt. Sarojini Naidu*
* The first Indian Chief of the Army Staff* : *General K.M. Cariappa*
* The first ever woman to become the Chief Minister of a State : *Smt. Sucheta Kripalani*
* The first Indian woman President of UN General Assembly : *Smt. Vijaylakshmi Pandit*
* The first Indian to become the President of International Court of Justice : *Dr. Nagendra Singh*
* The first Indian woman to swim across the English Channel : *Ms. Aarti Saha*
* The first Indian girl to become Miss Universe : *Miss Sushmita Sen*
* The first Indian girl to become Miss World : *Rita Faria*
* The first Indian to swim across the English Channel : *Mihir Sen*
* The first Field Marshal : *S.H.F.J. Manekshaw*
* The first Indian recipient of Victoria Cross : *Khudadad Khan*
* The first Indian to conquer Mt. Everest : *Sherpa Tenzing (May 29, 1953)*
* The first Indian Cosmonaut (man) : *Rakesh Sharma (April 3, 1984)*
* The first Indian Cosmonaut (woman) : *Kalpana Chawla (Nov. 19, 1997)*
* The first woman to climb Mt. Everest : *Miss Bachendri Pal (May 23, 1984)*
* The first ICS : *Satyendranath Tagore*
* The first to address the UN General Assembly in Hindi : *Atal Bihari Vajpayee*
* The first Newspaper : *Bengal Gazette (Jan 27, 1780)*
* The first Postage Stamp issued : *In 1852*
* The first Telegraph line laid : *In 1851 (Calcutta-Diamond Harbour)*
* The first Railways run : *April 16, 1853 (Bombay-Thane)*
* The first Electric Train run : *1925 (Bombay-Kurla)*
* The first Atomic Power Station : *Tarapore (Maharashtra)*
* The first passenger-cum-cargo ship made in India : *Harshavardhan*
* The first Satellite : *Aryabhatta (1975)*
* The first President of the Indian National Congress : *W.C. Banerjee*
* The first President of Indian Republic : *Dr. Rajendra Prasad*
* The first woman judge of the Supreme Court : *Ms Fatima Bibi*
* The first to climb Everest without oxygen : *Phu Dorjee (1987)*
* The first film (movie) : *Raja Harishchandra*
* The first film (talkie) : *Alam Ara*
* The first Metro Railway : *Calcutta Metro Railway*
* The first Test-tube baby, scientifically documented : *Born on August 6, 1986 at K.E.M. Hospital, Bombay*
* The first TV Centre : *At Delhi*
* The first Indian to get an Oscar : *Bhanu Athaiya*
* The first woman pilot in IAF : *Ms Harita Kaur Deol*
* The first woman to get Olympic Medal : *Karnam Malleswari*
* The first woman Foreign Secretary : *Chokila Iyer*

SUPERLATIVES (INDIA)

Highest, Biggest, Largest and Longest in India

* Award for Gallantry, highest : *Param Vir Chakra*
* Award, highest civilian : *Bharat Ratna*
* Bank, with largest number of branches : *State Bank of India*
* Road Bridge, Longest : *Bhupen Hazarika Setu (9.15 km)*
* Cattle Fair, Largest : *Sonepur (Bihar)*
* City, Most Populous : *Mumbai metropolis*
* Corridor, Longest : *Rameshwaram Temple corridor (4,000 ft.)*
* Desert, Largest : *Thar (Rajasthan)*
* Dam, Longest : *Hirakud Dam (Odisha)*

* Delta, Largest : *Sunderban's Delta*
* Dome, Largest : *Gol Gumbaj (Bijapur)*
* Dam, Highest : *Tehri Dam (261 m)*
* Gateway, Highest : *Buland Darwaja at Fatehpur Sikri (176 ft.)*
* Lake, Largest (Fresh water): *Wular Lake (Kashmir)*
* Literacy, Highest : *Kerala*
* Museum, Largest : *Indian Museum (Kolkata)*
* Mosque, Biggest : *Jama Masjid (Delhi)*
* Peak, Highest* : *K-2 (Pak-Occupied Kashmir)*
* Platform, Longest : *Shree Siddharoodha Swamiji Hubballi Railway Station Platform, Karnataka (1507 m. long)*
* Railway Bridge, longest : *Vembanad Rail Bridge (4,620 m)*
* River, Longest** : *The Ganges (2525 Km)*
* Rainfall, Highest (annual mean) : *Mowsynram near Cherrapunji (1178 cm)*
* Road Longest : *Grand Trunk Road (1,500 miles)*
* State, with maximum forest cover : *Madhya Pradesh*
* State, with maximum density of population : *Bihar*
* Statue, Tallest : *Statue of Unity (182 m)*
* Telescope, Largest in Asia : *Vainu Bappu Telescope (at Kavalur: Chennai) 2.34m*
* Tunnel, Longest (Road) : *Dr. Shyama Prasad Mukherjee Tunnel (J&K 9.28 km)*
* Tunnel, Longest (Railway) : *Pir Panjal Tunnel (11.21 kms) between Banihal and Qazigund stations in Jammu & Kashmir.*
* Tallest Minaret : *Qutub Minar (Delhi 72.5 m.)*
* Waterfall, Highest : *Kunchikal Waterfall (Karnataka: 455 m)*
* Zoo, Largest : *Zoological Gardens (Kolkata)*

* *Highest peak in the world is Mount Everest, which is in Nepal. K-2 is the second highest peak in the world. It is 8,611 metres high.*

** *Indus and Brahmaputra (each 2900 km). Both of them, however, cover a long distance outside India.*

TABLE OF PRECEDENCE

1. President
2. Vice-President
3. Prime Minister
4. Governors of States within their respective states
5. Former Presidents

5A. Deputy Prime Minister

6. Chief Justice of India, Speaker of Lok Sabha
7. Cabinet Ministers of the Union, Chief Ministers of States within their respective States
   Deputy Chairman NITI Aayog.
   Leaders of opposition in Rajya Sabha and Lok Sabha

7A. Holders of the Bharat Ratna Decoration

8. Ambassadors Extraordinary and Plenipotentiary and High Commissioners of Commonwealth Countries accredited to India, Chief Ministers of States outside their respective States
9. Judges of the Supreme Court
10. Deputy Chairman Rajya Sabha, Deputy Chief Minister of States, Deputy Speaker Lok Sabha, Members of the NITI Aayog, Minister of State of the Union and Other Minister in the Ministry of Defence.

BOOKS AND AUTHORS

FOREIGN

Book	Author
* As You Like It	*William Shakespeare*
* A Tale of Two Cities	*Charles Dickens*
* Ben Hur	*Lewis Wallace*
* Das Kapital	*Karl Marx*
* David Copperfield	*Charles Dickens*
* Hamlet	*William Shakespeare*
* Iliad	*Homer*
* Inferno	*A. Dante*
* In Memoriam	*Lord Tennyson*
* Ivanhoe	*Walter Scott*
* Julius Caesar	*William Shakespeare*
* Lady Chatterley's Lover	*D.H. Lawrence*
* Lajja	*Taslima Nasreen*
* Les Miserable	*Victor Hugo*
* Leviathan	*Thomas Hobbes*
* Lolita	*V. Nobokov*
* Lycidas	*John Milton*
* Mein Kampf	*Adolf Hitler*
* Moor's Last Sigh	*Salman Rushdie*
* Mother	*Maxim Gorky*

Book	Author
* Mother India	*Katherine Mayo*
* Nana	*Emile Zola*
* Odyssey	*Homer*
* Origin of Species	*Charles Darwin*
* Othello	*William Shakespeare*
* Paradise Lost	*John Milton*
* Paradise Regained	*John Milton*
* Path to Power	*Margaret Thatcher*
* Pickwick Papers	*Charles Dickens*
* Razor's Edge	*Somerset Maugham*
* Republic	*Plato*
* The Tempest	*William Shakespeare*
* Time Machine	*H.G. Wells*
* Tom Sawyer	*Mark Twain*
* Treasure Island	*R.L. Stevenson*
* Twelfth Night	*William Shakespeare*
* Unto This Last	*John Ruskin*
* Utopia	*Thomas More*
* Wealth of Nations	*Adam Smith*
* Wonder that was India	*A.L. Basham*

INDIAN

Book	Author
✶ Ain-i-Akbari	Abul Fazal
✶ Anand Math	Bankim Chandra Chatterjee
✶ Arthashastra	Kautilya
✶ A Suitable Boy	Vikram Seth
✶ Bhagwat Gita	Ved Vyas
✶ Chidambara	Sumitranandan Pant
✶ Devdas	Sarat Chandra Chatterjee
✶ Discovery of India	Jawaharlal Nehru
✶ Ganadevata	Tarashankar Bandopadhyaya
✶ Geet Govind	Jaya Dev
✶ Geetanjali	R. N. Tagore
✶ Glimpses of World History	Jawaharlal Nehru
✶ Godaan	Prem Chand
✶ Gul-e-Nagma	Firaq Gorakhpuri
✶ Harsh Charita	Bana Bhatta
✶ India Divided	Dr. Rajendra Prasad
✶ Justice of Peace ke Aansu	Janardan Prasad Singh
✶ The Judgement	Kuldip Nayyar

Book	Author
✶ Kadambari	Bana Bhatta
✶ Kagaz Te Kanwas	Amrita Pritam
✶ Kamayani	Jai Shankar Prasad
✶ Kitni Nawon Mein Kitni Bar	S. H. Vatsyayan
✶ Kumar Sambhav	Kalidas
✶ Mahabharata	Ved Vyas
✶ Malgudi Days	R.K. Narayan
✶ Meghdoot	Kalidas
✶ Mritunjaya	B.K. Bhattacharya
✶ Mudrarakshasa	Vishakhadatta
✶ Prison Diary	Jaya Prakash Narayan
✶ Raghuvansha	Kalidas
✶ Rajtarangini	Kalhana
✶ Ramayana	Balmiki
✶ Ramcharit Manas	Tulsidas
✶ Rukh Te Rishi	Harbhajan Singh
✶ Satyarth Prakash	Swami Dayanand
✶ Sur Sagar	Surdas
✶ The Guide	R.K. Narayan

IMPORTANT DATES AND DAYS OF THE YEAR

✶ JANUARY

5-11 Road Safety Week
12 National Youth Day
15 Army Day
15-21 Pin Code Week
23 National Day of Patriotism
26 Republic Day
30 Martyr's Day

✶ FEBRUARY

1-14 Oil Conservation Fortnight
14 Valentine's Day

✶ MARCH

4 National Safety Day
8 International Women's Day
15 Consumers' Day
16 Immunisation Day
21 World Forest Day
22 World Day for Water
24 World Meteorological Day
1-7 Preservation of Blindness Week

✶ APRIL

7 World Health Day
7-13 Handloom Week
14-20 Fire Service Week
18 World Heritage Day
22 World Earth Day

✶ MAY

1 May Day
5 National Labour Day
8 World Red Cross Day
11 National Technology Day
15 International Day of the Family
17 World Telecommunication Day
24 Commonwealth Day
31 World No-Tobacco Day

✶ JUNE

5 World Environment Day
21 World Yoga Day
26 International Day against Drug Abuse and Illicit Trafficking

✶ JULY

11 World Population Day

✶ AUGUST

1-7 World Breast feeding Week
10 Sanskrit Divas
15 Independence Day
20 Sadbhavana Divas

✶ SEPTEMBER

1-7 National Nutrition Week
5 Teachers' Day
8 International Literary Day
14 Hindi Diwas

23 World Deaf Day
27 World Tourism Day

✶ **OCTOBER**

2 V Gandhi Jayanti
V International Day of Non Violence
V Anti-Leprosy Day
4 World Animal Day
6 World Habitat Day *(Ist Monday)*
8 Indian Air Force Day
14 World Standard Day
15 International Day of Rural Women
16 World Food Day
24 United Nations Day
27 Infantry Day
28 World Thrift Day
31 Anti-Terrorism Day

✶ **NOVEMBER**

2 All Saints Day
14 Children's Day
15-21 National Cooperative Week
19-25 Quami Ekta Week
20 Child Rights Day
26 Constitution Day

✶ **DECEMBER**

1 World AIDS Day
3 World Day for the Disabled
4 Naval Day
7 Flag Day
8 SMRC Day
10 Human Rights Day
14 National Energy Conservation Day

INDIAN DEFENCE

- The Supreme Command of the Armed Forces is vested in the hands of the President of the Country.
- The responsibility for national defence, however, rests with the Cabinet. All important questions having a bearing on defence are decided by the Cabinet Committee on Political Affairs, which is presided over by the Prime Minister.
- The Defence Minister is responsible to Parliament for all matters concerning the Defence Services.
- All the administrative and operational control of Armed Forces are exercised by the Ministry of Defence. The three services—Army, Navy and Air Force function through their respective service head-quarters headed by the chief of Staff. The post of Chief of Defence Staff (CDS) was created in 2019.

Indian Army Commands

Command	HQ Location
Eastern Command	Kolkata
Western Command	Chandigarh
Northern Command	Udhampur
Southern Command	Pune
Central Command.	Lucknow
Training Command	Shimla
South-Western Command	Jaipur

Indian Air Force Commands

Command	HQ Location
Western Air Command	New Delhi
Sout-Western Air Command	Gandhinagar
Central Air Command	Allahabad
Eastern Air Command	Shillong
Southern Air Command	Thiruvananthapuram
Training Command	Bengaluru

Indian Navy Commands

Command	HQ Location
Eastern Naval Command	Vishakhapatnam
Western Naval Command	Mumbai
Southern Naval Command	Cochin

Commissioned Ranks in Defence Services

Army	Navy	Air Force
General	Admiral	Air Chief Marshal
Lieutenant-General	Vice-Admiral	Air Marshal
Major-General	Rear-Admiral	Air Vice-Marshal
Brigadier	Commodor	Air Commodor
Colonel	Captain	Group Captain
Lieutenant-Colonel	Commander	Wing Commander
Major	Lt.Commander	Squadron Leader
Captain	Lieutenant	Flight Lieutenant
Lieutenant	Sub-Lieutenant	Flying Officer

Internal Security Organisations of India

S. No.	Name of Organisation	Year of Creation	Headquarters
1.	Assam Rifles (A.R.)	1835	Shillong
2.	Central Reserve Police Force (CRPF)	1939	New Delhi
3.	Territorial Army	1948	In different States
4.	Indo-Tibetan Border Police	1962	New Delhi
5.	Home Guard	1962	In different States
6.	Coast Guard	1978	New Delhi
7.	Border Security Force (B.S.F.)	1965	New Delhi
8.	Central Industrial Security Force (CISF)	1969	New Delhi
9.	National Security Guard	1984	New Delhi
10.	Police	—	In different States

Army Institutes

1.	Sainik Schools upto +2 Level	33 places in India
2.	Rashtriya Indian Military College (prepare for entrance to N.D.A.)	Dehradun
3.	National Defence Academy (three services)	Khadakwasla, Pune
4.	Indian Military Academy (Army)	Dehradun
5.	Officers Training Academy (3 services) Short Courses	Chennai
6.	National Defence College	New Delhi
7.	The College of Combat	Mhow
8.	The College of Military Engineering	Kirkee
9.	Military College of Telecommunication Engineering	Mhow
10.	The Armoured Corps Centre and School	Ahmed Nagar
11.	The School Artillery	Deolali
12.	The Infantry School	Mhow and Belgaum
13.	College of Material Management	Jabalpur

Air Force Institutions

✶ Air Force Academy	Hyderabad	✶ Helicopter Training School	Hakimpet
✶ Flying Instructors School	Tambaram, Chennai	✶ The College of Air Warfare	Secunderabad
✶ Air Force Administrative College	Coimbatore	✶ Air Force Technical College	Jalahalli

UNITED NATIONS (UN)

- The United Nations (UN) is an association of states which have pledged themselves to maintain international peace and security and cooperate in solving international political, economic, social cultural and humanitarian problems towards achieving this end.
- Trygve Lie of Norway (1946-52) was the first Secretary-General of the UN.
- ***Origin:*** UN Charter was signed by 50 members on June 26, 1945. Poland signed the charter later to become one of the original 51 member-states. It officially came into existence on October 24, 1945.
- ***UN Charter:*** The Charter is the Constitution of the UN and contains its aims and objectives and rules and regulations for its functioning.
- ***Aims and Objectives:*** They are security, welfare and human rights.
- ***Headquarters:*** New York.
- ***Flag:*** The flag is light blue in colour, and emblazoned in white, in its centre is the UN symbol—a polar map of world embraced by twin olive branches open at the top.
- ***Official Languages:*** The official languages of the UN are: English, French, Chinese, Russian, Arabic and Spanish. However, working languages are English and French only.
- ***Present Membership:*** At present 193 countries are members of the UN. South Sudan is the latest entrant to this world organisation.

- ***Main Organs of the UN:*** There are six main organs:
  1. General Assembly
  2. Security Council
  3. Economic and Social Council
  4. Trusteeship Council
  5. International Court of Justice, and
  6. Secretariat.

1. *General Assembly:* It consists of representative of all members of the UN. Each member country has only one vote. It meets once a year and passes UN Budget. It is the main place for discussions and policy making in the UN.
2. *Security Council:* It is the Executive body of the UN and is mainly responsible for maintaining international peace and security. It has 15 members, 5 of which (USA, UK, France, Russia and China) are permanent members. The 10 non-permanent members are elected by General Assembly for two-year term and are not eligible for immediate re-election.
3. *Economic and Social Council:* It has 54 members elected by General Assembly.
4. *Trusteeship Council:* It looks after interest of the people in areas not yet independent and leads them towards self-government.
5. *International Court of Justice:* It has 15 judges, no two of whom may be nationals of the same state. They are elected by General Assembly and Security Council for a term of 9 years. The Court elects its President and Vice-President for a 3-year term.
6. *Secretariat:* It is the Secretariat of the UN and is headed by the Secretary General.

Some Important UN Agencies

UN Agencies	Headquarters	Year of Establishment
∗ United Nations Organisations (U.N.O.)	New York	1945
∗ International Monetary Fund (I.M.F.)	Washington D.C.	1945
∗ World Health Organisation (W.H.O.)	Geneva	1948
∗ Food & Agricultural Organisation (FAO)	Rome	1945
∗ International Labour Organisation (ILO)	Geneva	1919
∗ UNESCO	Paris	1946
∗ Universal Postal Union (UPU)	Berne	1874
∗ UNIDO	Vienna	1966
∗ International Atomic Energy Agency (IAEA)	Vienna	1957
∗ United Nations Development Programme (UNDP)	New York	1965
∗ UNICEF	New York	1946
∗ International Maritime Organisation (IMO)	London	1958
∗ World Meteorological Organisation (WMO)	Geneva	1950
∗ International Telecommunication Union (ITU)	Geneva	1845
∗ World Trade Organisation (WTO)	Geneva	1995
∗ International Development Association (IDA)	Washington D.C.	1960
∗ World Intellectual Property Organisation (WIPO)	Geneva	1967

Famous International Organisations

International Organisations	Headquarters	Year of Establishment
∗ International Court of Justice	The Hague	1945
∗ International Civil Aviation Organisation (ICAO)	Montreal	1947
∗ International Finance Corporation (IFC)	Washington	1956
∗ Arab League	Cairo	1945
∗ Commonwealth of Nations	London	1949
∗ International Bank for Reconstruction and Development (IBRD)	Washington D.C.	1944
∗ Organisation of Islamic Cooperation (OIC)	Jeddah (Saudi Arabia)	1969
∗ Red Cross	Geneva	1863
∗ Interpol	Lyons	1923
∗ Asian Development Bank (ADB)	Manila	1966
∗ North Atlantic Treaty Organisation (NATO)	Brussels	1949
∗ Association of South East Asian Nations (ASEAN)	Jakarta	1967

Organisation	Headquarters	Year
∗ South Asian Association for Regional Cooperation (SAARC)	Kathmandu	1985
∗ Asia-Pacific Economic Cooperation (APEC)	Singapore	1989
∗ Organisation for Economic Cooperation and Development (OECD)	Paris	1961
∗ Organisation of Petroleum Exporting Countries (OPEC)	Vienna	1960
∗ Commonwealth of Independent States (CIS)	Minsk	1991
∗ International Olympic Committee (IOC)	Switzerland	1894
∗ European Union (EU)	Brussels	Changed form of EEC Established in 1958
∗ Amnesty International (AI)	London	1961
∗ Shanghai Cooperation Organisation (SCO)	Shanghai	2002
∗ BRICS Development Bank	Shanghai	2014

AWARDS AND HONOURS

NATIONAL AWARDS

BHARAT RATANA

- Bharat Ratna is India's highest Civilian Award. It was first awarded in 1954.
- The actual award is designed in the shape of a *peepal* leaf with Bharat Ratna inscribed in Devanagri script in the Sun Figure.
- This is India's highest civilian award. It is given for exceptional work on art, literature, science and recognition of public service of the highest order.
- The emblem, the Sun and the rim are of platinum. The inscriptions are in burnished bronze.
- Government servants are not eligible for it. The table shows the recipients of the award:

Bharat Ratna Award Winners

No.	Name	Year
1.	Dr. S. Radhakrishnan	1954
2.	C. Rajagopalachari	1954
3.	Dr. C.V. Raman	1954
4.	Dr. Bhagwan Das	1955
5.	Dr. M. Visvesvaraya	1955
6.	Jawahar Lal Nehru	1955
7.	Govind Ballabh Pant	1957
8.	Dr. D.K. Karve	1958
9.	Dr. Bidhan Chandra Roy	1961
10.	Purushottam Das Tandon	1961
11.	Dr. Rajendra Prasad	1962
12.	Dr. Zakir Hussain	1963
13.	Dr. Pandurang Vaman Kane	1963
14.	Lal Bahadur Shastri	1966
15.	Indira Gandhi	1971
16.	V.V. Giri	1975
17.	K. Kamraj	1976
18.	Mother Teresa	1980
19.	Acharya Vinoba Bhave	1983
20.	Khan Abdul Ghaffar Khan	1987
21.	M.G. Ramachandran	1988
22.	Dr. B.R. Ambedkar	1990
23.	Dr. Nelson R. Mandela	1990
24.	Rajiv Gandhi	1991
25.	Sardar Vallabhbhai Patel	1991
26.	Morarji R. Desai	1991
27.	Maulana Abul Kalam Azad	1992
28.	Jehangir Ratanji Dadabhai Tata	1992
29.	Satyajit Roy	1992
30.	Shri Gulzari Lal Nanda	1997
31.	Mrs. Aruna Asaf Ali	1997
32.	Dr. A.P.J. Abdul Kalam	1997
33.	M.S. Subbalakshmi	1998
34.	C. Subramaniam	1998
35.	Jaya Prakash Narayan	1999
36.	Prof. Amartya Sen	1999
37.	Pt. Ravi Shankar	1999
38.	Gopinath Bardoloi	1999
39.	Lata Mangeshkar	2001
40.	Bismillah Khan	2001
41.	Bhimsen Joshi	2009
42.	C.N.R. Rao	2014
43.	Sachin Tendulkar	2014
44.	Pt. Madan Mohan Malaviya	2015
45.	Atal Bihari Vajpayee	2015
46.	Pranab Mukherjee	2019
47.	Nanaji Deshmukh	2019
48.	Bhupen Hazarika	2019

REPUBLIC DAY AWARDS

Padma Awards

They fall in line after the Bharat Ratna. They are also discontinued in 1977 along with the Bharat Ratna and award was started again in 1980.

There are three Padma Awards:

- ***Padma Vibhushan:*** This award is given for exceptional and distinguished service in any field, including service rendered by Govt. servants.
- ***Padma Bhushan:*** This award is given for distinguished service of a high order in any field, including service rendered by Govt. servants.
- ***Padma Shri:*** This award is given for distinguished service in any field, including service rendered by Government servants.

Gallantry Awards

- ***Param Vir Chakra:*** The highest award for bravery or some daring and pre-eminent act of valour or self-sacrifice in the presence of the enemy, whether on land, at sea or in the air.
- ***Mahavir Chakra:*** It is the second highest decoration and is awarded for acts of conspicuous gallantry in the presence of the enemy, whether on land, at sea or in the air.
- ***Vir Chakra:*** It is the third in order of awards given for acts of gallantry in the presence of enemy, whether on land, at sea or in the air.
- ***Ashok Chakra:*** This medal is awarded for the most conspicuous bravery or some daring or pre-eminent act of valour or self-sacrifice on land, at sea or in the air but not in the presence of enemy.
- ***Vishishta Sewa Medal:*** It is awarded to personnel of all the three Services in class I, II and III in recognition of distinguished service of the "most exceptional" and "exceptional" and a "high" order respectively. Prefixes Parma and Ati are added before first two categories of medals respectively.
- ***Jeewan Raksha Padak:*** Awarded for meritorious acts or a series of acts of a human nature displayed in saving life from drowning, fire and rescue operations in mines etc.

OTHER NATIONAL AWARDS

SAHITYA AKADEMI AWARDS

- These prizes are awarded annually to the authors of the most outstanding books of literary merit published in each of the 22 languages recognised by the Akademi.
- There are also two awards for Sanskrit and English. The award, in form of a casket containing an inscribed copper plate and a cheque of ₹ 1 lakh is given to the author or his/her heir.

DADA SAHEB PHALKE AWARD

- The award carries a cash prize of ₹ 10 lakh, a Shawl and Swarna Kamal. Mrs Devika Rani Roerich was the first person to receive Dadasaheb Phalke Award in 1969.
- The award for 2020 has been given to Asha Parekh.
- The award for 2019 has been given to Rajinikanth.

BHARATIYA JNANPITH AWARD

- Instituted in 22nd May, 1961, carries a cash prize of ₹ 11 lakh, a citation and a bronze replica of Vagdevi (Saraswati).
- Instituted by a literary organisation in India.

SARASWATI SAMMAN

- Given for outstanding literary works, value ₹ 15 lakh.

KALINGA PRIZE

- This award is given each year by the UNESCO and founded by former Odisha Chief Minister late Shri Biju Patnaik for popularisation of science.

INTERNATIONAL AWARDS

NOBEL PRIZES

- These Prizes were instituted in 1901 by a Swedish scientist, Dr. Alfred Nobel; the discoverer of Dynamite.
- Six prizes are awarded annually for (*i*) Chemistry, (*ii*) Physics, (*iii*) Medicine, (*iv*) Literature, (*v*) Peace and (*vi*) Economics—started since 1969.
- Five Indians so far have been awarded these Prizes, (*i*) Rabindranath Tagore for literature in 1913 for his work 'Gitanjali', (*ii*) C. V. Raman for Physics in 1930, (*iii*) Mother Teresa for Peace in 1979, (*iv*) Prof. Amartya Sen for Economics in 1998, (*v*) Kailash Satyarthi for Peace in 2014.
- In addition, four non-resident Indians have also been awarded the Nobel Prize. They are: (*i*) Hargobind Khurana for Medicine in 1968, (*ii*) Subramanian Chandrasekhar for Physics in 1983, (*iii*) Venkatraman Ramkrishnan for Chemistry in 2009, (iv) Abhijit Vinayak Banerjee for Economics in 2019.

GANDHI PEACE PRIZE

- The government instituted this ₹ 1 crore prize on the lines of the Nobel Peace Prize in 1995.
- It is the highest Civilian International award by the Govt. of India.

MAN BOOKER INTERNATIONAL AWARD

- The Man Booker International Prize was established in 2005, biannually rewarding an author for a body of work originally written in any language as long as it was widely available in English.
- From 2016, the prize became a translation prize, awarded annually for a single work of fiction, translated into English and published in the UK. Underlining the importance of translation, the £ 50,000 prize is divided equally between the author and the translator.

Highest Honours of Some Countries

Country	*Highest Honour*
India	Bharat Ratna
Pakistan	Nishan-e-Pakistan
Kuwait	Mubarak-Al-kabir Medal
Saudi Arabia	Shah Abdul Aziz Medal
Argentina	The Order of Sona Martin
Nicaragua	Augusto-Caesar Sandino Order
Vietnam	The Order of the Golden Star
Hungary	The Order of Banner
Britain	Member of British Empire, Victoria Cross
Japan	Order of Moulovenice Sun
Denmark	Order of Diana Brog
France	Legend of Honour
America	Presidential Medal of Freedom
Germany	Pore Lee Merit Iron Cross
The Netherlands	Netherlands Lion

SPORTS

OLYMPICS

- First of all these games were held by the Greeks in 776 B.C. on Mount Olympus in honour of the Greek God Zeus. In this way, the history of Olympic Games is about twenty eight hundred years old. These games continued to be held every four years until 394 A.D. when these games were stopped by a royal order of the emperor of Rome.
- The modern Olympic Games which started in Athens in 1896, are the result of the devotion and dedication of a French educator Baron Pierre de Coubertin and the first Olympic meet in the modern series was held in 1896 in Athens, the Capital of Greece. Since then, they are being held every four years except for breaks during world wars.
- The Olympic flag is white in colour with five coloured rings, each ring symbolic of a continent. Summer as well as Winter Olympics are held in the same year.
- The 2020 Olympic Games was held at Tokyo, Japan in 2021.
- The official Olympic Motto is *Citius, Altius, Swifter, Higher, Stronger*. The Head Office of International Olympic Committee (IOC) is at Lausanne (Switzerland).

COMMONWEALTH GAMES

- The Commonwealth Games are held every four years, in the year in which Asian Games are held. All the Commonwealth Countries (former colonies of Britain) can take part in it.
- The first Commonwealth Games were held in 1930 at Hamilton (Canada).
- There are currently 56 members of the Commonwealth of Nations, and 72 teams participated in the games.
- The 2022 Commonwealth Games, officially known as the XXII Commonwealth Games or Birmingham, 2022, held in Birmingham, England between 28 July to 8 August 2022.

ASIAN GAMES

- After the Second World War, most of the Asian Countries gained independence. On the lines of Olympic Games, Asian Games were planned every four years.
- India hosted the first Asian Games in 1951.

WORLD CUP CRICKET

- The first Cricket World Cup was organised in England in 1975. A separate women's Cricket World Cup has been held every 4 years since 1973.

List of Cricket World Cup

Year	Venue	Winner/Runner
1975	England	*West Indies beat Australia*
1979	England	*West Indies beat England*
1983	England	*India beat West Indies*
1987	India & Pakistan	*Australia beat England*
1992	Australia	*Pakistan beat England*
1996	India, Pakistan & Sri Lanka	*Sri Lanka beat Australia*
1999	England	*Australia beat Pakistan*
2003	South Africa	*Australia beat India*
2007	West Indies	*Australia beat Sri Lanka*
2011	India, Sri Lanka, Bangladesh	*India beat Sri Lanka*
2015	Australia, New Zealand	*Australia beat New Zealand*
2019	England	*England beat New Zealand*
2023	India	*To be held*

HOCKEY WORLD CUP

- The first Hockey World Cup was organised in Barcelona (Spain) in 1971. Women's Hockey World Cup has been held since 1974.

FOOTBALL WORLD CUP

- The Football World Cup is organised by FIFA (Federation of International Football Association). The World Cup is called 'Jules Rimet Cup' named after the name of FIFA President Jules Rimet. The first Football World Cup was organised in Uruguay in 1930.
- In 1942 and 1946, the Football World Cup was not played due to World War II.
- Brazil is the only nation to have participated in every World Cup so far.

IMPORTANT CUPS & TROPHIES

International

∗ *American Cup*	:	Yacht Racing
∗ *Ashes*	:	Cricket
∗ *Davis Cup*	:	Lawn Tennis
∗ *Derby*	:	Horse Race
∗ *Grand National*	:	Horse Streple Chase Race
∗ *Jules Rimet Trophy*	:	World Soccer Cup
∗ *King's Cup*	:	Air Races
∗ *Merdeka Cup*	:	Football
∗ *Swaythling Cup*	:	Table Tennis (Men)
∗ *Ryder Cup*	:	Golf
∗ *Thomas Cup*	:	Badminton
∗ *U. Thant Cup*	:	Tennis
∗ *Walker Cup*	:	Golf
∗ *Wightman Cup*	:	Lawn Tennis
∗ *Rothman's Trophy*	:	Cricket
∗ *European Champions Cup*	:	Football
∗ *Grand Prix*	:	Table Tennis
∗ *Edgbaston Cup*	:	Lawn Tennis
∗ *Grand Prix*	:	Lawn Tennis

National

- ✶ *Agha Khan Cup* : Hockey
- ✶ *Beighton Cup* : Hockey
- ✶ *Bombay Gold Cup* : Hockey
- ✶ *C.K. Naydu Trophy* : Cricket
- ✶ *Deodhar Trophy* : Cricket
- ✶ *Duleep Trophy* : Cricket
- ✶ *Durand Cup* : Football
- ✶ *Dhyan Chand Trophy* : Hockey
- ✶ *Dr. B.C. Roy Trophy* : Football (Junior)
- ✶ *Ezra Cup* : Polo
- ✶ *Guru Nanak Cup* : Hockey
- ✶ *Holkar Trophy* : Bridge
- ✶ *Irani Trophy* : Cricket
- ✶ *Indira Gold Cup* : Hockey
- ✶ *Murugappa Gold Cup* : Hockey
- ✶ *Nehru Trophy* : Hockey
- ✶ *Nixan Gold Cup* : Football
- ✶ *Rani Jhansi Trophy* : Cricket
- ✶ *Ranji Trophy* : Cricket
- ✶ *Rangaswami Cup* : Hockey
- ✶ *Ramanujan Trophy* : Table Tennis
- ✶ *Rene Frank Trophy* : Hockey
- ✶ *Rohinton Baria Trophy* : Cricket
- ✶ *Rovers Cup* : Football
- ✶ *Santosh Trophy* : Football
- ✶ *Subroto Cup* : Football

SPORTS TERMS

- ✶ ***Badminton:*** Mixed doubles; Deuce; Drop; Smash; Let; Foot work; Setting.
- ✶ ***Base Ball:*** Pitcher; Put out, Strike; Home; Bunt.
- ✶ ***Billiards:*** Cue; Jigger; Pot; Break; In Baulk; In Off; Cannons.
- ✶ ***Boxing:*** Upper cut; Round; Punch; Bout; Knock down; Hitting below the belt; Ring.
- ✶ ***Bridge:*** Finesse; Dummy; Revoke; Grand Slam; Little Slam; No Trump; Rubber.
- ✶ ***Chess:*** Bishop, Gambit; Checkmate; Stalemate.
- ✶ ***Cricket:*** L.B.W. (leg before wicket); Creases, Popping-creases; Stumped; Bye; Leg-Bye; Googly; Hattrick; Maiden over; Drive; Bowling; Duck; Follow-on; No ball; Leg Break; Silly point; Cover point; Hit-wicket; Late-cut; Slip; Off-spinner; In-swing.
- ✶ ***Football:*** Off Side; Block; Drop-kick; Penalty-kick (or goal kick); Corner-kick; Free-kick; Dribble; Thrown-in; Foul.
- ✶ ***Golf:*** Boggy; Foursome; Stymic; Tee; Put; Hole; Niblic; Caddie; Links; The green; Bunker.
- ✶ ***Hockey:*** Carried; Short Corner; Bully; Sticks; Off side; Roll in; Striking Circle; Under-cutting; Dribble.
- ✶ ***Horse racing:*** Jockey; Punter.
- ✶ ***Polo:*** Bunker; Chukker; Mallet.
- ✶ ***Tennis:*** Back hand drive; Volley; Smash; Half-volley; Deuce; Service; Let; Grand Slam.

Stadiums and Places Associated with Sports

Name of Stadium	Sports	Place
Narendra Modi Stadium	Cricket	Ahmedabad
Arun Jaitley Stadium	Cricket	Delhi
Jawaharlal Nehru Stadium	Athletics	Delhi
Shivajee Stadium	Hockey	Delhi
National Stadium	Hockey etc.	Delhi
Ambedkar Stadium	Football	Delhi
Brabourne Stadium	Cricket	Mumbai
Wankhede Stadium	Cricket	Mumbai
National Stadium	Hockey etc.	Mumbai
Eden Garden	Cricket	Kolkata
Green Park Stadium	Cricket	Kanpur
Keenan Stadium	Cricket	Jamshedpur
Nehru (Chepauk) Stadium	Cricket	Chennai
Barabati Stadium	Cricket	Cuttack
Lords, Oval, Leeds	Cricket	Britain
Hedingle Manchester	Cricket	Britain
Black Heath	Rugby Football	London
Henley	Boat race	England
Wimbledon	Lawn Tennis	London
Wembley Stadium	Football	London
White City	Dog-race	England
Aintree	Horse-race	England
Tentbridge	Cricket	England
Patnee Martlake	Boat-race	England
Tibankham	Rugby Football	England
Sandy Lodge	Golf	Scotland
Forest Hill	Tennis	New York
Brooklyn	Baseball	New York
Melbourne	Cricket	Australia

Name of Playing Compound of Different Games

Name of Compound	Related Sports
Court	Lawn Tennis, Badminton, Netball, Hand ball, Volleyball, Squash, Kho-Kho, Kabaddi
Diamond	Baseball
Ring	Boxing, Skating, Wrestling, Circus, Riding display
Course	Golf
Board	Table Tennis
Pool	Swimming
Alley	Bowling
Mat	Judo, Karate II
Arena	Horse Riding
Vellodrum	Cycling
Field	Polo, Football, Hockey
Track	Athletics
Pitch	Cricket, Rugby
Rink	Ice Hockey

CULTURAL ACTIVITIES

Dance

India has a very rich tradition of tribal, folk and classical dances.

Classical Dance

Dance	State	Famous Artists
• Bharat Natyam	Tamil Nadu	Yamini Krishnamurthy, Rukmini Devi Arundale, Swapna Sundari, Sonal Mansingh, Vaijanti Mala, Mrinalini Sarabhai, Chandralekha, Indrani, Ram Gopal, Bal Saraswati
• Kathakali	Kerala	Gopinath, K.K. Nayar, Kunju-Kurup, T.K. Chandu
• Kuchipudi	Andhra Pradesh	Sapna Sundari, Raja Reddy, Radha Reddy, Vedantam Satyanarayan, Vimpanti Chinna Satyam.
• Kathak	North India	Birju Maharaj, Gopi Krishna, Shambhu Maharaj, Sitara Devi, Vishnu Sharma, Durga Lal, Shobhana Narayan
• Odissi	Odisha	Kelucharan Mahapatra, Indrani Rehman, Madhavi Mudgal, Pratima Bedi, Samyukta Panigrahi, Sonal Mansingh, Debudas
• Manipuri	Manipur	Uday Shankar, Bipin Singh, Suryamukhi, Darohra Jhaveri

Famous Folk-Dance

- Andhra Pradesh: *Dandari, Banjara*
- Asom: *Bihu, Keli Gopal, Sataria*
- Bihar: *Chhau, Magahi, Durga dance*
- W. Bengal: *Kirtan, Kalatri, Asweabadh, Brita, Kalidance*
- Chhattisgarh: *Saila, Karama, Bhagoria*
- Gujarat: *Garba, Rasalila, Tippani, Dandia,*
- Haryana: *Damyal, Lahoor*
- Himachal Pradesh: *Dussehra dance, Hikat, Notio*
- Jammu & Kashmir: *Dumhal*
- Jharkhand: *Jhau, Ghumakudia, Jadur, Sarhul, Soharai, Karama, Vaima, Loojhari, Jat-Jatin, Vidayat*
- Karnataka: *Yakshagan, Dolu Kunitha*
- Kerala: *Mohini Attam, Padayuni*
- Madhya Pradesh: *Lota Nritya, Jawara*
- Maharashtra: *Tamasha, Dahi Handi, Gof, Deepak Dindi*
- Manipur: *Dhol Cholam*
- Meghalaya: *Nongakarem*
- Nagaland: *Bamboo dance*
- Odisha: *Chhau, Maya Shabari, Dalachai*
- Punjab: *Gidda, Bhangra, Panihari*
- Rajasthan: *Ghumar, Kathaputali, Tera Tali*
- Tamil Nadu: *Terukalathu, Kabalatam, Kargam, Pulivesham*
- Tripura: *Hazagiri*
- Uttar Pradesh: *Rasalila, Nautanki, Thali, Huraka, Dhurang, Jhumela, Bol.*
- Uttarakhand: *Kajari, Karan*
- Goa: *Dhode Modini*

Musical Instruments and Artists

- **Flute:** Hari Prasad Chaurasia, Panna Lal Ghosh, T.R. Mahalingam, N. Ramani, Vijaya Raghava Rao
- **Tabla:** Allah Rakha, Gudai Maharaj, Latif Khan, Zakir Hussain
- **Violin:** Lalgudi Jayaraman, L. Subramaniam, M.S. Gopal Krishnan, S. Subrahmaniam, V.G. Jog, N. Rajan
- **Shehnai:** Bismilla Khan, Imrat Khan
- **Sarod:** Ali Akbar Khan, Amjad Ali Khan, Alauddin Khan, Saren Rani, Brij Narayan
- **Sitar:** Pandit Ravishankar, Vilayat Khan
- **Santur:** Shiv Kumar Sharma
- **Rudraveena:** Zia Mohiuddin Dagar
- **Pakhawaj:** Govind Rao, Anokhe Lal, Kanthi Maharaj
- **Mridanga:** Palghat R. Raghu, U.S. Burman
- **Harmonium:** Purushottam Walawakar, M. Dhaulpuri
- **Guitar:** Pt. Vishnu Mohan Bhatt, Brij Bhushan Kalra
- **Ghatam:** T.H. Vinayakaram
- **Janjira:** V. Nagarajan
- **Symphony:** Jubin Mehta

❑ ❑ ❑

8

Multiple Choice Questions

1. Match List-I with List-II and select the correct answer from the codes given below the lists:

List-I	List-II
(*a*) Napoleon Bonaparte	1. 'A history is contemporary history'
(*b*) Jean Jacques Rousseau	2. 'Liberty what crimes are committed in thy name'
(*c*) Croce	3. 'Man is born free but every-where he is in chains.'
(*d*) Madame Roland	4. 'I am the Child of Revolution'

Codes :

	(*a*)	(*b*)	(*c*)	(*d*)
A.	1	2	3	4
B.	4	3	1	2
C.	3	4	2	1
D.	3	4	1	2

2. Abraham Lincon was elected the President of United States in:
A. 1862 B. 1860
C. 1875 D. 1855

3. Who was known as the 'Prince of Humanists'?
A. Francisco Petrarch B. Dante
C. Boccacio D. Erasmus

4. D-Day is the day when:
A. Germany declared war on Britain
B. US dropped the atom bomb on Hiroshima.
C. Allied Troops landed in Normandy
D. Germany surrendered to the allies

5. Whose teachings inspired the French Revolution?
A. Locke B. Rousseau
C. Hegel D. Plato

6. At a time when empires in Europe were crumbling before the might of Napoleon which one of the following Governor-Generals kept the British flag flying high in India?
A. Warren Hastings B. Lord Cornwallis
C. Lord Wellesley D. Lord Hastings

7. Which one of the following statements regarding Fascism in Italy is *not* true?
A. The Fascists came to power as a result of popular uprising
B. In 1926, all political parties except Mussolini's party were banned
C. The Fascists suppressed the Socialist movement
D. The Fascists were hostile to the Communists

8. The fall of Czar Nicholas-II is known as:
A. Bloody Sunday
B. Bolshevik Revolution
C. February Revolution
D. October Revolution

9. Industrial Revolution took place first in:
A. France B. Germany
C. United Kingdom D. Japan

10. The British Prime Minister at the outbreak of World War II was :
A. Churchill B. Baldwin
C. Attlee D. Chemberlain

11. The 'Great Depression' (1929) economic crisis was met by adopting the policy of
A. Stimulus B. Marshall Plan
C. New Deal D. Open Door

12. The slogan "No taxation without representation" was raised during the:
A. American War of Independence
B. Russian Revolution
C. French Revolution
D. Indian Freedom struggle

13. In the nineteenth century the people of Europe started moving from the villages to the cities due to the impact of :
A. Epidemics
B. War
C. Industrialisation
D. Population explosion in villages

14. The important cause of the Civil War in America was:
A. Abolition of slavery
B. Quest for freedom
C. Industrialisation
D. Rebellion by the native Americans

15. Industrial Revolution could not have come about without:
A. Merchant capitalism
B. The Enclosure Movement
C. The services of the proletariat class
D. An agricultural revolution

16. Consider the following statements :
The French Revolution came about mainly due to the:
1. Extreme poverty of the people
2. Impact of the works of great writers
3. Cruelty of the rulers
4. Impact of impulsive reaction
Which of the above statements are correct?
A. 1, 2 and 4 B. 2 and 3
C. 1, 3 and 4 D. 1, 2, 3 and 4

17. Asia's oldest and largest Buddhist monastery is situated in :
A. Tawang (Arunachal Pardesh)
B. Lhasa (Tibet)
C. Trincomallee (Sri Lanka)
D. Ulan Bator (Mongolia)

18. Who was the main architect of the Russian Revolution?
A. Karl Marx B. Lenin
C. Stalin D. Tolstoy

19. V.I. Lenin is associated with :
A. Russian Revolution of 1917
B. Chinese Revolution of 1949
C. German Revolution
D. French Revolution of 1789

20. Which one of the following statements is *not* correct?
A. Voltaire believed in Natural Religion
B. Rousseau wrote *Social Contract*
C. Montesquieu authored *The Spirit of Laws*
D. Necker believed in 'General Will'

21. 6th April, 1930 is well known in the history of India because this date is associated with..........
A. Dandi March by Mahatma Gandhi
B. Quit India Movement
C. Partition of Bengal
D. Partition of India

22. Which ruler enforced the system of 'Price Control' in India?
A. Mohammad Tughlak B. Razia Begum
C. Alauddin Khilji D. Sher Shah Suri

23. The concept of 'Din-e-Elahi' was founded by which king?
A. Dara Shikoh B. Akbar
C. Sher Shah Suri D. Shahjahan

24. Who are supposed to be the earliest inhabi-tants of India? Where did they come from?
A. Aryans from Central Asia
B. Dravidians from Mediterranean
C. Negroids from Africa
D. Bhils and the Santhals from West Asia

25. The one chief characteristic of temple architecture of the Gupta Age was :
A. Absence of dome
B. Huge size
C. Beautiful carvings
D. absence of a covered courtyard for the gathering of worshippers

26. The Rigveda consists of :
A. 1000 hymns B. 2028 hymns
C. 1028 hymns D. 1038 hymns

27. The central point in Ashoka's dharma was :
A. royalty to kings B. peace and non-violence
C. respect to elders D. religious tolerance

28. The social evil which was conspicuously absent during ancient India was :
A. *Sati*-System B. *Devadasi*-System
C. Polygamy D. *Purdah*-System

29. Which, among the following, can be accepted as a novelty introduced by Mughal emperors to their buildings?
A. Domes B. Minarets
C. Arches D. Attached gardens

30. The first ruler of India who defeated Muhammud of Ghur was :
A. Mularaja II of Gujarat
B. Prithviraja Chauhan of Delhi
C. Jayachand of Kannauj
D. Parmaldeva of Bundelkhand

31. What important event happened in India in 1911?
A. Bengal was partitioned
B. Non-Cooperation movement was launched
C. India's capital was shifted from Calcutta to Delhi
D. Mahatma Gandhi presided over the Congress session

32. The first phase of the Congress Party (1885-1905) was characterized by its efforts to secure:
A. limited independence
B. complete freedom
C. Indianization of services
D. constitutional reforms

33. The Muslim League demanded a separate homeland for the Indian Muslims openly for the first time at its annual session held in Lahore in the year :
A. 1931 A.D. B. 1936 A.D.
C. 1940 A.D. D. 1941 A.D.

34. Under whose governorship did the East India Company secure the Diwani Rights in Bengal, Bihar and Odisha from Emperor Shah Alam?
A. Lord Cornwallis B. Lord William Bentinck
C. Lord Clive D. Lord Wellesley

35. The Simon Commission was generally boycotted by the Indian political parties. What was the reason for this general non-cooperation?
A. the Commission aimed at dividing the people
B. it was an 'all white' Commission
C. it came after the Jallianwala Bagh carnage
D. it was an eye wash

36. Aligarh Muslim University was founded by :
A. Dr. Saifuddin Kitchlu
B. Mohammad Ali Jinnah
C. Sir Syed Ahmed Khan
D. Maulana Mohammad Ali

37. Ibn Batutah was an African traveller visiting India during the time of :
A. Alivardi Khan
B. Ala-ud-din Khalji
C. Iltutmish
D. Mohammad-bin-Tughlaq

38. The battle of Wandiawash was fought in :
A. 1726 B. 1760
C. 1818 D. 1857

39. The abolition of *Sati* by government regulation was at the time of :
A. Warren Hastings B. Lord Wellesley
C. Lord Bentinck D. Lord Ahmerst

40. Pick out the wrong combination :
A. Dilwara Temple : Mt. Abu
B. Pashupati Temple : Kathmandu
C. Padmanabh Temple : Bangalore
D. Minakshi Temple : Madurai

41. Match the following:
(*a*) Chanhudaro (*b*) Kalibangan
(*c*) Lothal (*d*) Surkotada
1. Alleged discovery of the skeleton of horse.
2. Bead making.
3. Traces of a dock and ship on seal.
4. Evidence of ploughing the fields.

The Correct code is :

	(*a*)	(*b*)	(*c*)	(*d*)
A.	2	4	3	1
B.	2	1	3	4
C.	1	2	3	4
D.	2	1	4	3

42. Match the Harappan settlements with the banks of rivers on which they were located :
(*a*) Harappa 1. Ravi
(*b*) Mohenjodaro 2. Indus
(*c*) Ropar 3. Sutlej
(*d*) Kalibangan 4. Ghaggar
(*e*) Lothal 5. Bhogava

Codes :

	(*a*)	(*b*)	(*c*)	(*d*)	(*e*)
A.	1	2	3	4	5
B.	1	2	3	5	4
C.	2	1	3	5	4
D.	2	1	4	3	5

43. The Goddess 'Kannagi' whose many temples were erected during the 'Sangam Age' was the goddess of:
A. Chastity B. Love
C. Prowess D. Wisdom

44. The Jain goal of life is to attain deliverance from the fetters of mudane existence, the way to which lies through three jewels. Which one of the following was not included among the 'three jewels' of Jainism?
A. Right faith B. Right action
C. Right knowledge D. Right conduct

45. The most striking feature of the Ashokan pillar is polish. Name the Ashokan pillar which is considered to be the most graceful of all Ashokan pillars.
A. Sarnath B. Rampurva
C. Laurya-Nandangarh D. Rummindei

46. Which are the correct statements?
1. The land grants, started in Satavahana period, paved the way for feudal developments in India.
2. Silk and spices were the Chief Indian export articles of Indo-Roman trade.
3. The Guptas issued the largest number of gold coins in ancient India.
4. The first memorial of a 'SATI' dated 510 A.D. is found at Eran in Madhya Pradesh.

A. 1 and 2 B. 1, 3, and 4
C. 1 and 4 D. 1, 2, 3 and 4

47. Who among the following patronised the 'Gandhara' (Indo-Greek style) School of Art?
A. Ashoka, the Great
B. Harsha Vardhana
C. Kanishka
D. Chandragupta Vikramaditya

48. The Sultanate of Delhi had five ruling dynasties. The dynasty having longest and shortest period were :
A. Ilbari and Khalji B. Tughlaq and Khalji
C. Tughlaq and Sayyid D. Ilbari and Lodis

49. Which one of the following events took place at the last during reign of Muhammad-bin-Tughlaq?
A. Introduction of token currency
B. Increase of land-revenue in Doab
C. Transfer of Capital from Delhi to Devagiri.
D. Conquest of Khurasan and Iraq

50. The most learned medieval Muslim ruler who was well versed in various branches of learning including astronomy, mathematics and medicine was :
A. Jalaluddin Khilji B. Sikander Lodi
C. Ghiyasuddin Tughlaq D. Muhammad-bin-Tughlaq

51. The 'Sufis' had 12 silsilas. They propounded the idea of Union with God through:
A. Love B. Rituals
C. Fasts D. Prayers

52. Match the following:
(*a*) Peshwa 1. Foreign affairs
(*b*) Panditrao 2. Audit and accounts
(*c*) Amatya 3. Providing grants to scholars
(*d*) Sumant 4. General supervision
5. Military affairs

Select the correct code :

	(*a*)	(*b*)	(*c*)	(*d*)
A.	2	3	4	5
B.	4	1	2	3
C.	4	3	2	1
D.	3	1	4	2

53. The Regulating Act of 1773 can be regarded as the first measure to :
A. assert the right of British Parliament to legislate for India
B. separate the legislature from the executive
C. separate the judiciary from the executive
D. centralise law-making

54. What was the exact constitutional status of the Indian Republic on 26th January, 1950?
A. A Democratic Republic
B. A Sovereign, Democratic Republic
C. A Sovereign, Secular, Democratic Republic
D. A Sovereign, Socialist, Secular, Democratic Republic

55. When the British obtained the grant of Diwani of Bengal, Bihar and Odisha they acquired the right to:
A. maintain law and order in these territories
B. administer civil justice and collect revenue in these territories
C. collect revenue and establish revenue administration in these territories
D. militarily defend these territories

56. Which of the following were responsible for the growth of nationalism in India during the British rule?
1. Economic exploitation of India.
2. Impact of western education.
3. Role of the Press.
Select the correct answer using the codes given below :
Codes:
A. 1, 2 and 3 B. 1 and 2
C. 2 and 3 D. 1 and 3

57. Which one of the following nationalist leaders has been described as being radical in politics but conservative on social issues?
A. G.K. Gokhale B. B.G. Tilak
C. Lala Lajpat Rai D. Madan Mohan Malviya

58. Provincial Autonomy in British India was envisaged by the :
A. Act of 1909 B. Act of 1919
C. Act of 1935 D. Act of 1947

59. Dyarchy means :
A. double government
B. a government in which the centre is very powerful
C. a government based on division of power between centre and provinces
D. None of the above

60. The Indian National Congress observed 'Independence Day' for the first time on 26th January in :
A. 1920 B. 1925
C. 1930 D. 1947

61. ....is situated near the banks of Sabarmati River
A. Bhavnagar B. Aurangabad
C. Ahmedabad D. Rajkot

62. Sericulture is:
A. science of the various kinds of serum
B. artificial rearing of fish
C. art of silkworm breeding
D. study of various cultures of a community

63. The most abundant constituents of earth's crust are:
A. Igneous rocks B. Sedimentary rocks
C. Metamorphic rocks D. Granite

64. Indian Standard Time is based on:
A. 80°E longitude B. 82½°E longitude
C. 110°E longitude D. 25°E longitude

65. Tides in the oceans are caused by :
A. Gravitational pull of the moon on the earth's surface including sea water
B. Gravitational pull of the sun on the earth's surface only and not on the sea water
C. Gravitational pull of the moon and the sun on the earth's surface including the sea water
D. None of these

66. Nagarjunasagar Project is situated on the river:
A. Tungabhadra B. Cauvery
C. Krishna D. Godavari

67. The difference between the Indian Standard Time and the Greenwich Mean Time is:
A. – 3½ hours B. + 3½ hours
C. – 5½ hours D. + 5½ hours

68. Which of the following dams is not on Narmada river?
A. Indira-Sagar Project
B. Maheshwar Hydel Power Project
C. Jobat Project
D. Koyna Power Project

69. Which of the following statements is **not true** about the availability of water on the earth, the crisis for which is going to increase in the years to come?
A. About 97.5 per cent of the total volume of water available on the earth is salty
B. 80 per cent of the water available to us for use comes in bursts as monsoons
C. About 2.5 per cent of the total water available on the earth is polluted water and cannot be used for human activities
D. Possibility is that some big glaciers will melt in the coming ten-fifteen years and sea level will rise by 3-4 metres all over the earth

70. Which of the following is **not** a cash crop?
A. Jute B. Paddy
C. Cashewnut D. Sugarcane

71. Through which States does Cauvery River flow?
A. Gujarat, M.P., Tamil Nadu
B. Karnataka, Kerala, Tamil Nadu
C. Karnataka, Kerala, Andhra Pradesh
D. M.P., Maharashtra, Tamil Nadu

72. Indian Standard Time is the local time of 82½°E which passes through :
A. Guntur B. Delhi
C. Allahabad D. Kolkata

73. The 17th parallel defines the boundary between:
A. North and South Korea
B. USA and Canada
C. North and South Vietnam
D. China and Russia

74. During the period of south-west monsoon, Tamil Nadu remains dry because:
A. the winds do not reach this area
B. there are no mountains in this area
C. it lies in the rain shadow area
D. the temperature is too high to let the winds cool down

75. Which country does top in producing cocoa?
A. Ivory Coast B. Brazil
C. Ghana D. Nigeria

76. The biggest reserves of thorium are in :
A. India B. China
C. Russia D. U.S.A.

77. The Girnar Hills are situated in which of the following states?
A. Gujarat B. Karnataka
C. Madhya Pradesh D. Maharashtra

78. During December 22nd the sun is vertically over:
A. Tropic of Cancer B. Tropic of Capricorn
C. The Equator D. None of the above

79. Photosphere is described as the :
A. Lower layer of atmosphere
B. Visible surface of the sun from which radiation emanates
C. Wavelength of solar spectrum
D. None of the above

80. Broadly, there are three layers of the earth of the crust, the mantle and the core. The crust forms what percentage of the volume of the earth?
A. 0.5% B. 2.5%
C. 7.5% D. 12.5%

81. The grassland of Argentina is known as :
A. Pampas B. Campos
C. Savanna D. None of the above

82. Different seasons are formed because :
A. Sun is moving around the earth
B. of revolution of the earth around the Sun on its orbit
C. of rotation of the earth around its axis
D. All of the above

83. Eskers and Drumlins are features formed by:
A. underground water B. running water
C. the action of wind D. glacial action

84. Match List-I and List-II and select the correct answer using the codes given below the Lists :

List-I *(Rivers)*	List-II *(Towns)*
(*a*) Ghaghara	1. Lucknow
(*b*) Brahmaputra	2. Hoshangabad
(*c*) Narmada	3. Ahmedabad
(*d*) Sabarmati	4. Guwahati
	5. Ayodhya

Codes :

	(*a*)	(*b*)	(*c*)	(*d*)
A.	4	5	1	2
B.	5	4	2	3
C.	5	4	3	1
D.	3	5	2	1

85. Which of the statements as regards the consequences of the movement of the earth is not correct?
A. Revolution of the earth is the cause of the change of seasons.
B. Rotation of the earth is the cause of days and nights.
C. Rotation of the earth causes variation in the duration of days and nights.
D. Rotation of the earth effects the movement of winds and ocean currents.

86. The world is divided into :
A. 12 time zones B. 20 time zones
C. 24 time zones D. 36 time zones

87. The 'Kiel' canal links the :
A. Pacific and Atlantic Oceans
B. Mediterranean Sea and Red Sea
C. Mediterranean Sea and Black Sea
D. North Sea and Baltic Sea

88. Match the following :

List-I	List-II
(*a*) Himadri	1. Outer Himalayas
(*b*) Shivalik	2. Inner Himalayas
(*c*) Himanchal	3. Middle Himalayas
(*d*) Sahyadri	4. Western Ghats

Codes :

	(*a*)	(*b*)	(*c*)	(*d*)
A.	1	2	3	4
B.	4	2	3	1
C.	2	1	3	4
D.	1	2	3	4

89. The term 'Regur' refers to:
A. Laterite soils
B. Black Cotton soils
C. Red Soils
D. Deltaic Alluvial Soils

90. Location of sugar industry in India is shifting from north to south because of:
A. cheap labour
B. expanding regional market
C. cheap and abundant supply of power
D. high yield and high sugar content in sugarcane

91. Consider the following statements :
1. Ozone is found mostly in the Stratosphere.
2. Ozone layer lies 55-75 km above the surface of the earth.
3. Ozone absorbs ultraviolet radiation from the Sun.
4. Ozone layer has no significance for life on the earth.

Which of the above statements are correct?
A. 1 and 3 B. 2 and 4
C. 2 and 3 D. 1 and 4

92. Purple Revolution is related to:
A. Saree Printing
B. Lavender Farming
C. Fine Arts
D. Performing Arts

93. Darjeeling and Dharamsala would be the right places to visit if one wanted to get a clear view respectively of :
A. Kanchanjunga and Dhauladhar ranges
B. Nandadevi and Dhauladhar ranges
C. Kanchanjunga and Nandadevi ranges
D. Nandadevi and Nanga Parvat

94. Atmosphere exists because:
A. The Gravitational force of the Earth
B. Revolution of the Earth
C. Rotation of the Earth
D. Weight of the gases of atmosphere

95. Victoria lake is located in the continent:
A. Africa B. Asia
C. North America D. South America

96. The famous Lagoon Lake of India is :
A. Dal Lake B. Chilka Lake
C. Pulicat Lake D. Mansarover

97. Where are most of the earth's active volcanoes concentrated?
A. Indian Ocean B. Pacific Ocean
C. Aral Sea D. Atlantic Ocean

98. Through which of the following states does the river Chambal flow?
A. U.P., M.P., Rajasthan
B. M.P., Gujarat, U.P.
C. Rajasthan, M.P., Bihar
D. Gujarat, M.P., U.P.

99. Which country is called the sugar bowl of the world?
A. Cuba B. India
C. Argentina D. USA

100. The area covered by forest in India is:
A. 46% B. 33%
C. 21.71% D. 23%

101. A closed economy is the one which :
A. does not permit emigration or immigration
B. permits emigration but no immigration
C. engages in no foreign trade
D. engages in no foreign and domestic trade or transit

102. In a developed economy the major share of employment originates in the :
A. primary sector
B. tertiary sector
C. secondary sector
D. any of the above

103. The Economic and Social Commission for Asia and Pacific (ESCAP) is located at :
A. Bangkok B. Kuala Lumpur
C. Manila D. Singapore

104. Commercial vehicles are not produced by which of the following companies in India?
A. TELCO B. Ashok Leyland
C. DCM Daewoo D. Birla Yamaha

105. In India, the Public Sector is most dominant in:
A. transport
B. steel production
C. commercial banking
D. organised term-lending financial institutions

106. The main argument advanced in favour of small scale and cottage industries in India is that:
A. cost of production is low
B. they require small capital investment
C. they advance the goal of equitable distribution of wealth
D. they generate a large volume of employment

107. The most serious economic problems of India are:
A. Poverty and unemployment
B. Stagnation, not poverty
C. Unemployment, not poverty
D. Underdevelopment, not poverty

108. Which of the following is not one of the three central problems of an economy?
A. What to produce
B. How to produce
C. When to produce
D. For whom to produce

109. If saving exceeds investment, the national income will:
A. fall B. rise
C. fluctuate D. remain constant

110. In which of the following industries in India are the maximum number of workers employed?
A. Sugar B. Jute
C. Textiles D. Iron and Steel

111. Terrace Cultivation is practiced mostly:
A. in urban areas B. on slopes of mountains
C. on tops of hills D. in undulating tracts

112. Which of the following is a Selective Credit Control method?
A. Bank Rate B. RBI directives
C. Cash Reserve Ratio D. Open market operations

113. Which of the following taxes is not shared by the Central Government with the States?
A. Union excise duties B. Customs duty
C. Income tax D. Estate duty

114. ICICI is the name of a:
A. Financial Institution
B. Chemical Industry
C. Cotton Industry
D. Chamber of Commerce and Industry

115. Structural Unemployment arises due to
A. Deflationary conditions
B. Heavy industry bias
C. Shortage of raw material
D. Inadequate productive capacity

116. Which of the following is the largest single source of the government's earning from tax revenue?
A. Excise duties B. Customs duties
C. Corporation tax D. Income tax

117. The largest public sector bank in India is:
A. Central Bank of India B. Punjab National Bank
C. State Bank of India D. Indian Overseas Bank

118. Which of the following statements best explains the term contraband goods?
A. Goods produced only for exports
B. Goods produced in joint sector only
C. Goods for the trading of which licence is not required
D. Goods that are forbidden, from export, import or even possession, by law

119. Price in the market is fixed by:
A. Stock exchange rates
B. The demand and supply ruling in the market at a particular time
C. The Finance Minister
D. None of the above

120. Devaluation of currency helps to promote:
A. National Income B. Savings
C. Imports at lower cost D. Exports

121. Balanced economic growth can be achieved only if:
A. All the sectors of economy grow at the same rate
B. Population growth is arrested
C. All the inter dependent sectors grow in harmony
D. Basic and heavy industries are assigned highest priority

122. First share market in India was established in:
A. Mumbai B. Delhi
C. Kolkata D. Chennai

123. 'MODVAT' stands for:
A. Ad Valorem tax on output
B. Deduction of cost of inputs from the value of output
C. Reduction in import duties
D. Imposition of tax on professions

124. The headquarters of ILO is at:
A. Washington B. Geneva
C. The Hague D. Manila

125. The term 'devaluation' means:
A. Reducing the value of a currency in terms of another currency
B. Increasing the value of a currency
C. Revising the value of a currency
D. None of the above

126. Per capita net availability of pulses has shown a tendency of:
A. Increase over time
B. Decrease over time
C. Constant over time
D. First increase then decrease

127. National Income is the same as:
A. Net national product at market price
B. Net domestic product at market price
C. Net national product at factor cost
D. Net domestic product at factor cost

128. Which one of the following is not an example of indirect tax?
A. Sales tax B. Excise duty
C. Customs duty D. Expenditure tax

129. The major aim of devaluation is to:
A. encourage imports
B. encourage exports
C. encourage both exports and imports
D. discourage both exports and imports

130. Structural unemployment arises due to:
A. deflationary conditions
B. heavy industry bias
C. shortage of raw materials
D. inadequate productive capacity

131. When was the Family Planning Programme officially started in India?
A. 1950 B. 1952
C. 1956 D. 1962

132. When was the Reserve Bank of India nationalised?
A. 1947 B. 1949
C. 1950 D. 1951

133. Which of the following is *not* a feature of the Indian economy?
A. High rate of population growth
B. Disguised unemployment
C. Lowest rate of adult literacy
D. High rate of exports

134. The 'Relative Deprivation' approach for measuring poverty has been adopted by:
A. developing countries
B. developed countries
C. under-developed countries
D. None of the above

135. One of the main factors that led to rapid expansion of Indian exports is:
A. Imposition of import duties
B. Liberalisation of the economy
C. Recession in other countries
D. Diversification of exports

136. Sustainable economic development means an increase in the rate of growth of real:
A. total and per capita product
B. total and per capita product and level of literacy rate
C. total and per capita product and life expectancy at birth
D. total and per capita product, taking into account the cost of degradation of the quality of environment in this process

137. Functional unemployment occurs when:
A. unemployed have no qualification for job
B. people frequently change their job
C. people were thrown out from job due to recession
D. None of these

138. Which among the following does **not** have a 'free trade zone'?
A. Kandla B. Mumbai
C. Visakhapatnam D. Thiruvanantpuram

139. Sun Belt of USA is important for which one of the following industries?
A. Cotton textile B. Petrochemicals
C. Hi-tech electronics D. Food Processing

140. Commercial banking system in India is
A. unit banking B. branch banking
C. mixed banking D. None of the above

141. Who gives recognition to political parties in India?
A. Parliament
B. President
C. Supreme Court
D. Election Commission

142. The Quorum of the Legislative Council is :
A. one-fourth of its total membership
B. one-third of its membership
C. one-tenth of its membership
D. 25

143. The Indian Constitution is:
A. federal
B. unitary
C. a happy mixture of the federal and unitary
D. federal in normal times and unitary in times of emergency

144. Universal adult franchise implies a right to vote to all:
A. adult residents of the State
B. adult male citizens of the State
C. residents of the State
D. adult citizens of the State

145. When a resolution prefering a charge against the President has been passed by a specified majority in the House, it is sent to the other House for investigation. If, as a result of such an investigation, a resolution is passed through a specified majority by the other House, declaring that the charge has been sustained, the President shall leave his office. The specified special majority must not be less than :
A. two-third of the members present and voting
B. one-third of the members present and voting
C. three-fourth of the members present and voting and two-third of the total membership
D. two-third of the total membership

146. Which one of the following judicial powers of the President of India has been *wrongly* listed?
A. he appoints the Chief Justice and other judges of the Supreme Court
B. he can remove the judges of the Supreme Court on grounds of misconduct
C. he can consult the Supreme Court on any question of law or fact which is of public importance
D. he can grant pardon, reprieves and respites to persons punished under Union Law

147. The Vice-president of India can be removed from his office before the expiry of his term if :
A. the Rajya Sabha passes a resolution by a majority of its members and the Lok Sabha agrees with the resolution
B. if the Supreme Court of India recommends his removal
C. the President so desires
D. None of the above

148. The Chief Justice of a High Court in India is appointed by the :
A. Governor of the State
B. Prime Minister of India
C. Chief Justice of the Supreme Court
D. President of India

149. Which of the following statements is constitu-tionally not true about the passing of the Union Budgets, and Finance Bill in India?
1. Under the law, Finance Bill should be adopted by both the Houses of the Parliament within 45 days of its introduction.
2. If the Finance Bill is not adopted within specified period, the government loses its authority to levy the taxes proposed in the budgets.
3. In the absence of full budget, a vote-on-account gives the power to the government to spend.
4. Government cannot raise revenues without a proper approval of the Finance Bill

A. Only 2 B. Only 3
C. Only 4 D. Only 1, 2 and 3

150. Normally, on whose advice the President's Rule is imposed in a State?
A. Chief Minister
B. Legislative Assembly
C. Governor
D. Chief Justice of High Court

151. Which Article of the Indian Constitution deals with Amendment procedure?
A. Article 368 B. Article 358
C. Article 367 D. All of these

152. Government is the agency through which the will of:
A. the state is expressed
B. the people is expressed
C. the head of the state is expressed
D. the majority is expressed

153. In a unitary system of government :
A. The centre is all powerful
B. The centre is weaker than the states
C. The centre and states stand at par
D. The states and centre are supreme in their respective spheres

154. In Cabinet System of Government the real executive authority rests with :
A. The Council of Ministers
B. The Prime Minister
C. The Constitution
D. The Parliament

155. The Head of the State under a parliamentary government:
A. is an elected representative
B. is a hereditary person
C. is a nominated person
D. may be any one of the above

156. In the event of a ministerial proposal being defeated on the floor of the legislature, under the parliamentary system :
A. the government waits for a general no-confidence motion
B. the minister concerned is taken to task by the Prime Minister
C. the minister is forced to resign
D. the whole Council of Ministers resign

157. The "due process of law" is an essential characteristic of the judicial system of:
A. UK B. France
C. USA D. India

158. Under the Constitution it is :
A. obligatory for the President to accept the advice of the Council of Ministers but is not obliged to follow it
B. obligatory for the President to accept the advice of the Council of Ministers
C. not obligatory for the President to seek or accept the advice of the Council of Ministers
D. obligatory for the President to seek the advice of the Council of Ministers if his own party is in power

159. Which one of the following statements is correct?
A. the Presiding Officer of Rajya Sabha is elected every year
B. the Presiding Officer of Rajya Sabha is elected for a term of two years at a time
C. the Presiding Officer of Rajya Sabha is elected for a term of six years
D. the Vice-President of India is the ex-officio Presiding Officer of Rajya Sabha

160. The introduction of "no confidence" motion in the Lok Sabha requires the support of at least:
A. 50 members B. 70 members
C. 60 members D. 80 members

161. The High Court comes under :
A. State List B. Union List
C. Concurrent List D. None of the above

162. Which one of the following has been wrongly listed as a Fundamental Duty of the Indian citizens?
A. to develop scientific temper, humanism and spirit of inquiry and reform
B. to work for raising the prestige of the country in the international sphere
C. to protect and improve the natural environment
D. to strive towards excellence in all spheres of individual and collective activity

163. Which one of the following is not a Fundamental Duty as outlined in Article 51A of the Constitution?
A. to abide by the Constitution and respect its ideals
B. to defend the country and render national service when called upon to do so
C. to work for the moral upliftment of the weaker sections of society
D. to preserve the rich heritage

164. The main characteristics of the Directive Principles of State Policy given in the Indian Constitution are :
A. not enforceable by any court
B. fundamental in the governance of the country
C. 'Like instruments, instructions, political manifesto and a code of moral precepts which have to guide governors of the country'
D. no law can be passed, which is opposed to these principles

165. Of the following which are true?
A. In a State, the Legislative Council is dominant with regard tó non-financial bills and the Legislative Assembly with regard to financial (money) bills
B. Vidhan Parishad can virtually block legisla-tion even if the same is passed by the Vidhan Sabha
C. In case of a tie between the two Houses, the Governor is duty-bound to call a joint session of the two Houses to have the issue settled on a majority verdict
D. If a Bill is twice approved by the Vidhan Sabha, it becomes law even if rejected by the Vidhan Parishad

166. Which one of the following types of emergency can be declared by the President?
A. Emergency due to threat of war and external aggresion
B. Emergency due to break-down of constitu-tional machinery in a State
C. Financial emergency on account of threat to the financial credit of India
D. all the three emergencies

167. The chairman of which of the following parliamentary committees is invariably from the members of ruling party?
A. Committee on public undertakings
B. Public accounts committee
C. Estimates committee
D. Committee on delegated legislation

168. Which of the following is not a formally prescribed device available to the members of parliament?
A. Question hour
B. Zero hour
C. Half-an-hour discussion
D. Short duration discussion

169. Which of the following is not a tool of executive control over public administration?
A. Power of appointment and removal
B. Line agencies
C. Appeal to public opinion
D. Civil services code

170. If the Speaker of the State Legislative Assembly decides to resign, he should submit his resignation to the:
A. Judges of the High Court
B. Deputy Speaker
C. Chief Minister
D. Finance Minister

171. Provision for free legal aid is mentioned in:
A. Fundamental Rights
B. Fundamental Duties
C. No Where
D. Directive principles of State policy

172. India is a Federal State because of:
A. dual judiciary
B. dual citizenship prevalent here
C. share of power between the Centre and the States
D. rigid Constitution

173. Residuary Subjects are those subjects which are:
A. contained in the State list
B. contained in the Union list
C. contained in the Concurrent list
D. not covered by any of the three lists

174. Which of the following writs can be issued, by the Supreme Court, to enforce Fundamental Rights?
A. Writ of Habeas Corpus
B. Writ of Mandamus
C. Writ of Quo Warranto
D. All of these

175. When the offices of both the President and the Vice-President of India are vacant, who will discharge their functions?
A. Prime Minister B. Home Minister
C. Chief Justice of India D. The Speaker

176. The Supreme Court tenders advice to the President of India on a matter of law or fact:
A. on its own
B. only when such advice is sought
C. only if the matter relates to some basic issue
D. only if the issue poses a threat to the unity and integrity of the country

177. Six months shall **not** intervene between two sessions of the Indian Parliament because :
A. it is the customary practice
B. it is the British convention followed in India
C. it is an obligation under the Constitution of India
D. None of the above

178. The States of the Indian Union can be recognised or their boundaries altered by:
A. the Union Parliament by a simple majority in the ordinary process of legislation
B. two-thirds majority of both the Houses of Parliament
C. two-thirds majority of both the Houses of Parliament and the consent of the legisla-tures of concerned States
D. an executive order of the Union government with the consent of the concerned State governments

179. The Basic Feature theory of the Constitution of India was propounded by the Supreme Court in the case of:
A. Minerva Mills Vs. Union of India
B. Golaknath Vs. State of Punjab
C. Maneka Gandhi Vs. Union of India
D. Keshavananda Vs. State of Kerala

180. Which one of the following writs is issued by a court in case of illegal detention of a person?
A. Habeas corpus B. Mandamus
C. Certiorari D. Quo-warranto

181. Name the instrument with the help of which a sailor in a submarine can see the objects on the surface of the sea.
A. Telescope B. Periscope
C. Gycroscope D. Stereoscope

182. 'Hemophillia' is the disease of ....
A. liver B. blood
C. brain D. bones

183. Vitamin A is abundantly found in ....
A. Brinjal B. Tomato
C. Carrot D. Cabbage

184. .... is not soluble in water.
A. Vitamin A B. Vitamin B
C. Vitamin C D. None of these

185. The blood vessels with the smallest diameter are called ....
A. capillaries B. arterioles
C. venules D. lymphatics

186. Out of the following .... has the greatest elasticity.
A. steel B. rubber
C. aluminium D. annealed copper

187. Cooking gas is a mixture of which of the following two gases?
A. Carbon Dioxide and Oxygen
B. Butane and Propane
C. Carbon Monoxide and Carbon Dioxide
D. Methane and Ethylene

188. The substance most commonly used as a food preservative is:
A. sodium carbonate B. tartaric acid
C. acetic acid D. benzoic acid

189. Normally, the substances that fight against diseases in human systems are known as:
A. dioxyribonucleic acids B. carbohydrates
C. enzymes D. antibodies

190. The SI unit of temperature is ....
A. Kelvin B. Celsius
C. Fahrenheit D. None of the above

191. One of the common fungal diseases of man is :
A. plague B. ringworm
C. cholera D. typhoid

192. A clear sky is blue because:
A. red light is scattered more than blue
B. ultraviolet light has been absorbed
C. blue light is scattered more than red
D. blue light has been absorbed

193. Jenner introduced the method of making people immune to :
A. small pox B. rabies
C. cholera D. polio

194. The largest cell in the human body is :
A. Nerve cell B. Live cell
C. Muscle cell D. Kidney cell

195. What is the device that steps up or steps down the voltage?
A. Dynamo B. Conductor
C. Inductor D. Transformer

196. The protein deficiency disease is known as :
A. Kwashiorker B. Cirrhosis
C. Eczema D. Clycoses

197. Iron deficiency causes :
A. rickets B. anaemia
C. cirrhosis D. goitre

198. Blood group of an individual is controlled by :
A. Haemoglobin B. Shape of RBC
C. Shape of WBC D. Genes

199. In a normal man the amount of blood pumped out by the heart per minute is about :
A. 1 litre B. 3 litres
C. 4 litres D. 5 litres

200. Red/green colour blindness in man is known as :
A. Protanopia B. Deutetanopia
C. Both A and B above D. Marfan's syndrome

201. The blue colour of the water in the sea is due to :
A. Reflection of the blue light by the impurities in sea water
B. Reflection of the blue sky by sea water and scattering of blue light by water molecules
C. Absorption of other colours by water molecules
D. None of the above

202. The image formed on the retina of the eye is:
A. upright and real B. larger than the object
C. small and inverted D. enlarged and real

203. Unit of loudness of sound is:
A. bel B. decibel
C. phon D. none of these

204. Oil rises up the wick in a lamp :
A. because oil is volatile
B. due to the capillary action phenomenon
C. due to the surface tension phenomenon
D. because oil is very light

205. The 'stones' formed in human kidney consist mostly of :
A. calcium oxalate
B. sodium acetate
C. magnesium sulphate
D. calcium

206. We hear the sound later, while the light is seen earlier:
A. because light's speed is more than that of sound
B. because lights travel in a straight direction while sound in a zigzag direction
C. because sound's frequency is lower than light
D. All of the above

207. Which part of an eye is transplanted?
A. Cornea B. Retina
C. Iris D. Sciera

208. The Universal donor group of blood is:
A. O B. A
C. B D. AB

209. The green colour of the leaf is due to :
A. Presence of Chloroplast
B. Presence of Chromium
C. Presence of Nicoplast
D. Presence of excess of oxygen

210. Voice of a child is more shrill than that of an elderly person because:
A. the pitch of the child's voice is higher than that of the person
B. the pitch is lower
C. the child is more energetic
D. None of the above

211. Camel uses its hump for :
A. storing water
B. storing fat
C. for balancing the body
D. temperature regulation

212. A man standing in a free falling lift releases a ball from his hand. The ball would be :
A. moving down B. moving up
C. stationary D. moving up and down

213. To change the quality of sound produced by an instrument we need to vary the:
A. pitch B. loudness
C. amplitude D. number of overtonnes

214. The disease caused by Asbestos is:
A. Emphysema B. Paralysis
C. Diarrhoea D. Dysentery

215. Sweetness of a sound depends upon its
A. wavelength
B. frequency
C. amplitude
D. periodicity and regularity

216. Bats can fly in the dark because :
A. they have a better vision in the dark
B. the pupils of their eyes are very big
C. they are guided by ultrasonic waves produced by them
D. any bird can do so

217. Blood is formed in the human adult by the :
A. heart B. spleen
C. kidney D. bone marrow

218. Pencil 'lead' is made up of:
A. graphite B. charcoal
C. lead oxide D. lampblack

219. The deficiency of which one of the following vitamins leads to bleeding of gums and loosening of teeth?
A. Vitamin D B. Vitamin C
C. Vitamin B D. Vitamin A

220. How much blood does a normal person have in his body?
A. 8 litres B. 4 to 5 litres
C. 10 litres D. 2 litres

221. Match List-I with List-II and select the correct answer using the codes given below the Lists :

List-I	***List-II***
(*a*) Visakhadatta	1. Mrichhakatika
(*b*) Shudraka	2. Ritusamhara
(*c*) Kalidasa	3. Kamasutra
(*d*) Vatsyayana	4. Devichandraguptam

Codes :

	(*a*)	(*b*)	(*c*)	(*d*)
A.	1	4	2	3
B.	4	1	3	2
C.	1	4	3	2
D.	4	1	2	3

222. In which one of the following langauges is the *Dalit* writing more conspicuous?
A. Punjabi B. Assamese
C. Marathi D. Odiya

223. The first writer to use Urdu as the medium of poetic expression was:
A. Amir Khusrau B. Mirza Ghalib
C. Bahadur Shah Zafar D. Faiz

224. The religious text of the Zoroastrians is named as:
A. Torah B. The Analects
C. Tripatika D. Zend Avesta

225. Name the music duo which composed music for Raj Kapoor's film 'Bobby'?
A. Laxmikant Pyarelal B. Shankar Jaikishen
C. Kalyanji Anandji D. Nadeem Shravan

226. Raja Harishchandra, an early Indian film, was produced by :
A. D.G. Phalke B. Ashok Kumar
C. Ardeshir Irani D. None of the above

227. All films are certified by .... before they are publicly exhibited.
A. Films Division
B. National Film Development Corporation (NFDC)
C. Directorate of Advertising and Visual Publicity (DAVP)
D. Central Board of Film Certificate (CBFC)

228. Who among the following was the director of the film 'Taal'?
A. Gulzar B. Shekhar Kapoor
C. Satish Shah D. Subhash Ghai

229. Who amongst the following actresses has played the leading role in the film Elizabeth?
A. Gwyneth Paltrow B. Cate Blanchett
C. Simi Garewal D. Kim Basinger

230. The film 'Train to Pakistan' is based on the novel of the same name, written by:
A. Bhishma Sahani B. Khushwant Singh
C. Amrita Pritam D. Khwaja Ahmed Abbas

231. Which of the following is a folk dance form of Jharkhand?
A. Pali B. Jhumar
C. Nati D. Chhau

232. The first feature film (talkie) to be produced in India was:
A. Hatimtai B. Alam Ara
C. Pundalik D. Raja Harishchandra

233. Who directed the film "Bombay"?
A. Shyam Benegal B. Meera Nair
C. Shekhar Kapoor D. Mani Ratnam

234. Late Iftekhar Ahmad was famous in which of the following fields?
A. Acting B. Singing
C. Music D. Literature

235. Who among the following is the director of the film 'Kaho Na Pyar Hai'?
A. Subhash Ghai B. Shekhar Kapoor
C. Ramesh Sippy D. Rakesh Roshan

236. The character played by Jim Carrey in the movie *Man on Moon* is based on:
A. Andy Kaufman B. Edwin Aldrin
C. John Glenn D. Neil Armstrong

237. A popular Hindi film-based on the famous Sanskrit play *Mrichhakatika*, was titled:
A. Meghadoot B. Amrapali
C. Utsav D. Shakuntala

238. Who composed the song 'Zara Yad Karo Kurbani'?
A. Javed Akhtar
B. Pradeep
C. Nusrat Fateh Ali Khan
D. Raghupati Sahay 'Firaq'

239. Who was the producer of the serial 'Mahabharat'?
A. Shyam Benegal B. B.R. Chopra
C. Ramanand Sagar D. Mani Ratnam

240. Which of the following is a folk dance of Rajasthan?
A. Garba B. Dandya
C. Jhumar D. Kathak

241. 'The Colonel' is the nickname of which Indian Test Cricketer?
A. Colonel C.K. Naidu B. Rahul Dravid
C. Mohinder Amarnath D. Dilip Vengsarkar

242. The term 'Grandmaster' is used in which of these games?
A. Judo B. Chess
C. Bridge D. Karate

243. The term "Derby" is related with which of the following?
A. Polo B. Swimming
C. Racing D. Horse Racing

244. With which game is Geet Sethi associated?
A. Basketball B. Chess
C. Snooker D. Tennis

245. Beighton Cup is related with which of the following?
A. Hockey B. Polo
C. Cricket D. Soccer

246. Match List-I with List-II and select the correct answer using the codes given below the Lists:

List-I	*List-II*
(*a*) Basketball	1. Lob
(*b*) Bridge	2. Revoke
(*c*) Golf	3. Pivot
(*d*) Tennis	4. Bunker

Codes :

	(*a*)	(*b*)	(*c*)	(*d*)
A.	2	3	1	4
B.	2	3	4	1
C.	3	2	1	4
D.	3	2	4	1

247. The head office of the International Cricket Council (ICC) is situated in :
A. Zimbabwe B. Australia
C. South Africa D. UAE

248. Match the following :

List-I	*List-II*
(*a*) Deodhar Trophy	1. Volleyball
(*b*) Durand Cup	2. Football
(*c*) Davis Cup	3. Cricket
	4. Tennis

Codes :

	(*a*)	(*b*)	(*c*)
A.	3	2	4
B.	3	1	4
C.	2	3	1
D.	1	2	4

249. Which of the following is called 'Grand Slam'?
A. Winning the highest number of medals in the Olympic games
B. Winning the men's singles title in Wimbledon Championship
C. Winning the Wimbledon Singles title successively for two years
D. Winning all the four championships Australian, French, Wimblendon and US

250. With which game is the term 'butterfly stroke' associated?
A. Swimming B. Cricket
C. Gliding D. Skiing

251. Who is the first Indian to win the 'International Grand Master' title in Chess?
A. Anupama Abhayankar
B. Bhagyashree Sathe Thipsay
C. Vishwanathan Anand
D. D.V. Prasad

252. The XXII Commonwealth Games were held in 2022 in:
A. Kuala Lumpur B. Bangkok
C. Victoria D. Birmingham

253. The term 'Tee' is associated with which of the following sports?
A. Golf B. Table Tennis
C. Polo D. Judo

254. The famous woman Tennis player who was stabbed during a match, is
A. Steffi Graf B. Monica Seles
C. Mary Pierce D. Martina Navratilova

255. The term 'Baseline' is related to which of the following?
A. Golf B. Hockey
C. Badminton D. Polo

256. In which Indian State did the game of Polo originate?
A. Manipur B. Rajasthan
C. Gujarat D. West Bengal

257. World Environment Day is Celebrated on :
A. June 9 B. June 11
C. June 5 D. June 13

258. Rafael Nadal is the well-known player associated with:
A. Hockey B. Cricket
C. Tennis D. Chess

259. Gagan Narang is the well-known player associated with :
A. Shooting B. Golf
C. Table Tennis D. Chess

260. Eden Garden, a famous Cricket stadium, is located in:
A. Kanpur B. Kolkata
C. Jamshedpur D. Pune

261. Maharaja Ranjit Singh Trophy is associated with :
A. Golf B. Hockey
C. Soccer D. Tennis

262. Neeraj Chopra is a distinguished athlete in which of the following games?
A. Swimming B. Weightlifting
C. Javelin Throw D. Archery

263. Cricket was an Olympic event at which of the following Olympics?
A. London, 1908 B. Amsterdam, 1928
C. Paris, 1900 D. Melbourne, 1956

264. WISPA competitions are associated with :
A. Squash B. Yatching
C. Boxing D. Billiards

265. Ryder Cup is the famous trophy of :
A. Golf B. Chess
C. Boxing D. Polo

266. Davis Cup is associated with the sport of :
A. Cricket B. Football
C. Tennis D. Hockey

267. 'Volley', 'Chop' and 'Drive Spine' are the term associated with :
A. Lawn Tennis B. Badminton
C. Table Tennis D. Golf

268. Lal Bahadur Shastri Stadium is located at :
A. Hyderabad B. Chennai
C. Ahmedabad D. Varanasi

269. The first winner of "Rajiv Khel Ratna Award" (Now Major Dhyanchand Khel Ratna Award) was :
A. Geet Sethi B. Sachin Tendulkar
C. Viswanathan Anand D. Karnam Malleswari

270. 2019 Cricket World Cup was held in :
A. England B. Sri Lanka
C. Bangladesh D. Australia

271. The first team event introduced in 1900 at Paris Olympics was :
A. Hockey B. Football
C. Cricket D. Baseball

272. Which of the following international tennis tournaments is held on grass court?
A. US Open B. French Open
C. Wimbledon D. Australian Open

273. Which cricketer is nicknamed as the pied piper of Punjab?
A. Yuvraj Singh B. Harbhajan Singh
C. Mohinder Amarnath D. Navjot Singh Sidhu

274. 'Merdeka Cup' is associated with ....
A. Golf B. Football
C. Squash D. Hockey

275. The first time athletes marched into the stadium behind their nation's flag in Olympics:
A. at St. Louis 1904 B. at London 1908
C. at Antwerp 1920 D. at Paris 1924

276. The "Dronacharya Award" is associated with:
A. Eminent Surgeons B. Famous Sports Person
C. Sport Coaches D. Expert Engineers

277. Which cricketer is nicknamed as 'Jumbo'?
A. Venkatesh Prasad B. Anil Kumble
C. Glenn McGrath D. Shane Warne

278. The first time the Olympic Games were organised by a private company at:
A. Montreal, 1976 B. Los Angeles, 1984
C. Atlanta, 1996 D. Rome, 1960

279. In which Asian Games Cricket was played first?
A. Guangzhou, 2010 B. Doha, 2006
C. Busan, 2002 D. Seoul, 1986

280. The term 'Penalty cick' is used in :
A. Hockey B. Football
C. Baseball D. Golf

281. "Green Revolution" began in India during the year:
A. 1972-73 B. 1977-78
C. 1980-81 D. 1967-68

282. Khmer Rouge is a dictatorial party of :
A. Cambodia B. Indonesia
C. Malaysia D. Thailand

283. Which country is not a member of SAARC?
A. Russia B. Bangladesh
C. Nepal D. Pakistan

284. The headquarters of WTO is located at :
A. Geneva B. Paris
C. The Hague D. Washington

285. The main function of the World Trade Organisation (WTO) is:
A. enforcing of Uruguay Round Agreements
B. facilitating multi-lateral trade relations of member countries and reviewing trade policies
C. administering trade dispute settlement procedures
D. None of the above

286. The Secretary-General of the UNO is appointed by the:
A. General Assembly B. Security Council
C. Trusteeship Council D. World Bank

287. The United Nations officially came into existence in 1945 on :
A. November 24 B. October 14
C. October 24 D. November 14

288. Which one of the following is true of the International Court of Justice?
A. The Judges of the Court are appointed according to the discretion of the Secretary General
B. No two Judges may belong to the same country
C. The Court consists of 20 Judges
D. The statute of the International Court of Justice is not an integral part of the UN Charter

289. Which of the following was not among the six founding countries of the European Community?
A. Belgium B. France
C. Germany D. UK

290. The smallest country in South America is:
A. Ecuador B. Guyana
C. Surinam D. Uruguay

291. In which year "Human Rights Resolution" was adopted by the U.N.?
A. 1945 B. 1946
C. 1947 D. 1948

292. Where is the headquarters of INTERPOL located?
A. Berlin B. California
C. Lyons D. Montreal

293. Parliament of which of the following countries is known as Great People's Khural?
A. Malaysia B. Mongolia
C. Thailand D. Indonesia

294. Numbers of major organs of United Nations are:
A. 3 B. 4
C. 5 D. 6

295. When is the UN Day celebrated?
A. October 24 B. January 24
C. June 24 D. September 24

296. Which one of the following organ of United Nations is known as the 'Policeman of the World'?
A. Security Council
B. International Court of Justice
C. The Secretariat
D. General Assembly

297. The members of the NAFTA include:
A. USA, Canada and Mexico
B. USA, Canada, Mexico and UK
C. USA, UK, Russia and Mexico
D. USA, Canada and Brazil

298. The sits of International Court of Justice is located at:
A. Vienna B. Paris
C. Hague D. New York

299. Which of the following is known as the Constitution of the UN?
A. UN Charter B. UN Assembly
C. UN Security Council D. UN Secretariat

300. The Headquarters of the Amnesty International is located at :
A. New York B. London
C. Geneva D. Addis-Ababa

301. Who is the author of the book 'PRISON DIARY'?
A. Bal Gangadhar Tilak B. Rajendra Prasad
C. Jai Prakash Narayan D. Jawahar Lal Nehru

302. Who is the author of 'Satanic Verses'?
A. Lewis Carrol B. Salman Rushdie
C. Parry Mason D. Mulk Raj Anand

303. Who wrote 'Gitanjali'?
A. Kalidas B. Gopal Das 'Neeraj'
C. Rabindra Nath Tagore D. Jawahar Lal Nehru

304. Who, among the following, scholars flourishing during the Gupta Age, was the author of *Dasakumara-Charita?*
A. Asanga B. Dignaga
C. Dandina D. Bhattin

305. The author of *Gitagovinda* was:
A. Halayudha B. Jayadeva
C. Kalhana D. Jona-raja

306. "Ingenious Pain" is a book/novel written by:
A. Andrew Miller B. Santa Monica
C. Ben Johnson D. Bill Gates

307. Who amongst the following is the author of the famous book "An Equal Music"?
A. Salman Rushdie B. Shasthivrata
C. Vikram Seth D. Kamla Markandeya

308. The famous Moorti Devi Award is given for excellence in which of the following fields?
A. Medicine B. Science & Technology
C. Social Service D. Literature

309. Who has written "Devdas"?
A. Tarasankar Bandyopadhyay
B. Bankim Chandra Chattopadhyay
C. Rabindranath Tagore
D. Sarat Chandra Chattopadhyay

310. "Ain-i-Akbari" is written by:
A. Todar Mal B. Abul Fazal
C. Sheikh Saadi D. Mirza Ghalib

311. "Alice in Wonderland" is written by :
A. Lewis Carrol B. Chester Bowles
C. Charles Dickens D. Jonathan Swift

312. "Mrichchhakatikam" is written by :
A. Vishakhadatta B. Vatsyayana
C. Sudraka D. Bana Bhatt

313. "My Experiments with Truth" is written by :
A. Jawaharlal Nehru B. M.K. Gandhi
C. Abul Kalam Azad D. Rajendra Prasad

314. Who wrote the book "India Wins Freedom"?
A. Maulana Abul Kalam Azad
B. Mahatma Gandhi
C. Sir Mohammad Iqbal
D. Abdul Gaffar Khan

315. Match List-I with List-II and select the correct answer using the codes given below the Lists :

List-I	*List-II*
(*a*) *Emma*	1. Graham Greene
(*b*) *Mother India*	2. E.M. Forster
(*c*) *Human Factor*	3. Jane Austen
(*d*) *Passage to India*	4. Katherine Mayo

Codes :

	(*a*)	(*b*)	(*c*)	(*d*)
A.	2	1	4	3
B.	3	4	1	2
C.	3	1	2	4
D.	4	2	1	3

316. 'Poverty and Un British Rule in India' is written by:
A. R.C. Dutt B. J.L. Nehru
C. D.B. Naoroji D. S.N. Sen

317. Name the author of the book *A Passage to England.*
A. E.M. Forster B. Nirad C. Choudhuri
C. Vikram Seth D. Eric Segal

318. The author of the book 'The Struggle in My Life' is:
A. Mandela B. J.L. Nehru
C. Tilak D. Gokhale

319. The Shanti Swarup Bhatnagar Award is given by which of the following organisations?
A. Council for Scientific and Industrial Research
B. Indian Council for Agricultural Research
C. Indian National Science Academy
D. Indian Space Research Organisation

320. Which of the following books is not written by Salman Rushdie?
A. The Satanic Verses B. Shame
C. Naked Face D. Midnight's Children

321. The different schools of modern socialism derive their strength primarily from the writings of ....?
A. Joseph Stalin B. Leo Tolstoy
C. Mao Tse-tung D. Karl Marx

322. Baba Amte is famous as a ....
A. Painter B. Singer
C. Politician D. Social Worker

323. Jaspal Bhatti, who died on October 25, 2012, was a famous:
A. Satirist B. Journalist
C. Politician D. Sportsperson and Coach

324. Mr. Yehudi Menuhin, was a famous:
A. Sitarist B. Cartoonist
C. Journalist D. Violinist

325. Sundarlal Bahuguna, a famous environ-mentalist, was associated with :
A. Chipko Movement
B. Narmada Bachao Andolan
C. Satyagraha Movement
D. Anti-corruption Movement

326. Mother Teressa's native place was :
A. Albania B. France
C. Greece D. Italy

327. The live polio vaccine which can be taken by mouth was developed by :
A. Albert Sabin B. Edward Jenner
C. Jonas Salk D. Selman Waksman

328. Which one of the following authors put forth the theory of the Drain of India's resources to England?
A. Raja Rammohan Roy
B. Bankim Chandra Chatterjee
C. G.G. Agarkar
D. Dadabhai Naoroji

329. The "Last Supper" is a famous renaissance painting. It was a masterpiece of :
A. Michael Angelo B. Leonardo da Vinci
C. Titian D. Raphael

330. Dhyanchand is associated with which sports?
A. Badminton B. Hockey
C. Tennis D. Football

331. 'Man is born free, yet every where he is in chains'. This was said by:
A. Voltaire B. John Stuart Mill
C. Rousseau D. Karl Marx

332. Who among the following was a prominent social reformer?
A. Baba Gurmukh Singh
B. Raja Mahendra Pratap
C. Bipin Chandra Pal
D. Jotiba Govind Phule

333. Whose real name was Gadadhar Chhattopa-dhyaya?
A. Swami Vivekanand
B. Ram Krishna Paramhansa
C. Dayanand Saraswai
D. Raja Ram Mohan Rai

334. Who was known as "Man of Destiny"?
A. Napoleon B. Nehru
C. Hitler D. Mussolini

335. Who discovered that mosquito served as a carrier of malaria?
A. Jonas Salk B. Ronald Ross
C. Louis Pasteur D. Robert Koch

336. Who was the first woman Governor of an Indian State?
A. Sushila Nayar B. Sucheta Kripalani
C. Sarojini Naidu D. Sulochana Modi

337. Who among the following founded the Bhartiya Jana Sangh?
A. Deen Dayal Upadhyaya
B. Veer Savarkar
C. Dr. Ram Manohar Lohia
D. Dr. Shyama Prasad Mukherjee

338. Who among the following President of India held his office for two successive terms?
A. V.V. Giri B. Dr. Rajendra Prasad
C. Dr. S. Radhakrishnan D. None of these

339. Ustad Amjad Ali Khan is an exponent of:
A. Flute B. Sitar
C. Sarod D. Tabla

340. Who is the first non-Indian to receive the Bharat Ratna?
A. Martin Luther King
B. Zubin Mehta
C. Mother Teressa
D. Khan Abdul Ghaffar Khan

ANSWERS

1	2	3	4	5	6	7	8	9	10
B	C	D	C	B	C	A	C	C	D
11	12	13	14	15	16	17	18	19	20
C	A	C	A	A	D	A	B	A	D
21	22	23	24	25	26	27	28	29	30
A	C	B	C	D	C	B	D	D	B
31	32	33	34	35	36	37	38	39	40
C	D	C	C	B	C	D	B	C	C
41	42	43	44	45	46	47	48	49	50
A	A	A	B	C	D	C	B	B	D
51	52	53	54	55	56	57	58	59	60
A	C	A	B	B	A	B	C	A	C
61	62	63	64	65	66	67	68	69	70
C	C	B	B	C	C	D	D	D	B
71	72	73	74	75	76	77	78	79	80
B	C	C	C	A	A	A	B	B	A
81	82	83	84	85	86	87	88	89	90
A	B	D	B	C	C	D	C	B	D
91	92	93	94	95	96	97	98	99	100
A	B	A	A	A	B	B	A	A	C

101	102	103	104	105	106	107	108	109	110
C	B	A	D	D	D	A	C	D	C
111	112	113	114	115	116	117	118	119	120
B	B	B	A	D	C	C	D	B	D
121	122	123	124	125	126	127	128	129	130
C	A	A	B	A	D	C	D	B	D
131	132	133	134	135	136	137	138	139	140
B	B	D	A	B	D	B	D	D	C
141	142	143	144	145	146	147	148	149	150
D	C	D	D	D	B	A	D	C	C
151	152	153	154	155	156	157	158	159	160
A	B	A	A	A	D	C	B	D	A
161	162	163	164	165	166	167	168	169	170
B	B	C	B	D	D	C	B	B	B
171	172	173	174	175	176	177	178	179	180
D	C	D	D	C	B	C	A	D	A
181	182	183	184	185	186	187	188	189	190
B	B	C	A	A	A	B	D	D	A
191	192	193	194	195	196	197	198	199	200
B	C	A	A	D	A	B	D	D	A
201	202	203	204	205	206	207	208	209	210
B	B	B	B	A	A	A	A	A	A
211	212	213	214	215	216	217	218	219	220
B	A	A	A	D	C	D	A	B	B
221	222	223	224	225	226	227	228	229	230
D	C	A	D	A	A	D	D	B	B
231	232	233	234	235	236	237	238	239	240
D	B	D	A	D	D	C	B	B	C
241	242	243	244	245	246	247	248	249	250
D	B	D	C	A	D	D	A	D	A
251	252	253	254	255	256	257	258	259	260
C	D	A	B	C	A	C	C	A	B
261	262	263	264	265	266	267	268	269	270
B	C	C	A	A	C	C	A	C	A
271	272	273	274	275	276	277	278	279	280
B	C	A	B	A	C	B	B	A	B
281	282	283	284	285	286	287	288	289	290
D	A	A	A	B	A	C	B	D	C
291	292	293	294	295	296	297	298	299	300
D	C	B	D	A	A	A	C	A	B
301	302	303	304	305	306	307	308	309	310
C	B	C	C	B	A	C	D	D	B
311	312	313	314	315	316	317	318	319	320
A	C	B	A	B	C	B	A	A	C
321	322	323	324	325	326	327	328	329	330
D	D	A	D	A	A	C	D	B	B
331	332	333	334	335	336	337	338	339	340
C	D	B	A	B	C	D	B	C	D

❐ ❐ ❐

BIHAR GENERAL KNOWLEDGE

1. Which of the following inscription provide information about the Pala rulers?
A. Munger copper-plate inscription of Devapala
B. Bhagalpur copper-plate inscription of Narayanpala
C. Bangarh copper-plate inscription of Vigrahapala
D. All of the above

2. The earliest source for the history of Bihar is:
A. Upanishads B. Atharvaveda
C. Samaveda D. Aranayaks

3. Which of the following inscriptions belong to the Mauryas?
A. Lauriya Areraj B. Lauriya Nandangarh
C. Rampurva D. All of the above

4. Which of the following texts provide information regarding the mahajanpads in Bihar?
A. Vinay Pitaka B. Anguttaranikaya
C. Kalpasutra D. Dighanikaya

5. Which aspect has been covered by the Arthashastra of Kautilya?
A. Political B. Economic
C. Social D. Religious

6. The Panchobha copper plate inscription belongs to:
A. Skandagupta B. Chandragupta
C. Samgramagupta D. Samudragupta

7. The story of which epic has been depicted on the brick wall of a Vishnu temple excavated from Aphsad in Gaya district?
A. Ramayana
B. Mahabharata
C. Srimadbhagvadgita
D. The story of Nal-Damyanti

8. Who excavated the Nalanda Mahavihara at Baragaon in Nalanda?
A. Mckenzie B. Wheeler
C. Spooner D. Cunningham

9. The excavations at Saraitila in Nalanda have yielded:
A. Buddhist Vihara of Mauryan times
B. Buddhist Vihara of Pala times
C. Temples of Gupta period
D. Buddhist Vihara of Shunga period

10. Which Jaina canon gives an account of Lichhavis of Vaishali?
A. Bhagvati Sutra B. Kalpsutra
C. Kathakosa D. Parisisthaparvana

11. The Buddhist canons Digha Nikaya and Vinaya Pitaka gives an account of:
A. Monarchy of Magadha and republic of Vaishali
B. Post-Mauryan Bihar
C. Both A and B
D. Neither A nor B

12. Which Buddhist text throws light on the political history of Bihar under the Guptas?
A. Dipavamsha
B. Mahavamsha
C. Aryamanjusrimulakalpa
D. Vinaya Pitaka

13. The Chalcolithic age remains have been found at:
A. Chechar (Vaishali) B. Chirand (Saran)
C. Sonpur and Maner D. All of the above

14. The evidences of the first appearance of human beings in Bihar are found at:
A. Munger and Nalanda
B. Gaya and Dehri
C. Chamaparan and Muzaffarpur
D. None of the above

15. Punch-marked coins which were found in abundance in Bihar were made of:
A. Gold B. Silver
C. Lead D. Copper

16. The early stone age site has been excavated at Paisara, located in the district of:
A. Munger B. Bhagalpur
C. Patna D. Gaya

17. From which neolithic site the antler bone tools have been unearthed?
A. Maner B. Barudih
C. Chechar D. Chirand

18. An ivory female-dancing figure with articulate limbs has been discovered at:
A. Champa B. Taradih
C. Maner D. Sonpur

19. An 80-pillared hall belonging to Mauryan period was excavated at:
A. Kurkihar B. Rampurva
C. Lauriya Areraj D. Kumrahar

20. Which of the following rulers did not issue a larger number of coins?
A. Palas B. Guptas
C. Mauryas D. Senas

21. Which text provides the crucial information about the Aryan expansion in North Bihar?
A. Rigveda B. Upanishads
C. Vayu Purana D. Satapatha Brahmana

22. The Aryans arrived in Bihar during:
A. Later Vedic period B. Rigvedic period
C. Mahajanapada period D. None of these

23. Which factor was responsible for the spread of the Aryans in Bihar as well as eastern India?
A. Extension of agriculture
B. Expansion of dynasties
C. Use of iron
D. Trade development

24. Which text mentions for the first time about the geographical area of Bihar?
A. Rigveda B. Shatapatha Brahmana
C. Vayu Purana D. Samaveda

25. The word Vratya mentioned in Atharvaveda refers to people of:
A. Anga B. Vajjis
C. Videha D. Magadha

26. Which of the following was an important state in the later vedic period in Bihar?
A. Vajji B. Videha
C. Magadha D. Anga

27. Who was the last ruler of Nanda dynasty and was a contemporary of Alexander?
A. Mahapadma Nanda B. Kalashoka
C. Pushyamitra D. Dhana Nanda

28. Which of the following Mahajanapadas was not situated in the region of modern Bihar?
A. Anga B. Vajji
C. Vatsa D. Magadha

29. In which regions of Bihar was the Anga Mahajanapada situated?
A. Bhagalpur and Munger
B. Muzaffarpur and Vaishali
C. Patna and Gaya
D. Hajipur and Siwan

30. The first capital of Magadha Mahajanapada was:
A. Pataliputra B. Girivraja
C. Gaya D. Champa

31. Which of the following ruling clan was not a part of Vajji republic?
A. Lichchavi B. Jnatrika
C. Chedi D. Videha

32. The capital of Lichchavi was:
A. Vaishali B. Kundagrama
C. Mithila D. Champa

33. Which river demarcated the Mahajanapadas of Magadha and Anga?
A. Assi B. Champa
C. Gandak D. Varuna

34. Which of the following Mahajanapadas in Bihar was a union of eight ruling clans?
A. Vajji B. Magadha
C. Anga D. All of the above

35. Patna and Gaya districts of Bihar were part of the Mahajanapada:
A. Anga B. Vajji
C. Asmak D. Magadha

36. The capital of Anga Mahajanapada was:
A. Gaya B. Girivraja
C. Vaishali D. Champa

37. Which of the following rulers permanently made Pataliputra the capital of Magadha?
A. Shisunaga B. Ajatashatru
C. Bimbisara D. Kalashoka

38. The founder of Nanda dynasty was:
A. Dhanananda B. Mahapadma Nanda
C. Munda D. None of the above

39. Bimbisara and Ajatashatru belonged to which dynasty?
A. Haryankas B. Sisungas
C. Nandas D. Brihadarathas

40. The last ruler of Haryanka dynasty was:
A. Udayin B. Anuruddha
C. Mundaka D. Nagadashka

41. Which dynasty established its rule after the fall of Haryanka dynasty?
A. Sisunaga dynasty B. Maurya dynasty
C. Nanda dynasty D. Gupta dynasty

42. Which of the following rulers established his capital at Vaishali?
A. Nagadashka B. Mahapadmananda
C. Shisunaga D. Kalashoka

43. Which ruler made a gift to Buddha of Venuvana (Bamboo-garden) near Rajagriha?
A. Bimbisara B. Ajatashatru
C. Shisunaga D. Udayin

44. Which of the following is considered as the real founder of Magadha dynasty?
A. Bimbisara B. Shisunaga
C. Jarasandha D. Mahapadma

45. Both Gautama Buddha and Mahavira died during the reign of:
A. Bimbisara B. Ajatashatru
C. Kalashoka D. Dhanananda

46. Which of the following rulers made Pataliputra the capital of Magadha for the first time?
A. Kalashoka B. Ajatashatru
C. Udayin D. Bimbisara

47. Who among the following was a contemporary of Gautam Buddha?
A. Nagarjuna B. Kanishka
C. Kautilya D. Mahavira

48. The concept of Anuvrata was advocated by:
A. Mahayana Buddhism B. Jainism
C. the Lokayata school D. Hinayana Buddhism

49. With which religion is Kaivalya associated?
A. Buddhism B. Jainism
C. Hinduism D. Sikhism

50. At which place did Gautama meet the five Brahmanas after achieving his enlightenment?
A. Sarnath B. Bodh Gaya
C. Kusinara D. Lumbini

51. Gautama gained enlightenment on the banks of the river:
A. Ganga B. Niranjana
C. Son D. Gandak

52. The famous Buddha disciple Sariputra was born in:
A. Gaya B. Vaishali
C. Patna D. Nalanda

53. The famous Mahabodhi temple was built at Bodh Gaya where:
A. Gautama Buddha was born
B. Gautama Buddha gave his first sermon
C. Gautama Buddha achieved englightenment
D. Gautama Buddha had died

54. The birth place of 12th Jaina Tirthankara was:
A. Champa B. Vaishali
C. Patna D. Gaya

55. Mahavira died at which place?
A. Vaishali B. Videha
C. Pavapuri D. Rajagriha

56. Mahavira's mother Trishala was a princess of:
A. Lichchavi B. Sarnath
C. Anga D. Videha

57. Mahavira's father Siddhartha was related to:
A. Kapilavastu B. Videha
C. Sarnath D. Vajji republic

58. Kundagrama, the birth place of Mahavira is situated in:
A. Patna B. Vaishali
C. Munger D. Champaran

59. The first Buddhist council was held at:
A. Rajagriha B. Vaishali
C. Pataliputra D. Kundalavana

60. The second Buddhist council was held during the reign of:
A. Ashoka B. Kalashoka
C. Kanishka D. Ajatashatru

61. Who was the founder of Ajivika sect?
A. Ajita Keshakambalin B. Makkhali Ghoshala
C. Pakudha Kaccayana D. Purana Kasyapa

62. Who was the founder of the Maurya dynasty?
A. Ashoka B. Chandragupta Maurya
C. Bindusara D. Dasaratha

63. Who helped Chandragupta Maurya in ascending the throne of Magadha?
A. Chanakya B. Seleucus
C. Megasthenes D. Radhagupta

64. The Greek ambassador Megasthenes lived in the court of:
A. Ashoka B. Bindusara
C. Chandragupta Maurya D. Kunala

65. During the reign of which Maurya King a 12-year long drought took place?
A. Ashoka B. Bindusara
C. Samprati D. Chandragupta Maurya

66. Who was the prime minister of Chandragupta Maurya?
A. Chanakya B. Radhagupta
C. Bhadrabahu D. Megasthenes

67. When did Ashoka invade Kalinga?
A. 298 B.C. B. 273 B.C.
C. 261 B.C. D. 232 B.C.

68. The Arthasastra is a treatise on which of the following?
A. Economics
B. Environment
C. Political Philosophy
D. Religion in Administration

69. Which one of the following edicts mentions the personal name of Ashoka?
A. Kalsi B. Rummindei
C. Bhabhru D. Maski

70. Who was the last ruler of Maurya dynasty in Bihar?
A. Brihadratha B. Samprati
C. Salisuka D. Kunala

71. The book written by Megasthenes is:
A. Arthasastra B. Indika
C. Mudrarakshasa D. Rajatarangini

72. Who was the successor of Bindusara?
A. Ashoka B. Tivara
C. Dasaratha D. Pushyamitra

73. Important evidence of the Maurya period has been found at which place?
A. Kumrahar B. Rajgir
C. Champa D. Sasaram

74. Who claimed that the affairs of the city of Pataliputra were conducted by a body consisting of 30 members which was divided into 6 boards of five members each?

A. Fa-hien B. Vishakhadatta
C. Taranath D. Megasthenes

75. The Greek ambassador Deimachus visited Magadha during the reign of:
A. Chandragupta Maurya B. Bindusara
C. Ashoka D. Brihadratha

76. Ptolemy Phillandelphus of Egypt sent Dionysius as his ambassador at the Mauryan court of:
A. Bindusara B. Chandragupta
C. Ashoka D. Dasaratha

77. Who built the famous temple named Gopika Kuha Bhawan in Nagarjuni Hills near Gaya?
A. Dasaratha B. Ashoka
C. Chandragupta D. Bindusara

78. The Mauryan palace excavated at Kumrahar was chiefly made of:
A. bricks B. stones
C. mud D. wood

79. During Ashoka's period there were 5 provinces after the addition of Kalinga. The capital of Kalinga (Prachyapatha) was at:
A. Pataliputra B. Tosali
C. Taxila D. Ujjaini

80. Which of the following edicts of Ashoka was not found in Bihar?
A. Lauriya Areraj B. Rummindei
C. Lauriya Nandangarh D. Rampurwa

81. In which district of Bihar, the edicts of Ashoka have been found?
A. Champaran B. Kaimur
C. Chhapra D. Bhagalpur

82. Which of the following sources mentions about the administration of Pataliputra?
A. Divyavadana B. Arthashastra
C. Indika D. Edicts of Ashoka

83. Which dynasty ruled Magadha after the fall of the Nandas?
A. Shungas B. Guptas
C. Mauryas D. Kushans

84. Megasthenes, who lived in the court of Chandragupta Maurya was the ambassador of:
A. Seleucus B. Alexander
C. Ptolemy D. Antiochus I

85. The central court of the Mauryas was situated at:
A. Pataliputra B. Avanti
C. Vaishali D. Suvarnagiri

86. Ashoka's Dhamma was:
A. a moral code
B. a religious law
C. an administrative system
D. a war code

87. The palace of Chandragupta Maurya was situated at:
A. Rajgriha B. Vaishali
C. Maner D. Kumrahar (Patna)

88. Who among the following had defeated the Hunas?
A. Chandragupta II B. Samudragupta
C. Skandagupta D. Ramagupta

89. Aryabhatta, the great mathematician and astrologer was related to which place?
A. Odantapura B. Pataliputra
C. Vaishali D. Nalanda

90. Gupta period coins have been found from which place?
A. Rajgir B. Vaishali
C. Sasaram D. Munger

91. Which Gupta ruler married Kumaradevi, a Lichchavi princess?
A. Chandragupta I B. Samudragupta
C. Chandragupta II D. Kumaragupta

92. The capital of Guptas was at:
A. Kanauj B. Ujjain
C. Pataliputra D. Allahabad

93. Nalanda University was established by the:
A. Mauryas B. Kushans
C. Palas D. Guptas

94. Nalanda University is famous for:
A. Medicine B. Philosophy
C. Buddhist Philosophy D. Physics

95. For how long did the Chinese pilgrim Fa-Hien stay in Pataliputra?
A. 3 months B. 1 year
C. 3 years D. 14 months

96. The Mahabodhi temple in Bodhgaya was established during the reign of:
A. Mauryas B. Palas
C. Guptas D. Later Guptas

97. The coronation ceremony Chandragupta-I took place at:
A. Prayag B. Banaras
C. Kanauj D. Pataliputra

98. The last ruler of the Later Guptas was:
A. Adityasena B. Jivitagupta II
C. Madhavagupta D. Kumaragupta III

99. In which one of the following inscriptions are Samudragupta's achievements mentioned?
A. Allahabad Pillar Inscription
B. Junagarh Rock Inscription
C. Mehrauli Iron Pillar Inscription
D. Hathigumpha Edict

100. In Sanskrit plays written during the Gupta period women and sudras speak:
A. Sanskrit B. Prakrit
C. Pali D. Sauraseni

101. Which one of the following is not a work of Kalidasa?
A. Ritusamhara B. Meghaduta
C. Kumarasambhava D. Dashakumaracharita

102. In Gupta period, the king's share of product was known as:
A. Bhaga B. Bhoga
C. Kara D. Hiranya

103. The largest grant of villages to temples and brahmanas was given by the ruling dynasty known as:
A. Guptas B. Palas
C. Rashtrakutas D. Pratiharas

104. Which university in Bihar was famous during the reign of Harshavardhan?
A. Vikramashila B. Gaya
C. Patna D. Nalanda

105. Which of the following authors stayed in Bihar and provided first hand information about the attacks of Bakhtiyar Khalji?
A. Minhas-us-Siraj B. Ziauddin Barani
C. Mullah Taqia D. Rizquallah

106. Which of the following books provide an account of land revenue in Bihar?
A. Tabakat-i-Nasiri B. Ain-i-Akbari
C. Akbarnama D. Tarikh-i-Firozshahi

107. The Arabic and Persian inscriptions in Bihar are predominantly found in:
A. Patna B. Sasaram
C. Bihar Sharif D. All of the above

108. Name the author of the book Corpus of Arabic and Persian Inscription of Bihar?
A. Cunningham B. Prof. Qyamuddin
C. Buchanan D. Z.A. Desai

109. The definite proof of minting of coins in Bihar comes from:
A. Tirhut-urf-Tughlaqpur B. Munger
C. Gaya D. Sasaram

110. Narsimhadeva was the king of:
A. Mithila B. Bhojpur
C. Sasaram D. Videha

111. Who founded the independent Karnat dynasty in Mithila?
A. Nanyadeva B. Narsimhadeva
C. Harisimha D. Devapala

112. Who founded the famous Odantapura Vihara?
A. Devapala B. Gopala
C. Rampala D. Narayanpala

113. Who was the last great king of Karnata dynasty?
A. Nanyadeva B. Harisimhadeva
C. Narsimhadeva D. None of the above

114. Who built the Sonapura Vihara in North Bengal?
A. Devapala B. Dharmapala
C. Gopala D. Vigrahapala

115. The Munger Copper Plate inscription belongs to which Pala King?
A. Devapala B. Gopala
C. Mahipala D. Dharmapala

116. The first important victory of Bakhtiyar Khalji in Bihar was:
A. Bihar Sharif (Oddantapuri)
B. Patna
C. Bhagalpur
D. Munger

117. Who destroyed the Nalanda University?
A. Mahmud Ghazni B. Bakhtiyar Khalji
C. Babar D. Muhammad Ghori

118. Who was the first ruler of Delhi Sultanate to invade Bihar?
A. Balban B. Alauddin Khalji
C. Aibak D. Iltutmish

119. At which place was Bakhtiyar Khalji buried?
A. Lakhnauti B. Munger
C. Bihar Sharif D. Rajgir

120. Who established the Turkish rule in Bihar?
A. Aibak B. Bakhtiyar Khalji
C. Iltutmish D. Malik Husam-ud-din

121. Which ruler established a mint-town at Tirhut which was also called Tughlaqabad-urf-Tirhut?
A. Ghiyasuddin Tughlaq
B. Firoz Tughlaq
C. Muhammad-bin-Tughlaq
D. Alauddin Khalji

122. Which Sultan ended the rule of Karnata dynasty?
A. Muhammad-bin-Tughlaq
B. Ghiyasuddin Tughlaq
C. Firoz Shah Tughlaq
D. Muhammad Tughlaq

123. Who defeated the Karnata dynasty ruler Harisimha Deva?
A. Ghiyasuddin Tughlaq B. Iltutmish
C. Firoz Tughlaq D. Alauddin Khalji

124. Which Sultan constructed a fort and a Jama Masjid in Darbhanga?
A. Firoz Tughlaq
B. Iltutumish
C. Ghiyasuddin Tughlaq
D. Muhammad-bin-Tughlaq

125. Which Sultan of Delhi conclusively controlled Bihar?
A. Tughlaqs B. Khaljis
C. Mamluks D. None of the above

126. In the 14th century Firoz helped in establishing the rule of which dynasty?
A. Karnata B. Vainvaar
C. Mitra D. Thakur

127. Who was the founder of Nuhani dynasty in Bihar?
A. Jalal Khan Nuhani B. Darya Khan Nuhani
C. Bahar Khan Nuhani D. Daulat Khan Lodhi

128. Who among the following was placed as the administrator of Bihar by Babar after removing Mahmud Lodhi?
A. Bahar Khan B. Jalal Khan
C. Farid Khan D. Hasan Khan

129. Who was deputed by Sikander Lodhi in 1495-96 as the head of Bihar?
A. Farid Khan B. Hasan Khan
C. Bahar Khan Nuhani D. Darya Khan Nuhani

130. The Sur dynasty was established by:
A. Sher Shah B. Hasan Khan
C. Muhammad Nuhani D. Darya Khan

131. Sher Khan's father Hasan Khan was a Jagirdar of:
A. Patna B. Gaya
C. Sasaram D. Arrah

132. Patna was made a provincial capital of Bihar by:
A. Ibrahim Lodhi B. Hasan Khan
C. Sher Shah D. Azim-us-Shaan

133. Sher Khan was appointed as the caretaker of which ruler of Bihar?
A. Darya Khan B. Jalal Khan
C. Hasan Khan D. Muhammad Nuhani

134. Sher Shah defeated Humayun in which of the following battles?
A. Kanauj or Bilgram B. Chausa
C. Both A and B D. None of the above

135. Who was the last Afghan ruler of Bihar?
A. Ibrahim Shah Sur
B. Ibrahim Lodhi
C. Dawood Khan Qararani
D. Sulaiman Qararani

136. Akbar merged Bihar and Bengal in Mughal empire in:
A. 1550 B. 1575
C. 1572 D. 1576

137. Who was the Governor of Bihar during Akbar's reign?
A. Munim Khan B. Baj Bahadur
C. Daud Khan D. None of the above

138. Who was the first Mughal ruler to be sworn in Patna?
A. Farrukhsiyar B. Bahadur Shah
C. Jahangir D. Shahjahan

139. Which Mughal ruler made his grandson as the Subedar of Bihar?
A. Akbar B. Shahjahan
C. Jahangir D. Aurangzeb

140. Who was the first Mughal Prince to be appointed as the governor of Bihar?
A. Prince Salim B. Prince Azim
C. Prince Parvez D. Prince Khurram

141. Raja Man Singh was appointed the governor of Bihar by:
A. Akbar B. Shah Jahan
C. Jahangir D. Aurangzeb

142. Who built the Shahi Idgah in Patna City?
A. Itiqad Khan B. Shaista Khan
C. Zulfiqar Khan D. Saif Khan

143. Who was the Dewan of Bihar when Prince Azim was the governor of Bihar?
A. Saadat Khan B. Safdarjung
C. Murshid Quli Khan D. Allahawardi Khan

144. Daud Khan was defeated by Akbar in the battle of:
A. Bahadurpur B. Munger
C. Rajmahal D. Chausa

145. The East India Company proclaimed the diwani rights of Bengal, Bihar and Odisha during the reign of:
A. Mir Qasim B. Shah Alam II
C. Farrukhsiyar D. Alivardi Khan

146. Who became the deputy Nawab of Bihar after the Battle of Plassey (1757)?
A. Mir Jafar B. Miran
C. Shujjat Khan D. Tabtabai

147. The first British traveller to visit Bihar was:
A. Bishop Heber B. Peter Mundy
C. John Marshall D. Raulf Fitch

148. Which Nawab of Bengal transferred his capital from Mushidabad to Munger?
A. Mir Jafar B. Siraj-ud-Daulah
C. Mir Qasim D. Alivardi Khan

149. In which year the Dutch established their first factory in Bihar?
A. 1620 B. 1651
C. 1609 D. 1632

150. In which year the Danes established their factory in Patna?
A. 1774 B. 1664
C. 1631 D. 1786

151. The Britishers established their first trading centre in 1620 Bihar at:
A. Munger B. Alamganj (Patna)
C. Purnea D. Champaran

152. Who among the following was the first to oppose the British rule in Bihar?
A. Ali Gauhar B. Haider Ali Khan
C. Kunwar Singh D. Mir Qasim

153. In which year was the Revenue Council of Patna established?
A. 1770 B. 1765
C. 1801 D. 1719

154. In which year did the company remove Dhiraj Narayan and replaced him with Raja Shitab Rai as the Naib Diwan of Bihar?
A. 1801 B. 1767
C. 1791 D. 1765

155. The Golghar in Patna was constructed during the reign of:
A. Warren Hastings B. Lord Hardinge
C. John Shore D. Lord Cornwallis

156. The first English magistrate of Patna was:
A. James Alexander B. Charles Francis Grand
C. Robert Palk D. John Vansittart

157. The battle of Buxar was fought on:
A. October 22, 1764 B. September 23, 1761
C. June 24, 1764 D. June 24, 1761

158. Who was the commander of British army in the battle of Buxar?
A. Clive B. Lord Hastings
C. Hector Munro D. Major Knox

159. Who emerged victorious in the battle of Buxar?
A. Shuja-ud-daulah B. East India Company
C. Shah Alam II D. Mir Qasim

160. Who was appointed as the Naib Diwan of Bihar by Robert Clive?
A. Omichand B. Shitab Rai
C. Raja Durlabh Rai D. Manik Chand

161. Which of the following is not related to Wahabi movement?
A. Syed Ahmad B. Shah Waliullah
C. Vilayat Ali D. Birsa Munda

162. In which year Wahabi movement was started?
A. 1820 B. 1830
C. 1840 D. 1850

163. Which of the following was/were the centres for the Wahabi Movement?
A. Patna B. Sittana
C. Both A and B D. None of these

164. Who led the Kol revolt?
A. Budhu Bhagat B. Sidhu and Kanhu
C. Birsa Munda D. Raja Porhat

165. Who led the Bhumij revolt?
A. Ganga Narayan B. Sidhu and Kanhu
C. Sayed Hasan D. Raja Porhat

166. Who among the following participated in the revolt of Tana Bhagat?
A. Ho tribe B. Munda tribe
C. Santhal tribe D. Oraon tribe

167. The Tana Bhagat movement was essentially a ________ movement.
A. religious B. political
C. social D. natural

168. The occupation of which of the following region led the HO uprising?
A. occupation of Singhbhum
B. occupation of Chhotanagpur
C. occupation of Kalahandi
D. None of the above

169. In which year Kol uprising began?
A. 1832 B. 1831
C. 1833 D. 1834

170. Who among the following was the leader of Ho tribals movement?
A. Raja Parhat B. Sidhu and Kanhu
C. Birsa Munda D. Budhu Bhagat

171. In which year Bhumij revolt started?
A. 1831 B. 1832
C. 1833 D. 1834

172. The term 'ulgulan' means:
A. Rebellion B. Courageous
C. Tribal movement D. Tribal song

173. Santhal uprising was led by:
A. Sidhu and Kanhu B. Birsa Munda
C. Budhu Bhagat D. None of them

174. Kunwar Singh was the King of:
A. Hamirpur B. Dheerpur
C. Jagdishpur D. Rampur

175. The leaders of the revolt of 1857 in Bihar was:
A. Maulvi Ahmadullah B. Tatya Tope
C. Nana Sahib D. Kunwar Singh

176. Who among the following had established an arms and ammunition factory at Jagdishpur?
A. Amar Singh B. Kunwar Singh
C. Pir Ali D. Harkishen Singh

177. Which region in Bihar was unaffected by the revolt of 1857?
1. Danapur 2. Patna
3. Ara 4. Muzaffarpur
5. Munger
Choose from the following options:
A. 4 and 5 B. Only 5
C. Only 4 D. 3, 4 and 5

178. The rulers of which state denied entry to Kunwar Singh in his state?
A. Rewa B. Azamgarh
C. Awadh D. Banda

179. Kunwar Singh fought his last war against which English captain?
A. Douglas B. Lugard
C. Le Grand D. Eyre

180. Who was the leader of Patna uprising in 1857?
A. Jaimangal Singh B. Inayat Ali
C. Vilayat Ali D. Pir Ali

181. Who arrested Amar Singh, the leader of revolt of 1857?
A. Lugard
B. Maharaja Jang Bahadur
C. Maharaja Rai Bahadur
D. Samuels

182. Kunwar Singh tried to meet which of the following leaders in October 1857?
A. Lakshmibai B. Liaqat Ali
C. Tatya Tope D. Begum Hazrat Mahal

183. Pir Ali, the leader of Patna rising was convicted and hanged on:
A. July 7, 1858 B. July 7, 1857
C. August 7, 1857 D. August 7, 1858

184. At which place in Bihar the revolt of 1857 started comprehensively for the first time?
A. Patna B. Munger
C. Muzaffarpur D. Rajgir

185. When did Kunwar Singh die?
A. 10 April, 1858 B. 23 April, 1858
C. 26 April, 1858 D. 20 June, 1858

186. Amar Singh initiated the guerilla war against the British in the hills of:
A. Rajgir B. Ranchi
C. Kaimur D. None of the above

187. The Zamindars of the following places helped the Company during the revolt of 1857?
A. Hathua B. Pandaul
C. Bettiah D. All of the above

188. Kunwar Singh captured which of the following districts on March 25, 1858?
A. Rewa B. Kanpur
C. Azamgarh D. Kalpi

189. Kunwar Singh helped Nana Saheb in the war of:
A. Lucknow B. Kanpur
C. Shahabad D. Jhansi

190. Who had invited Gandhiji in West Champaran district in Bihar?
A. Raj Kumar Shukla B. Mahadeo Desai
C. Rajendra Prasad D. Narhari Parikh

191. Which of the following Government Acts separated Odisha from Bihar province?
A. 1909 Act B. 1919 Act
C. 1935 Act D. 1948 Act

192. In Bihar, resolution for Non-cooperation Movement was passed in 1920 provincial meeting under the leadership of:
A. Rajendra Prasad B. Mazhar-ul-Haq
C. Shah Mohammad D. None of the above

193. In which year the period of Swarajist Movement started in Bihar?
A. 1920 B. 1922
C. 1921 D. 1923

194. The All India Congress Session in 1922, December was held in:
A. Patna B. Gaya
C. Bhagalpur D. Champaran

195. Which of the following movements is called first Civil Disobedience Movement?
A. Champaran B. Bhagalpur
C. Bardoli D. Gaya

196. Patna Yuvak Sangh was formed in:
A. 1929 B. 1926
C. 1928 D. 1927

197. Where was Anushilan Committee Branch established in Bihar?
A. Gaya B. Patna
C. Muzaffarpur D. Munger

198. When the British prince visited Bihar?
A. 1921 B. 1922
C. 1923 D. 1924

199. Who had formed Bihar Provincial Kisan Sabha (BPKS)?
A. Shahjanand Saraswati
B. Mohammad Zubair
C. Sri Krishna Singh
D. Rajendra Prasad

200. Champaran Satyagraha was against:
A. Tinkathiya system B. High rent
C. Outsiders D. Illegal transfer of land

201. When was Bihar Socialist Party established?
A. 1934 B. 1932
C. 1931 D. 1933

202. Who was the leader of Salt Satyagraha in Bihar?
A. Rajendra Prasad B. Jawaharlal Nehru
C. Gandhiji D. Professor Abdul Bari

203. Salt Revolt in Patna had started from which of the following dates?
A. 16th April, 1930 B. 18th April, 1930
C. 4th May, 1930 D. 3rd April, 1930

204. Which of the following physical features form the North-Western Part of Bihar?
A. Someshwar range B. Kaimur Plateau
C. Nawada hills D. Rajgir hills

205. In Bihar, Kaimur series of rocks are found in which district?
A. Bhojpur B. Aurangabad
C. Buxar D. Kaimur

206. Geologically southern plateau of Bihar was formed in the period.
A. Pre-cambrian B. Oligocene
C. Miocene D. Pleistocene

207. Mica deposits are found in which kind of rocks?
A. Dharwar B. Tertiary
C. Vindhyan D. Quaternary

208. The highest place of Bihar is:
A. Santpur B. Kaimur hills
C. Someshwar range D. Barabar hills

209. In which period was Ramnagar Dun formed?
A. Dharwar B. Quaternary
C. Vindhyan D. Tertiary

210. Bihar was maximum areal extent in which of the following natural regions?
A. Terai region of Shiwalik
B. North Gangetic Plan
C. South Gangetic Plan
D. None of the above

211. Chuars found in the Bihar plain are:
A. flooded plain B. levees
C. oxbow lakes D. highlands

212. In which district(s) of Bihar, gneiss, quartzite and schist rocks arc found?
A. Munger B. Gaya
C. Sheikhpura D. All of these

213. The capital of the Shungas was at:
A. Sialkot B. Rajagriha
C. Kannauj D. Pataliputra

214. Out of the total geographical area of India, Bihar comprises:
A. 3.76% B. 6.76%
C. 4.02% D. 2.86%

215. The total geographical area of Bihar is:
A. 94,162 sq.km B. 94,163 sq.km
C. 94,164 sq.km D. 94,165 sq.km

216. Bihar forms an international boundary with which country?
A. Bhutan B. Bangladesh
C. Nepal D. China

217. Which district of Bihar has the longest border with Nepal?
A. West Champaran B. Sitamarhi
C. Kishanganj D. East Champaran

218. The highest part of Ramnagar Dun is:
A. Someshwar fort B. Santpur
C. Gridhkut D. Barabar

219. The length of Bihar from east to west is:
A. 483 km B. 362 km
C. 401 km D. 415 km

220. Harha valley which is located in north-western Bihar is also known as:
A. Ramnagar Dun B. Dun Valley
C. Someshwar Range D. None of the above

221. Which of the following ranges form a boundary between India and Nepal?
A. Kaimur Hills B. Ramnagar Dun
C. Someshwar Ranges D. None of the above

222. Gogaville Bird Sanctuary is situated in which district of Bihar?
A. Arwal B. Aurangabad
C. Araria D. Banka

223. Mandar Vidyapeeth is situated in:
A. West Champaran B. Vaishali
C. Darbhanga D. Banka

224. The Indian Oil Refinery is located in which district of Bihar?
A. Begusarai B. Sitamarhi
C. Katihar D. Supaul

225. Ustad Bismillah Khan was a native of:
A. Ara B. Dumraon
C. Darbhanga D. Sasaram

226. Bela Industrial Area is located at:
A. Sitamarhi B. East Champaran
C. Darbhanga D. Purnea

227. Raxaul town is also known as:
A. Gateway to Nepal
B. Gateway to Bangladesh
C. Gateway to Bhutan
D. None of these

228. Vishnupad Temple was rebuilt by:
A. Ahilya Bai Holkar B. Sher Shah
C. Kunwar Singh D. Kameshwar Thakhur

229. Where is Tal soil found in Bihar?
A. In terai region
B. In plains
C. In desert
D. In backwater belt of river Ganga

230. Tal soil extends from Buxar to:
A. Banka B. Gaya
C. Bhagalpur D. Champaran

231. What are the major crops that can be grown of Balthar soil?
A. Rice B. Jowar and Bajra
C. Sugarcane D. Pulses

232. Lowest temperature in Bihar is found in:
A. Gaya B. Buxar
C. Rohtas D. Darbhanga

233. Which type of soil is predominantly found in the plains of Ganga?
A. Residual soil B. Alluvial soil
C. Both A and B D. None of the above

234. In which district of Bihar Balsundari soil is found?
A. Saharsa B. Darbhanga
C. Muzaffarpur D. All of the above

235. The old alluvial soil is found in which of the following districts of Bihar:
A. Nalanda B. Munger
C. Bhagalpur D. All of the above

236. Which district of Bihar records the highest temperature?
A. Aurangabad B. Gaya
C. Saran D. Siwan

237. The Bhagar soil in Bihar is found in:
A. Gaya–Bodhgaya–East Champaran Bhagalpur area
B. Purnea–Saharsa–Darbhanga–Muzaffarpur area
C. Gaya–Nalanda–Bodhgaya–Saharsa area
D. East Champaran–Nalanda–Gaya–Sasaram area

238. The Old alluvial soil in Bihar is found in:
A. Rohtas–Gaya–Patna–Munger–Bhagalpur area
B. Purnea–Saharsa–Darbhanga–Muzaffarpur area
C. Saharsa–Darbhanga–Muzaffarpur–Saran area
D. None of the above

239. In which area of Bihar the concentration of lime in the soil is found:
A. North Bihar plain
B. South Bihar plain
C. North-West Bihar plain
D. South-East Bihar plain

240. Consider the following statements about Norwesters.
(*i*) It is a cyclonic wind
(*ii*) It brings rainfall of about 10 cm in Bihar plain
(*iii*) It is useful for crops like mango, litchi, rice and jute.
(*iv*) It is a hot wind blowing from west.

Which of the above statement/s is/are wrong?
A. (*i*), (*ii*) and (*iii*) B. Only (*iv*)
C. (*i*) and (*iv*) D. (*iii*) and (*iv*)

241. In which of the following districts Khadar soil is found?
A. Bhagalpur and Araria
B. Patna and Nalanda
C. Purnea and Saharsa
D. None of the above

242. What is the older alluvium of Ganga plains called?
A. Bhabhar B. Bangar
C. Khadar D. Balsundari

243. Which district of Bihar gets highest rainfall?
A. Araria B. Kishanganj
C. Gaya D. Aurangabad

244. The local winds loo blowing in Bihar has following wind velocity:
A. 10-16 km/hr B. 10-14 km/hr
C. 8-16 km/hr D. 12-16 km/hr

245. The rainfall during monsoon in Bihar is due to:
A. Eastern monsoon B. South-east monsoon
C. Southern monsoon D. South-west monsoon

246. Which of the following crops is grown in red and yellow soil?
A. Pulses B. Sugarcane
C. Rice D. Wheat

247. Usar soil is found in which district?
A. Saran B. West Champaran
C. Siwan D. Nawada

248. Which of the following Wildlife Sanctuaries has hot springs?
A. Bhimbandh B. Vikramshila
C. Sanjay Gandhi D. Kaimur

249. The tropical seasonal swamp forests (canebrakes) are predominantly found in:
A. Gopalganj B. East Champaran
C. Sitamarhi D. West Champaran

250. A Wildlife safari is being established at which place?
A. Rajgir B. West Champaran
C. Sasaram D. Jamui

251. Bhimbandh Wildlife Sanctuary is famous for:
A. Tiger B. Elephant
C. Leopard D. Resident Birds

252. Find the wrong match:

	Wildlife Sanctuaries	District
A.	Valmiki	West Champaran
B.	Kaimur	Rohtas
C.	Vikramshila	Begusarai
D.	Bhimbandh	Munger

253. In which of the following wild life sanctuaries is Anupam lake situated?
A. Vikramshila B. Valmiki
C. Bhimbandh D. Kaimur

254. The largest wildlife sanctuary in Bihar is:
A. Bhimbandh
B. Valmiki
C. Sanjay Gandhi Udyan
D. Kaimur

255. Area of very dense forest is highest in:
A. West Champaran B. Siwan
C. Nawada D. East Champaran

256. The Vikramshila Gangetic Dolphin Sanctuary is located in:
A. Jamui B. Munger
C. Bhagalpur D. Vaishali

257. Kusheshwar Asthan Bird Sanctuary is located in:
A. Vaishali B. West Champaran
C. Samastipur D. Darbhanga

258. Gautam Buddha Bird Sanctuary is located in:
A. Rohtas B. Gaya
C. Nalanda D. Sasaram

259. Udaypur Vanya Prani Sanctuary is located in:
A. East Champaran B. Munger
C. West Champaran D. Rohtas

260. Baraila Jheel Salim Ali Jubba Sahni Bird Sanctuary is located in:
A. Vaishali B. Sheohar
C. Darbhanga D. Banka

261. The Bihar Government declared the Sanjay Gandhi Jaivik Udyan in Patna as protected forest in which year?
A. 1991 B. 1983
C. 1984 D. 1982

262. Nagi Dam Bird Sanctuary and Nakti Dam Bird Sanctuary are located in which district of Bihar?
A. Begusarai B. Siwan
C. Gaya D. Jamui

263. The Centre of Noise Pollution Control Board has been set up at:
A. Siwan B. Bhagalpur
C. Muzaffarpur D. Patna

264. The main vegetation of Bihar is:
A. Deciduous B. Tropical Evergreen
C. Mixed D. Alpine

265. In which of the following districts the Sal mixed deciduous forests are found?
A. Gaya B. Bhagalpur
C. West Champaran D. East Champaran

266. Which river is also known as Niranjana?
A. Gandak B. Phalgu
C. Sone D. Mahananda

267. Why is Bagmati considered as a dangerous river?
A. Due to its changing course
B. Due to its origin in the Himalayas
C. Due to its tendency to create floods
D. None of the above

268. ______ river emerges from Nampa of Nepal situated at Himalayan ranges.
A. Gandak B. Bagmati
C. Kamla D. Ghaghra

269. The North tributaries of the Ganga river are Gandak, Bagmati, Kosi Kalikosi and ______.
A. Son B. Karmanasa
C. Punpun D. All of these

270. Durgavati and Chandraprabha are important tributaries of which of the following rivers?
A. Karmanasa B. Punpun
C. Phalgu D. Saryu

271. Which pair of springs of Bihar along with their places is not correctly matched?

Springs	Places
A. Sita Kund	Rajgir
B. Rishi Kund	Munger
C. Surya Kund	Rajgir
D. Brahma Kund	Rajgir

272. Which river does not originate from Himalayas?
A. Bagmati B. Ganga
C. Kamla Balan D. Son

273. Triveni canal gets water from which river?
A. Son B. Kosi
C. Gandak D. Mayurakshi

274. Which of the following rivers of Bihar is almost dry in summer season?
A. Ganga B. Gandak
C. Punpun D. Kosi

275. Which of the following rivers has second longest length in the Bihar state?
A. Ganga B. Bagmati
C. Mahananda D. Burhi Gandak

276. Which river has the largest catchment area in Bihar?
A. Ganga B. Sone
C. Kiul Harohar D. Kosi

277. In which of the following districts river Ganga enters into Bihar?
A. Gopalganj B. Buxar
C. Rohtas D. Siwan

278. Which river is known as 'Sorrow of Bihar'?
A. Karmanasa B. Kosi
C. Son D. Subarnarekha

279. Which river is the sacred river for Hindus?
A. Punpun B. Phalgu
C. Karmanasa D. Sone

280. Name the bridge constructed over the river Ganga which connects Patna to Hajipur.
A. Mahatma Gandhi Setu
B. Hirakund Setu
C. Gopalganj Bridge
D. None of the above

281. Which river of Bihar does originate from the Someshwar hills and flows parallel to river Gandak?

A. Burhi Gandak
B. Gandak
C. Kamla
D. Bagmati

282. The deposits of manganese are found in the district(s) of:
A. Rohtas
B. Kaimur
C. Darbhanga
D. Patna and Gaya

283. Uranium is found in which of the following districts of Bihar?
A. Gaya
B. Rohtas
C. Munger
D. Banka

284. Gold is found in:
A. Munger
B. Jamui
C. Siwan
D. Saran

285. The deposits of Monazite are found in which districts of Bihar?
A. Siwan and Saran
B. Patna and Aurangabad
C. Gaya and Munger
D. Banka and Bhagalpur

286. Amjhor is famous for which of the following minerals?
A. Coal
B. Pyrite
C. Mica
D. Gold

287. Pyrite Phosphate and Chemicals Ltd. is located at:
A. Bihta
B. Amjhor
C. Jamui
D. Nawada

288. The least populous district of Bihar is:
A. Sheikhpura
B. Madhubani
C. Saran
D. Gaya

289. According to Census 2011, the child sex ratio of Bihar is:
A. 935
B. 938
C. 918
D. 925

290. Which among the following districts of Bihar has the lowest sex ratio?
A. Vaishali
B. Arwal
C. Saran
D. Siwan

291. Which among the following districts of Bihar has lowest population density?
A. Arwal
B. Madhubani
C. Saran
D. Kaimur

292. Which among the following districts of Bihar has the highest population density?
A. Sheohar
B. Siwan
C. Saran
D. Sitamarhi

293. The most populous district of Bihar is:
A. Patna
B. Madhubani
C. Saran
D. Gaya

294. As per Census 2011, the literacy rate of Bihar is:
A. 61.8%
B. 71.2%
C. 52.5%
D. 23.5%

295. As per Census 2011, the population density of Bihar is:
A. 223
B. 153
C. 1106
D. 123

296. According to Census 2011, what is the sex ratio of Bihar?
A. 918
B. 982
C. 972
D. 935

297. Which among the following districts of Bihar has the highest sex ratio?
A. Saran
B. Sheohar
C. Madhubani
D. Gopalganj

298. Which among the following districts of Bihar has the lowest child population?
A. Vaishali
B. Arwal
C. Saran
D. Siwan

299. According to Census 2011, the total population of Bihar is:
A. 10,40,99,452
B. 56,58,509
C. 68,70,997
D. 70,68,997

300. Highest production of wheat is recorded in which of the following districts?
A. Siwan
B. Rohtas
C. Kaimur
D. Muzaffarpur

301. Highest production of potato is recorded in which of the following districts?
A. Nalanda
B. Patna
C. Saran
D. Katihar

302. Sonaru Fish Seed Farm is being developed at which of the following places?
A. Badh
B. Muzaffarpur
C. Gaya
D. Fatuha

303. Which districts of Bihar has the highest population of goats?
A. Bhagalpur
B. West Champaran
C. Araria
D. East Champaran

304. Which district of Bihar is the leading produce of maize?
A. Katihar
B. Madhepura
C. Khagaria
D. Kaimur

305. The district of Bihar having the highest productivity (kg/hectare) of rice is:
A. Rohtas
B. Lakhisarai
C. Sheikhpura
D. West Champaran

306. A Fishery Research Centre has been established at which place:
A. Sonepur
B. Fatuha
C. Mithapur
D. Araria

307. The leading fish producing districts in Bihar are:
A. Kaimur, West Champaran, Madhubani
B. Madhubani, East Champaran, Darbhanga

C. Sitamarhi, Vaishali, Banka
D. Bhagalpur, Supaul, Saharsa

308. Which districts will be benefitted by the Budi Gandak–Noon-via-Ganga link scheme?
A. Samastipur, Begusarai, Khagaria
B. Jamui, Bhagalpur, Banka
C. Jamui, Banka, Lakhisarai
D. Kanpur, Rohtas, Aurangabad

309. The main cereal rops of Bihar are:
A. Groundnut, Coffee, Wheat
B. Sugarane, Tea, Barley
C. Rice, Wheat, Maize
D. None of the above

310. Which of the following district in Bihar is leader in terms of pulses production?
A. Patna B. Aurangabad
C. Nalanda D. Rohtas

311. Which of the following districts of Bihar has highest percentage of net sown area?
A. Siwan B. Gopalganj
C. Buxar D. Bhojpur

312. Which district of Bihar has the largest area under whcat cultivation?
A. East Champaran B. Rohtas
C. Kishanganj D. Siwan

313. Which district of Bihar has the largest area under rice cultivation?
A. Madhubani B. Samastipur
C. East Champaran D. Rohtas

314. Which district of Bihar has the largest area under maize cultivation?
A. Samastipur B. East Champaran
C. Begusarai D. Khagaria

315. Which district of Bihar has recorded highest productivity (kg/hectare) of sugarcane?
A. West Champaran B. Nalanda
C. Jehanabad D. East Champaran

316. Who has described agriculture as the Core Competence of Bihar?
A. APJ Abdul Kalam B. Pranab Mukherjee
C. Atal Behari Vajpayee D. M.S. Swaminathan

317. The marketing of dairy products in Bihar is done by which of the following organization?
A. KVIC B. COMFED
C. BIADA D. PMEGP

318. The medicine industry is situated in which of the following places?
A. Naryanpur B. Rampur
C. Bela D. Fatuha

319. The major implementing agency for Prime Minister Employment Generation Programme (PMEGP) is:
A. SIPB B. KVIC
C. KVI BOARD D. DIC

320. A Food Park is being established at which place?
A. Buxar B. Araria
C. Katihar D. Bettiah

321. In which year the Bihar State Milk Cooperative Federation was established?
A. 1984 B. 1981
C. 1980 D. 1983

322. Mukhyamantri Integrated Handloom Development Scheme was started in year:
A. 2011-12 B. 2012-13
C. 2013-14 D. 2014-15

323. The gun factory in Bihar is situated at which place?
A. Bhagalpur B. Sitamarhi
C. Munger D. Patna

324. In which five year plan was Barauni Oil Refinery in Bihar established?
A. Third B. Second
C. Fifth D. Fourth

325. In which district of Bihar the first Jute Park is being established?
A. Purnea B. Aurangabad
C. Begusarai D. Khagaria

326. At which place is Bihar Institute of Silk and Textiles located?
A. Nabinagar B. Fatuha
C. Bihta D. Nathnagar

327. The yarn produced under Mukhya Mantri Kosi Mulberry Scheme will be marketed under the brand name of:
A. Koshiki B. Mulberry Silk
C. Resham D. Tassar Silk

328. Which institute is the Cluster Monitoring and Technical Assistant (CMTA) for Bhagalpur Mega Handloom Cluster?
A. Rajendra Agriultural University, Pusa
B. NIFT, Patna
C. Bihar Institute for Silk and Textiles, Nathnagar
D. Bihar Agricultural University, Sabour

329. Match the corret pairs:

Cities	**Industry**
(*a*) Muzaffarpur	1. Tea
(*b*) Purnea	2. Tourism
(*c*) Kishanganj	3. Jute
(*d*) Gaya	4. Leather

Codes:

	(*a*)	(*b*)	(*a*)	(*d*)
A.	1	2	3	4
B.	4	3	2	1
C.	2	3	4	1
D.	4	3	1	2

330. In which of the following district of Bihar Castor Silk Development Project has been approved?
A. Purnea B. Katihar
C. Begusarai D. Kishanganj

331. The Plywood industry in Bihar is located in:
A. Hajipur B. Siwan
C. Muzaffarpur D. Motihari

332. Find out the incorrect pair:

A. Hajipur	Plywood
B. Purnea	Jute
C. Chakulia	Leather
D. Samastipur	Paper

333. Which city of Bihar is also known as Silk City?
A. Bhagalpur B. Purnea
C. Banka D. Madhubani

334. In which year was the sugar industry established in Bihar?
A. 1904 B. 1908
C. 1916 D. 1921

335. Which NGO is involved in the Tasar Silk Development at Chakai in Jamui?
A. Pahal B. Pradan
C. Prabandh D. Prarthna

336. The first diamond polishing unit in Bihar is being established at:
A. Patna B. Gaya
C. Muzaffarpur D. Samastipur

337. Mokama in Bihar is famous for:
A. Shoe factory B. Wagon of goods train
C. Brewery D. All of the above

338. The jute industry in Bihar is concentrated in which region:
A. North-western B. North-eastern
C. South-eastern D. Central

339. The Oil Refinery in Barauni was set up with the help of which country?
A. USA B. USSR
C. Britain D. Germany

340. The first radio station in Bihar was established at which place?
A. Muzaffarpur B. Patna
C. Darbhanga D. Sitamarhi

341. Abdul Bari Bridge is on the river Son at:
A. Koilwar B. Sonpur
C. Mokama D. Bhagalpur

342. The BSRTC was established in:
A. 1957 B. 1958
C. 1960 D. 1959

343. Which zone of Indian Railways lies in Bihar with its headquarters at Hajipur?
A. North-East Frontier Railways
B. East Central Zone
C. North-East Zone
D. Central Zone

344. Which two places in Bihar have international airports?
A. Patna and Muzaffarpur
B. Gaya and Bhagalpur
C. Patna and Gaya
D. Patna and Rajgir

345. Which National Highway in Bihar is a part of Golden Quadrangle project?
A. NH2 B. NH 31
C. NH 35 D. NH 38

346. The waterways present in river Ganga between Allahabad and Haldia is:
A. NW 2 B. NW 3
C. NW 1 D. NW 4

347. In which year was Bihar Rural Road Development Agency established?
A. 2004 B. 2003
C. 2002 D. 2001

348. A flying club is situated in which of the following places?
A. Nalanda B. Gaya
C. Patna D. Bhagalpur

349. Jaiprakash Narain International Airport is situated at:
A. Patna B. Nalanda
C. Bhagalpur D. Gaya

350. The capital of the Kanvas was at:
A. Ujjain B. Mathura
C. Pratishthan D. Pataliputra

351. Find the wrong pair:
A. Darbhanga – Nehru Setu
B. Bhagalpur – Vikramshila Setu
C. Mokama – Rajendra Setu
D. Patna – Gandhi Setu

352. In which of the following cities Vayudut service has been started?
A. Muzaffarpur B. Gaya
C. Raxaul D. Patna

353. Kataiya Hydro Power Project is located in which district of Bihar?
A. Supaul B. Katihar
C. Arwal D. Kishanganj

354. The highest installed capacity for power generation in Bihar is from:
A. Hydel Projects
B. Wind Projects
C. Thermal Power Projects
D. Nuclear Power Plants

355. In which district of Bihar an Ultra Mega Plant of 4000 MW capacity is being established?

A. Buxar B. Supaul
C. Katihar D. Banka

356. In which year was Bihar State Electricity Board established?

A. 2000 B. 1958
C. 1936 D. 1948

357. Find the wrong Match:

A. Nirmali Hydel Project Madhubani
B. Tejpura Hydel Projet Arwal
C. Rajpur Hydel Project Supaul
D. Amethi Hydel Projet Rohtas

358. Which of the following schemes have been launched by the central government for expanding the coverage of electricity supply?

A. IPDS B. DDUGJY
C. BRGF D. All of the above

359. Kosi Hydel Power Station is under the administration of:

A. BSHPC B. BREDA
C. BSEB D. None of the above

360. NABARD has identified how many districts in Bihar for promoting and financing women SHGs through positioning an anchor NGO in each identified district?

A. 15 B. 16
C. 17 D. 18

361. Which of the following reasons have been identified by NABARD for the dismal performance of SHGs in Bihar?

A. delays in opening SHG accounts
B. inadequate outreach in many regions
C. non-approval of repeat loans even when the first loans were repaired promptly
D. All of the above

362. Which of the following sectors are convered by RIDF?

A. Agriculture and Related sector
B. Social sectors
C. Rural connectivity
D. All of the above

363. Which district of Bihar has the highest participation of women in employment under MGNREGA?

A. Begusarai B. Darbhanga
C. Supaul D. Saharsa

364. The total number of Zila Parishads in Bihar are:

A. 36 B. 38
C. 41 D. 31

365. The chairperson of Zila Parishad is called:

A. Adhyaksha B. Mukhiya
C. Pramukh D. None of these

366. The Chairperson of Panchayat Samiti is called:

A. Mukhiya B. Adhyaksha
C. Pramukh D. Sarpanch

367. The Chairperson of Gram Panchayat is called:

A. Mukhiya B. Pramukh
C. Adhyaksha D. None of these

368. Bihar Panchayat Strengthening Project is being implemented with the help of:

A. SBI B. IMF
C. ADB D. World Bank

369. Which two cities of Bihar have received administrative approval for the implementation of Heritage City Development and Augmen-tation Yojana (HRIDAY)?

A. Ara and Sasaram B. Patna and Muzaffarpur
C. Gaya and Patna D. Gaya and Bodh Gaya

370. Which agency has been given the task of preparation of Detailed Project Report (DPR) for Patna Metro Rail Project?

A. CPWD B. DMRC
C. RITES Ltd. D. SE Railway

371. In which town of Bihar is Satyagraha Park being developed?

A. Motihari B. Bettiah
C. Ara D. Bhagalpur

372. Buddha Smriti Park is developed in which city of Bihar?

A. Vaishali B. Bhagalpur
C. Hajipur D. Patna

373. In which year was Bihar Urban Infrastructure Development Corporation (BUIDCO) established?

A. 2007 B. 2008
C. 2009 D. 2010

374. UIG and UIDSSMT are the sub-components of which of the following urban development programmes:

A. AMRUT
B. HRIDAY
C. Swachh Bharat Mission
D. Namami Ganga Scheme

375. The Namami Gange Scheme, a Central government programme aiming at the cleaning and rejuvenation of the river Ganga is being implemented in how many towns of Bihar:

A. 31 B. 20
C. 34 D. 35

376. The Support Programme for Urban Reforms (SPUR) is being implemented in 28 largest ULBs in Bihar with the support of:

A. USA B. Russia
C. France D. UK

377. Which three cities in Bihar have qualified to be developed under Phase I of Smart City Mission?
A. Patna, Bhagalpur, Muzaffarpur
B. Bhagalpur, Muzaffarpur, Gaya
C. Bhagalpur, Muzaffarpur, Biharsharif
D. Muzaffarpur, Biharsharif, Patna

378. The year for achieving the goals of Bihar Urban Agenda prepared by the state government is:
A. 2029 B. 2030
C. 2031 D. 2032

379. The first two towns in Bihar where property survey has been completed along with unique house numbering and number plate fixing:
A. Katihar, Banka B. Purnea, Banka
C. Katihar, Purnea D. Bhagalpur, Darbhanga

380. Which are the two mission cities in Bihar under the Urban Infrastructure and Governance (UIG) component of AMRUT?
A. Patna Urban Agglomeration, Bodhgaya
B. Gaya, Bodhgaya
C. Gaya, Jehanabad
D. Patna Urban Agglomeration, Gaya

381. JnNURM, a flagship programme for improving urban infrastructure in mission cities has been replaced by:
A. HRIDAY
B. Namami Gange Scheme
C. Swachh Bharat Mission
D. AMRUT

382. Which are the best three districts in Bihar in terms of availability of health infrastructure?
A. Sheohar, Sheikhpura, Sitamarhi
B. Jamui, Sheikhpura, Nawada
C. Bhagalpur, Banka, Bhojpur
D. Patna, Muzaffarpur, Darbhanga

383. In which district a new medical college Vardhamaan Ayurvigyan Sansthan, has been established?
A. Patna B. Samastipur
C. Bettiah D. Nalanda

384. Which of the following is incorrect?

A. IGIMS	Patna
B. Government Medical College	Bettiah
C. Narayan Medical college	Kishanganj
D. Vardhaman Ayurvigyan Sansthan	Nalanda

385. In which of the following districts of Bihar, Indira Gandhi Matritva Sahyog Yojana is operational?
A. East Champaran and West Champaran
B. Banka and Saharsa
C. Vaishali and Sitamarhi
D. Vaishali and Saharsa

386. Which of the following statement/statements is/are true regarding SABLA scheme?
A. It is a 100 per cent centrally sponsored shceme.
B. It is a comprehensive intervention for adolescent girls in the age group of 11-18 years.
C. It has a special focus on out-of-school girls.
D. All of the above

387. Consider the following statements regarding Janani Suraksha Yojana (JSY):
(*i*) It is an intervention for safe motherhood
(*ii*) It operates under National Health Mission
(*iii*) It is aimed at reducing maternal and neo-natal mortality by promoting institutional delivery among the poor women.

Which of the above statements are true regarding JSY?
A. (*i*) and (*ii*) B. (*ii*) and (*iii*)
C. (*i*) and (*iii*) D. All are true

388. Gargi Samhita mentions the attack of Greeks on Pataliputra. This attack took place during the reign of:
A. Vasudeva B. Dhanananda
C. Chandragupta II D. Pushyamitra

389. In which of the following district of Bihar the extent of institution delivery is highest?
A. Samastipur B. Purnea
C. Patna D. East Champaran

390. The bed occupancy rate means that the hospitals admit people with serious illness for their treatment. It reveals the availability of health infrastructure in a state. For Bihar as a whole, the bed occupancy rate is very high. Which of the following districts in Bihar has the highest bed occupancy rate?
A. Patna B. Bhojpur
C. Muzaffarpur D. Gaya

391. According to Manav Vikas Mission the target for Pupil-Teacher Ratio (PTR) in elementary education based on enrolment is:
A. 32 : 1 B. 40 : 1
C. 35 : 1 D. 30 : 1

392. The Mid-Day Meal Scheme (MDMS) covers the children belonging to classes:
A. I to VIII B. VI to VIII
C. I to V D. I to X

393. Bihar Education Project (Council) is the implementing agency for which of the following schemes:
A. Mid-Day Meal Scheme
B. Sarva Shiksha Abhiyan
C. Mission Gunwatta
D. None of the above

394. Pratham, a reputed non-government organization has been conducting learning assessment tests in every state, including Bihar. The results of these tests are presented in Annual Status of Education Report (ASER).

Consider the following results of ASER and identify which of the statement/statements is/are correct.

(*i*) In standard III, the percentage of students with satisfactory reading skills is lower in Bihar than the national average, while for mathematical skills it is nearly the same.

(*ii*) For standard V students, the percentage of students with satisfactory reading skills is same for both Bihar and India, however, for mathematics skills, the figures for Bihar are much higher.

A. Only (*i*) is correct
B. Only (*ii*) is orrect
C. None of them are correct
D. Both (*i*) and (*ii*) are correct

395. A high level committee has been constituted in Bihar under the chairmanship of Chief Secretary for the inclusion of which tribe in the category of scheduled tribe in Bihar.

A. Tharu B. Munda
C. Mal Pahariya D. Oraon

396. The Government of Bihar has decided to appoint Vikas Mitras at the Gram Panchayat and ward level for an effective implementation of various development and welfare schemes for a particular community. Name the community.

A. SC B. ST
C. Minorities D. Mahadalits

397. Which institution has been appointed as the nodal agency for imparting physical training to minority candidates for appearing in the examination of Bihar Police Service Recruitment?

A. Patna University
B. Mazharul Haque Arabi-Persian University
C. Magadha University
D. Tilka Manjhi University

398. The Government of Bihar has introduced reservation for women in panchayati raj institution and urban local bodies. How much reservation is provided?

A. 50 per cent B. 33 per cent
C. 51 per cent D. 75 per cent

399. In which of the following districts of Bihar, the state government operates AASRA, a 50-bedded special residential home for mentally challenged women and girls.

A. Samastipur B. Gaya
C. Siwan D. Patna

400. How much reservation is provided to women in direct recruitment for the posts of constable and in appointing junior inspector in the police force?

A. 33 per cent B. 50 per cent
C. 40 per cent D. 35 per cent

401. The objective of Samajik Punarvas Kosh Yojana which is in operation in all the districts of Bihar is:

A. to provide financial assistance to poor families at the time of marriage of girls who have attained the age of 18
B. to rehabilitate survivors of violene and human trafficking
C. to help mentally challenged women and girls
D. to provide free psychological legal of aid to victims and domestic violence

402. The state government operates speical schools for blind girls and a special school for deaf and dumb girls. These schools are respectively known as:

A. DRISHTI and KOSHISH
B. AASARA and SAHAYATA
C. DRISHTI and AASRA
D. SAHAYATA and KOSHISH

403. The state government has started a special school called KOSHISH, for deaf and dumb girls at:

A. Bettiah B. Motihari
C. Kishanganj D. Supaul

404. Which is the best district in terms of Mid-Day Meal Scheme Coverage?

A. Sitamarhi B. Sheohar
C. East Champaran D. Madhepura

405. Which of the following schemes are associated with drinking water and sanitation in Bihar?

A. Lohiya Swachhatta Yojana
B. Mukhyamantri Chapakal Yojana
C. Mukhyamantri Kshetra Vikas Yojana
D. All of the above

406. The head of state of Bihar, the Governor, is appointed by:

A. the President of India
B. the Chief Justice of India
C. Speaker of Lok Sabha
D. Speaker of Legislative Assembly

407. Governor holds office for a term of:

A. 5 years B. 4 years
C. 6 years D. 7 years

408. All the ministers are administered oath by:

A. Governor B. Chief Ministers
C. Speaker D. Deputy Chairman

409. Who was the first Governor of Bihar?

A. Sir James Sifton
B. Sir Maurice Garnier Hallett
C. Sir Thomas Alexander Stewart
D. Sir Thomas George Rutherford

410. Who appoints the Chief Minister?

A. Governor
B. President
C. Speaker of Legislative Assembly
D. Chairman of Legislative Council

411. After independence of India, who was the first Governor of Bihar?
A. Madhav Srihari Aney B. R.R. Diwakar
C. Jairamdas Daulatram D. Zakir Hussain

412. First Chief Justice of Patna High Court was:
A. Nand Lal Untwalia
B. D.P. Wadhwa
C. Vimal Chand Basak
D. Sir Edward Maynerd Champs Chamier

413. Bihar Public Service Commission (BPSC) is a body created by:
A. The Constitution of India
B. The extra constitutional provision
C. Legal provision
D. Administrative procedure

414. The Bihar Public Service Commission came into existence from:
A. 1st April, 1949 B. 1st April, 1950
C. 2nd April, 1953 D. 2nd April, 1951

415. The Bihar Public Service Commission initially began its functioning for the State of Bihar with its headquarters at:
A. Ranchi B. Patna
C. Gaya D. Muzaffarpur

416. Who was the first chairman of Bihar Public Service Commission?
A. Rajandhari Sinha B. Krishnakant Sahay
C. Bhupender Singh D. None of the above

417. The number of Divisions in Bihar are:
A. 6 B. 7
C. 8 D. 9

418. Gopalganj falls under which division:
A. Saran B. Tirhut
C. Magadha D. Patna

419. The total number of districts in Bihar are:
A. 27 B. 38
C. 37 D. 39

420. The sub-division is headed by SDM or SDO who is:
A. a newly recruited member of IAS
B. a member of state civil service
C. Both A and B
D. None of the above

421. Vaishali falls under which division:
A. Saran B. Tirhut
C. Bhagalpur D. Munger

422. A Panchyat Samiti is a local government body at which level?
A. Block level B. Village level
C. District level D. None of the above

423. What percentage of reservation has been provided to scheduled caste and scheduled tribe population in Panchayat election?
A. 1/2
B. 1/3
C. in proportion to their population
D. 1/5

424. The departments, not included under Panchayat Samiti work is:
A. Agriculture B. Education
C. Transport D. Social welfare

425. A Janpad Panchyat is constituted for each:
A. block B. village
C. district D. locality

426. Who is responsible for his work to the CEO of ZP?
A. BDO B. SDO
C. Sarpanch D. None of these

427. The schemes implemented by PRIs are financed by:
A. Backward Region Grants Fund (BRGF)
B. Grants from the Union Finance Commission
C. Grants from the State Finance Commission
D. All of the above

428. Panchayati Raj System was formalised in 1992 by which amendment to the Indian Constitution?
A. 73rd B. 74th
C. 75th D. 76th

429. Which of the following statement is true about panchayat election qualification:
A. must have 21 years age
B. must be qualified to be a member of legislature
C. Both A and B
D. None of the above

430. Which one of the following parts were added to the Constitution by 73rd Constitutional Amendment Act?
A. IXth B. Xth
C. XIth D. XIIth

431. The Panchayat Samiti is elected for a term of:
A. 5 years B. 3 years
C. 2 years D. 4 years

432. Zila Parishad has:
A. a President
B. a Vice President
C. a Chief Executive Officer
D. All of the above

433. The intermediate level of Panchayat is provided in which of the following state?
A. region with 10 lakh population
B. region with 15 lakh population
C. region with 20 lakh population
D. region with 25 lakh population

434. Bihar Panchayati Raj Act came in which year?
A. 2005 B. 2006
C. 2007 D. 2008

435. States appoints a finance commission to review the working of Panchayats:
A. every 2 year B. every 3 year
C. every 4 year D. every 5 year

436. The reservation for chairperson of Panchayats can be made by:
A. State B. Centre
C. Finance Commission D. Election Commission

437. The member of Block level Panchayat are:
A. ex-officials
B. elected by Gram Sabha
C. elected by Gram Panchayat
D. None of the above

438. The panchayat samiti is elected for a term of 5 years and is headed by:
A. A chairman and a deputy chairman
B. A chairman
C. A sarpanch
D. None of the above

439. How are the members of Zila Panchayat elected?
A. From the district on the basis of Adult Franchise
B. From the district on the basis of selection by the President
C. From the district on the basis of reommendation by the President
D. None of the above

440. Each Janpad Panchayat has a President, a Vice President and a:
A. Development Officer
B. Chief Executive Officer
C. Sarpanch
D. Both B and C

441. Which of the following statements is false about Karma dance?
A. It is performed mainly by tribes
B. It is mainly done at crop sowing and crop harvesting time
C. It is done to please Lord Karma
D. All of the above

442. The God worshipped in Karma dance form is:
A. Lord Rama B. Lord Krishna
C. Lord Indra D. Lord Karma

443. Find the incorrect match:

	Folk theatre	Main theme
A.	Bhakuli-Banka	Rural Life
B.	Domkuchh	Marriage
C.	Jat-Jatin	Child birth
D.	Kirtaniya	Krishna

444. Dhobia dance form is done in which region?
A. Bhojpur B. Gaya
C. Darbhanga D. Katihar

445. Hathiyar and Kalibanga are the two types of ________ dance.
A. Launda B. Chhau
C. Karma D. Kholdin

446. Sama Chakewa is organised in which month?
A. Kartik B. Magh
C. Phagun D. Shravan

447. Which of the following dance theatres has devotional theme?
A. Kirtaniya B. Jat-Jatin
C. Domkuchh D. Bhakuli-Banka

448. In which of the following festivals, Fagua songs are sung?
A. Holi B. Deepawali
C. Shravan D. Teej

449. Vidyapat dance is performed in:
A. Purnia B. Gaya
C. Siwan D. Saran

450. ________ dance is performed by ladies in moonlight in the month of Shravan to Kartik.
A. Jharni B. Jat-Jatin
C. Jogira D. Vidyapati

451. Pawadia dance form is performed on:
A. marriage B. child birth
C. gauna D. harvesting season

452. In which of the following regions, nunachar is sung?
A. Darbhanga B. Katihar
C. Nawada D. Gaya

453. Find the correct match:

	Dance Form	Occasion
A.	Kholdin	Child birth
B.	Karma	Harvesting
C.	Chhau	Holi
D.	Jogira	Marriage

454. Find the incorrect match:

	Dance Form	Occasion
A.	Jogira	Holi
B.	Kariya	Marriage
C.	Jharni	Muharram
D.	Launda	Child birth

455. Lalit Kala Manch is located at which place?
A. Gaya B. Patna
C. Muzaffarpur D. Darbhanga

456. Find the correct statement:
A. Chhau dance form has Veer Rasa and is performed at war time
B. It is perfomed by males only
C. It is basically performed in South Bihar
D. None of the above

457. The Chief markets of Tikuli are:
A. Varanasi B. Patna
C. Kolkata D. All of these

458. Shah Daulat's tomb in Maner is best example of:
A. Mughal style B. Turks
C. Afghan D. None of these

459. Patna Kalam was an offshoot of:
A. Mughal painting B. Afghan painting
C. Pala painting D. None of the above

460. Yaksh and Yakshini statues are the examples of finest sculpture of Mauryan period, which has been obtained from:
A. Patna B. Darbhanga
C. Gaya D. Bihar Sharif

461. The tradition of carpet making in Bihar dates back to:
A. Buddhist and the Mauryan period
B. Mughal period
C. Later Mauryan period
D. Afghan period

462. Sher Shah's tomb of Sasaram was built in which style?
A. Mughal style B. Afghan style
C. Jusks style D. Salve style

463. Manjusha Kala or Angika Art is another Bihari art form, practiced in the:
A. Vaishali region B. Magadh region
C. Anga D. None of the above

464. Madhubani painting depicts:
A. Nature and Hindu religious figures
B. Buddhist life
C. Marriage ceremony
D. None of the above

465. Tikuli works is a form of craft made from:
A. Broken glass B. Weeds
C. Applique D. Zari

466. Nalanda and Kurkihar has got evidence of which period?
A. Pala B. Mauryan
C. Post Mauryan D. None of these

467. Lacquer craft is famous for:
A. Bangles and stools B. Jewellery
C. Paintings D. Zari work

468. Which one is true?
A. Brass and stone statue gained prominence in Pala period
B. Dhiman and his son Vitthalpal had taken main role in its development
C. Both A and B
D. None of the above

469. Which is a very famous centre of wooden toy making?
A. Patna B. Gaya
C. Nawada D. Nalanda

470. Mandar hill features the unique image of which God from the Gupta period, in his man-lion incarnation?
A. Lord Vishnu B. Lord Shiva
C. Lord Ganesha D. None of the above

471. Patna Sahib is related to which of the following Sikh Gurus?
A. Guru Gobind Singh B. Guru Nanak
C. Guru Angad D. None of the above

472. In Saurath, in which month a fair on marriage is held?
A. Jayeshtha-Asharh B. Bhadrapada
C. Magha D. Kartik

473. Find the correct match:

	Fair		District
A.	Baunsi	-	West Champaran
B.	Saurath	-	Begusarai
C.	Brahmeshwamath	-	Buxar
D.	Simariya	-	Bhagalpur

474. Sonpur fair is held on which day?
A. Navami of Chaitra month
B. Kartik Purnima
C. Tryodashi of Chaitra Shukla
D. None of the above

475. Which one of the following fairs is celebrated by Tharu tribe?
A. Sahodhara B. Simaria
C. Saurath D. Baunsi

476. Singheswar fair is held in which district?
A. Supaul B. Madhepura
C. Katihar D. Purnia

477. Which of the following fairs is celebrated to Rama and Laxman arrival?
A. Buxar fair B. Sitamarhi fair
C. Sonpur fair D. None of these

478. When was Patna book fair held for the first time?
A. 1970 B. 1975
C. 1972 D. 1971

479. What does Mahalaya in Bihar mean?
A. Devpujan B. Govardhan
C. Pitrapaksha D. Ganeshapujan

480. Sitamarhi fair is celebrated for which occasion?
A. Saraswati Pooja B. Krishnashtami
C. Ramnavami D. Chhath

481. 'Jeutia' is celebrated on which day?
A. Ashwin Krishna Paksha Ashtami
B. Ashwin Shukla Paksha Ashtami
C. Kartik Krishna Paksha Ashtami
D. Kartik Shukla Paksha Ashtami

482. In which of the following places Loard Vishnu had taken holy bath?
A. Baunsi B. Simarya
C. Sitamarhi D. None of the above

483. In Chhath festival which God is offered Arghya?
A. Sun B. Vishnu
C. Shiva D. Rama

484. Which festival in Bihar is celebrated as a belief of the awakening of God after 4 months of sleep?
A. Chhath festival B. Govardhan
C. Mahalaya Amavasya D. Devotthan Ekadashi

485. Jeutia festival is celebrated by females for:
A. husband B. son
C. daughter D. none of these

486. Pitrapaksh fair in Gaya is held in which month?
A. Ashwin B. Kartik
C. Magh D. Chaitra

487. Brahmeshwarnath fair is basically:
A. an animal fair B. Jain's fair
C. Hindu's fair D. None of the above

488. Firangiya and Batohiya are written in which of the following languages?
A. Magadhi B. Maithili
C. Bhojpuri D. Angika

489. Which of the following languages is not a part of Munda language family?
A. Angika B. Vajjika
C. Maithili D. Nonc of thesc

490. Which among the following languages in Bihar is included in the Eighth Schedule of the Indian Constitution by the 92nd Constitutional Amendment Act, 2003.
A. Maithili B. Magadhi
C. Bhojpuri D. Urdu

491. Urdu was granted second language in Bihar in which year?
A. 1980 B. 1985
C. 1984 D. 1989

492. 'Varn Ratnakar' is the first written com-position of which language?
A. Maithili B. Magadhi
C. Bhojpuri D. Angika

493. When was 'The Patna Times' started?
A. 1912 B. 1924
C. 1944 D. 1916

494. Who is the first poet of Magadhi/Magahi?
A. Ishan B. Siyaram
C. Manoranjan Singh D. Nagarjuna

495. Who have researched widely on the dialects of Bihar?
A. V.S. Smith B. George Grierson
C. William Taylor D. Jyon Dren

496. Ambpali was written by whom?
A. Ram Briksha Benipuri B. Vachaspati Mishra
C. Nagarjuna D. Vidyapati

497. Who among the following is not a Magadhi poet?
A. Chaturbhuj Mishra B. Yogeshwar Singh
C. Suresh Dubey D. Dariya Das

498. 'Gautam' Mahakavya was written in Magadhi language by whom?
A. Yamuna Pathak B. Yogeshwar Singh
C. Harihar Pathak D. Sridhar Mishra

499. Who wrote 'Kaikeyi' and 'Rituvansh' in Bhojpuri language?
A. Kapilmuni Pathak B. Ratneshwar Pathak
C. Pt. Kedarnath Mishra D. Suman Sahay

500. 'Bidesiya' is a work of:
A. Bhikhari Thakur B. Kedarnath Mishra
C. Dariya Das D. Dharti Das

501. Which of the following languages is not a part of Aryan family?
A. Maithili B. Magadhi
C. Vajjika D. Bhojpuri

502. Tej Narayan Kushwaha has contributed to which language?
A. Angika B. Magadhi
C. Vajjika D. Maithili

503. Bhim Rao Ambedkar University is situated in which district?
A. Buxar B. Darbhanga
C. Muzaffarpur D. Nawada

504. In which year was Magadha University established?
A. 1976 B. 1903
C. 1962 D. 1980

505. Patna University was established in:
A. 1917 B. 1919
C. 1915 D. 1916

506. Khuda Baksh Oriental Library is situated in:
A. Munger B. Gaya
C. Bhagalpur D. Patna

507. IGIMS, Patna was established in which year?
A. 1984 B. 1990
C. 1980 D. 1983

508. Arabic and Persian Research Institute is situated in:
A. Darbhanga B. West Champaran
C. Patna D. Bhagalpur

509. Jawaharlal Nehru Medical College is situated in:
A. Banka B. Bhagalpur
C. Katihar D. Kishanganj

510. Bhitarwara Asharam related to Gandhiji is situated in which district of Bihar?
A. West Champaran B. Patna
C. East Champaran D. Sitamarhi

511. Gandhiji experimented satyagraha at which place for the first time?

A. Siwan B. Saran
C. East Champaran D. West Champaran

512. At which place the highest Buddhist Stupa in India is located?
A. Nalanda B. Rajgir
C. Vaishali D. Kesariya

513. Ahirauli related to Ahilya is situated in which district of Bihar?
A. Saharsa B. Buxar
C. Darbhanga D. Gopalganj

514. Bodhgaya is religious palace of which religion?
A. Buddhism B. Hinduism
C. Jainism D. Islam

515. Kabar Jheel Bird Santuary is located in which district?
A. Begusarai B. Sitamarhi
C. Jamui D. Banka

516. Matsyagandha Tourism complex is located in which district of Bihar?
A. Supaul B. Saharsa
C. Sitamarhi D. Bhagalpur

517. Goraul Sharif a muslim pilgrimage. is situated in which district:
A. Supaul B. West Champaran
C. Sitamarhi D. Patna

518. Jarasandh's Akhara is situated at which of the following places?
A. Patna B. Rajgir
C. Vaishali D. Bodhgaya

519. Padri Ki Haveli was constructed in which year?
A. 1705 B. 1771
C. 1707 D. 1772

520. The Kundeshwari Devi Temple at Kundghat is situated at which place?
A. Jamui B. Banka
C. Kaimur D. Bhojpur

521. Which of the following tourist sites is located in Nalanda?
A. Vajrasana B. Guneri
C. Venuvana Vihara D. Vikramshila

522. The Vishwa Shanti Stupa is located at which place of Bihar?
A. Hajipur B. Rajgir
C. Bodhgaya D. Maner

523. Which of the following is an incorrect pair?
A. Maniar Math – Gaya
B. Vasokund – Muzaffarpur
C. Mandar Hill – Banka
D. Bisram – Bhojpur

524. Which is the most famous treasure of Patna Museum?
A. Shiva Statue B. Buddha Statue
C. Didarganj Yakshini D. Vishnu Statue

525. The tomb of Yahiya Maneri is situated in:
A. Bettiah B. Gaya
C. Manersharif D. Rajgir

526. Dargah of Makhdum Hazrat Sultan Ahmed Charampose is situated in which district?
A. Bihar Sharif (Nalanda) B. Gopalganj
C. Sitamarhi D. Nawada

527. Who wrote several collections of Hindi poems including 'Umang'?
A. Gopal Singh Nepali B. Naval Kishore Dhawal
C. Ramnarayan Sharma D. Bhikari Thakur

528. Who was the author of Chandrakantha?
A. Devkinandan Khatri
B. Navin Vilochan Sharma
C. Kedarnath Mishra
D. None of the above

529. Veer Kunwar Singh University is in which district?
A. Bhojpur B. Gaya
C. Siwan D. Saran

530. Swami Sahjananda Saraswati had set-up an Ashram at which place?
A. Atrah B. Patna
C. Muzaffarpur D. None of the above

ANSWERS

1	2	3	4	5	6	7	8	9	10
D	B	D	B	A	C	A	D	B	A
11	**12**	**13**	**14**	**15**	**16**	**17**	**18**	**19**	**20**
C	C	D	A	B	A	D	A	D	A
21	**22**	**23**	**24**	**25**	**26**	**27**	**28**	**29**	**30**
D	A	C	B	D	B	D	C	A	B
31	**32**	**33**	**34**	**35**	**36**	**37**	**38**	**39**	**40**
C	A	B	A	D	D	D	B	A	D
41	**42**	**43**	**44**	**45**	**46**	**47**	**48**	**49**	**50**
A	C	A	A	B	C	D	B	B	A